# International Companion
# Encyclopedia of
# Children's Literature

# International Companion Encyclopedia of Children's Literature

*Edited by*
## PETER HUNT

*Associate Editor*
## Sheila Ray

## London and New York

First published 1996
by Routledge
11 New Fetter Lane, London EC4P 4EE
29 West 35th Street, New York, NY 10001

*Routledge is an International Thomson Publishing company*

Selection, editorial matter and chapters 10 and 48 © Peter Hunt
© 1996 Routledge

Typeset in Ehrhardt by Routledge
Printed and bound in Great Britain by
TJ Press (Padstow) Ltd, Padstow, Cornwall

*British Library Cataloguing in Publication Data*
A catalogue record for this book is available from the British Library

*Library of Congress Cataloging in Publication Data*
International companion encyclopedia of children's literature / edited by
Peter Hunt; associate editor, Sheila Ray.
p. cm.
Includes bibliographical references and index.
1. Children's literature–Encyclopedias. 2. Children's literature–History and
criticism. I. Hunt, Peter II. Ray, Sheila G. Bannister.
PN1008.5.I57 1996 95-33448
809'.89282'03–dc20

ISBN 0-415-08856-9

# Contents

Editor's Preface     xi
Contributors     xiii

1 Introduction     1
   *Margaret Meek*

**I THEORY AND CRITICAL APPROACHES**     **15**

2 Defining Children's Literature and Childhood     17
   *Karín Lesnik-Oberstein*

3 History, Culture and Children's Literature     32
   *Tony Watkins*

4 Ideology     41
   *Charles Sarland*

5 Linguistics and Stylistics     58
   *John Stephens*

6 Reader-Response Criticism     71
   *Michael Benton*

7 Psychoanalytical Criticism     89
   *Hamida Bosmajian*

8 Feminist Criticism: From Sex-Role Stereotyping to Subjectivity     101
   *Lissa Paul*

9 Illustration and Picture Books     113
   *Perry Nodelman*

10 A Note on Bibliography     125
   *Peter Hunt*

11 Intertextuality     131
   *Christine Wilkie*

**II TYPES AND GENRES**     **139**

12 Early Texts Used by Children     141
   *Margaret Kinnell*

13  Fairy Tales and Folk-tales                                                152
    *Ruth B. Bottigheimer*

14  Myth and Legend                                                          166
    *Maurice Saxby*

15  Playground Rhymes and the Oral Tradition                                 177
    *Iona Opie*

16  Poetry for Children                                                      190
    *Morag Styles*

17  Drama                                                                    206
    *Peter Hollindale*

18  The Development of Illustrated Texts and Picture Books                   220
    *Joyce Irene Whalley*

19  The Modern Picture Book                                                  231
    *Jane Doonan*

20  Popular Literature: Comics, Dime Novels, Pulps and Penny Dreadfuls       242
    *Denis Gifford*

21  Religious Writing for Children                                           267
    Catechistical, Devotional and Biblical Writing                          267
    *Ruth B. Bottigheimer*
    Moral and Religious Writing                                             273
    *Kate Montagnon*

22  Animal Stories                                                          282
    *Keith Barker*

23  Real Gardens with Imaginary Toads: Domestic Fantasy                     295
    *Louisa Smith*

24  High Fantasy                                                            303
    *C. W. Sullivan III*

25  Science Fiction                                                         314
    *Jessica Yates*

26  Shaping Boyhood: Empire Builders and Adventurers                        326
    *Dennis Butts*

27  The Family Story                                                        338
    *Gillian Avery*

28  School Stories                                                          348
    *Sheila Ray*

29  Pony Books                                                              360
    *Alison Haymonds*

30  Historical Fiction                                                      368
    *Janet Fisher*

31  Books for Younger Readers                                               377
    *Colin Mills*

32  Teenage Fiction: Realism, Romances, Contemporary Problem Novels  387
    *Julia Eccleshare*

33  Metafictions and Experimental Work  397
    *Robyn McCallum*

34  Major Authors' Work for Children  410
    *Marian Allsobrook*

35  Books Adopted by Children  422
    *Stuart Hannabuss*

36  Information Books  433
    *Peggy Heeks*

37  Children's Magazines  443
    *Marianne Carus*

## III THE CONTEXT OF CHILDREN'S LITERATURE  459

38  Children's Book Design  461
    *Douglas Martin*

39  Children's Book Publishing in Britain  472
    *Margaret Clark*

40  Children's Book Publishing in the USA  478
    *Connie C. Epstein*

41  Reviewing and Scholarly Journals  485
    *Gillian Adams*

42  Censorship  498
    *Mark I. West*

43  Prizes and Prizewinners  508
    *Keith Barker*

44  Translation  519
    *Ronald Jobe*

45  Radio, Television, Film, Audio and Video  530
    *Michael Rosen*

46  Story-telling  539
    *Mary Medlicott*

47  Libraries and Research Collections  546
    *Karen Nelson Hoyle*

48  What the Authors Tell Us  555
    *Peter Hunt*

## IV APPLICATIONS OF CHILDREN'S LITERATURE    571

49  Reading and Literacy    573
    *Geoffrey Williams*

50  Teenagers Reading: Developmental Stages of Reading Literature    584
    *Jack Thomson*

51  Teaching Fiction and Poetry    594
    *Geoff Fox*

52  Teaching Children's Literature in Higher Education    606
    *Tony Watkins*

53  Librarianship    615
    *Ray Lonsdale with Sheila Ray*

54  Bibliotherapy and Psychology    634
    *Hugh Crago*

55  Publishing for Special Needs    644
    *Beverley Mathias*


## V  THE WORLD OF CHILDREN'S LITERATURE    651

56  The World of Children's Literature: An Introduction    653
    *Sheila Ray*

57  Culture and Developing Countries    663
    *Anne Pellowski*

58  British Children's Literature: A Historical Overview    676
    *John Rowe Townsend*

59  Scotland    688
    *Stuart Hannabuss*

60  Wales    692
    *Menna Lloyd Williams*

61  Ireland    695
    *Valerie Coghlan*

62  The Nordic Countries    699
    *Boel Westin*

63  The Netherlands    710
    *Anne de Vries*

64  France    717
    *Jean Perrot*

65  Spain    726
    *Carmen García Surrallés and Antonio Moreno Verdulla
    with Marisol Dorao*

66  Portugal    731
    *Natércia Rocha*

67 Germany 735
German Children's Literature from the Eighteenth to the 735
Twentieth Century
*Hans-Heino Ewers*
The German Democratic Republic 744
*Bernd Dolle-Weinkauff*

68 Switzerland 748
*Verena Rutschmann*

69 Austria 752
*Lucia Binder*

70 Italy 757
*Laura Kreyder*

71 Greece 761
*Vassilis D. Anagnostopoulos*

72 Russia 765
*Ben Hellman*

73 Eastern Europe 774
*Sheila Ray*

74 Turkey 781
*Sheila Ray*

75 Hebrew and Israeli 783
*Zohar Shavit*

76 The Arab World 789
*Julinda Abu-Nasr*

77 Africa 795
English-Speaking Africa 795
*Jay Heale*
French-Speaking Africa 801
*Marie Laurentin*

78 The Indian Sub-Continent 807
*Manorama Jafa*

79 The Far East 823
*Sheila Ray*

80 China 830
*Wong Yoon Wah and Laina Ho*

81 Japan 837
*Teruo Jinguh*

82 Australia 843
*Rhonda M. Bunbury*

83 New Zealand 855
*Betty Gilderdale*

84  Canada                                                                862
    English–Speaking Canada                                               862
    *Alexandra West*
    French–Speaking Canada                                                868
    *Elvine Gignac-Pharand*
85  Children's Literature in the USA: A Historical Overview               871
    *Jerry Griswold*
86  Central and South America and the Caribbean                           882
    *Enrique Pérez Díaz*

# Editor's Preface

Children's literature, as a body of oral and written texts to be described, and as a subject of study to be investigated, is the confluence of many cultures and of many disciplines.

As a result, the essays in this volume not only present a huge range of material, they also represent a wide range of critical and theoretical attitudes and approaches. Children's books are at once the business of bibliographers and historians, librarians and teachers, theorists and publishers, reviewers and prizegivers, writers, designers, illustrators and publishers — and these and others are represented here. Each discipline has its own preoccupations and its own discursive techniques: the overall blend of voices demonstrates the growing interest in and profound commitment to a multi-faceted subject worldwide.

The *Encyclopedia* moves outwards from theoretical and critical bases, through types and genres, to the production and application of these oral, visual and written texts. The final section surveys the world picture; here the emphasis and the extent of the discussion has been determined by both the strength of children's literature in the countries and regions, and also by the extent of information available. Some countries have more sophisticated information networks than others; and in response to this, the selection has been pragmatic rather than political.

I would like to thank the many contributors and non-contributors who have helped me to navigate the world of children's literature by recommending and introducing me to writers – especially my Advisory Editor, Rhonda Bunbury, who gave me the benefit of her experience as President of the International Research Society for Children's Literature.

Many thanks are also due to Nancy Chambers, Geoff Fox, Margaret Kinnell, Margaret Spencer and Jack Zipes; to the School of English at the University of Wales, Cardiff for generous support in terms of time and materials, to Dr Alfred Whit for translations from the German and to my successive editors at Routledge: Alison Barr, Michelle Darraugh, Robert Potts, and Denise Rea.

# Contributors

Julinda Abu-Nasr, *Lebanese American University, Beirut*
Gillian Adams, *editor, Children's Literature Abstracts*
Marian Allsobrook, *Whitchurch High School, Cardiff*
Vassilis D. Anagnostopulos, *Author and Lecturer, Karditsa, Greece*
Gillian Avery, *Author, Oxford*
Keith Barker, *Westhill College, Birmingham*
Michael Benton, *University of Southampton*
Lucia Binder, *formerly of Internationales Institut für Jugendliteratur und Leseforschung, Vienna*
Hamida Bosmajian, *Seattle University*
Ruth B. Bottigheimer, *State University of New York at Stony Brook*
Rhonda Bunbury, *Deakin University*
Dennis Butts, *University of Reading*
Marianne Carus, *The Cricket Magazine Group, Peru Illinois*
Margaret Clark, *formerly of The Bodley Head*
Valerie Coghlan, *Church of Ireland College of Education, Dublin*
Hugh Crago, *University of New England*
Anne de Vries, *Dutch Library Centre, The Hague*
Enrique Pérez Díaz, *Author, Journalist, Poet, Havana, Cuba*
Bernd Dolle-Weinkauff, *Johann Wolfgang Goethe-Universität, Frankfurt-am-Main*
Jane Doonan, *Author and Lecturer, Bath*
Marisol Dorao, *University of Cádiz*
Julia Eccleshare, *Children's Book Correspondent, The Bookseller*
Connie C. Epstein, *formerly of William C. Morrow*
Hans-Heino Ewers, *Johann Wolfgang Goethe-Universität, Frankfurt-am-Main*
Janet Fisher, *Author and Lecturer, Quebec*
Geoff Fox, *University of Exeter*
Carmen García Surrallés, *University of Cádiz*
Denis Gifford, *founder of Association of Comics Enthusiasts*
Elvine Gignac-Pharand, *Laurentian University, (Ontario), Canada*
Betty Gilderdale, *Author and Lecturer, Auckland, New Zealand*
Jerry Griswold, *San Diego State University*
Stuart Hannabuss, *The Robert Gordon University*

Alison Haymonds, *Thames Valley University*
Jay Heale, *Children's Book Specialist, editor of 'Bookchat', Grabouw, South Africa*
Peggy Heeks, *Fellow of Loughborough University*
Ben Hellman, *University of Helsinki*
Laina Ho, *National University of Singapore*
Peter Hollindale, *University of York*
Karen Nelson Hoyle, *University of Minnesota*
Peter Hunt, *University of Wales, Cardiff*
Manorama Jafa, *Secretary General, IBBY India/AWIC*
Teruo Jinguh, *Shirayuri College, Tokyo*
Ronald Jobe, *University of British Columbia*
Margaret Kinnell, *Loughborough University*
Laura Kreyder, *Università della Calabria, Arcavacata*
Marie Laurentin, *Joie par les livres, Paris*
Karín Lesnik-Oberstein, *University of Reading*
Ray Lonsdale, *University of Wales, Aberystwyth*
Robyn McCallum, *Macquarie University*
Douglas Martin, *Douglas Martin Associates, Leicester*
Beverley Mathias, *National Library for the Handicapped Child,
     Wokingham (to be renamed REACH: National Resource Centre for Children with
     Reading Difficulties)*
Mary Medlicott, *Storyteller, London*
Margaret Meek, *University of London Institute of Education*
Colin Mills, *University of Exeter*
Kate Montagnon, *Ravenscroft Primary School, East London*
Antonio Moreno Verdulla, *University of Cádiz*
Perry Nodelman, *University of Winnipeg*
Iona Opie, *Author, Hampshire*
Lissa Paul, *University of New Brunswick*
Anne Pellowski, *Author, New York*
Jean Perrot, *University of Paris XIII*
Sheila Ray, *Children's Literature Consultant, Wales*
Natércia Rocha, *Author and Lecturer, Lisbon*
Michael Rosen, *Broadcaster, Lecturer, Author, London*
Verena Rutschmann, *Schweizerisches Jugendbuch-Institut, Zürich*
Charles Sarland, *University of East Anglia*
Maurice Saxby, *Author and Lecturer, Sydney, Australia*
Zohar Shavit, *Tel Aviv University*
Louisa Smith, *Mankato State University*
John Stephens, *Macquarie University*
Morag Styles, *University of Cambridge*
C. W. Sullivan III, *East Carolina University*
Jack Thomson, *Author and Lecturer, Ulladulla, NSW, Australia*
John Rowe Townsend, *Author and Historian of Children's Literature, Cambridge*
Wong Yoon Wah, *National University of Singapore*
Tony Watkins, *University of Reading*
Alexandra West, *University of Calgary*

Mark I. West, *University of North Carolina at Charlotte*
Boel Westin, *Stockholm University*
Joyce Irene Whalley, *formerly of the National Art Library, Victoria and Albert Museum, London*
Christine Wilkie, *University of Warwick*
Geoffrey Williams, *University of Sydney*
Menna Lloyd Williams, *Welsh Books Council, Aberystwyth*
Jessica Yates, *School Librarian, North London*

# 1

# Introduction

## *Margaret Meek*

### Acts of Definition

Encyclopedias are usually designed to assemble and to encompass, for the purposes of recognition and study, as much of what is known about a subject of interest and concern as the conditions of its production and publication allow. Children's literature is an obvious subject for this purpose. Its nature and social significance are most clearly discerned when activities associated with children and books are brought together. These activities may be as diverse as creating a book list, a publisher's catalogue, a library, an exhibition, a school's Book Week, a rare collection, a prize-giving ceremony, as well as the compilation of scholarly works of reference. Children's literature is embedded in the language of its creation and shares its social history. This volume is its first avowed encyclopedia, and thus, a representation of children's literature at a particular time.

The by-play of an encyclopedia is the view it offers of the world as reflected in its subject matter. Promoters and editors long for completeness, the last word on the topic, even when they know there is no such rounding off. Instead, there is only an inscribed event, which becomes part of the history of ideas and of language. When this moment passes for works of reference, we say the book has gone 'out of date', a description of irrelevance, calling for revision or reconstitution. But later readers continue to find in encyclopedias not simply the otherness of the past, but also the structures of values and feelings, which historians teach us to treat as evidence of the perceptions a culture has, and leaves, of itself. The appearance of this Encyclopedia in the last decade of the twentieth century, the end of a millennium and the traditional teleological judgement time, lets it become a significant mirror image of certain aspects of childhood and of a distinctive literature.

In this, as in other ways, the present volume differs from many of its predecessors. Earlier compilations of information about children's books were more heroic, written by individuals with a commitment to the subject, at the risk, in their day, of being considered quaint in their choice of reading matter. It is impossible to imagine the history of children's literature without the ground-clearing brilliance of F. J. Harvey Darton's *Children's Books in England* (1932/1982). But although Darton's account has a singleness of purpose and matching scholarship, it is not the whole story. There is more than diligence and systematic arrangement in John Rowe Townsend's careful revisions of *Written for Children*

(1965/1990), a text kept alert to change; it is still a starting place for many students. Over a period of forty years, Margery Fisher's contribution to this field included both a series of finely judged comments on books as they appeared, and a unique vision of why it is important to write *about* children's books, so that writing them would continue to be regarded as serious business. Better than many a contemporary critic she understood how, and why, 'we need constantly to revise and restate the standards of this supremely important branch of literature' (Fisher 1964: 9). *The Oxford Companion to Children's Literature* (Carpenter and Prichard 1984), however, shows how acts of definition are upheld by editors and their friends. Collectors, cataloguers, bibliographers and other book persons stand behind all works of summation, including those of the single author-as-editor-and-commentator.

By virtue of its anthologising form, this volume replaces the *tour d'horizon* of the classical encyclopedia with something more characteristic of the culture of its epoch, a certain deliberate untidiness, an openness. The writers brought together here are currently at work in different parts of the field of children's literature. Encompassing all their activities, their individual histories and directions, children's literature appears not as something which requires definition in order to be recognised or to survive, but as a 'total text', in what Jerome J. McGann calls 'a network of symbolic exchanges' (1991: 3), a diverse complexity of themes, rites and images. There are many voices. Each writer has an interpretative approach to a chosen segment of the grand design, so that the whole book may be unpacked by its searching readers, or dipped into by the curious or the uninitiated. Some of the writings are tentative and explorative; others are confident, even confrontational. As the counterpoint of topics and treatments emerges, we note in what is discussed agreement and difference, distinction and sameness. Thus the encyclopedia becomes not a series of reviews, but a landmark, consonant with and responsive to the time of its appearance.

Children's literature is not in this book, but outside, in the social world of adults and children and the cultural processes of reading and writing. As part of any act of description, however, a great number of different readers and writers are woven into these pages, and traces of their multiple presences are inscribed there. This introduction is simply a privileged *essai*, or assay, of the whole.

## Common Themes and Blurred Genres

Our constant, universal habit, scarcely changed over time, is to tell children stories. As Iona Opie tells us (see Chapter 15), children's earliest encounters with stories are in adults' saying and singing. When infants talk to themselves before falling asleep, the repetitions we hear show how they link people and events. As they learn their mother tongue they discover how their culture endows experience with meaning. Common ways of saying things, proverbs, fables and other kinds of lore, put ancient words into their mouths. Stories read to them become part of their own memories. Book characters emerge in the stories of their early dramatic play as they anticipate the possibilities of their futures.

The complexity of children's narrative understandings and the relation of story-telling to the books of their literature become clear from the records many conscientious adults have kept of how individual children grew up with books (Paley 1981; Crago and Crago 1983; Wolf and Brice Heath 1992). One of the most striking of these is Carol Fox's account of the effect of literature on young children's own story-telling, before they learn to read for themselves. In her book, *At the Very Edge of the Forest*, she shows how, by being read to, children learn to 'talk like a book'. This evidence outstrips the rest by showing how pre-school children borrow characters, incidents and turns of phrase from familiar tales and from their favourite authors in order to insert themselves into the continuous storying of everyday events. Children also expect the stories they hear to cast light on what they are unsure about: the dark, the unexpected, the repetitious and the ways adults behave. Quickly learned, their grasp of narrative conventions is extensive before they have school lessons. For children, stories are metaphors, especially in the realm of feelings, for which they have, as yet, no single words. A popular tale like *Burglar Bill* (1977) by Janet and Allan Ahlberg, invites young listeners to engage with both the events and their implications about good and bad behaviour in ways almost impossible in any discourse other than that of narrative fiction.

Narrative, sometimes foregrounded, always implied, is the most common theme in this Encyclopedia. Most writers engage with children's literature as stories, which gives weight to Barbara Hardy's conviction, sometimes contested but more often approved, that for self-conscious humans, narrative is 'a primary act of mind transferred to art from life' (Hardy 1968/1977: 12). (The same claim is made in various ways by Eco (1983), Le Guin (1980, 1981), Lurie (1990), Smith (1990), Bruner (1986), Barthes (1974) and others.) Stories are what adults and children most effectively share. Although myths, legends, folk and fairy tales tend to be associated particularly with childhood, throughout history they have been embedded in adult literature, including recent retellings as different as those of Angela Carter (1990) and Salman Rushdie (1990).

It is not surprising, therefore, that modern studies of narratology, their accompanying formalist theories and the psychological, linguistic, structural and rhetorical analyses developed from adult literary fictions are now invoked to describe the creative and critical practices in children's literature. Ursula Le Guin, whose renown as a writer of science fiction is further enhanced by her imaginative world-making for the young, acknowledges the continuity of story-telling in all our lives, and the vital part it plays in intellectual and affective growth.

> Narrative is a central function of language. Not, in its origin, an artefact of culture, an art, but a fundamental operation of the normal mind functioning in society. To learn to speak is to learn to tell a story.
>
> Le Guin 1989: 39

Narrative is not a genre. It is a range of linguistic ways of annotating time, related to memory and recollections of the past, as to anticipations of the future, including hypotheses, wishes, longing, planning and the rest. If a story has the imaginative immediacy of 'let's pretend', it becomes a present enactment. If an author tells a reader about Marie Curie's search for radium, the completed quest is rediscovered as a present adventure. While their experience is confined to everyday events, readers do not sort their imagining into different categories of subject-matter. Until they learn different kinds of writing conventions for different school subjects, children make narrative serve many of the purposes of their formal learning. The words used by scientists, historians, geographers, technologists and others crop up in biographies and stories before formal textbooks separate them as lessons.

Quite early, however, children discover that adults divide books into two named categories: fiction and non-fiction, and imply that books with 'facts' about the 'real' world are different from those that tell 'made up' stories. In modern writing for children this absolute distinction is no longer sustainable. Both novels and 'fact' books deal with the same subjects in a wide range of styles and presentations. Topics of current social and moral concern – sex, poverty, illness, crime, family styles and disruptions – discovered by reading children in newspapers and in feature films on television, also appear as children's literature in new presentational forms. The boundaries of genres that deal with actualities are not fixed but blurred. Books about the fate of the rainforests are likely to be narratives although their content emphasises the details of ecological reasoning.

Although stories are part of young children's attempts to sort out the world, children's literature is premised on the assumption that all children, unless prevented by exceptional circumstances, can learn to read. In traditionally literate cultures, learning to read now begins sooner than at any time in the past. Books are part of this new precocity because parents are willing to buy them, educators to promote them and publishers to produce them. At a very young age, children enter the textual world of environmental print and television and soon become at home in it. Encouraged by advertising, by governmental and specialist urgings, parents expect to understand how their children are being taught to read, and to help them.

They also want their children to have access to the newest systems of communication and to their distinctive technological texts. In England, the national legislation that sets out the Orders for literacy teaching begins with this sentence: 'Pupils should be given an extensive experience of children's literature.' No account of the subject of this Encyclopedia has ever before carried such a warrant.

Over the last decade the attention given to how children learn to read has foregrounded the nature of *textuality*, and of the different, interrelated ways in which readers of all ages make texts mean. 'Reading' now applies to a greater number of representational forms than at any time in the past: pictures, maps, screens, design graphics and photographs are all regarded as text. In addition to the innovations made possible in picture books by new printing processes, design features also predominate in other kinds, such as books of poetry and information texts. Thus, reading becomes a more complicated kind of interpretation than it was when children's attention was focused on the printed text, with sketches or pictures as an adjunct. Children now learn from a picture book that words and illustrations complement and enhance each other. Reading is not simply word recognition. Even in the easiest texts, what a sentence 'says' is often not what it means.

Intertextuality, the reading of one text in terms of another is very common in English books for children. Young children learn how the trick works as early as their first encounter with Janet and Allan Ahlberg's *Each Peach Pear Plum*, where they are to play I Spy with nursery characters. The conventions of intertextuality encourage artists and writers to exploit deliberately the bookish nature of books, as in John Burningham's *Where's Julius?* (1986) and Aidan Chambers's *Breaktime* (1978), both of which can be described as 'metafictive'.

Few children who have gone to school during the past twenty-five years in the West have learned to read books without also being proficient in reading television, the continuous text declaring the actuality of the world 'out there'. Book print and screen feed off each other, so there is a constant blurring of identifiable kinds. The voice-over convention of screen reading helps young readers to understand that the page of a book has also to be 'tuned'. Then they discover the most important lesson of all: the reader of the book has to become both the teller and the told.

Most of the evidence for children's reading progress comes from teachers' observations of how they interact with increasingly complex texts. But to decide which texts are 'difficult', or 'suitable' for any group of learners is neither straightforward nor generalisable. Children stretch their competences to meet the demands of the texts they really *want* to read.

## Distinctive Changes

Changes in the ways children learn and are taught to read indicate other symbiotic evaluations in children's literature. Marian Allsobrook describes children's literature as one of the 'numerous semi-autonomous cultures which have always existed alongside the dominant culture' (Chapter 34) and it has a continuous and influential history which is regularly raided for evidence of other social, intellectual and artistic changes. Encyclopedias are bound up in this tradition. Here, most writers give an account of their topic over time. This volume also extends the breadth of its subject to include the diversity of the scene at the time of its compilation. This includes textual varieties and variations such as result from modern methods of production and design and the apparently inexhaustible novelty of publishing formats.

Picture books exhibit these things best. However traditional their skills, authors and artists respond both to new techniques of book-making and to rapid changes in the attitudes and values of actual social living. The conventional boundaries of content and style have been pushed back, broken, exceeded, exploited, played with. Topics are now expected to engage young readers at a deeper level than their language can express but which their feelings recognise. In 1963, Maurice Sendak rattled the fundamentals of the emotional quality of children's books and the complacent idealised psychologies of the period by imaging malevolence and guilt in *Where the Wild Things Are*. Some contemporary critics said he threatened children with nightmares; in fact, Sendak opened the way for picture-stories to acknowledge, in the complexity of image–text interaction, the layered nature of early experiences, playful or serious, by making them *readable*.

Spatial and radial reading, the kinds called for by the original illustrated pages of Blake's *Songs of Innocence* (1789) and *Songs of Experience* (1794) are now in the repertoires of modern children who know Janet and Allan Ahlberg's *The Jolly Postman* (1986) and all the other works of their contemporaries discussed in these pages. Children's imaginative play, the way they grow into their culture and change it, is depicted in visual metafictions. In 1993 appeared Babette Cole's *Mummy Laid an Egg*, a picture story of two exuberant children who, when told by their parents the traditional fabled accounts of procreation, turn the tables on them. 'We don't think you really know how babies are made', they say. 'So we're doing some drawings to show you' (Cole 1993: np). Adult reactions to illustrations of this topic are always hesitant, despite contemporary convictions which support the idea of telling children the 'facts of life'. The sensitive delicacy of Cole's presentation of the children's exact and explicit understanding puts to rout any suggestion that this is a prurient book. Humour releases delight and increases children's confidence in understanding the metaphoric nature of language. It is also memorably serious.

Despite the attraction and distraction of many different kinds of new books, children still enjoy and profit from knowing myths, legends, folk and fairy tales. Some of these texts come in scholarly editions preferred by bibliophiles, but more often the versions are modern retellings, variable in quality and authenticity. Where the story is 'refracted' or told from a different viewpoint, the readers' sympathetic understanding undergoes a change. *The True Story of the 3 Little Pigs by A. Wolf* (Scieszka 1989) caught the imagination of young readers in just this way. It also lets them see how stories can be retold because they are something *made*. Neil Philip's exploration of the history of Cinderella (Philip 1989), Jack Zipes's collection of the versions of Little Red Riding Hood (Zipes 1983), Leon Garfield's *Shakespeare Stories* (1985) and his reworking of the texts of the plays to accompany animated films devised by Russian puppeteers, all show how multiple versions of traditional stories are matched by different ways of learning to read them.

A perceptive suggestion about versions of stories is made by Margaret Mackey. She points out that adults of a post-war generation have read popular and classic authors (Beatrix Potter, for example) in reprints of the original forms. Sequentially over time, they see reproductions of the texts and pictures on plates, mugs, calendars and aprons. The next generation that reads Raymond Briggs's *The Snowman* also encounters multiple versions of the pictures in different book formats, on video and film, wallpaper and sweaters *simultaneously*, and have the skill to choose from a number of versions the one they prefer. This commodification of children's literature is examined by Mackey in the case of *Thomas the Tank Engine* (1946) and its sequels. Forty years after their first appearance as books, the BBC produced animations of the stories. This generated 'a small industry of toys, games, pyjamas and so forth' (Mackey 1995: 43–44). This is how one part of the past of children's literature moves into the future.

> Those small children whose first fictional love is Thomas the Tank Engine are meeting a creation whose roots are deep in the certainties of a bygone era but whose branches and blossoms are so multifarious as to be confusing to the uninitiated. One of the striking things about the saga of Thomas the Tank Engine, as well as about other picture book characters who are the focus of industrial empires, is that they make it possible for very small toddlers to belong to the ranks of the initiated, and to know it. Their first approach to fiction is one of coming to terms with different versions, an experience which makes them experts in the settings and characters even as they learn the basic conventions of how story works.

Thomas's illustrations provide one single and small example of the way in which little readers learn the need to deal with plurality.

Mackay 1995: 44

General agreement that picture books exemplify and adorn the domain of children's literature is countered by arguments about the nature and worth of novels written for adolescents. This age group is usually subdivided into those who are discovering, usually at school, the kinds of writing related to 'subject' learning, and the pre-higher education teenagers (a word now less in use than it was when books were first deliberately written to distinguish them as readers) engaging with more complex subjective and social issues and making deliberate life choices. By this later stage, boys are often differentiated from girls in their tastes and reading habits. Critics of the bookish kind and teachers concerned that their pupils should tackle 'challenging' texts emphasise the importance of 'classic' literature, usually pre-twentieth century. Adolescents choose their reading matter from magazines commercially sensitive to the shifting identities of the young, and from the novels that connect readers' personal growth to a nascent interest in the world of ideas and beliefs, their nature and relevance. Adolescents are prepared to tackle sophisticated texts in order to appear 'in the know', adult fashion. At other times, both boys and girls, pressurised by examinations and the social complexities of their age groups, take time out to read the books they came to earlier, and to ponder the kind of world they want to live in.

To account for the range of texts, the diversity of topics, the differences between readers, and the vagaries of critical reactions in literature for adolescents, is to write a version of the history of social events of the last thirty years. It is also to to engage with the issues that emerge, including hypocrisy in social and political engagements, and global debates about how to protect the universe. As they confront incontinent streams of information in world-wide communication networks, young adults want to read about what matters. Dismayed by the single economic realism of their parents' generation, they salvage their imaginations by reading the chilling novels of Robert Cormier, where they discover the complexities of intergenerational betrayal in a book like *After the First Death* (1979). With some tactful help to encourage them to tolerate the uncertainties induced by unfamiliar narrative techniques, teenagers rediscover reading as an intellectual adventure. They learn to ask themselves 'Do I believe this? How reliable is this storyteller? What kind of company am I keeping in this book?' Good authors show them characters confronted by indecisions like their own in making choices. Happy endings are less in vogue than they once were.

Perhaps the most significant of the distinctive changes implied and dealt with in this Encyclopedia are those which differentiate readers and books in terms of gender, class and race. These issues and their ideological attachments go well beyond children's literature, but they have a part to play in books for readers more interested in the future than the past. As readers' responses are part of the adult involvement in writing for adolescents, and 'positive images' are now expected to be text-distinctive, then the influence of current thinking about these matters on authors of novels for adolescents is strong. Consider the effect of feminism on literature. 'Children' are no longer a homogeneous group of readers; they are constituted differently. In this volume Lissa Paul (Chapter 8) shows how the situated perspectives of boys and girls have now to be part of the consciousness of all writers and all readers. Girls have always read boys' books by adaptation, but boys have shown no eagerness, or have lacked encouragement, to do the same in reverse. Their tastes are said to be set in the traditional heroic tales of fable and legend and their reworkings as versions of Superman and other quest tales. Boys also seem to be more attracted to the portrayal of 'action' in graphic novels. Ted Hughes's modern myth, *The Iron Man* (1968) has a hero more complex than the Iron Woman, who, in her book of that name (1993), has little effective linguistic communication. She relies on a primeval scream.

At the end of the twentieth century, the most distinctive differences in children's books are those which reflect changes in social attitudes and understandings. In the late 1960s and early 1970s, the dominant white middle-class elite of children's book publishers in English-speaking countries was forced to acknowledge the presence in school classrooms of children who could not find themselves portrayed in the pictures or the texts they were given to read. In Britain, the Children's Rights Workshop asked publishers how many books on their lists showed girls playing 'a leading part', and let it be known that there were very few.

First attempts to redress the balance, the inclusion of a black face in a playground scene or an indistinct but benign 'foreigner' in a story, were dismissed as inept tokenism. In post-imperial Britain, two revisions were imperative: the renewal of school history texts to include the perspectives of different social groups, and the welcoming of new authors with distinctive voices and literary skill to the lists of books for the young. Topics, verbal rhythms and tones all changed, especially when a group of Caribbean writers went to read to children in schools. Consequently, as part of a more general enlightenment, local storytellers emerged, as after a long sleep, to tell local tales and to publish them. Now in Britain, children's literature represents more positively the multicultural life of the societies from which it emerges. At the same time, however, it is also the site for debates about 'politically correct' language to describe characters who represent those who have suffered discrimination or marginalisation.

Books of quality play their part in changing attitudes as well as simply reflecting them. But we are still a long way from accepting multicultural social life as the norm for all children growing up. Too many old conflicts intervene. Year by year, the fact that more and more people move to richer countries from poorer ones becomes evident. The next generation will encounter bilingualism and biliteracy as common, and the promotion of positive images of multicultural encounters is consequently important. Perhaps the isolation of monolingual readers of a dominant language such as English, who read 'foreign' literature in translation or not at all, will be less common.

Changes in the creation, production and distribution of children's books do not happen in a vacuum. They have been linked to the mutability of their economic environment at least since John Newbery offered *A Little Pretty Pocket Book* for 6d, or 'with ball or pincushion' for 8d in 1744. Publishing is as subject to market forces, take-over bids, the rise and fall in fashionable demand as other trading. 'Going out of print' is believed to be a more common occurrence now than ever before, but this may be an impression rather than a fact. Although their intrinsic worth is judged differently, all books are packaged to be sold. Publishers are involved in advertising deals, literary prizes, best-seller lists, and are careful when they select texts to carry their name. Authors also estimate their worth in pelf as in pages. Copyright laws are organised internationally but there too changes are current and continuous. It is interesting to note that when Geoffrey Trease wrote *Tales Out of School* in 1949, the 'outright purchase of juvenile copyright' (185) was still a common practice.

The number of outlets for children's books has increased; their locations are also different. This does not mean that the book in the shopping basket with the grocery beans is a lesser object of desire than one bought elsewhere. A bookshop may be a better place to choose from a wider range of books than a supermarket, but the popularity of books for the very young owes more to their availability than to the formal institutions intended to establish children's books as literature.

## Academic Attitudes

The first section of the Encyclopedia makes the claim, which the rest of the book is summoned to support, that children's literature is worthy of serious scholarly attention. The implication is that, like its adult counterpart, children's literature promotes and invites critical theory, notably in the study of the relation of texts to children's development as readers. The essays in this section document some recent moves in this direction so as to demonstrate the evolution of a discipline fit for academic recognition and institutionalised research.

Although many serious books about children's literature throw light on established ways of studying literature *tout pur*, conservative scholars and teachers, concerned about the dilutions of their topic specialisms and the blurring of canonical boundaries, have declared children's literature to be a soft reading option, academically lightweight. Once fairly widespread, this attitude has been increasingly eroded by those who have demonstrated in books for children both different kinds of texts and distinctive interactions between texts and readers. Scholars interested in the relation of literature to literacy, who ask questions about access to texts and exclusion from them, know that social differences in children's learning to read are part of any study of literary competences. Resistance to the notion of the 'universal child' and to common assumptions of what is 'normal' in interpretative reading provoke new questions, especially feminist ones, in ethnography, cultural studies and social linguistics. In all of these established disciplines there is a context for discussing the contents of children's books. But there is also the possibility for new perspectives which begin with books, children and reading. These have been slowly growing over time, but have not simply been accommodated elsewhere.

Shifts in this kind of awareness can be seen as far back as Henry James's recognition of the difference between *Treasure Island* and other Victorian novels for children. In 1949 Geoffrey Trease insisted that reviewers of post-war children's books needed new categories of judgement. For many years in the second half of this century in Britain, just to make children's books visible beyond the confines of specialist journals such as *Junior Bookshelf* and *The School Librarian* was something of a triumph. More support came from the London *Times Literary Supplement* in the 1960s, but children's literature remained a kind of appendage to serious publishing until the artists and authors who transformed it were backed by contracts, distribution and promotion so that they became socially recognisable. The world inside the books continued for a long time to be predominantly that of the literate middle classes. Critics thought that their obligation was to set the standards for the 'best' books, so as to separate 'literature' from ephemeral reading matter, comics and the like. If there was no evident body of criticism, no real acceptance of the necessary relation of literature to literacy, there were prizes for 'the best' books in different categories. Among these was 'The Other Award' to recognise what more conventional judges ignored or thought irrelevant: minority interests and social deprivation.

Academic research in children's literature is still a novelty if it is not psychological, historical or bibliographical – that is, detailed, factual, esoteric, fitting into the research traditions of diverse disciplines, especially those which establish their history, closed to those unschooled in the foundation exercises of the disciplines of dating. There is, I know, splendid writing about careful observations of children reading selected texts in hard-bound theses in some university libraries where education studies admit such topics. But who, besides competent tutors, admits as evidence the transcripts of classroom interactions which show readers breaking through the barriers of interpretation? Peter Hunt, reminding an audience in 1994 that the first British children's literature research conference was in 1979, suggested that this research enterprise has 'followed inappropriate models and mind-sets, especially with regard to its readership'. That is, 'we often produce *lesser* research when we should be producing *different* research' (Hunt 1994: 10). He advocates 'the inevitable interactiveness of "literature" and "the literary experience"' as worthy of analysis. Readers of the Encyclopedia will doubtless comment on this proposal.

Meanwhile, the most fully developed critical theory of children's literature is that of readers' responses to what they read. Michael Benton (Chapter 6) provides a full account of the history and the supporting adult studies of this approach. Most of the evidence for children's progress in reading and interpretation of literary texts comes from classrooms where teachers observe and appraise children's interactions with books as they read them. It is clear that individual children reveal 'personal patterns of reading behaviour irrespective of the books they read'. Benton's concern is to 'explore the ways in which we can learn from each other how children's responses to literature are mediated in by the cultural context in which they occur'. By foregrounding the readers' constitution of textual meaning, reading response theory has become the most frequently quoted theoretical position in relation to books for children. What it also makes clear is the lack of any fully grounded research on the nature of the development of these competences over the total period of children's schooling.

In contrast to the notion of 'response', critics who, like John Stephens (Chapter 5), derive their insights from social linguistics, stress the power of authors to make young readers 'surrender to the flow of the discourse'; that is, to become 'lost in a book'. Sociolinguists are concerned that, having learned to read, young people should be taught to discern the author's 'chosen registers', so as to discover how a text is composed or constructed. Then, the claim is, readers will understand, from their responses to the text, 'who is doing what to whom', and thus become 'critically' literate.

Even more challenging is Jacqueline Rose's assertion about the 'impossibility' of children's fiction ...

> the impossible relation between adult and child. Children's literature is clearly about that relation, but it has the remarkable characteristics of being about something which it hardly ever talks of. If children's fiction builds an image of the child inside the book, it does so in order to secure the child who is outside the book, the one who does not come so easily within its grasp.
>
> Rose 1984: 1

There are ways of countering this view, but none the less it has to be considered. Later, Rose offers a less controvertible utterance, probably the reason so many adult readers find solace in children's literature:

> Reading is magic (if it has never been experienced by the child as magic then the child will be unable to read); it is also an experience which allows the child to master the vagaries of living, to strengthen and fortify the ego, and to integrate the personality – a process ideally to be elicited by the aesthetic coherence of the book.
>
> Rose 1985: 135

Rose's examination of the textual condition of *Peter Pan*, the new tone of this criticism and the different paths she follows have opened up a number of possibilities for the theoretical consideration of children's books, even beyond the revelations that come from her social editing of the texts. One of these considerations is extended in Peter Hollindale's 'Ideology and the children's book'. Here children's literature is detached from the earlier division of those concerned with it into 'child people and book people', and firmly joined to studies of history and culture in the 'drastically divided country' that is Britain. Going beyond the visible surface features of a text children read in order to discover how they read it, Hollindale insists we 'take into account the individual writer's unexamined assumptions'. When we do that, we discover that 'ideology is an inevitable, untameable and largely uncontrollable factor in the transaction between books and children' (Hollindale 1988: 10). Thus we are bound to accept that all children's literature is inescapably didactic.

In the 1980s and 1990s, critics of children's literature have experimented with the take-over of the whole baggage of critical theory derived from adult literature and tried it for its fit. Most now agree that reading is sex-coded and gender inflected, that writers and artists have become aware that an array of audiences beyond the traditional literary elite are becoming readers of all kinds of texts. Moreover, before they leave school, children can learn to interrogate texts, to read 'against' them so that their literacy is more critical than conformist. Some theoretical positions are shown to have more explanatory power than others: intertextuality is a condition of much writing in English; metafiction is a game which even very young readers play skilfully (Lewis 1990). There are also experimental procedures, as yet untagged, which show artists and writers making the most of the innocence of beginning readers to engage them in new reading games.

If children's literature begets new critical theory and moves further into the academic circle it will become subject to institutional conventions and regulations which are not those of the old protectionist ethos. This may give new scholars more recognition, more power even, to decide what counts as children's literature and how it is to be studied. There will be no escape, however, from learning how children read their world, the great variety of its texts beyond print and pictures. Interactions of children and books will go on outside the academy, as has ever been the case, in the story-telling of young minds operating on society 'at the very edge of the forest', inventing, imagining, hypothesising, all in the future tense.

The contents of this Encyclopedia are a tribute to all, mentioned or not, who have worked in the domain of children's books during the twentieth century, and earlier. The hope is that, in the next millennium, by having been brought together here, their efforts will be continued and prove fruitful.

# References

Appleyard, J. A. (1990) *Becoming a Reader: the Experience of Fiction from Childhood to Adulthood*, Cambridge: Cambridge University Press.

Barthes, R. (1974) *S/Z: An Essay*, New York: Hill and Wang.

Bruner, J. (1986) *Actual Minds, Possible Worlds*, Cambridge, MA: Harvard University Press.

Carpenter, H. and Prichard, M. (1984) *The Oxford Companion to Children's Literature*, Oxford: Oxford University Press.

Carter, A. (1990) *The Virago Book of Fairy Tales*, London: Virago.

Cole, B. (1993) *Mummy Laid an Egg*, London: Cape.

Crago, H. and Crago, M. (1983) *Prelude to Literacy: A Pre-school Child's Encounter with Picture and Story*, Carbondale, IL: Southern Illinois University Press.

Darton, F. J. H. (1932/1982) *Children's Books in England: Five Centuries of Social Life*, 3rd edn, rev. B. Alderson, Cambridge: Cambridge University Press.

Eco, U. (1983) *Reflections on 'The Name of the Rose'*, trans. W. Weaver, London: Secker and Warburg.

Fisher, M. (1964) *Intent Upon Reading*, rev. edn, Leicester: Brockhampton Press.

Fox, C. (1993) *At the Very Edge of the Forest: The Influence of Literature on Storytelling by Children*, London: Cassell.

Garfield, L. (1985) *Shakespeare Stories*, London: Gollancz.

Hardy, B. (1968/1977) 'Narrative as a primary act of mind', in Meek, M., Warlow, A. and Barton, G. (eds) *The Cool Web*, London: Bodley Head.

Hollindale, P. (1988) 'Ideology and the children's book', *Signal* 55: 3–22.

Hunt, P. (1994) 'Researching the fragmented subject', in Broadbent, N., Hogan, A., Wilson, G. and Miller, M. (eds) *Research in Children's Literature: A Coming of Age?* Southampton: LSU.

Le Guin, U. (1981) 'Why are we huddling round the camp fire?', in Mitchell, W. J. T. (ed.) *On Narrative*, Chicago: Chicago University Press.

——(1989) *Dancing at the Edge of the World: Thoughts on Words, Women, Places*, London: Paladin.

Lewis, D. (1990) 'The constructedness of texts: picture books and the metafictive', *Signal* 62: 131–146.

Lurie, A. (1990) *Don't Tell the Grown-Ups: Subversive Children's Literature*, London: Bloomsbury.

McGann, J. J. (1991) *The Textual Condition*, Princeton, NJ: Princeton University Press.

Mackey, M. (1995) 'Communities of fictions: story, format, and Thomas the Tank Engine', *Children's Literature in Education* 26, 1: 39–52.

Paley, V. G. (1981) *Wally's Stories*, Cambridge, MA: Harvard University Press.

Philip, N. (1989) *The Cinderella Story: the Origins and Variations of the Story Known as 'Cinderella'*, London: Penguin.

Rose, J. (1984) *The Case of Peter Pan or The Impossibility of Children's Fiction*, London: Macmillan.

Rushdie, S. (1990) *Haroun and the Sea of Stories*, London: Granta.

Smith, F. (1990) *To Think*, New York: Teachers' College Press.

Townsend, J. R. (1965/1990) *Written for Children*, 5th edn, London: Bodley Head.

Trease, G. (1949) *Tales Out of School*, London: Heinemann.

Wolf, S. A. and Brice Heath, S. (1992) *The Braid of Literature: Children's Worlds of Reading*, Cambridge, MA: Harvard University Press.

Zipes, J. (1983) *Fairy Tales and the Art of Subversion*, New York: Wildman.

## Further Reading

Chambers, A. (1991) *The Reading Environment*, South Woodchester: Thimble Press.

Fry, D. (1985) *Children Talk About Books: Seeing Themselves as Readers*, Milton Keynes: Open University Press.

Scholes, R. (1989) *Protocols of Reading*, New Haven: Yale University Press.

Styles, M., Bearne, E. and Watson, V. (eds) (1994) *The Prose and the Passion: Children and Their Reading*, London: Cassell.

# Part I

# Theory and Critical Approaches

# 2

# Defining Children's Literature and Childhood

## Karín Lesnik-Oberstein

The definition of 'children's literature' lies at the heart of its endeavour: it is a category of books the existence of which absolutely depends on supposed relationships with a particular reading audience: children. The definition of 'children's literature' therefore is underpinned by purpose: it wants to be something in particular, because this is supposed to connect it with that reading audience – 'children' – with which it declares itself to be overtly and purposefully concerned. But is a children's book a book written by children, or for children? And, crucially: what does it mean to write a book 'for' children? If it is a book written 'for' children, is it then still a children's book if it is (only) read by adults? What of 'adult' books read also by children – are they 'children's literature'? As the British critic John Rowe Townsend points out:

> Surely *Robinson Crusoe* was not written for children, and do not the *Alice* books appeal at least as much to grown ups?; if *Tom Sawyer* is children's literature, what about *Huckleberry Finn*?; if the *Jungle Books* are children's literature, what about *Kim* or *Stalky*? and if *The Wind in the Willows* is children's literature, what about *The Golden Age*?; and so on.
>
> Townsend 1980: 196

Attempts to dismiss categorisation and definition of texts as a side issue which should not be an end in itself are very problematic when it comes to children's literature: how do we know which books are best for children if we do not even know which books *are* 'children's books'? For this is what 'children's literature' means in its most fundamental sense to every critic who uses the term: books which are good for children, and most particularly good in terms of emotional and moral values. We can see this view reflected in Canadian critic Michele Landsberg's belief that

> good books can do so much for children. At their best, they expand horizons and instil in children a sense of the wonderful complexity of life ... No other pastime available to children is so conducive to empathy and the enlargement of human sympathies. No other pleasure can so richly furnish a child's mind with the symbols, patterns, depths, and possibilities of civilisation.
>
> Landsberg 1987: 34

The meaning of children's literature as 'books which are good for children' in turn crucially indicates that the two constituent terms – 'children' and 'literature' – within the label 'children's literature' cannot be separated and traced back to original independent meanings, and then reassembled to achieve a greater understanding of what 'children's literature' is. Within the label the two terms totally qualify each other and transform each other's meaning for the purposes of the field. In short: the 'children' of 'children's literature' are constituted as specialised ideas of 'children', not necessarily related in any way to other 'children' (for instance those within education, psychology, sociology, history, art, or literature), and the 'literature' of 'children's literature' is a special idea of 'literature', not necessarily related to any other 'literature' (most particularly 'adult literature').

Having said this, one of the primary characteristics of most children's literature criticism and theory is that it assumes that the terms 'children' and 'literature' within 'children's literature' *are* separable and more or less independent of one another, and that they are directly related to other 'children' and 'literatures'; critics often make use of, or refer to, theories from education, psychology, sociology, history, art or literature, in buttressing their opinions. But in every case they transform the material from other disciplines to fit their own particular argument.

This complexity arises partly because the reading 'child' of children's literature is primarily discussed in terms of emotional responses and consciousness. Children's literature criticism, for instance, actually devotes little systematic discussion (but many random comments) to cognitive issues such as the correspondence between vocabulary lists composed by educational psychologists and the vocabulary levels in books, or to levels of cognitive development thought to be necessary to understanding the content of a book. These areas are regarded as the province of child psychologists, or as appropriate to the devising of strictly functional reading schemes which are not held to fall within 'children's literature'. This is the case even with the teachers' guides to children's literature (such as those of Lonsdale and Mackintosh 1973; Huck 1976; Sadker and Sadker 1977; Smith and Park 1977; Glazer and Williams 1979; and Norton 1983) which purport to be able to draw connections between psychological and educative investigations and children's books. (This exercise, even when it is seriously attempted, is in any case fraught with difficulties, and even in the best cases produces very limited results – one need only think of the ongoing debates in education on how to teach children the basic mechanics of reading itself.) In fact, in the actual discussion of works of children's literature, the critics' attention is primarily focused on whether and how they think the book will attract the 'child' – whether the 'child' will 'love' or 'like' the book.

But it is even more relevant to the problems of children's literature criticism that, although the idea that 'children's literature' might pose problems of definition is often accepted and discussed by critics, the idea that the 'child' might pose equal – if not greater – problems of definition is strenuously resisted. This is despite the fact that historians such as Philippe Ariès and anthropologists such as Margaret Mead and Martha Wolfenstein (1955) have argued in classic studies that – at the very least – definitions of 'childhood' have differed throughout history, and from culture to culture. As Ariès writes:

the point is that ideas entertained about these [family] relations may be dissimilar at moments separated by lengthy periods of time. It is the history of the idea of the family which concerns us here, not the description of manners or the nature of law ... The idea of childhood is not to be confused with affection for children: it corresponds to an awareness of the particular nature of childhood, that particular nature which distinguishes the child from the adult, even the young adult.

Ariès 1973: 8, 125

Ariès makes clear that the 'family' and 'childhood' are ideas that function within cultural and social frameworks as carriers of changeable social, moral, and ethical values and motives.

British theorist Jacqueline Rose further elaborates views such as those of Ariès with respect specifically to children's literature by applying them to contemporary processes within Western culture, rather than by tracing historical or cultural shifts. Rose argues that

children's fiction rests on the idea that there is a child who is simply there to be addressed and that speaking to it might be simple. It is an idea whose innocent generality covers up a multitude of sins ... *Peter Pan* stands in our culture as a monument to the impossibility of its own claims – that it represents the child, speaks to and for children, addresses them as a group which is knowable and exists for the book.

Rose 1984: 1

Rose points out that, to begin with, 'children' are divided by class, race, ethnic origins, gender, and so on, but her argument is more radical than that: to Rose, the 'child' is a construction invented for the needs of the children's literature authors and critics, and not an 'observable', 'objective', 'scientific', entity. Within Rose's argument the adults' needs are discussed within a Freudian terminology involving the unconscious, and Rose is therefore emphatically not arguing that this process of constructing the 'child', or books for it, can – or should – simply be stopped: it serves important functions which she is attempting to understand better in her terms. Children's literature and children's literature criticism have not, in fact, made much use of Rose's argument, and, indeed, in many ways they cannot, for the very existence of these fields depends utterly on a posited existence of the 'child': all their work is ostensibly on this 'child's' behalf. Yet, with or without Rose's argument, children's literature and its criticism continue to assume many different – and often contradictory – 'children', and this can only be accounted for by either accepting the notion of the 'child' as constructed (which, again, it should be noted, should not be taken to mean that it is superfluous or irrelevant: this use of 'construction' has to do with wider philosophical ideas about the way meaning works), or by maintaining that some critics are more correct about the child than others and adhering to their view.

The problems of children's literature criticism and theory, then, occur within the confines of the field of tension established by the contradictions and gaps between the assumption that 'children' and 'literature' have self-evident, consistent or logically derived meanings, and the actual use of 'children' and 'literature' within 'children's literature' in very specific, and often variable and inconsistent, ways. Attempts to define 'children's literature' and the reading 'child' thus also operate within this field of tensions. The British cultural theorist Fred Inglis argues that

> it is simply ignorant not to admit that children's novelists have developed a set of conventions for their work. Such development is a natural extension of the elaborate and implicit system of rules, orthodoxies, improvisations, customs, forms and adjustments which characterize the way any adult tells stories or simply talks at length to children.
>
> Inglis 1981: 101

Australian critic Barbara Wall agrees, and bases her whole analysis of children's books on 'the conviction that adults ... speak differently in fiction when they are aware that they are addressing children ... [This is] translated, sometimes subtly, sometimes obviously, into the narrator's voice ... [which defines] a children's book' (Wall 1991: 2–3). But British critic Nicholas Tucker points out that Inglis and Wall's type of view does not avoid the difficulty that: 'although most people would agree that there are obvious differences between adult and children's literature, when pressed they may find it quite difficult to establish what exactly such differences amount to' (Tucker 1981: 8).

Because it has been precisely the self-imposed task of children's literature critics to judge which books are good for children and why, all children's literature criticism and reviews abound with both implicit and overt statements concerning the definitions of 'children's literature', 'children' and 'literature'. When critics state in some way or another that this is a book they judge to be good for children this actually involves saying that the book is good because of what they think a book does for children, and this in turn cannot avoid revealing what they think children are and do (especially when they read). Joan Aiken, for instance, says she does not purposefully incorporate moral messages into her books because she feels that 'children have a strong natural resistance to phoney morality. They can see through the adult with some moral axe to grind almost before he opens his mouth' (Aiken 1973: 149), but Rosemary Sutcliff writes that 'I *am* aware of the responsibility of my job; and I do try to put over to the child reading any book of mine some kind of ethic' (Sutcliff 1973: 306). Pamela Travers, creator of *Mary Poppins* feels that 'You do not chop off a section of your imaginative substance and make a book specifically for children for – if you are honest – you have, in fact, no idea where childhood ends and maturity begins. It is all endless and all one' (Cott 1984: xxii), and E. B. White states that 'you have to write up, not down. Children are demanding ... They accept, almost without question, anything you present them with, as long as it is presented honestly, fearlessly, and clearly ... They love words that give them a hard time' (White 1973: 140). Austrian critic Maria Lypp, in line with Travers and White, argues that the adaptations children's authors introduce to children's literature depend on an 'asymmetrical relationship' which forms the 'code of children's fiction', but that there is an 'ideal of *symmetrical* communication' which implies true understanding between author and reader, and this becomes Lypp's prescriptive criterion for children's literature (Heimeriks and Van Toorn 1989: 370–372). However, Barbara Wall argues in contrast to Travers, White, and Lypp, that

> All writers for children must, in a sense, be writing down. If they write with an educated adult audience in mind – their own peers – their stories will surely be, at best not always interesting and probably often intelligible, and at worst positively harmful, to children, even when a child appears as a central character, as in *The Go-Between* or *What Maisie Knew*. Whenever a writer shows consciousness of an immature audience, in the sense of adapting the material of the story or the techniques of the discourse for the benefit of child readers, that writer might be said to be writing down, that is, acknowledging that there is a difference in the skills, interests and frame of reference of children and adults.
>
> Wall 1991: 15

But where Wall worries about harm to the child, Gillian Avery in turn believes that '[the child] has his own defence against what he doesn't like or doesn't understand in the book ... He ignores it, subconsciously perhaps, or he makes something different from it ... [Children] extract what they want from a book and no more' (Avery 1976: 33). This adult critics' defining of the 'child' cannot be formed or disrupted by any child's own voiced opinions or ideas because these are interpreted – selected or edited ('heard') – by adults for their purposes and from their perspectives. One aspect of this is reflected by Nicholas Tucker when he explains that

> Trying to discover some of the nature and effects of the interaction between children and their favourite books is by no means easy ... One simple-minded approach to the problem has always been to ask children themselves through various questionnaires and surveys, what exactly their books mean to them. Turning a powerful searchlight of this sort onto complex, sometimes diffuse patterns of reaction is a clumsy way of going about things, however, and children can be particularly elusive when interrogated like this, with laconic comments like 'Not bad' or 'The story's good' adding little to any researchers' understanding.
>
> Tucker 1981: 2

It may be noted at this point that children's literature's constant underlying assumption of the 'child' as a generic universality connects children's literature criticism all over the world. Children's literature criticism in different cultures is united by speaking of the 'child' as an existing entity – even though this 'existing entity' may be described differently in different cultures as it is described differently within cultures. The 'child' and its attendant 'children's literature' are often, in this sense, described as Western imports by critics from other cultures: Indonesian critic Sunindyo points out that

> as with other countries, Indonesian literature had its origins in an oral tradition ... The history of children's books in Indonesia at this time is to be found entirely within the history of Balai Pustaka, a government

publishing agency established in 1908 by the Government of the Netherlands East Indies [when Indonesia was a Dutch colony].

Sunindyo 1987: 44–45

Japanese critic Tadashi Matsui notes that in 1920s Japan the growth of 'large
cities with dense populations generated the birth of a middle class ... among
[whom] the ideas of European liberalism, the urban mode of living, free mass
education and a modern concept of the child were being fostered' (Matsui 1986–
1987: 14). Birgit Dankert, when noting the background to the development of
children's literature in Africa, draws attention to another aspect of response to
Western influences:

> In addition to many other cultural 'achievements', the former colonial
> powers also introduced children's books to Africa. These cultural imports
> elicited then (and elicit still today) the same ambivalent mixture of respect
> and rejection which characterises African reactions to so many other
> borrowings from former colonial powers ... If arguments in favor of
> children's books are brought up, then they resemble those of the early years
> of European children's literature: that children's books should educate, that
> they should preserve folk culture, that they should help guarantee Africa's
> transition to a culture of the written word, that they should support African
> cultural identity.

Hunt 1992: 112

The disparities between the various definitions of 'children's literature',
'children', and 'literature', are problematic to children's literature criticism
because they undermine the goal it sets itself. In this situation, children's literature
criticism's prescriptions or suggestions of reading for children become problematic, with critics attempting in different ways to assert the validity of their
particular views. Important social issues, such as racism, have led critics with the
same anti-racist orientation to differ utterly in their judgement of a book. For
instance, British critic Bob Dixon praises Paula Fox's *The Slave Dancer* (1973) as
being 'a novel of great horror and as great humanity ... [approaching] perfection
as a work of art' (Dixon 1977: 125), while American views have included Sharon
Bell Mathis's: 'an insult to black children' (Mathis 1977: 146), and Binnie Tate's
claim that it 'perpetuates racism ... [with] constantly repeated racist implications
and negative illusions [*sic*]' (Tate 1977: 152–153). The assumption that children's
books somehow affect children makes the issues crucial: does, or can, *The Slave
Dancer* perpetuate racism or does it counteract it (or does it do other things
altogether)? In each case children's literature critics inevitably ultimately resort to
one basic claim: that they know more about children or the child and how and why
it reads than the critics they disagree with.

In examining various attempts to define 'children's literature' we find a
constant assumption of the existence of the (reading) child (that is: the
assumption that there is such a thing as a unified, consistent, 'objective' 'child
reader') together with the capacity for knowing it that each critic claims for him-
or herself. This holds true for all children's literature critics, even if they claim
to be 'literary' critics of children's books, because the 'literary' is defined in

terms of how the book is supposed to affect the 'child'. Examining the processes of defining 'children's literature' and the 'child' which is essential to its project also illustrates the extent to which differences of opinion exist and threaten the coherence of children's literature criticism: in other words, how and why the definitions of children's literature and childhood matter so much to children's literature critics.

The first and most basic step critics take in defining 'children's literature' – and one which still receives primary emphasis in discussions around children's books – is to differentiate books used for didactic or educational purposes from 'children's literature'. F. J. Harvey Darton classically outlined this split that critics make between didactic books for children and children's 'literature': 'by "children's books" I mean printed works produced ostensibly to give children spontaneous pleasure and not primarily to teach them, nor solely to make them good, nor to keep them profitably quiet' (Darton 1932/1982: 1). To the children's literature critic the outstanding characteristic of 'children's literature' is that it is supposed to speak to the reading child through amusement and inherent appeal, and not through primarily didactic messages, which are described as being merely instructive, coercive, intrusive, or dull to the reading child. This also often comes to be the main means of indicating the 'literary' qualities of children's books. As Margery Fisher writes:

> We should not *expect* children's stories to be sermons or judicial arguments or sociological pamphlets. As independent works of art they must be allowed to appeal to the imagination, the mind, the heart on their own terms ... If a writer cannot say what he really feels, if he cannot be serious in developing a theme ... [If he has in any way to minimise] that approach to books for the young must eventually dilute their quality as mainstream literature.
>
> Haviland 1973: 273

This is how 'children's literature' defines 'literature': as something that in itself is good for children – that affects children better or more than non-literature – and this of course implies a world of assumptions about what the reading 'child' is and how it reads. Charlotte Huck sums up this view when she writes that 'good writing, or effective use of language ... will help the reader to experience the delight of beauty, wonder, and humor ... He will be challenged to dream dreams, to ponder, and to ask questions to himself' (Huck 1976: 4). This concept of the 'literary' causes many children's literature critics considerable problems in its own right. In attempting to preserve both an essential, coherent, consistent, 'child', and a concept of 'literature', critics find themselves struggling with statements which in their self-contradiction inadvertently betray the ways in which the 'child' and 'literature' mutually qualify and construct each other within children's literature criticism. Joan Glazer and Gurney Williams, for instance, first state that good children's books are characterised by 'strong materials – good plots, rich settings, well-developed characters, important themes, and artistic styles ... bold and imaginative language' (Glazer and Williams 1979: 34, 19), and that this 'freshness ... comes from the author. And in the author it begins with an understanding of who the child is' (22). Then they continue, however, by arguing that even if children don't like these books which are good for them, they may still be 'good literature ... built of strong materials ... the likes and dislikes of children do not determine the quality of literature ... Books must be judged as literature on their own merits. And children should be given excellent literature' (34).

'Children' in relation to reading have something to do with particular ideas about freedom and about emotion and consciousness, as Darton's statement implies; the 'child' develops as a concept produced by ideas of liberation from restriction and force, and is assigned various particular niches within cultural and societal structures. These ideas of literature and liberation are in fact derived from the ideals of Western liberal humanism, originating in classical Greek culture. This is clear if we compare Michele Landsberg, Charlotte Huck and Glazer and Williams's statements of the value of children's literature with the statement of the sixteenth-century humanist educationist Juan Luis Vives:

> poems contain subjects of extraordinary effectiveness, and they display human passions in a wonderful and vivid manner. This is called *energia*. There breathes in them a certain great and lofty spirit so that the readers are themselves caught into it, and seem to rise above their own intellect, and even above their own nature.
>
> Vives 1913: 126

There are not many clearer articulations of the power ascribed to literature in the intellectual, moral or emotional education of children that dominates the concern of children's literature critics despite all their protestations of resistance to education or the dreaded 'didacticism'.

We may, incidentally – with respect to this relationship between the 'child' and specific formulations of liberty or freedom – refer back to Tadashi Matsui's linking of 'the ideas of European liberalism, the urban mode of living, [and] free mass education' with 'a modern concept of the child', as well as to Birgit Dankert's statement on African children's literature, which highlights the complex status of children's literature. It is written of as if it can be a value-free carrier of an oral home culture (an 'innocent text'), when it is inevitable that as a product of a written culture's liberal arts educational ideals it carries these values with it, whatever the actual content of the book.

The Swedish critic Boel Westin echoes Darton while specifying further how this ostensible move away from didacticism is seen by the critics as moving from adult coercion to a consideration of the 'child':

> Well into the nineteenth century, [Swedish] children's books sought primarily to impress upon their young readers good morals, proper manners, and a sense of religion. In Sweden it was not until the turn of the twentieth century that children's literature began to respond to the needs of children rather than adults.
>
> Westin 1991: 7

'Children's literature' becomes defined as containing, both in form and content, the 'needs of children', and, therefore, this is how 'children's books' – written, published, sold, and usually bought, by adults – come to be spoken of as if the 'child' were *in the book*. As the New Zealand critic Sydney Melbourne states while discussing the portrayal of the Maori in children's books: 'What are we after? Not just cultural trappings – that's for sure. The essence of children? Yes ...' (Melbourne 1987: 102).

The intimate interconnections between definitions of reading children and children's literature are fully evident here: in many ways, critics define them as one and the same thing, and children's literature is often spoken of as if it had been written by children expressing their needs, emotions and experiences. As Lissa Paul writes when she compares the situations of women's writing and children's literature:

> as long as the signs and language of women's literature and children's literature are foreign, other, to male-order critics, it is almost impossible to play with meaning. So one of the primary problems feminist critics and children's literature critics have is how to recognize, define, and accord value to otherness.

> Paul 1990: 150

Paul discusses children's literature as if it were written by children and as if the situation were therefore the same as with books written by women, as she writes: 'But women make up more than half of the population of the world – and all of us once were children. It is almost inconceivable that women and children have been invisible and voiceless for so long' (150). In this way Paul submerges the fact that children's literature (when it is not written by women) may well be written by the very 'male-order critics' she is seeking release from (unless she is assuming, as many critics do, that writing children's literature involves becoming a child again). Myles McDowell, too, for instance, describes his 'child in the book' when he claims that

> Children's books are generally shorter; they tend to favour an active rather than a passive treatment, with dialogue and incident rather than description and introspection; child protagonists are the rule; conventions are much used; the story develops within a clear-cut moral schematism which much adult fiction ignores; children's books tend to be optimistic rather than depressive; language is child-oriented; plots are of a distinctive order, probability is often disregarded; and one could go on endlessly talking of magic, and fantasy, and simplicity, and adventure.

> McDowell 1973: 51

American critic and author Natalie Babbitt, on the other hand, argues with respect to these type of criteria – and her 'child in the book' – that children's books are neither necessarily less serious than adults' books, nor necessarily concerned with 'simpler' or 'different' emotions: 'there is, in point of fact, no such thing as an exclusively adult emotion, and children's literature deals with them all' (Babbitt 1973: 157). Babbitt then claims that there is also no genuine disparity in range or scope, 'Everyman' being just as present, for instance, in *The Wind in the Willows* as in, say, James Joyce's *Ulysses*. Furthermore, to Babbitt, there are few differences in content between adult and children's literature: 'war, disability, poverty, cruelty, all the harshest aspects of life are present in children's literature' (157), as is fantasy.

Language usage does not seem to Babbitt necessarily to distinguish children's literature from adult literature either:

> A children's book uses simple vocabulary geared to the untrained mind? Compare a little Kipling to a little Hemingway and think again. Opening sentence of *A Farewell to Arms*: 'Now in the fall the trees were all bare and the roads were muddy'. Opening sentence of *How the Rhinoceros Got His Skin*: 'Once upon a time, on an uninhabited island on the shores of the Red Sea, there lived a Parsee from whose hat the rays of the sun were reflected in more-than-oriental splendour'. So much for that!
>
> Babbit 1973: 157

One side-effect, incidentally, of the idea that 'children's literature' originated from a historical revelation of the 'child' and 'its needs' (John Locke and Jean-Jacques Rousseau are quoted as standard in this context as the 'discoverers' of childhood) is that many (although not all) critics tend to describe and define 'children's literature' in evolutionary terms: consciously or unconsciously 'children's literature' is described as progressing towards an ever better and more accurate inclusion of the 'child' in the book. As Boel Westin writes with respect to the history of Swedish children's literature:

> After the Second World War, new trends in child psychology and a freer educational approach, prompted by such figures as Bertrand Russell and A. S. Neill, gained widespread acceptance in Sweden. The child's urge to play and seek pleasure was now to be gratified at the different stages of growth. In children's literature the world was now to be portrayed through the eyes and voice of the child itself.
>
> Westin 1991: 22

Within this type of thinking the 'classics' of 'children's literature' are often described as being avant garde or exceptionally and anachronistically perspicacious with respect to the 'child'. Barbara Wall, for instance, explains the classic status of *Alice in Wonderland*, by arguing that

> Alice's became the first child-mind, in the history of children's fiction, to occupy the centre ... No narrator of a story for children had stood so close to a child protagonist, observing nothing except that child, describing, never criticising, showing only what that child saw.
>
> Wall 1991: 98

The children's literature critics' didactic–literary split continues and maintains its career as one of the ultimate judgements of the value – and therefore definition – of 'children's literature'. It is in these statements that the 'child' in the book – in all its various manifestations – is defined by each critic. Sheila Egoff, for instance, writes:

> May I suggest that the aim of children's writing be delight not edification; that its attributes be the eternal childlike qualities of wonder; simplicity,

laughter and warmth; and that in the worldwide realm of children's books, the literature be kept inside, the sociology and pedagogy out.

> Egoff 1987: 355

Yoko Inokuma, similarly, in discussing writing about minority groups in Japanese children's literature, argues that

> the didactic motive of the authoress is quite clear ... There is no doubt about the legitimacy of her motive. But both Korean and Japanese readers will find it difficult to identify themselves with the characters who are only one dimensional ... Finally ... his [Imao Hirano's] desire to enlighten Japanese children ... betrayed him into producing an autobiography of a mediocre literary value ... Books of high literary value are, after all, short cuts to the real understanding of and sympathy with minority groups.
>
> Inokuma 1987: 75, 76, 82

Inokuma's statement introduces a word which is a mainstay of children's literature critics: 'identification'. The idea of 'identification' as an explanation of how and why the 'child' reads in turn supports the assumption that the 'child' is in the good 'children's book': the 'child' is supposed to be inherently and voluntarily attracted to books in which it recognises itself. As the Israeli critic Adir Cohen claims:

> Writers have become aware that, for the child, a book is a source of satisfaction that derives from identification and participation, and an expansion of his own experience. They provide him with an opportunity for catharsis, self-knowledge, and broadening his psychic experience. The process of reading, identification, participation and relating brings the reader into the reality of the book in dynamic fashion.
>
> Cohen 1988: 31

But 'identification' is caught up in the same debates concerning the definition of the 'child'. Since the supposed process of 'identification' depends on the definition of the 'child' the critic employs; different definitions lead to different evaluations of a book's ability to lead to the child reader achieving 'identification', and this also involves different concepts of what 'identification' actually is and does. The whole discussion, however, emphasises the persistence and depth of the assumption of the existence of an essential 'child': how otherwise could the notion of 'identification' be thought to function with respect to children's fiction, which by definition has a complex relationship to 'reality'? An essential 'child' in fiction is still supposed to be recognised by the 'reading child' as 'real'.

Implicit and overt assumptions about the 'child' and children's literature thus permeate explanations of 'identification', as we saw already in Adir Cohen's statement. Donna Norton describes 'identification' as a 'process [which] requires emotional ties with the model; children believe they are like these models and their thoughts, feelings, and characteristics become similar to them' (Norton 1983: 20). American critics Judith Thompson and Gloria Woodard draw the conclusion from this premise that one limitation to [many] books, however, is their emphasis on, identification with, and relevance only to middle class children. For too many black children, they depict an environment removed from their immediate experience ... Identification for the young black reader rests in the central character's intimate knowledge of the black subculture.

Thompson and Woodard 1972: 23

But British critic Robert Leeson complicates this type of 'identification' as a description of the central mechanism of the emotional process of reading by pointing out that although he feels the 'child' needs 'to recognise himself or herself ... it is [also] argued that the working-class child does not want "only to read about itself" and likes to escape into a different world in its reading ... to escape and have vicarious pleasure and thrills' (Leeson 1977: 43). For Leeson, the good book for the 'child' offers not only the 'child' back to itself, but also needs to offer the 'child' that which is not itself. 'Identification' – despite its widespread and often unquestioned use – remains a problematic concept: it must assume a 'child in the book'; even if that 'child's' presence is assumed, 'identification' cannot account for reading which is not a perpetual reading of the self; and, finally, it cannot account therefore for other hypothetical processes in reading such as a possible learning of the new, or escapism, or what D. W. Harding has called 'imaginative insight into what another person may be feeling, and the contemplation of possible human experiences which we are not at that moment going through ourselves' (Harding 1967: 7).

The definitions of children's literature and childhood are thus enmeshed within the discourse of children's literature. They mutually qualify each other. Tension and problems arise within children's literature criticism because children's literature critics implicitly assume that there are independent, essential definitions of 'literature' and 'childhood' which only meet, to their mutual benefit, within children's literature and its criticism. Children's literature critics reveal this inherent assumption throughout their writings: besides the inherent contradictions and disagreements that I have touched on, this becomes most clear when critics attempt to divide themselves, for instance, into 'book people' and 'child people' (Townsend 1980: 199). Townsend argues that

most disputes over standards are fruitless because the antagonists suppose their criteria to be mutually exclusive; if one is right the other must be wrong. This is not necessarily so. Different kinds of assessment are valid for different purposes ... I would only remark that the viewpoints of psychologists, sociologists, and educationists of various descriptions have rather little in common with each other or with those whose approach is mainly literary.

Townsend 1980: 193–207

Townsend's suggestion, however, has not lessened the problem (for children's literature itself!) of differing 'children' – and thus conflicting interpretations of books – occurring within even the works of critics who regard themselves as belonging to the same 'camp'. Children's literature and children's literature criticism define themselves as existing because of, and for, 'children', and it is these 'children' who remain the passion of – and therefore the source of conflict for – children's authors and critics.

# References

Aiken, J. (1973) 'Purely for love', in Haviland, V. (ed.) *Children and Literature: Views and Reviews*, London: Bodley Head.

Ariès, P. (1973) *Centuries of Childhood*, Harmondsworth: Penguin.

Avery, G. (1976) 'A sense of audience – 2', in Fox, G. *et al.* (eds) *Writers, Critics, and Children: Articles from 'Children's Literature in Education'*, London: Heinemann Educational Books.

Babbitt, N. (1973) 'Happy endings? Of course, and also joy', in Haviland, V. (ed.) *Children and Literature: Views and Reviews*, London: Bodley Head.

Cohen, A. (1988) 'The changing face of Israeli children's literature: forty years of creativity', *Modern Hebrew Literature* new series 1: 25–31.

Cott, J. (1984) *Pipers at the Gates of Dawn: The Wisdom of Children's Literature*, London: Viking.

Darton, F. J. H. (1932/1982) *Children's Books In England: Five Centuries of Social Life*, 3rd edn, rev. B. Alderson, Cambridge: Cambridge University Press.

Dixon, B. (1977) *Catching Them Young*. Vol. 1: *Sex, Race and Class in Children's Fiction*, London: Pluto Press.

Egoff, S. (1987) 'Inside and out: a Canadian's view of trends in contemporary children's literature', in Lees, S. (ed.) *A Track to Unknown Water: Proceedings of the Second Pacific Rim Conference on Children's Literature*, Metuchen, NJ: Scarecrow Press.

Glazer, J. I. and Williams G, III (1979) *Introduction to Children's Literature*, New York: McGraw-Hill.

Harding, D. W. (1967) 'Considered experience: the invitation of the novel', *English in Education* 2, 1: 3–14.

Haviland, V. (ed.) (1973) *Children and Literature: Views and Reviews*, London: Bodley Head.

Heimeriks, N. and Van Toorn, W. (eds) (1989) *De Hele Bibelebontse Berg. De Geschiedenis van het Kinderboek in Nederland en Vlaanderen van de Middeleeuwen tot Heden [The Whole 'Bibelebonts' Mountain: The History of Children's Books in The Netherlands and Flanders from the Middle Ages to the Present]*, Amsterdam: Em. Querido.

Huck, C. S. (1976) *Children's Literature in the Elementary School*, 3rd edn, New York: Holt, Rinehart and Winston.

Hunt, P. (ed.) (1992) *Literature for Children: Contemporary Criticism*, London: Routledge.

Inglis, F. (1981) *The Promise of Happiness: Value and Meaning in Children's Literature*, Cambridge: Cambridge University Press.

Inokuma, Y. (1987) 'The present situation of stories about minority groups in Japan', in Lees, S. (ed.) *A Track to Unknown Water: Proceedings of the Second Pacific Rim Conference on Children's Literature*, Metuchen, NJ: Scarecrow Press.

Landsberg, M. (1987) *Reading for the Love of It: Best Books for Young Readers*, New York: Prentice-Hall.

Leeson, R. (1977) *Children's Books and Class Society: Past and Present*, Children's Rights Workshop (ed.) Papers on Children's Literature no. 3, London: Writers and Readers Publishing Cooperative.

Lonsdale, B. J. and Mackintosh, H. K. (1973) *Children Experience Literature*, New York: Random House.

McDowell, M. (1973) 'Fiction for children and adults: some essential differences', *Children's Literature in Education* 10: 551–563.

Mathis, S. B. (1977) '*The Slave Dancer* is an insult to Black children', in MacCann, D. and

Woodard, G. (eds) *Cultural Conformity in Books for Children: Further Readings in Racism*, Metuchen, NJ: Scarecrow Press.

Matsui, Tadashi (1986–1987) 'A personal encounter with Kodomo no kuni: a vanguard Tokyo periodical of the twenties and thirties', *Phaedrus: An International Annual of Children's Literature Research* 7, 2/3: 14–18.

Mead, M. and Wolfenstein, M. (1955) *Childhood in Contemporary Cultures*, Chicago: University of Chicago Press.

Melbourne, S. (1987) 'The portrayal of the Maori in New Zealand children's fiction', in Lees, S. (ed.) *A Track to Unknown Water: Proceedings of the Second Pacific Rim Conference on Children's Literature*, Metuchen, NJ: Scarecrow Press.

Norton, D. E. (1983) *Through the Eyes of a Child: An Introduction to Children's Literature*, Columbus, OH: Charles E. Merrill.

Paul, L. (1990) 'Enigma variations: what feminist theory knows about children's literature', in Hunt, P. (ed.) *Children's Literature: The Development of Criticism*, London: Routledge.

Rose, J. (1984) *The Case of Peter Pan or: The Impossibility of Children's Fiction*, London: Macmillan.

Sadker, M. P. and Sadker, D. M. (1977) *Now Upon A Time: A Contemporary View of Children's Literature*, New York: Harper and Row.

Smith, J. A. and Park, D. M. (1977) *Word Music and Word Magic: Children's Literature Methods*, Boston: Allyn and Bacon.

Sunindyo (1987) 'Publishing and translating in Indonesia', in Lees, S. (ed.) *A Track to Unknown Water: Proceedings of the Second Pacific Rim Conference on Children's Literature*, Metuchen, NJ: Scarecrow Press.

Sutcliff, R. (1973) 'History is people', in Haviland, V. (ed.) *Children and Literature: Views and Reviews*, London: Bodley Head.

Tate, B. (1977) 'Racism and distortions pervade *The Slave Dancer*', in MacCann, D. and .Woodard, G. (eds) *Cultural Conformity in Books for Children: Further Readings in Racism*, Metuchen, NJ: Scarecrow Press.

Thompson, J. and Woodard, G. (1972) 'Black perspective in books for children', in MacCann, D. and Woodard, G. (eds) *The Black American in Books for Children: Readings in Racism*, Metuchen, NJ: Scarecrow Press.

Townsend, J. R. (1980) 'Standards of criticism for children's literature', in Chambers, N. (ed.) *The Signal Approach to Children's Books*, London: Kestrel Books.

Tucker, N. (1981) *The Child and the Book: A Psychological and Literary Exploration*, Cambridge: Cambridge University Press.

Vives, J. L. (1913) *On Education: A Translation of the 'De Tradendis Disciplinis' of Juan Luis Vives*, intro. and trans. F. Watson, Cambridge: Cambridge University Press.

Wall, B. (1991) *The Narrator's Voice: The Dilemma of Children's Fiction*, London: Macmillan.

Westin, B. (1991) *Children's Literature in Sweden*, trans. S. Croall, Stockholm: The Swedish Institute.

White, E. B. (1973) 'On writing for children', in Haviland, V. (ed.) *Children and Literature: Views and Reviews*, London: Bodley Head.

## Further Reading

Egoff, S., Stubbs, G. T. and Ashley, L. F. (eds) (1969) *Only Connect: Readings on Children's Literature*, Toronto: Oxford University Press.

Hunt, P. (ed.) (1990) *Children's Literature: The Development of Criticism*, London: Routledge.

——(ed.) (1991) *Criticism, Theory and Children's Literature*, Oxford: Basil Blackwell.

Lesnik-Oberstein, K. B. (1994) *Children's Literature: Criticism and the Fictional Child*, Oxford: Clarendon Press.

Meek, M., Warlow, A. and Barton, G. (eds) (1977) *The Cool Web: The Pattern of Children's Reading*, London: Bodley Head.

Salway, L. (ed.) (1976) *A Peculiar Gift: Nineteenth Century Writings on Books for Children*, Harmondsworth: (Penguin) Kestrel Books.

Shavit, Z. (1986) *Poetics of Children's Literature*, Athens, GA: University of Georgia Press.

# 3

# History, Culture and Children's Literature

## *Tony Watkins*

Until the late 1970s, there was (outside Marxist criticism) a generally accepted view of the nature of history and its place in literary studies. Perkins (1991) points out that during most of the nineteenth century, literary history was popular and enjoyed prestige because it produced a more complete appreciation of the literary work than was otherwise possible. It functioned, too, as a form of historiography, revealing the ' "spirit", mentality or *Weltanschauung* of a time and place with unrivaled precision and intimacy' (Perkins 1991: 2). For much of the twentieth century, especially in Renaissance studies, history was seen as outside literature and as guaranteeing the truth of a literary interpretation: 'History ... was the single, unified, unproblematic, extra-textual, extra-discursive real that guaranteed our readings of the texts which constituted its cultural *expression*' (Belsey 1991: 26). In the traditional literary view of history and culture, there was no difficulty in relating text to context: history was singular and operated as a 'background' to the reading of a work of literature ('the foreground'); and culture was something which the work reproduced or expressed, or could be set against. Literary history was 'a hybrid but recognizable genre that co-ordinated literary criticism, biography, and intellectual/social background within a narrative of development' (Buell 1993: 216).

Such notions have, until recently, remained the dominant ones behind the histories of children's literature. Thus, John Rowe Townsend, in the fifth edition (1990) of his standard one-volume history of children's literature, *Written for Children*, writes 'While I have tried to see children's literature in its historical and social contexts, my standards are essentially literary' (xi). However, in the 1970s, there was 'a Turn toward History' (Cox and Reynolds 1993: 3) in American adult literary theory as it began to move away from the dominance of deconstruction. The consequent reconceptualisation of history and its relationship to literature had its roots in the work of such theorists and critics as Michel Foucault, Raymond Williams, Edward Said and Frank Lentricchia. In the 1980s, new terms associated with literary history (including 'the new history', 'cultural poetics' and, especially, 'the New Historicism') entered the critical vocabulary through the work of such critics as Stephen Greenblatt, Louis Montrose and Jerome McGann.

The '*new* historicism' is distinguished from the old by a lack of faith in the objectivity of historical study and, instead, an emphasis on the way the past is constructed or invented in the present. Felperin quotes the opening paragraph of Catherine Belsey's *The Subject of Tragedy* (1985):

History is always in practice a reading of the past. We make a narrative out of the available 'documents', the written texts (and maps and buildings and suits of armour) we interpret in order to produce a knowledge of a world which is no longer present. And yet it is always from the present that we produce this knowledge: from the present in the sense that it is only from what is still extant, still available that we make it; and from the present in the sense that we make it out of an understanding formed by the present. We bring what we know now to bear on what remains from the past to produce an intelligible history.

He comments: ' "history" is freely acknowledged to be a kind of story-telling towards the present, that is, a textual construct at once itself an interpretation and itself open to interpretation' (Felperin 1991: 89). The idea of a single 'History' is rejected in favour of the postmodern concept (Belsey 1991: 27) of 'histories', 'an ongoing series of human constructions, each representing the past at particular present moments for particular present purposes' (Cox and Reynolds 1993: 4).

The growth of radical alternative histories, such as women's history, oral history, and post-colonial rewriting of Eurocentric and other imperialist view-points, together with the more general blurring of disciplinary boundaries between historiography, sociology, anthropology and cultural studies, have all cast doubt on the validity, relevance or accessibility of historical 'facts' (Barker *et al.* 1991: 4). Cultural history draws closer to the concerns of the humanities and anthropology: 'The deciphering of meaning ... is taken to be the central task of cultural history, just as it was posed by Geertz to be the central task of cultural anthropology' (Hunt 1989: 12). With the emergence of the postmodern concept of 'histories' several questions have been put on the agenda of theory: for example, what valid distinctions can be made between the 'narrative' of history and the 'fiction' of texts? (Montrose (1989: 20) called for the recognition of 'the historicity of texts and the textuality of history'; see also White (1973).) What are the implications of our construction of the past from our present situation? What is the relationship between 'histories' and power?

The rise of newer forms of literary historicism is connected, in part, with social change and the effort to recover histories for blacks, women and minority groups within society. In turn, these social aims are linked with the recuperation of forgotten texts, including texts that have never been considered worthy of academic study. Such changes have, of course, benefited the academic study of children's literature.

The major influence in all this is that of Michel Foucault. As David Perkins puts it,

[Foucault] encouraged his readers to reject the traditional Romantic model of literary change as continuous development, to resituate literary texts by relating them to discourses and representations that were not literary, and to explore the ideological aspects of texts in order to intervene in the social struggles of the present, and these remain characteristic practices of present-day historical contextualism – of New Historicism, feminist historiography, and cultural criticism.

Perkins 1991: 4

Not everyone, however, would agree with the implied radical political stance of the new historicist movements. H. Aram Veeser, in his introduction to a 1994 collection of readings, asks of New Historicism, 'Is it liberal or Leftist? Literary or historical? Feminist or neuter? Reformist or radical? Canon-making or canon-smashing? Stabilizing or capsizing?' (Veeser 1994: 2) and points out that many believe that New Historicism is 'bent on neutralizing solidarity, subversion, disruption, and struggle' and that it 'entertained from the first the heresy of a good capitalism' (3). But he manages to give the following five-point definition of the assumptions held by New Historicists:

> 1) that every expressive act is embedded in a network of material practices;
> 2) that every act of unmasking, critique, and opposition uses the tools it condemns and risks falling prey to the practice it exposes;
> 3) that literary and non-literary 'texts' circulate inseparably;
> 4) that no discourse, imaginative or archival, gives access to unchanging truths or expresses unalterable human nature;
> 5) that a critical method and language adequate to describe culture under capitalism participate in the economy they describe.
>
> Veeser 1994: 2

Felperin argues that there are two broad schools of New Historicism, the American, sometimes called 'cultural poetics', and the British, often referred to as 'cultural materialism': 'Whereas cultural poetics inhabits a discursive field in which Marxism has never really been present, its British counterpart inhabits one from which Marxism has never really been absent' (Felperin 1991: 88). The radical nature of cultural materialism is made clear in books such as Dollimore and Sinfield's collection of essays, *Political Shakespeare*. In their foreword, the editors define cultural materialism as 'a combination of historical context, theoretical method, political commitment and textual analysis' (Dollimore and Sinfield 1985: vii). The historical context,

> undermines the transcendent significance traditionally accorded to the literary text and allows us to recover its histories; theoretical method detaches the text from immanent criticism which seeks only to reproduce it in its own terms; socialist and feminist commitment confronts the conservative categories in which most criticism has hitherto been conducted; textual analysis locates the critique of traditional approaches where it cannot be ignored. We call this 'cultural materialism'.
>
> Dollimore and Sinfield 1985: vii

Examples of how some of these new historicist ideas could be applied to children's literature are provided by the work of Mitzi Myers (Myers 1988; 1989; 1992). In a statement which blends something of the American and the British brands, Myers argues that a new historicism of children's literature would

> integrate text and socio-historic context, demonstrating on the one hand how extraliterary cultural formations shape literary discourse and on the other how literary practices are actions that make things happen – by shaping the psychic and moral consciousness of young readers but also by

performing many more diverse kinds of cultural work, from satisfying authorial fantasies to legitimating or subverting dominant class and gender ideologies ... It would want to know how and why a tale or poem came to say what it does, what the environing circumstances were (including the uses a particular sort of children's literature served for its author, its child and adult readers, and its culture), and what kinds of cultural statements and questions the work was responding to. It would pay particular attention to the conceptual and symbolic fault lines denoting a text's time-, place-, gender-, and class-specific ideological mechanisms ... It would examine ... a book's material production, its publishing history, its audiences and their reading practices, its initial reception, and its critical history, including how its got inscribed in or deleted from the canon.

Myers 1988: 42

Myers has also argued that 'Notions of the "child", "childhood" and "children's literature" are contingent, not essentialist; embodying the social construction of a particular historical context; they are useful fictions intended to redress reality as much as to reflect it' (Myers 1989: 52), and that such notions today are bound up with the language and ideology of Romantic literature and criticism (Myers 1992; see also McGann 1983).

These ideas have been applied by Myers to eighteenth-century children's authors such as Maria Edgeworth. The child constructed by Romantic ideology recurs as Wordsworth's 'child of nature' in such figures as Kipling's Mowgli and Frances Hodgson Burnett's Dickon in *The Secret Garden* (Knoepflmacher 1977; Richardson 1992) and, as one critic points out, 'many children's books that feature children obviously wiser than the adults they must deal with – like F. Anstey's *Vice Versa* or E. Nesbit's *Story of the Amulet* – would have been unthinkable without the Romantic revaluation of childhood' (Richardson 1992: 128).

The same crises in the humanities which resulted in radical questioning of the nature of history and the emergence of new historiographies of culture, including literary New Historicism, also brought forth cultural studies. It is difficult to define the field of cultural studies very precisely because, as Brantlinger argues, it has 'emerged from the current crises and contradictions of the humanities and social science disciplines not as a tightly coherent, unified movement with a fixed agenda, but as a loosely coherent group of tendencies, issues and questions' (1990: ix). Nevertheless, there are several points of similarity between the new literary historicism and cultural studies and their relevance to the study of children's literature. For example, it is possible to see such works as Grahame's *The Wind in the Willows* and Baum's *The Wizard of Oz*, not only operating as versions of the English and American national myth with their landscapes representing the 'real' England and the 'real' America, but becoming sites for ideological struggle and appropriation by, for example, the 'culture industries' (Watkins 1992).

In *Keywords*, Raymond Williams describes culture as 'one of the two or three most complicated words in the English language' (Williams 1976: 76). Culture is an ambiguous term: a problem shared, perhaps, by all concepts which are concerned with totality, including history, ideology, society, and myth. 'Cultural studies' is an equally ambiguous term, but most commentators would agree that cultural studies is 'concerned with the generation and circulation of meanings in industrial societies' (Fiske 1987: 254). An anthology published in 1992 suggests the following major categories of current work in the field:

> the history of cultural studies, gender and sexuality, nationhood and national identity, colonialism and post-colonialism, race and ethnicity, popular culture and its audiences, science and ecology, identity politics, pedagogy, the politics of aesthetics, cultural institutions, the politics of disciplinarity, discourse and textuality, history, and global culture in a postmodern age.
>
> Grossberg *et al.* 1992: 1

But the editors of the volume stress the shapeless nature of the field and the variety of methodologies in use: '[cultural studies] remains a diverse and often contentious enterprise, encompassing different positions and trajectories in specific contexts, addressing many questions, drawing nourishment from multiple roots, and shaping itself within different institutions and locations' (2–3). There are, for example, distinctions to be made between the British and American traditions of cultural studies. The British tradition may be traced back to the pioneering work of F. R. Leavis and Denys Thompson in the 1930s (Leavis and Thompson 1933), but, more particularly, it arises from the work of Raymond Williams (Williams 1958). The British tradition, it is claimed, believes that the study of culture involves both 'symbolic and material domains ... not privileging one domain over the other but interrogating the relation between the two ... Continually engaging with the political, economic, erotic, social, and ideological, cultural studies entails the study of all the relations between all the elements in a whole way of life' (Grossberg *et al.* 1992: 4; 14). From the later work of Raymond Williams, from the work of Stuart Hall and others at the University of Birmingham's Centre for Contemporary Cultural Studies, and from major bodies of theory such as Marxism, feminism, psychoanalysis and poststructuralism, the British tradition derived the central theoretical concepts of articulation, conjuncture, hegemony, ideology, identity, and representation. (See, for example, Williams 1975; 1976; 1977; 1989; Hall *et al.* 1980; Hall 1990.) But even British cultural studies is not a coherent and homogeneous body of work: it is characterised by disagreements, 'divergencies in direction and concern, by conflict among theoretical commitments and political agendas' (Grossberg *et al.* 1992: 10).

In the USA, a somewhat different inflection has been given to cultural studies by the 'new ethnography', rooted primarily in anthropological theory and practice (a 'postdisciplinary anthropology') which is, in turn, linked to work by feminists and black and postcolonial theorists concerned with identity, history and social relations. (Grossberg *et al.* 1992: 14).

In some of the cultural studies theorists, one can detect the following characteristics: first, a belief that reality can only be made sense of through language or other cultural systems which are embedded within history. Second, a focus upon power and struggle. In cultural terms, the struggle is for meaning: dominant groups attempt to render as 'natural' meanings which serve their interests, whereas subordinate groups resist this process in various ways, trying to make meanings that serve *their* interests. (Fiske 1987: 255). An obvious example is the cultural struggle between patriarchy and feminism; but, of course, divisions into groups in society can be along lines of race, class, age and so on, as well as gender. Third, cultural studies has tried to theorise subjectivity as a socio-cultural construction. Some theorists, under the influence of poststructuralist psycho-analytical thinking and Althusserian notions of ideology, replace the idea of the individual by the concept of the 'subject'. The 'subject' and his or her 'subjectivity' is a social construction: 'Thus a biological female can have a masculine subjectivity (that is, she can make sense of the world and of her self and her place in that world through patriarchal ideology). Similarly, a black can have a white subjectivity' (Fiske 1987: 258).

But, because subjectivity is a social construction, it is always open to change. All cultural systems, including language, literature and the products of mass communication, play a part in the construction and reconstruction of the subject. It is in this way, according to the Althusserian wing of cultural studies, that ideology is constantly reproduced in people.

This notion can be seen perhaps more clearly in the fourth characteristic of cultural studies – the way it views acts of communication, including the 'reading process'. As one theorist puts it when talking about the 'reading' of a television programme as cultural text: 'Reading becomes a negotiation between the social sense inscribed in the program and the meanings of social experience made by its wide variety of viewers: this negotiation is a discursive one' (Fiske 1987: 268). The relevance of this notion to children's literature is not difficult to perceive.

The fifth characteristic is that cultural studies is not exclusively concerned with popular culture to the exclusion of 'high' culture, or vice versa: 'Cultural studies does not require us to repudiate elite cultural forms ... rather cultural studies requires us to identify the operation of specific practices, of how they continuously reinscribe the line between legitimate and popular culture, and of what they accomplish in specific contexts' (Grossberg et al. 1992: 13). As a result, cultural studies does interest itself in the formation, continuation and changes in literary canons, including those of children's literature. For example, books originally denied inclusion in the canon of children's literature, such as Baum's Oz books, have later received recognition and have been included. Other books traditionally included in the canon of children's literature, such as Lewis's Narnia series, Tolkien's The Hobbit, and Kipling's Jungle Book have been criticised on the grounds that the values they contain are too exclusively male and white.

The sixth characteristic is the use of ideology as a central concept, either as a 'critical' concept or as a neutral concept. Materialist, political approaches deriving from Marxism and feminism obviously stress power as the major component of cultural text, power which is often hidden or rendered apparently 'natural' through the process of ideology. These approaches use what has been called the 'critical' concept of ideology which is 'essentially linked to the process of sustaining asymmetrical relations of power – that is, to the process of maintaining domination' (Thompson 1984: 4). If ideology is embodied in cultural text, the major task of the cultural critic is not only understanding the meaning of the text but also unmasking what appears as natural as a social construction which favours a particular class or group in society. This process of 'ideology critique' or ideological deconstruction is often carried out in literary studies using an approach, derived from Williams, involving a combination of textual analysis, theoretical method, study of historical context, and a political commitment to socialism and feminism.

However, ideology can also be used in a neutral sense (Ricoeur 1986) and this is reflected in the work of Fred Inglis, who has written at length on children's literature (for example, Inglis 1975; 1981). Inglis favours, not cultural materialism, but cultural hermeneutics. In *Cultural Studies* (1993), he argues in favour of making cultural studies 'synonymous with the study of values (and valuing)' (Inglis 1993: 190). The book is dedicated to the cultural anthropologist, Clifford Geertz, with his influential view that 'man is an animal suspended in webs of significance he himself has spun' and that those webs are what we call culture'. For Geertz, the analysis of culture, therefore, will be 'an interpretive one in search of meaning', and culture itself is defined as 'an assemblage of texts' and 'a story they tell themselves about themselves' (Geertz 1975: 5; 448). So the model of cultural analysis Inglis favours is the interpretative one which aims not to *unmask* texts, using such critical concepts as ideology or hegemony which deconstruct and demystify ideologies, but to *understand* intersubjective meanings (Inglis 1993: 148). He argues against the tendency within cultural studies to collapse 'both aesthetics and morality into politics' so that 'the study of culture translates into politics without remainder' (175; 181). He quotes Dollimore and Sinfield's statement (see above) that cultural materialism 'registers its commitment to the transformation of a social order which exploits people on grounds of race, gender and class' (Dollimore and Sinfield 1985: viii) but asks, using the same phrase which formed the title of his book about children's literature (Inglis 1981), 'What about the promise of happiness held out by art? What about art itself?' (Inglis 1993: 181).

Following Geertz's concept, Inglis defines culture as, 'an ensemble of *stories* we tell ourselves about ourselves' (Inglis 1993: 206) and argues that our historically changing identity is formed from experience and the 'narrative tradition' of which we are part. It is from this identity that we interpret the world. In a passage strongly relevant to the study of children's literature, (see, for example, Watkins 1994), he goes on to argue that

> the stories we tell ourselves about ourselves are not just a help to moral education; they comprise the only moral education which can gain purchase on the modern world. They are not aids to sensitivity nor adjuncts to the cultivated life. They are theories with which to think forwards ... and understand backwards.
>
> Inglis 1993: 214

Because of the variety within the cultural studies paradigm and the dynamic nature of the field, it is difficult to generalise about features which underlie such work in the study of children's literature. But the work of Fred Inglis (1981), Karín Lesnik-Oberstein (1994), Jacqueline Rose (1984), Marina Warner (1994) and Jack Zipes (1979), although in many respects very different, may be thought of as arising within a cultural studies framework.

# References

Barker, F., Hulme, P. and Iversen, M. (eds) (1991) *Uses of History: Marxism, Postmodernism and the Renaissance*, Manchester: Manchester University Press.

Belsey, C. (1991) 'Making histories then and now: Shakespeare from *Richard II* to *Henry V*', in Barker, F., Hulme, P. and Iversen, M. (eds) *Uses of History: Marxism, Postmodernism and the Renaissance*, Manchester: Manchester University Press.

Brantlinger, P. (1990) *Crusoe's Footprints: Cultural Studies in Britain and America*, New York: Routledge.

Buell, L. (1993) 'Literary History as a Hybrid Genre', in Cox, J. and Reynolds, L. J. (eds) *New Historical Literary Study: Essays on Reproducing Texts, Representing History*, Princeton, NJ: Princeton University Press.

Cox, J. N. and Reynolds, L. J. (eds) (1993) *New Historical Literary Study: Essays on Reproducing Texts, Representing History*, Princeton, NJ: Princeton University Press.

Dollimore, J. and Sinfield, A. (eds) (1985) *Political Shakespeare: New Essays in Cultural Materialism*, Manchester: Manchester University Press.

Felperin, H. (1991) ' "Cultural poetics" versus "cultural materialism": the two New Historicisms in Renaissance studies', in Barker, F., Hulme, P. and Iversen, M. (eds) *Uses of History: Marxism, Postmodernism and the Renaissance*, Manchester: Manchester University Press.

Fiske, J. (1987) 'British cultural studies and television', in Allen, R. C. (ed.) *Channels of Discourse: Television and Contemporary Criticism*, London: Routledge.

Geertz, C. (1975) *The Interpretation of Cultures*, London: Hutchinson.

Grossberg, L., Nelson, C. and Treichler, P. (eds) (1992) *Cultural Studies*, New York: Routledge.

Hall, S. (1990) 'The emergence of cultural studies and the crisis of the humanities', *October* 53: 11–90.

—— et al. (eds) (1980) *Culture, Media, Language*, London: Hutchinson.

Hunt, L. (ed.) (1989) *The New Cultural History*, Berkeley: University of California Press.

Inglis, F. (1975) *Ideology and the Imagination*, Cambridge: Cambridge University Press.

—— (1981) *The Promise of Happiness: Value and Meaning in Children's Fiction*, Cambridge: Cambridge University Press.

—— (1993) *Cultural Studies*, Oxford: Blackwell.

Knoepflmacher, U. C. (1977) 'Mutations of the Wordsworthian child of nature', in Knoepflmacher, U. C. and Tennyson, G. B. (eds) *Nature and the Victorian Imagination*, Berkeley: University of California Press.

Leavis, F. R. and Thompson, D. (1933) *Culture and Environment*, London: Chatto and Windus.

Lesnik-Oberstein, K. (1994) *Children's Literature: Criticism and the Fictional Child*, Oxford: Clarendon Press.

McGann, J. J. (1983) *The Romantic Ideology: A Critical Investigation*, Chicago and London: University of Chicago Press.

Montrose, L. A. (1989) 'Professing the Renaissance: the poetics and politics of culture', in Veeser, H. A. (ed.) *The New Historicism*, London: Routledge.

Myers, M. (1988) 'Missed opportunities and critical malpractice: New Historicism and children's literature', *Children's Literature Association Quarterly* 13, 1: 41–43.

—— (1989) 'Socializing Rosamond: educational ideology and fictional form', *Children's Literature Association Quarterly*, 14, 2: 52–58.

—— (1992) 'Sociologizing juvenile ephemera: periodical contradictions, popular literacy, transhistorical readers', *Children's Literature Association Quarterly* 17: 1: 41–45.

Perkins, D. (ed.) (1991) *Theoretical Issues in Literary History*, Cambridge and London: Harvard University Press.

Richardson, A. (1992) 'Childhood and romanticism', in Sadler, G. E. (ed.) *Teaching*

*Children's Literature: Issues, Pedagogy, Resources*, New York: The Modern Language Association.

Ricoeur, P. (1986) *Lectures on Ideology and Utopia*, New York: Columbia University Press.

Rose, J. (1984) *The Case of Peter Pan, or, The Impossibility of Children's Fiction*, London: Macmillan.

Thompson, J. B. (1984) *Studies in the Theory of Ideology*, Cambridge: Polity Press.

Townsend, J. R. (1990) *Written for Children: An Outline of English Language Children's Literature*, 5th edn, London: Bodley Head.

Veeser, H. A. (1989) (ed.) *The New Historicism*, London: Routledge.

—— (1994) *The New Historicism Reader*, London: Routledge.

Warner, M. (1994) *From the Beast to the Blonde: On Fairy Tales and Their Tellers*, London: Chatto and Windus.

Watkins, T. (1992) 'Cultural studies, new historicism and children's literature', in Hunt, P. (ed.) *Literature for Children: Contemporary Criticism*, London: Routledge.

—— (1994) 'Homelands: landscape and identity in children's literature', in Parsons, W. and Goodwin R. (eds) *Landscape and Identity: Perspectives from Australia*, Adelaide: Auslib Press.

White, H. (1973) *Metahistory: The Historical Imagination in Nineteenth-Century Europe*, Baltimore: Johns Hopkins University Press.

Williams R. (1958) *Culture and Society 1780–1950*, London: Chatto and Windus.

—— (1975) *The Country and the City*, St Albans: Paladin.

—— (1976) *Keywords: A Vocabulary of Culture and Society*, London: Fontana.

—— (1977) *Marxism and Literature*, Oxford: Oxford University Press.

—— (1989) *The Politics of Modernism: Against the New Conformists*, London: Verso.

Zipes, J. (1979) *Breaking the Magic Spell: Radical Theories of Folk and Fairy Tales*, London: Heinemann.

# 4

# Ideology

## *Charles Sarland*

## Introduction

Discourse on children's fiction sits at the crossroads of a number of other discourses. In the late twentieth century the most important among these, for the purposes of this chapter, are the discourses that surround the subject of 'literature' itself, and the discourses that surround the rearing, socialisation, and education of the young. Thus discussion of ideology in children's literature requires the consideration of a number of issues. The very use of the expression 'children's literature', for instance, brings with it a whole set of value judgements which have been variously espoused, attacked, defended, and counterattacked over the years. In addition, discussion of children's fiction – my preferred term in this chapter – has always been characterised by arguments about its purposes. These purposes, or in some cases these denials of purpose, stem from the particular characteristics of its intended readership, and are invariably a product of the views held within the adult population about children and young people themselves and their place in society. Since there is an imbalance of power between the children and young people who read the books, and the adults who write, publish and review the books, or who are otherwise engaged in commentary upon, or dissemination of the books, either as parents, or teachers, or librarians, or booksellers, or academics, there is here immediately a question of politics, a politics first and foremost of age differential.

But wider than this, the books themselves and the social practices that surround them will raise ideological issues. These issues may be related to specific debates in adult society, to do for instance with class, gender or ethnicity, or they may be instances of more general debate about the role of liberal humanist values in a capitalist democracy. In addition to all of this, there is a continuing debate about reader response (see Chapter 6), a debate which also impacts upon considerations of ideology in children's fiction. And finally, no consideration of ideology in children's fiction would be complete without a glance at the current developments by which children's fiction is becoming a commodity in a global market, controlled by a relatively small number of international publishers.

## Moral Purpose and Didacticism

It is useful, in the first instance, to recognise the historical nature of the debate, a debate that initially centred around questions of didacticism and moral purpose. In the 'Preface' to *The Governess or Little Female Academy* in 1749, Sarah Fielding wrote:

> Before you begin the following sheets, I beg you will stop a Moment at this Preface, to consider with me, what is the true Use of reading: and if you can once fix this Truth in your Minds, namely that the true Use of Books is to make you wiser and better, you will then have both Profit and Pleasure from what you read.
>
> Fielding 1749/1968: 91

Lest it should be thought that such overt moral purpose is a thing of the past, here is Fred Inglis: 'Only a monster would not want to give a child books she will delight in and which will teach her to be good. It is the ancient and proper justification of reading and teaching literature that it helps you to live well' (Inglis 1981: 4).

Contrary views have almost as long a history; for instance, Elizabeth Rigby writing in 1844 in *The Quarterly Review*, while admitting that no one would deliberately put what she calls 'offensive' books in the way of children, goes on:

> but, should they fall in their way, we firmly believe no risk to exist – if they will read them at one time or another, the earlier, perhaps, the better. Such works are like the viper – they have a wholesome flesh as well as a poisonous sting; and children are perhaps the only class of readers which can partake of one without suffering from the other.
>
> Hunt 1990: 21

The debate was lively in the eighteenth and nineteenth centuries, but for the bulk of this century it appeared largely to have been settled. Thus Harvey Darton, in 1932, could introduce his history with the words: 'By "children's books" I mean printed works produced ostensibly to give children spontaneous pleasure, and not primarily to teach them, not solely to make them good, nor to keep them *profitably* quiet' (Darton 1932/1982: 1, his emphasis).

For a considerable time, then, the question of values was left in abeyance. There was discussion about both how to write for children in ways that were not condescending, and about what the differences might be between fiction written for children and fiction written for adults, but considerations of moral purpose were not an issue. In the 1970s, however, the debate was revived, albeit in another form, and it was at this point that ideological considerations came to be labelled as such.

## Ideology

Ideology is a problematic notion. In the current general discourse of the electronic media, for instance, it is often considered that ideology and bias are one and the same thing, and that ideology and 'common sense' can be set against each other. This distinction continues into party political debate: 'ideology' is what the other side is motivated by while 'our' side is again merely applying common sense. In the history of Marxist thought there has been a convoluted development of usage of the term, not unrelated to the distinction just outlined. For the purposes of this chapter, however, ideology will be taken to refer to all espousal, assumption, consideration, and discussion of social and cultural values, whether overt or covert. In that sense it will include common sense itself, for common sense is always concerned with the values and underlying assumptions of our everyday lives.

Volosinov (1929/1986) encapsulates the position when he argues that all language is ideological. All sign systems, including language, he argues, have not only a simple denotative role, they are also and at one and the same time, evaluative, and thus ideological. 'The domain of ideology coincides with the domain of signs' (10). From this perspective it will thus be seen that all writing is ideological since all writing either assumes values even when not overtly espousing them, or is produced and also read within a social and cultural framework which is itself inevitably suffused with values, that is to say, suffused with ideology. In addition, in Marxist terms, considerations of ideology can neither be divorced from considerations of the economic base, nor from considerations of power (that is, of politics), and that too is the position taken here.

## Representation: Gender, Minority Groups, and Bias in the 1970s

In eighteenth- and nineteenth-century didacticism the promotion of values had often taken the overt form of direct preaching, while in the 1970s the specific form of the debate was to do with questions of character representation and character role. The analysis consisted in showing how children's fiction represented some groups at the expense of others, or how some groups were negatively represented in stereotypical terms. The argument was that by representing certain groups in certain ways children's books were promoting certain values – essentially white, male and middle-class, and that the books were thus class biased, racist and sexist. The fact that the protagonists of most children's books tended to be white middle-class boys was adduced in evidence. Black characters rarely made an appearance in children's fiction, and working-class characters were portrayed either as respectful to their middle-class 'betters', or as stupid – or they had the villain's role in the story. Girls were only represented in traditional female roles.

Geoffrey Trease (1949/1964) had led the way in drawing attention to the politically conservative bias of historical fiction, and had attempted to offer alternative points of view in his own writing. Nat Hentoff drew attention to the under-representation of teenagers in children's books, and saw the need to make 'contact with the sizeable number of the young who never read anything for pleasure because they are not in it' (Hentoff 1969: 400). Bob Dixon's work (1974) was characteristic of many attacks on the most prolific of British authors, Enid Blyton, and commentators were becoming increasingly aware of the white middle-class nature of many children's books, and of the sex-role stereotyping to be found within them. Zimet (1976) drew attention to the exclusion or the stereotypical presentation of ethnic minorities and women in children's fiction, and incidentally also in school textbooks, and espoused the use of positive images of girls and of ethnic minorities. Bob Dixon (1977), in a comprehensive survey, demonstrated the almost universally reactionary views on race, gender and class, together with a political conservatism, that informed most British children's books of the time, and Robert Leeson (1977) came up with similar findings. The Writers and Readers Publishing Co-operative (1979) drew attention to the racism inherent in a number of children's classics and one or two highly rated more modern books, and examined sex roles and other stereotyping.

In order to respond to what was seen as the bias in children's fiction, it was argued that books should be written with working-class, or female or black protagonists. In this way working-class, anti-racist and anti-sexist values would be promoted. Thus, in 1982 Dixon drew up what was essentially an annotated book list of 'stories which show a positive, overall attitude with regard to sex roles, race and social class' (Dixon 1982: 3), though he also insisted that the books should meet 'literary' standards that were essentially Leavisite. Such initiatives have multiplied in recent years and the practical outcome has been a proliferation of series aimed particularly at the teenage market, and the emergence of writers like Petronella Breinburg, Robert Leeson and Jan Needle in Britain, and Rosa Guy, Julius Lester, Louise Fitzhugh and Virginia Hamilton in the USA, who have offered different perspectives and attempted to redress the balance.

As has been indicated, the debate was essentially about representation, and 'literary standards' *per se* were not generally challenged. Thus more complex considerations of the ways in which ideology is inscribed in texts did not enter into the equation, nor did considerations of the complexity of reader response. What such initiatives did do, however, was to point out that all texts incorporated value positions, and that after all, as John Stephens has observed, 'Writing for children is usually purposeful' (Stephens 1992: 3)

It was therefore not long before questions were raised about the grounds of the judgements made about the quality of children's books, and that in turn relates to a wider consideration of such questions with regard to literary criticism as a whole.

## The Development of Criticism of Children's Fiction: the Leavisite Paradigm

The criticism of children's fiction has been something of a poor relation in critical studies. For the first two-thirds of twentieth century there was little written that addressed the subject, and in an interesting article Felicity Hughes (1978/1990) offers some analysis as to why this was the case. She argues that at the turn of the century Henry James and others encapsulated the view that for the novel to fully come of age as an art form it had to break free of its family audience. Since then the tendency has increased to view writing for children as a 'mere' craft, not worthy of serious critical attention. Reviewing and commentary focused on advising parents, librarians and other interested adults on what to buy for children, or on advising teachers on how to encourage and develop the reading habits of their pupils. And while critical judgements were offered about the quality of the books, the criteria for such critical judgements were assumed rather than debated. When surveys of the field were published they also tended to sacrifice discussion of critical criteria to the need for comprehensive coverage.

However, a developing body of work did start to emerge in the 1960s and 1970s which was directly concerned with confronting the problem and trying to establish criteria for judgement. Such work drew on two traditions, the Leavisite tradition in Britain, and the New Criticism in the USA. Foremost amongst such initiatives was a collection of papers edited by Egoff *et al.* (1969). Rosenheim (1969) and

Travers (1969), both from that collection, look specifically to New Critic Northrop Frye's mythic archetypes, as do Ted Hughes (1976), and Peter Hunt (1980). Wallace Hildick (1970) and Myles McDowell (1973) both address the question of the difference in writing for children and writing for adults, but both resort to Leavisite criteria for evaluating the quality of children's books, as does John Rowe Townsend (1971/1990). The Leavisite tradition perhaps reaches its apogee with Fred Inglis's *The Promise of Happiness*. Inglis's opening sentence directly quotes the opening of Leavis's *The Great Tradition* (1948): 'The great children's novelists are Lewis Carroll, Rudyard Kipling, Francis Hodgson Burnett, Arthur Ransome, William Mayne, and Philippa Pearce – to stop for a moment at that comparatively safe point on an uncertain list' (Inglis 1981: 1).

The tradition is not dead. Margery Fisher (1986) for instance, assumes that the definition of a children's classic is still essentially unproblematic. William Moebius (1986/1990) brings similar assumptions to bear upon picture books, and Peter Hunt's book on Arthur Ransome is still largely rooted in Leavisite practice in its judgements of quality and value (Hunt 1992).

One of the features of the tradition is its refusal to address questions of value at a theoretical level. Here is Townsend exemplifying the point.

> We find in fact that the literary critics, both modern and not-so-modern, are reluctant to pin themselves down to theoretical statements. In the introduction to *Determinations* (1934), F. R. Leavis expresses the belief that 'the way to forward true appreciation of literature and art is to examine and discuss it'; and again, 'out of agreement or disagreement with particular judgements of value a sense of relative value in the concrete will define itself, and without this, no amount of talk in the abstract is worth anything'.
>
> Townsend 1971/1990: 66

The values in question can be culled from a variety of sources. F. R. Leavis (1955) talks of 'intelligence', 'vitality', 'sensibility', 'depth, range and subtlety in the presentment of human experience', 'achieved creation' 'representative significance'. Inglis (1981) talks of 'sincerity' 'dignity', 'integrity', 'honesty', 'authenticity', 'fulfilment', 'freedom', 'innocence', 'nation', 'intelligence', 'home', 'heroism', 'friendship', 'history'. And Peter Hunt tells us that the virtues of Arthur Ransome are 'family, honour, skill, good sense, responsibility and mutual respect', and 'the idea of place' (Hunt 1992: 86). All of these terms and formulations are offered by their various authors as if they are essentially unproblematic, and they are thus rendered as common sense, naturalised and hidden in the discourse, and not raised for examination. We may have little difficulty, however, in recognising a liberal humanist consensus which runs through them, even if one or two of Inglis's choices are somewhat idiosyncratic. Nowhere, however, are we able to raise the question of the role that this liberal humanist discourse plays ideologically in a late capitalist world, and it is such a challenge that an ideological critique inevitably raises.

However, before moving on to such considerations, it is necessary to add that Inglis's book also marks a peak in the *educational* debate which has filled the pages of such journals as *English in Education* throughout the 1980s and into the 1990s, and which is also a debate between the Leavisites and the exponents of newer developments in structuralism and semiotics. As I have indicated above, the discourses of children's literature and education continuously overlap. Felicity Hughes (1976/1990) highlights Henry James's concern that the universal literacy that would follow from universal schooling would endanger the future of the novel as an art form, leading to inevitable vulgarisation, as the novel itself catered to popular taste – and children's literature itself catered to an even lower common denominator. As a result, and in order to try to return some status to children's literature, it was, and often still is seen as the training ground of adult literary taste. From such a perspective the distinction conferred by the term 'literature' is crucial, since by that means the Jamesian distinctions between the novel as an art form and other fiction as *commercial* entertainment is promoted.

It is perhaps ironic that the criticism of children's fiction should come of age at precisely the point when the newer perspectives of structuralism, semiotics, and Marxism were beginning to make their mark in literary criticism in Britain, and to undermine those very certainties after which Inglis was searching.

## The Ideological Debate in Literary Studies

### *Character and action: structuralist insights*

As already noted, the work of New Critic Northrop Frye (1957) had been influential in establishing a structuralist tradition in the criticism of children's fiction in the USA in the early 1970s. From Europe a different tradition began to make its influence felt in Britain in the later 1970s and 1980s, particularly with regard to the treatment of character and action. The Russian formalist, Vladimir Propp (1928/1968), suggested in his study of the Russian folktale that character was not the source of action, rather it was the product of plot. The hero was the hero because of his or her role in the plot. One can go back to Aristotle for similar insistence that it was not character but action that was important in tragedy (Aristotle 1965: 39) and such views were echoed by the pre-war critic Walter Benjamin (1970) and in Tzvetan Todorov's work (1971/1977).

The Leavisite tradition had, by contrast, tended to emphasise the importance of psychological insight in characterisation, and had seen characters themselves as the source of the action of the story, and it is easy to see how the work of authors such as Philippa Pearce, Nina Bawden, William Mayne, Maurice Sendak, Anthony Browne or Aidan Chambers, to take a list not entirely at random, lends itself to such approaches. By contrast the work of popular authors, such as Enid Blyton or Roald Dahl, more easily lends itself to structuralist analysis: their protagonists are heroines and heroes primarily because that is their plot role, not because there is anything in their psychological make up that makes them inherently 'heroic'.

Such structuralist approaches need not be limited to popular texts, and can be applied with equal usefulness to the work of authors at what is often regarded as the 'quality' end of the market. To take an example, the character of Toad in *The Wind in the Willows* (Grahame 1908) could be seen on the one hand as a rounded psychological creation, in turns blustering and repentant, selfish, self-seeking and replete with hubris. His exploits can then be seen entirely in terms of his personality. Structuralist analysis, on the other hand, might see him as comic hero, archetypal overreacher, functioning as the disruptive element in the social order that is necessary for the book's main plot to develop, and thus acting as a pivotal point for the articulation of the conflict between the uncertainties of the newer machine age, and the more settled life of the rural idyll, a conflict which is one of the major themes of the book.

Robert Leeson (1975/1980) led the attack on the application to children's fiction of the then prevailing tradition of adult literary criticism. He writes: 'these days, turning to adult lit-crit is like asking to be rescued by the *Titanic*' (209). He locates the debate about characterisation in a specifically ideological context, suggesting that enthusiasm for psychological characterisation is a bourgeois trait. The old tales, he argues, echoing Propp, didn't need psychology, they had action and moral. The claims made by traditional 'lit-crit' for such characterisation are elitist, and have little application for the general reader. J. S. Bratton, too, rejected the Leavisite tradition in her study of Victorian children's books: 'the liberal humanist tradition of literary criticism offers no effective approach to the material' (Bratton 1981: 19) although she draws on Frye as well as Propp in her resort to structuralism (see also Sarland 1991: 142).

The critique of the position which sees character as the source of meaning and action comes from a wider and more ideological perspective than that of structuralism alone, and structuralism itself has more to offer than insights about character and action. More widely, structuralism draws on semiotics to explore the whole range of codes that operate in texts and by which they construct their meanings; it also takes a lead from Lévi-Strauss (1963), who related structural elements in myths to structural elements in the society that gave rise to them. This becomes a central tool of ideological critique, allowing parallels to be drawn between ideological structures in the works and those in society at large.

### The underlying ground of ideological value

Marxist literary criticism analyses literature in the light of prevailing economic class conflict in capitalist society. This conflict is not slavishly reproduced in the ideological superstructure, of which literature is a part, but it is always possible to trace it in some form in individual work. The liberal humanist tradition, by contrast, sees not class conflict as the major determining structure in understanding history and society, but materialism itself. The ideological conflict then becomes materialism versus humanism and the paradigm distinction to be made about the work, *pace* Henry James, is that between art and commerce. Terry Eagleton (1976) and Catherine Belsey (1980) are among the major critics of the Leavisite tradition, identifying its liberal humanist roots, and analysing its escapist response to the materialism of bourgeois capitalism. Furthermore, they argue, by 'naturalising' its values as common sense, liberal humanism conceals its reactionary political role, though the idealist nature of its position is often clear enough in its claim of transcendent status for those same values and for a universal 'human nature' in which they inhere.

To take an example, a liberal humanist reading of *The Wind in the Willows* might see it as celebrating the values enshrined in notions of home and good fellowship, in opposition to the threatening materialism of the wide world with its dominant symbol of the motor car. A case might be made that the recurrent plots and sub-plots, all of which involve explorations away from, and successive returns to warm secure homes, culminating in the retaking of Toad Hall from the marauding weasels and stoats, have a universal appeal, since such explorations and returns are the very condition of childhood itself. An ideological perspective might note, by contrast, the resemblance of those secure warm homes to the Victorian middle-class nursery, and comment upon the escapism of the response to the materialism of the wide world. Such an approach might further recognise the underlying feudalist presuppositions that are hidden within the 'common sense' assumptions of the book, and might identify in the weasels and stoats the emergence of an organised working class challenging the privileges of property and upper-middle-class idleness. Jan Needle's re-working of the book, *Wild Wood* (1981), starts from just such a premise. In addition the celebration of fellowship is an entirely male affair, the only women in the book – the jailer's daughter and the bargee – have distinctly subservient roles, and claims for universality just in terms of gender alone begin to look decidedly suspect.

In her continuing ideological critique Belsey suggests that from the liberal humanist perspective people are seen as the sole authors of their own actions, and hence of their own history, and meaning is the product of their individual intentions. In fact, she argues, the reverse is true: people are not the authors of their own history, they are rather the products of history itself, or less deterministically, engaged in a dialectical relationship with their history – both product and producer. The grounds for Leeson's argument, above, are now clear, for a criticism that espouses psychological characterisation as a central tenet of 'quality', and that insists that the stories in which those characters find themselves should be rooted in the intentionality of those characters' psyches, is liberal humanist in assumption, and will fail to expose the ideological nature both of the fiction to which it is giving attention, and of the fiction that it is ignoring.

In liberal humanist criticism it is the author who takes centre stage, and Belsey identifies 'expressive realism' as literature's dominant form over the past 150 years: reality, as experienced by a single gifted individual is expressed in such a way that the rest of us spontaneously perceive it as being the case. Grahame's intention is assumed to be that readers should see childhood as a time and place of adventure within a secure framework, and readers are to take his word for it. The resort to the author's intention as the source of meaning in the work, known to its critics as the 'intentional fallacy', had already come under attack for circularity from the New Critics, since the primary evidence for the author's intention was usually the work itself. Belsey takes the argument one step further, suggesting that expressive realism operates to support liberal humanism, and thus, effectively, in support of capitalism itself. Ideological perspectives insist, in contrast, that texts are constructions in and of ideology, generally operating unconsciously, and it is the job of the critic to deconstruct the work in order to expose its underlying ideological nature and role. Thus, far from being the unique insight of an individual with a privileged understanding of the world, *The Wind in the Willows* can be seen as resting securely within a continuum of escapist response to developing bourgeois capitalism that stretches all the way from *Hard Times* to *Lady Chatterley's Lover*.

Peter Hollindale (1988) takes on a number of the perspectives outlined above, and applies them to his discussion of ideology in children's books. He distinguishes three levels of ideology. There is first of all an overt, often proselytising or didactic level, as instanced in books like *The Turbulent Term of Tyke Tyler* (Kemp 1977). Then there is a second more passive level, where views of the world are put into characters mouths or otherwise incorporated into the narrative with no overt ironic distancing. (There is a famous example of this from Enid Blyton's *Five Run Away Together* (1944), analysed by Ken Watson (1992: 31), in which the reader is implicitly invited to side with the obnoxious middle-class Julian putting down a member of the 'lower orders'.) Finally, there is what Hollindale calls an 'underlying climate of belief' which he identifies as being inscribed in the basic material from which fiction is built. It is possible to detect a hankering after the old transcendent certainties in Hollindale's work. None the less he does substantially shift the ground of the debate in regard to children's fiction, recognising the complexity of the issues.

### Circumstances of production

Within the Marxist tradition it has long been recognised that literature is a product of the particular historical and social formations that prevail at the time of its production (see for example Lenin, originally 1908, 1910, 1911/1978; Plekhanov 1913/1957; Trotsky 1924/1974). Children's books have not received such attention until comparatively recently. Bratton (1981) traced the relationship between Victorian children's fiction and its various markets – stories for girls to teach them the domestic virtues, stories for boys to teach them the virtues of military Christianity, stories for the newly literate poor, to teach them religion and morality. Leeson, in his history of children's fiction (Leeson 1985), suggests that there has always been a conflict between middle-class literature and popular literature, a distinction which can be traced in the content of the material, and related to the market that it found. He draws attention to the roots of popular fiction in folktale, which had political content which survived (somewhat subdued) into the written forms. Leeson thus raises a question mark over the perhaps somewhat more determinist analysis offered by Belsey and Eagleton.

More thorough exploration of the issues in contemporary children's fiction has come from feminist perspectives, with a collection of studies of popular teen romance fiction edited by Linda K. Christian-Smith (1993a). Christian-Smith herself (1993b) provides a particularly powerful analysis of the economic, political and ideological circumstances of the growth in production of romances for 'teenagers' or 'young adults', which is now a global industry, with most of the publishing houses based in the USA. She traces the relationship between the imperatives of 'Reaganomics', the emphasis on family values in the rise of the New Right in the 1980s, and the need to enculturate young women into the gendered roles that serve such interests. The collection as a whole analyses how such material both constructs and meets the needs of its market in a rich and subtle exegesis which I shall return to below.

In the meantime it is necessary to explore a further area which has important ideological implication, and that is the way in which the child reader is constructed by the texts he or she is reading.

## The Construction of the Reader

The initiatives of the 1970s to redress the balance in the bias of children's fiction took a straightforward view about the relationship between the text and the reader. At its simplest an almost directly didactic relationship was assumed. If you wrote books with positive characterisations of, and roles for, girls, ethnic minorities and the working class, then readers' attitudes would be changed and all would be well with the world. I do not suggest that anyone, even then, thought it would be quite that simple, and since the 1970s there has been something of a revolution in our understandings of how readers are constructed by texts. The insights of reader-response theoreticians like Wolfgang Iser (1978), applied to children's books most notably by Aidan Chambers (1980), had alerted us to some of the textual devices by which an implied reader is written into the text. Iser himself had drawn attention to the fact that texts brought with them a cultural repertoire which had to be matched by the reader. Macherey (1978) brought Freudian perspectives to bear on ways in which ideology operated in hidden ways in the text, and by extension, also in the reader, and Catherine Belsey drew insights from Althusser, Derrida and Lacan to further explore the ways in which the subjectivity of the reader is ideologically constructed.

It is Jacqueline Rose (1984) who offers the most thoroughgoing exposition of this view with respect to children's fiction. She argues that, by a combination of textual devices, characterisation and assumptions of value position, children's books construct children, both as characters and as readers, as without sexuality, innocent, and denied politics, either a politics between themselves or within wider society. As such they are seen as beings with a privileged perception, untainted by culture. More recently, John Stephens (1992), engages in a detailed analysis of a number of books to show how they produce ideological constructions of implied child readers. He concentrates particularly on narrative focalisation and the shifts, moves and gaps of narrative viewpoint and attitude, showing how such techniques imply certain ideological assumptions and formulations, and construct implied readers who must be expected to share them.

## Implied Readers and Real Readers

When real readers are introduced into the equation, however, the picture becomes more complicated, and it is here that the educational discourse overlaps with the discourse about fiction *per se*, for it is almost always within school that evidence is gathered, and intervention is proposed. The introduction of real readers has another effect, for it throws into relief some of the more determinist assumptions of the analysis offered above. The evidence comes under three headings: identification, the polysemous text, and contradictory readings.

## *Identification*

The notion of identification has been a contentious issue for some time. The assumption is that readers 'identify with' the protagonists, and thus take on their particular value positions. Readers are thus ideologically constructed by their identification with the character. D. W. Harding (1977) offered an alternative formulation of the reader as an observer in a more detached and evaluative spectator role, and both Geoff Fox (1979) and Robert Protherough (1983) suggest that such a straightforward notion as identification does not account for the evidence that they collected from children and young people. It is clear from their evidence that readers take up a range of positions of greater or lesser involvement, and of varied focalisation. The ideological initiatives of the 1970s presupposed an identification model of response, and subsequent commentators are still most fearful of what happens should a young person engage in unmediated identification with characters constructed within ideologically undesirable formulations. Such fears underlie Stephens's analysis (1992) and the work of Christian-Smith and her co-contributors (1993).

## *The polysemous text*

Roland Barthes (1974) alerted us to the notion that texts operated a plurality of codes that left them open to a plurality of readings, and Umberto Eco (1981) offers the most extensive analysis of that plurality. Specifically, with regard to ideology, Eco agrees that all texts carry ideological assumptions, whether overt or covert. But readers, he argues, have three options: they can assume the ideology of the text and subsume it into their own reading; they can miss or ignore the ideology of the text and import their own, thus producing 'aberrant' readings – 'where "aberrant" means only different from the ones envisaged by the sender' (22); or they can question the text in order to reveal the underlying ideology. This third option is, of course, the project that ideological critique undertakes. When real readers, other than critics, are questioned about their readings, it is clear that the second option is often taken up, and that 'aberrant' readings abound (Sarland 1991; Christian-Smith 1993a), though consensual readings also clearly occur. Texts, it seems, are contradictory, and so evidently are readings.

## *Contradictory readings*

Macherey (1977, 1978) and Eagleton (1976), both assume that the world is riven with ideological conflict. To expect texts to resolve that conflict is mistaken, and the ideological contradictions that inform the world will also be found to inform the fictional texts that are part of that world. Some texts, Eagleton argues, are particularly good at revealing ideological conflict, in that they sit athwart the dominant ideology of the times in which they were written. Eagleton looks to examples from the traditional adult canon to make his point.

Jack Zipes (1979) takes the argument one stage further and suggests that popular work too will be found to be contradictory. He links popular literature and film with its precursors in folktale and romance, and suggests that it offers the hope of autonomy and self-determination, in admittedly utopian forms, while at the same time affirming dominant capitalist ideology. In other words, while the closure of popular texts almost always reinforces dominant ideology, in the unfolding narratives there are always countering moves in which it is challenged. Zipes, then, denies the implications of Eagleton's work that only texts that sit athwart the prevailing ideology can be open to countervailing readings, and he denies too the implications of Belsey's work that popular forms sit within the classic expressive realist tradition, and as such demand readings that are congruent with the dominant ideology.

For example in Enid Blyton's *Famous Five* books, many of the plots are predicated on the refusal of the central female character, George, to accept her role as subservient, domesticated and non-adventurous, despite repeated exhortations to 'behave like a girl'. She even refuses to accept her 'real' name, which is Georgina. Countering this is the fact that Blyton only offers her the alternative of 'tomboy', an alternative that is itself determined by a predominantly male discourse; and the closures of the books re-establish traditional domestic order with the sexes acting according to conventional gender stereotype. (Zipes himself later turned his attention to children's fiction (Zipes 1983), and see also Sarland 1983.)

While this analysis is still essentially theoretical, supporting evidence is beginning to emerge from studies that have been done of readers themselves. The focus has been on popular fiction, and on teenagers. Popular fiction causes educationalists particular concern since it appears to reinforce the more reactionary values in society, particularly so far as girls and young women are concerned. The research evidence uncovers a complex picture of the young seeking ways to take control over their own lives, and using the fiction that they enjoy as one element in that negotiation of cultural meaning and value. Gemma Moss showed how teenage girls and boys were able to turn the popular forms of, respectively, the romance and the thriller to their own ends. She found unhelpful some of the more determinist ideological analysis that suggested that, by their reading of romance, girls were constructed as passive victims of a patriarchal society. The girls who liked the romances were tough, worldly wise working-class girls who were not subservient to their male counterparts. 'Girls didn't need to be told about male power, they were dealing with it every day of their lives' (Moss 1989: 7). The traditional assessment of 'teen romance' by most teachers as stereotyped drivel was applied to the girls' writing, too, when they chose to write in that form. However, Moss shows how the teenage girls she was working with were able to take the form into their own writing and use it to negotiate and dramatise their concerns with and experience of femininity and oppression. Romance offered them a form for this activity that was not necessarily limiting at all.

In *Young People Reading: Culture and Response* (Sarland 1991) I have argued that young people engaged in 'aberrant' readings of pulp violence and horror, readings which ran against the reactionary closure of such material, and they thus were able to explore aspirations of being in control of their own lives, and I further argued that the official school literature as often as not offered them negative perspectives on those same aspirations. Christian-Smith and her colleagues (1993) explore similar dualities and demonstrate the complexity of the problem. For instance, in her analysis of the Baby-Sitters Club books, Meredith Rogers Cherland shows how the characters are placed securely within feminine roles and functions, being prepared for domestic life and work in lowly paid 'caring' jobs. The 11-year-old girls who are reading them, however, 'saw the baby-sitters making money that they then used to achieve their own ends. They saw the baby-sitters shaping the action around them so that things worked out the way they wanted them to. They saw girls their age acting as agents in their own right' (Cherland with Edelsky 1993: 32). By contrast, horror, Cherland argues, which these girls were also beginning to read, casts women in increasingly helpless roles. In its association of sexuality with violence it seemed to offer the girls in Cherland's study a position of increasing powerlessness, living in fear and thus denied agency.

Research into the meanings that young people actually make of the books they are reading demonstrates the plural nature of the texts we are dealing with. While it was often claimed that texts within the canon had complexity and ambiguity, it was always thought that popular texts pandered to the lowest common denominator, and offered no purchase on complex ideological formulations. The evidence does not bear that out. Popular texts too are discovered to be open to more than one reading, and the deconstruction of those texts, and the readings young people bring to them, proves be a productive tool of analysis for exploring the ideological formulations which constitute them. There is yet to be a large mainstream study of what readers make of the more traditional central canon of children's fiction, though John Stephens and Susan Taylor's exploration of readings of two retellings of the Seal Wife legend (Stephens and Taylor 1992) is a useful start.

## Ideology and Children's Fiction

We have learned from the debate in literary studies that ideology is inscribed in texts much more deeply and in much more subtle ways than we at first thought in the 1970s. The initial emphasis in the criticism of children's books was on the characters, and addressed questions of representation. The relationship between reader and text was assumed to be one of simple identification. Literary merit was an unproblematic notion built upon Leavisite assumptions. This was set in question by reconsideration of characterisation itself, and then by the revolution in literary studies. Hollindale (1988) made an initial attempt to explore the complexity of the problem, and Stephens (1992) has taken it further. Stephens brings powerful ideological perspectives to bear upon the themes of children's fiction, the ways in which the stories are shaped, as well as the ways in which implied readers are constructed by the texts. He looks at a range of texts, including picture books written for the youngest readers, and examines specific titles by a number of writers in the central canon – Judy Blume, Anthony Browne, Leon Garfield, Jan Mark, William Mayne, Jan Needle, Rosemary Sutcliffe, Maurice Sendak and others. The debate has been informed by a rerecognition of the moral/ didactic role of children's fiction, now recoded as its ideological role. Unresolved conflicts remain between those who want to retain or renegotiate some literary criteria for judging the quality of children's fiction and those who are more sceptical of such judgements.

The overlap with the discourse of child rearing, and in particular, education, reveals another conflict, that between determinism and agency. One view of fiction is that it constructs readers in specific ideological formations, and thus enculturates them into the dominant discourses of capitalism – class division, paternalism, racism. Such views are not totally fatalistic, but do require of readers a very conscious effort to read against texts, to deconstruct them in order to reveal their underlying ideology. This then becomes the educational project. The opposing view is that readers are not nearly such victims of fiction as has been assumed, and that the fictions that are responsible for the transmission of such values are more complex than was at first thought. Evidence from the children and young people themselves is beginning to be collected in order to explore this complexity. The argument is that readers are not simply determined by what they read; rather there is a dialectical relationship between determinism and agency. With reference to her discussions of girls' reading, Cherland quotes J. M. Anyon:

> The dialectic of accommodation and resistance is a part of all human beings' response to contradiction and oppression. Most females engage in daily conscious and unconscious attempts to resist the psychological degradation and low self-esteem that would result from the total application of the cultural ideology of femininity: submissiveness, dependency, domesticity and passivity.
>
> Cherland with Edelsky 1993: 30

Applied to language itself, this analysis of a dialectic between individual identity and the ideological formulations of the culture within which it finds itself can be traced back to Volosinov. Within children's literature the dialectic will be found within the texts, and between the texts and the reader.

The collection of papers edited by Christian-Smith explores this dialectic in the greatest detail. There is initially the dialectic within the texts between feminine agency and patriarchy, traced by Pam Gilbert (1993) and Sandra Taylor (1993), who show how the female characters are agents of their own lives, finding spaces for decision making and autonomy within the gendered discourse of the culture, and in the case of younger characters, within the adult child power relationships of the family. They generally insist that boys treat them with respect, in an equal and caring relationship, yet they are trapped within stories that in their closure, suggest futures in domesticity, in poorly paid service and 'caring' jobs, and in monogamous heterosexual relationships.

There is, further, the dialectic between the mode of production, distribution and dissemination of the texts, and the fact that the girls themselves choose to read them despite whatever 'better' alternatives may be available (Christian-Smith 1993b; Willinsky and Hunniford 1993).

There is finally the dialectic in school itself as readers appropriate such texts as oppositional reading, and use them both to renegotiate their own gender roles in their writing (Moss 1993) and in their discussions (Willinsky and Hunniford 1993). Yet the schools' own rating of such reading as being beneath attention, and the tendency to regard the readers as therefore – and already – constructed by their reading in such a way that those readings do not merit serious attention, means that the young women and girls are themselves excluded from full educational opportunity (Taylor 1993, Davies 1993).

In Christian-Smith's collection *Texts of Desire: Essays on Fiction, Femininity and Schooling* (1993) ideological criticism of children's fiction has come of age. The collection as a whole addresses the complexity of the debate, analysing the ideologies of the texts themselves, the economic and political circumstances of their production, dissemination and distribution, the ideological features of the meanings their young readers make of them, and the political and economic circumstances of those young readers themselves. The focus of attention is the mass-produced material aimed at the female teen and just pre-teen market, but their study offers a paradigm for future exploration of children's fiction generally, if we are to fully understand its ideological construction within society.

## References

Aristotle (1965) 'On the art of poetry', in Aristotle, Horace and Longinus, *Classical Literary Criticism*, trans. Dorsch, T., Harmondsworth: Penguin.

Barthes, R. (1974) *S/Z*, New York: Hill and Wang.

Belsey, C. (1980) *Critical Practice*, London: Methuen.

Benjamin, W. (1970) *Illuminations*, Glasgow: Collins Fontana.

Blyton, E. (1944) *Five Run Away Together*, London: Hodder and Stoughton.

Bratton, J. S. (1981) *The Impact of Victorian Children's Fiction*, London: Croom Helm.

Chambers, A. (1980) 'The reader in the book', in Chambers, N. (ed.) *The Signal Approach to Children's Books*, Harmondsworth: Kestrel.

Cherland, M. R., with Edelsky, C. (1993) 'Girls reading: the desire for agency and the horror of helplessness in fictional encounters', in Christian-Smith, L. K. (ed.) *Texts of Desire: Essays on Fiction, Femininity and Schooling*, London: Falmer Press, 28–44.

Christian-Smith, L. K. (ed.) (1993a) *Texts of Desire: Essays on Fiction, Femininity and Schooling*, London: Falmer Press.

—— (1993b) 'Sweet dreams: gender and desire in teen romance novels', in Christian-Smith, L. K. (ed.) *Texts of Desire: Essays on Fiction, Femininity and Schooling*, London: Falmer Press.

Dahl, R. (1980) *The Twits*, Harmondsworth: Penguin.

Darton, F. J. H. (1932/1982) *Children's Books in England: Five Centuries of Social Life*, 3rd edn, rev. B. Alderson, Cambridge: Cambridge University Press.

Davies, B. (1993) 'Beyond dualism and towards multiple subjectivities', in Christian-Smith, L. K. (ed.) *Texts of Desire: Essays on Fiction, Femininity and Schooling*, London: Falmer Press, 145–173.

Dixon, B. (1974) 'The nice, the naughty and the nasty: the tiny world of Enid Blyton', *Children's Literature in Education* 15: 43–62.

—— (1977) *Catching them Young* 2 vols, London: Pluto Press.

—— (1982) *Now Read On*, London: Pluto Press.

Eagleton, T. (1976) *Criticism and Ideology*, London: Verso.

Eco, U. (1981) *The Role of the Reader*, London: Hutchinson.

Egoff, S., Stubbs, G. T. and Ashley, L. F. (eds) (1969) *Only Connect*, Toronto: Oxford University Press.

Fielding, S. (1749/1968) *The Governess or, Little Female Academy*, London: Oxford University Press.

Fisher, M. (1986) *Classics for Children and Young People*, South Woodchester: Thimble Press.

Fox, G. (1979) 'Dark watchers: young readers and their fiction', in *English in Education* 13, 1: 32–35.

Frye, N. (1957) *Anatomy of Criticism*, Princeton, NJ: Princeton University Press.

Gilbert, P. (1993) 'Dolly fictions: teen romance down under', in Christian-Smith, L. K. (ed.) *Texts of Desire: Essays on Fiction, Femininity and Schooling*, London: Falmer Press.

Grahame, K. (1908) *The Wind in the Willows*, London: Methuen.

Harding, D. W. (1977) 'Psychological processes in the reading of fiction', in Meek, M., Warlow, A. and Barton, G. (eds) *The Cool Web*, London: Bodley Head.

Hentoff, N. (1969) 'Fiction for teenagers', in Egoff, S., Stubbs, G. T. and Ashley, L. F. (eds) *Only Connect*, Toronto: Oxford University Press.

Hildick, W. (1970) *Children and Fiction*, London: Evans.

Hollindale, P. (1988) 'Ideology and the children's book', *Signal* 55, 3–22.

Hughes, F. (1976/1990) 'Children's literature: theory and practice', in Hunt, P. (ed.) *Children's Literature: The Development of Criticism*, London: Routledge.

Hughes, T. (1976) 'Myth and education', in Fox, G., Hammond, G., Jones, T. and Sterk, K. (eds) *Writers, Critics and Children*, London: Heinemann.

Hunt, P. (1980) 'Children's books, children's literature, criticism and research', in Benton, M. (ed.) *Approaches to Research in Children's Literature*, Southampton: University of Southampton Department of Education.

—— (ed.) (1990) *Children's Literature: The Development of Criticism*, London: Routledge.

—— (1992) *Approaching Arthur Ransome*, London: Cape.

Inglis, F. (1981) *The Promise of Happiness*, Cambridge: Cambridge University Press.

Iser, W. (1978) *The Act of Reading*, London: Routledge and Kegan Paul.

Kemp, G. (1977) *The Turbulent Term of Tyke Tyler*, London: Faber and Faber.

Leavis, F. R. (1948) *The Great Tradition*, Harmondsworth: Penguin.

—— (1955) *D. H. Lawrence: Novelist*, Harmondsworth: Penguin.

Leeson, R. (1975/1980) 'To the toyland frontier', in Chambers, N. (ed.) *The Signal Approach to Children's Books*, Harmondsworth: Kestrel.

—— (1977) *Children's Books and Class Society*, London: Writers and Readers Publishing Co-operative.

—— (1985) *Reading and Righting*, London: Collins.

Lenin, V. (1908, 1910, 1911/1978) 'Lenin's articles on Tolstoy', in Macherey, P. (ed.) *A Theory of Literary Production*, London: Routledge and Kegan Paul.

Lévi-Strauss, C. (1963) *The Structural Study of Myth*, Harmondsworth: Penguin.

McDowell, M. (1973) 'Fiction for children and adults: some essential differences', *Children's Literature in Education* 10: 50–63.

Macherey, P. (1977) 'Problems of reflection', in Barker, F., Coombes, J., Hulme, P., Musselwhite, D. and Osborne, R. (eds) *Literature, Society, and the Sociology of Literature*, Colchester: University of Essex.

—— (1978) *A Theory of Literary Production*, London: Routledge and Kegan Paul.

Marx, K. and Engels, F. (1859/1892/1971) *Historical Materialism*, London: Pluto Press.

Moebius, W. (1985/1990) 'Introduction to picturebook codes', in Hunt, P. (ed.) *Children's Literature: The Development of Criticism*, London: Routledge

Moss, G. (1989) *Un/Popular Fictions*, London: Virago.

—— (1993) 'The place for romance in young people's writing', in Christian-Smith, L. K. (ed.) *Texts of Desire: Essays on Fiction, Femininity and Schooling*, London: Falmer Press.

Needle, J. (1981) *Wild Wood*, London: André Deutsch.

Plekhanov, G. V. (1913/1957) *Art and Social Life*, Moscow: Progress Publishers.

Propp, V. (1928/1968) *Morphology of the Folktale*, Austin: Texas University Press.

Protherough, R. (1983) *Developing Response to Fiction*, Milton Keynes: Open University Press.

Rose, J. (1984) *The Case of Peter Pan or the Impossibility of Children's Fiction*, London: Macmillan.

Rosenheim, E. W. Jr (1969) 'Children's reading and adults' values', in Egoff, S., Stubbs, G. T. and Ashley, L. F. (eds) (1969) *Only Connect*, Toronto: Oxford University Press.

Sarland, C. (1983) 'The Secret Seven Versus The Twits', *Signal* 42: 155–171.

—— (1991) *Young People Reading: Culture and Response*, Milton Keynes: Open University Press.

Stephens, J. (1992) *Language and Ideology in Children's Fiction*, Harlow: Longman.

Stephens, J. and Taylor, S. (1992) 'No innocent texts', in Evans, E. (ed.) *Young Readers, New Readings*, Hull: Hull University Press.

Taylor, S. (1993) 'Transforming the texts: towards a feminist classroom practice', in Christian-Smith, L. K. (ed.) *Texts of Desire: Essays on Fiction, Femininity and Schooling*, London: Falmer Press.

Todorov, T. (1977) *The Poetics of Prose*, New York: Cornell University Press.

Townsend, J. R. (1971/1990) 'Standards of criticism for children's literature', in Hunt, P. (ed.) *Children's Literature: The Development of Criticism*, London: Routledge.

Travers, P. (1969) 'Only connect', in Egoff, S., Stubbs, G. T. and Ashley, L. F. (eds) *Only Connect*, Toronto: Oxford University Press.

Trease, G. (1949/1964) *Tales out of School*, London: Heinemann.

Trotsky, L. (1924/1974) *Class and Art*, London: New Park Publications.

Volosinov, V. N. (1929/1986) *Marxism and the Philosophy of Language*, Cambridge, MA: Harvard University Press.

Watson, K. (1992) 'Ideology in novels for young people', in Evans, E. (ed.) *Young Readers, New Readings*, Hull: Hull University Press.

Willinsky, J. and Hunniford, R. M. (1993) 'Reading the romance younger: the mirrors and fears of a preparatory literature', in Christian-Smith, L. K. (ed.) *Texts of Desire: Essays on Fiction, Femininity and Schooling*, London: Falmer Press.

Writers and Readers Publishing Co-operative (1979) *Racism and Sexism in Children's Books*, London: Writers and Readers.

Zimet, S. G. (1976) *Print and Prejudice*, Sevenoaks: Hodder and Stoughton.

Zipes, J. (1979) *Breaking the Magic Spell: Radical Theories of Folk and Fairy Tales*, London: Heinemann.

—— (1983) *Fairy Tales and the Art of Subversion*, London: Heinemann.

# 5

# Linguistics and Stylistics

## *John Stephens*

Because the contexts in which children's literature is produced and disseminated are usually dominated by a focus on content and theme, the language of children's literature receives little explicit attention. Yet style – which is the *way* things are represented, based on complex codes and conventions of language and presuppositions about language – is an important component of texts, and the study of it allows us access to some of the key processes which shape text production (Scholes 1985: 2–3). The assumption that what is said can be extricated from how it is said, and that language is therefore only a transparent medium, is apt to result in readings with at best a limited grasp of written genres or of the social processes and movements with which genres and styles interrelate.

The language of fiction written for children readily appears to offer conventionalised discourses by means of which to 'encode' content (both story and message). The ubiquitous 'Once upon a time' of traditional story-telling, for example, not only serves as a formal story onset but also tends to imply that particular narrative forms, with a particular stock of lexical and syntactic forms, will ensue. But the contents and themes of that fiction are representations of social situations and values, and such social processes are inextricable from the linguistic processes which give them expression. In other words, the transactions between writers and readers take place within complex networks of social relations by means of language. Further, within the large language system of English, for example, it is possible for young readers to encounter in their reading an extensive range and variety of language uses. Some textual varieties will seem familiar and immediately accessible, consisting of a lexicon and syntax which will seem identifiably everyday, but others will seem much less familiar, either because the lexicon contains forms or uses specific to a different speech community (British 'Standard' English versus USA 'Standard' English, for example), or because writers may choose to employ linguistic forms whose occurrence is largely or wholly restricted to narrative fiction, or because particular kinds of fiction evolve specific discourses. Books which may be said to have a common theme or topic will differ not just because that theme can be expressed in a different content but because it is expressed through differing linguistic resources. For example, a large number of children's books express the theme of 'growing up', but since that theme can be discerned in texts as diverse as Tolkien's *The Hobbit* and Danziger's *Can You Sue Your Parents for Malpractice?*, it cannot in itself discriminate effectively between texts of different kinds.

Writers have many options to select from. Thus fiction offers a large range of generic options, such as the choice between fantasy and realism, with more specific differences within them, such as that between time-slip fantasy grounded in the knowable world, or fantasy set in an imaginary universe. To make such a choice involves entering into a *discourse*, a complex of story types and structures, social forms and linguistic practices. That discourse can be said to take on a distinctive style in so far as it is distinguished from other actualisations by recurrent patterns or codes. These might include choices in lexis and grammar; use, types and frequency of figurative language; characteristic modes of cohesion; orientation of narrative voice towards the text's existents (that is, events, characters, settings). Aspects of such a style may be shared by several writers working in the same period and with a common genre, as, for example, contemporary realistic adolescent fiction, but it is usually more personal, as when we speak of the style of Kenneth Grahame, or William Mayne or Zibby Oneal, and at times we may refer to the distinctive style of a particular text, such as Virginia Hamilton's *Arilla Sun Down*. Because the patterns of a particular style are a selection from a larger linguistic code, however, and exist in a relationship of sameness and difference with a more generalised discourse, a writer remains to some degree subject to the discourse, and the discourse can be said to determine at least part of the meaning of the text. Moreover, a narrative discourse also encodes a reading position which readers will adopt to varying extents, depending on their previous experience of the particular discourse, their similarities to or differences from the writer's language community, their level of linguistic sophistication, and other individual differences. At a more obviously linguistic level, a writer's choices among such options as first/third person narration, single/multiple focalisation, and direct/ indirect speech representation further define the encoded reading position. Between them, the broader elements of genre and the more precise linguistic processes appear to restrict the possibility of wildly deviant readings, though what might be considered more probable readings depends on an acquired recognition of the particular discourse. If that recognition is not available to readers, the readings they produce may well seem aberrant.

The communication which informs the transactions between writers and readers is a specialised aspect of socio-linguistic communication in general. The forms and meanings of reality are constructed in language: by analysing how language works, we come nearer to knowing how our culture constructs itself, and where we fit into that construction. Language enables individuals to compare their experiences with the experiences of others, a process which has always been a fundamental purpose of children's fiction. The representation of experiences such as growing up, evolving a sense of self, falling in love or into conflict and so on, occurs in language, and guarantees that the experiences represented are shared with human beings in general. Language can make present the felt experiences of people living in other places and at other times, thus enabling a reader to define his or her own subjectivity in terms of perceived potentialities and differences. Finally, the capacity of language to express things beyond everyday reality, such as abstract thought or possible transcendent experiences, is imparted to written texts with all its potentiality for extending the boundaries of intellectual and emotional experience. Readers (and writers) often like to think of this as a kind of 'word magic' (for example, Sullivan 1985) – and numerous fantastic fictions so represent it – though it is in fact an explicable linguistic function.

The socio-linguistic contexts of text production and reception are important considerations for any account of reading processes. But beyond satisfying a basic human need for contact, reading can also give many kinds of pleasure, though the pleasures of reading are not discovered in a social or linguistic vacuum: as we first learn how to read we also start learning what is pleasurable and what not, and even what is good writing and what not. Our socio-linguistic group, and especially its formal educational structures, tends to precondition what constitutes a good story, a good argument, a good joke, and the better our command of socio-linguistic codes the greater is our appreciation. In other words, we learn to enjoy the process as well as the product. Writing and reading are also very individual acts, however, and the pleasure of reading includes some sense of the distinctive style of a writer or a text. One primary function of stylistic description is to contribute to the pleasure in the text by defining the individual qualities of what is vaguely referred to as the 'style' of a writer or text.

Stylistic description can be attempted by means of several methodologies. These range from an impressionistic 'literary stylistics', which is characteristic of most discussions of the language of children's literature, to complex systemic analyses. The latter can offer very precise and delicate descriptions, but have the limitation that non-specialists may find them impenetrable. This article works within the semiotic analysis developed in contemporary critical linguistics (Fairclough 1989; Stephens 1992a).

To discuss the textuality of children's fiction one has to begin by considering some assumptions about the nature of language on which it is grounded. Linguists recognise that language is a social semiotic, a culturally patterned system of signs used to communicate about things, ideas or concepts. As a system constructed within culture, it is not founded on any essential bond between a verbal sign and its referent (Stephens 1992a: 246–247). This is an important point to grasp, because much children's fiction is written and mediated under the contrary, essentialist assumption, and this has major implications both for writing objectives and for the relationships between writers and readers. As mentioned above, fantasy writing in particular is apt to assert the inextricability of word and thing, but the assumption also underlies realistic writing which purports to minimise the distance between life and fiction, or which pivots on the evolution of a character's essential selfhood, and it often informs critical suspicion of texts which foreground the gap between signs and things. The essentialist position has been conveniently (over-)stated by Molly Hunter:

> the belief underlying the practice of magic has a direct bearing on the whole concept of language ... The meaning of every word, it is argued, is innate to its sound and structure. Thus the word itself is the essence of what it names; and to capture that essence in speech is to be able to direct its power to a desired end.
>
> Hunter 1976: 107–108

Later in the same paper Hunter balances this position against a writer's more sober awareness 'that words may be defined only to the extent of ensuring their correct use in context' (109), describing the difference as a contradiction which 'all creative writing is an attempt to solve'. But a creative writer cannot resolve those incompatible assumptions about the nature of language and linguistic function. The following passages throw some light on this difference:

> The glade in the ring of trees was evidently a meeting-place of the wolves ... in the middle of the circle was a great grey wolf. He spoke to them in the dreadful language of the Wargs. Gandalf understood it. Bilbo did not, but it sounded terrible to him, and as if all their talk was about cruel and wicked things, as it was.
>
> *The Hobbit*, Tolkien 1937/1987: 91

> Charlie did not know much about ice ... The only piece he had known came from a refrigerated boat, and was left on the wharf, cloudy white, not clear, not even very clean. Charlie had waited until the boat went with its load of lamb carcasses, and then gone for it. By then it had melted. There was a puddle, a wisp of lambswool, and nothing more.

> He did not even think this was the same stuff. He did not think this place was part of the world. He thought it was the mouth of some other existence coming up from the ground, being drilled through the rock. The pieces coming away were like the fragments from the bit of the carpentry brace Papa used for setting up shelves. An iron thing would come from the ground, Charlie thought, and another Papa would blow through the hole to make it clear. Last time all the dust had gone into Charlie's eye, because he was still looking through. Papa had thought him such a fool.
>
> *Low Tide*, Mayne 1992: 163–164

The Tolkien and Mayne passages represent a principal character at a moment of incomprehension: Bilbo hears a foreign language, and has no actual referents for the verbal signs; Charlie perceives a physical phenomenon (the point at which pieces of ice break from a glacier into a river, though *glacier* is not introduced for two more paragraphs) and struggles with the socio-linguistic resources at his disposal to find meaning in it. A significant difference between the two is the implication that the Wargs' language communicates meanings beyond sense. On a simple level, this is to say no more than that it is obvious what the sounds made by a nasty horde of wolves signify. But Tolkien directly raises the question of comprehension – 'Gandalf understood it' – and uses his overt, controlling narrative voice to confirm that Bilbo comprehends something which is a linguistic essential: the language is inherently 'dreadful' (presumably in the fuller sense of 'inspiring dread'); and the 'as it was' confirms the principle that 'the meaning is innate to its sound' suggested by the lexical set 'terrible, wicked and cruel'. Mayne focuses on the other side of the sign/thing relationship, in effect posing a question often posed in his novels: can a phenomenon be understood if it cannot be signified in language? Tolkien's shifts between narration and Bilbo's focalisation are clearly marked; Mayne slips much more ambiguously between these modes, a strategy which serves to emphasise the gap between phenomena and language. The first paragraph is a retrospective narration of Charlie's single relevant empirical experience, but because that ice then differed in colour and form ('cloudy white', 'a puddle') the past experience does not enable him to make sense of the present. Instead, in the second paragraph Charlie produces a fantastic (mis-)interpretation on the premise that what he sees is visually isomorphic with another previous experience. The upshot is that, once again, he seems 'such a fool', though that is only a temporary state induced by linguistic inadequacy, and is set aside by the novel's congruence of story and theme. As a story, *Low Tide* is a treasure hunt gone wrong and then marvellously recuperated; a major thematic concern, articulated through the child characters' struggles to make sense of phenomena, language, and the relationships between phenomena and language, is a child's struggle towards competence in his or her socio–linguistic context.

The texts thus demonstrate two very different approaches to the semiotic instability of language. A third, and very common, approach is to exploit that instability as a source of humour, and this partly explains why nonsense verse is considered to be almost entirely the province of childhood. A rich vein of narrative humour also runs from the same source. In Sendak's *Higglety Pigglety Pop!*, for example, humour is created by exploiting the arbitrary relationship between signs and things or actions, specifically the instabilities which can result when significations slip, multiply, or change. In the following extract, Jenny, the Sealyham terrier, has undertaken the task of feeding a mysterious and uncooperative baby:

Jennie wiped her beard on the rug. 'If you do not eat, you will not grow.'

'NO EAT! NO GROW! SHOUT!'

Jennie sighed and neatly tapped the top off the soft-boiled egg. 'Baby want a bite?'

'NO BITE!'

'GOOD!' snapped Jennie, and she gulped the egg, shell and all.

Breakfast was disappearing into Nurse, and suddenly Baby wanted some too. 'EAT!' she cried, pointing to the cereal.

Jennie thanked Baby and gobbled up the oatmeal.

'NO EAT!' Baby screamed.

                                                        Sendak 1967/1987: 24

Signification in this extract pivots on the Baby's shouted 'EAT!', which in its immediate context is an expression of the Baby's desire, but becomes an instruction when Jennie chooses to interpret it as such. Subsequently, 'NO EAT!', which initially signifies the Baby's act of refusal, shifts to become another instruction. The first line of the extract is itself a succinct example of how context determines meaning. As a discrete utterance, 'Jennie wiped her beard on the rug' would seem to violate two normal social assumptions: female names do not normally collocate with beards, and 'rug' does not belong to the lexical set comprising objects on which beards might be wiped (towel; handkerchief; sleeve; etc.). In such an example, 'correct use in context' extends beyond other nearby words and the grammar which combines them into intelligible form to include the situation of utterance and cultural context. The situation of utterance – the knowledge that Jennie is a dog – clarifies the focus of reference, but at the same time foregrounds how the 'same' utterance can have a very different meaning in different contexts. The instability of reference emerges even when we know Jennie is a dog, because the primary association of *beard* is with human (male) facial hair, and hence is always to some degree figurative when transferred to animals or plants. In such ways, *Higglety Pigglety Pop!* is a richly subversive text, playing on meanings to such an extent as to suggest that if allowed free play, language will tend to be uncontainable by situation, hovering always on the boundary of excess. Such a view of language, however, tends to be uncommon in the domain of children's literature.

The issue of sign/referent relationship is of central interest here because it bears directly on linguistic function in children's fiction and the notion of desirable significances. The assumption that the relationship is direct and unproblematic has the initial effect of producing what might be termed closed meanings. The Tolkien example is especially instructive because it explicitly shows how language which is potentially open, enabling a variety of potential reader responses, is narrowed by paradigmatic recursiveness and essentialism. Writers will, of course, often aim for such specification, but what are the implications if virtually all meaning in a text is implicitly closed? The outcome points to an invisible linguistic control by writer over reader. As Hunt has argued, attempts to exercise such control are much less obvious when conveyed by stylistic features than by lexis or story existents (Hunt 1991: 109).

A related linguistic concept of major importance for the issue of language choice and writerly control is register, the principle which governs the choice among various possible linguistic realisations of the same thing. Register refers to types of language variation which collocate with particular social situations and written genres. Socially, for example, people choose different appropriate language variations for formal and informal occasions, for friendly disputes and angry arguments, and for specialised discourses: science, sport, computing, skipping rope games, role-play, and so on, all have particular registers made up of configurations of lexical and syntactical choices. Narrative fictions will seek to replicate such registers, but also, as with a wide range of writing genres, develop distinctive registers of their own. Genres familiar in children's fiction such as folk and fairy stories, ghost and terror stories, school stories, teen romance, and a host of others – use some readily identifiable registers. Consider the use of register in the following passage from Anna Fienberg's *Ariel, Zed and the Secret of Life*. It describes three girls watching a horror movie, but one of them (Ariel) is giggling:

When the girls looked back at the screen, the scene had changed. It was dusk, and shadows bled over the ground. A moaning wind had sprung up, and somewhere, amongst the trees, an owl hooted.

'Ooh, *look*,' hissed Lynn, her nails digging into her friend Mandy's arm. 'Is that him there, crouching behind that bush? Tell me what happens. I'm not looking any more.'

'The nurse is saying goodnight,' Mandy whispered, 'she's leaving. She'll have to go right past him.'

*The Monster From Out of Town* was, indeed, breathing heavily behind a camellia bush. His clawed hands crushed flowers to a perfumed pulp, which made you think of what he would do to necks ...

Ariel grinned. The monster's mask was badly made and his costume looked much too tight ...

Fienberg 1992: 9–10

The scene from the movie is presented in the conventional register of the Gothic (dusk, shadows, bled, moaning wind, an owl hooted), though the unusual metaphor 'shadows bled' reconfigures the conventional elements with the effect of foregrounding the Gothic trait of overwording (or semantic overload). By then switching the retelling to the audience's perceptions and responses, Fienberg builds in a common Gothic narrative strategy, that of determining emotional response to scene or incident by building it in as a character's response. The switch also enables a version of the suspense so necessary to horror ('him ... behind that bush'; 'the nurse ... leaving'; 'his clawed hands'). These narrative strategies set up the deflation occurring with Ariel's response and the register shift which expresses it: detached and analytic, she epitomises the resistant reader who refuses the positioning implied by the genre. The deflation has the effect of retrospectively defining how far a genre can depend on its audience's unthinking acceptance of the emotional codes implied by its register.

Fienberg is making an important point about how fiction works (her novel is pervasively metafictive), and it is a point which is well applied to modes of fiction in which register is much less obtrusive. It is easy to assume that realistic fiction is based on a neutral register, though this is not really so, and a stylistic account can help disclose how its registers position readers even more thoroughly than do obvious registers such as that of Gothic. This is readily seen in the tradition of realism in adolescent fiction in the USA, which developed in the 1960s out of a psychology of adolescence based in the work of Erik Erikson re-routed through the textual influence of Salinger's *The Catcher in the Rye*. Thus a first-person, adolescent narrator represents significant issues of adolescent development, such as 'experience of physical sexual maturity, experience of withdrawal from adult benevolent protection, consciousness of self in interaction, re-evaluation of values, [and] experimentation' (Russell 1988: 61). Cultural institutions, genre and style interact with a material effect, not just to code human behaviour but to shape it. A stylistic analysis offers one position from which we can begin to unravel that shaping process. Danziger's *Can You Sue Your Parents for Malpractice?* is thematically focused on the five concepts of adolescent development listed above; most are evident in the following passage:

[Linda] says, 'How can you stop a buffalo from charging?'

'Take away his credit cards,' my mother answers.

My father turns to her. 'You should know that one. Now that you're going back to work, I bet you're going to be spending like mad, living outside my salary.'

'Why don't you just accept it and not feel so threatened?' My mother raises her voice. She hardly ever does that.

I can feel the knot in my stomach and I feel like I'm going to jump out of my skin.

'Who feels threatened?' he yells. 'That's ridiculous. Just because you won't have to depend on me, need me any more, why should I worry?'

So that's why he's acting this way. He thinks it's the money that makes him important. Sometimes I just don't understand his brain.

'Why can't you ever celebrate anything?' she yells again.

I throw my spoon on the table. That's it. I'm leaving.

Linda follows me out. It's like a revolution. Nothing like this has ever happened before.

Danziger 1979/1987: 64

An important part of the register here is the first person and – as often – present tense narration, particularly in so far as it constructs a precise orientation of narrative voice towards a conventional situation. The function of present tense narration is to convey an illusion of immediacy and instanteity, suppressing any suggestion that the outcome is knowable in advance. Thus Lauren, the narrator, proceeds through specific moments of recognition and decision – 'I can feel ...'; 'So that's why ...'; 'That's it. I'm leaving'; 'It's like a revolution' – but each of these moments, as with the depiction of the quarrel itself, is expressed by means of a register which consists of the clichés which pertain to it. Linguistically, this has a double function. It is, now at the other end of the creative spectrum, another use of language which assumes an essential link between sign and referent; and in doing that through cliché it constitutes the text as a surface without depth, an effect reinforced by the way present tense narration severely restricts the possibility of any temporal movement outside the present moment. The outcome, both linguistically and thematically, is a complete closing of meaning: there is no interpretative task for a reader to perform, no inference undrawn. This closure even extends to the joke with which the passage begins.

Another way to describe this is to say that the metonymic mode of writing which characterises realistic fiction, and which enables particular textual moments to relate to a larger signifying structure (Stephens 1992a: 248–249), has been directed towards a closing of meaning. Another aspect of the metonymic process is that a narrative may draw upon recognisable scenes repeatable from one text to another and which constitute a 'register' of metonyms of family life. This example could be categorised as: situation, the parental quarrel; pretext, money; actual focus, power and authority. With perhaps unintentional irony produced by the present tense verb, the repeatability of the scene is foregrounded by Lauren's remark that 'Nothing like this has ever happened before.' It happens all the time, especially in post-1960s realist adolescent fiction, and its function, paradoxically, is to confirm a model whereby the rational individual progresses to maturity under the ideal of liberal individuality, doing so through the assurance that the experience is metonymic of the experience of everybody in that age group.

The presence of a narrative voice which interprets the scene for the benefit of readers is a characteristic of another linguistic aspect of texts, the presentation of scene and incident through the representation of speech and thought and the strategy of focalisation. These are important aspects of point of view in narrative, the facet of narration through which a writer implicitly, but powerfully, controls how readers understand the text. Because readers are willing to surrender themselves to the flow of the discourse, especially by focusing attention on story or content, they are susceptible to the implicit power of point of view. Linguistically, point of view is established by focalisation strategies and by conversational pragmatics. The first is illustrated in the following passage from Paula Fox's *How Many Miles to Babylon?*, which exemplifies a common textual strategy in children's fiction, the narration of incidents as they impact on the mind of a single focalising character. Most novels which are third-person narrations include at least one focalising character, and this has important implications for the kind of language used, because in the vast majority of books written for children there is only one such focaliser, who is a child (or ersatz child, such as Bilbo in *The Hobbit*). Further, as with first person narrators, readers will tend to align themselves with that focalising character's point of view.

> [James] *knew* he shouldn't go into the house – it wasn't his house. But that wasn't the reason why he wanted the street to be empty when he walked up the little path. What he knew and what he felt were two different things. He felt that going into that house had to be something he did secretly, as though it were night and he moved among shadows.
>
> The door was open enough to let him slip in without pushing it. Sunlight didn't penetrate the dirty windows, so he stood still until his eyes grew accustomed to the darkness. Then, as he smelled the dusty old rooms and the dampness of the wallpaper that was peeling off the walls, other things he felt came swimming towards him through the gloom like fish.
>
> Fox 1967/1972: 28

The text is shaped by the presence of represented thought and by direct or implied acts of perception. The narrative representation of thought – marked here by the verbs 'knew' and 'felt' – situates events within the character's mind but also enables a separate narrating voice. This narration is always evident here in such aspects of register as the quite complex left-branching syntax of the final sentence and lexical items such as 'penetrate' and 'accustomed', and by the use of analogies and figurative language. James is a 10-year-old, whose own linguistic level is shown to be a scant competence with a *Dick and Jane* reader (20), and there is no evident attempt at this moment to match linguistic level of narrative discourse to that of the character, though that does often happen. There is, nevertheless, an obvious contrast with the Danziger passage, which, despite having a much older main character (14), has access to a more limited range of registers. Figurative language is likewise less complex. Lauren's 'I can feel the knot in my stomach and I feel like I'm going to jump out of my skin' are cliché analogies, whereas in 'other things he felt came swimming towards him through the gloom like fish' the ground of the concrete/abstract comparison foregrounds the double meanings of 'swimming' and 'gloom', opening out the space between sign and referent and giving readers an opportunity to draw inferences which are not fully determined by the text but have room to include more personal associations.

The last sentence of the Fox extract is unusual in its complexity, however, because complex sentences, especially in conjunction with complex focalisation, tend rather to be the province of more difficult Young Adult fiction. In general, most fiction for children up to early adolescence is characterised by a lexis and grammar simplified relative to the notional audience: sentences are right-branching, and within them clauses are mainly linked by coordination, temporality or causality; and the use of qualifiers and figurative language is restricted. Even the passage cited from *Low Tide*, which has a very subtle effect (and Mayne is often thought of as a writer of 'difficult' texts), is entirely right-branching and contains very few qualifiers. There, as elsewhere, subtlety depends on textual strategies which open, rather than close off, signification.

The second linguistic construction of point of view is by means of represented conversation. Various modes are available to a writer (see Leech and Short 1981), and all appear in children's fiction. These modes range from reported speech acts, which are mainly an aspect of narrative, to direct speech dialogues, which readers must interpret in the light of their knowledge of the principles and conventions of conversation. Because the intermediate forms of indirect and free indirect speech representation allow both for subtle interplay between narratorial and character points of view and for narratorial control, they have tended to receive most attention in discussions of general fiction. With children's fiction, however, more attention needs to be paid to direct speech dialogue, both because it exists in a higher proportion and because of the general principle that the narrator in the text appears to have less control over point of view in dialogue. Leech and Short envisage a cline running between 'bound' and 'free' forms, where 'free' corresponds with closeness to direct speech (324). But point of view in such conversations is affected by two factors: the presence of narratorial framing, especially speech-reporting tags, that is, the devices for identifying speakers which may in themselves suggest attitudes; and the pragmatic principles which shape conversation. The following passage illustrates these factors.

When they reached [the others] they slipped in behind Rebecca and Sue Stephens, and Juniper saw Ellie standing on the pavement buttoned up in her old red coat, Jake beside her. They waved and smiled.

'Your mum looks like ... a pop star,' said Sue.

'No, someone in a TV series,' said Rebecca.

'It must be strange to have a mother looking like that,' went on Sue, still staring behind her.

'How would I know? I've only had her, haven't I? I don't know any different mother, so I don't know if it's strange or not.'

Sue kept on:

'Is that your dad? That one with the beard?'

'Shut up,' hissed Rebecca, then said very loudly and clearly, 'I liked your reading, Juniper. You were the best.'

'You sounded dead miserable but your arm didn't show. Nobody could tell. I expect Sir picked you because of being sorry for you. He's like that. What did you say?' asked Sue.

'I said Abbledy, Gabbledy Flook,' answered Juniper and then under her breath, Ere the sun begins to sink, May your nasty face all shrink, which came into her head out of nowhere, and wished herself away to a wide, pale beach with the sun shining down and a white horse galloping at the edge of the incoming tide, far, far away from the wind slicing down the pavement blowing up grit and rubbish as they made their way back to school.

Kemp 1982: 78–79

This exchange shows very clearly how meaning in conversations arises not from the simple sense of individual utterances but from the tenor of utterances in combination and as shaped by narratorial tagging. It also illustrates how a children's book makes use of the main principles which inform actual or represented conversations: the principle of cooperation, the principle of politeness and the principle of irony. In order to communicate in an orderly and productive way speakers accept five conventions which organise what we say to one another: an utterance should be of an appropriate size; it should be correct or truthful; it should relate back to the previous speaker's utterance (a change of subject and a change of register may both be breaches of relation); it should be clear, organised and unambiguous; and each speaker should have a fair share of the conversation, that is, be able to take his or her turn in an orderly way and be able to complete what s/he wants to say (Leech 1983; Stephens 1992b: 76–96). These conventions are very readily broken, and much of everyday conversation depends on simultaneously recognising and breaking one or more of them. In particular, many breaches are prompted by the operation of politeness in social exchange. Whenever conversational principles are breached, the product is apt to be humour, irony or conflict.

After a sequence of four utterances which more or less adhere to the principles of coherence and turn taking, but skirt the boundaries of politeness by drawing attention to Ellie's unusual appearance (shabby but beautiful, she doesn't conform to the girls' image of 'mother'), Kemp introduces a sequence built on crucial breaches of relation and politeness, beginning with Sue's 'Is that your dad?'. This is flagged contextually because readers know that Juniper's father is missing, and textually because of the cline in the speech reporting tags from the neutral 'said Sue' to the intrusively persistent 'Sue kept on', and the heavy tagging of Rebecca's interruption and shift of relation ('hissed Rebecca, then said very loudly and clearly'). Finally, of course, Juniper's escapist daydream cliché also serves as a narratorial comment on how painful she has found the exchange: indeed, the blowing 'grit and rubbish' becomes a metonym for the anguish at the heart of her being. Second, Sue's response to Rebecca's intervention is to apparently pursue relation but to breach politeness by turning attention to Juniper's missing arm. The upshot is Juniper's final spoken utterance – interrupting, impolite and nonsensical, it terminates the exchange and the discourse shifts into represented thought. Such an astute use of conversational principles is one of the most expressive linguistic tools available to a children's writer.

A stylistic examination of children's fiction can show us something very important, namely that a fiction with a high proportion of conversation and a moderately sophisticated use of focalisation has access to textual strategies with the potential to offset the limitations which may be implicit in a disinclination to employ the full range of lexical, syntactic and figurative possibilities of written discourse. But stylistic analysis is also never an end in itself, and is best carried out within a frame which considers the relationship of text to genre and to culture. Obviously enough, stylistics alone cannot determine the relative merits of Sue and Rebecca's preferences for 'a pop star' or 'someone in a TV series', and cannot determine whether a reader treats either category as prestigious or feels that both consign Ellie to a subject position without selfhood. The example illustrates two general principles in language analysis: that significance is influenced by the larger contexts of text and culture within which particular utterances are meaningful; and that particular language features or effects can have more than one function, simultaneously expressing both purposiveness and implicit, often unexamined, social assumptions.

Finally, attention to the language of children's fiction has an important implication for evaluation, adding another dimension to the practices of judging books according to their entertainment value as stories or to their socio-political correctness. It can be an important tool in distinguishing between 'restrictive texts' which allow little scope for active reader judgements (Hunt 1991: 117) and texts which enable critical and thoughtful responses.

## References

Danziger, P. (1979/1987) *Can You Sue Your Parents for Malpractice?*, London: Pan.

Fairclough, N. (1989) *Language and Power*, London and New York: Longman.

Fienberg, A. (1992) *Ariel, Zed and the Secret of Life*, Sydney: Allen and Unwin.

Fox, P. (1967/1972) *How Many Miles to Babylon?*, Harmondsworth: Puffin.

Hamilton, V. (1976) *Arilla Sun Down*, London: Hamish Hamilton.

Hunt, P. (1991) *Criticism, Theory, and Children's Literature*, Oxford: Basil Blackwell.

Hunter, M. (1976) *Talent Is Not Enough*, New York: Harper and Row.

Kemp, G. (1986/1988) *Juniper*, Harmondsworth: Puffin.

Leech, G. N. (1983) *Principles of Pragmatics*, London and New York: Longman

—— and Short, M. H. (1981) *Style in Fiction*, London and New York: Longman.

Mayne, W. (1992) *Low Tide*, London: Cape.

Russell, D. A. (1988) 'The common experience of adolescence: a requisite for the development of young adult literature, *Journal of Youth Services in Libraries* 2: 58–63.

Scholes, R. (1985) *Textual Power: Literary Theory and the Teaching of English*, New Haven and London: Yale University Press.

Sendak, M. (1967/1984) *Higglety Pigglety Pop! or There Must be More to Life*, Harmondsworth: Puffin.

Stephens, J. (1992a) *Language and Ideology in Children's Fiction*, London and New York: Longman.

—— (1992b) *Reading the Signs: Sense and Significance in Written Texts*, Sydney: Kangaroo Press.

Sullivan, C. W. III (1985) 'J. R. R. Tolkien's *The Hobbit*: the magic of words', in Nodelman, P. (ed.) *Touchstones: Reflections on the Best in Children's Literature*, vol. 1, West Lafayette, IN: Children's Literature Association.

Tolkien, J. R. R. (1937/1987) *The Hobbit*, London: Unwin Hyman.

## Further Reading

Billman, C. (1979) 'Verbal creativity in children's literature', *English Quarterly* 12: 25–32.

Hunt, P. (1978) 'The cliché count: a practical aid for the selection of books for children', *Children's Literature in Education* 9, 3: 143–50.

—— (1988) 'Degrees of control: stylistics and the discourse of children's literature', in Coupland, N. (ed.) *Styles of Discourse*, London: Croom Helm.

Kuskin, K. (1980) 'The language of children's literature', in Michaels, L. and Ricks, C. (eds) *The State of the Language*, Berkeley: University of California Press.

Stephens, J. (1989) 'Language, discourse, picture books', *Children's Literature Association Quarterly* 14: 106–110.

# 6

# Reader-Response Criticism

## *Michael Benton*

The importance of reader-response criticism in the area of children's literature lies in what it tells us about two fundamental questions, one about the literature and the other about its young readers:

- who is the implied child reader inscribed in the text?
- how do actual child readers respond during the process of reading?

The main advocates of reader-response criticism acknowledge the complementary importance of text and reader. They attend both to the form and language of poem or story, and to the putative reader constructed there, acknowledging, as Henry James put it, that the author makes 'his reader very much as he makes his characters ... When he makes him well, that is makes him interested, then the reader does quite half the labour' (quoted in Booth 1961: 302). Equally, they attend to the covert activity of the reading process, deducing the elements of response from what readers say or write, and/or developing theoretical models of aesthetic experience.

Whatever the particular orientation of the reader-response critic, one central issue recurs: the mystery of what readers actually do and experience. The subject of the reader's response is the Loch Ness Monster of literary studies: when we set out to capture it, we cannot even be sure that it is there at all; and, if we assume that it is, we have to admit that the most sensitive probing with the most sophisticated instruments has so far succeeded only in producing pictures of dubious authenticity. That the nature and dimensions of this phenomenon are so uncertain is perhaps the reason why the hunters are so many and their approaches so various. Accordingly, it is necessary to map the main historical development of reader-response criticism and, second, to outline the theoretical bases which its advocates share, before going on to consider how this perspective – whose concepts have been formulated largely in the area of adult literary experience – has been taken up by researchers interested in young readers and their books.

## A Shift of Critical Perspective

In the 1950s the criticism of literature was in a relatively stable state. In *The Mirror and the Lamp* (1953), M. H. Abrams was confidently able to describe 'the total situation' of the work of art as one with the text at the centre with the three elements of the author, the reader, and the signified world ranged like satellites around it. What has happened since has destabilised this model. In particular, reader-response critics have argued that it is readers who make meaning by the activities they perform on texts; they see the reader in the centre and thus the privileged position of the work of art is undermined and individual 'readings' become the focus of attention. This is not to say that the emphasis upon reading and response which emerged in the 1960s was entirely new. It had been initiated famously by I. A. Richards forty years earlier; but Richards's (1924, 1929) seminal work, with its twin concerns of pedagogy and criticism, influenced subsequent developments in criticism in two contrary ways. For, in one sense, Richards privileged the text, and the American New Critics, particularly, seized upon the evidence of *Practical Criticism* to insist that close analysis of the words on the page was the principal job of critic and teacher. Yet, in another sense, Richards privileged the reader; and subsequently, modern reader-response criticism has developed to give the reader freedoms that infuriate text-oriented critics. Hence, Stanley Fish writes: 'Interpretation is not the art of construing but the art of constructing. Interpreters do not decode poems: they make them' (Fish 1980: 327). Or, even more provocatively: 'It is the structure of the reader's experience rather than any structures available on the page that should be the object of description' (152). As Laurence Lerner (1983: 6) has pointed out, perhaps the most important division in contemporary literary studies is between those who see literature as a more or less self-contained system, and those who see it as interacting with real, extra-literary experience (that of the author, or of the reader or the social reality of the author's or the reader's world). Reader-response critics clearly fall within this second category.

Reader-response criticism is difficult to map because of its diversity, especially in two respects: first, there are several important figures whose work stands outside the normal boundaries of the term; and second, there is overlap but not identity in the relationship between German 'reception theory' and Anglo-American reader-response criticism. On the first issue, two highly influential writers, D. W. Harding and Louise Rosenblatt, began publishing work in the 1930s which was ahead of its time (for example, Harding 1937; Rosenblatt 1938/1970) and their explorations of the psychological and affective aspects of literary experience only really began to have an impact upon educational thinking (and hence upon children's experiences of poems and stories in school) when the educational and literary theorists began to rehabilitate the reader in the 1960s and 1970s. Subsequently, Harding's paper on 'Psychological approaches in the reading of fiction' (1962) and Rosenblatt's re-issued *Literature as Exploration* (1938/1970) have been widely regarded as two of the basic texts in this area.

It is an indication of the diversity and loose relationships which characterise response-oriented approaches to literature that Harding and Rosenblatt are reduced to complimentary footnotes in the standard introductions to reader-response criticism (Tompkins, 1980: xxvi; Suleiman and Crosman, 1980: 45; Freund, 1987: 158), and that writers in the German and Anglo-American traditions have, with the notable exception of Iser, little contact with or apparent influence upon one another. In a thorough account of German reception theory, Holub (1984) comments upon this divide and provides an excellent analysis of

Iser's work to complement that of Freund (1987), whose book summarises the Anglo-American tradition.

The development of reader-response writings since the 1960s has steadily forged a new relationship between the act of reading and the act of teaching literature which, as is illustrated later, has significant consequences for the way the relationship between young readers and their books is conceptualised. Prior to this time, during the 1940s and 1950s, the reader was hidden from view as the critical landscape was dominated by the American New Criticism, whose adherents took a determinedly anti-reader stance to the extent that, despite a concern for 'close reading', the major statement of New Criticism views – Wellek and Warren's *Theory of Literature* (1949) – makes no mention of the reader and includes only two brief references to 'reading'. Subsequently, the development of reader-response studies has seen the momentum shift periodically from literary theory to educational enquiry and practice almost decade by decade.

The 1960s were dominated by education, with the most influential work published by The National Council of Teachers of English (Squire 1964; Purves and Rippere 1968), culminating in two surveys, one English and the other American (D'Arcy 1973; Purves and Beach 1972). The 1970s saw the full bloom of reader-response theorising by literary critics of whom Holland (1975), Culler (1975), Iser (1978) and Fish (1980) were perhaps the most notable figures, all of whom were well represented in the two compilations of papers that stand as a summary of work in this area at the end of the decade (Suleiman and Crosman 1980; Tompkins 1980). During the 1980s the emphasis moved back to education, where the main concern was to translate what had become known about response – both from literary theory and from classroom enquiry – into principles of good practice. Protherough (1983), Cooper (1985a), Benton and Fox (1985), Scholes (1985), Corcoran and Evans (1987), Benton *et al.* (1988), Dias and Hayhoe (1988), Hayhoe and Parker (1990), Benton (1992a), Many and Cox (1992) have all, in their different ways, considered the implications for practice of a philosophy of literature and learning based upon reader-response principles. In Britain, one of the more heartening results of this development was that the importance of the reader's response to literature was fully acknowledged in the new National Curriculum as embodied in the Cox Report (1989) and in the official documents that ensued. Such has been what one standard book on modern literary theory calls 'the vertiginous rise of reader-response criticism' (Jefferson and Robey, 1986: 142), that its authors see it as threatening to engulf all other approaches.

What are the theoretical bases that such writers share? Reader-response criticism is a broad church as a reading of the various overview books demonstrates (Tompkins, 1980; Suleiman and Crosman, 1980; Freund, 1987). None the less, a number of principles can be said to characterise this critical stance. First is the rejection of the notorious 'affective fallacy'. In describing the 'fallacy' as 'a confusion of the poem and its results', and in dismissing as mere 'impressionism and relativism' any critical judgements based on the psychological effects of literature, Wimsatt and Beardsley (1954/1970) had left no space for the reader to inhabit. They ignored the act of reading. New Criticism, it could be said, invented 'the assumed reader'; by contrast, reader-response criticism deals with real and implied readers. Iser, Holland, Bleich and Fish operate from a philosophical basis that displaces the notion of an autonomous text to be examined in and on its own terms from the centre of critical discussion and substitutes the reader's recreation of that text. Reading is not the discovering of meaning (like some sort of archaeological 'dig') but the creation of it. The purpose of rehearsing this familiar history is its importance for children's reading. The central concerns of response-oriented approaches focus upon

1   what constitutes the source of literary meaning; and
2   what is the nature of the interpretative process that creates it.

Both issues are fundamental to how young readers read, both in and out of school.

The works of Iser on fiction and Rosenblatt on poetry, despite some criticism that Iser has attracted on theoretical grounds, have none the less had greater influence upon the actual teaching of literature and our understanding of children as readers than those of any other theoretical writers. No doubt this is because they avoid what Frank Kermode calls 'free-floating theory' and concentrate, in Iser's words, on 'an analysis of what actually happens when one is reading' (Iser 1978: 19). Iser's theory of aesthetic response (1978) and Rosenblatt's transactional theory of the literary work (1978, 1985) have helped change the culture of the classroom to one which operates on the principle that the text cannot be said to have a meaningful existence outside the relationship between itself and its reader(s). This transfer of power represents a sea-change in critical emphasis and in pedagogical practice from the assumptions most critics and teachers held even a generation ago. Yet it is evolutionary change, not sudden revolution – a progressive rethinking of the way readers create literary experiences for themselves with poems and stories. In fact, reader-response is the evolutionary successor to Leavisite liberal humanism. It is perceived – within the area of literature teaching – as providing a framework of now familiar ideas which are widely accepted and to which other lines of critical activity often make reference: the plurality of meanings within a literary work; the creative participation of the reader; the acknowledgement that the reader is not a *tabula rasa* but brings idiosyncratic knowledge and personal style to the act of reading; and the awareness that interpretation is socially, historically and culturally formed. All these ideas are ones that have had a sharp impact upon the study of texts and upon research into young readers' reading in the field of children's literature.

## Young Readers and Their Books

Reader-response approaches to children's literature which set out to answer the questions raised at the beginning of this chapter all have a direct relationship with pedagogy. Some are concerned with children's responses, mainly to fiction and poetry but latterly also to picture books, with the broad aim of improving our understanding of what constitutes good practice in literature teaching. Others employ reader-response methods in order to explore children's concepts and social attitudes. Others again, are text-focused and use concepts and ideas from reader-response criticism of adult literature in order to examine children's books, with the aim of uncovering their implied audience and, thence, something of the singularity of a specifically *children's* literature.

This diversity creates two problems: first, there is bound to be overlap. Many studies cover both textual qualities and children's responses as complementary aspects of a unitary experience which, as the foregoing discussion has argued, follows from the mainstream thinking of reader-response criticism. When considering a study under one or other of the headings below, therefore, its writer's principal orientation has been the guide. Second, there is bound to be anomaly. The nature and complexity of the studies varies greatly. In particular, there are two important collections of papers devoted to theoretical research and empirical enquiries in this area (Cooper 1985a; Many and Cox 1992). These are most conveniently considered between discussion of the first and second themes below to which most of their papers relate.

The discussion deals, in turn, with five themes: the process of responding; development in reading; types of reader behaviour; culturally oriented studies exploring children's attitudes; and text-oriented studies employing reader-response concepts.

### *The process of responding*

The stances of those enquirers who have explored the response processes of young readers vary as much as those of the literary theorists, but the most common one is that of the teacher-researcher attempting to theorise classroom practice. The range and combinations of the variables in these studies are enormous: texts, contexts, readers and research methods are all divisible into subsets with seemingly infinite permutations. Among texts, short stories, poems, fairy tales and picture books are favoured, with a few studies focusing upon the novel and none on plays. Contexts, in the sense of physical surroundings, also influence response. The 'classroom' itself can mean a variety of things and clearly there are crucial differences between say, monitoring the responses of thirty children within normal lesson time and four or five children who volunteer to work outside lessons. Most studies are small-scale enquiries run by individual researchers, perhaps with a collaborative element; hence, the focus is usually narrow when selecting the number, age–level, social background, gender and literacy level of the readers. Finally, reader-response monitoring procedures are generally devised in the knowledge that the medium is the message. The ways readers are asked to present their responses are fundamental influences upon those responses; they range from undirected invitations to free association or 'say what comes into your mind as you read', through various 'prompts' or guideline questions to consider, to the explicit questionnaire. Oral, written, or graphic responses and whether the readers are recording individually or in groups all provide further dimensions to the means of monitoring and collecting response data.

Guidance through this diversity is offered by two older books already mentioned (Purves and Beach 1972; D'Arcy 1973); and, more recently, by Galda (1983) in a special issue of the *Journal of Research and Development in Education* on 'Response to literature: empirical and theoretical studies', and by Squire's chapter 'Research on reader response and the national literature initiative' in Hayhoe and Parker (Squire 1990: 13–24). What follows does not attempt to be exhaustive but briefly to indicate the main lines that process studies have taken.

The process of responding became one of the main objects of enquiry during the 1980s. Studies of children's responses to poetry began to appear in articles or booklet form: Wade (1981) adapted Squire's (1964) work on short stories to compare how a supervised and an unsupervised group of middle-school children responded to a poem by Charles Tomlinson. Dixon and Brown (1984) studied the writings of 17-year-old students in order to identify what was being assessed in their responses; Atkinson (1985) built upon Purves and Rippere's (1968) categories and explored the process of response to poems by children of different ages. Several books also focused exclusively on young readers and poetry and, either wholly or in part, concerned themselves with the response process, notably Benton (1986), Dias and Hayhoe (1988) and Benton et al. (1988). The work of Barnes (1976), particularly, lies behind the enquiries of Benton (1986) into small group responses to poetry by 13 to 14-year-olds. What is characterised as 'lightly-structured, self-directed discussion' is seen as the means of optimising group talk about poems and as the most appropriate way for teacher-researchers to explore the process of response. Dias and Hayhoe (1988) build upon Dias's earlier work (1986) to develop responding-aloud protocols (RAPs) which, essentially, require individual pupils to think aloud as they attempt to make sense of a poem with the help, if needed, of a non-directive interviewer. Preparatory group discussions were used to build up confidence for the individual sessions. The RAP transcripts were then analysed to see how pupils negotiated meaning. Dias and Hayhoe claim that their study is 'designed to track the process of responding as it occurs' (1988: 51) and their methodology is a significant contribution to this end.

Similarly, the work of Benton and his co-authors (1988) focuses upon process. It shows three experienced teachers exploring how their students, aged 14 and above, read and respond to poetry. Rosenblatt's transactional theory underpins the approach, especially in Teasey's work which gives the hard evidence for the reader's 'evocation' of a poem through meticulous, descriptive analyses of aesthetic reading. Bell's data shows the emphases of the response process from initial encounter through group discussion, to an eventual written account, in such a way that what in mathematics is called 'the working' can be observed – in this case, the slow evolution over time and in different contexts of how young readers make meaning. Hurst's focus is upon the whole class rather than individuals. From studying the responses of pupils in a variety of classrooms and with different teachers and texts, he develops a model of three frames (story, poet, form), derived from Barnes' and Todd's (1977) notion of the 'cycles of utterances' that characterise group talk, as a means of mapping the episodes of a group's engagement with a poem. The three enquiries are set against a critical appraisal of the main theorists in the field from Richards to Rosenblatt and all contribute to the development of a response-centred methodology.

The process of responding to fictional narrative was first examined by Squire (1964) and Purves and Rippere (1968), whose early studies provoked many adaptations of their work with students of different ages and backgrounds. These studies all tended to categorise the elements of response, with Squire's list emerging as the most commonly quoted and replicated in studies of children's responses. Squire's study of adolescents responding to short stories described the six elements of response as literary judgements, interpretational responses, narrational reactions, associational responses, self-involvement and prescriptive judgements (Squire, 1964: 17–18). He showed that the greater the involvement of readers, the stronger was their tendency to make literary judgements; and that what he termed 'happiness-binding' (41) was a characteristic of adolescent readers' behaviour. Here, as in many studies of fiction reading, there is a noticeable move towards a broadly psychoanalytical explanation for the gratifications readers seek in fiction (compare Holland 1975). More recent studies include those of Fox (1979) whose phrase 'dark watchers' (32) is a memorable description of the imaginary, spectator role that young readers often adopt during reading; and Jackson (1980) who explored the initial responses of children to fiction which later he developed more fully throughout the secondary school age range (Jackson 1983). Several books also focused wholly or in part upon young readers' response processes, notably Protherough (1983), Benton and Fox (1985), and Thomson (1986). Drawing upon enquiries he conducted in Hull, Protherough suggests that there are five major ways in which children see the process of reading fiction: projection into a character, projection into the situation, association between book and reader, the distanced viewer, and detached evaluation. There is a developmental dimension and he argues that maturity in reading is connected with the ability to operate in an increasing number of modes.

Benton and Fox address the question of what happens when we read stories and consider that the process of responding involves the reader in creating a secondary world. This concept is elaborated with reference to children's accounts of their experiences with various stories. The reading experience is then characterised in two ways: first, as a four-phase process of feeling like reading, getting into the story, being lost in the book, and having an increasing sense of an ending; and second, as an activity consisting of four elements – picturing, anticipating and retrospecting, interacting and evaluating. This latter description has been taken up by others, notably Corcoran (Corcoran and Evans, 1987: 45–51).

Thomson's work with teenage readers offers a further description of the elements of response to fiction and cross-hatches this with a developmental model. The requirements for satisfaction at all stages are enjoyment and elementary understanding. Assuming these are met, his six stages are described as: unreflective interest in action, empathising, analogising, reflecting on the significance of events and behaviour, reviewing the whole work as the author's creation, and the consciously considered relationship with the author. Thomson's is a sophisticated and detailed account, firmly rooted in young readers' fiction reading, and drawing effectively upon the theoretical literature summarised earlier in this chapter.

As can be seen from this summary, studies of the process of responding tend towards categorisation of the different psychological activities involved and towards descriptions of what constitutes maturation in reading. Two collections of papers which should contribute more than they do to our understanding of the process of responding are Cooper (1985a) and Many and Cox (1992), although in their defence it has to be said that the former has a focus upon the theories that should guide our study of readers and the research methodologies that derive from them, and the latter is primarily concerned with reader 'stance' (Rosenblatt 1978) as the discussion of types of reader below indicates. Brief comment upon these two collections is appropriate before moving on to consider reading development.

Only some of the seventeen papers in Cooper's compilation bear upon the subject of children and literature. The first of the three parts of the book is helpful in relating theoretical issues of response to practice, especially the chapters by Rosenblatt, Purves and Petrosky. In Part 2, Kintgen's piece stands out, not only because its focus is poetry (a comparative rarity in such company), but because it faces up to the problems of monitoring responses, and attempts to describe the mental activities and processes of the reader. Kintgen's subjects (as with many researchers) are graduate students but the methodology here could readily transfer to younger readers. The four contributors to the final part of the book on classroom literature, whom one might expect to deal with children and their books, studiously avoid doing so, preferring instead to discuss theoretical and methodological issues such as the need to identify response research with literary pedagogy (Bleich), the use of school surveys (Squire), and the evaluation of the outcomes of literary study (Cooper 1985b).

Many and Cox (1992) take their impetus from Cooper's book and their inspiration from Rosenblatt (1978). The first part gives theoretical perspectives on reader stance and response and includes specific consideration of readings of selected children's books (Benton: 1992b) and of young readers' responses (Corcoran). The papers in Part two focus upon students' perspectives when reading and responding and tell us more about types of readers than about process; these are dealt with below. Part three deals with classroom interactions of teachers, students and literature. Hade explores 'stance' in both silent reading and reading aloud, arguing its transactional and triadic nature in the classroom. Zancella writes engagingly about the use of biography, in the sense of a reader's personal history, in responding to literature and how this influences the teacher's methods. Zarrillo and Cox build upon Rosenblatt's efferent/aesthetic distinction and urge more of the latter in classroom teaching in the light of their empirical findings that 'elementary teachers tend to direct children to adopt efferent stances towards literature' (245). Many and Wiseman take a similar line and report their enquiries into teaching particular books (for example, Mildred Taylor's *Roll of Thunder, Hear My Cry* (1976)) with efferent and aesthetic emphases to different, parallel classes. At various points, all these studies touch upon the issue of the process of responding; but, equally, they also relate to some of the other issues that are discussed in the remainder of this chapter.

### Development in reading

Of these issues, the question of how children develop as readers of literature is one of the most frequently raised. This has been approached in four main ways: personal reminiscences of bookish childhoods (Sampson, 1947; Inglis, 1981); the growth of the child's sense of story in relation to the Piagetian stages of development (Applebee 1978; Tucker 1981); the development of literacy, with the idea of matching individual and age-group needs to appropriate books (Fisher 1964; Meek 1982); and, deductions about development drawn from surveys of children's reading interests and habits (Jenkinson 1940; Whitehead *et al.* 1977).

While none of these writers would see their work as necessarily falling strictly under the reader-response heading, all are in fact listening to what children as readers say about their experiences and, in more recent years, are conscious of interpreting their findings against a background of reader-response criticism. This awareness is evident, for example, in the work of Tucker (1980) who, in a paper entitled 'Can we ever know the reader's response?' argues that children's responses are different from adults' (in, say, the relative emphasis they give to the quality of the writing as opposed to the pace of the plot) before he goes on to relate their responses to intellectual and emotional development as psychologists describe it (the subject of his subsequent book (Tucker 1981)). In the highly influential work of Meek, too, from *The Cool Web* (Meek *et al.* 1977) onwards, reader-response criticism has been one of her perspectives – evident, for example, in her 'Prolegomena for a study of children's literature' (1980: 35) and in her exploration of the relationship between literacy and literature in her account of the reading lessons to be found in picture books (Meek 1988). Or again, in the discussion of their findings of children's reading preferences at 10+, 12+ and 14+, Whitehead and his team speculate about the cognitive and affective factors involved in the interaction between children and their books. All are aware that response-oriented criticism should be able to tell us more about this interaction at different ages.

Developmental stages in literary reading are outlined by Jackson (1982), Protherough (1983), and Thomson (1986) on the basis of classroom enquiries with young readers as we have already seen; and there have been some small-scale studies of reading development focused upon responses to specific books. Hickman (1983) studied three classes, totalling ninety primary school-aged children, and monitored their spontaneous responses, variations in solicited verbal responses, the implications of non-responses, and the role of the teacher in respect of two texts: Silverstein's *Where the Sidewalk Ends* (1974) and McPhail's *The Magical Drawings of Moony B. Finch* (1978). She was interested in the age-related patterns of responses and in the influences of the class teacher. Cullinan *et al.* (1983) discuss the relationship between pupils' comprehension and response to literature and report the results of a study, conducted with eighteen readers in grades, 4, 6 and 8, which focused on readings of and taped responses to Paterson's *Bridge to Terabithia* (1977) and Le Guin's, *A Wizard of Earthsea* (1968). Their data confirmed that there are clear developmental levels in children's comprehension and they claim that: 'Reader-response provides a way to look at the multi-dimensional nature of comprehension' (37). Galda (1992) has subsequently reported on a four-year longitudinal study of eight readers' readings of selected books representing realistic and fantasy fiction in order to explore any differences in responses to these two genres. The 'realistic' texts included Paterson's *Bridge to Terabithia* (1977) and S. E. Hinton's *The Outsiders* (1968); the 'fantasy' texts included L'Engle's *A Wind in the Door* (1973) and Cooper's *The Dark is Rising* (1981). She considers reading factors, such as developing analytical ability; text factors, arguing that children find it easier to enter the world of realistic fiction than they do of fantasy stories; and concludes by advocating the 'spectator role' (Harding 1937; Britton 1970) as a stance that offers readers access to both genres.

## Types of reader behaviour

The third theme concerns different sorts of readers or readings. It would be too much to claim that there is an established typology of readers; there have been few studies that venture beyond generalised discussions such as that between 'interrogative' and 'acquiescent' reading styles (Benton and Fox 1985: 16–17), itself a tentative extension of Holland's (1975) notion of personal style in reading behaviour. One study that does make some clear category decisions is that of Dias and Hayhoe (1988: 52–58) in respect of 14- and 15-year-old pupils reading and responding to poems. Their 'Responding-aloud protocols' (RAPs), described earlier, revealed four patterns of reading: paraphrasing, thematising, allegorising and problem solving. They stress that these are patterns of reading not readers (57) but have difficulty throughout in maintaining this discrimination. None the less, theirs is the most sophisticated account to date of that phenomenon that most teachers and others concerned with children's books have noticed without being able to explain, namely, that individual children reveal personal patterns of reading behaviour irrespective of the nature of the book being read. The study of these four reading patterns under the sub-headings of what the reader brings to the text, the reader's moves, closure, the reader's relationship with the text, and other elements is one that needs to be replicated and developed in relation to other types of text.

Fry (1985) explored the novel reading of six young readers (two 8-year-olds; two 12-year-olds; two 15-year-olds) through tape-recorded conversations over a period of eight months. The six case studies give some vivid documentary evidence of individual responses (for example, on the ways readers see themselves in books (99)) and also raise general issues such as re-readings, the appeal of series writers like Blyton, the relation of text fiction and film fiction, and the developmental process. Many and Cox's (1992) collection of papers includes their own development of Rosenblatt's efferent/aesthetic distinction in respect of the stances adopted by a class of 10-year-olds in their responses to Byars's *The Summer of the Swans* (1970) and other stories. Enciso, in the same collection, builds upon Benton's (1983) model of the secondary world and gives an exhaustive case-study of one ten-year-old girl's reading of chapters from three stories in order to observe the strategies she uses to create her story world from these texts. Benton's development of the secondary world concept, after Tolkien (1938) and Auden (1968), is reappraised in Many and Cox (1992: 15–18 and 23–48) and has also been extended by the author to incorporate aspects of the visual arts, notably paintings and picture-books (Benton 1992). The concept as originally formulated appeared in the special issue of the *Journal of Research and Development of Education* (Agee and Galda 1983) along with several other articles that focus upon readers' behaviours. Beach (1983) looks at what the reader brings to the text and reports an enquiry aimed at determining the effects of differences in prior knowledge of literary conventions and attitudes on readers' responses through a comparison between high school and college English education students' responses to a short story by Updike. Pillar (1983) discusses aspects of moral judgement in response to fairy tales and presents the findings from a study of the responses of sixty elementary school children to three fables. The responses are discussed in terms of the principles of justice that distinguish them. This enquiry edges us towards the fourth theme, where reader-response methods are employed in culturally oriented studies.

### Culturally oriented studies

Children's concepts and social attitudes have been the subject of reader-response enquiries in three complementary ways: multicultural and feminist studies, which explore how far literature can be helpful in teaching about issues of race or gender; whole-culture studies, which consider children's responses to literature in the context of the broad range of their interests; and cross-cultural studies, which compare the responses of young readers from different countries to the same texts to identify similarities and cultural differences. An article and a book about each group must suffice to indicate the emphases and the degree to which reader-response theory and practice have been influential.

Evans (1992) contains several studies with explicitly cultural concerns, among which is 'Feminist approaches to teaching: John Updike's "A & P"' by Bogdan, Millen and Pitt which sets out to explore gender issues in the classroom via Updike's short story. They quote Kolodny (in Showalter 1985: 158) in support of the shift feminist studies makes from seeing reader-response in a purely experiential dimension to a more philosophical enquiry into how 'aesthetic response is ... invested with epistemological, ethical, and moral concerns'. The feminist position is stated explicitly: 'Reading pleasure can no longer be its own end-point, but rather part of a larger dialectical process which strives for an "altered reading attentiveness" to gender in every reading act' (Evans: 151). This dialectical response model is further elaborated and augmented by specific pedagogical suggestions to help young readers towards this new attentiveness.

Within the broadly, and somewhat uncomfortably, defined field of multicultural education, the most sophisticated use of reader-response criticism and practice is Beverley Naidoo's (1992) enquiry into the role of literature, especially fiction, in educating young people about race. Working with a teacher and his class of all-white 13 to 14-year-old pupils over a period of one academic year, Naidoo introduced a sequence of four novels to their work with increasingly explicit racial issues: *Buddy* (Hinton 1983), *Friedrich* (Richter 1978), *Roll of Thunder, Hear My Cry* (Taylor 1976) and *Waiting for the Rain* (Gordon 1987). Influenced by Hollindale's (1988) notion of 'the reader as ideologist', Rosenblatt's (1978, 1985) transactional theory and Benton's ethnographic approach to reader-response enquiries (Benton *et al.* (1988), Naidoo adopted an action-researcher role to develop 'ways of exploring these texts which encouraged empathy with the perspective of characters who were victims of racism but who resisted it' (22). Written and oral responses in journals and discussion were at the centre of the procedures. Many challenging and provocative issues are examined through this enquiry, including overt and institutionalised racism, whether teaching about race challenges or merely reinforces racism, the nature of empathy and the gender differences pupils exhibited. The cultural context, especially the subculture of the particular classroom, emerged as a dominant theme. The subtle interrelatedness of text, context, readers and writers, is sensitively explored in a study that shows how reader-response methods can help to illuminate the values and attitudes that readers sometimes hide, even from themselves.

The second group of whole-culture studies tends to focus upon adolescent readers. Stories and poems, especially those encountered in school, are seen as but one aspect of the cultural context in which teenagers live and in which books are low on their agenda after television, computer games, rock music, comics and magazines. Beach and Freedman's (1992) paper, 'Responding as a cultural act: adolescents' responses to magazine ads and short stories' widens the perspective from the individual reader's 'personal' and 'unique' responses to accommodate the notion of response as a cultural practice. They discuss the cultural practices required in adolescent peer groups and note the ways in which these are derived from experiences with the mass media, with examples from adolescents' responses to magazine advertisements and short stories. Particular points of interest in the responses of these 115 8th and 11th grade pupils are the gender differences, the tendency to blur fiction and reality when talking about the advertising images, and the low incidence of critical responses.

Reader-response criticism also influences Sarland's (1991) study of young people's reading. He takes seriously both Chambers's (1977) account of the implied child reader (discussed below) and Meek's (1987) plea for an academic study of children's literature which situates it within the whole culture of young people. Building on Fry's (1985) work, he considers the popular literature that children read both in relation to a culture dominated by television and video, and in relation to the 'official' literature read in school. By eliciting and analysing students' responses to such books as King's *Carrie* (1974) and Herbert's *The Fog* (1975), Sarland draws upon response-oriented theory and practice to discuss the importance of these texts to their readers and to begin to open up a subculture of which, at best, teachers are usually only hazily aware.

Cross-cultural studies are relatively uncommon for the obvious reason that they are more difficult to set up and sustain. Bunbury and Tabbert's article for *Children's Literature in Education* (1989; reprinted Hunt 1992) compared the responses of Australian and German children to an Australian bush-ranger story, Stow's *Midnite* (1967/1982). Using Jauss's notion of 'ironic identification', where the reader is drawn in and willingly submits to the fictional illusion only to have the author subvert this aesthetic experience, the enquiry considered a range of responses; while there are interesting insights into individual readings, it none the less ends inconclusively by stating: 'The best we can say is that the capacity to experience ironic identification extends along a spectrum of reading encounters which vary in intensity' (Hunt: 124). The study is ambitious in tackling two difficult topics whose relationship is complex: children's sense of the tone of a text and the effect of translation upon the readers' responses. To begin to open up such issues is an achievement in itself.

Chapter 6 of Dias and Hayhoe's (1988) book makes explicit the international perspective on the teaching of poetry that permeates the whole of this Anglo-Canadian collaboration. Views from Australia, Britain, Canada and the USA on good practice in poetry teaching all share the same principle of developing pupils' responses. Clearly, cross-cultural influences grow more readily and are more easily monitored in English-speaking countries than elsewhere; yet there is sufficient evidence here of cultural diversity to encourage other researchers to explore the ways in which we can learn from each other about how children's responses to literature are mediated by the cultural contexts in which they occur.

## Text-oriented studies

Studies of children's literature which directly parallel the work of, say, Iser (1974) or Fish (1980) in their close examination of particular texts are surprisingly rare. It is as if those who work in this field have been so concerned with pedagogy and children as readers that they have failed to exploit reader-response criticism as a means of understanding the nature of actual texts. Two concepts, however, which have received some attention are the 'implied reader' and the notion of 'intertextuality'. The first, developed by Iser (1974) after Booth (1961), for a time encouraged the search for the 'implied child reader' in children's books; the second followed from enquiries into how readers make meaning and the realisation of the complex relationships that exist between the readers, the text, other texts, other genres, and the cultural context of any 'reading'.

Although Chambers (1977/1985) and Tabbert (1980) gave the lead, the implied child reader remains a neglected figure in children's book criticism. In 'The reader in the book' Chambers takes Iser's concept and advocates its central importance in children's book criticism. He illustrates Roald Dahl's assumptions about the implied adult reader of his story 'The champion of the world' (1959) in contrast to those about the implied child reader of the rewritten version in the children's book *Danny: The Champion of the World* (1975), and argues that the narrative voice and textual features of the latter create a sense of an intimate, yet adult-controlled, relationship between the implied author and the implied child reader. He generalises from this example to claim that this voice and this relationship are common in children's books, and identifies both with the figure of the 'friendly adult storyteller who knows how to entertain children while at the same time keeping them in their place' (69). Much of the remainder of his article rests upon two further narrative features: 'the adoption of a child point of view' (72) to sustain this adult–author/child–reader relationship; and the deployment within the text of indeterminacy gaps which the reader must fill in order to generate meanings. These three characteristics – the literary relationship, the point of view, and the tell-tale gaps – are then exemplified in a critique of Boston's *The Children of Green Knowe* (1954).

Chambers's article is already regarded as a landmark in the development of criticism (Hunt 1990: 90), not least because it opened up one means of defining the singular character of a form of literature that is designated by its intended audience. That this lead has been followed so infrequently calls into question the seriousness of the whole critical enterprise in this field. Among the few who have exploited these concepts in relation to children's books is Tabbert (1980) who comments usefully on the notion of 'telling gaps' and 'the implied reader' in some classic children's texts and sees a fruitful way forward in psychologically oriented criticism, particularly in the methodology adopted by Holland. Benton (1992a) parallels the historically changing relationship between implied author and implied reader that is found in Iser's (1974) studies of Fielding, Thackeray and

Joyce, with a corresponding critique of the openings of three novels by children's authors – Hughes's *Tom Brown's Schooldays* (1856), Day Lewis's *The Otterbury Incident* (1948), and Garner's *Red Shift* (1973). The emphases, however, here, are upon the nature of the collaborative relationship and upon narrative technique rather than on the implied child reader. Shavit (1983: 60–67) extends Iser's concept to embrace the notion of childhood as well as the child as implied reader. After giving a historical perspective on the idea of childhood the discussion focuses upon various versions of 'Little Red Riding Hood' in order to explore 'how far they were responsible for different implied readers' (61). In particular, she argues that prevailing notions of childhood helped determine the changing character of these texts over several centuries from Perrault's version to those of the present day.

By far the most rigorous account of the implied reader is that of Stephens (1992), given from a position that is sceptical about a mode of reading which locates the reader only within the text and ignores questions of ideology. He argues that in critical practice the being or meaning of the text is best characterised as 'a dialectic between textual discourse (including its construction of an implied reader and a range of potential subject positions) and a reader's disposition, familiarity with story conventions and experiential knowledge' (59). His account of ideology and the implied reader in two picture books (Cooper and Hutton, *The Selkie Girl*, 1986; Gerstein, *The Seal Mother*, 1986) develops this argument and leads him to take issue with Chambers's view of the implied reader on ideological grounds. He says of Chambers's account that: 'his own ideology of reading demands a reified "implicated" reader, led by textual strategies to discover a determinate meaning' (67). Stephens's conceptualisation of the implied reader is significant both of itself and in helping to explain the paucity of critical effort in this area following Chambers's article. For it tells us that criticism has moved on and, in particular, that such concepts can no longer be regarded as innocent aspects of narrative.

Stephens, too, offers the fullest account to date of intertextuality in the third chapter of his book 'Not by words alone: language, intertextuality and society' (84–119). He outlines seven kinds of relationship which may exist between a particular text and any other texts and goes on to discuss various manifestations of intertextuality in children's literature, notably in fairy tales. Agee (1983: 55–59) concentrates on the narrower focus of literary allusion and reader-response and begins to explore the intertextual patterning of such books as *Z for Zachariah* (O'Brien 1977), *Jacob I Have Loved* (Paterson 1981) and *Fahrenheit 451* (Bradbury 1967). Stephens and Agee both approach the topic exclusively through the study of texts.

Meek (1988) keeps young readers constantly in view when she draws upon the intertext of oral and written literature, together with the Iserian concepts of the implied reader and indeterminacy gaps, in her brief but widely acclaimed paper 'How texts teach what readers learn'. Her main texts are picture books: the telling gaps in *Rosie's Walk* (Hutchins 1969) and *Granpa* (Burningham 1984) and the play of intertexts in *The Jolly Postman* (Ahlberg 1986) and the short story 'William's Version' (Mark 1980) are explored with great subtlety, and display, above all, the quality that distinguishes the best sort of criticism of children's literature: the ability to listen to children's responses to a book and to 'read' these with the same effort of attention that is afforded to the text themselves. Reader-response criticism accommodates both the reader and the text; there is no area of literary activity where this is more necessary than in the literature that defines itself by reference to its young readership.

# References

Abrams, M. H. (1953) *The Mirror and the Lamp: Romantic Theory and the Critical Tradition*, New York: Norton.

Agee, H. (1983) 'Literary allusion and reader response: possibilities for research', in Agee, H. and Galda, L. (eds) 'Response to literature: empirical and theoretical studies', *Journal of Research and Development in Education* 16, 3: 55–59.

—— and Galda, L. (eds) (1983) 'Response to literature: empirical and theoretical studies', *Journal of Research and Development in Education* 16, 3: 8–75.

Applebee, A. N. (1978) *The Child's Concept of Story: Ages Two to Seventeen*, Chicago and London: Chicago University Press.

Atkinson, J. (1985) 'How children read poems at different ages', *English in Education* 19, 1: 24–34.

Auden, W. H. (1968) *Secondary Worlds*, London: Faber.

Barnes, D. (1976) *From Communication to Curriculum*, Harmondsworth: Penguin.

—— and Todd, F. (1977) *Communication and Learning in Small Groups*, London: Routledge and Kegan Paul.

Beach, R. (1983) 'Attitudes, social conventions and response to literature', in Agee, H. and Galda, L. (eds) 'Response to literature: empirical and theoretical studies', *Journal of Research and Development in Education* 16, 3: 47–54.

—— and Freedman, K. (1992) 'Responding as a cultural act: adolescents' responses to magazine ads and short stories', in Many, J. and Cox, C. (eds) *Reader Stance and Literary Understanding: Exploring the Theories, Research and Practice*, Norwood, NJ: Ablex.

Benton, M. (1983) 'Secondary worlds', in Agee, H. and Galda, L. (eds) 'Response to literature: empirical and theoretical studies', *Journal of Research and Development in Education* 16, 3: 68–75.

—— (1992a) *Secondary Worlds: Literature Teaching and the Visual Arts*, Milton Keynes: Open University Press.

—— (1992b) 'Possible worlds and narrative voices', in Many, J. and Cox, C. (eds) *Reader Stance and Literary Understanding: Exploring the Theories, Research and Practice*, Norwood, NJ: Ablex.

—— and Fox, G. (1985) *Teaching Literature 9–14*, Oxford: Oxford University Press.

—— Teasey, J., Bell, R. and Hurst, K. (1988) *Young Readers Responding to Poems*, London: Routledge.

Benton, P. (1986) *Pupil, Teacher, Poem*, London: Hodder and Stoughton.

Bleich, D. (1985) 'The identity of pedagogy and research in the study of response to literature', in Cooper, C. R. (ed.) *Researching Response to Literature and the Teaching of Literature: Points of Departure*, Norwood, NJ: Ablex.

Bogdan, D., Millen, K. J. and Pitt, A. (1992) 'Feminist approaches to teaching: John Updike's "A & P"' in Evans, E. (ed.) *Young Readers, New Readings*, Hull: Hull University Press.

Booth, W. C. (1961) *The Rhetoric of Fiction*, Chicago: University of Chicago Press.

Britton, J. N. (1970) *Language and Learning*, London: Allen Lane and The Penguin Press.

Bunbury, R. and Tabbert, R. (1978) 'A bicultural study of identification: readers' responses to the ironic treatment of a national hero', *Children's Literature in Education*, 20, 1: 25–35.

Chambers, A. (1977) 'The reader in the book', *Signal* 23: 64–87.

Cooper, C. R. (ed.) (1985a) *Researching Response to Literature and the Teaching of Literature: Points of Departure*, Norwood, NJ: Ablex.

—— (1985b) 'Evaluating the results of classroom literary study', in Cooper, C. R. (ed.) *Researching Response to Literature and the Teaching of Literature: Points of Departure*, Norwood, NJ: Ablex.

Corcoran, B. (1992) 'Reader stance: from willed aesthetic to discursive construction', in Many, J. and Cox, C. (eds) *Reader Stance and Literary Understanding: Exploring the Theories, Research and Practice*, Norwood, NJ: Ablex.

—— and Evans, E. (eds) (1987) *Readers, Texts, Teachers*, Milton Keynes: Open University Press.

Cox, C. B. (1989) *English for Ages 5–16*, London: HMSO.

Culler, J. (1975) *Structuralist Poetics: Structuralism, Linguistics and the Study of Literature*, London: Routledge and Kegan Paul.

Cullinan, B. E, Harwood, K. T. and Galda, L. (1983) 'The reader and the story comprehension and response', in Agee, H. and Galda, L. (eds) 'Response to literature: empirical and theoretical studies', *Journal of Research and Development in Education* 16, 3: 29–38.

D'Arcy, P. (1973) *Reading For Meaning*, vol. 2, London: Hutchinson.

Dias, P. (1986) 'Making sense of poetry', *English and Education*, Sheffield: NATE, 20(2).

—— and Hayhoe, M. (1988) *Developing Response to Poetry*, Milton Keynes: Open University Press.

Dixon, J. and Brown, J. (1984) *Responses to Literature: What is Being Assessed?* London: Schools' Council Publications.

Encisco, P. (1992) 'Creating the story world', in Many, J. and Cox, C. (eds) *Reader Stance and Literary Understanding: Exploring the Theories, Research and Practice*, Norwood, NJ: Ablex.

Evans, E. (ed.) (1992) *Young Readers, New Readings*, Hull: Hull University Press.

Fish, S. (1980) *Is There a Text in this Class?*, Cambridge, MA: Harvard University Press.

Fisher, M. (1964) *Intent Upon Reading*, London: Brockhampton Press.

Fox, G. (1979) 'Dark watchers: young readers and their fiction', *English in Education* 13, 1: 32–35.

Freund, E. (1987) *The Return of the Reader: Reader-Response Criticism*, London: Methuen.

Fry, D. (1985) *Children Talk About Books: Seeing Themselves as Readers*, Milton Keynes: Open University Press.

Galda, L. (1983) 'Research in response to literature', *Journal of Research and Development in Education* 16: 1–7.

—— (1992) 'Evaluation as a spectator: changes across time and genre', in Many, J. and Cox, C. (eds) *Reader Stance and Literary Understanding: Exploring the Theories, Research and Practice*, Norwood, NJ: Ablex.

Hade, D. D. (1992) 'The reader's stance as event: transaction in the classroom', in Many, J. and Cox, C. (eds) *Reader Stance and Literary Understanding: Exploring the Theories, Research and Practice*, Norwood, NJ: Ablex.

Harding, D. W. (1937) 'The role of the onlooker', *Scrutiny* 6: 247–258.

—— (1962) 'Psychological processes in the reading of fiction', *The British Journal of Aesthetics* 2, 2: 113–147.

Hayhoe, M. and Parker, S. (eds) (1990) *Reading and Response*, Milton Keynes: Open University Press.

Herbert, J. (1975) *The Fog*, London: New English Library.

Hickman, J. (1983) 'Everything considered: response to literature in an elementary school setting', in Agee, H. and Galda, L. (eds) 'Response to literature: empirical and theoretical studies', *Journal of Research and Development in Education* 16, 3: 8–13.

Hinton, N. (1983) *Buddy*, London: Heinemann Educational.

Hinton, S. E. (1968) *The Outsiders*, New York: Dell.

Holland, N. N. (1968) *The Dynamics of Literary Response*, New York: Norton.

—— (1973) *Poems in Persons*, New York: Norton.

—— (1975) *Five Readers Reading*, New Haven and London: Yale University Press.

Hollindale, P. (1988) 'Ideology and the children's book', *Signal* 55: 3–22.

Holub, R.C. (1984) *Reception Theory*, London: Methuen.

Hunt, P. (ed.) (1990) *Children's Literature: The Development of Criticism*, London: Routledge.

—— (ed.) (1992) *Literature for Children: Contemporary Criticism*, London: Routledge.

Inglis, F. (1981) *The Promise of Happiness*, Cambridge: Cambridge University Press.

Iser, W. (1974) *The Implied Reader*, Baltimore: Johns Hopkins University Press.

—— (1978) *The Act of Reading: A Theory of Aesthetic Response*, Baltimore: Johns Hopkins University Press.

Jackson, D. (1980) 'First encounters: the importance of initial responses to literature', *Children's Literature in Education* 11, 4: 149–160.

—— (1982) *Continuity in Secondary English*, London: Methuen.

—— (1983) *Encounters With Books: Teaching Fiction 11–16*, London: Methuen.

Jefferson, A. and Robey, D. (1986) *Modern Literary Theory*, 2nd edn, London: Batsford.

Jenkinson, A. J. (1940) *What Do Boys and Girls Read?* London: Methuen.

Kintgen, E. R. (1985) 'Studying the perception of poetry', in Cooper, C. R. (ed.) *Researching Response to Literature and the Teaching of Literature: Points of Departure*, Norwood, NJ: Ablex.

Lerner, L. (ed.) (1983) *Reconstructing Literature*, Oxford: Blackwell.

Many, J. and Cox, C. (eds) (1992) *Reader Stance and Literary Understanding: Exploring the Theories, Research and Practice*, Norwood, NJ: Ablex.

—— and Wiseman, D. (1992) 'Analysing versus experiencing: the effects of teaching approaches on students' responses', in Many, J. and Cox, C. (eds) *Reader Stance and Literary Understanding: Exploring the Theories, Research and Practice*, Norwood, NJ: Ablex.

Meek, M. (1980) 'Prolegomena for a study of children's literature', in Benton, M. (ed.) *Approaches to Research in Children's Literature*, Southampton: Department of Education, Southampton University.

—— (1982) *Learning to Read*, London: Bodley Head.

—— (1987) 'Symbolic outlining: the academic study of children's literature', *Signal* 53: 97–115.

—— (1988) *How Texts Teach What Readers Learn*, South Woodchester: Thimble Press.

—— Warlow, A. and Barton, G. (eds) (1977) *The Cool Web*, London: Bodley Head.

Naidoo, B. (1992) *Through Whose Eyes? Exploring Racism: Reader, Text and Context*, London: Trentham Books.

Petrosky, A. R. (1985) 'Response: a way of knowing', in Cooper, C. R. (ed.) *Researching Response to Literature and the Teaching of Literature: Points of Departure*, Norwood, NJ: Ablex.

Pillar, A. M. (1983) 'Aspects of moral judgement in response to fables', in Agee, H. and Galda, L. (eds) 'Response to literature: empirical and theoretical studies', *Journal of Research and Development in Education* 16, 3: 39–46.

Protherough, R. (1983) *Developing Response to Fiction*, Milton Keynes: Open University Press.

Purves, A. C. (1985) 'That sunny dome: those caves of ice', in Cooper, C. R. (ed.) *Researching Response to Literature and the Teaching of Literature: Points of Departure*, Norwood, NJ: Ablex.

—— and Beach, R. (1972) *Literature and the Reader*, Urbana, IL: NCTE.

—— and Rippere, V. (1968) *Elements of Writing About a Literary Work*, Research Report No. 9, Champaign, IL: NCTE.

Richards, I. A. (1924) *Principles of Literary Criticism*, London: Routledge and Kegan Paul.

—— (1929) *Practical Criticism*, London: Routledge and Kegan Paul.

Rosenblatt, L. (1938/1970) *Literature as Exploration*, London: Heinemann.
—— (1978) *The Reader, The Text, The Poem: The Transactional Theory of the Literary Work*, Carbondale, IL: Southern Illinois University Press.
—— (1985) 'The transactional theory of the literary work: implications for research', in Cooper, C. R. (ed.) *Researching Response to Literature and the Teaching of Literature: Points of Departure*, Norwood, NJ: Ablex.
Sampson, G. (1947) *Seven Essays*, Cambridge: Cambridge University Press.
Sarland, C. (1991) *Young People Reading: Culture and Response*, Milton Keynes: Open University Press.
Scholes, R. (1985) *Textual Power: Literary Theory and the Teaching of English*, New Haven and London: Yale University Press.
Shavit, Z. (1983) 'The notion of childhood and the child as implied reader', in Agee, H. and Galda, L. (eds) 'Response to literature: empirical and theoretical studies', *Journal of Research and Development in Education* 16, 3: 60–67.
Showalter, E. (ed.) (1985) *The New Feminist Criticism: Essays on Women, Literature and Theory*, New York: Pantheon.
Squire, J. R. (1964) *The Responses of Adolescents While Reading Four Short Stories*, Research Report No. 2, Champaign, IL: NCTE.
—— (1985) 'Studying response to literature through school surveys', in Cooper, C. R. (ed.) *Researching Response to Literature and the Teaching of Literature: Points of Departure*, Norwood, NJ: Ablex.
—— (1990) 'Research on reader response and the National Literature initiative', in Hayhoe, M. and Parker, S. (eds) *Reading and Response*, Milton Keynes: Open University Press.
Stephens, J. (1992) *Language and Ideology in Children's Fiction*, London: Longman.
Suleiman, S. R. and Crosman, I. (eds) (1980) *The Reader in the Text*, Princeton, NJ: Princeton University Press.
Tabbert, R. (1980) 'The impact of children's books: cases and concepts', in Fox, G. and Hammond, G. (eds) *Responses to Children's Literature*, New York: K. G. Saur.
Thomson, J. (1986) *Understanding Teenagers Reading: Reading Processes and the Teaching of Literature*, Sydney: Methuen.
Tolkien, J. R. R. (1938) *Tree and Leaf*, London: Unwin Books.
Tompkins, J. P. (1980) *Reader-Response Criticism: From Formalism to Post-Structuralism*, Baltimore: Johns Hopkins University Press.
Tucker, N. (1980) 'Can we ever know the reader's response?', in Benton, M. (ed.) *Approaches to Research in Children's Literature*, Southampton: Department of Education, Southampton University.
—— (1981) *The Child and the Book*, Cambridge: Cambridge University Press.
Wade, B. (1981) 'Assessing pupils' contributions in appreciating a poem', *Journal of Education for Teaching* 7, 1, 40–49.
Wellek, R. and Warren, A. (1949) *Theory of Literature*, London: Cape.
Whitehead, F. et al. (1977) *Children and their Books*, London: Macmillan.
Wimsatt, W. K. and Beardsley, M. (1954/1970) *The Verbal Icon: Studies in the Meaning of Poetry*, London: Methuen.
Zancella, D. (1992) 'Literary lives: a biographical perspective on the teaching of literature', in Many, J. and Cox, C. (eds) *Reader Stance and Literary Understanding: Exploring the Theories, Research and Practice*, Norwood, NJ: Ablex.
Zarillo, J. and Cox, C. (1992) 'Efferent and aesthetic teaching', in Many, J. and Cox, C. (eds) *Reader Stance and Literary Understanding: Exploring the Theories, Research and Practice*, Norwood, NJ: Ablex.

# 7

# Psychoanalytical Criticism

## *Hamida Bosmajian*

Because the child and childhood hold a privileged position in most psycho-analytical theories, the elective affinity between children's literature and psychological criticism seems even more natural than the affinity between psychology and literature in general. Psychoanalytic theory adds to the literary text a 'second dimension – unfolding what might be called the unconscious content of the work' (Holland 1970: 131), but the condensations and displacements at work in the author–text–reader relation are problematised in children's literature because of the double reader: adult/child.

Children's fiction might be impossible because it rests on the assumption that there is a child who can be addressed when, in actuality, 'children's fiction sets up the child as an outsider to its own process, and that aims, unashamedly, to take the child in' (Rose 1984: 2). The implied author, even in first-person narration by a child character, is a displacement of the contexts of personal and collective values and neuroses. Furthermore, while the analyst is supposedly the most reliable reader-interpreter of stories told in a psychoanalytic dialogue by the analysand-author, the reader of adult literature may or may not be a reliable interpreter of the text. In children's literature the implied reader is, moreover, highly unreliable and, therefore, most easily 'taken in'. Thus, the authorial self is in a sense liberated, in that the textual strategies and gaps that constitute the subtext of the work escape the implied reader, the child. The author can experience therapeutic release without anxieties over the scrutiny of an adult's psychoanalytical critique.

The nemesis for the projection of the naïve implied reader is the adult reader as psychoanalytic critic of children's literature who exposes the gaps, substitutions and displacements of the author and appropriates the author's text as a symptom of individual or cultural neuroses that underlie and undermine values associated with growth and development. While psychoanalytic critics of adult literature amplify the reader's appreciation of the text, those same critics will, in the case of children's literature, conceal their interpretation from the child and, therewith, both censor and protect the author. The child may be imaged as myth of origin – as father of the man and mother of the woman – but in children's literature the adult is in control.

The correspondences between author–text–reader and analysand–psycho-analytic dialogue-analyst break down, for author–reader are not in a dialogical relation, no matter how intensely the reader *responds*, nor can the critic-interpreter make enquiries of a character in a narrative, as an analyst can in the psychoanalytic situation. While critics act as if one could ask about Alice's relation with her parents as she develops from pawn to queen in *Through the Looking Glass*, they forget that she is a linguistic construct, a trope for the unresolved problems of her author (Greenacre 1955). It is important that psychoanalytic critics are aware of the ambivalences inherent in their method and do not seize one aspect of a psychoanalytical theory as a tool for interpretation, thereby reducing the text to universals about human development (compare Hogan 1990; Knoepflmacher 1990; Phillips and Wojcik-Andrews 1990; Steig 1990; Zipes 1990).

The following discussion will focus on defining those psychoanalytic theories that have influenced the criticism of children's literature. Frequently such criticism relies on the informal developmental psychological knowledge of the interpreter without reference to any specific theory. This is especially true of realistic narratives for young adults. The strongest psychoanalytic tradition of criticism can be found in the interpretation of folktales and *märchen* and, to a lesser extent in fantasy literature. While Freud, Jung and their disciples have been important in interpretations of children's literature, the poststructuralist influence has not been as prevalent. Quite dominant, however, is the influence of psychological criticism that relates the development of the child character to the social context depicted in psychologically realistic narratives. Perhaps because of the deep issues involved in psychoanalytic criticism, critics of children's literature occasionally seem to screen discussions of psychoanalytical issues with analyses of social contexts, even where the topic is announced as being psychoanalytical (Smith and Kerrigan 1985).

## Freudian Criticism

Classical Freudian criticism interprets the work as an expression of psychopathography, as a symptom whose creation provided therapeutic release for the author. In 'The relation of the poet to daydreaming' (1908), Freud saw the crucial relationship between child–play/poet–language: 'every child at play behaves like an imaginative writer, in that he creates a world of his own or, more truly, he arranges the things of this world and orders it in a new way that pleases him better ... Language has preserved this relationship between children's play and poetic creation' (1908/1963 9: 144), just as it does between dream and text.

Freud assumed that all psychoneurotic symptoms are generated by psychic conflicts between a person's sexual desires and the strictures of society. The conflict is expressed through substitutions and displacements, just as in literature a metaphor's tenor and vehicle condense two disparate ideas into one image that hides and reveals what is not articulated. Similarly, displacement substitutes socially acceptable modes for desires that are forbidden. Substitutions thus function as censors in dreams and daydreams, in play and in texts. Freud's first triad of unconscious, pre-conscious and conscious defines the unconscious as a non-verbal, instinctual and infantile given and as dominated by the pleasure principle. The desires and conflicts (oral, anal, oedipal) of childhood persist throughout the adult's life and can be made conscious only by being first raised to the level of the pre-conscious which facilitates the dynamic of consciousness and repression through condensation and displacement. Freud later modified his first triad with the paradigm of id, ego and superego, in part because he suspected a greater simultaneity in the dynamics of the psyche. The revised triad places the embattled ego between the deterministic forces of the id and the internalised strictures of society. It is here where we find the cause of the pessimism in Freudian psychoanalytic theory: the ego's inevitable discontent.

Crucial for Freudian critics of children's literature is the importance Freud gave to the child in the psychoanalytic process. Though the Oedipus complex has been accepted as part of child development, Freud's insistence on the polymorphous sexuality of the infant (1962/1975: 39–72) is somewhat more troubling for most critics of children's literature, for if such sexuality is displaced in the text but communicates itself sub-textually to the child-reader, then the author has transferred his infantile sexuality and communicates it to the child. Texts such as Dahl's *Charlie and the Chocolate Factory* (see Bosmajian 1985), Sendak's *In the Night Kitchen* might fall into this category.

Freud's profound appreciation of the psychological importance of language was bound to lead him not only to interpretations of everyday language phenomena in the processes of repression and substitution, but also to interpretations of major authors of European literature. In 'The occurrence in dreams of materials from fairy tales', Freud notes that fairy tales have such an impact on the mental life of the child that the adult will use them later as screen memories for the experiences of childhood (1913/1963: 59).

'The serious study of children's literature may be said to have begun with Freud', acknowledges Egan in his discussion of *Peter Pan* (1982: 37). Psychoanalysts have indeed been the precursors of the study of children's literature, which explains the powerful but dubious influence of Bruno Bettelheim's *The Uses of Enchantment* (1975), a discussion of familiar tales along infantile and adolescent psychosexual development. Bettelheim sees the child's libido as a threat to both a meaningful life and the social order; therefore, the child needs fairy tales to order his inner house by acquiring a moral education through the tales (5), for, as the stories unfold, they 'give conscious credence and body to the id pressures and show ways to satisfy these that are in line with ego and superego' (6). Literary critics have strongly critiqued Bettelheim not only for his a-historicality and reductionism of Freud's theories (Zipes 1979), but also for his punitive pedagogy, for being 'oddly accusatory towards children' (Tatar 1992: xxii) and for displacing his 'own real life fantasies, particularly of the dutiful daughter who takes care of her father's needs' (xxv) into his interpretative work.

## Jungian Criticism

Jungian criticism discovers archetypes that are the basis for the images in a text. Pre-consciously, or consciously, the author connects with archetypal patterns of which the narrative becomes a variable whose content will somehow relate to the issue of the ego's integration with the self. Jung's concept of the therapeutic process begins with the recognition of the loss of an original wholeness, possessed by every infant, a wholeness lost through self-inflation and/or alienation of the ego. On a mythic level, the ego would experience a dark night of the soul followed by a breakthrough that establishes, not an integration with the self, but a connection with the transpersonal self. The end of Jungian analysis is not a complete individuation of the ego, but rather the analysand's recognition that growth is a life-long process, a quest, during which conscious and unconscious connect primarily through symbols and archetypes.

Jung assumed a personal unconscious consisting of memories and images gathered during a life-time, for the archetypes, as experienced by the individual, are in and of the world. This personal unconscious is raised to consciousness when the analysand connects the personal with the collective unconscious. The collective unconscious is an *a priori* existence of 'organising factors', the archetypes understood as inborn modes of functioning, rather like a grammar that generates and structures the infinite variables of symbol formations whose recurrence is to be understood again as archetypal (Jung 1964: 67). Archetypes are 'without known origin; and they reproduce themselves in any time or any part of the world – even where transmission by direct descent or "cross-fertilisation" through migration must be ruled out' (69). Jung, too, believed that dreams are meaningful and can be understood (102) as their specific images connect with archetypes whose force can suddenly overwhelm the dreamer. Such an experience contrasts with the conscious use of representing archetypes through culturally defined images and motifs. Jung's own metaphoric use of archetypal images such as shadow, anima or animus and self, blurred the distinction between archetype as a grammar and archetype as symbol.

Jung, whose theory has been criticised for demanding a vast amount of knowledge of myth, did not perceive the unconscious as an instinctual and libidinal battleground, although he posited a 'primitive psyche' in the child which functions in dreams and fantasies comparable to the physical evolution of mankind in the embryo (1964: 99). In Jung's 'Psychic conflicts in a child' (1946/1954: 8–46), the child-patient, obsessed with the origin of babies, fantasised that she would give birth if she swallowed an orange, similar to women in fairy tales whose eating of fruit leads to pregnancy. The child-patient was eventually enlightened by her father, but Jung concludes that, while false explanation are not advisable, no less inadvisable is the insistence on the right explanation, for that inhibits the freedom of the mind's development through concretistic explanations which reduce the spontaneity of image-making to a falsehood (34).

Because the essential nature of all art escapes our understanding, Jung did not perceive literature as psychopathography. We can interpret only 'that aspect of art which consists in the process of artistic creation' (1931/1966: 65). While he admits that literary works can result from the intentionality of the author, they are also those that 'force themselves on the author', reveal his inner nature, and overwhelm the conscious mind with a flood of thoughts and images he never intended to create: 'Here the artist is not identical with the process of creation; he is aware that he is subordinate to his work or stands outside it, as though he were a second person' (73). An author may, for a time, be out of fashion when, suddenly, readers rediscover his work, because they perceive in it archetypes that speak to them with renewed immediacy (77). We can, therefore, only discuss the psychological phenomenology in a work of literature.

It is evident how readily children's literature, especially when it has components of fantasy, connects with Jungian theories. Marie Louise von Franz (1977, 1978) has written comprehensive studies of fairy tales which the Jungian critic tends to see as 'allegories of the inner life' that meet 'the deep-seated psychic and spiritual needs of the individual' (Cooper 1983: 154). The problem with such criticism is that it reduces images in fairy tales to fixed allegorical meanings without regard for historical and social contexts, as the Jungian critic basically explains metaphor with metaphor. Northrop Frye's discussion of archetypes in terms of convention and genre is an attempt to avoid such reductionism (1957). What makes the Jungian approach attractive to interpreters of children's literature is that the theory assumes an original wholeness that can be regained after alienation is overcome. This coincides with the comic resolution of so many narratives for children and young adults.

In Jungian literary criticism children's literature is often seen as privileged, just as the 'primitive psyche' of the child is in Jungian psychoanalysis. 'Children's literature initiates us into psychic reality, by telling about the creatures and perils of the soul and the heart's possibilities of blessing in images of universal intelligibility' (Hillman 1980: 5). At its best Jungian criticism is able to integrate the author's and the reader's needs as exemplified in Lynn Rosenthal's interpretation of Lucy Boston's *The Children of Green Knowe* (1980).

## Ego Psychology and Object Relations Theories

The generation of psychoanalysts that was influenced by, reacted against and revised Freud, distinguishes itself by overcoming Freud's pessimism regarding the ego's inevitable discontent. While the new focus does not deny the existence of the unconscious, it emphasises the possibility of healthy growth and development in the ego's self-realisation in relation to its environment. Karen Horney and Abraham Maslow, Melanie Klein and Donald Winnicott describe possibilities for growth through constructive management of the id's pressures. Each insists that the developing psyche of the child responds to environmental conditions with a positive urge to self-actualisation that is thwarted only by hostile environments. From the perspective of ego psychology, author and reader participate in a shareable fantasy that constructively breaks down 'for a time the boundaries between self and other, inner and outer, past and future, and ... may neutralise the primal aggressions bound up in those separations' (Holland 1968: 340). Psychoanalytic literary critics have, however, also been concerned that ego psychology tends to be in one direction only, 'namely from the ego as a publicly adjusted identity' (Wright 1984: 57).

### Karen Horney and Abraham Maslow

According to Horney, the goal of psychoanalysis is the patient's discovery of the possibility of self-realisation and the recognition that good human relations are an essential part of this, along with the faculty for creative work and the acceptance of personal responsibility (1950: 334). Persistent denial of childhood conflicts and their screening with defensive self-delusions block self-realisation. Irrational expectations or 'neurotic claims' such as self-idealisation obscure not only self-hate, but also 'the unique alive forces' that each self possesses and that are distorted by the self-illusions. The therapeutic process weakens the obstructive forces so that the constructive forces of the real self can emerge (348). The constructive forces in ego psychology become known as the 'Third Force'.

Bernard Paris has applied 'Third Force' psychology to several canonical novels whose self-alienating characters fit Horney's descriptions of neurotic styles, while self-activating characters express their 'Third Force' as defined by Maslow (Paris 1974: 29). For Maslow, the 'Third Force' is our 'essentially biologically based inner nature', unique to the person but also species-wide, whose needs, emotions and capacities are 'either neutral, pre-moral or positively good' (1968: 3). Neuroses result when our hierarchically organised basic needs are not met (21). When one level of needs is satisfied, the needs of another level emerge as persons define themselves existentially. During that process the person has 'peak experiences', epiphanic moments that afford glimpses into the state of being fully actualised and can have the effect of removing symptoms, of changing a person's view of himself and the world, of releasing creativity and generally conveying the idea that life is worth living in spite of its difficulties (101). Maslow admits that not all peak experiences are moments of 'Being recognition' (100), but he insists that people are 'most their identities in peak experiences' (103) where they feel most self-integrated.

The development of the ego as self-reliant and socially accepted is perhaps most evident in the young adult novel whose comic resolution integrates the young person with socially acceptable norms. Frequently such narratives include the figure of the social worker or therapist who aids the process, or the young protagonist plans to become a therapist so as to 'help kids in trouble'. Such problem narratives are accessible to young readers through stories that occasionally seem like case studies. The young adult novel that projects the genuine misfit as a worthwhile subject is a rarity. The largely middle-class context of young adult novels generally furthers the optimism implied in ego psychology.

### Melanie Klein and D. W. Winnicott

According to Klein, because the ego is not fully integrated at birth, it is subject to splitting and fragmentation as it projects states of feeling and unconscious wishes on objects or absorbs qualities of the object through introjection where they become defined as belonging to the ego.

Like Freud, Klein saw the 'exploration of the unconscious [as] the main task of psycho-analytic procedure, and that the analysis of transference [was] the means of achieving this' (1955/1975a: 123). Her analysands were primarily children whose inability to freely associate verbally led Klein to develop the psychoanalytic play technique already begun by Anna Freud (1925/1975b: 146).

The use of simple toys in a simply equipped room brought out 'a variety of symbolical meanings' bound up with the child's fantasies, wishes and experiences. By approaching the child's play in a manner similar to Freud's interpretation of dreams, but by always individualising the child's use of symbols, Klein felt she could gain access to the child's unconscious (1975a: 137). She discovered that the primary origin of impulses, fantasies and anxieties could be traced back to the child's original object relation – the mother's breast – even when the child was not breastfed (138).

In commenting on the influence of Klein on literary theory, Elizabeth Wright regrets that Klein's demonstration of fantasy as a precondition of any engagement with reality has been neglected by literary critics who have instead focused on the aesthetic of ego psychology (1984: 83–84). It is through the structure of fantasy that the child acts out not only real or imagined damage, but also the desire for reparation. Klein saw the monsters and menacing figures of myths and fairy tales as parent displacements exerting unconscious influences on the child by making it feel threatened and persecuted, but such emotions 'can clear our feelings to some extent towards our parents of grievances, we can forgive them for the frustrations we had to bear, become at peace with ourselves' so that 'we are able to love others in the true sense of the word' (1975b: 343).

In criticisms of children's literature, Klein's approach can reveal how the text enables the actualisation of the ego intentionally or how it falls short of it. For example, an interpretation of Bianco's *The Velveteen Rabbit* reveals it as a fantasy of unresolved ambivalence between the need to be loved and becoming independent, that is, real. Because 'the story never acknowledges the Rabbit's desire to grow away from the object of his attachment, and hence never acknowledges the basis for his entry into the depressive position, it cannot credit him with working through it' (Daniels 1990: 26). The Kleinian perspective also offers insight into the relation of fantasy to guilt and reparation as exemplified in White's *Charlotte's Web* (Rustin 1987: 161).

While Klein focused on play as a means to the end of the therapeutic process, D. W. Winnicott saw play as intrinsically facilitating healthy development and group relationships. Even psychoanalysis is an elaborate playing 'in the service of communication with oneself and others' (1971: 41). In his studies of babies and children, Winnicott retained the psychoanalytic attention to inner reality along with an emphasis on the child's cultural and social context. Crucial in his discovery is the concept of the 'transitional object': 'one must recognise the central position of Winnie-the-Pooh' (xi). By transitional object and transitional space Winnicott designates the intermediate area of experience between the thumb and the teddy bear, between oral eroticism and true object relationships. Identifying the mother's breast as part of itself, the baby must develop the ability of the 'not me' through substitutions which are transitions between the illusion of identification and the acceptance of the 'not me'. The baby's relationship with the transitional object has special qualities: the infant assumes right but not omnipotence over the object which can be loved and changed, even mutilated by the infant. Gradually, the infant will be able to detach itself from the object which becomes consigned to a limbo, rather than being introjected by the infant (1–5). The object is not a signifier for some hidden unconscious content, but a crucial partner in the game of intersubjectivity as the playing infant tests out the me/not me.

Winnicott's concept of the transitional object not only lends itself to the interpretation of content images in narratives, but also to the text itself. Both author and reader can claim the text as transitional object. Small children do indeed appropriate a book as object – loving it, adding to it, mutilating it. An especially Winnecottian book would be Margaret Wise Brown's *Good Night Moon*, which has been cited as an example of child's having just learned the distinction between animate and inanimate objects. 'Good night, bears' (toys) and 'good night, kittens' is acceptable, but saying good night to chairs and mittens provokes shrieks of laughter in the child (Applebee 1978: 41) who does not yet accept the object 'bear' as inanimate. *Good Night Moon* is, for a certain age, a transitional object containing many transitional objects that assuage bedtime anxieties as the child connects with all of them, thus assuring itself of the 'me' before the lights go out at bedtime.

## Jacques Lacan: The Return to Freud Through Language

For Freud the subconscious is the irreducible radical of the psyche, its universal, whose paradox it is that nothing raised from it remains unconscious: we can only be conscious of *something*. Thus the unconscious is replaced by the comprehensible mental acts of the ego, be they dreams, symbolisation's or linguistic utterances. As Wright points out, for Jacques Lacan 'the dictum "the unconscious is structured like a language"' is borne out in that 'every word indicates the absence of what it stands for, a fact that intensifies the frustration of this child of language, the unconscious, since the absence of satisfaction has not to be accepted. Language imposes a chain of words along which the ego must move while the unconscious remains in search of the object it has lost' (Wright 1984: 111). The unconscious as a language allows Lacan to revise Freud's self-sufficiency of the unconscious with social interaction. How this comes about through the development of the infant and how this relates to the perception of the text as psyche – a major shift away from the author's or reader's psyche – has special relevance to interpreters of children's literature.

Lacan distinguishes three stages in the infant's development: the imaginary, the symbolic and the real. In the imaginary or mirror stage, which can happen at the age of six months, the infant receives the *imago* of its own body (*Ecrits*, 1977: 3). Having seen itself only as fragmentary, the infant perceives in the mirror a symbolic 'mental permanence of the I', but this perception prefigures alienation, for the mirror stage is a spatial illusion of totality (4), an imaginary identification with reflection. The mirror stage, which is pre-verbal, conveys the illusion that the image will respond to the child's wishes, as did the mother–breast–infant identification. The symbolic stage is the stage of language, a stage that will form the subject henceforth only in and as dialogue. The implied assumption that language may have definitive authority is undermined or deconstructed by Lacan's argument that every utterance is permeated by the unconscious in the sense that wholeness, meaning, and gratification of wishes are perpetually deferred. The real, not to be confused with 'external reality', describes what is lacking in the symbolic – 'it is the residue of articulation or the umbilical cord of the symbolic' (ix-x) (translator's note).

The literary text, then, is an image of the unconscious structured like a language. 'The lure of all texts', comments Wright, 'lies in a revelation, of things veiled coming to be unveiled, of characters who face shock at this unveiling' (1984: 121). When this phenomenon is given utterance in the reader-interpreter's language, meaning is inevitably deferred. In contrast to Freudian interpretation, we have here no unearthing of authorial neuroses. The Lacanian consequences for reader and text is the realisation that

> the selves we see ourselves as being are as fictional [made up of language] as the stories of written fiction – limited images like those we see in mirrors when we first became conscious of our separateness – so fiction can be read in terms of the way it echoes our basic human activity of inventing ourselves and becoming conscious of the limitation of our invention. All we usually call reality is in fact fiction, and always less complete than the actual real world outside our consciousness.
>
> Nodelman 1992: 93–94

Perry Nodelman discusses how Cinderella becomes a fixed subject at the end of the story rather than the multifaceted one she was. As she completes her stage of becoming, she has actually lost wholeness in her state of being (94). An analysis of *Charlotte's Web* shows how Lacan's imaginary and symbolic stage work through the 'Miracle of the web' in that Wilbur perceives himself and is perceived as transformed through the ability of words to reorient desire by demonstrating 'that things are desirable because they are signified and, therefore, significant' in and through language (Rushdy 1991: 56). Another Lacanian interpretation applies the concept of the subject being created by disjunction and discontinuity to Russell Hoban's *The Mouse and His Child* where the mouse child, submerged to the bottom of a pond, is jubilant when it sees itself reflected in the labelless Bonzo dog food can: 'He sees himself suddenly whole, apparently co-ordinated and in control' (Krips 1993: 95). The directive 'be happy' is in *The Mouse and His Child* as authoritative as Charlotte's five single word texts in the web, in that it creates the illusion of desire fulfilled, even as desire is deferred.

## Psychoanalytic Theory and the Feminist Critique

The patrimony psychoanalytic criticism received from Freud has exerted a deep 'anxiety of influence' on the feminist critic (Gilbert and Gubar 1979: 45–92; Gallop 1982), primarily because of Freud's definition of female sexuality and his centring of the male myth of Oedipus, both of which reduce the female to an addendum. Revisionary readings of Freud, particularly those by French feminists influenced by Lacan, both appropriate and retain his powerful influence. Feminist readings of Jung underwent less radical revisions (Lauter and Rupprecht 1985). Even without specific reference to ego-relations and object psychology, the feminist critic, by delineating the struggle of the female in a patriarchially constructed world, finds in the concept of self-actualisation an ally in her attempt at social transformation.

While not denying the existence of the subconscious, feminist psychoanalytic criticism, including the feminist criticism of children's literature, privileges the concept of social construction in the development of the female. Nancy Chodorow's *The Reproduction of Mothering* has been especially influential in its synthesis of psychoanalysis and the sociology of gender where 'the reproduction of mothering occurs through social structurally induced psychological processes' and is 'neither a product of biology nor of intentional role training' (1978: 7). Here the critic of children's literature finds a female focus, especially for the mother–daughter relation (Barzilai 1990; Murphy 1990; Natov 1990). The focus on the body–self relations allows the feminist critic to explore unique female experiences that have been neglected in the study of literature. The focus on the social construction of female and male children, especially since the nineteenth-century middle-class self-definition of gender roles and the family, has guided feminists to valuable contextual insights into the history of children's literature and its readers.

A major issue in feminist criticism is the problematics of the female writer's precursors which has led Gilbert and Gubar to revise Bloom's 'anxiety of influence' (Bloom 1973) with 'anxiety of authorship' by which the female writer questions her claim to be a writer (Gilbert and Gubar 1979: 48–49). It remains to be seen if the important role of female writers in children's literature and the status of children's literature as a field of study might be understood as defences against the pressures of the male dominated literary and critical tradition.

## Conclusion

The revisions and transformations by which psychoanalytical theories and criticisms continue to construct themselves have retained so far the concept of the unconscious and its powerful influence on the ego's development and struggle in the world. Children's literature, whose language signifies the substitutions and displacements necessitated in that struggle, intimates and makes acceptable the dream of desire. It is a great irony of our psychoanalytic age that the psychological self-help narratives for young readers abandon consideration of the powers of the id in favour of the social adjustment of the young ego and that they do so, usually, in the language of low mimetic accessibility where the mode of romance and poetry is gone. That phenomenon is itself worthy of psychoanalytical interpretations of authors, texts and readers.

## References

Applebee, A. N. (1978) *The Child's Concept of Story*, Chicago: University of Chicago Press.
Barzilai, S. (1990) 'Reading 'Snow White': the mother's story', *Signs* 15, 3: 515–534.
Bettelheim, B. (1976) *The Uses of Enchantment*, New York: A. A. Knopf.
Bloom, H. (1973) *The Anxiety of Influence*, New York: Oxford University Press.
Bosmajian, H. (1985) '*Charlie and the Chocolate Factory* and other excremental visions', *The Lion and the Unicorn* 9: 36–49.
Chodorow, N. (1978) *The Reproduction of Mothering. Psychoanalysis and the Sociology of Gender*, Berkeley: University of California Press.
Cooper, J. C. (1983) *Fairy Tales: Allegories of the Inner Life*, Wellingborough: Aquarian Press.
Daniels, S. (1990) '*The Velveteen Rabbit*: a Kleinian perspective', *Children's Literature* 18: 17–30.
Egan, M. (1982) 'The neverland of id: Barrie, *Peter Pan*, and Freud', *Children's Literature* 10: 37–55.
Franz, M.-L. von (1977) *Individuation in Fairy Tales*, Zurich: Spring.
—— (1978) *An Introduction to the Psychology of Fairy Tales*, Irving, TX: Spring.
Freud, S., (1908/1963) 'The relation of the poet to daydreaming', *Character and Culture*, trans. J. Strachey, New York: Macmillan.

—— (1913/1958) 'The occurrence in dreams of material from fairy tales', *Character and Culture*, trans. J. Strachey, New York: Macmillan.

—— (1962/1975) *Three Essays on the Theory of Sexuality*, trans. J. Strachey, New York: Harper Collins.

Frye, N. (1957) *Anatomy of Criticism*, Princeton: Princeton University Press.

Gallop, J. (1982) *The Daughter's Seduction: Feminism and Psychoanalysis*, Ithaca, NY: Cornell University Press.

Gilbert, S. and Gubar, S. (1979) *The Madwoman in the Attic: The Woman Writer and the Nineteenth Century Literary Imagination*, New Haven: Yale University Press.

Greenacre, P. (1955) *Swift and Carroll: A Psychoanalytic Study of Two Lives*, New York: International Universities Press.

Hillman, J. (1980) 'The children, the children!' *Children's Literature* 8: 3–6.

Hogan, P. (1990) 'What's wrong with the psychoanalysis of literature?', *Children's Literature* 18: 135–140.

Holland, N. (1968) *The Dynamics of Literary Response*, New York: Oxford University Press.

—— (1970) 'The 'unconscious' of literature: the psychoanalytic approach', in Bradbury, N. and Palmer, D. (eds) *Contemporary Criticism*, Stratford-upon-Avon Series 12, New York: St Martin's.

Horney, K. (1950) *Neurosis and Human Growth: The Struggle Toward Self-Realization*, New York: Norton.

Jung, C. G. (1931/1966) 'On the relation of analytical psychology to poetry', *The Spirit in Man, Art, and Literature. Collected Works* vol. 15, trans. R. F. C. Hull, New York: Random House.

—— (1946/1954) 'Psychic conflicts in a child', *The Development of Personality. Collected Works* vol. 17, trans. R. F. C. Hull, New York: Random House.

—— (1964) 'Approaching the unconscious', *Man and His Symbols*, New York: Doubleday.

Klein, M. (1975a) *Envy and Gratitude*, New York: Delacorte.

—— (1975b) *Love, Guilt and Reparation*, New York: Delacorte.

Knoepflmacher, U. C. (1990) 'The doubtful marriage: a critical fantasy', *Children's Literature* 18: 131–134.

Krips, V. (1993) 'Mistaken identity: Russell Hoban's *Mouse and His Child*', *Children's Literature* 21: 92–100.

Lacan, J. (1977) *Ecrits*, trans. Alan Sheridan, New York: W. W. Norton.

Lauter, E. and Rupprecht, C. S. (1985) *Feminist Archetypal Theory. Interdisciplinary Revisions of Jungian Thought*, Knoxville: University of Tennessee Press.

Maslow, A. (1968) *Toward a Psychology of Being*, New York: D. Van Nostrand.

Murphy, A. (1990) 'The borders of ethical, erotic, and artistic possibilities, *Little Women*, *Signs* 15, 3: 562–585.

Natov, R. (1990) 'Mothers and daughters: Jamaica Kincaid's pre-oedipal narrative', *Children's Literature* 18: 1–16.

Nodelman, P. (1992) *The Pleasures of Children's Literature*, New York: Longman.

Paris, B. J. (1974) *A Psychological Approach to Fiction*, Bloomington: Indiana University Press.

Phillips, J. and Wojcik-Andrews, I. (1990) 'Notes toward a Marxist critical practice, *Children's Literature* 18: 127–130.

Rollin, L. (1990) 'The reproduction of mothering in *Charlotte's Web*', *Children's Literature* 18: 42–52.

Rose, J. (1984) *The Case of Peter Pan, or the Impossibility of Children's Fiction*, London: Macmillan.

Rosenthal, L. (1980) 'The development of consciousness in Lucy Boston's *The Children of Green Knowe*', *Children's Literature* 8: 53–67.

Rushdy, A. H. A. (1991) ' "The Miracle of the Web": community, desire and narrativity in *Charlotte's Web*', *The Lion and the Unicorn* 15, 2: 35–60.

Rustin, M. and Rustin, M. (1987) *Narratives of Love and Loss: Studies in Modern Children's Fiction*, New York: Verso.

Segel, E. (1986) ' "As the Twig Is Bent ..." ', gender and childhood reading', in Flynn, E. A. and Schweikart, P. (eds) *Gender and Reading*, Baltimore: Johns Hopkins University Press.

Smith, J. and Kerrigan, W. (1985) *Opening Texts: Psychoanalysis and the Culture of the Child*, Baltimore: Johns Hopkins University Press.

Steig, M. (1990) 'Why Bettelheim? A comment on the use of psychological theories in criticism', *Children's Literature* 18: 125–126.

Tatar, M. (1992) *Off with Their Heads! Fairy Tales and the Culture of Childhood*, Princeton: Princeton University Press.

Winnicott, D. W. (1971) *Playing and Reality*, New York: Tavistock/Routledge.

Wright, E. (1984) *Psychoanalytic Criticism*, New York: Methuen.

Zipes, J. (1979) *Breaking the Magic Spell: Radical Theories of Folk and Fairy Tales*, Austin: University of Texas Press.

—— (1990) 'Negating history and male fantasies through psychoanalytic criticism', *Children's Literature* 18: 141–143.

# Further Reading

Bloch, D. (1978) *'So the Witch Won't Eat Me' Fantasy and the Child's Fear of Infanticide*, New York: Grove Press.

Jung, C. G. (1964) *Man and His Symbols*, New York: Doubleday.

Tucker, N. (1981) *The Child and the Book: A Psychological and Literary Exploration*, New York: Cambridge University Press.

# 8

# Feminist Criticism: From Sex-Role Stereotyping to Subjectivity

## *Lissa Paul*

'A Cinderella story: research on children's books takes on new life as a field of literary study': that was the headline for an article on the rise of academic children's literature criticism, published 13 February 1991, in the *Chronicle of Higher Education* (the newspaper for American universities, similar to the *Times Higher Educational Supplement* in Britain). Although the article, by Ellen K. Coughlin, nicely sketches several of the current poststructuralist, including feminist, lines in children's literature criticism, it is the headline that is arresting. The teasing, metaphoric association with the rags-to-riches image of Cinderella stories inadvertently discloses the uneasy relations between children's literature, feminist theory and the academy.

Cinderella herself is, after all, the subject of a great deal of feminist critique. Most of us – women, children and feminist critics, I imagine – don't want to be seen valuing riches. Or princes for that matter. The implication in the Cinderella reference in the headline is that as 'the province of library schools and education departments' (Coughlin 1991: 5), children's literature criticism ranks low on the academic hit parade. Now associated with high-order poststructuralist theory and with English departments, children's literature criticism moves up in the respectability ratings.

If the destabilisation of hierarchical orders is one of the mobilising features of feminist theory then there is probably something hypocritical and arrogant about disenfranchising librarians, teachers – and children – from the ranks of stake-holders in the field of children's literature studies. It is not coincidental that librarians and teachers tend to be women and that the education of young children is not regarded as the serious business of scholars (a hold over from the New Criticism).

A pair of articles in *Orana*, an Australian children's literature journal, neatly problematise the gender equity issues as raised often by critics from education, library science and psychology. In 'Sexism and children's literature: a perspective for librarians' (1981), Christine Nicholls recognises that 'sexism is a type of colonialism', but she then goes on to suggest that solutions to the problem include the use of 'white out' and the abandonment of books no longer in accord with contemporary definitions of gender equity. Hugh Crago (a psychologist and a fine children's literature critic) offers a sensitively worked out corrective. In 'Sexism, literature and reader-response: a reply to Christine Nicholls', he reminds Nicholls (and the rest of us) that responses to texts are subject to large fluctuations, especially in fluid forms like fairy tales where versions, translations and illustrations all contribute to shaping the interpretative possibilities of texts. He also foregrounds the idea there is really no such thing as 'the one-way cause and effect relationship' (Crago 1981: 161) between reader and text – something implicit in the Nicholls article and in a great many like it.

There are two points worth foregrounding here. One is that the emphasis on sex-role stereotyping and sexism found most often in education and library science journals is connected with an honest front-line attempt to create a more female-friendly climate, especially in schools. That connection between theoretical change and political change is true to the roots of feminist theory in the women's movements of the 1970s. To dismiss librarians and teachers as the 'rags' phase of the Cinderella story is to participate in a hierarchical ordering of critical values. As a feminist critic, I don't want to do that.

The other point worth keeping in mind is that current poststructuralist discussions, especially those on semiotics, deconstruction, ideology and sub-jectivity, make it possible to develop language and strategies that speak – to borrow a phrase from Carol Gilligan – 'in a different voice'. As an academic feminist children's literature critic, feminist admonitions to remember our histories and value members of our communities constantly sound in my mind.

Children's literature offers to children the promise of inclusion in a literate community (something regarded as culturally valuable, at least nominally). The critical apparatus surrounding children's books offers an intellectual under-standing of what inclusion means and how it might be achieved. In an ideal world anyway. What feminist theory has done for children's literature studies – and for all fields of literary study – is to insist on the right to be included, but not just as honorary white men. As a result, not only have our interpretations of texts changed, but also our production of them and our access to them – as I'll try to demonstrate throughout this article.

The current wave of academic children's literature criticism rose in the early 1970s at the same time as the rise of what is known as the 'second wave' of feminist theory in this century. In the 1990s both feminist criticism and children's literature criticism are established participants in the academy with all the requisite structures in place to support establishment status – refereed journals, professional associations, graduate degree programmes.

Signs of the common ground between children's literature criticism and feminist theory are marked in two special issues of children's literature journals. The *Children's Literature Association Quarterly* ran a special section, edited by Anita Moss, in the Winter 1982 edition: 'Feminist criticism and the study of children's literature'. In that early collection of essays there were several reviews of books of feminist literary criticism, each sketching possible critical lines children's literature critics might find worth exploring. Virginia Wolf, for instance, writes about alternatives to the heroic quest in science fiction; and Lois Kuznets about texts that value communities rather than kingdoms.

In December 1991, *The Lion and the Unicorn* published an issue called 'Beyond sexism: gender issues in children's literature'. By this time the lessons of feminist theory are internalised, and critics are actively constructing a feminist tradition in children's literature (see especially essays by Judith John, W. Nikola-Lisa, Lynne Vallone and the essay by Lois Kuznets discussed below). Note the switch, incidentally, from 'feminist criticism' to 'gender' studies. That shift marks the subtle inclusion of gay and lesbian studies into the fray. It also marks the popular use of a code word to try prevent feminist studies from becoming a pink-collar ghetto. And it hints at the speed with which feminist theory is changing – something I'll try to track.

In keeping with feminist critic Jane Gallop's cryptic caution to remember that 'history is like a mother' (1992: 206–239), I'm going to focus on three broad areas of academic children's literature criticism influenced (unanxiously) by feminist theory: the rereading of texts for previously unrevealed interpretations; the reclaiming of texts that had been devalued or dismissed; and the redirection of feminist theory into providing a welcoming climate for texts by people margin-alised by patriarchal colonial societies. The titles in each of my three sections in this essay, 'Rereading', 'Reclaiming' and 'Redirection' take their cue from Adrienne Rich's ideas that feminist poetics are about 'revision' (Rich 1976).

## Rereading

The desire for feminist rereading comes from an understanding of the ways ideological assumptions about the constitution of good literature (or criticism for that matter) work. By the early 1970s, feminist critics like Kate Millett had made it common knowledge that assumptions about good literature had been predicated on the belief that the adult white male was normal, while virtually everyone else was deviant or marginal. And so was born a critical desire to see if a feminine literary tradition, and feminine culture could be made visible. By using techniques from deconstruction (derived largely from Derrida) and from contemporary discussions of ideology (from Althusser and Pierre Bourdieu) and subjectivity (largely derived from Lacan), feminist critics began to look at the ways ideological assumptions are played out in the text. They searched for a feminine tradition of 'other' stories: mother, daughter, sister stories (Chodorow, Hirsch); a preference for survival tactics over honour (Gilligan); a search for a 'both/and' feminine plot rather than an 'either/or' oedipal plot (Hirsch); a preference from multiplicity, plurality, jouissance and a valuing of pro-creations, recreations and new beginnings (Cixous, Gallop, Rich). Feminist children's literature critics also participate in this recovery of a female literary tradition (Paul 1987/1990; 1990). The following small sketches of reinterpretation, rehabilitation and re-creation demonstrate the range of ways in which that tradition is being revealed.

### *Reinterpretation*

Feminist reinterpretations of familiar classics like *The Secret Garden* and *Little Women* turn stories we thought were about struggles to conform to the social order into stories about women's healing and successful communities of women (Bixler, Nelson, Auerbach). *Little Women* – as read by Edward Salmon (a nineteenth-century authority on children's literature) in his 1888 obituary of Alcott in *Atalanta* – is a story about instructing girls to be 'the proper guardians of their brothers' and to be 'all-powerful for good in their relations with men' (449). But for Nina Auerbach, in *Communities of Women* (1978), it is the story of 'the formation of a reigning feminist sisterhood whose exemplary unity will heal a fractured society' (37). The critical rereading turns it from a story about women learning how to serve men into a story of women supporting each other.

## *Rehabilitation*

The rehabilitation of works by Mary Wollstonecraft, Maria Edgeworth and other 'lady moralists' of the Georgian and Romantic periods, is one of the major success stories of academic feminist children's literature criticism. Although I am going to focus on criticism by Mitzi Myers, credit also goes to Anita Moss and Lynne Vallone.

As Mitzi Myers pointedly states, texts by Georgian 'lady' moralists as rendered in standard overviews of children's literature, suffer from 'something like the critical equivalent of urban blight' (Myers 1986: 31). John Rowe Townsend dismisses these women as ranging 'from the mildly pious to the sternly moralistic' (1974: 39). Harvey Darton refers to 'the truculent dogmatic leanings of Mrs Sherwood and Mrs Trimmer' and the 'completely dogmatic' Mary Godwin (1982: 156, 196).

Myers offers different readings. She participates in what feminist critic Elaine Showalter calls 'gynocriticism', that is, criticism that attends to 'the woman as producer of textual meaning, with the history, themes, genres, and structures of literature by women' (Showalter 1985: 128). What Myers asks is how those Georgian women found autonomy and influence in a world where those freedoms were denied. Her answers transform lady moralists scorned for their conformity, into the founding mothers of a feminist pedagogical tradition.

In Georgian England, where there were few roles for (upper class) women except as wives, mothers and governesses, Mary Wollstonecraft, Maria Edgeworth and other women like Mrs Trimmer and Mrs Sherwood transformed their roles. They constructed 'an almost unrecognised literary tradition', one that 'accepts and emphasises the instructive and intellectual potential of narrative' (Myers 1986: 33). Maria Edgeworth, for example, creates female protagonists as 'desiring' subjects, not just objects of desire. And Mary Wollstonecraft, in her 'Mrs Mason' stories, redefines power in unpatriarchal terms 'as pedagogic and philanthropic power' (43).

The autonomy, creativity and integrity of those Georgian women would not have been possible without the eyes of Mitzi Myers and her knowledge of feminist theory. They would have remained in the footnotes of what is now beginning to look like a masculinist tradition of children's literature.

## *Re-creation*

Although I've focused so far on the way academic critics construct feminist traditions in children's literature, I'm mindful of the ways authors living through the second wave of feminism are changing what we read. Author Ursula Le Guin chronicles the change most dramatically. In *Earthsea Revisioned* (1993), the published version of lecture she gave in Oxford in 1992, Le Guin records the influence of gender politics on her *Earthsea* quartet. The first three *Earthsea* novels published between 1968 and 1972, are in the genre of the traditional heroic fantasy, something Le Guin defines as 'a male preserve: a sort of great game-park where Beowulf feasts with Teddy Roosevelt, and Robin Hood goes hunting with Mowgli, and the cowboy rides off into the sunset alone' (Le Guin 1993: 5).

Le Guin does not apologise for the male-order, hierarchical world in the first three novels. But twenty years after their publication she recognises things about that world that she didn't understand when she made it. With the insights of contemporary feminist theory, she understands that at the time, she was 'writing partly by the rules, as an artificial man, and partly against the rules, as an inadvertent revolutionary' (7). In her revolutionary mode, in a partly conscious attempt to create a hero from a visible minority, Le Guin made Ged and all the good guys in the *Earthsea* books black, and the bad guys white. Nevertheless, the good guys were standard male-order heroes anyway. They lived lives of 'continence; abstinence; denial of relationship' (16). And they worked in a world predicated on 'power as domination over others, unassailable strength, and the generosity of the rich' (14).

But in *Tehanu*, the fourth and final *Earthsea* book, published seventeen years after the third, Le Guin scraps male-order heroism. She creates Tenar, a feminist pro-creative, recreative hero: 'All her former selves are alive in her: the child Tenar, the girl priestess Arha ... and Goha, the farmwife, mother of two children. Tenar is whole but not single. She is not pure' (Le Guin 1993: 18). The traditional male hero, the dragonslayer and dragonlord, marked by his capacity to defeat evil, to win, and to receive public adoration and power, is nowhere in sight. In the new mythology Le Guin creates, the dragon is transformed into a familiar, a guide for a new female hero: 'The child who is our care, the child we have betrayed, is our guide. She leads us to the dragon. She is the dragon'. Le Guin moves out of the hierarchical ordering of the heroic world, and into a new world where the search is for wildness, a 'new order of freedom' (26).

The feminist tradition created in the span that includes Mitzi Myers's rereading Wollstonecraft, and Le Guin revisioning *Earthsea*, is one that celebrates maternal pedagogies, disorder, wildness, pro-creation, re-creation and multiplicity: a large cultural shift in a short space of time.

## Reclaiming

One of the most significant feminist projects of the last twenty-five years has been the reissuing of long out-of-print books by women authors. Many have been gathering dust on library shelves for dozens, sometimes hundreds of years. Most had long since ceased to make any money for anyone. But Virago and other feminist presses that grew up with the second wave of feminism, have put many of these books back into circulation. Now easily available in good quality paperback editions they are read for pleasure, not just among scholars, though scholars were often the first to create the demand for these books by finding them, writing about them and bringing them to university course lists and to public attention.

Though there is no exactly comparable resurrection of authored fiction in children's literature (Angela Brazil is as unlikely to be reissued as Talbot Baines Reed), there is one class of texts enjoying a new lease on life as a direct result of the second wave of feminism: fairy tales. In fact, the shift in fairy tale fashions over the last twenty-five years provides a virtual paradigm for shifts in feminist poetics.

In the 1970s, with the rise of the second wave of feminist theory, there was increasing discomfort with the gender dynamics in popular Grimm, Andersen and Perrault fairy tales (though Simone de Beauvoir had already drawn attention to passive Grimm heroines twenty years earlier in *The Second Sex*). Girls and women play dead or doormats (as in 'Snow White', 'Cinderella', and 'Sleeping Beauty') or are severely mutilated (as in 'The Little Mermaid').

The move was on for female heroes (I'll use the term in preference to 'heroines' – who tend to wait around a lot). Unfortunately, the female heroes of the early 1970s tended not to be of a different order, as is Tenar in Le Guin's *Tehanu*. They tended to be more like men tricked out in drag. The stories were the same as those with male heroes in them. But instead of being about boys seeking adventure, profit, and someone to rescue, girls were in the starring roles. They rescued instead of being rescued. Like television situation comedies that colour middle-class families black, most of those tales died natural deaths. *The Paper Bag Princess* by Robert Munsch is a dubious exception. It is still in print, and the princess uses the feminist tactic of deceit to defeat the dragon and rescue the prince. But as the prince suffers from the traditionally feminine vice of vanity, s/he is essentially rejected for a lack of machismo.

When revisionist tales virtually disappeared in the late 1970s, reclaimed tales looked like a more viable alternative. But in the first collections of reclaimed tales, the preference for male characteristics in female heroes was still much in evidence. In the introduction to *Tatterhood and Other Tales*, for example, Ethel Johnston Phelps states a preference for stories with 'active and courageous girls and women in the leading roles', ones who are 'distinguished by extraordinary courage and achievements' (1978: vx). In other words, she prefers the same old male type, who, as Valerie Walkerdine suggests, is 'gender-neutral, self-disciplined, and active' (120). That is, the preferred hero is still a man.

The one voice that begs to differ belongs Angela Carter. Her two collections of reclaimed fairy tales for Virago are so good they are difficult to put down. She doesn't just present tales about the unrelieved glory of women – a male-order project anyway. Instead, she tries 'to demonstrate the extraordinary richness and diversity of responses to the same common predicament – being alive – and the richness and diversity with which femininity, in practice is represented in "unofficial" culture: its strategies, its plots, its hard work' (Carter 1991: xiv). One of her favourite stories from this collection was apparently 'Tongue meat', a Swahili story that tells of a languishing queen who only revives when fed 'tongue meat', something that turns out to be a metaphor for stories. The tales of girls and women that Angela Carter revives are exactly that kind of 'tongue meat'. They establish an alternative feminist tradition – one that hadn't been visible before.

While it is true that fairy tales seem to have enjoyed the most dramatic revival as a result of twinned interests in women's studies and children's literature studies, other reclamation projects are also taking place. The texts being rediscovered by feminist critics are important because they provide a historical context for our own ideological assumptions about gender, about what constitutes good literature, and about what is worth remembering, circulating and retaining for study.

One of the most compelling studies of women's texts lost and found is, 'Lost from the nursery: women writing poetry for children 1800–1850', by Morag Styles (1990). Styles came to write the article because she casually noticed how few women were represented in poetry anthologies for children, especially poets who published before 1900. As she began to explore, she discovered consistent patterns working to obliterate women poets from the record.

In early anthologies Styles found that poems which had quickly become popular in their own time, like 'Twinkle twinkle little star', or 'Mary had a little lamb', rapidly became separated from their authors as they entered anthologies. They were usually attributed to the anonymous authors of oral tradition. So while generations of children learned to say 'Twinkle twinkle little star', few knew it was by Jane Taylor, or that Sara Hale wrote 'Mary had a little lamb', or that 'The months of the year' was by Sara Coleridge.

The systematic exclusion of these women from the children's literature canon accords precisely with the ideological reasons for their exclusion from the literary canon – and from positions of power and influence. Styles explains that 'the colloquial domestic writing of some women whose concern in literature for children (and often for adults) is with relationships, affection, friendship, family life often located in the small-scale site of the home' (Styles 1990: 203) was devalued, lost and forgotten in a world where large scale adventures and public rhetoric were valued. So the voices of Jane and Anne Taylor 'talking lovingly and naturally' in their poetry collections were lost. And Dorothy Wordsworth, with her 'private, colloquial and domestic' poetry (202), was relegated to a footnote in her brother's life.

By bringing the domestic cadences of women 'lost from the nursery', to our eyes and ears again, Styles provides a climate that warms to the domestic scene and to the softer, more direct, colloquial cadences of the female voice. She teaches us to listen with different ears to the different voice of women's poetry for children.

Although I've focused on two specific feminist reclamation efforts, fairy tales and poetry, both are part of a much larger feminist agenda, and I don't want to leave this section without mentioning other ways in which feminist children's literature critics are gradually recovering a female literary tradition.

By revealing the constructions of gendered patterns of childhood reading, academic feminist critics are beginning to locate the origins of ideological constructions of gender. Two studies of nineteenth-century girls' books and boys' books were published within a year of one another: *Girls Only?: Gender and Popular Children's Fiction in Britain, 1880–1910*, by Kimberley Reynolds in 1990, and *Boys will be Girls: The Feminist Ethic and British Children's Fiction, 1857–1917*, by Claudia Nelson in 1991. The sudden focus on that late nineteenth- and early twentieth-century time period is more than coincidental. It marks a critical recognition of that period as the time when colonial and patriarchal values were being actively inscribed in the culture. In widely circulating publications like the *Girl's Own Paper*, girls were apparently encouraged to accept simultaneously characteristics gendered feminine – 'purity, obedience, dependence, self-sacrifice and service' – and, an 'image of feminine womanhood ... expanded to incorporate intelligence, self-respect, and ... the potential to become financially dependent'. The result was a set of 'contradictory tendencies characteristic of femininity: reason and desire, autonomy and dependent activity, psychic and social identity' (Nelson 1991: 141). Those contradictions still haunt women today.

Other critics participate in the recovery of more recent histories of the relations between gender and reading. Lois Kuznets, in 'Two Newbery Medal winners and the feminine mystique: *Hitty, Her First Hundred Years*' and *Miss Hickory* (1991) looks at how two doll stories reflect the shifting ideological values of their times: *Hitty*, the 1930 winner, reflects the valuing of the independent woman who flourished in the 1920s; while *Miss Hickory*, the 1947 winner, reflects the post-war 'feminine mystique', something we now read as revealing a sadly repressed woman.

Relations between public success and childhood reading are being recounted in several reading memoirs published in the late 1980s and early 1990s. The women writing them at the height of, or late in, their professional careers seem to be offering clues that might be of use to librarians and teachers interested in creating a more supportive academic environment for girls. In *My Book House as Bildung*, Nancy Huse reconstructs her childhood reading of Olive Miller's *My Book House* as a way of establishing a maternal pedagogical line that influenced her choice of an academic career. And in the children's literature journal, *Signal*, Nancy Chambers has published several reading memoirs by well-known women who are active in a range of children's literature fields. Among them are ones by children's book editor Margaret Clark; author Jane Gardam; and Susan Viguers writing about her children's literature expert mother. All reveal how childhood reading enabled them to enter public worlds of letters on bridges built from private, domestic literate environments.

The tunes – to borrow a phrase from Margaret Meek (1992) – of women's texts are different from the ones established in the canon as being of value. What feminist theory has revealed, especially in reconstructions of a female literary tradition, is that the disproportionate emphasis placed on adventure, power, honour and public success squeezed out feminine valuing of maternal, domestic voices, ideas of sisterhood and stories about the lives of women. While only the feminist fairy tales may have found popular readership, scholarship teaches us to value domestic scenes and colloquial voices, and to remember our histories. It enables us to make familiar the new texts that come our way. The scholarship enables us to appreciate their difference.

## Redirection

The second wave of feminism began in the late 1960s when a whole generation of white, well-educated 'baby-boomer' women found that they were still relegated to making the coffee and stuffing envelopes. They were still excluded from the dominant discourses. The consciousness-raising groups of the 1970s began as means of mobilising collective voices in order to gain inclusion.

The right to be included: that became a basic tenet of feminist theory. So feminist theory changed to become increasingly inclusive: the feminist studies of the 1970s grew into gender studies in the 1980s. In the 1990s another change is happening as gender studies become aligned with post-colonial and cultural studies. Critics like Gayatri Spivak and Tinh T. Minh-ha, recognising the similarities between political power plays and gender power plays, have helped feminist criticism shed its Eurocentric, middle-class look. For children's literature critics, there is an increased awareness of the way primitives and children are frequently (t)roped together. In keeping with feminist agendas, this new theoretical line is changing both the readings and the text.

It is true that there is nothing in children's literature or children's literature criticism as yet that is as dramatic as the acknowledgement in Marina Warner's novel *Indigo*, that it was a work of post-colonial theory, *Colonial Encounters* by Peter Hulme, that spurred her to write the novel. But there are changes, as children's literature increasingly includes the images and voices of people of colour. I'm thinking especially of writers for children like John Agard, Grace Nichols, James Berry and Joy Kogawa who probe at the ways patriarchal powers have screwed up, how they've ruined the environment in favour of profit, and how they locked-up people designated as 'other' on the grounds that if they were foreign they were dangerous.

The unpicking of the child/primitive trope is also the subject of academic study. Stephen Slemon and Jo-Ann Wallace, professors at the University of Alberta in Canada taught a graduate course together called, 'Literatures of the child and the colonial subject: 1850–1914'. In an article they wrote together about their experience 'Into the heart of darkness? Teaching children's literature as a problem in theory' (1991), they discuss their struggle with the construction of the child in pedagogical and institutional terms. They write about the child who, like the 'primitive' is treated, 'as a subject-in-formation, an individual who often does not have full legal status and who therefore acts or who is acted against in ways that are not perceived to be fully consequential' (20). Post-colonial discourse illuminates ways in which authority over the 'other' is achieved in the name of protecting innocence. The ideological assumption is that primitives and children are too naïve (or stupid) to look after themselves so need protecting – like rain-forests.

The critical lessons in feminist/post-colonial theory increasingly have to do with ideology and with constructions of the subject. That's quite different from what used to be the common feature of children's literature and children's literature criticism – the notion of the identity quest, with its attendant assumption that there was such a thing as a stable identity. Instead, contemporary critical emphasis is on the ways we are constructed by the socialising forces pressuring us in all aspects of our lives: relationships with parents and families, class, gender and cultural patterns and expectations.

The implications for the unpicking of the child/primitive trope are part of something provoking a new crisis of definition in children's literature and children's literature criticism and teaching. While children's literature is predicated on the notion that children are essentially blank or naïve and in need of protection and instruction, then issues of suitability or unsuitability are important. But as children become differently constructed in the light of feminist and post-colonial theory, so does children's literature. Distinctions between them and us no longer become categorising features and suitability recedes as an issue.

The effects of this ideological shift begin to become apparent in criticism and in texts. Critics who work in feminist theory, post-colonial studies and children's literature all find themselves interested in common grounds: in the dynamics of power, in ideology, in the construction of the subject. And authors produce texts in which child/adult categories are no longer the significant ones. Jane Gardam's books, for example, appear in Abacus editions that don't make adult/child distinctions. And Angela Carter's Virago fairy tales are catalogued in the library not with children's literature or women's literature – but as anthropology.

The second wave of feminist theory has profoundly changed what we read and how we read. New texts and reclaimed texts have changed the canon so that more people are included and the 'dead white male' is less dominant. There is an increased awareness and valuing of maternal pedagogies and traditions of women's writing. Tastes have developed for colloquial, domestic voices pitched in higher registers and speaking in other cadences.

It is true that by the time this text is in print, the second wave of feminist theory will be long over. But it has created something else, something not fully defined yet. An article on feminist theory and children's literature written in 2006 would look radically different from this one – perhaps closer to the wild world of Le Guin's imaginings.

# References

Auerbach, N. (1978) *Communities of Women: An Idea in Fiction*, Harvard: Harvard University Press.

Beauvoir, S. de (1953) *The Second Sex*, New York: Random House.

'Beyond sexism: gender issues in children's literature' (1991), *The Lion and the Unicorn* 15, 2.

Bixler, P. (1991) 'Gardens, houses, and nurturant power in *The Secret Garden*', in McGavran, J. (ed.) *Romanticism and Children's Literature in Nineteenth Century England*, Athens, GA: University of Georgia Press.

Carter, A. (ed.) (1991) *The Virago Book of Fairy Tales*, London: Virago.

—— (1992) *The Second Virago Book of Fairy Tales*, London: Virago.

Chodorow, N. (1978) *The Reproduction of Mothering: Psychoanalysis and the Sociology of Gender*, Berkeley, CA: University of California Press.

Cixous, H. (1991) *Coming to Writing and Other Essays*, Cambridge MA: Harvard.

Clark, M. (1991) 'Early to Read', *Signal* 65: 112–119.

Coughlin, E. K. (1991) 'A Cinderella story: research on children's books takes on new life as a field of literary study', *Chronicle of Higher Education* 13 February: 5–7.

Crago, H. (1981) 'Sexism, literature and reader-response: a reply to Christine Nicholls', *Orana* 17, 4: 159–162.

Darton, F. J. H. (1982) *Children's Books in England: Five Centuries of Social Life*, 3rd edn, rev. B. Alderson, Cambridge: Cambridge University Press.

'Feminist criticism and the study of children's literature' (1982), special section of *Children's Literature Association Quarterly* 7, 4.

Gallop, J. (1992) *Around 1981: Academic Feminist Literary Theory*, New York: Routledge.

Gardam, J. (1991) 'A writer's life and landscape', *Signal* 66: 179–194.

Gilligan, C. (1982) *In a Different Voice: Psychological Theory and Women's Development*, Cambridge MA: Harvard University Press.

Hirsch, M. (1989) *The Mother/Daughter Plot: Narrative, Psychoanalysis, Feminism*, Bloomington: Indiana University Press.

Hulme, P. (1986) *Colonial Encounters: Europe and the Native Caribbean, 1492–1797*, New York: Methuen.

Huse, N. (1988) '*My Book House* as Bildung', *Children's Literature Association Quarterly* 13, 3: 115–121.

John, J. G. (1990) 'Searching for great-great grandmother: powerful women in George MacDonald's fantasies', *The Lion and the Unicorn* 15, 2: 27–34.

Kuznets, L. (1982) 'Defining full human potential: *Communities of Women, An Idea in Fiction*', and *Toward a Recognition of Androgyny, Children's Literature Association Quarterly* 7, 4: 10.

—— (1991) 'Two Newbery Medal winners and the feminine mystique: *Hitty, Her First Hundred Years* and *Miss Hickory*', *The Lion and the Unicorn* 15, 2: 1–14.

Le Guin, U. K. (1993) *Earthsea Revisioned*, Cambridge: Children's Literature New England in association with Green Bay Publications.

Meek, M. (1992) 'Transitions: the notion of change in writing for children', *Signal* 67: 13–32.

Millett, K. (1977) *Sexual Politics*, London: Virago.

Moss, A., 1988) 'Mothers, monsters, and morals in Victorian fairy tales', *The Lion and the Unicorn* 12, 2: 47–59.

Munsch, R. (1980) *The Paper Bag Princess*, Toronto: Annick Press.

Myers, M. (1986). 'Impeccable governesses, rational dames, and moral mothers: Mary Wollstonecraft and the female tradition in Georgian children's books', *Children's Literature* 14: 31–59.

Nelson, C. (1991) *Boys Will Be Girls: The Feminine Ethic and British Children's Fiction, 1857–1917*, New Brunswick: Rutgers.

Nicholls, C. 'Sexism and children's literature: a perspective for librarians', *Orana* 17, 3: 105–111.

Nikola-Lisa, W. (1991) 'The cult of Peter Rabbit: a Barthesian analysis', *The Lion and the Unicorn* 15, 2: 61–66.

Paul, L. (1987/1990) 'Enigma variations: what feminist theory knows about children's literature', in Hunt, P. (ed.) *Children's Literature: The Development of Criticism*, London: Routledge.

—— (1990) 'Escape claws: cover stories on *Lolly Willowes* and *Crusoe's Daughter*', *Signal* 63: 206–220.

Phelps, E. J. (1978) *Tatterhood and other Tales*, New York: The Feminist Press.

Reynolds, K. (1990) *Girls Only? Gender and Popular Children's Fiction in Britain, 1880–1910*, New York: Harvester Wheatsheaf.

Rich, A. (1976) 'When we dead awaken: writing as re-vision', *On Lies, Secrets, and Silence: Selected Prose 1966–1978*, New York: Norton.

Salmon, E. (1888) 'Miss L. M. Alcott', *Atalanta* 1, 8: 447–449.

Showalter, E. (1985) 'Toward a feminist poetic', *Feminist Criticism: Essays on Women, Literature, and Theory*, New York: Pantheon.

Slemon, S. and Wallace, J. (1991) 'Into the heart of darkness? Teaching children's literature as a problem in theory', *Canadian Children's Literature*, 63: 6–23.

Styles, M. (1990) 'Lost from the nursery: women writing poetry for children 1800 to 1850', *Signal* 63: 177–205.

Townsend, J. R. (1974) *Written For Children: An Outline of English-language Children's Literature*, Harmondsworth: Penguin.

Vallone, L. (1990) 'Laughing with the boys and learning with the girls: humor in nineteenth-century American juvenile fiction', *Children's Literature Association Quarterly*, 15, 3: 127–30.

—— (1991) ' "A humble spirit under correction": tracts, hymns, and the ideology of evangelical fiction for children, 1780–1820', *The Lion and the Unicorn* 15, 2: 72–95.

Viguers, S. T. (1988) 'My mother, my children, and books', *Signal* 55: 23–32.

Walkerdine, V. (1990) *Schoolgirl Fictions*, London: Verso.

Warner, M. (1992) *Indigo: or Mapping the Waters*, London: Chatto and Windus.
Wolf, V. (1982) 'Feminist criticism and science fiction for children', *Children's Literature Association Quarterly* 7, 4: 13–16.

# Further Reading

Auerbach, N. and Knoepflmacher, U. C. (1992) *Forbidden Journies: Fairy Tales and Fantasies by Victorian Women Writers*, Chicago: University of Chicago Press.

Barrs, M. and Pidgeon, S. (1993) *Reading the Difference: Gender and Reading in Primary School*, London: Centre for Language in Primary Education.

Conway, J. K. (1990) *The Road from Coorain*, New York: Vintage.

Hookes, B. (1992) 'Representing whiteness in the black imagination', in Grossman, L., Nelson, C. and Treichler, P. (eds) *Cultural Studies*, New York: Routledge.

Miller, J. (1990) *Seduction: Studies in Reading and Culture*, London: Virago.

Myers, M. (1987). ' "A taste for truth and realities": early advice to mothers on books for girls', *Children's Literature Association Quarterly* 12, 3: 118–123.

—— (1991) 'Romancing the moral tale: Maria Edgeworth and the problematics of pedagogy', in McGavran, J. (ed.) *Romanticism and Children's Literature in Nineteenth-Century England*, Athens, GA: University of Georgia Press.

Vallone, L. (1990) 'Laughing with the boys and learning with the girls: humor in nineteenth-century American juvenile fiction', *Children's Literature Association Quarterly* 15, 3: 127–130.

Warner, M. (1994) *Managing Monsters: Six Myths of Our Time*, The Reith Lectures, London: Vintage.

# 9

# Illustration and Picture Books

## *Perry Nodelman*

This is Mr Gumpy.

From *Mr Gumpy's Outing* by John Burningham. Copyright © 1971 John Burningham. Reprinted by permission of Jonathan Cape and Henry Holt and Co. Inc.

I open a book. I see a picture of a man, standing on a path in front of a house. Under the picture, printed words appear: 'This', they tell me, 'is Mr Gumpy.'

What could be more straightforward, more easily understood? And for good reason: the book, John Burningham's *Mr Gumpy's Outing* (1970), is intended for the least experienced of audiences – young children; and therefore, it is a 'picture book', a combination of verbal texts and visual images. We provide children with books like this on the assumption that pictures communicate more naturally and more directly than words, and thus help young readers make sense of the texts they accompany.

But are pictures so readily understood? And are picture books really so straightforward? If I try for a moment to look at the picture of Mr Gumpy without engaging my usual assumptions, I realise that I'm taking much about it for granted.

Burningham's image does in some way actually resemble a man, as the words 'man' or 'Mr Gumpy' do not; it is what linguists identify as an 'iconic' representation, whereas the words are 'symbolic', arbitrary sounds or written marks which stand for something they do not resemble. Nevertheless, if I didn't know that what I'm actually looking at – marks on a page – represented something else, I would see nothing in the picture but meaningless patches of colour. I need some general understanding of what pictures are before I can read these patches as a person, apparently named Mr Gumpy, living in a real or fictional world which exists somewhere else, outside the picture.

Even so, my previous knowledge of pictures leads me to assume that this man is different from his image. He is not four inches tall. He is not flat and two-dimensional. His eyes are not small black dots, his mouth not a thin black crescent. His skin is not paper-white, nor scored with thin orange lines. I translate these qualities of the image into the objects they represent, and assume that the four-inch figure 'is' a man of normal height, the orange lines on white merely normal skin.

But before I can translate the lines into skin, I must know what skin is, and what it looks like. I must have a pre-existing knowledge of actual objects to understand which qualities of representations, like the orange colour here, do resemble those of the represented objects, and which, like the lines here, are merely features of the medium or style of representation, and therefore to be ignored.

For the same reason, I must assume that the sky I see above the man does not end a few inches above his head – that this is a border, an edge to the depiction, but not a representation of an edge in the world depicted. And I must realise that the house is not smaller than the man and attached to his arm, but merely at some distance behind him in the imaginary space the picture implies.

But now, perhaps, I'm exaggerating the degree to which the picture requires my previous knowledge of pictorial conventions? After all, more distant real objects do appear to us to be smaller than closer ones. But while that's true, it's also true that artists have been interested in trying to record that fact – what we call perspective – only since the Renaissance, and then mostly in Europe and European-influenced cultures. Not all pictures try to represent perspective, and it takes a culture-bound prejudice to look at visual images expecting to find perspective and therefore, knowing how to interpret it.

Children must learn these prejudices before they can make sense of this picture. Those who can accurately interpret the relative size of Mr Gumpy and the house do so on the expectation that the picture represents the way things do actually appear to a viewer. Applying that expectation might lead a viewer to be confused by Burningham's depiction of Mr Gumpy's eyes. These small black dots evoke a different style of representation, caricature, which conveys visual information by means of simplified exaggeration rather than resemblance. In order to make sense of this apparently straightforward picture, then, I must have knowledge of differing styles and their differing purposes, and perform the complex operation of interpreting different parts of the pictures in different ways.

So far I've dealt with my understanding of this image, and ignored the fact that I enjoy looking at it. I do; and my pleasure seems to be emotional rather than intellectual – a sensuous engagement with the colours, shapes, and textures that leads me to agree with Brian Alderson (1990: 114), when he names *Mr Gumpy's Outing* as one of 'those picture books which have no ambitions beyond conveying simple delight'. But Alderson forgets the extent to which experiencing that simple delight depends on still further complex and highly sophisticated assumptions about what pictures do and how viewers should respond to them.

These particular assumptions are especially relevant in considering art intended for children. Ruskin famously suggested in 1857 that taking sensuous pleasure in pictures requires adults to regain an 'innocence of the eye' he described as 'childish' (quoted in Herbert 1964: 2). The implication is that children themselves, not having yet learned the supposedly counterproductive sophistication that leads adults to view pictures only in terms of their potential to convey information, are automatically in possession of innocent eyes, automatically capable of taking spontaneous delight in the colours and textures of pictures.

But according to W. J. T. Mitchell (1986: 118), 'This sort of "pure" visual perception, freed from concerns with function, use, and labels, is perhaps the most highly sophisticated sort of seeing that we do; it is not the "natural" thing that the eye does (whatever that would be). The "innocent eye" is a metaphor for a highly experienced and cultivated sort of vision.' Indeed, I suspect my own pleasure in the way Burningham captures effects of light falling on grass and bricks relates strongly to the impressionist tradition the picture evokes for me – a tradition that built a whole morality upon the pleasure viewers could and should take in just such effects.

Could I have the pleasure innocently, without the knowledge of impressionism? I suspect not; as Arthur Danto asserts (1992: 431), 'To see something as art requires something the eye cannot descry – an atmosphere of artistic theory, a knowledge of the history of art: an artworld'. The 'simple delight' sophisticated adults like Brian Alderson and me take in this picture is not likely to be shared by children unaware of the ethical value of an 'innocent eye', untutored in the 'artworld'.

Nor is the picture the only thing I've read in the context of previous assumptions. There are also the words. 'This is Mr Gumpy', they say. But *what* is, exactly? The paper page I'm looking at? The entire image I see on it? Of course not – but I must know conventions of picture captioning to realise that these words are pointing me towards a perusal of the contents of the image, in order to find somewhere within it a depiction of the specific object named.

And besides, just *who* is telling me that this is Mr Gumpy? It's possible, even logical, that the speaker is the person in the picture – as it is, for instance, when we watch TV news broadcasts; and then, perhaps, he's telling us that Mr Gumpy is the name of the watering can he's holding? It's my prior knowledge of the narrative conventions of picture books that leads me to assume that the speaker is not the figure depicted but someone else, a narrator rather than a character in the story, and that the human being depicted is the important object in the picture, and therefore the most likely candidate to be 'Mr Gumpy'.

As does in fact turn out to be the case – but only for those who know the most elementary conventions of reading books: that the front of the book is the cover with the bound edge on the left, and that the pages must be looked at in a certain order, across each double-page spread from left to right and then a turn to the page on the other side of the right-hand sheet. And of course, these conventions do not operate for books printed in Israel or Japan, even if those books contain only pictures, and no Hebrew or Japanese words.

In other words: picture books like *Mr Gumpy's Outing* convey 'simple delight' by surprisingly complex means, and communicate only within a network of conventions and assumptions, about visual and verbal representations and about the real objects they represent. Picture books in general, and all their various components, are what semioticians call 'signs' – in Umberto Eco's words (1985: 176), 'something [which] stands to somebody for something else in some respect or capacity'.

The most significant fact about such representations is the degree to which we take them for granted. Both adults and children do see books like *Mr Gumpy* as simple, even obvious, and as I discovered myself in the exercise I report above, it takes effort to become aware of the arbitrary conventions and distinctions we unconsciously take for granted, to see the degree to which that which seems simply natural is complex and artificial.

It's for that reason that such exercises are so important, and that thinking of picture books in semiotic terms is our most valuable tool in coming to understand them. According to Marshall Blonsky, 'The semiotic "head", or eye, sees the world as an immense message, replete with signs that can and do deceive us and lie about the world's condition' (1985: vii). Because we assume that pictures, as iconic signs, do in some significant way actually resemble what they depict, they invite us to see objects *as* the pictures depict them – to see the actual in terms of the fictional visualisation of it.

Indeed, this dynamic is the essence of picture books. The pictures 'illustrate' the texts – that is, they purport to show us what is meant by the words, so that we come to understand the objects and actions the words refer to in terms of the qualities of the images that accompany them – the world outside the book in terms of the visual images within it. In persuading us that they do represent the actual world in a simple and obvious fashion, picture books are particularly powerful deceivers.

Furthermore, the intended audience of picture books is by definition inexperienced – in need of learning how to think about their world, how to see and understand themselves and others. Consequently, picture books are a significant means by which we integrate young children into the ideology of our culture.

As John Stephens suggests, 'Ideologies ... are not necessarily undesirable, and in the sense of a system of beliefs by which we make sense of the world, social life would be impossible without them' (1992: 8). But that does not mean that all aspects of social life are equally desirable, nor that all the ideology conveyed by picture books is equally acceptable. Picture books can and do often encourage children to take for granted views of reality that many adults find objectionable. It is for this reason above all that we need to make ourselves aware of the complex significations of the apparently simple and obvious words and pictures of a book like *Mr Gumpy's Outing*. As Blonsky says, 'Seeing the world as signs able to deceive, semiotics should teach the necessity to fix onto *every* fact, even the most mundane, and ask, "What do you mean?"' (1985: xxvii).

What, then, do John Burningham's picture and text mean? What have I been lead to assume is 'natural' in agreeing that this *is*, in fact, Mr Gumpy?

Most obviously, I've accepted that what matters most about the picture is the human being in it: it encourages a not particularly surprising species-centricity. But it does so by establishing a hierarchic relationship among the objects depicted: only one of them is important enough to be named by the text, and so require more attention from the viewer. Intriguingly, young children tend to scan a picture with equal attention to all parts; the ability to pick out and focus on the human at the centre is therefore a learned activity, and one that reinforces important cultural assumptions, not just about the relative value of particular objects, but also about the general assumption that objects do indeed have different values and do therefore require different degrees of attention.

Not surprisingly, both the text and the picture place the human depicted within a social context. He is *Mr* Gumpy, male and adult, his authority signalled by the fact that he is known only by his title and last name and that he wears the sort of jacket which represents business-like adult behaviour. The jacket disappears in the central portions of the book, as visual evidence that Mr Gumpy's boat trip is a vacation from business as usual, during which the normal conventions are relaxed. Then, at the end, Mr Gumpy wears an even fancier jacket as host at a tea party which, like the meals provided to children by adults at the end of children's stories from 'Little Red Riding Hood' through Potter's *Peter Rabbit* (1902) and Sendak's *Where the Wild Things Are* (1963), confirms the benefits for children of an adult's authority.

But despite the absence of this visual sign of his authority in many of the pictures, Mr Gumpy always remains *Mr* Gumpy in the text – and he is always undeniably in charge of the children and animals who ask to accompany him on his ride, always entitled to make the rules for them. Apparently, then, his authority transcends the symbolism of the jacket, which might be donned by anybody and therefore represents the status resident in a position rather than the power attached to an individual person. Mr Gumpy's authority must then emerge from the only other things we know about him: that he is male and adult, and that as the text makes a point of telling us, he 'owned' the boat.

Apparently it is more important for us to know this than anything about Mr Gumpy's marital status or past history or occupation – about all of which the text is silent. Both by making ownership significant and by taking it for granted that adult male owners have the right to make rules for children and animals, who don't and presumably can't own boats, the book clearly implies a social hierarchy.

Nor is this the only way in which it supports conventional values. A later picture shows us that one of the children, the one with long hair, wears a pink dress, while the other has short hair and wears shorts and a top. In terms of the behaviour of actual children, both might be girls; but a repertoire of conventional visual codes would lead most viewers to assume that the child in shorts is male – just as we assume that trouser-wearing figures on signs signal men's washrooms, skirt-wearing figures women's washrooms. But whether male or not, the wearer of shorts behaves differently from the wearer of the dress. A later picture of the aftermath of a boating accident shows the one wet child in shorts sensibly topless, the other equally wet child still modestly sodden in her dress. This picture takes for granted and so confirms that traditionally female attire requires traditionally constraining feminine behaviour.

The story revolves around Mr Gumpy eliciting promises that the children not squabble, the cat not chase the rabbit, and so on, before he allows them on to his boat; the creatures break their promises, and the boat tips. My knowledge of the didactic impulse behind most picture book stories leads me to expect that an ethical judgement is about to be made: either Mr Gumpy was wrong to demand these promises, or the children and animals were wrong to make them.

Curiously, however, the book implies no such judgement. The pictures, which show Mr Gumpy as a soft, round man with a pleasant, bland face, suggest that he is anything but the sort of unreasonable disciplinarian we ought to despise; and even though the breaking of promises leads to a spill, nothing is said or shown to insist that we should make a negative judgement of the children and animals. After all, exactly such outbreaks of anarchy are the main source of pleasure in most stories for young children, and therefore to be enjoyed at least as much as condemned. Mr Gumpy himself is so little bothered that he rewards the miscreants with a meal, and even an invitation to come for another ride.

Not accidentally, furthermore, the promises all relate to behaviour so stereotypical as to seem inevitable: in the world as we most often represent it to children in books, on TV, and elsewhere, cats always chase rabbits – and children always squabble. In centring on their inability to act differently, and the fun of the confusion that ensues when they don't, this story reinforces both the validity of the stereotypes and the more general (and again, conservative) conviction that variation from type is unlikely.

But why, then, would Mr Gumpy elicit promises which, it seems, could not be kept? This too the text is silent on; but the silence allows us to become aware that his asking the children and animals to do what they are not sensible enough to do reinforces the story's unspoken but firm insistence on his right to have authority over them. If they ever did mature enough to keep their word, then we couldn't so blindly assume they were unwise enough to need his leadership. Someone else might be wearing that jacket at the final tea party.

*Mr Gumpy's Outing* thus reinforces for its implied young readers a not uncommon set of ideas about the similarity of children to animals, the inevitability of child-like irresponsibility in both, and the resultant need for adult authority. In accepting all this as natural, readers of *Mr Gumpy's Outing* and many other apparently 'simple' picture books gain complex knowledge, not just of the world they live in, but also of the place they occupy as individual beings within it – their sense of who they are.

This latter is important enough to deserve further exploration. Like most narrative, picture book stories most forcefully guide readers into culturally acceptable ideas about who they are through the privileging of the point of view from which they report on the events they describe. Knowing only what can be known from that perspective, we readers tend to assume it ourselves – to see and understand events and people as the narrative invites us to see them. Ideological theorists call such narrative perspectives 'subject positions': in occupying them, readers are provided with ways of understanding their own subjectivity – their selfhood or individuality. But, as John Stephens suggests, 'in taking up a position from which the text is most readily intelligible, [readers] are apt to be situated within the frame of the text's ideology; that is, they are subjected to and by that ideology' (1992: 67).

All stories imply subject positions for readers to occupy. Because picture books do so with pictures as well as words, their subject positions have much in common with what Christian Metz (1982) outlines as the one films offer their viewers. The pictures in both offer viewers a position of power. They exist only so that we can look at them: they invite us to observe – and to observe what, in its very nature as a representation, cannot observe us back.

In *Mr Gumpy's Outing*, Burningham makes the authority of our viewing position clear in the same way most picture book artists do: by almost always depicting all the characters with their faces turned towards us, even when that makes little sense in terms of the activities depicted. Indeed, the picture in which Mr Gumpy stands with his back to his house while smiling out at us makes sense only in terms of the conventions of photography or portrait painting; as in family snapshots, he is arranged so as to be most meaningfully observable by a (to him) unseen viewer who will be looking at the picture some time after it was made. In confirmation of the relationship between this image and such snapshots, the caption tells us, 'This *is* Mr Gumpy', in the same present tense we use to describe photographic images of events past (for example, 'This *is* me when I *was* a child'). The story that follows switches to the more conventional past tense of narratives.

In making their faces available to an unseen observer, the characters in *Mr Gumpy's Outing* imply, not just the observer's right to gaze, but also their somewhat veiled consciousness of an observer – and therefore, their own passive willingness, even desire, to be gazed at. Like the actors in a play or movie, and like characters in most picture books, they share in a somewhat less aggressive form the invitation to voyeurism that John Berger (1972) discovers in both pin-up photographs and traditional European paintings of nudes. Their implied viewer is a peeping Tom with the right to peep, to linger over details, to enjoy and interpret and make judgements.

But meanwhile, of course, the power such pictures offer is illusory. In allowing us to observe and to interpret, they encourage us to absorb all the codes and conventions, the signs that make them meaningful; they give us the freedom of uninvolved, egocentric observation only in order to enmesh us in a net of cultural constraints that work to control egocentricity. For that reason, they encourage a form of subjectivity that is inherently paradoxical. They demand that their implied viewers see themselves as both free and with their freedom constrained, and both enjoy their illusory egocentric separation from others and yet, in the process, learn to feel guilty about it.

Interestingly, *Mr Gumpy* confirms the central importance of such paradoxes by expressing them, not just in the position of its implied viewer, but also in the ambivalence of its story's resolution. Are we asked to admire or to condemn the children and animals for being triumphantly themselves and not giving in to Mr Gumpy's attempts to constrain them? In either case, does their triumphantly being themselves represent a celebration of individuality, or an anti-individualist conviction that all cats always act alike? And if all cats must always act in a cat-like way, what are we to make of the final scene, in which the animals all sit on chairs like humans and eat and drink out of the kinds of containers humans eat and drink from? Does this last image of animals and children successfully behaving according to adult human standards contradict the apparent message about their inability to do so earlier, or merely reinforce the unquestionable authority of the adult society Mr Gumpy represents throughout?

These unanswerable questions arise from the fact that the story deals with animals who both talk like humans and yet cannot resist bleating like sheep – who act sometimes like humans, sometimes like animals. While such creatures do not exist in reality, they appear frequently in picture books, and the stories about them almost always raise questions like the ones *Mr Gumpy* does. In the conventional world of children's picture books, the state of animals who talk like humans is a metaphor for the state of human childhood, in which children must learn to negotiate between the animal-like urges of their bodily desires and the demands of adults that they repress desire and behave in social acceptable ways – that is, as adult humans do. The strange world in which those who bleat as sheep naturally do, or squabble as children naturally do, must also sit on chairs and drink from teacups, is merely a version of the confusing world children actually live in. *Mr Gumpy* makes that obvious by treating the children as exactly equivalent to the other animals who go on the outing.

The attitude a picture book implies about whether children should act like the animals they naturally are or the civilised social beings adults want them to be is a key marker in identifying it either as a didactic book intended to teach children or as a pleasurable one intended to please them. Stories we identify as didactic encourage children towards acceptable adult behaviour, whereas pleasurable ones encourage their indulgence in what we see as natural behaviour. But of course, both types are didactic.

The first is more obviously so because it invites children to stop being 'child-like'. In the same way as much traditional adult literature assumes that normal behaviour is that typical of white middle-class males like those who authored it, this sort of children's story defines essentially human values and acceptably human behaviour as that of adults like those who produce it.

But books in the second category teach children *how* to be child-like, through what commentators like Jacqueline Rose (1984) and myself (1992) have identified as a process of colonisation: adults write books for children to persuade them of conceptions of themselves as children that suit adult needs and purposes. One such image is the intractable, anti-social self-indulgence that Mr Gumpy so assertively forbids and so passively accepts from his passengers. It affirms the inevitability and desirability of a sort of animal-likeness – and child-likeness – that both allows adults to indulge in nostalgia for the not-yet-civilised and keeps children other than, less sensible than, and therefore deserving of less power than, adults.

That picture books like *Mr Gumpy* play a part in the educative processes I've outlined here is merely inevitable. Like all human productions, they are enmeshed in the ideology of the culture that produced them, and the childlikeness they teach is merely what our culture views as natural in children. But as a form of representation which conveys information by means of both words and pictures, picture books evoke (and teach) a complex set of intersecting sign systems. For that reason, understanding of them can by enriched by knowledge from a variety of intellectual disciplines.

Psychological research into picture perception can help us understand the ways in which human beings – and particularly children – see and make sense of pictures; Evelyn Goldsmith (1984) provides a fine summary of much of the relevant research in this area. The *gestalt* psychologist Rudolph Arnheim (1974: 11) provides a particularly useful outline of ways in which the composition of pictures influences our understanding of what they depict, especially in terms of what he calls 'the interplay of directed tensions' among the objects depicted. Arnheim argues (11) that 'these tensions are as inherent in any precept as size, shape, location, or colour', but it can be argued that they might just as logically be viewed as signs – culturally engendered codes rather than forces inherent in nature.

In either case, the relationships among the objects in a picture create variations in 'visual weight': weightier objects attract our attention more than others. In the picture of Mr Gumpy in front of his house, for instance, the figure of Mr Gumpy has great weight because of its position in the middle of the picture, its relatively large size, and its mostly white colour, which makes it stand out from the darker surfaces surrounding it. If we think of the picture in terms of the three-dimensional space it implies, the figure of Mr Gumpy gains more weight through its frontal position, which causes it to overlap less important objects like the house, and because it stands over the focal point of the perspective. Meanwhile, however, the bright red colour of the house, and the arrow shape created by the path leading toward it, focus some attention on the house; and there is an interplay of tensions amongst the similarly blue sky, blue flowers and blue trousers, the similarly arched doorway and round-shouldered Mr Gumpy. Analysis of such compositional features can reveal much about how pictures cause us to interpret the relationships among the objects they represent.

Visual objects can have other kinds of meanings also: for a knowledgeable viewer, for instance, an object shaped like a cross can evoke Christian sentiments. Because picture books have the purpose of conveying complex information by visual means, they tend to refer to a wide range of visual symbolisms, and can sometimes be illuminated by knowledge of everything from the iconography of classical art to the semiotics of contemporary advertising. Consider, for instance, how the specific house Burningham provides Mr Gumpy conveys, to those familiar with the implications of architectural style, both an atmosphere of rural peacefulness and a sense of middle-class respectability.

Furthermore, anyone familiar with Freudian or Jungian psychoanalytical theory and their focus on the unconscious meanings of visual images will find ample material for analysis in picture books. There may be Freudian implications of phallic power in Mr Gumpy's punt pole, carefully placed in the first picture of him on his boat so that it almost appears to emerge from his crotch; in the later picture of the aftermath of the disastrous accident, there is nothing in front of Mr Gumpy's crotch but a length of limp rope. Meanwhile, Jungians might focus on the archetypal resonances of the watering can Mr Gumpy holds in the first few pictures, its spout positioned at the same angle as the punt pole in the picture that follows and the teapot he holds in the last picture, its spout also at the same angle. The fact that this story of a voyage over and into water begins and ends with Mr Gumpy holding objects that carry liquid, and thus takes him from providing sustenance for plants to providing sustenance for other humans and animals, might well suggest a complex tale of psychic and/or social integration.

Nor is it only the individual objects in pictures that have meaning: pictures as a whole can also express moods and meanings, through their use of already existing visual styles which convey information to viewers who know art history. Styles identified with specific individuals, or with whole periods or cultures, can evoke not just what they might have meant for their original viewers, but also, what those individuals or periods or cultures have come to mean to us. Thus, Burningham's pictures of Mr Gumpy suggest both the style of impressionism and the bucolic peacefulness that it now tends to signify.

In addition to disciplines which focus on pictures, there has been an extensive theoretical discussion of the relationships between pictures and words which is especially important in the study of picture books. Most studies in this area still focus on the differences Lessing (1776/1969) pointed out centuries ago in *Laocoön*: visual representations are better suited to depicting the appearance of objects in spaces, words to depicting the action of objects in time. In a picture book like *Mr Gumpy*, therefore, the text sensibly says nothing about the appearance of Mr Gumpy or his boat, and the pictures are incapable of actually moving as a boat or an animal does.

But pictures can and do provide information about sequential activity. In carefully choosing the best moment of stopped time to depict, and the most communicative compositional tensions among the objects depicted, Burningham can clearly convey the action of a boat tipping, what actions led the characters to take the fixed positions they are shown to occupy, and what further actions will result. Furthermore, the sequential pictures of a picture book imply all the actions that would take the character from the fixed position depicted in one picture to the fixed position in the next – from not quite having fallen into the water in one picture to already drying on the bank in the next. Indeed, it is this ability to imply unseen actions and the passage of time that allow the pictures in picture books to play the important part they do in the telling of stories.

Nevertheless, the actions implied by pictures are never the same as those named in words. The bland statement of Burningham's text, 'and into the water they fell', hardly begins to cover the rich array of actions and responses the picture of the boat tipping lays out for us. W. J. T. Mitchell (1986: 44) concludes that the relationship between pictures and accompanying texts is 'a complex one of mutual translation, interpretation, illustration, and enlightenment'. Once more, *Mr Gumpy's Outing* reveals just how complex.

Burningham's text on its own without these pictures would describe actions by characters with no character: it takes the pictures and a knowledge of visual codes to read meaning into these simple actions. Without a text, meanwhile, the pictures of animals that make up most of the book would seem only a set of portraits, perhaps illustrations for an informational guide to animals. Only the text reveals that the animals can talk, and that it is their desire to get on the boat. Indeed, the exact same pictures could easily support a different text, one about Mr Gumpy choosing to bring speechless animals on board until the boat sinks from their weight and he learns a lesson about greed. So the pictures provide information about the actions described in the words; and at the same time, the words provide information about the appearances shown in the pictures.

If we look carefully, in fact, the words in picture books always tell us that things are not merely as they appear in the pictures, and the pictures always show us that events are not exactly as the words describe them. Picture books are inherently ironic, therefore: a key pleasure they offer is a perception of the differences in the information offered by pictures and texts.

Such differences both make the information richer and cast doubt on the truthfulness of both of the means which convey it. The latter is particular significant: in their very nature, picture books work to make their audiences aware of the limitations and distortions in their representations of the world. Close attention to picture books automatically turns readers into semioticians. For young children as well as for adult theorists, realising that, and learning to become more aware of the distortions in picture book representations, can have two important results.

The first is that it encourages consciousness and appreciation of the cleverness and subtlety of both visual and verbal artists. The more readers and viewers of any age know about the codes of representation, the more they can enjoy the ways in which writers and illustrators use those codes in interesting and involving ways. They might, for instance, notice a variety of visual puns in *Mr Gumpy's Outing*: how the flowers in Burningham's picture of the rabbit are made up of repetitions of the same shapes as the rabbit's eyes, eyelashes and ears, or how his pig's snout is echoed by the snout-shaped tree branch behind it.

The second result of an awareness of signs is even more important: the more both adults and children realise the degree to which all representations misrepresent the world, the less likely they will be to confuse any particular representation with reality, or to be unconsciously influenced by ideologies they have not considered. Making ourselves and our children more conscious of the semiotics of the pictures books through which we show them their world and themselves will allow us to give them the power to negotiate their own subjectivities – surely a more desirable goal than repressing them into conformity to our own views.

# References

Alderson, B. (1990) 'Picture book anatomy', *Lion and the Unicorn* 14, 2: 108–114.
Arnheim, R. (1974) *Art and Visual Perception: A Psychology of the Creative Eye*, Berkeley: University of California Press.
Berger, J. (1972) *Ways of Seeing*, London: BBC and Penguin.
Blonsky, M. (1985) *On Signs*, Baltimore: Johns Hopkins University Press.
Burningham, J. (1970) *Mr Gumpy's Outing*, London: Cape.

Danto, A. (1992) 'The artworld', in Alperson, P. (ed.) *The Philosophy of the Visual Arts*, New York and Oxford: Oxford University Press, 426–433.

Eco, U. (1985) 'Producing signs', in Blonsky, M. (ed.) *On Signs*, Baltimore: Johns Hopkins University Press.

Goldsmith, E. (1984) *Research into Illustration: An Approach and a Review*, Cambridge: Cambridge University Press.

Herbert, R. L. (ed.) (1964) *The Art Criticism of John Ruskin*, Garden City, NY: Doubleday Anchor.

Lessing, G. E. (1766/1969) *Laocoön: An Essay upon the Limits of Poetry and Painting*, trans. E. Frothingham, New York: Farrar Straus and Giroux.

Metz, C. (1982) *The Imaginary Signifier: Psychoanalysis and the Cinema*, Bloomington, IN: Indiana University Press.

Mitchell, W. J. T. (1986) *Iconology: Image, Text, Ideology*, Chicago: University of Chicago Press.

Nodelman, P. (1992) 'The other: orientalism, colonialism, and children's literature', *Children's Literature Association Quarterly* 17, 1: 29–35.

Potter, B. (1902) *The Tale of Peter Rabbit*, London: Frederick Warne.

Rose, J. (1984) *The Case of Peter Pan, or The Impossibility of Children's Fiction*, London: Macmillan.

Sendak, M. (1963) *Where the Wild Things Are*, New York: Harper and Row.

Stephens, J. (1992) *Language and Ideology in Children's Fiction*, London and New York: Longman.

## Further Reading

*Children's Literature* 19 (1991). New Haven: Yale University Press. (An issue of this journal devoted to discussions of picture books.)

Gombrich, E. H. (1972) 'Visual image', *Scientific American* 227: 82–94.

Kiefer, B. Z. (1995) *The Potential of Picture Books: From Visual Literacy to Aesthetic Understanding*, Englewood Cliffs, NJ and Columbus, OH: Merrill.

Moebius, W. (1986) 'Introduction to picturebook codes', *Word and Image* 2, 2: 63–66.

Nodelman, P. (1988) *Words About Pictures: The Narrative Art of Children's Picture Book*, Athens, GA: University of Georgia Press.

—— (1992) *The Pleasures of Children's Literature*, New York: Longman.

Schwarcz, J. H. (1982) *Ways of the Illustrator: Visual Communication in Children's Literature*, Chicago: American Library Association.

Schwarcz, J. H. and C. (1991) *The Picture Book Comes of Age*, Chicago and London: American Library Association.

# 10

# A Note on Bibliography

## *Peter Hunt*

In 1975, Brian Alderson, in a paper presented before The Bibliographical Society, made the following observations:

> Although in the past this Society has enjoyed one or two addresses on detailed aspects of children's books ... there has been little attempt ... to put forward a rationale of the bibliographer's role in the study of books for this large section of the reading public ... Now while I do not wish to suggest that a more professional grasp of bibliographical skills will itself enable the study of children's books to gain greater maturity, there can be no doubt that scientific bibliography is able to play as important a role in supporting the very varied activity that is taking place among children's books as it does in the field of literary studies elsewhere ... Implicit in all that I have been saying so far is the contention that, at the nuts-and-bolts level, there is much elementary bibliographical work still to be done.
>
> Alderson 1977: 203

Twenty years later, in a review in the *Children's Books History Society Newsletter* of what he dismissed as 'sub-critical ego-trips' which characterise 'much professorial or assistant professorial writing', he lamented, 'Oh dear, so much bibliographical groundwork to be done, and all we get is floss' (Alderson 1995: 17).

The impression that little has been achieved in the bibliography of children's literature in twenty years is undoubtedly false, although the fact that *comparatively little* has been achieved in the context of other aspects of critical and practical activity surrounding children's books is undoubtedly true. However, this is a characteristic of all literary studies, as John Harwood pointed out in his swingeing attack on the literary-theoretical/critical establishment, *Eliot to Derrida: The Poverty of Interpretation*:

> Few in the field of literary studies question the value of good biography, or a scholarly edition of a writer's works, letters, manuscripts or diaries. We are not constantly assailed by warnings that the demise of editing or bibliography will bring about the end of civilisation as we know it. In contrast, doubts about the value of theory and interpretation are endemic in the profession, and it is these activities which are characteristically satirised by sceptical outsiders. Despite the efforts of some theorists to problematise them, the 'service industries' seem remarkably crisis-free. In the mid-1980s,

theorists were talking about a 'return to history' as if no one had done any historical work since the advent of Derrida.) Literary works, manuscripts, letters and diaries are better edited than ever before ...

Harwood 1995: 25–26

In the case of children's literature, resources are, of course, directed towards education and librarianship as well as literary and bibliographical studies; consequently the resources available to bibliography is disproportionately small for both the influence of the subject, and the amount of work which could be done. A good deal of work, then has been the result of privately financed enterprise, or has been supported by the major research collections (see Chapter 47). Juvenile bibliography might thus seem to be a poor relation, a paradox compounded by the flourishing collector's market for children's books.

The 'core' books in the area are ageing, and increasingly in need of revision as detailed bibliographical work changes the historical map. However, nothing has been published that matches the work of Darton (1932/1982), Muir (1954), Thwaite (1963/1972) or the specifically bibliophile, but widely available, 'collector's guides' of Quayle (1971; 1983) (as against the avalanche of theory and 'popular' history). (One attempt to supplement them has been Mary V. Jackson's *Engines of Instruction, Mischief and Magic: Children's Literature in England from its Beginning to 1839* (1990), which was not critically well-received.)

F. J. Harvey Darton's *Children's Books in England* (1932/1982) laid an important foundation (although its organisation may seem somewhat arcane to the lay reader), and the revised edition contains extensive bibliographies, from fables to magazines (these may be supplemented by Thwaite 1963/1972: 283–313).

Similarly, no series has emerged to replace the Oxford University Press Juvenile Library, which produced facsimiles of, for example, Sarah Fielding's *The Governess* (ed. Jill E. Grey 1968), Isaac Watts's *Divine Songs* (ed. J. H. P. Pafford 1971) and John Newbery's *A Little Pretty Pocket Book* (ed. M. F. Thwaite 1966).

The journal that most seriously addressed scholarly concerns, *Phaedrus* (which began as a Newsletter in 1973 and ended as an International Annual) did not survive the 1980s (it merged with *Die Schiefertafel* in 1989), and even by 1977 its editor, James Fraser, was lamenting his disillusion with the fact that the 'groundswell of serious discussion and superior research' had not been stimulated. (Fraser 1977: 2). The most 'respectable' of children's literature journals, the Yale annual *Children's Literature*, although rarely concerned with children, has published, in the most liberal definition, two articles which have a primarily bibliographic approach in the last ten years.

While the situation is better in the USA, in Britain the establishment of major collections, notably the Opie Collection in the Bodleian Library, Oxford, and the Renier Collection of Historical and Contemporary Children's Books at the Bethnal Green Museum of Childhood in London has not been backed up by the funding necessary to adequately document them, or to provide a viable research base. None the less, Tessa Chester of the Renier Collection has produced a number of valuable 'Occasional Lists' of different types and genres of books (the first was on Struwwelpeter (Chester 1987)). An interesting article on Peter Opie's accession diaries by Clive Hurst appears in Avery and Briggs's *Children and their Books: A Celebration of the Work of Iona and Peter Opie* (1989: 19–44).

However, the major world collections are being documented: important contributions have been Gerald Gottlieb's *Early Children's Books and their Illustrators* (1975), and the catalogue of the Osborne Collection in Toronto (St John 1975); others include Florida State University's catalogue of the *Shaw Childhood in Poetry Collection* (1967).

Equally, there has been a steady output of historical and bibliographically orientated work, both within such specialist journals as *The Library*, *The Book Collector*, *Bodleian Library Record*, *Papers of the Bibliographical Society of America*, *Antiquarian Book Monthly* and *The Private Library* and elsewhere. In Britain, the Children's Book History Society began a series of occasional papers with *After Henry*, an exploration of English ABCs (Garrett 1994), while the Provincial Booksellers Fairs Association's catalogue of an exhibition mounted at Oxford, *Childhood Re-Collected* (Alderson and Moon 1994) is characteristic of some high-quality work on the scholarly/commercial border. Many other exhibitions of early books have been mounted by individual collectors and societies, but most of the catalogues, booklets and articles associated with them are available through only the most specialist of outlets.

In the USA, the UCLA Occasional Papers have included work on children's literature, such as Alderson's description of an eighteenth-century collection from Warwickshire (1989) and Andrea Immel's *Revolutionary Reviewing: Sarah Trimmer's 'Guardian of Education' and the Cultural Politics of Juvenile Literature* (1990). The Lilly Library has, similarly, produced catalogues of exhibitions, such as Linda David's *Children's Books Published by William Darton and his Sons* (1992), and of material from the Jane Johnson nursery collection (Johnson 1987). The burgeoning de Grummond Collection of Children's Literature at the University of Southern Mississippi, Hattiesburg, occasionally includes scholarly articles in its journal, *Juvenile Miscellany*. A major step forward in work on American children's literature has been Gillian Avery's *Behold the Child: American Children and their Books 1621-1922* (1994).

There is much work to do unravelling the intricacies of the early book trade, but progress is being made. Booksellers who have been examined include Joseph Cundall (McLean 1976), James Lumsden (Roscoe and Brimmell 1981); James Burns (Alderson 1994), William Godwin (William St Clair, 'William Godwin as children's bookseller' in Avery and Briggs 1989: 165–179) and John Newbery (Townsend 1994; Roscoe 1973). Outstanding have been Marjorie Moon's work on Tabart and Harris: *Benjamin Tabart's Juvenile Library: A Bibliography of Books for Children Published, Written and Sold by Mr Tabart 1801–1920* (1990), and *John Harris's Books for Youth 1801–1843* (1992).

Some authors, such as Beatrix Potter (Linder 1971) and Carroll (Guiliano 1981) have been well served bibliographically; others, such as Arthur Ransome, are just beginning to have their work explored in detail (for example, Wardale 1995). Other studies include work on George MacDonald (Shaberman 1990) and Richmal Crompton (Schutte 1993; and see also Cadogan with Schutte 1990), while Hans Andersen's *Eventyr* have been explored by Alderson (1982). A wider range of reference is found in Robert Kirkpatrick's *Bullies, Beaks and Flannelled Fools: An Annotated Bibliography of Boys' School Fiction 1742–1990* (1990).

However, it is clear that, despite the occasional specialist work, such as Dennis Butt's study of Mrs Hofland (Butts 1992) or M. Nancy Cutt's on Mrs Sherwood (Cutt 1974), there are vast tracts of the history of children's literature untouched by bibliographers.

The same is true of illustration, although there are some excellent outlines of its history, notably by Whalley and Chester with their *A History of Children's Book Illustration* (1988) (and also Muir, 1971/1985; Whalley 1974; Ray 1976; Martin 1989), while *The Dictionary of 20th Century British Book Illustrators* (Horne 1994) is a standard work. There are useful volumes on American (Mahoney *et al.* 1947 *et seq.*), and Australian art (Muir, 1982). There have also been individual bibliographical studies of Thomas Bewick (Roscoe 1953), the Brocks (Kelly 1982) Heath Robinson (Lewis 1973), William Nicholson (Campbell 1992) and many others.

The same principle, of excellent work in some areas and much that could be explored, could be extended to other types and genres. Thus in folklore, Neil Philip's exemplary editing and work on sources and analogues in *The Penguin Book of English Folktales* (1992) could well be extended. Similarly, book collectors have been served by Joseph Connolly's *Modern First Editions: Their Value to Collectors* (1988).

In 1966, Fredson Bowers wrote in his book *Textual and Literary Criticism*: 'I could wish that critics knew more, and knowing would care more, about the purity of the texts they use' (7). This is an even more unfashionable view now, among theorists, than it was then. Bibliographers may well see their work as fundamental to the whole project of children's literature studies, in establishing the true history, and in establishing the true texts – and it is a position difficult to argue with if one wants children's literature to stand beside other literatures. None the less, bibliographical studies often sit uneasily with the other disciplines involved with children's literature: on the one hand they seem to be concerned with irrelevant minutiae; on the other to be linked to a particularly solipsistic and monetarily oriented trade – book collecting. And if theory has not sufficiently taken on board bibliographical concerns, then the reverse seems equally to be true.

However, it is clear that in academic, historical, and bibliographical terms there is an immense amount of work to be done, in collecting, clarifying, and documenting the often bewildering output of children's literature. How successful the bibliographers are in this endeavour may well provide an accurate barometer for the progress and status of children's literature studies as a whole.

# References

Alderson, B. (1977) *Bibliography and Children's Books: The Present Position*, London: The Bibliographical Society, reprinted from *The Library* 32, 3: 203–213.

—— (1982) *Hans Christian Andersen and his 'Eventyr' in England*, Wormley: Five Owls Press for International Board on Books for Young People, British Section.

—— (1989) *The Ludford Box and 'A Christmass Box': their Contribution to Our Knowledge of*

*Eighteenth Century Children's Literature*, UCLA Occasional Papers 2, Los Angeles, UCLA.

—— (1994) 'Some notes on James Burns as a publisher of children's books', in Blamires, D. (ed.) *Bulletin of the John Rylands University Library of Manchester*, 76, 3: 103–126.

—— (1995) 'A widish, widish world', *Children's Books History Society Newsletter* 51: 17.

—— and Moon, M. (1994) *Childhood Re-Collected: Early Children's Books from the Library of Marjorie Moon*, Royston: Provincial Book Fairs Association.

Avery, G. (1994) *Behold the Child: American Children and Their Books 1621–1922* London: Bodley Head.

—— and Briggs, J. (1989) *Children and their Books. A Celebration of the Work of Iona and Peter Opie*, Oxford: Clarendon Press.

Bowers, F. (1966) *Textual and Literary Criticism*, Cambridge: Cambridge University Press.

Butts, D. (1992) *Mistress of Our Tears: A Literary and Bibliographical Study of Barbara Hofland*, Aldershot: Scolar Press.

Cadogan, M. with Schutte, D. (1990) *The William Companion*, London: Macmillan.

Campbell, C. (1992) *William Nicholson: The Graphic Work*, London: Barrie and Jenkins.

Chester, T. R. (1987) *Occasional List no. 1: Struwwelpeter*, London: The Renier Collection of Historic and Contemporary Children's Books, Bethnal Green Museum of Childhood.

Connolly, J. (1988) *Modern First Editions: Their Value to Collectors*, London: Macdonald Orbis.

Cutt, M. N. (1974) *Mrs Sherwood and her Books*, London: Oxford University Press.

Darton, F. J. H. (1932/1982) *Children's Books in England: Five Centuries of Social Life*, 3rd edn, rev. B. Alderson, Cambridge: Cambridge University Press.

David, L. (1992) *Children's Books Published by William Darton and his Sons*, Bloomington, IN: The Lilly Library.

Florida State University (1967) *Shaw Childhood in Poetry Collection*, 5 vols., Detroit: Gale Research.

Fraser, J. (1977) 'Editor's comment', *Phaedrus* 4, 2: 3.

Garrett, P. (1994) 'After Henry', Children's Books History Society, Occasional Paper 1, London: Children's Books History Society.

Gottlieb, G. (1975) *Early Children's Books and their Illustrators*, New York: Pierpont Morgan Library.

Guiliano, E. *Lewis Carroll. An Annotated International Bibliography 1960–77*, Brighton: Harvester Press.

Harwood, J. (1995) *Eliot to Derrida: The Poverty of Interpretation*, London: Macmillan.

Horne, A. (1994), *The Dictionary of 20th Century British Book Illustrators*, Woodbridge: Antique Collectors' Club.

Immel, A. (1990) *Revolutionary Reviewing: Sarah Trimmer's 'Guardian of Education' and the Cultural Politics of Juvenile Literature*, UCLA Occasional Papers 4, Los Angeles: UCLA.

Jackson, M. V. (1990) *Engines of Instruction, Mischief and Magic: Children's Literature in England from its Beginning to 1839*, Aldershot: Scolar Press.

Johnson, E. L. (1987) *For Your Amusement and Instruction: the Elizabeth Ball Collection of Historical Children's Materials*, Bloomington, IN: The Lilly Library.

Kelly, C. M. (1975) *The Brocks: A Family of Cambridge Artists and Illustrators*, London: Skilton.

Kirkpatrick, R. (1990) *Bullies, Beaks and Flannelled Fools: An Annotated Bibliography of Boys' School Fiction 1742–1990*, privately published.

Lewis, J. (1973) *Heath Robinson, Artist and Comic Genius*, London: Constable.

Linder, L. (1971) *A History of the Writings of Beatrix Potter*, London: Warne.

McLean, R. (1976) *Joseph Cundall: A Victorian Publisher*, Pinner: Private Libraries Association.

Mahoney, B. E. *et al.* (1947/1958/1968/1978) *Illustrators of Childrens Books 1744–1945* (and supplements to 1978), Boston: The Horn Book.

Martin, D. (1989) *The Telling Line: Essays on Fifteen Contemporary Book Illustrators*, London: MacRae.

Moon, M. (1990) *Benjamin Tabart's Juvenile Library: A Bibliography of Books for Children Published, Written and Sold by Mr Tabart 1801–1920*, Winchester: St Paul's Bibliographies.

—— (1992) *John Harris's Books for Youth 1801–1843*, rev. edn, Folkstone: Dawson.

Muir, M. (1982) *A History of Australian Children's Book Illustration*, Melbourne: Oxford University Press.

Muir, P. (1954) *English Children's Books, 1600–1900*, London: Batsford.

—— (1971/1985) *Victorian Illustrated Books*, London: Batsford.

Philip, N. (1992) *The Penguin Book of English Folktales*, London: Penguin.

Quayle, E. (1971) *Collector's Book of Children's Books*, London: Studio Vista.

—— (1983) *Early Children's Books. A Collector's Guide*, Newton Abbott: David and Charles.

Ray, G. N. (1976) *The Illustrator and the Book in England from 1790 to 1914*, New York: Pierpont Morgan Library.

Roscoe, S. (1953) *Thomas Bewick: A Catalogue Raisonné*, Oxford: Oxford University Press.

—— (1973) *John Newbery and his Successors, 1740–1814: A Bibliography*, Wormley: Five Owls Press.

—— and Brimmell, R. A. (1981) *James Lumsden and Son of Glasgow, their Juvenile Books and Chapbooks*, Pinner: Private Libraries Association.

St. John, J. (1975) *The Osborne Collection of Early Children's Books, 1476–1910*, Toronto: Toronto Public Library.

Schutte, D. (1993) *William: The Immortal: An Illustrated Bibliography*, privately published.

Shaberman, R. (1990) *George MacDonald: A Bibliographical Study*, Winchester: St Paul's Bibliographies.

Thwaite, M. F. (1963/1972) *From Primer to Pleasure in Reading*, 2nd edn, London: Library Association.

Townsend, J. R. (1994), *Trade & Plumb-Cake for Ever, Huzza! The Life and Work of John Newbery 1713–1767*, Cambridge: Colt Books.

Wardale, R. (1995) *Ransome at Sea: Notes from the Chart Table*, Kendal: Amazon Publications.

Whalley, J. I. (1974) *Cobwebs to Catch Flies: Illustrated Books for the Nursery and Schoolroom, 1700–1900*, London: Elek.

—— and Chester, T. R. (1988) *A History of Children's Book Illustration*, London: John Murray with the Victoria and Albert Museum.

# 11

# Intertextuality

## *Christine Wilkie*

The term 'intertextuality' is now common in literary discourse. It is used most often and most simply to refer to literary allusions and to direct quotation from literary and non-literary texts. But this is only one small part of the theory, which has its origins in the work of Julia Kristeva (1969) and Mikhael Bakhtin (1973).

Kristeva (1969: 146) coined the term 'intertextuality' when she recognised that texts can only have meaning because they depend on other texts, both written and spoken, and on what she calls the intersubjective knowledge of their interlocutors, by which she meant their total knowledge – from other books, from language-in-use, and the context and conditions of the signifying practices which make meanings possible in groups and communities (Kristeva 1974/1984: 59–60). The literary text, then, is just one of the many sites where several different discourses converge, are absorbed, are transformed and assume a meaning because they are situated in this circular network of interdependence which is called the intertextual space.

Kristeva was keen to point out that intertextuality is not simply a process of recognising sources and influences. She built on the work of Bakhtin, who had identified the word as the smallest textual unit, situated in three coordinates: of the writer, the text and exterior texts. For the first time in literary history, the literary text (the word) took on a spatial dimension when Bakhtin made it a fluid function between the writer/text (on the horizontal axis) and the text/context (on the vertical axis). This idea replaced the previous, Formalist notion that the literary text was a fixed point with a fixed meaning. Bakhtin described this process as a dialogue between several writings, and as the intersection of textual surfaces: 'any text is a mosaic of quotations; any text is the absorption and transformation of another' (in Kristeva 1980/1981: 66).

The theory of intertextuality has also been refined and extended by Jonathan Culler (1981), and by Roland Barthes (1970/1975), who have included the reader as a constituent component of intertextuality. Culler described intertextuality as the general discursive space in which meaning is made intelligible and possible (1981: 103), and Barthes invented the term 'infinite intertextuality' to refer to the intertextual codes by which readers make sense of literary works which he calls a 'mirage of citations'. They dwell equally in readers and in texts but the conventions and presuppositions cannot be traced to an original source or sources. 'The "I" which approaches the texts [says Barthes] is already a plurality of

other texts, of infinite, or more precisely, lost codes (whose origins are lost)'
(Barthes 1975/1976: 16).

The idea that texts are produced and readers make sense of them only in
relation to the already embedded codes which dwell in texts and readers (and in
authors too, since they are readers of texts before they are authors), has
ramifications which challenge any claim to textual originality or discrete readings.
In this sense, then, all texts and all readings are intertextual. This brings us close to
Genette's use of the term 'transtextuality' (1979: 85–90), by which he is referring
to *everything* that influences a text either explicitly or implicitly.

This dynamic model of intertextuality has peculiar implications for an
intertextuality of children's literature because the writer/reader axis is uniquely
positioned in an imbalanced power relationship. Adults write for each other, but it
is not usual for children to write literature for each other. This makes children the
powerless recipients of what adults choose to write for them and, *de facto*,
children's literature an intertextual sub-genre of adult literature. The writer/
reader relationship is also asymmetric because children's intersubjective knowledge cannot be assured. A theory of intertextuality of children's literature is,
therefore, unusually preoccupied with questions about what a piece of writing (for
children) presupposes. What does it assume, what *must* it assume to take on
significance? (See Culler 1981: 101–102.) For these reasons the interrelationship
between the components of intertextuality, of writer/text/reader – text/reader/
context, are quite special when we are addressing a theory of intertextuality of
children's literature.

By now it should be clear that the theory of intertextuality is a dynamic located
in theories of writing, reader-response theory and the production of meaning, and
intersubjectivity (the 'I' who, is reading is a network of citations). It is also a theory
of language inasmuch as Bakhtin had identified the word as the smallest textual
link between the text and the world, and because the reading subject, the text and
the world are not only situated in language, they are also constructed by it. So, not
only do we have a notion of all texts being intertextual, they become so because
they are dialectically related to, and are themselves the products of, linguistic,
cultural and literary practices; and so too are readers and writers.

Culler (1975: 139), has described the urge towards integrating one discourse
with another, or several others, as a process of *vraisemblance*. It is the basis of
intertextuality. Through this process of *vraisemblance* we are able to identify, for
example, the set of literary norms and the salient features of a work by which to
locate genre, and also to anticipate what we might expect to find in fictional worlds.
Through *vraisemblance* the child reader has unconsciously to learn that the
fictional worlds in literature are representations and constructions which refer to
other texts that have been normalised, that is: those texts that have been absorbed
into the culture and are now regarded as 'natural'.

At the level of literary texts (the intertext) it is possible to identify three main
categories of intertextuality: (1) texts of quotation: those texts which quote or
allude to other literary or non-literary works; (2) texts of imitation: texts which
seek to paraphrase, 'translate' and supplant the original and to liberate their
readers from an over-invested admiration in great writers of the past, and which
often function as the pre-text of the original for later readers (Worton and Still

1990: 7); and (3) genre texts: those texts where identifiable, shared, clusters of codes and literary conventions grouped together in recognisable patterns which allow readers to expect and locate them, and to cause them to seek out like texts.

Texts of quotation are probably the simplest level at which child readers can recognise intertextuality. Examples are works such as Janet and Allan Ahlberg's *The Jolly Postman* (1986), John Prater's *Once Upon a Time* (1993), Jon Scieszka's *The Stinky Cheese Man* (1992) and his *The True Story of the 3 Little Pigs!* (1989), and Roald Dahl's *Revolting Rhymes* (1987). All these fictions are characterised by their allusive qualities. They make explicit assumptions about previously read fairytales: 'Everyone knows the story of the Three Little Pigs. Or at least they think they do' (Scieszka 1989: first opening), and 'I guess you think you know this story. You don't, the real one's much more gory' (Dahl 1987: 5). So, as well as assuming familiarity with an 'already read' intertext the 'focused texts' are at the same time foregrounding their own authenticity; that is, they purport to be more authoritative than the texts they are quoting and are thereby undermining the 'truth' of their pre-texts. They cleverly destabilise the security of their readers by positioning them ambivalently in relation to (1) what they think they know already about the fairy tales and (2) the story they are now reading. At the discursive level, then, these particular examples of texts of quotation are doing much more than simply alluding to other texts; they are challenging their readers' 'already read' notions of the reliable narrator by an act of referring back which says it was all a lie. And *The Jolly Postman* is, at the very least, breaking readers' 'already read' boundary of fictionality by presenting them with a clutch of touchable, usable, readable literary artefacts from and to characters of fiction, which are themselves facsimile versions of their real-life counterparts.

Every text of quotation which relocates the so-called primary text in a new cultural and linguistic context must be by definition a parody and a distortion. All the examples I have given parody the telling of traditional tales: *Once Upon a Time* (Prater 1993), 'Once upon a time' (Scieszka 1992: passim), and 'Once upon a bicycle' (Ahlberg 1986: first opening). But the challenge to authority and problems of authenticity for these quotation texts of fairy tales lies in the fact that the tales themselves are a collage of quotations, each of which has assumed a spurious 'first version' authenticity but for which the ur-text does not exist, or at least, cannot be located. The situation of fairy tales in contemporary culture is analogous to Barthes's notion of 'lost codes'. The tales are intelligible because they build on already embedded discourses which happened elsewhere and at another time; they are part of the sedimented folk memory of discourse and they function now by the simple fact that other tales like them have already existed.

Children's exposure to other media such as film, television animations, and video, means increasingly, that they are likely to encounter these media adaptations of a children's fiction before they encounter the written text and to come to regard it as the 'original' from which to approach and on which to base, their (later) reading of the written version. This has particular implications for a theory of intertextuality because it raises questions about whether the nature of the later reading is qualitatively and experientially different if the ur-text happens to have been a Disney cartoon version of, say, 'Snow White'. Children's intertextual experience is peculiarly achronological, so the question about what sense children make of a given text when the intertextual experience cannot be assumed, is important.

Disney adaptations of fairy tales are particularly interesting to an intertextuality of children's literature because, as touchstones of popular culture, they reflect the way in which each generation's retellings have assumed and foregrounded the dominant socio-linguistic and cultural codes and values at a particular moment in history: for example Disney's foregrounding Snow White's good looks over qualities of moral rectitude and goodness claimed for her by earlier, written versions.

But it is not only the stories which change in the repeated intertextual quotations – the intertextual context of the reading and their reception also changes. For example, contemporary, feminist, post-Freudian readings of Carroll's *Alice's Adventures in Wonderland* (1866), or Hodgson Burnett's *The Secret Garden* (1911), make them different kinds of texts from what was previously possible. Similarly, a contemporary child reader's readings of, say, a modern reprint of the original tales of Beatrix Potter will be quite different from that of its intended readers. In their reading of *Jemima Puddle-Duck* (1908), for example, today's child readers are less likely than child readers from the earlier part of the century to recognise the ingredients of duck stuffing for what they are. This is not because, like Jemima, they are simpletons, but because their stuffing today is more likely to be from a packet. Their probable inability to recognise the ingredients of duck stuffing removes an opportunity to anticipate Jemima's fate well in advance of narration. And, not only do contemporary-child readers have an intertextual familiarity with Beatrix Potter's character, Jemima Puddle-Duck and her Potter co-star, Peter Rabbit, from a proliferation of non-literary artefacts, including video adaptations, they can also now read about them in series adaptations in Ladybird books (1992). Ladybird has developed a very powerful position in Britain as a publisher of low-priced, hardback, formula books – especially retellings of traditional tales – with simplified language and sentence constructions. They are a good example of the texts of imitation I described earlier. For some children in Britain they will be the only written version of traditional tales they have encountered. Comparison between the Ladybird and original versions of *Jemima Puddle-Duck* reveals linguistic and syntactic differences that make assumptions about their respective implied readers; and there are other syntactic, micro-discursive and linguistic differences which encode different socio-linguistic climates and – by extension – imply different language-in-use on the parts of their respective readerships. What we see in operation in these two texts is the tension and interplay between two idiolects and two sociolects: the uses of language in each text and their situation in, and reception by their respective socio-historic contexts and readers. Each is operating as a textual and intertextual paradigm of its time, but the first-version text can only be 'read' through a network of late-twentieth-century intertexts.

Susan Cooper's *The Dark is Rising* quintet (1966–1977), and Alan Garner's *The Owl Service* (1967), are texts which rely for their fullest reading on a reader's knowledge of Arthurian and Celtic myth, especially of the *Mabinogion*. Together these texts are examples of the type of two-world fantasy genre where child readers can come to recognise, and to expect, such generic conventions as character archetype, stereotype and the archetypal plot structures of quest and journeys. The novels allude only obliquely to their mythical sources, even though myth is integral to their stories. So, even in readings that do not rely on knowledge of the myth, readers might intuit the echoes of myth as they read and absorb the novels' more subtle messages and connections.

Similarly, Robert Cormier's *After the First Death* (1979), and Jill Paton Walsh's novels *Goldengrove* (1972) and *Unleaving* (1976), allude to lines from Dylan Thomas's poem 'A refusal to mourn the death, by fire, of a child in London' (After the first death, there is no other) and Gerard Manley Hopkins's 'Spring and fall' (Márgarét, áre you grieving/Over Goldengrove unleaving?). In each case, a perfectly coherent reading of the text is possible without the reader's knowledge of the intertextual poetic allusions; but the potential for a metaphoric reading is enhanced by the reader's previous knowledge of them. In the case of Paton Walsh's *Goldengrove*, for example, the metaphor for metaphysical transience first mooted by Hopkins in his image of the Goldengrove unleaving, is employed again by Paton Walsh as the name of the fictional house, 'Goldengrove', from which the book takes its title. This is the place of symbolic and literal change where the two teenage characters spend their (significantly) late-summer vacation of maturation and realisation. The image is extended in numerous other references: changing body-shapes, changed sleeping arrangements, changed attitudes to each other, and not least, in repeated references to the falling leaves of late summer. It also invokes and parodies the style and content of Virginia Woolf's *To The Lighthouse* (1927), with a polyphony which moves effortlessly between several viewpoints, and positions its readers accordingly. This polyphonic, multilayered structure, which is also a feature of the Cormier novel, is particularly interesting to an intertextuality of children's literature because it breaks the intertextual discursive codes and conventions of the single viewpoint and linear narrative that are usually typical of the genre.

Young readers who come to these novels by Cooper, Garner, Cormier and Paton Walsh with an explicit knowledge of their intertexts will have a markedly different experience of reading. They will experience what Barthes has described as the 'circular memory of reading' (Barthes 1975: 36). This describes a reading process where the need consciously to recall and to refer back to specific, obligatory intertexts now being quoted as metaphor and/or metonymy in the focused texts, restricts the reader's opportunity for free intertextual interplay at the point of reading. The reading experience is, therefore, simultaneously centrifugal and centripetal as the reader seeks to refer to the 'borrowing' and at the same time to integrate it into a new context. It is the essence of this kind of reading to deny readers an opportunity for linear reading as they move in and out of the text to make connections between it and the intertext(s).

Another Paton Walsh novel, *A Parcel of Patterns* (1983), is a fictionalised account of the bubonic plague's destruction of the inhabitants of the Derbyshire village of Eyam. It uses many secondary signals to ground the events in their historic context and to ensure that readers locate the events in these pretextual happenings by, for example, the use of paratextual devices such as the words of the publisher's introduction:

Eyam (pronounced Eem) is a real village in Derbyshire and many of the events in this evocative novel are based on what actually happened there in the year of the Plague.

Paton Walsh 1983

Another example is the use of direct quotation from historic artefacts, not least, from the inscription of the great bell of Eyam 'SWEET JESU BE MY SPEDE' (54). The book reinforces the historic authenticity of its subject matter by a consistent capitalisation throughout of the word Plague, and by use of an invented dialect which pastiches what we know about the dialect of sixteenth-century Derbyshire.

In contrast, Robert Westall's novel *Gulf* (1992), is embedded in the events of the 1991 Gulf War which began after the Iraqi invasion of Kuwait and the retaliation by the United Nations. *Gulf*, unlike *A Parcel of Patterns*, assumes (for its Western readers) a shared, contemporary, intertextual experience. This makes recovery of the pre-text more likely and it therefore calls for little explanation and contextualisation. But the novel's foregrounded meaning centres on the need for its readers to see the connection between the out-of-body experiences of the narrator's younger brother, Figgis, and the experiences of a young Iraqi boy soldier whose life he shares. The detail of the geography and history of Iraq is an intertextual experience that cannot be assumed; so the narrative deals with it by way of explanation, 'I looked up Tikrit in our atlas; it was north of Baghdad. Then I read in the paper it was where Saddam Hussein himself came from' (Westall 1992: 47). This is an example of the way in which texts written for children sometimes have a felt need to be overreferential; the need to fill intertextual gaps to mobilise a positive reading experience in its young readers.

Literature for children has to tread a careful path between a need to be sufficiently overreferential in its intertextual gap filling so as not to lose its readers, and the need to leave enough intertextual space and to be sufficiently stylistically challenging to allow readers free intertextual interplay. It is on the one hand a formally conservative genre that is charged with the awesome responsibility to initiate young readers into the dominant literary codes of the culture. On the other hand, the genre has seen the emergence of what we now confidently call the 'new picture books' and the 'new young adult' novel. Picture book writers such as John Scieszka, Maurice Sendak, the Ahlbergs, Ruth Brown, David McKee, Anthony Browne, John Burningham; young adult writers like Robert Cormier, Aidan Chambers and Peter Hunt, and books like Gillian Cross's *Wolf* (1990), Berlie Doherty's *Dear Nobody* (1991), Nadia Wheatley's *The Blooding* (1988), Aidan Chambers's *Breaktime* (1978), and Geraldine McCaughrean's *A Pack of Lies* (1988), are challenging conventional literary forms of children's literature and breaking the codes.

A theory of intertextuality of children's literature points the way forward for a genre that acknowledges the lost codes and practices and underlying discursive conventions by which it functions and is defined, and urges the breaking of ranks. Some of the children's writers I have mentioned here have demonstrated how this is beginning to happen. They have been prepared to take risks with their writing and with their young readers. Some of these books, such as Scieszka's *The Stinky*

*Cheese Man*, Chambers's *Breaktime*, Cormier's, *After the First Death*, and *Fade* (1988), and McCaughrean's *A Pack of Lies,* have a metafictional dimension which causes readers to pay attention to the fabric and artifice of these texts as works of literature, and to the textuality of the world to which they allude; it also causes readers to recognise how they are being (have been) textually constructed in and by this intertextual playground. Since both using codes and breaking codes are sites for intertextual interplay, the work of these writers is a legitimate site on which to mobilise the construction of a child-reader intersubjectivity that is intertextually aware.

## References

Bakhtin, M. (1973) *Problems of Dostoevsky's Poetics,* trans. R. W. Rostel, Ann Arbor, MI: Ardis.

Barthes, R. (1970/1975) *S/Z,* trans. R. Miller, London: Cape.

—— (1975/1976) *The Pleasure of the Text,* trans. R. Miller, London: Cape.

Culler, J. (1975) *Structuralist Poetics: Structuralism, Linguistics and the Study of Literature,* London: Routledge and Kegan Paul.

—— (1981) *The Pursuit of Signs: Semiotics, Literature, Deconstruction,* London: Routledge and Kegan Paul.

Dahl, R. (1987) *Revolting Rhymes,* London: Jonathan Cape.

Genette, G. (1979) *The Architext: An Introduction,* trans. J. E. Lewin, Berkeley and Los Angeles: University of California Press.

Kristeva, J. (1969) *Semiotiké,* Paris: Editions du Seuil.

—— (1974/1984) *Revolution in Poetic Language,* trans. M. Waller, New York: Columbia University Press.

—— (1980/1981) *Desire In Language: A Semiotic Approach to Literature and Art,* trans. T. Gora, A. Jardine, and L. Roudiez, Oxford: Blackwell.

Paton Walsh, J. (1983) *A Parcel of Patterns,* Harmondsworth: Kestrel (Penguin).

Prater, J. (1993) *Once Upon a Time,* London: Walker.

Scieszka, J. (1989) *The True Story of the 3 Little Pigs!,* New York: Viking.

—— (1992) *The Stinky Cheese Man,* New York: Viking.

Worton, M. and Still, J. (eds) (1990) *Intertextuality,* Manchester: Manchester University Press.

## Further Reading

Ahlberg, J. and Ahlberg, A. (1985) *The Jolly Postman,* London: Heinemann.

Bloom, H. (1973) *The Anxiety of Influence,* New York: Oxford University Press.

—— (1975) *A Map of Misreading,* New York: Oxford University Press.

Hunt, P. (1988) 'What do we lose when we lose allusion? Experience and understanding stories', *Signal* 57: 212–222.

Rifaterre, M. (1984) 'Intertextual representation: On Mimesis as interpretive discourse', *Critical Inquiry* 11, 1: 141–162.

Stephens, J. (1990) 'Intertextuality and the wedding ghost', *Children's Literature In Education* 21, 1: 23–36.

—— (1992) *Language and Ideology in Children's Fiction,* London: Longman.

Valdes, M. J. (ed.) (1985) *Identity and the Literary Text,* Toronto: University of Toronto Press.

# Part II

# Types and Genres

# 12

# Early Texts Used by Children

## Margaret Kinnell

### Origins: from Caxton to Puritanism

It has been said that children's book publishing began in earnest in 1744, when John Newbery issued *A Little Pretty Pocket Book*, 'intended for the Instruction and Amusement of Little Master Tommy and Pretty Miss Polly' and offered for sale on its own at 6d or with ball or pincushion at 8d (Darton 1982: 1–5). However, this is to assume that early children's literature encompassed only books aimed mainly at pleasing the reader. The span was very much wider and a literature read by children therefore began much earlier. Many of the texts used by children in the centuries between the introduction of printing and the development of the serious business of children's book publishing in the mid-eighteenth century were far from light-hearted; they were a mixture of courtesy books, school books and religious texts. Children also took what they could from the diverse range of cheap paper pamphlets, the chapbooks. These began circulating in earnest in the seventeenth century after the Star Chamber was abolished in 1641 and political and religious ideas could be expressed in relative freedom. Along with the sermons and tracts were published the 'small merry books' which Samuel Pepys collected (Spufford 1981: passim).

Many of these were enjoyed by children and young adults; there were no distinctions between readership ages in the popular literature circulating in the seventeenth and early eighteenth centuries. The young John Bunyan read avidly of *George on Horseback* or *Bevis of Southampton* and later repented of his laxity: 'for the Holy Scriptures, I cared not' (Spufford 1981: 7). The story of Bevis predates the invention of printing – manuscript versions were known as early as the thirteenth century – and his famous battle with the giant Ascapart was depicted in a graphic woodcut in William Copland's edition, published around 1565. Certainly, Shakespeare knew the tale. Richard Johnson's *The Seven Champions of Christendom*, first published in 1596, *Tom Hickathrift*, *Old Mother Shipton*, and *The King and the Cobbler* are further examples of similarly popular tales which sprang from an earlier, largely oral, culture and were taken around the country by the travelling pedlars. This literature survived well into the nineteenth century in better produced formats, and was remarked upon by Wordsworth among others as of continuing significance for children. The early, rough, uncut paper books with their crude woodcut illustrations provided much of the reading matter for the mass of the population in the seventeenth and early eighteenth centuries, adults and children alike. John Clare, born in 1793, noted how his father was 'very fond of the superstitious tales that are hawked about the streets for a penny' (Spufford 1981: 3): tales which included *Guy of Warwick*, *History of Gotham*, *Robin Hood's Garland* and *Old Mother Bunch*. These became the province of children as adult reading tastes shifted and, like the nursery rhymes which evolved from an adult-oriented oral literature, provided the basis for a specifically children's literature.

The chapbooks and ballads which so appealed to Bunyan, and which he acknowledged were also read by his fellows, were commonly available even to the yeoman class. However, despite this widespread availability, literacy levels were low; by the mid-seventeenth century only around 30 per cent of men could read fluently, and even fewer women. (Cressy 1980: passim.) Nevertheless, that more and more children were learning to read in Britain can be seen from the increasing numbers of schools in towns and the larger villages. By the end of the seventeenth century even poorer children in these areas had access to some rudimentary schooling, although pupils would usually be removed from school as soon as they were old enough to earn for their families, perhaps as early as 7 or 8. Social class differentiated those children who received little more than the barest introduction to reading – using a basic primer or horn book – from those who were taught to write and learn further from the better produced school books, bound in sheepskin or calf. Horn books, which provided the earliest exposure to reading for many children, have been dated from the fifteenth century; several are shown in contemporary portraits, hanging by a ribbon from the waists of young children. This type of 'book' was usually made from a bat-shaped piece of wood, to which was pasted the alphabet and sometimes the Lord's Prayer, and covered with a transparent piece of horn. Versions in lead, alloy, bone and even silver have also been found and the horn book frequently served as a battledore for play between lessons. Primers – small booklets which contained the alphabet, the Lord's Prayer, catechism and collects – were also commonly available: Thomas Tryon, born in Oxfordshire in 1634, learned to read by using one and then sold one of his sheep to learn writing from a master 'who taught some poor people's children to read and write'.

More substantial, real, books for the education of well-to-do children included the books of courtesy like *Stans Puer ad Mensam* (*c.*1479) and Hugh Rhodes's *Boke of Nurture* (*c.*1545), which were intended as much for the instruction of parents and tutors as their charges, and schoolbooks – Latin and Greek grammars, spelling books, arithmetic books and so forth – provided the mainstay of reading for older schoolchildren. More boys than girls attended school during this period, and boys' reading and writing skills were generally further advanced. While most of what was offered would have seemed hard labour to a child, as few books were illustrated by more than a crude woodcut frontispiece, some writers did attempt to provide a little lighter material. John Hart's *A Methode, or Comfortable Beginning for all Unlearned* (1570) contains the first known printed picture alphabet and Francis Clement's *Petie Schole* (1576), one of the earliest English spelling books, offered some verses written for 'the litle children [*sic*]'. However, until the late seventeenth century, most schoolchildren had little by way of diversion through their schoolbooks. One of the most significant changes to this can be seen in the publication in English of John Amos Comenius's *Orbis Sensualium Pictus* (1659).

Although not a children's picture book by modern standards, this was the first lavishly illustrated picture encyclopedia for children and is evidence of a new acceptance that children learn best through books designed to stimulate them. Towards the end of the seventeenth century writers were beginning to write more sympathetically for children; Thomas Lye's *The Child's Delight* (1671), a spelling book, is one example.

Not all of the schoolbooks used by children in this early period were therefore lacking in imaginative stimulus. The old fables, especially the compilation known as *Aesop's Fables* which was first printed in English by Caxton in 1484, were also much used in schools. One of the earliest English translators was Robert Henryson, whose version has survived in an edition published in 1570; John Brinsley produced another translation in 1624 and in 1692 Roger L'Estrange provided one of the most comprehensive renditions in a magnificent collection of 500 tales from Phaedrus, Avian and La Fontaine, as well as 'Aesop'. While the older animal fables were not Christian in origin, the morals preached in them were approved by all religious persuasions, and editions of Aesop were used widely in schools and in the home. The need to illustrate the fables to make them more accessible to a child had, however, not been fully realised; John Locke, writing in *Some Thoughts Concerning Education* (1693) argued that 'if his *Aesop* has pictures in it, it will entertain him much the better, and encourage him to read when it carries the increase of knowledge with it' (Axtell 1968: 259). Locke's treatise contained a range of advice on the teaching of reading and the kind of books best suited to young children; his remarks on the importance of presenting it in as attractive a format as possible, reflected the changing mood of the times. Samuel Croxall's illustrated edition of *Fables of Aesop and Others*, published in 1722, was the product of this intention that children's reading books should be both morally profitable and also pleasurable; John Newbery later borrowed heavily from Croxall in his preface to *Fables in Verse for the Improvement of the Young and the Old* (1757). The evolution of Aesop from a collection of somewhat florid moral fables to the neat tales published by Newbery exemplifies the paradox that the history of children's literature has always been characterised by continuity mixed with far-reaching change.

This paradox is especially evident in the tenacious hold on children's books of morality, especially the Puritan morality which pervaded much of seventeenth-century writing. In Thomas White's *A Little Book for Little Children* (*c.*1660), readers are warned to 'read no ballads and foolish books, but a Bible, and the Plainmans pathway to Heaven'. Children were exhorted not only to read scripture; they were also directed to adult devotional books. Arthur Dent's *The Plaine Mans Pathway to Heaven; wherein every man may clearely see whether he shall be saved or damned* (1610) was an important Puritan text and was used by children beside other classics such as John Foxe's *Actes and Monuments* (1563), usually known as the *Book of Martyrs*.

An even more significant book, designed specifically for children, and which continued in publication into the nineteenth century, was James Janeway's *A Token for Children: Being an Exact Account of the Conversion, Holy and Exemplary Lives, and Joyful Deaths of Several Young Children*. Published in two parts between 1671 and 1672, the book contains moral tales of young children who died young of unspecified illness, or the Plague, and who lecture their families and companions for their lax religious observance. The preface to Part 1 asks the reader: 'How art thou now affected, poor Child, in the reading of this Book? Have you ever shed a tear since you begun reading?' Children were given Janeway to improve their souls as much as their reading. Books such as this were not intended for amusement, although by the time John Harris was publishing Janeway in 1804 along with other 'pious little works' in a gift box, its original impact had degenerated somewhat, largely because other lighter material served as an antidote. To the seventeenth-century child, there was little choice. John Bunyan's *Pilgrim's Progress* (1678) remains as the best loved classic of the Puritan period, and Bunyan's allegory was recognised by him as having a special appeal to children, but this too was a work of devotion rather than imagination. Children's delight at Christian's adventures on his journey to the Celestial City was not intended to obscure the moral meaning.

Abraham Chear, one of the most popular of the Puritan writers, whose work was used in many others' books, had his verse published in *A Looking Glass for the Mind* (1672), a book of poems and elegies which went into four editions by 1708. This book is remarkable only for its popularity; like many others of its kind it was bought by parents seeking to educate their children for a good life and a holy death. Publishers, though, were realising the worth of the market for these 'good godly books' and by the 1670s many more were being published. Benjamin Keach was one of the most prolific of the Puritan authors; his *War with the Devil* (1673), which describes the fight for a young man's soul between Conscience, Truth, the Devil and Christ, was still being published in the mid-eighteenth century, when it was advertised as 'necessary to be read by all Christian families'. Another much read author was Nathaniel Crouch, editor and publisher as well as writer; his pseudonym was 'R.B.' – Richard Burton. *The Young Man's Calling* (1678), *Youth's Divine Pastime* (3rd edn, 1691) and *Winter Evening Entertainments* (1687) were conventional in tone and contained much that was repackaged from other works: riddles, stories, morals.

There were those in addition to Bunyan who stood above the mediocrity of Puritan religious tracts. William Ronksley's work, for example, displayed considerable interest in the child as reader. His *The Child's Weeks-Work: or, A Little Book so nicely suited to the Genius and Capacity of a Little Child ... that it will infallibly Allure and Lead him on into a way of Reading* (1712) was moral in its intention but so well composed with neat rhymes for every day of the week that the child would have undoubtedly been charmed by it. Isaac Watts also wrote at the turn of the century, at the point when Puritanism was losing some of its ferocity in dealing with children. Like Ronksley, Watts wrote gentle verse; his *Divine Songs attempted in Easie Language for the Use of Children* (1715) continued as a staple of the nursery through to the Victorian period and was lovingly parodied by Carroll in *Alice's Adventures in Wonderland* (1865). The duty children owed to parents was his particular theme, but the lesson is easily read and could be liltingly spoken:

> How doth the little busy bee
> Improve each shining hour,
> And gather honey all the day

From every opening flower . . .
In works of labour, or of skill,
I would be busy too;
For Satan finds some mischief still
For idle hands to do . . .

By the beginning of the eighteenth century, therefore, books for children were becoming more child oriented: in the tone, the language and the subject matter. While death and damnation were still important concerns, so too were the more prosaic concerns of family life. Watts was writing in the Puritan tradition, but his verse was accessible to everyone, and remained a staple of schoolroom and nursery for two centuries.

## Publishing for Children: the Early Eighteenth Century

There was growing commercial interest in publishing books for children that not only taught them but also provided some amusement, as the numbers of children in the British population increased during the eighteenth century. The child population was to reach its peak in the early nineteenth century, but the intense commitment to educating the children of the middle classes which was evident during this period as academies and small private schools sprang up across the country stimulated the market for schoolbooks and lighter reading. Nathaniel Crouch's *Winter Evening Entertainments* was an early example of the transition to more child centred material as publishers identified the potential for selling books to parents and schools. The chapbook publishers – John Marshall and William and Cluer Dicey were two of the earliest London publishers to specialise in small books for children, many of them religious or moral tracts – produced material at the cheaper end of the market to satisfy this demand. Children also borrowed from adult books. Daniel Defoe's *Robinson Crusoe* was published in 1719 and Jonathan Swift's *Gulliver's Travels* in 1726. Chapbook versions which were written for children appeared later and adaptations became a genre in their own right, with the Robinsonnade evolving into a European-wide phenomenon through numerous versions of the story. One of the earliest examples to appear was Peter Longueville's *The Hermit: or, the Unparalleled Sufferings and Surprising Adventures of Mr Philip Quarrl* (1727). Joachim Campe's *Robinson the Younger* appeared in 1781, and a superior version – *The New Robinson Crusoe* – was issued by John Stockdale in four volumes with twenty-two woodcuts in 1788.

Of the books being published specifically for children, Mary Cooper's *The Child's New Plaything* (1742) and *Tommy Thumb's Pretty Song Book* Voll 2 [*sic*] (1744) are two of the most interesting. Several of the traditional nursery rhymes which were intended simply to amuse children appeared for the first time in print in this latter volume, a tiny book printed in red and black with neat copper engravings. The verses are an odd mixture of ribald drinking songs and old favourites. Lady Bird, Lady Bird, fly away home, for example, sits somewhat uncomfortably beside Fidlers Wife:

We are all a dry/With drinking ont
We are all a dry/With drinking ont

The piper kisst/The Fidlers wife
And I cant sleep/For thinking ont.

Thomas Boreman, who published a set of ten miniature books, the *Gigantick Histories*, between 1740 and 1743, also considered a new venture of books for amusement as well as instruction worthy of some investment, and there are isolated examples of other publishers issuing significant items for children.

One of the more important was the first English translation of Charles Perrault's fairy tales: Robert Samber's *Histories, or Tales of Past Times. Told by Mother Goose* (1729). Fairy tales became established not only in the productions of the mainstream publishers; the chapbook publishers took them up and distributed them widely beside the moral and religious tracts. The *Contes de Fées* of the Countess d'Aulnoy, translated as her *Diverting Works* (1707), became popular in chapbooks, and included 'The yellow dwarf', 'Goldylocks' and 'The white cat'. Madame de Beaumont's *Le Cabinet des Fées* (1785–1789) was also published in English versions and her adaptation of 'Beauty and the beast' became a staple of chapbook literature.

## John Newbery: 1744–1767

However, what all of these endeavours lacked was a coherent approach to the development of a specifically children's literature. Before the mid-eighteenth century, book publishing for children lacked seriousness of purpose. John Newbery's publishing activities changed this; he developed the children's side of his business through a sustained and forceful exploitation of the market. Newbery began as a provincial bookseller and newspaper proprietor and also dealt in patent medicines, activities which continued to be significant elements in his complex business empire. However, soon after his move to London from Reading he produced *A Little Pretty Pocket Book* (1744). Verses with wood blocks of children at play comprise most of this slight but significant offering, which became one of the best known of all the early children's books. His *Lilliputian Magazine* (1751–1752) was more substantial, although less successful, and continued the Newbery mixture of light-hearted material – jests, songs, riddles – and more moral tales. There followed *A Pretty Book of Pictures for Little Masters and Misses* (*c*.1752), and *Nurse Truelove's New Year's Gift* (*c*.1753), similarly light-hearted in tone and content. Binding in Dutch floral boards was also his trademark and the overall quality of their production marked out his books from the cruder reading materials of the previous century.

Perhaps his most famous book – and certainly the one which drew the admiration of Charles Lamb – was *The History of Little Goody Two-Shoes* (1765). This tale of the 'trotting tutoress', Margery Meanwell, encapsulated all of Newbery's emphasis in his books on the mercantile class, a group in society to whom trade and good sense meant everything. Margery progresses from penury to a good marriage through hard work, thrift and the use of her talents: a tale with true moral sense for the middle-class children at whom it was directed.

Newbery also contributed to the burgeoning schoolbook market with a series of lesson books, *The Circle of the Sciences* (1745–1748), and books like Oliver

Goldsmith's *An History of England, in a Series of Letters from a Nobleman to his Son* (1764). (Goldsmith probably also wrote *Goody Two-Shoes*). Indeed, most of Newbery's output for the youth market was intended for schools or for home tutoring; only sixteen or so were mainly for entertainment. His schoolbooks were generally weightier and more expensive: the *Account of the Constitution and Present State of Great Britain* (1759) cost 2 shillings. The more light-hearted items cost less and were usually printed in several editions: 'Abraham Aesop's' *Fables in Verse* was priced at 6d and was in its sixth edition by 1768. However, at a time when chapbooks were being sold for 1d, even these were expensive by the standards of the day. Newbery was intent on selling to the middle classes and aspiring artisans, not the mass of the labouring population.

Newbery's great talent was his understanding of the new market for children's books and schoolbooks: exploiting that market required tenacity of purpose and the development of a class of books which appealed to both parents and children. Advertising and distribution was also essential to ensure a good volume of sales. By marketing his books through the important provincial newspapers of the day, and using the newspaper distribution outlets, Newbery maximised the penetration of his books into rural areas from his famous shop at the Bible and Sun in St Paul's Churchyard, London, which was the focus for his activities. Newbery's later years were his busiest period; between 1755 and 1767, when he died, he published around 390 adult and children's books, although his contribution to the development of a children's publishing trade has tended to obscure his many other business activities. He probably made more as a purveyor of quack medicines than from the children's books, and his newspaper interests and magazine publishing were also of considerable value.

## Educational Theorists and Children's Books

John Newbery's output was largely dependent on the school and home tutoring market, with his educational items selling to the proprietors of the increasing numbers of academies and private schools springing up throughout the country and to parents eager to enhance their children's education. The education of the young was becoming of increasing significance as social expectations developed, and the middle classes – including women – had more time for the leisurely pursuit of reading. Good schooling was becoming a necessity. The hallmark of a gentleman, and increasingly a gentlewoman, was not only a thorough grounding in basic reading and writing skills but also a knowledge of the classical or modern languages, arithmetic, geography – even a little science such as astronomy or mechanics. John Locke was not offering new ideas in *Some Thoughts Concerning Education* when he recommended a carefully judged curriculum designed to meet the needs of pupils on the basis that knowledge should be impressed on young and untouched minds: the *tabula rasa* or blank sheet principle. His argument, which he had begun in the *Essay Concerning Human Understanding* (1689), was, however, hugely influential. At least fourteen editions of his educational treatise were published between 1693 and 1772 and provided a focus for writers and publishers in their provision of a literature to feed the demand from schools and parents (Pickering 1981: passim).

His emphasis on a carefully judged and rational approach to writing for children was echoed in one of the first books to expound upon schooling for girls: Sarah Fielding's *The Governess: or Little Female Academy* (1749), in which her aim was 'to endeavour to cultivate an early inclination to benevolence and a love of virtue in the minds of young women'. Ellenor Fenn, writing towards the end of the century, was also intent on controlling and containing the natural behaviour of children and impressing virtues upon them, although a lightness of touch was also evident in her work. In *Cobwebs to Catch Flies* (*c.*1783) she appealed to parents as much as to children: 'if the human mind be a *tabula rasa* – you to whom it is entrusted should be cautious what is written upon it'. Lady Fenn also produced books and 'schemes for teaching under the idea of amusement'. One of these, *The Infant's Delight*, was sold with 'a specimen of cuts in a superior stile for children: with a book containing their names, as easy reading lessons [*sic*]'.

Sarah Trimmer, hugely influential as a critic as well as a writer of children's books and who credited Locke with inspiring the increase in books published for children at the end of the eighteenth century, was especially concerned with the moral impact of writing for children. Her *Fabulous Histories. Designed for the Instruction of Children, respecting their Treatment of Animals* (1786), later better known as *The History of the Robins*, aimed to teach children their duty towards brute creation. In *Prints of Scripture History* (1786), and numerous other pious works, she provided children with a grounding in sound religious teaching. Her *Little Spelling Book for Young Children* (2nd edn, 1786) and *Easy Lessons for Young Children* (1787) were also popular and went into several editions.

The relationship between religious principles, morality and a child–centred literature, which had begun with the Puritan writers, continued in the eighteenth century through the impact of a number of female authors. Like Sarah Trimmer, they considered that reading matter should improve young minds while making the reading light and easy: another of Locke's dictums. Anna Barbauld, whose *Lessons for Children from Two to Three Years Old* (1778) and *Hymns in Prose for Children* (1781) expressed a sensitivity for her readers which was quite remarkable, nevertheless aimed mainly to 'inspire devotional feeling early in life'. *Evenings at Home* (1792–1796), a collection of amusing tales, moral pieces and verse, compiled in collaboration with her brother, John Aikin, similarly mixed morality with amusement. In common with many of the writers of this period she was herself deeply involved in educating children; following her husband's untimely death she ran a small school.

Mary Pilkington, who worked as a governess and wrote around fifty books for children, also combined a firm didactic line in her work with more amusing and adventurous material. Her *Biography for Girls* and *Biography for Boys*, both published in 1799, contained cautionary tales of children whose later lives were fixed through their youthful misdeeds, while *New Tales of the Castle* (1800), modelled on Madame de Genlis's *Tales of the Castle* (1785), featured a French noble family fleeing the Revolution – altogether a more thrilling story line.

Mary Wollstonecraft had also worked as a governess before turning to writing as a career; her publisher, Joseph Johnson, made something of a specialism out of didactic literature for children. In *Original Stories from Real Life* (1788) she used the setting of a girls' school for her series of moral tales, but was rather less inspiring than Sarah Fielding. Her contemporary, Dorothy Kilner's, *Anecdotes of a Boarding School; or an Antidote to the Vices of those Useful Seminaries* (c.1783) set out the dangers of boarding schools even more explicitly, but only served to make them exciting places for her readers: 'we all get out of bed, and play blindman's buff, or dance about in the dark: then if we hear any noise, and think anybody is coming, away we all run helter-skelter, to get into our beds'. Dorothy Kilner also wrote about less privileged education in *The Village School* (c.1795) and produced simple lesson books for children which included *Short Conversations* (c.1785). Her most entertaining story was *The Life and Perambulation of a Mouse* (c.1783–1784), where play again featured: 'After the more serious employment of reading each morning was concluded, we danced, we sung, we played at blind-man's buff, battledore and shuttlecock, and many other games equally diverting and innocent.'

Her sister-in-law, Mary Ann Kilner, was also a popular writer, although less prolific. *The Adventures of a Pincushion* (c.1780) and *The Memoirs of a Peg-Top* (c.1781) went into many editions; the combination of sound common sense, amusing detail and imaginative writing seems to have appealed to parents.

Locke was not the only influential theorist; his emphasis on the impression of virtue on young minds and the need to treat children as rational creatures, was only one strand of thought. Following the translation of Jean Jacques Rousseau's *Emile* into English in 1763, in which it was judged that children's (or rather boys') education should be related to their status as reflective creatures of the natural world, writers adopted new methods of imparting morality. Children had to learn rationality through experience. Maria Edgeworth, whose best known story – 'The purple jar' – first appeared in *The Parent's Assistant* (1796), was one of Rousseau's most faithful disciples in imparting this ideology. Rosamund is offered a gift by her mother, and instead of choosing the sensible pair of new shoes opts for a purple jar in the apothecary's shop. Her old shoes let her down and she finally has to acknowledge that mother knows best and to 'hope, I shall be wiser another time'. The idea that children learn best through acting out a lesson was one which many writers adopted from Rousseau. French writers from this school were imported and achieved a wide readership, including Rousseau's friend the Marquise D'Epinay whose *Conversations of Emily* was published in English in 1787.

Another English Rousseauist was Thomas Day; his *Sandford and Merton* (1783–1789) became one of the most popular sets of tales for boys during this period and was widely adapted and reissued well into the nineteenth century. Harry Sandford and Tommy Merton have a series of largely unconnected adventures in the original version, unexciting material by later standards, but one of the first attempts to depict recognisably real boys exploring a friendship through active incident. Day's *Little Jack* (1788) was equally firm in its Rousseauism, with its depiction of the hero's natural upbringing in his 'little hut of clay' and allusions to the Crusoe tale of survival through ingenuity and tenacity.

## Fun and Frivolity

It might appear that an emphasis on earnest moral teaching and the influence of the educational theorists had driven all that was frivolous from children's reading. Newbery's greatest contribution to children's publishing had been his introduction of lighter-hearted literature. *Tommy Thumb's Pretty Song Book Voll II* had also stood as an early example of sheer amusement for children, together with a few other items which have survived. *The Famous Tommy Thumb's Little Story Book* was issued by Stanley Crowder and Benjamin Collins (*c.*1760), and, like *The Top Book of All* (*c.*1760), contained verse and light material, including the game of 'The wide mouth waddling frog'. Riddles were especially popular with adults in the seventeenth century and owed their survival to their continuation in innovative children's books such as these.

Despite the prevalence of moral tales and didacticism, there were, therefore, items to amuse and divert children towards the end of the century in addition to the chapbook literature of the period. *Mother Goose's Melody* was probably published *c.*1780: at about the same time as *Nancy Cock's Pretty Song Book* was published by John Marshall. *Mother Goose's Melody*, a 96-page Newbery book in two parts – with fifty-one songs and lullabies in Part One – is particularly important because of the number of times it was to be reprinted in Britain and America. (Opie and Opie, 1951/1980: 33). Issued by John Newbery's successors (a 1791 edition was issued by Francis Power, John Newbery's grandson) this was, at 3d, a cheap little book by Newbery standards and hence likely to be widely bought. *Gammer Gurton's Garland*, published in Stockport in 1784, was a further important example of an early published collection of nursery rhymes.

Books containing moral material in a light-hearted guise were also becoming commonplace. For example, adaptations of the *Goody Two-Shoes* tale were published: *The Entertaining History of Little Goody Goosecap* (1780) was John Marshall's version, with *The Renowned History of Primrose Pretty Face* (1785) following a similar theme – a profitable marriage is the reward for virtue and probity. Children's publishers also dealt in the production of maps and games; books were not the only educational materials to provide amusement. John Wallis was one of the most successful of these; his *Chronological Tables of English History for the Instruction of Youth* (1788) and *The New Game of Life* which he issued in collaboration with Elizabeth Newbery in 1790, were instructional games with counters and dice – and a set of neatly printed instructions.

By the late eighteenth century publishing for children had become a sufficiently profitable undertaking for several major London publishers and many provincial chapbook publishers to be issuing a range of children's items: for instruction *and* amusement. The firm of William Darton began business in 1787, when William Darton set up as an engraver and printer. The firm was to specialise in neatly engraved books for children and to produce some of the finest coloured books in the early nineteenth century. The Newbery tradition was carried on by Elizabeth Newbery, who took over one arm of the business when her husband (nephew to John) died in 1780. She specialised particularly in the education market, but also continued with many of the earlier Newbery items, and also collaborated with other publishers. Her Catalogue of 1800 indicates the range that was now available to parents, schools – and children – by the end of the eighteenth century. In addition to the 400 or so more substantial items, including schoolbooks and moral tales, she offered thirteen one-penny and fourteen two-penny chapbooks as makeweights. Vernor and Hood, Joseph Johnson, John Nourse who specialised in French books for school and home, and John Marshall, were some of the other firms engaged in the London trade. Children's books were also being produced in provincial publishing centres: Newcastle was one of the earliest chapbook centres to specialise in children's works, but there were also small provincial presses across the country, from Wrexham to York and from Alnwick to Wellington.

The quality and variety of production had also improved immeasurably. Much of the credit for this is due to the development of illustration techniques, through the work of John and Thomas Bewick who perfected the art of wood engraving, and the increasing use of copper engravings in the more expensively priced children's books (Whalley and Chester, 1988: 27–28). William Blake was a major illustrator, but his own children's book, *Songs of Innocence* (1789) was only widely known much later.

By 1800, the children's book trade was well established and children had a wide-ranging literature at their disposal. Not all of it was just for entertainment, but increasingly it was being written with their developmental needs in mind. From their origins in the formal writing of the early schoolbooks, Puritan texts, popular literature and fables, children's books had emerged as a class of literature. The book trade was poised to develop this even further and to exploit the technical innovations of the next century.

## References

Axtell, J. L. (1968) *The Educational Writings of John Locke*, Cambridge: Cambridge University Press.

Cressy, D. (1980) *Literacy and the Social Order*, Cambridge: Cambridge University Press.

Darton, F. J. H. (1982) *Children's Books in England: Five Centuries of Social Life*, 3rd edn, ed. B. Alderson, Cambridge: Cambridge University Press.

Opie, I. and Opie P. (1951/1980) *The Oxford Dictionary of Nursery Rhymes*, Oxford: Oxford University Press.

Pickering, S. F. (1981) *John Locke and Children's Books in Eighteenth Century England*, Knoxville, TN: University of Tennessee Press.

Roscoe, S. (1973) *John Newbery and his Successors 1740–1814: A Bibliography*, Wormley: Five Owls Press.

Spufford, M. (1981) *Small Books and Pleasant Histories: Popular Fiction and its Readership in Seventeenth Century England*, Cambridge: Cambridge University Press.

Whalley, J. I. and Chester, T. R. (1988) *A History of Children's Book Illustration*, London: John Murray/The Victoria and Albert Museum.

## Further Reading

Jackson, M. V. (1989) *Engines of Instruction, Mischief and Magic: Children's Literature in England from its Beginnings to 1839*, Aldershot: Scolar Press.

Opie, I. and Opie P. (1974) *The Classic Fairy Tales*, Oxford: Oxford University Press.

Plumb, J. H. (1975) 'The new world of children in eighteenth century England', *Past and Present* 67: 64–95.

Summerfield, G. (1984) *Fantasy and Reason: Children's Literature in the Eighteenth Century*, London: Methuen.

# 13

# Fairy Tales and Folk-tales

## *Ruth B. Bottigheimer*

### Tales about Fairies and Fairy Tales

Tales about fairies are elaborate narratives that depict the fairy kingdom and elfland; the leprechauns, kobolds, gnomes, elves, and little people (Briggs 1976, 1978) that populate its stories are authors of unintelligible actions that often have no moral point and frequently lead to troublingly amoral consequences and conclusions. Based on surviving Celtic lore, tales about fairies flowered in ornate seventeenth-century versions composed during the reign of Louis XIV by the French *précieuses* and their followers. Their fairies and giantesses, invented for literate adult aristocratic French audiences, soon found favour among children. A representative example, Mme d'Aulnoy's *Yellow Dwarf*, opens with a princess disdainful of her suitors and continues with an unfortunate promise of betrothal to a physically deformed yellow dwarf. When the princess finally meets and falls in love with the valorous and virtuous King of the Gold Mines, a worthy suitor, the yellow dwarf kills him and the princess swoons and dies in sympathy. The tale ends in a manner hardly calculated to delight seventeenth- and eighteenth-century moralists: 'The wicked dwarf was better pleased to see his princess void of life, than in the arms of another' (1721 vol. 1, story VII; here Opie 1974: 80).

Humble people had also become familiar with the fairy world, and in the same period used simple stories of the fairy world to frighten children. John Locke decried this practice and urged readers of his *Thoughts on Education* to eschew hobgoblins and their ilk altogether (Locke 1693: 159). Despite his influence in other educational questions, his advice was often ignored, and tales about fairies specifically for children began to appear after 1700 as part of the chapbook trade (Darton 1932/1982: 94).

Fairy tales, unlike tales about fairies, more often than not, do not include fairies in their cast of characters and are generally brief narratives in simple language that detail a reversal of fortune, with a rags-to-riches plot that often culminates in a wedding. Magical creatures regularly assist earthly heroes and heroines achieve happiness, and the entire story is usually made to demonstrate a moral point, appended separately, as in Perrault, or built into the text, as in Grimm.

In terms of the history and development of children's literature, tales about fairies and fairy tales postdate the earliest writing for children – instructional manuals, grammars, school texts and books of courtesy. Bible stories, too, regularly preceded the appearance of fairy tales, and in the eighteenth century were often intermixed with them, as in Mme Leprince de Beaumont's *Magasin des Enfans* (1756).

The magic of modern fantasy fiction is an offspring of the joint parentage of tales about fairies and fairy tales; born in the second half of the nineteenth century, fantasy fiction matured in the twentieth century.

Both tales about fairies and fairy tales demonstrate the phenomenon of readership boundary cross-over. The content of tales about fairies that were originally composed by and for adults often passed, in simplified form, into the domain of children's reading. Mme d'Aulnoy's *Yellow Dwarf* provides an example of this process: published with its tragic conclusion throughout the eighteenth century for adults and for children, it was altered to end happily for nineteenth-century child readers (Warner 1994: 253).

For centuries, discrete narratives, whether tales about fairies, fairy tales or secular tales, had been embedded within overarching story-telling narratives, like that provided by the pilgrimage in the *Canterbury Tales*. The French *précieuses'* tales about fairies maintained this narrative tradition, but Perrault's *Contes* broke with it. His structural innovation, the free-standing fairy tale, became the norm in children's literature, although the embedded fairy tale periodically returned, for example, in Sarah Fielding's eighteenth-century novel, *The Governess*, and in a nineteenth-century English reformulation of *Grimms' Tales* into a twelve-night cycle between Christmas and Twelfth Night told by Gammer Gurton.

### France

Charles Perrault's *Contes du Temps Passé* (1697) and Madame d'Aulnoy's *Contes des Fées* (4 vols., 1710–1715) sowed the seeds for early modern and modern fairy tales and tales about fairies. At a very early point tales about fairies and certain kinds of fairy tales were identified as the products of women's imaginations; and indeed there seem to be qualitative differences between the tales women tell and those that men recount (Holbek 1987: 161 ff.). Whether children were ever significant contributors to the fairy tale tradition, as the Abbé de Villiers suggested in 1699 (Warner 1991: 11) is doubtful.

For the French book buying public in the eighteenth century, fairy tales existed in three forms. The first consisted of chapbooks of the *bibliothèque bleue*, which foraged among seventeenth- and eighteenth-century tales about fairies and fairy tales in search of fodder for their hungry presses and for an even more ravenous humble public, and delivered French tales about fairies and fairy tales to a semi-literate and illiterate public in France (Tenèze 1979: 283–287). It was a population that provided nurses who told fairy tales to children put in their care and who were, in part, responsible for the myth of fairy tale orality. The second form comprised fantasy tales about fairies. These tales, with little or no moral or moralising component, had been composed for adult readers and often offered distinctly dystopic views of the human condition. Hence, their suitability for children was highly problematic. There existed a third form, however, intensely moralised fairy tales that were intended for child readers. Enlightenment pedagogy remained dissatisfied with magic in any form, and by the late 1770s and early 1780s Rousseau and Locke had 'gradually alienated the child from the world of Perrault's fairies

... and Mme Leprince de Beaumont's "Beast", and indeed, Mme de la Fite had openly attacked the highly moralised fairy tales of Mme Leprince de Beaumont' (Davis 1987: 113).

In nineteenth-century France the market for fairy tales for children was limited to Perrault (Caradec 1977: 53 ff.) and a few translations of *Grimms' Tales*. In general, France's educational system, and hence its book market, was firmly closed against fantasy.

*Germany*

The fairy tale in Germany derived almost completely from the French tradition. For a century, translations and borrowings had enabled German booksellers to repeat the French model: the writings of Charles Perrault, Charlotte de la Force, Suzanne de Villeneuve, Marie-Catherine d'Aulnoy and the *Cabinet des Fées* supplied middle- and upper-class German adults and children with tales about fairies and fairy tales, and the *bibliothèque bleue* had delivered chapbook versions of the same material (Grätz 1988: 83 ff.) to the lower orders.

The French had ascribed fairy tales to women's authorship, despite the manifest participation by many men such as Perrault. German intellectuals took a circuitous route to arrive at the same conclusion. First, they developed a theory of the fairy tale (Märchen) that linked it with ancient history, which they defined as the childhood of the human race. Then the childhood of the human race was equated with childhood *per se*. Because of fairy tales' simple structure and plot lines (so different from the tales about fairies of the *précieuses*) J. G. Herder further equated fairy tales with nature. And finally, because a body of gender theory had developed in eighteenth-century Germany that defined women as the incarnation of nature, fantasy and non-rational cerebration, and because – in the same theory – women's natural state was motherhood, the establishment of the two fairy tale correlates, childhood and nature, forged a theoretical linkage between fairy tales and women. (A belief in that conclusion endures in many quarters to the present day.) Enlightenment pedagogues thus denigrated fairy tales as stories told by ignorant nursemaids, or by women, who were understood to be incapable of intellection, and sought, unsuccessfully, to eradicate fairy tales from the nursery and classroom. None the less, fairy tales entered the precincts of some privileged German homes just as they had in England: Mme de Beaumont's *Magasin des Enfans* was translated into German as *Lehrreiches Magazin für Kinder* and published for girls' reading in 1760, and Sarah Fielding's *Governess*, with its fairy tale inclusions, was translated into German and published in the following year.

With the rise of German Romanticism, fairy tales were proposed as a paradigm for educating the imagination (Steinlein 1987: 115 ff.), and when Wilhelm and Jacob Grimm published their *Kinder- und Hausmärchen* (1812 *et seq.*), they labelled it a child-rearing manual (Grimm 1812: preface). The collection eventually contained over two hundred tales, culled from friends, acquaintances, country informants, children's almanacs and old books. The 'Twelve Brothers' (no. 9) may be taken as typical. Twelve brothers face relinquishing their patrimony and losing their lives should their mother bear them a sister. When that happens, they flee to the forest and vow blood vengeance on every girl they might encounter in the future. A full complement of fairy tale situations ensues, and although the tale ends happily, the sister is first exposed to the threat of her brothers' violence and her mother-in-law's hatred.

Even before Wilhelm and Jacob published their collection, Albert Ludwig Grimm had turned against Enlightenment children's literature and had issued a call for a revival of the tales like 'Cinderella', 'Hansel and Gretel', and 'Snow White' ('Aschenpittchen', 'Hänsel und Gretel', 'Schneewittchen') which he included in *Kindermärchen* (1808), his collection of children's fairy tales. In a later book, *Linas Märchenbuch* (1827), A. L. Grimm scolded Jacob and Wilhelm Grimm for the 'unchild-like style of their fairy tales'.

Eventually, fairy tales came to form the nucleus of German romantic children's literature: Wilhelm Hauff's *Märchen Almanacke* (1822–1828), E. T. A. Hoffmann's fairy tales (especially the Nutcracker cycle) (Ewers 1984: 195), and the fairy tales of Contessa and Fouqué.

The runaway fairy tale bestseller of the mid-to-late-nineteenth century in Germany, however, was Ludwig Bechstein's *Deutsches Märchenbuch* [*German Fairy-tale Book*] (1845 *et seq.*). Bechstein's tales differed from contemporaneous collections of fairy tales by his playful prose style, by the loving and unified families they depicted, and above all, by the ethic of self-reliance they described in their characters and fostered in their readers. Bechstein's twelve brothers, for example, are overjoyed rather than inclined to homicide when they find their sister in their midst. His fairy tales exemplified bourgeois behavioural norms and social expectations, while *Grimms' Tales* expressed values that paralleled those of an agrarian proletariat. However, with the wholesale republication and recirculation of sixteenth- and seventeenth-century German chapbooks in nineteenth-century Germany, the ethic of *Grimms' Tales* was reinforced, and that of Bechstein's *Deutsches Märchenbuch* denigrated, with consequential results for German children's literature (Bottigheimer 1990: 84–85; 1992: 473–477).

In the late nineteenth century *Grimms' Tales* began to dominate the fairy tale market in German children's literature. Their eventual hegemony owed much to newly developed nationalist theories of pedagogy, but even after these were displaced in the mid-twentieth century, *Grimms' Tales* reigned supreme until they were attacked as fundamentally flawed in the aftermath of German university unrest in 1968. They re-emerged, however, with much of the stories' primitive violence removed, a process that had occurred twenty years before in West Germany's then sister state, the German Democratic Republic.

### Britain

English Puritans had been deeply antipathetic to tales about fairies, which they considered relics of pagan, pre-Christian thought. In their view, tales about fairies and fairy tales were non-Christian in content and anti-Christian in intent. 'And yet, alas!' one committed Christian wrote, 'how often do we see Parents prefer Tom Thumb, Guy of Warwick, Valentine and Orson, or some such foolish Book ... Let not your children read these vain Books ... Throw away all fond and amorous Romances, and fabulous Histories of Giants, the bombast Achievements of Knight Errantry' (Fontaine 1708: vii).

Popular taste did not concur with Puritan antipathy, however, and when *Tales of the Fairies* (1699) was published in England, and when Galland's *Mille et Une Nuits* (12 vols, 1704–1717) was translated into English as *Arabian Nights*, chapbook purchasers immediately signalled their approval of magic by buying them in large numbers. Similarly, subsequent translations of Madame d'Aulnoy's *Contes des Fées*, which appeared in English translation as *Diverting Works* (1707) and *A Collection of Novels and Tales* (1721) became well-known in English: for example, 'The Yellow Dwarf', 'Finetta the Cinder-girl', and 'The White Cat'.

In 1729 Robert Samber translated Perrault's fairy tales as *Histories, or Tales of Past Times* and completed the early eighteenth-century inventory of tales about fairies and fairy tales in England. In his dedication to the Countess of Granville, mother of Lord Carteret, Samber discussed the fairy tale as an improvement on Aesop's fables: 'stories of human kind', he wrote, 'are more effectively instructive than those of animals' (A 3v). Perrault's fairy tales', he continued, were 'designed for children' yet the stories themselves 'grow up ... both as to their Narration and Moral' because 'Virtue is ever rewarded and Vice ever punished in these tales' (A 4r). Samber meant his book to be morally instructive, and he licensed no 'poor insipid trifling tale in a tinkling Jingle' with a 'petty Witticism, or insignificant useless Reflection'. Samber bridged the cultural gap between France and Britain by giving some of Perrault's characters English names (Red Riding Hood's Christian name became Biddy, and the bad girl in 'The Fairy' was called Fanny), by defining an ogre ('a giant that has long teeth and claws, with a raw head and bloody bones, that runs away with naughty little boys and girls, and eats them up' (43)), and by offering a recipe for Sauce Robert in 'Sleeping Beauty' (51).

Eighteenth-century English fairy tales specifically for children also existed in chapbooks. Their format dispensed with frame tales and particularised vocabulary to produce simplified narratives like 'Bluebeard', 'Red Riding Hood', and 'The Blue Bird' along with 'Aladdin' and 'Sindbad' to a broad reading public (Summerfield 1984: 45, 55, 57).

When children's literature was formally and self-consciously instituted in the mid-eighteenth century, fairy tales remained an integral component of the moral lessons composed for children. Thomas Boreman's tiny four-penny book, *The History of Cajanus, the Swedish Giant* (1742) offered a tongue-in-cheek biography of a seven-foot tall Finnish giant, capable of remarkable fairy tale-like acts. Sarah Fielding also used tales about fairies for *The Governess* – 'the story of the cruel giant Barbarico, the good giant Benefico, and the pretty little Dwarf Mignon' and 'Princess Hebe ... To cultivate an early Inclination to Benevolence, and a love of Virtue, in the Minds of young Women' (Fielding 1749: A 2r). Mrs Teachum, the governess of the title, viewed fairy tales with some alarm and cautioned that 'Giants, Magic, Fairies, and all sorts of Supernatural Assistances in a Story, are only introduced to amuse and divert ...' and presented them as 'figures of a sort' that stood for virtuous or vicious conduct (Fielding 1749: 68).

Fairy tales had long been securely harnessed to moral education, as the full title of Henry Brooke's 1750 collection indicated: they contained 'many useful Lessons [and] Moral Sentiments' (cited in Kamenetsky 1992: 222). And although the word 'moral' was absent from its title, *Robin Goodfellow, a Fairy Tale* (1770) did the same.

In this period a new visual code was in the process of being established in Europe, in part codified by Lavater's study of physiognomy. Lavater aimed to demonstrate that character could be read from countenance, and in children's literature that perception translated into an equation of virtue with beauty. One stylistic consequence was that the authors of fairy tales for girls increasingly described the facial appearance of characters in their books.

Mme Leprince de Beaumont, whose arrival in England coincided with the commercial development of books for children, elevated tales about fairies and fairy tales to religious company in her *Magasin des Enfants* (1756). 'La Belle et la Bête' appeared between the stories of 'Adam and Eve', and 'Noah'. Like her predecessor, Sarah Fielding, she employed the device of a frame tale: conversations between pupils and a governess. Eleanor (or Ellenor) Fenn, the author of *The Fairy Spectator* (1789), in the guise of Mrs Teachwell, used fairy tales for equally high moral ends. By the late eighteenth century, primers began to include fairy tales as reading exercises for children, and children's magazines mixed fairy tales into a pot-pourri of rhymes, stories, and anecdotes (MacDonald 1982: 45, 110). Even the thoroughly amoral tales of *The Thousand and One Nights* were transformed by the earnest efforts of English educators into books with titles like Cooper's *Oriental Moralist* (1790). The stories themselves, quite different from the unobtrusive, almost logical metamorphoses of Western convention, restocked the European inventory of the fantastic with new magic objects, enchanted places and a dazzling array of startling transformations (Jan 1974: 35). In the *Enchanted Mirror, a Moorish Romance* (1814), for example, the properties of traditional magic mirrors were adapted to the requirements of moral improvement, so that this one returned viewers' gazes with images of how they *were* rather than how they appeared (cited in Pickering 1993: 188), a further indication of the formative power of physiognomic thought on literature.

Despite the scoffing dismissal of fairy tales by official pedagogy in the eighteenth century – the Edgeworths commented in 1798 that they did not 'allude to fairy tales, for we apprehend these are not now much read' (cited in Opie 1974: 25) – fairy tales continued to grow in popularity (Pickering 1993: 187). Even Sarah Trimmer, who would later turn against fairy tales, acknowledged in *The Guardian of Education* that she had enjoyed them as a child (Goldstone 1984: 71).

The most frequently published individual fairy tale, 'Cinderella', provided a satisfying rags-to-riches plot that answered a longing felt in many segments of society: for example, among the newly literate but still poor buyers of chapbooks, as well as among the the middle-class children who aspired to inclusion in yet more elevated social classes. The 'Cinderella' paradigm was as evident in *Goody Two-Shoes* (1765) as it was in *Primrose Prettyface* (1785) but the tale contained within itself not only the hopeful promise of social elevation, but also disturbing possibilities for frightening social inversion. The French Revolution of 1789 and the bloody executions of the 1790s aroused suspicion about 'Cinderella' plots suggesting rags-to-riches and evoked violent reaction. Sarah Trimmer now criticised fairy tales, and especially Cinderella, whom she 'accused of causing ... the worst human emotions to arise in the child' (Goldstone 1984: 71), and conservative educators excised first Cinderella plots and then fairy tales themselves from books of moral improvement. One result was that post-1820 editions of *The Governess* appeared shorn of their fairy tale interludes.

These attacks on fairy tales echo those that occurred a hundred years before, but a telling distinction separated criticisms of fantasy for children at the beginning and at the end of the eighteenth century. A hundred years before, John Locke had warned against elves, gnomes and goblins (in tales about fairies), but by the end of the century, it was fairy tales that came under attack, as in Mrs Trimmer's essay, 'Mother Goose's fairy tales', in her magazine *The Guardian of Education* (1803: 185–186).

Enlightenment pedagogical principles left little room for imaginative constructs (Steinlein 1987: 115) and led to the 'censorship of everything fanciful', yet many authors recognised that imaginative tales induced a love of reading in children, and that, furthermore 'much good advice and information can be conveyed in a Fable and a Fairy Tale' (dedication of *Oriental Tales* [1802] cited in Jackson 1989: 195–196).

All of the practices and controversies that centred on fairy tales marked the genre in nineteenth-century English children's literature. For instance, the question of the educational value of fairy tales versus their putatively damaging consequences met head on in the Peter Parley–Felix Summerly debate. Samuel Griswold Goodrich's Peter Parley books (1827 *et seq.*) grew directly out of eighteenth-century utilitarian principles and were relentlessly useful and didactically informative. Sir Henry Cole, under the pen name of Felix Summerly, opposed Goodrich's objections with the playful fantasy of stories in his *Home Treasury* (1843–1845) (Darton 1932/1982: 219–251). This debate was never resolved, and both of these trains of thought survived into the twentieth century.

The maternality that had been imputed to fairy tales by both French and German theoreticians, if one may dignify the rank sexism that passed for reasonable fact with that word, lived on in the titles of fairy tales for children. Perrault's tales were attributed to Mother Goose and Mme d'Aulnoy's to Queen Mab or Mother Bunch, and along the way, other fictive female relatives took their place among the authors of fairy tales: Aunt Friendly, Aunt Louisa and Mme de Chatalain.

National identity played a far smaller role in the project of valorising fairy tales in England than it did in Germany and in other countries that were either emerging from domination by foreign governments, like Finland and Norway, or amalgamating from disparate units, like Italy and Germany. But the dynamics of the publishing trade played a very large part in determining the contents of the scores, perhaps hundreds, of fairy tale collections that English booksellers purveyed to the English child.

Chapbooks remained a feature of nineteenth-century fairy tales for English children. Ross's Juvenile Library delivered small two-penny 48-page books like *Fairy Tales of Past Times from Mother Goose* (1814–1815) into young hands. The wolf became Gaffer Wolf, Blue Beard's wife used part of the estate she inherited on the death of her uxoricidal husband to marry her sister to a young gentleman and to buy military commissions for her brothers.

Moralisation continued to mark nineteenth-century fairy tales, but it was far more limited than it had been in the eighteenth century. For example, Cruikshank used 'Cinderella' as an anti-drink platform and Charles Dickens credited fairy tales with inculcating 'forbearance, courtesy, consideration for the poor and aged, kind treatment of animals, the love of nature, abhorrence of tyranny and brute force' (cited in Townsend 1974: 92).

Translations of other national fairy tale collections poured into England, enriching its store of available fairy material. In 1749 *The Fairy Tales of all Nations* entered England from a German collection that was itself based on French publications, and in 1823 Edward Taylor continued the importation of German fairy tale narrative when he translated and published the first of two volumes of the Grimm's tales as *German Popular Stories*. Illustrated by Cruikshank and provided with scholarly notes, its lively stories enchanted children, and the Grimm's scholarly reputation overcame the objections of doubting parents. In 1848 Taylor also translated Giambattista Basile's Neapolitan *Pentamerone* (1634, 1636 *et seq.*), which like *German Popular Stories*, was illustrated by Cruikshank. He edited both the German and the Italian fairy tales heavily to remove objectionable features, some violent episodes in the case of Grimm, sexual references in the case of Basile.

Hans Christian Andersen's Danish tales entered the English tradition in 1846 and soon gathered a large and enthusiastic English following. Norse material entered in 1857 when the *Heroes of Asgard* was printed, and Asbjørnsen and Moe's enchanting Norwegian fairy tales were translated in 1859 as *East o' the Sun and West o' the Moon*. There had also been imports from other parts of the British Isles, like Crofton Croker's Irish fairy tales (1825–1828) and various collections of Scottish tales.

Each of the translations listed above represented a form of republication, but true republication began in earnest with renamed and reprinted collections of stories and fairy tales containing material taken from English-language books already published in England. Benjamin Tabart's *Popular Tales* (1804 *et seq.*) was one such early republication, and the genre flourished increasingly as the century wore on. The *Fairy Tales of All Nations* (1849) reappeared as *The Doyle Fairy Book* (1890), while Mrs D. M. Craik's *Fairy Book* (1863) retold stories from Perrault, d'Aulnoy and Grimm.

When Andrew Lang's colour Fairy Books appeared between 1889 and 1910, they codified fairy tale narrative in English. The formative importance of Lang's books for the English can hardly be overestimated, for they became a mother lode for many twentieth-century 'authors' of fairy tales for children. Lang himself firmly believed that fairy tales represented an 'uncontaminated record of our cultural infancy' (cited in Rose 1993: 9), and all twelve of his fairy volumes – Blue, Brown, Crimson, Green, Grey, Lilac, Olive, Orange, Pink, Red, Violet, and Yellow – were 'intended for children', whom he hoped would like 'the old stories that have pleased so many generations' (*Blue Fairy Book*: preface).

Concurrent with Lang's colour Fairy Books were Joseph Jacobs's *English Fairy Tales* (1890) and *More English Fairy Tales* (1894) which were followed by *Celtic Fairy Tales* (1892, 1894) and *Indian Fairy Tales* (1892), but ultimately Lang's fairy tales, with their more accessible prose style, dominated English fairy tale tellings and writings.

The nineteenth century had also seen a return to tales about fairies. John Ruskin can be said to have initiated the movement with his extraordinary fantasy, *The King of the Golden River* (1851). The story's three German-named protagonists, Hans, Schwartz and Gluck, suggest Germanic imaginative ancestry for the book, while its elaborate plot and magical devices link it to French tales about fairies, that flourished in the seventeenth and eighteenth centuries.

Charles Kingsley's *The Water-Babies* (1863), another quasi-tale about fairies, united adventure tale qualities to fairyland characteristics and 'seems like a prospectus for future generations of children's fiction' (Carpenter 1985: 38). The alternative reality it delineated came alive in George MacDonald's classic tales about slightly allegorised fairy-tale-like worlds, *At the Back of the North Wind* (1871), *The Princess and the Goblin* (1872), and *The Princess and Curdie* (1882). With these books, nineteenth-century tales about fairies had transformed themselves into forms that would serve as models for nineteenth- and twentieth-century high fantasy.

In the twentieth century, fairy tales in England's children's literature derived largely from the canon established in the nineteenth century. Modern fairy tales of that pattern can be said to have originated with 'Uncle David's nonsensical story' in Catherine Sinclair's *Holiday House* (1839) (Townsend 1974: 93).

### USA

America's English-language children's books were almost exclusively of English parentage until about 1850, yet fairy books remained conspicuously absent from children's reading, because American intellectuals, and especially the teachers among them, rejected their magic as contradictory to the enlightened rationalism that underlay and guided American political thought. Consequently, they equated tales about fairies and fairy tales with Old World superstition, and held their kings and queens to be antithetical to the concepts of equality on which the new country had been founded. Hence, Perrault's fairy tales remained unavailable in any American printing until Peter Edes's Haverhill edition of 1794, two full generations after their introduction into England.

### Italy, Spain, Portugal

In Italy Basile's tales were published throughout the seventeenth and eighteenth centuries in Naples and several times in the eighteenth century in Bologna. Every printing of fictional narrative provided material for the Italian chapbook trade, and many of Basile's tales found their way into the cheap press and thence to the semi-literate and illiterate population, where they reinforced existing oral tradition and created new narrative lines.

In Spain and Portugal, however, religious regulation and a rigid system of imprimaturs proscribed publication of tales of magic from the early seventeenth century until the beginning of the nineteenth century.

## Readership

From the eighteenth century onward, frontispiece illustrations always included both boys and girls listening raptly to a woman telling, or sometimes reading, fairy tales, or to a man, who was usually shown reading aloud. In the eighteenth and the first half of the nineteenth century, the frontispiece was the only illustration to have formed an integral part of books whose illustrations were otherwise sold separately and only bound in when the text was taken to the bindery for finishing. Picturing boys as well as girls in these pictures, the first a potential buyer would see, can be construed as a marketing device to double the potential buyership, for, in fact, there is much evidence that eighteenth-century fairy tales and tales about fairies were the particular province of girls. Even in the subscription list of Thomas Boreman's *History of Cajanus* (1742), which dealt with a male giant, a breed more generally associated with boys' interests (Wardetzky 1993: 172–198), girls none the less outnumbered boys by a slight margin. In France Mme L'Heritier remembered that fairy tales and tales about fairies were for girls, fables for boys (cited in Warner 1991: 13). Shortly thereafter, Richard Steele, as Isaac Bickerstaff, described the reading habits of his godson and his sister. The boy, he said, read fables, and Betty, his sister, read fairy tales (*Tatler* 95, cited in Macdonald 1982: 106). England's Sarah Fielding confirmed Mme L'Heritier's observation when she produced *The Adventures of David Simple* (1744) a character with whom boys and young men could easily identify, 'a moral Romance' (A 2r) without a single reference to faerie; in *The Governess*, however, she embedded 'Fable and Moral', but her 'fable' included stories of fairy magic.

This pattern of a highly gender-specific readership was broken with the mixed content of *Grimms' Tales*. Along with traditional fairy tales of magic and reversal of fortune that culminated in a wedding, the Grimms included religious tales, nonsense tales, folk-tales, aetiologies, moral tales, burlesques and animal tales. In expanding the 'fairy tale' canon to embrace many forms of the brief narrative (*Märchen*), the Grimms successfully incorporated both boys and girls into their readership. But when, in the twentieth century, the genre in effect contracted to a small corpus of girl tales like 'Cinderella', 'Sleeping Beauty', 'Red Riding Hood' and 'Beauty and the Beast', readership boundaries similarly contracted to a primarily female audience.

## Folk-tales

The definition of folk-tales is more fluid than that of fairy tales and tales about fairies. The term 'folk-tale' normally embraces a multitude of minor genres, like nonsense tales, aetiologies, jests, burlesques, animal tales and neverending tales, but there is good reason to incorporate a discussion of chapbook romances within a consideration of folk-tales in children's literature. *Guy of Warwick, Valentine and Orson*, and *Bevis of Southampton* typify medieval romances that were borne by printing presses into the modern world and carried further on the backs of chapmen to new readers, both young and old. In their medieval original forms their dragons, giants, kings, queens, wicked mothers and faithful fairies provided a cast of characters that fit into the schema of the modern fairy tale, but their sheer length distinguished them from the modern fairy tale. When romances were refashioned for chapbook distribution, however, they were shortened drastically, but kept their familiar panoply of royalty, giants and dragons. Romances required dragons, as the adventure-filled *Seven Champions of Christendom* indicates. Newly assembled in 1596–1597, it included an obligatory dragon, but did without heroic romantic involvement, as befitted its cast of seven national saints as protagonists. *Fortunatus*, another medieval romance, included Oriental magic in the form of a bottomless purse of gold and a hat that could cause him to be transported anywhere in the world. Thus romances were ready made for chapbook wear.

Another set of tales, *Jack and the Giants, Tom Hickathrift, Robin Hood* and *Tom Thumb* embody and thematize the confrontation of small, weak, poor but witty hero against a large, strong, rich, but stupid real or metaphorical giant. The early eighteenth-century chapbook Jack, 'brisk and of a level wit', could irreverently best a clergyman as well as cunningly defeat a giant. He used the common tools of a Cornish miner – horn, shovel and pickaxe – to dig a pit and decoy the giant Cormilan into it, and after killing him, he gained the giant's treasure. Amazing adventures follow hard upon one another – Jack kills several more giants, releases maidens from captivity, succours a virtuous prince and gains magical objects, including a coat that confers invisibility, a cap that furnishes knowledge, a sword that splits whatever it strikes and seven-league boots. With these, Jack overcomes the Devil himself and is made a knight of the Round Table. A second part recounts more encounters with English giants, all of whom Jack gorily vanquishes, their heads being sent to King Arthur as announcement and proof of his valour. Jack himself ends his days married to a duke's daughter and rewarded 'with a very plentiful Estate' where they 'lived the Residue of their Days in great Joy and Happiness' (Opie 1974: 51–65).

Jack, Robin, and the two Toms are true folk heroes who rise from penury to esteem, and whose stories bear many close resemblances to fairy tales. Each of these tales became 'folk-tales' by virtue of their wide chapbook circulation among the 'folk'; and numerous English memoirs – Boswell's, Johnson's, William Cowper's – mention them as beloved, even inspiring, childhood reading. Some, adapted for nineteenth- and early twentieth-century children, have been reprinted.

The term 'folk-tale' suggests an intimate relationship with the folk, and nineteenth-century scholars therefore defined all of these minor genres as belonging peculiarly to unlettered country dwellers. Either as an example of cultural infancy or an artefact of individual maturation, fairy and folk-tales' association with children remained unchallenged until J. R. R. Tolkien disputed the belief that children understood fairy tales better than adults do (Tolkien 1947/1986: 31–62). Unlike fairy tales, nearly all folk-tales enjoy a truly ancient literary lineage. Some folk-tales appear in the Indian *Panchatantra* or in the Bible. Other animal tales derive from classic collections like *Aesop's Tales*, and many burlesques and jokes appear in the text or in the margins of medieval manuscripts.

Children must have overheard folk-tales when they were told in small groups or were alluded to in theatrical productions, but they first made formal contact with children when Latin translations of *Aesop's Tales* were adapted as classics by monastic schools and used as textbooks, a function they continued to serve well into the early modern period.

Animal tales also circulated as part of court literature from the Carolingian period into the high middle ages, when they flowered in Reynard cycles in England, Germany and France. From the thirteenth century onward, preachers integrated Aesopic fables into sermons. It is reasonable to assume that children came into contact with fables in both of these milieus, even though court and church literary traditions would have affected different segments of the population. In the sixteenth century Steinhöwel, Luther, Erasmus and Waldis all prepared fable collections whose contents eventually found their way into school readers, and in the seventeenth century, La Fontaine's humorous and psychologically subtle reworking of Aesopic material became foundational for European children's literature; German writers, like Hagedorn, Gleim, Herder and Lessing, embraced the genre enthusiastically in the eighteenth century, and produced not only collections of tales but also theory about them. Aesopic material, unlike fairy tale magic, was approved for general use in both Catholic and Protestant countries, and hence it joined Bible stories as a source of knowledge shared in common by children all over Europe.

By the eighteenth century, then, the only folk-tale genre to have survived for children's reading was the fable, and it had done so in large part because its brief texts with miniaturised plots could be easily edited to produce a moral acceptable within the reigning social code: a single fable might – and did – have very different morals attached to it at different times, in different places, and for different readerships.

Folktales as a whole, as opposed to the sub-genre of fables, flowered as a component of children's literature in the nineteenth century. The chief source was *Grimms' Tales*, the majority of whose tales derived from folk-tale genres. Clever Gretel, a good example, is a cook who helps herself so generously to the dinner she is preparing for her master and his guest, that not enough remains for their meal. By an ingenious ruse, she scares off the guest and simultaneously blames him for the missing chicken. Generations of little girls have delighted in her clever cover up, and their brothers have similarly enjoyed the antics of Brother Jolly who sinfully transgresses one prohibition after another only to be rewarded with free entry into heaven. The folk-tale component of fairy tale collections expanded with the publication of Ludwig Bechstein's *Deutsches Märchenbuch* (1845 *et seq.*), which incorporated many tales from the *Panchatantra*, like 'The Man and the Serpent' (no. 57).

By the end of the nineteenth century many people believed so unquestioningly in the appropriateness of folk-tales for children, that new stories were collected or composed directly for them. Some of the *Uncle Remus* tales by Joel Chandler Harris (1880 *et seq.*) fit this paradigm. As animal tales whose plots encompass the eternal enmity and repeated encounters between Brer Rabbit and Brer Fox, the Uncle Remus stories bear a close resemblance to the tales of the medieval Reynard cycle that form the basis of so many of the animal tales in *Grimms' Tales*.

A distinctly American folk-tale cycle was composed by the American poet Carl Sandburg in his three volumes of Rootabaga stories (1922, 1923 and 1930). They begin with railroads and continue with a nonsense cast of characters and actions that express mid-Western humour, at once gentle and outlandish. Here, as in other examples of folk-tales in children's literature, generic boundaries remain fluid.

# References

*Arabian Nights Entertainments* (4 vols, 1705-1708), London: Andrew Bell.

[Aulnoy, Marie-Catherine, Mme d'] (3 vols, 1721–1722) *A Collection of Novels and Tales, Written by that Celebrated Wit of France, the Countess d'Anois in Two Volumes*, London: W. Taylor and W. Chetwood.

—— *Les contes des fées* (4 vols, 1710–1715), Paris: Claude Barbin.

[Boreman, T.] (1742) *The History of Cajanus, the Swedish Giant, from his Birth to the Present Time. By the Author of the Gigantick Histories*, London: Thomas Boreman.

Bottigheimer, R. (1990) 'Ludwig Bechstein's fairy tales: nineteenth century bestsellers and *Bürgerlichkeit*', *Internationales Archiv für Sozialgeschichte der deutschten Literatur*, Tübingen: Max Niemeyer 55–88.

—— (1993) 'Sixteenth-century tale collections and their use in the *Kinder- und Hausmärchen*', *Monatshefte* 84, 4: 472–490.

Briggs, K. (1976) *A Dictionary of Fairies*, Harmondsworth: Penguin.

—— (1978) *The Vanishing People*, London: Batsford.

Caradec, F. (1977) *Historie de la littérature enfantine en France*, Paris: Albin Michel.

Carpenter, H. (1985) *Secret Gardens: The Golden Age of Children's Literature From 'Alice in Wonderland' to 'Winnie-the-Pooh'*, Boston: Houghton Mifflin.

[Cooper, J.] (1790) *The Oriental Moralist or The Beauties of the Arabian Nights Entertainments translated from the original & accompanied with suitable reflexions adapted to each story by the Revd Mr Cooper Author of the History of England &c &c &c*, London: E. Newbery.

Darton, F. J. H. (1932/1982) *Children's Books in England. Three Centuries of Social Life*, 3rd edn, rev. B. Alderson, Cambridge: Cambridge University Press.

Davis, J. H. Jr (1987) *The Happy Island: Images of Childhood in the Eighteenth-Century Théâtre d'Education*, New York: Peter Lang.

Ewers, H.-H. (1984) *Kinder- und Jugendliteratur der Romantik*, Stuttgart: Phillip Reclam Jun.

[Fielding, S.] (1744) *The Adventures of David Simple: Containing an Account of his Travels Through the Cities of London and Westminster, In the Search of A REAL FRIEND. By a Lady. In Two Volumes*, London: A. Millar.

—— (1749) *The Governess; or Little Female Academy. Being the History of Mrs Teachum, and her NINE GIRLS. With their Nine Days of Amusement. Calculated for the Entertainment, and Instruction of young LADIES in their Education.* By the Author of David Simple. London, A. Millar.

[Fontaine, N.] (1708) *The History of Genesis*, London: Andrew Bell.

Goldstone, B. P. (1984) *Lessons to be Learned: A Study of Eighteenth Century Didactic Children's Literature*, New York: Peter Lang.

Grätz, Manfred (1988) *Das Märchen in der deutschen Aufklärung: Vom Feenmärchen zum Volksmärchen* Stuttgart: Metzler.

Grimm, W. and Grimm, J. (2 vols, 1812, 1815, *et seq.*) *Kinder- und Hausmärchen*, Berlin: Reimer.

—— (2 vols, 1823, 1826) *German Popular Stories*, trans. E. Taylor, London: C. Baldwin (1823); J. Robins [1826].

Holbek, B. (1987) *Interpretation of Fairy Tales*, Folklore Fellows Communications 239, Helsinki: Academia Scientarum Fennica.

Jackson, M. (1989) *Engines of Instruction, Mischief, and Magic: Children's Literature in England from its Beginnings to 1839*, Lincoln, NB: University of Nebraska Press.

Jan, I. (1974) *On Children's Literature*, New York: Schocken.

Kamenetsky, C. (1984) *Children's Literature in Hitler's Germany*, Athens, OH: Ohio University Press.

Lang, A. (*c.*1889) *The Blue Fairy Book*, London: Longman, Green.

Leprince de Beaumont, M. (1756) *Magasin des Enfans, ou Dialogues entre une sage governante et plusieus de ses élives de la première dislimitive ... on y donne un Abrégés de l'Historie Sacrée, de la Fable, de la Geographic*, London: J. Haberkorn.

Locke, J. (1693) *Some Thoughts Concerning Education*, London: J. Churchill.

MacDonald, R. K. (1982) *Literature for Children in England and America from 1646 to 1774*, Troy, NY: Whitston.

Opie, I. and Opie, P. (1974) *The Classic Fairy Tales*, London: Oxford University Press.

Perrault, C. (1697) *Histoires ou Contes du Temps Passé*, Paris: Claude Barbin.

—— (1729) *Histories, or Tales of Past Times*, London: L. Pote and R. Montague.

Pickering, S. F., Jr (1993) *Moral Instruction and Fiction for Children, 1749–1820*, Athens, GA: University of Georgia Press.

Rose, J. (1993) *The Case of Peter Pan, or the Impossibility of Children's Fiction*, Philadephia: University of Pennsylvania Press.

Steinlein, R. (1987) *Die domestizierte Phantasie: Studien zur Kinderliteratur, Kinderlektüre und Literaturpädagogik des 18. und frühen 19. Jahrhunderts*, Heidelberg: Carl Winter.

Summerfield, G. (1984) *Fantasy and Reason: Children's Literature in the Eighteenth Century*, Athens, GA: University of Georgia Press.

Tenèze, M. L. (1979) 'Bibliothèque bleue', *Enzyklopädie des Märchens* 2 283–287.

Tolkien, J. R. R. (1947/1986) *The Tolkien Reader*, New York: Ballantyne.

Townsend, J. R. (1974) *Written for Children*, New York: Lippincott.

Wardetzky, K. (1993) *Märchen-Lesarten von Kindern*, Berlin: Lang.

Warner M. (1991) *The Absent Mother, or Women Against Women in the 'Old Wives Tale'*, Hilversum, Verloren.

—— (1994) *From the Beast to the Blonde: On Fairytales and their Tellers*, London: Chatto and Windus.

# 14

# Myth and Legend

## Maurice Saxby

Speaking about his collaboration with Leon Garfield when they were reframing some of the ancient Greek myths as *The God Beneath the Sea* Edward Blishen said, 'It was like working with a sort of radium of story'. (Blishen 1979: 33). It is this 'original tremendous *concentrate* of story' (33) embedded in myth and legend that, as Sir Philip Sidney expressed it, 'holdeth children from play, and old men from the chimney corner'. The very impulse that gave birth to myth and legend makes them the right and proper fare for all children, especially for those growing up in a technological and rational society.

At the heart of mythology – *mythos*, a story – is imagination, creativity, the urge to understand, to explain and to embellish. Throughout the ages all cultures have developed a body of myth and legend, at first as an oral tradition, then ultimately fixed in clay, stone, papyrus, vellum or paper and elevated to literature – if not always to sacred lore and belief. While folk- and fairy tale, myth, legend and epic hero tales are all threads of one vast story it would seem that myth, a universal phenomenon, is the progenitor. The folk-tale, 'Little Red Riding Hood', for example, in the version where Red Riding Hood is released from the stomach of the wolf to be reborn could well be a remnant of a nature myth explaining the setting and the rising of the sun.

For myth grows out of the need to form hypotheses and create explanations for natural phenomena: how the world came into being; the formation of rivers, lakes, mountains and other geographical features; why spring always follows winter just as the dawn always rises to herald the new day that will end with sunset. More than that, it seeks to explain what lies beyond the dawn and the sunset, beyond the edge of vision, beyond the immediately observable and knowable: what worlds, celestial kingdoms or nether regions exist beyond the horizon, above the sky or beneath the earth. Myth deals with imponderables: where, how and why did life as we know it originate; what supernatural being/s pre-existed human life; from whence did mortals come and whither are they bound. Just as imperative are questions about human nature and behaviour. What is the nature of 'good' and 'evil'? When does folly slide over into sin? What fearful consequences follow disobedience of the 'Law'? Are the wages of sin always the death of the spirit?

So myth postulates life before birth and an after life. It fashions a pantheon of deities, demi-gods, nymphs, satyrs and a multitude of other supernatural creatures. It seeks to explain the ways of the gods, the relationship of those gods with humanity and the consequences of divine anger. It chronicles the human longing for immortality, the passionate search for the water of everlasting life and eternal youth, the hope of bliss beyond the sufferings and trials of earthly life and the fear of eternal damnation.

The form and tone of the *mythos*, the environmental details, the characteristics and attributes of the local deities, spirits and the human participants in the drama vary with the culture that gave the stories birth. The myths of ancient Greece, which have most influenced the Western world, reflect the pure light, the blue skies, the lofty mountains, the plains and olive groves that shaped the lives of its people. Those of the Vikings are starker, harsher, grimmer and icier as befits a landscape of forests, passes and ravines, bordered by sometimes perilous seas. The myths of India and the east are more exotic, colourful and flamboyant; those of the Australian Aborigines express a spirituality embedded in the land itself. Myth and legend, being truly multicultural, introduce children to a diversity of national temperaments and to different ways of confronting universal and ongoing questions about life and human nature.

But because all races throughout time have been awed by the unknown and the unknowable, that wonder, when expressed through myth is elevated to religion. Gods not only demand obedience, reverence and worship but at times they require propitiation and appeasement. Here again the ancient Greeks were more light-hearted and less reverent than, say, the Egyptians or Sumerians. Because the Greek immortals frequently trafficked with mortals (Zeus fathered heroes such as Perseus and Heracles who were thus demigods) they were not always treated with the respect demanded by the gods of other nations. And Hera, the wife of Zeus, was often driven by jealousy and rage to shrewishness. So by exposure to a rich array of mythology young readers gain an insight into human nature and are confronted with the essence of the divine and the supernatural.

Because of this, mythology gives rise to ceremony and ritual, an ongoing necessity in human behaviour. Even when ritual is minimalised, as it is in some religious groups or sects, it tends to be replaced by even more rigid rules and regulations, often more stringently enforced than what was abandoned.

Moreover, myth is rich in symbols, and human existence is governed largely by metaphor. Even vehicles are controlled by road signs and highway symbols. So the odyssey in myth, legend and epic is often dangerous and demanding, even with its detours and resting places, but leads ultimately to home and fulfilment. It is an image of a universal life experience, but on a vast scale. In all cultures the heroic journey involves rivers that must be breasted, bridges to cross, mountains to climb: all symbols of life's progress. The monsters – be they dragons, trolls or demons – are local expressions of a universal fear and uncertainty. On life's journey each mortal, like the superheroes of myth and legend often encounters a tutelary figure or receives unexpected aid from the Immortals, often in human guise. The powers of darkness that lurk by the wayside can be vanquished only if the traveller does not faint, is of unshakeable faith and wields the sword of understanding and action fashioned long ages ago and passed on from generation to generation. The slain dragon yields its gold to the victor, and if the conqueror has the resolution of a Sigurd and plucks out the heart of a Fafnir and tastes its blood upon the tongue, that individual will then understand the call of the birds, comprehend what the beasts are saying and grow wise in the ways of nature.

At some crisis point or points all humanity, like Cuchulain (hero of the great Irish saga, known as the Ulster Cycle, collected between about 100 BC and AD 100) will be confronted by a dark and brooding shadow whose menace chills the soul. It is the same shadow, the black side of his nature that Ged is forced to face in Ursula Le Guin's mythic novel, *A Wizard of Earthsea*. Cuchulain leaps his salmon leap at the monster shadow and disperses it with his sword. Ged stares down his shadow through the power of the mind. Both stories carry an urgent message for today's readers.

The border between myth and legend is ill-defined. Traditionally legend is story passed down by word of mouth from former times and popularly accepted as historical. However, in the passage of time detail is added, the protagonist glorified and raised in heroic status. The superheroes, often of semi-divine origin, create their own legend within the myth of their race: Theseus, Perseus, Jason, Heracles, Odysseus and their company from Greece; Gilgamesh from Sumeria; Sigurd and Vainamoinen from old Scandinavia; Moses and Samson of the Old Testament; Beowulf, Arthur and Cuchulain from ancient Britain; Roland of France; El Cid of Spain and Maui of the Pacific are but a few. All have elements of the supernatural woven into their mythic life stories.

So, too, have many of the saints, prophets, seers and holy ones. Miracles of healing are attributed to saints such as Catherine of Siena, and Guanyin, the Chinese Goddess of Mercy. Siddharta, a prince from north India and the future Buddha, is conceived after musical instruments play celestial music without the aid of human hands, trees have burst spontaneously into flower, and rivers have ceased to flow in order to witness the miracle that is taking place. The death of the wise and charitable Countess Cathleen of Ireland drives away the pestilence that has scourged her country, and she joins the hosts of heaven, sanctified by love. Joan of Arc of France is elevated to sainthood because she obeys implicitly her heavenly voices. The German saint, Hildegard of Bingen (1098–1179), was a visionary whose music is still played today and whose poems are now believed to be prophetic warnings against the pollution and contamination of a selfish world:

> There issues forth an unreality
> An overpowering, dark cloud of menace,
> That withers the earth's green shoots,
> And shrivels fruit upon the bough
> Fruit that was meant to give the people food.
>
> Saxby 1990: 118

Both Catherine and Hildegard are examples of practical, strong-minded women who challenged evil and corruption as they saw it, even in the Church, to the Pope himself.

Stories of the saints, martyrs, wise and holy men and women have long been passed down by word of mouth and then enshrined in written literature because of their inspirational quality: holiness backed up by steadfastness of purpose, resolute action and nobility of spirit. They still have a much-needed place in the literature for the children of a cynical and materialistic age. They are the prototypes for the plethora of tales of the supernatural, the fighting fantasies and those spurious stories of apocalyptic battles between the powers of light and the demons of doom that currently pervade children's literature. From these archetypes have evolved the swaggering celluloid supermen of Hollywood, the witches, wizards and warlocks of pulp fiction. Only rarely does the synthetic hero have the enduring quality of those who were given literary permanence in heroic literature.

The ongoing quest for 'stars' in the contemporary media, be they sports persons, entertainers or even humanitarians is also indicative of the same urge to worship that has give lasting life to the legendary folk heroes from around the world: Robin Hood, William Tell, Boadicea, Pochahontas, Davy Crockett or Lady Godiva. They are all larger-than-life characters whose exploits have perhaps been romanticised but who for that very reason stir the popular imagination and fulfil an ongoing human need to reverence the spark of nobility within ordinary people. Such heroes, because they belong to a specific family, society, tribe or region provide a sense of identity for those whose roots are in that culture as well as a cross-cultural reference in a world where internationalism is seen as desirable; but not at the cost of losing pride in one's country.

Myth and legend perhaps provide the most potent form of literature that can be offered to children – for a variety of reasons. Not only are they archetypes, but they generate linguistic power, stir the imagination, ease anxiety and help bring about inner harmony and much-needed emotional and spiritual wholeness.

So called 'high' fantasy such as that of J. R. R. Tolkien's *The Hobbit*, and especially his *Lord of the Rings* trilogy, sometimes described as 'mythological epic' creatively synthesises elements from myth and legend (the journey, battle and pursuit) with medieval romance and boys' adventure literature. The Australian, Patricia Wrightson, in her *Book of Wirrun* takes her Aboriginal hero on an epic journey across Australia. The creatures he encounters such as the water spirit, the Yunggamurra, although derived from Aboriginal mythology are universally recurring images.

From the epic hero tale comes adventure and survival literature – from *Robinson Crusoe* to Ann Holm's *I am David*, Ian Serraillier's *The Silver Sword*, Ivan Southall's *Ash Road* or Cynthia Voigt's *Homecoming*. Each involves a journey of sorts, a disaster, and survival through grit, determination and moral integrity. In all such novels there is a moral dilemma and a social problem just as there is in heroic literature. So the seeds of the contemporary problem novel are to be found in traditional literature. Children immersed in that literature absorb not only the structure and pattern of story which thus enables them to appreciate the most demanding contemporary writing but they are empowered linguistically.

Apart from the ringing tone and heightened language of the better retellings – to which we will return later in the chapter – our vocabulary and usage are enriched, unconsciously, by references to myth and legend: a jovial chap; a mercurial disposition; the Midas touch; even brand names such as Cyclops or Excalibur.

Even more importantly the ancient tales demonstrate the universality and ongoing nature of the human condition. The televised cry of the distraught mother of an abducted child, 'Please give me back my daughter!' echoes the story of Demeter's search for Persephone, carried off by Hades, the black monarch of the Underworld to his nether kingdom, so swiftly that only Hecate, the queen of black magic and evil ghosts saw her go.

When night fell and Persephone failed to return home, her mother sent out a search party; and Demeter joined the searchers, lighting torches from the fires of the volcano, Etna, so as to search through nine long, grief-filled days and nights. She ate no food, she didn't wash, and she took no rest. On the tenth night, when no moon shone, Hecate came out of the cave and appeared before the bereft mother.

Saxby 1990: 26

Medea's slaying of her children because Jason has cast her aside for another woman who would advance his fortunes in the ancient city of Corinth is an archetypal story of what is happening all too frequently in our own culture. Perseus leaves home and goes forth to slay the Medusa because an evil Polydectes lusts after his mother and sends Perseus on a dangerous errand. Perseus, like any jealous but protective son, uses his grizzly trophy to render Polydectes impotent by turning him into stone.

The ancient Greeks knew all about catharsis – the purging of the emotions by being party to true tragedy, which evokes both pity and terror. Such potent stories reflect an ongoing temper of mind and are products not just of a particular period or a specific culture. No other stories offer children the same imaginative or emotional depth, the same insight into the human condition and the essential truth of universal experience. They provide children with something of the same kind of experience that adults find in *King Lear* or *Crime and Punishment*. Whereas the protagonists of the fairy tale live 'happily ever after' the heroes (male or female) of myth and legend don't necessarily triumph in the end. They have harder choices to make than Jack climbing his beanstalk. For they are often dogged by misfortune or traits of character. Pride – or hubris – always leads to nemesis; the downfall of the hero, as it does with Roland of France. But as with Roland his ultimate triumph is not as important as his persistence, courage and integrity. Without being overtly didactic the stories of myth and legend have an inherent moral. Icarus flies too close to the sun and plummets to the sea. Orpheus looks back (remember Lot's wife!) and must return from the Underworld bereft and alone. A taboo has not been heeded. So Orpheus is doomed to wander an earth which has lost its sweetness. Yet he endures; singing to the end: and his lyre is set among the stars.

We might well ask as did Paul Hazard:

How would heroism be kept alive in our ageing earth if not by each fresh, young generation that begins anew the epic of the human race? The finest and noblest of books intended for children tell of heroism. They are the inspiration of those who, in later life, sacrifice themselves that they may secure safety for others.

Hazard 1947: 170

So it is with Beowulf – or King Arthur, who some say:

sleeps still in Avalon, while his wounds heal, awaiting the call to the upper world as king in the hour of his country's need. Others say that he sleeps in the fiery cradle of Etna or at Snowdon in Wales, or at Glastonbury. Perhaps he rests in the hearts of all noble men. Hic Iacet Arthurus, Rex Quondam que Futurus – Here lies Arthur, the Once and Future King.

Saxby 1989: 141

This is the hope that myth and legend sets before us: that we all, if we pursue our odyssey to the end, will find ourselves and thus be saved: and in saving ourselves we save the world. It is thus that the world is being constantly redeemed and renewed.

Plato, in *The Republic*, states that the ultimate goal of education should be to create in children an active imagination, because imagination, he claims, is the means through which we recreate the world, and we each rediscover the meaning and significance of life, experience the joy of being alive. Plato would educate children through myth, through story and through folklore. Aristotle claims that the friend of wisdom is also the friend of myth.

In more recent times, Joseph Campbell, the author of *The Hero with a Thousand Faces* maintains that myths are metaphors or fields of reference to what ordinarily can't be known or named. He says that they are guiding signs to a deep, rich, satisfying inner life, a vivifying spiritual experience. Campbell points out that in medieval times the tallest building in any city was the tower of the church, temple or mosque whereas today it is an office block – to which could be added, the television tower. In forsaking myth for technology and commerce a society runs the risk of being inwardly impoverished. We can now bring Mount Olympus into close range with our giant telescopes; listen through our headsets to the music of the spheres; read and print out the pronouncements of the oracle from the computer screen. Hermes has been replaced by the fax machine.

Yet the awesome wonder of the old tales remains; but only if the versions and retellings remain true to the spirit of the originals, as far as we can trace them. The prototypes of many myths and legends, however, have come down to us in fragmented form and are not accessible or even suitable for use with children.

In ancient days tales of heroes were often sung by minstrels and gathered by poets in the form of an epic: a long narrative verse cycle clustered around the exploits of a named hero who embodied the cultural symbols and qualities which the society held dear. The first known and recorded epic would appear to be the legend of Gilgamesh sung to the harp by Sumerians and recorded in clay some 3,000 years before Christ. It exalts the wondrous exploits of Gilgamesh, King of Uruk, and celebrates his friendship with Enkidu. It probes the mysteries of life and whatever is beyond it. *The Epic of Gilgamesh*: an English version with an introduction by N. K. Sanders (1980) is a source book for retellings such as that in Maurice Saxby's *The Great Deeds of Superheroes*, the introduction to which, 'We all need heroes' includes a comprehensive table charting the heroic pattern in myth and legend (Saxby 1989: 6–12). (A companion volume, *The Great Deeds of Heroic Women* (Saxby 1990) retells stories of goddesses, saints, warrior women and strong females who became legends in their own time.) The Gilgamesh story has been used by Ludmila Zeman as the basis for two rich and lavish picture books, *Gilgamesh the King* (1992) and *The Revenge of Ishtar* (1993), illustrated in Sumerian art style. The text, which is pitched at the newly independent reader, is pared down to an accessible level without being impoverished.

Myths and legends from ancient Greece used with children today come largely from Homer's epic poems, the *Iliad* and the *Odyssey* (*c.*850 BC) telling the story of the Trojan War and its aftermath. After the fall of Troy, between 600 and 700 BC, Hesiod, Homer, Pindar and other Greek writers collected and wrote down the myths of the gods and the legendary stories of the heroes. Apollonius of Rhodes (*c.*305–235 BC) and Apollodorus (fl. *c.*AD 100) also gave us versions of the stories. Other sources are the odes of Pindar (*c.*502–446 BC) and the Greek dramatists, Sophocles (born *c.*496 BC) and Euripides (born *c.*480 BC) as well as the *Metamorphoses* of the Roman poet, Ovid in the first century BC. Many of the common myths have been pieced together from several sources – fragments of poems and references in plays – and there are variant versions, even among the writers of the ancient world, as detailed by Robert Graves in *The Greek Myths*. Yet when they are retold faithfully the Greek tales are staggering in their imaginative power and psychological insight and are always intensely dramatic. Lillian Smith (1953: 66) has said that 'to read them is to experience the wonder of the morning of the world'. It is also to experience the aspirations, joys, terrors, defeats, triumphs and the creative energy of humankind throughout the ages.

As few today can read ancient Greek we are dependent on translations such as those of E. V. Rieu, whose *Iliad* and *Odyssey* would seem to capture the swift stateliness of Homer's narration along with the detail of everyday life in ancient Greece. For young readers there is poetry and dignity as well as swift narrative action in Rosemary Sutcliff's *The Black Ships Before Troy: The Story of the Iliad* (1993), combining as it does, the drama of human emotion and that of a ferocious naval and military campaign. Alan Lee's universal 'Greek' style illustrations both here and in Sutcliff's *The Wanderings of Odysseus* (1994) harmoniously complement the text; and with the 'picture story' format of the book add tremendously to the reader appeal. Remarkably, most retellings of the *Odyssey* including that of Barbara Leonie Picard for the Oxford Myths and Legends series retain a third person narrative throughout. In Homer, however, when Odysseus in Part II is presented to Alcinous, King of Phaecia the hero narrates in the first person his adventures from his imprisonment on Calypso's isle to his arrival at the palace of Alcinous. One of the few recent children's versions to retain this structure is by Robin Lister (1987). Lister and his illustrator, Alan Baker have collaborated successfully here and in *The Story of King Arthur* (1988) to produce eye-catching illustrations and euphonious texts of two of the world's most potent stories.

One of the first to recognise the literary merit of the Greek tales for children was Nathaniel Hawthorne. In *A Wonder Book* (1851) he retells them in lush but vivid prose, treating them more as fairy tales than as high drama. He adds his own detail, giving Midas a daughter whom he calls Marygold and who is turned into gold by her father along with everything else he touches.

Hawthorne's cavalier treatment of the text motivated Charles Kingsley to restore the purity of the tales. In his introduction to *The Heroes* (1856) Kingsley wrote, 'Now, I love these old Hellens heartily', and so proclaimed his enthusiasm for the language as well as the story. His version is lofty in idealism yet homely in detail, poetic in expression yet dramatic in action. The stories as he tells them reflect his belief that we 'call it a "heroic" thing to suffer pain and grief, that we may do good to our fellow men'.

Later Padraic Colum in *The Golden Fleece and the Heroes Who Lived before Achilles* (1921) used the technique of having Orpheus sing the stories to the heroes as they sailed in search of the golden fleece. His retelling is poetic and full of wonder. Yet he is not in awe of the gods, but treats them with familiar respect.

Since Hawthorne, Kingsley and Colum versions of the Greek stories have proliferated. For the reteller it is easy to seize upon a tailor-made story and recount it in facile, easily digestible prose. Sheila Egoff dismisses most modern retellers, such as Roger Lancelyn Green in *Tales of the Greek Heroes* (1958) and Doris Gates in *The Warrior Goddess: Athena* (1972) as 'faceless and styleless' (Egoff 1981: 214). While Green is certainly no stylist, and he lacks Kingsley's 'awesome wonder', he tells the stories clearly and dramatically, preserving traditional story lines and making them accessible to young readers. Through his collections he has provided a basic introduction to a wide range of traditional literature: *King Arthur and His Knights of the Round Table* (1953), *Tales of the Greek Heroes* (1958), *The Tale of Troy* (1958), *Myths of the Norsemen* (1960), *The Luck of Troy* (1961) and *Tales of Ancient Egypt* (1967).

Current publishing projects to keep the Greek and Roman myths and legends alive for a contemporary audience have had mixed success. Anthony Horowitz's retellings for *The Kingfisher Book of Myths and Legends* (1985) are workmanlike and make for easy if not inspired reading. Most disappointing are Geraldine McCaughrean's versions for *The Orchard Book of Greek Myths* (1992). Here the tragedy of Persephone is reduced to melodrama through banal dialogue and trite narrative. Persephone, captured by Pluto [Hades] cries out: ' "Who are you? What do you want of me? Oh let me go! Help me, somebody! Mother, help me!" '; in the Underworld Persephone sobs: ' "I want to go home! I want my mother!" '; and Demeter calls: ' "Persephone darling! Time to go home!" ' (McCaughrean 1992: 16).

Of the recent picture story books based on myths and legends those retold and illustrated by Warwick Hutton – *Theseus and the Minotaur* (1989), *The Trojan Horse* (1992) and *Perseus* (1993) – remain faithful to the traditional storyline but are told simply and directly as adventure stories in language adapted to the ability of newly independent readers. Hutton's illustrations are modern interpretations of classical Greek design.

The source for retellings of the Norse myths is, in the main, two thirteenth-century Icelandic sagas compiled after Iceland had been Christianised for over one hundred years: the so-called *Elder Edda* of thirty-four poems, sometimes referred to as the *Iliad* of the North, and the *Younger Edda*, a prose collection written partly by Snorri Sturluson who lived between about 1179 and 1241. The dramatic succinctness yet the imaginative power of these stories has been faithfully retained in Dorothy Hosford's *Thunder of the Gods* (1952) while her earlier *Songs of the Volsungs* (1949) is a prose adaptation of William Morris's verse drama *Sigurd the Volsung*; his version of the ancient *Volsunga Saga* of Sigmund and his son Sigurd. Hosford's account of the Death of Balder is told with stark directness and moving simplicity yet with the pathos and intensity of the old Eddas.

Kevin Crossley-Holland, a later reteller, has by his own admission, not hesitated to develop hints of action in the Eddas, flesh out dramatic situations and add snatches of dialogue, to hone some sound or meaning. Hence his *Axe-Age*,

*Wolf-Age: A Selection from the Norse Myths* (1985) and *Northern Lights: Legends, Sagas and Folk-tales* (1987) have a hard glittering edge as befits the 'fatalism, courage, loyalty, superstition, cunning, melancholy, a sense of wonder, curiosity about all that's new' which in his foreword to *The Faber Book of Northern Legends* (1977) he claims as the 'most pronounced strain in the make-up of the Germanic heroic peoples, as revealed through their prose and poetry' (Crossley-Holland 1977: 20). This author's sombre yet ringing prose version (1982) of *Beowulf* the Anglo-Saxon poem, dating back to before AD 1000 is extended to become an atmospheric horror-hero story by Charles Keeping's chilling black and white drawings. (Rosemary Sutcliff has also retold the story of Beowulf in prose as *Beowulf: Dragon Slayer* (1966), while Ian Serraillier tells the tale in verse, *Beowulf the Warrior* (1954)). As with Keeping's illustrations for Leon Garfield and Edward Blishen's sagas of creation and the early Greek world, *The God Beneath the Sea* (1970) and *The Golden Shadow* (1973), there is an overtone of sexuality which is often latent but at times explicit in the early stories themselves.

Also at times chilled by northern mist and tempest is the *Kalevala: The Land of Heroes* fragments of heroic songs collected by a nineteenth-century Finnish folklorist and poet, Elias Lonnrot. These songs tell of Vainamoinen the Wise, Ilmarinen the Smith and the hare-brained rogue, Lemminkainen, and of their feud with Mistress Louhi, the sorceress of the bitter North. Ursula Synge has retold the stories in lyric prose in *Kalevala: Heroic Tales from Finland* (1977); and a striking picture book for young children, *Louhi Witch of North Farm* (1986) has text by Toni de Gerez and ice-cold pictures by Barbara Cooney.

Since Caxton printed Mallory's *Morte d'Arthur* in 1485 the Arthurian romances have attracted many scholarly retellings as well as popularised chapbook versions. Robin Hood stories taken from early ballads and oral sources have also proliferated. From America has come Howard Pyle's grandly medieval cycle of both the Robin Hood (1883) and Arthurian stories (1903). But perhaps the finest modern interpreter of the old hero tales from the Middle Ages has been Rosemary Sutcliff. Her Arthurian trilogy remains one of the most accessible and poetic yet scholarly versions for children and adults – *The Sword and the Circle: King Arthur and the Knights of the Round Table* (1981); *The Light Beyond the Forest: The Quest for the Holy Grail* (1979); and *The Road to Camlann: The Death of King Arthur* (1981). Her *Tristan and Iseult* (1971) pares away accretions to the romantic love story to lay bare in taut narrative the stark tragedy of the star-crossed lovers.

A latter-day Celtic revival was perhaps fuelled by the publication in 1949 of a translation of the thirteenth-century Welsh classic, *The Mabinogion* by Gwyn Jones and Thomas Jones. Here the story is dense and concentrated, and daunting to young readers. More easily digestible are the tales from the *Mabinogion* included in Barbara Leonie Picard's *Hero Tales from the British Isles* (1963) and Gwyn Jones's *Welsh Legends and Folktales* (1955). Gwyn Jones and Kevin Crossley-Holland collaborated to tell in measured prose *Tales from the Mabinogion* (1984) with strong, stylised illustrations by Margaret Jones.

A comprehensive analysis of available editions of myths, legends and fairy tales up to 1976 is Elizabeth Cook's *The Ordinary and the Fabulous* (2nd edn, 1976), while Mary Steele in 1989 compiled *Traditional Tales: A Signal Bookguide* which details then available collections of legend and hero tales, Norse myths, Irish myths, Welsh legends, Greek legends, Robin Hood stories and Traditional tales from around the world.

Perhaps one of the most useful references to world mythology is the Hodder and Stoughton series of some twelve titles ranging from *Gods, Men and Monsters from Greek Mythology* (1977) to *Warriors, Gods and Spirits from Central American Mythology* (1983). Each volume sets the stories in their cultural and historical context, the retellings are dramatic, vivid and arresting; the illustrations colourful and energetic. For children exploring world mythology they provide an invaluable resource. Similarly Penelope Farmer's *Beginnings: Creation Myths of the World* (1978) and John Bailey's *Gods and Men: Myths and Legends from the World's Religions* (1981) although spare and tightly told are useful springboards for further research.

Each year new versions of mythic and heroic literature are published for the children's market. Geraldine McCaughrean in 1989 produced a lively and dramatic retelling of the story of a hero whose exploits were the subject of medieval manuscripts of the twelfth and thirteenth centuries in Latin, Hebrew, Arabic and Spanish, *El Cid*. In 1992 appeared Margaret Hodges's adaptation of the Cervantes novel *Don Quixote and Sancho Panza* (1605–1615) as a 'literary' hero tale. Among notable picture book additions to the field is Margaret Early's *William Tell* (1991).

The loom of myth and legend is seemingly never still, even today. The *mythos* of south-east Asia, Third World countries, the Middle East, Australia and Papua New Guinea, for example, are slowly being woven from their oral sources. In time they will take their place with those from Europe, the Near East and the old world to provide children the world over with a fabric which is both timeless and multicultural.

## References

Blishen, E. (1979) 'The impulse to story', in Saxby, M. (ed.) *Through Folklore to Literature*, Sydney: IBBY Publications.

Campbell, J. (1988) *The Hero With a Thousand Faces*, London: Paladin.

Cook, E. (1976) *The Ordinary and the Fabulous*, 2nd edn, Cambridge: Cambridge University Press.

Crossley-Holland, K. (1977) *The Faber Book of Northern Legends*, London: Faber.

Egoff, S. (1981) *Thursday's Child: Trends and Patterns in Contemporary Children's Literature*, Chicago: American Library Association.

Graves, R. (1960) *The Greek Myths*, London: Penguin.

Hazard, P. (1947) *Books, Children and Men*, trans. M. Mitchell, Boston: American Library Association.

McCaughrean, G. (1992) *The Orchard Book of Greek Myths*, London: Orchard.

Saxby, M. (1989) *The Great Deeds of Superheroes*, Sydney: Millennium.

—— (1990) *The Great Deeds of Heroic Women*, Sydney: Millennium.

Smith, L. (1953) *The Unreluctant Years: A Critical Approach to Children's Literature*, Chicago: American Library Association.

Steele, M. (1989) *Traditional Tales: A Signal Bookguide*, South Woodchester: Thimble Press.

## Further Reading

Armour, R. A. (1986) *Gods and Myths of Ancient Egypt*, Cairo: The American University in Cairo Press.

Brunel, P. (ed.) (1992) *Companion to Literary Myths, Heroes and Archetypes*, London: Routledge.

Butler, B. (1975) *The Myth of the Hero*, London: Rider.

Cotterell, A. (ed.) *The Illustrated Encyclopedia of Myths and Legends*, London: Marshall.

Davidson, H. R. E. (1964) *Gods and Myths of Northern Europe*, Harmondsworth: Penguin.

Larve, G. A. (1975) *Ancient Myth and Modern Man*, Englewood Cliffs, NJ: Prentice-Hall.

Lévi-Strauss, C. (1978) *Myth and Meaning*, London: Routledge.

Murray, H. A. (ed.) (1960) *Myth and Mythmaking*, Boston: Beacon Press.

Sirk, G. S. (1970) *Myth, Its Meaning and Functions in Ancient and Other Cultures*, Cambridge: Cambridge University Press.

Willis, R. (1993) *World Mythology: the Illustrated Guide*, London: Duncan Baird.

# 15

# Playground Rhymes and the Oral Tradition

## *Iona Opie*

The traditional verbal lore available to children up to the age of about eleven includes nursery rhymes, nonsense and satirical verse, riddles, spooky narratives, verses to chant at particular times of the year, trickery and repartee, formulas with which to regulate relationships, counting-out rhymes, and the songs and dialogues that accompany various kinds of games.

A child's first experience of the charms of tradition is in the form of a lullaby (the word means 'lull to bye-byes', that is, to sleep). Lullabies must be the most instinctive music in the world; a woman with a child in her arms automatically rocks it and sings. Even today, the song may be only a repetition of meaningless hushing syllables sung to a spontaneous tune, but more often than not a young mother will sing a lullaby handed down in her own family, possibly for generations. The tune is more important than the words, for if the tune is soothing, the infant cannot know whether it is being bribed into quietness (Dinna mak' a din,/An' ye'll get a cakie/When the baker comes in) or threatened (Baby, baby, naughty baby/Hush you squalling thing, I say). Nor can it be frightened by the story line of the best known of all lullabies, Hush-a-bye, baby, on the tree top,/When the wind blows the cradle will rock,/When the bough breaks the cradle will fall,/Down will come baby, cradle and all.

Lullabies come under the heading of nursery rhymes, that comprehensive collection of songs and verses which assist grown-ups in pacifying and entertaining children from birth to the age of about 5. Known as Mother Goose rhymes in the eighteenth century after the influential nursery rhyme booklet *Mother Goose's Melody*, (*c*.1765), probably compiled by Oliver Goldsmith, they have retained the appellation in the USA. In England the term 'nursery rhymes' began to be used soon after the turn of the century, promoted by Ann and Jane Taylor's immensely successful *Rhymes for the Nursery* (1806), and James Kendrew of York's pirated edition of 1812, which was entitled *Nursery Rhymes, for the Amusement of Children*. The earliest record of the term having entered the language is in *The British Review*, August 1815, when the reviewer of Wordsworth's *The Excursion* took to task those who were currently condemning his poems as being 'beneath the dignity of what they call poetry, and as worthy only of being celebrated in nursery-rhymes'.

The huge diversity of the nursery rhyme corpus (there are 800 rhymes in *The Oxford Nursery Rhyme Book* (Opie and Opie 1955) includes verses suited to every practical purpose as well as songs to take the imagination soaring. There are baby games to play with the child's features, fingers and toes, dandling rhymes and knee rides; and occasional rhymes to chant when it is raining or snowing, or when a ladybird or snail is encountered. Alphabet and number rhymes, riddles, tongue twisters, rhymed proverbs and rhymes of advice are for people approaching school age. However, the lines which have caused nursery rhyme books to be called 'poets' primers' are from evocative, magical songs like 'How far is it to Babylon?', 'I have four sisters beyond the sea', and 'Tom, he was a piper's son', with its refrain of 'Over the hills and far away'. These, and the long ballad-like songs such as 'A fox jumped up one winter's night', are for aesthetic pleasure alone, and lucky is the family who has at least one performer who can say or sing some of them from beginning to end.

Most people, even those who disclaim any repertoire, will find that they know about twelve nursery rhymes, which are in such common use that they seem to be 'in the air' and no one can remember how they first came to know them. These are the rhymes most illustrated in ephemeral children's books, and used to decorate babies' toys and children's china. Typically, they are narratives which pack a whole drama into four or six lines, and describe characters which have entered the English language: everyone understands an allusion to the Grand Old Duke of York's march or Mother Hubbard's cupboard. They include 'Hey diddle diddle, the cat and the fiddle', 'Hickory, dickory, dock' (with its limerick-like structure), and a group of histories, each beginning Little Somebody-or-other and each containing six dactylic lines, which may have originated in a seventeenth-century craze similar to the later limerick craze. The best-known of these are 'Little Miss Muffet', 'Little Polly Flinders', and 'Little Jack Horner', but other less skilful attempts have survived, such as 'Little Poll Parrot' and 'Little General Monk' (General Monk was a famous Cromwellian soldier who died in 1669).

Two of the chief characteristics of nursery rhymes are their brevity and strongly-marked rhythm; in fact these may be said to be necessary qualifications for a verse to enter the nursery rhyme canon, since they ensure memorability. In a desperate need to pacify or divert a squalling infant an adult needs to recall instantly the rhyme that will do the trick.

Another effect of the emphatic syllables is to implant the rhythms of the English language in minds too young to understand all the words (and some of the words are distinctly archaic). Rhymes with trochaic lines, like Baa, baa, black sheep and Humpty Dumpty sat on a wall, are the simplest for 2-year-olds to master, and are favourites for reciting to admiring grandparents.

The overwhelming majority of nursery rhymes were not in the first place composed for children. They are for the most part fragments of songs and ballads originally intended for adult delectation. For instance, the ballad of the 'Moste Strange weddinge of the ffrogge and the mowse' was registered at Stationers' Hall in 1580, and went through various transmogrifications before, in the early nineteenth century, Grimaldi made famous the version with the refrain Rowley, powley, gammon and spinach which is still popular today. 'Lavender's blue' and 'One misty moisty morning' were, in the second half of the seventeenth century, black-letter ballads written by anonymous literary hacks.

Anonymity is, by definition, a requirement of traditional verse, which is handed down by word of mouth without thought of authorship. The few authors of nursery rhymes whose names are known are never credited with their productions. Who cares to know that Sir Charles Sedley wrote 'There was a little man, And he woo'ed a little maid' (1764), and Septimus Winner 'Oh where, oh where has my little dog gone?' (1864); or, among the few compositions written for children, that Jane Taylor wrote 'Twinkle, twinkle, little star' (1806) and Sarah Josepha Hale 'Mary had a little lamb' (1830). 'Wee willie winkie' was the first verse of a poem about a 'waukrife laddie that winna fall asleep', written by William Miller, published in 1841, and immediately commandeered for inclusion in nursery rhyme books, stripped of its Scotticisms and unacknowledged.

A large number of nursery rhymes have not been found recorded before the nineteenth century, when folklore of every kind began to be taken seriously and investigated, but haphazard references from the Middle Ages onwards confirm the existence of some of them. A phrase of 'Infir taris' is recorded about 1450; 'White bird featherless' appears (in Latin) in the tenth century; the germ of 'Two legs sat on three legs' may be seen in the works of Bede. Agricola (b. 1492) learnt the German version of 'Matthew, Mark, Luke, and John' from his parents. The whole of 'I have a young sister far beyond the sea' had been set down by 1450. A French version of 'Thirty days hath September' belongs to the thirteenth century. A game of 'falling bridges', on the lines of 'London Bridge', seems to have been known to Meister Altswert in the late fourteenth century.

References in the sixteenth and seventeenth centuries to verses now known in the nursery exist in some number. Almost certainly one in nine of the rhymes were known by the mid-seventeenth century. At least a quarter, and very likely over half the rhymes are more than 200 years old. However, before the emergence of nursery rhyme literature in the eighteenth century, the glimpses we get of the existence of children's lore are by the way; a clergyman (1671), wishing to illustrate a theological point, quotes 'A apple pie'; an ageing lexicographer (1611), attempting to define the Italian word *abomba*, recalls part of a rhyme from his childhood, 'as we use to say Home againe home againe market is done'; a pamphleteer (1606), reporting a murder trial, reveals that children regularly repeated a Cock a doodle doo couplet; and a playwright (*c.*1559) introducing a clown singing old songs ('Tom a lin' among them) makes him admit they were learnt from his fond mother As I war wont in her lappe to sit.

It is the difficulty of dating the nursery rhymes precisely, and their anonymity, that has made them so suitable for ingenious historical 'interpretations'. As early as 1708 Dr William King was speculating light-heartedly on the identity of Old King Cole in his satirical *Useful Transactions in Philosophy*. Sixty years later the jesting editor of *Mother Goose's Melody* gave birth to a new set of propositions, still sometimes taken seriously (for instance, that the old woman tossed in a blanket was composed in derision of Henry V when, during the Hundred Years War, he conceived new designs against the French).

The game of fitting historical events to the rhymes has been especially popular in the present century, and Katherine Elwes Thomas's *The Real Personages of Mother Goose*, published in 1930, provided shadow personalities for most of the best known rhyme characters (best known in the present day, be it noted, but not likely to have been known at the time of their supposed historical origin): thus Bo-peep became Mary, Queen of Scots; Jack Sprat, Charles I; Old Mother Hubbard,

Cardinal Wolsey; Tommy Tucker, also Cardinal Wolsey and so on. Amusing and often detailed 'solutions' to the rhymes continue to be invented, usually in universities (for example, the equation of Humpty Dumpty with Dr Chillingworth's tortoise-like siege machines of the ancient Roman type, tried out during the siege of Gloucester in 1643, a theory Professor David Daube put forward in *The Oxford Magazine* of 16 February 1956). This is ingenuity for ingenuity's sake; but the inventor must also feel some satisfaction if, as with the current craze for horrific 'urban legends', he can watch his story spreading to a public gullible enough to repeat it in earnest.

Like other oral traditions, nursery rhymes have also been disseminated in print. Once it was allowed that books for children should contain entertainment as well as instruction, nursery songs were naturally considered candidates for inclusion. At the beginning of the eighteenth century, in the reign of Queen Anne, appeared a primer, *A Little Book for Little Children*, by T.W. (*c*.1712), which contained 'A was an Archer and I saw a Peacock with a fiery tail', as well as three well-known riddle verses. The first considerable nursery rhyme book was *Tommy Thumb's Pretty Song Book*, published in two volumes by M. Cooper 'According to Act of Parliament', probably in 1744. Only 'Voll. II' survives, in a unique copy in the British Library. Measuring only $3 \times 1\frac{3}{4}$ inches, it nevertheless contains thirty-nine rhymes which (with three exceptions) are as familiar to the child of today as they were to the young Boswells and Cowpers and Gibbons, its readers at the time: 'There was a little Man, And he had a little Gun', 'Who did kill Cock Robbin?', 'Bah, Bah, a black sheep', 'Hickere, Dickere Dock'. Nearly every rhyme is illustrated with a pleasant and appropriate little woodcut. The far-sighted publisher was Mary Cooper, whose imprint also appears on works by Gray, Fielding, and Pope.

The publication of illustrated nursery rhyme books has continued unabated until the present day, when superb Mother Goose picture books are a mainstay of the children's books market and it seems to be the ambition of every established illustrator to 'do a Mother Goose'. There has also been a constant flow backwards and forwards between oral tradition and literature. Consider only two examples: Lewis Carroll's use of nursery rhymes in the Alice books, and Robert Burns's use of traditional songs as a basis for his own lyrics. Burns's song 'My love, she's but a Lassie yet' was written for the third part of Johnson's *Scots Musical Museum* (1790); but a verse of it (We're all dry with drinking on't (see Chapter 12) had already appeared, most unsuitably, nearly fifty years before in *Tommy Thumb's Pretty Song Book*.

When children go to school they encounter a quite different oral tradition. It might be said that while nursery rhymes echo the voice of the adult, being adult approved, and adult transmitted, school rhymes echo the voice of children out on their own in a potentially unfriendly world. The rhymes pass with lightning speed from one child to another, and have a quite different character. They have a different cadence, and a difference purpose, which is often mockery. Schoolchildren will chant: Good King Wenceslas/Knocked a bobby [policeman] senseless/Right in the middle of Marks and Spencers [a British chain of shops], and: Julius Caesar the Roman geezer/Squashed his wife in a lemon squeezer. They parody the rhymes their parents taught them at home:

Mary had a little lamb
She also had a bear;
I've often seen her little lamb
But I've never seen her 'bear'.

Humpty Dumpty sat on a wall
Eating black bananas.
Where do you think he put the skins?
Down his best pyjamas.

Their mockery includes rhymes which can be recited *sotto voce* to make fun of a teacher. The most popular is one which was already known in 1797, when it appeared in the song book *Infant Amusements*:

Mr — is a very good man,
He tries to teach us all he can,
Reading, writing, arithmetic,
And he doesn't forget to use the stick.
When he does he makes us dance
Out of England into France,
Out of France into Spain,
Over the hills and back again.

Schoolchildren have preserved the ancient art of riddling in its true form (to be found, for instance, in the predominantly eighth-century riddles in the *Exeter Book*), in which some creature or object is described in an intentionally obscure manner. Characteristically, children continue to take delight in amusements once enjoyed, and now discarded, by adults. For instance, in the mid-1950s a 13-year-old boy from Knighton, in Radnorshire, wrote down a riddle, 'What goes up a tree with its head turned downwards? A nail in your boot', which was printed in the adult-oriented *Booke of Meery Riddles*, 1629: 'What is it that goes to the water on the head? It is a horse-shoe naile'. Another riddle in the same work, 'What is that: goeth through the wood, and leaveth on every bush a rag? It is snow', was known to a 15-year-old girl in Kirkcaldy in 1952, though with the answer 'A sheep':

Round the rocks
And round the rocks
The ragged rascal ran,
And every bush he came to,
He left his rags and ran.

Usually, however, what the present-day schoolchild means by 'a riddle' is really a conundrum, whose wit depends on a pun. Many conundrums still popular today have been found in literature of the first half of the nineteenth century, a typical example being 'What is the difference between a warder and a jeweller? One watches cells and the other sells watches.'

Whereas the playground narratives of the mid-twentieth century made fun of death and decay, children today apparently prefer to retell the explicitly sexual stories they learn from their older brothers. On certain occasions at home, however, and especially at Hallowe'en, they like to frighten each other with spooky tales, told softly, in which the tension builds up until the last word is suddenly and frighteningly shouted. The best known such tale is undoubtedly,

> In the dark, dark wood, there was a dark, dark house,
> And in that dark, dark house, there was a dark, dark room,
> And in that dark, dark room, there was a dark, dark cupboard,
> And in that dark, dark cupboard, there was a dark, dark shelf,
> And in that dark, dark shelf, there was a dark, dark box,
> And in that dark, dark box, there was a GHOST!

In the remoter parts of Britain children mark the seasons by going round to their neighbours and chanting traditional verses, in expectation of some small reward in money or kind. For instance, on Exmoor and in the Bredon Hills, at least until the 1950s, the custom of Lent Crocking was still carried out at Shrovetide. Children with soot-blackened faces went round the farmhouses, and after singing, 'Tippety, tippety tin, Give me a pancake and I will come in. Tippety, tippety toe, Give me a pancake and I will go', they crept in – if the door was left open – threw a load of broken crocks on the floor and tried to escape unseen. If the householders caught them they had their faces further blackened with soot, were given a pancake and allowed to go.

It is difficult to know how many of the little songs asking for a gift in exchange for seasonal good wishes are still extant. Perhaps those collected in the 1950s as material for *The Lore and Language of Schoolchildren* (Opie and Opie 1959) have disappeared in response to a new social climate in which children have more money at their disposal, and are more protected and escorted. Of the various celebrations conducted by children on their own initiative, at Christmas and New Year, on St Valentine's Day and May Day, at All Souls and in the weeks before Guy Fawkes Day, the most likely to have survived is probably May Day (especially in Manchester), when little groups of girls chose a queen, visited their neighbours with the maypole they had decorated, and sang a song such as,

> Around this merry maypole
> And through the livelong day
> For gentle — —
> Is crowned the Queen of May.
> With hearts and voices ringing
> We merrily dance today,
> For gentle — —
> Is crowned the Queen of May.

The Hallowe'en custom 'Trick or Treat', which flourishes in the USA as an occasion for children to dress up in fancy dress and go round the neighbourhood asking for sweets and other goodies (the implied threat seldom if ever being carried out) has been reimported to Britain. It is a development of a darker Celtic belief that evil spirits were abroad on the eve of All Saints' Day and that 'guising' [disguising] oneself was a way of avoiding danger. Some of the more jocular rhymes celebrating the night linger on in Scotland:

> This is the nicht o' Halloween
> When the witches can be seen,
> Some are black and some are green,
> And some the colour o' a turkey bean.

Human society has a tendency to split into antagonistic groups, and children are no exception. Other schools and localities, members of other religions or political parties, and supporters of other football teams, are seen as peculiar, unpleasantly different and possibly threatening. The rhymes children shout at these outsiders are no less irritating for being traditional, and seem designed to lead to a skirmish. Those attending Forfar Academy used, in the 1950s, to be harassed by: Academy kites, ye're no very nice,/Ye bake yer bannocks wi' cats and mice. Recognisably the same formula had been used, a hundred years before (as M. A. Denham reported in *Folk-lore of the Northern Counties*, 1858) to denigrate the inhabitants of a Northumberland village:

> The Spittal wives are no' very nice,
> They bake their bread wi' bugs and lice:
> And after that they skin the cat,
> And put it into their kail-pat,
> That makes their broo' baith thick and fat.

Even artificial groups created in schools, as for instance teams denominated the Red and the Blue, raise a partisan spirit, and enthusiastic supporters yell the following adjustable encouragement:

> Red, red, the bonnie red,
> The red that should be worn;
> Blue, blue, the dirty blue,
> The blue that should be torn.

The armoury of the schoolchild is filled with verbal weapons of attack and defence which are of importance for survival in the milieu of the playground. They are effective because they have been tested by time (though the children are not aware they are old) and because they are immediately available in situations when there is no time for original thought. Well-established rhymes of an insulting nature can be launched on the spur of the moment against anyone felt to be obnoxious. A person who is 'being silly' is told,

> You're daft, you're potty, you're barmy,
> You ought to join the army.
> You got knocked out
> With a brussel sprout,
> You're daft, you're potty, you're barmy.

Someone thought to be staring too hard (an intrusion on privacy which is universally resented) is warned, Stare, stare, like a bear,/Then you'll know me anywhere; and the accused one may reply, I'm looking at you with your face so blue/ And your nose turned up like a kangaroo. Liars, especially, are vilified (Liar, liar, your pants are on fire), and can only defend themselves with solemn oaths

(Wet my finger, wipe it dry, Cut my throat if I tell a lie). Cowards, cry-babies and sneaks have been ritually taunted with their failings for a hundred years and more: Cowardy, cowardy, custard is part of the title of a pantomime of 1836; Cry, baby, cry is quoted in an essay by Charles Lamb in *The London Magazine*, April 1821; and 'Tell tale tit' appeared in *Tommy Thumb's Pretty Song Book*, vol. 2, 1744 (Spit Cat, Spit, Your tongue shall be slit, And all the Dogs in our Town Shall have a bit.)

If, in the past, more notice had been taken of the minor delights of childhood, the same sort of antiquity could probably be claimed for many of the catches with which schoolchildren amuse and tease each other. A correspondent to *Notes and Queries*, 1905, showed that the lines Adam and Eve and Pinch-me/Went down to the river to bathe;/Adam and Eve were drowned,/Who do you think was saved? were already 'a schoolboy's catch for the innocent new boy' in 1855. The trick dialogue beginning 'I went up one pair of stairs' and ending 'I saw a monkey', with the dupe having to answer 'Just like me' after each statement, was recorded by J. O. Halliwell in *The Nursery Rhymes of England*, 1844.

Rhyme and assonance give an almost spell-like authority, and this is exploited in the solemn oaths and imprecations children use to regulate their social life. When swearing to the truth they will chant, with hands crossed over heart, Cross my heart and hope to die,/Drop down dead if I tell a lie. They will confirm a bargain by linking little fingers and reciting, Touch teeth, touch leather,/Can't have back for ever and ever. As with swopping, so with giving. Something given must not be asked for again, and the answer to one who does so is the centuries old formula (which once more directly consigned the asker to the Devil), Give a thing, take a thing,/Dirty man's plaything. The ability to keep a secret is tested with a rhymed ritual:

> Can you keep a secret?
> I don't suppose you can.
> You mustn't laugh or giggle
> While I tickle your hand.

And even the quick-fire exclamations needed for claiming something found are often thought to need the reinforcement of rhyme: Finders keepers,/Losers weepers!

Regulatory rhymes are also needed to organise the playing of games. At the outset of a game of He (or Tig, Tag or Touch, according to locality) the players must form up in a line or circle and the 'boss' of the game counts along the line the number of counts prescribed by the stressed syllables of some little rhyme such as the following, which has fifteen counts:

> Errie, orrie, round the table,
> Eat as much as you are able;
> If you're able eat the table,
> Errie, orrie, *out*!

When the word 'out!' falls on a person they must stand aside, and the survivor – on whom the count has never fallen – has to take the disliked role of chaser. This procedure is known as 'dipping'. Sometimes the dipping can be extended by using fists (as in One potato, two potato, three potato, four,/Five potato, six potato, seven potato, More! when one fist is put behind the player's back on 'More!') or by counting-round on feet in a similar fashion. However, the most enjoyable verses incorporate an element of choice (which, if the player is quick-witted, can be adjusted to avoid the count landing unfavourably). One such is My mother and your mother, an old-established favourite in Scotland, where an Edinburgh version was recorded amongst *The Rymour Club Miscellanea*, vol. 1, 1906–1911:

> My mother and your mother
> Were hanging out the clothes,
> My mother gave your mother
> A punch on the nose.
> What colour was the blood?
> Shut your eyes and think.
> *Blue.*
> B–L–U–E spells blue, and out you go
> With a jolly good clout upon your big nose.

The most interesting of these rhymes are perhaps the mysterious rigmaroles that the children sometimes refer to as Chinese counting. They are gibberish, yet sound as if they might contain some hidden meaning. A widespread favourite in Britain during the 1950s and 1960s went like this:

> Eenie, meenie, macca, racca,
> Air, rie, dominacca,
> Chicka pocka, lollipoppa,
> Om pom push.

Yet this construction is in none of the nineteenth-century folk-lore collections and can only be traced back (except for precursors of the last two lines) to the 1920s. During the first three decades of the twentieth century, indeed, far the best known counting jingle was:

> Eenie, meenie, minie, mo,
> Catch a nigger by his toe,
> If he squeals, let him go,
> Eenie, meenie, minie, mo

whose predecessors in the nineteenth century were composed of completely meaningless syllables. An example is the following from the *Northumberland Glossary*, vol. 2, 1854:

> Any, many, mony, my,
> Barcelony, stony, sty,
> Harum, scarum, frownum ack,
> Harricum, barricum, wee, wo, wack.

Other groups of variants exist. Those beginning 'Inty, minty, tippety, fig' have always had a more lively existence in America than in Britain. Those beginning 'Zeenty teenty' were popular in Scotland in the nineteenth century and remain in circulation. The starting point, or inspiration, or source of occasional words in 'Zeenty teenty' and its associates, would appear to be versions of the 'shepherd's score', so called, the numerals reputedly employed in past times by shepherds counting their sheep, by fishermen assessing their catch, and by old women minding their stitches. In the north of England this score is still known, not only to old folk but to children when dipping; though the scores vary, in a typical example the first ten numerals are 'An, tan, tethera, methera, pimp, sethera, lethera, hothera, dothera, dick'. However, the relationship between the children's rhymes and the shepherds' scores is not close.

The games of children are accompanied by verses and songs which, later in life, are remembered with affection – and a certain puzzlement, for most of the older songs have been corrupted in their passage through oral tradition into a kind of surrealist poetry. A singing game like 'The wind blows high' is losing popularity in its old ring form, as a mating game, since girls, now the custodians of the singing game tradition, are beginning to find it unnatural to play the roles of both sexes. The power of the story is, however, undeniable:

> The wind, the wind, the wind blows high,
> The rain comes scattering down the sky,
> He is handsome, she is pretty,
> She is a girl of London City,
> He comes a-courting of one, two, three,
> And may I tell you who it be?
>
> *Tommy Johnson* says he loves her,
> All the boys are fighting for her.
> He takes her in the garden, he sits her on his knee,
> And says, Pretty girl, will you marry me?
>
> Pick up a pin and knock at the door,
> And say has *Tommy* been here before?
> She's in, she's in, she's never been out,
> She's in the parlour walking about.
> She comes down as white as snow,
> With a baby in her arms all dressed in silk.

The story of the girl of London City has, however, not been relinquished. The first verse, with its haunting tune, has been turned into a skipping song; it functions very well, with the skipper calling the next player into the rope at 'May I tell you who it be?'

The main custodians of the oral literature of childhood are female. Mothers and grandmothers purvey nursery rhymes; and it is the girls who cherish and pass on the singing games and the multitude of rhymes used in the skipping, ball-bouncing and clapping games. Whether this is because females have a stronger sense of tradition, or because they have a stronger appreciation of rhyme and rhythm, is not clear. Certainly it is generally assumed that they enjoy repetitive words and actions.

When skipping in a long rope ceased being a boys' game and came into the possession of girls, towards the end of the nineteenth century, it was increasingly ornamented with rhymes which regulated the movement of the players through the rope. The rhymes may be custom-made, like 'All in together, girls', which brings players into the rope, and sends them out again, one by one; a version of this was in circulation *c*.1900, and it is still a favourite today:

> All in together, girls,
> Never mind the weather, girls,
> When it is your birthday,
> Please jump in [later, 'jump out']
> January, February, March ...

Or they might foretell the future, like the ever-popular,

> Raspberry, strawberry, apple tart,
> Tell me the name of your sweetheart,
> A, B, C ...

which, in the 1890s, was a divination formula for use in a game of battledore and shuttlecock. Or they might be old songs, sung once through for each skipper. The following, in the 1870s simply a set of words for the Sultan Polka, was being used for skipping by the 1890s (Gomme 1898: 203):

> Dancing Dolly had no sense,
> For to fiddle [more often 'She bought a fiddle'] for eighteen pence;
> All the tunes that she could play,
> Were 'Sally get out of the donkey's way'.

Some of the words girls chant while juggling two balls against a wall have instructions built into them – 'Oliver Twist' for instance:

> Oliver Twist
> Can you do this? [clap]
> If so, do so [clap]
> First your knee [touch knee]
> Next your toe [touch toe]
> Then under you go [lift leg over ball]

The actions named must be performed; then the rhyme is repeated and the hands clapped before the knee, and so on, is touched; then all actions are performed 'Standstills' without lifting a foot; then 'Dancing Dollies', doing a kind of dance; lastly, 'Faraways', when the player stands further away from the wall and the ball is allowed to bounce once before the action.

Another regulatory rhyme is Plainsie, clapsie,/Round the world to backsie,/Highsie toosh, lowsie toosh,/Touch the ground and under. But most of the ball-bouncing rhymes have the same character as the rest of children's oral literature; everyday life and fantasy are inextricably mixed, and the whole is suffused by an air of defiant gaiety. They chant Mademoiselle she went to the well, Robin Hood and his merry men,/Went to school at half past ten, Winnie the witch fell in a ditch,/Found a penny and thought she was rich, and many other rhymes, some of which are borrowed from the disciplines of skipping and counting-out.

If the totality of children's experience of oral literature is to be covered, mention must be made of the dialogues which precede some of the side-to-side catching games, and of the strange, archaic-seeming scenarios of the acting games. In

'Sheep, sheep, come home', for instance, a game also traditional in German-speaking countries and in Italy, a player in the role of shepherd calls 'Sheep, sheep, come home' and the sheep reply 'We are afraid'. 'What of?' says the shepherd. 'The wolf,' say the sheep. The shepherd deludes them, saying 'The wolf has gone to Devonshire, Won't be back for seven year, Sheep, sheep come home'. The sheep run towards the shepherd and the wolf springs out and tries to catch one of them, who becomes the next wolf.

The acting game of 'Fox and chickens' is possibly the weirdest of this weird genre. The actors are the fox, the mother hen, and the chickens, who form up in single file behind the hen, holding on to each other. They march up to the fox, who is crouching on the ground, and chant:

> Chickany, chickany, crany crow,
> I went to the well to wash my toe,
> When I came back a chicken was dead.

Then the hen asks 'What are you doing, old fox?' and he replies in a gruff voice, 'Picking up sticks.' 'What for?' 'To make a fire.' 'What do you want a fire for?' 'To cook a chicken.' 'Where will you get it?' 'Out of your flock.' As the fox says this he springs up and tries to seize the last chicken in the line. When he catches her, he takes her back to his den, and the whole scene is gone through again and again until all the chickens have been caught. The game has been known under many names, through many centuries – it seems to be referred to a number of times as far back as the Middle Ages – and in many countries of the world. In the older versions the sinister crouching figure, who is sometimes a hawk or wolf, and is sometimes sharpening a knife, raises a dark, mythological shadow.

Oral traditions are subject to change, and children's rhymes are no exception. Words take the place of other words, usually through misunderstandings, as when the old Scottish singing game I lost my lad and I care nae became I lost my lad in the cairnie and then Rosa love a canary. Shifts in taste and contemporaneity account for other changes. Thus in 'Mary, Mary, quite contrary' the line Sing cuckolds all on a row became, more politely, And pretty maids all in a row; and a 1956 parody of 'The yellow rose of Texas' was found, when collected as a ball-bounce chant in 1975, to have shed its dramatis personae – the Yellow Rose herself and Davy Crockett – in favour of Batman and Robin, and Cinderella.

Often the change in the lore is caused by a change in use. Take the old courting game All the boys in our town, for instance, in which, during the nineteenth century, each turn at choosing from the ring was prefaced by as many as twenty-four lines of song. Revived as a skipping game, the chant was necessarily shortened and became only eight brisk lines. Songs have a tendency to split or coalesce in an almost biological manner. An example is the clapping sequence Under the bram bushes, under the sea, which was originally a students' song formed from two popular songs, 'Harry Harndin's A cannibal king', 1895, and Cole and Johnson's 'Under the bamboo tree', 1902. The central verse of this amalgamation developed into the clapping verse, 'bamboo tree' became 'bram bushes', and 'When we are married happy we will be' proliferated into a variety of forms of which this Leeds, 1973, version is typical: True love for you, my darling,/True love for me;/And when we are married,/We'll raise a family,/With a boy for you,/and a girl for me,/

I tiddley om pom, pom pom (which itself carries echoes of Vincent Youmans' song 'Tea for two', 1924). The custodians of oral lore have a careless and carefree way with their inheritance.

## References

Gomme, A. B. (1894, 1898) *Traditional Games of England, Scotland, and Ireland*, 2 vols, London: David Nutt.

Opie, I and Opie, P. (1955) *The Oxford Nursery Rhyme Book*, Oxford: Oxford University Press.

—— (1959) *The Lore and Language of Schoolchildren*, Oxford: Oxford University Press.

## Further Reading

Douglas, N. (1916) *London Street Games*, London: St Catherine Press.

Newell, W. W. (1883) *Games and Songs of American Children*, New York: Harper Brothers.

Opie, I. and Opie, P. (1951) *The Oxford Dictionary of Nursery Rhymes*, Oxford: Oxford University Press.

—— (1969) *Children's Games in Street and Playground*, Oxford: Oxford University Press.

—— (1985) *The Singing Game*, Oxford: Oxford University Press.

Ritchie, J. T. R. (1964) *The Singing Street*, Edinburgh and London: Oliver and Boyd.

—— (1965) *Golden City*, Edinburgh and London: Oliver and Boyd.

# 16

# Poetry for Children

## Morag Styles

### 'Country Rhimes' or 'Fingle-fangles': What is Poetry for Children?

I am tempted to say that there is no such thing as poetry for children. There is plenty of poetry *about* children; and some of the best poetry ever written is about *childhood*; at some time or other most poets explore that inviting furrow – their own youth and growing up. A great body of the so-called canon of children's verse was never intended for the young at all, but was verse which adults thought *suitable for children*. The gatekeepers of the canon are the anthologists.

Of course, poets have written specifically for children, some choosing to divide their time between their different audiences; others specialising in juvenile poetry. The latter group has, however, been marginalised by influential editors of the past and present. Coventry Patmore, writing in *The Children's Garland* (1862, subtitled 'from the best poets') firmly states, 'I have excluded nearly all the verse written expressly for children and most of the poetry written about children for grown people' (p. c). Here is Neil Philip in 1990: 'I have also been cautious with poems written specially for children, preferring on the whole work which makes itself available to a young reader *without any sense of talking or writing down*' (my emphasis) (15).

Such views are not uncommon. Poems by Shakespeare, Wordsworth and Tennyson, who never wrote for children, have been collected more frequently in prestigious anthologies of the last hundred years than work by Stevenson, Lear or Rossetti. Look at distinguished general anthologies of the nineteenth and twentieth century and consider the omissions. Where are the poets writing for children? Where are the women? Most anthologies of the past and present are testimonies to the preferences of elite groups of academically educated men. Poetry by women, working-class people, ethnic minorities and *those who specialise in writing for the young* are often treated as second class. A large body of the poetry actually favoured by children (so the evidence would suggest) has been ignored by anthologists. The tension between the improving instincts of adults and what children choose to read is nowhere more keenly demonstrated than in the anthologising of verse for the young.

Some of these adult poems have been adopted by children themselves, a healthy trend which shows young readers' powerful drive to shape their own literature. Children have always poached from the adult canon; Kaye Webb's *I Like This Poem* (1979), a collection of the declared favourite poems of children (although, no doubt, a privileged group of children), includes much that was written before the twentieth century. Traditionalists do not have anything to worry about; children today simply like a varied diet.

Some of the most popular themes for children remain fairly constant – nature, magic, the sea, the weather, school and family life, adventure – and anything that makes them laugh. One of the most powerful topics is the exploration of childhood itself. Many poets write for children because they want (often unconsciously) to understand the 'child in themselves'. At worst this can be self-indulgent and full of nostalgia; at best it reaches the tenderness of Rossetti, the gentle scrutiny of Stevenson, or Rosen's funny and unpretentious accounts of everyday life. Adults will always view children through the 'distorting lens' of their own dreams, hopes, memories and prejudices: this has led to some of the most moving and most sentimental poetry ever written.

Until the middle of the eighteenth century, most verse for children was didactic and severe, expressed through in lessons, fables (with morals, of course) and hymns. For those who could get their hands on it, what a contrast the rude, crude and dramatic verse available in the chapbooks must have made. By the early nineteenth century, significant numbers of poets writing for children aspired to entertain rather than educate young readers. Harsh moral tales in verse began to develop into the extravagances of cautionary verse; light-hearted poems about the imaginary doings of animals became popular; cradle songs and tender expressions of love between children and parents began to be expressed in poetry for the young. The Victorian period also ushered in some fine humorists, and nonsense verse became a substantial part of children's fare. By then common forms included limericks, narrative poems, ballads, songs and nursery rhymes. It was virtually all in rhymed, metrically regular verse; free verse was not predominant until the latter half of the twentieth century. Anthologies of different poets have rivalled single-poet collections since this period: poets regularly included are Burns, Clare, Cowper, Goldsmith, Keats, Pope, Shelley and Scott.

A sea-change occurred in the 1970s when poetry for children moved into the city: the earlier gentle and often rural lyricism turned into something more earthy, harking back, perhaps, to the bawdiness of the chapbooks. This poetry is closer to the 'real world' as many children – not just middle-class children – may experience it. Gone, largely, are descriptions of neat nurseries, countryside idylls and sweet fancies. Nature may still be central, but it is more likely to come in the shape of muscular poetry about animals by writers like Ted Hughes, or hard-hitting descriptions of how human beings have destroyed the environment. Humour is widespread, but serious concerns are not neglected.

As for content, there are few unmentionables left. The late twentieth-century's attitude to childhood in poetry is refreshingly robust – too much so for some tastes. Iona Opie's recent study of children's behaviour without adults present, *The People in the Playground* (Opie 1992), may have convinced some tender-hearted commentators that children are by and large hardy and resilient and require a literature which takes account of that.

Contemporary poetry for children also favours the vernacular and tends to be informal and unstructured. All the popular forms of the past are still evident; but children's poetry also features raps, song-lyrics, dub poetry, haiku, concrete verse, dialect poetry, dramatic monologues and realistic conversation poems. The recitation of beautiful poems was once highly valued; now the oral performance of poetry might be a rap accompanied by a reggae backing or a tongue-twister, *as well as* 'The daffodils'. Another recent development is the recognition of *children as poets*; contemporary poetry is very accessible to children and they are encouraged by teachers, poets and annual competitions to try their hands at writing it themselves. Publication of this poetry demonstrates the high standards that can be achieved.

Poetry for children, then, is defined by the age: contemporary poetry emphasises the need to love, value, amuse and protect small people, and has a liberal tolerance of their private brand of humour; the poetry of the Puritan age believed its function was to save the souls of children by admonishing them to virtue, Godliness and obedience. As John Bunyan wrote in 1686:

> I do't to show them how each Fingle-fangle,
> On which they doating are, their Souls entangle.

## 'Ancient and Wiser Tongues': Poetry for Children to 1900

Before the eighteenth century most published poetry relating to the young is *about* children or *good for* children, rather than to entertain or feed the imaginations of children, although there are some glorious lullabies written, perhaps surprisingly, by men. Thomas Dekker's (1570?–1632) A cradle song is tender and loving: Golden slumbers kiss your eyes/Smiles awake you when you rise; so is George Wither's (1588–1667) A Rocking Hymn: Sweet baby, then, forbear to weep/Be still my babe; sweet baby, sleep. These were the exceptions in an age when literature for children, where it existed at all, tended to be harsh, didactic, religious and moralistic. Popular culture in the form of chapbooks provided the children and their parents with a more robust diet of rhymes, jokes, ballads, heroic tales and extracts from contemporary writing.

One of the earliest examples of poetry for children is John Bunyan's (1628–1688) variously titled *Country Rhimes for Children: or A Book for Boys and Girls:* or *Divine Emblems* (1686). Zachary Leader sums up Bunyan and other writers for the young in this period: 'At the heart of the Puritan attitude towards childhood lies a rock-hard belief in original sin' (Leader 1981: 6). Writing in the preface to *Divine Emblems* Bunyan showed, however, that he *was* aware that children needed to like the taste of the medicine, if they were to imbibe it:

> Wherefore good Reader, that I save them may,
> I now with them, the very Dottrill play.
> And since at Gravity they make a Tush
> My very Beard I cast behind the Bush.
> And like a Fool start fing'ring of their Toys,
> And all to show them they are Girls and Boys.

Even so, it is stern stuff. Around the same period, Abraham Cheare (d. 1668) addressed the recipients of his poetry affectionately enough: 'Sweet John', 'My pretty Child', but *A Looking Glass for Children* (1672), reads harshly today: Hath

God such comliness display'd/and on me made to dwell/'Tis pity, such a pretty Maid/as I should go to Hell. Poetry for children, then, was mainly devotional writing, lullabies, fables or lessons in verse until the beginning of the nineteenth century. Fortunately, there were some excellent hymnists.

Isaac Watts (1674–1748), author of well known hymns like 'Jesus shall reign where're the sun', published *Divine Songs Attempted in easy Language for the Use of Children*, in 1715. As Pafford, editor of a recent edition makes clear, this was 'an early and outstanding attempt to write verses for children which would give them pleasure, but at the same time point and urge to the paths of virtue' (Pafford 1715/ 1971: 1). Watts urged kindness in education and understood the power of verse in learning: 'what is learnt in Verse is longer retained in Memory, and sooner recollected ... this will be a constant Furniture'. Although he is little read today, Watts was extremely popular in his own lifetime and for more than a century after his death: *Divine Songs* had run to 550 editions by 1918. One of his most famous poems, How doth the little busy bee/Improve each shining hour/And gather honey all day/From every opening flower was notably parodied by Lewis Carroll.

Charles Wesley (1707–1788), brother of the evangelist John Wesley, followed the same tradition by writing some of the most beautiful hymns in the English language, including 'Hark! the herald-angels sing'. His *Hymns for Children* appeared in 1763.

Another talented writer of hymns was Christopher Smart (1722–1771), perhaps best remembered for 'My cat Jeoffrey' (from *Jubilate Agno*), who wrote *Hymns for the Amusement of Children* (1771), while in prison for debt:

> A lark's nest, then your playmate begs
> You'd spare herself and speckled eggs;
> Soon she shall ascend and sing
> Your praises to the eternal King.
>
> 'Hymn for Saturday'

Smart's verse displays a humanity and a sweetness of touch that was singularly lacking elsewhere, although his hymns never deviate from praising God. Anna Barbauld (1743–1825) was one of the best writers for children of the eighteenth century. Her work conformed to the standards of her day: anything too fanciful was repressed, and moral tales were her forte. However, her *Lessons for Children* (1778) demonstrated a new approach to the teaching of reading, and her *Hymns in Prose* (1781) made her justly famous:

> Come, let us go forth into the fields; let us see how the flowers spring; let us listen to the warbling of birds, and sport ourselves upon the new grass. The winter is over and gone, the buds come out upon the trees, the crimson blossoms of the peach and the nectarine are seen, and the green leaves sprout.

We have to move to the middle of the nineteenth century to consider our last notable hymnist, Cecil Frances Alexander (1818–1895) who was married to the Archbishop of Armagh. She wrote many verses for children despite a busy family and pastoral life. Some of her hymns, such as 'Once in Royal David's city' and 'All

Things Bright and Beautiful' have worldwide popularity. Her maxim for writing hymns (reported by her husband) was simple: 'It must be *sung*; it must be *praise*; it must be *to God*,' (Alexander 1896: xxv). Her publications include *Hymns for little Children*, (1848) and *Moral Songs* (1849).

As we have seen, the main concern of most eighteenth-century writers for children was didactic. The admonitions in Nathaniel Cotton's (1705–1788) *Visions in Verse* (1751) are not exactly welcoming; nor was there much fun in John Marchant's (fl. 1751) *Puerilia*, 1753: I must eye my Copy duely/And exactly cut my Strokes/Ev'ry Letter joining truely/So my writing better looks. Dorothy Kilner's (1755–1836) *Poems on Various Subjects for the Amusement of Youth* (1785) offered some amusement as well as directives on how a God-fearing child should behave, and she is an early exponent of something close to cautionary verse.

> How with smacks he each mouthful seem'd eager to taste,
> And the last precious drop was unwilling to waste.
> But ye Graces! how can I the sequel relate?
> Or tell you, ye powers! that he lifted his plate?
> And what must have made a Lord Chesterfield sick,
> Why his tongue he applied the remainder to lick.
>
> 'The Retort to Master Richard'

The first poet of genius to write for children was William Blake (1757–1827), though it could be argued that he was really more interested in writing for other adults *about* childhood in order to challenge the prevailing ideology of his day. However, a glance at the title poem of *Songs of Innocence* (1789) makes it clear that whatever else Blake was trying to achieve in his poetry, he was also keen to communicate with the young: And I wrote my happy songs/Every child may joy to hear. The subject matter of Blake's poetry was consistent with that of other children's writers of his day: hymn-like poems glorifying God through nature, cradle songs, references to children's games, birds and animals, even social comment. But, as Heather Glen suggests in *Vision and Disenchantment* (1983), what Blake was doing in these poems was initiating a debate on eighteenth-century morality. He did not go along with the didactic purposes of his contemporaries and his poems frustrate the notion that there should be an unequivocal moral line presented to children. Deceptively simple, they hide complexities of irony, and the expectations of the reader are frequently subverted. For example, the child leads the adult in 'The voice of the ancient bard' and the sheep lead the shepherd in 'The shepherd'; the adult acquiesces with youth's desire for freedom and experience in 'Nurse's song', and the children find school a cruel diversion from the joys of nature in 'The School Boy': But to go to school in a summer morn/O! it drives all joy away. Unlike almost all the juvenile literature of this period, there is no clear authorial voice instructing the reader what to think.

*Songs of Innocence* (1789) and *Songs of Experience* (1794), can be seen as cunningly contradicting adult dominance and replacing it with the wisdom of innocence and naturalness, qualities which, in Blake's mind, were associated with the state of childhood (a similar view was taken up by Wordsworth and Coleridge in *Lyrical Ballads* (1798)), and although his enlightened ideas were too advanced for his age, his work has had a profound influence on poetry for children.

The visionary and humanising influence of the Romantic movement exerted a huge impact on writing for children, if not, perhaps, immediately. Wordsworth and his companions contributed to changing views of childhood: There was a time when meadow, grove and stream/The earth and every common stream/To me did seem/Apparelled in celestial light/The glory and the freshness of a dream ... It is an open question whether the spirit of the Romantics directly influenced writers of poetry for the young in the early nineteenth century. On the one hand there was some liberalism in juvenile poetry. William Roscoe's (1753–1831) *The Butterfly's Ball and Grasshopper's Feast* (1807) and its eight imitations (in the same a year), were entirely free of moralising. Catherine Ann Dorset (1750–1817) wrote one of these, *The Peacock at Home* (1808), which was better than its precursor, though few know her name today:

> Worms and frogs en friture for the web-footed fowl,
> And a barbecued mouse was prepar'd for the Owl;
> Nuts, grain, fruit and fish, to regale every palate,
> And groundsel and chickweed serv'd up in a sallad.

Roscoe and Dorset sold 40,000 copies of their two books within the year. Ann Taylor (1782–1866) and Jane Taylor (1783–1824), best known for *Original Poems for Infant Minds* (1804), with other writers, including Adelaide O'Keefe, also heralded a kinder approach to children in poetry, as this extract from 'Evening' demonstrates:

> The moon through your curtains shall cheerfully peep;
> Her silver beams rest on your eyes
> And mild evening breezes shall fan you to sleep
> Till bright morning bid you arise.

The Taylors' most famous poems were probably 'My Mother' from *Original Poems* and 'The Star' (Twinkle, twinkle ...) from *Rhymes for the Nursery* (1806). As Percy Muir observed: 'Here, at last, were books that children surely chose for themselves, albeit with the undoubted approval of their elders' (Muir 1954: 91).

The originality of the Taylors did not lie in willingness to abandon admonitions to virtuous behaviour in children – in fact, the Taylors were the seminal developers of the moral tale in verse, and their poetry, for all its new gentleness, still demonstrated unswerving moral conviction. It could be argued that in the early part of the nineteenth century, the type of poetry written for children was dominated more by the tone and content of *Original Poems* and its successors than by the Romantics. Lucy Aikin included Wordsworth in the second edition of her anthology *Poetry for Children* (1825); after that Romantic poetry was, and continues to be, regularly anthologised. Coleridge's *The Rime of the Ancient Mariner* has long been part of the children's canon.

Certainly, many tried their hands at writing in the Taylors' style. Elizabeth Turner (1775–1846) wrote *The Daisy* (1807) subtitled 'Or, Cautionary Stories in Verse ...'. Here is a characteristic example, from 'The giddy girl who will go near the well':

> One morning, intending to take but a peep,
> Her foot slipt away from the ground;

Unhappy misfortune! the water was deep,
And giddy Miss Helen was drown'd!

Other successful examples from this period are Sarah Martin's (1768–1826), *The Comic Adventures of Old Mother Hubbard and her Dog* (1805), and the rather insipid *Poetry for Children* (1809) by Charles Lamb (1775–1834) and Mary Lamb (1764–1847).

Dorothy Wordsworth (1771–1855), wrote poems for children which were only for family consumption and were not published in her lifetime. They display an endearing playfulness and homeliness, as this extract from her poem, 'The cottager to her infant', makes clear:

The kitten sleeps upon the hearth,
The crickets long have ceased their mirth;
There's nothing stirring in the house
Save one wee, hungry, nibbling mouse,
Then why so busy thou?

Roger Lonsdale's collection of eighteenth-century verse reveal that there were many talented scribblers, often women, whose work never gained public attention (Lonsdale 1989). Dorothy Wordsworth is a prime example.

Mary Howitt (1799–1888) who translated Hans Christian Andersen's fairy tales with her husband, William, wrote dozens of books for children including *Hymns and Fireside Verses* (1839), *Tales in Verse for the Young* (1836) and *Sketches of Natural History* (1834) which contained the famous, 'Will you come into my parlour, said the Spider to the Fly'. Later, there was the jolly Aunt Effie, Jane Euphemia Browne (1811–1898), author of the much-loved *Aunt Effie's Rhymes for Little Children* (1852): Oh, where do you come from/You little drops of rain/Pitter patter, pitter patter/ Down the window pane? Elizabeth Hart (1822–1888) was still writing in this genre in 1868: *Poems written for a Child*, was a collaboration with her sister-in-law, Menella Bute Smedley (1820–1877).

Charlotte Smith (1749–1806), a fine poet by any standards, wrote *Conversations Introducing Poetry to Children Chiefly on the Subject of Natural History* (1804), where a mother and her son and daughter discuss poetry, natural history and manners. It is hard going for the contemporary reader, but there are moments of sublime poetry, as this extract from The Humble Bee shows:

Where poppies hang their heavy heads,
Or where the gorgeous sun-flower spreads
For you her luscious golden beds,
On her broad disk.

To live on pleasure's painted wing,
To feed on all the sweets of spring,
Must be a mighty pleasant thing,
If it would last.

Felicia Hemans (1793–1835) has suffered from the declining popularity of poems such as *Casabianca* with its once-famous opening: The boy stood on the burning deck, although plenty of lesser nationalistic verse has survived. In fact, Felicia

Hemans was one of the most prolific, popular and highly regarded poets of her day. *Hymns for Childhood* (1833) was her best known book for children. She had five boys herself whom she brought up on her own, after her husband had left her. Charlotte Smith also supported *her* twelve children by writing, when her husband brought them to near ruin: she wrote her most famous book of poetry, *Elegaic Sonnets* (1784) in debtor's prison. These are just two examples of women who were successful writers against the odds, and whose work deserves to be better known today.

Sara Coleridge (1802–1852) devoted much of her life to the work of her famous father, Samuel Taylor Coleridge, but she did write books for children, one a collection of poetry, *Pretty Lessons in Verse for Good Children* (1834), including the delightful 'Months of the year': January brings the snow/Makes our feet and fingers glow. Her title exemplifies the continuing current of didacticism in books for children at that time: even a Romantic poet's daughter still speaks of 'lessons … for good children', although they will be 'pretty lessons'!

The Taylors' influence is also evident in the work of a later poet, Christina Rossetti (1842–1897). *Sing-Song* (1872), is the best of a sub-genre of poetry where affection between mothers and babies could be tenderly expressed:

> Mother's arms under you,
> Her eyes above you
> Sing it high, sing it low
> Love me, – I love you.

Walter De la Mare wrote admiringly of Rossetti's 'imaginative truth', though he rather spoiled his praise by going on to say that 'Christian Rossetti was that still rarer thing, a woman of genius' (de la Mare 1930: x). *Goblin Market* (1862), a most original, sensuous, long narrative poem, was not composed for the young, although it has been frequently anthologised, illustrated and marketed for them. Rossetti's biographer describes it as a 'combination of the grotesque, the fairy tale, the erotic and the moral', Jones 1991: 91. Did children actually like the poem or was it considered suitable for them because it was full of goblins? Christina's friend, Jean Ingelow (1830–1897) also wrote regularly anthologised poetry.

Kate Greenaway (1846–1901) is known for her charming illustrations, but she wrote her own poetry for *Under the Window* (1879) and *Marigold Garden* (1885). Edith Nesbit (1858–1924) is a much better writer and famous for her fiction, but her poetry for children, *Songs of Two Seasons* (1891), *Flowers Bring and Songs Sing* (1893), has been forgotten. Her forte was nature poetry with a delicate touch, which is evident from this extract from 'The way of the wood' in *A Pomander of Verse* (1895):

> Sweet chestnuts droop their long, sharp leaves
> By knotted tree roots, mossed and brown,
> Round which the honeysuckle weaves
> Its scented golden wild-wood crown.

In the same period in America, Eliza Follen (1787–1860), a prominent abolitionist and editor of the periodical, *Child's Friend*, produced *New Nursery Songs for all Good Children* (1832), *Little Songs* (1833), and *The Lark and the Linnet*

(1884), while Clement Clarke Moore, a Hebrew scholar (1779–1863) established his place in history by publishing *A Visit from St Nicholas* (often known as *The Night before Christmas*) in 1823. One of the many women writing for children to fall into obscurity was Sara Hale (1788–1879), a journalist who wrote for various periodicals and who edited *Boston Ladies' Magazine* and *The Juvenile Miscellany* during the 1830s. She was author of the enduringly popular 'Mary's lamb' and *Poems for Our Children* (1830). Eugene Field (1850–1895), a literary columnist in Chicago, wrote poems of modest accomplishment, many of which are still anthologised today. His best known collections are *A Little Book of Western Verse* (1889) and *With Trumpet and Drum* (1892), but it was his poem, 'Wynken, Blynken and Nod' that was published in many picture book versions: Wynken, Blynken, and Nod one night/Sailed off in a wooden shoe/Sailed on a river of misty light/Into a sea of dew. Henry Wadsworth Longfellow's (1807–1882) *The Song of Hiawatha* (1885) still enthrals children in Britain and America over a century later.

Robert Browning's (1812–1889) *The Pied Piper of Hamelin* first put in an appearance in *Dramatic Lyrics* (1842), and was immediately adopted by the juvenile market. Elizabeth Barrett Browning wrote the passionate, but now forgotten, 'The Cry of the Children'. (F. G. Kenyon edited a volume, *The Brownings for the Young*, in 1896.) But it was 'between 1865 and 1875 [that] the entire course of juvenile poetry was altered by two bachelor writers who had little in common except an elfin lightsomeness and a love of other people's children' (Shaw 1962: 431); 1846 was actually the year when Edward Lear (1812–1888) published *A Book of Nonsense*: the other bachelor was, of course, Lewis Carroll (1832–1898).

Lear was first and foremost an artist who struggled all his life to earn a precarious living as a professional painter specialising in landscapes. The nonsense verse came about as a refuge from the trials and irritations of his life – epilepsy, lack of funds, an eccentric personality and regular bouts of severe depression. Like many of those writing after him who chose to express themselves primarily in nonsense, Lear felt somewhat alienated from society. The urge to comment sardonically on the conventional world and escape from its restrictions is evident in the verse: 'My life is a bore in this nasty pond/And I long to go out in the world beyond'. Friendship with children and writing for them gave him a welcome respite from his problems.

Lear made the limerick form his own, though it really began some years before with *Anecdotes and Adventures of Fifteen Gentlemen* by Richard Scrafton Sharpe (1775–1852). Nonsense verse was already a thriving form in chapbook culture and there were talented humorists with verbal facility before Lear's time, like the brilliant Thomas Hood (1799–1845): Ben Battle was a soldier bold/And used to war's alarms/But a cannon-ball took off his legs/So he laid down his arms. Hood's robust humour works perfectly in his parody of Ann Taylor's loving, but sentimental poem, 'My mother'. The original reads: Who fed me from her gentle breast/And hushed me in her arms to rest/And on my cheek sweet kisses prest/My Mother: Hood's version reads: Who let me starve, to buy her gin/Till all my bones came through my skin/Then called me ugly little sin/My Mother'. Hood was a popular humorist of his day with a strongly developed social conscience (he was a friend of Dickens). After his death, his children collected his poems for the young in *Fairy Land* (1861). He is best known for his *Comic Annual* (1830–1839), and 'I remember, I remember' in *Friendship's Offering* (1826).

But it took a poet of Lear's originality to bring nonsense verse to a head and explore its possibilities with an inventiveness and playfulness which was quite stunning, equalled only, perhaps, by Lewis Carroll. Lear was also a talented musician (he set some of his good friend Tennyson's poetry to music) and this ear for musical language is one of the reasons why the verse is so good. He also drew gloriously quirky pictures to accompany many of his poems.

Lear's *Nonsense Songs* was published in 1871, the same year as *Jabberwocky* and *The Walrus and the Carpenter* appeared in *Alice through the Looking Glass* which Harvey Darton (writing about *Alice in Wonderland* as well) described as 'the spiritual volcano of children's books … the first unapologetic … appearance in print … of liberty of thought in children's books' (Darton 1932/1982: 260). Carroll was also an accomplished parodist: he plays deliciously with Watts's verse and with Jane Taylor's 'Twinkle, twinkle, little star': Twinkle twinkle little bat/ How I wonder what you're at. Most of Carroll's best verse is contained in the two *Alice* novels: his verse collection, *Rhyme? and Reason?*, is surprisingly dull.

Later parodists included Hilaire Belloc (1870–1953) who wrote *The Bad Child's Book of Beasts* in 1896 – a book which sold out of its first print run in four days. It shows that children have always been quick to recognise what they liked and Belloc has been a favourite on nursery shelves ever since: the sheer, wicked, tongue-in-cheek, over-the-top quality of the verse makes it very satisfying. *More Beasts for Worse Children* followed in 1897 and *Cautionary Tales for Children* in 1907. Harry Graham (1874–1936) writes in the same style, in books like *Ruthless Rhymes for Heartless Homes* (1899), although he is nastier than Belloc: Father heard his children Scream/So he threw them in the stream/Saying as he drowned the third/'Children should be seen, not heard!'. *When Grandmama Fell off the Boat* (1986), is a recent collection of the best of Harry Graham. A later master of this art is the American humorist, Ogden Nash (1902–1971), as in *Parents Keep Out* (1951). All three owe a debt to poets like Jane and Ann Taylor who explored some of the possibilities of this genre in 1804.

Three men stood out as the century drew to a close: William Brighty Rands, William Allingham and Robert Louis Stevenson. William Brighty Rands (1823–1882) is best known for *Lilliput Levee* (1869) and *Lilliput Lyrics* (1868): there are too many mentions of the prettiness and kisses of little girls for my taste, but the verse is lively and amusing. *Rhymes for the Young Folk* (1886) by William Allingham (1824–1889) is very appealing: January/Bitter very/February damp, Sir/ March blows/On April's nose/May has caught the cramp, Sir. *The Fairies* came out in 1883 and the gorgeous picture book, *In Fairyland*, illustrated by Richard Doyle in 1870.

Robert Louis Stevenson (1850–1894) was, perhaps, the first poet for the young to write effectively 'as if by a child in the first person'. *A Child's Garden of Verses* (1887) first appeared as *Penny Whistles* in 1885. John Rowe Townsend identifies a 'shifting perspective … between the author as a child and the author as a man' (Townsend 1987: 122). Indeed, it is clear that Stevenson himself was aware of this and spoke to Edmund Gosse of his unusual ability in remembering what it felt like to be a child:

> At evening when the lamp is lit,
> Around the fire my parents sit;
> They sit at home and talk and sing,
> And do not play at anything.

'The Land of Story Books'

Perhaps it was because Stevenson's Edinburgh childhood was dogged by poor health and confinement to house and bed, a lonely life cut off from normal activities, that he had such empathy for children. His poems still mesmerise them today, with their memorable images, evocative rhythms and narrative suggestion. Most moving of all *to adults* is the poem 'To any reader' – it is about childhood and growing up, and what adults lose and try to hold on to: So you may see, if you will look/Through the windows of this book/Another child, far, far away/And in another garden, play. Stevenson made no claims for himself as a poet: 'These are rhymes, jingles; I don't go in for eternity' ( Stevenson 1883: 285). He was wrong.

## 'The Ordinary Rituals of Life': Poetry for Children in the Twentieth Century

Walter de la Mare's (1873–1956) first book of poetry for children, *Songs of Childhood*, was published in 1902, and followed by many others, the most popular of which was, perhaps, *Peacock Pie* (1913). Most of his work for children can be found in *Collected Rhymes and Verses* (1944). He is also famous for one of the finest anthologies 'for the Young of all ages', *Come Hither* (1923). His gift was to write with a tremendous eye for detail, and he emphasised the importance of the particular. Like Blake and the Romantics, de la Mare shared a wonder at the beauty of the world, but in his case he rarely chose to tackle the harsh or unpleasant side of life. His poetry, though a little out of vogue at present, has timeless qualities: is there a better narrative poem than 'The listeners'?

> 'Is there anybody there?' said the Traveller,
> Knocking on the moonlit door;
> And his horse in the silence champed the grasses
> Of the forest's ferny floor:
> And a bird flew up out of the turret,
> Above the Traveller's head:
> And he smote upon the door again a second time;
> 'Is there anybody there?' he said.

Rudyard Kipling is better known as a novelist, but some of the poems in *Puck of Pook's Hill* (1906) and *Rewards and Fairies* (1910), such as 'If' are part of our culture, although it is worth remembering that the stalwart principles of character enumerated in that poem are directed only at boys! The children's song from *Puck*, is better-known as a hymn.

> Father in heaven who lovest all,
> Oh, help thy children when they call;
> That they may build from age to age,
> An undefiléd heritage.

After the First World War, light verse became popular. Rose Fyleman (1877–1957), whose many fairy books include *Fairies and Chimneys* (1918) is, surprisingly, still anthologised, although her verse is cloyingly sweet. A much better poet is Eleanor Farjeon (1881–1965) whose first collection, *Nursery Rhymes of London Town*, appeared in 1916. *The Children's Bells* (1957), contains her personal selection gleaned from the many books of verse she wrote for the young, and Anne Harvey recently collected some of her lesser known poems in *Something I Remember* (1987).

Nearly forty years after *A Child's Garden of Verses*, A. A. Milne (1882–1956) published *When We Were Very Young* (1924) and *Now We Are Six* (1927). There is no doubt that Milne's depiction of childhood is full of delight for many children. There is also, at worst, arch, adult knowingness and sentimentality. If the impetus for Stevenson's poetry was capturing moments of his childhood, rendered as faithfully as it is possible for an adult to do, Milne's came from a different source. As his son, Christopher Milne put it:

> Some people are good with children. Others are not. It is a gift. You either have it or you don't. My father didn't – not with children, that is ... My father was a creative writer and so it was precisely because he was *not* able to play with his small son that his longings sought and found satisfaction in another direction. He wrote about him instead ... My father's most deeply felt emotion was nostalgia for his own happy childhood.
>
> Milne 1974: 36

What cannot be denied is that Milne has stood the test of time because the poetry *is* good. Years of writing for the magazine *Punch* trained a facility for well-crafted verse which Milne combined winningly with well-observed concerns of childhood. Ironically, Milne regarded himself as largely a writer for adults, so did T. S. Eliot, who produced one whimsical book for children *Old Possum's Book of Practical Cats* (1939).

Outstanding among more recent poets have been James Reeves (1909–1978), with collections such as *The Wandering Moon* (1950) and *The Blackbird in the Lilac* (1952); his work has been collected in one volume, *Complete Poems for Children* (1973). No longer in vogue and mostly out of print are his near contemporaries, publishing for children in the 1960s, such as Leonard Clark (1905–1981) (*Near and Far* (1968)); Robert Graves (1895–1985) (*The Penny Fiddle* (1960)); E. V. Rieu (1887–1972) (*The Flattered Flying Fish and other poems* (1962)); Ian Serraillier (1912–1995) (*Happily Ever After* (1963)); Edward Thomas (1878–1917) (*The Green Road; Poems for Young Readers* (1965)); John Walsh (1911–1972) (*The Roundabout by the Sea* (1960)); and Russell Hoban (b. 1925) (*The Pedalling Man* (1968)).

Eminent American poets of the century include Laura Richards (1850–1943) whose *Tirra Lirra* (1913), draws on her many collections. Of the poets whose writing is mostly directed at adults, Elizabeth Coatsworth, e. e. cummings, Emily Dickinson, Rachel Field, Robert Frost, Langston Hughes, Myra Cohn Livingstone, Edna St Vincent Millay, Carl Sandburg, Theodore Roethke, May Swenson, John Updike and William Carlos Williams provide, perhaps, the most often anthologised and most distinguished poetry for the young. Frost and Sandburg made selections of their poems for children, *You Come Too* (1959) and *Wind Song* (1960) respectively; while Emily Dickinson *A Letter to the World* (1968) and Langston Hughes *Don't You Turn Back* (1969) have recently had selections published. In Britain the poetry of Edmund Blunden, W. H. Davies, Thomas Hardy, John Masefield, Elizabeth Jennings and R. S. Thomas was (and is) often chosen for children.

Before the sweeping changes that were to take place in the mid-1970s, two very distinctive poets produced their first collections for children: Ted Hughes (*Meet My Folks* (1961)), and Charles Causley (*Figgie Hobbin* (1970)).

In the early 1970s a new type of poetry hit the market in the rumbustious form of Michael Rosen: *Mind Your Own Business* came out in 1974 and was immediately successful. Rosen is probably the best-selling poet for children today, but his work caused a stir with many critics. Is it really *poetry*? He employs a form of free verse close to the the the rhythms of speech. Is it subversive? Could it be regarded as quality literature for the young? Rosen mocks his detractors: 'Is it a poem? Is it a story? Is it a film? Is it a banana?' (Styles 1988: 89). His poetry is certainly a departure from the past – it centres on the everyday experiences of children, sometimes exaggerated, written in ordinary language, peppered with jokes, insults and slang. It is cheeky, sometimes rude, often poking its tongue out at adult proprieties. Most critics failed to notice the serious side of Rosen which has always been interspersed with the humour. Rosen is a prolific writer and anthologist: *You Can't Catch Me* (1981), *The Hypnotiser* (1988), *Mind the Gap* (1992), are just a tiny sample of his many collections for children.

John Rowe Townsend calls it 'urchin verse': 'here is family life in the raw, with its backchat, fury and muddle, and instead of woods and meadows are disused railway lines, building sites and junkheaps' (Townsend 1987: 303). Simply reading the titles of the 1970s and 1980s shows how much poetry had changed: it had become irreverent, street-wise, informal and assertive. Certainly a flurry of collections by a talented group of poets using similar subject matter to Rosen quickly followed *Mind Your Own Business*, but their backgrounds, perspectives on childhood, styles of writing and chosen forms are distinctive and varied.

Kit Wright teamed up with the cartoonist, Posy Simmonds to produce lively, child-friendly poems in *Rabbiting On* (1978), but he was already an established poet, his verse stylish and carefully crafted. Wendy Cope, a witty, best-selling poet for adults, revealed a playful voice for the very young in *Twiddling Your Thumbs* (1987). Vernon Scannell's poetry had been used in schools for years, before he published *The Clever Potato* (1988), aimed at children. John Mole, *Boo to a Goose* (1987) and Libby Houston *All Aboard* (1993) were both published poets long before turning their attention to children.

Roger McGough comes from the performance tradition of the radical, Liverpool poets of the 1960s. So does Adrian Henri, *The Phantom Lollipop Lady* (1986) and Brian Patten *Gargling With Jelly* (1985). All three use a lot of humour, but the pain and tenderness associated with their adult work is there too; so is the satire. McGough's inventive imagination and skilled word play is on full display in *You Tell Me* 1979 (with Michael Rosen) and *Sky in the Pie* (1983). Adrian Mitchell is also well known on the performance circuit: his combination of compassion, social concern and the comic touch makes for memorable poetry as in *Nothingmas*

*Day* (1984). Gareth Owen was interested in the street life of children in *Salford Road* (1979) and *Song of the City* (1985), but his inspiration came from having worked in education; so did Mick Gowar's in *Swings and Roundabouts* (1981). Allan Ahlberg, an ex-teacher, used contemporary school life in *Please Mrs Butler* (1983) and *Heard it in the Playground* (1990), as did Judith Nicholls in *Magic Mirror* (1985).

Another exciting development since the 1980s has been the growing popularity of Caribbean British writers. John Agard produced *I Din Do Nuttin'* in 1983; *Say It Again, Granny* (1986), uses Caribbean proverbs as the basis for poetry which is both witty and wise. Grace Nichols published her first collection for children, *Come on into my Tropical Garden* in 1988: Me mudder chase bad-cow/with one 'Shoo'/she paddle down river/in she own canoe/Ain't have nothing/dat me mudder can't do. James Berry's impressive *When I Dance* (1988), demonstrated fine writing, an empathy for young people's feelings and a lively sense of fun, both in dialect and standard English. These three poets have also compiled ground-breaking anthologies, particularly in terms of introducing young readers to poetry from other cultures. Jackie Kay's original *Two's Company* and other talented voices like that of Valerie Bloom, Faustin Charles and Benjamin Zephaniah, show how contemporary children's poetry is blossoming into an experimental phase in terms of language, forms and themes.

Children have never had it so good in terms of accessible, amusing, racy poetry, but it is not all light-hearted. There's often a dark undertone in McGough which he describes as 'the shadow round the corner' and he is prepared to deal with child abuse, depression and death in his poetry. The skill lies in delicate yet honest treatment of harrowing issues. Wright also feels that children 'can take some stiffening' and tenderly explores mental handicap, bereavement and the cruelties of whaling in amongst the laughter. Agard, Berry and Kay touch on racism in their poetry. Rosen and Mitchell tackle bullying, sexism, rejection and loss. Henri reflects on a war-time childhood and Patten considers the aftermath of a nuclear war. Owen writes of poetry as a means of hanging on to memories, teaching us not to forget: 'always too in the further recesses of my mind I have a hope that there's another soul out there who will say "That's how it was … for me"' (Styles and Triggs 1988: 89). It is simply inaccurate to characterise contemporary poetry for children as humorous and slight. In some respects it has never been stronger.

All these poets have in their various ways 'tuned into childhood' with intimacy and honesty, reflecting, I think, a basic respect for and recognition of young readers in all their complexity. One reason for this is the regular contact with children they gain through school visits and performances. These are poets who *know what children enjoy*, who are close to their audience; most of them divide their time between writing for adults and children, something that certainly isn't common in the world of fiction; many of them have also edited significant anthologies for children. All of them have continued to publish popular new collections into the 1990s.

Some of their American counterparts are John Ciardi, Eloise Greenfield, Mary Ann Hoberman, David McCord, Eve Merriam, Jack Prelutsky, Nancy Willard and Charlotte Zolotow. Their poetry tends to have a quieter and less realistic flavour than that of British poets, with the exception of Shel Silverstein (*A Light in the*

*Attic* (1982)), Karla Kuskin (*Any Me I Want To Be* (1972)), and Nikki Giovanni (*Spin a Soft Black Song* (1971) whose spunky verse is anything but tame. Interestingly, 'urchin verse', as Townsend defines it, which does so well in Britain, is hardly known in America.

There are also a clutch of humorists on both sides of the Atlantic who sell well: for example, William Cole (*Oh Such Foolishness* (1980)), Roald Dahl (*Revolting Rhymes* (1982)), Spike Milligan (*Unspun Socks from a Chicken's Laundry* (1981)), Colin McNaughton (*There's an Awful Lot of Wierdos in our Neighbourhood* (1987)), Colin West (*A Step in the Wrong Direction* (1984)); and 'Dr Seuss' (*Green Eggs and Ham* (1960)). None would be called, or perhaps call themselves poets, but their verse is much appreciated by children.

The late twentieth century has seen the development of outstanding pictorial texts such as Charles Keeping's version of *The Highwayman* (1981) or Michael Foreman's *A Child's Garden of Verses* (1985), and collaborations between poets and artists such as Michael Rosen and Quentin Blake, or Ted Hughes and Leonard Baskin – reminding us of famous collaborations of the past, such as Rossetti and Hughes or Milne and Shepard.

The current climate of popularising poetry may lead to a wider audience: despite the huge range available, it remains a minority interest and only a small number of people read, write and buy it. Equally, although poetry for children has come a long way, how much of it is still the well-meaning preferences of adults foisted on children?

## Poetry Internationally

The discussion thus far has related to poetry for children in Britain, with America, Canada (poets like Anne Corbett and Dennis Lee) and Australia (Max Fachen, Norman Lindsay, Doug MacLeod) following roughly parallel tracks in this century. It is worth noting that poetry written for children is not so widespread outside Britain: and most countries do not have a native tradition of published children's poetry. Young readers interested in poetry borrow from accessible adult works. There are a few anthologies which deal specifically with international poetry: for example, *Can I Buy a Slice of the Sky* (edited by Grace Nichols) (1991), *I Like That Stuff* (edited by Morag Styles) (1984), and *Poetry World* (1985) edited by Geoffrey Summerfield. Indeed, most good editors spread their nets widely, as with Charles Causley's *The Sun, Dancing* (1984) or Naomi Lewis's *A Footprint in the Air* (1983). There is generally more interest in the poetry of ethnic minorities within most cultures, but there is still a long way to go before we reach a genuinely international outlook or a representation of poetry *in all its voices*.

## References

Alexander, W. (ed.) (1896) *Poems of Cecil Frances Alexander*, London: Macmillan.
Darton, H. (1932/1982) *Children's Books in England. Three Centuries of Social Life*, 3rd edn, rev. B. Alderson, Cambridge: Cambridge University Press.
de la Mare, W. (ed.) (1930) *Christina Rossetti: Poems*, Newtown: Gregynog Press.
Glen, H. (1983) *Vision and Disenchantment*, Cambridge: Cambridge University Press.

Jones, K. (1991) *Learning not to be First: the life of Christina Rossetti*, Oxford: Oxford University Press.

Leader, Z. (1981) *Reading Blake's Songs*, London: Routledge.

Lonsdale, Roger (ed.) (1989) *Eighteenth Century Women Poets*, Oxford: Oxford University Press.

Milne, C. (1974) *The Enchanted Places*, London: Methuen.

Muir, P. (1954) *English Children's Books 1600 to 1900*, London: Batsford.

Opie, I. (1992) *The People in the Playground*, Oxford: Oxford University Press.

Pafford, J. H. (ed.) (1971) *Divine Songs Attempted in Easy Language for the Use of Children* by Isaac Watts [facsimile of 1715 edn], London: Oxford University Press.

Milne, C. (1974) *The Enchanted Places*, London: Methuen.

Patmore, C. (1862) *The Children's Garland*, London: Macmillan.

Philip, N. (ed.) (1990) *A New Treasury of Poetry*, London: Blackie.

Shaw, J. M. (1962) *Childhood in Poetry*, Detroit: Gale Research.

Townsend, J. R. (1897) *Written for Children*, 3rd edn, London: Penguin.

Webb, K. (ed.) (1979) *I Like This Poem*, Harmondsworth: Penguin.

## Further Reading

Hall, D. ( 1985) *The Oxford Book of Children's Verse in America*, Oxford: Oxford University Press.

Morse, B. (1992) *Poetry Books For Children, A Signal Bookguide*, South Woodchester: Thimble Press.

Opie, I. and Opie, P. (1973) *The Oxford Book of Children's Verse*, Oxford: Oxford University Press.

—— (1977) *Three Centuries of Nursery Rhymes and Poetry for Children*, Oxford: Oxford University Press.

St John, J. (1975) *Osborne Collection of Early Children's Books*, Toronto: Toronto Public Library.

Shaw, J. M. (1962) *Childhood in Poetry*, vols 1–5, Detroit: Gale Research Company.

Styles, M. (1990) 'Lost from the nursery: women writing poetry for children 1800–1850', *Signal* 63: 177–205.

—— and Cook, H. (eds) (1988) *There's a Poet Behind You*, London: A. and C. Black.

—— and Triggs, P. (1988) *The Books For Keeps Guide to Poetry 0–16*, London: Books For Keeps.

# 17

# Drama

## *Peter Hollindale*

'Children's literature' is a term which asks for subtle and flexible definitions, but as commonly used it has the almost universal common features of adult authorship, child readership, professional publication and a stable text. If these criteria are applied to drama, and we think of an equivalent 'dramatic literature for children', then the field is a very narrow one. It begins only in the late nineteenth century, falls into relative inertia in the years between the two World Wars, and gathers momentum only after 1945. Even now, many plays for children achieve only local performance, remain unpublished, and fail to win a regular place in the repertoire.

On the other hand, if we detach the word 'drama' from the constraints of 'dramatic literature for children' and interpret it more generously, we find that far from being the youngest and most ill-supplied of literary art forms for children, it is actually the oldest, the most fundamental to child development, and the one in which children as performers if not as originators have engaged most nearly on equal terms with adults. Children encounter their 'dramatic literature' only by attending the performance of a children's play. But they encounter 'drama' whenever they play, act out stories, imitate other people, experiment with social roles, pretend to be someone else whom they admire or fear or love. John O'Toole, in his book *Theatre in Education* (1976), defines drama as 'the symbolic representation at first hand of the working out of relationships involving human beings', and he gives examples of this process at work in children's dramatic play.

> Children in their own dramatic play act out stories and explore worlds where the outcome is in their hands; they create their own conventions: 'You've got to lie down, you're dead' ... We must all have seen children externalising their fears and anxieties by playing bears, exploring the implications of conflict and morality in games of cowboys and Indians, learning to copy adult behaviour playing Mummies and Daddies – and sometimes doing all three at once (children in wartime will endlessly play fighters and bombers, tanks and ambushes). All the time they are unconsciously developing their ability to co-exist and work co-operatively, discovering and extending the limits of mutually acceptable behaviour, learning about leaders and roles, acceptance and rejection; often with tears, exasperation and boredom.
>
> O'Toole 1976: 18

Two of the greatest and most significant early works of dramatic literature for children incorporate their authors' awareness of this broader meaning and necessity for drama. At the very beginning of J. M. Barrie's *Peter Pan* (1904) we see John and Wendy 'playing Mummies and Daddies':

> *John* (*histrionically*): We are doing an act; we are playing at being you and Father. (*He imitates the only father who has come under his special notice*) A little less noise there.
>
> *Wendy*: Now let us pretend we have a baby.
>
> *John*: (*good-naturedly*): I am happy to inform you, Mrs Darling, that you are now a mother.
>
> Barrie 1995: 89

Arguably the whole of *Peter Pan* is concerned with the dramatic games of children at play, and Peter himself is given over entirely to a life of acting and performance. And in Frances Hodgson Burnett's *A Little Princess* (1902) Sara Crewe, reduced to household slavery and confined to a rat-infested garret by the odious Miss Minchin, finds consolation for her plight in dramatic romance, and pretends that her attic is a cell in the Bastille:

> *Sara*: I pretend I have been here for years – and years and years – and years – and everyone has forgotten all about me, and Miss Minchin is the jailer. And I pretend that there's another prisoner in the next cell, – that's Becky [the scullery maid], you know, – I've told her about it – and I knock on the wall to make her hear, and she knocks like this, – you know. (*Knocks three times on wall; listens a moment*). She's not there; if she were she'd knock back. Ah!
>
> *Ermengarde*: Ah, it's just like a story.
>
> *Sara*: It is a story; everything is a story – you're a story, I'm a story. Miss Minchin's a story. (*Rats squeak*).
>
> Bedard 1984: 91

*A Little Princess* was first produced in 1902 – initially as *A Little Unfairy Princess* – and published in Moses (1921).

In these seminal dramatic texts the continuum of drama is affirmed, from childhood play and pretence and acting through to works of dramatic literature composed by adults for children. O'Toole points to the widespread use of dramatic metaphors in media reportage, citing 'tragic mistake', 'dramatic rescue', and 'common farce', which he says 'reflect the closeness of drama to reality in our lives' (O'Toole 1976: 19). He might have added that theatrical metaphors figure largely in the everyday phrases used by adults to control child behaviour: 'Don't act so silly'; 'Stop dramatising'; 'There's no need to make a scene'. In using such terms, we implicitly recognise the continuity of drama in children's lives, from playing to watching a play, from 'acting stupidly' to acting on the stage. Drama for children is both something that you watch and something that you do, and so important is it that we have 'educational drama' to make sure it is done well. 'Dramatic literature' such as *Peter Pan* and *A Little Princess* is only part of a much larger spectrum of activity, one in which it is necessary to define our terms.

## Definitions

The British Arts Council pamphlet of guidance on drama education, *Drama in Schools* (1992), defines drama as an educational experience in terms of three activities: making, performing and responding. Virtually all the encounters a child can have with drama come under one or more of these headings, and all are essential if the adult is to gain life-long pleasure from drama, whether in the theatre or through film and television. Children at play in early childhood are already 'making' drama, when they improvise stories and games with rules and allotted parts: a child putting her teddy to bed is starting to engage in creative dramatics. At school, experiences of 'structured play' and early ventures in classroom improvisation begin to formalise the natural impetus to play. When stories are 'acted out', the child is performing. Whether or not there is an audience is unimportant. Many teachers regard drama as a process, not a product, and view premature involvement in theatrical performance, however informal and domestic, as actively harmful. However, thousands of children begin to perform for a friendly public of peers, parents or the local community at a very early stage. Later there will probably be full-scale school productions. Simultaneously, the child is 'responding' to drama, on television and possibly in the theatre, and should be aided to develop a critical response. *Drama in Schools* observes: 'Responding to the plays they see, or take part in, is also an essential part of pupils' drama education' (Arts Council 1992: 5).

John and Wendy in *Peter Pan*, and Sara Crewe in *A Little Princess*, are already making, performing and responding. They invent the scenarios of their mini-dramas, act them out, and also show awareness of the fictive convention they are using. When Wendy says 'let us pretend', and Sara says 'it is a story', they are imaginatively committed to their dramatic play while reserving part of themselves as aware spectators of its inventedness. They are 'responding to the plays they ... take part in', and so are learning to be an audience. The children in the theatre audience for productions of plays are learning the same lessons both directly and at one remove, in an advanced, sophisticated experience of dramatic play: the experience of children's theatre.

Clearly we need subsidiary terms to denote these varied experiences of making, performing and responding to drama. Moses Goldberg, in *Children's Theatre: a Philosophy and a Method* (1974) proposes three terms which broadly correspond to the three key activities, all of them under the inclusive heading of 'children's drama'. 'Creative dramatics' is Goldberg's term for 'an informal activity in which children are guided by a leader to express themselves through the medium of drama. Its goal is not performance, but rather the free expression of the child's creative imagination though the discipline of an art form' (4). The activities of 'creative dramatics' lead directly on from spontaneous play. They may include improvised dialogue, movement and dance, mime and puppetry, the acting out of stories and dramatised response to poetry and music. Their aims are not only imaginative and artistic but personal, including the development of self-confidence and social awareness. Most of what happens in creative dramatics is an advanced and structured version of what children naturally do for themselves.

'Recreational drama' is the term Goldberg proposes for 'a formal theatrical presentation where the development and experience of the performers is as or more important than the aesthetic enjoyment of the audience' (5). He includes 'school pageants, camp skits, or recreation department programs in which children act for other children' (5), and in Britain its most important manifestation is the school play.

'Children's theatre' is Goldberg's title for 'a formal theatrical experience in which a play is presented for an audience of children' (5). Its purpose is to entertain, and to encourage enjoyment of theatre as an art form. Although children may appear in child roles in such plays, the assumption is that most parts will be played by adults, and usually by professional actors. Children who appear may be professionals themselves, perhaps attending drama schools and hoping for a career in theatre; they will not be acting because someone thinks it will be good for them. Such professional performances are classified by Goldberg as 'Youth Theatre' if they are designed for the 14–18 age group.

These are useful distinctions. However, in Britain the term 'Youth Theatre' is used rather differently, and defined by the Standing Conference of Young People's Theatre (SCYPT) as 'theatre *done by young people themselves*, usually led by a teacher or under the auspices of a Young People's Company' (England 1990: 1): that is, it is a branch of recreational theatre.

Because theatrical companies and professional actors are now widely involved in the educational process, not just in mounting productions for children's aesthetic pleasure but in visiting schools and other youth venues for educational purposes, and not just as performers but with a professional identity which straddles acting and teaching, two other terms have come into common use to designate activities which Goldberg's categories do not fully cover. They are 'Young People's Theatre' and 'Theatre in Education'.

'Young People's Theatre' refers to 'a performance by professional actors in an educational context, or in any space where young people form the audience, such as youth clubs or community centres. It is frequently based on social issues'. 'Theatre in Education' (TIE) is

> work done by professional actor-teachers in a school context. The primary aim is to use theatre and drama to create a wide range of learning opportunities across the whole curriculum. Typically TIE works with one class for at least half a day and in addition to performance, the programme involves some active participation on the part of the pupils.

(I am indebted for these descriptions to the British Centre of ASSITEJ (Association Internationale du Théâtre pour l'Enfance et la Jeunesse) which has done a great deal in recent years to promote ideas and activity across national frontiers in all branches of theatre for the young.)

These categories cover almost everything that currently occurs in the field of children's drama, with one exception: dramatic performances of professional quality by children designed for audiences of adults (or for both adults and children). Nowadays these are rare, but not unknown. The film (and some stage productions) of Alan Parker's *Bugsy Malone* (1984) is perhaps the most successful and well known achievement of this kind in recent years. In the past, however, quasi-professional performances by children for adults have been an important feature of our theatre history. It should also be remembered that the boundary between recreational drama and children's theatre is ill defined. Summer productions in London by the National Youth Theatre have been intended for the personal development of the student participants, but they achieve professional standards of production and in the past have included many actors marked for future distinction, including Derek Jacobi, Helen Mirren and Daniel Day Lewis.

## Drama in Children's Literature

In both Britain and the USA children's theatre effectively begins in the late nineteenth century, first with Christmas pantomimes for a family audience, and dramatisations of well-known children's novels, and then at the turn of the century with *Peter Pan* and the start of an original dramatic literature. Children's novelists, however, have long been aware of the broader place that drama has in children's lives, creating plots and episodes which reflect the varied experiences of drama set out above. A classic early example can be seen in the 'duke and king' chapters of Mark Twain's *Huckleberry Finn* (1884), notably the duke's hilarious travesty of Hamlet's soliloquy, To be or not to be (chapter 21) which so arouses Huck Finn's admiration.

Almost every level of child drama from the crudest 'creative dramatics' to professional performances is reflected in modern stories. Louise Fitzhugh's *Harriet the Spy* (1964) has a wonderful episode in which Harriet's class, at the behest of an enthusiastic drama teacher, improvises a dance for the Christmas pageant, with the children cast as items in the festive dinner (including brown leotards for those who play the gravy). Harriet's teacher is the model of all that is worst in creative dramatics:

> 'I want you to feel – to the very best of your endeavour – I want you to feel that one morning you *wake up* as one of these vegetables, one of these *dear* vegetables, nestling in the earth, warm in the heat and power and magic of growth, or striving tall above the ground, pushing through, bit by bit in the miracle of birth, waiting for that glorious moment when you will be ...'
> 'Eaten', Harriet whispered ...
>
> Fitzhugh 1964/1975: 93

A school play, a revival of the Victorian melodrama *Sweeney Todd*, is the occasion of Gillian Cross's *The Dark Behind the Curtain* (1982), in which the old story summons up the restless ghosts of maltreated Victorian children, while dramatics in more opulent schools are important in the lives of Antonia Forest's Marlow family, in, for example, *Autumn Term* (1948) and *The Cricket Term* (1974). The Lake District teenagers of Geoffrey Trease's Black Banner series mount a production in *Black Banner Players* (1952). Outside school, the hero of Jean Ure's *A Proper Little Nooryeff* (1982), has to come to terms with his embarrassing gift for ballet. Pamela Brown's *The Swish of the Curtain* (1941) achieved enormous popularity with its varied dramatic experiences of pantomime, open-air performances, theatrical competitions and a visit to Stratford-upon-Avon. Perhaps the most committed theatrical stories of all were those of Noel Streatfeild, who had herself been an actress for many years before she became a successful writer. Most famously in *Ballet Shoes* (1936), but also in such stories as *Curtain Up* (1944) and *The Painted Garden* (1949), she depicted the lives and tribulations of young people taking their first steps in show business. There are many popular images of 'making, performing and responding' in modem children's fiction.

There is also an informal theatre history. Through contemporary children's books we can track back children's involvement in drama, as spectators but especially as performers, across the centuries to the beginnings of modern theatre history. Frederick Grice's *Aidan and the Strollers* (1960) depicts a band of travelling actors in England in 1825, while another company of strolling players, this time in the eighteenth-century, supplies the family background in Leon Garfield's *Devil-in-the-Fog* (1966). The world of eighteenth-century provincial theatres and of Drury Lane in Sheridan's time is evoked with documentary precision in Margaret Jowett's *Candidate for Fame* (1955). In Lucy Boston's *The Children of Green Knowe* (1954), the boy treble Alexander Oldknow sings the part of Cupid in the masque *Cupid and Death* for Charles II in Restoration England. Not surprisingly, the heady politics of Tudor England and the achievements of Shakespeare's theatre have proved most attractive of all for children's writers, in such books as Geoffrey Trease's *Cue for Treason* (1940), Rosemary Sutcliff's *Brother Dusty-Feet* (1952), Margaret Jowett's *A Cry of Players* (1961), and Antonia Forest's *The Player's Boy* (1970). Surprisingly little has been made in stories of the children's companies which flourished in Tudor and early Stuart England, but a factual account appeared in Elfrida Vipont's *A Child of the Chapel Royal* (1967). Set even earlier in time, the mystery-play cycles of medieval England provided the background for Dennis Hamley's *Pageants of Despair* (1974). And the very beginnings of Western drama are celebrated in the Athenian dramatic contests and festivals of Geoffrey Trease's *The Crown of Violet* (1952). The child characters of these and many other stories are deeply involved in drama centuries before a children's dramatic literature came into being, and so were their counterparts in life.

## From the Beginnings to the Nineteenth Century

The beginnings of children's drama, like the beginnings of modern European drama itself, lie with the Roman Catholic Church. The dramatic content of Christian worship became evident very early in church history: from the fourth century onwards the central rite of Christian observance was the Mass, which is highly dramatic in conception and form. As early as the tenth century there are European records of solemn processions of children through the church in celebration of Holy Innocents' Day (28 December). Liturgical drama was a natural development in the Middle Ages from the core observances of services and processions, and as it took shape so the drama moved outside the church itself into the precincts and the churchyard, and eventually into the neighbouring market places. E. K. Chambers, in *The Medieval Stage* (vol. 2, 1903), refers to Palm Sunday processions, elaborations of the usual processions before Mass, going round the churchyard carrying palms. 'At the doors of the church', he says, 'the procession was greeted by boys stationed upon the roof of the porch' (5). Perhaps the first recorded example in England of children's participation, as audience, in a dramatic event is a chronicle description of a 'representation of the Lord's resurrection' in St John's Churchyard, Beverley, about 1220. Richard Axton, in *European Drama of the Early Middle Ages* (1974), describes the event:

> The Beverley play was performed by masked actors, as usual ... The play at Beverley was apparently 'in the round', since the crowd, gathered together, the writer says, by delight or curiosity or devotion ... formed a ring ... Some boys climbed into the church tower to get a good view of the costume, actions and dialogue.
>
> Axton 1974: 162–163

Although firm documentation of medieval drama before the fifteenth century is sparse, it is generally believed that a gradual process of secularisation took place in the thirteenth and fourteenth centuries, culminating in the great mystery play cycles such as those at York, Wakefield and Chester, which were performed annually at the recently established feast of Corpus Christi. The descendants of those enthusiastic boy theatre-goers at Beverley would have seen these plays each year, and not a few would have taken part in them.

Boys as performers rather than spectators, however, had the greatest role in furthering children's drama. It was the boy choristers of medieval England whose Elizabethan successors provided the most curious and remarkable achievement of professional child theatre. For the first decade of the seventeenth century the theatre of Shakespeare's London was augmented by two fashionable and gifted children's companies, the Children of Paul's, who were the boy choristers of St Paul's Cathedral, and the Children of the Chapel Royal, the choristers of the monarch's private chapel. Major dramatists wrote major plays for these boys, who were mostly aged between 10 and 15; their playwrights included Ben Jonson, John Marston, Thomas Middleton, and Beaumont and Fletcher. So successful were they that they seriously undermined the economic prosperity of the adult companies, including Shakespeare's own. These boys are the 'little eyases', whom Rosencrantz describes to Hamlet in a famous scene:

> there is, Sir, an eyrie of children, little eyases, that cry out on the top of question, and are most tyrannically clapped for't. These are now the fashion, and so berattle the common stages – so they call them – that many wearing rapiers are afraid of goose quills and dare scarce come thither.
>
> *Hamlet* Act 2 scene 2

Hamlet asks, 'What, are they children? Who maintains 'em?', to which the answer is that some brilliantly entrepreneurial choirmasters maintained 'em, to no little profit. 'Do the boys carry it away?' asks the Prince. 'Ay, that they do, my lord', says Rosencrantz, and ay, that they did. But the gifts that made possible their unique achievement – their appearance of knowing innocence, their musical ability, their grammar school training, their powers of iconoclastic parody directed at the adult world – can all be traced back to earlier manifestations of child drama in medieval and Tudor England. The two great children's companies were only the final achievement of a very long history of child theatre, and its quality should not be underestimated. Not for nothing were choristers so prominent in this phase of children's performance theatre. Drama and music, brought together at the outset in liturgical plays, formed an inseparable theatrical union which depended on the boys' contribution, especially at the Christmas festival. Something of their place in ecclesiastical music drama is conveyed by E. K. Chambers's account of the liturgical drama *Officium Pastorum* at Rouen in the Middle Ages: 'After the Te Deum five canons or vicars, representing the shepherds, approached the great west door of the choir. A boy *in similitudinem angeli* perched *in excelsio* sang them the "good tidings", and a number of others *in voltis ecclesiae* took up the *Gloria in excelsis*' (41).

Choristers in less pure and saintly guise prefigured the parodic gifts of the children's companies through the Boy Bishop ceremonies of the medieval church. For twenty-four hours, starting at Vespers on Holy Innocents' Eve (27 December) choir boys or schoolboys replaced their elders and conducted all the services, except perhaps Mass. On Childermass Day (28 December) the boy chosen by his fellows to be Bishop preached a sermon, and after dinner he and his fellows processed through the streets, receiving gifts and offerings. This widespread custom is recorded at York as early as 1221, and continued in many parts of England until it was suppressed by Henry VIII after the Reformation.

The third strand of dramatic experience which made up the pattern of early children's drama was the belief of Renaissance teachers in the educational advantages of acting. Regular performances of Latin comedies by Terence and Plautus were part of the curriculum in many sixteenth-century English grammar schools, and similar scholastic productions took place across Europe, notably in the Jesuit colleges which were founded from the middle of the century onwards. The hopes and aims of modern drama teaching were anticipated by these Tudor schoolmasters: they included not only cultural experience, and training in Latin, but the development of eloquence, poise, good movement and general self-confidence. One schoolmaster, Nicholas Udall, wrote the first true English comedy, *Ralph Roister Doister*, for performance by his pupils at Eton (probably between 1534 and 1541), and theatrical performances by choristers and schoolboys were a regular feature of life at court. No doubt all this drama incurred much righteous disapproval, and in the Induction to his play *The Staple of News*, Ben Jonson puts into the mouth of his gossips the selfsame public indignation which is now directed at progressive education and 'misuse of taxpayers' money'.

> They make all their scholars playboys! Is't not a fine sight to see all our children made interluders? Do we pay our money for this? We send them to learn their grammar and their Terence and they learn their playbooks! ... I hope ... we shall have good painful ministers to keep school and catechise our youth and not teach them to speak plays, and act fables of false news, in this manner, to the supervexation of town and country, with a wannion [with a vengeance]!
>
> Jonson 1631/1975: 106–107

Alas, it was not to last. The brief heyday of the great children's companies was, as we have seen, the climax of much diverse activity over several centuries, but with their closure, shortly followed by the Puritan ascendancy, children's drama became marginalised for the next two hundred years.

Even so, from the late eighteenth century onwards it is possible to find distinguished forerunners of modern children's theatre and creative dramatics. A key figure in the birth of modern children's drama was Stephanie, Comtesse de Genlis, whose plays for children under the title *Théâtre a l'Usage des Jeunes Personnes* were first published in 1779–1780. Madame de Genlis, who followed the educational theories of Rousseau, made theatre a central experience for the children she taught, not only writing plays for them to perform but taking them to the Comédie Française. Jonathan Levy, in the introduction to his invaluable anthology *The Gymnasium of the Imagination: A Collection of Children's Plays in English 1780–1860* (1992), notes that her strategies 'became the basis of a new dramaturgy for playwriting for children'.

> [T]he premises of this new dramaturgy are threefold: first, that children's plays should be based not on the struggle between good and evil, but rather on the struggle between good and not-yet-good; second, (a corollary), that in children's plays real evil will not be shown and that, when wickedness of any kind is shown, unless it is clearly reformed and repentant by the final curtain, it will be shown to be inept or else will be so outrageously overwritten as to be unbelievable; and third, that the sensibility that suffuses plays for children should be one of triumphant sweetness and light.
>
> Levy 1992: 2–3

Under these general principles a century of inconspicuous but valuable playwriting for children ensured that theatre as making and performing secured an active presence in both school and home. Indeed, many of the plays written at this period were intended for domestic performance by families, with parents and children taking part together. In their common belief that the imaginative experience of children's drama could contribute to the moral and social education of children, it is possible to see these plays as the precursors of the present-day Young People's Theatre and Theatre-in-Education. Levy separates their subjects into five categories: 'dramatic proverbs and other moral tales; history plays, including sacred history; sentimental comedies; fairy tales and Eastern tales; and familiar dialogues' (7–8).

Naturally, many of the plays written under such voluntary constraints are of minor literary and dramatic merit, although important figures made their contribution. William Godwin, the husband of Mary Wollstonecraft and father of Mary Shelley, published his *Dramas for Children* in 1809. But the most distinguished of English language children's dramatists in this century of activity was Maria Edgeworth. Edgeworth's *Little Plays* (1827) are only a small part of her prolific output, but they are tried and tested, having been written for and performed by the younger children of her father's enormous family, and they are full of humour, lively and convincing dialogue, practical observation of real people, and humane moral intelligence. These little plays deserve a continuing place in the repertoire of children's theatre.

Alongside this private drama for school and home, the major public event of children's theatre before the close of the nineteenth century was the emergence of pantomime in the Victorian period as a children's entertainment. As a distinctive dramatic convention pantomime appeared in Britain early in the eighteenth century, forming a combination of popular story (initially from classical mythology, but by the beginning of the nineteenth century increasingly from fairy stories) with the traditional Italian harlequinade. A 'transformation scene' joined together the two parts of the entertainment. With the freeing of the theatres from restrictive legislation in 1843, this developed into the complex theatrical phenomenon which persists in its ambiguities to the present day. On the one hand, pantomimes became specifically associated with Christmas, and closely rooted in local communities for whom they were specially written. As Christmas entertainments they naturally became established as performances for children. On the other hand, the parallel and similar form of the 'burlesque' was emphatically *not* for children, but unavoidably affected pantomime conventions. There were also complaints that inappropriate and vulgar material was spilling over into pantomime from the newly flourishing music halls, as this nineteenth century commentator confirms:

> We may say of present day pantomime that the trail of the music hall is over it all ... The objection to music hall artists on the stage is ... that they have the effect of familiarising general audiences, and children especially, with a style and kind of singing, dancing and business which, however it may be relished by a certain class of the population, ought steadily to be confined to its original habitat.

> Mander and Mitchenson 1973: 35

Over a hundred years later, pantomime is still for many children the main or only family experience of theatre, but it habitually displays the same uncomfortable blend of fairy tale, burlesque and risqué music hall turns. In this way children's theatre becomes the pretext for variety acts, replete with innuendo, aimed at grown-ups. In the USA, pantomime enjoyed brief popularity but disappeared at the turn of the century, having performed the useful service of establishing a base for children's theatre. In Britain it persisted, providing incentive, partly by adverse reaction, towards new experiments in theatre for children. Bernard Shaw, in an article 'Grimaldi is dead, why not bury him?' in *The Era* (30 December 1937), observed: '*Peter Pan* was an attempt to get Christmas pieces out of their groove. *Androcles and the Lion* was another.'

## *Peter Pan* **and After**

In his study, *Fifty Years of 'Peter Pan'* (1954), Roger Lancelyn Green describes Barrie's masterpiece as 'really the first absolutely straight play for children – and assuredly the best and most popular' (1–2). First produced in 1904 in London, and the following year in New York, it achieved annual Christmas revivals for half a century, and in its original or adapted forms continues to be widely popular. Disney's cartoon version (1953), and more recently Steven Spielberg's *Hook* (1991), have brought versions of the tale to a wider audience. Spielberg has acknowledged his fascination with the story, and I would argue that his blockbuster film *E.T.: the Extra Terrestrial* (1984), even more than *Hook*, embodies a powerful indirect reworking of the story. Not for nothing is the mother in *ET* heard reading *Peter Pan* aloud to the youngest child at a crucial moment in the film.

*Peter Pan* survives in many forms, but the story we know best began life as a play, being converted to prose narrative only later: the reverse of the process which produced stage versions of Hodgson Burnett's *Little Lord Fauntleroy* (1888) and *A Little Princess* (1902), and of Kenneth Grahame's *The Wind in the Willows* (1908). From its beginnings the most usual evolution of children's theatre has been from novel or story into play or film, a sequence which continues to the present day through film and television drama. Many of the most memorable experiences of drama for modern children have been television adaptations of such books as John Masefield's *The Box of Delights* (1935), Frances Hodgson Burnett's *The Secret Garden* (1911), Philippa Pearce's *Tom's Midnight Garden* (1958), and more recently Peter Dickinson's 'Changes' trilogy (1968–1970) and Jill Paton Walsh's *Torch* (1987). But *Peter Pan* was play first and play foremost, exploiting the resources of theatrical lighting, visual and sound effects (most famously the ticking crocodile) and circus-like spectacle such as flying.

Lancelyn Green notes that *Peter Pan*'s only significant predecessor as children's theatre, the play *Bluebell in Fairyland* by Seymour Hicks (which was first produced in 1901 and which supposedly prompted Barrie to the writing of a fairy play) had 'only half escaped from pantomime or operetta' (2). *Bluebell in Fairyland* was a fantasy or dream play, which in itself provided the model for numerous successors, but it relied heavily on pantomime effects. Nor is *Peter Pan* itself at all free of them: the tradition of having Peter Pan played by an actress obviously reflects the pantomime's 'principal boy'. But with these two plays the leap was made from pantomime to true drama as the proper sphere of children's theatre, and *Peter Pan* is a central work not only for its mythopoeic originality but for its pioneering creation of a genre.

The years up to the First World War produced one other masterpiece, the allegorical fairy story *The Blue Bird*, by the Belgian symbolist poet Maurice Maeterlinck, which was first performed in Britain in 1909. Unfortunately this subtle and moving story is difficult to stage and has rarely been produced (though it is one of the works commemorated in Noel Streatfeild's *Ballet Shoes*). Far less distinguished but more accessible and readily stageworthy was *Where the Rainbow Ends* (1911) by Clifford Evans and John Ramsey, the story of a quest by supposedly bereaved children for their lost parents, whom they find in a magic land. Bearing traces of *Peter Pan*, this play is also noticeably imbued with the febrile patriotism which by 1911 was already creating psychological preconditions for the war. Nevertheless, it retained its popularity for many years. Shaw's *Androcles and the Lion* (1913), allegedly written as a counterblow to *Peter Pan*, is a satirical play of sporadic genius but not really a work for children at all; its shortcomings as children's theatre are very evident if it is compared with the witty and entertaining *Androcles and the Lion* (1963) by the gifted American children's dramatist Aurand Harris, which is written in the style of Italian *commedia dell'arte*.

For children's theatre the interwar years were chiefly distinguished by the work of actor-managers and educators with special interests in children's aesthetic development. Not all of them wrote plays, and even those who did, like the gifted and influential American writer and director Charlotte Chorpenning, are remembered less for the competent and popular plays they wrote as for their practical theatre initiatives. In Chorpenning's case these stretched over many years at the Goodman Theatre of the Art Institute of Chicago. In Britain much the same was true a few years later of Brian Way, and their achievement belongs most closely not with the dramatists but with great pioneers of educational drama such as Caldwell Cook (whose book *The Play Way* (1917), is an important milestone) and above all of Peter Slade, whose book *Child Drama* (1954), and inspiring gift for matching practice with theory, supplied a powerful influence for the following generation. Along with several founders of sometimes short-lived but none the less important children's theatre companies, such as Bertha Waddell's Scottish Children's Theatre, innovators such as these laid the foundations for post-war work.

In the dramatic literature itself, two works by A. A. Milne stand out from the interwar years. One was *Toad of Toad Hall* (1929), a cunningly selective and theatrically proven dramatisation of *The Wind in the Willows*; the other was the more original *Make-Believe* (1921). Milne was modest about this play, believing himself to be overshadowed by *Peter Pan*. 'The difficulty in the way of writing a children's play', he observed, 'is that Barrie was born too soon. Many people must have felt the same about Shakespeare. We who come later have no chance' (Milne 1922: xiii). Even so, *Make-Believe* is undeservedly neglected. It is three plays in one, of which the third act, 'Father Christmas and the Hubbard Family', is a spirited and ingenious comedy in its own right, and it is also in its modest fashion metadrama for children, with much to teach through entertainment about the nature of theatre.

The years since 1945 have produced much valuable if short-lived work under the headings described earlier, not least in the field of documentary drama produced through Young People's Theatre and Theatre in Education. Some individual works, such as David Pownall's play about American Indians, *The Dream of Chief Crazy Horse* (1975), stand out as dramas of lasting value, but much is quite properly 'occasional' work, and not for that reason to be decried. Few professional dramatists have devoted themselves wholly or regularly to children's theatre. Most prominent among them was Nicholas Stuart Gray who wrote a series of inventive dramatisations of well-known fairy tales such as *The Imperial Nightingale* (1956) and *New Clothes for the Emperor* (1957), skilfully devised for performance by or for children, and offering worthwhile experiences in either performing or responding. It is a sad indication of the Cinderella status of children's drama that had Gray chosen to write primarily in fiction he would undoubtedly be more famous than he is.

Alan Ayckbourn is a rare example of a commercially successful dramatist who has frequently returned to children's theatre, not least with his imaginative vehicle for audience participation, *Mr A's Amazing Maze Plays* (1989), but also in other accomplished works, often comic and always thought-provoking, such as *Invisible Friends* (1991) and *Ernie's Incredible Hallucinations* (1991). Adrian Mitchell is another talented writer who has kept faith with children in the midst of other activity, with effective plays such as *Tamburlane the Mad Hen* (another play which puts itself at the mercy of its child audience), which first appeared in the anthology *Playspace* (1971), and *You Must Believe All This* (1981), which is based on Charles Dickens's *Holiday Romance*, and most recently in a version of Kipling's *Jungle Book*, *Mowgli's Jungle* (1992). Robert Bolt's *The Thwarting of Baron Bolligrew* (1966), a somewhat laboured performance by the author of *A Man for All Seasons*, has proved highly popular despite its evident defects – which perhaps indicates the continuing shortage of good texts.

The post-war years have produced two clear masterpieces, in addition to the fine work of the American Aurand Harris. One is *Reynard the Fox* (1958), by the Belgian Arthur Fauquez, which gives to children's theatre a classic equivalent of Chaucer's 'Nun's Priest's Tale'. The other is Mary Melwood's *The Tingalary Bird* (1964), the work of an English dramatist, which is much better known in the USA and which has deservedly been widely anthologised there. *The Tingalary Bird* is an absurdist drama, brilliantly conceived and uncompromisingly at one with mainstream post-war theatre, yet wholly accessible to children (and once again requiring participant decisions from its youthful audience). One of its American editors, Roger L. Bedard, correctly noted Melwood's use of absurdist techniques and made the necessary distinction. 'The absurdist, however, attempted to portray man's entrapment in an illogical, hostile, impersonal and indifferent existence. There are no such pretensions in *The Tingalary Bird*: it is more fantastic than brooding, more humorous than menacing' (Bedard 1984: 495).

Such occasional achievements apart, the picture of post-war children's dramatic literature is a varied and confused one, with greater activity than ever before but relatively little manifest excellence or corporate agreement about the rules and objectives of the game. Some children's novelists have written plays, among them L. M. Boston with *The Horned Man* (1970) and Joan Aiken with *Winterthing* and *The Mooncusser's Daughter* (1975), but these are not remotely their best achievements. Some writers have devoted their careers to writing and producing for children – notably David Wood, whose *The Gingerbread Man* (1977) is his best-known contribution to a theatre of would-be non-didactic entertainment for the young. By contrast the work of David Holman is openly didactic, taking a strong view on a range of political and especially environmental and conservationist concerns: it is well exemplified by *Solomon's Cat* (1993). Such writers have honourably furthered the cause without creating anything which seems likely to endure. Ted Hughes, whose writing for children ranks with his finest achievements, has produced competent plays in his collection *The Coming of the Kings* (1970), but they do not rival his fiction and poetry.

Some television plays intended for an adult audience have become part of children's theatre, either because of opportune casting or appropriate theme: they include Willy Russell's *Our Day Out* (1977) and Don Taylor's *The Roses of Eyam* (1976).

Current activity is energetic and dedicated, but achievement is patchy and idiosyncratic. Some of the best work, with greatest innovative possibilities, has lain in the plays specially written for the British National Youth Theatre, notably Peter Terson's play about football supporters, *Zigger Zagger* (1967) and Paul Thompson's Brechtian political drama, *The Children's Crusade* (1975). There is some resemblance here to the Elizabethan children's companies: these are works written without condescension for a theatre of young players expected to perform them with distinction. Not only at this exalted level, but throughout the education system, recent years have seen excellent work in the fields of making and performing. Appropriate experience of response, however, depends too heavily on the chance of visits to dedicated theatres and the small number of dedicated theatre companies. Too many children miss them altogether. And our 'dramatic literature for children', more prolific than ever before, is fragmentary in nature and in dire need of the serious critical attention and institutional support which are given to children's poetry and children's fiction. Until that happens, drama will remain the Cinderella of children's literature, when it is arguably the most important children's art form of all, the one they are sure to live with, through the media of film and television, all their lives.

## References

Axton, R. (1974) *European Drama of the Early Middle Ages*, London: Hutchinson.

Barrie, J. M. (1995) *Peter Pan and Other Plays*, ed. P. Hollindale, Oxford: Oxford University Press.

Bedard, R. L. (ed.) (1984) *Dramatic Literature for Children: A Century in Review*, New Orleans: Anchorage Press.

Chambers, E. K. (1903) *The Medieval Stage*, vol. 2, Oxford: Oxford University Press.

England, A. (1990) *Theatre for the Young*, London: Macmillan.

Fitzhugh, L. (1964/1975) *Harriet the Spy*, London: Collins.

Goldberg, M. (1974) *Children's Theatre: A Philosophy and a Method*, Englewood Cliffs, NJ: Prentice-Hall.

Green, R. L. (1954) *Fifty Years of 'Peter Pan'*, London: Peter Davies.

Jonson, B. (1631/1976) *The Staple of News*, ed. D. R. Kifer, London: Arnold.

Levy, J. (1992) *The Gymnasium of the Imagination: A Collection of Children's Plays in English 1780–1860*, Westport, CT: Greenwood Press.

Milne, A. A. (1922) *Second Plays*, London: Chatto and Windus.

Moses, M. J. (ed.) (1921) *Treasury of Plays for Children*, Boston: Little, Brown.

O'Toole, J. (1976) *Theatre in Education*, London: Hodder and Stoughton.

## Further Reading

Arts Council (1992) *Drama in Schools*, London: Arts Council.

Bolton, G. (1979) *Towards a Theory of Drama in Education*, Burnt Mill, Harlow: Longman.

Caldwell Cook, H. (1917) *The Play Way*, London: Heinemann.

Chambers, A. (1982) *Plays for Young People to Read and Perform*, South Woodchester: Thimble Press.

Gair, R. (1982) *The Children of Paul's: The Story of a Theatre Company 1553–1608*. Cambridge: Cambridge University Press.

Hornbrook, D. (1989) *Education and Dramatic Art*, Oxford: Blackwell.

—— (1991) *Education in Drama: Casting the Dramatic Curriculum*, London: Falmer Press.

Redington, C. (1983) *Can Theatre Teach?* Oxford: Pergamon.

Shapiro, M. (1977) *Children of the Revels*, New York: Columbia University Press.

Slade, P. (1954) *Child Drama*, London: University of London Press.

# 18

# The Development of Illustrated Texts and Picture Books

*Joyce Irene Whalley*

Children learn to read pictures before they learn to read words. Pictures also form the earliest records of man's attempts at communication: cave paintings, church murals, stained glass windows – all testify to the importance placed on pictorial representation. It is surprising therefore to realise how long it took for due significance to be placed on the illustration of children's books. Early books for the young were not without pictures, but they were not illustrated books.

What is the difference? A good illustrated book is one where the accompanying pictures enhance or add depth to the text. A bad illustrated book is one where the pictures lack relevance to the text, or are ill placed and poorly drawn or reproduced – these are books with pictures rather than illustrated books. In this outline study of illustrated children's books we shall trace the rise of the importance of pictures and the improvement in standards of illustration, until on occasions the pictures assume greater significance than the text – or even replace it.

The emphasis in this study is on books for children's leisure reading, not text books. Nevertheless, the first illustrated book of any significance for children was in fact a Latin text book. This was *Orbis Sensualium Pictus*, by Johann Amos Comenius, published in 1658. There had been many Latin text books before this, but Comenius, an educationalist from Moravia, was among the first to realise that children best remember things they have *seen* rather than merely read about. His book was translated into English by Charles Hoole in 1659. It consisted of a picture at the top of every page, with the name of each object depicted in it listed below in Latin and then in English. The crude little woodcut illustrations covered a great variety of topics, both familiar and unfamiliar, and so provided the widest range of pictures for the young then available. The book was popular throughout Europe and remained in use in schools for many years. A popular imitation in English was James Greenwood's *The London Vocabulary*, which by 1771 had reached its sixteenth edition.

But the point about all these books, to our eyes at least, is that the illustrations were so crude. This was not because good illustration was impossible in the seventeenth and eighteenth centuries, although England did not have a school of illustrators such as existed in France at the time. There were, however, many competent engravers who rendered their French models very finely, as we can see from contemporary adult books. But the models for children's book illustration were taken from the lower end of the market, from chapbooks and broadsheets, selling to a partially literate readership at a fraction of the cost of the better class adult book. This fact is in itself indicative of the attitude at that time to children's books, their production and illustration.

It is appropriate here to consider the methods available in the seventeenth and eighteenth centuries for the actual reproduction of illustrations, which were of course largely manual processes. For children's books in particular, the most important method of reproducing illustration was by woodcut – a process that goes back to the late fifteenth century. In this method, everything that was not required to print was cut away on the block so that the resulting illustration was one of mass rather than line. Such illustrations lacked subtlety, especially in the small size common in children's books. But the method was cheap and the blocks could go through the press at the same time as the type, so that in an illustrated book text and pictures could be printed together. Children's books have always been required to be cheaper than adult books, and in a society where such books were little regarded, this form of simplified – or crude – illustration was considered quite suitable. It was also the method used in the production of chapbooks and broadsheets, which themselves lay at the cheaper end of the market.

A superior form of illustration, and one used in technical books and the more expensive eighteenth-century adult works, was engraving. This is an intaglio process, by which the line of the drawing is engraved onto a copper plate, which is subsequently inked for printing. To reproduce this incised inked line, the plate has to be put under great pressure in a printing press, and cannot therefore go through at the same time as the type, which is raised. As a result, any book using engraving as a means of illustration either had to go twice through the press, or else it had its illustrations and text printed separately (this was the more common method). Engraving was certainly used in children's books, especially in the more expensive ones produced towards the end of the eighteenth century. It was also used by John Harris and William Darton in the mainly didactic works produced by them in the early decades of the nineteenth century. Engraved illustration permitted the reproduction of far greater detail in a picture, and a good engraver could produce very fine effects of line as well as of mass, giving much greater variety to the illustrations.

But the use of this more expensive process of illustration indicates that a change had taken place in the course of the eighteenth century in the whole attitude to children and their books. This change was initiated to a large extent by one man, John Newbery, who in 1744 set up his shop in St Paul's Churchyard, London, where he produced a wide range of children's books. He was not the first to do this – Thomas Boreman had preceded him in this new approach to children's books. But Newbery was the first to appreciate, and to exploit commercially, the market in illustrated children's books. He realised that his new product had to be reasonably cheap and so his books were small – no disadvantage in young eyes – and certainly illustrated, but by the cheapest method, namely the woodcut. Few names of the artists employed by Newbery are known, and many of the pictures he published were used again and again, in his own or other publishers' books. This was made possible by the general nature of the pictures: two children in a garden, a coach and horses, a lady and a child in a room. Such basic pictures could easily have stories written round them, though of course there were even at that date illustrations specially commissioned for specific books.

By the end of the eighteenth century the idea of illustrated books for children had become established and some of their authors had become well known – although others still preferred to hide behind such phrases as 'by the author of ...' or 'by a lady'. These books tended to emphasise religious and moral matters (not good illustrative material), or social behaviour which was seen as the key to prosperity. By contrast, the early nineteenth century turned towards more factual themes. Children's books were of course written by adults and for the most part bought by adults for their children. It is surprising, therefore, that such poor quality material was for so long allowed to circulate among the young by people who would not have tolerated similar standards in their own books. Moreover it was the most scorned type of reading – the chapbook – which in the end effected the revolution in children's books.

The chapbook was a small, crudely illustrated booklet of about 2½ × 4 inches, which could be easily carried in the chapman or pedlar's pack as he traversed the countryside selling ribbons, pins, ballads and other small items to villages and farmsteads. The middle-class child probably only obtained sight of these cheap booklets through the servants' hall, but whether the child saw them or not, they certainly flourished among the poorer and semi-literate members of the population. Their content was varied: folktales, nursery rhymes, ballads, riddles, short entertaining or moral tales. All these continued to flourish as a substratum of literature, ready to surface when the time was right and a change had taken place in children's reading, when fairy tales, folktales and nursery rhymes were once again permitted in the nursery.

But while the crude woodcut illustration continued to prevail in the cheaper productions for children, certain improvements were taking place. By the early nineteenth century the rationalism so much in favour for children's literature was being supplemented by an appreciation of new discoveries of all kinds. The publishers William Darton and John Harris caught the public mood admirably in the books they produced over the next few decades. Nearly always didactic in content, these books sought to bring to children an awareness of the wider world beyond the British Isles, as well as to explore in depth the wonders of their own country. The titles of such works are themselves revealing. John Harris produced a number of travel books specifically for 'Little Tarry-at-Home Travellers', while there were also such works as *Scenes of British Wealth* (1823), *Rural Employments* (1820) and *City Scenes; or A Peep into London for Children* (1828). Publications of this sort demanded, and got, plenty of illustration. But since detail was essential in these pictures, engraving was the method most frequently employed to reproduce them. This often meant that the books contained texts which were separated from the pictures. These were usually grouped together, two or three to a plate, for the technical reasons described earlier. This was not a very satisfactory arrangement for the young child. Nevertheless, these books, often with the pictures hand coloured, were a popular if rather expensive contribution to children's reading. The names of the artists employed are rarely known – it would appear that many quite well known illustrators were prepared to contribute pictures to children's books, but at this period the standing of juvenile publishing was not such as to openly attract the named artist. Much work remains to be done on the identity of artists working for both William Darton and John Harris.

By the 1830s there were various methods of illustration in use in children's books, which were now being produced in considerable quantity. The didactic books still led the field, but there were also religious and moral tales, now often by named authors, and it was certainly accepted that for the most part children's books should be illustrated. The earlier engraving had been done on copper-plate, which had a limited life. By the 1820s onward, it was found that the use of steel plates gave longer runs, and so steel engraving frequently took the place of copper in the more popular works, such as the 'Keepsakes' and gift books of the period. Though cheaper and longer lasting, steel engraving had one disadvantage; it gave an appearance of coldness and lack of subtlety to the illustrations where it was employed. Lithography, the invention of Alois Senefelder at the end of the eighteenth century, was also used in children's books, but less frequently in Britain than on the European continent. It had the same disadvantage as engraving, in that it too needed to go through the printing press separately from the text, so that books illustrated by lithography were expensive and usually had far fewer illustrations. There remained the woodcut, but by the 1830s the improved version of white-line wood engraving pioneered by Thomas Bewick was almost universally used in preference to the cruder woodcut. Thomas and his brother John had both themselves illustrated children's books, but it was in the 1830s and 1840s that their method of engraving on wood became more widely used in children's books.

The 1840s saw great developments in the field of children's books, in content and in production. Edward Lear's *Book of Nonsense*, and the first translations of Hans Andersen's *Fairy Tales* both appeared in 1846. The *Fairy Tales* of the Brothers Grimm had appeared with Cruikshank's illustrations as early as 1823–1826, although their circulation was probably not widespread until later. But equally important for the acceptance of nonsense and fairy tale in the nursery, was the advent of Henry Cole and Joseph Cundall. Henry Cole was a man who had a finger in many pies baked in the mid-nineteenth century, including such outstanding events as the Great Exhibition of 1851. But he was also a father, and as such was appalled at the state of children's books when he came to provide them for his own family. Under the pseudonym 'Felix Summerly' he instituted the Home Treasury series. In this he published fairy tales and nursery rhymes, commissioning well known artists of the day, many of whom he knew personally, to illustrate them. He also commissioned special covers for his books. Joseph Cundall, with his interest in producing well-designed books, was the right man to work with Henry Cole. Such productions should have been outstanding, but it must be confessed that to modern eyes the Home Treasury series often appears somewhat dull. The cover designs were based on various traditional arabesque patterns, taken from older bindings, and were usually printed in gold on coloured paper, but they were not eye-catching, especially for children. The illustrations were of good quality, relevant and attractive – but (no doubt because of the cost) very few in number. These booklets were certainly very tasteful productions, but left to themselves children do not necessarily exhibit good taste, preferring a brightly coloured cover to a well-designed one. Nevertheless, a precedent had been set by which all aspects of a book designed for children should be given the same degree of attention previously allocated to adult books. Moreover, Henry Cole's standing ensured wide publicity for these new ideas – he was known to be a friend of the Prince Consort, and later became the first Director of the South Kensington Museum (later the Victoria and Albert Museum).

By the end of the 1840s, well known book artists were no longer reluctant to put their names to their work in children's books. The establishment of popular illustrated papers during this period, *The Illustrated London News* and *Punch* among them, ensured a regular demand for good illustrators and engravers, thus encouraging a native school to flourish.

By the 1850s many of the artists whose names were to become well known in the next decade were already producing notable work. In 1851 the *Punch* artist Richard Doyle produced illustrations to accompany John Ruskin's text *The King of the Golden River*, so getting the new decade off to a good start. Others working in the 1850s were Hablot K. Browne (Phiz), one of the Dickens's illustrators, and 'Alfred Crowquill', a pseudonym for the two Forrester brothers. George Cruikshank's work spanned a large part of the nineteenth century, starting with his illustrations for the Brothers Grimm's tales in the 1820s, but in the middle of this decade he started to issue his own Fairy Library.

Whereas almost all the children's book illustrators of this period used wood engraving, Cruikshank used etching. This method, like engraving, is an intaglio process, but uses acid to bite the line on the plate rather than a burin or graver; it too can give a fine detailed picture as we can see from Cruikshank's own pictures for his *Cinderella* of 1854. Also using etching, and writing and illustrating his own stories, was Charles Henry Bennett, another *Punch* illustrator.

Having now reached the middle of the nineteenth century, it is a suitable point to consider the state of children's books, and how they differed from those of the beginning of the century. In the first place there were far more of them. The prosperous middle class now provided an extensive reading public, while the tremendous technical improvements made good quality illustrated books more widely available and relatively cheaper. The subject matter too had changed. Entertainment was much more to the fore, and nonsense, folk and fairy tales, as well as longer stories, were now provided for children's reading. Other more subtle trends are noticeable in the illustrations of the period. Following the popularity of Heinrich Hoffmann's *Struwwelpeter* in 1844, there was a fashion for a more primitive or archaicising style, which would certainly amuse the young, and a tendency to facetiousness. We can also see the beginning of the cult of childhood, as the illustrators start to depict coy, quaint or sentimental children – something almost unthinkable at the beginning of the century. Obviously didactic, religious and moral books continued to be published – after all, even today children's books still have an underlying moral tone, even if it is scarcely noticeable.

The best illustration was still uncoloured, although some books were issued in two kinds: plain or coloured. The colouring at this date, in children's books at least, was still by hand. But experiments were taking place to produce a commercially acceptable form of colour printing – it was in fact already available, but it was expensive. Colour became much more widely used from the 1850s onward, especially in the popular 'toy books'. The toy book had nothing to do with toys, but was basically a publishers' description of a paper-covered picture book. In its earliest manifestations it consisted of about eight pages, with a minimum of text and a picture on each page, which was usually blank on the back. Various artists obviously worked on the 'toy books' but few early publications can be attributed to known illustrators, and some must have been done by hack workers employed for the job. But these booklets were cheap and colourful, and covered a wide range of topics in a very basic way, whether it was a summary account of the story of Red Riding Hood or Robinson Crusoe, or a brief description of the wonders of the world. These books were at first hand-coloured, often by children employed as cheap labour, but they were also among the earliest to bring colour printing – of a sort – to the mass market of child readers. In the hands of a master they could indeed become works of art in their own right, as we shall see towards the end of the century.

As we move into the 1860s we reach the peak period of British book illustration for children and adults alike, since by now the illustrators worked equally for both the juvenile and the adult market, boldly putting their names with those of the authors on the title page. Indeed not only were some artists their own story writers, as we have seen, but sometimes the artist could even dominate the book – Harrison Weir, the famous animal artist, was one such example; the text had now become subsidiary to the pictures.

Not only did Britain now produce black-and-white illustrators of very high calibre, but these also had the satisfaction of being much in demand, so that security further encouraged them to work to the highest standards. The spread of popular illustrated papers continued, while the increase in the actual reading public, and a middle class with more leisure, all encouraged the production of books of all kinds. This was the era of Dickens, Wilkie Collins and Trollope, and also of the gift book (the Victorian equivalent of the 'coffee-table' book) – and all these works were lavishly illustrated, providing plenty of work for the book artist.

Although colour was now more prevalent and improving in quality, it is interesting to note that the best illustrators of the period still preferred to work in black and white, in the method of wood engraving derived from Thomas Bewick. But we should always remember that in the production of these illustrations two sets of hands were at work – the artist who drew the original art work, and the engraver who engraved it on the block ready for printing. But here too in Britain at this period a good school of engravers had developed, the best-known often working for the firm of the Dalziel Brothers. Artists already mentioned, such as Richard (Dicky) Doyle, C. H. Bennett, and 'Crowquill', all produced outstanding children's books during this decade. There were new names, too, at least as far as children's books were concerned, who were often already artists in their own right. One of these was John Millais, with his illustrations for books such as *Little Songs for me to Sing* (1865), or Arthur Hughes, who produced the evocative drawings for George Macdonald's *At the Back of the North Wind* (1869), as well as other similar high quality illustrations, all usually set spaciously on the page.

The book was now considered as a work of art in itself, and layout and cover were, in the best instances, receiving as much care as the text and illustrations. Illustration could also be much more sophisticated too, as we see in the often dramatic work of Ernest Griset. Griset was for long a rather neglected artist, though much appreciated in his own time. His illustrations to a work like *The Purgatory of Peter the Cruel* (1868), in which the incidents are sometimes shown from an unusual view point, such as that of a fly or a frog, and his melodramatic designs for Aesop's *Fables* or *Robinson Crusoe* (reminiscent of Gustav Doré), put him high on the list of mid-century illustrators.

But surely dominating the mid-1860s and early 1870s we must consider the two Alice books by Lewis Carroll. Here we have perhaps for the first time an artist and a writer working together to produce a definitive form of an illustrated story. Others have since tried to interpret Carroll's *Wonderland* creatures, but surely no one has portrayed them so memorably as their first illustrator, Sir John Tenniel. Subsequent artists have also given permanent form to a writer's imagination (Shepard's illustrations for A. A. Milne's Winnie-the-Pooh books spring to mind), but here in a book for children was the first complete interpretation of a fantasy world, which has survived more than a century of change in children's books.

Would the Alice books have survived to the same degree if they had been unillustrated? It is an interesting speculation, since it can also be applied to other books where text and pictures complement each other so perfectly – in Beatrix Potter's work for example. Certainly Lewis Carroll depicted his creatures verbally with great care, but readers would have been left to imagine the exact form of the *Wonderland* creatures without Tenniel's guide. This is perhaps the great mark of a good book illustrator, in that the visual forms they give to the text linger in the mind, whereas those of lesser illustrators (and there have been many of Alice alone) do not.

Some of the finest children's books date from the 1860s, a notable period for British book illustration, when known illustrators worked with book designers to produce works for children which were as fine inside as out, and as good reading as viewing. But Sir John Millais, Arthur Hughes, Ernest Griset and others were all producing high quality black-and-white work during this period, just at the moment when colour printing and photography were about to be applied to children's books in such a way that, for a time at least, progress would seem to go backwards rather than forwards. For it is very rare that any new process immediately reaches its peak – there has to be a period of trial and development.

In the last quarter of the nineteenth century, technical developments were increasing in all fields of book production and helped to satisfy the immense growth in children's reading. This increase in readership was brought about by the various Education Acts, starting with that of 1870. With the expansion of literacy went also the further development of the illustrated journal, widening in scope and reaching lower down the social scale – with the consequent need for ever cheaper productions.

At the end of the century there was a conscious effort to reduce costs, which led to the employment once again of hack artists – often unnamed as in the past – together with poor quality paper and type, as we can see from those journals and cheap books which have survived. In colour printing, especially the three-colour process, there was both good and bad, and on the whole, the good was much more expensive. Fortunately the 'toy book', in the hands of publishers such as Darton, Routledge and Warne, ensured that the standard was largely maintained, aided by the arrival on the scene in the last quarter of the nineteenth century of a great triumvirate of illustrators, Walter Crane, Randolph Caldecott and Kate Greenaway, together with the remarkably competent colour printer, Edmund Evans.

Of the three artists mentioned, Randolph Caldecott was probably most truly a book illustrator. Walter Crane was certainly more prolific, but his other work in the decorative arts tended to spill over into his books, making him more of a book decorator than an illustrator. This is particularly evident in his 'toy books', where contemporary motifs – the fan, the sunflower, the general air of japonaiserie – manifest themselves on nearly every page. If we look at Crane's *Sleeping Beauty*, for example, we find the whole of the centre page spread covered in illustration and design, and looking more like a decorative tile than a book picture. The same is equally true of his illustrations to *Goody Two-Shoes* and *Aladdin*.

By contrast, Randolph Caldecott made great use of space in his illustrations, allowing his line to speak for itself, and his pictures to enhance the (often traditional) texts he chose to illustrate. In *The Queen of Hearts* for example, the simple basic nursery rhyme is 'expanded' by the pictorial comment of the cat who has seen the knave steal the tarts – no text is used, or indeed needed. The same is equally true of his other 'toy books', such as *The House that Jack Built* or *The Three Jovial Huntsmen*.

Kate Greenaway, however, was to some extent in a category of her own, and for the most part she chose to write and illustrate her own poems – *Under the Window* and *Marigold Garden* are perhaps her best known books. She 'invented' a style of dress and a 'never-never' period of her own, in which she placed her elegantly clad and immaculately clean children. Her work was highly stylised and very popular – although not very well drawn (her figures tend to have no bodies under their clothes) – and this popularity has remained firm to the present day. These books were not cheap, with their fine colour printing and high-quality illustrations, but they formed a small if influential section of the children's book market.

By contrast there was a great outpouring of muddy coloured and indifferently illustrated works, often printed in Germany (Bavaria for the most part), which have survived in large quantities to show how widespread they were. These frequently contained not the traditional nursery rhymes or folk-tales used by Caldecott and Crane, but *ad hoc* verses and short tales made to accompany pictures – one can hardly call them illustrations. The use of photographic methods and of the three-colour process led to a lowering of standards, while at the same time providing school and Sunday School prizes and Christmas and birthday gifts in plenty. Such books demanded little from the child, and indicated their level of approach by their titles: *Our Little Dots* or *Little Chicks* are examples – and their poorly drawn and indifferently coloured pictures matched their titles.

In the early years of the twentieth century the highly sophisticated type of work by Kate Greenaway, for example, was carried to extremes by the productions of several artists whose books lie on the border line between those for children and those for adults. Kate Greenaway's books had been intended for children, with their simple rhymes and games, but illustrators like the Frenchman Edmund Dulac, Kay Nielson from Denmark, and Arthur Rackham offered a fantasy world which was scarcely that of the child. Of the quality of their illustrations to well known works like *Cinderella*, Hans Andersen and others, there can be no doubt, and the lavishness of production ensured that the books were duly treasured, but they stand to one side of the general production of children's books.

Although the names of Rackham, Neilson and Dulac may be linked together as indicating a particular type of lavish book for children, their styles were very different. Of the three, Rackham was possibly the most significant because of the stories he chose to illustrate, and also because his very personal style invited imitation. Even today it is possible to describe a woodland scene as 'Rackham-esque', and the picture which arises in the mind's eye is revealing. For Rackham made good use of line as well as colour, at the same time using both to convey a twilight fairy world, based on the factual (trees, flowers, buildings), but to which his art added an air of fantasy, sometimes even of the grotesque and the eerie. Although a frisson of fear does not come amiss to some children, as Charles Lamb pointed out in his essay 'Witches and other night fears' (*Essays of Elia*, 1823) the more sensitive child may be greatly alarmed by illustrations, even in so-called children's books. Both Nielson and Dulac relied more on a subtle use of colour rather than line, and both made use of oriental and other exotic touches to conjure up the romance in the children's books they illustrated.

Almost contemporary with these illustrators, and with a stronger touch of the real world, was Beatrix Potter. This writer, like Charles Henry Bennett, was also her own illustrator, and as a result her artistic creations have a homogeneous quality with her text. Unlike the fine (and expensive) colour books mentioned above, Beatrix Potter was determined that her books should be of a size and price to suit children – she saw her books as quite definitely aimed at the child reader, and many of her stories were first tried out on young relatives or friends. She was particularly concerned that picture and text should match each other on the page, and that both should progress from page to page with the story. Although she used only back-and-white sketches in her privately printed *The Tale of Peter Rabbit* (1901), the commercial edition subsequently issued by Frederick Warne (1902) was coloured, and the vast majority of the pictures in her subsequent books were in colour. Where black-and-white was used, it was usually subservient to the colour pages. Beatrix Potter based her art on the real world – she made many detailed studies of animals, flowers and scenes before she began to illustrate each story. Her tales are of course fantastic – but in quite a different way from those artists whom we have just been considering. There it is the trappings of their art that give rise to the fantasy – it lies in the colour, the line, the mystery. But Beatrix Potter takes identifiable places and animals, and, without comment, gives them lives and speech which make them live and move in a world which is both ours and theirs. It is probably this mixture, together with the concern for the physical make up of the little books, that has kept her work among the foremost of the twentieth-century illustrated books.

But the first two decades of the twentieth century saw a great outpouring of books of all kinds for children in Britain. The Education Acts of the previous century and the provision of a public library service all ensured a good reading public – though not necessarily a public for good books. There was much 'run of the mill' illustration in weekly comics and in the popular Christmas annuals and 'bumper books'. But a lot of good work was also being provided for children, often in black-and-white to ensure relative cheapness. The Robinson brothers produced a wide range of good quality illustrations during the last decade of the nineteenth century and the first two of the twentieth century. William Heath Robinson in particular gave new interpretations to the work of Hans Andersen and others, as well as illustrating his own stories for children. Although his best work is perhaps in his black-and-white drawings, he too was a subtle master of the three-colour process. One interesting feature of early twentieth-century illustration was the use of silhouette: it was to be found in works as diverse as Rudyard Kipling's illustrations to his own *Just So Stories* (1894), W. Heath Robinson's edition of Hans Andersen's tales, and Arthur Rackham's illustrations to C. S. Evans's retelling of *Cinderella* (1919).

European contributions came from Hoffman, and Wilhelm Busch, whose *Max und Moritz* cartoons were to influence a wide range of later illustrators. From the USA, Howard Pyle was important on both sides of the Atlantic at the end of the century, together with his pupils Maxfield Parrish and Jessie Willcox Smith.

There were indeed many prolific and competent artists working for the children's market in the decades before the First World War, besides those who catered more for the luxury trade. Interestingly, most of their work was done in black and white, though their range within this limitation was quite remarkable. Among such artists was H. J. Ford, who provided the illustrations for Andrew Lang's widely read twelve colour fairy books, which began with *The Blue Fairy Book* in 1889 and ended with *The Lilac Fairy Book* in 1910. Norman Ault and the Brock brothers were also working in the early decades of the century along similar lines, while an artist of rather greater stature and imagination was Leslie Brooke, whose *Johnny Crow's Garden*, published in 1903, was deservedly popular. Having noticed at the beginning of this chapter the influence of continental artists on British book making, it is interesting to note at this period some examples of influences working in the opposite direction. This was especially true of Maurice Boutet de Monval, whose books were influenced by Greenaway, although his colours are more sutle, and he has a charming sense of humour. He in turn greatly influenced the work of Henriette Willebeek Le Mair, a Dutch artist, with her flat pastel colours and rather flat ornamental pictures. Her work was very popular in the first decades of the twentieth century, especially accompanied by nursery rhymes, and several of her books have been recently reprinted.

In the late nineteenth century and the early years of the twentieth century there were almost as many women illustrators as men; notable were the Scot Jessie M. King, Anne Anderson, Jessie Wilcox Smith and Mabel Lucie Attwell. But the immediate future lay with what was almost a throw back to an earlier style. The work of William Nicholson, Cecil Aldin and John Hassall carried with it overtones of the chapbook style of the 1890s. Simple masses and flat colours, set on a spacious page, were quite striking when they first appeared, as we can see in such work as Nicholson's *An Alphabet* (1898) and Aldin and Hassall's *Two Well-worn Shoe Stories* (1899). It was to some extent this simpler style which was to appeal to the book makers of the 1920s and 1930s, though all too often these lacked the courage to allow the use of blank spaces which had contributed so much to the success of the earlier artists' work. But the 1914–1918 war made a break which though not immediately apparent in the children's books of the 1920s, soon asserted itself, and a new era of children's book illustration began to develop.

## Further Reading

Alderson, B. (1986) *Sing a Song for Sixpence: the English Illustrative Tradition and Randolph Caldecott*, Cambridge: Cambridge University Press in association with the British Library.

Barr, J. (1986) *Illustrated Children's Books*, London: British Library.

McLean, R. (1972) *Victorian Book Design and Colour Printing*, 2nd edn, London: Faber.

Muir, P. (1985) *English Children's Books 1600–1900*, 4th imp., London: Batsford.

Whalley, J. I. (1975) *'Cobwebs to Catch Flies': Illustrated Books for the Nursery and Schoolroom, 1700–1900*, London: Elek.

—— and Chester, T. R. (1988) *A History of Children's Book Illustration*, London: John Murray, with the Victoria and Albert Museum.

# 19

# The Modern Picture Book

## *Jane Doonan*

### Development

One of the most fertile areas of growth in children's literature has been in the development of the picture book, once the prerogative of the young, which in its modern form is capable of engaging the interest of children well above the age of infancy and learner-reader.

The story-telling of the traditional picture book puts the words in charge, even though the design of the whole is conceived in visual terms. The illustrations are almost always congruent with the text, engaged at best in a responsive interplay which illuminates, amplifies, exemplifies, and extends it. The artist's style is graphic rather than painterly both as a result of its historical roots in book and journal illustration, as well as in the limitations imposed by available printing methods. The subject matter and themes are those which amuse, educate and socialise a young child.

Perceptions about childhood, perceptions about the picture book and the nature and structure of publishing have changed considerably since the First World War. The story-telling of the modern picture book exploits more fully the potential of the interdependent complexities of the form itself: words, pictures, layout, the physical object from cover to cover with its turning pages. The relationships between words and pictures range from an obvious congruency through to that of a highly ironic one in which words and images may seem to be sending contradictory messages, and a challenge lies in resolving the differences to make a composite text with a satisfying conclusion; at its most extreme, the nature of the relationship is permanently unclear and a high degree of toleration of ambiguity is required of the reader-beholder. There is a delight in parodic and satirical modes most frequently displayed in reworkings of folk- and fairy tales. The metafictional elements which may be found in contemporary fiction have their picture book counterparts, as writers and artists question notions of how stories are told and meanings are made. Conventions and techniques are subverted; boundaries are broken between fictional characters and the very picture books in which they feature, and between the picture book maker and the audience; too much or too little information is given for issues within the verbal and visual stories to be resolved once and for all. Artists exploit the abstract elements of picture making – line, shape, colour and their ordering – together with the choice of materials and historical style, to allude to complex psychological states through images which function as the visual equivalent of simile, metaphor, and of intertextuality. Painterly styles, new graphic materials and means are reproduced on the picture book page through the advances of print technology; examples may be found of expressionism, symbolism, surrealism, romanticism, pop art and of techniques as varied as cloissonisme and collage. Themes includes most matters of life and death, from an individual viewpoint to the survival of the planet. The pedagogic role of the picture book has been extended to include its use to create readers and to help literary and aesthetic development.

By the mid-1920s the characteristics of the modern picture book begin to take shape in Europe and America. William Nicholson, with *Clever Bill* (1926) and *The Pirate Twins* (1929) pioneered the use of offset colour lithography. Picture and narrative are unified by paralleling events, and by the line of his assured drawings and handwritten script. Edward Ardizzone's *Little Tim and the Brave Sea Captain* (1936) is also an early example of offset litho, which gives the images a softer effect than the earlier method of printing directly onto the paper. The handwritten script ebbs and flows against, around, above and below the sketchily drawn water colour illustrations, which at times tilt with the tide. Suspense is built into the turn of the page. Little Tim's limitless energy is caught in gestural poses, and his staying power was such that his series of adventures lasted until the 1960s.

A rich use of colour glides into the picture book through Kathleen Hale's soft waxy crayons in a series which began with *Orlando the Marmalade Cat: A Camping Holiday* (1938). With the freedom of its layout, the inventive ways of showing different events happening simultaneously over the picture plane, and the punning details, Hale's picture books look fresh even today. The adventures of Little Tim, Orlando and Babar (see below) were all originally printed in books of folio size giving a sense of substance to the characters.

A deepening of the treatment of themes is also apparent. Jean de Brunhoff made his six Babar picture books between 1931 and 1937 with themes which explore family relationships as well as political ones. In the Peaceable Kingdom of Babar, an enterprising elephant, the welfare of everyone is important, goodness triumphs, and death is presented and accepted as a natural part of life. Munro Leaf and Robert Lawson took a pacifist stance with their picture book about a bull who preferred flowers to fighting, in *The Story of Ferdinand* (1936). Against the political background of Europe at the time, Ferdinand was a subversive model for children. The most meticulous comic strip, Hergé's Tintin series, began in 1929, showing sustained, well plotted pictorial stories, while the adventures of Rupert the Bear, founded by Mary Tourtel in cartoon form (1920) were reissued in annual form a decade later and given a multimedia story telling layout, page by page. The structure of these two forms are combined, reworked and expanded for the modern picture book.

Mass produced semi-educational picture books appeared in the 1930s in Russia, France and Germany, and were designed with the intention to delight as well as to instruct children. The English extension of these movements came through Puffin picture books, founded under the editorship of Noel Carrington in 1941.

In the 1930s, the American picture book became increasingly colourful, innovative, and diverse. Publishers had at their disposal an enormous number of fine artists including many immigrants. Wanda Gág, with her *Millions of Cats*

(1928), combines a handwritten text with firmly contoured sturdy, black and white drawings. Feodor Rojankovsky, a Russian émigré, moved from Paris where he had illustrated calendars and wild animal stories for Père Castor books, to America in 1941. There he made more exuberant and dramatic picture books of his own like *The Tall Book of Mother Goose* (1942) and *The Three Bears* (1948). Ingri and Edgar Parin d'Aulaire, with *The Magic Ring* (1931) established their chosen medium, stone lithographs, as a brilliant new way of getting colour into picture books, a process which involved them in doing their own separations, and which gave the finished work a hand drawn look. Roger Duvoisin in *Donkey-Donkey* (1933), first displayed his gift for animal characters whose looks clearly express feelings, and which finds its ultimate expression later in tales of a misguided goose, *Petunia* (1950) and in *The Happy Lion* (1954). Jean Charlot introduced sculptural forms and Mexican imagery in *The Sun, the Moon and a Rabbit* (1935), whilst Boris Artzybasheff, a linearist, made a Russian narrative spectacle of a picture book with *Seven Simeons* (1937).

After the Second World War there was a gradual refinement in offset lithography, and by the late 1950s the full possibilities of how the technology might serve in the development of picture books with more painterly qualities were realised, in Britain, through the vision and enterprise of the children's book editor for the Oxford University Press. Mabel George commissioned Brian Wildsmith, a daring colourist, to paint plates for an edition of the *Arabian Nights*, and then sent them to an Austrian fine-art printer for reproduction. The results led her to launch what has come to be seen as a marker for the modern picture book: Wildsmith's *ABC* (1962). Other artists whom she commissioned included Victor Ambrus and Charles Keeping.

Over the years an increasing number of awards for children's books and book illustration have been instituted which acknowledge talents, raise public awareness, and increase sales: awards include the American Library Association's Randolph Caldecott Medal (instituted in 1938), the British Library Association's Kate Greenaway Medal (1955), the Hans Christian Andersen Award (1966) given by the International Board on Books for Young People to an illustrator in recognition of an entire body of work, and the Australian Children's Picture Book of the Year Award; prizes are awarded at the Biennale of Illustrations Bratislava and the Bologna Children's Book fair.

In the 1970s and 1980s the picture book suffered from massive overproduction resulting in far too many indistinguishable products. As a result of the growing demands of international cooperation in the book market, pictures can be printed in one single large print run and sold to different countries where texts in the relevant languages are then attached. Nevertheless there are two advantages for the consumer: the cost is reduced, and at best, the originality of vision of the most creative artists, writers and designers is made available to all.

## The Modern Picture Book: its Makers and Characteristics

The following modified list has a twofold purpose. It nominates individual illustrators whose body of work rewards study; and it identifies picture books which exhibit strongly the diverse characteristics of the modern picture book form as well as some which sustain the earlier tradition.

*Janet and John Ahlberg*, artist and writer, staked out a pictorial territory, a historic era of the 1940s and 1950s of England. Janet Ahlberg's detailed pictures, are replete with images which exude atmosphere, nostalgia, and amuse parents as well as children, as in *Peepo!* (1981), a book-as-toy. At their most innovative, the Ahlbergs created *The Jolly Postman* (1986). The eponymous hero delivers the mail between folk- and fairy tale characters on a fictive level, and literally delivers them to the reader, enclosed in envelopes within the picture book pages themselves: a birthday card to baby bear, a formal warning to the Big Bad Wolf from a firm of solicitors, a commemorative booklet about Cinderella's wedding, a mail order catalogue for witches and so on. Thus the oral fairy tale genre is delivered in a host of written discourses and language registers and the Ahlbergs increased the art and devices of the novelty book.

*Anno [Mitsumaso Anno]*. There is a a strong mathematical element manifested through play upon perspective, paradox and logic, and which gives Anno's picture books a potential readership well beyond that of childhood while nevertheless intriguing and delighting children. He takes his viewers travelling through time, space and cultures in his wordless Journey books through Britain, Italy and the USA. From a bird's eye perspective, the picture-plane teems with busily peopled identifiable scenes. References to literature and painting – Shakespeare and Sendak, Constable and Courbet – are scattered among the craftsmen and artisans, pageants and parades. *Anno's Aesop* (1987) is a metafictive multidimensioned work of art about telling stories, interpreting pictures, and the practices of parenthood. A book within a book, it carries a facsimile of *Aesop's Fables* retold and illustrated by Anno, and a separate text of the 'readings' of those fables by a preliterate father fox to his son: four story-tellers at work, and Anno is deliberately playing fast and loose with at least twenty-five literary or graphic conventions.

*Jeannie Baker* provides examples of the development of collage technique, used, in the following instances, to support the environmental theme. With cut paper, clay, hair, string, fabric, feathers and found objects she produces collage constructions which are then expertly photographed to produce a three-dimensional effect. *Where the Forest Meets the Sea* (1988) reveals a child's imagination at work as he explores the tropical rainforest in North Queensland. Time merges on the page; past and future inhabitants of the territory are visible ghostly presences. Baker's wordless picture book *Window* (1991) graphically depicts the gradual devastation of the Australian countryside in a twenty-four year span, as we watch a baby grow to adulthood and in turn become a parent. With vision allied to great technical skill Baker shows how nature feeds off nature, and how each new generation is unable to learn from the mistakes of the preceding one.

*Quentin Blake*. Originally a cartoonist, Blake has illustrated many notable picture books with his spritely pen. His awareness of the potential of the form may be seen in *The Story of the Dancing Frog* (1984).The framework, in the present, in sepia monochrome shows a mother telling a story to her child; the main text is the child's visualisation (in colour) of her mother's words. As well as distinguishing the structure of the story within the story, the monochrome passages act as a device to hold back the narrative thrust, and promote a reflective quality. He has collaborated on several occasions with Russell Hoban. In *How Tom Beat Captain Najork and his Hired Sportsmen* (1974), they tease the reader-viewer by withholding precise information about the three games which are central to the story, thus drawing attention to our dependency upon sufficient information to bridge narrational gaps. Their story *Monsters (1989)*, for example, is essentially postmodernist and raises questions about the relationship between creator and creation, the nature of reality, and of the creative process itself. Young thinkers can cut their philosophical teeth on all of these multilayered works.

*Raymond Briggs.* Briggs has been consistently diverse in both graphic technique, and in thematic range, particularly in the cartoon picture book. His work spans the concerns of the complete age range. *Fungus the Bogeyman* (1978) is a tour of an alternative society with a novella-length text delivered in hundreds of fragments of dozens of styles of discourse. In *The Snowman* (1978) he uses a wordless picture strip form for his lyrical account of a small child's dreams, and the reality of the morning's thaw. With gentle satire he challenges the traditional view of Father Christmas, showing him at work and on holiday. In other picture books, satire takes on an increasingly darker dominant mode, notably in *Gentleman Jim* (1980), a bleak vision of consumerism and bureaucracy, and the apocalyptic *When the Wind Blows* (1983). The theme of the power of irreconcilable differences over love and goodwill, is shaped with wit and vigour for two distinct audiences in *The Man* (1992) and *The Bear* (1994), both of which show the development and inevitable deterioration of a pair of would-be friendships, and witness Briggs's refusal to sentimentalise. In *The Man*, a boy harbours a thoroughly demanding manikin who challenges his (and our) assumptions over a range of social issues. In *The Bear*, for younger beholders, a little girl tries but fails to domesticate her magnificent polar visitor.

*Anthony Browne* is a major international picture book maker. His pictorial style is characterised by surrealistic and fantastic imagery, the recurring major image of a gorilla and a mode of depiction which, with its intense care to selected details and textures, gives the quality of non-photographic realism. Browne works on the very boundaries of form, and theme, and his illustrations are rich with the visual equivalent of transtextual and intertextual allusions. His visual interpretation of *Hansel and Gretel* (1981) accords with a Freudian analysis of the tale, and employs a symbolic mode which includes sets of images to represent the children's conflicting feelings about their mother, who shares the same facial features as those of the witch. His own tale of transformation, *Gorilla* (1983) shows the complex psychological relationship between a child and her father, while a picture book for the very young, *Bear Hunt* (1979) reworks Crockett Johnson's *Harold and the Purple Crayon* (1957) to social and political ends. In *Zoo* (1992), Browne compares the behaviour of powerful animals rendered powerless, and literally trapped in cages, with specimens of mankind, free but metaphorically trapped in brutish responses to each other and the immediate environment.

*Marcia Brown* has made very individual versions of traditional tales in traditional media. *Cinderella* (1954) a picture story book, illustrated in water colour and crayon, has witty drawings, coloured chiefly in rose and blue, their spirit matched by the Bembo text type. *Once a Mouse* (1961) is an Indian fable of transformations, illustrated in wood-cut, with colour. Intended for a young child, this is a distinguished picture book, rich in visual interest and contrast.

*John Burningham* has provided a series of benchmarks of excellence. *Borka, the Adventures of a Goose with no Feathers* (1963) is an exemplar of a painterly book, the picture plane alive with rich textures and gestural sweeps of the brush, with colour used structurally – coral flows the Thames. *Mr Gumpy's Outing* (1970) (explored in detail by Perry Nodelman in Chapter 9) shows the close linking of pictures to movement of the text, as he offsets large colour plates against smaller hatched sepia drawings which act as a commentary. In the late 1970s he exploited the bifurcated nature of the form differently, with *Come Away from the Water, Shirley* (1977).This book has two sets of pictures on each opening; to the left, pale drawings of and for the adults together with their spoken words, contrasting with opposing full page vibrantly hued spreads of the child's imaginary world. Burningham withholds information as to how the two sequences of images are related and his picture book narratives become increasingly challenging from there on. In *Granpa* (1984), an exploration of the relationship between a little girl and her grandfather, two typefaces and sepia drawings and colour spreads are used to carry threads of conversation between the two voices and to portray memories, imaginings, and events of the present. The gap between words and images widens so far in *John Patrick Norman McHennessy – The Boy Who Was Always Late* (1987) a story about story-telling, that their relationship remains wholly indeterminate.

*Eric Carle.* The physical attributes of the page itself is often a feature which is intrinsic to the narrative in Carle's picture books. He provides examples of skilful collage technique, a concept book, and a book-as-toy, in *The Very Hungry Caterpillar* (1969), in which the caterpillar eats its way through images of food, piercing a hole through the page as he goes. A child's finger inserted in the hole mimics the caterpillar, and enables the translation of the text from word to action. Solving clues, the shapes of which are mirrored by cut-out pages, takes the beholder on a mysterious journey to find a surprise present in *The Secret Birthday Message* (1972). Imaginative application of thermography (a process which uses non-toxic, chip-proof ink) enables children to feel with their fingers as well as see with their eyes the web being built in *The Very Busy Spider* (1985).

*Philipe Dupasquier* has produced a number of wordless books with interestingly varied narrational devices. In *The Great Green Mouse Disaster* (with Martin Waddell, 1987), a hotel is reduced to chaos by an invasion of mice and every room is shown simultaneously. For this visual assault course the viewer may look at a whole opening at a time, or take one room at a time in a series of reviewings of the whole book. With twelve words, twelve major illustrations, and an abundance of detailed strip pictures, Dupasquier forms the picture book into an autobiographical visual calendar, recording the effects of the passage of a year upon the seasonal activities of his family and the appearance of the landscape, in *Our House on the Hill* (1987).

*Monique Felix* plays a poststructuralist game with her concept books about a little mouse trapped in a book by introducing an interplay between the physical object and a fictional escape by the image. To take one example from her highly original series; in *Alphabet* (1992) the mouse eats its way through the pages, liberating random lower-case letters, and meets up with a similarly trapped mouse doing the same with capitals which together they gradually sort into order. The front case (cover) of the book is literally 'nibbled away', further factualising the fantasy.

*Barbara Firth* and the writer Martin Waddell have achieved a notable partnership. Their collaboration *Can't You Sleep Little Bear?* (1988), a perfect example of the traditional bed-time book, now appears in eighteen languages. It features Little Bear who is afraid of the dark until he is given the sight of the huge benevolent moon from the safe vantage of Big Bear's arms. The bears are skilfully anthropomorphised by pose and human expressions. Their territory is pictured in a sure soft pencil and fluid water paint, on grainy paper, the whole having a tactile, sensuous quality. In Caldecott style the visual narrative is not as simple as it first appears, displaying several transtextual jokes.

*Michael Foreman* is both a picture book maker as well as an illustrator of modern and classic texts. The main thrust of his earlier work is political. In *The Two Giants* (1967), one called Sam the other Boris, the world is systematically made a sadder place until they learn to be friends. He later developed this pacifist theme in a satire, *Moose* (1971). *War and Peas* (1974) is a thinly disguised pictorial parable about surplus food enjoyed by rich nations, and a starving Third World. Mixed media artwork includes a landscape with giant collages of cakes and jellies, mountainous sponges and chocolate sundae skyscrapers. He has combined historical writing and autobiographical visual recollections in his illustrated story, *War Boy: A Country Childhood* (1989). *War Game* (1993) a moving and complex companion volume, set in the First World War, inspired by and dedicated to his four young uncles who died in the fighting, has multiple sources of visual and textual information, and a sombre double irony in its title.

*Fiona French* brings the art of other times and places to the traditional concerns of picture books. Her virtuosity is demonstrated in, for example, the adaptation of Egyptian friezes for *Huni* (1971), witty allusions to seventeenth-century Dutch painting for *Hunt the Thimble* (1978), electronic-type graphics for *Future Story* (1983), a radical version of *Snow White in New York* (1986) set in the 1930s, and Ethiopian geometrics lending Noah an archaic quality in *Rise, Shine!* (1989).

*Jane Hissey's* picture story book texts have satisfying plots with a small central mystery, and the visual narratives display ingenuity and felicitous details as in *Little Bear's Trousers* (1987). She offers an entirely credible nursery microcosm which is humorous because it takes itself so seriously – a quality which has echoes of the Kingdom of Babar. Her crayon medium mimics texture, which has particularly strong associations for young viewers: soft velvet pile, fur and felt, old worn carpeting, glistening jam, the gleam on a beady eye.

*Shirley Hughes* innovates form, using traditional materials. *Up and Up* (1979) showing the fantasy adventure of a little girl who wants to fly, demonstrates that with graphic brilliance, the wordless strip cartoon can sustain complex ideas. *Chips and Jessie* (1985) is a multimedia metafictive picture book with a fresh synthesis of words, pictures and strip cartoon techniques. In one notable passage the story is carried by layout, picture, narrative text, speech balloons and further written amplification.

*Pat Hutchins* always has devices to draw in her young beholder, such as running stories in addition to the main one in the illustrations for *You'll Soon Grow Into*

*Them, Titch* (1983). Her classic masterpiece, *Rosie's Walk* (1968), is like a pantomime sketch, which showed what could be accomplished in the contrast between word and image and complicity between artist and child; there is one sentence and an ironic visual sequence in the story of a hen who struts round the farm unaware of the presence of a predatory fox. Rosie – he's behind you!

*Robert Ingpen. The Idle Bear* (1986) is picture book to stretch a child's intellect, imagination and toleration of ambiguity. Two tattered teddy bears, one a realist and the other a philosopher, face each other and engage in Pinteresque dialogue. The twelve page openings take the reader/viewer through a 40-year life span in the presented world of the bears as naturally as the apparent drifts and shifts of their conversation. Ideas explored by the text from the stance of old age, are all reflections of how we make sense of our lives through memory, affections, and through language. Deft, sure drawing braces the rich pastel medium of the illustrations. The philosophical musings of Ted, the Idle Bear's companion, continue in *The Age of Acorns* (1988).

*Ezra Jack Keats* is closely associated with the collage technique. Given that all painting is a delicate balance between illusion and reality, solid objects occupying deep space, which in reality are only shapes on a flat surface, collage demands special means of expression for the artist. The materials of the collage elements have their own character, but at the same time the beholder is asked to see them as part of the composition. Keats's great skill in seizing the unique possibilities of patterned paper is apparent in *The Snowy Day* (1962), and *Whistle for Willie* (1964).

*Charles Keeping* created truthful picture books which made no concessions to received opinion about what is suitable for children. *Joseph's Yard* (1969) and *Through the Window* (1970) which explored themes of jealousy and loss respectively, are painterly, with intense colour, gestural obsessive patterning and vigorous handling of outline. Keeping's style later became more linear, though still with allusive colour, as in the tale of a subway busker, *Sammy Streetsinger* (1984). For his interpretation of Alfred Noyes's poem *The Highwayman* (1981) Keeping limits his pictorial means to sepia monochrome and his opulent confident line which leaves every tracing to contribute to the vitality of the drawing as a whole. The sexual undertones surface in this tale of tenderness, betrayal, sacrifice and butchery.

*Satoshi Kitamura* transforms the inherently constrained form of alphabet and counting books. *What's Inside? The Alphabet Book* (1985), which involves the learner in a guessing game, has complex relationships between layout and compositions. These exert a particularly strong influence on the dynamics of the picture book, which exhibits a strong kinship to jazz music. *When Sheep Cannot Sleep: The Counting Book* (1986) combines narrative, folk lore, and numbering; *Acorn to Zoo: An Alphabet Picture Book* (1992) is in effect also a dictionary, a visual dictionary, and a source for story telling, as nearly 400 figures and objects come together in twenty-six highly imaginative situations. An intuitive fine pen line, sculptural shapes and an outstanding sense of colour and tone characterise Kitamura's pictorial style.

*David McKee* refuses to take for granted how stories 'should' be told, pictures viewed, and books held. *Not Now, Bernard* (1980) is a satire on parenting, and a brief study in child psychology. *I Hate My Teddy Bear* (1982) with a sparse dialogue between two children and then their teddies, is illustrated in a surreal manner. The children play against a background showing disconnected fragments of the lives of those around them, whilst in places, changing viewpoints oblige the beholder to turn the book through different angles. Mental agility and delight in ambiguity are viewing requirements.

*Nicolas Mordinoff* illustrated *The Two Reds* (1950), William Lipkind's tale about a boy and a cat, in a style showing the influence of modern art, and which was highly innovative at the time. Pictorial impact is made through bold images, strong flat-colour masses, and a line with direct expression.

*Helen Oxenbury.* Over the past two decades Oxenbury has produced a variety of illustration with shifts in style and techniques while working within the Caldecott tradition. Her early work as in Ivor Cutler's eccentric *Meal One* (1971) about a robust relationship between a mother and son, shows a preoccupation with surface texture, as well as her many other strengths: fluent drawing, organisational skill, inventiveness with composition, technical mastery of viewpoint and convincing characterisation. More recently her name has become associated with board books, big and small, and picture books for the youngest viewers. For these she uses instantly recognisable forms, drawn and modelled in soft pencil line and colour wash. In her collaboration with the poet Michael Rosen, for *We're Going on a Bear Hunt* (1989), Oxenbury alternates drawings of sketch-like immediacy with water colour paintings, which vary in scale to match the drama of events.

*Kveta Paconska* gives an example of the European aesthetic tradition with *The Little Flower King* (1991). The simple fairy tale of a quest for a wife by the eponymous hero is a textual springboard for artwork which effortlessly and joyfully crosses the age range: the artist takes the line for a walk with the adventurousness of Klee, and charges the images with the lyricism of Chagall.

*Jan Pienkowski* is an artist-designer who both makes and seizes upon technical innovations in colour processing, in advanced print technology, and in paper engineering. In *The Golden Bird* (1970) and *The Kingdom Under the Sea* (1971) he unites the black silhouette, a characteristic technique of his, with his own experiments on marbling paper, which for these books is reproduced facsimile. His silhouette illustrations of *Christmas* (1984) and *Easter* (1989) use a bronze powder technique for the gold printing which enriches the page. Pienkowski has also designed hugely entertaining pop-up books such as *Haunted House* (1979) which even produces naturally made noises to add to the scary effects.

*Tony Ross* is a prolific interpreter of folk- and fairy tales and a maker of his own parodic dead-pan variant of the genre. One of his best, *Puss in Boots: The Story of a Sneaky Cat* (1981) achieves a fine balance between tradition and innovation. The shapes of the pictures, the viewpoints and the scale constantly change to reflect the daring energy and ingenuity of the events of the tale.

*Maurice Sendak*, through his originality of vision and his technical skill has a oeuvre which is unmatched in its thematic range and graphic styles. In his self-styled trilogy he explores childhood as a state of being, and shows how through fantasy children achieve catharsis for their feelings. *Where The Wild Things Are* (1963) was a breakthrough for form and theme. The spare text, its punctuation, the format, layout, symbolic imagery, scale of the pen and wash illustrations, wordless pages, colour saturations and tones, interdependently created a small boy's rage and its release. *In The Night Kitchen* (1971), a more complex work in every way, is a celebration and candid acceptance of the curiosity, sensuality and sexuality of children, taking shape in a dream, with New York of the 1930s transformed into a fantasy kitchen. *Outside Over There* (1981) a study in sibling rivalry, is Sendak's tribute to Mozart, a reworking of a fragment of a folk-tale, a pictorial record of the Northern Romantic tradition, and an example of how far it is possible to explore – historically, culturally and psychologically – inside the covers of a picture book.

*Lane Smith* exploits the effects of using new materials in a technically incorrect way. He alternates oil paint glazes with water-based acrylic sprays, layer upon layer, which through their reactions form strange surface textures and sometimes collage elements are added. In his postmodernist interpretation of *The True Story of the 3 Little Pigs! By A. Wolf, as told to Jon Scieska* (1989) the crackles, bubbles, and swirls of the paint act as a visual metaphor for the wolf's energy. In *The Big Pets* (1991) a dreamscape, the images of animals loom, move mysteriously, their edges lost in the layered depths and dark, muted hues.

*Chris Van Allsburg* invites his viewers to become highly active creators and narrators in *The Mysteries of Harris Burdick* (1985). The contents of the picture book purport to be a series of picture plates to fourteen stories left at a children's book publisher by the mysterious Harris Burdick. Each picture, in intense tonal drawing, heavily shadowed and mysteriously lit, has a title and one line of text and appears to allude to a genre. His illustrations are permeated with a dream-like stillness and intensity, whether in monochrome as in *The Garden of Abdul Gasazi* (1979) or in muted opaque colour, as in *The Wreck of the Zephyr* (1985).

*David Weisner* draws upon stylistic allusions to animated cartoons, the silent films, the wide screen, and superhero comic books for *Tuesday* (1991) his visual burlesque of a night raid on a small town by squadrons of frogs on aerodynamic lily pads. The text comprises a few words and the monitoring of the hours in minutes in numerals. The layout mimics the pace of the action. Vertical picture strips are superimposed on double spread 'bleeds' to give simultaneous presentation of isolated incidents; horizontal strips, close ups, zooms and long shots echo cinematic techniques. A clean outline, luminous colour and meticulous detailing gives the images a quality of hallucinatory ordinariness which contrasts strongly with the events portrayed.

*Brian Wildsmith* is as much a painter as an illustrator. His early work, like *Fishes* (1968), a concept book, rejoices in rich surfaces, layered, scored, scratched, spattered in bejewelled colours. With vision, he takes an old story and gives it a new twist in his environmentally aware picture book, *Professor Noah's Spaceship* (1980). Wildsmith integrates different styles painting for a structural purpose. Earthy hues and brush strokes, fine or bold, suggest an equivalence for the natural world of fur, feather and forest, whilst saturated chemical-dye hues and geometric patterning on hard-edge forms are used for mankind's technological obsessions. Wildsmith has also developed the split-form picture book, where alternate leaves throughout the book are only half-page width. He uses this device to make new double spreads as the pages turn, and to forward a narrative thrust, not in its more traditional mode, to promote bizarre effects. In *Give a Dog a Bone* (1985) the split page also contributes a guessing game to the tale of a stray dog's search for food.

*Lisbeth Zwerger.* With the minimum of pictorial means – pen and wash, traces of pencil under-drawing, and the ability to exploit the relationships between figure and ground – Zwerger supports, dramatises and amplifies folk- and fairy tales. Settings are reduced often to only a line, or a change of tone in the background wash. The focus of the composition is on the character, brought into being by a lively line and lack of superfluous details. The latter quality encourages speculation as well as bringing a beautiful economy to the page. *The Swineherd* by Hans Christian Andersen (1982), *Little Red Cap* by the Brothers Grimm (1983), and *The Selfish Giant* by Oscar Wilde (1984) all show how consistently well Zwerger is able to honour and interpret traditional texts.

## Further Reading

Alderson, B. (1986) *Sing a Song for Sixpence*, London: Cambridge University Press in association with the British Library.

Bader, B. (1976) *American Picturebooks from Noah's Ark to The Beast Within*, New York: Macmillan.

Bennett, J. (1979) *Learning to Read with Picture Books*, South Woodchester: Thimble Press.

Doonan, J. (1992) *Looking at Pictures in Picture Books*, South Woodchester: Thimble Press..

Fever, W. (1977) *When We Were Very Young*, London: Thames and Hudson.

Graham, J. (1990) *Pictures on the Page*, Sheffield: NATE.

Hunt, P. (1991) *Criticism, Theory and Children's Literature*, Oxford: Blackwell.

Hurlimann, B. (1967), *Three Centuries of Children's Books in Europe*, trans. and ed. by B. W. Alderson, London: Oxford University Press.

—— (1968) *Picture-Book World*, trans. and ed. by B. W. Alderson, London: Oxford University Press.

Kingman, L. (ed.) (1978) *The Illustrator's Notebook*, Boston: The Horn Book.

Lewis, D. (1990) 'The constructedness of texts: picture books and the metafictive', *Signal* 62: 131–146.

Martin, D. (1989) *The Telling Line*, London: MacRae.

Meek, M. (1988) *How Texts Teach what Readers Learn*, South Woodchester: Thimble Press.

Moss, E. (1985) *Picture Books for Young Children 9-13*, 2nd edn, South Woodchester: Thimble Press.

Nodelman, P. (1988) *Words About Pictures*, Athens, GA: University of Georgia Press.

Pullman, P. (1989) 'Invisible pictures', *Signal* 60: 160–186.

Schwarcz, J. H. (1982) *Ways of the Illustrator*, Chicago: American Library Association.

Sendak, M. (1988) *Caldecott & Co.*, New York: Farrar, Straus and Giroux.

Whalley, J. I. and Chester, T. R. (1989) *A History of Children's Book Illustration*, London: John Murray in association with the Victoria and Albert Museum.

# 20

# Popular Literature: Comics, Dime Novels, Pulps and Penny Dreadfuls

*Denis Gifford*

### British Children's Comics: 150 Years of Fun and Thrills

The familiar British weekly comic magazine of today, usually comprising some thirty-two pages of strip cartoons, most in colour, some in black-and-white, can trace its ancestry back to an experiment produced for Christmas 1874, and forty years further back to a four-page annual edition dated 1831. And the regular comic characters can trace themselves back to a one-off experimental strip designed with no more ambition than to fill a page in a weekly humour magazine published in the summer of 1867. Both these casual (at the time) events took place long enough ago to secure Britain's claim as founder of the feast of fun that fills the world with laughter.

To take these two events in chronological order, first came the vehicle. *Bell's Life in London and Sporting Chronicle*, a weekly which began on 3 March 1822, introduced a regular pictorial feature called The Gallery of Comicalities in 1827. This series of caricatures, illustrated jokes and humorous engravings was contributed by such favourite contemporary cartoonists as George Cruikshank, Robert Seymour and Kenny Meadows. The pictures were so popular that thirty-four of these cartoons were gathered together and reprinted as a full page of pictures on Sunday, 2 January 1831: the first cartoon page in British newspaper history. This was so successful – and economical! – that a further fifty-four cartoons were reprinted in the edition dated 12 March 1831, with the interesting editorial note that the engravings 'cost the proprietors two hundred and seventy guineas'. If true, this would imply that the average fee paid per picture was five guineas, a good deal higher than the fee a comic artist would receive half a century later, when two shillings would be considered a good price per panel!

An enterprising publisher named George Goodyer now enlarged on Bell's idea and, assembling four broadsheet pages from back numbers of Bell's weekly, published them as a one-shot entitled *The Gallery of 140 Comicalities* on 24 June 1831. Goodyer charged the steep price of threepence for this bumper budget of cartoons, editorially reckoning that the total cost to him was £735. His profits can be estimated by the mathematically minded, as we know his total sales to have been 178,000 copies. Another publisher, William Clement Jr, saw even more potential in this pictorial format, and turned *The Gallery of Comicalities* into an annual series, running it from Part II (1832) to Part VII (1841). This regular cartoon paper becomes a good contender for the title of the first comic, for among the myriad cartoons can be found primitive strips, tiny two-picture episodes usually in the form of cartooned comparisons or contrasts. Indeed, in Bell's first full-page Gallery of Comicalities can be found a captionless two-picture strip entitled 'Before and After the Election', reprinted from an issue of *Life in London* of 1830.

Bell's weekly and its reprints represent the mainstream of popular journalism, but at the same time the wealthier end of the market purchased caricature prints, plain or hand coloured, and issued by the print houses in limited editions.

The original idea of using the lithographic printing system to issue a regular cartoon magazine rather than single sheets of pictures seems to have been born in Scotland. Number one of *Glasgow Looking Glass*, dated 23 July 1825, was issued and most probably illustrated by John Watson of the Lithographic Press Office, 189 George Street: 'Price Common Impression, One Shilling, Best Ditto, 1s 6d'. It even included an eight-picture serial strip entitled 'History of a Coat, Part 1'. This monthly was followed by *Northern Looking Glass*, a four-page pictorial drawn by William Heath, who later went to London to draw *The Looking Glass* for Thomas McLean, the famous print publisher of 26 Haymarket. Heath drew the first seven issues (January–July 1830), after which Robert Seymour was given the credit. *The Looking Glass* was 'designed and drawn on stone'.

The father of what most students of the comic would recognise as true British comic art was *c.*J. Grant. He drew cartoons in the Thomas Hood style of pictorial pun, but with a common touch: for example, the phrase 'Making a Deep Impression' is illustrated by a slapstick scene showing a top-hatted toff flopping into a puddle of mud. 'Every Man to His Post' shows a bottle-brandishing drunk clutching a horse hitching post. William Makepeace Thackeray, writing about Grant, saw his drawings as 'outrageous caricatures' with 'squinting eyes, wooden legs, and pimpled noses forming the chief points of fun'. They were beneath that great literary gentleman, but that was, and is, their point. In Grant's lively London line can be seen the start of an art appealing to, and belonging to, the working and lower class. Grant's 'pimpled noses' are archetypes for Ally Sloper's.

Grant described himself as 'A.A.E.' which stood for 'Author, Artist, Editor' on the byline of a fortnightly broadside which he drew from 1 January 1834. *Every Body's Album and Caricature Magazine*, published by the lithographic printer J. Kendrick of 54 Leicester Square, London, had a good run and in its welter of caricatural contents can be found a comic strip with speech balloons, 'Adventures of the Buggins's', a short serial strip that ran from number 36 to number 37 (July 1835).

The first comic paper to match all the features of the modern comic (low price, regular weekly publication, mass circulation via newsagents, editorial and artistic content) was called *Funny Folks* (12 December 1874). Like the other essential of the comic, the regularly appearing character, the first comic evolved by accident. James Henderson, publisher of *The Weekly Budget*, a family magazine, designed *The Funny Folks Budget* as a pull-out supplement to his Grand Christmas Number. It was to be an all-cartoon section and was advertised as a special one-off edition. However, so striking was it in its large tabloid format, and so intriguing to the readers of *The Weekly Budget* readers, that it was immediately turned into a separate publication in its own right. Curiously, although it laid down a formula clung to by British comics for the next seventy-five years (eight pages, four of cartoons and four of text, in tabloid newspaper size), *Funny Folks* never developed a continuing hero. The few strips it ran were, like the cartoons which dominated its content, topical, even political, following the promise of the magazine's subtitle: 'The Comic Companion to the Newspaper'. Thus we see the first important point a student of the comic should always remember, that originally comics were intended as light entertainment for the adult reader, and not for children.

And so we come to our second essential to the comic, the continuing cartoon character. The first true comic strip hero (after one or two minor false starts) starred in a full-page cartoon episode entitled 'Some of the Mysteries of Loan and Discount'. He was created by the astoundingly talented Charles Henry Ross, a prolific author of serial stories, novels and plays, a journalist, an editor, an actor and a cartoonist; and his name was 'Ally Sloper'. Ally was supposed to have been an abbreviation of Alexander, but in fact the name was designed as a pun, a favourite form of verbal humour of the period. Being forever workshy and penniless, Ally Sloper was one who 'sloped' up the 'alley' – that is to say, he slipped around the corner with great alacrity whenever the landlord came to collect his rent!

Charles Ross was already drawing a regular comic strip page in the weekly joke magazine, *Judy*, which had been founded in 1867 as a rival to the successful humorous journal, *Punch* (1841). Having now hit by sheer chance on a character who would stand repetition, Ross reintroduced Ally Sloper in his subsequent contributions to *Judy*, probably to save himself the trouble of continually creating new comic heroes. Sloper took the public's fancy as his efforts to avoid hard work and make a comfortable living became ever more outrageous. An annual cartoon publication, a burlesque almanac entitled *Ally Sloper's Comic Kalendar* was introduced from December 1873, followed by a mid-year special, *Ally Sloper's Summer Number* (1880). Eventually Ross sold his character to the famous Victorian engravers and publishers, the Dalziel Brothers, and a complete weekly comic was built around the old reprobate: *Ally Sloper's Half-Holiday* from 3 May 1884.

Ross's original image of Sloper, crude but full of action, was lost when the artwork for his adventures was taken over by W. G. Baxter. This brilliant comic draughtsman established the vast Sloper Family, including the sexy chorus girl Tootsie Sloper, who ran the fashion features, depicting them in the bumper Christmas Holiday issues in huge centre spreads of Yuletide activities. Unhappily Baxter died far too young, suffering, it is said, from the curse of drink that so befuddled his cartoon hero, and for the remainder of his long comic career Sloper was drawn, in the Baxter image, by W. F. Thomas.

Sloper's comic life in his own weekly ran for some forty years. In addition he was the first strip character to be merchandised, and can be found to this day in such venerable collectibles as china busts (with removable top hats!), ashtrays, a pocket watch, a glass sauce-bottle and a brass doorstop. It was the last of these antiques that became the model for the annual (but now defunct) Ally Sloper Award, instituted in 1976 as a mark of appreciation towards veteran comic artists. Although Sloper died officially in 1923, he has refused to lie down, being revived by two comic publishers in 1948, and again as the title for the first British comic magazine for adults (1976).

The true boom in comic weeklies began on 17 May 1890 when an enterprising young publisher named Alfred Harmsworth produced Number One of *Comic Cuts*. Harmsworth modelled his weekly paper so closely on James Henderson's *Funny Folks* that he even filled it with cartoons and strips that had already been published in the past by Henderson! Harmsworth himself had been an editorial employee of Henderson, and well knew that most of his employer's cartoons were reprinted from back numbers of the American comic weeklies, *Judge*, *Life* and *Puck*. Henderson, however, had a perfect right to do this, as he had financial arrangements with the American publishers; Harmsworth had not. In consequence it was not long before Harmsworth was advertising in *Comic Cuts* for British cartoonists to contribute to his new paper. Henderson had moved in with a writ! Thus, through Harmsworth's undoubted perfidy, a brand new market for British cartoonists was opened up. Contributions poured in and were used to fill the four illustrated pages of the eight-page *Comic Cuts*, plus the additional pages of *Illustrated Chips*. The runaway success of Harmsworth's new comic had virtually forced him to produce a companion comic, and *Illustrated Chips* was launched on 26 July 1890. Both papers succeeded beyond Harmsworth's expectations, not because of the quality of their cartoons (or indeed of their paper itself, which was of the lowest quality and dyed pink), but because both papers cost exactly half the price of his rival Henderson's comics: Harmsworth sold his comics for a halfpenny each, instead of one penny!

The halfpenny comic boom continued through to the new century, and through it many new cartoonists were discovered. None was greater than a youthful Nottingham lithographer named Tom Browne (1870–1910). Browne scorned the closely cross-hatched style of cartooning so prevalent in the old-established humorous weeklies such as *Punch*, and favoured the new, simple style popularised by Phil May. Applying this formula of linework plus solid blacks to strip art, Browne began freelancing the occasional comic strip to such London weeklies as *Scraps*: his first ever, entitled 'He Knew How To Do It', appeared in the issue of 27 April 1890. A prophetic title: Tom Browne certainly 'knew how to do it', and soon abandoned lithography in Nottingham for a studio in Blackheath, London, from whence he turned out as many as five different front-page series a week, plus posters, postcards, advertising art, illustrations and water colour paintings. His most popular and famous characters in comics were Weary Willie and Tired Tim, who first appeared as casual tramp heroes in a one-off strip described as Weary Waddles and Tired Timmy in *Chips* for 16 May 1896. Immediately popular with editors and readers alike, these classic comic heroes, one short and fat, the other tall and thin, remained on page one of *Chips* through the comic's entire life, right to the final edition on 12 September 1953. This fifty-eight year run is something of a record, but one which Tom Browne did not live to see. He died in 1910, some five years after giving up his characters and, indeed, comic work altogether. But he had lived long enough to know that his bold black-and-white style of art, and his working-class type of hero, plus his slapstick, action-packed comedy, had set the style, the standard, and indeed the look of British comic art, for half a century to come.

Incidentally, it is a sad sidelight on British comic history that the cartoonist who drew Weary Willie and Tired Tim from 1907 to their very last appearance, was never once permitted to sign his work. His name was Percy Cocking, and he continued the classic Tom Browne style of comic drawing to the very end.

Harmsworth's huge financial success led to many smaller publishers entering the comic market, each with one or more titles, and all modelled on the originals. Indeed they invariably featured tramp double-acts on their front pages, virtually carbon copies of Tom Browne's Willie and Tim. Indeed, the more prosperous publishers hired Browne to create these front page characters for them, such as C. Arthur Pearson: Airy Alf and Bouncing Billy appeared on number 1 of *The Big Budget* (19 June 1897), a huge penny comic divided into three pull-out parts of eight pages each.

At this time all British comics were being published for an adult market: even Harmsworth's price of one halfpenny was a sum beyond the pocket of the average working-class child. Thus all the early comic heroes are adult, and all the themes of their adventures are adult – tramps stealing from shopkeepers and ending up in prison, for example. The first comic paper to feature children as heroes was *Larks*, published as a halfpenny comic by the proprietors of *Ally Sloper's Half Holiday* (one penny). The Balls Pond Road Banditti was a gang of juvenile delinquents whose weekly adventures took them around such landmarks of Victorian London as the British Museum and the Albert Memorial. They were drawn on the front page by Gordon Fraser, an artist whose name still graces a greetings card publisher. The Banditti can be considered the cartoon ancestors of the *Beano*'s gang of destructive schoolboys, The Bash Street Kids. Although obviously popular with young readers, it would be some years before British comics became the sole property of children. Even then, the heroes of the strips remained predominantly adult with just the occasional strip concerning itself with the antics of schoolboys and schoolgirls.

The first coloured comics were simply printed in black ink on coloured paper. *Chips*, for example, was almost always printed on pink paper, and despite a brief flirtation with red ink on white paper, reverted in the final decade of its existence to its traditional form. The first British comic to be printed in full colour was the special autumn issue of *Comic Cuts*, published 12 September 1896. This brave failure, an enterprise of Alfred Harmsworth in answer to the coloured comic supplements which were being published as part of the New York Sunday newspapers, failed mainly because the printing costs raised the price of a coloured edition from a halfpenny to one penny. However, Harmsworth continued to experiment spasmodically with special coloured editions of his several weekly comics, but it would be his business rivals, the relatively small firm of Trapps and Holmes, who would publish the first regular weekly comic printed in full colour. Called, appropriately, *The Coloured Comic*, it appeared on 21 May 1898 with the usual tramp partnership on the front – Frog Faced Ferdinand and Watty Wool Whiskers – but after about a year was reduced to being printed black on coloured paper, thus continuing to justify its title, to the publishers at least!

Alfred Harmsworth was, however, the first to publish a really successful coloured comic weekly, launching *Puck*, a twelve-page penny comic, on 30 July 1904, 'To gladden your eye on bright wings of colour and fancy'. But by the end of the year the comic had completely changed in character, and with it the whole nature and concept of the British comic. Puck begins as a weekly magazine for adults, modelled closely on the American Sunday supplements. Even its name was stolen from the American humorous weekly, while many of its characters in the comic strips are also stolen. There was The Newlyweds, but by a British artist, not George McManus. There was Buster Brown complete with dog and resolutions, redrawn as Scorcher Smith. Some weeks there was a full-page cover cartoon; other weeks a decorative drawing of a lovely lady. But the key to the comic was contained in 'Puck Junior', a section within the comic intended for the younger members of the family. This quickly took over the entire twelve-page comic (except for some of the serialised fiction pages). Johnny Jones and the Casey Court Kids (guest stars from Harmsworth's well-established *Chips*) took over the front page, and by Christmas 1904 the whole pictorial content of *Puck* was geared to children.

And so the first comic weekly designed for children was evolved. It became such a success that almost all comic papers published in Great Britain from then on have been designed for the juvenile market. The special appeal remained for adults – they bought the comic for their children, children still seldom being able to afford the necessary penny. Thus a new style of comic was born, one which appealed to the adult eye as a well-drawn, well-designed, well-printed paper which would have nothing objectionable in its contents for children to see, a style of comic quite separate from the halfpenny knockabouts of *Chips* and its companions, which would remain working class, despite the lowering of the age of its readership, for their entire lives.

James Henderson, Harmsworth's old employer and now business rival, was the next publisher to attempt a coloured comic. Taking inspiration from Harmsworth's methods, he succeeded in printing a full colour comic at half *Puck*'s price – one halfpenny! This was *Lot-O-Fun*, which started on 17 March 1906 and ran for a total of 1,196 weekly issues, most of them featuring George Davey's clever fantasy strip 'Dreamy Daniel', about a tramp whose weekly dreams took him to the wild west with Buffalo Bill, and on adventures with many other contemporary heroes, real and imaginary. *Lot-O-Fun* finally closed when Harmsworth, now trading as the Amalgamated Press, bought Henderson out and killed off all his publications, one by one. This shameful practice would be repeated throughout the history of British comics, first with the disappearance of the Trapps and Holmes comics, then with the independent Target Comics of Bath in the 1930s, the J. B. Allen *Comet* and *Sun* in the 1940s, and the Hulton Press comics, *Eagle* and *Girl*, in the 1950s.

British comics were now separated into two distinct classes, the 'penny blacks' and the 'tuppenny coloureds'. The 'black' comics, distinguished by being printed on different coloured newsprint, were aimed at the working-class market – the child at the council school, while the coloureds concentrated on the younger child of middle-class families. The age-range of the comics was considerable. *Chick's Own* (25 September 1920) catered specifically for the very young child just learning to read. All its words were hyphenated into syllables. Next came *The Rainbow* (14 February 1914) for the school beginners aged five to seven, followed by *Sparkler* (20 October 1934) for the 8-year-olds and upwards. Of the many titles covering these age groups *Rainbow* is the most important, and was the most successful, being the pioneer 'nursery comic', as the group came to be called. It was also the first British comic to sell one million copies every week, including one copy which was delivered to Buckingham Palace tucked in the King's *Times*! This enabled the editor to emblazon his comic with the headline, 'The Paper for Home and Palace!'

The front page stars of *Rainbow* were the Bruin Boys, a gang of anthropomorphic animals who lived at Mrs Bruin's Boarding School, and the star of the gang was Tiger Tim. Tim and his chums had been created as early as 1904 for *The Daily Mirror*, then transferred to *The Monthly Playbox* (November 1904), the first coloured comic supplement to a magazine, the sumptuous shilling monthly *The World and His Wife*. This section continued to be given away until May 1910, when it transferred to a fortnightly juvenile educational magazine, *The New Children's Encyclopedia*, to afford much-needed comic relief. The enormous popularity of Tiger Tim and the (then) Hippo Boys encouraged the editor of the newly conceived comic *Rainbow* to feature them on his front page in full colour. Their popularity was so huge that a second comic, *Tiger Tim's Weekly* (31 January 1920), was created, but still this was not enough. Finally a weekly comic just for girls was designed, using the old *Playbox* title, and from 14 February 1925 the hitherto unsuspected twin sisters of Tiger Tim and Company, Tiger Tilly and the Hippo Girls, cut their comic capers.

Once again the darker side of British comic publication is cast across the comedy. None of this immense commercial success benefited Julius Stafford Baker (1869–1961), the cartoonist who created the characters. (He also created Casey Court, the large panel of slum kid comedy that appeared in *Chips* from 1902 to the final issue – again without continued benefit to his income.) Baker was dismissed from the *Rainbow* front page after only a few issues, for being 'too American' in style. Tiger Tim was taken over by Herbert S. Foxwell (1890–1943), who redesigned the character and related the style of drawing more to the traditions of British children's book illustration – amusing but decorative. Foxwell continued the cover strips to the mid-1930s, but was then lured away with greatly increased money to *The Daily Mail* to draw their weekly comic supplement starring their long-established children's strip hero, Teddy Tail (a humanised mouse). Tiger Tim and his pals are, incidentally, the oldest continuing heroes in British comics: they continued to appear in the nursery comic *Jack and Jill* and celebrated their eightieth birthday in 1984.

The 1930s were the Golden Age of British comics and there was even a handsome black-and-orange penny comic called *Golden*, to prove it. The two styles of comic art, nursery and slapstick, had developed to perfection, building on the pioneering work of Tom Browne, Stafford Baker, and others. Of all the many weeklies produced during the decade, the finest has to be *Happy Days* (1 October 1938), a nursery-plus comic printed in full colour photogravure showcasing the two finest Golden Age artists in comics, Roy Wilson (1900–1965) and Reg Perrott (1916–1948?). Wilson had started his comic career as assistant to the slapstick artist, Don Newhouse, but had speedily overtaken his tutor on such excellent penny comic series as Pitch and Toss, a fat-and-thin pair of silly sailors, and Basil and Bert, a monocled secret service agent and his lower-class assistant. Wilson loved to draw funny animals, and his characters Chimpo's Circus on the ever-varied covers of *Happy Days* are his comedy masterpieces. The editor thought so much of this artwork that Wilson was actually allowed to sign his name!

*Happy Days* was the Amalgamated Press's answer to *Mickey Mouse Weekly*, the first full colour photogravure comic which started on 8 February 1936. It was published by the hitherto exclusively adult-magazine publisher Odhams Press, in collaboration with the Walt Disney organisation. Many of the interior strips were American-originated Sunday and daily strips, but the wonderful full-tabloid cover pictures featuring Mickey and his Gang were painted by Wilfred Haughton, who had been the first artist in England to draw the movie mouse for merchandising. Every year from 1931 to the mid-1940s he drew single-handedly the 128-page *Mickey Mouse Annual*. These are collectors' items today, and it is hard to believe that Haughton was actually discharged from the comic for refusing to bring his characterisations of Mickey and friends into line with the modernised style of the Disney Studio. Also working on the pages produced in England for *Mickey Mouse Weekly* was Reg Perrott, a young comics artist who favoured adventure strips and serials. His historical adventure, 'Road to Rome' is a masterpiece in line and wash, followed by his first full-colour serial, the western 'White Cloud'. Moving to the Amalgamated Press comic *Happy Days*, Perrott drew another great colour serial, 'Sons of the Sword', in which cinemascopic panels were used for the first time. Perrott's early death, not long after his demobilisation from the Royal Air Force, robbed British comics of their finest adventure strip artist.

As the 1930s closed, a new publisher entered the comic market, and immediately became the most successful of them all. This was the Scottish publisher, D. c. Thomson of Dundee. Thomson had been issuing very successful boys' story-papers (*Adventure*, *Wizard*, etc.) since the 1920s and now entered comics for the first time with *The Dandy* (3 December 1937), produced in their story-paper format: twenty-eight pages, half-tabloid size, with a full-colour front page. It was an instant success, and its two leading strip stars, Korky the Cat on the cover and Desperate Dan the tough cowboy inside, are still running today. Their original artists, James Crichton and Dudley D. Watkins (1907–1969), are both long dead, but their characters and drawing styles live on. Watkins was only eighteen when he was hired as a staff artist by Thomson, who lured him to Dundee from his native Nottingham, and he would stay with the Scots firm all his life, dying in mid-strip at his drawing-board. Towards the end of his career he became the only Thomson artist allowed to sign his artwork.

*The Beano*, a companion comic to *The Dandy*, was introduced on 30 July 1939, and included stories told purely in pictures – Thomson's had discarded the traditional British style of printed captions underneath every panel (trade term: 'the libretto'). (The Amalgamated Press continued to support their strips with libretti until well after the Second World War). Today the captionless strip is standard, improving the visual drama of the strip but removing much of the traditional reading matter of the comic. D. C. Thomson were also the first to use the American term 'comics' to describe their strips ('All Your Favourite Comics Inside!'), while the Amalgamated Press clung to the word 'comic' (for example, *The Knock-Out Comic*) as descriptive of the whole publication. Finally they too bent to Americanisation with the publication of their *Cowboy Comics* in May 1950. *The Beano*, like its partner, continues to be published to this day, and is Britain's top-selling comic. Of its original heroes, only Lord Snooty and his Pals – another

Dudley Watkins creation – survive. Dropped by the comic in 1992, Snooty was swiftly snapped up by the *Sunday Times* comic supplement.

The Amalgamated Press quickly produced rivals to the Scottish comics, similar in format but differing in character. *Radio Fun* (15 October 1938) depicted famous BBC stars in clever caricature adventures by Roy Wilson and others, and was modelled on the successful pioneer comic in this genre, *Film Fun*, which had been running since 17 January 1920. *Knockout* (4 March 1939) also featured famous heroes, but fictional ones, adapting the story-paper characters Sexton Blake, a detective whose origins go back to the 1890s, and Billy Bunter, the fat schoolboy who first appeared in *The Magnet* in 1908. The look of the comic, however, was designed by Hugh McNeill (1910–1979), a brilliant and highly personal humorous artist. His slightly zany, very funny characters, Our Ernie, Mrs Entwhisle's Little Lad, and Deed-a-Day Danny, were the real stars of the comic. *Knockout* artists (including myself) were encouraged to model their comic style on McNeill.

The years of the Second World War were drab ones for the comics. A national paper shortage helped kill off many of the less successful titles; others suffered from reduced content (down to twelve pages from twenty-eight) and frequency (down from weekly to fortnightly). But the blacked-out 1940s also saw the birth of the British comic book. Gerald G. Swan, a market salesman no longer able to import American comic books, turned himself into a publisher and issued his own. *New Funnies* (January 1940) was the first, sixty-four pages for sixpence, but, unlike the American comics, only the cover was in colour. Further titles followed (*War Comics*, *Thrill Comics*) and even a nursery comic complete with hyphens, *Kiddyfun*. Many other small publishers flourished during the war, including A. Soloway (*Comic Capers*, *All Star*), Martin and Reid, (*Jolly Chuckles*, *Jolly Western*) and the Philipp Marx Group (*The New Comics*, *The Miniature Comic*). Of these minor publishers soon L. Miller and Son would emerge as the most prolific and longest lived. This firm began by reprinting American comic books from Fawcett Publications. When their best-seller, *Captain Marvel Adventures*, had to be discontinued as a consequence of the law-suit between Fawcett and National-D. *c.* Comics (who claimed that Captain Marvel plagiarised their Superman), Miller converted his comic to an all-British superhero, *Marvelman* (6 February 1954). Billy Batson became Micky Moran, his magic cry changed from 'Shazam!' to 'Kimota!' (more or less the word 'Atomic' spelled backwards!). *Marvelman* caught on immediately with comic-hungry children, and was soon joined by *Young Marvelman*, replacing *Captain Marvel Junior*, and *The Marvelman Family*, in which Kid Marvelman replaced Mary Marvel, the All-American superheroine. Don Lawrence, whose artwork rapidly became among the best in British comics, began his career in the *Marvelman* comics.

The 1950s began superbly with *Eagle*, launched on 14 April 1950. This large-format comic in full colour photogravure had been designed by a cleric, the Reverend Marcus Morris, and drawn to his specifications by a failed pilot with his head in the stars, art student Frank Hampson. Hulton Press, publishers of the best selling weekly magazine, *Picture Post*, took it on and *Eagle* rapidly flew to become top comic in the country. Its circulation soon touched the magic million mark once achieved by the pre-war *Rainbow*. 'Dan Dare, Pilot of the Future' was the leading strip, and Hampson quickly turned this science-fiction adventure into a true saga, his artwork improving week by week. Young readers loved the serial for its apparent accuracy, achieved by the unprecedented idea of Hampson's to build scale models of Dare's spacecraft, the futuristic cities of Mars, and so on, so that these would appear authentic from all angles when drawn into the comic. The success of *Eagle* against the hide-bound traditions of the Amalgamated Press and D. C. Thomson comics was to a great extent due to the fact that the entire art and editorial staff of the comic had never worked in either comics or strip cartoons before.

Frank Hampson and his many followers (Frank Bellamy, John Burns, Ron Embleton) changed the face of the British adventure strip. Meanwhile over in the funnies this was being done by a new cartoonist, Leo Baxendale. His strips for *Beano*, including 'The Bash Street Kids' and 'Little Plum', stood out against the standard and somewhat mechanical slapstick comic art in a way that was both new and very funny. (*Beano* had finally gone into 100 per cent picture format on 5 March 1955). Baxendale was lured away from Thomson's by Odhams Press to create the characters and do much of the drawing for a new comic, *Wham* (20 June 1964). His crazy style can still be seen in many modern British comics, although he himself has not drawn for them for many years. After producing an unsuccessful annual of his own (*Willie the Kid*), Baxendale drew for newspapers and Dutch comics, and gathered evidence for a daring law-suit against his former publishers to claim royalties on his many characters which continued to perform (depicted by lesser pens), without benefit to him as creator. Finally settling out of court, Baxendale was more fortunate than Frank Hampson, who died in near poverty despite the fact that his Dan Dare continued to be a comic star when *Eagle* was revived in the 1980s.

In the 1990s British comics are still published in many titles, but are usually tied in some way with television or video games and toys. Old favourites (*Beano*, *Dandy*) continue, while others (*Victor*, *Beezer*) vanish. *2000 AD* (26 February 1977) has succeeded as a cult comic for older readers through the hideous exploits of its ultra-violent anti-hero, Judge Dredd, and is a science-fiction variation of Britain's most violent comic, *Action* (14 February 1976), notorious as the only children's comic ever to be banned.

The surprise here was that *Action* was published by Fleetway/IPC, the company that had inherited the fun factory created by Alfred Harmsworth. An outcry in the tabloid newspapers led to television exposure, and finally refusal by W. H. Smith, the nation's largest wholesaler, to handle the comic. The last issue to be printed (number 37) was not released and has become something of a collector's item. Two months later the publisher issued the first of a 'new series' of *Action*, but it failed to please the 'tough-kid' market it had been created for, and, like its ancestor, it too was wound up; it was incorporated with the war comic, *Battle*, as *Battle Action*.

Comics began in Britain as picture publications for adults, and it is perhaps fitting that they should now have come full circle after some eighty years as children's publications. *Action*'s error was in depicting violence for a juvenile market. *2000 AD*, modelled on what had been successful in *Action*, and what teenagers enjoyed in the cinema – the new breed of science-fiction – gradually became the best-produced comic in the country, always raising its standards of script writing, artwork, colour printing and paper. American editions were produced, and a film starring Judge Dredd released in 1995. Many other sci-fi-plus-violence followed *2000 AD*: *Tank Girl* added sex to violence successfully, and W. H. Smith gave way to commercial pressure.

The British adult comic had a rebirth in the late 1960s under the influence of the American 'underground' comic which had been pioneered by cartoonists like Robert Crumb with his comic/erotic *Zap Comics*. These were reprinted in Britain and much emulated in many one-off or short run comics, drawn and published by amateurs in London and the provinces. The best and longest-lasting of these local cartoonists is Hunt Emerson from Birmingham, who began with his *Large Cow Comix* (1974), and became an internationally admired creator. His style owes much to George Herriman and his vintage American page 'Krazy Kat', but Emerson's style and sense of humour are now all his own (perhaps spoiled for some by his obsession with obscenity).

The most successful comic ever published in Britain is *Viz* (December 1979), which began as a very small circulation amateur comic, and now sells over 1,000,000 copies bi-monthly. Some of its characters, such as The Fat Slags have been animated, shown on television and released on video. Its style is a mixture of American 'underground' and the British *Beano*, and if the humour of its young artists is not 'adult' in the true sense of the word, it is definitely highly unsuitable for children!

## American Comics and Comic Books

Superficially, the American comic book is virtually the same as when it began in 1933, a sturdy monthly magazine of comedy and adventure strips told purely in pictures, the textual detail being carried in 'speech balloons' and descriptive boxes within the pictures. The fictional stories, always dominant in the British comic, supported by a single illustration, were never more than a page or two in the American comic books, and were there only to pacify the US Post Office into allowing comics to receive a low-price subscription postal permit.

The history of the American comic book which was to become such an influence on the world's comic publishing style, begins in a remarkably similar fashion to the British comic and more especially the European. American comic books have their roots in reprints from magazine and newspaper publication. The first appears to be a book entitled *Scraps*, published in 1849 by the cartoonist himself, D. C. Johnston of Boston. This was a mixture of cartoons and sequential striplets in the form of 'scrap sheets', but whether they were originally issued as separate sheets is not known.

The first comic books intended for children were issued before 1876 by the Broadway publishing house of Stroefer and Kirchner, who had links with Germany, where for some time the large size picture-story sheets had been published as *Münchener Bilderbogen* in Munich. Two sets of twenty numbered sheets were issued both loose and bound in two hardback volumes. Translated into English they were also reprinted in Britain by Griffith and Farran of St Paul's Churchyard. Titles and artists included strip stories such as 'Scenes from Fairyland' by Thomas Hosemann, 'Puck and the Peasant' by H. Scherenberg, and

'Munchhausen's Travels and Adventures' by W. Simmler. The books were entitled *Illustrated Flying Sheets for Young and Old* and sold for $1.25 a volume ($2 for colour). The same publisher also issued the pioneering picture strip books written and drawn by Wilhelm Busch, the German credited with creating the modern comic strip with Max und Moritz (1865).

More natively American was *Stuff and Nonsense* (1884) a collection of cartoons and strips drawn by Arthur Burdett Frost for the magazine *Harper's Monthly*, published as a hardback book by Charles Scribner's Sons. The book was divided into two parts: 'Stuff' being the strips, such as 'Ye Aesthete, Ye Boy and Ye Bullfrog', and 'Nonsense' being the single cartoons. (This book also had a British edition, being reprinted by John C. Nimmo no fewer than three times, and again in 1910 by George Routledge.) The same year saw the start of strip and cartoon reprints from *Life Magazine* (then a weekly humorous publication unrelated to the photo-journal of today), starting with *The Good Things of Life* (1884) and followed by *The Spice of Life* (1888).

Joseph Keppler, a Viennese cartoonist, emigrated to New York and started *Puck*, a German-language humorous weekly, in September 1876. An English-language edition followed six months later and by 1880 Frederick Burr Opper, who became one of the founding fathers of the American strip cartoon, had joined the staff. The following year a rival weekly, *Judge*, appeared, to be followed in 1883 by *Life*. In this illustrated trio can be found the work of all the men who founded American strips: Richard F. Outcault who gave the world The Yellow Kid, often considered the first newspaper strip hero (1896), Rudolph Dirks, who created The Katzenjammer Kids in the likeness of the German bad boys Max und Moritz, and George Herriman, who would evolve the most surrealistic character ever seen in the funnies, Krazy Kat (1910).

The beginnings of the American newspaper strip can be seen in the translations of the well-established *Imagerie d'Epinal*, published in France by Pellerin et Cie from the 1830s. These single sheets of stories for children, printed on extremely thin standard Pellerin paper, and illustrated in twelve to sixteen pictures, were translated and distributed in the USA from 1888 by the Humoristic Publishing Company of Kansas City. (Sets have also been found in Britain, which suggests that they were also sold there.) A total of sixty different sheets were issued beginning with 'Impossible Adventures', the wild boastings of an old braggart in the style of Baron Munchhausen. Echoes of many strips yet unborn may be found in these sheets, from fantastic adventures (no. 1: 'Impossible adventures'), fairy tales (no. 59: 'Cinderella'), science-fiction (no. 22: 'King of the moon'), and illustrated 'classics' (no. 36: 'Don Quichotte' [*sic*]). Unfortunately it has proved impossible to discover whether these sheets were sold singly, or in sets, and at what price.

These Anglo-French sheets did not introduce any continuing characters, but their French-printed fullness of colour, alongside the *Münchener Bilderbogen*, acted as inspiration to the press barons, who were seeking to expand their already flourishing empires.

The first paper to pioneer cheap colour printing in the USA was the *Chicago Inter-Ocean*. This paper introduced a family supplement in colour on 18 September 1892, and the following year added a detachable children's-section,

*The Youth's Department.* In the spring of 1894, cartoonist Charles Saalburg introduced 'The Ting-Lings', a weekly full page escapade in which a crowd of pint-sized Orientals wreaked topical havoc. In May 1897 they even crossed to Britain and helped Queen Victoria to celebrate her Diamond Jubilee, an event reprinted 'at a tremendous price' in the woman's weekly, *Home Chat*.

Occasionally these juvenile strips would be reprinted in books, such as *Funny Folks* (1899), a compilation of forty strips by Franklin M. Howarth selected from *Puck*, and *Little Johnny and the Teddy Bears* (1907), a full-colour book reprinting John R. Bray's strip from *Judge*.

More influential than the magazine strips, however, were the Sunday newspapers. The circulation war between New York press barons William Randoph Hearst and his *New York Sunday Journal* and Joseph Pulitzer's *New York Sunday World*, led to ever burgeoning weekly packages of several sections. Then, using the new colour printing press, Pulitzer introduced his Sunday *Comic Weekly* in *The New York Sunday World* (21 May 1893), and two years later this supplement included Outcault's single-panel series, 'Hogan's Alley'. Among the crowds in that panel lurked a dumb, moronic, oriental character soon to be known colloquially as The Yellow Kid, who made his comments, not by talking, but via slangy scrawl on his bright yellow night-gown, his only clothing! This series eventually evolved into a strip and has come to be thought of (erroneously) as the origin of American comics. This is not to decry the Kid's enormous popularity: he was merchandised in many collectable forms; he was the first comic strip hero to have his own regular magazine (*The Yellow Kid*, published at five cents by Howard Ainslee), and a book written about him, *The Yellow Kid in McFadden's Flats* by E. W. Townsend (popular author of the Chimmie Fadden tales), illustrated by Outcault (1897). The success of the strip led to the cartoonist being lured away with a considerable pay hike by the legendary press baron, William Randolph Hearst. Buster made his Hearst debut in the *New York World* comic section on 14 January 1906. A historic contest over the copyright of the character ensued, with the courts deciding that whilst Outcault, had every right to Buster Brown, his original employer had equal rights in Buster's name! Thus both the *New York Herald* and the *New York World* could run new adventures of the bad boy but only *World* could have Outcault, while the *Herald* had to find a new cartoonist, and only the *Herald* could call their page 'Buster Brown', the *World* having to be content with a rather anonymous 'He': as in 'He's At It Again!', 'He Makes a New Resolution', and so on. This legal decision was reestablished a few years later when a similar situation arose with cartoonist Rudolph Dirks. He kept drawing his twin terrors' tales for another newspaper, still calling them Hans and Fritz, but under the title 'The Captain and the Kids', while the other pair went under their original title, 'The Katzenjammer Kids', now drawn by Harold Knerr!

On 12 December 1897, the *Sunday World* published the grandfather of all American comic books, *The Children's Christmas Book*, a free supplement which had sixteen pages, eight of them in full colour, and featured strips and cartoons by George Luks, whom Pulitzer had hired to continue his strips about The Yellow Kid after Outcault had been lured away.

In 1900 the first reprint books of newspaper strips began to appear. Carl Schultze, who signed himself 'Bunny', drew a regular half-page set entitled 'The

Herald's Vaudeville Show'. This was issued in book form as *Vaudevilles and Other Things* by Isaac Blanchard, using an oblong format to cope with the half-page broadsheet format of the original strips, and a cardboard cover, newly drawn by 'Bunny', necessitated by the awkward shape of the book. This became the standard format for the newspaper reprint comic book through the first quarter of the twentieth century. 'Bunny' replaced his comic vaudeville with a regular character, Foxy Grandpa, and by December 1900 the first reprint book was issued by his own company. Some twenty followed and the character also appeared in a play, some very early movies, and was revived in the comic book *Star Comics* as late as 1937.

The history of American comics now makes its radical departure from the well-established European format. The broadsheet newspaper supplement, originally four pages in full colour (although frequently only front and back), given away every Sunday (and sometimes on a Saturday where no Sunday edition was issued), became standardised throughout the country, and syndicates were formed to supply papers with strips. Characters emerged and became regularised, such as 'Buster Brown', the classic naughty boy whose middle-class pranks and regular 'resolutions' established him as the nation's number one comic star. Buster was drawn by the same R. F. Outcault who gave America The Yellow Kid – a remarkable switch of social strata as well as of style. Buster books were assembled out of the strips and sold, not only in the USA, but throughout the Empire, thanks to British editions published by Chambers of London and Edinburgh.

The Buster Brown books, enormously popular despite their huge awkward oblong format, began at Christmas 1903 with *Buster Brown and his Resolutions*, probably the most popular of the series, leading to a total of thirty-five books in all, some of which were not by Outcault. (Buster was father to Scotland's Oor Wullie by Dudley D. Watkins (*Sunday Post Fun Section* from 1936) and grandfather to England's Dennis the Menace (*Beano* from 1951).)

The cardboard-covered comic book containing reprints of Sunday strips became well and truly established when William R. Hearst entered the field on 23 November 1902. At the top of his *New York Journal* supplement appeared this startling announcement: 'The popular characters of the comic supplement have been published in book form. Your newsdealer can get them for you. They are the best comic-books that have ever been published.' A historic moment, and the first use of the term 'comic book'. Out came no fewer than five books, all priced at fifty cents. They were *Happy Hooligan*, Fred Opper's tramp in a tin-can hat; *The Katzenjammer Kids* by Rudolph Dirks; *The Tigers* by James Swinnerton, the first in the funny animals field; *Alphonse and Gaston and their Friend Leon*, the funny Frenchmen, another Opper creation; and *On and Off Mount Ararat*, a Noah's Ark with animals, also by Swinnerton. But these hard-to-handle landscape-format books were child's play compared to the first Mutt and Jeff comic book. Published by Ball and Co. in 1910, this featured one strip per page and measured 5 inches high by $15\frac{1}{2}$ inches wide!

'Mutt and Jeff' is frequently credited with being the first daily newspaper strip, but in fact it was preceded by several others, including 'A. Piker Clerk' by Clare Briggs (1904) and A. D. Condo's 'The Outbursts of Everett True' (1905). Harry Conway Fisher, better known as 'Bud', began his series as a tipster strip, having his hero, Augustus Mutt, forever losing his shirt on sure things. Jeff, shortened from

Jefferson, was an escapee from the lunatic asylum who teamed up with the lanky gambler some time into the series. Bud Fisher was the first cartoonist to personally copyright his creation, and thus was able to move from newspaper to newspaper without copyright prosecution, finally becoming the richest cartoonist in the world with such spin-offs as the longest run of any cinema animated-cartoon series (via the Fox Film Corporation). He even gave up drawing the strip, although his signature was ably forged by a string of assistants including Al Smith, who finally took it over in recent times.

The main publishers of cardboard comic books became Cupples and Leon of New York. They added 'Mutt and Jeff' to their chain, which by the 1920s included George McManus's 'Bringing Up Father' (one of the first American strips to be reprinted in England by the *Daily Sketch*), Harold Gray's 'Little Orphan Annie' (later to inspire 'Belinda Blue-Eyes' in the *Daily Mirror*) and Sidney Smith's family saga, 'The Gumps' (models for another *Daily Mirror* strip, 'The Ruggles'). These and many other square comic books were quickly established as the popular format, selling at twenty-five cents and containing reprints of forty-six newspaper strips apiece. These, being daily strips, did not come in colour, which helped keep the price down, but it would be the addition of full colour that would see the end of Cupples and Leon comic books and establish the format that remains supreme to this day.

The first attempt at a new-look style of American comic was published on 16 January 1929 by George T. Delacorte Jr, head of Dell Publications. It was entitled *The Funnies* and followed the newly popular tabloid (or half broadsheet) comic supplements of several newspapers. Under the joint editorial control of Harry Steeger and Abril Lamarque (billed as Comic Art Editor), this twenty-four-page comic sold at ten cents and looked like a Sunday supplement crossed with a British comic paper: between the strips appeared several pages of text stories, puzzles and features. Its resemblance to the giveaway Sunday comics would prove its downfall: why should children pay for what came free with dad's newspaper? Dell tried many ways to expand sales – increased pages (up to thirty-two), decreased price (down to five cents), but it was all to no avail. *The Funnies* wound up after thirty-six issues, and it was good-bye to 'Frosty Ayre' by Joe Archibald, 'Rock Age Roy' by Boody Rogers, and all the other original strips that the Comic Art Editor had supervised.

The true father of the modern American comic book did not appear until 1933, and even then it took a while to catch on. The now familiar format was devised by Max Gaines and Harry Donenfield, who worked for the Eastern Colour Printing Co. By folding a tabloid comic section in half, they came up with a handy sixty-four page booklet measuring $7\frac{1}{2}$ by $10\frac{1}{2}$ inches. Into this they packed miniaturised reprints of popular syndicated strips including 'Reg'lar Fellers', 'Joe Palooka' and the ubiquitous 'Mutt and Jeff'. The result, entitled *Funnies On Parade*, was not sold but given away as promotion by the company Proctor and Gamble. They produced two further booklets: *Century of Comics* was a one-hundred page edition; *Famous Funnies* was also a success, so they decided to try selling their comic on news-stands at ten cents a time. *Famous Funnies Series One* (1934) led to a regular monthly run, finally expiring at number 218 in July 1955.

The next step was an all-original comic book, which came from Major Malcolm Wheeler-Nicholson, a pulp magazine writer, in February 1936. Entitled *New Fun*, subtitled 'The Big Comic Magazine', this ten cent monthly initially made the mistake of printing in Dell's failed *Funnies* format, a large tabloid. However, after six issues and a retitle to *More Fun*, it reduced to the *Famous Funnies* format; subtitled 'The National Comics Magazine', it ran to 127 editions. Its partner, *New Comics*, began in the now popular small size in December 1936, and with a name change to *New Adventure Comics*, later *Adventure*, reached its 503rd edition before closing in September 1983.

Wheeler-Nicholson did not remain at the helm, however. He lost control quite early on and the series was taken over by the same Harry Donenfield who had started *Famous Funnies*. The company was known variously as National Periodicals and D.C. Comics, under which style it continues to this day as America's leading comic book publisher.

Comic books became the newest form of children's publishing, and sixty-four-page magazines (sixty-eight-page if you include the higher-quality paper covers) began to flood the market. Several (*Popular Comics, Super Comics*) stuck to the old *Famous Funnies* formula of reprinting popular newspaper strips, but others (*Funny Pages, Funny Picture Stories*) preferred the 'all new' approach. Specialised comic books began to appear (*Western Picture Stories, Keen Detective Funnies*), and finally, in June 1938, Donenfield issued number one of the comic book that would set the seal on the form and set the style that would take the American comic book around the world, conquering all other national variations.

*Action Comics* number one, seeking some new character, encountered a failed newspaper strip that two young friends had been trying to get off the ground for five years. The partnership, stemming from schooldays, was that of Jerry Siegel, writer, and Joe Shuster, cartoonist; the strip was called 'Superman'. It told the far-fetched yarn of an alien shot from his exploding home planet, Krypton, and growing up on Earth as the adopted child of homespun farming folks. When his powers continue to expand ('Faster than a Speeding Bullet! Able to Leap Tall Buildings at a Single Bound!'), he conceives the idea of changing himself into Superman, and clad in cloak and costume he zips into action to save the world from gangsters, spies and assorted mad scientists. The concept, considered 'unreal' by many newspaper editors and even his eventual publisher, hit home with the young readership and soon *Action Comics* was outselling its rivals. Very soon, Superman was being featured in a radio serial, a movie serial, a novel, and all the other manifestations of modern commercialisation. This success was sustained into television series, feature films (among the world's largest grossing), and animated cartoons – and gone for ever (almost) was the reliance on reprinting old newspaper strips. But although the publishers prospered, Siegel and Shuster made little more than the price of their comic pages. Siegel soldiered on, but Shuster lost his eyesight, and if it had not been for the pressure by fellow comic artists and fans, they would never have received the life pension eventually awarded to them by the company.

Superman soon conquered Britain, which first imported the original comic books, and then reprinted the daily strip which was syndicated to American newspapers. This began in the British boys' story paper *Triumph* in July 1939, with the strips pasted up into a four-page centre section. The covers, although only printed in blue and orange, showed the new hero in action, and were drawn by

John (Jock) McCail, a Scottish illustrator. After the war, Superman comics were reprinted in Australia and exported to Britain before receiving British publication in their own right. In 1959 the traditional comic weekly *Radio Fun* began reprinting the strips, and later several smaller publishers tried their hands. Superman became the most copied comic character in history, by both his own publishers (Bob Kane's 'Batman') and his rivals.

Fawcett Publications, whose original paperback magazine *Captain Billy's Whizbang* had founded their fortune, entered the comic book field with *Whiz Comics* and their own superhero Captain Marvel. This red-suited strongman was soon outselling Superman, whose publisher brought a copyright suit. This dragged on for so long in the courts that it outlasted the comic's best-selling years; eventually, Fawcett decided that it was easier to get out of the comic book business altogether, and capitulated without the legal decision being finalised. But in their wartime years, Fawcett's comics had spread where National-D.C.'s had failed to penetrate, and in England a small publisher, Leonard Miller and Son issued cut down versions of Captain Marvel (and his sister, Mary Marvel and Hoppy the Marvel Bunny!).

The war years were important to American comic books: they became required reading for the armed forces and millions of copies were issued to the military post exchanges. Publishers upgraded their content to embrace not only more adult-oriented stories, often based on crime and detection, but added pretty pin-up girls. These girls graced every kind of comic from superheroes to college boy capers, and especially, perhaps, science-fiction comics such as *Planet*, published by Fiction house, a former pulp magazine purveyor. Fiction House comics, including the Tarzan-like series *Jungle Comics* with its leopard-skin-clad ladies swinging around the trees, were the nearest thing to illustrated erotica many a young soldier had ever seen. These comics were also on sale at America's local news-stands, and were naturally bought by youngsters not yet in their teens. It was the beginning of a new wave of comic books and eventually a new wave of adult criticism which, after the war, would lead to the temporary downfall of the whole comic book business.

Frederick Wertham, a psychologist, wrote a series of articles focusing on the comic book as a corrupter of childhood; his *Seduction of the Innocent* (British edition 1955) blamed comics for leading children into crime and sexual depravity. The illustrations from horror comics in the book made a convincing case; Senate hearings followed, and horror comic publishers rapidly went out of business – although their legacy is still with us. It was a dark decade for the American comic book, leading to an uninteresting period of 'approved' comics, subject to the seal of an industry-owned censoring board.

Thus the American comic book has grown from localised reprints to world domination in less than sixty years. Early examples can command thousands of dollars from collectors, there are specialist shops selling them in Britain, and there are regular comic markets and annual comic conventions where dealers, artists and fans congregate to spend small fortunes on 'rare' comics, original artwork, and even to dress up as their favourite fantasy heroes for prizes (comics, of course!).

## Dime Novels, Pulps and Penny Dreadfuls

Erastus Flavel Beadle, father of the American dime novel, a pocket-sized paperback of 128 pages of thrilling fiction selling at ten cents (later reduced to five cents) was born in Otsego County, New York, in 1821. His own father, Irvin P. Beadle, had been a ballad hawker who set up as a printer and issued the best-selling *Dime Song Book*, a compilation of the ballads he had been hawking for years. By 1840 Erasmus was a printer in Buffalo, and in 1852 published number one of a children's story magazine, *The Youth's Casket*. But it was in June 1860 that his great idea of popular novels at affordable prices took shape with the first volume in his series of The Choicest Works of the Most Popular Authors, otherwise billed as 'Dollar Books for a Dime'. It was entitled *Malaeska, the Indian Wife of the White Hunter*, and was a reprint of the 'Prize Story' from the magazine, *The Ladies Companion*, written by Mrs Ann Sophia Winterbottom Stephens and first published in 1839. The *Beadle's Dime Library* reissue sold 65,000 copies within a few months.

The title and source of this tattered milestone in popular literature sound romantic, but consider this moment from page 10:

> 'Touch but a hair of her head, and by the Lord that made me, I will bespatter that tree with your brains!' Thus spake William Danorth, white hunter. Many a dusky form bit the dust and many a savage howl followed the discharge of his trusty gun!

Here, in fact, was the dauntless American hero in action, the lone frontiersman opening up an untamed continent, fighting savage odds with rifle, dagger and bare fist and rescuing a beauteous bride along the way. The very stuff at the heart of James Fenimore Cooper's work, the spirit of whose Hawkeye bestrides the thousands of popular paperbacks that now followed in his trail.

Not that every dime novel hero was a wilderness scout. Number two of Beadle's series was entitled *The Privateer's Cruise* and starred the heroically named Harry Cavendish ('God of my fathers! Every soul will be lost!'), and his staunch chum O'Hara, the Irishman who acted as comic relief with his brogue.

Editor for Beadle's books was Orville J. Victor, whose wife Martha Victoria wrote the fourth novel in the series. *Alice Wilde, the Raftsman's Daughter* introduced further comic relief in the shape of rustic Ben Perkins ('That ar log bobs round like the old sea-sarpint!'). Editor Victor was responsible for the first great publicity campaign for a dime novel, posting the countryside with advertisements demanding 'Who is Seth Jones?'. He turned out to be a white hunter in fringed buckskin, hero of *Seth Jones or the Captives of the Frontier*, who introduced himself thus: 'How de do? How de do? Ain't frightened, I hope? It's nobody but me, Seth Jones, from New Hampshire!'. A 19-year-old schoolmaster from Ohio, Edward Ellis, was paid $75 for the book. The first edition sold 60,000 copies and it finally reached half a million sales, being translated into eleven languages. Ellis never went back to school, writing 150 volumes of juvenile stories, plus many biographies and histories before his death in 1916.

Beadle himself died in 1894. He had moved from Buffalo to New York in 1858 and formed a partnership with Robert Adams, publishing joke books and almanacs as well as a string of cheap magazines, such as *Girls of Today* and *The Young New Yorker*. The success of their dime novel library encouraged further publications, and out came 'Beadle's Boy's Library of Sport, Story and Adventure' (*Snow Shoe Tom or New York Boys in the Wilderness*), 'Beadle's Pocket Library' (*Roaring Ralph Rocked the Reckless Ranger*) and the even cheaper – hence more popular with working-class youngsters – 'Beadle's Half Dime Library'. This series would run to over a thousand titles.

Naturally other American publishers jumped on the dime novel bandwagon. Ten Cent Novelettes (1863) came from Boston with *The Brave's Secret*; Ten Cent Romance (1867) came from New York with *The Mountain Trapper*. The most successful publisher may have been George P. Munro, whose Ten Cent Novels (1867) began with *The Patriot Highwayman*, and who died thirty years later a multimillionaire.

The bloodthirsty descriptions that bespattered dime novels soon began to bother the 'better classes', notably when in 1874 Jesse Pomeroy, a sadistic murderer, claimed to be prompted by 'literature of the dime novel type'. Beadle and his editors immediately formulated a set of writer's rules which were sent to all their authors:

> We prohibit all things offensive to good taste, in expression or incident, subjects or characters that carry an immoral taint, the repetition of any occurrence which, though true, is better untold, and what cannot be read with satisfaction by every high-minded person, old and young alike.

Moving away from Fenimore Cooper-style frontiersmen, dime novel heroes began a new trend when somebody had the bright idea of dramatising real life 'folk' heroes. Daniel Boone, Davy Crockett and especially Kit Carson were soon starring in ten-cent libraries of their own. 'Kit Carson, Mountain Man' apparently wrote his own reports of his adventures, which were then edited by Jessie Benton Fremont into readable narratives. Published in the early 1840s, these formed the foundation for wilder versions adapted for the excitement-hungry readers of weekly story-papers. These were the broadsheets of fiction published in the big cities for family consumption, containing exciting and romantic fiction in serialised chapters. Compiled, these episodes were reprinted (both with and without permission) as dime novels, such as *Kit Carson, the Prince of the Gold Hunters*.

It was in *The New York Weekly* at Christmas 1869 that the greatest of all wild western heroes of the combined fact-fiction genre made his gun-toting bow. The title was *Buffalo Bill, King of the Border Men*, the hero was Colonel William F. Cody, and the author Colonel Ned Buntline. Buntline's real name was Edward Zane Carroll Judson, born 1822 in Philadelphia, who had started writing hack fiction for *The Knickerbocker Magazine* in 1838 at the age of sixteen. His many early titles included *The Black Avenger of the Spanish Main, or The Fiend of Blood* – a typical title for a typical tale of bloodthirsty buccaneering. Buntline met Cody in Nebraska, saw the possibilities in the Indian scout's meat-hunting enterprises, and formed a partnership that would prove one of the most prosperous of the day. It is safe to say that the ensuing worldwide popularity of the dime novels and magazine serials made Buffalo Bill the box-office attraction that he shortly became. However, although Buntline profited by $20,000 in the deal, he and Cody fell out over how the profits should be shared. As a result he was fired by Cody, who hired another 'Colonel', Prentiss Ingraham. The dime novels continued without interruption or noticeable change in literary style: 'I could see his eyeballs start in agony from his head, the beaded sweat, blood colored, ooze from his clammy skin, each nerve and tendon quivering like the strings of a harp struck by a maniac hand!' Ingraham would write 600 novels before he died in 1904, and is said to have completed a 35,000 word book in one day and a night.

Western heroes continued to reign supreme. There was 'Deadwood Dick, the Rider of the Black Hills', created for Beadle and Adams by Edward L. Wheeler, for the first issue of their new Pocket Library (1884). Wheeler, a city man all his life, described Dick thus: 'A youth of an age somewhere between 16 and 20, trim and compactly built with a preponderance of muscular development and animal spirits, broad and deep of chest, with square iron-cut shoulders, limbs small yet like bars of steel'. Dick was clearly designed to appeal to the younger reader, who might not care for Buffalo Bill and his flowing gold moustache. Wheeler's titles also had youth-appeal, being invariably alliterative, such as *Deadwood Dick at Danger Divide*.

Another army officer, a Major Sam Hall, created another western hero in Buckskin Sam, who starred in a dime novel with perhaps the unlikeliest title of them all: *Ker-Whoop Ker-Whoo! or the Tarantula of Taos*. The Major was a specialist in colloquial dialogue: 'Woop-la! Shove out a bar'l o' bug-juice afore I bu'st up yer she-bang!'

With the untamed frontiers taking up so much paper and print, dime novel publishers looked eastward for their next heroes. They came up with the detective, a hero who first saw public print through the open-eye trademark of Allan Pinkerton and his detective agency (motto 'We Never Sleep'). Pinkerton's casebook of reminiscences was an early best-seller and became a plot source for many of the dime detective writers.

First of the new breed of city dicks was 'Old Sleuth', created by Harlan P. Halsey for *The Fireside Companion*, a family story paper in 1872. Halsey used the pen-name of 'Old Sleuth', and was thus able to write about other detectives he 'knew', such as *Old Electricity the Lightning Detective* (1885). Old Sleuth, however, was not in fact old. He was a young detective who regularly assumed the disguise of an old man. The gimmick caught on, and in 1881 arrived 'Old Cap Collier' in a 'real life mystery' entitled *The Bashful Victim of the Elm City Tragedy*. Not content, as was his predecessor, with one disguise, the Cap had a repertoire of eighteen, ranging from 'Fat Dutchman' to 'Masked Cavalier', although how frequently this latter was used in modern New York is unknown. He was also adept at turning his clothes inside out in an instant. There would be over 700 novels of the Old Cap published by 1898.

But the great Master of Disguise was undoubtedly Nick Carter, who made his detecting debut in *The New York Weekly* in 1886. *The Old Detective's Pupil* was subtitled 'The Mysterious Crime of Madison Square', and it was credited, as would be all the Nick Carter stories, to Nick Carter himself. The author was in fact John Coryell, who wrote the weekly stories for three years and withdrew into romance. The task was taken on by Frederick Marmaduke Van Rennsselaer Dey, who proceeded to write one thousand Nick Carter stories (as 'Nick Carter'), over forty million words, before shooting himself in 1922. Dey's stories began with number one of the *Nick Carter Library* (1891), which turned into the *New Nick Carter Library* (1897), soon to be renamed *Nick Carter Weekly*. With other title changes this ran right through to 1915 when publishers Street and Smith turned it into a 'pulp', the current craze, called *Detective Story Magazine*. Nick Carter was billed as editor.

Nicholas Carter owed little to the classic English detective, Sherlock Holmes. A handsome young man, son of one Sim Carter (murdered by gangsters), he is never seen without his smart bow-tie, unless he is in one of his many disguises. These, arrayed around the lettering in the title of his *Weekly*, included that of a hunchback involving a false hump that lay 'deeper than the coat or the flowered waistcoat that covered it. It was deeper than the shirt beneath the heavy, coarse woollen undershirt he wore, in fact, so that if the occasion should arise to remove his coat, as was likely to happen, the hump was still there'. Carter, nicknamed 'Little Giant' (he was not much more than five feet tall), was strong enough to tear four packs of cards in half and 'lift a horse with ease, and that, too, while a heavy man is seated in the saddle'. Nick is the longest lived of any fictional detective in the world, spanning radio, films and television with ease, and entering the James Bond era of Secret Agents in a new series of paperbacks.

In 1882 one, Frank A. Munsey, a telegraph operator, left Augusta, Maine, for the lights of New York City, with a long-standing ambition to publish a weekly children's magazine of uplifting fiction. And on 2 December of that year number one of *Golden Argosy* went on sale. It was subtitled 'Freighted with Treasures for Boys and Girls', and within its eight pages carried the opening chapter of 'Do and Dare, a Brave Boy's Fight for a Fortune'. This serial was written by Horatio Alger Jr, an author whose basic theme – if a poor boy perseveres he will win fame and fortune – would eventually fill 118 books, sell 250 million copies, and inspire juvenile weeklies (*Brave and Bold, Might and Main, Wide Awake Weekly* and others). But meanwhile Munsey's children's paper was not doing too well. He had more success with a new adult title, named *Munsey's Magazine*. He worked on the first, shortening its title to *Argosy*, increasing its pagecount and generalising its fiction, until in 1896 a thick, new *Argosy* was born, with 192 pages printed on the cheapest possible paper, coarse, bulky stuff known as pulpwood in the trade. Its value for money at ten cents acted as inspiration to other publishers, especially as *Argosy*'s circulation rose to half a million. The pulp magazine was born.

Pulp magazines, counting 128 pages or more, with their cheap paper bound into art paper covers sporting ever more exciting artwork, would last for sixty years before shrinking in size (to Pocket Digest proportions) and number (from hundreds to tens) by 1957. From assorted fiction they started to specialise into themes: westerns, detectives, adventure, fantasy, horror, science-fiction and even erotica (*Snappy Stories* was the first in 1912). Pulps were only briefly for the young, who quickly took to the half-price (five cent) story weeklies. These continued into the 1920s averaging sixteen pages of cheap paper bound within thin art paper colour covers. The boys' heroes were cowboys, outlaws (*Jesse James Stories*), college boys like William Patton's 'Frank Merriwell' in *Tip Top Weekly* (from 1896), and incredible inventors whose extraordinary sci-fi adventures were recorded by 'Noname' in *The Frank Reade Library*. Inventor Reade was first read about in *Irwin's American Novels*, when he fought Red Indians with his incredible *Steam Man of the Prairies* (1865).

This was the origin of a genre which would eventually flower under editorial genius Hugo Gernsback in his monthly pulp *Amazing Stories* (1926). But as for the juvenile reader, he would soon be wooed away from nickel novels by the 'all in color for a dime' illustrations of the comic books.

The bloodstained saga of the Penny Bloods later known (both popularly – by their readers – and unpopularly – by those who disdained them) as the Penny Dreadfuls, has its roots in the records of the eighteenth-century's worst criminals, known as *The Newgate Calendar*. The prime edition of this seems to be *The Malefactor's Register or New Newgate and Tyburn Calendar*, an illustrated collection published by Alex Hogg in book format, but which had a cheap edition in penny parts, published once a week. Pirate publishers quickly pounced on the series and printed their own, including one James Catnach of Seven Dials, a noted publisher of broadsides of many kinds, including criminal confessions known as 'Goodnights'. There followed *The Tell-Tale* (1823), *Legends of Horror* and *The Terrific Register* (both 1825). This last ran two years (104 penny parts) and in number eleven featured Sawney Bean and family, 'The Monster of Scotland' and king of the cannibals, while *The Tell-Tale* saw the first English reporting of the man who might have been Sweeney Todd: 'Horrible Murder and Human Pie-Makers' (1825).

The 'father of the Penny Dreadfuls' was Edward Lloyd, a farmer's boy from Surrey. He was not more than a youth when he came to London and set up as a bookseller, from whence it was but a small step to becoming his own publisher. He was twenty-one when he issued number one of his first partwork, *Lives of the Most Notorious Highwaymen*. It ran for sixty weeks, but well before it expired, Lloyd had started three more popular pennyworths: *The Gem of Romance*, *The History of Pirates of All Nations* and *The Calendar of Horrors*. Criminal history could not provide enough material for Lloyd's profitable presses, and so a new industry was launched, fiction-hacking at a halfpenny a line.

Lloyd's leading hack, who also acted as editor on many of the weekly parts, was Thomas Peckett Prest, a relation of the Archdeacon of Durham. Although Prest relished blood and thunder (he wrote some 200 series with titles like *Mary Bateman the Yorkshire Witch* (1840), *The Maniac Father or the Victim of Seduction* (1842), and the classic *Varney the Vampire or the Feast of Blood* (1847)), he was also sufficiently well educated to successfully write pirate versions of current bestsellers by Charles Dickens, as well as the now 'standard' version of the Sweeney Todd story, *The String of Pearls* (1840).

The villain as hero was popular in both 'proper' fiction and penny parts. Dick Turpin, who died on the gallows in 1739, was raised to high stardom by W. Harrison Ainsworth in his 1834 novel, *Rookwood*. The ride to York on Bonnie Black Bess is said to have been an author's invention, and it seems to have been the key to the story's popularity. It featured ever after in the many rewrites of Turpin's career, and was the centrepiece of action in a number of stage and circus dramatisations as well as early films. Turpin weeklies and libraries were being published into the 1930s, and the hero and his horse were illustrated in *Thriller Picture Library* (a pocket comic) as late as 1957.

Several of the hack writers found a fair living churning out Dreadfuls before ascending to better things. One such was George William MacArthur Reynolds whose partworks included the plagiarised imitation, *Pickwick Abroad* (1838). Son of a sea captain, Reynolds spent some time in Paris where he read Eugene Sue's popular partwork *The Mysteries of Paris*. Inspired, he returned to England and commenced his own *Mysteries of London* (1845), a long-runner which wove into its fictional narrative factual reports on the evils of the nation's capital. Five years later Reynolds founded his own Sunday journal, *Reynolds's Weekly Newspaper*, a title which would run, latterly supported by the Co-operative movement, until it turned into the tabloid *Sunday Citizen* in the 1960s.

The change from penny parts to penny magazines came about in 1866 when Edwin J. Brett, operating as the Newsagents Publishing Co., and publisher of some of the 'fiercest' (to use a contemporary term) Dreadfuls of the day, including *The Wild Boys of London* (which was eventually suppressed by the police), issued number one of *Boys of England*. There were already plenty of religious-based weeklies and monthlies for boys and girls, especially 'Mr' Samuel Orchard Beeton's *Boy's Own Magazine* which began in 1855. But these were either too 'goody-goody' for a young taste corrupted by Dreadfuls, or were too expensive: Beeton's magazine cost sixpence a month, and was therefore thoroughly middle-to-upper class.

*Boys of England*, sixteen pages of stories, serials, illustrations and competitions (prizes ranged from fifty pairs of ducks to a hundred concertinas!), was at the beginning not far removed from a Dreadful; the lead story was 'The Skeleton Crew'. But in time, as the Victorian era progressed, Brett boasted on his front page that the weekly was 'subscribed to by HRH Prince Arthur, the Prince Imperial of France and Count William Bernstorff'. It was the start of a publishing gold rush as publisher after publisher put out penny weeklies for boys. Brett's main rival, William Laurence Emmett, also of Penny Dreadful fame, issued his *Young Gentleman's Journal* (1867). Brett answered with *Young Men of Great Britain* (1868), and Emmett counterpunched with *Young Gentlemen of Great Britain*. Finally both men issued virtually identical papers on the same day: Brett's *Rovers of the Sea* and Emmett's *Rover's Log* (1872).

Brett holds the distinction of publishing the first boys' weekly printed in full colour. This was the slightly fabulous *Boys of the Empire*, but after a year he had to revert to standard monochrome printing. However, the paper led to another Brett battle. A rival, Melrose, revived the *Boys of the Empire* title in 1900, seven years after Brett's paper collapsed. Immediately Brett rushed a *Boys of the Empire (New Series)* on to the bookstalls, and beat Melrose by two weeks. The battle of the bloods ended with surrender, and Melrose's paper changed to *Boys of Our Empire* on 29 June 1901, while Brett's added the subtitle, 'An Up-To-Date Journal', as it incorporated another of his failed weeklies.

The modern boys' weekly was born in 1893 when Alfred Harmsworth, who had created the boom in comics with his *Comic Cuts* (1890) now tackled the story paper field. He used the same tactic, known as the 'Harmsworth Touch'. He priced his paper as he did his comic, at half the current market price: one halfpenny. *The Halfpenny Marvel* was also launched on a spearhead of anti-Dreadful publicity. Number one carried the slogan, 'No more Penny Dreadfuls! These healthy stories of mystery, adventure, etc, will kill them!' An editorial exclaimed: 'The Penny Dreadful makes thieves of the coming generation and so helps fill our jails! If we can rid the world of even one of these vile publications, our efforts will not have been in vain.' Soon *The Marvel* (as it would later be known when Harmsworth raised the price to one penny) proclaimed an unsolicited tribute from the Revd C. N. Barham of Nottingham: 'So pure and wholesome in tone', said the Revd. But on the cover of that issue was a picture of Greek bandits at work, with this caption: 'The gaoler screwed up the horrible machine until the brigand's bones were nearly broken and he shrieked aloud for mercy, though none was shown'. Small wonder a contemporary critic wrote, 'Harmsworth has killed the Penny Dreadful by inventing the Ha'penny Dreadfuller!'

Although Harmsworth's ha'porths revolutionised the market for cheap reading matter for boys, with smaller hack publishers issuing halfpenny weeklies as fast as they were able, it would not be until the turn of the century that the weeklies began to settle into the formula still remembered by readers of what came to be popularly called 'tuppenny bloods'. These were the more sumptuous successors to the ha'penny (penny by the 1900s; penny-halfpenny by 1918) weeklies with more pages (leaping from eight to sixteen to twenty-eight to thirty-two), coloured covers (from black on pink paper to mixtures of red and blue, to four-colour photogravure), and very often a Grand Free Gift, which might be anything from a booklet about pirates to a tin jumping frog. The formula changed from one long story, or a serial or two, to 'Seven Star Stories', a favourite headline of the 'Big Five'.

These were the D. C. Thomson weeklies, which began issuing from Dundee, Scotland, in 1921 with number one of *Adventure*. Instant success soon brought on *Rover* (1922), *Wizard* (1922), *Skipper* (1930) and *Hotspur* (1933), with only *Vanguard* (1923) falling quickly by the way. Each paper had a character of its own via its choice of heroes: 'Dixon Hawke' was *Adventure*'s answer to Harmsworth's Sexton Blake; 'The Wolf of Kabul' was *Wizard*'s empire-builder, and 'The Chums of Red Circle' was the innovative school story in *Hotspur*. This rival to *Magnet*'s long-running Greyfriars, home of the bulging Billy Bunter from 1908, was unique in that during its 1,197 episodes boys arrived at school, rose from form to form, and in six years or so left as other boys came in to replace them (masters, however, stayed on for ever!)

The Second World War saw the demise through paper shortage of many of the British boys' weeklies (by then, fortnightlies). The Amalgamated Press was left with one, *Champion*, while Thomson lost only one, *Skipper*. After the war some of the papers went over to serial strips and became comics (*The New Hotspur*, 24 October 1959); others died and were incorporated into comics (*Tiger and Champion*, 26 March 1955). The last of them all to go was *Rover*, joining *Wizard* (revived as a comic) from 20 January 1973. Some heroes continued as strips ('The Wolf of Kabul'); some went into paperbacks ('Sexton Blake') – but it was the end of an enjoyable and nostalgically remembered era.

## Further Reading

Crawford, H. (1978) *Crawford's Encyclopedia of Comic Books*, New York: World.
Daniels, L. (1991) *Marvel*, London: Virgin.
Gifford, D. (1971) *Discovering Comics*, rev. 1991, Princes Risborough: Shire.
—— (1975) *Happy Days: 100 Years of Comics*, London: Jupiter.
—— (1975) *The British Comic Catalogue, 1874–1974*, London: Mansell.
—— (1976) *Victorian Comics*, London: George Allen and Unwin.
—— (1984) *The International Book of Comics*, rev. 1990, London: Dean/Hamlyn.
—— (1985) *The Complete Catalogue of British Comics*, London: Webb and Bower.
—— (1987) *Encyclopedia of Comic Characters*, London: Longman.
—— (1988) *Comics at War*, London: Hawk.
—— (1990) *The American Comic Book Catalogue, 1884–1939*, London: Mansell.
—— (1991) *Christmas Comic Posters*, London: Blossom.
—— (1992) *Space Aces*, London: Green Wood.
—— (1992) *Super Duper Supermen*, London: Green Wood.
Godstone, T. (1970) *The Pulps*, New Rochelle: Chelsea House.
Goulart, R. (1972) *Cheap Thrills*, London: Arlington House.
—— (1975) *The Adventurous Decade*, New Rochelle: Arlington House.
Haining, P. (1974) *The Penny Dreadful*, London: Gollancz.
Horn, M. (ed.) (1976) *The World Encyclopedia of Comics*, New York: Chelsea House.
James, L. (1963). *Fiction for the Working Man*, Oxford: Oxford University Press.
Kurtzman, H. (1991) *From 'Aaargh' To 'Zap'*, New York: Prentice-Hall.
Lupoff, D. and Thompson, D. (1970) *All in Color for a Dime*, New Rochelle: Arlington House.
—— (1973) *The Comic-Book Book*, New Rochelle: Arlington House.
Pumphrey, G. (1955) *Children's Comics*, London: Epworth.
Reynolds, Q. (1965) *The Fiction Factory*, New York: Random House.
Robinson, J. (1974) *The Comics*, New York: Putnam.
Rollington, R. (1913) *The Old Boy's Books*, London: Simpson.
Rovin, J. (1985) *The Encyclopedia Of Super Heroes*, New York: Facts on File.
Server, L. (1993) *Danger Is My Business*, New York: Chronicle.
Simon, J. and Simon, J. (1990) *The Comic Book Makers*, New York: Crestwood.
Summers, M. (1940) *A Gothic Bibliography*, London: Fortune.
Turner, E. S. (1948) *Boys Will Be Boys*, London: Joseph.
Waugh, C. (1947) *The Comics*, New York: Macmillan.
Wertham, F. (1955) *Seduction of the Innocent*, London: Museum Press.

# 21

# Religious Writing for Children

In its early stages of development, children's literature was closely associated with religion; it had a strong didactic purpose and was influenced by religious requirements and perceptions. The production of manuscripts and early printed books was a costly business and the products far too valuable to be purely for children's entertainment. Formal provision for the acquisition of literacy developed in conjunction with religious institutions and it is not surprising, therefore, that the earliest children's books were intended to propound and support prevailing beliefs. Although children's books gradually became less overtly didactic, they have continued to prescribe what are regarded as morally and socially acceptable behaviour and attitudes. Even as the barriers around topics previously considered unsuitable for books for young people have been pushed back, 'right' and 'wrong' have continued to be clearly signalled.

Although these essays look at religion in children's literature from the viewpoint of countries which regard themselves as primarily Christian, the points which are made can be paralleled in countries where other religions predominate, although timescales may vary. For example, in a survey of the children's literature available in Kuwait in the mid-1980s, religion was the prevalent theme, with books containing explanations of religious rites and stories from the Koran (Ramadan 1988).

## Catechistical, Devotional and Biblical Writing

### Ruth B. Bottigheimer

#### Catechisms and Bibles before 1900

Catechisms for children represent the oldest form of religious instruction. Known since the early middle ages, catechisms multiplied dramatically in the sixteenth and seventeenth centuries in conjunction with the Protestant and Catholic Reformations. Early catechisms were directed indiscriminately at 'the simple', a concept that – in the words of Richard Barnard's *Two twinnes: or, two parts of one portion of scripture* (1613) – included adult 'babes in knowledge' together with young 'babes in yeares'. In the eighteenth century and after, children were often distinguished as a separate, educable group. Catechesis as a pedagogical practice affected only a small proportion of Jewish children (cf. Abraham Jagel's *Catechismus Judaeorum, c.*1587 *et seq.*).

According to Isaac Watts's *Discourse on the Way of Instruction by Catechisms* (1730), catechisms, were 'the best Summaries of Religion for Children'. Simple and brief, Cotton Mather's *The A, B, C of Religion* read in its entirety:

Q. Who Made You and all the World?

A. The Great GOD made me, to serve Him.

Q. Who Saves the Children of Men from all their Miseries?

A. Jesus Christ, who is both God and Man, saves them that Look unto Him.

Q. What will become of You, when You Dye?

A. If I obey Jesus Christ, my Soul will go to the Heavenly Paradise; and He will afterwards Raise me from the Dead. If I continue Wicked, I shall be Cast among the Devils.

The most durable genre for children, apart from catechisms, was the Bible story collection which had first appeared in the high middle ages when Peter Comestor composed the *Historia Scholastica* (*c.*1170) in Latin for students at the University of Paris. Entering Latin grammar school curricula and adult devotional literature in the later middle ages, the *Historia Scholastica*'s stories provided Europe with a common set of Bible narratives. Most books of Bible stories were rooted in Reformation attempts to familiarise children (and unschooled adults) with Biblical material.

Bible story collections written solely for children emerged in the mid-seventeenth century and were the first extended prose narratives composed specifically for child readers. They thus predated the emergence of fiction specifically intended for children by about fifty years. Children's Bible histories, which claimed to be true stories composed by 'the Holy Penman' himself, differed from contemporaneous chapbooks, which were written for a mixed audience and whose prose mixed 'true reports' of prodigious experiences with fanciful fictions like *Tom Thumb*, *Robin Hood* and *Fortunatus*.

In France, Nicolas Fontaine's *L'Histoire du Vieux et du Nouveau Testament* (1670 *et seq.*) provided virtually the only Bible story collection for Catholic children until the nineteenth century, when additional titles appeared. In Germany, Johann Hübner's *Zweymahl Zwey und funffzig Biblische Historien* (1714 *et seq.*) dominated the eighteenth century and was only slowly displaced by competing versions in the late eighteenth and nineteenth centuries. In England, Bible story collections began in 1690 but proliferated only in the mid-eighteenth century when John Newbery, and later his heirs and rival publishers, repeatedly printed *The Holy Bible Abridged* (London 1757 *et seq.*), which was followed in the later eighteenth century by *The Bible in Miniature*, *A Concise History of the Old and New Testaments*, *The Holy Bible Abridged*, *A New History of the Holy Bible*, *The Children's Bible* and *The History of the Holy Bible Abridged*. The genre appeared in Switzerland and the USA in the late eighteenth century, but south of the Alps and Pyrenees only after 1945.

The principal developments in the history of Bible story collections were their shift from negative to positive exempla at the beginning of the eighteenth century, their slow reduction in the number of female characters in the course of the eighteenth century, and their increasing emphasis on New Testament stories in the nineteenth century. Eighteenth-century writers assumed that all children shared a 'common spiritual inheritance', as did Isaac Watts in his *Discourse on the Education of Children and Youths* (1725). Yet educators also prescribed different forms of education for different classes, one consequence of which was that authors of Bible story collections between 1750 and 1850 built social expectations about anticipated child readerships into their editing. A century-long two-tier tradition of Bible stories resulted (*c.* 1750–1850), in which differing topics or differing treatments of the same topics appeared in the two tiers. For example, children's Bibles for the well-off largely ignored work, while those for the poor advocated work as spiritually beneficial.

From the sixteenth-century onward authors explored numerous prose and verse forms to familiarise children with the Bible. Like Bernard's *Two twinnes*, Henoch Clapham's *Briefe of the Bible* (London 1596) addressed 'all yovng ones in Christs Schoole', that is, the untutored of all ages. A lengthy interpretative recapitulation accompanied each six-line versified chapter summary. For the story of Joseph and Potiphar's wife, the commentary read thus:

> *Ioseph*, placed in *Potiphar* the Eunuch his house, is for his beautie, lusted after by his inordinate eyed Mistress. She, having no blush in her fore heade, wooeth *Ioseph* to Sinne; but he avoideth her alluring presence. Her lust, for that cannot be properlie called Love, it turned into Hate. She therefore pulling his Garment from him, accuseth him to her Husband, for a wanton Hebrewe, and an Assailer of the Marriage-bed. He believing her, cast *Ioseph* into Prison.

In the nineteenth century, Bible story collections proliferated in England and America, and offered scores of approaches for micro-readerships of different ages, educational levels, confessions, or denominations. Bible story collections for Jewish children also began to appear in the nineteenth century, the first English example of which was Moses Mordecai Büdinger's *The Way of Faith; or, The Abridged Bible* (London 1848).

There were also sub-genres. *The Child's Bible* (London 1677), whose title misleadingly suggests story content, was simply a concordance of 'all the Words that are found in the Old and New Testament (excepting some of the most unusual proper Names)', that grouped common nouns by their number of syllables. Postils, specialised excerpt collections whose content was arranged according to liturgical Bible reading throughout the church year, familiarised communicants with the words and meaning of specific Bible verses. Bible excerpts, like postils, preserved Biblical language, appeared in a verse a day format for the calendar year, and bore fanciful titles like William Mason's *Crumbs from the Master's Table; or, select sentences, doctrinal, practical, and experimental* (London 1831) or *Scripture Gems* (1835). Bible summaries concentrated not on Bible language but on abbreviated Bible content, often in minuscule thumb Bibles. Prose thumb Bibles, like *Biblia; or a practical summary of the Old and New Testaments* (London 1727), initially intended for adults, were manifestly read by children. Versified early Bible summaries, like John Taylor's *Verbum Sempiternum* (London 1614) galloped through the Old Testament, allotting only sixteen lines to the fifty chapters of Genesis:

> Jehovah here of Nothing, all things makes,
> And Man, the chief of all, his God forsakes.
> Yet by th' Almighty's Mercy 'twas decreed,
> Heaven's Heir should satisfie for Man's misdeed.
> Men now live long, but do not act aright,
> For which the flood destroys them all but eight;
> *Noah*, his Wife, their Sons, with those they wedd:
> The rest all perish'd in that watery Bed.
> Read here of *Abraham*'s numberless increase,
> And of their journeying, and his own decease.
> Of *Israel*'s going into *Egypt*'s Land,
> Of their Abode, their Entertainment, and
> Of *Joseph*'s Brethren, faithless and unkind,
> Of his firm faith, and ever-constant mind.
> He pardons them that did his death devise;
> He sees his Children's Children, and he dies.

*Verbum Sempiternum*, which remained in print for nearly two centuries, provided a model for Benjamin Harris's *Holy Bible in Verse*, which substituted a rollicking tetrameter for Taylor's pentameter:

> This book contains a full relation
> Of God Almighty's wise Creation,
> Who by his Power in six Days,
> The Earth did frame and Heav'n raise.

First printed in London *c.*1712, it was imported to Boston in 1717. Nathaniel Crouch also versified Bible material in *Youth's Divine Pastime* (2 vols) and used trimeters. A second volume (1720) turned towards violent death and lurid sex as it recounted stories like Lot's incest, in which his daughters made him 'drunk with Wine,/And then both with him lye;/He being ignorant of this,/Their wanton policy.'

Bibles edited for children in the seventeenth and eighteenth centuries were usually illustrated. On occasion, however, pictures alone were printed to elicit spontaneous tellings of Bible stories. Such picture albums, of varying graphic and aesthetic merit, were directed at adult buyers all over central, western and northern Europe for use in the family circle. One early example that may stand for many was *The History of the Old and New Testament described in Figures* (London *c.*1670). Typical for the late eighteenth century was Sarah Trimmer's *Series of Prints from the Old Testament* (London 1797), which was soon joined by her publisher's *New Series of Prints for Scripture History* (1803 *et seq.*) and – in the chapbook market – by the twenty-four page *New Pictorial Bible*.

Hieroglyphic Bibles, like Elisha Coles's *Youth's Visible Bible* (London 1675), became popular in the USA in the late eighteenth and early nineteenth centuries.

The full title of an early import, published by Isaiah Thomas in Worcester, Massachusetts in 1788, advertised its intent:

> *A curious hieroglyphick Bible: or select Passages in the Old and New Testaments represented with Emblematical Figures for the Amusement of Youth Designed chiefly to familiarize tender Age in a pleasing and diverting Manner, with early Ideas of the Holy Scripture to which are subjoined, a short account of the Lives of the Evangelists, and other pieces.*

Coles united hieroglyphics to Latin instruction in his 1675 book (published in London) with the forbidding title, *Nolens Volens; or, You shall make Latin whether you will or no ... Together with the youth's visible Bible.*

In some Latin schools, boys encountered Sebastian Châteillon's *Dialogorum Sacrorum libri quattuor* (London 1577), which reformulated those parts of the Bible that lent themselves to dialogic presentation. Thus Châteillon's dialogues began not with Creation, but with the serpent's conversation with Eve, while Sodom included Lot's altercation with the lowering mob, though it excised his daughters' discussion of inebriating him in order to become pregnant by him.

Scripture catechisms inculcated a knowledge of Bible content, in two modes. Protestants favoured prescribed responses, while Catholics tended to allow content summaries. One of the earliest Protestant scripture catechisms was Eusebius Pagit's *Historie of the Bible briefly collected by way of question and answer* (London 1613). It had grown out of Pagit's nightly practice for twenty-six years of reading Scripture to his assembled servants and family, making 'such observations as [he] thought fit for their capacities and understanding', and questioning them 'daily [to take] an account how they understood and retained [Bible content] in memorie'. Bible catechisms continued into the eighteenth century, for example with Ambrose Rigge's *Scripture Catechism for Children. Collected out of the whole Body of the Scriptures, for the instructing of Youth with the Word of the Lord in the Beginning ... that they might be taught our children, and Children's children ... Presented to Fathers of Families, and Masters of Schools, to train up their Children and Scholars, in the Knowledge of God and the Scriptures* (London 1702). Historical catechisms, like some Bible story collections, could on occasion be interconfessional, as when the English Protestant publisher T. Cooper adapted the Jesuit Abbé Claude Fleury's *Catechisme Historique* for Anglican children. The genre survived into the nineteenth century with *A Brief Historical Catechism of the Holy Scriptures, designed for the Use of Children and Young Persons* (York 1815), which its author William Alexander proudly announced had small format and clear facts, so that even the poorest classes might buy, and understand, it.

Bible subjects also made their way into English chapbooks like those printed and distributed by the English firm of Dicey. Individual stories, like Joseph and Potiphar's wife sold well, while cheap reference works like *A Family Index to the Bible* (Northampton 1739) entered modest households at small cost (two pence apiece or one shilling and six pence per dozen).

English publishers supplied American printers in the seventeenth and eighteenth centuries, a situation confirmed by the title of Cotton Mather's catechism, *Spiritual Milk for Boston Babes in either England* (1662; first British edition 1646). Mather's *Spiritual Milk* lived on in the eighteenth century in editions of the enormously influential *New-England Primer* (*c.*1686 *et seq.*) assembled by the transplanted London printer, Benjamin Harris. Until the nineteenth century, the majority of American children's religious books, including children's Bibles, originated in England and appeared on the western side of the Atlantic with a lag of one or two generations. For example, John Taylor's 1614 *Verbum Sempiternum* was printed in Boston in 1693; and Newbery's 1757 *Holy Bible Abridged* appeared in Boston in 1782 and in Worcester (Massachusetts) in 1786. The printing of American children's religious books differed from English ones, however, in one important respect. Whereas in England such printing centred almost exclusively in London, in the USA it was scattered among small provincial presses like those in Leicester in Massachusetts, Bridgeport, New London, and New Haven in Connecticut, Sag Harbor, Cooperstown, and Buffalo in New York State, as well as in regional printing centres like Boston, Worcester, New York and Philadelphia.

### Devotional literature before 1800

John Foxe's *Actes and Monuments*, which soon came to be known as *Foxe's Book of Martyrs* was first published in England in 1563, and soon made its way into abridged editions for children, its horrifying reports of martyrdoms affirming Protestant identity, in part by vilifying Catholics. (It remained in print in illustrated editions well into the twentieth century.)

James Janeway, one of the first writers to recognise that a message can be most effectively communicated by exploiting children's love of story, published *A Token for Children* (1671–1672), which contained accounts of the 'Conversion, holy and exemplary lives and joyful Deaths of several young Children'. The children, some of them of very tender years, set an example to their families by their piety and, as it approaches, welcome death as the way to everlasting bliss, while their sorrowing families look on, full of awe and admiration. Similar books were published throughout the eighteenth century and provided a model for some of the nineteenth-century evangelical writing for children.

John Bunyan offered doctrinal doggerel in *A Book for Boys and Girls: or, Country Rhimes for Children* (1686), using the already established pattern of illustrating divine truths and moral ideas through everyday and familiar objects. However, children appear to have been much more attracted to the earlier *Pilgrim's Progress* (1678), which not only told a good story, but used familiar figures and images from popular traditional tales. *Pilgrim's Progress* has been published in countless editions for children.

The *Divine Songs* of Isaac Watts (1715), verses in which he emphasised moral virtues in order to 'beautify [children's] Souls', also enjoyed a long-lasting popularity and were still widely known when Lewis Carroll parodied some of them in *Alice's Adventures in Wonderland* (1865). Although much devotional literature was didactically grim, some used a toy book format. For example, a rotating dial in Nathaniel Crouch's *Delights for the Ingenious* (1684) guided readers to appropriate moral verse. At home and in school children encountered verse and prose with religious and devotional intent. Rhyming ABC books taught that 'A is our Advocate, Jesus his name;/B is a Babe, in weakness who came'. In the mid-eighteenth century Jeanne Marie Leprince de Beaumont mixed Bible stories with fairy tales and interleaved both with edifying conversations in her *Magasin des Enfans* (1756).

Drama also proffered religious and devotional messages. At the French court of Louis XIV the pious Marquise de Maintenon encouraged girls to act in Bible dramas, a practice that François Fénelon codified in his *Traité de l'éducation des filles* (1687) where he discussed girls' dramatising appropriate Bible stories. In the eighteenth century Mme de la Fite's *Drames et contes moraux* (1778 *et seq.*) were part of an English education as were Maria Edgeworth's *Little Plays for Young People*, Hannah More's *Sacred Dramas* (1782), the Comtesse de Genlis's *Théâtre à l'Usage des Jeunes Personnes* (1785), and Mark Anthony Meilan's *Holy Writ Familiarized to Juvenile Conceptions* (1791).

Magazines and miscellanies also included religious and devotional material, and with evangelical and Anglican support the religious component blossomed in the nineteenth century.

Allegories, which followed the pattern set by *The Pilgrim's Progress* and which were written especially for children, were enacted in symbolic space by archetypal characters, without linear plots; people's actions were surely and simply eponymous, their names predictive for their individual fates. Mrs Sherwood's *Infant's Progress From the Valley of Destruction to Everlasting Glory* (1821) exemplifies this genre. Her histories were structured by sequential events that impinged on their stories' characters, shaped their fates, and generated their attributes, for example, 'chaste' Joseph. Moral narrative amalgamated the characteristics of allegories and histories by retaining allegorical naming (Squire Allworthy, Peter Prudence, Betsey Goodchild, Anthony Greedyguts and Marjory Meanwell) within an essentially historical narrative structure. Allegories, histories and moral narratives shaded one into the other and shared a single aim – to produce good Christian children.

## Moral and Religious Writing

### Kate Montagnon

#### Evangelical writing for children 1800–1900

In historical terms broad trends can be discerned in religious, devotional and moral writing for children. In the seventeenth century, religious and spiritual development was fostered by allegorical books; in the eighteenth century, educational progress led child heroes and heroines to wealth and fame, although books were class-specific, with appropriate messages – the rich man in his castle, the poor man at his gate. In the nineteenth century as a single-class religious prose began to emerge, evangelism became a major influence in the development of children's literature. Evangelical Christians, who saw the written word as a potential path to salvation, were interested in souls not stories, and thus a friendly critic praised Mrs O. F. Walton's *A Peep Behind the Scenes* (1877) for its godliness in clearly teaching 'the three Rs – Ruin, Redemption and Regeneration'. Evangelicals turned to publishing to serve a new literate class among the poor – a class they had helped to create by founding Sunday Schools. Anxious that literacy should not foment evil, they supplied pious tracts to supplant vulgar chapbooks. Fiction, still regarded by some as sinful lying, might be acceptable if it highlighted Biblical truths, and much of the early evangelical material for children was in the form of eight-page tracts, which told stories that exhorted readers to repentance or holy living. These were distributed by pedlars, some of whom were 'Christian pedlars' who dealt (or were supposed to deal) only in religious tracts; one series, the 'Cheap Repository Tracts' sold over two million copies in the mid-1790s, and bound copies were used in schools and wealthier homes.

Initially the tract writers aimed their production at adults, but as early as 1803, the Religious Tract Society (founded in 1799) considered the possibility of producing tract stories for children. The first, which appeared in 1809, were reprints of tracts for adults; however, by the 1820s both the Religious Tract Society and many others were producing tracts specifically for children. (With child mortality still high, there was a continuing impulse to 'save' children before death.) Children at Sunday School could be taught to carry the message of salvation home to their parents – a scenario that was developed in numerous tracts. The tracts also reflect a growing interest in children and childhood; and although evangelicals have traditionally been seen as opposed to the romantic view of childhood (as they insisted on the corruption of individual sin rather than on inherent childhood grace), they were not immune to childish charm and prettiness. A number of periodicals also sprang up; William Carus Wilson, notorious as the model for Mr Brocklehurst in *Jane Eyre*, edited *The Children's Friend* – which contains the customary holy deaths of children. Such magazines elevated English values, purveyed the message that it was better to be pious than rich, and included grotesque narratives and pictures of heathen barbarity. Death was luridly prominent with titles like 'You are not too young to die' and 'The dying Sunday scholar'.

The main purpose of the tract or evangelical story was not to entertain but to exhort. Since the writers sought to appeal not to the imagination but to the religious conscience of their readers, the stories follow set patterns and there is little difference between one tract and another on the same theme. In some, particularly the early *Cheap Repository Tracts* of Hannah More (and others, from 1795), virtue is rewarded and vice punished in this life: honest servants gain promotion and (limited) wealth, while lazy or dishonest children come to bad ends. In others, Christians in poor circumstances lead lives of contentment and usefulness, and in many cases the witness of their lives and conversation impresses others and brings them to salvation. Old cottagers are content because they have 'Christ with their crust and their crust with Christ' – and it is clear that the stories served to teach social subordination as well as evangelical principles. Thus although the circumstantial details of many tracts and tract-style books seem to attempt realism, there is a blindness (deliberate or otherwise) concerning social conditions. The houses of the poor are well kept or ramshackle according to the spiritual state of the tenant, and not according to the quality of the landlord. Christians may be poor but they are clean and neat and never uncomfortable. Very revealing is an example like 'The Lancashire collier girl' (More 1798: 2: 20–31) who goes down the mine at 9-years-old to earn money for her parents. Because her father is in the mine, and she has a careful supervisor, the author says, the work cannot be too hard for her to sustain.

While assessing the tracts it is important to remember, as J. S. Bratton has pointed out, that these stories were written by naïve writers for naïve readers (25). Not only is the formula story effective for such readers, but the themes of 'rags to riches' and set-piece dramatic death-bed scenes were popular in secular fiction too. Tract writers were thus very much in tune with the popular imagination of the time, and contributed to mainstream popular culture, and many of the stories and series remained in print throughout the nineteenth century.

Of the *Cheap Repository Tracts* some of the stories are merely pious: 'The cottage cook', for example, is about a widow who finds consolation in teaching girls cooking and dressmaking, and thus raising good wives for working men, but others are more racy. In 'The two wealthy farmers', Sir Dashall Squeeze blows his brains out; in 'The Cheapside apprentice' the hero confesses 'It was at the Dog and Duck I first saw the infamous Miss West; she was many years older than myself, but her person was as lovely as her heart was wicked . . . ' (More 1798: 2: 3).

Legh Richmond was an Anglican clergyman, and his book, *Annals of the Poor*, is a collection of stories about his parishioners on the Isle of Wight. Although not originally intended for children, one story, 'The young cottager' is about the conversion and death of a 10-year-old, Little Jane. It later became popular as a children's book, and large numbers were distributed as Sunday School prizes. Legh Richmond toured the country distributing copies, and noted with satisfaction that it had proved 'useful' to many children.

Mrs Sherwood's *Little Henry and his Bearer* (1814) is set in India, where the author lived for some time. Henry is first neglected and left to the care of servants, and then rescued and converted by an English girl; Henry in turn converts his servant and then dies. Apart from the details of the setting, the story is interesting as an example of a favourite tract theme, that of the child who converts an adult: in teaching his servant about Christ, Henry is carrying out the chief duty of an evangelical Christian. He is also transcending the subordinate role of childhood – a child's dream that children's stories often seek to fulfil. Here in a surprising context is an early example of the liberation of childhood:

> Here are two persons, who have been nearly fifty years in the world, sitting together talking of their finery and painted toys; while a little creature, who eight years ago had not breathed the breath of life, is endeavouring to impart divine knowledge to the Heathen.

Mrs Sherwood's most famous tract is *The History of the Fairchild Family* (1818, 1842, 1847). Henry, Lucy and Emily on occasion lie, steal, and even get drunk on cider, and are taken to task by their parents, all to show how sinful the human heart is without God's grace. Punishment is severe: Henry is completely excluded from the family for days because he will not learn his Latin. When the children quarrel, they are taken to see the remains of a murderer on a gibbet – the man has been hanged for killing his brother, and their father warns them that they may fall into such sin if they persist in quarrelling. It is difficult to judge the appeal of this book at a distance from the moral climate in which it was written. Nineteenth-century commentators, who had been given the book as children, suggest that they enjoyed the naughtiness and perhaps gained a frisson from the gibbets and corpses. Alongside her severity, Mrs Sherwood makes the Fairchild family's life sound appealing, with details of outings and food. Certainly, the preface to a facsimile edition of the 1870s claims that it was difficult to find an original edition, 'it has been so often read and re-read that most of the early editions have long ere this been thumbed out of existence' (Sherwood nd: ii).

The tractarians, in providing a mass of reading material for the newly literate, helped to set a trend for later literature in which the themes of death, repentance, and poverty overcome by virtue remained important.

Even as children's literature became more liberal, evangelicalism remained a strong force: even the sceptical Alice stories have an Easter message attached. However, some writers were overtly critical: Charlotte M. Yonge, for example, commented that Mrs Sherwood's moral lessons 'reflect the shifting opinions of a very untaught and conceited though pious mind' (Yonge 1869: 308).

There were, however, two major changes in evangelical writing. The first was caused by the rapid growth in popularity of fairy stories – although the usual response was to rewrite them as Christian allegories. Charlotte Tucker, writing as A.L.O.E (A Lady of England), for example, published a collection of moralised fairy stories, *Old Friends with New Faces*, in 1858. This treatment of the tales was distasteful to many – notably Charles Dickens, who wrote a forceful riposte to George Cruikshank's teetotal version of some of the tales, in 'Frauds on the fairies', published in *Household Words*, in 1853. Other Christian writers used the fairy tales to present their message in a way more acceptable to their contemporaries; notable among these were Charles Kingsley with *The Water Babies* (1863) and George MacDonald with *At the Back of the North Wind* (1871).

The second change was a response to the effects of industrialisation and poverty, concern for which had been expressed through such writers as Kingsley and Dickens. The setting of the stories shifted to the towns, and child protagonists became slum dwellers and 'street arabs'. Characteristic was *Jessica's First Prayer* (1867) by Hesba Stretton (Sara Smith), a direct attack on the religiosity of the wealthy which uses the device of the adult converted by the child. Here, however, Jessica succeeds not because of her grasp of doctrine but because of the childish simplicity of her faith. Daniel Standing, the chapel caretaker who is converted, explains his conversion to the minister: 'She's come often and often of a morning, and looked into my face with those dear eyes of hers and said "Don't you love Jesus Christ, Mr Dan'el?" ' (Stretton 1867: 89). A move has been made away from the story which presents an evangelically correct doctrinal position in order to educate the reader, to one where the correct doctrine to grasp is essentially that of a romantic view of childhood.

Stretton's later books, populated by appealing waifs, were influenced by Dickens, and many other writers followed suit. In Mrs O. F. Walton's novel of theatrical children, *A Peep Behind the Scenes*, Rosalie learns about Jesus from a picture of the Good Shepherd and teaches her mother and various members of the cast of her drunken father's travelling show. Mrs Walton's greatest success was

*Christie's Old Organ* (1882), in which the waif who brings the organ grinder to conversion goes on to be a lay-preacher.

The 'waif' stories had a long life; writers like 'Brenda' (Mrs G. Castle Smith) produced books, like *Froggy's Little Brother* (1875), which survived well into the twentieth century. One notable example is *The Basket of Flowers*, a translation from the German of Christopher von Schmid (1823), which was still being offered as a Sunday School prize in the 1950s.

The influence of these books (which became known as 'rewards') was pervasive, and should not be underestimated in literary and cultural terms.

### The twentieth century

In the twentieth century, the division between mainstream children's literature and literature produced for religious reasons began to sharpen. Religious books, including evangelical stories, are still written for children but now reach a smaller audience; they are written by the faithful for the faithful, published by specialist publishers and sold through specialist outlets, often to be distributed as Sunday School prizes. Few parents see religious content as essential or even desirable in their children's reading. naïve offerings of writers motivated by faith rather than talent are not acceptable where children have access to more choice.

While catechisms and prayer books are the responsibility of the specialist publishers, the Bible is still an important source of inspiration for mainstream writers and illustrators. Developments in colour printing have resulted in a wide range of attractive illustrated collections of Bible stories and picture books.

In 1938 Dorothy P. Lathrop won the first Caldecott Medal for her illustrations in *Animals of the Bible*, while in the early 1990s Jane Ray won much acclaim for her picture books, *The Creation* (1992), which portrayed a pregnant Eve, *Noah's Ark* (1990) and *The Story of Christmas* (1991), in which the Virgin Mary is seen to be breastfeeding the Baby Jesus. Walter de la Mare's *Stories from the Bible* (1929) and Margherita Fanchiotti's *Stories from the Bible* (1955) are just two of the many distinguished retellings by major writers. The life of Christ and lives of the Saints also feature in mainstream publishing as in Eleanor Graham's *The Story of Jesus* (1959), illustrated by Brian Wildsmith, and Eleanor Farjeon's *Ten Saints* (1936), with illustrations by Helen Sewell.

New editions of John Bunyan's *The Pilgrim's Progress* have been published throughout the twentieth century, although it is no longer as central to children's lives as it clearly was in the nineteenth-century (Louisa M. Alcott's *Little Women* (1868) is only one of many books which attest to its influence). Bunyan's story was retold in *The Land of Far-Beyond* (1942) by Enid Blyton, who felt the language of the original was too difficult and the ideas too hard for twentieth-century children. When this book was reissued in 1973, with illustrations by the Greenaway Medallist, Pauline Baynes (who also illustrated C. S. Lewis's Narnia books) it was severely criticised by Brian Alderson, who compared it unfavourably with earlier retellings by Mrs Sherwood, A.L.O.E and Frances Hodgson Burnett which he felt had conveyed the allegoric force of the original (Alderson 1973: 13).

One controversial re-visioning (rather than re-telling) of a Biblical text was Julie Vivas's *The Nativity* (1988), while ingenious glosses on Biblical narratives have included Nicholas Allan's *Jesus' Christmas Party* (1991) and Margaret Gray's *The Donkey's Tale* (1984).

It is in the field of fiction that the greatest division between mainstream and religious writing is seen. Evangelical Christian publishing is essentially on the edges of the children's book market. In the past, Christian writers produced books in which the religious message reflected general popular taste: this is no longer the case. For the first fifty or sixty years of the twentieth-century, however, evangelical fiction for children, supported by the Sunday School movement with its buying of prizes as a reward for good attendance and by the fact that the books appeared to be good value for money, continued to appear.

Some of the authors conveyed their message in the popular genres of the time. Amongst the flood of writers of girls' school stories in the period before 1930 was Dorothy Dennison. Many of her books are conventional school stories but a few were published by the Religious Tract Society, and in these an evangelical interest is forced into the standard framework. For example, *Rumours in the Fourth Form* (nd, but published in the 1920s) has a chapter, 'Rosemary hears the call', in which the heroine is invited to accompany a friend to a Bible class, an experience which causes her to repent her dishonest behaviour and to become a reformed character. It is such books that led Judith Humphrey to suggest that the worth of a book 'varies in direct proportion to its evangelistic message' (Humphrey 1994: 220).

One of the most popular evangelical writers in recent years has been Patricia St John; her earliest stories, beginning with *Tanglewood's Secret*, published by the Scripture Union in 1948, use some of the romantic devices typical of nineteenth-century evangelical publishing, but she also writes stories with a tougher edge, set in trouble spots of the world. Set in war-torn Lebanon, *Nothing Else Matters* (1978) describes scenes she knew from her experience as a missionary. Although Patricia St John does not reach the wide audience enjoyed by, for example, Hesba Stretton a century earlier, her books have been very popular with Christian readers and have been translated into other languages.

A major influence on evangelical writing for children in the latter part of the twentieth century has been the popularity of the Chronicles of Narnia of C. S. Lewis. Recognising the appeal and Christian content of *The Lion, the Witch and the Wardrobe* (1950) and its successors, many writers have tried to emulate Lewis's example, creating imaginary worlds in which the fairy tale forces of good and evil represent God and Satan. In an age when few believe in the direct interventions of Providence or acknowledge their need of salvation, such books are seen as a way of educating non-Christian readers in the ways of God without appearing to preach directly. Some of the imitations of Narnia have been poorly written, but Pauline Fisk's *Midnight Blue* (1990) was awarded the prestigious Smarties Prize, both as the best book for 9 to 12-year-olds and as the best children's book of the year.

*Midnight Blue* was published by Lion Publishing, established in 1971 and almost unique in the twentieth century as a new imprint aiming to publish Bible stories and books that 'help children to find out about Christianity'. Other specialist imprints include Pickering and Inglis, and the Victory Press. Those publishers established in the nineteenth century realised the market was changing. The Religious Tract Society became, first the United Society for Christian Literature and, in 1930, the Lutterworth Press. The Society for the Promotion of

Christian Knowledge (SPCK), although it continued to use the SPCK imprint, established the Triangle and Sheldon Presses in the 1960s. Thus, both societies chose names which do not advertise their religious connections, and began to publish a wider range of titles.

When Burns and Oates, a leading Catholic publisher, asked the agnostic Charles Keeping to illustrate two of their books in the 1960s, 'it was made clear that he was at liberty to regard Biblical stories simply as stories' (Martin 1993: 33). Faith in Print, an initiative of the Christian Book Promotion Trust, was set up in 1971 to promote good quality, readable children's books; its advisory panel includes representatives of the Anglican, Roman Catholic and Free Churches, and its *Young People's Book List 1994/95* draws on mainstream as well as specialist publishers, with recommendations including E. Nesbit's *The Railway Children* (1906) and Anne Holm's *I am David* (1965).

In twentieth-century Britain it is very unusual to find a book such as Cecily Hallack's *Adventure of the Amethyst* (1937) coming from a mainstream publisher, in this case Macmillan. The production is in the best traditions of the 1930s, with black and white line drawings scattered through the well-spaced text. At first glance it appears to be a holiday adventure story about a family of middle-class children, typical of the period. The children ride, explore the Sussex village and its surroundings and even find a secret room in the large house to which they have just moved. But in this story the secret room is an old Catholic chapel containing a long lost statue of the Virgin, and the adventures are subservient to the story of how the children are converted to Roman Catholicism under the guidance of a Canadian bishop recuperating in the area after an air crash. Catholic beliefs and ceremonial are described and discussed at great length as the children move from being 'heathens', through baptism to confirmation.

In contrast to this, a species of all-purpose religion prevails in most mainstream books. Children's fiction generally encourages the kind of qualities that are promoted by all religions – honesty, truthfulness, integrity, sympathy for others, particularly the weaker or less fortunate, patience, positive action as opposed to idleness, hard work, helpfulness and so on. God is only approached through prayer in times of stress when characters are cut off by the tide or lost in caves or underground passages or, occasionally, in times of illness or bereavement when close friends and relatives are involved. There is often an implication that people usually go to church on Sundays, and particularly at Christmas and Easter, school prayers are taken for granted, but there is little mention of specific religious content, customs or beliefs.

Christmas may be an important occasion in a book, but it could well be replaced by a similar festival from the calendar of any other religion. The performance of a nativity play may be a set piece or may be used to point a simple moral message. For example, in Barbara Robinson's *The Best Christmas Pageant Ever* (1974), a family of badly behaved children of whom most of the local mothers disapprove, join the Sunday School and take all the best parts in the Christmas play – and people's attitudes towards them begin to change as the play comes to have more meaning than ever before. In 1966 Alan Garner and William Mayne collaborated on *Holly from the Bongs: A Nativity Play*, produced in Goostrey in Cheshire in 1965 and subsequently published, illustrated by coloured photographs of the production, as what must be one of the most distinguished literary nativity plays ever to be written.

The parish church or the vicarage family feature in numerous twentieth-century British children's books, almost as a form of shorthand since certain facts can be taken for granted about both. Churches may feature as worthy of being saved but there is little mention of their spiritual significance. Nor are the churches or vicarage families always idyllically rural. In K. M. Peyton's *Marion's Angels* (1979), the plot centres on a campaign to save an old rural church from becoming a ruin, but Janet McNeill's church in *The Battle of St George Without* (1966) is set in a run-down city area. Noel Streatfeild's vicarage family move from the inner London parish of *The Bell Family* (1954) to a very different kind of parish in *New Town* (1960).

Historical novels are often set in periods of religious conflict or at times when religious minorities were persecuted, but there is little discussion of the issues involved in such conflicts. Geoffrey Trease's *The Red Towers of Granada* (1966) tells of the attitudes towards Jews in medieval Europe. Barbara Willard's *The Grove of Green Holly* (1967) and Elizabeth Speare's *The Witch of Blackbird Pond* (1960) are both set against a background of Puritan bigotry, one in England, the other in New England, and Meriol Trevor's *Lights in a Dark Town* (1964) is set in nineteenth-century Birmingham at the time when Cardinal Newman was leading the Roman Catholic revival.

One of the few writers who does explore religious issues more deeply is Antonia Forest. In her stories about the Marlow family, the Marlows themselves are Protestant, although there is a Catholic grandmother whose rosary and bedroom furnished with an altar and prie-Dieu fascinate one of the children, but the neighbouring friends, the Merricks, are Catholics and Patrick, the son, frequently discusses Catholic doctrine and ceremonial with the Marlow girls. One of Nicola's best friends at school is Miranda, a Jewish girl. The different beliefs permeate most of the books in the series but *End of Term* (1959) has the performance of a school nativity play as its focus and this sparks off more religious discussions than usual.

Elfrida Vipont, winner of the Carnegie Medal for *The Lark on the Wing* (1950), writes about Quaker schools and Quaker families in her Larks and Springs sequence, published between 1948 and 1969, and few readers can remain unaware of the Quaker beliefs, which come through clearly in the books but do not dominate them. Although children have been made more aware of Judaism through reading stories set in the period of the Second World War, few of these describe Jewish beliefs or customs. Leila Berg's *A Box for Benny* (1958), which incorporates several Jewish customs as an integral part of the story, is a rare find. Sydney Taylor's *All-of-a-Kind Family* (1951) and its sequels, with their details of Jewish food and festivals, are based on her own childhood in New York at the turn of the century. The books in which Adèle Geras draws on her Jewish heritage are also set in the past; *Voyage* (1983) describes the hardships faced by European Jews emigrating to the USA in the early twentieth century, *The Girls in the Velvet Frame* (1979) is set in Jerusalem in 1913, and the short stories which make up *Golden Windows and other Stories of Jerusalem* (1993) are set in the years from 1910 to 1954.

In Britain, with the coming of a multi-ethnic society, there is more interest in religions other than Christianity. Many of the books published for young people are information books, some of which are presented as narratives, with emphasis on colourful feast days and festivals such as the Jewish Chanukah, the Chinese New Year, Diwali and Eid-ul-Fitr. Celebrations, a series published by A. and C. Black, which includes titles such as *Diwali* by Chris Deshpande (1985) and Lynne Hannigan's *Sam's Passover* (1985), is typical of this kind of publishing, aimed at 8- to 10-year-olds, focusing on one particular child or family and illustrated by colour photographs.

At the end of the twentieth century, publishers must produce books which meet the demands of the market place if they are to survive. In the past Christian authors wrote books with a religious message that reflected popular taste. Popular taste has changed and whether there will be room for a self-consciously Christian fiction in the twenty-first century or whether it was simply a phenomenon of two hundred years' duration remains to be seen.

## References

Alderson, B. (1973) 'Miss Blyton in the way of progress', *The Times* 2 May: 13.

Bratton, J. S. (1981) *The Impact of Victorian Children's Fiction*, London: Croom Helm.

Humphrey, J. (1994) My God, it's the Head', in Auchmunty, R. (ed.) *The Chalet School Revisited*, London: Bettany Press.

Martin, D. (1993) *Charles Keeping: An Illustrator's Life*, London: MacRae.

More, H. (1798) *Cheap Repository Tracts*, 3 vols, London: Rivingtons.

Ramadan, K. (1988) 'Children's books in Kuwait', *Bookbird* 26, 2: 8–9.

Sherwood, M. M. (nd) *The History of the Fairchild Family*, London: Ward, Lock.

Stretton, H. (1876) *Jessica's First Prayer*, London: Religious Tract Society.

Yonge, C. M. (1869) 'Didactic Fiction', *Macmillan's Magazine*, 20: 302–310.

## Further Reading

Bottigheimer, R. B. (1996) *The Bible for Children from the Age of Gutenberg to the Present*, New Haven: Yale University Press.

Cutt, M. N. (1974) *Mrs Sherwood and her Books for Children*, Oxford: Oxford University Press.

—— (1979) *Ministering Angels, a Study of Nineteenth Century Evangelical Writing for Children*, Wormley: Five Owls Press.

Demers, P. (1993) *Heaven Upon Earth. The Form of Moral and Religious Children's Literature to 1850*, Knoxville: University of Tennessee Press.

Greene, I. (1995) *The Christian's ABC: Catechisms and Catechizing in England, c.1540–1740*, Oxford: Oxford University Press.

Jones, W. (1850) *The Jubilee Memorial of the Religious Tract Society 1799–1849*, London: Religious Tract Society.

Milligan, E. H. (1988) 'Elfrida Vipont as children's writer', *Friends' Quarterly* 25, 2: 66–76.

Pickering, S. F., Jr (1993) *Moral Instruction and Fiction for Children, 1749–1820*, Athens, GA: University of Georgia Press.

# 22

# Animal Stories

## *Keith Barker*

The predominance of animals in children's books comes as no surprise when looking at the way Western civilisations treat both children and animals. Countries in other parts of the world take a far less sentimental attitude towards both groups, as did pre-industrial revolution Britain and Europe. Indeed, de Mause (1976: 274, 280) has suggested that not only did pet animals roam freely throughout early European dwellings, providing a health hazard for crawling infants, but that bestiality was also rife. However, in recent centuries animals and children have been linked together in terms of their privileged and protected position in the culture so inextricably that since the nineteenth century children's books have strongly featured animal characters either exhibiting strong human characteristics or showing empathy for such traits.

One of the earliest works adopted by children uses animals to convey to young readers messages about life. Whether Aesop, the Greek slave who lived at around 550 BC on Sanos, was the author of the fables that bear his name is doubtful; however, what is not in any doubt is the way they have been seen from the earliest printed version in English (translated and printed by Caxton in 1484) to the present day. Originally they were not intended for children but Caxton and further adapters have geared them towards a child audience. Roger L'Estrange, in his comprehensive collection of 1692, wrote that they were produced for the 'hearing, learning and telling of little stories' while John Newbery included four of the fables in his first book for children in 1744.

Another Newbery publication, *The History of Little Goody Two-Shoes* (1765), also features animal characters as prominent forces in the story. Jumper the dog, Ralph the raven, Tippy the lark and Willy the lamb help Mrs Margery when she takes on the role of village postmistress.

Traditional rhymes also continued to be dominated by animal characters, who sometimes displayed human characteristics but sometimes remained resolutely animals. Tucker says that they

> may sometimes be dressed in the height of fashion, like the three young rats with black, felt hats, or else come closer to the birds or beasts of everyday life, passively awaiting the next milking, or laying eggs to order. Cats and dogs are equally adaptable, wearing petticoats, playing the fiddle and visiting the

queen on one page, and frightening mice, sipping milk or lying quietly by the
fire on the next.

Tucker 1981: 44

Animals have continued to be a major feature of rhyme for children, from the very
popular *Comic Adventures of Old Mother Hubbard and her Dog* (1805) and *The
Monkey's Frolic* (1825) to Edward Lear's owl and pussycat (1867) and to
contemporary verse. They have always been an important component of alphabet
books, from early Shaker alphabets to the present day, having been used by, among
others, Brian Wildsmith, Wanda Gág, Satoshi Kitamura and Celestino Piatti.

Early children's books used animals as a device which is still employed in
modern writing for children. Animals in this type of story are really only seen as a
way of portraying human characteristics to young readers in a way they will not
find threatening or disturbing but which will teach them a lesson in human (rather
than animal) nature. This device reached its apotheosis in Victorian times, and is
most ably demonstrated in one of the most famous early children's books, Sarah
Trimmer's *Fabulous Histories. Designed for the Instruction of Children, respecting
their Treatment of Animals* (1786). The didactic purpose of these stories was
obvious from the preface in which Mrs Trimmer wrote that her young readers
should be

> taught to consider them, not as containing the real conversations of Birds
> (for that it is impossible we should ever understand) but as a series of
> FABLES, intended to convey moral instruction applicable to themselves, at
> the same time that they excite compassion and tenderness for those
> interesting and delightful creatures, on which such wanton cruelties are
> frequently inflicted, and recommend universal Benevolence.

Darton 1932/1982: 158

The book contains two major sets of characters, whose stories are interwoven. The
story of the human family is designed to teach those sentiments described above.
Cruelty to animals was a favourite Georgian theme. As Gillian Avery says:

> So universal was the moralising on the subject that we are led to conclude
> the chief recreation of Georgian youths was spitting cockchafers, pulling the
> wings off flies, stripping birds of their feathers, flogging donkeys and horses,
> and thinking up ingenious ways to torment kittens and dogs.

Avery 1965: 37

The animal aspect of *Fabulous Histories* is designed to explain human foibles and
virtues to a child audience. The Robin family contains father, mother and four
children: Robin, Dicky, Pecksy and Flopsy. Pecksy is held as a shining example of
what a good daughter should be: unattractive in appearance but sweet and dutiful
in nature. At all times she submits to the better knowledge of her parents, unlike
the other children who all come to unfortunate ends. The Robin parents
themselves demonstrate every good quality which the author feels is important.
They are good and loving parents, devoted to each other as a couple and know their
proper station in life. Father is fond of moralising sermons and sends the young on
their way from the nest with the following words:

Let none of your own species excel you in any amiable quality, for want of your endeavours to equal the best; and do your duty in every relation of life, as we have done ours by you. To the gay scenes of levity and dissipation prefer a calm retirement, for this is the greatest degree of happiness to be found.

Avery 1975: 50

It is interesting that one of the most famous exponents of the animal story, Beatrix Potter, encountered *Fabulous Histories* in her youth and described it as a 'stodgy fat book' which she hated.

Other books of this period contained animals as important elements. Dorothy Kilner's *The Life and Perambulations of a Mouse* (1783) is light years away from Mrs Trimmer's moralising. Master Nimble the mouse does comment on human foibles in his journey, it must be admitted, but he remains a mouse, raiding larders and eating the food of both rich and poor alike. The whole spirit of the book is akin to later works in this field, most notably from writers like Beatrix Potter and Dick King-Smith.

Further stories about animals continued to be published into the next century: they were normally dressed up as a moral fable. Titles like *The Rambles of a Butterfly* (1819), *The Adventures of Poor Puss* (1809) and *Further Adventures of Jemmy Donkey; interspersed with biographical sketches of the Horse* (1821) demonstrate this. The popular writer A.L.O.E ['A Lady of England', Charlotte Maria Tucker] produced *The Rambles of a Rat* (1857), in which the humanised rats Ratto, Whiskerandos and Oddity tell their stories which are interspersed with an examination of human eccentricities.

However, a subtle difference emerged during the Victorian period in the attitude of these books to animals. The Victorians were probably the first real animal-loving generation in Britain and in their writings only the ignorant or ill-educated were shown abusing animals. The culmination of this attitude was shown in the first major children's book about animals, *Black Beauty* (1877).

Anna Sewell's book is still in print in several editions. Often it is abridged and the more moralising aspects of the story are cut but its message remains undiluted. Margaret Blount (1974: 249) describes it as 'perhaps the last of the moral tales, the last great first person narrative in the listen-to-my-life style'. It was Anna Sewell's only book (although her mother had written many moral tracts and fables), written in the later years of her life as a semi-invalid. Its major theme is kindness to horses and although much of the story is not relevant today (transport has been superseded by less stately methods), it can still be read for its compassion (the author also condemns war and fox hunting), for the power of the narrative voice and for the almost folktale-like plot. The narrative voice is, of course, human which may make it more easy for reader identification. Black Beauty, although well born, descends to becoming a London cab horse by falling into bad hands. His rescue and his return to happiness and security through the offices of Joe, previously a stable lad, introduce the reader to a colourful array of characters, both human (good and bad: the kindly Jerry Barker to the drunken Reuben Smith) and animal (Peggy, Captain, Lizzie, and most particularly, Ginger). *Black Beauty* demonstrates one type of animal story and probably the rarest type produced (most of them are originally written for adults and then adopted by children), the story of an animal told entirely from that character's viewpoint.

The Victorian and Edwardian eras saw not only a flowering of talent writing for children but also a period when animal characters featured prominently in these stories. Even fantasy writers like Lewis Carroll and A. A. Milne employ animals to act out their plots (although Pooh and his friends are technically toys, they display many of the characteristics of the 'human beings as animals' which is a major feature of the animal story).

Rudyard Kipling created two supreme examples of the animal story in which a human being is able to communicate with creatures. *The Jungle Book* (1894) and *The Second Jungle Book* (1895) introduce the reader to a myriad of wild animals and to the complex social structure of their world. Inspired by a sentence in Rider Haggard's *Nada the Lily*, Kipling created a world approximate to an Eden in which the animals inhabit an idyllic home, yet are still prey to the complexities of reality, such as killing, death and old age. The boy Mowgli is saved from the clutches of the tiger, Shere Khan, by Mother and Father Wolf and is brought up as one of their cubs (parallels can be drawn with the Tarzan stories). He is introduced to the patterns of jungle life, their rituals and to the influence of animals such as Baloo, the sage, and Bagheera. The animals' conversation is almost a formal transcript of Urdu, with their references to 'thou' and addressing Mowgli as 'Little Brother'. Mowgli himself discards the human world and refers dismissively to the squalid life of the Indian villagers dwelling around the jungle. The relationship between animals and the human, Mowgli, is central. As Robson notes:

> Mowgli spends his whole life among animals. But as he approaches manhood he begins to find that he is not like the animals. A central symbol for this is Mowgli's eyes. They are a source of his power over the beasts, who cannot meet his gaze ... Mowgli has passed through a preliminary training which in many ways is like that suitable to animals. But a time comes when he must move beyond his animal 'brothers' and realise the truth about himself, and accept the responsibility of being a man, and the recognition that it sets him apart.
>
> Robson 1987: xvii–xviii

'The spring running', the last story in the Mowgli cycle and the last of the sequence which Kipling wrote, is almost unbearably poignant as Mowgli, young and healthy, returns to his animal friends who are growing old and dying. Kipling is not afraid to show that in the animal world there is death and murder.

The two jungle books also contain a number of other fablesque creations, such as 'Rikki-Tikki-Tavi', the famous story of a mongoose. Kipling extended his use of the animal fable in his *Just So Stories* (1902), written for and loved by younger children, with favourites like 'The elephant's child' in which human foibles are depicted through animal characters.

The tradition which Kipling embodies of portraying realistic situations in the animal kingdom while also adopting the fantasy of animals talking and communicating with humans continues in the work of one of its greatest exponents, Beatrix Potter. Potter's early life has been well documented. A lonely child who found her only comfort in the world of natural history and who kept a coded diary in her adolescent years would seem a ripe candidate for the imaginative world of writing for children.

It is difficult today to separate the truth of Beatrix Potter's writing from the commercialism which has surrounded it for so long. The illustrations, which were designed to fit naturally into the complexities of the text, can be tainted with the anthropomorphism that is a great danger of the humanised animal story. As Nicholas Tucker says

> In all her stories, in fact, Beatrix Potter describes a half-human, half-animal world, populated by partly-clothed animal characters who have courtesy titles and surnames, and visit each other exactly as humans do, but who also mix the gentilities of polite conversation with offhand references to a more savage state. This type of ambiguity enables her characters to flit between human and animal roles, according to the needs of the plot.
>
> Tucker 1981: 62–63

Indeed, danger is never too far away in Potter's stories, as it is in real life. Tom Kitten is the potential filling for a roly poly pudding in *The Tale of Samuel Whiskers* (1908), while in *The Tale of Jeremy Fisher* (1906) the hero, a frog, ends up in the mouth of a trout, only to be saved by his mackintosh. However, the author does prevent her child readers from seeing too much realism: unlike later writers who use a similar technique (Dick King-Smith, for instance), sex and death are almost taboo subjects.

Many comments have been made on Potter's refusal to write down to children and on her insistence that she introduced at least one complex word into each of her books. She also tried to ensure that the physical appearance of her books was child-centred, as Alison Lurie has noted:

> One special attraction of these books was that Beatrix Potter portrayed the world from a mouse's – or rabbit's – or small child's-eye view. The vantage-point in her exquisite water-colours varies from a few inches to a few feet from the ground, like that of a toddler. Indeed, when I first came across the Peter Rabbit books, I had no idea Beatrix Potter was a grown-up woman: I thought of her as a little girl. Certainly she was small enough to look at hollyhocks and tables and big dogs from below and to see everything in close-up. In her illustrations a cabbage leaf, the pattern of moss on a stump, a painted china cup, or a spool of red thread are seen with a short-range clarity of focus that is physiologically possible for most of us in early childhood.
>
> Lurie 1990: 94–95

Others have seen much of the writer's own life in the stories. Humphrey Carpenter has described the early stories as bitter comments on life while *The Tale of Pigling Bland* (1913), published the year of the writer's late marriage, is a comment on her escape from her frustrating life as the spinster daughter of repressive parents. Earlier, *The Tale of Two Bad Mice* (1904) can be seen as a parody of Potter and her fiance breaking up a conventional Victorian life. *The Tale of Peter Rabbit* (1902), the writer's first and most famous book, written initially as a letter to her governess's child, is a variation on the giant-killer folk-tale in which Peter outwits the gigantic Mr McGregor. However, it cannot be denied that much of the books' appeal rests in their nostalgia, as is witnessed in the high sales of Potter merchandise and the tourism generated in her adopted home, the English Lake District.

In America, meanwhile, a different series of animal stories began to emerge. Joel Chandler Harris was a newspaperman who began to collect the folk-tales told by slaves in the Southern states. *Uncle Remus, his Songs and Sayings* was first published in 1880 and was followed by seven more volumes, many of which had the wily character of Brer Rabbit as their hero. Brer Rabbit is an obvious descendant of folk heroes from Africa, including Anansi and Wakaima, who use their wits rather than any physical strength to get them out of dangerous situations. Nor do the stories shirk the extremities of violence in animal life: Brer Bear is stung to death by bees, Brer Wolf scalded in a chest and Brer Fox's head is served up in a stew to his wife and children.

Harris used the Grimm brothers' methods of collecting stories, and his assemblage of Afro-American folk-tales was the largest of its time. However, he also chose to set them down in an almost phonetically rendered dialect which has meant that many children since have come to the stories, particularly the famous ones like 'The tar baby', through adaptations. In more recent years the books have become associated with an unacceptable attitude towards black slavery, as represented mainly through the character of Uncle Remus, who looks back with nostalgia to what he sees as the golden days of slavery while telling his stories to a solitary white child. Julius Lester, who has produced his own adaptation of the Brer Rabbit stories, says

> the telling of black folktales, and indeed tales of all cultures, was a social event bringing together adults and children. That folktales are now considered primarily stories for children is an indication of our society's spiritual impoverishment. Traditionally, tales were told by adults to adults. If the children were quiet, they might be allowed to listen. Clearly, black folktales were not created and told for the entertainment of little white children, as the Uncle Remus tales would lead one to believe.
>
> Lester 1987: xv

Another British landmark in fantasy writing of the golden age of children's literature, which involves the use of anthropomorphism, is Kenneth Grahame's *The Wind in the Willows*, written for Grahame's own son and published in 1908 to almost complete indifference. In Grahame's world, animals and humans exist side by side with each other, sometimes being of the same size and at other times existing in their natural dimensions. It is also a world very much of its period, which often encourages a feeling of nostalgia in its adult readers.

There are a number of strands to the story. The most attractive from the child reader's point of view is almost certainly the story of Toad, the *nouveau riche* braggart who closely resembles the unattractive aspect of children's nature and who is given the author's freedom to race around the countryside in his bright new car. This may well be why A. A. Milne chose to call his stage adaptation of Grahame's book *Toad of Toad Hall* (1929) and to make that animal's adventures the centre of the work. Another strand now seems to the modern reader mawkish and set firmly in its own time: the pantheism which Grahame felt was so important and which reaches its apotheosis in the chapter 'The piper at the gates of dawn'. Between these two strands is Grahame's own mixture of anthropomorphism in which he transforms three animals, Mole, Ratty and Badger into characteristics of the ideal Edwardian gentleman. Humphrey Carpenter has said of Grahame:

> In many ways he was writing specifically about the *bachelor* Arcadia, unencumbered by women. Mole's first meeting with the Water Rat, their picnic together with its catalogue of good food, and their homeward row during which Mole makes a fool of himself by grabbing the oars and upsetting the boat, is a perfect expression of the delights of the all-male life as enjoyed by Grahame in the company of such friends as Furnivall, Quiller-Couch, and his Fowey boating acquaintance Edward Atkinson – a life without many responsibilities, but certainly not without etiquette. The shy, slightly effeminate, and privately rebellious Mole, bursting out from his private confines, is both coming to terms with his own nature as he 'entered into the joy of running water' (a phrase strikingly reminiscent of *The Water-Babies*) and is being initiated into the outdoor, gently muscular world that Kingsley, Furnivall, and the other Christian Socialists knew so well, a world which offered them a form of Escape which was quite adequate for high days and holidays.
>
> Carpenter 1985: 156

This is very much an all-male world: the few women who appear, either as animals or as humans, are subsidiary to the males, as Margaret Meek has pointed out:

> The world of the River Bank is a men's club, with Fortnum and Mason picnics for luncheon, and suppers in warm kitchens underground without the problems of shopping or washing up. When the Otter child goes missing, his father 'lonely and heartsore' watches by the ford where he taught the little one to swim. Mrs Otter appears only as the 'they' of 'the Otters', who insisted Rat should stay to supper, and 'keep it up late with his old comrade'. To believe in the artistic success of *The Wind in the Willows* one has to enter this enchanted circle of friends.
>
> Meek 1991: 24

Alison Prince has said 'the theme of homecoming occurs as repeatedly in Grahame's work as his other favourite topic – that of escape. At first sight, they appear to be opposites, but in fact the escape is often away from something alien and unhomely to the welcome cosiness of a private nest' (Prince 1994: 70). These two elements are both strongly in *The Wind in the Willows* in the shape of the adventurous Ratty and the timid Mole, with that perfect Edwardian gentleman, Badger, as the still centre of the book. The characters have long been a part of popular lore, both through cartoon versions of the story (often confined to the Toad episodes) as well as sequels such as William Horwood's *The Willows in Winter* (1993) and Jan Needle's fascinating reworking of the plot, *Wild Wood* (1981).

While Grahame was indulging in a peculiarly English type of whimsy, Jack London was producing a very different kind of animal story. These are authentically raw and credible novels in which the harsh lives of animals in the wild are depicted with a ferocious attention to detail. *White Fang* (1905) and *The*

*Call of the Wild* (1903) both have wolf heroes. *White Fang* describes a Canadian wolf's life in a way which readers can appreciate but not feel is a parallel with their own lives. Margaret Blount, who calls *White Fang* 'to me the most outstanding dog book of all' has said of its power:

> what gives the book a different sort of drama, changing it from a brilliant animal story into a psychological study of great power, almost a case history, is the meticulous detailing of the way in which circumstances mould character – in this instance turning a natural young animal into an outcast and an enemy of every creature that walked, ran, or flew. White Fang, like a human child, has parents, ancestry, cubhood and youth; forces work on him inevitably to alienate him from his own kind and turn him into the ferocious killer that he later becomes. He is only redeemed by the sharp intelligence that enables him to survive, which is, at the end, recognised by Weedon Scott, the human who loves and tames him.
>
> Blount 1974: 254–255

Other stories in this vein have shown animals in real life situations. Henry Williamson's *Tarka the Otter* (1927), although not written for children, was soon adopted by them while Sheila Burnford's *The Incredible Journey* (1960) shows two dogs and a cat travelling four hundred miles to reach their Canadian home.

Indeed, the USA and Canada seem to be have been pre-eminent in producing this type of animal story in the years between the two world wars, having been led by the Canadian founder of the Woodcraft Movement, Ernest Thompson Seton, author of *Wild Animals I have Known* (1900). Marjorie Kinnan Rawlings's *The Yearling* (1938) and Mary O'Hara's *My Friend Flicka* (1941) used the affection felt by children towards these animals to show the difficulty of their family relationships. Dhan Gopal Mukerji, an Indian writer who lived in the USA, produced a number of realistic animal stories of which, *Gay-Neck, the story of a Pigeon* (1927), won the Newbery Medal. One of the most famous animal books of this period is now mainly known through its adaptation as a film by Walt Disney, Felix Salten's *Bambi* (1928). In this story of the life and death of a deer, the animals in the forest live realistic lives but talk to each other with the morality of a respectable society. However, the author does capture the brevity and tensions of animal life.

While this type of writing was produced in Britain, as exemplified by Sir John Fortescue's *The Story of a Red-Deer* (1897), more often the animals became anthropomorphised. One important example is Alison Uttley's series of books about Little Grey Rabbit, which began with *The Squirrel, the Hare and the Little Grey Rabbit* (1929) and concluded more than thirty books later with *Hare and the Rainbow* (1975), published a year before the writer's death. Uttley always jealously asserted that her contribution was more important than that of the books' first artist, Margaret Tempest, but it is the illustrations which are the most distinctive aspect of the books. Little Grey Rabbit is shown in a neat dress, keeping house most successfully for boastful Hare and vain Squirrel, all three living in cosy domesticity. However, Alison Uttley also manages to squeeze in a few pointers about country lore, as she does in her other series of animal books, the Sam Pig stories. She strongly denied that she had tried to humanise animals:

Animals are mysteries, a race apart ... They are too noble to be humanised in story and fable, they are too great for our small civilisations, and yet only by a humanisation shall we know them and learn to love them.

To humanise is to attempt to bring animals and nature itself into our lives, a way known to ancient man, who felt that the rocks and earth were alive and full of power and living substance ...

Far from the machine age, the animals are older and wiser than we in the best sense of the word, inhabitants of earth alongside humanity, struggling to survive, yet waging no wars, and using no poisons, as they struggle on through life to silent death.

Uttley 1970: 116–117

Nevertheless, her books did open the way for other, more popular, writers to adopt a similar style of anthropomorphism. This can be seen in the animal stories of Enid Blyton (whose popularity Uttley resented) and, more recently, in the highly commercialised work of Jill Barklem's Brambly Hedge series.

In the years between the First and Second World Wars, picture books were also using animals as main characters. Jean de Brunhoff's *The Story of Babar, the Little Elephant* (1934) made a huge impact in both Britain and North America. A. A. Milne wrote the preface to the English edition of the book which used a hand-written text and a large format to tell its story of Babar's escape from the forest after his mother is killed. He is adopted by a rich old lady and becomes the toast of the town but the call of the wild becomes too strong for him and he returns to the forest where he and his wife Celeste are crowned King and Queen of the Elephants. A number of sequels followed, written first by de Brunoff and after his death by his son, Laurent, but the originality of both the format and the animal characters disintegrated. In time the figure of Babar has become a marketable product, probably known more through the cartoon versions and his appearance on calendars and diaries than through the original books.

Another stunning picture book which appeared in the 1930s was Kathleen Hale's *Orlando the Marmalade Cat* (1938) which achieved many of its visual effects through the use of lithography. The book and its sequels achieved other effects through the witty use of puns and through its sense of domesticity which does not deny the feline characters their breed's special qualities. Margaret Blount has said:

The Orlando books are holidays from life as it is, giving another species a chance of being dominant without suggesting that they are out to manipulate humans by being more human than they. The cats are always catlike, never really humanised, however much they enjoy civilised living. Dining out, they sit on their chairs as cats do, not as those cat-headed people in *The Poll Parrot Picture Book* who all have their feet in shoes, on the floor. Orlando, kissing Grace, gives her an eye-closing lick and greets her with the 'half-purr, half-mew' that cats use to each other but very rarely to humans; and although Grace has her apron, fur coat, mouse tippet and cornflower hat, Orlando wears, and needs to wear, nothing.

Blount 1974: 273–274

Lengthier fantasies were also being written about animals. Hugh Lofting began to tell stories about his famous characters to his own children; *The Story of Doctor Dolittle* was first published in America in 1920 and was soon followed by *The Voyages of Doctor Dolittle* (1922), a story more obviously geared to children and which was a Newbery Medal winner. Dolittle lives in the English village of Puddleby-on-the-Marsh and learns to attend to sick animals by speaking to them in their own language which is taught to him by Polynesia, his parrot. The charm and simplicity of the books, coupled with their almost naïve drawings, soon made them highly popular and they continued to be published after Lofting's death. Again, the story is often known more through versions in other media as is Dodie Smith's *The Hundred and One Dalmatians* (1956), remembered by many through its Disney version (*One Hundred and One Dalmatians* (1961)).

One American writer, E. B. White, the humorist famed for his contributions to the *New Yorker*, created two fascinating books in which animals play a prominent role (and one featuring birds, *The Trumpet of the Swan* (1970)). In *Stuart Little* (1945) the hero is a mouse who is born to a human family. The sad, often tragic, story tells of his adventures and love for a bird, as he is able to fit into neither human nor animal world. As Margery Fisher notes:

> E. B. White has faced the implications of his fantasy head on ... The story that begins as a cheerful if edgy fantasy darkens until it becomes distressingly poignant. Stuart ... can never belong either in the human or the animal world. It is not easy to read the book without a feeling of distaste at the idea of a mouse being born to a human mother. If this is to be overcome, it can only be by recognising the sober meaning under the riddling humour of the book.
>
> Fisher 1975: 334

In *Charlotte's Web* (1952), White does not shirk the realities of animal life. 'Where's papa going with that axe?' is the first line of the book and Fern's papa is about to finish off Wilbur, the runt of a pig litter on their farm. Fern manages to save Wilbur's life and with the guidance of Charlotte, the spider who lives with him, he even manages to win a prize at the fair. Wilbur is afraid of dying, but Charlotte's death reinforces the cycle which is a vitally important part of animal existence. (Animals are also used in picture books which try to help children through the trauma of death, such as Susan Varley's *Badger's Parting Gifts* (1984) and two books dealing with the death of pets, Judith Viorst's *The Tenth Good Thing about Barney* (1971) and Hans Wilhelm's *I'll Always Love You* (1985).)

A writer whose work can be compared with White's in its attitude to realistic depictions of animal life is Dick King-Smith, an ex-farmer. His books are rare in that they are enjoyed by children and praised by adults. He is a prolific writer whose early work probably best represents an unsentimental approach to animals. His creatures communicate with each other with words but otherwise are animals, living short and often bloody lives. King-Smith himself says

> You've got to be careful you don't cross the invisible dividing line and make the animal do things it couldn't possibly do – for instance, the idea of animals dressed up in human clothes, the Rupert Bear concept, that's absolutely

anathema to me because that's whimsy. But if somehow you can steer a way between leaving the animal as an animal and still make it recognisably human, that seems to me to be the trick.

Powling 1987: 13

King-Smith achieves this in a large number of his books, notably *The Sheep-Pig* (1980), which won the *Guardian* award, in which a pig becomes a champion sheep herder, *Magnus Powermouse* (1982) where a baby mouse emerges as large as a rat through the use of growth pills and *The Hodgeheg* (1987), a miniature masterpiece about a hedgehog who talks backwards after being hit by a lorry.

King-Smith's work is one of the success stories of recent years, as is that of Colin Dann whose *The Animals of Farthing Wood* (1981) spawned a number of sequels and has more recently achieved worldwide fame through a cartoon version. Another well known animal hero who also appears in other formats is Michael Bond's Paddington Bear who first appeared in *A Bear Called Paddington* (1958) which uses irony to show an innocent let loose in a world he takes at face value.

However, the most successful single post-war animal story is probably Richard Adams's *Watership Down* (1972). This book's publishing history is now legendary. Rejected by practically every major publisher, it was finally published by the small British publishing house of Rex Collings. It became a worldwide success, won both the *Guardian* award and the Carnegie Medal and is one of those rare books read by both children and adults. Adams devised the story on long car journeys with his children and acknowledges his debt to the animal stories of Ernest Thompson Seton. Its intricate depiction of a rabbit community and the characterisation of its (mainly male) protagonists have enough contact with realism to make the book seem entirely credible.

One set of animal stories which have their roots in realism but often seem to belong to a bygone age are pony stories. These began in 1929 with *Moorland Mousie*, became established as a genre during the 1930s (Joanna Cannan's *A Pony for Jean* (1936) and Enid Bagnold's *National Velvet* (1930) are notable examples) and have continued to be popular on both sides of the Atlantic. The Whitehead (1977) survey of children's reading discovered the reading of this genre was extensive among 10- to 12-year-olds but dropped at 14+. Authors of this type of book include the Pullein-Thompson sisters, Monica Edwards, Ruby Ferguson and, of a different type, K. M. Peyton. Mary Cadogan and Patricia Craig have characterised the main features of these stories as follows:

> The stock type of pony story features a central character who longs for a pony but can't afford one; usually she is connected with a group of superior girls – relatives or school-fellows – who do have ponies but are not 'natural' riders like the deprived heroine. She, however, by luck, pluck, or sheer determination, gets hold of a horse, a seemingly inferior animal which turns out to be a champion.

Cadogan and Craig 1976: 353

Nevertheless, the most constant encounters with animals in modern children's literature is through the picture book. Almost invariably these animals are used in an anthropomorphic way to mirror children's own behaviour. William Steig, author of *Dominic* (1977) and *Abel's Island* (1976) has said why he uses this technique:

> I think using animals emphasises the fact that the story is symbolic – about human behaviour. And kids get the idea right away that this is not just a story, but that it's saying something about life on earth ... When you write about a dog, you're really writing about a child, because a dog's mature when it's only a year old.

Cott 1984: 104

Many writers throughout the world continue to do this. Steven Kellogg, Leo Lionni, Max Velthuijs and Pamela Allen are only a few of the most respected of such writers. A large number use the same characters through a number of picture books: Gene Zion's Harry, Mary Rayner's Pig family, Gabrielle Vincent's Ernest and Celestine, Arnold Lobel's Frog and Toad, Lynley Dodd's Hairy Maclairy and Graham Oakley's church mice. A significant proportion use animals to show children their behaviour in a different shape. Russell Hoban's books about Frances are domestic mini-dramas while Rosemary Wells's books about sibling rivalry such as *Noisy Nora* (1976) and *Stanley and Rhoda* (1978) have often been used by adults to help children examine their own feelings. Nor are more sophisticated techniques ignored: Anthony Browne in his award-winning books, *Gorilla* (1983) and *Zoo* (1992), and in *King Kong* (1994) uses his formidable technique to explore animal/human connections, while the Australian artist Graeme Base adopts that most traditional of animal genres, the alphabet book, to stunning effect in *Animalia* (1987). However, the classic animal picture book of the post-war years is almost certainly Pat Hutchins's *Rosie's Walk* (1968), a seemingly straightforward depiction of a hen going for a walk around a farmyard, pursued by a fox, which continues to intrigue and entrance each new generation of readers.

The animal story seems to relate to children, and to adults, cross-culturally; and it seems to adapt to cultural preoccupations, for example, contemporary books with an ecological theme. Whatever the other interests of future generations. it is highly unlikely the animal story will ever die.

## References

Avery, G. (1965) *Nineteenth Century Children: Heroes and Heroines in English Children's Stories 1780–1900*, London: Hodder and Stoughton.

—— (1975) *Childhood's Pattern: A Study of the Heroes and Heroines of Children's fiction 1770–1950*, London: Hodder and Stoughton.

Blount, M. (1974) *Animal Land: The Creatures of Children's Fiction*, London: Hutchinson.

Cadogan, M. and Craig, P. (1976) *You're a Brick, Angela! A New Look at Girls' Fiction from 1839–1975*, London: Gollancz.

Carpenter, H. (1985) *Secret Gardens: A Study of the Golden Age of Children's Literature*, London: George Allen and Unwin.

Cott, J. (1984) *Pipers at the Gates of Dawn: The Wisdom of Children's Literature*, Harmondsworth: Viking.

Darton, F. J. H. (1992/1982) *Children's Books in England: Five Centuries of Social Life*, 3rd edn, rev. B. Alderson, Cambridge: Cambridge University Press.

de Mause, L. (1976) *The History of Childhood*, London: Souvenir Press.

Fisher, M. (1975) *Who's Who in Children's Books*, London: Weidenfeld and Nicolson.

Lester, J. (1987) *The Tales of Uncle Remus*, London: Bodley Head.

Lurie, A. (1990) *Don't Tell the Grown-Ups: Subversive Children's Literature*, London: Bloomsbury.

Meek, M. (1991) 'The limits of delight', *Books for Keeps* 68: 24–25.

Powling, C. (1987) 'Dick King-Smith', *Books for Keeps* 45: 12–13.

Prince, A. (1994) *Kenneth Grahame: An Innocent in the Wild Wood*, London: Allison and Busby.

Robson, W. W. (1987) Introduction, in Kipling, R., *The Jungle Book*, Oxford: Oxford University Press.

Tucker, N. (1981) *The Child and the Book: A Psychological and Literary Exploration*, Cambridge: Cambridge University Press.

Uttley, A. (1970) *The Ten O'Clock Scholar and Other Essays*, London: Faber.

Whitehead, F. *et al.* (1977) *Children and Their Books*, London: Macmillan.

## Further Reading

Barker, K. (1991) *Dick King-Smith*, Swindon: School Library Association.

Goldthwaite, J. (1987) 'Sis Beatrix', *Signal* 53: 117–137; 54: 161–177.

Hunt, P. (1994) *The Wind in the Willows: A Fragmented Arcadia*, New York: Twayne.

Paul, L. (1988) 'Dumb bunnies: a re-visionist re-reading of *Watership Down*', *Signal* 56: 113–122.

Taylor, J. (1986) *Beatrix Potter: Artist, Storyteller and Countrywoman*, Harmondsworth: Warne.

Thwaite, M. F. (1963) *From Primer to Pleasure*, London: The Library Association.

# 23

# Real Gardens with Imaginary Toads: Domestic Fantasy

## *Louisa Smith*

Children's literature of the fantastic suggests either high drama – battles between the powers of lightness and darkness – or stuffed animals capering about a nursery world after hours. Generally the chief human actors in these fantasies are children imbued with the key attribute of being parent free; parents, after all, would get in the way by providing cautions which would inhibit the child characters from stepping through wardrobes or time travelling, or worse, chuckling indulgently when children mention that their stuffed animals talk. Introducing fantasy into children's real worlds, making the unbelievable believable while the central characters are surrounded by everyday settings and activities, takes a skilled author. An intact family unit almost defeats the concept of fantasy, but it commonly points out the fundamental conflict between fantastic and rational views of the world, or between (stereotypically) the child's view and the adult's.

Domestic settings have been traditional in fairy tales, where 'magic' operates in everyday life to right a wrong. Parents – or, frequently, step-parents – in such tales can be the cause of the problem, even if the setting is some remote kingdom in some remote time. However, when a book is set in an actual place, and in an actual time, with a real family, then the suspension of disbelief is harder to achieve. Considerations such as how observant (or sympathetic) are the parents, how siblings react, how the magic is introduced, and what results are allowed in the real world when the fantasy departs enter the picture. When the fantasy occurs largely or completely in a 'secondary' world, such as C. S. Lewis's Narnia, or L. Frank Baum's Oz, or A. A. Milne's Hundred Acre Wood where links with normality are relatively insignificant or irrelevant, or make their point peripherally, the author has the luxury of creating a world complete with its own rules, borrowing only that reality necessary to relate the action to children. Fantasy set more solidly in 'reality' has to be more circumspect; it may be given an ambiguous status, as in Mary Norton's Borrowers sequence (from 1952) with its complex frame of hearsay evidence; or it may simply be discounted as a dream, as in John Masefield's *The Box of Delights* (1935), or it may take on a mystical status as in Lucy Boston's *The Children of Green Knowe* (1954).

The fantastic mode in domestic life can be employed to solve real problems imaginatively or to provide an escape (as in William Mayne's *A Game of Dark* (1971)), or to confront child protagonists with situations which require brave and intelligent responses. Rather than being a means of imaginative liberation for the child, it can be, and frequently is, the vehicle for moral teaching, made all the more relevant by fantasy's proximity to reality.

There are two very broad categories of domestic fantasy: first, where parents provide and/or accept the magic, and second, where children discover a magic being or thing which has the power to change their lives, but which parents fail to notice.

Under the first category, five books each with a different approach to fantasy will be discussed, to stand for hundreds of others of the same type: *A Bear Called Paddington* (1958) by Michael Bond, *Mary Poppins* (1934) by P. L. Travers, *The Ogre Downstairs* (1974) by Diana Wynne Jones, *Vice Versa* (1893) by F. Anstey, and *Freaky Friday* (1972) by Mary Rodgers.

The parents who are the most aware and accepting of the fantastic being are Mr and Mrs Brown in *A Bear Called Paddington*. Almost immediately upon the discovery of a small talking bear on the Paddington station platform in London, they agree to take him home to live with them. Neither seem to question the reality of a talking bear from Peru; they accept their daughter Judy's plea (and indeed Paddington's Aunt Lucy's request) that they look after him. As Mrs Brown says, 'We shall expect you to be one of the family, shan't we, Henry?' (Bond 1958: 12). He moves in, shares the Brown family activities, provides amusement by his good intentions, his improbable command of English and his habit of staring people down, and is introduced to British life, places, and characters. As Margery Fisher suggests:

> the central absurdity works simply because it is taken completely for granted. Though Paddington remains an animal in appearance and movement, he is more like another child in the family, whose peccadilloes are excused because he is different. Incongruity is the moving force of the stories.
>
> Fisher 1975: 269

The premise, according to Paddington, that 'things are always happening to me. I'm that sort of bear' (Bond, 1958 et seq.) has sustained the fantasy through more than fifty books.

Humour is important too, as is the case with Mary Poppins. Left abruptly without a nanny for their four children, Mr and Mrs Banks engage Mary Poppins who arrives without references because, as she observes imperiously, it isn't fashionable to give them. In quick succession, Jane and Michael observe her flying in on the wind, sliding up the banister, pulling items out of an empty carpetbag and ladling different tasting medicines out of the same bottle. In contrast, the adults appreciate her orderliness and her matter-of-fact managing of the nursery.

On their first outing with her, Michael and Jane visit Mary Poppins's Uncle Wigg and find him bobbing around on the ceiling, buoyed up by his own good humour. On the bus ride home, Michael and Jane try to talk about the experience. Mary Poppins responds, 'What, roll and bob? How dare you. I'll have you know that my uncle is a sober, honest, hardworking man, and you'll be kind enough to speak of him respectfully. and don't bite your bus ticket! Roll and bob, indeed – the idea' (Travers 1945: 46). This establishes the pattern of subsequent outings – something out of the ordinary happens and Mary Poppins denies it, and takes offence at the suggestion that it did. The parent Banks are kept in the dark; when Jane tries to tell her mother about shopping with the Pleiads, for example, Mrs Banks replies: 'we imagine strange and lovely things, my darling' (193). The parents employ Mary Poppins and in the sequels continue to welcome her back, even though Mrs Banks declares at the end of the first book that 'I certainly shan't have her back if she does want to come' (203).

The appeal of the books, beyond the humorous situations, may also lie in what Patricia Demers identifies as Michael and Jane's attachment to Mary Poppins.

> The bond between her and the children is cemented as much by her brusqueness as by her firm yet sympathetic adult presence. Neither bored with her charges, nor infantilized by their demands, Mary Poppins is clearly at home in the nursery, and entirely capable of dealing with their curious questions.
>
> Demers 1991: 86

Certainly the fantasy, often unexpected, enlivens their lives, but it is coupled with the assurance that they will return home, that Mary Poppins will remain unchanged, every hair in place, vain, curt and reliable. The only threat is her possible departure which is softened when it occurs by her promise of a return.

Although both books are clearly comedies, the incongruence between the fantasy and the 'reality' is emphasised in both *A Bear Called Paddington* and *Mary Poppins* by the setting – a real London. In Diana Wynne Jones's *The Ogre Downstairs*, the setting of a rural market town has a similar effect, and there is further displacement because the book reads like a realistic 'problem' novel and the fantasy merges into realistic problem solving.

This book features a combined family, three children of the mother and two sons of the father. The step-father is referred to as 'the Ogre' by the mother's three children. The joining of the two families has not gone smoothly; daily battles and small indignations occur. The mother's children are sloppy, the father's neat. The father is reduced to bellowing for silence; he frequently retreats to his study. The mother has headaches. In an attempt to pacify the children, the father gives two chemistry sets, one each to the younger boys.

The first accident with the chemicals results in flight, the second reduces the size of one of the father's children; this is followed by a transformation of one boy into the other: each literally learns what it is like to be in each other's shoes; then one child becomes invisible, and inanimate objects come alive. Finally, the mother departs in desperation, and the children are left to explain the chemistry sets to the ogre. At this point, Wynne Jones ingeniously links fantasy and reality, for miraculously, he believes them, and together they set about to right their living conditions. The children learn to like each other, to understand the father, and he them; the mother returns, and the last use of the chemistry set turns certain household objects into gold which sell for huge amounts of money at auction allowing the family 'to move into a larger house almost at once, where, they all admitted, they were much happier. Everyone had a room to himself' [*sic*] (Jones 1975: 191).

The technique of transformation is also used in *Vice Versa* and *Freaky Friday* to accomplish similar ends as in *The Ogre Downstairs*, an understanding of what it is like to be someone else – focusing particularly on the adult–child divide. In *Vice Versa*, the emphasis is on the father learning how awful it is to be a child attending a public (that is, in Britain, a private boarding) school; in *Freaky Friday*, the mother actuates the transformation so that the daughter can understand how difficult she is making her mother's life.

*Vice Versa* is subtitled 'a lesson to fathers'. The father, Paul Bultitude, is pompous and overbearing. He finds his son a trial and can hardly wait for him to return to his school appropriately called, Grimstone. On their parting interview, Dick, the son requests some extra pocket-money which the father denies. Then Dick asks if he can keep the Garuda stone his uncle had given his now dead mother. Again the father refuses. Finally Dick asks if he could leave school after this term and the father, still holding the stone, refuses pontificating that 'I only wish, at this very moment, I could be a boy again, like you. Going back to school wouldn't make me unhappy, I can tell you' (Anstey 1893: 22). He gets the wish. What changes is his body, however, not his mind, and so he thinks of himself as the father, certain that he can convince adults who he really is. Dick meanwhile uses the stone to change his mind into his father's body. Paul (as Dick) is hauled off to school where he is roundly mistreated by the staff and other boys, and learns what it is like not to have money. Meanwhile, Dick thoroughly enjoys himself, treats his younger brother and sister to pantomimes, and plays with them. When the transformation is reversed after a week, the father has a whole new view on Dick's education and reflects that 'his experiences, unpleasant as they had been, had had their advantages: they had drawn him and his family closer together' (366).

While Dick learns that being an adult with money is desirable, the opposite occurs in *Freaky Friday*. Annabel Andrews thinks it is hard being 13 but after a day in her mother's body, is happy to remain herself. Only at the end of the book, does the reader learn that the mother was, in some unexplained way, responsible for the change. While the book focuses on the daughter struggling to cope with her mother's appointments and chores, the mother has gone out and had her hair cut and bought new clothes, and had the braces taken off her teeth. Much of the humour in this book is based on what Annabel doesn't know; just as in *Vice Versa* Paul, the father, has problems with school friends and school codes and classroom material.

It has probably not escaped the reader's attention that only one of the books mentioned was written by an American. In general terms, British fantasy, both domestic and 'high' tends to be rooted in places: literature is often attached to a real or realistic place. As Peter Hunt has pointed out:

> not only do the complex layers of history embedded (as it were) in the landscape enrich the texture of stories, but the meanings of the landscapes themselves provide a subtext for the journeys: places mean. The American tradition of fantasy journey seems to be – at least to an Englishman like myself – one reaching outwards and westwards; it is a linear matter. Because there is little to dig down into, American fantasy tends to be set in secondary worlds ... The English, in contrast, are re-treading ancestral ground. Their reference points are more concrete, deep-rooted cultural symbols which seem to lie, sometimes literally, underfoot.
>
> Hunt 1987: 11

Thus American fantasy writers set their work in different countries, as for example, Nancy Bond's *A String in the Harp* (1984) is set in Wales, or reference it to a different time/place such as Eleanor Cameron's *The Court of the Stone Children* (1973).

Perhaps the most notable exception is E. B. White's *Charlotte's Web*, which provides an interesting shift of perspective, and which suggests that fantasy is the province of the younger child. While Wilbur the pig lives with the Arabels, as a family member, he does nothing out of pig-ordinariness. Once in the barn, surrounded by animals and observed by Fern, he communicates in understandable English along with the rest of the animals. The only human to comprehend this communication is Fern and when she tries to explain to her mother, her mother seeks advice from the family doctor who soothes Mrs Arabel by suggesting that Fern will grow out of it. By the end of the book, this process is already taking place as Fern shifts her interest to a boy, Henry Fussy; the adults, as far as they know, are scarcely touched.

Some major classic writers fall within my second category of domestic fantasy, in which the children are responsible for discovering the magic being or thing – a good number of which are dug out from the past.

For example, the children in E. Nesbit's *Five Children and It* unearth the Psammead in a sand pit in a realistically described Kent where the children are spending the summer. A survivor from the neolithic age, the Psammead is described as 'old, old, old, and its birthday was almost at the very beginning of everything' (Nesbit 1902: 11). The Psammead has the magical ability to grant a wish a day; each chapter presents another wish gone wrong. The children wish to be beautiful and no one recognises them, they ask for money and get non-negotiable gold coins. When they finally request their mother's return, they get it right and vow never to wish for anything again. They retain the knowledge of the adventures and are, it is assumed, wiser about what is essential to happiness.

The fantasy is kept well in its place; magic effects wear off at sunset, and both parents are absent; when they return at the end of the book, truthful Jane tries to explain: ' "We found a Fairy," said Jane obediently. "No nonsense, please," said her mother sharply.' (288). As in *The Phoenix and the Carpet* (1904) and *The Story of the Amulet* (1906), the children know better than the adults.

Roger Lancelyn Green has cited the influence on Nesbit of F. Anstey's *The Brass Bottle* and *Vice Versa*, and of Mrs Molesworth's novels, especially *The Cuckoo Clock*. Published in 1887, *The Cuckoo Clock* is characteristic of the way in which domestic fantasy developed. It features a magic cuckoo crafted by Griselda's great-grandfather which introduces her to various adventures. As Rosenthal has observed:

> Far from separating her from reality, Griselda's forays into the world of fantasy have a direct and immediate impact on her daily life; her two worlds begin to interlock as in 'real' life she begins to obey her aunts' instructions and do her lessons despite her distaste for 'musting.'
>
> Rosenthal 1986: 190

The Psammead and the Phoenix and the Cuckoo are all argumentative 'adult' characters who generally have a good moral, or moralising, effect on the children.

By contrast, Puck, called forth by accident by Una and Dan on Midsummer Eve in Kipling's *Puck of Pook's Hill* (1906) is intended to educate more subtly. The setting, around Kipling's own house, Bateman's in Sussex, England provides a lovingly recreated backdrop for the author's attempt to demonstrate that history could be as exciting as a fairy tale. Puck brings to the children characters from Britain's past and their presence is deftly hidden from the adults who carry on their lives around them.

Both William Mayne and Penelope Lively select a character from a particular time; Mayne's *Earthfasts* (1967) presents a Napoleonic drummer boy and Lively's *Ghost of Thomas Kempe* (1975), a seventeenth-century alchemist. Both of these characters, out of their familiar time of reference, continue to operate as though they were in their respective centuries. Each interacts with a present day boy and, conventionally, for some time, no adult will believe the young people; in the case of *The Ghost of Thomas Kempe*, this disbelief provides the humour. Kempe never materialises, unlike Nellie Jack John, the drummer boy, who, unable to return to his own time is accepted by the local people (once he has been washed, and his skin conditions have been treated). Mayne's bold acceptance of the supernatural into the real world (the book also contains a house-spirit, the Boggart) is an important variation on the normally confrontational nature of domestic fantasy.

Linking past with present has also been achieved ingeniously in the USA. Nina, in Eleanor Cameron's *The Court of the Stone Children* (1973) also meets the physical presence of a child from the past, Domique, who has been transported to a San Francisco museum which has reconstructed the period rooms of her chateau. Displacement is more common, as with Nancy Bond's *A String in the Harp* (1984). An American family mourning the unexpected death of the mother, moves to Aberystwyth in west Wales, and the father buries himself in his work. His three children adjust to living in a foreign country with varying degrees of success; Peter, who is most unhappy, discovers a harp key which starts to show him life from the Arthurian period.

> He had thought he'd be safe with other people around – it had always come when he was alone before – but he was helpless to stop it … The study vanished. In its place, Peter saw the country called the Low Hundred lying flat under the hammering rain … The Key sang a wild and ominous song that wove through the gale inexorably, showing Peter a series of painfully vivid images.
>
> Bond 1984: 66

Bond uses the intrusion of the supernatural into everyday life as both threat and challenge, as Susan Cooper (using similar materials) did in her 'The Dark is Rising' sequence (from *Over Sea, Under Stone* (1965)). Here, Peter's sisters first notice that he is drifting off, going blank; eventually, they can see some of what Peter is seeing, and the links to the Welsh epic *The Mabinogion* and specifically to Taliesin, whose harp key Peter has found, are made explicit.

Once again, the fantasy has a direct effect on reality. By the end of the book, Peter is not reluctant to spend another year in Wales even it it means 'another year of rain and freezing cold houses and a language that's got no vowels and a bunch of kids who don't know how to play football' (Bond 1984: 256). Because the children have had to confide in their father and because he has taken time to re-examine his children, the newly configured family is on stronger footing. As C. W. Sullivan suggests, 'without the traditional Welsh materials, *A String in the Harp* would be just another adolescent problem novel; the traditional materials make it a novel about understanding on many levels, levels which would not be present without those traditional materials.' (Sullivan 1986: 37)

Possibly the most subtle and complex use of mythological elements in a modern setting has been by Alan Garner, who had used the device of an intrusive other world in *The Weirdstone of Brisingamen* (1960), *The Moon of Gomrath* (1963), and *Elidor* (1965), before writing *The Owl Service* (1967). Based on Welsh mythology and also set in modern Wales, in Llanymawddwy, a valley near Aberystwyth, this book would also fit Sullivan's description of just another adolescent problem novel without the fantasy.

Alison, Gwyn and Roger brought together by circumstance are fated to live out the triangle myth of Lleu Llaw Gyffes in the Fourth Branch of *The Mabinogion*. As Neil Philip states in *A Fine Anger*: 'As often in Garner's writing, children must learn to cope with their parents' failure to confront their problems' (Philip 1981: 67). Philip sees Garner's use of the myth as a symbolic alternative to the weighty pages of psychological analysis which would be necessary to straighten out the complex relationships among children and adults in the book. As Garner has said:

> A prime material of art is paradox, in that paradox links two valid yet mutually exclusive systems that we need if we are to comprehend reality: paradox links intuitive and analytical thought. Paradox, the integration of the nonrational and logic, engages both emotion and intellect ... and, for me, literature is justified only so long as it keeps a sense of paradox central to its form.
>
> Garner 1983: 5

Reality needs a touch of the fantastic.

Throughout the domestic fantasy books which deal with the older child, choices are made, and one of the most difficult confronts Winnie Foster at the age of eleven in a book by an American author with an American setting, *Tuck Everlasting* (1975) by Natalie Babbitt: she has the choice of living forever in the company of an enchanting young man, or of remaining ordinary. The story is set in 1880 in New England; the Tuck family drank from a spring, which Winnie has also discovered, eighty-seven years before and have not aged a day since. They kidnap Winnie to stop her from drinking or telling anyone, and then set about to convince her about the importance and necessity of death. Winnie makes her decision: when she returns home with a bottle of water from the spring, instead of drinking it and gaining eternal life, she pours it on a toad. When the Tucks return eighty years later, they find Winnie's gravemarker and the toad – which continues to live after being run over by a car.

In domestic fantasy, then, some of the books, such as *Earthfasts* and the Paddington series retain the magic, in others the magic is undone, sometimes remembered, as in Mary Poppins, sometimes forgotten, as in *Puck of Pook's Hill*. But it remains as a possibility in everyday life, a chance of escape, a method of coping with or transforming the everyday world. In domestic fantasy, both the tensions and the possibilities of children's fiction, the benefits of imaginary toads, are at their most potent.

# References

Anstey, F. (1893) *Vice Versa: A Lesson to Fathers*, London: Smith, Elder.
Bond, M. (1958) *A Bear Called Paddington*, London: Collins.
Bond, N. (1984) *A String in the Harp*, New York: Athenaeum.
Demers, P. (1991) *P. L. Travers*, Boston: Twayne.
Fisher, M. (1975) *Who's Who in Children's Books*, New York: Holt, Rinehart and Winston.
Garner, A. (1983) 'Achilles in Altjira', *Children's Literature Association Quarterly* 8, 4: 5–9.
Green, R. L. (1979) 'Introduction' in Nesbit, E. (ed.) *Five Children and It*, Harmondsworth: Penguin.
Hunt, P. (1987) 'Landscapes and journeys, metaphors and maps: the distinctive features of English fantasy', *Children's Literature Association Quarterly* 12, 1: 11–14.
Jones, D. W. (1975) *The Ogre Downstairs*, New York: E. P. Dutton.
Nesbit, E. (1902/1979) *Five Children and It*, London: T. Fisher Unwin/Harmondsworth: Puffin/Penguin.
Philip, N. (1981) *A Fine Anger*, London: Collins.
Rosenthal, L. (1986) 'Writing her own story: the integration of the self in the fourth dimension of Mrs Molesworth's *The Cuckoo Clock*', *Children's Literature Association Quarterly* 10, 4: 187–191.
Sullivan, C. W. (1986) 'Nancy Bond and Welsh traditions', *Children's Literature Association Quarterly* 11, 1: 33–36.
Travers, P. L. (1934/1945) *Mary Poppins*, New York: Reynal and Hitchcock.

# Further Reading

Atterbury, B. (1980) *The Fantasy Tradition in American Literature: From Irving to Le Guin*, Bloomington: Indiana University Press.
Dusinberre, J. (1987) *Alice to the Lighthouse*, New York: St Martin's Press.
Hunt, P. (1992) 'Winnie-the-Pooh and domestic fantasy', in Butts, D. (ed.) *Stories and Society, Children's Literature in its Social Context*, London: Macmillan.
Kuznets, L. (1994) *When Toys Come Alive*, New Haven: Yale University Press.
Lochhead, M. (1977) *The Renaissance of Wonder in Children's Literature*, Edinburgh: Canongate.

# 24

# High Fantasy

## *C. W. Sullivan III*

The literary or compound term 'high fantasy' is enormously evocative, and like most evocative terms, it is pluralistic in meaning and, therefore, difficult to pin down with a neat or precise definition. 'High' can refer to style, subject matter, theme, or tone. It can also refer to the characters themselves – their elite or elevated social status or the moral or ethical philosophies which they espouse or exemplify. It can even refer to the affective level of the story itself. 'Fantasy', as a literary term, refers to narrative possibilities limited, at least initially, only by the author's own imagination and skill as a story-teller. When combined, high fantasy identifies a literary genre which includes some of the most universally praised books for young readers.

Fantasy, or the fantastic element in literature, has been most usefully defined by Kathryn Hume. In her book, *Fantasy and Mimesis: Responses to Reality in Western Literature,* Hume argues that any work of literature can be placed somewhere on a continuum one end of which is mimesis and the other fantasy. All literature, Hume suggests

> is the product of two impulses. These are *mimesis,* felt as the desire to imitate, to describe events, people, and objects with such verisimilitude that others can share your experience; and *fantasy,* the desire to change givens and alter reality – out of boredom, play, vision, longing for something lacking, or need for metaphoric images that will bypass the audience's verbal defences.
>
> Hume 1984: 20

Fantasy itself, she continues, '*is any departure from consensus reality*' (21, italics in original). The relative proportions of the two elements – mimesis and fantasy – in a specific work will determine that work's place on the continuum.

The departure from consensus reality, or the inclusion of what most critics have referred to as the 'impossible', in high fantasy places books in that sub-genre quite close to the fantasy end of Hume's continuum, because high fantasy contains a great deal of material which is not a part of contemporary consensus reality. Unlike science fiction, however, which departs from contemporary consensus reality by extrapolating that reality into the near or far future where it has been significantly changed by discovery, invention, and development, high fantasy departs from contemporary consensus reality by creating a separate world in which the action takes place. In *Critical Terms for Science Fiction and Fantasy: A Glossary and Guide to Scholarship,* Gary K. Wolfe defines high fantasy as that fantasy 'set in a secondary world ... as opposed to Low Fantasy which contains supernatural intrusions into the "real" world' (1986: 52).

J. R. R. Tolkien was one the first critics to articulate the importance of the secondary world; in 'On fairy-stories' (1947), he delineated the concept and stressed the importance of its cohesiveness.

> What really happens is that the story-maker proves a successful 'sub-creator.' He makes a Secondary World which your mind can enter. Inside it, what he relates is 'true': it accords with the laws of that world. You therefore believe it, while you are, as it were, inside. The moment disbelief arises, the spell is broken; the magic, or rather art, has failed. You are then out in the Primary World again, looking at the little abortive Secondary World from outside.
>
> Tolkien 1966b: 37

Tolkien realised the importance of the reality and cohesiveness of the secondary world not from writing *The Hobbit*, which is, along with *The Lord of the Rings*, certainly an excellent example of the secondary world taken seriously, but from his study of ancient epic, especially *Beowulf*.

In '*Beowulf:* The Monsters and the Critics' (1936), published a year before *The Hobbit*, Tolkien defended the reality of the monsters against those who would see them only as symbolic or metaphoric constructs. The *Beowulf* poet, Tolkien argues, 'esteemed dragons ... as a poet, not as a sober geologist' (1966a: 11). 'A dragon is no idle fancy', he continues (15), and 'the monsters are not an inexplicable blunder of taste; they are essential, fundamentally allied to the underlying ideas of the poem, which give it its lofty tone and high seriousness' (19). Tolkien the academic scholar knew that before *Beowulf* could be taken seriously as a poem the monsters had to be taken seriously as monsters, monsters which actually existed within the world created by the artist; Tolkien the high fantasy writer knew that before a work of high fantasy could be taken seriously the author had to create a world that was real, a world of logical internal cohesiveness, within the pages of the story.

Writers and critics since Tolkien have, consciously or unconsciously, echoed his sentiments on the need for the author and the reader to take seriously the fantastic elements of the secondary world. Ursula Le Guin has asserted:

> I think 'High Fantasy' a beautiful phrase. It summarises, for me, what I value most in an imaginative work: the fact that the author takes absolutely seriously the world and the people which he has created, as seriously as Homer took the Trojan War, and Odysseus; that he plays the game with all his skill, and all his art, and all his heart. When he does that, the fantasy game becomes one of the High Games men play.
>
> Cameron 1971: 137

And it is not coincidence that Le Guin, like Tolkien, draws upon ancient epic for analogues by which to explain high fantasy.

The secondary world of high fantasy can not be totally fantastic, however, or the reader would not be able to understand a word of what was written. There have to be elements of the secondary world which the reader can recognise and understand, and no small amount of critical effort has been expended over the years in enumerating the traditional sources on which high fantasy has drawn for its reality. The roots of high fantasy, and the literatures which continue to be a source of everything from general inspiration to specific character names, can be traced back to the most ancient of traditional literary impulses in Western Europe: myth, epic, legend, romance and folk-tale.

Some of the most imaginative aspects of modern high fantasy have come from the oldest of stories. The continuing battles between the dragon and the dragon slayer can be traced through the St George legends and Sigurd's slaying of Fafnir in the *Volsunga Saga* to the battles between Thor and the Midgard Serpent in the Norse myths; and the avuncular magician/tutor who guides the young prince or hero to manhood and triumph has his origins in the stories of Merlin, himself based on the Celtic druids. The contemporary fantasy hero looks back through a myriad of folktale and legendary heroes to the epic heroes: Beowulf, Achilles, and Odysseus; and the 'larger than life' aspects of the hero's task or quest and those supernatural powers which are effective in the fantasy world come from myth and epic as well.

If much of the content and many of the concrete items come from myth, epic, and legend, the essential structure of high fantasy is taken from the magic tale, the *Märchen*.

> The *Märchen* is, in fact, an adventure story with a single hero ... The hero's (or heroine's) career starts, as everyone else's, in the dull and miserable world of reality. Then, all of a sudden, the supernatural world involves him and challenges the mortal, who undertakes his long voyage to happiness. He enters the magic forest, guided by supernatural helpers, and defeats evil powers beyond the boundaries of man's universe. Crossing several borders of the Beyond, performing impossible tasks, the hero is slandered, banished, tortured, trapped, betrayed. He suffers death by extreme cruelty but is always brought back to life again. Suffering turns him into a real hero: as often as he is devoured, cut up, swallowed, or turned into a beast, so does he become stronger and handsomer and more worthy of the prize he seeks. His ascent from rags to riches ends with the beautiful heroine's hand, a kingdom, and marriage. The final act of the *Märchen* brings the hero back to the human world; he metes out justice, punishes the evil, rewards the good.
>
> Dégh 1972: 63

Although not all high fantasies contain each and every element in Dégh's outline, each tale contains most of them; and sometimes, as in the case of the death and rebirth of the hero, the action may be metaphoric rather than realistic.

The society of high fantasy is drawn from medieval romance as is much of the material culture and technology. The people live in castles and manor houses, the transport (unless magical) is by horse on land and by sailing ship at sea, both the domestic and military technologies (except for wizardry) are essentially frozen at a level which would be recognisable to a medieval Briton, and the ideals are a distillation of those which have come down to the twentieth century as the Arthurian tradition – the dream of Camelot. And although most of the main characters are from the upper classes – kings and queens, princes and princesses, wizards, knights and ladies – there is always the chance that the orphan will prove himself worthy (in which case, he, too, will join the elite at the end of the tale). In addition to these rather concrete materials, medieval romance also provides high fantasy with something more abstract, its style.

What separates the good from the bad in high fantasy has less to do with the material on which the writer draws than it does on how he or she tells the story. Ursula Le Guin argues that the 'style is, of course the book ... If you remove the style, all you have left is a synopsis of the plot' (1982: 84). Style is especially important in high fantasy, Le Guin continues, because to 'create what Tolkien calls a "secondary universe" is to make a new world. A world where no voice has ever spoken before; where the act of speech is the act of creation. The only voice that speaks there is the creator's voice. And every word counts' (1982: 85). The elevated and sometimes formal style of the medieval romance is certainly appropriate to the actions being described. As Dainis Bisenieks comments, 'There is no pretending, as in some modern novels, that inconsequence is the rule of life; the tales of Faerie are of those who walk with destiny and must be careful what they are about' (1974: 617). Chronologically more recent than myth and epic, medieval romance may be the most observable ancestor of and influence on high fantasy.

It was, in fact, the interest of the English romantics in the medieval which led directly to the writing of high fantasy. Whereas myth, epic, legend, romance, and folktale contain most of the elements which are found in modern high fantasy, they are traditional narrative forms from ages in which the distinctions between the mimetic and the fantastic were less formalised than they are now. In the seventeenth and eighteenth centuries, the scientific method, with its emphasis on rationalism and experimentation, began to take hold; and the literary world, like the scientific and technological worlds, attempted to ban the fantastic as unsuitable for modern, educated tastes. The prose which grew during that period – history, biography, newspaper reporting, and the essay – reflected the interest of the times in things factual.

The romantics, rejecting or bypassing the rational orientation of the previous centuries, looked to the medieval and beyond for their inspiration, bringing back to popularity the vast resources of the fantastic in the Celtic and Scandinavian literatures as well as reinvigorating classical pieces such as *The Iliad* and *The Odyssey*. Reawakened interest in pre-Renaissance literatures, along with the popularity of gothic fiction and a century of tales imported from the Middle East, the Far East and South America, contributed to the conditions in which high fantasy could be created. In addition, other intentionally fantastic literature was appearing in Britain in the latter half of the nineteenth century. John Ruskin's *The King of the Golden River*, Lewis Carroll's Alice books, Charles Dickens's *A Christmas Carol*, Charles Kingsley's *The Water-Babies* and George MacDonald's numerous books, among other works, while not high fantasies themselves, certainly helped set the stage for the creation of that form. That creation began with William Morris.

Morris, well-known for his interest in all aspects of the medieval and especially his literary inclinations toward the Arthurian materials and his interest in the Icelandic sagas, is generally acknowledged to be the first to have brought the elements of traditional narrative together in novel form to create a secondary world within which to set fantastic tale told in a high style (Carter 1973: 25). There were certainly tales which a modern reader would call fantastic written and told before Morris wrote *The Wood Beyond the World* (1895), but they were not deliberate attempts to create a logically cohesive secondary world.

We have no way of knowing what cultures previous to the renaissance thought was mimetic and what they thought was fantastic; those categories were not then the mutually exclusive categories we consider them today. In fact, they may not have been mutually exclusive for British culture (and by extension American culture) until some time in the late seventeenth or early eighteenth century. The novel, developed from the factual prose of the seventeenth and eighteenth centuries, was initially mimetic, if at times certainly exaggerated; and Morris was the first to consciously break from that realistic tradition and create the world in which the action of *The Wood Beyond the World* is set.

Morris's story begins in Langton on Holm, certainly an English-sounding place name, with a hero named Golden Walter who is, we are told, the son of Bartholomew Golden of the Lineage of the Goldings. Walter, following a disastrous first marriage, decides to depart on one of his father's ships and see something of the world. After seven months of travel and several encounters with a mysterious trio – a woman, a young girl and a dwarf – Walter receives word that his father has died and sets out for home. The ship is blown off course, and Walter leaves a world at least objectively like our own for a secondary world in which he will encounter aspects of the fertility goddess. Having seen the old goddess destroyed and having himself slain the dwarf, Walter will marry 'the maid' (a goddess as well), descend from the wilderness to the secondary world's major city, and become king.

*The Wood Beyond the World* contains elements from all of the traditional sources. The old goddess's sacrifice so that the young goddess can marry and assume her role as fertility figure is a variant of a pattern common in ancient mythology. Golden Walter's taking his father's last name as his first is evidence of Morris's interest in Scandinavian traditions. The journey across the ocean to a vastly different world is based on voyage literature from a variety of Western European literary traditions, including the legend and the folk-tale. The technology of wooden sailing ships, the descriptions of clothing, and the swords, knives, and bows and arrows are all found in medieval romance. The language of the novel, including such words as 'mickle' for 'much' and 'wot' for 'know,' has a late-medieval ring to it, and Morris's overall style is reminiscent of the medieval romances he is known to have studied. Although he wrote many other books, William Morris and *The Wood Beyond the World* deserve their initial place in the development of high fantasy.

The possibilities for fantasy broadened considerably in the late years of the nineteenth century and the early years of the twentieth. Kenneth Grahame's *The Wind in the Willows*, Beatrix Potter's various animals and their adventures, J. M. Barrie's *Peter Pan*, A. A. Milne's Pooh books, and L. Frank Baum's Oz books, to name but a few of the most famous, opened the door wide for fantasy written and marketed for the young reader. Another major publishing series was undertaken by Howard Pyle; his most famous works, *The Merry Adventures of Robin Hood* (1883), and *The Story of King Arthur and His Knights* (1903), reinvigorated traditional British legends. It was also during this time that the educational system began to reach children at almost all socio-economic levels and to teach them to read; simultaneously, the publishing industry developed faster and cheaper printing techniques, ensuring that the enlarged reading public would have books and magazines to read. Almost simultaneously, the next steps in the development of high fantasy were taken by a re-teller, T. H. White, and a creator who made high fantasy his own domain, J. R. R. Tolkien

White's *The Sword in the Stone* (1939), the first section of what was to become *The Once and Future King*, is a high fantasy novel written for young readers. In that book, White tells the story of the child Arthur, covering those years between his birth and his drawing the sword from the stone to become King of England. Unlike the *Märchen* pattern or *The Wood Beyond the World*, there is no transition in White's book from the ordinary world to the secondary world; when the reader opens the book, the story begins with the orphan, Arthur, in what is both the ordinary world, for him, and the secondary world in which both he and the reader will discover the existence of the impossible. Merlin is there in both his specific role, as Merlin the Magician, and in a generic role as the avuncular guide and wisdom-giver who superintends the Hero's growth. At the end of *The Sword in the Stone*, Arthur emerges from his protective isolation, having conquered the challenges of growing up, to become the High King.

White's retelling of the Arthurian materials signalled important developments in high fantasy. First, as there is very little of the youth of Arthur preserved in medieval manuscripts, White tells the story of Arthur's youth from his understanding of the traditional tale; that is, White's invention or rendition of Arthur's early years is patterned after the early years of all the heroes in all the tales known. Second, White makes the Arthurian materials fantastic. Instead of merely retelling the stories in modern prose, White augments descriptive passages and action as the novel framework allows, but also adds a larger component of the impossible to make his telling 'more fantastic' (especially to a modern audience) than the original. Third, White adds humour to the high fantasy novel, but while he has fun *with* the magic, he never makes fun *of* the magic; the characters who do make fun of the magic are the 'dolts' of the book, and White makes fun of *them*. By rounding out the Arthurian materials in these ways, White transformed them from medieval romances into high fantasy and made both the Arthurian materials and high fantasy accessible to young readers.

As White was finishing the first steps in the reinvigoration of the Arthurian legends begun by Pyle, J. R. R. Tolkien was beginning to map the boundaries of the secondary world. Although not Arthurian, Tolkien's *The Hobbit*, like White's fantasy, is a large book written for children which tells a fantastic tale full of gentle humour, genuine danger and serious magic. It is also a book which displays a carefully crafted secondary world. Bilbo Baggins's front porch, where the action of *The Hobbit* begins, is in an even less-familiar world than Arthur's foster home in *The Sword in the Stone* (even if it superficially resembles an idealised Merrie England) and Bilbo undertakes a *Märchen*-like journey not through a fantastic and legendary Britain but into a Middle Earth of wizards, dwarves, elves, trolls, giants, shape-changers and dragons in which even he only half believed and understood very little of when the story opened. By the end of the novel, with the dragon slain, the treasure recovered, and order restored, Bilbo knows a great deal more about the secondary world than he did at the beginning – and so does the reader.

*The Hobbit* was published in 1937 as a children's book and was an immediate success. Allen and Unwin, the book's publishers, soon began urging Tolkien to write 'another Hobbit', even though he had a greater interest in the mythological materials which would be published as *The Silmarillion* some years after his death (Helms 1981: ix). In 1953 and 1954, however, Tolkien completed and Allen and Unwin published, in their regular listings and not as a children's book, *The Lord of the Rings*. That enormous book, usually presented in three volumes, drew *The Hobbit* into its own tremendous aura, and the earlier, smaller volume became, as the Ballantine paperback's cover announces, the 'enchanting prequel to *The Lord of the Rings*'. Today, the two are stocked together in the fantasy or even the Tolkien section of most bookstores and are read by virtually all age groups; this is true of much high fantasy, that whatever age group it might have been written for, it is, in fact, read by all.

It is important to remember, however, that Tolkien began his career in high fantasy with a book that he thought of – as did his publishers – as a children's book. Picking up on the idea that *The Hobbit* was a 'prelude' to *The Lord of the Rings*, a number of critics have suggested, as Randall Helms does, that *The Hobbit* can be seen as a 'mid-wife' to the birth of *The Lord of the Rings* out of the material that was to become *The Silmarillion* (1981: 80). Elsewhere Helms states:

> Taken in and for itself, Tolkien's children's story deserves little serious, purely literary criticism. But we cannot take *The Hobbit* by itself, for it stands at the threshold of one of the most immense and satisfying imaginative creations of our time, *The Lord of the Rings*.
>
> Helms 1974: 80

But relegating *The Hobbit* to prelude status allows critics to ignore that book's value as a children's book and as high fantasy, and it could lead them to miss some of its influence on Tolkien's later fiction and on fantasy literature in general.

. *The Hobbit* contains three major characteristics which help identify it as a children's book: intrusions by the author, a plot about growing up, and word or language play. These characteristics, as Lois Kuznets notes in 'Tolkien and the rhetoric of childhood', are found not only in *The Hobbit* but are a part of the general rhetoric found in various classics of children's literature (1981: 150–151). Tolkien, however, may have drawn on sources other than children's literature for those characteristics. Authorial intrusion was certainly a part of the ancient literatures he studied; there are numerous incidents of authorial intrusion in *Beowulf* and in *Sir Gawain and the Green Knight*, two poems with which Tolkien was very familiar. The plot about growing up could also have come from those sources; both Beowulf and Gawain learn from their experiences and return home, as does Bilbo, significantly changed. And Tolkien, as a student of language, was himself delighted by words and word play, and as a student of Scandinavian and Celtic traditions, he knew how highly those peoples valued words, stories, and songs. Moreover, Tolkien did not begin with a list of characteristics of children's literature; he began with a story he was telling his son at bedtime.

Thus Tolkien began with the tale itself. Numerous critics have commented on the structural similarities of the plots of *The Hobbit* and *The Lord of the Rings* as if that were a defect in Tolkien's writing (see Helms 1981, Nitzsche 1979, and Petty 1979); but what they usually fail to note is that Tolkien's plot structure is the structure of the *Märchen* or magic tale, the legend and the epic. Folk-lore and mythology scholarship has repeatedly shown that traditional stories share traditional characteristics, and Tolkien wanted to tell a traditional story. Unlike the tales he had studied, which were in existence in oral tradition long before they were written down, the tales he published, with the exception of the early parts of *The Hobbit*, were written down without a specific pre-existing orality.

Some of Tolkien's sources, however, lie in the traditional stories from pre-Christian northern Europe and are easily traceable. The names of the dwarves come directly from Sturluson's *Prose Edda*, wherein the inquisitive reader will discover, among other things, that Gandalf means 'sorcerer elf'. The dragon, Smaug, with his soft underside, is very like the Midgard Serpent, the dragon in *Beowulf*, and Fafnir, in *The Volsunga Saga*; and Bilbo's theft of Smaug's cup is reminiscent of a similar scene in *Beowulf*. Beorn, the shape-changer, also comes from Scandinavian legend and folk-tale. Dain's reputation as a generous lord and Fili and Kili's death protecting Thorin can both be traced to Scandinavian prototypes. Gandalf's role as wizard and guide for Bilbo may be patterned after Merlin's similar role in the Arthurian stories and more generally based on the Celtic druids. The traditional hero of the story, Bard, certainly takes his name from Celtic sources and his role in the novel from the traditional hero tale. And there is much more.

Tolkien's use of these obvious Scandinavian and Celtic materials does not make his tale derivative, however. In *The Celts*, Gerhard Herm describes the education of a Bard or Druid and notes that the Bard had to learn 'all of the old stories circulating that the public invariably wished to hear again and again, in the same traditional form' (1979: 239). Tolkien would have known, from his own studies of the ancient tales, that the traditional story-teller was not inventing new stories but retelling old ones, that the art of the story-teller was not, like that of the modern novelist, in inventing something new but in re-telling something old and re-telling it very well. Tolkien took the traditional materials he knew, including the dragons which had held his attention since childhood, and retold them as *The Hobbit*. What Tolkien was able to do was to call on a lifetime's study of northern European languages, histories, legends, mythologies, literatures, and the like; to simmer them together until the whole was distinct from the origins as well as greater than the sum of its parts; and to synthesise a cohesive secondary world for his high fantasy which was both original and resonant with the echoes of hundreds of years of pre-Renaissance European culture – especially the Celtic and Scandinavian sources which have influenced so much post-Tolkien high fantasy (Sullivan 1989).

The reader who moves from *The Hobbit* to *The Lord of the Rings* moves from a novel with a single plot and a limited number of characters to a novel with several plots and an enormous number of characters, from a novel which follows the folk-tale format quite closely to a novel which has the folk-tale format as its base but also contains much of the structure and content of legend as well as elements of myth, and from a novel in which there is a finalising conclusion to a novel which points to events both previous and subsequent to the story told within its pages and whose conclusion is, at best, a temporary victory for the main characters. In short, *The Lord of the Rings* is written for a more mature and experienced reader who can deal with its complex and highly textured story.

If the initial publication of *The Hobbit* and, later, *The Lord of the Rings* were important steps in the development of high fantasy, their paperback publication was crucial to high fantasy's current status. That publication of *The Hobbit* and *The Lord of the Rings* in the mid-1960s created a popular market for high fantasy, and for fantasy in general, which continues to this day. As Ruth Nadelman Lynn's *Fantasy Literature for Children and Young Adults: An Annotated Bibliography* (1989) illustrates, there are many books which might fall under the general heading of fantasy. Her chapter entitled 'High fantasy (heroic or secondary world fantasy)' runs approximately eighty pages and is divided into three sections: alternate worlds or histories, myth fantasy, and travel to other worlds.

All three sections contain books immediately recognisable as children's or young adults' books as well as books usually considered adult reading. The first section contains Tolkien's *The Hobbit* and Lloyd Alexander's Prydain books as well as Richard Adams' *Shardik* and Gene Wolfe's Torturer series. The second section contains Natalie Babbit's *Tuck Everlasting* and White's *The Sword in the Stone* as well as Terry Bisson's *The Talking Man* and Evangeline Walton's Mabinogion tetralogy. And the third section contains L. Frank Baum's *The Wizard of Oz* and Andre Norton's Witch World series as well as Greg Bear's *The Infinity Concerto* and Jonathan Swift's *Gulliver's Travels*.

Not only is Lynn's definition of high fantasy more inclusive than most, the second set of works mentioned for each section includes books written and marketed for an adult audience. The reader who moves easily and naturally from *The Hobbit* to *The Lord of the Rings* moves just as easily from any of the obvious children's or young adults' books in Lynn's bibliography to many if not most of the adult books also listed there. The fact that adults read *The Hobbit* and young readers work their way through *The Lord of the Rings* points up a major feature of this kind of writing: high fantasy appeals to a kind of reader rather than a reader of a certain age. High fantasy's reliance on traditional form and content makes it accessible to the younger readers and, at the same time, invests it with thematic significance for the older readers who will appreciate it on a different level.

The popularity of *The Hobbit* and *The Lord of the Rings* not only created a popular interest in high fantasy, it also created an academic interest in fantasy. That interest supports one major scholarly organisation, the International Association for the Fantastic in the Arts, as well as dozens of fantasy subgroups within other scholarly organisations. The fantastic is the subject of articles appearing in a variety of academic journals, and there are fantasy literature courses on most university campuses in the USA.

But the most important thing that Tolkien did in those two books was to set the standard by which other high fantasy would be judged. Numerous book covers pronounce this or that offering to be 'in the Tolkien tradition' or 'the next *Lord of the Rings*' or the author to be 'the next Tolkien,' but in truth, few even merit comparison and the vast majority fall far short. Even C. S. Lewis's Narnia series, which is itself a classic high fantasy and must be ranked with Tolkien's books, seems, at the very least, a bit too preachy when compared to the more subtle ethics and morality in *The Hobbit* and *The Lord of the Rings*.

Any listing of books by genre opens the doors for debate, and a category as narrow as high fantasy has very disputable borders. Still, some of the following books, in addition to the ones mentioned above, may well be listed among the twentieth-century classics of high fantasy when literary history passes judgement: Peter Beagle's *The Last Unicorn*, John Bellairs's *The Face in the Frost*, Marion Zimmer Bradley's *The Mists of Avalon*, Gillian Bradshaw's Arthurian trilogy, Emma Bull's *The War for the Oaks*, Joy Chant's *Red Moon and Black Mountain*, Susan Cooper's The Dark is Rising series, Jane Louise Curry's *The Sleepers*, Charles de Lint's *Moonheart*, Stephen R. Donaldson's *Chronicles of Thomas Covenant*, Alan Garner's *The Owl Service*, Barbara Hambly's *Dragonsbane*, Guy Gavriel Kay's *Tigana*, Louise Lawrence's *The Earth Witch*, Ursula Guin's Earthsea books, R. R. MacAvoy's *Tea with the Black Dragon*, Patricia McKillip's *The Forgotten Beasts of Eld*, Kenneth Morris's *The Fates of the Princes of Dyfed* and *Book of the Three Dragons*, Rosemary Sutcliff's Celtic and Iron Age novels, and Roger Zelazny's Amber series.

The current popularity of high fantasy and the quality of the best books in that genre today are due in large part to Tolkien's being in the right place at the right time – twice. From the 1920s to the early 1950s, he was in the right place and time to acquire the education and interests that inform *The Hobbit* and *The Lord of the Rings*. In the 1960s and after, he, in the person of his books, was in the right place and time to influence a whole generation of readers and writers who took his works as the model for high fantasy. What Tolkien had succeeded in doing, as reading the books aloud clearly demonstrates, was wedding the oral tale's style and content to the novel's format, creating an epic every bit as large as *The Iliad* and *The Odyssey*. Those who would be Virgil to his Homer are fortunate to have a climate hospitable to high fantasy.

The future of high fantasy lies in the past. Because it is a form which draws so heavily on the past for virtually all of its context, content, and style, there can be little literary innovation in the genre. Rather, the best high fantasies to be written will be written by those authors who, like Tolkien, can most successfully synthesise their knowledge of the traditional narratives and the cultures in which they were popular and who can also tell a story well.

## References

Bisenieks, D. (1974) 'Tales from the "perilous realm": good news for the modern child' *Christian Century* 91: 617–618, 620.

Cameron, E. (1971) 'High fantasy: *A Wizard of Earthsea*', *The Horn Book* 47: 129–138.

Carter, L. (1973) *Imaginary Worlds*, New York: Ballantine Books.

Dégh, L. (1972) 'Folk narrative', in Dorson, R. (ed.) *Folklore and Folklife*, Chicago: University of Chicago Press.

Helms, R. (1974) *Tolkien's World*, Boston: Houghton Mifflin.

—— (1981) *Tolkien and the Silmarils*, Boston: Houghton Mifflin.

Herm, G. (1979) *The Celts*, New York: St Martin's Press.

Hume, K. (1984) *Fantasy and Mimesis: Responses to Reality in Western Literature*, New York: Methuen.

Kuznets, L. (1981) 'Tolkien and the rhetoric of childhood', in Isaacs, N. D. and Zimbardo, R. A. (eds) *Tolkien: New Critical Perspectives*, Lexington: University of Kentucky Press.

Le Guin, Ursula (1982) 'From Elfland to Poughkeepsie', in Wood, S. (ed.) *The Language of the Night*, New York: Berkeley Books.

Lynn, R. N. (1989) *Fantasy Literature for Children and Young Adults: An Annotated Bibliography*, 3rd edn., New York: R. R. Bowker.

Nitzsche, J. C. (1979) *Tolkien's Art: A 'Mythology for England'*, Boston: Houghton Mifflin.

Petty, A. C. (1979) *One Ring to Bind Them All: Tolkien's Mythology*, University, AL: University of Alabama Press.

Sullivan, C. W. III (1989) *Welsh Celtic Myth in Modern Fantasy*, Westport, CT: Greenwood Press.

Tolkien, J. R. R. (1966a) *'Beowulf:* the monsters and the critics' (1936), in Nicholson, L. (ed.) *An Anthology of Beowulf Criticism*, Notre Dame: University of Notre Dame Press.

—— (1966b) 'On fairy-stories' (1947), *The Tolkien Reader*, New York: Ballantine.

Wolfe, G. K. (1986) *Critical Terms for Science Fiction and Fantasy: A Glossary and Guide to Scholarship*, Westport, CT: Greenwood Press.

## Further Reading

Attebery, B. (1982) *The Fantasy Tradition in American Literature*, Bloomington, IN: Indiana University Press.

—— (1992) *Strategies of Fantasy*, Bloomington: Indiana University Press.

Carpenter, H. (1977) *J. R. R. Tolkien: A Biography*, Boston: Houghton Mifflin.

Donaldson, S. R. (1986) *Epic Fantasy in the Modern World*, Kent, OH: Kent State Libraries.

Manlove, C. (1983) *The Impulse of Fantasy Literature*, Kent, OH: Kent State University Press.

Schlobin, R. (ed.) (1982) *The Aesthetics of Fantasy Literature*, Notre Dame: University of Notre Dame Press.

Shippey, T. A. (1983) *The Road to Middle Earth*, Boston: Houghton Mifflin.

Thompson, R. (1985) *The Return from Avalon*, Westport, CT: Greenwood Press.

# 25

# Science Fiction

## *Jessica Yates*

Not every genre of children's literature has a corresponding adult genre – school stories being one example – and it is only recently that the horror novel and murder mystery have returned to children's literature. Historical novels for adults and children both have an honourable and independent pedigree; but while children's fantasy enjoys a far longer and more distinguished tradition than adult fantasy, which only became a commercial genre after Tolkien's success in the 1960s, children's science fiction (SF) is considered the poor relation both of adult science fiction and children's fantasy. In this chapter I shall discuss why this is so, and demonstrate how, since the 1950s, writers specialising in children's and teenage science fiction have raised the literary standard of the genre.

The story of the development of children's fantasy is well known (Green 1969/ 1980: 1–16), and authors choosing a supernatural mode for their children's books would choose fantasy or mild forms of the ghost story, not science fiction. Although the term 'science fiction' was not coined until the late 1920s as an improved version of Hugo Gernsback's first name for the genre – 'scientifiction' (Clute and Nicholls 1993: 311, 1076), the genre had been recognisably in existence for several decades as 'scientific romance', a term applied to the work of Verne and Wells, and science fiction plots were also familiar in the 'pulp' literature read by adults and teenagers. So just as it can be argued that the first modern science fiction novel is Mary Shelley's Gothic novel *Frankenstein* (1818) – not only because of its now-typical SF motif of the artificial man, but because of its theme of the man who desires to rival nature through science – so one might look for proto-juvenile SF among the fantasy classics of the nineteenth century.

Science-fictional motifs may appear, therefore, in work whose overriding ethos is magical. Although the story of *The Cuckoo Clock* (1877) includes a voyage to the moon, it remains a children's fantasy; in Kipling's *Puck of Pook's Hill* (1906) the agency which brings characters out of the past is magical. In general we find that children's fiction employing time travel to and from the past will be fantasy, and to the future, science fiction. Although I would not claim Carroll's Alice books as SF, we can still note the somewhat scientific basis for their events: mathematics, the logical aspects of language, and the challenge to the laws of physics in the looking-glass world.

My candidate for the first modern children's SF novel – the counterpart to *Frankenstein* for adults – is *The Water-Babies* (1863) by Charles Kingsley. The branch of science known as Natural History forms the background, and one of the messages of this deceptively entertaining, but highly didactic work, is that technology is right, if rightly used. Kingsley, by profession a clergyman and by interest not only a writer but an amateur naturalist, was excited by the controversies of the time, especially Darwinism, and corresponded with Huxley and Darwin. In *The Water-Babies* he attempted a synthesis of children's belief in fairies, the doctrines of Christianity and the new theories of evolution and the origin of species, and was much more successful in communicating his ideas about the wonder of God's creation in this fantastic form, than in his pamphleteering and adult novels.

According to his unique theology, the world is governed by a Goddess who appears in several guises: as Mrs Bedonebyasyoudid, embodying the natural and moral law and punishing transgressors; Mrs Doasyouwouldbedoneby, embodying God's love for Creation; Mother Carey, who supervises the process of Creation; and the Irishwoman who carries out good deeds on earth, and intervenes in Tom's story to start him on his quest. All four beings share one consciousness and represent Mother Nature; they are also described as fairies: Kingsley says that 'the great fairy Science ... is likely to be queen of all the fairies for many a year to come'. The reverse-evolutionary fable of the Doasyoulikes, and the myth of Prometheus and Epimetheus, instruct Tom that humans were meant to use their brains and that technology is better than abstract science, which doesn't improve the quality of life. When Tom has completed his quest he returns to earth to become 'a great man of science', using technology to improve the state of the world.

Two short stories anticipate SF more directly. Hans Andersen wrote a prophecy of Americans seeing Europe by airship, 'In a thousand years' time' (1853), in which he predicted the Channel tunnel between France and England, an 'electro-magnetic cable under the ocean' and the destruction of 'ancient eternal Rome'. It is certainly science fiction, but more a satirical essay than a children's story.

E. Nesbit, who established the fantasy convention that magic must have particular rules, embedded a tiny piece of science fiction in her time fantasy *The Story of the Amulet* (1906). The children have been searching in the past for the other half of the Amulet, and Cyril suggests that they go into the future where they will remember how they found it. Although they do find the whole Amulet in the British Museum, they do not remember how it was united. Walking out of the Museum into a clean and sunny London full of happy people, they find a sad boy expelled for one day from school for throwing litter. The boy's mother shows them her lovely house, and calls their own time 'the dark ages'. Her son is named Wells 'after the great reformer ... We've got a great many of the things he thought of '.

The one pure science fiction novel by a classic children's author before the first World War, although it has not achieved classic status, is *The Master Key* (1901) by L. Frank Baum, subtitled ' "An Electrical Fairy Tale" founded upon the mysteries of electricity and the optimism of its devotees. It was written for boys, but others may read it.' (Baum included scientific devices in his Oz books, and Tiktok of Oz is a robot.)

Baum's son Robert, the dedicatee of *The Master Key*, was an electrical gadgeteer, and inspired this story of how Rob, a teenage experimenter, one day connects all the wires in his bedroom together and accidentally summons the

Demon of Electricity, a kind of genie, who offers him a series of electrical gifts in order to move the human race on to the next stage of civilisation. Pseudo-scientific (and thus magical), the gifts include food tablets to do away with food preparation and eating time, a stun-gun for self-defence without killing, a fly-anywhere device strapped to the wrist, and a mini-television to show current world events. Rob is trapped by cannibals and pirates, saves the King of England and President of France from conspirators, and intervenes in a war between Turks and Tatars. Having risked his life several times by failing to realise the dangers caused by his impulsive use of these gadgets, Rob returns them to the Demon and persuades it to wait until mankind is ready to be trusted with them. Sadly, this professional, entertaining novel has remained out of print for many years, only re-issued in a collector's edition in 1974, as its dated political allusions have made it impossible to reprint for children as originally published.

These few books demonstrate that there has been no tradition of children's science fiction comparable to children's fantasy. Kipling and Nesbit could no doubt have written in the genre had they wished: Kipling wrote adult SF, Nesbit, adult supernatural stories; perhaps they did not find the Vernian yarn a congenial model, and believed that the Wellsian scientific romance was too pessimistic to import into children's literature. Since children willingly accepted magic, there was no need for a pseudo-scientific explanation for supernatural events – compare Nesbit's treatment of invisibility in *The Enchanted Castle* (1907) with H. G. Wells's in *The Invisible Man* (1897).

Thus the juvenile SF published from the late nineteenth century onwards, comparable in popular appeal to other children's genres like the historical novel or adventure yarn, had no market leaders who combined popularity with quality, and whose names are recalled today. The best authors in the developing SF genre had the sound commercial sense to write for the widest possible audience: adults and their teenage children; lesser authors imitated their plots and wrote more directly for youngsters. If Verne, an author for adults who did not exclude younger readers, is the genre's Henty, there are no equivalents to, say, Angela Brazil, Frank Richards or Robert Louis Stevenson.

Jules Verne (1828–1905) rightly takes a pre-eminent place in the early history of children's SF. A professional writer, he published over sixty novels, which he described as '*Voyages extraordinaires*'. The most famous in the SF vein are *Journey to the Centre of the Earth* (1863), *From the Earth to the Moon* (1865), *Around the Moon* (1870), and *Twenty Thousand Leagues Under the Sea* (1870). Speedily translated into English, they were often abridged for the young, and technical details cut. In their full versions they display awareness of political issues as well as authenticity in the fields of geography and practical science.

H. G. Wells (1866–1946), with Verne the co-creator of science fiction, is more obviously an author for adults and his early SF novels have become classics recommended to teenagers moving on to adult literature, whatever their genre preferences. These classics are *The Time Machine* (1895), *The Invisible Man* (1897), *The War of the Worlds* (1898), *When the Sleeper Wakes* (1899, revised as *The Sleeper Awakes* 1910), and *The First Men in the Moon* (1901). With the horror novel *The Island of Dr Moreau* (1896) he provided many classic ideas to open up the genre:

alien invasion, adventures on other planets, genetic manipulation, future totalitarianism, and naïve, over-reaching scientists.

Other yarns in the science fiction area which have become popular classics for teenagers are *The Lost World* (1912) and *The Poison Belt* (1913) by Arthur Conan Doyle, *The Scarlet Plague* (1914) by Jack London; and most memorably the works of Edgar Rice Burroughs. Burroughs learned from Rider Haggard the plot motif of the unattainable Goddess-Woman, and more practically the way to sell books by writing a series of novels about the same characters, some linked by book-to-book cliff-hangers. Most famous for his Tarzan yarns, Burroughs wrote three sets of planetary romances, the first set on Barsoom (Mars), the second set in Pellucidar, the land 'at the earth's core', and the third on Venus, and also wrote *The Moon Maid*, set in several future epochs. Clearly a writer for adults, with his recurrent heterosexual theme of the hero in search of his kidnapped lady love, Burroughs's sagas appeal to youngsters who are beginning to be curious about sex.

Here then were the themes which were to be recycled by juvenile publishing in four distinct formats: the dime novel; the boys' paper; the hardback, often in series form; and the comic.

Science fiction was part of the repertoire of boys' thrillers (Turner 1975). Dime-novel SF developed from the American dime novel western. Set in the Wild West, a major series featured Frank Reade Junior with his amazing transports such as the Steam Man and Steam Horse, and others like airships and submarines. Written in the 1880s and 1890s under the pseudonym of Noname, they were probably the work of Luis Senarens, who, according to his entry in the *Encyclopaedia of Science Fiction*, was characterised by 'sadism, ethnic rancour, factual ignorance ... On the positive side, he led the dime novel away from eccentric inventiveness into a developmental stream that culminated in modern Children's SF' (Clute and Nicholls 1993: 1083).

From Frank Reade Junior's status as boy inventor, and a rival series featuring Tom Edison Jr in the early 1890s, Clute named this type of story an 'Edisonade' by analogy with 'Robinsonade' (Clute and Nicholls 1993: 368–370), and shows that the problem-solving type of SF plot derives from this tradition: the archetypal myth figure of Trickster becomes the Competent Man, in the hands of writers like Robert Heinlein. Other story-types featuring in dime novels included the lost-race story, usually involving a hunt for treasure, and the marvel tale of strange peoples and adventures in Antarctica, or on other planets. The dime novel may have influenced Burroughs and Doyle (Clute and Nicholls 1993: 336).

Boys' papers were predominantly a British phenomenon, deliberately set up to provide a higher moral tone than the penny dreadfuls. Several of Verne's novels were serialised in the *Boy's Own Paper*, this being often their first appearance in any English publication. One dominant story line, an obsession of Lord Northcliffe's, was invasion of Britain in the near future, and it frequently appeared in the boys' papers he published before the First World War (Turner 1975: 176–186). Space adventures, future catastrophe and lost-world themes also appeared (Turner 1975: 187–199). Science-fictional themes turned up in the story papers published by D. C. Thomson, with such characters as Morgyn the Mighty and Wilson the Incredible Athlete.

In 1934 *Scoops*, a newspaper-style boys' magazine devoted solely to science fiction, was launched in Britain, combining new SF with reprints; but it only lasted for twenty issues. To sum up, boys' papers 'played an important role in the history of SF ... by creating a potential readership for the SF magazines and by anticipating many Genre-SF themes' (Clute and Nicholls 1993: 149). George Orwell's critique 'Boys' weeklies' includes a reference to 'Death-rays, Martians, invisible men, robots, helicopters and interplanetary rockets' which he considered new plot ideas; Frank Richards's riposte corrected him by pointing out the work of Verne, and Verne's predecessors (Orwell 1940/1970: 460–493).

Turning now to the conventional hardback format, we find as yet no classic authors, but the genre was paid some significant attention by Edward Stratemeyer, who published two important series of juvenile SF, the Great Marvel and the Tom Swift series (*Fortune Magazine* 1934/1969: 41–61; Donelson 1978). Stratemeyer supplied synopses and then published novels by a stable of writers under his house names. Roy Rockwood's Great Marvel series, the first six written by Howard Garis, describe the adventures of two boys with a professor who invents spaceships and other futuristic travelling devices. Titles included *Through Space to Mars* (1910).

Much better known, and commercially very successful, was the Tom Swift series written by 'Victor Appleton' (mostly by Garis) from 1910 to 1941, in which a boy inventor realises the potential of, and copes with the problems caused by, his futuristic inventions, such as a giant magnet. A second series about Tom Swift Jr, written by 'Victor Appleton II' and including off-planet adventures, ran from 1954 to 1971, and two more series have appeared in the 1980s and 1990s. They are fast paced and addictive, packed with science and pseudo-science, and promote an optimistic view of technology and atomic power. The plots generally involve criminals or spies trying to steal Tom's latest invention. Reading Tom Swift was thus a formative experience for thousands of teenagers who took their ideas about science and science fiction from the series. There was some stereotyping of female characters and foreigners, although it seems to have been well-intentioned.

In Britain, Dr Gordon Stables, a stalwart adventure story-writer in the Ballantyne tradition, and regular contributor to the *Boy's Own Paper*, wrote several Vernean yarns: *The Cruise of the Crystal Boat* (1891), *The City at the Pole* (1906), and a future-war novel *The Meteor Flag of England* (1905). Throughout the first part of the twentieth century SF juveniles continued to be published in the Burroughs and Verne traditions, featuring survivors from Atlantis, lost worlds, and super-criminals. The Burroughsian yarns of American Carl Claudy are especially remembered: two youths under the patronage of an eccentric scientist have rather frightening adventures in stories with such titles as *The Mystery Men of Mars* (1933).

The 'mad scientist' motif also turns up in several fantasies of the period with SF overtones. In Hugh Lofting's *Doctor Dolittle in the Moon* (1929) the doctor is brought to the moon by a giant moth. The journey was airless but the moon has an atmosphere to which the Doctor and his friends adapt, enjoying the release from earth gravity. The doctor learns to communicate with the moon plants, and finds that moon life is a utopia where vegetable and animal life live in harmony, supervised by the one moon man. The moon people plan to keep the doctor with them for ever, and as originally written Dolittle was intended to stay on the moon, but Lofting's public would not allow him to 'kill off' the doctor, so he returned in a sequel.

Norman Hunter's *Professor Branestawm* books are classics of nonsense humour. Their science-fictional content deserves a mention, as humour is otherwise distinctly lacking in the genre. Hunter wrote *The Incredible Adventures of Professor Branestawm* in 1933, following it with *Professor Branestawm's Treasure Hunt* (1937); there was then a gap of over thirty years until Hunter retired and a new market appeared for the books, whereupon several more Branestawm collections were published. In these short stories the Professor usually invents a machine to solve a problem, and the machine goes wrong, resulting in chaos.

A precursor of British juvenile SF in the 1950s was Professor A. M. Low's *Adrift in the Stratosphere* (1937), with its near-earth plot and emphasis on problem-solving; its preposterous story and lucky escapes also render it unintentionally quite amusing.

It seems that the first SF comic strip was 'Le roi de la lune', published in the early nineteenth century by Jean-Claude Pellerin (reproduced in Gifford 1984: 12). It is a moral tale about naughty children being taken to the Moon for punishment to fit the crime: a cross between *The Water-Babies* and Dante's *Inferno*! In the twentieth century, once comics had developed into adventure stories told in pictures, and were no longer 'funny' nor indeed 'comic', the potential for depicting SF's impossible scenarios was relished by artists, writers and readers. Apart from comic book versions of SF novels such as *The Invisible Man*, there were two main types of SF story: the space opera; and the super-hero tale. The latter, in monthly comic book form, has been the most popular comic book type in the USA for decades. Because of the indiscriminate distribution of comic strips in newspapers and comic books in shops, SF comics have generally been aimed at a universal audience of juveniles and adults, until the graphic novel became commercially viable in the 1980s.

High points in the SF comic strip were 'Buck Rogers in the 25th Century', which began in 1929 as a daily strip, and then became a Sunday page. An American air-force pilot is transported five hundred years into the future, makes friends with female soldier Wilma Deering, who becomes his regular companion, and has typical space-opera adventures. A serial film (1939), TV serials, and a modern film (1979) followed. Other important strips were 'Brick Bradford' (from 1933), who uses a Time Top to travel to the past and future, and 'Flash Gordon' (from 1934) which went on to radio and other spin offs, including a film (1980). Gordon's girlfriend is always Dale Arden, and his arch-enemy is Ming the Merciless of the planet Mongo. Superman (from 1938) is, of course, the most famous. SF has continued to flourish in comics, and the worldwide influence of Superman, Dan Dare and the Marvel Comics Group superheroes like Spider-Man, the Incredible Hulk, and the X-Men cannot be underestimated.

As we move into the 1940s, it is obvious that children's SF has made no contribution to the body of 'classic' children's literature. Only writers familiar with the conventions of the genre would have had the knowledge and motivation to write good juvenile SF, such as the writers of adult SF published in J. W. Campbell's *Astounding* magazine. Campbell was an intellectual who constantly challenged his stable of writers with new ideas, and it was one of his men, Robert

Heinlein, who took juvenile SF in hand with *Rocketship Galileo* in 1947. Crudely plotted in its snap solutions to chapter-end cliff-hangers, and its happy ending, it remains a brilliant transformation of the Tom Swift 'can-do' plots, with fresh colloquial dialogue, varied and exciting episodes, and factual but lucid technical details. From 1947 to 1958, Heinlein published one juvenile a year.

Heinlein's basic plot is the initiation of a teenage male into his adult career as space pioneer, colonist or politician, and the books share a common background with some of his adult fiction – the unrolling colonisation of space. He intended not only to entertain but to educate his readers in citizenship – that is, Heinlein-style, politically of the right, non-pacifist and libertarian, supporting revolution in colonies on planets such as Mars and Venus. But his novels, for all their terse titles – *The Star Beast* (1954), *Between Planets* (1951), *Farmer in the Sky* (1950) – address complex political issues; *Citizen of the Galaxy* (1957) is even a homage to Kipling's *Kim*! Heinlein's view of gender roles is also unexpected – women may be doctors, pioneers, pilots, or even soldiers and survivalists.

His *Starship Troopers* (1959), was rejected by his juvenile publisher as being too violent and militaristic; published for adults, it won the Best SF Novel Hugo award.

Heinlein's influence on children's SF (and on the young adult novel) was immense, establishing its literary credentials and establishing classic plot motifs. He co-scripted *Destination Moon*, the first post-war SF film, and his Space Patrol, an ethical organisation run on naval lines, moulded Gene Roddenberry's vision of the cult TV and film series *Star Trek*.

One of Heinlein's early disciples was Lester del Rey, with such books as *Marooned on Mars* (1952), *Attack from Atlantis* (1953), and *Moon of Mutiny* (1961) about a teenage space pilot with the gift of calculating courses without a computer.

In the 1950s, Isaac Asimov wrote a series of short thrillers about David 'Lucky' Starr, a 'Space Ranger'; Asimov's second wife, Janet, who also wrote SF, collaborated with him on the Norby Chronicles in the 1980s. These are humorous tales which are far-fetched even for SF, and might best be called science fantasy.

Arthur C. Clarke, a British author writing for the American market, using American genre conventions, wrote two juveniles. *Islands in the Sky* (1952) describes Clarke's vision of space satellites between earth and the moon, but the balance between predicted fact and story is weighted towards non-fiction, and the book is a near documentary. *Dolphin Island* (1963) is much better, a story enhanced by Clarke's personal experience of underwater exploration. Both books are set during the twenty-first century, a time of world peace. *Of Time and Stars* (1972) is a collection of his short pieces selected for young readers.

Ray Bradbury, another of SF's all-time great authors, wrote no SF juveniles, but made two selections from his adult short stories for the juvenile market, *R is for Rocket* (1962) and *S is for Space* (1966), the latter including the chilling 'Zero hour' in which aliens seduce the USA's children into abetting their conquest of earth with the promise of late nights and plenty of TV.

James Blish made *A Life for the Stars* (1962), the second volume of his *Cities in Flight* quartet, a Heinleinian rite-of-passage story about a teenager press-ganged aboard a city just before its take-off into space. He also wrote *The Star Dweller* (1961) and *Welcome to Mars!* (1967) – both optimistic and rather intellectual.

Harry Harrison, one of today's leading SF writers for adults, has written a few juveniles, such as the very simply written *The Californian Iceberg* (1975), and the humorous *The Men from P.I.G. and R.O.B.O.T.* (1974). With *Spaceship Medic* (1970), however, Harrison produced a book which deserves classic status. When a meteorite holes a spaceship travelling to Mars, nearly all the ship's officers are killed and the ship's doctor assumes command; he appoints new officers, corrects the ship's course, copes with solar storm and mutiny, and works out an antidote for the meteor-borne plague which strikes the ship. All this is done with only knowledge, experience, devotion to duty (and drugs to keep him awake!).

Other noteworthy books of this genre include Alan Nourse's *Star Surgeon* (1960), which innovatively makes an alien the hero, and the book is propelled by a powerful plea for racial equality.

Two characteristics of post-Second World War children's SF are that, compared with children's fantasy, the author needs to have produced a substantial body of work to achieve classic status; second, specialist juvenile SF writers take over from adult SF writers. Some are forgotten, like 'John Blaine', author of more than twenty 'Rick Brant Science Adventures' between 1947 and 1968.

However, the first woman on the scene has remained popular, and has become the *grande dame* of SF. Taking an androgynous pen name, Andre Norton, Alice Mary Norton (who has also written as 'Andrew North') has written prolifically. Norton's SF novels usually share a far-future setting where humans (Terrans) mix with alien races; intergalactic law is enforced by the Patrol in a never-ending conflict with the Thieves' Guild. Norton is uninterested in the nuts and bolts of engineering her faster-than-light ships, and she has imported several fantasy motifs into her SF, especially motifs from the sword-and-sorcery sub-genre: the quest; the magic token; enhanced mental powers such as telepathy (which in Norton's universe may occur between people and animals as well as interpersonally); and archaic dialogue to suggest the lifestyle of less advanced cultures. With her research into anthropology and archaeology, Norton gives depth to the varied cultures in her worlds, as in *The Beast Master* (1959), while scenes in *Android at Arms* (1971) recall Tolkien. Norton's lengthy novels do not suit modern teenage taste, nor does the absence of a love interest, or its delay to the last page (romance, however, flourishes in her Witch World fantasies).

We turn now to children's SF in Britain (and a few French titles) immediately after 1945. These were conventional genre-books with SF motifs added: the most popular type was the space thriller, optimistic in mood, reflecting the feeling that now the war was over, Britain, probably co-operating with the USA, would build on wartime rocketry developments and start exploring the Solar System. The most well known authors of this period were W. E. Johns, Patrick Moore, Angus MacVicar and Hugh Walters, and I should also mention Paul Berna's *Threshold of the Stars* (France 1954) and its sequel *Continent in the Sky* (1955), about a space station and lunar exploration.

Johns, the creator of Biggles, wrote ten books about a traditional group of explorers: war hero, teenage son, eccentric professor and doctor, who make contact with Martians. Free of the Empire ethos which some have criticised in the Biggles books, the books are 'ripping yarns' and are also a vehicle for serious criticism of the arms race: in *The Quest for the Perfect Planet* (1961) the professor searches for a place to shelter refugees if Earth blows up.

Patrick Moore, a popular astronomer, has published over twenty children's SF novels, including *Mission to Mars* (1955); Angus MacVicar, Scottish novelist and scriptwriter, had some of his children's SF about the Lost Planet serialised on radio and children's television in the 1950s – a series which has obvious messages about the Cold War; while Hugh Walters specialised in children's SF writing a single series about astronaut Chris Godfrey from 1957 to 1981. With their straightforward plots, incorruptible heroes, and internationalist ethos, Walters's SF is the best of its kind and Britain's nearest rival to Heinlein in terms of an unfolding vision of the future. The Tom Swift tradition of improbable technology was continued in E. C. Eliott's *Kemlo* series published from 1954 to 1963.

During this period some fine literary fantasies, precursors of today's 'science fantasy', were published by non-SF-genre authors. The plot of T. H. White's *The Master* (1957) is familiar from James Bond thrillers: a mad scientist with mesmeric powers and a secret weapon plans to rule the world; two children accidentally trapped in his island fortress destroy him, thanks to their pet dog. *The Little Prince* (*Le Petit Prince* (1943)) is a unique classic fable, illustrated by its author Antoine de Saint-Exupéry, and other examples are Garry Hogg's *In the Nick of Time* (1958) (inspired by J. W. Dunne's *An Experiment in Time*), Meriol Trevor's *The Other Side of the Moon* (1956), and *Merlin's Magic* (1953) by 'Helen Clare' (Pauline Clarke) – a family treasure-hunt guided by Merlin and the god Mercury, with clues and adventures from literature and legend.

With the most memorable British children's SF of the period being actually 'science fantasy', the way of writing genre SF had to change. A radical shift away from 'space opera' was driven by new developments in adult SF and world politics. The influence of John Wyndham's four great disaster novels, *The Day of the Triffids* (1951), *The Kraken Wakes* (1953), *The Midwich Cuckoos* (1957) and *The Chrysalids* (1955) on British children's SF cannot be overestimated. With Orwell's *1984* (1949), and Nigel Kneale's television Quatermass trilogy, the 1950s were an exciting, if doom-ridden time for the genre.

In the new model of children's SF, historical, political and religious issues would be centre stage; Donald Suddaby is an important transitional figure here, writing both space and disaster fiction in books like *Prisoners of Saturn* (1957), and *The Death of Metal* (1952), while David Severn's *The Future Took Us* (1956) is a vital pivotal work, a chilling vision of post-holocaust Britain in AD 3000, where machines, especially the wheel, are banned.

The major British figures to emerge in the field in the 1960s and 1970s have been John Christopher, Peter Dickinson, Nicholas Fisk, and Louise Lawrence. Christopher's first juveniles, the Tripods trilogy – *The White Mountains* (1967), *The City of Gold and Lead* (1967) and *The Pool of Fire* (1968) are a tribute to H. G. Wells: suppose the Martians had won? His masterpiece is the Winchester trilogy: *The Prince in Waiting* (1970), *Beyond the Burning Lands* (1971) and *The Sword of the Spirits* (1972) in which man-made geological disasters have returned Britain to a medieval city-state culture. *The Guardians* (1970) is probably the first to use Orwell's motifs of the escape from the city and the forbidden romance/friendship, in a world divided between the Conurbs and the Country. *A Dusk of Demons* (1993) reverts to the classic post-holocaust dark ages formula.

Peter Dickinson enjoys a literary career that spans children's and adults' books, and has written fantasy, historical novels and political young-adult fiction. The Changes trilogy – *The Weathermonger* (1968), *Heartsease* (1969) and *The Devil's Children* (1970) uses the device of a future suspicious of machines; *The Devil's Children* is interesting as a positive view of an ethnic minority group (Sikhs), written shortly before educationalists began to make demands for such books. Elsewhere, Dickinson uses the biological sciences as science fact to back his fiction, as in *Emma Tupper's Diary* (1971), *Eva* (1988) and its companion piece *A Bone from a Dry Sea* (1992).

Nicholas Fisk specialises in shorter SF for the under-13s: catchy titles like *Antigrav* (1978) and *Wheelie in the Stars* (1976) indicate his approach. His work can be deceptively light-hearted when dealing with matters of life and death, for example in *Trillions* (1971) in which a fanatical general decides to use nuclear weapons to destroy an alien mineral. *Grinny* (1973) and its sequel *You Remember Me!* (1984) deal with alien invasion, while *A Hole in the Head* (1991) produces a cure for the hole in the ozone layer.

Louise Lawrence is Britain's leading woman SF writer for teenagers, and she confronts her protagonists with inescapable moral choices, beginning with *Andra* (1971) and *The Power of Stars* (1972). Her next SF novels were published only in the USA, until she returned to Britain with *Children of the Dust* (1985) a powerful anti-nuclear novel inspired by her children's involvement with the peace movement. Throughout the 1980s she produced a fine sequence of novels: *The Disinherited* (1994) is an escape/forbidden romance set in a future gripped by the ultimate energy crisis and the greenhouse effect.

British-born Monica Hughes, now a Canadian citizen and probably the leading woman SF writer for children today, has taken advantage of new freedoms to make girls her leading characters, and does not share the British prejudice against space adventures. Her Isis trilogy (from *The Keeper of the Isis Light* (1980)) is a study in prejudice and superstition with leading roles for girls, and many of her books, such as *The Golden Aquarians* (1994), are concerned with the need for peace and reconciliation.

From the mid-1970s the mood in the USA has been individualistic, breaking away from the formulae of Heinlein and Norton. Outstanding examples have been Jay Williams's Danny Dunn series; Laurence Yep's *Sweetwater* (1973), set on a colonised planet; Robert C. O'Brien's *Mrs Frisby and the Rats of NIMH* (1971) about laboratory rats with increased intelligence, and his proto-feminist, post-holocaust *Z for Zachariah* (1975); and Virginia Hamilton's trilogy about four children with psychic gifts, beginning with *Justice and Her Brothers* (1978). Sylvie Engdahl explored deep religious and philosophical questions with books such as *Enchantress from the Stars* (1970), while H. M. Hoover backs up her suspenseful plots with anthropological research.

Canadian-born Douglas Hill made an important contribution to British children's SF with new sagas derived from memories of Heinlein and Flash Gordon (such as the *Last Legionary* quartet (1979–81)) at a time when the genre seemed to be becoming somewhat rarefied. From the late 1970s, non-SF-genre children's authors were turning to the genre, such as Ann Schlee (*The Vandal* (1979)), Penelope Lively (*The Voyage of QV66* (1978)), Jan Mark (*The Ennead* (1978)) Rosemary Harris (*A Quest for Orion* (1978)), John Rowe Townsend (*The Xanadu Manuscript* (1977)), Robert Westall (*Futuretrack 5* (1983) and *Urn Burial* (1987)).

SF has come to address many contemporary issues. The anti-nuclear protests of the early 1980s found a voice in Robert Swindells's *Brother in the Land* (1984), Gudrun Pausewang's *The Last Children* [*Die Letzen Kinder von Schewenborn*] (1983, English trans. 1989), and Dr Seuss's *The Butter Battle Book* (1984). Religion has been discussed through Madeleine L'Engle's complex series of five books beginning with *A Wrinkle in Time* (1962), Fay Lapka's *Dark is a Colour* (Canada 1990), while specialist religious presses have published overtly Christian SF, such as Wendy Green's *The Great Darkness* (1983). Politically correct SF has been provided by Robert Leeson's *Time Rope* quartet (1986).

Not only a stimulus for young and reluctant readers (such as Bob Wilson's *Ging Gang Goolie, it's an Alien* (1988)) SF motifs have found their way into the picture book, often with comic intent, for example Jeanne Willis's *Dr Xargle's Book of Earth Tiggers* (1990).

In a study of the genre in 1969, Sheila Egoff denied that there was any literature in the genre (390); in 1981, she lamented the lack of 'such distinguished and defining practitioners' as Sutcliff and Cooper (in history and fantasy) (Egoff 1981: 133). Contemporary SF, says Peter Nicholls, resembles Victorian juveniles in its 'ethically intransigent and propagandist' tendency (Clute and Nicholls 1993: 216). And yet there are very many excellent and subtle books around – often written by authors 'moonlighting' from other genres. There is a rich tradition in Australasia: Margaret Mahy's *Aliens in the Family* (1986), Robin Klein's *Halfway Across the Galaxy and Turn Left* (1985), Lee Harding's *Displaced Person* (1979), and Caroline MacDonald's *The Lake at the End of the World* (1988) set in New Zealand in 2025 when the Earth's surface is almost completely polluted. Gillian Rubinstein is becoming Australia's leading specialist in the genre, with titles such as *Space Demons* (1986) (about computer games) and *Beyond the Labyrinth* (1988). In the USA, the genre continues to flourish, with writers like Annabel and Edgar Johnson, William Sleator, Pamela Sargent, Pamela Service, Clare Bell, Jane Yolen and Lois Lowry; in Britain Gwyneth Jones and Jean Ure have produced fine trilogies (*Inland* (1987–1990) and *Plague 99* (1990–1994) respectively) which add to the classic canon, while fantasy writer Terry Pratchett's comic trilogy about 'nomes', beginning with *Truckers* (1989) has reached a mass audience of thousands who would not call themselves SF fans.

Thus although children's SF could not boast a 'quality' writer between Verne and Heinlein, and has had an immense influence through comics, it cannot be dismissed as 'sub-literary'. In order to be fairly compared with other genres it should be seen to include science fantasy, and the genre has attracted many distinguished practitioners who have extended the range of ideas and issues that can be addressed in children's literature.

# References

Clute, J. and Nicholls, P. (eds) (1993) *The Encyclopaedia of Science Fiction*, 2nd edn, London: Orbit.

Donelson, K. (1978) 'Nancy, Tom and assorted friends in the Stratemeyer syndicate then and now', *Children's Literature* 7: 17–44.

Egoff, S. (1969) 'Science Fiction', in Egoff, S. Stubbs, G. T. and Ashley, L. F. (eds) *Only Connect*, Toronto: Oxford University Press.

—— (1981) *Thursday's Child: Trends and Patterns in Contemporary Children's Literature*, Chicago: American Library Association.

Fortune Magazine (1934/1969) 'For it was indeed he', in Egoff, S., Stubbs, G. T. and Ashley, L. F. (eds) *Only Connect*, Toronto: Oxford University Press.

Gifford, D. (1984) *The International Book of Comics*, London: Hamlyn.

Green, R. L. (1969/1980) 'The Golden Age of Children's Books', in Egoff, S., Stubbs, G. T. and Ashley, L. F. (eds) *Only Connect*, 2nd edn, Toronto: Oxford University Press.

Orwell, G. (1940/1970) *The Collected Essays, Journalism and Letters of George Orwell* Vol. 1. *An Age Like This 1920–1940*, ed. S. Orwell and A. Angus, London: Secker and Warburg.

Turner, E. S. (1975) *Boys Will Be Boys*, 3rd edn, London: Joseph.

# Further Reading

Aldiss, B. W. (1973) *Billion Year Spree: the History of Science Fiction*, London: Weidenfeld and Nicolson.

Berger, L. S. (ed.) (1994) *Twentieth-Century Young Adult Writers*, Chicago: St James Press.

Watson, N. and Schellinger, P. E. (eds) (1991) *Twentieth-Century Science Fiction Writers*, 3rd edn, Chicago: St James Press.

# 26

# Shaping Boyhood: Empire Builders and Adventurers

## *Dennis Butts*

### Origins of the Adventure Story

Romances of the Middle Ages, such as the tales of Robin Hood and the story of Bevis of Hampton, seem to have been the earliest forms of adventure stories British children enjoyed. Richard Baxter, the famous seventeenth-century preacher, lamented his youth 'bewitched with a love of romances, fables and old tales' (*Reliquiae Baxterianae*, quoted in Ure 1956: 10), and in 1709 Richard Steele described his 8-year-old godson's acquaintance with 'Guy of Warwick', whose brave deeds included killing a dragon and repelling Danish invaders.

As more children learned to read, their appetite for adventure stories grew, and, as well as devouring the romances circulated in chapbooks, they turned to Defoe's *Robinson Crusoe* (1719) and Swift's *Gulliver's Travels* (1726). Defoe's novel may have been intended originally as a tale about Christian Providence, and Swift's work as a political satire, but both were often read by children as exciting stories about shipwrecks and adventures at sea. Many readers have seen Crusoe's development of his desert island, particularly with the help of his black servant Man Friday, as a parable of the way British colonisation worked, and thus connected the ideology of imperialism with the adventure story almost from its beginnings. Defoe's work was so popular that it inspired a whole series of imitations throughout Europe, which were called 'Robinsonnades', including versions edited specifically for children. A Swiss pastor, Johann Wyss, (1743–1818) produced the most famous adventure story for children modelled upon *Robinson Crusoe* in *The Swiss Family Robinson*, first translated into English in 1814.

In 1814 Sir Walter Scott (1771–1832) produced his first historical romance *Waverley* in which he showed that exciting adventures need not only be set on desert islands, but could be just as thrilling when set in the past. Many of his novels were enthusiastically read by children, and his success helped to establish the form of the historical novel. James Fenimore Cooper (1789–1851), the American novelist, followed Scott's example in such stories as *The Pioneers* (1823), and in writing about the adventures of his fellow Americans struggling against treacherous foes and the natural elements he discovered the value of placing the action of his stories on the exotic frontiers of North America.

Defoe, Scott and Cooper did not write specifically for children, but their books were enjoyed by them, and other writers were eager to provide similar stories designed for young readers. Agnes Strickland's *The Rival Crusoes, or the Shipwreck*

(1826) is a typical example of a 'Robinsonnade'. Mrs Hofland's *The Stolen Boy* of 1830, about the adventures of a young boy who is captured by Red Indians in Texas, illustrates the growth of stories with exotic backgrounds; and Mrs J. B. Webb's *Naomi, or the Last Days of Jerusalem* (1841) reveals the growing interest in historical tales.

This appetite for adventure stories coincided with Britain's emergence from the Napoleonic Wars as a great military and naval power, with an expanding empire and a growing enthusiasm for foreign enterprises. The exploits of Clive in India and of Wolfe in Canada had whetted boys' thirst for adventure in the late eighteenth century, and the more recent triumphs of Nelson and the Duke of Wellington had raised patriotic feeling to great heights. The rise in popularity and to some extent the contents and form of adventure stories may be seen as an expression of this feeling and of the growth of popular interest in the British Empire which rapidly expanded in the nineteenth century.

Captain Frederick Marryat (1792–1848) played the decisive role in establishing the popularity and forms of the adventure story for children. After a distinguished career as naval officer, he became the extremely popular author of such seafaring novel's as *The King's Own* (1830).

In response to a request from his own children to write a story like *The Swiss Family Robinson*, Marryat, who was annoyed by that book's inaccuracies, produced *Masterman Ready: or, the Wreck of the Pacific* (1841–1842), the story of a family who are wrecked on a desert island but protected by the wise advice of an old seafarer. Despite a tendency to moralise typical of the period, Marryat produced an interesting 'Robinsonnade', which can still surprise us with its broad-minded discussion of imperialism and its unexpectedly poignant ending. The book's success encouraged Marryat to continue writing for children, and he produced a Cooper-like tale, *The Settlers in Canada* (1844), about the adventures of an immigrant family who settle near Lake Ontario, despite the threats of Red Indians and wild animals.

Then in 1847 Marryat published his best book, *The Children of the New Forest*, a historical novel about the adventures of the four Beverley children who are orphaned during the English Civil War. Marryat vividly describes how the children are taken into hiding in the New Forest by a poor forester who teaches them how to survive by hunting and farming, and evade capture by parliamentary troopers. Marryat's story-telling is not without faults, but in his account of the children's learning to survive on their own in the forest (rather like an inland 'Robinsonnade'), the story of the maturing of Edward Beverley, the rather rash, eldest teenager, and in his treatment of the historical situation with a picture of growing understanding and tolerance, Marryat produced a near masterpiece. With *The Children of the New Forest*, the first historical novel for children which has endured, and with his stories of shipwreck and of British settlers struggling to survive in Canada, Marryat laid down the foundations of the nineteenth-century adventure story for children.

Meanwhile the British Empire continued to expand. In 1815 it had hardly existed. Although the West Indies supplied Britain with sugar, Australia was regarded as little more than a convict station and on the African continent Cape Colony was the only part inhabited by white people, and they were mainly Dutch.

Canada was largely unexplored, and New Zealand was inhabited by natives only. India was the one major possession overseas Britain cared about, although three-quarters of that was ruled by native princes and the rest by the East India Company.

But new forces were at work and during the nineteenth century Britain vastly extended its overseas territories, forming the New Zealand Colonisation Company, consolidating its control of India, and acquiring the whole of Burma and huge areas of Africa including Uganda, Nigeria and Zanzibar. The Empire over which Queen Victoria reigned in 1897 was four times greater than at her accession sixty years earlier.

Improvements in communications by railways, steamships and the electric telegraph, together with the availability of cheaper newspapers made the British public more aware of affairs overseas, and newspaper reports from Special Correspondents, such as W. H. Russell of *The Times* helped to sharpen the public consciousness of such events as the Charge of the Light Brigade, the Indian Mutiny, the Zulu War, and the Relief of Mafeking during the second Boer War.

The eighteenth-century explorations of Captain Cook and Mungo Park, the wanderings of Charles Waterton in South America, the dramatic encounter of Livingstone with Stanley in Africa in 1871, and the travels of such men as Sir Richard Burton, all intensified interest in adventures in exotic places. When the domestic economic situation seemed to offer only the grim alternatives of unemployment or dreary factory work, many began to look overseas. As well as searching for opportunities of trading with British colonies, hundreds of thousands of Britons emigrated to America, Australia, Canada and South Africa, because there was more scope for enterprise and even excitement there. In the process, links between Britain and its great Empire overseas were gradually extended and strengthened.

Many Victorian children, particularly boys, shared their parents' interests in the Empire, expecting to work there when they left school, in commerce, the armed forces or as public servants. (Girls would expect to become the loyal companions and helpmates of their husbands according to the conventions of the age, of course.) The United Services College at Westward Ho! in Devon, was actually founded to help prepare boys to serve in such countries as India, and it is no coincidence that Rudyard Kipling (1865–1936), 'the poet of imperialism', was a pupil there. Thus the British public's interest in thrilling deeds in faraway places, normally within the hegemony of British imperialism, helped create a cultural climate in which boys and girls wanted to read adventure stories in which the heroes and (less often) the heroines were young people like themselves.

Like Captain Marryat, many of the writers who contributed to the proliferation of adventure stories from the middle of the nineteenth century, had also enjoyed exciting lives before settling down to writing. Captain Mayne Reid (1818–1883), after an adventurous life which included serving with distinction in the American War against Mexico, began to produce such stories as *The Desert Home* (1851). R. M. Ballantyne (1825–1894), after years working for the Hudson's Bay Company in Canada, wrote a whole series of adventure stories, such as *Snowflakes and Sunbeams: or the Young Fur Traders* (1858) and his popular 'Robinsonnade', *The Coral Island: A Tale of the Pacific Ocean* (1858). W. H. G. Kingston (1814–

1880), the third of Marryat's mid-nineteenth-century successors, tended to specialise in sea stories, such as *Peter the Whaler: His Early Life and Adventures in the Arctic Regions* (1851). Many children, of course, continued to enjoy adventure stories written for adults such as *Westward Ho!*, an Elizabethan romance by Charles Kingsley (1819–1875).

Kingston was succeeded as editor of the significantly named periodical *The Union Jack: Tales for British Boys*, a penny weekly devoted to adventure stories, by G. A. Henty (1832–1902), who became the most prolific writer of boys' adventure stories in the last decades of the nineteenth century. A war correspondent who had travelled widely, and covered most of the major conflicts in Europe from the Crimean to the Franco-Russian War as well as various colonial expeditions, Henty began writing full-time for children when his poor health made strenuous travelling impossible. He was soon producing four books a year, ranging from historical works, such as *With Clive in India: or the Beginnings of Empire* (1884) to stories based upon recent or even contemporary events, such as *The Dash for Khartoum: A Tale of the Nile Expedition* (1892).

Henty was enormously popular, with sales of his books reaching 150,000 annually, according to his publisher Blackie. In view of this kind of success, it is not surprising that by the end of the century almost every publishing house in Britain was eagerly providing adventure stories for a young reading public which was growing in size not only because of the expansion of the public (that is, private) schools but also of the national state schools, after education had been made compulsory for all children by a Parliamentary Act of 1870.

Even the Religious Tract Society, originally founded to disseminate religious works, launched a weekly periodical, the *Boy's Own Paper*, in 1879 to cater for a new generation of readers by serialising adventure stories by such writers as Ballantyne and Kingston. So popular was the magazine that within five years its circulation had reached a quarter of a million, and over half a million within ten years.

Other periodical publishers followed suit. In the years between 1855–1901 over a hundred secular magazines for boys were published in Britain, the majority after the 1870 Education Act – *Young Folks* in 1871, *Young England* in 1880, *Chums* in 1892 and *The Captain* in 1899, to name some of the most famous examples. Most of them attracted the major writers of adventure stories at this time, including Ballantyne, Kingston and Stevenson. They were well produced on good quality paper, and copiously illustrated.

Alongside these periodicals produced by the respectable, middle-class publishers, however, there also existed penny magazines of a more sensationalist character. Edwin J. Brett (1828–1895) dominated this field with his *Boys of England* launched in 1867, featuring the boisterous adventures of Jack Harkaway, but Brett had notable rivals in the brothers George and William Emmett with melodramatic serials in their periodical *Sons of Britannia*, launched in 1876.

In the 1890s Alfred Harmsworth, later Lord Northcliffe (1865–1922), started a series of weekly periodicals selling at only one halfpenny each, such as *The Halfpenny Marvel* in 1893, *The Union Jack* (reviving Henty's old title) in 1894, and *Pluck*, also 1894. *The Halfpenny Marvel* specialised in stories about buried treasure and adventures at sea, while the *Union Jack* concentrated more on stories about how Britain obtained her colonies. *Pluck* also contained tales of daring deeds in imperial settings, and serials based upon such topics as General Gordon and the Siege of Khartoum. The weekly fiction found in *Pluck* and the *Union Jack*, with their stories about youthful heroes in romantic parts of the British Empire, extended and reinforced familiarity with the form and imperialistic values of the adventure genre which had developed from the middle of the century. 'Dr Jim of South Africa,' for example, which appeared in *Pluck* in 1896, actually featured Dr Jameson, the instigator of the notorious Jameson Raid into the Transvaal in 1895, in a plot similar to many boys' adventure stories of the previous forty years.

## The Genre

What were the characteristics of the boys' adventure story as it developed in the nineteenth century? How were they shaped by individual writers, such as Stevenson, and how were they developed in the twentieth century?

The most important feature of the genre is its combination of the extraordinary and the probable, for if the events in a story are too mundane, they fail to excite, but a sequence of completely extraordinary events fails to be credible. Whether an adventure story deals with shipwrecks or heroic battles, the events have to seem to arise naturally from the context of the story to retain the young reader's confidence. The remarkable adventures that H. Rider Haggard (1856–1925) describes in *King Solomon's Mines* (1885) are carefully led up to step by step, the illusion of reality being created by the narrator's low-key introduction of himself, his quasi-scholarly footnotes about the African vegetation and wild life, and his modest unwillingness to make any dramatic claims about his own part in the treasure hunt. The unfolding of more and more extraordinary events is done so gradually and skilfully as to suspend (or at least reduce) the reader's sense of disbelief.

This sense of the probable is usually achieved by choosing as hero a normal and identifiable teenage boy, generally from a respectable but not particularly wealthy home. Peter Lefroy, the 15-year-old son of a clergyman in Kingston's *Peter the Whaler*, is a typical example. Neither particularly clever nor stupid, the hero has plenty of common sense and that spirit often called 'pluck'. Under the influence of evangelism, the heroes of the early books are apt to be rather pious at times (in the novels of Marryat and Ballantyne, for example), but, though the hero is always keen to do what is right, by the beginning of the twentieth century he is often portrayed in more secular and fiercely nationalistic terms, like Yorke Harberton in Henty's *With Roberts to Pretoria* (1902), who is introduced as

> a good specimen of the class by which Britain has been built up, her colonies formed and her battlefields won – a class in point of energy, fearlessness, the spirit of adventure, and a readiness to face and overcome all difficulties, unmatched in the world.

The beginning of the story usually depicts the young hero in a minor crisis which reveals an early glimpse of his pluck. Charley Kennedy demonstrates his spirit with a display of horse-breaking in Ballantyne's *The Young Fur Traders* and David

Balfour shows his courage in dealing with his Uncle Ebenezer at the beginning of Stevenson's *Kidnapped* (1886).

Usually as the result of a domestic crisis, sometimes because of the death of a parent or a decline in the family fortunes, the hero leaves home and undertakes a long and hazardous journey – to seek other relations, or to repair his fortunes elsewhere. The whole family emigrate after losing their estate in Marryat's *The Settlers in Canada*, but it is also common for the hero to be an orphan as in G. M. Fenn's *Nat the Naturalist* (1883), or to lose his father early in the story, as Dick Varley does in Ballantyne's *The Dog Crusoe* (1861).

The settings of adventure stories are usually unfamiliar and often exotic. Those in Britain focus on out-of-the-way places such as the New Forest or the Scottish Highlands, but normally the hero's journey takes him even further, sometimes overseas to European wars, but more frequently to the desert or bush of Africa, the snowy wastes of Canada or the jungles of South America. These unusual and dangerous locations, as well as adding drama to the story, often act in a quasi-symbolical way to reinforce the sense of moral obstacles which the young hero struggles to overcome.

The hero often acquires a faithful companion during the journey, sometimes in the shape of a surrogate father, such as the old servant Jacob Armitage in Marryat's *The Children of the New Forest*, or sometimes a friendly native, following the precedent of Man Friday, who can speak the language and knows the local customs, such as Makarooroo in Ballantyne's *The Gorilla Hunters* (1861). Although average in many ways, the hero often possesses some special asset which proves invaluable on his journey. Henty's heroes often have a remarkable facility for acquiring foreign languages as well as an extraordinary aptitude for disguise, while Captain Good's possession of false teeth and an *Almanack* prove to be unexpectedly useful physical assets in *King Solomon's Mines*.

As the hero continues his journey, all kinds of complications and difficulties threaten the Quest – shipwreck, attacks by cannibals, treachery. In Rider Haggard's *Allan Quatermain* (1887), for instance, the hero canoes down a dangerous river, rescues a missionary's daughter from kidnappers, is swept under a volcanic rock, and survives an attack of giant crabs, before finally becoming engulfed in a civil war. The story thus rises by a series of minor crises to a great climax, which is often a ferocious battle against bloodthirsty antagonists.

Normally the hero survives, and the end of the story sees him rewarded with wealth and honour. This is sometimes more than the conventional 'happy ending', however, as if the author, having shown how the hero has proved himself through enduring various trials on his quest, and discovered his real worth, deserves symbolic proof of this. The young hero generally discovers the truth about his family, and so his real identity, in such stories as Kingston's *In the Eastern Seas* (1871) and Stevenson's *Kidnapped*. More usually, however, the hero returns home laden with great wealth to be warmly greeted by his family and sometimes to marry.

Religious didacticism is not so apparent in adventure stories produced in the second half of the nineteenth century as in earlier books. But their authors took their responsibilities seriously, guiding their young readers towards such virtues as loyalty, pluck and truthfulness, nearly always within the ideological framework of

Victorian *laissez-faire* capitalism, a hierarchical view of society, and strict gender divisions. Girls occasionally play a minor role in adventures, and there were even some women writers of adventure stories, such as Anne Bowman (1801–1890). (Later writers such as Bessie Marchant (1862–1941) actually showed girls enjoying adventures.) But the nineteenth-century genre was dominated by male values.

One of the strongest features of the genre was its belief in the rightfulness of British territorial possessions overseas, and the assumption that the British empire was an unrivalled instrument for harmony and justice. Occasionally a writer, such as Marryat, discussed the system, but most nineteenth-century writers of adventure stories accepted the values of British imperialism quite uncritically. G. A. Henty was not afraid to criticise aspects of British policy in his stories, but it is always within an unquestioning acceptance of the legitimacy of British rule. Indeed, he often prefaced his tales with a letter addressed to his readers – 'My Dear Lads', he calls them – in which he drew attention to the heroic feats in the story which followed, and which helped to create the British empire. The imperialist statesman Winston Churchill (perhaps deliberately?), echoed the title of one of Henty's books *A Roving Commission* (1900) in the subtitle of his early autobiography *My Early Life: A Roving Commission* (1930), and he was also a great admirer of Rider Haggard's stories.

In their use of formulaic plots and stereotypical characters adventure stories owed a great deal to the structure of traditional folk- and fairy tales. Propp has shown how Russian folk-tales contain many features also found in western European stories, such as 'Jack the Giant Killer' and the English 'Dick Whittington', in which a young hero, often with the help of a companion and a magical gift such as a ring, leaves home to perform some great feat before returning triumphant to his family. In *The Hero with a Thousand Faces* Joseph Campbell argues that such tales, with their mixture of realism and the extraordinary, their narrative of the hero's journey as quest, and their happy ending, also have much in common with the myths of Greece and other ancient cultures; and he suggests that they remain powerful because they express the unconscious fears and desires which lie beneath the surface of much conscious behaviour. In *The Uses of Enchantment*, Bruno Bettelheim also vigorously defends the psychological value of folk- and fairy tales, particularly for young people.

Despite their surface realism, many nineteenth-century adventure stories are based upon the pattern of folk-tales, transformed by Victorian ideologies and reflecting contemporary attitudes towards race and gender, but popular because they satisfied some of the same human and psychological needs as traditional tales. The use of a narrative structure which depends upon a familiar pattern also has other advantages: the young readers may actually be encouraged in their reading of narrative as they recognise familiar patterns of story telling, and also obtain aesthetic satisfaction in learning to appreciate the ways different writers vary the expected formula or use it to express a personal vision.

The finest writer within the tradition of the Victorian adventure story was Robert Louis Stevenson (1850–1894), and the structure of the folk-tale is clearly visible behind many of his books. In both *Treasure Island* (1883) and *Kidnapped* Stevenson portrays heroes who are young boys when their fathers die. In *Treasure Island* Jim goes off on a voyage in search of buried treasure, and in *Kidnapped*

David leaves home in search of his surviving relations. Both heroes take ships, visit remote islands, and return triumphantly. The story pattern is a familiar one.

But Stevenson uses and develops these formulaic elements with imagination and seriousness. He introduces considerable variety into his heroes' journeys, describing the way an apparently loyal crew reveal themselves as mutinous pirates in *Treasure Island*, and transforming David Balfour's role from that of hunter into that of victim in *Kidnapped*. Indeed both stories are full of imaginative touches with an enduring resonance – the Black Spot, Jim's visit to the apple-barrel, David's climb up the stair tower, and his miseries on the isle of Earraid, among many.

Less interested in imperialism than his contemporaries, Stevenson achieved the most radical variation in the adventure story formula, however, in his treatment of the faithful companions and the predictable villains. Most strikingly in the relationships between Jim and Long John Silver in *Treasure Island*, and David and Allan Breck Stewart in *Kidnapped*, Stevenson exploits the familiar elements to portray the ambiguities of human behaviour. For Silver is the leader of the pirates and ostensibly the villain of *Treasure Island*; but he consistently looks after Jim Hawkins, and they become, in a wonderful stroke of irony, like father and son. Conversely David dislikes Allan's flamboyant Jacobite values in *Kidnapped*, and they bitterly quarrel in the flight across the heather, but when they draw swords on each other they are forced to recognise their fundamental brotherhood. Stevenson was preoccupied with the contradictions and complexities of human behaviour, seeing it constantly changing, and therefore all the more difficult to make judgements about. He is constantly challenging the reader's response and powers of moral assessment. Who is really good or bad, he asks the reader. Which is better – cool, rigid principles or erratic principles and genuine love? Stevenson's work demonstrated how the traditional structure of the adventure story could be a magnificent instrument for raising serious issues.

So powerful was the tradition created by Captain Marryat and his successors that it continued through the last years of the nineteenth century into the twentieth century, with such writers as Captain F. S. Brereton (1872–1957) and 'Herbert Strang,' the pseudonym of the collaborators George Herbert Ely (1866–1958) and James L'Estrange (1867–1947), who produced such works as *With Drake on the Spanish Main* (1907).

The only work of this kind which seems to have endured, however, is *Moonfleet* (1898) by J. Meade Falkner (1858–1932), a tale of smugglers and treachery in eighteenth-century England, more reminiscent of Stevenson than the imperialistic writers.

New developments were discernible. Richard Jefferies (1848–1887), with *Bevis: The Story of a Boy* (1882), the account of a boy's exploits exploring and sailing near his father's farm, successfully demonstrated how a realistic domestic setting was no obstacle to a tale of engrossing adventures. Thomas Hardy's one children's book, *Our Exploits at West Poley* (serialised in America 1892–1893), about some teenage boys' exploration of a cave in the Mendips, also portrayed realistic adventures combined with humour at a time when tales of imperial heroics dominated the scene.

British boys' adventure stories were read throughout the Empire, and known through translations in most European countries, including Germany, which in Karl May (1842–1912) had its own highly popular author of Cooper-like adventures. A different kind of boys' adventure story had long been popular in North America, however. Even the early didactic books of Jacob Abbott (1803–1879) portrayed his young hero Rollo in realistic situations of danger, for example, when he is caught in a storm while sailing to visit relations in Europe. That tradition was extended by 'Oliver Optic' (the pseudonym of W. T. Adams (1822–1897)), whose story *The Boat Club* (1854), about two rival bands of rowers on a New England lake, became immensely popular. *The Story of a Bad Boy* (1868) by T. B. Aldrich (1836–1907) gave the emerging genre a more humorous flavour, helping to prepare the way for *The Adventures of Tom Sawyer* (1876), by 'Mark Twain' (the pseudonym of S. L. Clemens (1835–1910)). Despite its comic beginning, this famous book's power depends enormously upon such traditional adventure story ingredients as Tom and Huck's involvement with a murder and their subsequent discovery of a treasure chest.

Many Americans were deeply influenced by the contents and form of British adventure stories. Howard Pyle (1853–1911), for example, produced *The Merry Adventures of Robin Hood* in 1883 and his first historical novel *Otto of the Silver Hand* in 1888; and later works such as Esther Forbes's *Johnny Tremain* (1943) and Scott O'Dell's *Island of the Blue Dolphins* (1960) show the continuation of that tradition. The success of 'dime novels', works of cheap, sensationalist American fiction which began to appear in the 1860s, also contributed to the enduring popularity of tales of frontier and pioneering life with heroes like Buffalo Bill, although perhaps only E. S. Ellis (1840–1916), with such books as *The Boy Hunters of Kentucky* (1889) and *On the Trail of the Moose* (1894), seems to have made much impact on British readers.

## New Developments – The Twentieth Century

The great scientific and technological changes which took place in the first years of the twentieth century had an enormous influence on the development of the boys' adventure story. The invention of the motor car and particularly the rapid evolution of powered flight, with von Zeppelin's airship of 1900 and Blériot's journey across the Channel in 1909, all began to affect the content of such stories. The outbreak of the First World War, with the advent of airship and aeroplane attacks, bombing raids, and the emergence of flying heroes such as Billy Bishop and von Richthofen accelerated these developments.

Some of Herbert Strang's books, such as *The King of the Air* (1908), tried to exploit the new technology. But the writer who reflected these changes most clearly was Percy F. C. Westerman (1876–1960); after writing historical novels in the manner of G. A. Henty, he began to introduce aviation into such stories as *The Secret Battleplane* (1918) and *Winning his Wings: a story of the R.A.F.* (1919).

From now on flying stories, with their formulaic elements of young hero, his introduction to the skills of aviation, and subsequent encounter with an enemy, whether in peacetime or war, became an important sub-genre of the adventure story. From the 1930s W. E. Johns (1893–1968) came to dominate the field, eventually becoming even more popular than Westerman. Johns had served as an airman in the First World War, and had experience of bombing raids and of being shot down and taken prisoner. When he eventually left the Royal Air Force, he began to contribute to magazines, and in 1932 published 'The white Fokker', his first story about 'Biggles', the nickname of the pilot James Bigglesworth, who was to become his most enduring creation. In the magazine stories collected in such books as *Biggles of the Camel Squadron* (1934) Johns successfully conveyed the way many flyers, with their strange mixture of flippancy and idealism, behaved during the First World War. When Johns had exhausted his war experiences, he turned his knowledge of aviation to producing more conventional adventure plots, dealing with the adventures of Biggles and his war-time companions as, for example, they foil criminals or search for treasure in the Brazilian jungle. But although Johns wrote primarily to give entertainment to his young readers, like earlier writers of adventure stories he was always conscious of the need to educate them too – 'I teach a boy to be a man', he said, 'I teach sportsmanship according to the British idea ... I teach that decent behaviour wins in the end as a natural order of things. I teach the spirit of team work, loyalty to the Crown, the Empire and to rightful authority' (quoted in Trease 1965: 80). By the time of his death Johns had written over a hundred books about Biggles, who remains popular.

The events of the First and Second World Wars influenced more than the technical content of adventure stories, however. The massive loss of life, eclipsing anything seen in the nineteenth century, clearly affected society's attitude to wars in general, and, after the shocks of the Somme and Gallipoli, Dunkirk and Singapore, many found it increasingly difficult to believe in the incontestable superiority of British arms. The growth of international organisations, such as the United Nations, and radio and television's revelation of the world as a global village, together with the swift liquidation of the British Empire from 1947 onwards also removed the imperial basis of many enterprises. The ideology of an expanding and self-confident British empire, which had underpinned the rise of the nineteenth-century adventure story, was gradually eroded, and its replacement by a troubled, multiracial and democratic humanism sought new forms of story-telling.

Despite the popularity of such writers as Westerman and Johns, even in the 1930s some writers had found it impossible to produce stories with the same formulaic confidence as their Victorian predecessors. Geoffrey Trease, for example, in such historical tales as *Bows Against the Barons* (1934) had tried to write more realistically about 'Merrie England' and portrayed Robin Hood's battles against the aristocracy as tragically doomed. Arthur Ransome (1884–1967) developed the tradition of the realistic adventure story created by Jefferies and Hardy by writing about the adventures that ordinary middle-class children might credibly experience, especially when sailing, in such books as *Swallows and Amazons* (1930). Katherine Hull (1921–1977) and Pamela Whitlock (1920–1982) followed suit with *The Far Distant Oxus*, in 1937, a story set on Exmoor.

The historical story took on a new lease of life in the 1950s, perhaps inspired by Trease's pioneering work. Gillian Avery, Hester Burton, Cynthia Harnett, Kathleen Peyton, Rosemary Sutcliff and Barbara Willard all produced interesting and often distinguished work, frequently taking different perspectives on history from earlier writers, and engaging with the lives of the underprivileged, for example, rather than the great and well-born. Rosemary Sutcliff (1920–1992) chose a disabled hero in her Bronze Age *Warrior Scarlet* (1958), and Leon Garfield portrayed the life of an eighteenth-century pickpocket in *Smith* (1967). More recently Jan Needle has produced a powerful account of the navy in Nelson's time from the point of view of two pressed sailors in his dark *A Fine Boy for Killing* (1979).

The character of realistic contemporary adventure stories has also changed dramatically since the Second World War, for when total war came to involve women and children at home as well as men at the front, children were quite likely to become involved in dangerous events. Ian Serraillier's *The Silver Sword* (1956) about the journey of a group of Polish children through war-torn Europe was an early example, and other writers such as Jill Paton Walsh and Robert Westall (1929–1993) have also produced successful stories with Second World War settings.

As society has changed since the war, and adult fiction begun to deal with sex and violence more explicitly, so, too, have children's books, narrowing the gap between 'teenage' and adult novels particularly. Authors such as Bernard Ashley and Farrukh Dhondy have dealt with racism in their stories, and children's writers have also begun to deal with issues involving the Third World and problems such as terrorism. Gillian Cross has used the traditional framework of an explorer's search for a lost Aztec city in Bolivia to discuss the values of so-called 'primitive' people in her *Born of the Sun* (1983), for example, while in *AK* (1990) Peter Dickinson takes us inside the mind of a child guerrilla struggling to live in a country, once part of the British Empire, but now torn apart by civil war.

The flying stories of the 1930s, which replaced the sea stories of the previous century have now been replaced by tales of space travel set in the future. Although the use of the folk-tale formula, with a fearless young hero and the successful fulfilment of a hazardous quest has almost disappeared from other adventure stories, being replaced by increasing social realism and psychological doubt, this pattern can still be found in much science fiction. Douglas Hill's *Planet of the Warlord* (1981), for instance, describes the hero's journey, with a female companion, in a spaceship across the galaxy, to find and destroy the warlord who annihilated his own planet.

While apparently dealing with civilisations of the future, however, many science fiction stories, such as John Christopher's *The White Mountains* (1967) or Robert Westall's *Future Track 5* (1983) actually offer a critique of trends in contemporary society, and explore such issues as the advantages and disadvantages of new technology, or the needs of the individual as against the welfare of a whole community. Monica Hughes writes about the dangers her young Canadian heroine faces in *Ring-Rise Ring-Set* (1982) as her technological society struggles to deal with the problems of a new Ice Age, and in the process reflects her concern for a better relationship between science and nature. Louise Lawrence's *Moonwind* (1986), another story about space travel, in which two teenagers win a month's stay at the American moon base, is even more radical in its conclusion, showing Gareth preferring to die and join the world of spirit in company with Bethkahn, a female from another planet, rather than return to the materialism and violence of Earth.

Changes in British society in the closing years of the twentieth century are reflected in the growing importance of women writers and of girls as protagonists or equal partners within recent adventure stories. Along with the introduction of such themes as racism, the environment, and debates about the meaning of political freedom, they show how much the modern adventure story has changed from the self-confident, imperialistic, and male-dominated tales of the Victorian age. Although opportunities for deeds of adventure remain, Western society is changing, and it is inevitable that adventure stories should reflect these changes.

## References

Trease, G. (1965) *Tales Out of School*, 2nd edn, London: Heinemann.
Ure, P. (ed.) (1956) *Seventeenth-Century Prose*, Harmondsworth: Penguin.

## Further Reading

Bettelheim, B. (1976), *The Uses of Enchantment: The Meaning and Importance of Fairy Tales*, London: Thames and Hudson.
Campbell, J. (1971) *The Hero with a Thousand Faces*, Bollingen Series XVII, Princeton, NJ: Princeton University Press.
Fisher, M. (1976) *The Bright Face of Danger*, London: Hodder and Stoughton.
Green, M. (1980) *Dreams of Adventure, Deeds of Empire*, London: Routledge and Kegan Paul.
—— (1991) *Seven Types of Adventure Tale: An Etiology of a Major Genre*, University Park: Pennsylvania University Press.
Howarth, P. (1973) *Play Up and Play the Game: The Heroes of Popular Fiction*, London: Eyre Methuen.
Propp, V. (1975) *Morphology of the Folktale*, 2nd edn, Austin: University of Texas Press.
Richards, J. (ed.) (1989) *Imperialism and Juvenile Literature*, Manchester: Manchester University Press.

# 27

# The Family Story

## *Gillian Avery*

It is a curious fact that few authors of juvenile domestic tales have felt equal to depicting a complete family. In American books of the last century it is the mother (or perhaps a spinster aunt) who holds the home together. A happy home circle with both a Pa and a Ma as shown by Laura Ingalls Wilder has always been exceptional. In the last quarter of the twentieth century, domestic security is seemingly unknown, and children struggle to survive against a background of problem parents.

In Britain, Victorian writers ostensibly set great store by family values, but nevertheless preferred to keep mothers in the background, while fathers were distant and often feared; children were shown leading a tightly knit existence in nursery and schoolroom. This remoteness from the adult world continued into the second half of the twentieth century, with parents relegated to the background while children enjoyed their own adventures. By the 1980s adults pose the same threat that they do in the American book.

Nevertheless the Victorians produced some excellent writing. But its appeal was limited. For this the elaborate English social stratification must be blamed. The early and mid-Victorians felt bound to draw attention to class difference, to the duties which fell upon the privileged, and the need for the lower orders to stay in their own station. The late Victorians were more relaxed, but liked to describe prosperous nurseries where the young lived in isolation. It resulted for a long time in class-conscious children's books aimed at specific sectors of society.

One book, however, did step out of the usual English mode and circulate more widely. It was also unusual in presenting family life with parents who both play an equally active part in their children's upbringing. This was *The History of the Fairchild Family* by Mary Martha Sherwood (1775–1851), the first part of which was published in 1818, and which was the first realistic domestic tale for the young. The book was designed to show 'the importance and effects of a religious education'. The Calvinistic doctrine that is imparted in Mr Fairchild's lengthy homilies and prayers, and the methods he uses to bring his children into a state of grace, make it a curiosity now. Nevertheless it remained part of juvenile culture in well-conducted families for at least eighty years and was read in homes that were certainly not Calvinist.

Underlying the religious instruction is an attractive account of family life and of likeable, frequently naughty children. Indeed, the forbidding chapter head, 'Story of the constant bent of man's heart towards sin' is a prelude to an entirely convincing story of mischief. The little Fairchilds, with their squabbles and attempts to resist authority, are in fact far more lifelike than the two children in Catherine Sinclair's *Holiday House* (1839), a book expressly written to show 'that species of noisy, frolicsome, mischievous children, now almost extinct'. Harry and Laura Graham are boisterous tearaways, but they are more like engines of destruction than children. Besides, this is no normal family; their parents are dead and they live with their grandmother but are brought up by a ferocious nurse, with a houseful of servants to clear up after them.

There were several capable early and mid-Victorian writers of domestic fiction, among them Harriet Mozley, sister of John Henry Newman, who wrote *The Fairy Bower* (1841) in reaction to the stereotype characterisation of the moral tales prevalent in the early decades of the century. She was, she says in the preface, trying to show families as they really were. Elizabeth Sewell (1815–1906) used fiction with some skill to convey religious instruction in a family setting, as in *Amy Herbert* (1844) and *Laneton Parsonage* (1846). Annie Keary (1825–1879), less solemn than either Mozley or Sewell, wrote a handful of vigorous stories about families, including *The Rival Kings* (1857) which powerfully describes the implacable hatred that children can feel for each other – a theme which few juvenile authors have cared to investigate.

But it was Charlotte Yonge (1823–1901) who was regarded as the doyenne of the domestic writers at the time. Family chronicles such as *The Daisy Chain* (1856) and *The Pillars of the House* (1873) were intended for the schoolroom girl. She loved to create vast families, often with a complicated cousinhood, from a background such as her own – upper class, devoutly Anglican, high principled, bookish. Her characterisation is nearly always convincing, unexpectedly so when she describes unruly boys, or boisterous girls, such as the turbulent young Merrifields of *The Stokesley Secret* (1861) or the rebellious Kate Caergwent in *Countess Kate* (1862). But for all her concern for the sanctity of the family, Miss Yonge did not often choose to show a complete one. In *The Daisy Chain* the mother is killed early in the story in a carriage accident; in *Magnum Bonum* (1879) it is the father who has been removed, and the mother, too young and immature for the role, has to bring up her brood alone. In *The Pillars of the House* the thirteen Underwood children are orphaned. The dying father lives long enough to bless the new-born twins; ' "My full twelve, and one over, and on Twelfth-day" '. The mother, her mind gone, dies a year later, and the eldest brother takes on the role of father. The immensely high standards of behaviour that Yonge expected of her young characters, the lofty idealism, the crises of conscience, are to be found in much mid-Victorian fiction.

Juliana Horatia Ewing (1841–1885) was one of the best of the later Victorian writers of family stories, though her style was too subtle and leisurely to be generally popular. (Like Charlotte Yonge, she delineated characters better than she constructed plots.) Brought up in a well-born, well-read but penurious clerical family, she wrote for readers who understood that sort of background. G. M. Young, in *Victorian England* (1936) recommended *Six to Sixteen* (1875) as containing one of the best accounts of a Victorian girlhood. *A Flat Iron for a Farthing* (1872) and *We and the World* (1880) describe equally well the early years of very different boys, in the first a rather 'precious' only child is depicted with affectionate humour; in the second two rumbustious Yorkshire brothers. In shorter stories such as *A Great Emergency, Mary's Meadow* and *A Very Ill-Tempered Family*, all written in the 1870s, she anticipates E. Nesbit's style.

Mary Louisa Molesworth (1839–1921) was more preoccupied with social status than either of the two former writers. She was always careful to stress that her characters were the children of gentlefolk, and dwelt much upon the marks that identified them as such. She wrote over a hundred books, and is remembered for stories such as *Carrots* (1876), about sheltered and protected children, very young for their age. All that is required of them is that they should be happy and contented, and above all childlike. Fathers and mothers lead their own lives downstairs; it is nurse and the other siblings who impinge on young lives. (Americans tended to view this arrangement with amazement if not abhorrence. Eleanor Gates's *The Poor Little Rich Girl* (1912) describes how the 7-year-old daughter of a wealthy New York couple suffers at the hands of her nurse, and longs only to be with her parents.)

The turn of the century brought a new development, a view of children preoccupied with their own imaginative games in a world where adults are, with a few exceptions, uncomprehending aliens. In the wake of Kenneth Grahame's nostalgic essays *The Golden Age* (1895) and *Dream Days* (1898), there was a torrent of verse and prose proclaiming that it was children alone who held the key to the universe. The ideal child was the imaginative child. E. Nesbit (1858–1924) made her adults shadows in the wings while her child characters, centre stage, played out their fantasies. The child like Albert-next-door who does not want to dig for buried treasure is dismissed with contempt. In *The Story of the Treasure-Seekers* (1899) and its sequels, the six Bastable children have no mother, and a father so broken by business failure that he plays very little part in their life. They are genteelly poor, but there is always a presence in the kitchen to bring them meals and to clear up the mess. In *The Railway Children* (1906) Father has been wrongly imprisoned, Mother writes feverishly to support them all, while the three children devise more practical schemes than the Bastables' to rescue the family fortunes. The neatly happy outcome to everyone's troubles has always made this book popular.

' "I think it would be nice" ', says one of the Railway Children, ' "to marry someone very poor, and then you'd do all the work, and see the blue wood smoke curling up among the trees from the domestic hearth as he came home from work every night" '. But this was much more the American style. English writers for many years to come assumed a middle-class background free from domestic responsibility. In Enid Blyton's Famous Five stories (1942–1963) the children can be certain that everything will be provided for them – the picnic baskets will always be filled by a kindly retainer – while they solve mysteries and capture international gangs of criminals. Nesbit provided even the struggling Railway family with someone to cook and clean.

This was also to be the case with Noel Streatfeild (1895–1986). Her talented children come from middle class backgrounds, and however straitened the circumstances, there are loyal and loving servants to prop up the often scatty mothers. The great difference is that her best-remembered juvenile characters do not play; with single-minded purpose they are inching their way forward in their chosen sporting or artistic careers; Sebastian, the musical prodigy in *Apple Bough* (1962), for instance, can rarely be persuaded to put down his violin. Streatfeild's first book, *Ballet Shoes* (1936) was published in an era when the holiday adventure story reigned (Arthur Ransome's *Pigeon Post*, Joanna Cannan's *A Pony for Jean*, and M. E. Atkinson's *August Adventure* were published in the same year). Holiday adventures certainly involved families, but in these books fathers are abroad or invisible and if there are mothers they are merely a source of supplies. Parents and guardians have a far larger presence in Streatfeild stories, and the children are in touch with reality. In *Ballet Shoes* the three Fossil girls (all foundlings, none of them related) contribute to the household expenses through stage earnings at an age when the Swallows and Amazons and their kind are still absorbed in a play world. The happy optimism, the warmth of the home background, the glamour of the stage world which the author could still see through naïve, teenage eyes, made it an instant best-seller, the first book about an English family to be popular with American readers.

Until at least the 1960s a middle-class viewpoint was taken for granted in the English family story. To the authors it represented normal life; working-class characters occasionally stray in, but they are a different species. Enid Blyton gave them names like Sniffer and Nobby and made them exclaim 'Cor!' and 'Coo!'. The three boat-builders' sons, the 'Death and Glories', in Arthur Ransome's *Coot Club* (1934) are called Joe, Pete and Bill which to a 1930s reader would subtly convey their origins (as, for example, the names Tamzin, Rissa, Roger, Meryon and Diccon would to 1950s readers of Monica Edwards's stories about adventures with ponies). Eve Garnett's *The Family from One End Street* (1937) was initially rejected by eight publishers who felt the setting was unacceptable. It was indeed a new departure to show a happy family where the father was a dustman and the mother a washerwoman. Seventy years before, there had been a fashion for street waif stories, such as *Jessica's First Prayer* (1867), but these had a strong religious message and such homes as the waifs knew were certainly not happy. Garnett did not dwell on the darker aspects of poverty; this is a cheerful book where the struggles of a chronically hard up family are material for picturesque comedy; it is not an exercise in realism.

The 1960s saw the beginning of social realism and a new theme, the child alone in the world. John Rowe Townsend's *Gumble's Yard* (1961), while in effect a watershed, has curious echoes of the holiday adventure story, though one with an urban setting. Here are children foiling a criminal gang, and a 15-year-old narrator from the same officer mould as Arthur Ransome's John Walker and his kind – articulate, authoritative, responsible. But these children have been abandoned by the people supposedly in charge of them, their uncle Walter, a loutish petty criminal, and his feckless, almost mentally defective girlfriend. To avoid being taken into care, they try to make a home for themselves in a derelict building. In the new style, the book lacks a happy ending; Walter comes back, but there is no expectation that he can hold down a job for long. In the sequel, *Widdershins Crescent* (1965), Walter returns to crime, and the children are left to bring themselves up.

There were still to be some books where the family circle was unbroken, and the parents properly concerned for their young. In Philippa Pearce's *A Dog so Small*

(1962), Ben who yearns for a dog with such passion that he creates an invisible one, is surrounded by a family who are affectionate and anxious for his happiness, but uncomprehending. Only his grandfather understands a little of the longing that he conceals. One of the most poignant and deeply felt books of its time, it is also remarkable for its classlessness. The background in fact is similar to *One End Street*, but for almost the first time an English writer succeeds in presenting it from within and not as a phenomenon which has to be explained to readers.

In the later twentieth century authors increasingly choose to show children alienated from their parents. Brian Fairfax-Lucy, drawing on memories of his own childhood, and Philippa Pearce in their joint *The Children of the House* (1968) showed four neglected and unloved children in a great country house. Edward and Jane in Penelope Lively's *Going Back* (1975) are only happy when their father is far away and they are alone with the servants. Donald in William Mayne's *A Game of Dark* (1971) hates his sick father with an obsessive intensity that comes to take complete possession of him. Michelle Magorian's *Goodnight Mister Tom* (1981) describes how a half-starved, terrified child finds a proper home at last. His crazed mother has beaten and abused him; it is only when he is evacuated from London that he encounters affection. With Ruth Thomas's *The Secret* (1990) we are back with the merely feckless mother. Mrs Mitchell, a single parent, goes off for a weekend with her boyfriend and, injured in a road accident, fails to come back. Her two increasingly panic-stricken children are also terrified of being taken into care and try to conceal her absence.

Fashion has now made it difficult to write unselfconsciously about happy families. Helen Cresswell has achieved it through farce. In her Bagthorpe saga (1977–1989) the eccentric Bagthorpes lurch from one zany domestic adventure to the next. The social setting in fact is not dissimilar from the pre-war story – literary father, talented children, jolly uncle, attendant dog – but the comedy has transformed it.

American family stories, certainly in the nineteenth century, had a far wider appeal than their English counterparts. They were not bedevilled by class considerations, and there was a sense of the domestic circle gathered round the hearth (even if the father in fact was often missing). Children in the American home were not segregated from adult life, they had responsibilities, and if it was a farming family, their help was vital. The books are often full of practical detail; frequently, life centres round the kitchen – represented as the source of warmth, comfort and food, but a region unknown to the inhabitants of Victorian nurseries. There are lavish descriptions of food, which the austerely reared British children brooded over with intense pleasure.

The earliest writer to celebrate American domesticity was Catharine Maria Sedgwick (1789–1867) in whose *A New-England Tale* (1822) we find the charismatic female orphan who was to become so popular with American writers. We also find the granite-hewn spinster, a miracle of domestic skills (another very popular character). In *Redwood* (1824) we can note the start of an American tradition of portraying fathers as insignificant, if not far worse. Mr Lenox, a New England farmer, is in fact industrious and frugal. But his wife is much his superior. She is the driving force in the home, and this is how it was to be in the majority of American books. Sedgwick wrote several books for children, all remarkable for degraded fathers. ' "He a father!" ' says a son in *The Boy of Mount Rhigi* (1847), ' "He makes me lie for him, and steal for him; and if I don't he tries to drown me".' Huckleberry Finn's father, it will be remembered, is much the same.

The fathers who show up best are the pioneers and the farmers. William Cardell (1780–1828), of whom little is known except that he was a schoolmaster, wrote two books which are among the earliest to describe the life of settlers. *The Story of Jack Halyard, the Sailor's Boy, or The Virtuous Family* (1825) begins on a New Jersey farm. ' "Of all men, I think, " said Mr Halyard, "the American farmers are the most independent, and the most happy".' (For years to come writers were to express the same view.) But Mr Halyard dies, and Jack has to make his own way in life; we leave him prosperous enough to buy back the farm. *The Happy Family; or Scenes of American Life* (1828) describes with much practical detail a family's trek over the mountains from Massachusetts to Ohio. Here they build a log-house and become self-sufficient. Cardell takes his family beyond this, to the point where they are comfortably wealthy, with a fine house and a horse and carriage, but for many the log-house and the farm represented the perfect life, where families could live in harmony and godly simplicity. Writers often were to use farm life to bring about conversion and a proper sense of values in spoilt city children. Later examples include Dorothy Canfield Fisher's *Understood Betsy* (1917). Here an over-protected 9-year-old is sent to a Vermont farm where she becomes, in the words of her relations there, both smart and gritty. In Betsy Byars's *The Midnight Fox* (1968) Tom, initially terrified by even the cows and chickens on Aunt Millie's farm, gradually learns to love animals.

The orphan theme was also to be very popular with American authors. Susan Warner (1819–1885), who wrote what she supposed was Sunday school fiction under the name of Elizabeth Wetherell, specialised in these. Her first book, *The Wide, Wide World* (1850), clearly derives from Sedgwick. It is an immensely long account of the moral development of an orphan, readable for its descriptions of domestic life. The father is discarded without regret at an early stage; the mother dies, and Ellen (given to outbursts of stormy weeping) is brought up and taught domestic skills by her flinty-hearted Aunt Fortune, a paragon housewife. (There was a similar scenario in *A New England Tale*.) The book was very popular with girls; not only was there highly charged emotion, there was also between 13-year-old Ellen and her spiritual mentor – the young man she calls her 'brother' – a romantic if not erotic relationship, never hitherto found in a Sunday book. In *Queechy* (1852) the author (never good at controlling a plot) succeeds in bringing her heroine to a nubile age so that she can melt into the arms of a wealthy English aristocrat. Warner did not often introduce parents into her fiction; but when she did they could be harsh instruments of oppression as in *Melbourne House* (1864), where little Daisy Randolph is the only God-fearing member of a worldly but also cruel family.

The Warner style had a profound effect on Martha Finley (1828–1909), who wrote as Martha Farquharson. Her *Elsie Dinsmore*, the first of a long series which went on until 1905, appeared in 1867, and would seem to be modelled on *Melbourne House*, though the setting is a never-never-land in the ante-bellum South, where the protagonists, all plantation owners, live in sumptuous luxury. Apparently disapproving of the freedom with which Warner heroines allowed themselves to be caressed by male strangers, Finley keeps it within the family. In the Dinsmore books it is the father (only 17 when he begot Elsie) who is the lover. He is insanely possessive, violent and tender by turns, and though he eventually and painfully allows Elsie to marry, readers insisted that the husband should be shed so that she could return to father.

Orphan stories continued into the twentieth century. In Kate Douglas Wiggin's *Rebecca of Sunnybrook Farm* (1903) the fatherless heroine is sent to live with two spinster aunts. Her Aunt Miranda is a termagant spinster in the Aunt Fortune mould, and indeed the book has more than a passing likeness to *The Wide, Wide World*, though Rebecca is lively and literary rather than tearful and godly. Jean Webster's *Daddy Long-Legs* (1912) places its heroine (literary, like Rebecca) in an orphanage, whence an unknown benefactor (later to fall in love with her) sends her to college. Eleanor Hodgson Porter's *Pollyanna* (1913) is a ray of sunshine, again afflicted with a vinegarish aunt, who sees good everywhere and transforms the lives of those around her. Frances Boyd Calhoun's *Miss Minerva and William Green Hill* (1909) is a curious variant, with Tom Sawyer and Pollyanna rolled into the person of one small boy, a wrecker but a charmer, also saddled with an aunt.

The prolific Jacob Abbott (1803–1879) wrote about more normal family life. From his accounts of country children English readers first learnt about such New England pleasures as maple sugaring, sleigh riding, camping in the woods. His books are an American version of Maria Edgeworth's Harry, Lucy, Rosamond and Frank tales, and like her he aimed to produce sensible, alert and independent children, though as this was America he expected more in the way of work from them. However, it is not the parents who are so influential in the moulding of character as the older children whom he shrewdly introduces as mentors. In the Rollo series which began in 1834, Jonas the hired boy teaches little Rollo useful skills; in the ten Franconia stories (1850–1853) there is a Swiss boy whom the children call Beechnut, with a wonderful talent for planning unusual games and amusements. There are also ingenious punishments, for Abbott was a school-master, albeit a benign and enlightened one.

Rebecca Clarke (1833–1906) who wrote under the name of Sophie May, continued in the Abbott style. Her stories have more religious content, and show children (the younger of whom talk in winsome baby fashion) being gently and rationally guided into good behaviour. Female influence here is dominant; there are mothers, aunts, sisters, grandmothers, but fathers rarely appear. *Little Prudy* (1863) was followed by a steady stream of stories about Prudy (who grows up and has children of her own), Dotty Dimple and Flaxie Frizzle.

Far less didactic and never sentimental, but also with something of the Abbott flavour, is *Doings of the Bodley Family in Town and Country* (1876) by Horace Scudder (1838–1902). This gentle saga of Nathan, Philippa and Lucy Bodley, their father and mother, the hired man, and various household animals including Mr Bottom the horse, contained much from Scudder's own childhood. Later Bodley books became travelogues and have fewer domestic events. Lucretia Hale's *The Peterkin Papers*, first published in book form in 1880, brought a new element of farce into the family story. The Peterkin family muddle everything, and are unable to bring common sense to the smallest domestic problem.

The febrile atmosphere created by Warner and Finley for girls' reading gave way to the straightforward good sense of Louisa Alcott (1832–1888). ' "I do think that families are the most beautiful things in all the world" ', she makes Jo exclaim in *Good Wives*, and the quartet of books about the March family, beginning with *Little Women* (1868), is the supreme celebration of family affection. ' "It seems as if I should be homesick for you even in heaven" ', says the dying Beth. It would be impossible to guess from *Little Women* that Alcott's own childhood had been over-shadowed by the irresponsibility of her father, who at one stage had contemplated abandoning his family. Mr March is revered, even though he is superfluous to the story and is rarely seen even when he returns from the Civil War. It is 'Marmee' upon whom the whole household depends. (It was to be the same in *Eight Cousins* (1875) where no fathers are ever seen; they are either too busy, or, in the case of Uncle Mac, dare not open their lips.) *Little Women*, dashed off in six weeks, brought Alcott instant fame, and also money to prop up the needy family. But she came to resent having to provide what she termed 'moral pap' for the young. *Little Women* and *Good Wives* were written from the heart; in her other books we can often detect a note of weariness.

*What Katy Did* (1872) and *What Katy Did at School* (1873) by Susan Coolidge (Sarah Chauncey Woolsey (1835–1905)) have been kept continuously in print in Britain since their first publication. (The third book in the cycle is an unmemorable travelogue.) But they are almost unknown to American children. The first may have been inspired by Charlotte Yonge's *The Daisy Chain*, in that a widowed father, also a doctor, is left to bring up a large brood of children. But the Carr children are far more absorbed in play than is usually the case in American books, and the heroine's metamorphosis, via a spinal injury and 'the School of Pain', from a self-willed tomboy into a serious-minded adolescent, is again in the English style. The second book is about boarding school life, one of the earliest examples of a genre to become very popular in Britain, but always a rarity in America.

*The Five Little Peppers and How They Grew* (1881) and its sequels by Margaret Sidney (Harriet M. Lothrop (1844–1924)) were far better received by American readers. Though the Peppers are poor they are a 'noisy happy brood' and make their little house 'fairly ring with jollity and fun'. The widowed Mrs Pepper 'with a stout heart and a cheery face' holds the home together. Good things come winging to them, and a rich family, enraptured by their spirit, carries them all off to live in a mansion. *Mrs Wiggs of the Cabbage Patch* (1901) by Alice Hegan Rice (1870–1942) is a more serious account of poverty. Mrs Wiggs is another widow who holds the family together (Mr Wiggs having 'traveled to eternity by the alcohol route'); like Mrs Pepper her philosophy lies 'in keeping the dust off her rose-colored spectacles'.

Booth Tarkington's *Penrod* (1914), followed by two sequels, shows the Bad Boy (a favourite character with American authors) in a prosperous middle class setting with unlimited leisure for play and make believe. The *mise-en-scène* and characterisation in Richmal Crompton's *Just William* (1922) and subsequent volumes follow Penrod too closely to be merely coincidence. Penrod Schofield is well-meaning but is a powder keg who wrecks every occasion – dancing-classes, parties, pageants, his grown-up sister's flirtations. And as William was to do, he crumbles when faced with the femininity of little girls.

Middle-class families leading stable, secure lives, their doings described in episodic fashion as in *Penrod*, featured in many authors' works before the 1960s. Beverly Cleary's chronicles of life in Portland, Oregon, began with *Henry Huggins* in 1950 and continued through the 1980s. Cleary's most famous character, Ramona the Pest, who first appears in *Henry and Beezus* (1952) is the archetypal awful little sister. (Dorothy Edwards's *My Naughty Little Sister* (1952) was the English counterpart.) Elizabeth Enright's books about the Melendy family began in 1941 with *The Saturdays*. Here there is no mother, but a devoted old retainer in the Streatfeild style. Eleanor Estes, beginning with *The Moffats* (1941), described New England village life of a quarter of a century before. The Moffats's father is dead; Mama is a kindly and efficient, though unobtrusive presence. In Madeleine L'Engle's *Meet the Austins* (1960) there are two wise and loving parents; the sweetness is cloying.

The Little House books of Laura Ingalls Wilder (1867–1957) which began with *Little House in the Big Woods* (1932) and finished with *Those Happy Golden Years* (1943) are remarkable for their portrayal of the parents. It is a rarity, as has been said, for there to be two parents, even more so to give them such a dominant position. This pioneer family of the 1870s and 1880s is seen uncritically through a child's eyes. Even so, the character of Pa emerges – restless, reluctantly held back from further adventuring by the greater prudence of Ma. The journeys, the joyful triumph when a new home is established, the sense of security when they sit round the fire with the door safely barred against the dangerous world outside, the strength of the family's love for each other, all described without a trace of sentimentality, make this series the most satisfying of all accounts of happy family life.

The search for a home has always been a favourite theme with American writers. Gertrude Chandler Warner's *The Boxcar Children* (1942), which describes four orphans setting up house in an abandoned railway truck, was so successful that the author followed it with eighteen more. Cynthia Voigt's *Homecoming* (1981), far more sophisticated, describes the weary trek made by four abandoned children to find the grandmother who may take them in. Dicey, the resolute sister who leads them, is a heroine of a particularly American sort: strong-willed and independent.

Such girls have been a feature of family stories. In the previous century there were heroines like Elizabeth W. Champney's *Witch Winnie* (1889), a high-spirited, though fundamentally serious prankster; or like Gypsy Breynton in the series by Elizabeth Stuart Phelps (1844–1911) – an engaging tomboy whose skills win the admiration of even her brother. There is something of Gypsy in Leslie of Katherine Paterson's *Bridge to Terebithia* (1977), a girl who can outrun all the boys. This girl is also imaginative, and with her special friend Jesse she creates a secret kingdom.

American heroines can be craggy or cussed. There is the single-minded Harriet of Louise Fitzhugh's *Harriet the Spy* (1964), or Claudia in E. L. Konigsburg's *From The Mixed-up Files of Mrs Basil E. Frankweiler* (1967) who runs away with her brother and successfully camps out in New York's Metropolitan Museum of Art. On a more serious level is the 14-year-old Mary Call Luther in Vera and Bill Cleaver's *Where the Lilies Bloom* (1969), who holds the family together when the father dies. Here is the flinty spinster in embryo: 'I sure would hate to be the one to marry you, Mary Call ... You're enough to skeer a man, standin.'

Home life in the last third of the century is more often shown as shattered, if not posing appalling problems, as in Marilyn Sach's *The Bear's House* (1971) where Fran Ellen's only refuge from abject squalor and a demented mother is a fantasy world. Two black writers have elected to show black families 'united in love and pride, of which the reader would like to be a part', as Mildred D. Taylor said of her own *Roll of Thunder, Hear My Cry* (1976). Virginia Hamilton's *M. C. Higgins, the Great* (1974) creates another family welded together in the face of hardship. Otherwise the brightest message seems to be 'If you take the letters in the word DIVORCES and rearrange them, they spell DISCOVER', as the concluding sentence in Paula Danziger's *The Divorce Express* (1982) avers.

## Further Reading

Andrews, S. (ed.) (1963) *The Hewins Lectures 1947–1962*, Boston: Horn Book.

Avery, G. (1975) *Childhood's Pattern: A Study of the Heroes and Heroines of Children's Fiction 1770–1950*, Leicester: Hodder and Stoughton.

—— (1994), *Behold the Child: American Children and their Books 1621–1922*, London: Bodley Head.

Baym, N. (1978) *Woman's Fiction: A Guide to Novels by and about Women, 1820–1870*, Ithaca, NY: Cornell University Press.

Manthorne, J. (1967) 'The lachrymose ladies' *Horn Book Magazine*, Part 1, 43, 3, 375–384, Part 2, 43, 4, 501–13, Part 3, 43, 5, 623–631.

Meigs, C., Eaton, A., Nesbitt, E. and Viguers, R. (1953) *A Critical History of Children's Literature*, New York: Macmillan.

Townsend, J. R. (1983) *Written for Children: An Outline of English-Language Children's Literature*, Harmondsworth: Kestrel Books.

# 28

# School Stories

## *Sheila Ray*

Attendance at school for some years between the ages of 5 and 18 is a common experience, and one well within the comprehension of readers of children's books. Many books written for children have scenes set in, or references to, school, but the term 'school story' is generally used to describe a story in which most of the action centres on a school, usually a single-sex boarding school. In his essay, 'Boys' weeklies', first published in 1940, George Orwell suggested that the school story is peculiar to England because in England education is mainly a matter of status (Orwell 1962: 182). It is certainly true that the genre is dominated by British writers, who are responsible for most of the examples quoted in this essay.

The world of school is a microcosm of the larger world, in which minor events and concerns loom large and older children, at least, have power, responsibilities and an importance they do not have in the world outside. Despite the rules and regulations, children enjoy a certain kind of freedom. A school story offers a setting in which young people are thrown together and in which relationships between older and younger children, between members of the peer group and between children and adults can be explored. Events and relationships can be imbued with an air of excitement and the possibilities for humour are never far away. Through reading an entertaining story, children can 'test the water', learn how people may react in specific situations and see what lies ahead.

School stories for girls differ from those for boys. Even before the advent of feminism, writers must have realised, albeit subconsciously, the advantages of setting a story in an all girls' school, where females are leaders and decision takers. In the boys' school story, there are few references to home life, but the story for girls usually reflects close links between home and school. The boys' story and the girls' story have developed in parallel, but separately, partly because they have reflected educational developments in the real world.

In Britain, the Education Act of 1870 marked the first official step towards education for all, but even before this schools catering for every level of society were being established in increasing numbers. Two early, full-length books for children, Sarah Fielding's *The Governess* (1749) and *Mrs Leicester's School* by Charles and Mary Lamb (1808), each used a small girls' school as a framework for a collection of short stories, but the first genuine story of school life, which looks at the experience from the child's point of view, is, according to Mary Thwaite, Harriet Martineau's *The Crofton Boys* (1841) (Thwaite 1972: 153). Hugh finds learning difficult and thinks that life will be easier when he joins his older brother at Crofton School; alas, his high expectations are disappointed. These school stories by Fielding, the Lambs and Martineau are still remembered because of their distinguished authorship; there were others, now long forgotten.

In the 1850s, Thomas Hughes set the pattern for what came to be regarded as the traditional school story. *Tom Brown's Schooldays* (1857), which became a children's classic, grew out of Hughes's admiration for Dr Arnold, the Headmaster of Rugby School, an important figure in the development of the English 'public' (that is, private) school system. Preaching the doctrine of muscular Christianity, in vogue in the mid-nineteenth century, the book follows Tom Brown and his friends through their schooldays: Tom arrives as a new boy, passes through a period when he makes the headmaster 'very uneasy' and eventually becomes the most senior boy, a credit to the school. The book has survived because of the fresh, lively style, its concern with everyday school activities, the convincing characters, including the archetypal bully, Flashman, and the still relevant themes.

Published in the following year, Dean Farrar's *Eric, or, Little by Little* (1858) was also based on the author's own schooldays at King William's College on the Isle of Man, but it has dated badly. The author was more interested in his hero's moral development, and Eric, through a series of disastrous misunderstandings, gradually changes from an appealing, basically honest, schoolboy to a sad runaway approaching death. Happily for the school story, Hughes proved to be the more influential writer of the two.

The 1870 Education Act, as well as marking the start of the move towards universal literacy, helped to create a larger market for children's books and magazines; the latter, being cheaper and more accessible, were widely read. Most famous of the many launched in the late nineteenth century were the *Boy's Own Paper* (*BOP*) (1879) and the *Girl's Own Paper* (*GOP*) (1880).

Talbot Baines Reed, whose story, 'My first football match', appeared in the first issue of the *BOP*, quickly established himself as a successful writer of school stories; his most famous, *The Fifth Form at St Dominic's* (1887), was serialised in the *BOP* in 1881–1882. Although the world it portrays has long since disappeared, the characters, their feelings and attitudes, still ring true. Baines Reed was an excellent story-teller; he even manages to make the Nightingale Scholarship examination, described in great detail, sound as exciting as a football match. The themes and incidents which he used were to become the staple ingredients of school stories; the arrival of the new boy and his adjustment to school ways, school matches, the school magazine, conflict between juniors and seniors, concerts, friendships and rivalries, and villainies and blackmail.

The *GOP*, although it contained stories set in girls' boarding schools, did not produce a woman author of the status of Baines Reed. The female equivalents of Rugby's Dr Arnold were Miss Beale and Miss Buss, whose ideas on the education of girls led to the foundation of schools such as Cheltenham Ladies College (1853) and Roedean (1885), which were modelled on boys' public schools, and the high schools, which provided a good, academic education for girls on a daily basis. It was, however, some time before fictional versions of these schools appeared in print. Late nineteenth-century writers for girls wrote from their own experience which was of girls being taught at home or in small schools which were an extension of home. Fictional versions of the latter can be found in Charlotte

Yonge's *The Pillars of the House* (1893), Mrs Molesworth's *The Carved Lions* (1895), in which Geraldine is sent to Green Bank, a small school of twenty to thirty girls, while her brother goes to Rugby, and *Pixie O'Shaughnassy* (1903) by Mrs George de Horne Vaizey. Most of these schools were established in ordinary houses in urban surroundings, a far cry from the gracious stately homes and turreted castles which later became the norm. The plot of Frances Hodgson Burnett's *A Little Princess* (1905) hangs on the fact that the school attended by Sara Crewe is situated in a house in a London terrace. In all these books, however, school is just a small part of the heroine's experiences, and the authors of them were not attempting to write school stories.

The first woman writer who can be compared to Talbot Baines Reed is L. T. Meade. Like Baines Reed, she was a very prolific writer; she edited a magazine, *Atlanta*, and wrote many kinds of fiction, but it was in her stories about girls at school that she found the best outlet for her talents, and she paved the way for her twentieth-century successors. At first glance, it is difficult to see why L. T. Meade is not regarded as the first major writer and populariser of girls' school stories, a role usually ascribed to Angela Brazil; a closer examination of her work, however, shows that, although she uses some of the plots and characters associated with the typical girls' school story, there is a difference between her work and that of the writers who flourished in the 1920s and 1930s. Although Lavender House in *A World of Girls* (1886), Briar Hall in *A Madcap* (1904) and Fairbank in *The School Favourite* (1908) are similar to some of the small schools created by Angela Brazil soon afterwards, Meade is much more concerned with the moral development of her characters. The girls who belong to the secret society in *The School Favourite* are bound by a code of honour which requires them to be obedient, to work hard, to love each other and to do 'a little deed of kindness to some one every day'. In *A World of Girls*, although the heroine, Hester, is clever and hardworking and one of the main themes is the prize essay competition, much of the story is taken up with emotional relationships and with questions of honesty and truthfulness.

Evelyn Sharp's *The Making of a Schoolgirl* (1897) shows the prevailing attitudes to girls' schools, particularly those of the brothers whose sisters attended them, but it puts much more emphasis on the fun side of school, with humorous and sometimes ironic descriptions of school activities and academic achievement. Beverly Lyon Clark rightly describes it as 'brilliant' (Clark 1989: 6).

Between 1899 and 1927, a number of books set in boys' schools, written for adults as much as for children, gave a status to the school story for boys which has never been enjoyed by that for girls. These were usually based on the author's own schooldays and included Rudyard Kipling's *Stalky and Co.* (1899), Horace Annesley Vachell's *The Hill* (1905) and P. G. Wodehouse's *Mike* (1909); later, in the same style, came Alec Waugh's *The Loom of Youth* (1917) and Hugh Walpole's *Jeremy at Crale* (1927). Of these, the most famous is *Stalky and Co.*, of which John Rowe Townsend says, 'After the knowingness of *Stalky* it was difficult ever again to assert the innocent values of the classical school story' (Townsend 1987: 100). Kipling turns the traditional formula on its head: Stalky, M'Turk and Beetle are three natural rebels who have no respect for the school spirit. The irony is that while they are smoking, breaking bounds, collaborating on their prep and generally setting themselves up against authority, they are clearly in the process of becoming just the kind of resourceful and self-disciplined young men that the public schools aimed to produce.

The only similar books by women writers, drawing on their own experiences and writing mainly for adults, are *The Getting of Wisdom* (1910) by Henry Handel Richardson (despite her name, a woman) set in Australia, and Antonia White's *Frost in May* (1933). These were not of enough status to give the girls' school story a more positive image: if Virginia Woolf or Ivy Compton-Burnett had gone to one of the newly emerging girls' public schools and subsequently used her experience in her writing, critical attitudes to girls' school stories might have been very different.

Authors of children's books elsewhere in the Anglo-Saxon world showed little interest in writing school stories: two exceptions are very different in spirit from the stories being published in Britain at the same period. Susan Coolidge's *What Katy Did at School* (1873) was an exception in describing Katy and Clover Carr's adventures at the New England boarding school to which they are sent for a year to be 'finished'; much of the interest centres around the silliness of the other girls in their relationships with the students at the nearby boys' college, a topic ignored by British writers. In Ethel Turner's *Seven Little Australians* (1894) lively Judy Woolcot is sent to boarding school as a punishment.

The heyday of the girls' school story was in the 1920s and 1930s. It came in various forms, in serials and short stories in magazines, annuals and miscellaneous collections as well as in books, all of which were published in great quantities for the growing and apparently insatiable market. Like most popular fiction, school stories emphasised what were seen as middle-class virtues such as good manners, the need for self-discipline, a sense of responsibility and a respect for authority.

By far the most popular girls' writer before 1940 was Angela Brazil (1869–1947), whose name is known to many who have never read her books. She published her first school story, *The Fortunes of Philippa*, in 1906, her last, *The School on the Loch*, in 1946. Although her books reflected events in the outside world – the two World Wars, for example – her underlying attitudes changed very little during forty years. Her fictional schools range from small day schools to large boarding schools; her stories are episodic, describing everyday school activities, but are usually underpinned by plots about missing heiresses, the restoration of family fortunes or the successful achievement of some important goal. Her books contain a lot of information about literature, geography, history, botany, music and the visual arts (Freeman 1976: 20). Schoolgirl readers of Angela Brazil and her successors do not seem to have demanded an exciting plot; rather, they were fascinated by the minutiae of school organisation and a lifestyle which was probably somewhat different from their own experience.

Readership surveys of the period show that Angela Brazil was a favourite author among girls from both middle-class, and working-class backgrounds. In 1933, *The Bookseller* described her as a 'juvenile bestseller' (McAleer 1992: chapter 5). In 1947 she was still the most popular writer for girls according to a survey carried out in north-west England (Carter 1947: 217–221).

Although a few of Brazil's books are linked through the reappearance of characters from an earlier book, most of them are free-standing. Her three most outstanding successors, Elsie Jeanette Oxenham (1880–1960), Dorita Fairlie Bruce

(1885–1970) and Elinor M. Brent-Dyer (1894–1969), all achieved their popularity through the production of series.

Elsie Jeanette Oxenham, the daughter of the journalist and author, John Oxenham, may have had ambitions to write for adults. Her early stories were mildly romantic family tales, but in 1913 she published *Rosaly's New School*, which has a strong school interest, and, in the following year, *Girls of the Hamlet Club*, the first story in the long sequence of Abbey stories, into which most of her books eventually linked. The mainly day-school in *Girls of the Hamlet Club* has recently opened its doors to less wealthy girls who live in the nearby hamlets. Cicely Hobart comes to the area to be near her maternal grandparents, who had not approved of their now dead daughter's marriage, goes to the school and is appalled by the snobbery and the way in which the hamlet girls are outsiders. She befriends them, organises them into the Hamlet Club, with the motto, 'To be or not to be', and arranges country rambles and folk dancing sessions for them. Cicely meets, and is accepted by, her grandparents, and also unites the school by persuading the Hamlet Club to provide a programme of dances when the official school play has to be cancelled because of illness. In *The Abbey Girls* (1920), the Hamlet Club members visit the Abbey, where Mrs Shirley is caretaker; they meet her daughter, Joan, and Cicely arranges for Joan to have a scholarship to the school. Joan sacrifices this to her cousin, Joy, whom she feels needs the discipline of school. Fortunately, Joy is eventually reconciled with her grandfather (he too had disapproved of his daughter's marriage), and both girls are able to go to the school, join the Hamlet Club and in due course become May Queens. In Oxenham's last book, *Two Queens at the Abbey* (1959), Joy's twin daughters are crowned joint Queens. In many of the Abbey books, school is peripheral to the main interest, which centres on the Abbey and the girls who come to live with Joy in the house which she has inherited from her grandfather. However, they were clearly enjoyed in much the same way as school stories.

Dorita Fairlie Bruce wrote three series, the Dimsie, the Springdale and the Maudsley High/St Bride's books, each consisting of six to twelve titles. Her first book, *The Senior Prefect* (1920) was later retitled *Dimsie Goes to School*; the Dimsie series chronicles the career of Daphne Isabel Maitland (Dimsie) as she moves through the Jane Willard Foundation, becomes prefect and head girl, and it then follows her into marriage and motherhood. Bruce's last published book, *Sally's Summer Term* (1961), was part of a trilogy and, like Oxenham's later books, is very much poorer than her earlier work.

The books of Elinor M. Brent-Dyer have lasted much better and are still available, in paperback editions, in the 1990s. Her first book, *Gerry Goes to School*, appeared in 1922, but it was *The School at the Chalet* (1925) that launched her on the road to success. In this, a young English woman, Madge Bettany, establishes a school in the Austrian Tyrol, with her younger sister, Jo, as its first pupil. The school flourishes, evacuating to the Channel Islands and then the English/Welsh border during the Second World War, and returning to Switzerland afterwards. In the final book, *Prefects of the Chalet School* (1970), Jo's own daughters are senior pupils, looking forward to university and adulthood.

Although the school story is generally thought of as being set in a boarding-school, there were also stories about day-schools. Winifred Darch (1884–1960) concentrated on these; her books, from *Chris and Some Others* (1920) to *The New Girl at Graychurch* (1939) are all free-standing. Some of her fictional schools are the newly established county high schools, in one of which she taught, which educated both children who passed the 11+ examination and were given scholarships, and those whose parents could afford modest fees. Most of her books have strong plots, and many contain detailed accounts of school plays; they are also fascinating social documents, reflecting the snobbish and class-conscious attitudes of the period. In *The New School and Hilary* (1926), for example, Hilary, who has to leave her expensive independent school on the death of her father, and Judith Wingfield, a successful ex-pupil of the same school, both arrive at a new county high school for girls, Hilary as a pupil, Judith as a young teacher. The school is rather despised in the town, but through their combined efforts and a successful production of *As You Like It*, it is established as a real asset among the local people.

In the 1920s and 1930s, a high proportion of British girls joined the Girl Guide movement, which recruited from all sections of society. It offered girls some of the same opportunities as an all-girls' school, an environment in which friendships and competition flourished, and in which they could develop skills and interests, and experience leadership. Many of the fictional schools had Guide companies; Catherine Christian, editor of *The Guide* magazine in the 1940s, specialised in Guide stories and in at least two of her books, *The Marigolds Make Good* (1937) and *A Schoolgirl from Hollywood* (1939), the plot develops from the fact that schools which have grown slack or fallen on hard times, are brought up to standard with the help of the Guides in their midst.

There were many popular stock characters, such as the 'wild' Irish girl; another was the Ruritanian princess who, sent to an English boarding school for safety, was frequently kidnapped (Trease 1964: 107). Elinor Brent-Dyer's *The Princess of the Chalet School* (1927) and F. O. H. Nash's *Kattie of the Balkans* (1931) both use this theme; a typical set piece has the brave English girl who has rescued the princess riding in state to receive the grateful thanks of the Ruritanian citizens. Authors were well aware of their readers' fantasies and did their best to fulfil them.

The Ruritanian theme was also used by boys' writers. In A. L. Haydon's *His Serene Highness* (1925), Prince Karl of Altburg arrives at Compton Prior, a famous boys' public school, and earns the respect of his fellow pupils by beating up one of the school bullies. He is kidnapped and it then transpires that he is only a look-alike cousin of the real Karl and has been sent to Compton Prior as a decoy. However, the real Prince Karl does visit the school to thank both his cousin, and the English schoolboys who had saved his life. Apart from this, the book is typical of its time, with a subplot concerning two rival gangs of younger boys, each trying to make the other believe that the school is haunted.

Harold Avery, Richard Bird, Hylton Cleaver, R. A. H. Goodyear, Gunby Hadath and Michael Poole were the most prolific among the many authors who supplied the steady demand for stories set in boys' public schools, but none of them achieved the popularity of the writers for girls already mentioned, with the exception of Frank Richards (1876–1961), whose work appeared in *The Gem* (1907–1939) and *The Magnet* (1908–1940). It is estimated that Charles Hamilton, using over twenty pseudonyms, of which 'Frank Richards' is the best known, wrote over sixty million words (Richards 1988: 266). As Martin Clifford, he created Tom Merry and St Jim's for *The Gem*; as Frank Richards, writing in *The Magnet*, he launched Greyfriars and the Famous Five of Harry Wharton, Frank Nugent, Bob Cherry, Johnny Bull and Hurree Jamset Ram Singh together with the bounder, Herbert Vernon-Smith, and the famous fat boy of the Remove, Billy Bunter.

In 1919, as Hilda Richards, he introduced Billy's sister, Bessie Bunter, to Cliff House in the *School Friend*; the Cliff House stories were then taken over by other writers and the characters developed into more realistic personalities with Bessie herself becoming a still fat but loyal and popular friend. The other famous girls' school in magazine fiction was Morcove, a boarding school on Exmoor; the Morcove stories, which appeared in *Schoolgirls' Own* (1921–1936), were also written by a man, Horace Phillips, using the pseudonym of Marjorie Stanton.

Many school stories in the 1920s and 1930s were badly written with banal and carelessly constructed plots, unconvincing characters and situations, and a lack of attention to detail. It is not surprising that the genre was poorly regarded by adults who cared about what children read. There were few outlets for the criticism of children's literature and the fact that some school stories might be better than others was easily overlooked in view of the amount of material that was being published.

The years of the Second World War provided a watershed, after which the gaps between school, domestic and adventure stories began to close. The changes are well illustrated by looking at the work of Geoffrey Trease, who is both a critic and a writer of children's books. He paid tribute to A. Stephen Tring's *The Old Gang* (1947) as a 'good story about Grammar School day-boys which broke new ground' (Trease 1964: 111) and he himself began a series of books about day schools with *No Boats on Bannermere* (1949). He wrote this because two girls whom he met when he gave a talk to a group of school children in Cumberland in 1947 at a 'book week' asked him for stories about real boys and girls going to day schools (Trease 1974: 149). Later, beginning with *Jim Starling* (1958), E. W. Hildick published a series of books set in and around Cement Street secondary modern school, in which school is seen as an integral part of the boys' lives.

The boarding school story was not dead, even for boys. Anthony Buckeridge's schoolboy, Jennings, first appeared in a radio play on the BBC's *Children's Hour* in 1948; *Jennings Goes to School* (1950) followed, the first in a series of books about the pupils of Linbury Court, a preparatory school for boys. The humour of these, which sometimes borders on farce, made them very popular and Buckeridge shows a good understanding of how small boys talk, and very shrewdly invented his own, dateless, slang. In 1955, William Mayne, educated at a choir school himself, published *A Swarm in May*, the first of three books set in a Cathedral choir school. In most of his books, however, the children attend day schools. The day schools are still largely single-sex, but there is more communication between boys and girls, and sometimes co-operation is important to the plot as in Trease's Bannerdale books and in William Mayne's *Sand*.

There are few examples of stories set in mixed boarding schools. Enid Blyton set her first series of school stories about the 'Naughtiest Girl' in the mixed Whyteleafe School with its two headmistresses, Miss Belle and Miss Best (an echo of Miss Beale and Miss Buss or, more probably, names which lend themselves to the nicknames, Beauty and the Beast?). Whyteleafe is also a progressive school with a School Meeting at which all the children are involved in making rules and deciding on appropriate awards and punishments. It seems likely that Enid Blyton was aware of the existence of progressive, mixed, independent boarding schools such as Dartington, Bedales and Summerhill, but almost certainly she chose to set her first school stories in one because they first appeared as serials in *Sunny Stories*, a magazine intended to appeal to both sexes. However, the girls-only school was far more popular with the girl readers (who were in the majority), and after Whyteleafe came St Clare's and Malory Towers, both girls' schools. Beginning with *The Twins at St Clare's* (1941) and *First Term at Malory Towers* (1946), the careers of the O'Sullivan twins and Darrell Rivers respectively are chronicled, from the time they arrive as new girls until their final term. Darrell is one of Blyton's most attractive and convincing characters.

If Enid Blyton was influenced largely by the demands of her market, Mabel Esther Allan was genuinely interested in the theories of A. S. Neill, who founded Summerhill, when she created several co-educational boarding establishments among her numerous fictional schools. She acknowledges his influence: 'All my schools were progressive ones, where pupils relied on self-discipline and not imposed discipline. Many of them were co-educational' (Allan 1982: 16). *The School on Cloud Ridge* (1952) is about a co-educational school, *Lucia Comes to School* (1953) about an equally progressive (but all-girls) school, where potholing, walking and cycling take the place of organised games. Lucia, half Italian, arrives at Arndale Hall to find that it is nothing like the schools described in the English school stories she has read, but although the rules are made by the girls themselves and school work is done on a flexible learning basis, she still has to learn to fit in with the other girls.

Although Blyton and Allan use many of the conventions and situations pioneered by earlier writers, their style and attitudes are very different. Their schoolgirls have more freedom and their outlook is more modern. This is also true of Nancy Breary who, between 1943 and 1961, and writing about more traditional schools, produced a succession of humorous stories, skilfully ringing the changes on standard plots and characters.

Three outstanding writers for girls in this period were Mary K. Harris, Antonia Forest and Elfrida Vipont. Mary Harris specialised in school stories; her first, *Gretel at St Bride's* (1941) is a fairly conventional boarding school story although Gretel is an unusual heroine, a refugee from Nazi Germany. Her last, *Jessica on Her Own* (1968) is centred on a secondary modern day school.

Elfrida Vipont's work included a sequence of five novels about an extended Quaker family. In *The Lark in the Morn* (1948), Kit Haverard goes to 'the great Quaker school for girls at Heryot'. In a later book, Kit's niece, Laura, fails to pass the 11+ examination for the local grammar school, refuses to be sent to Heryot and settles in well at the nearby secondary modern school for girls, where her acting talent flourishes. In both books Elfrida Vipont, who won the Library Association Carnegie Medal for the second book in this sequence, *The Lark on the Wing* (1950), uses their school experiences as an important element in the careers of her central characters but their family and out of school life are not excluded.

Antonia Forest's sequence of novels about the Marlow family began with a school story, *Autumn Term* (1948), in which 12-year-old twins, Nicola and Lawrie, arrive at Kingscote, a traditional girls' boarding school, in the wake of their four sisters, the eldest of whom is head girl. The sequence includes three more school stories and five books set in the school holidays, giving a rounded picture of the lives of the twins as they grow from 12 to over 14.

By 1960 it was felt that the traditional school story had run its course and certainly few new titles were appearing. Elsie Jeanette Oxenham's last book was published in 1959, Dorita Fairlie Bruce's in 1961; these are so weak compared with their authors' earlier work that they seem to provide an appropriate death knell. There was, however, a continuing demand for school stories, particularly from girls, and titles stayed stubbornly in print. The last Chalet School book was published posthumously in 1970, but in 1967 paperback editions of earlier titles were successfully launched and have continued to sell in their thousands each year since.

If interest in writing school stories petered out in the 1960s, it was clear by 1970 that some major children's writers might find still the enclosed world of school an ideal framework within which to explore matters of concern to young people. Penelope Farmer's *Charlotte Sometimes* (1969) marks the beginning of this revival; in a satisfying time travel story, the author explores the question of identity through Charlotte who goes to school some time in the 1960s and wakes up one morning to find she has changed places with Clare who was a pupil in 1918. How, Charlotte wonders, can the schoolgirls and teachers in 1918 accept her as Clare, and why is Clare so readily accepted in the 1960s?

Later, Barbara Willard's *Famous Rowena Lamont* (1983), Michelle Magorian's *Back Home* (1985) and Ann Pilling's *The Big Pink* (1987) were all to use the conventions of the boarding school story to explore the problems of growing up and adjustment, but they also break away from the accepted pattern. Rusty, the heroine of *Back Home*, for example, is one of the few schoolgirl heroines to be expelled. In Frances Usher's *Maybreak* (1990) the conventions are essential to the fast-moving plot. There were even two new series set in girls' boarding schools, Anne Digby's Trebizon books, launched in 1978, and Harriet Martyn's stories about Balcombe Hall, which began in 1982.

Two books published in the USA in the 1970s contrast with the British school story, where, despite the developments in the genre, integration and the triumph of good over evil continued to be the norm. Robert Cormier's controversial book, *The Chocolate War* (1974) is set in the all-boys Catholic day school, Trinity. It is a sad, pessimistic story; Brother Leon, in charge of the annual fund-raising event, which involves the selling of twenty thousand boxes of chocolates, is helped by The Vigils, a powerful secret society led by the corrupt bully, Archie Costello. Jerry Renault, a new boy with hidden strengths, refuses to participate and is trapped into a fight which he cannot win, his downfall and humiliation brought about with the compliance of Brother Leon. The school setting is essential to the story and makes the triumph of evil over good all the more horrifying.

Rosemary Wells's *The Fog Comes on Little Pig Feet* (1972) is based on the author's experiences. Rachel lasts two weeks at North Place, a private New England girls' boarding school, where she is appalled by the lack of freedom, the snobbery and the corruption; favourable treatment can apparently by bought by rich fathers for their rebellious or under-achieving daughters. Instead of settling down in time-honoured fashion, Rachel is allowed to return home.

In the 1970s, British authors set stories for younger children in primary schools, which offer an environment in which children from different cultural and ethnic backgrounds come together naturally; against this background, racial attitudes and sex roles can be examined, and both these topics were of new importance in the 1970s. Gene Kemp's *The Turbulent Term of Tyke Tiler* (1977), set in a state primary school, won the Carnegie Medal; the reader assumes from the evidence that Tyke is a boy and only at the end of the book does it become clear that she is a girl. In the late 1970s Mabel Esther Allan began a series of books about Pine Street primary school. Samantha Padgett, bright and intelligent, a natural leader at Pine Street, moves on to a secondary comprehensive in *First Term at Ash Grove* (1988) and has to prove that she can cope with the new challenges. The setting may be different; the message is the same.

In 1976 Anna Home, in charge of children's drama programmes at the BBC, was looking for a series which would reflect contemporary school life rather than 'the traditional worlds of Bunter and Jennings' (Home 1993: 102). Grange Hill School, created and peopled by Phil Redmond, proved an ideal vehicle for looking at contemporary issues such as bullying, serious illness, death, broken homes, teenage pregnancy, smoking and drugs, while presenting a rounded picture of school life. When *Grange Hill* was first shown, it was seen as anti-authoritarian by adults; skilfully crafted, its underlying purpose is to look at school from the child's viewpoint and while reflecting the real world, it supports traditional values. The popularity of the first series led, not only to its continuation but also to books, based on the series, by Phil Redmond and Jan Needle, while Robert Leeson used the characters in original stories.

Since the 1970s, writers of school stories have had to take account of the fact that children mature earlier and are more worldly-wise. They tend to write about pre-pubertal children and concentrate on either boys or girls. In *Flour Babies* (1992), Anne Fine writes humorously about boys engaged in a school science project; in *Goggle-Eyes* (1989) she creates a traditional girls' day school as a framework within which to examine contemporary problems such as divorce and conservation. Set in the same sort of schools, Jean Ure's Peter High books and Mary Hooper's School Friend series reflect the continuing popularity of series among girl readers and make good use of traditional themes while showing awareness of the realities of life in the 1990s. Allen Sadler's *Sam's Swop Shop* (1993) finds boys raising money for essential school equipment rather than charity as would have been the case in the past, but some problems are perennial. *The Present Takers* (1983) by Aidan Chambers and, a decade later, Jan Dean's *Me, Duncan and the Great Hippopotamus Scandal* (1993) both show that bullying, a theme which provided a memorable scene in *Tom Brown's Schooldays*, still looms large in the lives of many schoolchildren.

In stories about older children, school may provide a background for light romances as in the popular American series such as Sweet Valley High. Adèle Geras, on the other hand, faces the problems of growing sexuality head-on in her Egerton Hall trilogy. Set in the early 1960s, this tells the stories of three friends who have gone through a girls' boarding school together and, now in the sixth-form, are preoccupied by sex and impending adulthood. Each of their lives parallels that of a fairy tale heroine (Geras 1990: 20–21). Megan, heroine of *The Tower Room* (1990) is the Rapunzel figure; Alice in *Watching the Roses* (1991) is Sleeping Beauty, while Bella of *Pictures of the Night* (1992) is Snow White, complete with wicked step-mother and the apple which nearly chokes her to death. The trilogy is a significant literary achievement which shows how far the school story has come since its first manifestation over two hundred years ago.

At the end of the twentieth century, school, whatever its nature, remains an attractive setting for a story for young people, providing a stable and safe environment in which children from different backgrounds can meet, develop relationships and share experiences. School stories continue to appeal to children at the age when the peer group is all important, when they are seeking independence and curious about what lies ahead. The genre has a special appeal for girls, who enjoy stories and series in which the characters are seen to mature; boys are more likely to read for the enjoyment of the moment – Jennings is always 11, Bunter forever in the Remove.

School stories have been criticised for their unreal picture of school life, but authors have responded to changes in society, and time-honoured themes are adapted to new circumstances. School stories, with a few exceptions, provide a positive picture of one of the almost universal experiences of childhood and, perhaps most important of all, show a respect for intellectual and personal achievement, preparing readers to play a responsible role in society.

# References

Allan, M. E. (1982) *To Be An Author*, Heswall: published by the author.

Carter, G. A. (1947) 'Some childish likes and dislikes', *Library Association Record* 49, 99: 217–221.

Clark, B. L. (1989) 'Introduction', in Sharp, E. (ed.) *The Making of a Schoolgirl*, New York: Oxford University Press.

Freeman, G. (1976) *The Schoolgirl Ethic: The Life and Work of Angela Brazil*, London: Allen Lane.

Geras, A. (1990) 'Fairy Frameworks', *Books for Keeps* 65: 20–21.

Home, A. (1993) *Into the Box of Delights: A History of Children's Television*, London: BBC Books.

McAleer, J. (1992) *Popular Reading and Publishing in Britain 1914–1950*, Oxford: Clarendon Press.

Orwell, G. (1962) *Inside the Whale and Other Essays*, Harmondsworth: Penguin.

Richards, J. (1988) *Happiest Days: The Public Schools in English Fiction*, Manchester: Manchester University Press.

Thwaite, M. F. (1972) *From Primer to Pleasure in Reading*, 2nd edn, London: Library Association.

Townsend, J. R. (1987) *Written for Children*, 3rd edn, London: Penguin.

Trease, G. (1964) *Tales Out of School: A Survey of Children's Fiction*, 2nd edn, London: Heinemann.

—— (1974) *Laughter at the Door*, London: Macmillan.

# Further Reading

Auchmuty, R. (1992) *A World of Girls*, London: Women's Press.

Avery, G. (1991) *The Best Type of Girl: A History of Girls' Independent Schools*, London: Deutsch.

Cadogan, M. and Craig, P. (1985) *You're a Brick, Angela!: The Girls Story 1939–1985*, 2nd edn, London: Gollancz.

Kirkpatrick, R. J. (1990) *Bullies, Beaks and Flannelled Fools: An Annotated Bibliography of Boys' School Fiction 1742–1990*, London: published by the author.

Löfgren, E. M. (1993) *Schoolmates of the Long-Ago: Motifs and Archetypes in Dorita Fairlie Bruce's Boarding School Stories*, Stockholm: Symposion Graduale.

McClelland, H. (1981) *Behind the Chalet School*, Bognor Regis: New Horizon.

Quigley, I. (1982) *The Heirs of Tom Brown: The English School Story*, London: Chatto and Windus.

Reynolds, K. (1990) *Girls Only? Gender and Popular Children's Fiction in Britain, 1880–1910*, Hemel Hempstead: Harvester Wheatsheaf.

# 29

# Pony Books

## *Alison Haymonds*

The pony book continues in the long tradition of literature celebrating the love affair between the British and the horse, yet it has always been relegated firmly to the sidelines. Like all popular fiction with mass appeal, the quality of the stories is variable, but there are pony books which merit comparison with any books in the canon of children's literature.

The genre, which first appeared in the 1920s and 1930s, and then developed and flourished during the post-war boom in riding, is part of a much wider range of horse stories, which can be divided into four categories:

1 The anthropomorphic horse story in which the horse replaces the human hero and tells the story or is the centre of consciousness. The most famous examples are *Black Beauty* and *Moorland Mousie*. This type of story has almost died out, but can still be found in the Australian writer Elyne Mitchell's Silver Brumby series (from 1958).
2 The wild horse story, mainly American, which owes much to the influence of Western movies and generally features a boy taming a horse. It has many examples, including Will James's *Smoky* (1926), *My Friend Flicka* (1943) and the long-running *Black Stallion* series (from 1941), and is still popular in the USA.
3 The adventure story which includes ponies – Pamela Whitlock and Katharine Hull, Mary Treadgold, Monica Edwards and Monica Dickens are key names in this category.
4 The pony story which is realistic, domestic, and based in Britain; the humans are of equal importance to the horses, and the relationship between girl (or occasionally boy) and pony is the driving force of the book. Joanna Cannan, Primrose Cumming, the Pullein-Thompsons, K. M. Peyton and Patricia Leitch are among the major writers.

This final category is the one commonly perceived to be 'the pony story'. As a genre, it lacks the universality of school stories or family stories. It ignores the world outside the stable yard, and most of the traditional conventions of storytelling – love and villainy, conflict and mystery. Its readership is as limited as its scope, mainly female, adolescent, and pony mad, for the passion for ponies and pony books seems to be a uniquely female phenomenon. In the formula pony book, the girl is the central character with the pony filling an ambiguous role, which is closer to the traditional heroine both as victim and object of desire. Ponies are not completely personified but they are treated as three–dimensional characters and their physical appearance and personality are described in great detail.

Pony stories, like other types of formulaic fiction – school stories, westerns, and romances – have certain narrative conventions. The following sequence of situations can be found in almost all formulaic pony books: a young girl, lacking in confidence and self esteem, longs for a pony but cannot afford one; she finds a special pony, longs to own it, and acquires it by chance or by saving money; she discovers the economic problems of keeping a pony, learns to ride, school and look after it properly and, in the process, gains confidence and a skill; something threatens the status quo, often lack of money, and it seems the girl may lose the pony; however, in the end, she rides it to success in a show.

The books contain detailed advice on horsemanship and riding and also come complete with a set of situations, values and assumptions: the setting is British and rural - the female hero and her family have often moved to the country from the town; country life is 'better' than city life; the heroine's family is short of money, or has lost money, and her parents are often in 'artistic' jobs – writers, artists, and potters. There is a strong code of behaviour attached to horses and horse riding which mirrors the traditional English code of fair play, sportsmanship and good manners.

Books like *A Pony for Jean* (Joanna Cannan 1936), *Wish for a Pony* (Monica Edwards 1947) *A Pony of Our Own* (Patricia Leitch 1960), *Dream of Fair Horses* (Leitch 1975), *Jackie Won a Pony* (Judith M. Berrisford 1958), *A Pony in the Family*, (Berrisford 1959) *Jill's Gymkhana* (Ruby Ferguson 1949), *Fly-by-Night* (K. M. Peyton 1968) and *For Love of a Horse* (Leitch 1976) though written over a period of forty years and quite different in tone and quality, are all formula stories. There is also a vast amount of literature which though not adhering to that rigid formula can still be classified as pony books; books which describe children with ponies of their own, running or helping at riding stables, pony trekking, rescuing ponies, and taking part in other pony-centred adventures. Very often a series of books about a particular girl rider starts with the formula novel then progresses to less pony-centred stories, such as Monica Edwards's Romney Marsh and Punchbowl books.

It is hardly surprising that the genre has been frequently criticised as narrow, middle class and unchanging: Elaine Moss observed that 'Horse and pony books . . . tend to be thought of by trendy journalists as middle-class, static, irrelevant to today's social pattern' (Moss 1976: 30). Marcus Crouch complained: 'Pony stories were from the beginning middle-class. Young riders owned their ponies by unchallenged right; there was no vulgar show of money, and Pony Club subscriptions were paid by some unseen and disembodied daddy' (Crouch 1972: 152). Margery Fisher promotes the pony story to 'the upper-middle-class' and points out the problem of updating the genre: 'When the Great House has become a home for backward children, it is not easy to write of it unselfconsciously, as if at the present time, with Cook in residence, and yet it is too soon for this kind of story to become a period piece. The arbitrary addition of topical detail hardly helps' (Fisher 1961: 312). Yet the pony story succeeds in what it sets out to do and remains popular because it stays within the small, highly specialised society of horse lovers. Although the world of horses is perceived as upper class and privileged, the families in these stories are not always middle class – less so in recent books – and seldom well off (which is why the children long hopelessly for ponies). Pony books are obsessed with lack of money, not wealth, and with the care, riding and love of horses – and these concerns are as relevant in the 1990s as they were in the 1940s.

Pony stories owe a good deal to traditional fairy tales with their stories of the transformation of gauche girls and neglected ponies and the recurring pattern of motifs and conventional events. They also bear a resemblance to the novel of 'education', the *bildungsroman*, for the female hero gains confidence and a purpose in life by acquiring a pony. Perhaps they are even closer to the formula love story – girl meets pony, girl loses pony, girl gets pony – for these stories are about intense emotional relationships in which the object of affection happens to be a pony. They are also books of instruction for they are crammed with closely detailed information about buying and riding horses, their tack, grooming and diet, as well as the specialised language of equitation.

This didactic streak has descended directly from the forerunners of the genre. Although *Black Beauty* (1877) is generally regarded as the first in the field, there were many moral books told from the animals' point of view written earlier in the nineteenth century (Avery 1965: 38). One of the first was *Memoirs of Dick, the little poney: supposed to be written by himself; and published for the instruction and amusement of little masters and mistresses*, published in 1799. Dick's story – he is stolen by gypsies and passed between cruel and kind owners until he ends his days in a 'fertile field' – was the pattern for many autobiographical pony stories, which remained popular for a century and a half.

The greatest of these, Anna Sewell's *Black Beauty*, was intended for simple working folk who had daily contact with horses 'to induce kindness, sympathy, and an understanding treatment of horses' (Chitty 1971: 187), but from the first was read enthusiastically by children. Exciting, dramatic, with its strong, simple style, and memorable characters, *Black Beauty* set a standard which future pony books found hard to match, but its values and attitudes to animals still influence the genre. Anna Sewell preached a new compassionate understanding between horse and owner, and judged people on their treatment of animals, regardless of money or class.

For the next fifty years, pony stories tended to be labelled as nature-study books, like *Skewbald the New Forest Pony* (1923), one of the publisher Black's animal stories series told from the animal's point of view, sober books which concentrated on accurate country lore rather than exciting plots. (*Skewbald* was written by Allen W. Seaby (1867–1953), Professor of Fine Art at Reading University (1920–1933); he wrote a series of stories about British native ponies, including *Exmoor Lass* (1928), *Dinah the Dartmoor Pony* (1935), *Sons of Skewbald* (1937), *Sheltie* (1939), *Mona the Welsh Pony* (1948), and a book on *British Ponies* (1936).) This reflected the growing interest in native breeds of ponies as did the next pony classic, *Moorland Mousie* (1929). This realistic story of an Exmoor pony was autobiographical, full of tips on horsemanship and horse management and memorably illustrated by the great horse artist Lionel Edwards. It was a direct imitation of *Black Beauty*, but was written specifically for children by 'Golden Gorse', the pseudonym of Muriel Wace. The grand-daughter of a crown equerry to Queen Victoria, Muriel Wace, like most of the pony story writers who followed her, was brought up with ponies, and Mousie and Tinker Bell were based on real Exmoors.

Perhaps it was no coincidence that *Moorland Mousie* was published in the same year that the Pony Club was established with the express aim of 'interesting young people in riding and sport and at the same time offering the opportunity of higher instruction in this direction than many of them can obtain individually' (*The Pony Club Year Book* 1994: 68). This started a trend for stories of instruction thinly disguised as fiction with young riders being taught the finer points of horsemanship, like 'Golden Gorse's' *Janet and Felicity, the Young Horse-Breakers* (1937), and *Riders of Tomorrow* (1935), by Captain J. E. Hance, former captain and riding master of the Royal Horse Artillery. Captain Hance had served in India and was one of the many military men who came back from the Empire imbued with a passion for horses. They were immensely influential in all sports and organisations involving horses, including the Pony Club, and introduced Indian words like 'gymkhana' and 'jodhpur' into the language.

It was adolescent girls who were most receptive to this new obsession for horses and the emergence of the girl rider changed the character of the pony book. The focus of attention shifted from the pony to the pony owners and early books like *The Ponies of Bunts and the Adventures of the Children Who Rode Them* (1933), and their sequels, lively true stories, written as fiction and illustrated with black and white photographs, reflected the new trend. But the book which did most to influence the formula was a classic story originally intended for adults by its author Enid Bagnold. Despite this, *National Velvet* (1935), has always been read by children, particularly after the enormous success of the film version in 1944. The plot has all the motifs which became familiar in countless pony books: the pony-mad girl who cannot afford a pony wins an unmanageable horse in a raffle, loves and trains it and eventually comes first in a major race, the Grand National. Although it has been criticised for its caricature of a working-class family, *National Velvet* was among the first books to put into words that passionate yearning for horses by adolescent girls which characterises the genre:

> 'I tell myself stories about horses', [Velvet] went on, desperately fishing at her shy desires. 'Then I can dream about them. Now I dream about them every night. I want to be a famous rider, I should like to carry despatches, I should like to get a first at Olympia, I should like to ride in a great race, I should like to have so many horses that I could walk down between the two rows of loose boxes and ride what I chose'.
>
> Bagnold 1935: 71

Another pony-mad girl echoed these sentiments more prosaically in a book published in the following year. Joanna Cannan's *A Pony for Jean* (1936), now regarded as the pioneer of the new type of pony novel, was written specifically for children, and owed much to E. Nesbit in tone and humour. Like *National Velvet*, it concentrated on the pony-owner rather than the pony, telling the story of Jean Leslie, 'nearly 12', who moves to the country when her father loses his money, and is given a neglected pony, 'The Toastrack', by her horsey cousins who regard her as hopeless as her mount. Jean learns to ride by trial and error, nurtures and trains the pony, romantically renamed Cavalier, and wins the jumping class at the local gymkhana. It is the prototype for hundreds of pony books and is still one of the best of the genre. It had the benefit of an experienced author, Joanna Cannan, who shared her young readers' passion for ponies and who (according to her daughter Josephine Pullein-Thompson) had 'longed and longed to have her own pony to ride' when she was young. Her pony books, which include two sequels to *A Pony for Jean*, are distinguished by their humour, and a tone which shifts between chatty informality and deliberate literariness.

Joanna Cannan passed on her love of horses and her writing talent to her three daughters and started a pony-book dynasty. Josephine Pullein-Thompson and her twin sisters Diana and Christine, began writing books in their teens and have continued for almost half a century, selling 11 million books all over the world. The name Pullein-Thompson has become synonymous with pony stories and this family, above all other writers in the genre, can be credited with popularising the pony book.

The early Pullein-Thompson books had an innocent ebullience and lively style missing in the later ones. They bear the influence of Victorian children's writers, showing their human characters receiving a moral education from animals. The books are about spoilt, bad-mannered children who are not fit to own ponies, learning kindness and humility through proper horsemanship, or ordinary children who are 'broken in' as they school their ponies. These were the themes of Josephine Pullein-Thompson's first and best stories, *Six Ponies* (1946), *I Had Two Ponies* (1947), and *Plenty of Ponies* (1949). Josephine ran a riding school with her sisters, rode in major competitions and was a Pony Club District Commissioner, and her zeal to instruct is clear, but her books are still readable and full of lively and believable children. In later years she concentrated on less successful adventure stories and a Pony Club series but has returned to more straightforward stories of horsemanship, like *The Prize Pony* (1982).

Diana and Christine have not confined themselves to pony stories. Diana, who has written adult fiction and non-fiction, has found it hard to match her early books, such as *I Wanted a Pony* (1946), *A Pony for Sale* (1951) and *Janet Must Ride* (1951), although one of her last pony stories, *Cassidy in Danger* (1979), is a satisfying return to form. Christine, who is the most prolific of the three, has endeavoured, more than most pony writers, to keep her books abreast of the times, notably in the series featuring the show jumper David Smith. Her hunting trilogy starting with *We Hunted Hounds* (1949) is also noteworthy, but has suffered, like others in the genre with a hunting theme, from the sharp decline in public support for the sport.

With such a huge output, the sisters' standard is variable, but their love and knowledge of horses is undeniable. They have joined forces since their first book written together, *It Began with Picotee* (1946), to write a series of sequels to *Black Beauty*.

Another pioneer of the pony book was Primrose Cumming whose first book *Doney* (1934) was published when she was still in her teens. Her fantasy, *Silver Snaffles* (1937), in which the heroine, Jenny, passes Alice-like through the wall of the stable into a utopian world of talking horses who teach her horsemanship, successfully bridged the gap between the talking-horse story and the new type of pony book. Primrose Cumming experimented more than most with the genre, writing about the great working horses, as well as ponies. Her best books have a strong sense of the English countryside. *The Wednesday Pony* (1939), based on real characters, tells the story of a butcher's children and one of the great equine characters in children's fiction, Jingo, the high-stepping harness pony who turns out to be the horse of their dreams. *The Silver Eagle Riding School* (1938), and its sequels, in which the three Chantry sisters discover the problems and pleasures of running their own stables, was one of the first of many 'working' pony stories which proliferated in the 1950s with the arrival of careers books for girls. Primrose Cumming, conscious of the limitations of the genre, wrote her last pony book in 1969 and concentrated on girls' picture books and comics for more than twenty years.

The flood of pony stories was temporarily stemmed by the Second World War. Mary Treadgold's Carnegie Medal winner, *We Couldn't Leave Dinah* (1941), an adventure story rather than a pony book, was one of the very few books to acknowledge the war, with its exciting story of children trapped on an occupied Channel Island. As peace broke out, there was an astonishing resurgence of popularity in riding among children grown blasé about the machine age. Once the pastime of the favoured few, riding became everybody's sport, and there were more and more children to enjoy it for the birth rate rose sharply until 1947. There was an ever-increasing number of riding schools and more children could afford their own ponies, particularly the native breeds which were cheap and easy to keep. This interest was encouraged by the flourishing Pony Club and whetted by the new phenomenon, television. In 1947, the BBC televised the Royal International Horse Show at White City for the first time and soon Lieutenant-Colonel Harry Llewellyn, Pat Smythe and their famous horses, Foxhunter, Prince Hal and Tosca, became household names. Any book with 'pony' in the title would find thousands of eager readers and, in the 1950s, a large number of indifferent pony stories were trotted out to meet the growing demand.

Equestrian experts in horse-breeding and riding, like Pamela Macgregor-Morris, Lady Kitty Ritson and Pat Smythe, and writers of adult books, like Catherine Cookson and Monica Dickens, tried their hand at the genre with varying degrees of success. Kitty Barne, better known for more serious children's fiction, wrote a classic pony book, *Rosina Copper* (1954), based on the true story of an Argentine polo pony. M. E. (Mary Evelyn) Atkinson, author of the popular Lockett family holiday adventure books, and Lorna Hill, who wrote the Sadler's Wells series, both produced indifferent pony stories, lured, perhaps, by the deceptive simplicity of the genre. However, young readers preferred the Jill series, starting with *Jill's Gymkhana* (1949), by Ruby Ferguson, most of which are still in print. Regarded as trivial by the more serious minded, the books about Jill, her ponies and her pals, have the jolly, hearty, middle-class tone more typical of school stories and lack the didactic streak of the genre.

Many young riders felt a compulsion to write as well as ride and joined the growing ranks of pony book authors. This large number of young writers is unique to the genre and seems to be part of the pony-mad phase. Primrose Cumming and the Pullein-Thompsons were not the only early starters. Among the youngest published writers were Moyra Charlton, who was 11 when she wrote *Tally Ho, the*

Story of an Irish Hunter (1930), and Daphne Winstone, who wrote *Flame* (1945) when she was 12: others included April Jaffe (14), who wrote *Satin and Silk* (1948), and the 15-year-olds Lindsay Campbell (*Horse of Air* (1957) and Bernagh Brims (*Runaway Riders* (1963)). In 1936, 15-year-old Shirley Faulkner-Horne wrote a book of instruction, *Riding for Children*, and schoolgirls Katharine Hull and Pamela Whitlock, 15 and 16 respectively, sent the manuscript of a book they were writing together to Arthur Ransome. With his encouragement, *The Far-Distant Oxus* was published the following year (1937). A sub-*Swallows and Amazons* with ponies, this book and its two sequels were the forerunner of the adventure plus pony stories in which the ponies were incidental.

Arguably the finest writer in the genre, K. M. (Kathleen) Peyton, started writing at the age of 9 and her first story was published when she was 15. *Sabre, The Horse from the Sea* (1948), written under her maiden name Kathleen Herald, was followed by *The Mandrake* (1949) and *Crab the Roan* (1953). Although she went on to greater things, including a Carnegie Medal, and other kinds of books, she never lost her all-consuming interest and continues to write pony stories. Even her admired *Flambards* series (from 1978), though by no stretch of the imagination pony books, is permeated with her love of horses. Her best pony book, *Fly-by-Night*, was written in 1968 when the popularity of the genre was losing its impetus, killed, suggested Marcus Crouch 'by sheer exhaustion of possibilities and also, perhaps, by affluence, for children who have a pony hardly need the vicarious experiences offered by pony stories' (Crouch 1972: 152). If *Fly-by-Night* marked the end of the golden age of pony books, it also demonstrated how it was possible to transform the old formula without flouting the conventions. The plot is almost identical to *A Pony for Jean* – but heroine Ruth Hollis's family is not wealthy and middle class; they live on a housing estate and they are plagued by money worries. In this and other books by Kathleen Peyton, like *Darkling* (1989), the responsibilities as well as the pleasures of owning horses are stressed, and in *Poor Badger* (1990), a classic 'pony rescue' story, the ethics of taking someone else's pony, however badly treated, are seriously discussed.

Another exponent of the more realistic pony stories of the 1960s was Vian Smith; one of the few male writers of pony stories and probably the only good one, he is as knowledgeable about human behaviour as he is about animals. *Come Down the Mountain* (1967), the story of a girl's determination to save a neglected racehorse and the effect it has on her family and the community in which they live, is an exceptional book by any standards.

The downward trend in pony stories continued in the 1970s, enlivened only by the first of the twelve Jinny books by Patricia Leitch. Her earlier books had followed in the tradition of the Pullein-Thompsons, although *Janet – Young Rider* (1963), with its working-class family, reflected far more accurately the preoccupations of its period. *Dream of Fair Horses* (1975), heavily influenced by *National Velvet*, is still a remarkable work of imagination with serious things to say about the dangers of trying to possess living beings. But Leitch set her own seal on the genre with the series about Jinny and her Arab horse Shantih (starting with *For Love of a Horse* in 1976). Still deservedly popular, these books, set in the Highlands, follow the growth and development of Jinny through a continuous series of adventures linked together by the mysterious Red Horse, painted on her bedroom wall, which represents the life force.

In the 1980s and 1990s, there has been a slight resurgence of interest in pony books. Today there are more horses in Britain – about 750,000 – than at the outbreak of the First World War (Lean 1994: 8) and riding is as popular as ever. There is still a demand for pony books around the world, and they sell particularly well in Germany and Scandinavia. However there is a shortage of new writers like Caroline Akrill with her lively trilogy – *Eventer's Dream* (1981), *A Hoof in the Door* (1982), *Ticket to Ride* (1983) – about aspiring eventer Elaine and the eccentric, aristocratic and impoverished Fane family. More recently the ubiquitous American Saddle Club series has appeared, full of thinly disguised instruction on the care of the horse with some teenage romance to sugar the pill, but the writers could learn a lot from earlier pony books about the art of combining fact and fiction. Established authors are still in print and some older stories, most recently Christine Pullein-Thompson's, are being updated and reissued. Publishers have now turned their attention to younger readers and new pony books are aimed at the under-10s. It seems there is still life in the genre and while adolescent girls continue to have a passion for ponies, the pony book will survive.

## References

Bagnold, E. (1935) *National Velvet*, London: Heinemann.

Chitty, S. (1971) *The Woman who Wrote Black Beauty: A Life of Anna Sewell*, London: Hodder and Stoughton.

Crouch, M. (1972) *The Nesbit Tradition, the Children's Novel in England 1945–1970*, London: Benn.

Fisher, M. (1961) *Intent Upon Reading*, London: Brockhampton Press.

Lean, G. (1994) 'Horsiculture curbed to save countryside', *Independent on Sunday* 3 July: 8.

Lindstam, B. (1982) 'The horse story as love story', *Barn och Kultur* 28, 1: 16–20.

Moss, E. (1976) 'On the tail of the seductive horse', *Signal* 19: 27–30.

Poll, B. (1961) 'Why children like horse stories', *Elementary English* 7, 38: 473–474.

The Pony Club Year Book (1994) London: The British Horse Society.

Strickland, C. (1986) 'Equine fiction in the 1980s', *School Library Journal* 32, 10: 36–37.

Treadgold, M. (1982) 'For the love of horses', *Books for Your Children* 17, 1: 16–17.

# 30

# Historical Fiction

## *Janet Fisher*

Historical fiction, paradoxically, must be based on fact, which makes it different from other fiction. Its task is more difficult because of that mixture; having said that, it must be like other fiction by creating a world into which the reader can be drawn, a credible world with characters he or she can relate to, the only difference being that that world is in the past.

It is not enough to know the facts to write such a story; the difficulty is to place them in the plot, so that the historical background is clear, the place is evident, and any unfamiliar terms are self-explanatory. There is the great problem of the language the characters speak; modern idioms cannot be used, neither can 'gadzookery'; both can easily destroy a carefully created atmosphere. Many writers overcome this by a rearrangement of the words, which has the effect of making the prose sound authentic without being incomprehensible; for example, Joan W. Blos in *A Gathering of Days* (1979).

> I Catherine Cabot Hall aged 13 years 6 months 29 days, of Meredith in the state of New Hampshire, do begin this book. It was given to me yesterday, my father returning from Boston Massachusetts, where he had gone ahead to obtain provisions for the months ahead. My father's name is Charles; Charles Hall; I am daughter also of Hannah Cabot Hall, dead of a fever these four long years.
>
> Blos 1979: 5

The field can be divided into two categories: those books which use real historical figures and those whose characters are wholly imaginary. A device often used is to tell the story of a real figure, for example, King Alfred, through the eyes of an imaginary one as in C. W. Hodges's *The Namesake* (1964). Other stories have glimpses of real figures, for example Fairfax and Cromwell in *Simon* (1957), by Rosemary Sutcliff. In the early years of the genre real figures appeared frequently, but increasingly as the emphasis has moved from a political to social history, lives of ordinary, imaginary people have been told.

Some writers, for example Cynthia Harnett, use a wealth of detail to make the story live, others such as Gillian Avery use characterisation and leave an impression of a period; a few, like Rosemary Sutcliff, paint so vivid a picture with words the reader can inhabit the past. A sense of place is vital and it is notable that the great writers in this genre have made a particular place their own: Rosemary Sutcliff – Hadrian's Wall, Barbara Willard – Ashdown Forest, Sussex,

Laura Ingalls Wilder – the Prairies, and Hester Burton – Suffolk. Political views can colour a book, often to its advantage, witness Geoffrey Trease's stories of revolution. Illustrations are more important than in most other genres, adding as they can to the period flavour, and in many books a map is vital (although often missing!).

There are writers, and Leon Garfield is the best example, who write of the past but not in a way that can be considered as pure historical fiction. Anthea Bell in *Twentieth Century Children's Writers* (Kirkpatrick 1978), says that 'history sits lightly on these novels' (313). Garfield's characters inhabit a world lightly drawn from the eighteenth century but his chief concern is with them and not with the period. He has set his own standards and defies categorising.

Historical fiction, then, is a genre in which many of the best stories for children have been written: for example, *The Eagle of the Ninth, The Iron Lily, The Bronze Bow, The Little House in the Big Woods, The Machine Gunners, Viking's Dawn, The Stronghold* and *A Thousand for Sicily.*

Before the 1930s in Britain, historical novels were largely written for adults, with one or two noticeable exceptions, such as Captain Marryat's *The Children of the New Forest* (1847). Writers such as Sir Walter Scott, Charles Kingsley and Robert Louis Stevenson wrote historical adventures much enjoyed by adults and children alike. G. A. Henty wrote adventure stories for boys from 1881 onwards, with well researched historical backgrounds. They were patriotic stories full of daring deeds. They read stiffly now and some of the sentiments expressed are no longer fashionable. Rudyard Kipling's *Puck of Pook's Hill* (1906) was and still is much admired. Rosemary Sutcliff freely admitted her debt to Kipling and his influence on her writing can be seen in the rich prose she used. These early books were in the main adventures or historical romances, rather than an attempt to create a living past.

In 1934 Geoffrey Trease wrote *Bows Against the Barons* and changed the nature of the genre. He painted a picture of a man fighting injustice and oppression, not the swashbuckling Robin Hood of legend, but a revolutionary character, one to whom children could relate, a real living person who just happened to be in the past, full of colour and vigour. Many of Trease's stories are historical adventures, but this and several other books are much more than that. Trease's left-wing views permeated his writing and his best stories burn with revolutionary zeal. It is difficult not to rush out and join Garibaldi after reading *Follow My Black Plume* (1963)! Trease's considerable output is always well researched; a great many of his stories involve a journey by a young man, usually accompanied by a girl, often disguised as a boy. The best of these is *The Red Towers of Granada* (1966), which has a bold dramatic opening, and a journey from Nottingham to Toledo, full of detail and colour, against a background of the treatment of Jews and lepers.

In the USA in 1932 *The Little House in the Big Woods* by Laura Ingalls Wilder was published. This first book of a magnificent series took the story of her family's move west in the late nineteenth century. The stories are full of the details of everyday life, the fight for survival in which the provision and preparation of food dominate. Place is all important. *The Long Winter* (1940) makes the reader see the snow on the bedcovers and feel the lethargy the long intense cold of the winter brings.

Elizabeth Coatsworth had also written of settlers, but *Away Goes Sally* (1934) is a more comfortable story of a house being moved on runners in a Maine winter. Although there are other stories about Sally, they do not have the sweep of the Wilder stories.

In the USA the Newbery medal had already been awarded to historical fiction, in 1929 to Eric P. Kelly for *The Trumpeter of Krakow*, telling in stately prose of an episode in Polish history, and in 1936 it was awarded to Carol Ryrie Brink for *Caddie Woodlawn*. (It is interesting to compare this book with the Wilder stories and note the same preoccupation with food, in this case turkeys.) In 1943 Elizabeth Janet Gray won with *Adam of the Road*, a lively tale of Chaucerian England, which today lacks a period feel, and Esther Forbes won in 1944 with *Johnny Tremain*. Like Trease's *Bows Against the Barons*, this dealt with revolution, in this case the American War of Independence. The complex background is slowly drawn against Johnny's gradual involvement in the conflict.

In Britain, the 1950s saw the flowering of differing talents who were to dominate the scene, and during this period three authors of historical novels won the Carnegie medal; Cynthia Harnett for *The Woolpack* in 1951, Ronald Welch for *Knight Crusader* in 1954 and Rosemary Sutcliff for *The Lantern Bearers* in 1959.

Cynthia Harnett's interest was in the everyday life of ordinary people and it is this wealth of detail which makes her books so interesting, if at times a little indigestible. *The Writing on the Hearth* (1971) has as well, politics, witchcraft and sorcery which speed the story along, and the reader sees also the growth of the Oxford colleges. William Caxton appears in *A Load of Unicorn* (1959), a story of resistance to change by the scriveners to his newfangled printing methods. Rosemary Sutcliff began her writing career with *The Queen Elizabeth Story* in 1950, followed by *The Armourer's House* (1951) and *Brother Dusty-Feet* (1952), her first story to deal with comradeship between young men. *Simon* (1953), deals with a friendship in a fair minded account of the Civil War. *The Eagle of the Ninth* (1954) is based on two episodes of Romano-British history, using which she constructed her picture of the British tribes under a Roman army of occupation, and in which the greatness of her talent emerges. There is a portrait of a friendship again, this time between Esca, the freed slave, and Marcus, who go north to find the lost eagle of his father's regiment; also a recurring theme from this point on, of a young man coping with some kind of handicap. *The Silver Branch* (1957), and *The Lantern Bearers* (1959), linked stories, continue these themes, the latter being almost an adult book in which Aquila overcomes the bitterness at his father's murder and the abduction of his sister and comes to maturity with the beginning of Britain.

Rosemary Sutcliff had a talent for making the past come alive through her descriptions, dialogue and a sense of place. In a few words she painted the landscape for the reader, for example, 'the wind from the east laying the moorland grasses over all one way' (133). Many of the books are set in the north of England, on Hadrian's Wall, but she also memorably used the Sussex Downs in *Warrior Scarlet* (1958) and *Knight's Fee* (1960). Carolyn Horowitz talks about Rosemary Sutcliff's 'acute sense of place ... a feeling of belonging to a certain landscape becomes a vital part of the plot structure. By the time the novel is finished the reader feels homesick, not only for a certain essence of country and climate, but for another time' (142).

The brotherhood of men fighting a common enemy features in *Blood Feud* (1976), and *Frontier Wolf* (1980); a rare heroine appears in *A Song for a Dark Queen* (1978), Boadicea's story told in subtly singing language by her harper. *Warrior Scarlet* tells of Drem, who, physically handicapped, fails his wolf slaying test, and *Knight's Fee*, is a story of the making of a knight set amidst the Sussex downs. Often from a few known facts, Rosemary Sutcliff created a past so vivid that she stands head and shoulders above the rest.

Ronald Welch also wrote of battles but as a military historian. In his best book *Knight Crusader* (1954) the complicated political background of the Crusades is well set but it is the scorching heat of the Middle East on knights in full armour, that the reader remembers. Welch wrote a number of stories of young men under all sorts of fire from bows and arrows to tanks.

Henry Treece made the Vikings, a subject no one else of stature has tackled, very much his own field. In his three books covering the life of Harald Sigurdson, *Viking's Dawn* (1955), *The Road to Miklagard* (1957) and *Viking's Sunset* (1960), the ethos and brotherhood of the Vikings is expounded in a style evolved especially for the series; it is a little stiff to read at first until one is used to the rhythm of his prose. In *The Queen's Brooch* (1966), he wrote a powerful and dramatic story of a Roman tribune involved in Boadicea's uprising and subsequent defeat by Suetonius. This stands well alongside Rosemary Sutcliff's stories of Roman Britain, although Treece's is a less romantic view.

Gillian Avery chose a more recent period for her domestic comedies set in Victorian England, using the narrow confines of the lives of middle-class children to make sharp observations on their place. There is no wealth of detail in these books, but an impression of what it was like to be a Victorian child. *The Warden's Niece* (1957), in which Maria runs away to join her uncle, who is warden of an Oxford college, and *James Without Thomas* (1959), show her gifts to the full, her dialogue being particularly entertaining and humorous.

In 1956 Ian Serraillier was the first to use the Second World War and its aftermath as a backdrop in a book which has become a classic, *The Silver Sword*. Based on fact, it tells of a journey across post-war Europe by four Polish children searching for their parents; a stark and heart-wrenching tale. *Rifles for Watie* (1957) by an American, Harold Keith, follows Jeff, drawn into the American Civil War by high ideals, only to find that good and bad and right and wrong are more subtle concepts than he supposed. *Across Five Aprils* (1964), by Irene Hunt looks at the same subject from a different viewpoint, that of an Illinois farming family waiting for letters from the front. Both stories are moving accounts of the horror and muddle of war. Elizabeth George Speare won the Newbery Medal twice; first in 1959 with *The Witch of Blackbird Pond*, a portrayal of an independent girl in the fiercely Puritan New England of 1687, who befriends a Quaker accused of being a witch. It gives a fair picture of the bigotry of the time and of the less-than-just rule from England. It was among the first and is still one of the best books on this subject. *The Bronze Bow*, which won the 1962 Newbery, in which the author chose the unusual territory of Israel at the time of Christ, makes it easy to understand the impact of Jesus on a boy bitter at the death of his father at the hands of the Romans, as he listens to His teaching, and why events followed their tragic course.

Other American writers at this time included Jean Fritz, whose *Brady* (1960) observes a boy unable to keep a secret, but whose involvement in the underground railway for slaves teaches him how. Ann Petry in *Tituba of Salem village* (1964) also deals with a slave. Patricia Clapp went back to early settlers with *Constance* (1968), based on her family's history, covering the years 1620–1626 in a diary in which the young Constance confides.

The 1960s and 1970s became known as the golden age of historical fiction for children, in Britain, not only with specialist children's writers working, but also writers working across the breadth of children's fiction. In 1960 Frederick Grice was one of the first to use twentieth-century history when he took the northern England of the 1920s for *Bonnie Pit Laddie*, an episodic tale of a pit strike which brought a community to its knees. It tells of the ordinary working man, his poverty and hunger with a raw sense of injustice reminiscent of Trease's early work. Hester Burton took another form of injustice for *Time of Trial* (Carnegie Medal 1963), which tells of the trial and imprisonment of a bookseller in eighteenth-century London for his political views. It is a deep, thoughtful book requiring maturity from the reader. *No Beat of Drum* (1966) is a sombre, harsh story of a labourer deported to Australia for his part in a demonstration to get better wages.

As with Rosemary Sutcliff, a special countryside is important in Hester Burton's work, in her case the Suffolk area with its vast skies. Her most vivid book is *Castors Away!* (1962). Set against the battle of Trafalgar, it is above all a family story in which Tom goes off to war and Nell is left to cope at home. Many of Hester Burton's stories are illustrated by Victor G. Ambrus who matches her prose superbly. *A Grenville Goes to Sea* (1977) showed that she did not need to write at length to create a period exactly. Richard Grenville, coming from a long line of seafarers, is unwilling to admit his fear of heights, but conquers it in this brief tale full of the life of a midshipman in Nelson's navy.

Barbara Willard made the Ashdown Forest in Sussex her own in her Mantlemass novels. She takes women as her main characters, although as Margaret Meek states,

> this is a period which seems to offer them only dependent roles. Dame Elizabeth in the first book *The Lark and the Laurel* (1970), established the Mantlemass fortune and makes a woman of Cecily who becomes a legend in her turn. Catherine insists on choosing where her heart is. Ursula holds the family together when its fate is doubtful, and finally Cecilia rejects the New World and stays in the ruins with the prospect of a different kind of rebuilding. They are a formidable tribe expecting no pity or excuses, tender and loving and much more clear-sighted than the men. Above them towers Lilias, a Master of iron, more than a match for the men she works with and commands.
>
> Meek 1980: 805

Through all the stories the reader senses life driven on by the seasons, despite the great events going on outside the forest which occasionally touch their lives like the ripples on a pond.

In the 1960s Mollie Hunter wrote graphically of Scottish history in *The Ghosts of Glencoe* (1966), and *The Pistol in the Greenyards* (1965), rearranging words to give the rhythm of the Scottish tongue without the use of dialect. Her finest book is *The Stronghold* (Carnegie Medal 1974), in which she went further back in time to create her idea of how a broch, a stone fortress found only in the Orkneys, came to be built. Peter Hollindale points out that this book covers a moment when 'history is altered by a single original mind' (112). The hero, a crippled member of an early tribe finds his distinction not in the traditional warrior field, but in the design of the stronghold which saves his tribe from the Roman invaders. The hold of the old religion of the Druids is powerfully described and the sacrificial scene is a high point in the story.

K. M. Peyton also began to write at this time and published three powerful stories of the sea and the Essex coast. The sea and naval history do not seem to attract writers and Mrs Peyton moved away from this subject to horses. She won the Carnegie Medal for *The Edge of the Cloud*, the second book of her Flambards trilogy in 1969, which caused some controversy, as the books do not have the depth of the earlier novels. *Windfall* (1962), *The Maplin Bird* (1964), and *Thunder in the Sky* (1966), share a background of sailing in coastal waters and of the hand-to-mouth existence this life meant. The third story uses the transport of ammunition in the First World War as its backdrop.

Pioneering stories usually come from America, but in 1967 Eleanor Spence wrote the first of three novels about Australia, *The Switherby Pilgrims*, in which Arabella Braithwaite takes ten orphans from England to New South Wales in the 1820s. The hardships of the 'better life' are well drawn.

Increasingly in the 1960s and 1970s the Second World War was used as a setting. Two outstanding examples are by Jill Paton Walsh: *The Dolphin Crossing* (1967), an exciting and moving story of two boys from different backgrounds brought together by the events of Dunkirk, and *Fireweed* (1969), set in the Blitz again examining class differences which, with an unhappy ring of truth, separate the young couple. Jill Paton Walsh also wrote of other periods; memorably of the Plague in *A Parcel of Patterns* (1983), in which the difficult language suits the period of the tragic story, and *Grace* (1991), which speculates, as a novel, on the effect that the bravery of a nineteenth-century heroine, Grace Darling had on the rest of her life.

*The Machine Gunners* (Carnegie Medal 1975) by Robert Westall showed the effect of war on a group of youngsters in Newcastle. It is a raw, gutsy tale about a boy, Chas, who finds a machine gun in a wrecked German aeroplane and decides to 'have a go' at the Germans. Westall wrote several other stories of war, including *The Kingdom by the Sea* (1990), and *Blitzcat* (1989), using his favourite cat theme to depict the chaos of war. In a calm, but no less telling style, David Rees recreated a night of bombing in Exeter in 1942 in *The Exeter Blitz* (Carnegie Medal 1978); in it, Colin Lockwood is separated from his family and witnesses the destruction of the city from the cathedral tower: the low-key style makes it all the more horrific. Susan Cooper also wrote realistically of the tension caused by bombing and its effect on three children in *Dawn of Fear* (1972).

Hans Peter Richter's chilling trilogy tells of another side of the Second World War. In *Friedrich* (1971) there is an episodic chart of the progress of anti-Semitism seen through the eyes of a German boy observing his neighbour. Hans's story, through his time in the Hitler Youth to his army career is continued in *I Was There*

(1973), and *The Time of the Young Soldiers* (1976), in a cold, stark style which suits the subject exactly.

*Carrie's War* was based on Nina Bawden's own experience as an evacuee and paints a picture of an uncomfortable and unforgettable experience. Other novels with a similar theme, for example, Hester Burton's *In Spite of All Terror* (1968), Gordon Cooper's *A Certain Courage* (1975), Alan Spooner's *Rainbow Cake* (1981) and Alison Prince's *How's Business* (1987), show different experiences of evacuation. *When Hitler Stole Pink Rabbit* (1971), draws on Judith Kerr's own experience as a refugee in France and England.

Elliot Arnold in *A Kind of Secret Weapon* (1970), with its passionate plea for resistance against tyranny, and *Bright Candles* (1974) by Nathaniel Benchley, tell of the courage of resistance workers in occupied Denmark. For a younger age group *What About Me?* (1974) by Gertie Evenhuis shows Dirk's endeavours to be part of his father's work, not glossing over the stark nature of the situation and its dangers.

Many other periods were written about. Shakespeare's theatre, for example, featured in two deep and literary stories by Antonia Forest, *The Player's Boy* (1970), and *The Player and the Rebels* (1971), in which the theatre and Shakespeare's plays really come alive and send the reader back to the original. Barbara Smucker, a Canadian, wrote movingly of the underground railway for slaves using real figures, in *Underground to Canada* (1977). Gillian Cross dealt with the effect of the building of the railway on a small Sussex village where the hostility between the villagers and the navvies flares into violence, in *The Iron Way* (1979). Peter Carter's stark tale of the Peterloo Massacre, *The Black Lamp* (1973), lacks the warmth to make it a rounded picture but again shows the resistance to change. *The Slave Dancer* (Newbery Medal 1974), by Paula Fox, tells in a series of economically worded episodes, of one boy's experiences on a slave ship. Marjorie Darke took the topic of the Suffragettes in *A Question of Courage* (1975), in a powerful and emotional story of a working-class girl caught up in the movement.

Mildred D. Taylor wrote of her family's life in Mississippi of the 1930s in her trilogy, *Roll of Thunder, Hear My Cry* (1976), *Let the Circle be Unbroken* (1981), and *The Road to Memphis* (1990). The dignity of the Logan family in the face of the bigotry of the whites is magnificently drawn. Another American, Joan W. Blos gives an account of a year in the life of a 14-year-old girl on a New Hampshire farm in 1830 in *A Gathering of Days* (Newbery Medal 1980), a marvellous evocation of the period.

In the 1970s there was a burst of stories for children aged between 6 and 8. This proved to be a difficult venture partly because of the difficulty of setting the historical scene in a few words, and only a few writers succeeded. Penelope Lively was one of these with *Fanny's Sister* (1976), a perfect vignette of Victorian life.

The 1980s saw a falling off of the output: although Rosemary Sutcliff, Geoffrey Trease and Barbara Willard were still writing, there were few names coming along behind. Michelle Magorian showed promise in *Goodnight Mister Tom* (1981), an overlong story of an evacuee and his relationship with an old man; Elsie McCutcheon produced *Rat War* (1985), a perceptive story of a boy conquering his fear, set in the stringencies of post-war Britain. Joan Lingard also wrote of the war in *File on Fraulein Berg* (1980), showing how easily fear leads to suspicion, and *Tug of War* (1989), and *Between Two Worlds* (1991), stories of refugees, based on family history. In the USA, Pam Conrad wrote *Prairie Songs* (1985), a book which minces no words in telling of the tragedy of the doctor's wife who could not adjust to life in a 'soddy'. Patricia MacLachlan wrote of another woman's arrival in the American west in *Sarah, Plain and Tall* (Newbery Medal 1986), observed by Anna and Caleb in beautiful spare prose. There are, too, few wasted words in *Isaac Campion* (1986), Janni Howker's raw memory of an old man's early life in the north of England. Raw in a different way is Christa Laird's *Shadow of the Wall* (1989), based on the last few months of Dr Janus Korczak in the Warsaw Ghetto, a quite outstanding re-creation of courage and inspiration. Geraldine McCaughrean went right back to the Mystery plays for a humorous story of Gabriel in *A Little Lower Than the Angels* (1987).

Three very different books represent the 1990s. Michael Morpurgo's *Waiting for Anya* (1990), in which Jo's village conspires to save the Jewish children hidden in the hills is an exciting rounded story which shows the maturing of his writing. Judith O'Neill also fulfilled early promise in *So far from Skye* (1992), a deeply satisfying novel of emigration to Australia in the nineteenth century. Katherine Paterson goes back to the Industrial Revolution in Massachusetts in her portrayal of a girl's fight for better conditions in *Lyddie* (1991).

There were few books in the 1980s about medieval times, and a burgeoning in the number of books about twentieth-century history, particularly about the Second World War. With this shift there has also been a change from the observation of great political events to a concentration on the life of the ordinary family, on how they lived and how the great events touched their lives.

Although there has been a distinct falling off in the number of historical stories published since the 1980s, it is encouraging to note that Margery Fisher in her journal *Growing Point*, reviewed over twenty historical novels for children in 1991. It is to be hoped that the books mentioned in this essay, which are evidence of the depth and breadth of the genre, will provide a rich heritage, a way of illuminating the past for future generations.

## References

Hollindale, P. (1977) 'World enough and time: the work of Mollie Hunter', *Children's Literature in Education* 8, 3: 109–119.

Horowitz, C. (1969) 'Dimensions in time: a critical view of historical fiction for children', in Field, E. W. (ed.) *Horn Book Reflections*, Boston: Horn Book.

Kirkpatrick, D. L. (ed.) (1978) *Twentieth Century Children's Writers*, New York: St Martin's Press.

Meek, M. (1980) 'The fortunes of Mantlemass', *The Times Literary Supplement* 18 July: 805.

Sutcliff, R. (1983), *Bonnie Dundee*, London: Bodley Head.

## Further Reading

Butts, D. (1977) *Good Writers for Young Readers*, London: Hart-Davis.

Egoff, S., Stubbs, G. T. and Ashley, L. F. (eds) (1969) *Only Connect: Readings on Children's Literature*, Toronto: Oxford University Press.

Fisher, J. (1994) *An Index of Historical Fiction for Children and Young People*, Aldershot: Scolar Press.

Meek, M., Warlow, A. and Barton, G. (eds) (1967) *The Cool Web: the Pattern of Children's Reading*, London: Bodley Head.

Sutcliff, R. (1983) *Blue Remembered Hills*, London: Bodley Head.

Trease, G. (1971) *A Whiff of Burnt Boats*, London: Macmillan.

—— (1974) *Laughter at the Door*, London: Macmillan.

Welch, R. (1972) 'Attention to detail: the workbooks of Ronald Welch', *Children's Literature in Education* 8: 30–39.

# 31

# Books for Younger Readers

## *Colin Mills*

The history of books for the young is a fascinating and intricate narrative about the tension between entertainment and didacticism; the need to socialise the young into dominant values; the twentieth-century concern for the inner life of the young child. We still hear arguments about the perceived dichotomy between pleasure and the business of learning in the debate in the 1980s and 1990s in Britain, the USA and Australia as to the most 'suitable' books for children learning to read in school classrooms. More than one contemporary commentator has seen similarities between the arguments of those like Mrs Trimmer in the early nineteenth century about the need to protect young children and the debates about the 'suitable' content of books for the young in the 1980s. The concerns of the latter-day Janeways and Trimmers have resonated in modern times: books for the young have been the arena for debates about the inculcation of attitudes and stances towards racism, sexism and views about those with disabilities, or those who are, in some way, 'different'. The contemporary arguments perhaps reached their most dramatic pitch when there were letters to *The Times* and a parliamentary discussion about the compulsory removal from London schools of a book which featured a little girl growing up (quite happily) with a gay male couple (Bosche 1987). Another puzzling and depressing aspect of that contentious debate was that the term 'real books', as opposed to structured schemes specifically designed to teach reading, became a term of abuse (Meek 1992).

If before 1850 books written for the young were judged largely on extra-literary merits – books were there 'to preach, teach, exhort and reprimand' (Egoff 1980: 412), the watershed was probably the publication, in 1865, of Carroll's *Alice in Wonderland*. This moved imaginative writing to the foreground and became a touchstone for subsequent writing for the young (see Butts 1992: x). There have been three periods in which major classics for younger children were produced. The middle decades of the nineteenth century saw the publication of *Alice in Wonderland*, the works of Edward Lear and Robert Louis Stevenson. The late Victorian and Edwardian years saw the early flowering of A. A. Milne, J. M. Barrie, Kenneth Grahame and Beatrix Potter. The post-Second World War period saw an expansion of themes and genres and the most extraordinary emergence of writers and artists for the young.

Two key factors influenced expansions in creative activity for younger children in these 'golden ages'. One was the gradual spread of state education – from the earliest Sunday School movements to universal primary schooling – which meant that more children were learning to read. There was an accompanying 'professionalism' of the adult interest in books through the rapid growth of teacher training and of school libraries. Rose's (1984) is a fascinating account of the relationship between schooling and literature. The second factor was the growth of innovative techniques in printing and publishing and the rise in new technologies which made for mass production. More care and attention could be given to the physical format of texts for the young. Developments in the form and production of the picture book in the post 1950 years are a prime example.

After *Alice in Wonderland*, *The Wind in the Willows* and the works of E. Nesbit, twentieth-century fiction for the young was able to develop what the Rustins term 'a diversity of modes of exploration of central life experiences, reflecting the complexity of society as it is experienced by child readers' (Rustin and Rustin 1987: 21). Increasingly sophisticated insights into childhood gave rise to more sensitive depictions of children's lives and feelings. It was realised that young children may be small, but their emotions are large. A post-Freudian generation of adult readers have seen the symbolic possibilities within literature for the young.

The twentieth-century development of a whole field of literature for young children was one element in an emergent culture of childhood in Western society. The language used to talk about stories for children parallels and draws upon the discourses of psychology, child development, educational theory, psychoanalysis and social policy. Whereas ages and stages can be unhelpful and over-simplifying, it is appropriate in this survey to think in terms of the years of infancy (birth to 5); the early years (5 to 7) and of the newly independent (7 to 10).

## Birth to Five

Interest in the earliest years of child development, drawing upon educationalists such as Froebel and Pestalozzi and psychologists such as Piaget and Vygotsky have changed our perceptions. Children are no longer seen as passive recipients of adult knowledge but as active agents, learning about their environment through a continuous process of assimilation and adjustment to novel experience and emotions. It is now widely acknowledged that books play a crucial part in early learning by providing strong and accessible images of the world.

Books with clearly defined, uncluttered pictures and bright primary colours like those of the Dutch artist, Dick Bruna, are appealing to very young children. Dorothy Butler's work is an outstanding account of the ways in which books play a part in children's development from their earliest days. There are startling, yet very practical accounts of how books such as Bruna's alphabet books can make an impact upon children as young as eight months. (Butler 1980: 28, and see Butler's excellent bibliography which includes all the classic alphabet, concept, animal and counting books).

During the past twenty years, there has been a growth in the number of books designed to stimulate children's senses and to encourage investigation. The British artist, Janet Ahlberg, who with her husband Allan, has achieved success in many areas, produced several books popular with the very youngest children which illustrate the power of books in the child's exploration of the world. *The Baby's Catalogue* (1982) uses the textual format of the trade catalogues which are often the first written texts that a child will encounter. *Peepo!* (1981) shows family life in the 1940s through the eyes of a very young child – with 'peepholes' in the pages: books can be 'toys', with holes in their pages apparently being eaten by hungry caterpillars (*The Very Hungry Caterpillar* 1970). These books, and others with more complex paper engineering, are both practical and beautiful objects.

Artists and publishers have recognised that books for this age group need to be sturdy and flexible. From the mid-1970s, there was growth in the production of 'board books'; the Bodley Head's series, which included Betty Young's *Farm Animals* (1980), is a particularly innovative example. Talented artists such as John Burningham, Brian Wildsmith, Rodney Peppe and Helen Oxenbury have brought their individual talents to the production of alphabet books.

Stories and pictures about everyday objects help the child to see the world represented in books. Children of this age respond to language in terms of sound, and since the early days of publishing this has been recognised in the provision of collections of rhymes, lore, tales and literature which is essentially playful with language. Nursery rhymes are often the first and one of the most potent forms of storytelling and appeared, of course, in the earliest books for children. The most comprehensive, and one of the most popular of modern collections is Raymond Briggs's *The Mother Goose Treasury* (1966). Briggs depicts the blend of the old and the new in that his pictures have clarity and vigour that appeals to modern lookers and listeners. An American equivalent is Alice and Martin Provensen's *The Mother Goose Book* (1976).

Research into children's early literary competence and their development as readers has emphasised the importance of listening to stories and rhymes, and children's early play with consciously patterned forms of language. The work of Fox (1993) is an eloquent statement of the insoluble links between literature and literacy. Mills (1994a) gives a detailed account of current research on these relationships between stories, early texts and literacy. Much research into children's early reading has emphasised the sense of pleasurable play that children gain from books. Reading enhances their experiences and understanding. Dorothy Neal White's classic New Zealand study of the role of books in young children's lives, *Books Before Five* (1954), gives many insights into the connections between literary and lived experience: 'The experience makes the book richer and the book enriches the personal experience even at this level. I am astonished at the early age this backward and forward flow between book and life takes place' (13).

## Five to Seven

Children's developing awareness of the structure of stories, and the importance of them hearing stories read is obviously crucial to their growth as readers as they get older. Stories that are memorable are often ones that come out of an oral tradition. Of particular value and enjoyment at this stage of childhood are collections of folk and fairy stories that have been shaped by centuries of retelling; these stories are powerful in their content too, dealing as they do with themes of archetypal significance, feelings and fantasies that are part of the inner experience of childhood.

When reading is new to children, stories are inextricably linked with their play.

The fantastic has its roots in the workaday, and the domestic: playthings, toys, animals are anthropomorphised as friends. Novice readers have to understand stories as a particular kind of imaginative activity. An important category of books is made up of those which seem particularly good at teaching the game of reading. Books such as *Where's Spot?* (1980) by the British artist, Eric Hill, or *Each, Peach, Pear, Plum* (1984) by the Ahlbergs, invite children to join in, predict, set up expectations about what will happen next. A story such as John Burningham's *Come Away from the Water, Shirley* (1977) shows that a story may, literally, have two sides. Books that 'teach the game of reading' are often made for sharing – and this notion of learning reading as 'apprenticeship' has been imported into the vocabulary of the school-based teaching of reading in Britain (Harrison and Coles 1992), the USA (Goodman 1986), Canada, and Australia (Brown and Mathie 1990). The significant picture book author-artists who have emerged since the 1960s have stimulated a refined critical appreciation (see, for example, Lewis 1990). They match the craft of the story-teller shower with the literary possibilities available to the young. Some books for this age range are all pictures, such as Shirley Hughes' *Up and Up* (1979), Jan Ormerod's *Sunshine* (1983), and Pat Hutchins's *Changes, Changes* (1971). They enable the child to control the whole process of taking meaning from books from the very beginning. The picture book is not mere preparation for 'real' literary experience; artists have managed to place narrative patterns as old as story-telling into the contemporary universe of school, play, families and cultural contexts which are accessible to modern children.

Five- to seven-year-olds have a taste for realism and an insatiable curiosity about how things are, and what people do. It is, however, simplistic to label stories which deal with the homely and the accessible as 'realism'. The best stories for 5- to 7-year-olds slow down, and turn into art, the action, sounds, sights, feelings of childhood. The universal experiences – birthdays, starting school, having a baby brother or sister, losing a tooth, being left awake at night – can shown to be the same for everyone. Form is important. When one reads stories by the best writers in the genre – Ted Greenwood's stories *Ginnie* (1979); Dorothy Edwards's *My Naughty Little Sister* (1969 and sequels) (one of the very few nameless characters of all fiction), the Frog and Toad stories of Arnold Lobel (from *Frog and Toad are Friends* (1970)) – one sees how deceptively simple techniques can work. The length of chapters, and the interplay of episodes help story-tellers to catch the slowness of childhood time. Events often happen all in a day and can be held in the head. Crude divisions into 'realism' and 'fantasy' ignore the fact that, for children at this age, the line between the two is not a clear one; the fabulous often lies just beneath the surface of the ordinary.

In stories for the young, first pages tend to be crucial parts of the invitation. In a classic story like Helen Morgan's *Mrs Pinny and the Blowing Day* (1991) theme, plot, image and action cohere for the young reader-listener.

Stories are often the means through which children from 5 to 7 can come to confront, and begin to understand, their fears and anxieties. This feature of literature can sometimes be taken to extremes. In the USA in the 1960s and 1970s there was a strong feeling that children's books could be, in some ways, a cure for childhood problems. In a sense, this returns us to the origins of children's books and the view that they should somehow socialise children. But it is certainly the case that fears and anxieties can be miniaturised, or made manageable through stories. Tucker (1981: 62–66) provides a reading of Beatrix Potter's stories in which he shows how she dealt with complex ideas relating to childhood fears, including ideas about pursuit, and children's anxieties about being preyed upon, through pastoral settings and humanised animals.

A fine example of the ways in which anxieties can be contained, domesticated and turned into fine literature for children from 4 to 7 are Russell Hoban's stories about Frances the badger. With her mother and father, baby sister and her best friend, she goes through experiences that are familiar to young readers. Occasionally the parents' patience wears thin, and Frances has to learn that some things have to be accepted for the way they are. *Bedtime for Frances* (1960) in which she is constantly awoken by imagined sounds, shapes and stirrings, is a superb example of a story which shows how fears can be articulated and dealt with.

At this age, family relationships usually remain central to a child's preoccupations. Sensitive writers help children with the serious business of dealing with adults, who, in the main, set the boundaries and devise the rules. As children do not have a great deal of power or control over their lives, there is often a great appeal in 'miniaturised' stories. They will enjoy stories such as Mary Norton's *The Borrowers* (1952 and sequels), or Patricia Cleveland-Peck's *The String Family At Home* (1986). The appeal of these kind of stories is not hard to see. Societies of people who are small and at the mercy of adults, offer possibilities for modes of behaving and surviving the whims of the powerful.

During this stage, 'bridging books' are particularly important: those where the pictures are still a vital cue to understanding, but where the text becomes more central. Several innovative series are worth noting here: in Britain, Jan Pienkowski and Helen Nicholls's Meg and Mog Stories (1972 on) and in the USA Harriet Ziefert's stories about the Small Potato Club (1986 on) are good examples. The role of the collaborative adult, supporting and modelling reading is still crucial. Adults are still important as a physical presence, discussing stories, helping children relate them to their own lives, considering alternative versions and making judgements – all this in the role of partners in the telling, two-thirds of the triangular relationship adult, child and author (Dombey 1988).

## Seven to Ten

The most potent change that comes about between these ages in Western society, is that children have an extended and more diverse relationship with the social world. Friends, teachers, groups or gangs, clubs or societies have an increased importance to them. They develop more sophisticated modes of thinking, experience a wider range of emotions. Their stamina in terms of literacy and literary competence increases. Children's own social groups become much more important to them. These groups, evolve their own myths, rituals, passwords, formulaic games and rhymes. Many significant writers have skilfully integrated the jokes and superstitions within children's games and culture into stories and poems. The work of the British poets Michael Rosen and Allan Ahlberg are good examples of demotic language meeting mainstream literature.

From the 1970s onwards, writers for this age group have explored sometimes complex aspects of young children's lives. The dynamic nature of friendships is well caught by such American writers as Beverley Cleary – who began her long series of domestic stories with *Henry Huggins* (1950) and Louise Fitzhugh (with the rather more complex *Harriet the Spy* (1964)). British writers such as Gene Kemp, in her Cricklepit stories (*The Turbulent Term of Tyke Tyler* (1977) *et al.*), and Chris Powling (for example, *The Conker As Hard As A Diamond* (1984)) have caught the banter and felt life of primary (elementary) school classrooms particularly well. Children's experience of places, including the secret ones that adults do not know about, is a special feature of this age group classically pinned down in Clive King's *Stig of the Dump* (1970).

The domestic can still be an appropriate setting for children's stories, but such settings can lead out to fantastic explorations, in classics such as E. Nesbit's stories and C. S. Lewis's Narnia tales. Domestic settings can also lead inwards to explorations of relationships, to the interplay between children, their siblings and their parents. Of particular note here is the work of the British writer, Philippa Pearce. *A Dog So Small* (1962) deals with a solitary child's longing for a fantasy companion. *The Battle of Bubble and Squeak* (1978) deals with sibling rivalry, and relationships between step-parents and children. Pearce's work shows how books for this age range can become more complex and sophisticated in their moral viewpoint and in the range of themes that can be addressed. *Tom's Midnight Garden* (1958) and *The Way to Sattin Shore* (1983) are subtle yet very readable explorations of time, of past secrets and of the relationships between the young and the old.

Two other writers deserve special mention here to show how simple seeming stories can give developing readers the challenges they need. One, Margaret Mahy, is a New Zealander who has produced an impressive body of work since 1969, from picture books to novels. Her collection of short stories, *The Great Chewing Gum Rescue* (1982), for example, shows a writer at the peak of her power. In Britain, Jan Mark has been versatile and represents the best of the new wave of writers for the young to have emerged in the last two decades. *The Dead Letter Box* (for 8- to 12-year-olds) shows how ideas about friendship and communication can be folded in an accessible storyline.

One of the fascinating features of children's reading of literature in this age group is that it shows greater understanding of the ways in which literature works for them (Meek 1988). It is also possible to probe the development of children's grasp of the sorts of textual devices that writers use; children's comprehension of rituals within stories build upon their prior reading, and can lead to more sophisticated texts. These are learned behaviours, and parents, teachers, adults play an important part in developing them (see Mills 1994b).

Children's sense of humour becomes more sophisticated. They enjoy the possibilities of logic and common sense being turned on their heads. Like Alice, children at this stage have to battle their way, without a map, through an adult world which often appears ridiculous. Writers have often drawn upon the comic potential of that process of growing up (although not always for the benefit of children). A. A. Milne's Pooh stories, and many others since, show how easy it is for immature minds to misconstrue things. Children of 9 or 10, who are just past that kind of misapprehension themselves, can be onlookers on the action of childhood. Much of the best humour in books for this age group can come when adult pomposity, or adults' obliviousness of children, is observed. A classic example is the American Florence Parry Heide's *The Shrinking of Treehorn* (1971) where parents and teachers are earnestly unhelpful; as in many of the best books, there is a powerful metaphor beneath the hilarious surface.

Much of the sharpest and wittiest content has appeared in picture books over the last twenty years. Gifted artists have shown that the form is no longer the preserve of very young children, demonstrating its particular ability to catch the irony and the tang of contemporary childhood. Maurice Sendak's *In the Night Kitchen* (1970) tells a tale that has dark edges, by drawing upon the conventions of strip cartoons, movies and American art of the 1930s. Other artists have exploited the picture book's potential in showing the multifaceted nature of stories in pictures. Often, as in Raymond Briggs's *Father Christmas* (1973) and *Father Christmas Goes on Holiday* (1975) the humour lies in the gap between pictures and texts: what is left unsaid. And there are many other artists whose work is worth exploring in this context: from the USA: Tomi Ungerer, William Steig and James Stevenson; from Britain, Quentin Blake, Michael Foreman and Anthony Browne. Elaine Moss's study (1992) is a thorough and thoughtful account of what picture books contribute to children's reading in middle childhood.

Books for children in this age group reflect some of society's concerns and shifting consciousness. For a long time, there was a gender imbalance in terms of which characters in books were active and assertive. It is now possible (though still too rare) to see girls at the centre of plots, engaging and acting rather than sitting on the sidelines. Gene Kemp's award-winning *The Turbulent Term of Tyke Tyler* plays tricks with the readers' perceptions of how girls and boys behave. Similarly, Mary Hoffman's *Beware Princess!* (1986) offers a stimulating postmodern reading within a classic genre.

The young can possess varied frameworks to interpret how boys and girls 'naturally' are. There has also been much more effort made by writers, artists and publishers to reflect the multicultural nature of British and American society in stories for children. Other diverse and pluralistic cultures need a similar diversity in their reading matter for the young (Whitehead 1988).

Since the 1960s there has been a practice of 'packaging' fiction for young children into series. Long-held assumptions about the need for structure and linguistic control often stifle quality. However, during the 1980s and 1990s there have been some highlights, such as books, by Jane Gardam (*Bridget and William* (1981)), Bernard Ashley (*Dinner Ladies Don't Count* (1981)) and Barbara Willard (*Smiley Tiger* (1984)). Meguido Zola's *Moving* (1983) is a superb example of a book with potentially complex ideas and feelings – the shifting of communities and alienation – dealt with in an accessible way. Particular attention should be drawn to Judy Blume's *Freckle Juice* (1984). It is a splendid example of a sharply contemporary, fine-tuned kind of writing for 7- to 10-year-olds that American women writers are particularly adept at. Phyllis Green's *Eating Ice Cream with a Werewolf* (1985) is another fine (and underrated) example of the unpatronising verve these writers bring. The quality of books at this level might be indicated by the fact that Kevin Crossley-Holland's *Storm* published in Heinemann's Banana Books series had the distinction of winning the Carnegie Medal in 1985. Hobson

(1992: 213–222) gives an excellent summary of British, American and Australian series.

During the mid-1980s and into the 1990s, writers for this age group showed signs of interest in new forms and challenging content. This should not be overstated. The relative lack of innovation has always been a contrast to the adventurous themes and modes of presentation that picture books provide. Artists who are also story-tellers seem to be more willing to exploit new forms of telling for a generation who know the conventions of television, video narrative and cartoons. Attention here can be drawn to Shirley Hughes's *Chips and Jessie* (1985), a book which combines visual and verbal techniques in a highly original way. Poets, who are always concerned with form, are often highly innovative when they tackle extended stories. Roger McGough's *The Great Smile Robbery* is a superb example of virtuoso insouciance (aided by the interpolated illustrations). Sometimes ingenuity can take the book into an uncategorisable area, such as Jon Scieszka and Lane Smith's *The Stinky Cheese Man* (1992).

## Critical Shifts

Our developing awareness of the kinds of literary competence that children bring to the early texts they read, and the refined appreciation of the ways these texts 'work' for children, have stimulated new critical awareness and insight.

Until the late 1970s, criticism of children's books had tended to focus upon the surface features of texts: plot, action and characterisation. Perspectives from literary theory, cultural studies, and the kinds of analysis used in the study of adult fiction have given a fresh charge to critical writing about books for the young (see Hunt 1990). Chambers's critical work is significant in that he is a children's author as well as a critic. His *The Present Takers* (1983) was one of the most challenging books to appear in the 1980s and can be appreciated by 9- to 11-year-olds.

A good example of the kind of illumination that new theoretical perspectives can offer to books for the young is Chambers's discussion of the concepts of the author's voice, and 'the bond with the author'. First pages are important for this, as children are drawn in and reassured by the authorial tone of voice. Whereas objections to the work of Enid Blyton, for instance, had been put down to sexism, racism or class-based attitudes, Chambers's shifting to concepts such as 'side taking' on the part of an author gives a much needed critical edge to our discussions. Her 'subversive charm' writes Chambers, is 'made all the more potent for being couched in a narrative style that sounds no more disturbing than the voice of a polite maiden aunt telling a bedtime story over cocoa and biscuits' (Chambers 1985: 45). Chambers writing on Blyton, possibly the most influential and widely read of writers for the young, gives us a glimpse of the ways of 'seeing through' the manner in which texts do their work upon young children.

That kind of exciting criticism links well with pedagogical concerns. In a seminal work aptly titled *How Texts Teach What Readers Learn*, Margaret Meek, a literary critic and educator, shows how authors for the young create 'a shared cultural understanding' with their readers. Writers, she claims, teach reading as something pleasurable, and help with 'the early untaught lessons' that all good readers understand (Meek 1988: 31). That kind of appreciation has shifted quality literature from a reward children get for learning to read, to the reason for learning to do it in the first place.

More important, the new critical shifts outlined here put an enormous amount of trust in readers and writers. Adults have always mediated, for both good and questionable reasons. Perhaps as we come to understand more clearly the ways in which literature works its spell with the young, the power will be with the writers and with those who are their true readers.

# References

Bosche, S. (1987) *Jenny Lives with Eric and Martin*, London: Gay Men's Press.

Brown, H. and Mathie, V. (1990) *Inside Whole Language: A Classroom View*, Rozell, NSW: Primary English Teaching Association.

Butler, D. (1980) *Babies Need Books*, Sevenoaks: Hodder and Stoughton

Chambers, A. (1985) *Booktalk*, London: Bodley Head.

Dombey, H. (1988) 'Partners in the telling' in Meek, M. and Mills, C. (eds) *Language and Literacy in the Primary School*, Lewes: Falmer Press.

Egoff, S. (1980) 'Precepts, pleasures and portents: changing emphases in children's literature', in Egoff, S., Stubbs, G. T. and Ashley, L. F. (eds) *Only Connect: Readings on Children's Literature*, 2nd edn, Toronto: Oxford University Press.

Fox, C. (1993) *At the Very Edge of the Forest: The Influence of Literature on Storytelling by Children*, London: Cassell.

Goodman, K. (1986) *What's Whole in Whole Language?* Leamington: Scholastic.

Harrison, C. and Coles, M. (eds) (1992) *The Reading for Real Handbook*, London: Routledge.

Hobson, M. *et al.* (1992) *Children's Fiction Sourcebook*, Aldershot: Ashgate.

Hunt, P. (1990) *Children's Literature: The Development of Criticism*, London: Routledge.

Lewis, D. (1990) 'The constructedness of texts: picture books and the metafictive', *Signal* 62, 131–146.

Meek, M. (1988) *How Texts Teach What Readers Learn*, South Woodchester: Thimble Press.

—— (1992) 'Transitions: the notion of change in writing for children', *Signal* 67, 13–33.

Mills, C. (1994a) 'Texts that teach', in Wray, D. and Medwell, J. (eds) *Teaching Primary English: The State of the Art*, London: Routledge.

—— (1994b) 'Making sense of reading', in Bourne, J. (ed.) *Thinking Through Primary Practice*, London: Routledge/Open University.

Moss, E. (1992) *Picture Books 9–13*, South Woodchester: Thimble Press.

Rose, J. (1984) *The Case of Peter Pan, or the Impossibility of Children's Fiction*, London: Macmillan.

Rustin, M. and Rustin, M. (1987) *Narratives of Love and Loss: Studies in Modern Children's Fiction*, London: Verso.

Tucker, N. (1981) *The Child and the Book: A Psychological and Literary Exploration*, Cambridge: Cambridge University Press.

Watson, V. (1992) 'The possibilities of children's fiction' in Styles, M. *et al.* (eds) *After Alice: Exploring Children's Literature*, London: Cassell.

White, D. N. (1954) *Books Before Five*, Wellington: New Zealand Council for Educational Research.

Whitehead, W. (1988) *Different Faces: Growing Up with Books in a Multicultural Society*, London: Pluto Press.

## Further Reading

Butts, D. (ed.) (1994) *Stories and Society: Children's Literature in its Social Context*, London: Macmillan.

Leeson, R. (1985) *Reading and Righting*, London: Collins.

Lurie, A. (1990) *Don't Tell the Grown-Ups: Subversive Children's Literature*, London: Bloomsbury.

# 32

# Teenage Fiction: Realism, Romances, Contemporary Problem Novels

## *Julia Eccleshare*

The demarcation of reading by age is always a tricky one, perhaps especially so when it comes to teenage fiction. What is at issue is not so much the teenage of the reader as the teenage or 'young adulthood' of the characters. The expectation is that teenagers should read about the things that they themselves are doing or would enjoy doing if only they could. For this reason, teenage fiction has evolved as the most narcissistic of all fictions as, in its current form at least, it seems primarily directed towards mirroring society and in so doing offering reassurance about ways of behaving.

The concept of young adults as a separate group to be addressed and instructed was put forward by the educationalist Sarah Trimmer as long ago as 1802. She drew a dividing line at 14 and suggested that 'young adulthood' should last until 21. As far as publishing specifically for that readership was concerned no direct action was taken, but writers wrote for them naturally, seeing them as an eager audience and one that needed to be well influenced.

In the absence of a definable teenage culture there were obvious settings or situations which would appeal directly to adolescent readers. School stories like Thomas Hughes's *Tom Brown's Schooldays* (1857) and Talbot Baines Reed's *The Fifth Form at St Dominic's* (1887) were successes at the time of their publication and (particularly *Tom Brown's Schooldays*) have remained classics of their genre. R. M. Ballantyne's *Coral Island* (1858) and Robert Louis Stevenson's *Treasure Island* (1883), *Kidnapped* (1886) and *The Black Arrow* (1889) offered adventure to readers of all ages but the strength of young male characters such as Jim in *Treasure Island* and David Balfour in *Kidnapped* made them popular with contemporary and subsequent generations of teenagers. Stevenson wrote directly for his 12-year-old stepson, Lloyd, which may add to his success with the young. Mark Twain's *Tom Sawyer* (1876) and its sequel *Huckleberry Finn* (1884) are the obvious American counterparts.

The two most recent precursors of the teenage novel, like their nineteenth-century predecessors, were published for adults, but both have had a significant influence on adolescent readers. William Golding's *The Lord of the Flies* (1954) shatters any illusions about childhood innocence. For this reason it appeals powerfully to readers who have begun to recognise this loss in themselves. J. D. Salinger's *The Catcher in the Rye* (1954) has made an even greater impact, because the stream-of-consciousness, first person narrative of Holden Caulfield, with its detached and critical view of the adult world is not only in itself liberating but has also been imitated in many subsequent novels.

The notion of teenagers as a separate group of readers with their own tastes and demanding a style of writing that is directed specifically at them was not adopted by publishers until relatively recently and, even then, it took a long time to establish an identity and, perhaps most importantly of all, to find a suitable space in libraries and bookshops. Naming this invention was a further difficulty. 'Teenager', 'Young Adult' ... what was this audience to be called?

And then there was the further problem that everyone knew that readers younger than the magic age of 13 would be reading these books. Did publishers have a responsibility not to include 'unsuitable' material for them, or was it enough to have overt labelling warning that this was *intended* for teenagers? As books for teenagers became increasingly daring in terms of explicit writing about sex in the 1970s and violence in the 1990s the naming and marketing of the books was a significant issue.

Before the concretisation of teenage fiction into named series, acknow-ledgement that teenagers wanted books about their own experiences had come gradually and had started (not surprisingly because 'teenagers' themselves were first recognised there) in the USA. Post-war teenagers were a far more vociferous and independent group than their predecessors and their experiences had never been explored in fiction. 'Teenage' became a separate fashionable entity, and so did its fiction. From the mid-1950s on, and increasingly with the social liberation of the 1960s and 1970s, books for 'young adults' were making their mark, attracting serious writers who recognised the potential market of intelligent, sophisticated readers who needed books that would acknowledge their growing awareness of the complex emotions and events they were experiencing. Writers needed to understand the dilemmas that were posed to this generation by their new freedoms and to offer sensible discussion of choices without too much moral instruction.

Initially, the prime thrust of books for the new teenage market was romance, the range of books reflecting contemporary mores and as well as eternal truths. *Fifteen* by Beverley Cleary, one of the first novels directed wholly at teenagers, was published in 1956 in the USA but not until 1962 by Penguin in Britain – and then as the second title in their newly launched series for teenagers, Peacocks. It is an unpretentious, straightforward romance, which is unashamedly about a girl's desire for a boyfriend, the arrival of said boyfriend and their ensuing, developing relationship during the year. Cleary treads a delicate path between the mundane and the romantic, and the book's very 'decency' made it possible for it to fit on to the Peacock list of the time.

The reserve and modesty of books such as *Fifteen* was followed by a wave of books which were considerably more sophisticated and complex. While many still dealt with the very first steps in a relationship, others were tackling the more serious problems like teenage pregnancy, always a possible result of too much teenage romance. K. M. Peyton is a romantic writer to her fingertips but she is also a realist. Her stories about the delinquent Pennington who has a rare talent for playing the piano started in *Pennington's Seventeenth Summer* (1970) with not much more than background romance. But they progressed through *The Beethoven*

*Medal* (1971) in which Pennington continues on his wayward and brilliant career to *Pennington's Heir* (1974) in which girlfriend, now very young wife, Ruth struggles with a baby and nappies under the shadow of the grand piano, against a background of crashing minor chords. Realistic possibly, but certainly Ruth was a very unliberated heroine by the standards of the next two decades.

Teenage fiction emerged almost simultaneously with the first soundings of the women's liberation movement but it remained unaffected by it for a long time, even though the majority of novels written at the time were written by women and directed predominantly at girls.

Honor Arundel's approach of using the popular romance with some elements of reality thrown in was similar to K. M. Peyton's. The books of both were an important bridge between magazine romance and literary love stories such as *Jane Eyre* and *Wuthering Heights*. Emma, her best known heroine, first appeared in an uncomplicated adventure *Emma's Island* (1968). As an orphan on a remote Scottish island she has all the qualities necessary for romance and, of course, as she grows up she falls in love. In *Emma in Love* (1970) Arundel describes the stages of first joy and then disillusionment that Emma goes through until she finally recognises that there will be other boys. But Arundel was well aware that love has its price and she was not afraid of confronting the issues of sex and even single parenthood, as in *The Longest Weekend* (1969) in which Eileen struggles to cope with her 3-year-old daughter and her suffocatingly 'understanding' parents.

Good teenage romances have persisted, looking at every possible angle of love and relationships. But fiction was several years behind the enormous fashion and popular-music upheavals of the mid-1960s. Reading retained its 'middle-class' conservative image and was in danger of offering very little to anyone other than the committed reader.

The mid-1970s brought a wave of more hard-hitting novels to Britain. Imports from liberated Scandinavia, such as Gunnel Beckman's *Mia* (1974) and its sequels, talked openly about sex between teenagers. Bodley Head's New Adult list on which they appeared was incredibly controversial at the time and did much to shape the identity of subsequent teenage fiction. 'Nice' stories lost out to novels which gave a less romantic picture of the realities of contemporary teenage life.

Lynne Reid Banks used her romance *My Darling Villain* (1977) to tackle parental control and particularly parents' views about class head on. Fifteen-year-old Kate, nice and very middle class, is allowed to give her first adult party, which is gate-crashed by some less-than-middle-class lads. After the ensuing chaos one of them, Mark, stays behind to tidy up, and they start going out together: but Mark's working-class background is deplored by Kate's parents. The way in which attitudes about both class and race are discussed by Lynne Reid Banks makes *My Darling Villain* – the title itself gives it away – a notably dated book but the theme of loving against parental wishes is perennially popular.

Perhaps the most controversial, at the time of publication at least, was Judy Blume's *Forever* (1975). The joys and disappointments of first love are shown through the story of Michael and Katherine; more importantly, the joys and disappointments of their first sexual encounter are described explicitly and easily, making *Forever* readily accessible to pre-teens, too. For such frankness Judy Blume has been heavily censored throughout the USA but *Forever* has an important place in the canon of teenage fiction and Blume's boldness of purpose and her directness of style were recognised and applauded in many circles at the time.

Admitting that sex among teenagers does take place was an important breakthrough for both writers and readers. For the first time, writers were beginning to acknowledge fully the reality of teenage relationships and to recognise the pressures that teenagers are under and the choices they have to make. As with their romantic predecessors, experiences were predominantly retold from the girl's point of view. Boys' feelings about sex and relationships were rarely explored except as a shadowy foil to whatever the girl at the centre of the story was thinking. The knowledge that girls are the prime readers of romances and the expectation that therefore the stories should be told from their point of view survives today and most teenage romances are still told from the girl's angle.

Alan Garner fared better than most in *Red Shift* (1973). He was absolutely up-to-date in making Tom and Jan's failure to have a satisfactory sexual relationship the centre point of his story. Because of his parallel and mirroring historical narratives – one set in Celtic Britain and one in the English Civil War – the pertinence of the central story was easily missed and that, combined with Garner's elusive and cryptic style, made the book have less impact than it should. Garner's male perspective was refreshing, as was his superior writing in an area not always noted for this quality.

For both of these reasons Aidan Chambers, too, was an important contributor to the teenage books of the time. A boy's sensitivities were described by him in *Breaktime* (1978). Like Garner, Chambers is a demanding writer. His account of Ditto's sexual initiation and the subsequent reassessment of his life, and especially of his relationship with his father, is retold in a complex but thrilling narrative which offers insight into ways of reading literature as well as speaking openly about sex. In *Dance on My Grave* (1982) Chambers is bolder in both subject matter and style. Hal has known for some time that he is gay but he has not acknowledged it openly. When Barry appears, the two recognise their need for one another, but also acknowledge that they may not be faithful forever.

The telling of *Dance on My Grave* is introverted and complex. Jean Ure's *The Other Side of the Fence* (1986) is more accessible but the point of the story – that Richard's girlfriend Jan turns out to be a Polish boy – is not revealed until the very end, making the story didactic rather than instructive. Both books mark a brief window during which gay sex could be written about before widespread knowledge of AIDS made such fictions even more controversial and harder to tackle.

In *Hey, Dollface* (1979) Deborah Hautzig writes far more plainly about Val's developing feelings for Chloe. Written in the first person by Val, *Hey, Dollface* describes how the friendship becomes romantic and physical though, after discussion, the girls decide not to become lovers.

Such openness about relationships marked an important change in the way teenagers and the kind of books they might want to read were perceived. But the upsurge of writing about teenage sex and the conviction that physical attraction was the impetus for all teenage relationships began to distort the realities of society. Ursula Le Guin's *A Very Long Way From Anywhere Else* (1976) was an excellent antidote providing a welcome respite for teenagers who were quite happy having strong but wholly platonic friendships. Owen and Natalie are both intelligent, strongly motivated people set on different paths for further study. Their relationship is stimulating and enriching, each helping the other to discover what it is that they really believe in. Both find it hard to cope with the sexual expectations pushed on them by the media, their peers and even their parents. Paul Zindel, too, has recognised that a common purpose may lead to powerful friendships which have nothing to do with sex. In *My Darling, My Hamburger* (1969) he makes his point about teenage relationships in a story which revolves around two couples who are treating being 'a couple' in quite different ways. He harks back to the theme in *A Begonia for Miss Applebaum* (1989) in which Henry and Zelda tell the story of their befriending of Miss Applebaum in alternate chapters, revealing much of their thoughts about each other and their developing emotions as they find out about the life of their amazing teacher and come to terms with her death.

Margaret Mahy has an exceptional understanding of just how emotionally charged teenagers are. She sees this as relating to many things, including the supernatural, as much as necessarily being bound up with preoccupations about sex. In *The Catalogue of the Universe* (1985) she captures the importance of Tycho and Angela's friendship. Their need for one another that is based on under-standing and intellectual harmony rather than anything overtly physical.

Once the sexual side of relationships had became a recognised and accepted part of teenage writing, the complexities of such relationships rather than their shock qualities could be discussed in an interesting way. Berlie Doherty's *Dear Nobody* (1992) takes a hard look at a girl's choices when she discovers that she is pregnant. Helen decides to keep the baby and the anguish that causes is resolved only at the end, but her steadfast belief in the rightness of her decision is painfully explored in her diary entries. Chris's responses are understandably different – he is mostly concerned with not losing Helen – but at least he is credited with a viewpoint and, even if he is clearly not as mature as Helen, he is at least concerned and caring.

The arrival of AIDS and changing attitudes to sexual freedom, especially the advent of vociferous feminism, have caused a slowing down in the number of books where 'the relationship' is the centre of the narrative. Writers are crediting teenagers with deeper understanding and good sense about the world and the issues which loom large in it.

Beyond the limitations of peer relationships, books for teenagers are an excellent vehicle for exploring all kinds of relationships with other members of the family or other age groups. Recognition of the developing intellectual and emotional powers of adolescent readers as they move out of a relatively safe world in which decisions are made for them and into one of infinite variety and choice has encouraged thoughtful and wide-ranging analysis. Closest in terms of subject matter to relationship with their peers are the numerous books ·which reflect relationships within families and, especially, the breakdown of traditional, close-knit families. To acknowledge parental failing is an extraordinarily difficult thing and many stories have served as valuable conduits for analysing the pain and trauma that can be caused.

The extent to which unhappiness and self-examination became a predominant theme reached an all time high in the late 1970s and was in danger of belittling teenage readers in a misguided attempt at social realism. Too many books were devoted to the fragility of traditional family values. Teenage readers were in grave danger of being sold very short by the dearth of high-quality writing and thinking in what was being offered to them. It needed writers of distinction to add an extra dimension to the genre. Robert Westall's *The Scarecrows* (1981) painfully traces 13-year-old Simon's traumatic emotional ride as he rejects his stepfather and conjures up spirits from the past whose powers threaten to overwhelm him. Westall borders on the emotionally savage in his version of how a teenager reacts to the replacement of his father by another man. Such emotional force combined with powerful imagery turns subject matter which, in fiction at any rate, was becoming depressingly routine into a book of enormous power and importance.

Anne Fine has tackled family break-ups head on in both *Madame Doubtfire* (1989) and *Goggle-Eyes* (1992). Her wit, insight and subtlety set her books apart from the rest and do much to redress the balance and show just how well this hoary chestnut of a theme can be handled. In *Madam Doubtfire* she carries off the preposterous notion that the estranged father, desperate to spend more time with his children, can come back disguised as a housekeeper who takes charge of the children while the mother is working. The implausibility of the deception is deftly handled with the children acknowledging and distancing themselves from the intrigue in almost equal, and perfectly convincing, measure. In *Goggle-Eyes*, Kitty Killin tells Helly Johnson everything she needs to know about mothers having new and unwanted boyfriends who, as both girls know, may all too easily become unwanted stepfathers. Huddled in the school lost-property cupboard, the two girls share their grief at the loss of the parents they first loved. Helly's story remains untold as the forceful Kitty unravels her own story about the horrors of Goggle-Eyes and her eventual conversion to him and to his mother's relationship with him.

Paula Danziger's books are read by many who are not yet into adolescence but much of what she writes about concerns how teenagers come to terms with parental failure and especially with the breaking up of marriage. Like Anne Fine, Paula Danziger's ability to write humorously about traumatic feelings and events enables her to inform her readers about important emotional developments without ever preaching to them. In both *Can You Sue Your Parents for Malpractice?* (New York 1979; London 1986) and *The Divorce Express* (New York 1982; London 1986) the titles alone indicate Danziger's lightness of touch on what can all too easily become a portentous and didactic subject area.

Cynthia Voight takes a completely different approach in *Homecoming* (New York 1981; London 1983). There is little humour but much warmth in this long and profoundly moving story about four children who are abandoned in a car park by their mother who can no longer cope with the problems of being a single parent without adequate support. Dicey, the oldest, leads the others on a journey to find their grandmother. Their trek takes them many miles to Maryland and their experiences on the way are a convincing mixture of meetings with people, some good and some bad. Most importantly, the journey is an opportunity for the characters of the children and their interaction with one another to be developed. From the starting point of the break up of the traditional family Cynthia Voight has written a story that is full of hope about sibling support and their ability to redefine a family in the absence of parents.

*Homecoming* is the first in a series of interconnected novels through which

Cynthia Voight allows each of the four Tillerman children further room for development. The personal growth of her characters, and particularly of the two boys when they go in search of the father they know they need in *Sons From Afar* (1989), makes them fascinating models for all adolescents, not just those who are needing fictional role models to help them resolve their own problems.

Jan Mark's understanding of teenage confusions is equally acute and, like Voight, she writes about characters developing in all kinds of ways rather than merely as survivors of situations. Mark is particularly sharp in her observations about friendships and their importance to adolescents both at school and at home. *Thunder and Lightnings* (1976), her first book, revolves around the friendship between the bright newcomer Andrew and Victor, considered locally to be stupid. Their exchanges are spare and reflect both the initial unease and the subsequent comfortableness that the two feel with one another. In *Man in Motion* (1989) Lloyd, like Andrew, is newly arrived in a new home with a new school and no friends. At first he is at a complete loss to know how to make friends and is puzzled that his sister seems to find the whole thing so easy. But gradually things change and Lloyd finds himself with friends for a whole range of activities and not enough time to devote to his own passion – American football. Lloyd learns how to juggle his loyalties so that he can keep faith with all his friends and have time to do what he really wants.

Exploring the complexities of something as comparatively simple as friendships is every bit as important as delving into the more obviously traumatic areas of the problem novels mentioned above. Robert Cormier's picture of teenage interaction is far bleaker than anything Jan Mark describes. In *The Chocolate War* (1975) Cormier writes of the merciless persecution of one boy by the powerful secret society in an American Catholic high school in which corruption is rife. Cormier's novel is almost unremittingly bleak in both style and content. It offers the reader little comfort, though some insights into the cruelties which teenagers can inflict upon one another. Later, in *Beyond the Chocolate War* (1985), Cormier modifies the bleakness of his message, though the style remains as taut and telling. In it Jerry Renault, victim in *The Chocolate War*, is semi-recovered from his ordeal and returns to school to face up to his tormentor who is revealed as a demonic character who reaches a nasty end.

Cormier is never frightened of showing how evil teenagers can be and he expands on this in *We All Fall Down* (1992). Four teenagers 'trash' a house in an act of mindless violence. The damage to the property is bad enough but worse is that they push 14-year-old Karen down the cellar steps leaving her smashed and helpless. The repercussions on all involved – the trashers, Karen and her family, and the mysterious 'avenger' who watches it all – are skilfully and carefully unravelled revealing much about the different characters' motives and allowing the reader to act as judge of each for themselves. *We All Fall Down* is a book of tremendous force and the lurid description of the trashing is haunting, but somehow Cormier weaves in a morality which, combined with the sheer quality of his writing, separates his books from the excesses of the recent, highly successful American products Point Horror and Point Crime. Both series pull no punches and have been decried for their apparent endorsement of remorse-free violence. Some teenagers clearly like to be frightened and for those such books provide a legitimate thrill. The danger lies in the chilling amorality of stories which may make them unreasonably frightening for unwitting readers.

While relationships may be centre stage for many during the years of physical and emotional changes, vital world issues are also deeply important. The incredible response among teenagers to issues concerning the environment and the needs of those in developing countries, as was revealed in the success of first Live Aid and then Band Aid, also needed to be reflected in fiction. Different issues dominate at different times and books which deal with them can be important stories of the moment rather than becoming classics. Robert Swindells's *Brother in the Land* (1984) was just one of a number of books published within a five-year span which dealt with what, at the time, seemed a perfectly likely event – the dropping of a nuclear bomb. The prospect of the destruction of the world and speculation as to what might survive and how led to some undisciplined and morbid writing. Many seemed to assume that the sheer gravity of the subject matter was enough to make a book on the subject good. *Brother in the Land* is an exception and the fact that it is as readable and poignant today proves the point. In the aftermath of the nuclear destruction moral order breaks down, survival depends on selfishness. Or so Danny thinks, until he finds a crumb of reassurance in the behaviour of a handful of the other survivors. Robert Swindells wrote a book reflecting the mood of the moment but his understanding of how people behave in extremis has made it a book to last.

The picture book format of Raymond Briggs's *When the Wind Blows* (1982) might not make it immediately look like a book for teenagers but the comic strip layout of text and pictures does little to soften the intensity of the tragedy that unfolds through the story. Jim and Hilda, a retired couple, try hard to follow the government's instructions about what to do in the event of a nuclear war. Briggs's point was that such guidance was fatuous and would do nothing to help people if a bomb really was dropped. Jim and Hilda are not directly hit by a bomb but they are affected by radiation sickness. Watching them slavishly trying to do as they have been told while all the time turning greener, weaker and with less hair is almost too painful to bear but it is a frighteningly powerful way of conveying the impact of the atomic bomb while also serving as a hard-hitting attack on government policy in supporting a nuclear programme.

Other books of the same period such as Louise Lawrence's *Children of the Dust* (1985) reflected just how pessimistic current thinking then was. Set after the dropping of the bomb *Children of the Dust* describes a horribly mutated race as the sole survivors in a bleak new world.

When Joan Lingard wrote the first of what was to become a quintet of books about Protestant Sadie and Catholic Kevin, the 'troubles' in Northern Ireland had only just begun. In *The Twelfth Day of July* (1970) the two teenagers meet against the background of the annual Orange Day celebration in Belfast. They rapidly become a modern version of 'star crossed lovers' in *Across the Barricades* (1972) facing increasing hostility from friends and family – with the exception of Kevin's sister. Realistically, Joan Lingard moves the couple from Belfast in *Into Exile* (1973) and from then on the political situation in Northern Ireland recedes into the background as the story of the young couple's early married life unfolds. Sectarian hostilities happen the world over and even if the Northern Ireland situation is resolved the Kevin and Sadie books offer shrewd insight into a long episode in the history of the country as well as describing what it might feel like growing up anywhere where there is civil war.

Martin Waddell, under the pseudonym Catherine Sefton, has also written about the problems of growing up in Northern Ireland where the sectarian war is part of the everyday background. Living with such accepted prejudice it is hard for adolescents to form their own opinions and learn tolerance. In *Island of the Strangers* (1983) a group of children from the city clash with a gang from the seaside town they are visiting. The conflict is based on crude preconceptions. The resolution depends on the growing maturity of the individual characters and their awareness that the individual may be more important than a cause or belief.

Apartheid, like the threat of a nuclear holocaust, was a live issue for many teenagers and traces of it will remain for many years to come. Toekey Jones's *Skindeep* (1985) still deserves reading as it exposes not only the well-documented gulfs within South African society but also the hypocrisy and false thinking on which apartheid operated since the friendship that develops between the two teenagers is 'allowed' because Dave is a 'pass White'. In *Python Dance* (1992) Norman Silver explores how Ruth, living as a privileged White in 1960s Johannesburg, begins to question the assumptions of her background. Stepping outside her own world she learns the grim truth of how the Blacks, whom she has been brought up to despise, live.

As with apartheid, the extremism of General Pinochet's regime in Chile exists no longer but James Watson's *Talking in Whispers* (1983) a fast-paced adventure story in which Andres witnesses the ultimate in censorship – the burning of books – and plays an important part in exposing the secret service's shooting of an eminent opponent of the junta, remains as a powerful reminder of an episode in Chile's history and also as a picture of any repressive regime at any time.

The wars that have most recently affected Britain directly have been used as source material by Jan Needle and Robert Westall. Both exploit the particular to describe something much greater: the realities of conflict as set against the propaganda that is generated about them. Jan Needle set *A Game of Soldiers* (1985) in the Falklands War. Sarah, Thomas and Michael come face to face with a wounded soldier and soon discover the realities of the pain, fear and suffering of war which contrasts sharply with the jingoistic patriotism that was being written about it at the time. Robert Westall did much the same for the Gulf War, though with a quite different kind of story in *Gulf* (1992), in which an English boy 'turns into' an Iraqi boy soldier.

Books of this kind pick up on teenagers' commitment to issues that do not affect them directly but which they know about superficially from newspaper and television reporting. Contemporary domestic issues, too, have been treated seriously for teenagers as in Ian Strachan's *Throwaways* (1992) which describes the pathetic existence eked out by children who have been abandoned by their parents because they can no longer afford to feed them. Sky, Chip and Dig soon learn (as did Danny in *Brother in the Land*) that integrity can and must survive against all odds if they are themselves to survive as people rather than to merely exist. Robert Swindells's *Stone Cold* (1993), with its central theme of homelessness and its chilling account of the terrible dangers that the young who live rough may encounter, gives insights into a world which it is all to easy to keep at arm's length.

Like readers of all ages, teenagers need a mixture of fictions to sustain their literary interests. Self-knowledge is a spur to growth, but so too is a wider understanding of the all aspects of society, present, past and in the future. While the impetus for teenage fiction may have come from the need to provide a vociferous band of readers with amusing stories about themselves, it is now a vehicle for telling the same readers about the world as it really is. Indeed as novels become increasingly bleak, partly because of the bleakness of social issues such as homelessness, unemployment and the rest, there are serious concerns about what may and may not be suitable fictional fare.

Whatever the direct subject matter of teenage fiction, what remains important is the steady flow of good-quality writing for an eager but easily distracted age group.

## Further Reading

Chambers, A. (1985) *Booktalk*, London: Bodley Head.
Eccleshare, J. (1984–1993) *Children's Books of the Year*, London: Andersen Press.
Landsberg, M. (1988) *The World of Children's Books*, London: Simon and Schuster.
Moss, E. (1970–1980) *Children's Books of the Year*, London: Hamish Hamilton.
—— (1986) *Part of the Pattern*, London: Bodley Head.
Yates, J. (1986) *Teenager to Young Adult*, London: School Library Association.

# 33

# Metafictions and Experimental Work

## Robyn McCallum

The term 'metafiction' is used to refer to fiction which self-consciously draws attention to its status as text and as fictive. It does this in order to reflect upon the processes through which narrative fictions are constructed, read and made sense of and to pose questions about the relationships between the ways we interpret and represent both fiction and reality (Waugh 1984: 2). Although they are not interchangeable, there is considerable overlap between contemporary categories of metafiction and experimental fiction. Texts which are experimental are often also metafictive, and vice versa. As categories of fiction both are, to some extent, context bound, definable in relation to other forms of narrative fiction – the category 'experimental' changes through time, socio-historical context, and critical conceptions of what constitutes the mainstream. With children's literature this category can shift between 'literary' and popular, neither of which is exempt from experimentation, depending on which aspects of a text are the focus of attention: the discursive and stylistic techniques, narrative technique and structures, content, social, ideological, intellectual and moral concerns and so on.

A key distinction between metafictive and experimental texts and the majority of fiction written for children lies in the kinds of narrative and discursive techniques used to construct and inscribe audience positions within texts. Briefly, the narrative modes employed in children's novels tend to be restricted to either first person narration by a main character or third person narration with one character focaliser (Stephens 1991: 63). Texts tend to be monological rather than dialogical, with single-stranded and story-driven narratives, closed rather than open endings, and a narrative discourse lacking stylistic variation (Moss 1990; Hunt 1988). These are strategies which function to situate readers in restricted and relatively passive subject positions and to implicitly reinforce a single dominant interpretive stance. Restrictions on narrative point of view in particular frequently have the effect of restricting the possible interpretive positions available to implied readers (Stephens 1991: 63; 1992b: 27).

Metafictive and experimental forms of children's writing generally use a broader range of narrative and discursive techniques: overly obtrusive narrators who directly address readers and comment on their own narration; disruptions of the spatio-temporal narrative axis and of diegetic levels of narration; parodic appropriations of other texts, genres and discourses; typographic experimentation; mixing of genres, discourse styles, modes of narration and speech representation; multiple character focalisers, narrative voices, and narrative strands and so on.

These are strategies which distance readers from a text and frequently frustrate conventional expectations about meaning and closure. Implied readers are thereby positioned in more active interpretive roles. By foregrounding the discursive and narrative structuring of texts, metafictions can show readers how texts mean and, by analogy, how meanings are ascribed to everyday reality.

## Metafiction and Readers

Although the use of metafictive and experimental narrative forms in children's fiction has recently received positive criticism (Moss 1985; Lewis 1990; Moss 1990, 1992; Hunt 1992; Stephens 1991, 1992b, 1993; Mackey 1990), the genre can still generate resistance and scepticism. A common response is that it is too difficult for children. Metafictive texts often draw attention to their own artifice through the parody or inversion of other texts, genres and discourses. These strategies depend upon a reader's recognition of the parodied text, genre, or discourse, and hence assume certain levels of literary and interpretive competence. As inexperienced readers, children may not have learned the cultural and literary codes and conventions necessary to recognise metafictive devices. However, as Hunt has observed 'it may be correct to assume that child-readers will not bring to the text a complete or sophisticated system of codes, but is this any reason to deny them access to texts with a potential of rich codes?' (1991: 101). Furthermore, Mackey argues that metafictive children's texts can 'foster an awareness of how a story works' and implicitly teach readers how texts are structured through specific codes and conventions (1990: 181).

The instructive potential of metafiction has been emphasised by many theorists (of both adult and children's texts). Hutcheon's description of the activity of a reader of metafiction also aptly describes the activity of an inexperienced child reader: that is, 'one of learning and constructing a new sign-system, a new set of verbal relations' (1980: 19). By involving readers in the production of textual meanings, metafictions can implicitly teach literary and cultural codes and conventions, as well as specific interpretive strategies, and hence empower readers to read more competently: more explicit forms often seek to teach readers conventions and strategies with which to interpret metafictions as well as other more closed texts.

There are two main aspects of metafiction which are important for reading development. First, developmental studies suggest that mature readers 'read with a more reflective and detached awareness of how the processes of fiction are operating as they read' (Mackey 1990: 179). Metafictive narratives construct a distance between an audience and the represented events and characters and can potentially foster such an awareness (Stephens 1991: 75). Second, there is a demonstrated relationship between play-oriented activities, such as verbal puns, jokes and rhymes, role play and story-telling, and the acquisition of language and of complex cognitive and social skills (Vygotsky 1934/1962; Britton 1970/1972). Underlying much metafiction for children is a heightened sense of the status of fiction as an elaborate form of play, that is a game with linguistic and narrative codes and conventions. Janet and Allan Ahlberg exemplify this kind of writing for quite young children, by producing narratives which are parodic reversions of familiar childhood texts (for example Allan Ahlberg's *Ten in a Bed* (1883).

A second objection to metafiction (for children and adults) is that as a radically self-reflexive and playful genre it is ultimately self-indulgent and solipsistic. To assume that fiction can be self-reflexive in any simple way, however, is to confuse the signifying and referential functions of the linguistic signs that constitute a text – that is, it is indicative of a failure to distinguish between signs and things. It is precisely this distinction that theorists such as Britton see as important in the encouragement of an 'openness to alternative formulations of experience' associated with the move out of egocentricism (1970/1972: 86), and which metafictions frequently foreground and exploit. We use language and narrative to represent, mediate and comprehend reality, as well as to construct fictions. By 'laying bare' the artifice through which fictional texts mean, metafictions can also lay bare the conventions through which what we think of as 'reality' is represented and ascribed with meanings.

## Defining Metafiction

Metafiction tends to be defined in two main ways: as a distinctive sub-genre of the novel, defined in opposition to literary realism; or as an inherent tendency of the novelistic genre (Ommundsen 1989: 266). Waugh (1984) and Lewis (1990) both stress the relation between metafiction and the classic realist text. Metafictions appropriate and parody the conventions of traditional realism in order to construct a fictional illusion and simultaneously expose the constructedness of that illusion (Waugh 1984: 6). Our understanding of a metafiction will depend to some extent upon the conventions and intertexts which it parodies, but more specifically upon assumptions about the verbal sign inscribed within these conventions. The narrative conventions of realist fiction work to mask the gap between linguistic signs and their fictive referents and to construct an illusion of an unmediated relation between signs and things. In doing so, these conventions obscure the fictionality of referents and imply a reading of fiction as if it were 'real'. In metafiction, however, the ontological gap between fiction and reality is made explicit; that is, the fictionality of the events, characters and objects referred to is foregrounded.

While the relations between metafiction and literary realism are important, to define one in opposition to the other excludes from consideration a vast number of (often ostensibly 'realist') texts which have self-reflexive elements but which are not 'systematically self-conscious' (Ommundsen 1989: 265), as well as early forms of metafictive writing. Hutcheon has stressed that the use of self-reflexive narrative strategies is part of a long novelistic tradition: 'Art has always been "illusion" and it has often, if not always, been self-consciously aware of that ontological status' (1980: 17). Anita Moss's (1985) inclusion of early writers such as Nesbit and Dickens acknowledges this tradition in children's literature.

Much of the critical discourse around children's metafiction has been situated within a theoretical frame which opposes metafiction and realism and has focused on recent and unambiguously 'metafictive' examples. However, an approach which proceeds from an opposition between mainstream children's writing and 'counter texts' – texts which don't fit unproblematically into the category of children's literature – excludes all but the most explicitly self-conscious forms and, by implication, suggests a simplistic correlation between metafiction and subversion (for example, Moss 1990: 50). On the other hand, to over-emphasise the novelistic potential for self-reflexivity at the expense of specific identifiable metafictive narrative techniques and discursive strategies is to reduce the possibilities of critical insight and analysis. In other words, both aspects need to be taken into account: the specific strategies through which metafictions play with literary and cultural codes and conventions, and the historicity and conventionality of these metafictive textual practices.

## Postmodernism, metafiction and experimental picture books

Metafiction is a mode of writing which has recently flourished within a broader cultural movement referred to as postmodernism (Waugh 1984: 21) with which it shares some common features: narrative fragmentation and discontinuity, disorder and chaos, code mixing and absurdity of the kind which appears in the picture books of John Burningham, Chris Van Allsburg, Anthony Browne, David Wiesner, David Macaulay and the novels of William Mayne and Terry Pratchett.

Two recent studies have focused on postmodern features of contemporary picture books (Lewis 1990; Moss 1992). The tendency toward parody, playfulness and openness in many recent picture books constitutes a metafictive potential: picture books comprise two inherently different modes of representation – verbal and visual – the relations between which are always to some extent more or less dialogical. Words and pictures interact so as to construct (and defer) meanings, rather than simply reflecting or illustrating each other. The visual and verbal components of a picture book can thus imply a dialogue between text and picture and readers – for example, Burningham's Shirley books or Van Allsburg's *The Mysteries of Harris Burdick*.

The combination of two sign systems clearly provides a way of problematising the representational function of visual and verbal signs and of foregrounding the ways in which the relations between signs and things are structured by culturally inscribed codes of representation and signification. The extent to which meanings are socially and culturally constructed, and hence open to challenge, is a concern addressed in many of Browne's picture books, for example *A Walk in the Park* (1977) or *Willie the Wimp* (1984). Browne characteristically uses surrealist visual elements to foreground the gap between signs and things (for example, his construction of settings out of pieces of fruit and other odd objects). Similarly, Wiesner's pictures in *Tuesday* (1991) are constructed out of a bricolage of visual quotations. Van Allsburg uses realist pictorial conventions to represent fantastical situations, blurring textual distinctions between the fantasy and reality.

## Metafictive and Experimental Narrative Techniques

Though we can make broad distinctions between implicit and explicit forms of metafiction and between texts which reflect on their own narrative processes and those which reflect on their linguistic construction, metafictive strategies tend to be used in combination, which means that individual texts have a curious habit of refusing classification. For this reason, rather than attempting to classify texts, I have organised the discussion which follows around specific metafictive and experimental strategies.

### Intertextuality and parody

The term intertextuality covers the range of literary and cultural texts, discourses, genres and conventions used to construct narrative fictions. In metafictions these are often foregrounded so as to heighten their conventionality and artifice. Intertexts include specific literary texts, as well as generic and discursive conventions – such as Leon Garfield's parody of nineteenth-century narrative genres in *The Strange Affair of Adelaide Harris* (1971) – and cultural texts and discourses – such as Terry Pratchett's parodic appropriations of department store jargon in *Truckers* (1989). The relationship between the focused text and its intertexts in metafiction is frequently parodic, though not always – for example, references to the work of John Fowles in Caroline Macdonald's *Speaking to Miranda* (1990) indicate interpretive possibilities to readers (McCallum 1992). A common metafictive strategy is the production of a re-version of a specific text – such as Jan Needle's *Wild Wood* (1981), a re-version of *The Wind in the Willows* – or of well-known fairy stories, or folk-tales. Overt forms of intertextuality have three main effects: they foreground the ways in which narrative fictions are constructed out of other texts and discourses; they work to indicate possible interpretive positions for readers, often distancing readers from represented events and characters; and they can enable the representation within a text of a plurality of discourses, voices and meanings.

### Narratorial and authorial intrusions

There is a strong tradition of intrusive narrators who by drawing attention to their story-telling function seek to validate the status of their narrative as 'truth'. A common self-reflexive narrative strategy is to use narratorial intrusions to comment on the processes involved in story-telling and to implicitly or explicitly foreground the fictionality of the narrative. In implicit forms of metafiction, such as Edith Nesbit's *The Story of the Treasure Seekers* (1899) the narrator draws attention to the act of narration through direct address to readers, discussion of narrative choices about material, tone, register, diction and order, self-conscious parody of conventionalised narrative discourses, and references to the relations between 'life' and fiction. Anita Moss (1985) argues on these grounds that the novel is an explicit form of metafiction. However, although the narrative is self-reflective and readers may go on to infer the status of Nesbit's text as a literary artefact, this is not a position constructed within the text. More explicit forms of metafiction, such as Terry Jones's *Nicobobinus* (1985) Gene Kemp's *Jason Bodger and the Priory Ghost* (1985) or Aidan Chambers's *Breaktime* (1978) overtly parody the intrusive narrator so as to break the fictional illusion. In the final paragraph of *Nicobobinus* the narrator, Basilcat, discloses that the whole narrative – including himself – is a fiction. Anachronistic narratorial intrusions in *Jason Bodger* also break the fictional frame by alerting readers to the gap between the time of narration and the time of the story.

In experimental fictions narratorial and authorial intrusions often function quite overtly to position readers in relation to a text. An authorial note at the end of Kemp's *I Can't Stand Losing* (1987/1989) almost demands that readers take a moral stance in relation to the text. Kemp morally censures the behaviour of the main character, thereby confirming the implied reader position constructed through the novel and implicitly undermining the contrived fictionality of the ending of the novel. Jan Mark's *Finders Losers* opens with a note addressed to a narratee which describes the relationship between the narrative and the narratee (and by analogy the text and its readers) in terms which constitute the story and its meanings as being constructed by the narratee rather than as being artefacts of the text: 'By the time you have read all six [stories] you will know exactly what happened on that day, and why, but you'll be the only one who does' (1990: 6). The second person pronoun usually refers to a narratee, but is also used to directly address an implied reader (as in 'choose your own adventure' novels). When it is used more extensively – as it is in Peter Dickinson's *Giant Cold* (1984) and the opening of Peter Hunt's *Backtrack* (1986) – its referential function can be more ambiguous, having a disruptive effect on the relations between text and reader.

### Narrative forms: mystery, fantasy, games and readers

Hutcheon describes specific narrative forms which can function as internalised structuring devices to represent reading positions and strategies (1980: 71–86). The mystery is a common device whereby a character's quest to solve a central mystery is represented as analogous to a reader's struggle with the text (Stephens 1993: 102). Combined with an extensive use of character focalisers whose viewpoints are limited, partial and selective and who consistently misinterpret events, this strategy can be used to construct implied readers in a position of superior knowledge, as in Garfield's parody of Conan Doyle in the character Selwyn Raven, in *The Strange Affair of Adelaide Harris*. Further, Stephens has shown how Mayne uses these strategies in *Salt River Times* (1980) and *Winter Quarters* (1982) to express an 'analogy between interpreting human situations and reading fictions' (1993: 102). A variation on this structuring device is the construction of a mystery which remains unsolved, for example Hunt's *Backtrack* or Gary Crew's *Strange Objects* (1990). The focus becomes, not so much the mystery itself, but the interpretive processes and discourses through which characters attempt to produce solutions.

Fantasy and game genres are also used as internalised structuring devices which point to the self-referentiality of a text. A fantasy text constructs an autonomous universe with its own rules and laws. Metafictive fantasies draw attention to the temporal and spatial structuration of this world – its geography, history, culture – and the role of readers in the act of imagining it and giving shape to the referents of words (Hutcheon 1980: 76). In this way, the reading of metafictive fantasies is 'emblematic' of the reading of fiction in general (81).

The 'choose your own adventure' novel is a relatively recent popular genre which explicitly constructs readers as 'players' in a fictional game and as active participants in the construction of the story. Readers construct characters from an assortment of traits and roles, and at each narrative juncture readers are offered a choice, usually from two or three possible narrative paths leading to a range of possible endings – see for example Steve Jackson's and Ian Livingstone's *The Warlock of Firetop Mountain* (1982). This is a highly conventionalised and codified genre, which can potentially teach its readers specific narrative conventions, as well as implicitly reinforce social codes. It is not, in itself, particularly metafictional, though it does clearly have a metafictive potential which has been exploited by writers such as Gillian Rubinstein and Pratchett. In *Beyond the Labyrinth* (1988) Rubinstein's main character attempts to transpose the rules and conventions of the Fighting Fantasy fiction which he is reading on to life. In *Only You Can Save Mankind* (1992) Pratchett inverts and parodies the conventions of computer games. Both writers are concerned with the interrelationships between the ways in which we perceive, think and behave in game fictions and in life. Pratchett's novel implicitly suggests that the modes of action and interpretation used in both fiction and life are very similar; Rubinstein makes more clear-cut distinctions between them.

### Narrative disruptions and discontinuities

Disruptions to the causal, logical or linear relationships between narrative events, characters and narrators, and between primary and secondary narratives have the effect of foregrounding the narrative structuring of texts. There are two main strategies for disrupting narratives: narrative metalepsis, and the representation of heterotopias. Metalepsis refers to the transgression of logical and hierarchical relations between different levels of narration (Genette 1980: 234–235; McHale 1987/1989: 119); heterotopias are fictional 'spaces in which a number of possible orders of being can coincide' (Stephens 1992a: 52).

A classic example of narrative metalepsis occurs in Browne's *Bear Hunt* (1979). By literally drawing his way out of each predicament, Bear functions as both a character constructed within the text and as an authorial figure who actively creates and changes the discourse of the text. By transgressing his narrative function, Bear disrupts the conventional hierarchy of relations between character, narrator and author. A more subtle use of metalepsis occurs in Diana Wynne Jones's *The Spellcoats* (1979) where through the process of narrating her story, Tanaqui realises that the act of narration is itself a performance which can influence events in the world. Implicit here is an awareness that any narration of a past simultaneously re-constructs (and fictionalises) that past, but Tanaqui's narratorial role literally shifts from scribe to that of author. What begins as retrospective narration of past events (that is a secondary narrative) becomes a narrative which simultaneously shapes and changes events in the present (that is a primary narrative).

The relationships between authors, primary narrators, secondary narrators and characters are usually hierarchical. By inverting or transgressing these hierarchical relations, metalepsis can be used to articulate questions about authority, power, and freedom, such as who has control of the story and its characters – the narrator, her narratees, an author, his readers, or the socio-cultural context within and through which stories are told, heard, interpreted and appropriated. In *A Step off the Path* (1985) Hunt makes extensive use of metalepsis to articulate complex concerns with forms of textual and cultural appropriation and displacement. This is a multistranded novel, in which a story told by a character (Jo) in one narrative strand is a version of events occurring in another strand. The story concerns a group of knights (descendants of their Arthurian namesakes) who exist on the margins of mainstream society and culture. The novel hinges on a discrepancy between these knights, and their 'fictional' counterparts represented in the popular medieval romance fictions of mainstream culture, out of which Jo's narrative is constructed. Furthermore, these fictions also inform and obscure the perceptions and interpretations of other characters in the primary narrative. The point is that by appropriating the stories and culture of one social group and re-writing it as 'romance' (that is, fiction or myth), the dominant culture effectively writes this group out of 'history' and out of the present. With his representation of the knights, then, Hunt inverts the usual direction of metaleptic transgression, so that the primary narrative disrupts and transgresses the secondary narrative.

Fantastic children's literature is characterised by widespread representation of heterotopias (Stephens 1992a: 52). Diana Wynne Jones and Peter Hunt both construct temporal heterotopias in which a number of possible time zones co-exist in order to overtly play with the relations between history and the temporal structuring of narrative. Jones's *Witch Week* is premised on the possibility that parallel alternative worlds are constructed through spatio-temporal divergences which occur at decisive points in history – for example events such as battles, 'where it is possible for things to go two ways' (1982/1989: 171). This works self-reflectively to represent the kinds of narrative choices which writers make in constructing fictions (Waterhouse 1991: 5). In *The Maps of Time* (1983) Hunt takes this idea a step further: narrative paths diverge as characters perceive and imagine events as occurring differently.

Macaulay's picture books quite overtly play with narrative and temporal linearity. He uses a recursive narrative structure in *Why the Chicken Crossed the Road* (1991). *Black and White* (1990) is an elaborate play with perception, representation and interpretation. It consists of four narrative strands. Each is represented using different narrative and pictorial techniques, and they become visually mixed in the latter part of the text as the visual frames are broken by images which mirror and spill over into adjacent frames. The four narratives are linked by repeated images and 'story' elements, which imply that the four stories might constitute aspects of the same story. However, readers' attempts to construct a single logical chronological narrative are frustrated through the confusion of logical, temporal and causal relations between the four strands. Ultimately the text refuses interpretive closure. What we get is layering of different but similar fictions, interwoven into and endlessly reflecting each other.

### Mise en abyme *and self-reflective devices*

The term *mise en abyme* refers to a representation or narrative segment, which is embedded within a larger narrative, and which reflects, reproduces or mirrors an aspect of the larger primary narrative (Prince 1987/1988: 53; McHale 1987/1989:

124–125; Hutcheon 1980: 54–56). It usually functions to indicate ways in which 'the larger narrative might be interpreted' (Stephens 1993: 105). Narrative aspects which might be reflected include: the story or themes of the primary narrative; its narrative situation – such as the relationship between the narrator and narratee; or the style of the primary narrative text (McHale 1987/1989: 124–125).

In realist novels a story, photo, painting or drawing will often function as a *mise en abyme* to reflect the thematic concerns of the primary narrative. For example, in Zibby Oneal's *The Language of Goldfish* the main character, Carrie, executes a series of abstracted drawings based on 'the idea of making patterns in which the real object disappeared' (1980/1987: 31), descriptions of which are analogous with Carrie's experience of a dissolution of selfhood which she both desires and fears as she retreats from adolescence and growing up. Lois Lowry also uses this device in *A Summer to Die* (1977). Self-reflective visual images, such as mirrors, paintings and intertextual quotations are also a common metafictive strategy in the picture books of Browne and Van Allsburg, where they work to foreground the nature of the text as representation, and to blur the distinctions between textual fantasy and reality.

Stories narrated within the primary narrative by a character or a secondary narrator which reflect the story or themes of the primary frame-narrative can also function as *mise en abyme* devices. For example, in Paula Fox's *How Many Miles to Babylon?* (1967) the stories which James tells reflect larger thematic concerns with the role of story-telling in the recuperation of the past and the construction of a subjectivity. Russell Hoban plays with the recursiveness of the 'story-within-story-within-story' structure in repeated descriptions of 'Bonzo Dog Food' labels in *The Mouse and His Child* (1967). Stephens has discussed the use of *mise en abyme* in three of Mayne's novels *Salt River Times, Drift* (1985) and *Winter Quarters*, where he sees the device as functioning to replicate the relations between reader and text (1993: 108). Similarly, the representation of relations between a narrator and her narratees in Hunt's *A Step off the Path* replicates a range of text/reader relations.

Self-reflective images are also used to mirror the narrative processes in texts. Thus the narrator of Price's *The Ghost Drum* (1987) is a cat chained to a pole around which it walks, telling stories, winding up the chain (that is, the story) as it goes. Similarly, the image of story-telling as 'weaving' is represented literally in *The Spellcoats* where the narrator's story is literally woven into a coat.

### The linguistic construction of texts and the world

There are four main strategies whereby metafictive novels can be self-conscious about their existence as language: parodic play on specific writing styles; thematised wordplay, such as puns, anagrams, clichés; variation of print conventions and the use of marginalia, footnotes and epigraphs – strategies which draw attention to the physicality of texts; and deliberate mixing of literary and extra-literary genres, such as the journal, letter, newspaper items, historical documents, and so on.

Pratchett's *Truckers* is a metafictive fantasy novel about a group of 'nomes' who live under the floorboards of a large department store. Their social system, culture and religion is a bricolage of appropriated signs and discourses associated with department stores, mixed with parodic forms of Biblical and religious discourse. Pratchett constantly plays on the slippage between signifiers and signifieds, foregrounding the gap between signs and things (in the meanings the nomes ascribe to 'Bargains Galore' for instance). By foregrounding the construction of the represented world and, hence, the construction of the text, Pratchett also draws attention to the ways in which representations of the world outside the text are similarly constructed and ascribed with meanings. The stories in Alhberg's *The Clothes Horse* (1987) are constructed out of a play with the literal meanings of commonplace figures of speech, such as 'clothes horse' or 'jack pot'.

The combination of typographical experimentation and overt genre mixing is widespread in recent popular children's fiction, but as Stephens has suggested, 'seems to be settling into its own formulaic conventions: two or three clearly delineated genres or modes ... are juxtaposed in order to suggest restricted perspective and to complicate otherwise flat, everyday surfaces' (1992a: 53). In novels such as Libby Gleeson's *Dodger* (1990) or Aidan Chambers's *The Toll Bridge* (1992) the metafictive and experimental potential of genre mixing is repressed through the combination of these strategies with an implicit authorial position and with realist conventions. The discourse is treated as a transparent medium which simply conveys information, rather than as a specific linguistic code which constructs and inscribes this information with meaning. Novels such as Hunt's *Backtrack*, Chambers's *Breaktime* or Crew's *Strange Objects* consistently foreground their own textuality. Extra-literary genres and discourses are combined so as to effect abrupt shifts in the diegetic levels of narration, disrupt relations between fiction and reality within the textual frame, and draw attention to the discursivity of extraliterary genres.

### Multistranded and polyphonic narratives

Two common experimental strategies which can also be used metafictionally are multistranded and polyphonic narration. Multistranded narratives are constructed of two or more interconnected narrative strands differentiated by shifts in temporal or spatial relationships, and/or shifts in narrative point of view (who speaks or focalises). In polyphonic narratives events are narrated from the viewpoints of two or more narrators or character focalisers. These are strategies which enable the representation of a plurality of narrative voices, social and cultural discourses, perceptual, attitudinal and ideological viewpoints. In doing so they can work to efface or destabilise a reader's sense of a single authoritative narratorial position, and thereby situate readers in more active interpretive positions. These are not in themselves metafictive strategies though they can be used as such, particularly in texts which use multiple narrators or focalisers to represent different versions of the same events, such as Mayne's *Drift*.

One of the most common narrative structures used is interlaced dual narration. The narratives of two narrators or character focalisers are represented as two parallel strands interlaced together in alternating chapters or segments. This can work to overtly structure a novel as a 'dialogue' between two social, cultural, historical or gendered positions, as in Hunt's *Going Up* (1989), Caroline Macdonald's *The Lake at the End of the World* (1988), Jenny Pausacker's *What*

*Are Ya?* (1987), Jan Mark's *The Hillingdon Fox* (1991) or Dickinson's *A Bone from a Dry Sea* (1992). However, like typographic and generic forms of experimentation, interlaced dual narration has also settled into its own formulaic conventions and is frequently structured so as to privilege one dominant authoritative position.

These narrative forms are at their most innovative when combined with other experimental narrative features, such as intertextuality, complex shifts in narrative point of view, and indirect and effaced modes of narration (see Stephens 1992b and Hunt 1991: 100–117). Two of the most sophisticated examples of polyphonic multistranded narration to date are Alan Garner's *Red Shift* (1973) and Jill Paton Walsh's *Unleaving* (1976).

### Postmodernist historiographic metafictions

Historiographic metafiction refers to novels which self-reflexively mix fictive and historical modes of representation so as to pose questions about the relationships between fiction, history and reality (Hutcheon 1989: 50). Represented historical material may refer to either actual or fictive events – the texts and documents represented in Hunt's *Backtrack* are almost entirely fictional, whereas those in Crew's *Strange Objects* are a mixture of actual and fictive. It is the physical incorporation of the discursive style of history writing, rather than their actual historicity, that is characteristic.

Intellectual historians such as White (1987) and LaCapra (1980) have focused on the relations between representation, in particular narrative representation, and our capacity to know and understand the past. To the extent that the past is only accessible via its documents, archives and artefacts, our knowledge of that past is always mediated and determined by prior textualisations or representations. Potentially the past is, therefore, only knowable as text, and is thereby always already implicated in problems of language, discourse and representation. Historiographic metafictions highlight concerns with interpretation and representation by incorporating 'historical' texts and discursive conventions. For example, Hunt plays with the conventional historicist assumption that the closer an account of an event is to that event in time, the more accuracy and credibility it has, by including a transcript of an Inquest Report in which he steadfastly refuses to disclose information, thereby drawing attention to the discursive strategies which structure the report. The primary narrative of *Backtrack* centres on two characters, Jack and Rill, who attempt to solve a mysterious train crash which occurred seventy years earlier. The mystery remains unsolved and the lack of narrative resolution draws attention to the discourses whereby the mystery is constructed and whereby Jack and Rill attempt to solve it: namely, historical research, conjecture and reconstruction, and conventionalised generic narrative codes – the espionage plot, and the crime of passion plot. A subsequent blurring of the status of these discourses, as fiction and/or history, foregrounds their conventionality and the extent to which fiction and history are both culturally inscribed categories of discourse and not always easily distinguishable from each other. The narrative forms for representing and structuring events are common to both history writing and fiction, and that these are forms which impart meaning as well as order (Hutcheon 1989: 62). The possibility remains that the act of

narration, in either fictive or historical writing, might construct and thereby
construe its object.

## Conclusions

An increasingly noticeable phenomena has been the appropriation of experimental
and metafictive narrative techniques into mainstream children's literature, an
occurrence which blurs the distinctions between experimental and non-experimental, between the mainstream and the marginal. However, a key distinction
between experimental and non-experimental writing for children lies in the
audience positions constructed within texts. As experimental and metafictive
features become more superficial aspects of a texts construction, and hence more
conventionalised and formulaic, the range of interpretive positions inscribed in
texts become increasingly restricted. Many of the techniques and strategies which I
have described are not in themselves 'experimental' or 'metafictive', though they
have the capacity to function in these ways when used in combination either with
each other, or with particular discursive and narrational modes. Metafictive and
experimental forms of children's writing generally utilise a wide range of narrative
and discursive strategies which distance readers from texts, and construct implied
readers who are more actively involved in the production of meanings. By drawing
attention to the ways in which texts are structured and to how they mean,
metafictions can potentially teach readers specific codes and conventions and
interpretive strategies with which to read and make sense of other, more closed,
fictions. Furthermore, to the extent that we use language and narrative to
represent and comprehend reality, as well as to construct fictions, metafictions can,
by analogy, show readers how representations of reality are similarly constructed
and ascribed with meanings.

## References

Britton, J. (1970/1972) *Language and Learning*, Harmondsworth: Penguin.

Genette, G. (1980) *Narrative Discourse*, Oxford: Blackwell.

Hunt, P. (1988) 'Degrees of control: stylistics and the discourse of children's literature', in
 Coupland, N. (ed.) *Styles of Discourse*, London: Croom Helm.

—— (1991) *Criticism, Theory and Children's Literature*, Oxford: Blackwell.

—— (ed.) (1992) *Literature for Children: Contemporary Criticism*, London: Routledge.

Hutcheon, L. (1980) *Narcissistic Narrative: The Metafictional Paradox*, New York:
 Methuen.

—— (1989) *The Politics of Postmodernism* London: Routledge.

Jones, D. W. (1982/1989) *Witch Week*, London: Mammoth.

Kemp, G. (1987/1989) *I Can't Stand Losing*, Harmondsworth: Penguin.

LaCapra, D. (1980) 'Rethinking intellectual history and reading texts', *History and Theory*
 19, 3, 245–276.

Lewis, D. (1990) 'The constructedness of texts: picture books and the metafictive', *Signal*
 61, 131–146.

McCallum, R. (1992) '(In)quest of the subject: the dialogic construction of subjectivity in
 Caroline Macdonald's *Speaking to Miranda*', *Papers: Explorations into Children's
 Literature* 3, 3: 99–105.

McHale, B. (1987/1979) *Postmodernist Fiction*, London: Routledge.

Mackey, M. (1990) 'Metafiction for beginners: Allan Ahlberg's *Ten in a Bed*', *Children's Literature in Education* 21, 3, 179–187.

Mark, J. (1990) *Finders Losers*, London: Orchard Books.

Moss, A. (1985) 'Varieties of children's metafiction', *Studies in the Literary Imagination* 17, 2: 79–92.

Moss, G. (1990) 'Metafiction and the poetics of children's literature', *Children's Literature Association Quarterly* 15, 2: 50–52.

—— (1992) 'Metafiction, illustration, and the poetics of children's literature', in Hunt, P. (ed.) *Literature for Children: Contemporary Criticism*, London: Routledge.

Ommundsen, W. (1989) 'Narrative navel gazing: or how to recognise a metafiction when you see one', *Southern Review* 22, 3: 264–274.

Oneal, Z. (1980/1987) *The Language of Goldfish*, London: Gollancz.

Prince, G. (1987/1988) *A Dictionary of Narratology*, Aldershot: Scolar.

Stephens, J. (1991) 'Did I tell you about the time I pushed the Brothers Grimm off Humpty Dumpty's wall? Metafictional strategies for constituting the audience as agent in the narratives of Janet and Allan Ahlberg', in Stone, M. (ed.) *Children's Literature and Contemporary Theory*, Wollongong: New Literatures Research Centre.

—— (1992a) 'Modernism to postmodernism, or the line from Insk to Onsk: William Mayne's *Tiger's Railway*', *Papers: Explorations into Children's Literature* 3, 2: 51–59.

—— (1992b) *Language and Ideology in Children's Fiction*, London: Longman.

—— (1993) 'Metafiction and interpretation: William Mayne's *Salt River Times, Winter Quarters* and *Drift*', *Children's Literature* 21: 101–117.

Vygotsky, L. S. (1934/1962) *Thought and Language*, ed. and trans. E. Hanfmann and G. Vakar, Cambridge, MA: MIT Press.

Waterhouse, R. (1991) 'Which way to encode and decode fiction', *Children's Literature Association Quarterly* 16, 1: 2–5.

Waugh, P. (1984) *Metafiction: The Theory and Practise of Self-Conscious Fiction*, London: Methuen.

White, H. (1987) *The Content of the Form: Narrative Discourse and Historical Representation*, Baltimore: Johns Hopkins University Press.

# 34

# Major Authors' Work for Children

## *Marian Allsobrook*

Established authors, when they address the child reader, often have in mind a particular individual, occasion and objective. This may give the narrative a frame or determine its texture, especially its field of reference. The author's voice, intimate and personal in some texts, may invite ironic exploration of the material set before the young reader.

The work is often completed alongside a major text and reflects the writer's preoccupations at the time, to the extent of sharing textual features; however, it is often one in which an author may feel inclined to seek diversion, relax or experiment in a newly encountered readership. For a variety of reasons publication may be delayed.

Early works in England by major authors for children sought to guide the child into the adult world. Chaucer, in *Tretis of the Astrolabie* (1391), for example, instructs his young son in the medium of 'light Englissh' since the adult sources in Latin would be less accessible. Comparing the astrolabe's rings to the 'webbe of a loppe' [spider] Chaucer constructs the meshes of a text which supports technical substance as it empowers the young reader. A title attributed to this work, *Bread and Milk for Children*, illustrates the tendency to revise/recharacterise titles of works for children, reflecting both a concern for commercial profit and ideological tensions as authors and publishers sought to reconcile instruction with entertainment.

Caxton's translation of *Aesop's Fables* in 1484 generated a sequence of fabulist works by major authors for more than five centuries in Britain. His advice to 'lytel John' to read Chaucer, Gower, Hoccleve and others would seem to include literate children in an adult readership. Recent studies indicate increased estimates of general literacy levels and that the child reader by the late fourteenth century was no longer an anomaly. Lydgate wrote *Isopes Fabules*, moral beast fables; he is also attributed with the fifteenth-century verse translation of *Stans Puer ad Mensam*, an influential courtesy book, to be followed in 1513 by the widely used *Latin Aesop*, translated by Erasmus, who in 1532 produced the similarly popular *Lytil Book of Good Maners for Children*. In 1659 the first illustrated book for children, the *Visible World*, of Comenius (1592–1670) became available in English.

That the combined impact of printing in Britain (1474) and of the sixteenth-century European Reformation increased literacy levels is reflected in the sudden huge increase in sales of popular chapbooks during the decades of 1640–1660, a period free of censorship in Britain during which a new reading public had been created. Bunyan (1628–1688), competing for readership with the chapbook writers, sought to capture children's attention in his *Divine Emblems* or *Book for Boys and Girls* (1686), described as a sort of 'after-glow' to the *Pilgrim's Progress* two years earlier. (Hill 1988: 266). Homely Biblical emblems first appear in the *Pilgrim's Progress Part II*; both that work and the children's verses demonstrate Bunyan's preaching technique with its emphatic repetition of key phrases and key words.

Bunyan's chapbook rivals, readily adapting romances and other traditional stories of giants, duelling and enchantment, required him to combine his spiritualising with a sharper urban wit which distinguished the text from the blander *Divine Songs* (1715) by Isaac Watts (1674–1748), whose verses were profoundly influenced by Bunyan's text and enormously popular. In Watts, piety mingles with a sense of national superiority not found in Bunyan's vigorous preaching, which is much more varied in its response to nature. The shift of tone is strongly evident in the contrast between Bunyan's Verse upon the disobedient child (XLVII) and Watts's *Cradle Hymn*. Bunyan laments that the bantling, like a predatory bird, once brought up, turns on parents to 'pick out their eyes'. Watts's child, blessed with a loving mother, and the infant Christ as a role model, contains no trace of ingratitude or predatory self-interest.

The tradition of the fable, established by the sixteenth century in English works for children, brought ironic texture to the verse and prose of such major authors who also wrote for children as Bunyan, Gay, Swift, Richardson, Blake and Kipling; Lear, Carroll and Beatrix Potter reworked the fabulist material for children influentially. In some cases the attempt to offer suitable reading material for children involved revision of an existing adult text; elsewhere sources were inventively adapted and parodied.

Apart from his Aesop, Richardson produced three early works for young readers, including *Letters of Advice to a nephew* (1731), *The Apprentices' Vademecum* (1733) and *Familiar Letters* (1741). Protestant introspection and courtesy books shaped his work, while the influence of the theatre is pervasive. In *Clarissa*'s closing pages Richardson comments, 'Even the pulpit has lost a great part of its weight.' By reference, quotation, comparison and dramatisation within the letter form, Richardson alludes extensively to the contemporary theatre; he uses its techniques to enhance his instruction and exploits its ability to persuade and influence.

However, his printing and ideological innovations also have significance for those investigating children's books since he not only draws the reader into the text by exploring the 'interior self' (Watt 1974: 176) but extends non-verbal meaning on the page. Experimenting with ciphers and varying print-forms in *Clarissa*, as the first edition reveals, Clarissa's Ode to wisdom by a lady set to her own music, folds out of the book to allow the reader to play the composition at the keyboard. Her 'angry passions' are composed in musical notation and in a print that resembles handwriting. In Volume IV (8 June), Richardson includes accusatory forefingers to draw attention to the expressions in a letter which have kindled Lovelace's fury. Such printerly extension of meaning on the page anticipates the inventive techniques employed by modern authors for children, particularly in picture books.

Whereas the adult or original epistolary form of Richardson's three major novels enabled the reader to stand in as 'recipient' or 'correspondent', his authorised shortened versions, *The Paths of Virtue Delineated or the History in miniature of the celebrated Pamela, Clarissa Harlowe and Sir Charles Grandison, Familiarised and Adapted to the Capacities of Youth* (1756) dispensed with the letters, while retaining the use of dramatised episodes.

Richardson's novels kindled a consuming interest in Europe for sixty years among writers busy on translation, parody and prequel. Richardson's *Aesop*, dismissively treated by the author himself, was possibly loved into extinction by child owners. Richardson spoke of the 'alluring force' of woodcuts, lavishly illustrating the fables at extra expense; not only did he revise *L'Estrange's Fables* (1692) but he commented on Croxall's version of L'Estrange, editing out both political and sexual suggestions, in accordance with the feminised codes within his texts, as Ian Watt (1974: 169) has pointed out. G. Lessing, translating Richardson's *Aesop* into German in 1757, acknowledged feminised codes when praising Richardson's knowledge of the education of the human heart and of the promotion of virtue. Richardson's collaborative literary production must have been unique. Eagleton characterises him as the 'engagingly modern deconstructionist adrift in an infinity of texts', and describes Richardson's texts for adults and for young readers as 'plural, diffuse kits of fiction' (Eagleton 1982: 21–22), the result of a process of ceaseless revision responding both to readers and to fellow authors as he reworked, or authorised abridged versions of, his texts.

The Richardsonian novel, originating in Puritan tract, popular romance and fable, addresses a deeply anxious response to processes of urban change; in 'draughts so small', the abridged versions for young readers are, though changed in narrative form, true to the author's spirit, if less highly charged with sexual intensity. Such sequel-generating texts, since they encode mythical qualities (like *Robinson Crusoe*) appear talismanic in their generative capacity, according to Watt (1974: 247).

Chapbook versions adapted or imitated *Pamela*; shilling versions of Richardson's novels were sold by the publisher Francis Newbery from 1769. Mary Wollstonecraft translated Mme de Cambon's *Kleine Grandison* (1782) in 1790 as *Young Grandison*, while Berquin's version appeared in 1791 as *Little Grandison*. Jane Austen dramatised material from the original novel with her niece in 1800 (Kirkham 1983: 27).

Both Swift (1667–1745) and Gay (1685–1732) wrote fables for children, Gay's influenced by Montaigne; Goldsmith (1730–1774) and Charles Lamb (1775–1834) wrote for children at publishers' request. Christopher Smart (1722–1771) wrote hymns for children. Goldsmith produced an epistolary *History of England* (1764) and was at least partially responsible for *Goody Two Shoes* (1765), one of the most successful children's stories.

Educational and moral aims, determining form and content in children's literature by major authors worked both for and against the interests of women writers. Many, like Mary Wollstonecraft, sought intellectual recognition by distancing themselves from derided romance forms, pursuing rational or educational discussion 'symptomatic of a desire felt by many women writers to free themselves and their offspring too, from weaknesses regularly associated with their sex – being too emotional, too fickle, too affectionate, too doting' (Briggs 1989: 229). Inglis discusses the tendency of European social life to concentrate very gradually on the family and the virtues of domesticity, drawing attention to the 'growth of affective individualism' in the eighteenth century, while factors such as two great revolutions and Romanticism wrought changes (Inglis 1981: 41–43). If, as McKillop suggests (263), one of Richardson's achievements in his fiction was to make domesticity interesting, the women writers achieved recognition for the children 'discounted from history for centuries' (Inglis 1981: 83). The feminising of fiction, started by Richardson two generations earlier, had provided an area in which the scale and significance of childhood could be explored and acknowledged.

In her *Original Stories from Real Life* (1791) Mary Wollstonecraft places her two motherless child heroines in the charge of a discerning relative who relates stories to them to shape and improve their minds. She commented in a letter to her publisher: 'If parents attended to their children, I would not have written the stories.' Drawing on personal experience of revolutionary Paris and of oppression in England, Wollstonecraft acknowledged children as characters; she also gave value to the depersonalised poor and recognised the discounted nobility of their endurance.

Charles Lamb wrote for Godwin, Mary Wollstonecraft's husband, who himself pseudonymously produced *Fables Ancient and Modern* (1805) under the name Edward Baldwin. Lamb wrote the comic poem *The Queen of Hearts* (1805), *Adventures of Ulysses* (1808) and *Prince Dorus* (1811); he may have written more for Godwin. Collaborating with his sister Mary (1764–1847), he wrote six of the enduring *Tales from Shakespeare* (1807); this work was commissioned by Godwin. Other shared works, *Poetry for Children* and *Mrs Leicester's School* appeared in 1809.

In all their work for children, the Lambs sought freedom from didacticism, writing with an interest in a child's perception and a child's developing awareness: Arabella (*Mrs Leicester's School*) voyaging from the East Indies and befriended by the first mate nicknamed Betsy, discusses the cruelty of harpooning and the power of nature while observing the animated behaviour of creatures on board. The ship is not only a miniature world, but an Ark which empowers the child through friendship. Many of the child characters in this work are outsiders, exiles, bereaved or unchristened, observing clear-sightedly the adult world into which they must be initiated. Mary Lamb's Elizabeth, having learnt her alphabet from the letters on her mother's gravestone, tells her uncle how Mama had taught her to spell.

Like Wollstonecraft and the Lambs, Maria Edgeworth deserves greater recognition for her achievements in children's literature. She emerges from the critics' revisionist scrutiny as skilled in using her father's influence advantageously to promote feminist views without offence, unlike Wollstonecraft. Praised by Yeats in 1891 as the most 'finished and famous' Irish novelist, she proves herself 'a thorough mistress of ... multiple discursive practices' (Myers 1992: 139) in fiction for both adults and children. Writing at first for her younger siblings and encouraged by her father, she produced the first sociological fiction, employing the *bildungsroman* as a means to explore the 'idealist pattern of wish-formulation and wish-fulfilment that might be termed maternal romance' (Myers 1992: 140). She initiated not only the regional novel, but also the prototypes of several related genres of American women's writing, the female *bildungsroman*, and narratives of manners and customs.

In 1796 she produced *The Parent's Assistant*, tales drawing on the authentic detail of observation and experience, while working on *Castle Rackrent*, her 'memoir-novel'. Although much of her work, for example *Belinda* (1801) seems female-centred, the strongly masculine tone of *Castle Rackrent* (1800) has caused her to be described as the least feminine of female novelists. The vibrantly individuated voices of her characters in that novel are found in the *Moral Tales* for younger readers, in which the diverse speech patterns of a female Quixote, a mannish bibber, Quakers and Welsh working women provide textual play. While educational aims shape Edgeworth's work for children, her texts are animated by the vulnerable of European society, peasants, struggling émigrés, displaced soldiers.

*Castle Rackrent* influenced Walter Scott (1771–1832) whose historical novels created the precedent for the popularity of the fictional treatment of history in children's literature. By 1888 Scott had been voted the third most popular boys' author. He produced only one work specifically for children, *Tales of a Grandfather* (1827–1830), a history of Scotland and of France.

In this respect his literary output resembled that of Dickens, whose *A Child's History of England* (1852–1854) is probably his least familiar work. Thackeray's fairy tale, *The Rose and the Ring* (1855) however, has not suffered eclipse and displays the fiction-making powers evident in his major novel of the same period, *The Newcomes* (1853–1855), which first appeared in periodical numbers. Like Dickens, Thackeray (1811–1863) wrote seasonal fiction at Christmas. In both narratives he achieves a densely allusive texture: in the adult work he conveys 'that increased sense of social life as something registered, lived and validated in newsprint' (McMasters 1991: 162); Thackeray's frame of reference included literature, art, European and colonial society, business and the press. In both works the ironic wit and parody, the suppleness of the narrative role charge the text with verbal energy. In *The Newcomes*, the reader is bombarded with a multiplicity of encoded meanings, including three other languages besides infantile and adult English, Cockney and London Jewish variants; characters study the 'meaning' of large canvases or of named novels. In the children's text, a pantomime fiction for a child absent from the Twelfth Night party Thackeray's daughters enjoyed in Rome, the manipulative governess Gruffanuff, and the benign fairy Blackstick, together serve as counterparts to the 'wicked fairy', Lady Kew, whose dynastic reign of terror darkens *The Newcomes*. In *The Rose and the Ring* magical properties operate with apparent haphazardness, causing bewildering experiences of love; the fairy tale conventions of godmother denied her invitation to the royal christening and concealed identity of the beggar-maid reappear in a pantomime medium of exuberant intertextuality and wordplay topical in its allusions to the theatre, Christmas and the Crimea. Italian vegetable names and parody of both major bards and minor authors in the guise of self-deprecating authorial pretension, move frequently from prose dialogue to blank and rhyming verse. Barbara Wall describes his 'wild breathlessness', as that of a narrator, 'little more than a grown-up boy', engaging the double audience of children and adults (51).

The fairy tale was also used inventively by Dickens (1812–1870), who defended it against propagandist exploitation by the illustrator Cruikshank, champion of temperance. In a satirical essay, 'Frauds on the fairies' (1853), Dickens ridiculed the profane versions of 'sacred' texts which had instilled gentleness and mercy in generations of young listeners and readers; Dickens was incensed by the 'intrusion of a Whole Hog of unwieldy dimensions into the fairy flower garden', protesting that within a generation or two children would not know how to distinguish the authentic fairy tale from the propagandist versions. 'The world is too much with us, early and late', intoned Dickens. 'Leave this precious old escape from it, alone.' Dickens wrote his own examples of the genre: 'The golden fagots' appeared in *Household Words* (15 June 1850) and 'The magic fishbone' in 1868.

In *A Child's History of England* Dickens builds a conspiratorial alliance with the young reader who is coaxed into perceiving the early Britons as savages civilised by the Romans and converted by the Saxons into the English nation. Bold outlines – Henry VIII is a 'blot of blood and grease upon the history of England', Judge Jeffries a 'great crimson toad, sweltering and swelling with rage' as he looks down from a Wapping window – and formulaic interventions – 'I daresay you think as I do' – encourage the reader to view events through the individual lens superimposed by Dickens. This is especially noticeable in the barbarous tendencies attributed by Dickens to the Irish: he combines graphic details of revenge with heavily directive authorial comment: one king has a 'wild kind of name spelt in more than one wild kind of way'. Alternatively, he voices scepticism when introducing detail he considers unreliable. Dickens, however, by placing the child centrally in so many of his adult and family fictions, and by reworking the fairy tale elements, achieved far more on behalf of child readership there, where the child's vision exists, than in what he wrote specifically for children.

Reworking folk and fairy tale for children, Browning (1812–1889) and Ruskin (1819–1900) produced very different narratives: Browning's father had previously written a version of the Pied Piper story derived from the fifteenth century or even earlier; this was only one of several versions with which Browning was familiar. He dedicated his poem, *The Pied Piper of Hamelin* (1842) to the son of the actor Macready in 1842. Its auspicious progress as an anthologised narrative began in 1862, when it was first included by Coventry Patmore in a book of verse for children. Ruskin's prose fiction, written for the child who later briefly became his wife, was intended as consolation after the deaths of her three sisters from scarlet fever. Ruskin assuages doubts about materialism and Philistinism in a restorative text, *The King of the Golden River* (1841), about a quest for spiritual riches in keeping with his championing of heroic and social idealism.

Much more disparate elements from widely diverse sources reworked by Mark Twain (Samuel Clemens 1835–1910) generated important new forms of fiction through parody of Shakespeare, burlesque and use of the vernacular. In his regionalism he had been influenced also by Bret Harte's 'new realm of discourse', the world of hard-living, subversive vagabonds (Ruland and Bradbury 1991: 192). Regionalism provided new possibilities for humorous and dramatic discourse incorporating the 'stretchers' or tall tales of mockery and ironic dialect. His writing drew on the West and the rural Mississippi Valley, but was charged with the energy of the rapidly changing world of industrialised spread of population and wage slavery (replacing black slavery) once the two coasts had been linked by rail in

1869. Twain both criticised and celebrated American culture in burlesque and pessimistic irony in the adult fantasy *A Connecticut Yankee in King Arthur's Court* (1889), in *Pudd'nhead Wilson* (1894) and *What is Man?* (1906), and in the classic American boy's story *The Adventures of Tom Sawyer* (1876).

Less to the taste of the American public and lacking Twain's vigorous humour, Hardy's commissioned fiction for children failed to find publication for some ten years. *Our Exploits at West Poley* (1883) written for the American periodical *Youth's Companion*, eventually appeared in *The Household* in six instalments beginning in November 1892. As in his adult fiction, man is dwarfed by a landscape which inscribes the secrets of the human condition. Hardy (1840–1928) empowered his two boy heroes to seize destiny and redirect it (the stream that generates mill-power in two rural villages): in their exploits they explore the organic subterranean world of the Mendip caves where nature's supremacy is challenged. They bring upon themselves moral and intellectual decisions difficult to address. Hardy's child characters are found in his poetry rather than in his adult fiction. Defoe, in *A Tour of the Whole Island of Great Britain* (1724–1726) mentioned the little river that drives twelve mills within a quarter mile of the Mendips, and Hardy chose this secret place, a hidden landscape, to attract young readers, painstakingly creating a featured, speaking landscape. Steve possesses the fatal ingenuity and enterprise of Henchard, the Mayor of Casterbridge, in the book which Hardy was writing during that period. Wilful decisions in youth bring fatal consequences in the adult fiction. Henchard's role has parallels with the harsh miller who seeks to reaffirm his mastery by cruelty to his apprentice. Hardy's text for children allows the oppressed to outwit the master; in the adult text, Henchard's rival is the boyish Farfrae, whose light-footed dancing and tender singing voice are illuminated by Hardy's proto-cinematic devices, or visual compositions, which capture all the tensions present in each narrative.

Both Wilde (1854–1900) and Kipling (1865–1936) have made important contributions to children's literature, Wilde drawing upon the fairy tale tradition and Kipling in part upon the fable tradition. Wilde composed fairy tales for his sons, believing this to be a father's duty. He read them Verne, Stevenson and Kipling, authors whom he admired, and told them of huge disconsolate carp in Lough Corrib, where the family home was situated; these would not stir from the depths unless he called them with traditional Irish songs. The redemptive patterning of tales like 'The happy prince ' and 'The star child' reflects ideas in *De Profundis* (1905). Egotists are roused to experience compassion and are reconciled with nature. 'The remarkable rocket' parodies Wilde's major concerns of egotism and philistine materialism with the wit of his major dramatic work (1892–1895): it draws on folk and fairy tale, including Andersen and Grimm, Lewis Carroll, art history and contemporary controversies such as the Ruskin–Whistler trial (1877). Nine fairy tales were originally published in two volumes: *The Happy Prince* (1888) and *The House of Pomegranates* (1891), the latter consisting of elegies rather than parables, opposing scientific material existence with the redemptive pastoral world of the artist. Pessimistic elements in the protagonist's trials and transfigurations in 'The star child' are echoed in the mythic *Dorian Gray* (1890) and *Salome* (1894).

Kipling, remarkable both for his range of fiction, his pioneering of the short story, his fables, historical fiction, travel writing, and for his achievement as a modernist, provoked widely differing critical responses. *The Jungle Book* (1894) and *The Second Jungle Book* (1895) were termed stronger than Aesop, yet Beerbohm cruelly caricatured him. Wilde rated him 'a genius who drops his aspirates and our first authority on the second rate' (Green 1971: 59). J. M. Barrie criticised his coarse journalese, calling him the man from Nowhere in 1890. His work, particularly his relish for jargon, was parodied and his reputation as a prophet resented. Yet T. S. Eliot recognised him as a major writer in 1919 and Henry James acknowledged his power of attracting readers of all social classes. The vigour of his style brought a new power to literature at the close of the century, but, to the Aesthetic movement, appeared an unwelcome and disruptive force. To Chesterton, the *Just So Stories* (1902) were 'a great chronicle of primal fables', their animals 'walking portents'. Brecht admired and copied Kipling and C. S. Lewis identified him as primarily the poet of work, bringing to literature new areas of language. Lewis judged him the first journalist since Defoe to bring a sense of news to the service of fiction.

Apart from *The Jungle Books*, and *Just So Stories* his influential novels *Captains Courageous* (1894), *Stalky and Co.* (1899), and *Kim* (1900) (all of which have had a somewhat ambiguous status between adults' and children's literature) demonstrate his linguistic facility, deserving greater attention from students of modernism. His later historical fictions *Puck of Pook's Hill* (1906) and *Rewards and Fairies* (1910) summon up England's ancestral spirits. In his adult works, especially his short stories, children and the child's vision receive detailed attention; *Wee Willie Winkie* (1895) also maps the world of the British woman's sojourn in India. Overall, Kipling expresses a larger vision than that of little England and confounds charges of aggressive imperialism.

P. G. Wodehouse (1881–1975) started by writing school stories for the magazine *The Captain*; of these the most significant was *Mike* (1909). One of his characters, Psmith, proved so popular that he was transferred to Wodehouse's adult fiction.

Old Possum's male world is piratical, clubbable, dandyish and streetwise, a world of double lives and legendary reputations. T. S. Eliot (1888–1965) celebrates the secret, devilish dimensions of the cat's personae in *Old Possum's Book of Practical Cats* (1939), (a book seldom mentioned in evaluations of his work) creating fable characters. Like children, these characters inhabit their own subculture at odds with dominant values. A relish for naming and for terms of address permeates the text, which extends rather than re-works the fable form. Diabolical aspects are explored in names like Firefrorefiddle, the Fiend of the Fell, Mistofflees and Griddlebone; other names, like the fiendish epithets, resonate with suggestions of transformation, trickery, tumbling, tormenting and disarray. One female character only appears, preoccupied with educational reform and control, as if the child dedicatees might recognise a nanny or governess in The Gumbie Cat. Eliot's felicitous dancing and marching rhythms contrast markedly with his adult verse of the period, such as Four Quartets (1943).

Masefield (1878–1967) and Ransome (1884–1967) combined writing for children with a wide range of professional work as journalists. Extensive travel and a fondness for sailing were, however, expressed in remarkably different ways. Masefield as poet, editor, anthologiser and populariser of story telling and poetry in performance exerted a considerable influence upon generations of children to whom *The Midnight Folk* (1927) and *The Box of Delights* (1935) appealed. The contribution of such works to modernism is now attracting critical interest. In Ransome's series *Swallows and Amazons* (from 1930), Hunt recognises classic patterns of displacement and closure (Hunt 1991: 131) which motivated less inventive imitators to exploit the holiday adventure sequence. Ransome's first writing for children, his ghost-writing and early journalism preceded his time spent in Russia after which his career became established with the publication of *Old Peter's Russian Tales* (1916) for children and *Six Weeks in Russia* (1919) for adults. In the 1938 edition to the Russian tales he wrote that 'fairy stories ... live for ever with a life of their own', deprecating his role as editor transmitting the stories to the child in every reader of whatever age and distinguishing Russia as the country where 'hardly anybody is too old for fairy stories' (Ransome 1916/1984: 7). In his stories wise fools succeed and innocents outwit the witch Baba Yaga the Terrible with her iron teeth and appetite for children's flesh. The two child listeners move with their uncle Peter in to the forested landscape of the tales: they share the peasants' preoccupations and, at the end, enjoy a christening.

Isaac Bashevis Singer (1904–1991) shares some of that territory in his Yiddish stories. As journalist and writer Singer has achieved the most varied and expressive portrayal of Jewish life in modern fiction, drawing on the singularity and perversity of what he has observed. Fascinated by the process of translation, he has published four volumes of stories for children and an essay 'Are children the ultimate literary critics?' Like Ransome he writes for the 'serious' children – the adults – as well as for younger readers, often re-working medieval superstition with dark humour and tragic vision. Many of his adult stories employ a dangerously unreliable devil-narrator, while in 'Gimpel the fool' (Singer 1982: 3–14) his fables centre on the shabby *shtetl* which dominates so much modern Yiddish literature. The combined spirituality and vulgarity of the *shtetl* are at odds with modern technology and Western materialist individualism. In his *Preface to Stories for Children* Singer observes that children see through 'the hype and judge the text on the criteria of clarity, logic and narrative impact' (Singer 1984: 332). Among the re-worked biblical tales, the witches and festivals, the animal fables, letters, oaths, recipes, verses and prayers as well as Yiddish provide the multiple voices of Polish peasant communities and Jewish culture.

Among the wide-ranging dramas, novels, travel and autobiographical works of Graham Greene (1904–1991), his children's books appear uncharacteristically conventional, though the dangerous edge is present in the notion of the venture into the unknown. *The Little Train*, fist published in 1946 and followed by three similar books, depicts an adventure allowing the child-reader release from the familiar. Adventure is then reined in to guarantee a calm closure, or peaceful bedtime. The rural retreat is privileged above the city, where the main station like a 'terrible cave of demons' appals the little train; a castle glimpsed en route is identified as one where a king was put to death.

Of the same period, the poet Cecil Day Lewis (1904–1972) translator, editor and Establishment figure after early membership of the Left Book Club, became Poet Laureate in 1968 after occupying the Chair of Poetry at Oxford from 1951–1956; of his two fictions for children, *Dick Willoughby* (1933) and *The Otterbury Incident* (1948), the latter proved more enduring. In 1944 he wrote *Poetry for You* to popularise poetry among children, a book which maintains a strong sense of the young reader in its relaxed style and its reiterated appeal: 'older people tell you . . .' and 'have you made up your mind?' Recommending de la Mare's collection *Come Hither* (1923) for the 'lucky ones who do' like poetry, he also advises children to compile their own anthologies by copying favourite poems into a 'smart-looking manuscript book' (Lewis 1944: 110).

Another Poet Laureate, Ted Hughes (1930–   ) preoccupied with nature, later with legends of creation, writes plays, poems and fiction for children, reworking the fable in two significant forms, *Meet My Folks* (1961) and *What Is The Truth?* (1984), a 'farmyard fable for the young'. He derives amusement in *Meet My Folks* from the close identification of human characters with specific creatures. The collection ends hauntingly with a vision of a more symbiotic relationship between the rising generation and nature. These poems, celebratory rather than facetious, are likely to appeal individually. The much more ambitious *What is the Truth?* presents a mosaic collection of poetic fables interspersed in a portentous dialogue, affirming the Creator's presence in all living forms. In *Ffangs the Vampire Bat and The Kiss of Truth* (1986), he creates a promising fable character, Attila the Fighting Cock, whose brief adventures usher in the unfortunate Ffangs. Female characters are manipulated into passivity, as an incomplete truce is uneasily negotiated. A revenge fable element is discernible in the specific actuality of life-forms in *Crow* (1970) and in some of the *Moortown* (1979) poems, both for adults. In both *The Iron Man* (1968) and *The Iron Woman* (1993) bewildered child-heroes encounter a monstrous, but benign agent, primed to challenge a global threat humans are more or less blind to; though the ferrous couple are allowed a mutual polishing, Iron Woman remains barren, clumsy and destructive, crushing and uprooting whole trees. Relying on the energy of a post-primal scream, Hughes permits women momentary power, although food production and electronic communication instantly fail without male involvement. An 'ecological fantasy' rendered 'too didactic' (Alderson 1993: 31), it contains austere illustrations, rather adult for a children's book; these contrast with the large-scale, soft-edged pictures of *What Is The Truth?* which suggest a child's close-up view of living forms.

Hughes has authorised the publication of most of Sylvia Plath's work, including *The Bed Book* for children, which first appeared in 1976. Plath (1932–1963) wrote both prose and poetry; some of her most famous poems were addressed directly to her own children, such as 'You're', 'Morning Song', while others voice a mother's thoughts: 'Words for a nursery', 'For a fatherless son', 'Nicholas and the candlestick'. *The Bed Book* invites the child, who is directly addressed, to range imaginatively in fantastic bed-vehicles. Plath explores a child's inventiveness within adult constraints in humorously affectionate and rhyming verse, which allows the child-reader all the tricks and treats of adventure with a reassuring circularity of narrative direction which prepares the child for sleep.

The singular literary experience of Salman Rushdie (1947–   ), has prompted him to articulate protest against 'Silence Laws' in a children's book: *Haroun and the Sea of Stories* (1990), a fantasy of exuberant humour. Its vitality renders solemn didacticism elsewhere quite inert by contrast. The teasing game played by the author with the reader, so conspicuous in *Midnight's Children* (1981) where Rushdie's 'chutnification' of history is achieved (Rushdie 1981: 442) is evident in the children's text. *Haroun*, like *Midnight's Children*, is best described as magic realism. It employs bold patterns of opposition and refraction: Sengupta, the shadow people, the dark factory ship and web of night in turn confront the radiant source, the fertile stream of Rashid's story-telling. In *Midnight's Children*, Rushdie's Shandyean resonances are clear in the pervasive sense of the instability of the text and in the narrator's preoccupation with his nose; *Haroun* is similarly allusive, though its fields of reference are more popularly accessible. The living and transforming power of Logos, the word, is most ironically affirmed in the case of Haroun's creator.

This survey has necessarily neglected many authors who have worked in both the adult and children's fields with equal distinction. Equally, in the last thirty years the interchange between writing for children and writing for adults has increased, perhaps as the distinctions between the two kinds of writing have become finer, witness the work of Jill Paton Walsh, Nina Bawden, Penelope Lively, Jane Gardam, and others, whose association with children's literature has not damaged their reputations.

If Caxton's invention opened up – with the recognition of the uses of literacy – a great division between childhood and adult experience for which children had to be prepared, it is all the more appropriate that his early printing of *Aesop* in translation should have proved so regenerative and enduring a contribution to children's literature. The male authors notable in this field have defined themselves in many cases as writers for children by reference to the fable tradition, a tradition which has remained sensitive and accessible to continual reworking. The feminising of fiction extended the range and scale of children's literature, providing new opportunities for the revaluation of childhood and its relationship to adult experience.

The texts for children considered here exemplify and derive significance from the expression of the numerous semi-autonomous cultures which have always co-existed alongside the dominant culture. From within these subordinate mental worlds every past and future juvenile Edgeworth, Kipling, Eliot and Rushdie springs.

## References

Alderson, B. (1993) 'Myth with metal fatigue' [review of *The Iron Woman* by T. Hughes], *The Times* 16 August, 31.

Briggs, J. (1989) 'Women writers: Sarah Fielding to E. Nesbit' in Avery, G. and Briggs, J. (eds) *Children and their Books*, Oxford: Clarendon Press.

Day Lewis, C. (1944) *Poetry For You*, London: Blackwell.

Eagleton, T. (1982) *The Rape of Clarissa*, Oxford: Blackwell.

Green, R. L. (ed.) (1971) *Kipling: The Critical Heritage*, London: Routledge and Kegan Paul.

Hill, C. (1988) *John Bunyan and His Church*, London: Oxford University Press.

Hunt, P. (1991) *Criticism, Theory and Children's Literature*, Oxford: Blackwell.

Inglis, F. (1981) *The Promise of Happiness: Value and Meaning in Children's Fiction*, Cambridge: Cambridge University Press.

Kirkham, M. (1983) *Jane Austen, Feminism and Fiction*, Brighton: Harvester Press.

McKillop, A. D. (1936) *Samuel Richardson, Printer and Novelist*, Chapel Hill: University of North Carolina Press.

McMasters, R. D. (1991) *The Cultural Frame of Reference*, Toronto: McGill-Queen's University Press.

Myers, M. (1992) 'Daddy's girl as motherless child: Maria Edgeworth and maternal romance: an essay in re-assessment' in Spender, D. (ed.) *Living By The Pen, Early British Women Writers*, New York: Teachers College Press.

Ransome, A. (1916/1987) *Old Peter's Russian Tales*, London: Cape.

Ruland, R. and Bradbury, M. (1991) *From Puritanism to Post-Modernism: A History of American Literature*, New York: Viking Penguin.

Singer, I. B. (1982) *The Collected Stories*, London: Cape.

—— (1984) *Stories for Children*, New York: Farrar, Straus, Giroux.

Wall, B. (1991) *The Narrator's Voice*, London: Macmillan.

Watt, I. (1974) *The Rise of the Novel*, London: Chatto and Windus.

# 35

# Books Adopted by Children

## *Stuart Hannabuss*

It has always been difficult to define exact boundaries between children's literature and the broader domain of reading material read by adults. This has arisen for many reasons, some based on what the reading material intrinsically happens to be, and others on social and cultural factors. Adoption occurs when children 'take over' a work (book, cartoon, film or video) and make it their own, so that it becomes generally associated in the public mind as 'a work for children' or 'a work that children are expected to enjoy'. This process may entail making the work their own to the general exclusion of adult readers (who will then read it only for nostalgia, as story-tellers, or as children's book specialists), or it may remain popular with both adults and children.

There are times when adults encourage children to read particular books, making it easier by producing versions attractive or intelligible to them. This may be motivated by the desire to present 'great literature' or 'good books' to children, for imaginative, educational and moral reasons. Such works may be retold or abridged or censored or updated or provided with new illustrations: this may be regarded as adaptation. Adopting and adapting are complementary aspects of the process of reading provision which takes place in a diverse cultural setting where strict divisions between children's and adult reading are ultimately impossible to make. The cross-over between adults and children has arguably been greater in recent decades because of television, video, and computer games.

Some books written for adults, like *Robinson Crusoe* and *Gulliver's Travels* (particularly the journey to Lilliput), end up being liked by children. Some books written for children, like *The Hobbit*, end up being liked by adults, particularly those taken up with Tolkien exegesis. There are also many works, like Sue Townsend's *The Diary of Adrian Mole*, written about children rather than for them, and which appeal – or fail to appeal – to both groups. Distinctions are fraught with problems about what 'child', 'juvenile', 'young adult', and 'adult' categories actually mean, both demographically and in terms of reading, and these change historically. During the nineteenth century, the works of Charlotte M. Yonge or Evelyn Everett Green were widely read by women and girls alike; in the same way, the works of Ballantyne and Henty were read by men and boys alike. In the twentieth century the work of Terry Pratchett and Steven Spielberg has equal impact on child and adult audiences.

Distinctions may arise from publishing conventions, for example, when Anne McCaffrey's Dragon fantasy series is marketed as juvenile in one country and adult in another, and there is similar ambiguity over the work of Alan Garner, William Mayne, John Gordon and Sylvia Engdahl. Issues of this type are particularly interesting in popular generic writing, like westerns and science fiction and horror. Difficulties of classification also arise because writers may write for overlapping readerships, as with much of Jean Plaidy's historical fiction (even though there are works, like *The Young Elizabeth*, which are advertised for young readers). Writers known mainly for their work for adults (like E. B. White, Rumer Godden, J. B. S. Haldane, Eric Linklater, Howard Spring, Ray Bradbury, Roy Fuller, H. G. Wells, and T. H. White) have all produced significant works for children, like E. B. White's *Stuart Little*, or which children have adopted, like H. G. Wells's *The Time Machine*.

Fundamental to whether a book is a children's book are the expectations about what intellectual and emotional experience the implied reader can bring in reading response, and it enables us to contrast works as different as, on the one hand, the Paddington and Babar books and, on the other, Russell Hoban's *The Mouse and his Child* and Richard Bach's *Jonathan Livingston Seagull*. Marcus Crouch argues that Mary O'Hara's *My Friend Flicka* and Eric Knight's *Lassie-Come-Home* 'betrayed by their extreme emotionalism that they were really books for adults' (Crouch 1962: 93). Other criteria sometimes used for differentiating adult and children's books are (1) the inclusion of concrete events rather than abstract discussion; (2) the use of happy endings; (3) firm moral frameworks; and (4) a distinctive style and vocabulary, and suggest that children have adopted works like *The Sword in the Stone* and *20,000 Leagues Under the Sea* because such characteristics can be found in them; such works as T. H. White's *Mistress Masham's Repose* and Frank Herbert's Dune series despite the fact that many of them cannot; and that works like *The Pilgrim's Progress* and Homer's *Odyssey* have been adapted because ways of mediating them have been found.

Another critical factor in evaluating adoption and adaptation is dialectical. Children may like a work *despite* adults *and/or because* of adults; liking and disliking works is often influenced by what children read or have to read (an important distinction) at school. A deeper level of this dialectic hinges on 'the impossibility of children's fiction' owing to the fact that it must always be an adult construct (see Rose 1984: *passim*). So in books as ostensibly simple as those about Babar, Tintin and Peter Pan, there are ideological and psychological resonances unrecognised by children, even though the works are regarded as children's books. The dialectic is also given a commercial and elitist spin because of the division between 'book people' and 'child people'.

Successive layers of meaning in a work do not prevent its being adopted by children; for example, in Henry Williamson's *Tarka the Otter*, the action and empathy of the story grip the reader, even if the intricate poetry and meanings of the tragic denouement, which the book shares with the author's complex and mature vision of nature (evident in his large adult output), elude many child readers. (Mark Twain's *Huckleberry Finn* presents similar challenges.)

There are many writers of adventure stories adopted by children for their ability to tell an exciting fast-moving adventure and create plausible heroes. Among them are John Buchan, Alistair MacLean, John Masefield, C. S. Forester and Conan Doyle with his tales of Sherlock Holmes. Margery Fisher, in *Intent*

*Upon Reading*, refers to *Robbery Under Arms*, *Lorna Doone*, and *King Solomon's Mines* as works likely to go on appealing to children for their ability to tell a good story about heroes and danger and victory: 'and that is why children have appropriated many modern writers who do not write for them' – and she cites Buchan, Masefield, Hammond Innes, C. S. Forester and Nevil Shute (Fisher 1964: 207). Of course, those layers of meaning may make it improbable that an adult work is adopted, while some children's books – *Alice in Wonderland*, *The Water Babies*, and *The Wind in the Willows* – contain inaccessible meanings or sub-texts.

## Adoption and the Common Cultural Pool

Adoption entails taking over something from somewhere else. Yet it may be fair to say that both children's and adult literature derive historically from a common cultural pool of folk and fairy tales, myths and legends, the ingredients of oral tradition and folklore. Equally, only if children were regarded as distinct from adults in the past could the notion of adoption, in this sense, be meaningful. Themes common to adults and children (like monsters, magic and tragedies) appear in early chapbooks, and influence the contents of eighteenth-century books. It is clear that adaptation often preceded adoption, as can be seen from fairy stories like Perrault's, and conceptions of the child, as innately sinful or good were influential factors on what was provided as distinctly for children's reading during the eighteenth and nineteenth centuries, and in consequence what became available for adoption.

Evidence about responses to early children's books is elusive, though some can be found in autobiographies and diaries, records of child nurture and some (exceptional) contemporary criticism. It may also be inferred from children's books themselves. Currently, research into reading response by writers like Protherough, Fry and Applebee helps us to identify reasons for adoption. They range from the excitement of the forbidden to active identification with exciting storylines and characters. Comparisons between heroes as widely separated as Jason and Rambo, Gulliver and Indiana Jones, Beowulf and E.T. the Extra-Terrestrial, typically show how adoption crosses both historical tradition and types of media, and ultimately show this derivation from a common cultural pool.

Comparisons can also be made between adult and children's books which emerge from the same cultural (and even anthropological) tradition: the quest in *Don Quixote* and in the works of Sid Fleishman and early Alan Garner; religious allegory in *The Pilgrim's Progress* and Arthur Calder-Marshall's *The Fair to Middling*; the Arthurian cycle in Malory and T. H. White; the evil in mankind in the Faustus legend, James Watson's *The Partisan*, the works of Leon Garfield, and William Golding; and rites of passage in Brobdingnag with Gulliver, in the love triangle in *The Owl Service*, and in Ged's initiation into magic in *A Wizard of Earthsea*. These comparisons emphasise the extent of the common tradition between adult and children's books without which a comprehensive understanding of the process of adoption cannot be obtained.

Any area of generic fiction, such as fantasy, crosses easily between readerships, adult and child, general reader and cult/specialist. (This is also true – perhaps for a related reason – of hobby- and sport-orientated magazines.) Such materials contain many themes and styles of treatment which characterise the genre itself rather than any specific appropriateness for children. Talking beasts are in Genesis and *Animal Farm*, Robert C. O'Brien's *Mrs Frisby and the Rats of NIMH*, the Narnia books and *Watership Down*; dystopias exist in the work of Kafka and Huxley as well as in John Christopher and Peter Dickinson; supernatural events are as common in Christopher Pike as in James Herbert and Stephen King. Given the common cultural inheritance of these works, and in the case of popular fiction a strong array of textual similarities, it becomes essential to ask whether the process of adoption is in fact one where children's and adult writing are taking place not in two areas but in three: children's, adult's, and both together.

Where the boundaries come will always be a matter of context and interpretation. Does 'Dr Who' lie somewhere between Nicholas Fisk and Philip Dick? What makes *Shane* family viewing/reading, while the Edge and Sudden Western series of George C. Gilman remain, and probably should remain, on the adult shelves in a library? What makes Mary Norton a fantasist for children with her Borrowers books, while Andre Norton, with her speculations into future societies, and the effects on identity and evolution of shape-shifting, is a writer for both adults and young people? Why should 'B.B.' and Meindert DeJong, Rene Guillot and Margery Sharp be clearly tellers of animal stories for the young, yet Gavin Maxwell and T. H. White be for everyone? What happens between the preoccupations of *Tom Brown's Schooldays* and George MacDonald Fraser's 'sequels' about Flashman? What characteristics of story-telling – language, plotting, style – make Wanda Gág a reteller of folk and fairy tales for children, Nathaniel Hawthorne and Charles Perrault (in the original) writers for much older readers, and Rosemary Sutcliff, Andrew Lang, and Roger Lancelyn Green writers for both groups?

Behind answers to these questions will lie some of the reasons for successful and willing adoption by children of these works. Some tales are too complex structurally or emotionally (like those of the Kalevala or Weland or Undine or Scheherezade). Some stories use irony or self-parody, qualities usually reserved for older readers and adults with a frame of reference and experience, and a repertoire of speech acts and intentionalities, large enough for them to understand oblique modes of narration. Probably these account partly for why Norton Juster's *The Phantom Tollbooth* and the work of Reiner Zimnik and Wilhelm Hauff will never be universally popular with children, and why the more adventurous works of Raymond Briggs are popular only with older readers. Reasons for rejection at one age may be reasons for acceptance at another. Adoption of the reading materials of an older age group with which the reader wishes to be identified may in itself be a motivation for adopting particular works (thus 'adult' reading at puberty).

## Adoption and Generic Fiction

One of the major sources of works for adults adopted by children is the field of popular adult fiction. From their inception many adventure stories appeal both to children and to the child in every adult (see Turner 1948). It is easy to see how adventure stories were adopted by children because there was action and not introspection, straightforward resolutions and a clear-cut morality. Examples include Rider Haggard's *King Solomon's Mines*, Anthony Hope's *The Prisoner of Zenda*, A. E. W. Mason's *The Four Feathers*, John Buchan's *The Thirty-Nine Steps*, Edgar Wallace's *Sanders of the River*, and Baroness Orczy's tales of the Scarlet Pimpernel. These stories may have been adopted because of the stereotypes they contain, and raise the question as to how far children adopt any story which is two-dimensional (and, by that token, the extent to which any story which children adopt is necessarily simpler than any adult story). In these more ideology-conscious times children are actively discouraged from adopting books such as these, many of which are sexist, racist or otherwise politically incorrect.

Influential on these popular works were the historical novels of Sir Walter Scott and Alexandre Dumas, and some have been taken over by and for children. Many children's writers tell us that they read Scott and Dumas when young. From Scott we might identify *Rob Roy*, with its Highland dramatics, and *Guy Mannering*, with its young hero Bertram and its happy resolution, as being typical. From Dumas derived the saga of the three musketeers, with debonair swashbuckling and an easy identification with heroes and of villains, and the engrossing but long-winded tale of delayed revenge in *The Count of Monte Cristo*. The cladding is often gadzookery but the story motifs, the good/bad iconography, and the satisfaction of simple vengeance provide the underlying appeal. It is useful to compare these books with twentieth-century counterparts, like Alistair MacLean, whose *The Guns of Navarone* and *Where Eagles Dare* have a similar appeal. 'Buddy' movies carry on the motifs to the present day. It is useful, too, to ask why some of these works appeal more to boys than to girls, and whether roles and socialisation affects their choices.

Science fiction and fantasy is a particularly fertile domain for locating works for adults adopted by children. This may be because so many works incorporate themes and ideas widely used in mainstream children's books. Many authors write undifferentiatedly for both readerships. Whereas adult writers include J. G. Ballard, Philip José Farmer, Joanna Russ, Olaf Stapledon, Stanislas Lem and Yevgeny Zamyatin; and children's writers include Peter Dickinson, Nicholas Fisk, Tanith Lee, C. S. Lewis (*pace* the *Perelandra* series), Ursula Le Guin and Madeleine L'Engle; Ben Bova, Alan Nourse and Robert Heinlein seem to have set themselves in the middle, while Robert Sheckley and Dean Koontz have been placed there by equal numbers of adult and young fans.

Any aficionado of the genre, certainly one over 12, might have read all these, and be more preoccupied with discriminating between good and bad examples of each, or between 'sword and sorcery' fantasy and technopunk 'fact-fiction', rather than between books for adults and those for children. Cultural differences also exist between countries in their views of how serious such works can be as commentaries on the human condition. Where differences do lie between children's and adult works, it is usually a matter of complexity or explicitness.

Particular titles stand out as being adopted by children, by teachers and by children's publishers, like *Farmer in the Sky, Citizen of the Galaxy*, and *Starship Troopers*, all by Robert Heinlein, and some of Harry Harrison's novels like *Spaceship Medic*. The versatile Robert Silverberg, with stories like *The Face of the Waters* and *Kingdoms of the Wall*, explore futuristic catastrophes and journeys of personal pain and self-discovery that are common narrative coinage for children and adults. Similarly poised are the Star Trek television programmes and films, with the sixty-plus spin-off novels and the rapidly growing series based on George Lucas's Star Wars.

Animal stories offer other insights into the process of adoption. Isabelle Jan considers the form, from Jack London's *White Fang* to Kipling's *The Jungle Book*, arguing that 'animals are ideal partners and accomplices' and friendships with them are partnerships 'with a being who, like [the child reader], is an outsider, yet in front of whom he can show off, like Mowgli': this is a 'pretext for the invasion of a free society based on different relationships from those ... familiar to children ... free from restraints from adults'. She goes on: 'as an intruder in the animal societies of his book, the child has the unique experience of perfect psychological balance' (Jan 1973: 86–87). We find this kind of relationship in many successful children's books, like *Black Beauty*, *Charlotte's Web*, and *National Velvet*, but we also find it in many animal books intended for adults but adopted by children, and this is why they are adopted.

Examples include Mary O'Hara's *My Friend Flicka*, John Steinbeck's *The Red Pony*, Barry Hines's *Kes*, and Gavin Maxwell's *Ring of Bright Water*. The realism, pathos, integrity of the animals and the painfully growing self-awareness of these stories, and in O'Hara the high emotion, stay well within the experiential and emotional compass of most young people, and satisfy Jan's criteria. In considering what animal stories children adopt, a look at the most commercially successful corpus of talking animals, those of Walt Disney, is also informative. Why works like *Bambi* and *The Rescuers*, *The Jungle Book*, and the rest have been so widely popular, and what the Disney adaptations have entailed is highly relevant.

Another area is that of the western, where traditional writers like Zane Grey and Max Brand, Ernest Haycox and J. T. Edson continue to attract wide child readerships. Adoption can be interpreted here in two ways. The first is when children adopt a particular work or theme or hero as their own in a work originally intended for adults. The second is when books intended for children in the first place deal with a similar theme or event as any adult book in the same genre might. Demonstrating the first is Jack Schaefer's *Shane*, adopted perhaps because a small boy is the lens through which this stark story of a frontier war between ranchers and sod-busters is portrayed. In the same vein is Owen Wister's *The Virginian*, probably one of the most influential of books in the genre, creating the romantic image of the cowboy, instinctively noble, a man among boys, and winner in the gripping fight with the villain Trampas. In this and in countless films characterisation and iconography is thoroughly accessible to the child reader/ viewer. It offers familiarity and simple gratifications, more simple indeed than can be found in some works ostensibly for children like Elliott Arnold's *The Spirit of Cochise*, Scott O'Dell's *Island of the Blue Dolphins*, Hal Borland's *When the Legends Die*, and Jean Stafford's *The Mountain Lion*, which ask much more of a reader in terms of constructing coherent meanings. This is a good instance of where adoption of popular adult fiction may serve as a light relief to the more demanding works which young people find on their library shelves. The motive to adopt such books is also based on the wish to assert adult privileges, and access a range of materials which, in writers like Dee Brown and Brian Holmes, deal with adult themes in an adult way.

## Adoption, Adaptation and Mediation

Some adult books are adopted by children. Some adult books are *adapted for* children, and this is often because adults believe that such books should be made available to children. In some cases, like *Robinson Crusoe*, the motivation to get children to read it was partly to provide them with a good example of independence, rationality, diligence, and triumph over a hostile environment, very much in keeping with contemporary ideology. There were numerous editions and versions for children, including John Harris's in 1821, 'A new and improved edition, interspersed with reflections, religious and moral.' Similarly, versions of *The Swiss Family Robinson* were extended to include a wealth of natural history illustrations (for instruction) and further episodes of adventure and bravery (for moral improvement). W. H. G. Kingston's 1889 edition omitted 'the long sententious lectures found in the original, and [incorporated] some slight alterations calculated to enliven the narrative'.

Often, then, story types and themes are 'adopted' by writers for children and given new forms, re-contextualised in terms of contemporary needs and conceptions about what children should read and how they should behave. So sermons might be interpolated into an adventure story ('powder and jam'), illustrations supplied to enhance didactic impact, or death-bed repentances taken out as too melodramatic or lugubrious. Such 'adoption' points not merely to what authors and publishers see as timely commercial advantage: what is adopted in this way, and how texts are adapted and distributed to young readers, are implicitly ideological statements, ideologically informed acts of mediation. Accordingly, acts of adoption and adaptation throughout the history of children's literature inform us about prevailing cultural and ideological paradigms of each period – views that children were innately sinful, eighteenth-century rationality, views of natural nurture from Rousseau and Thomas Day, the Evangelical movement's stress on personal grace, and, in the twentieth century, the policing of racism, sexism and ageism in children's books. Without denying opportunities for spontaneous choice and response in children's reading, it is as illogical to analyse the process of adoption out of context, and detach adoption from dominant contemporary ideologies, as it is to decouple them from the shaping effect of changes in the publishing trade.

The urge to make children 'good', general to early children's books, was also an important impetus behind adaptations. Sentiments like this lay behind Mrs Trimmer's distrust of fantasy and her insistence on moral exhortation, even through myths and fairytales. Later works, like Jean Ingelow's *Mopsa the Fairy* or Christina Rossetti's *Speaking Likenesses*, show how influential nineteenth-century children's writers adapted the themes and sentiments of fantasy and folklore for moralistic purposes.

Humphrey Carpenter convincingly argues that many writers during that period were so successful (that is, they adapted their manner of writing so that their works were adopted by children) because their work appeared to present to children a world separate from, and even opposed to, the world of adults (Carpenter 1985). E. Nesbit parodied earnest moralising in her witty no-nonsense stories of play and magic, accounting for their popularity then and now. Adoption by children is always more likely to occur if readers can identify the authentic tone of their own culture in a work, and if the illusion of the reader's having ownership of the text's referential world can be created and sustained. This aspect of adoption is of particular importance in understanding the appeal of comics and magazines for the young, and of the many 'nameless' writers of sub-culture spin-offs in horror and fantasy.

The assumption of an adaptation is that, regardless of any enjoyment children might get out of the work, there is a strong probability that children would not spontaneously adopt it for themselves. Reasons might be pragmatic, when adults think that the work would simply bore children. Reasons might also be enlightened, when adults feel that a book is well worth reading but may not be accessible in its adult form. Many myths and legends have been adapted in this way, making tales with obscure characterisation and complex motivation like Tristan and Iseult, Daedalus and Icarus, and the stories of the Gorgon and the Minotaur and even of Gilgamesh intelligible through re-tellings by such as Andrew Lang, Roger Lancelyn Green, James Reeves, and Ian Serraillier. In this way Kevin Crossley-Holland brought as complex a tale as *Beowulf* to children, and Rosemary Sutcliff the tragic death of Boudicca. Writers and adapters of this quality know that books for children are not simply books for adults but on a reduced scale. If adaptation is going to work, and lead to adoption, then not just style and vocabulary may have to be simplified, but the images and event-structures translated into an acceptable texture and sequence which children can understand and accept as natural. The popularity of such works as *The Pilgrim's Progress* demonstrates how pervasive was the social pressure to read them; for example in Isaiah Thomas's 1789 edition the dictation is 'To the Youth of America'. Rosenbach comments that this work, not originally intended for the young, was one of the most popular and influential children's books in America. He claims that Bunyan was popular even though he was a Puritan because

> he nevertheless in this work succeeded in reconciling religion and romance, so that a century later Richard Graves in the Spiritual Quixote [another suitable adaptation, this time from the original of Cervantes] compared the adventures of Christian with those of Jack the Giant Killer ... In this respect the work of Bunyan is in striking contrast to the Janeway school [which preached at children and regarded them as innately evil, 'limbs of Satan'].
>
> Rosenbach 1971: 96

If there are dominant ideologies shaping the process of adoption and adaptation, then these ideologies take institutionalised social forms in order to implement their ideas: the Church in general, and organisations like the Religious Tract Society and the Society for the Propagation of Christian Knowledge in particular.

Another major channel of influence is education, through and by means of which much spontaneous and enforced adoption of books (intended for children and for adults, as well as adapted for children) took and still takes place. Education includes intellectual and emotional development, may entail socialisation to the point of indoctrination, may open imaginative doors to the 'best' books, and much else. Availability is a powerful shaper of what is adopted: what is bought for schools and libraries, as well as what is approved of as suitable reading by teachers and librarians and parents.

It is a debate which impels us to examine what is a 'classic' in children's reading, and the extent to which classics represent what children should most be encouraged to adopt. Classics are of two kinds here: first, books intended for children, like Marryat's *The Children of the New Forest* or George MacDonald's *At the Back of the North Wind*; second, works not necessarily written for children but regarded as 'worth reading'. By that token, Huxley's *Brave New World* and Orwell's *1984*, with their provocative dystopianism, appear on English syllabi in schools and colleges. Crises of identity and courage are explored in works like Crane's *The Red Badge of Courage* and Hemingway's *The Old Man and the Sea*, prejudice and personal danger in Harper Lee's *To Kill a Mocking-Bird*, the fragility of relationships between human beings and animals in *Kes*, and the nature of evil in Stevenson's *Dr Jekyll and Mr Hyde* and Golding's *Lord of the Flies*. Such works are adopted by a society as being suitable for children and young people to adopt for themselves. So mediated through teaching curricula, they become part of a common framework of cultural reference in the mind of the 'educated' adult.

Many such works are selected for their portrayal and analysis of growing up. *Huckleberry Finn*, with its rich mixture of the picaresque and the ironic, its exposure of humbug and its self-awareness, is a good example of this. McCullers's *The Member of the Wedding* moves into a world where the central character half-understands the complex actions and motivations of the others, observing adult affairs with a mixture of bravado and unease. Henry James's *What Maisie Knew* superimposes on the act of observing an autodiegetically styled barrier of understanding, reflecting what the heroine can actually know, and know she knew, layers of discourse which only a sophisticated reader can penetrate.

This refracted view of events, the reader watching the characters as they watch themselves watching the other characters, moves into emotional and sexual dangers in Richard Hughes's *A High Wind in Jamaica* and L. P. Hartley's *The Go-between*. Research is needed to define the extent to which exposure to such books, in the context of education, leads young people to adopt them, or to reject 'children's books'. Here, adoption may consist of anything from an opportunistic absorption of what young people think they need to say in order to pass academic courses to a deeply experienced internalisation of the events and emotions and their resonances. It is also useful to consider what so-called children's books are used in schools alongside these works – for example Ursula Le Guin's *A Very Long Way from Somewhere Else* or James Vance Marshall's *Walkabout*, and the influence of reading materials wholly outside adult culture.

Thus adoption cannot be fully understood without comparing what children and young people are formally asked to read with what they choose to read. Surveys of reading and popular taste often highlight large differences: between being asked to read *Lord of the Flies* while reading *The Silence of the Lambs* in private; studying *The War of the Worlds* for an exam and understanding it better for having seen Spielberg's *Close Encounters of the Third Kind*.

It is valuable to examine popular cultural trends among children and young people, and trace them through to what adoptions are made: movie hits tell us much about texts which get adopted. The concept of 'a good read' is now that of an encounter with a multi-representational package: book, film-of-book, book-of-film, television adaptation, graphic novel, cartoon, computer game, interactive program. CD-I (interactive compact disk) and virtual reality films are now becoming commercially available. Computer game heroes are being adopted as favourites by children and adults alike, and increasingly evident in successful popular books for young people are inter-textual references to these other media and characters in them, or even representations of themselves in other media. These serve as cross-media prequels and sequels which they 'know' the readers already know.

The issues of censorship, particularly for film and video versions of these stories, are profound, and hint at the ways in which any type of adoption (or its attempted prevention) predicates views about childhood, socialisation, morality, and imaginative health. For instance, recent MUDS (Multi-User Dungeons, virtual reality developments of Dungeons and Dragons) may be based on Narnia, Dune and the universe of Star Trek, but their ability to represent characters in simulated sex, or to 'change' the user's gender in order to explore new sexual experience, has led to the design of systems (for example where the virtual world is based on the Land of Oz or Yellowstone National Park) with problematic implications.

Arguably, marketing and merchandising cross-media products by global multi-media companies and conglomerates is having a more irresistible effect on what children and young people adopt than can books alone. This is certainly so in the information field, where topics and layouts and texts reveal a heavy influence of televisual presentation. It is no longer convincing to characterise adoption and adaptation as approaching each other from across a divide between adults and children, although some proof of this will always remain in terms of the way in which books and films like *Mary Poppins* and characters like Babar and Paddington Bear will always be for children. Neil Postman's thesis of the cultural fusion between children and adults, turning them into 'adultified children' and 'childified adults' is one of many modern factors which changes the context and increases the complexity of adoption, but the essential challenge of what to encourage children to read, and discourage them from reading, remains very much the same.

## References

Applebee, A. (1978) *The Child's Concept of Story*, Chicago: University of Chicago Press.
Carpenter, H. (1985) *Secret Gardens: A Study of the Golden Age of Children's Literature*, London: Allen and Unwin.
Crouch, M. (1962) *Treasure Seekers and Borrowers*, London: Library Association.
Fisher, M. (1964) *Intent upon Reading*, 2nd edn, Leicester: Brockhampton Press.
Fry, D. (1985) *Children Talk About Books: Seeing Themselves as Readers*, Milton Keynes: Open University Press.
Jan, I. (1973) *On Children's Literature*, London: Allen Lane.
Postman, N. (1982) *The Disappearance of Childhood*, New York: Delacorte Press.
Protherough, R. (1983) *Developing Response to Fiction*, Milton Keynes: Open University Press.
Rose, J. (1984) *The Case of Peter Pan*, London: Macmillan.
Rosenbach, A. S. W. (1971) *Early American Children's Books*, New York: Dover.

Tucker, N. (1981) *The Child and the Book: A Psychological and Literary Exploration*, Cambridge: Cambridge University Press.

## Further Reading

Bettelheim, B. (1976) *The Uses of Enchantment: The Meaning and Importance of Fairy Tales*, New York: Knopf.

Bold, C. (1987) *Selling the Wild West: Popular Western Fiction, 1860 to 1960*, Bloomington: Indiana University Press.

Cawelti, J. G. (1976) *Adventure, Mystery, and Romance: Formula Stories as Art and Popular Culture*, Chicago: University of Chicago Press.

Coles, R. (1986) *The Moral Life of Children*, Boston: Atlantic Monthly Press.

Dixon, J. (ed.) (1986) *Fiction in Libraries*, London: Library Association.

Hannabuss, S. (1989) *Managing Children's Literature*, Bradford: MCB University Press.

—— and Marcella, R. (1993) *Biography and Children*, London: Library Association.

Hawes, J. M. and Hiner, N. R. (eds) (1991) *Children in Historical and Comparative Perspective*, New York: Greenwood Press.

Hollindale, P. (1992) 'Ideology and the children's book', in Hunt, P. (ed.) *Literature for Children: Contemporary Criticism*, London: Routledge.

Kinnell, M. (ed.) (1991) *Managing Fiction in Libraries*, London: Library Association.

Louv, R. (1991) *Childhood's Future*, New York: Doubleday.

Palmer, J. (1991) *Potboilers: Methods, Concepts and Case Studies in Popular Fiction*, London: Routledge.

Turner, E. S. (1948) *Boys Will Be Boys*, London: Joseph.

Twitchell, J. B. (1985) *Dreadful Pleasures: An Anatomy of Modern Horror*, New York: Oxford University Press.

—— (1992) *Carnival Culture: The Trashing of Taste in America*, New York: Columbia University Press.

# 36

# Information Books

*Peggy Heeks*

## Definitions

Public libraries have, for decades, divided their stock into 'fiction' and 'non-fiction', with not only separation on the shelves but in many cases different borrowing regulations also. Implicit here, perhaps, is a value judgement, with fiction being regarded as a slight indulgence and non-fiction reading as a commendable activity. There are certainly practical reasons for this separation. Since the highest proportion of books borrowed from public libraries are fiction, it is convenient to group them together. The remaining categories, using Melvil Dewey's classification, are non-fiction, although they contain several sections which bear considerable relationship to fiction, such as poetry, plays, myths and folk-tales, which all offer aspects of the literary experience, and which are dealt with elsewhere in this encyclopedia.

Throughout their history, information books have been concerned with more than delivering facts, and this point will be discussed later in this chapter. The term 'information books' has its limitations, but it is the term most widely used in the field of children's books, as publishers' catalogues and library shelves show.

Just as there is some ambiguity about definitions of information books and non-fiction, so there is a need to examine the distinction between facts, information and knowledge. Facts are raw data. Facts are processed to provide information – for example, chronologically in dictionaries of dates, geographically in guidebooks, by both systems in railway timetables. The processing makes the accessing of facts easier. Knowledge arises when intelligence and understanding are brought to bear on the information. The distinction is lost when, as has happened in some curriculum statements, 'knowledge' is confused with remembrance of facts. *A Language for Life* was helpful in this respect.

> It is a confusion of everyday thought that we tend to regard 'knowledge' as something that exists independently of someone who knows. 'What is known' must in fact be brought to life afresh within every 'knower' by his own efforts.
>
> Department of Education and Science 1975: 50

One cannot, therefore, equate information with knowledge. Information books serve as the tools which can help readers to knowledge.

## Purposes Served

Traditionally, information books have set out to present facts about a specific subject. There is a long history of publications of this kind, but it is significant that those of earlier centuries attempted to coax children into learning. *Orbis Pictus* (1658) by J. A. Comenius, is often cited as one of the earliest examples of an information book, with its pictures of hundreds of familiar objects and scenes. However, this was more than an enjoyable browsing book: a major purpose of the author was to improve readers' knowledge of Latin, with each picture being given both its Latin and vernacular name. Some of John Newbery's works can also be regarded as having a concern for more than stories – witness the title of one of his works advertised in 1756: 'A Little Lottery-Book for Children; Containing a new Method of playing them into a Knowledge of the Letters, Figures etc.'

The long sequence of Peter Parley books, originated by Samuel Goodrich of New England, are tales of history, travels, nature, and so also have a claim to be early information books. *Tales of Peter Parley about America*, a rather rambling history, appeared in 1827, and was followed by some 120 other titles, covering a wide range of places and subjects. The style was conversational, the approach digressive, and the books achieved considerable sales. Goodrich's aim was 'to feed the young mind upon things wholesome and pure, instead of things monstrous, false and pestilent' (Sloane 1953: 68).

These early books are a reminder that non-fiction may offer pleasure as well as instruction, an imaginative experience as well as information. This duality is apparent as one studies the publications of this present century, but it is noticeable that non-fiction today seems to be serving a range of purposes not apparent three decades ago.

### The fact bank

Children need quick-reference books as much as adults, books so arranged that basic information on a specific subject can be accessed quickly. Many of these titles are likely to be bought for home use, as well as forming significant sections of school and children's libraries. The core categories are atlases, dictionaries and encyclopedias, and in all three there are publications available which cover the various stages of childhood. So, for example, a publisher may move from an introductory atlas for 7-year-olds, which works its way from interpretation of photographs and plans to simple maps, to an atlas with some world coverage but showing major features only, and end with an atlas aimed at 13-year-olds, which gives almost as much detail as an adult work. Similarly, some publishers produce a series of dictionaries, beginning with those which are almost picture books, and ending with works of 30–40,000 entries which include notes on etymology, usage and pronunciation.

As knowledge has expanded, it has become ever more difficult to produce a comprehensive children's encyclopedia. At the lower end of the market – in terms of age-level, price and quality – there are a number of single-volume works, which should, perhaps, be more accurately be described as general-knowledge books. The multi-volume works represent a considerable publishing investment and are therefore to be undertaken with considerable caution. Examples of current sets which have proved valuable in practice include (in rising order of reading age) *Children's Britannica*, first published in 1960, *Oxford Children's Encyclopedia*, dating from 1991, and *The World Book Encyclopedia*, which first appeared in 1917 and has undergone several major revisions resulting, latterly, in much greater coverage of non-American items. Comparison of the present *Oxford Children's Encyclopedia* with the *Oxford Junior Encyclopedia* of 1964 shows the great change in presentation and approach over the thirty-year period.

### The information giver

Expectedly, the traditional role of the information book has been the straightforward one of presenting information on a given topic. Typical examples from the 1950s and 1960s are the Methuen *Outlines* series and Faber's *Your Book* series. Although the form still continues, it has met criticism for the deadening effect that these fact-filled pages tend to have.

> On and on go these sentences of controlled length, jogging by like sales managers on a Sunday morning, building no tensions, generating no excitements. 'Factbooks' are typical of so many series in that they are neat packages, uniform in style, and also in lack of any apparent enthusiasm on the part of their creators.
>
> Haigh 1981: 22

> At times of budget constraints, fact-filled books are seen as good value for money, and it has been interesting to see some publishers known for this area in the 1950s rebuilding information lists in the 1980s.
>
> Heeks 1985: 60

### Shaper of attitudes

This has become an increasingly large category, working throughout the age groups. *Round the World: Families* (published jointly by Save the Children Fund and Macmillan Education 1981) is an example for young children, which emphasises the unity among the variety of lifestyles round the world and aims to enlarge tolerance and understanding. At the upper end, one can cite *Vanishing Species* (Watts 1992), just one of many titles available on environmental issues. The concern for racial equality can be seen mirrored in Black's *Strands* series of the mid-1970s, which attempted to show the everyday life of British families from different cultural backgrounds.

### Communicator of experience

Sometimes books in this category spring from the perceived needs of children – for example *Our New Home* (Hamish Hamilton 1993) – sometimes from the perceived needs of society – for example Black's *Beans* and *Worldwide* series, which reflect the experiences of children around the world. Perhaps the most successful books in this category stem from an author's desire to communicate an experience of personal importance. Examples can be found among winners of *The Times Educational Supplement*'s Information Book Awards, such as *Spiders* by Ralph Whitlock (1975) and *Being Born* by Sheila Kitzinger and Lennart Nilsson (1987).

### Practical guide

Many books on hobbies, crafts and scientific subjects come into this category. These are books which are tested in use and judged by practical outcomes, and the perceived audience is likely to be the child and the parent, rather than the teacher mediating the book.

### Criteria

We have noted some of the main purposes served by information books which indicates the wide range of this area of children's literature, and leads one to realise that any set of criteria will have to be used flexibly. It is in this context that the following points for consideration are offered.

- The standing of the publisher, the qualifications and experience of the author, and the reputation of the illustrator are useful initial guides.
- The purpose of the book, and (where appropriate) its relevance to one's own purposes are major factors. One cannot judge a book's success until one knows what the author is setting out to achieve. Questions about the scope of the book arise here. Does it set out to give an overview of a broad subject area, or to look closely at one specific subject area?
- The accuracy and currency of the information given is an obvious matter for concern. It may be necessary here to get a view from a subject expert, or make comparisons with other information sources. Since a high proportion of information books are team compilations, or are supervised by a panel of consultants, mistakes in a title from a reputable publisher should be few.
- Subject coverage needs to be assessed in the light of the anticipated use. Is the subject treated too superficially, or in too much detail? One sometimes needs to question how far complex material can be simplified. Some topics – for example those involving political issues or scientific concepts – resist summarising, which may merely distort or misrepresent the facts as known.
- The viewpoint of the author is important. A good information book will avoid stereotypes of age, gender and race, will indicate (as appropriate) the existence of different points of view, and encourage the reader to think critically about the issues raised.
- The organisation of material should help the book fulfil its purpose. A non-fiction book designed to communicate experience is likely to need a different arrangement from one principally concerned with information retrieval. However, most non-fiction needs a contents page which offers a clear guide to the book's coverage, and an index which will lead to information worth having. The quality, and manner of construction, of indexes varies greatly, so it is necessary to check a sample of entries. It is reasonable to expect an information

book to have an organic shape – which, again, will be linked to its purpose and its subject. In some cases the subject suggests the order of content quite naturally, as in the lifecycle of an animal, the history of a form of transport. Often an author will proceed from the particular to the general, in line with the way in which children develop understanding. A concluding section which summarises what has gone before and helps the reader reflect on the content as a whole may be helpful.

- The reading level of the text should match that of the expected audience: in some cases it may be necessary to use a standard instrument for measuring reading level. However, beyond such compatibility, one looks for a text which will encourage the reader, for language which has life and vitality, for a personal voice telling of something new and interesting. One needs to consider how much information the author expects the reader to absorb, and at what pace. It is sometimes helpful for a book to have a two-level text, where some information is conveyed simply through captions and/or summaries, with more detailed information presented in some complementary form.

- Both the style of illustration chosen and the illustrations themselves should advance the author's purpose. For example, diagrams may be required to supplement the information which can be drawn from photographs: cartoons can serve to make a point or arrest the reader's attention, but it is unlikely that they can stand alone as information carriers. Illustrations can decorate, reinforce or extend a text, so an initial task is establishing the purpose they are trying to fulfil. As illustrations have tended to occupy a greater proportion of space – a movement linked with advances in printing technology – so the need for assessment of their quality and value has increased.

- Page layout should encourage the reader and make the search for information easier. This implies a page which is not over-crowded, where the typeface is appropriate to the readership, captions are clearly related to illustrations, and the organisation of the page is quickly apparent.

- The overall physical production should generate a sense of pleasure or excitement. Information books come in many different shapes, sizes and textures, and this individuality is part of the reader's enjoyment. The book as object needs to be carefully designed to send messages to its anticipated audience.

## Readership

Information books are called on to satisfy the needs of two quite different readerships: the adult, whether librarian, parent or teacher, who is the likely buyer, and the children who will be reading and using the books.

Children's librarians recognise that information books have an important role to play in their stock, serving the recreational interests of library clients, providing a source for answering reference enquiries, and supporting school work. It would be expected that a children's library would have a reference section, containing atlases, dictionaries and encyclopedias; beyond these categories one finds few quick-reference books produced entirely for children so, in practice, the section might also contain material designed for the adult market – a dictionary of dates, for example, or a field guide to wild birds. At one time, there was a perceived shortage of information books for children under seven years (Heeks 1982: 3), but this has been partly overcome by publication of books which can be described as induction guides to everyday life. Typical examples are *Linda Goes to Hospital* by Barry Wade (Black 1981); *My First Book of Time* by Claire Llewellyn (Dorling Kindersley 1981) and *Clare's New Baby Brother* by Nigel Snell (Evans 1992).

Parents have long been interested in buying books to assist their children's education, an interest usually manifested in a search for a reasonably priced encyclopedia to help with homework tasks. More recently, in Britain, a new market has emerged, focused on learning needs of young children. So, for example, the Headstart series from Hodder and Stoughton covers key skills of number, reading and writing. In the past such topics would have been covered by textbooks and mediated by teachers rather than parents.

In schools, information books have been widely used for the past three decades to supplement textbooks and direct experience. In the pre-teen years school work has often been based around centres of interest, an approach usually called the project or topic method which, typically, involves work across a number of subject disciplines and promotes information-gathering skills. The comparison of different sources has generated a wide demand for information books. The National Curriculum which came into effect in England and Wales in 1989 tended to narrow the range of subjects studied in schools, but to increase the range of resources required within each subject.

It is some years since a thorough study of the reading interests of English children was undertaken but there is some indication of an increase in popularity of non-fiction. A benchmark study by A. J. Jenkinson published in 1940, found that the four categories of sport, travel, biography and technical books

> do not at any age in either type of school attract much attention. Not one of them ever reaches the level of 3 per cent of the total amount of attention given to reading books out of school.
>
> Jenkinson 1940: 184

By 1972 Margery Fisher, in looking at the assumption that there are more readers of fiction than of non-fiction, was declaring that 'statistics suggest otherwise'. No sources, however, are quoted (Fisher 1972: 9). Meanwhile the results of a major survey, *Children's Reading Interests* published in 1975, show non-fiction reading as a minority activity – no more than 14.5 per cent of the sample's total reading (Whitehead *et al.* 1975: 23). A slightly later study of 7 to 9-year-olds found that 19 per cent of 7 to 8-year-olds, and 13 per cent of 9-year-olds enjoyed non-fiction, but with boys showing a greater preference for information books than girls in both age groups (Southgate *et al.* 1981: 214, 223).

A less formal study, of 12-year-olds in one English school, found that non-fiction reading by boys amounted to 71 per cent of their total reading, with the figure for girls reaching 53 per cent (Davies 1991: 18). These results are similar to those of a survey of 15-year-olds in 1980, and covering 349 schools in England, Wales and Northern Ireland (Department of Education and Science 1983), which showed that 52 per cent of respondents enjoyed reading non-fiction: 56 per cent of the boys; 48 per cent of the girls. For 35 per cent of boys and 23 per cent of girls (28 per cent overall) non-fiction was preferred to fiction. While the majority of students said that they derived satisfaction from reading, a critique of both primary and secondary school surveys from the Assessment of Performance Unit concluded that 'This pattern of performance suggests that a substantial number of pupils have difficulty in gaining more than very simple information when they have to rely on reading alone' (Bald 1987: 47).

While it is easy to identify the main categories of buyers of information books, it is difficult to estimate the size of the market. Guidelines from The Library Association (Kinnell 1992: 42–43) suggest that thirteen items of stock per pupil is the minimum number required to meet current needs, and the implication of the calculation is that about 80 per cent of stock would be subject-related. The IFLA standard for children's libraries is three books per child. Usually fiction outnumbers non-fiction in such libraries, but the most recent Library Association guidelines give no specific recommendation on this point (Library Association, 1991: 24–26). Total expenditure on stock for children's libraries and School Library Services (which act as local support services to individual schools) can be tracked from annual surveys by the Library and Information Statistics Unit at Loughborough University. These originally covered England and Wales only, but have now been extended to cover the whole of Britain (Fossey *et al.* 1992). However, these figures do not show the proportion of funds being spent on non-fiction, and can, therefore, principally serve as a basis for estimates of expenditure on information books.

## The Publishing Context

As teaching by the textbook became enriched by an emphasis on children finding out facts for themselves from a variety of sources, so the demand for information books grew. One saw, in Britain, the success of publishers such as Watts and Wayland who virtually confined their lists to non-fiction and others, such as A. and C. Black, who relied heavily on their non-fiction lists to support other aspects of children's literature. This emphasis on an active role for learners grew throughout the 1960s: linked with it during the 1970s and 1980s was the information skills movement which sought to develop children's information-handling skills. Publishers consequently worked hard to design books which made information retrieval easy and which involved greater reader-participation, stimulating children to start their own lines of enquiry and observation.

The educational demand was fed by increased production, partly managed by the growth of series publishing. This enabled an economy in design and in marketing as books were issued in series with a common theme or readership, a common price, a common editor and common design features. The system made (and makes) selection and selling easier, as customers build up loyalty to a series. The disadvantages in terms of quality and individuality have been well-documented, for example in Ralph Lavender's article 'The fatal lure of the series' (Lavender 1979: 30), but the economic advantages to publishers are so considerable that series publishing is likely to continue for the foreseeable future.

Improvements in printing technology have enabled publishers to consider increasingly the international rather than national market, and, to a certain extent, this has reduced the range of subject coverage to those suitable for global use. More recently, recession has brought constraints in institutional book budgets. In these circumstances, the information book market remained relatively buoyant as schools trimmed down purchases of fiction in favour of the non-fiction which supported school work.

A new factor in the market for much of Britain has been the introduction of a national curriculum, but changes in its content leave publishers particularly vulnerable, with the strong possibility of having titles out of date almost as soon as published. Information books have a short backlist life in any case, with three years regarded as a reasonable lifespan, but the situation today is even less secure.

## The Critical Context

Although the criticism of children's literature in general has expanded over the last few decades, criticism of children's information books is in a relatively primitive state, and they are rarely considered. Surveys such as *The Year's Work in Children's Literature Studies* tend to include little material on non-fiction for children. Perhaps because its form is often closer to that of the story, biography seems to be the area where children's literature critics are most comfortable. The Carnegie Medal, awarded by the British Library Association, has been presented for only four non-fiction books since 1936; similarly the choice of *Abraham Lincoln: A Photobiography* for the American 1988 Newbery award was an exception. The lack of an agreed critical approach to non-fiction is exemplified in a report from the Kate Greenaway Medal judges for 1993 on the one non-fiction title short-listed.

> Stephen Biesty's work caused lively disagreement. Some of the panel were full of praise, others dismissed it as technical graphics, and not comparable to others in this category, but eventually it was voted on to the shortlist.
>
> Spencer 1993: 350

The major review journals in the children's literature field reserve most of their space to works of the imagination. For Britain, the most consistent attention is given in the journals *Books for Keeps* and *School Librarian*; overall, non-fiction is 'noticed' rather than critically reviewed, and suffers from being produced in quantity but receiving little critical attention. *Ways of Knowing* (Heeks 1982) was an attempt to record some works of quality as well as provide the basis for book assessment workshops: in *Matters of Fact* of a decade earlier, Margery Fisher offered a commentary built around ten subject lists in the expectation that her critical technique could then be applied to other subject areas (Fisher 1972).

While criticism of non-fiction books themselves is sketchy, the knowledge of the non-fiction reader is another missing area. This category of children's literature lacks the illumination which has come for children's fiction from such works as *The Implied Reader* (Iser 1975). A brief attempt to relate Iser's work to the information book field was made in a 1977 article for *The Times Educational Supplement* (Heeks 1977: 18).

# Trends

The most obvious change in information books during the past forty years has been the increase in importance of illustrations. A generation accustomed to taking in the visual images of television expects a similar approach in its books. This is as apparent in the 'coffee-table' books for adults as in the highly illustrated books for children. This has brought a shift in the respective roles of text and illustration. In the past, pictures supplemented the explanations given in the text. Now, in many cases, the text seems largely an appendage, a device for connecting the illustrations. Colour work of high quality is now available at a relatively modest cost, and information books have become visually exciting as exemplified in the productions of Dorling Kindersley.

At one stage the colour photograph had become a cliché, especially when text had to be skewed to fit the findings of picture researchers. There are now, though, signs of more variety of illustration. There is a continuing tradition of the factual picture book. One can trace a line from Père Castor's picture books of the 1930s, via the post-war Puffin picture books to the 1970s/1980s work of artists such as Aliki, Anno and Juliette Palmer and thence the 1993 offerings from Walker Books, the Read and Wonder series. These factual books are written by established picture book authors, and then given to illustrators used to the rhythm and freedom of stories.

Other publishers, for example Macdonald, have built on the tradition of bringing fact and fiction together in one subject book, a form which has had a long – and chequered – history. The factual framework restricts the story, while the fictional form makes information retrieval difficult. The search for more variety has led to criticism of 'the tyranny of the double-page spread', which breaks up the organic shape of the book and tends to lead to a crowded page opening, oppressive to the reader. In 1983 Geoff Fox suggested that the form seemed to be 'nearing abolition' (23), but it is significant that nearly a decade passed before Oxford University Press began publishing its Young Oxford Books, deliberately organised in chapters rather than double-page spreads.

The economics of publishing is making publishers much more cautious, and has even led to what appear to be sponsorship deals, for example, a book on car building featuring the work of one particular car manufacturer, and so, indirectly, serving as an advertisement for that company. Following the stages of one product in one factory gives an immediacy to the text, but is bound to raise questions on the appropriateness of this approach.

Just as the earliest information books sought to make facts palatable, so publishers today seek to arouse children's curiosity by a range of devices. There is less evidence that publishers have succeeded in judging how children will make information their own, and find space within the text to add their own observations and reflections. In essence, we are not yet clear whether information books are in the business of presenting facts or communicating with readers.

# References

Bald, J. (1987) 'Days of reckoning', *The Times Educational Supplement* 20 March: 47.

Davies, M. (1991) 'Words apart', *The Times Educational Supplement* 19 July: 18.

Department of Education and Science (1975) *A Language for Life* (The Bullock Report), London: HMSO.

Department of Education and Science, Assessment of Performance Unit (1983) *Language Performance in Schools: Secondary Survey Report No. 2*, London: HMSO.

Fisher, M. (1972) *Matters of Fact*, Leicester: Brockhampton Press.

Fossey, D. R., Marriott, R. and Sumsion, J. (1992) *A Survey of Library Services to Schools and Children in the UK, 1991–1992*, Loughborough: Loughborough University, Library and Information Statistics Unit.

Fox, G. (1983) 'Welcome idiosyncrasies', *The Times Educational Supplement* 11 November: 23.

Haigh, G. (1981) 'Workmanlike means dull', *The Times Educational Supplement* 6 November: 22.

Heeks, P. (1977) 'Scavenging across the border', *The Times Educational Supplement* 21 October: 18.

—— (1982) *Ways of Knowing*, South Woodchester: Thimble Press.

—— (1985) 'Being told and finding out', *The Times Educational Supplement* 4 November: 60.

Iser, W. (1975) *The Implied Reader*, New York: Johns Hopkins University Press.

Jenkinson, A. J. (1940) *What Do Boys and Girls Read?*, London: Methuen.

Kinnell, M. (ed.) (1992) *Learning Resources in Schools: Library Association Guidelines for School Libraries*, London: Library Association Publishing.

Lavender, R. (1979) 'The fatal lure of the series', *The Times Educational Supplement* 16 November: 30.

Library Association (1991) *Children and Young People: Library Association Guidelines for Public Library Services*, London: Library Association Publishing.

Sloane, W. (1953) *English Children's Books in England and America in the Seventeenth Century*, New York: King's Crown Press.

Southgate, V., Arnold, H. and Johnson, S. (1981) *Extending Beginning Reading*, London: Heinemann Educational.

Spencer, J. (1993) 'Harder choice from longer Carnegie/Greenaway Lists', *Library Association Record* 95, 6: 350.

Whitehead, F., Capey, A. C. and Maddren, W. (1975) *Children's Reading Interests*, London: Evans/Methuen Educational.

# 37

# Children's Magazines

*Marianne Carus*

## Introduction

According to a recent survey, 48 million children (ages 2–17) in the USA and Canada read magazines. Of course, children would not just read the quality magazines described in this article, but also comics and other mass magazines, and also religious and school periodicals, none of which are discussed here. Still, an amazing 75 per cent of all children in the USA and Canada read periodicals. There is no doubt that children's magazines, with their immense variety of content, seem to be the one form of reading best suited for our fast-paced times. The word 'magazine', derived from the Arabic *makhazin*, literally means 'a storehouse for various goods' – a great selection of different literary genres, fiction, non-fiction, fantasy, poetry, activities, puzzles, crafts, illustrations, and photographs. The relatively short selections, the lively variety of subject matter and format attract children to reading, children who have many different interests and tastes, and who may shy away from reading longer and more forbidding books.

The variety of reading levels in most magazines suits different age groups of readers. Beautiful illustrations and/or colour photographs make magazines attractive even to reluctant or non-readers. Indeed, magazines are the best vehicles of introducing children to the worlds of literature and art, nature, science and history, and for helping a great majority of children develop into enthusiastic, lifelong readers. Magazines are bridges to books, bridges to literacy.

Textbooks and other books that inform and teach cannot cope with the speed of changes and developments in today's technology and all other sciences. Magazines can publish the latest discoveries in their pages, and explain them in the context of existing research.

Another important role magazines play for children everywhere is that they build a community of readers. Children who read magazines are in touch with the world as well as with each other and with the editors of their magazines. Most children's periodicals publish and answer their readers' letters and encourage a constant stream of feedback from their audience. Because of this interaction with children, this close reader–editor relationship, magazines are never fixed or static. They are 'alive', ready for change, expansion, dialogue, communication, and adjustment to their readers' wishes. And because of this intimate relationship with their audience, magazine editors have valuable data about the interests, tastes, and preferences of today's children. Therefore, periodicals can play an important role in shaping the way societies look at and interact with their youngest members.

Most children's magazines also provide a vital creative outlet for their young readers – a chance for children to explore the world of the arts firsthand. A great majority of children's magazines sponsor creative writing, drawing, or other contests and encourage children's efforts by publishing the prize-winning contributions. Such contests provide many children with their only chance of exercising and developing their natural writing or other artistic abilities.

Young authors and illustrators regard their work for children's magazines as an important part of their creative development, and many already established authors and artists welcome periodicals as a way to showcase their work for thousands and often millions of children.

The 1990 exhibit of quality children's periodicals from all over the world on the occasion of the 22nd IBBY (International Board on Books for Young People) Congress in Williamsburg, Virginia, USA, was the first of its kind in the history of children's literature. Organised by *Cricket* magazine, the exhibit consisted of 280 magazines from fifty-five nations, an excellent and solid international representation. The great variety of quality children's magazines collected for the exhibit, and the diversity of editorial goals and missions showed only too clearly what an important part children's periodicals have played and are still playing in each country's history of children's literature – a part just as important as the development of children's book publishing.

The best contemporary magazines keep an important balance between education, information, and entertainment. A magazine has to be fun and offer features that excite children's interest immediately. However, if there is *just* entertainment and no stories or articles of literary substance, magazines become throwaways like comic books. Unfortunately after the Second World War many countries throughout the world were flooded with American and French comics. Many literary magazines that had flourished in these countries ceased publication with the advent of these strip features. The Second World War and other wars and revolutions had other far-reaching effects on the development of children's magazines, often changing ownership, editorial mission, and content.

The number of children's magazines is steadily growing despite great economic difficulties all over the world, and quality magazines everywhere have become powerful tools in starting young people on an inspiring and most rewarding lifetime of reading.

# Europe

## *Austria*

Most of the Austrian quality children's magazines are membership or club magazines. They are *Freundschaft* [*Friendship*], *Jungösterreich* [*Young Austria*], *Kleines Volk* [*Little People*], *Panda Club*, and *Spatzenpost* [*Sparrow Post*]. These magazines are widely used in schools.

Then there are independent magazines like *Topic* (11–16) with stories about politics, social and cultural affairs, science, and the environment, and general-interest magazines with a religious focus like *Weite Welt [Wide World]* (8–14). *Das Knickerbocker-Bandenblatt*, started in 1993, entertains 8 to 12-year-olds with detective stories, science fiction, and adventure.

Several magazines, published by banks and regularly given away to customers, have become quite popular and threaten the existence of commercially produced children's magazines.

### Belgium

A quality, general-interest, cultural education magazine in Belgium is *TOP* (12–15). It is written in Dutch and was started in 1973.

### Bulgaria

The magazine *Slaveiche* (3–8), founded in the early 1900s, was not regularly issued until 1957. Its focus is literature and art, and the prominent Bulgarian poet Petko R. Slaveyko is considered to be the magazine's godfather.

*Kartinna Galerija [Art Gallery]* was founded in 1925 and is still broadening 10 to 14-year-olds' knowledge of art and literature.

### Byelorussia

*Vyasyolka* (5–10) is a general-interest magazine that publishes the best works of Byelorussian writers and those of neighbouring republics. Children's letters are included.

### Czech and Slovak Republics

Even before the fall of the totalitarian socialist regime and Czechoslovakia's split into the Czech and Slovak Republics, children's magazines were published in both the Czech and Slovak languages and even in Polish, Ukrainian, and Hungarian for children of ethnic minorities in the border regions of the country. Several magazines have long traditions and have survived all changes, even though the number of issues printed has rapidly decreased. This is not caused by a lessening of their high standards (on the contrary, they have more colour, better paper, more variety of content), but by a rise in prices and an increase in imported mass magazines, mainly cartoons and comics. In the Czech language there are *Sluníčko [Little Sun]*, founded in 1967 for children under 6; *Mateřídouška [Thyme]* (6–8), founded by the Czech poet Frantisek Hrubín in 1945; and *Ohníček [Bonfire]*, which has been entertaining 9 to 11-year-olds for forty-five years. They all publish poems, good stories, fantasy, fairytales, competitions and children's drawings.

*ABC Mladých Techniküa Přírodovědcu [ABC for Young Technicians and Natural Scientists]* (10–15) has been published for thirty-seven years and is very popular. *Studio Pastelka [Studio Crayon]* is a new, clever and imaginative magazine for pre-school children and their parents.

The Slovak periodicals are *Vcielka [Little Bee]* for the youngest age group,

*Zornička* [*Morning Star*] (7–9), and *Ohník* [*The Little Fire*] (9–11). They are all general-interest magazines. *Slniečko* [*Little Sun*] (7–12), a literary magazine, was founded in 1927.

Children's magazines in the Czech and Slovak Republics are illustrated by the best artists, and many of them consider their work for magazines an important part of their artistic development.

### Denmark

The Danish *Krible Krable* (9–13) started in 1989 and was inspired by the American literary magazine *Cricket*.

### Estonia

*Noorus* (14–18) is a general-interest magazine, as is *Täheka* [*Star*] (6–10), which also publishes children's letters and contributions. *Trukitahed* [*Print*] (12–14) publishes literature and illustrations created by students. All three magazines are written in Estonian.

### Finland

Finland has several quality magazines for children of all ages. *JP* (10–14) started publication in 1938 as a boys' magazine, but is now written for both boys and girls. *Koululainen* (7–15) and *Nuorten Sarka* (8–17) are both over fifty years old. The latter is a science, nature, crafts and music magazine with children's contributions and letters. *Leppis* [*Ladybird*] (4–9) started publication in 1987. It now licenses many features from the French Bayard magazines.

### France

For almost 200 years, French children's magazines have been a part of French family life and have played an important role in the development of French children's literature. Many of the great French authors of the last century were first published in magazines, for example, la Comtesse de Sègur, Jules Verne, and Jean Macé, who was a pioneer in making science plausible for children. Today there are approximately 135 magazines for children from 2 to 18 years. Several quality magazines are published by Bayard Presse; for example, *Pomme d'Api* [*Small Apple*] (3–7), was started in 1966 as the first French magazine for children under 7 years of age. It is a general-interest magazine, as is *Astrapi* (7–11). *Popi* (18 months–3 years) wants to help very young children develop visual and language skills with simple stories, pictures, and games. *Les Belles Histoires* [*Beautiful Stories*] (3–7) publishes quality literature, as does *J'Aime Lire* [*I Love to Read*] (7–10), which encourages beginning readers and includes children's contributions. *Je Bouquine* [*I Read*] (10–14) has good literature and book and film reviews. *Okapi* (10–15) and *Images Doc* (8–12) focus more on non-fiction, geography, history, science and sports.

*Wapiti* (7–12) and *Wakou* (3–7), published by Le Groupe Milan, are quality journals about animals and nature. *Diablo* (7–9) and *Mikado* (9–12), also from Le Groupe Milan, include science, history, sports, and activities. *Toupi* [*Spinning Top*] is for 2 to 4-year-olds.

### Germany

By far the most sophisticated magazine in Germany today is *Der Bunte Hund* [*The Motley Dog*] (6–16). It introduces contemporary, young, and established authors and illustrators and discovers important new ones. The other magazines are *Stafette* [*Horse Messenger*], *Bimbo*, and *Floh* [*Flea*] (10–15), which is the oldest still-existing youth magazine. It was founded in 1875 and used to be called *Jugendlust*. *Flohkiste* [*Fleabag*] (two editions: 6–7 and 8–9) originated from the same magazine. Both are used in schools. *Geschichte mit Pfiff* [*History with Pizzazz*] (10+) focuses on the history of mankind through the ages and is very popular in schools. Then there are *Mücke* [*Mosquito*] (8–11) and *Mücki* [*Little Mosquito*] (6–8). Surviving magazines from the former DDR are *Benjamin*, *Bummi*, *ABC Zeitung* [*ABC Paper*], and *Mosaik*.

### Great Britain: England

The children's magazine situation in England at present is very disappointing, especially in view of Great Britain's long and venerable history in children's literature. In the late nineteenth and early twentieth centuries, many quality magazines were published, such as *Chatterbox* and *Aunt Judy's Magazine*. Famous contributors included Lewis Carroll, George Cruikshank, Randolph Caldecott and of course Juliana Horatio Ewing. A. A. Milne was an enthusiastic reader of *Aunt Judy's Magazine*. Also published were *Good Words for the Young*, with which George MacDonald was closely associated, and later the *Young Elizabethan* and *Puffin Post*.

Puffin Post (9–13), founded by Kaye Webb in 1963 as the magazine for the Puffin Club, includes stories, articles, and illustrations by some of England's best writers and illustrators. *Puffin Flight* replaced the Junior Puffin Club magazine *The Egg* in 1987. It is for 5 to 8-year-olds and is based on Puffin paperbacks. Both Puffin magazines are now available only through schools and the Puffin Book Club. *Play and Learn*, 'the monthly discovery magazine', is highly educational and claims to keep children informed about the world around them in a thoroughly entertaining way.

### Great Britain: Wales

*Sbondonics* (7–11), published by the Welsh Books Council, is written in Welsh. It has book reviews, puzzles, a cartoon strip, and children's contributions and letters.

### Greece

In the latter part of the nineteenth century many children's magazines flourished in Greece. The most successful and lasting one was *I Diaplasis Ton Pedon* [*Children's Formation*] which survived for seventy-eight years until 1957. It was considered a bridge between Greek and foreign juvenile literature, and Greek authors declared that their careers began with contributing to this magazine. Several quality magazines, published at the turn of the century, died after the Second World War because of the invasion of American and French comics. In 1977, the literary magazine *To Rodi* [*The Pomegranate*] (9–13) was started. It died in 1982 but was started again in 1993. Another magazine that started in 1979, gave up in 1983, and started again in 1990, is *Synergasia* [*Co-operation*] (9–13). It promotes Greek children's literature and an awareness of the environment.

### Iceland

The Icelandic magazine *Aeskan* [*Youth*] (6–15) has been published continuously since 1897. It promotes education and a healthy lifestyle. *ABC* (6–15) is a general-interest magazine and includes children's contributions and letters.

### Italy

*Il Giornalino* [*The Little Journal*] (7–14), a general-interest magazine, was created in 1924. *Giovani Amici* [*Young Friends*], founded in 1934, features fairy tales, stories, and games, and has children's letters and contributions. Both *La Rana* [*The Frog*] (6–13) and *Panda* (published by the World Wildlife Federation) concentrate on nature and environmental issues. *Primavera* [*Spring*], for teens, tries to help young people understand current events, each others' feelings, their professional development, and use of free time. The European Language Institute (ELI) publishes specific magazines for students learning English, French, German, Spanish, Italian, Russian and Latin, in four levels of difficulty. The same institute publishes *Cronos*, a history magazine. A new Italian general-interest magazine is *Peter Pan* (8–14).

### Lithuania

*Genys* [*Woodpecker*] (6–12) and *Zvaigzdute* [*Little Star*] are general-interest magazines. Magazines published after 1991 are *Aha* and *Zaliasis Laikrastis* [*Green Magazine*] (8–12), which emphasises nature and the environment. Three new magazines began publication in 1994: *Naminukas*, *Penvi* [*Five*], *Vaikai Vanagai* [*Children-Hawks*] (6–12). All of them are general-interest magazines.

### Malta

There are two general-interest magazines in Malta: *Taghna T-tfal* [*Children's Own*] (5–10), written in Maltese; and *Young Falcon* (7–13), which is the only English-language magazine in Malta.

## The Netherlands

In Holland, just as in many other countries in Europe, many children's magazines flourished in the 1800s. At the turn of the century, every denomination had its own periodical. But after the Second World War, all of Europe, including Holland, was flooded with comics from the USA and from France. Still today, mass-market magazines and comics have the largest share of the children's magazine market in Holland. However, two quality magazines have survived since their founding in 1919: *Okki* (7–8) and *Taptoe* (8–12). Both are general-interest magazines. For pre-schoolers there is *Bobo*, which publishes contributions by well-known authors and illustrators.

A brand-new venture started in 1993, *MikMak* is a literary magazine for ages 8 to 12, which publishes famous authors and artists.

*Fryske Bernekrante* (8–12) is available in the Frisian language spoken by 35,000 people in the northern region of The Netherlands.

## Norway

The only Norwegian children's magazine independent from special organisations is *Norsk Barneblad* (8–13). It was founded in 1887 and still publishes literature, science and nature articles, music, news, and children's letters and contributions.

## Poland

Most former eastern-bloc countries are struggling to save publications that were formerly published and supported by the Communist government and are now privately owned. It remains to be seen in the next few years how many will be able to survive. The two main periodicals in Poland are *Mis* [*Teddy Bear*] (3–7), founded in 1957, and *Swiat Mlodych* (11–15), founded in 1949. The latter also publishes a monthly edition for children of Polish origin living abroad. Both are general-interest magazines.

## Spain

At present, most of the quality children's magazines in Spain are published in collaboration with French publishers, especially Bayard Presse. *Caracola* [*Snail*] (4–7) is a Spanish version of the French *Pomme d'Api*, some of whose pages are created in Spain. *Reportero Doc* is a Spanish version of Bayard's *Images Doc*, and *Gente Ce* a version of Bayard's *Okapi*. *Camacuc* (6–14) and *Cavall Fort* (10–15) are general-interest magazines in the Catalan language. *Ipurbeltz* (8–11) is written in Basque to provide Basque literature for children.

## Sweden

Even though there were children's periodicals in Sweden as early as 1766, the golden age of children's magazines in Scandinavia was the period from 1870–1915.

Many were religious, many educational, some advocated the protection of animals, temperance or socialism. *Lyckoslanten* [*The Good Luck Penny*] (5–14) was founded in 1925 by a savings-bank director in order to promote thrift among school children. *Folkskolans Barntidning* [*The Elementary Schoolchild's Magazine*], founded in 1892, successfully adjusted to modern times and is still published today – since 1950 under the name of *Kamratposten* [*The Pal Paper*] (8–14). It is a general-interest periodical. For horse-loving teenagers there is *Min Häst* (6–16) and, for all animal lovers, *Zoo* (6–12).

### Switzerland

An interesting survey made by the Swiss Institute of Children's Literature in 1980 established that only twenty-four of the 115 most read periodicals were actually published in Switzerland: of these, eleven were in German, eight in French, three in Italian, and two in Romansh. The two most important German-language Swiss magazines, *Schweizer Jugend* [*Swiss Youth*] (10–16) and *Spick* (9–14), have excellent content and graphics. *Le Petit Ami des Animaux* [*The Little Friend of Animals*] was founded in 1918 and has been published in French continuously since that time. Its focus is on pet care and animals.

*Yakari* (6–10), thirty years old, is published simultaneously in French and German (literature, fantasy, science, crafts), and *Chabottin* in French, German, and Italian. *L'Aviöl* (7–15), began publication in 1919. It is a general-interest magazine written in Romansh.

### Ukraine

*Barvinok* (6–10), written in Ukrainian, teaches readers about Ukrainian history, traditions, and folk literature. Children's contributions and letters are included.

### Former Yugoslavia

There are several Slovene-language youth periodicals in Yugoslavia published in Ljubljana. *Ciciban*, almost fifty years old, *Kuriček* [*The Little Messenger*] (8–12), a literary magazine, *Pionir* for teenagers, first published in 1945, and *PIL-Pionirski List* (7–15), a general-interest magazine. *Pionieri* (8–13) was founded in 1939 to foster the language of the Slovak minority in Yugoslavia.

# North America

### Canada

The first Canadian magazine, *The Snow Drop*, was launched in 1847 and ceased publication in 1853. Since then, more than seventy Canadian children's periodicals, some in English, some in French, have come and gone. *Pik* was published in Inuktitut by the government of the Northwest Territories from 1972–1985. In 1976 *Owl*, an environmental magazine (7–12), was launched, and in 1979 *Owl's* junior version, *Chickadee* (3–9), was founded. Both magazines have licensed editions in Quebec: *Hibou* and *Coulicou*. Their focus is on nature and science, and they aim to inspire involvement and enquiry in their young readers. Other French-language Canadian magazines are *Vidéo-Presse*, a general-interest magazine for early teens, and *Je Me Petit-Débrouille* (7–14) with a focus on science experiments, computers, games, and puzzles. *Chalk Talk* (5–14) and *Rain Coast* are published in British Columbia.

## United States

The longest-lived of all USA children's periodicals, *The Youth's Companion*, was published from 1827 to 1929. Many other American children's magazines were published in the nineteenth and early twentieth centuries, but the most esteemed and most loved of all was *St Nicholas*, published by Scribner's Monthly from 1873–1940, and edited by Mary Mapes Dodge from 1873–1905. She was committed to publishing only the best in literature and illustration for children. Among the contributors to *St Nicholas* were Rudyard Kipling, Louisa May Alcott, Frank R. Stockton, Mark Twain, Howard Pyle, Palmer Cox, and many other luminaries.

Today several hundreds of magazines are published in the USA. Many are short-lived, and several new ones appear every year. A few endure. The oldest is *Boys' Life*, which was founded in 1911 by the Boy Scouts of America. It is still published today for 7 to 17-year-old Cub or Boy Scouts, and its mission is to bring good reading to all boys and to support the principles of Scouting. It publishes children's contributions and letters.

The publishers Scholastic produce a long line of classroom periodicals for all age groups.

*Highlights for Children* (2–12) was founded in 1946. It is an educational general-interest magazine and publishes original children's contributions and letters.

The Children's Better Health Institute publishes six general-interest magazines for ages 2 to pre-teen: *Turtle, Humpty Dumpty, Children's Playmate, Jack and Jill, Child Life, Children's Digest,* and *US Kids*. Several of these titles were founded by other publishers but were taken over by the Children's Better Health Institute and now emphasise education about good health. The Children's Television Workshop publishes *Sesame Street* (2–6), *Kid City* (6–10), and *3-2-1 Contact* (8–14). *Sesame Street, 3-2-1 Contact,* and *Ghostwriter* (7–10) are prepared in conjunction with television programmes for children. The *Sesame Street* television characters appear regularly in the magazine.

Cobblestone Publishing publishes *Cobblestone, Faces, Calliope* (all 9–15), and *Odyssey* (8–14). *Cobblestone* focuses on American history. *Faces, the Magazine About People*, publishes biographies and articles on anthropology. *Calliope* includes articles on world history and Western and Eastern civilisations. *Odyssey* is about space and astronomy. It publishes children's contributions and letters.

The National Wildlife Foundation publishes two magazines: *Ranger Rick* (6–12), founded in 1967, and *Your Big Backyard* (3–5). Both magazines want to inspire a greater understanding and appreciation of the natural world.

Carus Publishing Company publishes four magazines. *Babybug* (6 months–2 years) is a board-book magazine for babies. *Ladybug* (2–6) develops young children's imagination and creates in them a love for reading. *Spider* (6–9) offers excellent illustrations and quality literature for beginning readers, and *Cricket* (9–14), now over twenty years old, publishes the best literature from the USA and from all over the world. Original stories and poems by Isaac B. Singer, William Saroyan, Rosemary Sutcliff, James Herriot, Richard Wilbur, John and Roy Fuller, Joan Aiken, and Lloyd Alexander have appeared in its pages. *Cricket* introduces all genres: fiction, fantasy, non-fiction, science, nature, history, poetry, and translations of original stories from foreign languages. The Cricket League, with children's competitions in poetry, essays, drawing, and photography, was inspired by the St Nicholas League. Children's letters and League contributions are published in *Spider* and *Cricket*.

There are several relatively new magazines just for girls: *Hopscotch, the Magazine for Young Girls* (6–12) is a general-interest magazine. *New Moon Magazine* (8–14) is edited by 8 to 14-year-olds and has a sixteen-page newsletter for parents. *American Girl* (7+) features characters from the Pleasant Company doll collection. It is a general-interest magazine with activities and children's letters.

Several adult magazines in the USA have started publications of children's magazines in their particular fields. There is *Sports Illustrated for Kids* (8–13) with emphasis on all kinds of sports. *National Geographic World* (8–14) has photo essays on geography, nature, and social sciences, with children's contributions and letters. *Zillions* (8–14), published by the Consumer's Union, is a junior consumer education magazine which also publishes children's letters. *Field & Stream, Jr.* (9–12) passes on the hunting and fishing traditions to boys and girls, and *Outside Kids* (8–14) informs about camping and outdoor life. *Crayola Kids Magazine* (3–8) emphasises crafts, colouring, drawing, and other creative activities.

*YSB*, an acronym for *Young Sisters and Brothers* (11–18) is an entertaining and informative periodical for African-American teens. *Skipping Stones* (7–14) is a multicultural, multilingual environmentally aware quarterly.

There are several magazines that only publish children's creative efforts. The best of these are: *Stone Soup* (6–13), which publishes fiction, poetry, book reviews, and art by children; *Merlyn's Pen: The National Magazine of Student Writing* (12–16); and *Merlyn's Pen Senior Edition* (15–18). The last two publish fiction written by teens in the USA, and every contributor receives a response from an editor within ten weeks.

## Russia

The news about children's magazines in Russia is not good; new magazines are short-lived. The situation can be traced directly to the internal economic and political instability of the country. Many publishing houses that previously led a carefree existence because of state subsidies have gone bankrupt. There are very few publishers that have survived or found foreign sponsors.

*Murzilka* (6–11), one of the oldest magazines in Russia, was founded in 1924. A general-interest magazine with emphasis on literature, it publishes classical and contemporary Russian and foreign literary works, history, science, sports articles, children's competitions, and letters. *Kolobok* (3–9) is a general-interest magazine with songs and children's contributions and letters. *Druzhba* [*Friendship*] (7–18) is a general-interest magazine and has children's contributions and letters. *Kostyor* [*Bonfire*] (9–13), another general-interest magazine, includes children's contributions and letters. *Vesyoliye Kartinki* [*Merry Pictures*] (3–7) is a general-interest magazine with emphasis on Russian and foreign contemporary authors and Russian folk-tales. *Yuni Khudozhnik* [*Young Artist*] (10+) emphasizes art and photographs and publishes children's letters. *Yuni Naturalist* [*Young Naturalist*] (10–16) began publication in 1928 and was the first children's magazine in the former USSR devoted entirely to ecological education and the history of life on earth. Children's contributions and letters are included. *Vokrug Sveta* [*Around the World*] (11+) publishes stories and articles about travels and adventures. *Yuni Tekhnik* [*Young Scientist*] (11–17) emphasises science, astronomy and science fiction. It publishes children's contributions and letters.

## Africa

In Africa the high cost of publishing, especially of production and printing, caused by the need to import most of the production equipment, printing presses and materials, has resulted in the demise of many children's periodicals throughout the years. New magazines are appearing all the time, but their life spans are usually quite short.

In Botswana, *Moso*, a general-interest magazine, publishes children's contributions and competitions. *Ngouvou* [*Hippopotamus*] (8–16) is the only children's magazine in Congo. It is a general-interest magazine with children's contributions and letters. In Egypt, the general-interest magazine *Sadouk El Donia* (10–14) is written in Arabic and publishes children's contributions and letters. The two magazines in Ghana are *Playpen* (7–14) and *The Child* (5–16). *Playpen* concentrates on education and also publishes children's contributions, whereas *The Child* publishes all original stories and illustrations. In Kenya *Rainbow* (10–16) was started in 1976 to provide English-language material for children. It now contains only material from local authors and illustrators. Nigeria has three magazines: *Asha* (12–17) is a general-interest magazine with children's contributions and letters; *The Junior Group Magazine* (6–16) encourages children's contributions and is also a general-interest magazine. *Binta* (8–18), a general-interest magazine, was founded two years ago.

In December 1993, Jacqueline Kergueno of Bayard Presse, France, founded a French-language magazine called *Planet Jeunes* (12–18). Many contributing authors and artists are French-speaking Africans. *Planet Jeunes* is distributed in all French-speaking African countries.

In South Africa, the best general-interest magazines for young readers are *T-Mag* (for teens) and *Junior Bob*. *T-Mag* has articles in English and in Afrikaans. *Junior Bob* (8–12) is always built around a theme. There are separate English and Afrikaans editions, using the same artwork. *Toktokkie* (7–13), excellently produced, focusing on wildlife, also has separate English and Afrikaans editions. *Skipper* (6–17), with articles in both languages, concentrates on the environment and wildlife. *Youngtime* (6–14) encourages children to read, learn, and think, and includes children's contributions. Four new South African children's magazines are *Bright Owls*, *In Touch*, *Kids*, and *Learn and Teach*.

In Tanzania, *Malihai* (15+) is published twice a year. It focuses on nature and environmental education, and accepts readers' contributions and letters, while in Zimbabwe, *Action* (8–16) is an environmental health magazine.

## The Middle East

The most significant change in children's and youth magazines in Iran occurred after the Islamic revolution in 1979. Before, most articles published in magazines were translations from foreign magazines. Comic strips were prevalent. After the revolution, only works by Iranian authors, poets and illustrators were published, including realistic short stories about the life of Iranian children, written by young Iranian authors. This totally changed the entire children's literature of this period. The appearance of realistic stories and novels is one of its important aspects. Another is the high quality of Iran's science, technology, and mathematics magazines for teens, especially compared to the magazines in Western countries, including the United States, where teen periodicals are much more frivolous and superficial, discussing fashion, makeup, dating, and pop culture.

*Keyhan Elmi Baraye Nowjavanan* [*Scientific Keyhan for Young People*] (13–17) and *Fonoun* [*Technology*] (9–16) acquaint young people with the scientific method, presenting articles on science, technology, the environment, and social sciences. *Kavosh* (12–17) introduces the applied sciences. *Ayesh*'s (12–17) mission is to help develop creativity in aspiring young poets, writers, and artists. The *Roshd* magazines, all with general-interest content, are graded according to school-age children. Many magazines in Iran are supported by foundations, the Ministry of Education, or the Institute for the Intellectual Development of Children and Young Adults.

One magazine, *Kushesh*, was founded in 1988 by the Hobbies and Toys Center in Tehran and focuses on art, crafts, puzzles, etc. Between 1991 and 1994, four new quality magazines appeared in Iran. They are all general-interest magazines: *Soroush Koudakan*, *Umid Ayandeh* [*Hope of the Future*], *Soureh Nowjavanan*, and *Salam Bacheda* [*Hello Children*].

In contrast, the only magazine available at present in Iraq is the government owned general-interest magazine, *Majalati* (5–14).

The quality magazines in Israel are *Kulanu* (8–12), *Kulanu Alef Bet* (6–8), and *Pilon*. They are general-interest magazines.

In Syria, the Ministry of Culture founded the magazine *Ousama* (for boys 9–12), also of general interest.

A new magazine in Turkey is *Kirmizifare* [*The Red Mouse*] (8–12). It provides quality literature and illustrations. Two older general-interest magazines are *Dogan Kardes* (9–14) and *Bando* (7–14).

*Majed* (6–16) is a general-interest quality magazine published in United Arab Emirates and available in most Arab countries.

# Asia

## China

Most children's magazines in China are government owned. *Children's Literature Monthly* (10–16), now over thirty years old, is the nation's most influential and authoritative literary magazine. The stories and articles in it are representative of the best in the field and have won many awards and prizes. One of the aims of *CLM* is to discover new Chinese writers, poets, and artists. *CLM* is also the first children's magazine to publish foreign children's literature in translation. *Futurity*, another literary children's magazine, publishes longer stories and short novels. It also pays attention to the international literary scene and offers translations of foreign works. *Orient Juvenile* (10–15) aims at improving children's language and writing skills and raising their level of literary understanding. The magazine publishes fiction, non-fiction, poetry, artwork, fairy tales, and children's contributions.

There are also several magazines for very young children, including *Baby Pictorial* (2–4), *Little Friends* (3–8), which is over sixty years old; and *Baby's Pictorial* (1–3). Science-oriented magazines are *Science Magazine for Juveniles* (10–15), introducing current science news to children; *We Love Science* (10–15), and *Children's Scientific Pictorial* (7–11). A teen magazine, *Teenagers in China and Abroad*, written in English, reaches out to teens in other countries.

## India

The first magazine for children in India, entitled *Digdarshan*, was published in the Bengali language in 1818. It published only twenty-six issues, but was succeeded by another magazine in Bengali called *Balakbandhu*. The Bengali language children's periodicals continue to be the most energetic among all Indian periodicals. Today there are about 300 magazines for children published in all the Indian languages and dialects. There are approximately 200 magazines in Hindi, the best of which are *Nandan* (7–16) and *Chandamama* (9+), with traditional literature and folk-tales. *Parag* and *Balbharti* (both 9+) experiment with contemporary literature and have greater variety. *Champak*, supported by UNESCO, offers mostly articles on science and also includes children's observations of scientific subjects.

The quality magazines in English are *Children's World* (6–16), *Cub*, *Target*, and *Tinkle* (all 8–14). There are also English versions of *Champak* and *Chandamama*. *Cub* publishes articles on wildlife and excellent colour photographs.

There are over 100 million schoolchildren in India between the ages of 6 and 17, a vast readership for so many quality magazines.

## Japan

A famous literary magazine in Japan published from 1918–1936 was *Akaitori* [*Red Bird*], which had outstanding illustrations and quality stories. Fukuinkan shoten publishes three magazines: *Takusan no Fushigi* [*A World of Wonder*] (8–12) is a general-interest magazine; *Kagaku no Tomo* [*Children's Science Companion*] (4–7) has articles on natural science, science, social science, history, geography, and astronomy, and includes children's letters; *Kodomo no Tomo* [*Children's Companion*] (4–7), founded in 1956, has just one literary story with quality illustrations in each issue.

*Kobotachi* (5–12) focuses on environmental education, good quality stories, book reviews, and children's contributions and letters.

Froebel kan publishes two magazines: *Kinda Ohanashi* [*Illustrated Stories for Children*], with quality literature and illustrations, and *Kinda Bukku* [*Nature-kinderbook*], a nature magazine for children.

*Ohisama* [*Sun*] (4+), with a focus on literature, was founded in 1994. *Ohanashi Chairudo* [*Stories for Children*] is also a literary magazine; Child honsha is the publisher. *Gakken Ohanashi Ehon* [*Gakken Illustrated Stories*], published by Gakushukenkyu sha, concentrates on illustrated stories, as does *Kodomo no Sekai* [*World of Children*], published by Shiko-sha since 1947. *Wanda Bukku* [*Wonder Book*] was founded 1968 and is published by Sekaibunka-sha. Its focus is literature. *San Chairudo* [*Sun Child*], published by Child honsha, is a science magazine.

### Korea

*Haksaeng Kwahak* [*Student's Science*] (10–15) concentrates on science, science fiction, astronomy, fantasy, and puzzles, and also publishes children's letters.

### Mongolia

*Zalgamzhlagch* [*The New Generation*] (6–8), a general-interest magazine, was founded in 1926. Two other magazines are *Pioneriin Udirdagch* [*Pioneer Leader*] (9–12), and *Pioneriin Unen* [*Pioneer Truth*] (8–14).

### Singapore

In the last five years, magazine publishing has been flourishing in Singapore, and locally published children's magazines are now providing an alternative to magazines imported from overseas. English is the official language used in schools and administration, but the Singapore government also recognises Chinese, Malay and Tamil as official languages. The literacy rate of 10-year-olds and above was 86.8 per cent in 1987.

*Bookworm Digest* (9–14) and *Funland* (9–13), in English, are general-interest magazines and include children's contributions. *Singapore Scientist*, an adult magazine in English, has a large 'young scientist' section for 10 to 18-year-olds. *Zoo-Ed* (8–13) is another science magazine written in English. *Young Generation* (5–14) is the only bilingual (English/Chinese) general-interest magazine in Singapore, and *Nadim* the only quality magazine in Malay.

*Taiwan*

For the young children in Taiwan there are two general-interest magazines: *Seedling* (3–8) and *Wisdom* (8–12). *The Children's Magazine* (6–12) and *Youth Juvenile Monthly* (12–18) also are general-interest magazines with contributions by children. *Little Newton Magazine* and *Copel Science Magazine* (both 9–15) are science magazines.

*Thailand*

*Chaiyapruk Cartoon* (6–12) was started in 1977. It is a general-interest magazine and includes cartoons and children's contributions.

## Australasia

Four quality magazines published by the New South Wales Department of School Education in Australia are distributed through schools. They are all general-interest magazines with emphasis on literature: *Countdown*, *Blast Off*, *Orbit*, and *Touchdown*. Each title is for a different age group, within the range of 6–14. Other Australian magazines are *Eyespy* (8–12), which presents environmental and natural science to children and also publishes children's contributions and letters. *Puffinalia* (6–16) is based on the Puffin Club that was started by Kaye Webb in Britain in the 1960s.

In Indonesia, *Bintang Kecil* (6–10) is a general-interest magazine.

The Department of Education in Wellington, New Zealand, publishes *School Journal*, an excellent literary magazine for 7 to 13-year-olds. It was founded in 1907 and continues to be used in classrooms. It is published for four different age levels.

## Central and South America

Compared to other areas, there are very few quality children's magazines in Central and South America. In Bolivia there is *Chaski* (6–14), a general-interest magazine, which includes literature, fantasy, and science, and also publishes children's contributions. *Chiquirin* is published in Guatemala. In Uruguay, *El Grillo* [*The Cricket*] (10–12) is a school publication, as are *La Nave Oikos* [*The Ship Oikos*] (9–15) and *Moñita Azul* [*Little Blue Monkey*] (3–12). *Arco Iris* (Rainbow) (8–12) was founded in Venezuela in 1986. It is a general-interest magazine and includes children's letters. In Brazil, the Brazilian Society on the Progress of Science publishes *Ciência Hoje das Crianças* [*Children's Science Today*], for 8 to 12-year-olds.

# Part III

## The Context of Children's Literature

# 38

# Children's Book Design

## *Douglas Martin*

### Historical Introduction

Children's books and toys are grounded in a popular oral and craft tradition but are brought to a wider audience through mass production. Stories may have a long journey from the fireside – and pictures from the kitchen table – before their appearance on the printed page and packaged for the supermarket shelf; and book design is simply an inseparable and enabling part of this process.

Drawing, writing and copying on whatever materials came to hand must have gone on for the instruction and entertainment of children from the earliest times, and, although survivals are understandably scant, it is not hard to reconstruct imaginatively many of the forms this activity must have taken and its links with speech and reading, storytelling and the making of records. Features which interest the designer of children's books appear in abundance in manuscripts and early printed books, long before the first true children's books are to be found.

The theory and practice of book design was better understood within the monastic scriptoria than it is in most modern publishing houses, and the study of that tradition (Alexander 1992) is fast becoming as rewarding and relevant for the designer as the typographic history of the Gutenberg era. Medieval scribes and illuminators undertook an everyday task like 'ruling the page for writing' with a know-how – a geometry become instinctive – that their modern counterparts lack when faced with the same decisions in a desk-top situation. Words and pictures were related to each other and inventive solutions found to functional and decorative questions in manuscripts, with a freedom which is particularly apposite to children's book design.

Recent attention has focused on another fascinating group of publications, the blockbooks (Mertens *et al.* 1991), which are roughly contemporaneous with the invention of printing from moveable type. At their most exuberant they present reading matter through a variety of cartoon frame conventions with all the range and dexterity of Uderzo or Briggs. These little-known blockbooks extend the historic repertoire that stimulates modern designers and illustrators, and which includes such materials as manuscript illuminations and woodcut illustrations, writing manuals and decorated initials, playing cards and broadsheets, pattern papers and gift bindings, printed games and novelty books, signs on buildings and vehicles, packaging and printed ephemera. Encounters with all these colourful and intriguing items in their heyday must have figured large in the child's world, regardless of the prevalent state of literacy; and to the leisure environment of more recent generations. it is only necessary to add those letters, symbols and pictures which are made in light and on the electronic screen.

The *Orbis Pictus* of Comenius (1659) is acknowledged as the forerunner of the modern textbook and of the picture book as well, but it may provide a fresh angle of approach to stress that Comenius's visionary plan as an author could not have been realised without his genius as a book designer. The basis of his layout is that parts of a picture are numerically keyed to two parallel texts (Latin and vernacular) on each opening. Terms correspond across the columns in roman and italic, with other typographic 'voices' assigned to the few essential linking words. Devising pictorial content and composition, planning each topic to fit two facing pages, and writing to length, are additional triumphs of authorship: in twentieth-century terms it is evident that Comenius was working to a tight plan or grid.

Provision was made in the *Orbis Pictus* for all possible modes and speeds of readership and study, in a book which acknowledges no dividing line between learning and enjoyment. This uncommon fusion of design skills resulted in an exemplar for books of its kind for generations to come; and later publishing history is full of similar examples where a successful formula has been widely adapted or imitated. Until recent times an author or publisher of a book which presented visual complexities would have looked naturally to the printer for help; and it is the declining competence of this resource which has seen the rise of the professional designer, just as the practical builder made way for the architect in the design area.

Artists and book illustrators have often worked closely with book printers, but such alliances did most to expand the visual potential of the children's book during the nineteenth century, when the figure of the publisher emerged as a more vigorous entrepreneur as well. Although much has been written about the great Victorian illustrators and their work, such historians as Ruari McLean, in his standard works and in his account of the publisher Joseph Cundall and his circle have provided a fuller context for some of the more elaborate productions of that fertile age. The Home Treasury series, conceived and edited by Henry Cole and published by Cundall, was, in McLean's opinion, outstanding in design terms (McLean 1976: 4–12).

The pioneering American book designer Bruce Rogers wrote about his work with a directness that is still valid and readable today, and he had this to say about the relatively late emergence of typographic design as an occupation:

> It is only within the past two or three decades that the book designer has emerged and established himself as a professional, frequently with his own facilities for carrying out his designs for his clients.

> It is still the practice in many publishing houses and large printing-offices for the elements of a book to be planned and ordered piecemeal by different departments. This is a regrettable procedure which can hardly result in satisfactory book making. The book should always be considered as a whole and all instructions for materials and design should emanate from one desk.
>
> Rogers 1943/1979: 4

Although book design as most modern practitioners would understand it did not gain recognition until the beginning of the twentieth century, there is nevertheless a long history of books without a known designer which can in no sense be regarded as undesigned. Manuscripts and early printing often point to immediate solutions as well as offering a longer-term yardstick. There is a wealth of data on record here about the reading process itself over the centuries, and our eyes have not changed. The same stories and lessons are re-told with greater or lesser sophistication. Conventions concerning the content and structure of the book slowly evolve; some features retain their worth, others become archaic. Standards of raw materials and techniques of manufacture progress and regress. The book remains unique and inimitable, and the designer has a definable role in promoting its culture from childhood onwards.

## The Practice of Book Design

Book design is a behind the scenes activity, employing relatively few in-house or freelance designers at multifarious levels. Designing demands self-motivated expertise, sustained through teamwork involving at least two functions within any publishing house: editorial and production, and – if the work involves the design of jackets and publicity material – with the sales organisation as well. The editorial function entails creative involvement with author and illustrator from the outset, and the production department is responsible for specifying materials and monitoring manufacture. Design may be combined with other tasks in a small firm or with running a studio for a larger organisation, whereas freelance consultants normally work for several publishing houses in different capacities.

The design process starts with an initial reading of the text and a briefing on the publisher's intention for it, from which the experienced designer will sense what work will be necessary to help the book reach and serve its intended public. A high proportion of books published present few complexities or fall naturally into established series, but over-regimented design procedures have been shown to have limited application and success, for each book is different and none so elementary as not to benefit from considered design. At the other extreme a manuscript may need to be extensively re-worked to address its true market, and the designer sometimes has to take the initiative for presenting the author's material visually and thereby transforming it into a marketable product.

Some confusion may arise if the roles of book designer and book illustrator are too closely identified. Designers do not as a rule aspire to imaginative illustration, while illustrators, although appreciative of the contribution good typographic design has to make, are usually thankful to leave it to the specialist. This distinction may help to highlight that precise interface between author and illustrator in which the children's book designer operates: striking a balance between the primacy of language and that of the pictorial image; mediating between those who think and express themselves in words and those who think and create in a visual language. This elusive goal is well stated as the purpose of the Emil/Kurt Maschler Award which is given 'for a work of imagination for children in which text and illustration are integrated so that each enhances yet balances the other'.

## Reading and Typography

Typographic design is an activity which most readers would prefer not to have to define, since it involves asking what makes the printed page actually work for themselves. The process of becoming literate progressively relegates the mechanics of typography to the subconscious, and the only reason for delving into it here is to reveal how relatively straightforward it is for the designer to 'lay down a trail' which will be followed unerringly through reading and reference. Robert Escarpit offers a philosophical synthesis which supports a designer's view of these matters, but there is space here for only one key passage from his extended argument: 'Reading reactivates the sound content as well as the intellectual content, but the two reactivations do not necessarily coincide or coexist. The letter as a "delayed speech tool" can very well be separated from the letter as an "information tool"' (Escarpit 1966: 31–32).

For the child at the point of learning to read, the word is an arrangement of single characters, like the carriages of a toy train, to be put in the right order by trial and error; to get the sum of the letters right and only later to deduce the more familiar words from their massed effect. For this reason the space between letters should be uniform, that is to say rarely increased or reduced from that set as standard by the typeface manufacturer (early 'Monotype' hot metal specimens are easily found and provide an excellent guide), and word spacing should be particularly even and only slightly more generous than for adult use.

I want to sound a note of caution here, because it is not always realised that typesetters frequently modify their parameters to meet advertising preferences in text composition, which are seldom in tune with the best requirements for continuous reading. For many years the fit of letters and words has been far too close for optimum legibility, and the pendulum now seems set to swing over far in the opposite direction. The habituation argument (Burt 1959, and other mainstream studies) – that we read best what we are most exposed to – is of course a strong one; but there are certain danger signals for all to detect. For example, wherever adjoining letters or punctuation actually touch or fuse, or misreadings are caused by quirky spacing or word breaks, then typographic malpractice is sure to be reducing the ease of reading.

Unfortunately it has to be pointed out that the lobby that would put the reader first – despite being the custodian of a 6,000-year-old tradition of the book – is a small one in terms of the communications industry where trends in typographic systems, software and fashion are set by agencies and magazine publishers whose criteria for the use of type are different. It is for this reason as much as any that sans serif and other monotonous typefaces are still sometimes wrongly specified for lengthy texts, and why unsuitable column widths are adopted, either for ragged or justified setting.

Many of these type designs and typesetting conventions are not necessarily bad in themselves, and there are certain book contexts in which they may yield the best solution, but great judgement is called for in these areas. From time to time reading matter may be dressed up in formats with which children are assumed to be more familiar – for instance a textbook may be disguised as a magazine or comic – and such experiments in presentation (extended in a different direction by graphic novels) may work provided writer and editor can sustain a sufficiently high level of input. Book designers relish well-conceived experiments of this kind; but they should always be viewed as parallels rather than as possible replacements for the book, which has its own logic and integrity. Similarly, the children's book ought not to worry about being an adult book scaled up or down, as is sometimes alleged, any more than the adult book should fear the converse. Each learns from and invigorates the other.

It is gradually coming to be accepted that, once children can cope with the mechanics of reading, at any age, a dramatic drop in apparent type size is not only possible but actively desirable. This visual acuity can only be compared, at the opposite extreme of depth of field, to children's phenomenal ability to recognise the make of oncoming motor cars. A carefully judged drop in typesize, recommended at this stage in reading development, draws attention away from the identity of the single letter, the particular squashed fly on the page, in order to concentrate on the recognition of words and word groups. And so, for the purpose of continuous reading, the journey towards adult obliviousness of the design of the typeface that is being read is well under way.

As for adults, it is true that the recurrence of an eccentrically designed character (of the kind designers call 'spot letters' and which sometimes mar otherwise functional typefaces) can become a major source of subjective distraction for the young reader. Experienced book designers develop an eye for those aesthetic qualities in a particular typeface which determines its suitability for sustained and pleasurable reading, and shun the hundreds of available versions which fail to meet these exacting standards. The ease and quality of reading is further conditioned and enhanced, at a level which should remain subconscious for the reader, by the careful matching of type, paper, ink and print quality; and this is also very much the designer's concern.

On the surface it might sound a reasonable idea that during the crucial initial learning stages the teachers' writing on the blackboard, the type found in books, and the letter shapes the children are taught to write should all share the same generic shapes and directness so that writing, lettering and print are seen to have the same purpose and to belong together, as advocated in a recent survey (Sassoon 1993). But outside a strictly controlled classroom environment this is wishful thinking, since in practice the child is at the same time faced with an incredible range of letter forms in the high street and on television, on the cereal packet and in the comic. In fact, I don't think that this typographic Babel confuses children in the least, for they identify flash cards of all but extreme examples where the rules for letter recognition have been broken in any case, and find it fascinating to compare the countless inventive variations which can be made from the same letter shape. Children rarely find difficulty in making the distinction between rational typefaces for continuous reading and those for display – types for use and types for fun. They also appreciate typographical jokes!

Teachers and librarians are often keen to find out just which typefaces and sizes of type are best for a particular age group; but it is not easy to explain how in typography everything depends on everything else and that it is necessary to relate these questions to such matters as the size of the book, the length and nature of the text, and a host of other factors. The desire to confirm such hypotheses as 'sans serif typefaces are more readable than seriffed ones', or 'that the ideal size for 6 to 8-year-olds is 14–18 pt' is the reef on which a great deal of legibility research has foundered.

Common-sense decisions about page and type sizes can be arrived at by trying to see a situation through the users' eyes – and not eyes alone but other senses too. For instance, the size of a book has much to do with how it is likely to be used on the floor, bed or table. This could lead to the radical but valid deduction that, since most paperback novels are folded in half backwards to be read comfortably in bed, then the back margins should be increased massively to facilitate this. So far no publisher has been persuaded to make a change along these lines, but there has been a big response to a recent suggestion that many picture books are larger than their artwork or function demands.

Some – like Kathleen Hale's *Orlando* in its original format – need vast scale so that it is almost possible to walk into that particular world. In contrast to this and to the standard picture-book formats for floor and table-top use, Eric Carle's German publisher issued a version of *The Very Hungry Caterpillar* measuring only 125 mm × 90 mm, which rather set a fashion for miniature versions of established titles, and which works because the very young child has to take the book in both hands to turn the pages and discover what happens. The 9 pt size of type is absolutely splendid in the conditions which have been created: most children are intrigued by very small type, and the argument that this may tire their eyes may well have been overstated. At the opposite extreme a 96 pt type size would be perfectly acceptable in an alphabet book. In other words, the apparent size and style of type is selected in response to the page size, the number and level of the words and the nature of the artwork.

In some instances a bold or a sans serif typeface would still prove a natural choice to accompany a strong black line with primary colour infill – artwork of the Leo Lionni, Dick Bruna, Roger Hargreaves kind – but most book designers have agreed for some time that the machine-age aesthetic of the sans serif has failed their readers, and represents the typographic equivalent of the high-rise apartment block. Leading designers of typefaces have largely rejected modernism, and now favour more humanistic and user-friendly letter forms. The craft revival of calligraphy in all its aspects and not just as a model for everyday handwriting, has gained ground and this too is significant because it encourages the appreciation of the tones, textures and finishes of materials – whether natural, recycled or otherwise.

Children have an eye for the imperfections of the handmade, and this may well have been better accommodated by the crude, hand-coloured productions of Jemmy Catnach (Hindley 1878) and his like than by the current mechanical precision of letter form, colour register and glossy paper. The gap in attainment between the child's own efforts and the polished but soulless industrial artefact is one which children's book artists have striven to bridge over the ages, frequently working closely with a skilled colour printer. But as printers have become larger and more specialised, this direct link has been taken over by designers and production experts employed by the publisher. In recent times Janet and Allan Ahlberg have shown, paradoxically, that meticulous attention to the detail of production can still communicate this human touch.

What we think of as an illustrator's personal style can be viewed as a triumph of apparent spontaneity in the face of the levelling effects of printing, and it is interesting to look at the instantly recognisable handwriting of such different artists as Ardizzone, Blake or Steadman in this light. The nostalgia factor in children's literature is not unrelated to these visual qualities, for there is a deliberate cultivation of a period idiom at work in Sendak, Ardizzone and countless younger artists. It seems to cast a longer shadow as cultural changes otherwise accelerate for the young, while the canon of 'children's classics' appears to consolidate from one generation to the next and in the lists of set books for the schools. This persistence of tradition may appear to challenge the adage that there is a wholly fresh children's book audience for each age-group every three years or so, but history is a dimension the designer is compelled to work in for a host of reasons: the descent of the materials already in existence that the typographer constantly reassembles; the predilections of our illustrators; and the market itself.

Jan Pieńkowski is another artist fascinated by the expressive potential of printing and materials technology – he has worked creatively with paper engineers on *Robot* and *Haunted House* and others – and it is a pity we have no fitter title than 'novelty books' for such achievements. Picture books can and should involve as many of the senses as possible. Children smell paper and ink, and hear books as they snap, rustle and squeak. And so all these matters have much to do with the reading experience and the practice of typography (and also with theatre, with which book design and illustration have much in common).

## The Layout of the Page

Planning the basic page is as important as the choice of format and typeface, and the decisions this involves need to be taken concurrently to avoid a flawed solution. It is worth time and effort to get this underlying scheme right each time, for the book's entire structure down to the smallest detail will depend upon it. These decisions include fixing sizes of type, length of line, spacing between words, interlinear spacing, margins and column separation, and standard gaps between recurrent elements. Many finer points of spacing and arrangement should be covered by the publisher's house style; but detailed individual layouts and instructions are usually needed for the traditional parts of the book, levels of heading, and complexities within the text.

To create optimum reading conditions when the book is held open in use, the text areas need to be carefully positioned on the page according to a margin scheme or grid. There are certain rules of thumb for doing this and a corpus of geometrical and arithmetical theory stretching back to antiquity, but most typographers I know rely on instinct when making the critical decisions. Designing a book resembles chess in that players are familiar with the opening gambits, but after that the opportunities for creative strategy become limitless since no two books are alike in the demands they make of the accomplished designer.

Designing any book begins with reading the text in sufficient depth to highlight its audience and special requirements. In the case of a novel or other straightforward text for continuous reading, it should be possible to specify a functional reading page without more ado except perhaps to pause and question the desirability of some appropriate form of illustration. For if children's fiction is to be promoted in its key bridging role, then illustration can frequently offer the most effective and least patronising way of doing this where intended reading ages or interest levels differ from adult norms. However, the illustration of new novels has been gradually phased out over the years on economic grounds, and designers have frequently been exercised to maintain good typographic standards.

However, an encouraging recent tendency has been towards a more equitable distribution of costs and care and attention between the 'bookblock' or inside, and the outer jacket or cover, of casebound and paper-covered books alike. This can be seen as a recognition that glossy and colourful covers are no longer enough if the contents are visually uninviting; and that the reader now has more exacting expectations of the book as a leisure purchase. In concrete terms this is leading to improved print and paper quality, lively use of newly introduced typeface designs, more generous and practical paperback margins, and greater sophistication in the approach to text design as a whole. Many other categories of children's book have of course pioneered excellent structural features, visual exposition through colour printing, and value for money generally; but this latest design development has been stressed above all for the hope that it holds out to the beleaguered novelist or creative writer. But for most branches of children's book design, thankfully, the question of illustration still arises at the initial reading stage if not earlier. At a practical level, the scale and weight of the text page and a particular illustrator's style have to be adapted and attuned to each other, and so it becomes pointless to proceed until an artist has been selected and briefed. No category of books other than those for children uses such a wide range of illustrative styles and techniques to so many different ends, or lays down such varied visual-verbal pathways for the reader to follow. Therefore the field is particularly open to those book designers who are drawn to these issues, who will generally find that authors and illustrators welcome the creative involvement of a skilled typographer.

In complete contrast to the situation with unillustrated fiction, it is natural for picture book artists to wish to tell a story in a sequence of tableaux as Hogarth did for *The Rake's Progress*, and to resent having to leave suitable holes in the picture surface for the words. Brian Wildsmith remains the master craftsman of the wordless picture book, where questions and answers are stimulated in sum and in detail through the pictures, and he has continued to pioneer and augment the mechanics of picture book design.

Syntax and word order as preserved by Gutenberg's linear discipline are challenged by the multi-track possibilities opened up through the comic strip; and these developments have found personal echoes in the work of the Ahlbergs, Raymond Briggs, Shirley Hughes, Posy Simmonds and Jan Pieńkowski among many others. The aleatorical message structures of computer-generated graphics are breaking though into printed advertising almost as these words are being written, and so, new as these methods are, they are likely to shape the child's televisual environment and thus create their own resonances within the picture book world.

The final area I would like to consider is the design of non-fiction informational or reference titles, however complex. Book printers refer to straightforward novels or biographies as 'sausages' – wherever you slice them open the texture is uniform

– and this describes an essential precondition for continuous reading. It facilitates several recognisable modes of reading: vocalisation or reading aloud; the assimilation of pure intellectual meaning or apparent dialogue with another mind; study and recapitulation; the sporadic perception of typography as shape devoid of semantic content; and broken or fitful reading leading to a final break in concentration. These may be likened to alternating states of sleep, with the added awareness that one is travelling on a single track and relying on the system to give only vital signals and to keep the line clear of obstruction. In contrast, informational or reference books – from the telephone book to the *Orbis Pictus* to the latest Dorling Kindersley encyclopedia (where a central image or 'icon' is wrapped with surrounding information of descending importance towards the periphery) are invariably multi-track.

The designer's first task should be to draw a map of all the possible ways in which a book can be handled in reference use, and how its content may be presented on typical double-page spreads. Sketch designs are usually prepared for discussion with author and editor so that questions of structure and sequence, relative importance and location, can be reviewed before the manuscript and selection of illustration are finalised. The logic of design enables the signposting of a book to be organised as well as passenger circulation at an international airport, which is a comparable task.

Once the text has been typeset and all the illustrations assembled, there follows a 'scissors and paste' stage where each page is planned and fixed with meticulous attention to detail. The experienced designer will have an overall programme in mind which yields that degree of variety within conformity which corresponds to the pleasurable assimilation of the material in question. For a book of any complexity, creative input is taking place alongside tedious labour, and the computer can assist with one but not the other and certainly can't distinguish between them! This is accordingly an expensive operation, but the high reputation of many titles and series rests on how well this hidden design work has been carried out.

## Jacket and Binding Design

Typography has always had two distinct tones of voice; a quiet one for the private reader, and a shout for the proclamation of advertising and news headlines. This is reflected in the printer's historical division of typefaces into text and display. These groups were designed differently to work at contrasted optical distances: 14 pt and below for text to be read at the normal distance of about thirteen inches; 18 pt and above for those to be visible from arm's length to infinity. Text types are self-effacing introverts whereas display characters draw attention to their own dress and eccentricities. Inside the covers of a book the latter are admitted in very small numbers if at all – perhaps to provide titling or a period touch or even a carnival atmosphere where appropriate – but they really come into their own with the design of book jackets and paperback covers.

The dust wrapper was protective in origin but now exists to get the book into the right hands, in the bookshop primarily, but also when housed on library, school and domestic bookshelves. Therefore it is a poster or advertisement for the book, and potentially the centrepiece of point of sale material for a leading title. The jacket ought to tell instantly what kind of book it surrounds, and for children in particular it should not promise more than it will deliver. There are two schools of thought about jacket design: one states that the book designer must be responsible for the jacket to preserve the unity of the book; and the other that the jacket is not an integral part of the book and the purchaser should be encouraged to discard it as soon as possible to reveal the binding design. In other words: 'The true clothing of the book is its binding, the dustwrapper is merely a raincoat' (Tschichold 1991: 162).

This is the minority view, but I subscribe to it if only to encourage more adventurous binding materials and design for children's books. A solution which meets all needs, widely adopted for picture books, is to repeat the design of the printed paper cover as a dust wrapper. There are many less explored ways of redirecting design attention towards the permanent covering of the book, and alleviating the current situation where lavish full-colour jackets are used to conceal abysmally perfunctory binding styles of dispiriting drabness. As with other areas of product design, there are signs that a materials revolution will soon involve the designer in specifying the precise finishes and properties of papers and coverings for children's books, that are to be durable and aesthetically pleasing. With luck we'll then see less of materials which imitate others, and of the glossy finishes to papers and non-woven coverings, paints and inks, varnishes and laminates which were the hallmarks of the first plastics age.

Now that the book is able to share some of its educational and cultural burden with younger sectors of information technology, all the signs are that its status as a cultural object will rise alongside other quality media. Design holds many of the keys to such a transformation, and a massive new approach towards turning competing series of the classics of world literature into desirable possessions was to be observed in the bookshops by 1993. New trends in the total re-design of adult lists, both cased and paper covered, began rather earlier than that, and children's reference and resource books have gone from strength to strength. At the time of writing the mainstream of children's book design is moribund and ripe for new initiatives. There are a number of exceptionally talented younger designers and illustrators on the scene and I am sure that children, as always, are ready to be shown that books, the oldest branch of information technology, are still the most efficient and vital and the most fun.

# References

Alexander, J. J. G. (1992) *Medieval Illuminators and Their Methods of Work*, New Haven and London: Yale University Press.

Burt, C. (1959) *A Psychological Study of Typography*, Cambridge: Cambridge University Press.

Cornenius, J. A. (1659) *Orbis Pictus*, facsimile of first English edition introduced by Sadler, J. E. (1968), London: Oxford University Press.

Escarpit, R. (1966) *The Book Revolution*, London: Harrap.

Hindley, C. (1878) *The Life and Times of James Catnach (Late of Seven Dials), Ballad Monger*, London: Reeves and Turner.

McLean, R. (1976) *Joseph Cundall: A Victorian Publisher*, Pinner: Private Libraries Association.

Mertens, S., Purpus, E. and Schneider, C. (eds) (1991) *Blockbücher des Mittelalters. Bilderfolgen als Lektüre*, Mainz am Rhein: Philipp von Zabern.

Rogers, B. (1943/1979) *Paragraphs on Printing: Elicited from Bruce Rogers in talks with James Hendrickson on the Functions of a Book Designer*, New York: Dover.

Sassoon, R. (1993) 'Through the eyes of a child: perception and type design', in Sassoon, R. (ed.) *Computers and Typography*, Oxford: Intellect Books.

Tschichold, J. (1991) *The Form of the Book: Essays on the Morality of Good Design*, London: Lund Humphries.

## Further Reading

Baudin, F. (1989) *How Typography Works (and Why it is Important)*, London: Lund Humphries.

Glaister, G. A. (1960/1979) *Glaister's Glossary of the Book*, 2nd edn, London: Allen and Unwin.

McLean, R. (1980) *The Thames and Hudson Manual of Typography*, London: Thames and Hudson.

Martin, D. (1989a) *An Outline of Book Design*, London: Blueprint Publishing and The Publishers Association.

—— (1989b) *The Telling Line: Essays on Fifteen Contemporary Book Illustrators*, London: MacRae.

Peacock, J. (1989) *Book Production*, London: Blueprint Publishing and The Publishers Association.

Sutton, J. and Bartram, A. (1990) *Typefaces for Books*, London: The British Library.

Wilson, A. (1967) *The Design of Books*, London: Studio Vista.

# 39

# Children's Book Publishing in Britain

## *Margaret Clark*

The publishing of books is – and always has been – a matter of buying and selling: the publisher buys from authors and artists the right to reproduce their work in printed form (and, increasingly, towards the end of the twentieth century, in other ways – audio, visual, electronic). The publisher then sells, through many channels, as many copies of that work as customers can be persuaded to acquire. Where publishing differs from other commercial enterprises is in the nature of what is bought and sold. No book is exactly the same as another; nor is a book indispensable to survival, nor (some would claim) a necessary ingredient of a happy life. For some centuries possession of books was the privilege of a minority and in England it was only in 1870 that Forster's Education Act offered to everyone the opportunity of learning to read. Most publishers, therefore, have been motivated by desires other than that of making money, and this is especially true of the publishers of children's books.

For while Allen Lane, the creator of Penguin Books in the 1930s, could claim a missionary zeal in making available to the reader in search of self-education scholarly works at Woolworth prices (Flower 1959: 5–6), the publisher of children's books is inspired by two equally strong motives – a passionate belief in the pleasure to be gained by reading fiction (whether a picture-book story, a fairy tale or a teenage novel) and a constant aspiration to teach, to inform, to influence young minds. As the esteemed historian of children's books, F. J. Harvey Darton (himself a member of a publishing family), put it, 'children's books were always the scene of a battle between instruction and amusement, between restraint and freedom, between hesitant morality and spontaneous happiness' (1932/1982: vii).

The distinction between books published for adults and those published for children is not always acknowledged by their readers, and it could be said that William Caxton was the first publisher of a children's book in England, since he printed an edition of Aesop's *Fables* in 1484. In the following centuries alphabet books were published in the form of primers and horn-books, but one of the first people to publish books with the declared intention of entertaining, while instructing, young readers was John Newbery (1713–1767), who personally designed, and very often wrote, the books that he published and sold from his shop at 65 St Paul's Churchyard in London. *A Little Pretty Pocket Book*, a miscellany of 'instruction and amusement', was published in about 1744. No copy of the first edition has survived – a common feature of children's books is that favourites wear out with constant handling. The book was followed by nearly thirty other publications, although this represented only a small proportion of Newbery's total output. Publishers specialising in children's books alone have been few – which is why, in the twentieth century, Sebastian Walker's enterprise in founding Walker Books in 1978 was so notable.

By 1800 some 600 books for children were being published annually, a figure that had increased tenfold by 1992, when the total number of books in print – as recorded by Whitaker – had reached 30,000, issued by over 1,000 publishers.

John Newbery and his successors shared not only a love of reading but a care for the *appearance* of books – the design, the typeface, the paper, the binding, the jacket. The same interests were the motivation of the many individuals who, in the nineteenth century, set up their own, mostly family-owned, firms. But whereas, in John Newbery's time, the publisher had been both bookseller and often printer, publishing now became concerned solely with the acquisition of material, its editing and advertising, while printing and bookselling developed as separate activities.

Finding material has always been a matter of serendipity for the publisher, who is dependent on a sharp eye for the needs of the marketplace, an instinct for spotting potential in what may look unpromising, a wide circle of acquaintances with similar interests, and – once the list is established – an image that will entice authors to submit their work. This kind of networking is demonstrated in the way some nineteenth-century publishers went about their business.

George Bell, for instance, had known Mrs Gatty as a childhood friend, and thus became the publisher of her *Aunt Judy's Magazine* in 1866. Edmund Evans was an engraver and printer who, knowing Kate Greenaway's father, saw her work, recognised its appeal and persuaded George Routledge to publish her first book *Under the Window* in 1879. Routledge had started off as an apprentice to a Carlisle bookseller (direct experience of selling is still invaluable to a publisher) and went on to publish the Toy Books of another Evans protégé, Randolph Caldecott. Routledge's partner was his brother-in-law, Frederick Warne, who set up on his own in 1865. The artist Leslie Brooke was so pleased with Warne's successful publication of his illustrations to Andrew Lang's *Nursery Rhyme Book* (1897) that thereafter he would work for no one else. He, in turn, encouraged Warne to publish Beatrix Potter, whose *Tale of Peter Rabbit* had first been privately printed at the author's expense.

Publishing had become highly competitive, with children's books an important part of the business, though not always a profitable one. Although they may have long lives, popular books being bought by every generation, and although copies wear out and need constant replacement, the costing of children's books is different from that of adult books. Traditionally, they have always been priced more cheaply, the margin for profit and allowance for overheads being kept as low as possible. This is partly to do with perception of the books – most are, after all, shorter than adult books – but it mostly results from the desire of both publisher and author that the books, through the adult intermediary of parent, librarian or teacher, should be accessible to as large an audience as possible.

In the case of England's best-known children's book, *Alice's Adventures in Wonderland*, published by Macmillan in 1865 at a price of 7s 6d (in today's decimal currency 37.5 pence) Lewis Carroll pleaded for a cheap edition, writing on 15 February 1869, 'The only point I really care for in the whole matter (and it *is* a source of very real pleasure to me) is that the book should be enjoyed by children – and the more in number, the better' (Hudson 1954/1976: 129). And by 1887 Macmillan felt confident enough of the book's selling power to issue a cheap edition at one-third of the original price.

Often the pricing of a book is crucial to its chances of success. Put very simply, the unit cost of production decreases as the number of copies goes up, but estimating the print quantity accurately is difficult, since all the copies must be sold within a set period of time. Unless this happens, the publisher has no chance of even recouping the costs of production – the bills for which have to be paid often before the book is on the market. If the publisher has not reached the point of making a profit, then the cost of keeping copies in a warehouse (which has to be heated, lit and staffed) will become a drain on cash resources, and the publisher has the choice of 'remaindering' copies (selling off at a loss) or 'pulping' them, that is, turning them back into the paper from which they were made.

Included in the price, as well as the cost of paper, printing and binding, selling and distribution, and the bookseller's discount (which, starting at 35 per cent, fluctuates according to the quantity of books involved), is a small percentage for promotion. Unlike adult books, books for children are rarely promoted individually: money will be put into the production and distribution of a well-annotated, illustrated catalogue, including backlist titles, or a publicity campaign (posters, competitions, displays of artwork) for a group of books by the same author or with a similar theme.

The home market for publishers in Britain is self-evidently small: the British Isles occupy a tiny part of the global map. Again by tradition, the market for books in the English language was, until the 1970s, divided between those parts of the world that once made up the British Empire, and the USA and its dependencies. A publisher in London would have the exclusive right to sell the British edition of a book in the former territory and lease to an American publisher the right to publish a separate edition in the latter – and vice versa. Other parts of the world, notably Europe, were regarded as 'open market', where both editions could compete.

This agreement was challenged and declared illegal by the US State Department in 1976, as an anti-Trust act, and it has subsequently been eroded by the development of indigenous publishing in Australia, Canada, New Zealand and the Republic of South Africa – although those markets are still important to British children's book publishers. Nevertheless, the inevitable diminution of the export market, where at one time at least half an edition of a children's book might be sold, while at home public spending on books in schools and libraries has been cut back, has meant that publishers have had to look for other ways to sell their lists – through book clubs, school bookshops or book fairs, even by electronic transmission direct to the home.

An additional source of revenue for the publisher is the sale of translation rights in books originated in Britain, and, in the case of picture books printed in colour, the organising of 'co-editions' – that is, printing several editions at once, only the text (printed in black) needing to be changed into another language. As long ago as 1787 a visitor to the Leipzig Book Fair, L. F. Gedike, wrote:

No other form of literary manufactory is so active as book-making for young people of all grades and classes. Every Leipzig Summer and Winter Fair throws up a countless number of books of this kind like a flooding tide.

Muir 1954: 67

In the second half of the twentieth century the Children's Book Fair in Bologna, usually held in April, became the chief marketplace for the buying and selling of rights, although many children's book publishers also visit the Frankfurt Book Fair in the latter half of the year. While publishers in Germany and Scandinavia once depended on British authors for a regular supply of fiction, this has changed. In 1994 it was reported that Western Europe was no longer the rich source of partners for co-productions, and the countries of Eastern Europe, Taiwan and South Korea had become the 'growth markets'.

Until the final decade of the twentieth century, children's books, like adult books, were published at 'net prices': that is, the publisher stipulated the price below which the book could not be sold. The Net Book Agreement of 1900 (revised in 1957) was devised to ensure that booksellers who kept a wide range of books were not put out of business by price-cutting of a limited number of fast-moving titles. Partly as a result of a trade recession, this Agreement was abandoned in October 1995. School textbooks, by contrast, were issued at 'non-net prices' because, in 1920, when the practice began, such books were normally bought in bulk (one for each pupil in a class) and the risk to the bookseller of holding large stocks was reduced. The bookseller or distributor was able to vary the price in proportion to the costs involved, which varied with the quantity ordered.

The 'new' trade of textbook publishing dates back to the 1870s, when primary education in England became universal. Publishing of this kind – to meet a specific need – could be very lucrative. Among others, Edward Arnold set up his own business in 1890, starting with nine English and arithmetic textbooks. Once a book was adopted in schools, its sales were predictable for any number of years and the profit generated could help subsidise other, more risky projects. For example, in the 1920s Basil Blackwell in Oxford published a history series for elementary schools. Within two years, the series was selling at the phenomenal rate of 1,000 copies per week and this enabled the firm to publish children's books of entertainment, including the children's annual *Joy Street*, to which Hilaire Belloc, G. K. Chesterton and A. A. Milne were contributors.

As methods of teaching began to change in the second half of the twentieth century, so the pattern of educational publishing changed. Books of information – so-called 'children's books' written to stimulate curiosity rather than teach by rote – became the stock of the new school libraries which provided a source of reference for project work as well as fiction to promote the enjoyment of reading.

Although children's books for the most part are bought by adults rather than their ultimate readers, two developments in the twentieth century brought books within the reach of children's own spending power. Book tokens, devised by the publisher Harold Raymond in 1932, became a popular form of birthday and Christmas present. Paperback editions, of which the first were Puffin Picture Books, edited by Noel Carrington, and Puffin Story Books, edited by Eleanor Graham, were initiated by Allen Lane in 1941. Chosen with care, and produced at pocket-money prices (6d, or 2.5p), they were responsible for making readers of many children who grew up in Britain in the spartan years of the Second World War. Puffins had the field to themselves for nearly thirty years, reprinting in long print-runs titles that had originally appeared in hardback on other publishers' lists. By the 1990s, most children's publishers had their own paperback imprints. And by this time publishing was dominated by the big conglomerates, whose main business might not be books at all, but who had swallowed the small family firms driven to the wall by recession and the reluctance of individualistic publishers to adapt to changing economic conditions.

The publisher's role, therefore, is different. The job of the editor (which I once sentimentally defined as providing the sunshine without which few living things can thrive and which the author, working in isolation, needs to call on whenever required) has given way in importance to the vital work (now called 'input') of the marketing and rights executives. The publisher can no longer afford to back editorial 'hunches', or wait for the unsolicited manuscript that might prove a bestseller like *Watership Down*, but must seek books that meet market needs. Children's publishers study demography, analyse the ethnic make-up of the average classroom, make partnerships with film producers, and look for books that will satisfy children more familiar with computer games than the printed page.

At the same time, the publisher's role can be seen as returning to where it began – for new technology has changed the face of the British printing industry, which was ravaged by recession in the 1980s, with over 350 companies going out of business. Now printing facilities can be found within the publisher's office and authors are producing manuscripts not in typed form but on a disc format. The publisher can show a jacket design to an author on a computer screen, meaning that changes can be made without great expense. With children's picture books and information books – where the placing of illustration in relation to the text is such an important part of the publishing process – computer technology enables the publisher, the author and the illustrator to work on the design together, as artwork and text are moved at will around the screen in front of them. Such freedom is a boon undreamed of by John Newbery, and while pessimists may fear that one day the electronic image will replace the book, most publishers regard them as complementary, the former a means of enlarging an experience that only the latter can give.

# References

Flower, D. (1959) *The Paper-Back, Its Past, Present and Future*, with a foreword by Sir Allen Lane, London: Arborfield.

Harvey Darton, F. J. (1932/1982) *Children's Books in England: Five Centuries of Social Life*, 3rd edn, rev. Alderson, B., Cambridge: Cambridge University Press.

Hudson, Derek (1954/1976) *Lewis Carroll: An Illustrated Biography*, new ill. edn, London: Constable.

Muir, Percy (1954) *English Children's Books 1600–1900*, London: Batsford.

## Further Reading

*Dictionary of Literary Biography*, Vol. 106, *British Literary Publishing Houses, 1820–1880* (1991) Detroit: Gale Research.

*Dictionary of Literary Biography*, Vol. 112, *British Literary Publishing Houses, 1881–1965* (1991) Detroit: Gale Research.

Mumby, F. (1930/1974) *Publishing and Bookselling: A History from the Earliest Times to the Present Day*, 5th edn, rev. Norrie, I., London: Cape.

Norrie, I. (1982) *Mumby's Publishing and Bookselling in the Twentieth Century*, London: Bell and Hyman.

Roscoe, S. (1973) *John Newbery and his Successors, 1740–1814*, Wormley: Five Owls Press.

# 40

# Children's Book Publishing in the USA

## Connie C. Epstein

The first books specifically intended for children produced in the USA were largely devoted to the teaching of proper morals. Catechisms that pointed out duties and prepared the young for a proper death, they have been described by one historian as published in the 'gloomy tradition of the Puritans'. Some publishers managed to lighten their juvenile offerings with titles such as John Newbery's *Goody Two-Shoes* obtained from England, but as copyright was virtually non-existent they were almost entirely pirated editions. Not until early in the nineteenth century did a broader-based literature for children begin to develop with the publication of *Peter Parley's Tales of America* in 1827. Written by Samuel G. Goodrich, the many Peter Parley books that followed told adventurous tales about figures in American history, selling a total of seven million copies by the time of the Civil War in 1860.

As the country gradually recovered from the war, which ended in 1865, juvenile publishing entered a sustained period of growth that saw the emergence of a number of influential writers. A Boston schoolteacher named William Taylor Adams took the pen-name of Oliver Optic and began to write adventure story series in groups of six titles each, achieving annual sales of 100,000 copies until his death in 1897. Daniel Lothrop (still a distinguished name in American publishing) started his career as a publisher in 1868 and established the business primarily with books that appealed to children. Perhaps the most successful of them was the beloved *The Five Little Peppers and How They Grew* written by his second wife under the pseudonym Margaret Sidney in 1880. At Appleton, another leading nineteenth-century children's book publisher, an editor became interested in some poems and legends written in black dialect that were appearing in the Atlanta, Georgia, newspaper the *Constitution*. Approaching the writer, a staff editor by the name of Joel Chandler Harris, the Appleton editor arranged for the publication in 1880 of *Uncle Remus: His Songs and Sayings* and thus was credited with discovering a classic.

Some have called these years a flowering of American children's literature because of the number of enduring books, still being read, that were produced at this time. In 1866, the editor of the popular children's magazine *St Nicholas*, Mary Mapes Dodge, wrote *Hans Brinker or The Silver Skates* and set new standards of excellence. In 1868, Louisa May Alcott started what has turned out to be a long-lasting American tradition of realistic family stories for children with the publication of *Little Women*. In 1876, Mark Twain's *The Adventures of Tom*

*Sawyer* appeared, and this picture of a boy growing up in a small mid-Western town soon came to define boyhood for the nation at large. Nevertheless, American publishers still relied primarily on sales of well-known titles that they acquired one way or another from Britain, including Appleton's financial coup of picking up a supply of discarded sheets from a printing of *Alice's Adventures in Wonderland*. Not until 1894, in fact, did the number of domestic juvenile titles exceed those coming from European sources when the totals reached 370 and 297 respectively while approximately 5,400 books were being published overall.

By the turn of the century, juvenile output had climbed to 482 titles, one of which may prove to be the most timeless of all: *The Wizard of Oz* by L. Frank Baum. An innovative departure from the realistic content of other American juvenile writers, this wildly imaginary fantasy was still a home-grown product, firmly rooted in the USA through its opening setting of the tornado-ridden Kansas prairie. By combining the English fondness for word play with the American appetite for outdoor adventure, Baum developed an original style and form that stands alone in the literature of both countries. During these years, the publishing community was also coming of age in its recognition of the need for copyright regulation, supporting the passage of an International Copyright Law in 1891. The first steps were modest, however, with only a simple announcement of the intention to publish enough to establish copyright and no payment to the original copyright holder required.

The next advance came in the second decade of the twentieth century when several companies decided that the juvenile market had become large enough to warrant special staff attention. Until this time, children's books had been included here and there in the offerings of a publisher's general trade list and were sometimes overlooked, losing sales in the process. But now these firms began to appoint editors with the specific responsibility of producing an independent list of children's books, thus identifying these titles more clearly and selling them more effectively. This pioneering juvenile editor had to perform as a book designer, publicity director and sales manager, while carrying out the basic duties of manuscript acquisition and preparation. But as the market share of children's books slowly increased within the company, publishers began to provide their juvenile editorial departments with these services.

This structural change turned out to have a far-reaching effect on the business and was set in motion by three developments that occurred almost simultaneously on three different fronts in the aftermath of the First World War. By that time, the trend toward separate children's rooms in public libraries, presided over by a specialist in library services for children, was well established, creating more demand for original books in addition to new editions of familiar classics. Then, in 1919, a promotion known as Children's Book Week was launched by Frederic Melcher, editor of the trade magazine *Publisher's Weekly*, and Franklin Mathiews, librarian of the Boy Scouts of America; children's librarian Anne Carroll Moore of the New York Public Library started the first full year of her children's book review page in the *Bookman* magazine; and Louise Seaman (later Bechtel) became the first children's book editor at Macmillan Publishing.

During the ten years that followed, other publishing companies also set up juvenile departments, and the books that resulted more than justified their existence. In 1922, May Massee became the second children's book editor with her own list, at Doubleday Doran, and she quickly drew attention with the publication of such books as *The Poppy-Seed Cakes* by Margery Clark, illustrated by Maud and Miska Petersham. At the same time, Melcher established the Newbery Medal for the best children's book of the preceding year, inaugurating with the first winner, *The Story of Mankind* by Hendrik van Loon, an award with both literary and commercial weight. Other influential editors starting their careers in this period included Virginia Kirkus at Harper Brothers in 1926 and Elisabeth Bevier (later Hamilton) at Harcourt, Brace in 1928. The new books that they produced were enthusiastically supported by children's librarians, so much so that such a pre-eminent journal of criticism as *The Horn Book Magazine* devoted its August 1928 issue to an appreciation of Seaman's editorship, giving fourteen editorial pages to a reproduction of her autumn catalogue. Truly, editors and librarians seemed to have entered into what some in retrospect call 'a benign conspiracy'.

The first setback to these years of steady growth came in 1932 with the onset of the great depression. As managements trimmed staff in response to hard times, Massee apparently was let go at Doubleday, relocating soon after at Viking where she organised a new department. Kirkus also left Harper when it merged its juvenile department into the general trade department, ironically the year after she acquired *Little House in the Big Woods* by Laura Ingalls Wilder, an all-time bestseller for the company. Nevertheless, fifteen children's book departments remained in place and growth resumed shortly, with more companies deciding to compete in the juvenile market as trained personnel became available.

By 1938, output of new children's books had more than doubled since Seaman's early days, reaching a total of 1,041 titles, and both reviewers and buyers were beginning to complain about overproduction. In the same year, Frederic Melcher instituted the Caldecott Medal for the best picture book of the preceding year, thus giving official recognition to the art of illustration and to the illustrator as a key member of the team creating the picture book. Because of the interest of Massee and other editors in the graphics of their books, a number of gifted artists arriving from Europe were finding an outlet for their work in American children's books and producing landmark titles. One of these artists was the prolific Kurt Wiese, who is remembered for his visual interpretation of many enduring stories, including the classic *The Five Chinese Brothers* by Claire Huchet Bishop. But home-grown talent was developing as well, for the year before, in 1937, Dr Seuss burst upon the scene with *And to Think That I Saw It on Mulberry Street* on the Vanguard list, selling 31,600 copies in six years, and the picture book was never quite the same again. Another distinctively American artist to emerge was Glen Rounds, whose 1936 debut title *Ol' Paul, The Mighty Logger* is credited by publisher Vernon Ives with single-handedly saving his year-old company Holiday House from an early demise.

Two schools of thought on the most appropriate content for children's books were taking shape during this period, and each was often highly critical of the other. Some called this differing point of view the 'milk bottles versus Grimm' controversy, as it seemed to pit proponents of everyday realistic material against those of the fantastical themes found in more traditional storytelling. Lucy Sprague Mitchell of the Bank Street College of Education, whose staff was working directly with children and reading in her Writers Laboratory, pressed hard for what she called the 'Here and Now' in children's books. But Anne Carroll Moore, still a critical arbiter of great influence, found many of the stories coming out of this programme prosaic and uninspiring, including Margaret Wise Brown's beloved *Goodnight Moon* whose appeal for very young children was unrecognised by many at the time of its publication in 1947. Closely allied with these realistic stories were the informational books written in narrative style that had begun to appear, an early example being *The Earth for Sam* by W. Maxwell Reed, published in 1930 by Harcourt editor Bevier, a former school library supervisor who was keenly aware of the need for lively, accurate juvenile non-fiction.

Again, however, children's book publishing encountered a slow period with the entrance of the country into the Second World War in 1941 and the diversion of national resources to the wartime effort. Especially difficult for publishers was the rationing of paper, now in short supply, and within three years new book production had dropped a third to a total of 645 titles. Nevertheless, more talented editors continued to join the business, and more successful companies continued to emerge. In 1941, Ursula Nordstrom took over the children's book department at Harper Brothers, expanding the staff from three to twenty-five and annual sales from a few hundred thousand to ten million over the next twenty-five years. Shortly after, in 1942, the innovative imprint of Golden Books made its debut, opening up an additional mass market by producing inexpensive books priced at only twenty-five cents and selling them through general retail outlets. Proving itself quickly, the experiment managed to achieve annual sales of 39 million in five years. Another influential children's editor starting her career at this time was Margaret K. McElderry, who succeeded Elisabeth Hamilton at Harcourt in 1946. With thirty or so editors now holding this position, the need for a professional organisation was becoming apparent, and in 1945 the Children's Book Council was founded by publishers as a centre for cooperative projects benefiting the whole industry.

As what some have called the boom decade of the 1950s started, 1,400 new children's books were being published annually, and juvenile publishing had achieved the status of 'big business'. With this success came keener competition and diversification as companies began to look for new writing and artistic talent to add to their lists and for new markets to cultivate. At Harper, two major finds came to widespread recognition with the publication in 1952 of *Charlotte's Web* by E. B. White and Ruth Krauss's *A Hole Is to Dig* with illustrations by Maurice Sendak. At Random House, attention turned to innovative market strategy, which led to the launching in 1950 of its history and biography series known as Landmark Books and the opening up of sales outlets outside the traditional book market. In fact, the series format proved to be so well suited to the expanding school market for trade books that some publishers, such as Franklin Watts with its First Book series, began to specialise in this kind of publishing exclusively.

Then suddenly, when the Soviet Union became the first country to orbit earth successfully with its unmanned satellite Sputnik in 1957, the school market for children's books surged into the forefront of juvenile publishing. Convinced that American schools needed help if students were to be able to compete internationally, Congress passed the National Defense Education Act in the next year, making federal funds available to schools for the purchase of library books in the fields of science and mathematics. What followed was a vast outpouring of non-fiction, bringing overdue attention to creative non-fiction writers, but also sparking the publication of hasty work designed to capitalise on the demand that seemed to materialise overnight. Still, out of this period emerged a number of pioneering authors, Herbert S. Zim for one, who showed how the van Loon tradition of lively narrative non-fiction could be used to interest young readers in subjects previously thought too complex for them.

During these same years, the business of publishing children's books also began to diversify geographically. Early on, like all of American publishing, it had been centred almost entirely on the east coast: first in Boston, then shifting to Philadelphia around 1820, and finally settling in New York in the late nineteenth century. Now, however, a process of decentralisation from east to west began to take place with such ventures as the launching of Parnassus Press by Herman Schein in California in 1957 for the purpose of providing a showcase for western talent overlooked by the eastern establishment.

In the early 1960s, growth moved ahead steadily, the annual output of new books reaching 2,300 titles in 1963, and then once more a federal government programme sent the industry into a dizzying upward spiral. In 1965, the Elementary and Secondary Education Act was passed, again making money available to schools for the purchase of library books, and publishers were caught unprepared for the buying frenzy that followed. Book inventories were sold out; new printings were delayed at overloaded printers; and some publishers reported as much as a third of their backlist temporarily out of stock. If a publisher did not have a children's book department it tried to organise one now and share in what seemed an unlimited market. Unfortunately by the time companies were finally able to gear up for this new level of business, the money to support the legislation had begun to dry up and in the decade of the 1970s the boom of the Great Society turned into a bust.

One specific casualty of this downturn, accelerated by the isolationist reaction to the trauma of the Vietnam War, was the market for books from other countries published in translation, which had been on the rise since 1945. By 1973, internationally minded editors were reporting a drop in sales for translated novels clearly rooted in a foreign culture, even when they received outstanding reviews. Faring only slightly better were the translated picture-books, which usually were not tied to a specific setting. Apparently these editors concluded Americans were now more interested in erasing the cultural differences found within the country than in learning about them.

Disillusioning and disruptive as the cycle was, however, in time it further broadened and diversified children's book publishing. Until now librarians had been the dominant influence on editorial programmes in hard cover if not mass-market houses, because they were the primary buyers; their approval could make or break a book. But as library budgets tightened and book purchases dropped, the public began to turn elsewhere for new titles, and the phenomenon of the special children's bookstore appeared. By 1985, these stores were numerous enough to form their own professional organisation known as the Association of Booksellers for Children (ABC), and in five years its membership grew from forty to 800.

Although many ABC members were former librarians and teachers, their buying patterns differed to some extent, weighted more toward picture books and younger readers, and in recent years a number of publishers have emphasised this portion of their list accordingly. For some editors, the single most important change of the last fifteen years has been the expansion of the partnership between juvenile editor and children's librarian to include the children's bookseller.

Out of this expansion has come a second boom period of the 1980s, producing an annual output of over 5,000 new titles, wider public consumption, and business consolidation. In order to increase their market share of the industry as quickly as possible, corporations have acquired additional juvenile imprints and brought them together under joint management. Today Penguin and William Morrow both own six imprints, managed by four and six editors respectively, Simon & Schuster follows with five, while Harcourt and Putnam each has four. Though smaller in number, the remaining children's book publishers are now vastly bigger in terms of both book production and staff. In just seventy-five years, the lone self-sufficient children's book editor had matured into a broad-based manager with the title of publisher or editorial director, supported by separate departments of production, marketing, and sales. One of the first companies to set up a specialised sales force for its juvenile books was Random House, in 1983, and others such as Bantam Doubleday Dell have followed suit more recently.

Not surprisingly, American juvenile publishing has become more international in flavour as a result of these expansionary times. At least three major British companies have established branches in the USA, bringing their own books with them, in order to participate in the market directly. At the same time, half a dozen or so of the country's most prominent publishers – HarperCollins, Viking Penguin, Bantam Doubleday Dell, Grolier – are now owned by British, German and French global corporations. Although the number of books acquired from other countries has not increased noticeably, the interest in so-called multicultural books, with which children from newly arriving ethnic groups can identify, has risen sharply. Some are now projecting that 30 per cent of preschool-age children will be non-English speaking by the year 2000, and a new market is developing rapidly for books that will meet their needs. Instead of buying books from foreign publishers for the purpose, however, American editors are trying to produce them domestically, creating more opportunities for foreign-born writers and illustrators now living in the United States.

In response to the growing prestige of the Bologna Children's Book Fair, which celebrated its thirtieth birthday in 1993, more American editors have come to attend it regularly. Primarily offering an opportunity to join international co-productions of picture books, however, it has not proved to be a major sales outlet. Companies, in any case, have tended to view exports as a marginal extra since, so far at least, they represent a small percentage of the domestic market. Still, subsidiary rights directors now go to the Fair also and are putting more time and thought into selling the foreign rights to their books to other countries. Furthermore, as American colour printing has improved and become more affordable, picture books produced in the USA are attracting more international interest.

Another current trend is the continued spread of juvenile publishing throughout the country, perhaps in reaction to the corporate consolidation taking place in New York City. A 1993 listing of major companies for a national writer's organisation included eighty imprints based in twenty different cities, ranging from Portland, Oregon, in the north-west to Gretna, Louisiana, in the south. The number of small presses with children's lines is on the rise too, successfully publishing to narrow 'niches' with regional titles about local history, customs, and environment or with books that focus on specific topics such as African-American culture. No longer is one centre able to satisfy the interests and concerns of an increasingly diverse market.

But once again, in the 1990s, the publishing industry appears to be pausing and catching its breath while it reckons with the effects of a persistent global recession. Cuts in state public education funds are reducing purchases by school libraries, the largest sector of the juvenile market. Competition from the spread of the so-called superstores being developed by national book chains is hurting the business of the personal independent children's bookstore, forcing some to close. Nevertheless, if the pattern of past history holds true, then this quiet period should be followed by an upward spurt, aided by present-day population growth. Not only is children's book publishing a cyclical business, it is directly affected by demographics as well.

# 41

# Reviewing and Scholarly Journals

## Gillian Adams

The history of journals and reviews provides a revealing window on the process of canon formation, the use of children's and youth literature in teaching, and the development of critical theory and practice as regards children's literature. The initial choice of books for review, criticism, and use in the classroom has much to do with their eventual inclusion in the canon of significant children's literature. Nevertheless, knowledge of the subject is fragmentary, particularly for the earlier periods, with the exception of 1865–1881 in the USA (Darling 1968); much research remains to be done.

The story begins with the perception by the eighteenth-century book trade in England that children's literature could be a profitable commodity, but that it was necessary to publicise it. The earliest book lists and book reviews, if only in miniature, were the notices and book lists by John Newbery. His advertisement for his first children's book, *A Little Pretty Pocket Book*, appeared in the *Penny London Morning Advertiser* of 18 June 1744 (Chambers 1974: 161; Darton 1932/1982: 1). Further promotional material and book lists were included in his *The Lilliputian Magazine* (1751), *The Gentleman's Magazine*, and works like *The History of Little Goody Two-Shoes* (Darton 1932/1982: 122–135). Other publishers quickly espoused Newbery's practices.

There is a difference between promotional material, which contains not only information about a book but sometimes early positive responses to it, reviews, which range from purely descriptive annotations to perceptive analyses, and sustained bibliographical, historical and critical discussion. It is helpful, nevertheless, to think of writing about children's literature as a continuum rather than in terms of rigid categories such as advertisements, reviews, and criticism. Particularly for earlier periods, material put out by publishers can be a valuable source of information.

After 1800, children's books began to receive brief notices in literary reviews such as the *Critical Review, British Critic* and *Monthly Review*. The first sustained critical article on children's literature appeared in the *Quarterly Review* in 1844, unsigned but attributed to Elizabeth Rigby. The article consists of a plea for the importance of imaginative rather than didactic literature and is reprinted in Haviland (1974: 8–18). In a format well-known to readers of library journals, Rigby concludes with an annotated book list of 'books of direct amusement'. As the nineteenth century progressed, more sustained reviews and critical articles began to appear in journals like *The Bookman, Fortnightly Review, Macmillan's Magazine,* and *The Nineteenth Century* (see the bibliography in Pellowski 1968: 354–382). John Ruskin's remarks on what he considered appropriate reading for children, which appeared in his periodical *Fors Claviger* (1871–1884) and elsewhere, were particularly influential (Thwaite 1963: 226).

The first systematic reviews of children's books are in Mrs Sarah Trimmer's magazine *The Guardian of Education* (1802–1806), in which she hoped 'to counteract the pernicious influence of immoral books' such as *Robinson Crusoe* and Perrault's tales (Thwaite 1963: 102–103; Darton 1932/1982: 96–97). Although Mrs Gatty in her introduction to the first issue of *Aunt Judy's Magazine* (1866–1873) said it was 'intended for the use and amusement of children' (Haviland 1974: 19), it is clear from its contents that it included adults in its audience, and Mrs Gatty's book reviews of children's books were intended for the whole family. Under Charlotte Yonge's editorship (1851–1893), *The Monthly Packet*, an Anglican magazine for girls, also gave advice on choosing books (Haviland 1974: 20).

As in Britain, reviews of children's books appeared in literary periodicals in the USA in the nineteenth century. In New York, *The Literary World: A Gazette for Authors, Readers and Publishers* (1847–1853) includes juveniles in its 'Recent publications', and early issues contain reviews with extensive quotations of works by authors like Jane Taylor and Isaac Watts. (Detailed information on the period from 1865–1881 is available in Richard Darling's book on children's book reviewing in literary, scholarly, religious, pedagogical, children's, and book trade periodicals (Darling 1968).) Horace E. Scudder's *Riverside Magazine for Young People* (1867–1870) published reviews and critical articles, as well as a column, 'Books for young people', 'a series of informal notes, intended for children's elders' (Haviland 1974: 21). Scudder's interest in literature for children continued when he became editor of the *Atlantic Monthly*, which under his editorship also published articles about children's books. Journals with an extensive circulation like *The Nation*, *The New Statesman*, *Scribner's Monthly*, and *The Catholic World*, also reviewed children's books (see Pellowski 1968: 401–484).

Although lists of the best books, sometimes accompanied by discussion of selected titles and the general state of children's literature and publishing, had appeared in publications for children such as *St. Nicholas*, *The Academy*, and for adults, such as the *Book Buyer*, *Bookman*, *Dial*, *Education*, *Independent*, *Littell's Living Age*, *North American Review*, *Spectator*, and *Woman's Home Companion*, 1882 is the first year in the USA when material on the reviewing of children's books was routinely gathered in one place. In that year Carolyn M. Hewins put out her first book list in *Publisher's Weekly*: 'Books for the young: a guide for parents and children' (Haviland 1974: 30; Darling 1968: 11). Since that time *Publisher's Weekly* has continued to publish one-paragraph reviews of about five to fifteen children's books, most of them fiction, in every issue. It is most useful for its articles about authors (usually based on an interview) and about national and international children's book publishing; it publishes special children's books issued twice a year. H. W. Wilson published in 1909, as a supplement to its regular catalogue, *The Children's Catalogue*, still extant today. Other useful book trade publications are *CBC Features*, *Kirkus Reviews*, and *A. B. Bookman's Weekly*. *CBC Features*, put out by the Children's Book Council in New York, contains about four articles, often by well-known children's authors. *Kirkus Reviews*, a prepublication service widely used by bookstores, has an entire section devoted to children's and young adult books in each issue. Reviews, running to a sometimes lengthy paragraph and including a discussion of the illustrations, try to give some indication of a book's future popularity so that orders can be sent in ahead of time. *A. B. Bookman's Weekly*, directed largely at book dealers, runs articles of interest to collectors and bibliophiles and has a special children's book issue once a year.

Among London book trade publications is *Books for Keeps: The Children's Book Magazine*, edited by Chris Powling for the School Bookshop Association. It is a review journal of children's books, formerly called *Children's Books* and incorporating *British Book News Children's Supplement*. There is also *CBF News*, formerly *CCB News*, put out by the Children's Book Foundation. It was once a section incorporated with the Book Trust's *Book News* (London 1979– ) but is now available separately to members of the Book Trust. Primarily consisting of news and announcements, it does reprint acceptance speeches for awards.

In the first half of the twentieth century, literary periodicals such as *The Bookman* (New York 1891–1934) and the *Saturday Review of Literature* (New York 1924–1952) carried regular columns and sustained critical essays as did the Sunday supplements to *The New York Times* and the *New York Herald Tribune* (Pellowski 1968: 398). At present the *New York Times Book Review* publishes a special section on children's books twice a year, with some quite substantial illustrated reviews written by authors, members of the staff, and other people in the field. There is usually a general essay on the subject, and an outstanding historical or critical book on children's literature may also be reviewed. Every issue usually has two to four shorter reviews of children's books. These reviews are worth checking when beginning to write a critical article about a children's author.

A crucial date for English children's books, according to Frank Eyre (1971: 26–27), and for 'intelligent reviewing, reaching a wider public' is the introduction in 1949 of a periodic, special 'Children's books supplement' to the *Times Literary Supplement*. It marked a new phase, not only introducing literate parents to new and better children's books but granting recognition to fine writers for children. The new status gained for children's books improved the willingness of publishers to risk capital on better books that went beyond the usual formulas.

In Canada, *Quill and Quire* (1935– ), like the *Times Literary Supplement* and the *New York Times Book Review*, has provided sustained reviews, particularly since it incorporated *Canadian Books for Young People*, once a separate periodical. Serious reviewing of children's books in Australia began with the establishment of the *Australian Book Review* in 1961. Its reviews were dominated by Dennis Hall (Haviland 1974: 342). The annual children's book issue has contained short articles on the history and criticism of Australian children's books. In 1965 both the national newspaper, *The Australian*, and the *Australian School Librarian* (ceased publication), began publishing regular reviews of children's books. Now *The Age* also provides articles and reviews.

## Library Publications

The further development of regular reviews and articles at the beginning of the twentieth century in the USA was carried on by librarians, and it was the librarians who published the first journal that included discussions of literature for children and adolescents as a matter of principle. Reviews in library publications of books for children and adolescents, and of books for adults working with children and books, appear sporadically at first but grow in volume as the years pass. A classic example of the process is provided by *Library Journal*, sometimes called *American Library Journal*, which was founded in 1876 as the official organ of the American Library Association. The first discussion of fiction for young people in libraries is in the April 1877 issue (Kite 1877), followed by a long article on reading matter in the public library and the public schools by Charles Francis Adams (Adams 1877). In 1882 the *Journal* began printing a 'Yearly report on boys and girls reading' by Carolyn Hewins. As time went on, articles and commentary appeared with increasing frequency until in 1942, *Library Journal* introduced a monthly review column, 'Junior books appraised'. In 1954 the column and other features were combined into a bi-monthly magazine, issued with the *Library Journal*, called *Junior Libraries*, which changed in 1961 to *School Library Journal*. The journal became so large that since January 1975 it has been issued as a totally separate publication.

By 1929 the American Libraries Association had formed a separate Children's Services Division and Young Adult Services Division which began the American Association of School Libraries (AASL) Newsletter, *Top of the News*. In January 1947 there was a change in editorial policy and the newsletter began to accept advertising and to publish more than short notices, moving by the end of the year to a magazine of sixty-four or more pages with a table of contents and longer articles. The first of these included an article about children's books for African-Americans. Succeeding volumes expanded in size and sophistication until in the fall of 1987 the name was changed to *Journal of Youth Services in Libraries*. *JOYS* now publishes substantial, well-argued articles about children's literature and librarianship and has particularly useful reviews of books for adults working with children. AASL began a separate newsletter, *School Libraries*, in 1951, which also became a journal. Its last issue was in 1973.

*The Catholic Library World* was also founded in 1929 and includes articles about children's literature in almost every issue. Although the *Wilson Library Bulletin* (1939–1995) put out monthly by H. W. Wilson and Co. dealt with libraries in general, it contained some reviews in each issue, occasionally ran an article about children's literature, and sometimes devoted an entire issue to children's literature or school libraries. Other journals useful to librarians in the USA are *Booklist, Books for Children, Bulletin of the Center for Children's Books, Children's Book Review Service,* and *Children's Literature Review, Excerpts from Reviews, Criticism, and Commentary on Books for Children and Young People* (Gale Research). (For descriptions of these journals see Meacham 1978; Reetz 1994; and Hearne 1991).

In England, the children's library movement really began in 1919, when a new Public Libraries Act lifted prior tax limitations and local authorities could spend as they saw fit for book purchases and library service (Pellowski 1968: 353). *The*

*School Library Review*, the official organ of the School Libraries Section of the Library Association, was founded in 1936, when it was issued once a term 'for private circulation among members of school staffs or these directly in touch with school libraries'. It managed to put out one volume (3, March 1941–December 1943) during the war years. Early issues have reviews and book lists, but not in the regular pattern in which they occur in later issues. By the 1950s, the journal had united with *The School Librarian*, put out by the School Library Association, and was published three times a year; it now appears quarterly. Five or six feature articles are followed by an extensive section of signed, critical children's and adolescent book reviews grouped by age level, and by reviews of works for adults dealing with children.

## Educational Publications

In the USA, journals primarily for teachers are an important source of articles and reviews, some well worth reading. The year 1912 saw the first issue of *English Journal*, published from September to May by the National Council for the Teaching of English (NCTE). *English Journal* is directed toward teachers of adolescents in the USA and, although its primary focus is material that adults ask adolescents to read rather than material marketed to children and adolescents for reading for pleasure, as early as the first issue there is a discussion of what adolescents read out of school and how teachers can help to make such reading of the best quality (Bates 1912). Another article in that issue asks a crucial question that occurs again and again in discussions of teaching reading: 'Have we aimed at the wrong thing, taught for knowledge rather than for power?' (Lewis 1912: 11). The issue ends with three detailed reviews of books for teachers and a number of 'Book notices' that include plays and stories for children. These notices begin to be annotated by the third issue. Later issues in this first year have articles discussing Oliver Optic and advocating folk-tales, myths and medieval lore for the first years of secondary school. There is also much discussion of how to properly teach poetry. As the years have passed and reading levels in the USA have declined, more and more children's literature for younger and younger children, even picture books, has been addressed by this journal in its search for ways to get adolescents interested in reading. As well as feature articles, current issues contain extensive essay reviews and annotated bibliographies.

Another official publication of the NCTE began in 1924 as *The Elementary English Review* under the editorship of C. C. Certain of Detroit. The first issue contained articles on teaching literature, staging plays, interpreting poetry, and 'The creation of Dr Dolittle' by Hugh Lofting. After the second issue, the journal included a regular book review section. In September 1975 the journal was renamed *Language Arts*; it now appears eight times a year, and centres on the theory and practice of teaching reading and writing in the elementary school. The present journal includes reviews and annotated bibliographies of children's books and audio-visual media, including selected textbooks. Some articles deal directly with children's literature, and from time to time there have been issues devoted to the subject. Since the recent promotion of 'real books' in the classroom, renewed attention has been paid to children's literature.

The year 1924 also saw the beginning of *Childhood Education*, published for the International Kindergarten Union. From the first issue it has contained reviews of books for both children and teachers. It is now put out by the Association for Childhood Education International (a USA organisation) and appears five times a year. It contains feature articles on subjects like picture books and its reviews include magazines, newspapers, films and software.

The NCTE also put out the *CLA Bulletin*, now the biannual *Journal of Children's Literature* (1994– ), focused on issues relating to children's literature and pedagogy. In 1972 the NCTE's Assembly on Literature for Adolescents began a typescript *ALAN Newsletter*, since 1979 a standard journal, *The ALAN Review*, which appears three times a year. It contains several feature articles, usually on authors, and its useful reviews of hard cover and paperback books come on file cards which can be cut out of the journal. Another NCTE publication is *College English* which, although primarily devoted to issues centred on teaching at the university level, particularly rhetoric and composition, has from time to time published critical articles about children's literature.

The other association in the USA that has a large membership and many publications is the International Reading Association; its major journal is *The Reading Teacher*. A typescript without reviews in 1948, in September 1952 it became a fully-fledged journal, edited by Nancy Larrick, with themed issues, book reviews, columns, and advertisements. Today it provides themed essay reviews of recent children's books as a regular feature. The IRA also produces *The Journal of Reading, Reading Research Quarterly*, and as of the end of 1992, eighty-two other journals and newsletters, including *The Dragon Lode* (1983– ), a journal put out by its Children's Literature and Reading special interest group. *The Dragon Lode* has two or three short feature articles, book reviews, and announcements.

A journal of high quality for those concerned with using non-fiction in their teaching is *Appraisal* (1967– ), issued by the Children's Science Book Review Committee, which is jointly sponsored by the Harvard Graduate School of Education and the New England Round Table of Children's Literature. *Appraisal* has one longer article, sometimes critical sometimes informational, at the beginning of each issue followed by fifty to seventy reviews, for young adults as well as children, in two separate paragraphs, one by a librarian, the other by a scientific specialist. (For educational journals, some no longer published, see Meacham 1978, Hearne 1991, Reetz 1990, and *Children's Literature Abstracts*). In general, the early numbers of the older journals are of greater interest to those concerned with children's books themselves; the focus in their articles on the problems that still trouble us today is a reminder of how little is new. The greater and greater emphasis in later journals on how literature should be taught and how responses should be manipulated not only makes for some dull reading but may be responsible, at least in part, for the scorn with which some academics view the educational establishment in the USA. The 'real books' movement has improved matters somewhat, but fine books have already been basalised. Education journals rarely publish sustained critical analysis.

The early history of reviewing and criticism in journals put out by the book trade, library associations, and educational associations demonstrates that *The Horn Book Magazine* did not appear in 1924 out of the blue as is sometimes claimed, but was part of an extended evolutionary process. Nevertheless there is a divide between the primarily adult-centred or child-centred publications already mentioned and journals devoted solely to a discussion and review of children's literature, and the founding of *The Horn Book Magazine* marks that divide in the USA. This critical review journal, founded by Bertha Mahony, was the outgrowth of the lists she had been compiling with her colleague Elinor Whitney during her years of work at the Bookshop for Boys and Girls. Both Aidan Chambers and Ann Durell, in their articles celebrating the fiftieth anniversary year, stress that the journal was at its inception a publicity device in the Newbery tradition and was primarily intended to sell books. Although in its beginnings the journal was consumer-orientated, rather than critical or scholarly, 'by 1925 the magazine was demonstrating an interest in authors and illustrators that was to make it a serious tool for the study of children's literature' (Durell 1974: 667). By the 1950s, *The Horn Book Magazine* was publishing serious literary evaluations, more serious than those few that appear in it today, perhaps because *The Horn Book Magazine* no longer accepts unsolicited articles. At present, the middle section of every issue is devoted to detailed one-paragraph reviews written by the editor and members of the editorial staff, and much space is given over to award acceptance speeches, portraits of the award winners, and bibliographical essays. Its focus, then, has returned to the selling of children's books. *The Horn Book Magazine* also publishes *The Horn Book Guide*, devoted solely to reviews.

The first British journal dedicated solely to children's book reviewing appeared twelve years after *The Horn Book Magazine*. It was *The Junior Bookshelf: A Review of Children's Books* and, like *The School Library Review*, began in 1936. Six issues a year contain over a hundred signed, critical reviews of new titles for children and of some secondary literature. Since 1971 there have been one or two topical essays per issue.

By the beginning of the 1960s the situation of criticism in Britain had been much improved. Margery Fisher's bi-monthly journal *Growing Point*, founded in 1962, was the first independent reviewing journal of books for children and young people directed at parents rather than librarians. Although *Growing Point* did publish reviews by others, Fisher wrote most of them herself and kept the journal going single-handedly for exactly thirty years. Fisher died 24 December 1992 (see *Children's Literature Abstracts* for the many tributes to her). *Growing Point* was followed in 1965 by Anne Wood's *Books for Your Children: The Parent's Guide*, which appears three times a year.

## Critical Journals

None of the British journals mentioned above answered the need for a forum for more sustained critical discussion. In January, 1970, Nancy Lockwood Chambers, the former editor of *Children's Book News*, issued the first number of *Signal*, which appears three times a year. *Signal* is a unique journal, unconnected to any educational or other institution or to a publishing house, although Chambers works with teachers, librarians, academics, and members of the book trade, and their ideas and comments appear in the pages of her journal. Her audience is the general reader, and the articles she publishes have interesting ideas, fluently expressed; the editing is brilliant. The influence of *Signal* extends far beyond its relatively small subscriber base: two of its articles have won the Children's Literature Association literary criticism award, and the journal has been a leader in the movement away from basal readers and back to real books. It is a rare critical book or article now that does not cite material from *Signal*. Chambers has also published the *Signal Selection of Children's Books* and is building a list of books and pamphlets derived and developed from *Signal* material.

*Signal* was quickly followed, in March 1970, by *Children's Literature in Education*, which was established by the late Sidney Robbins, a professor at the University of Exeter, as the result of the conference on Recent Children's Fiction and its Role in Education. The first two issues of the journal contained papers from the conference. In 1977 the journal added a North American editor, Joan Blos, and since 1982 the journal has been edited jointly by a North American editor (Anita Moss 1982–95; followed by Dr Margaret Mackey) and a UK editorial team, chaired by Geoff Fox. *Children's Literature in Education* emphasises both the literary and the educational and is not interested in the academic apparatus of literary criticism for its own sake. Recently the journal has published articles that are based on new developments in critical theory, but it avoids excessive jargon and insists on lively writing. The journal also publishes reviews of books about children's literature.

As in Britain, the USA lacked a forum for sustained critical discussion of children's literature, aside from *The Horn Book Magazine*, which could be viewed as a strictly commercial venture in spite of some important articles that appeared in it. Although she was a published Shakespearean scholar, when Francelia Butler joined the faculty at the University of Connecticut in 1965, she was asked to teach the courses in children's literature because her male colleagues refused to do so. Resolved to legitimise the subject, Butler formed the Children's Literature Association, won affiliation and later division status for children's literature with the Modern Language Association, and, in 1972, founded the annual of the Association, *Children's Literature*. The first issue was published by a local minister at Butler's expense, but the journal rapidly won the respect of professionals and academics. In 1992, on Butler's retirement from the University of Connecticut, editorial operations were transferred to Hollins College, with Elizabeth Keyser and R. H. W. Dillard as editors, but the journal continues to be published by Yale University Press (Glassner 1993). The most academic of the children's literature journals, *Children's Literature* demands that articles be carefully researched and be significant contributions to the field. Scholarly books about children's literature are reviewed.

Somewhat less academic than *Children's Literature*, the *Children's Literature Association Quarterly* started in 1974 as a newsletter, and from its first numbered issue (1, 1) until Winter, 1980 (4, 4) bore the title *Quarterly Newsletter*. Since 1983, the editorship of the journal has changed every five years, with a shift in emphasis as well as place of publication. Most issues contain a themed special section with a guest editor. The journal includes reviews of books about children's literature.

*The Lion and the Unicorn* was begun in 1977 to provide more room for the good writing being generated by the still relatively new field of children's literature criticism. The journal was put out by its editors, Roni Natov and Geraldine

DeLuca, with the help of the Brooklyn College Publication Office until 1985, when it was taken over by Johns Hopkins University Press; it is now edited by Louisa Smith and Jack Zipes. From January 1997 two issues per yer will be theme-centred and one will be general. Essays tend to vary in scope and quality, but a number of significant articles have appeared in the journal. There is an extended interview with a children's or youth author in every issue. Some issues contain reviews of books about children's literature. With the exception of *Signal*, all the critical journals mentioned are becoming increasingly academic, with more and more footnotes and longer and longer lists of references. The question of whether the studies that they contain are excessively academic and technical and whether they may result in reader backlash has recently been raised (Hunt 1992).

## Recent Journals

The presence of five major critical journals, *Signal* and *Children's Literature in Education* in Britain, and *Children's Literature, The Children's Literature Association Quarterly*, and *The Lion and the Unicorn* in the USA, not to mention the numerous publications put out by library and educational associations and the book trade in both countries, did nothing to inhibit the creation of new journals in the 1980s and 1990s. Of these, the most significant in Britain is the *International Review of Children's Literature and Librarianship*, founded in 1986 and edited by Margaret Kinnell. Issued three times a year, this substantial journal, despite the title, is not limited to library services but includes historical research into and sophisticated critical assessments of literature for children and adolescents. The focus is international. From 1996 it has become an annual publication.

Other recent journals appearing in Britain have been *Bookmark, Bookquest: Reviews of Children's Books, Children's Books History Society Newsletter; Children's Books in Scotland, Children's Books in Ireland, Dragon's Teeth: The Anti-Racist Children's Books Magazine* (a quarterly issued by the National Committee on Racism in Children's Books), *Pori* (formerly *Dragon's Tale*), put out by the Welsh National Centre for Children's Literature (Welsh text); and *Youth Library Review*, the official journal of the Youth Libraries Group of the Library Association, with a focus on librarianship rather than literature.

Finally, there are the journals devoted to a single author. Perhaps the oldest of these in Britain is *Jabberwocky: The Journal of the Lewis Carroll Society* (1969– ). It includes reviews and letters to the editor as well as articles. Some other journals are the *Abbey Chronicle* (Elsie J. Oxenham and affiliated school stories), *Beatrix Potter Newsletter, Mixed Moss: Journal of the Arthur Ransome Society, Mallorn* (Tolkien) and *Souvenir* (Violet Needham and related topics).

The USA also has its single author journals, the oldest and most distinguished of which is *The Baum Bugle*, founded in 1956 by the bibliophile Justin Schiller. It has a large circulation for this kind of periodical, 3,000, and covers any aspect of the Oz books: films, games, and theatrical events, as well as bibliographical and critical questions. There are also a number of publications centred on authors who wrote for both children and adults, for example Jack London and Mark Twain. The most valuable of these is *Mythlore: A Journal of J. R. R. Tolkien, C. S. Lewis, Charles Williams, and the Genres of Myth and Fantasy Stories.* It has been issued quarterly by the Mythopoeic Society since 1969, and, since it became a refereed journal, the quality of the submissions to it has improved. Even issues from the 1980s, however, contain some worthwhile essays.

Other USA journals of interest are the *Interracial Books for Children Bulletin* or *Bulletin of the Council on Interracial Books for Children* (appears irregularly), *Children's Folklore Review* (a refereed journal issued by the Children's Folklore Section of the American Folklore Society), *Dime Novel Round-up*, *Five Owls*, and the *New Advocate*. *Five Owls* was begun by its present editor, Susan Stan, in 1986 and contains one or two feature articles; most of the journal is devoted to annotated theme bibliographies and reviews. It is directed at librarians, teachers, and parents. *The New Advocate* began in 1981 as *The Advocate*, which died in 1986, and was reborn as *The New Advocate* in 1988. The journal appears quarterly, is multiculturally oriented, and is starting to move into the niche once held exclusively by *The Horn Book Magazine*. *The New Advocate* is handsomely produced and illustrated, and it is aggressively promoted by Christopher Gordon, a Boston commercial publisher of education textbooks and aids. Gordon also puts out *Perspectives*, containing primarily reviews, and an annual, *FanFare* (1993– ), the first issue of which was devoted to recent poetry for children. Not to be neglected are the reviews devoted to non-print media (although of the journals listed in Meacham 1978, nearly fifty have ceased publication). Among those still current are *Media Review Digest*, *Media and Methods*, and *Theatre, enfance et jeunesse* (Paris 1963– ). An important new journal is *Youth Theatre Journal* (Blacksburg, Virginia 1986– ).

## Canada

According to Sheila Egoff, Canada does not have a journal 'that supplies the comprehensive and comparative reviewing necessary to evaluate our books in the context of an international children's literature' (1990: 308). *Emergency Librarian* (Winnipeg, 1974– ) has reviews of children's paperbacks and books about children's literature, as well as author profiles in every issue, often based on interviews. The first and to date only journal devoted to serious criticism, *CCL: Canadian Children's Literature/Littérature canadienne pour la jeunesse: A Journal of Criticism and Review* was founded in 1975. As well as printing reviews of children's books and occasionally reviews of critical books about children's literature, *CCL* has carried historical and analytical articles which recently have been of the highest quality. The 'News from the North' column by Sarah Ellis in *The Horn Book Magazine* also provides useful information about Canadian children's literature. (For *CM: Canadian Materials for Schools and Librarians*, *Des livres et des jeunes*, *Lurelu*, *Notable Canadian Children's Books/Un choix de livres canadiennes pour la jeunesse*, *School Libraries in Canada*, and other sources of reviews, see Egoff 1990: 308, Hearne 1991: 116; Reetz 1994.)

## Australia

The older Australian journals (which are described in Reetz 1994), are *Access* (Australian School Library Association), *Magpies: Talking about Books for*

*Children, Orana: Journal of School and Children's Librarianship* (formerly *Children's Libraries Newsletter*), and *Reading Time: The Journal of the Children's Book Council of Australia*. Journals initiated after 1989 are *LINES, The Literature Base, Papers: Explorations into Children's Literature*, and *Viewpoint: On Books for Young Adults* (particularly directed at secondary school teachers and librarians). Of these, the most promising is *Papers*, described in the editor's comments prefacing the first issue as 'a journal which will give researchers into the historical background of children's literature, academic theoreticians and literary critics an outlet for their material'. Also helpful is the column by Karen Jameyson, 'News from down under', in *The Horn Book Magazine*. (For *Children's Literature Association of New Zealand: Yearbook* see Reetz 1994.)

## Some International Journals

Space does not permit a discussion of the major children's literature journals in languages other than English. A description of them can be found in Reetz 1994 and in some cases in the chapter devoted to the country of publication in International Youth Library 1991.

In 1949 the International Youth Library (IYL) was founded in Munich by Jella Lepman, and the International Board on Books for Young People (IBBY) began organising soon after. IBBY's journal is *Bookbird*, which began publication in Vienna in 1962; it carries informational articles about authors, illustrators, and children's books from all over the world. The journal has had a series of homes through the years, but is now *Bookbird: World of Children's Books*, and is edited by Meena Khorana, Morgan State University, Baltimore, Maryland. Among the publications of the IYL is *The White Ravens: A Selection of International Children's and Youth Literature*. This annual contains reviews of 300 to 400 recent books which are particularly recommended for translation into other languages.

Other recent international journals of interest are *Merveilles et Contes [Marvels and Tales]* (1987– ) and *JACL: Journal of African Children's Literature* (1989– ). *Merveilles et Contes* is a semi-annual with text in English, French, Spanish, German, or Italian, with an English summary. Although not exclusively devoted to children's literature, every issue contains at least one article on the subject, as well as reviews of scholarly books. *JACL* moved from Nigeria to the USA with its editor, Osayimwénse Osa, in 1990. Its subject is literature for and about black children all over the world.

It is fitting that this survey should end with a discussion of *Phaedrus: An International Journal of Children's Literature Research*. Edited by James Fraser, *Phaedrus* was initiated in the autumn of 1973 in an effort to acquaint scholars with the nature and extent of international children's literature research. The intent was to complement *Children's Literature Abstracts*, which had just published its first issue that spring, and which emphasised professional journals of children's literature and library service. In spite of valiant efforts to cover the international field and experiments with different publishers and journal frequencies, *Phaedrus* finally ceased publication in 1988 after the publication of a joint issue with *Die Schieffertafel*.

The problems of access to international periodicals that *Phaedrus* and *Children's*

Literature Abstracts attempted to address in 1973 have yet to be solved. The most helpful printed bibliography to date is Linnea Hendrickson's (Hendrickson 1987), which is in the process of revision. It is limited, however, to books and articles in English. The on-line/CD-Rom data bases, *ERIC* and *MLA*, cover only a limited number of children's literature journals. Perhaps the eventual answer lies in *CLIP* (Children's Literature in Periodicals), an international indexing project initiated by the Swedish Institute for Children's Books in the autumn of 1992 and including children's book institutions in Austria, Denmark, Finland, France, Germany, Holland, Norway, and Switzerland. *CLIP* will begin in 1996 with fifty to a hundred current periodicals and gradually expand back in time and beyond northern Europe. The data base will be in English.

The *Professional Periodicals in Children's Literature* (Reetz 1994) contains descriptions with addresses of over two hundred periodicals, but it is not complete. Although updates appear every few years, they are in danger of being out of date shortly after publication, given the fluidity of periodicals. With desktop publishing, it is easy for a newsletter to become a bulletin and then grow into a fully-fledged journal. Particularly in the USA, where those working in higher education must publish in order to receive promotion and tenure, the flood of articles reaching editors of existing journals can be overwhelming. On the other hand, libraries all over the world are facing budget cuts, and rather than taking on new periodicals, many are terminating the ones to which they already subscribe. Specialised journals in other disciplines have started to publish on-line on the Internet, and on-line publication may be the wave of the future for some children's literature journals. Just as the first years of the twentieth century saw the beginnings of what was to become a flood of children's literature journals, its closing years may signal the beginning of a decrease in the number of such journals that appear in print.

# References

Adams, C. F. (1877) 'The public library and the public schools', *American Library Journal* 1, 12: 437–441.

Bates, H. (1912) 'The school and current fiction', *The English Journal* 1, 1: 15–23.

Chambers, A. (1974) 'Letter from England: in a great tradition', *The Horn Book Magazine* 50, 5: 161–164.

*Children's Literature Abstracts* (1973- ) ed. G. Adams, Austin: IFLA, Children's Libraries Section.

Darling, R. L. (1968) *The Rise of Children's Book Reviewing in America, 1865-1881*, New York and London: R. R. Bowker.

Darton, F. J. H. (1932/1982) *Children's Books in England. Three Centuries of Social Life*, 3rd edn, rev. Alderson, B., Cambridge: Cambridge University Press.

Durell, A. (1974) 'Pollen in the wind', *The Horn Book Magazine* 50, 6: 665–670.

Egoff, S. and Saltman, J. (1990) *The New Republic of Childhood*, Toronto: Oxford University Press.

Eyre, F. (1971) *British Children's Books in the Twentieth Century*, New York and London: E. P. Dutton.

Glassner, S. S. (1993) 'Francelia Butler: the intrepid lady of children's literature', *Teaching and Learning Literature*, Jan/Feb: 4–7.

Haviland, V. (1974) *Children and Literature: Views and Reviews*, New York: Lothrop, Lee and Shepard.

Hearne, B. (1991) 'Research in children's literature in the US and Canada: problems and possibilities', in International Youth Library (ed.) *Children's Literature Research: International Resources and Exchange*, Munich: K. G. Saur.

Hendrickson, L. (1987) *Children's Literature: A Guide to the Criticism*, Boston: G. K. Hall.

Hunt, P. (1992) ' "Tread softly for you tread on my dreams": academicising Arthur Ransome', *International Review of Children's Literature and Librarianship* 7, 1: 1–10.

International Youth Library (ed.) (1991) *Children's Literature Research: International Resources and Exchange*, Munich: K. G. Saur.

Kite, W. (1877) 'Fiction in public libraries', *The American Library Journal* 1, 8: 35–36.

Lewis, W. D. (1912) 'The aim of the English course', *The English Journal* 1, 1: 9–14.

Meacham, M. (1978) *Information Sources in Children's Literature*, Westport, CT: Greenwood Press.

Pellowski, A. (1968) *The World of Children's Literature*, New York and London: R. R. Bowker.

Reetz, M. (1994) *Professional Periodicals in Children's Literature: A Guide*, Munich: Internationale Jugendbibliothek.

[Rigby, E.] (1844) 'Children's books', *Quarterly Review* 74: 1–3, 16–26.

Thwaite, M. F. (1963) *From Primer to Pleasure*, London: The Library Association.

## Further Reading

Salway, L. (1976) *A Peculiar Gift: Nineteenth Century Writings on Books for Children*, Harmondsworth: Kestrel (Penguin).

Silverman, J. (1980) 'A rack of journals: research in children's literature', *Children's Literature* 8: 193–204.

Weedman, J. (1986) 'Literary criticism of children's books: the significant journals', *Public Library Quarterly* 7, 1/2: 35–44.

# 42

# Censorship

## *Mark I. West*

Most discussions of the relationship between censorship and children's literature focus on attempts to ban controversial children's books from libraries, but a recounting of such attempts tells only one part of a far larger story. A children's book can be censored in many different ways. Even before its actual publication, a book can be subjected to censorship pressures. A cautious editor may require that potentially controversial passages be deleted from the book before clearing it for publication. Sometimes further deletions are made by the publisher of the paperback edition, especially if the paperback publisher markets books through the schools. Once a book is in print, efforts may be made to restrict children's access to it. These efforts can include banning it from libraries, but there are other ways that restrictions can be imposed. A parent group may pressure their local bookstore not to sell it, or a worried librarian may not allow children to check it out without parental permission. A school principal may prohibit teachers from using it in the classroom, or a religious organisation may instruct its members not to allow their children to read it.

Just as the censorship of children's literature takes many forms, there are numerous reasons why some adults try to censor certain children's books. For many would-be censors, their religious beliefs lead them to call for the censorship of children's books that, in their view, are sinful or that conflict with the precepts of their religion. Other would-be censors are motivated by political concerns. Some conservatives advocate the censorship of children's books that do not conform to their conception of 'family values', while some liberals support the censorship of children's books that they view as being racist or sexist. Often censorship cases are initiated by adults who feel strongly about one particular issue. A mother who believes that children should eat nothing but health foods, for example, may call for the censorship of a children's book that features cake and candy, or an advocate of the rights of small people might seek to censor children's books that present dwarfs in a negative light. Given the diverse reasons behind the censorship of children's literature, no overarching generalisations can be applied to every censorship case involving a children's book. Nevertheless, if these cases are viewed from a historical perspective, discernible patterns emerge.

Many of the early efforts to censor children's literature were tied to the growing acceptance of the idea of childhood innocence. Jean-Jacques Rousseau, one of the earliest proponents of this idea, presented his views on the subject in his book *Emile*, which first appeared in print in 1762. 'Let us lay down as an incontrovertible rule', Rousseau wrote, 'that the first impulses of nature are always right; there is no original sin in the human heart, and the how and why of the entrance of every vice can be traced' (Rousseau 1762/1974: 56). Rousseau believed that books contributed to the corruption of children, which is one of the reasons why he argued that children should not be taught to read until they reached the age of ten. He also felt that severe limits should be imposed on children's reading materials, a point he elaborated on in *Emile*:

> I hate books; they only teach us to talk about things we know nothing about ... Since we must have books, there is one book which, to my thinking, supplies the best treatise on an education according to nature. This is the first book Emile will read; for a long time it will form his whole library ... What is this wonderful book? Is it Aristotle? ... No; it is *Robinson Crusoe*.
>
> Rousseau 1762/1974: 147

By the beginning of the nineteenth century, Rousseau's notion of childhood innocence had gained a considerable following in both Britain and the USA. Not all of these people agreed with some of Rousseau's more extreme positions, but most supported his argument that children should be sheltered from books that could, in their view, have a corrupting influence. This development led to a tradition of self-censorship among children's authors. From the early nineteenth century until well into the twentieth century, most children's authors tried to make sure that their books contained nothing that could be considered corruptive. These authors automatically assumed that they could not refer to sexuality, mention certain bodily functions, graphically describe violent acts, portray adults in a negative light, use swear words, criticise authority figures or address controversial social issues.

Since most children's authors practised self-censorship, the publishers of conventional children's books seldom saw any need to censor the manuscripts that were submitted to them. Sometimes, however, publishers decided to reprint children's books that pre-dated the era of childhood innocence, and these books often included material that publishers found objectionable. Many nineteenth-century publishers, for example, decided that some of the bawdy passages from Jonathan Swift's *Gulliver's Travels* were inappropriate for children and excised them from juvenile editions of the book. The most frequently censored passage, according to a survey conducted by Sarah Smedman, was the one in which Gulliver extinguishes a fire in the Lilliputians' palace by urinating on it. This incident was deleted or rewritten in nearly every children's edition published during the second half of the nineteenth century (Smedman 1990: 84–85).

Although few children's authors deliberately violated taboos, occasionally authors included scenes or passages that gave their publishers pause. Beatrix Potter's publisher, for example, twice pressured Potter to delete material from her books. When Potter sent her publishers the original manuscript version of *The Tailor of Gloucester*, it contained a picture of rats having a party in the mayor's cellar. The publisher insisted that this picture be cut because it showed a rat drinking out of a suspicious-looking black bottle. Potter thought that this objection was silly, but she reluctantly went along with the change in part because she was a beginning author and felt slightly intimidated. The book, minus the picture of the rats' party, came out in 1903 (Linder 1987: 117). A few years later, however, Potter took a more defiant approach when her publisher wanted to censor a line from *The Tale of Tom Kitten*. At one point in the story, Tom falls off a wall and loses his clothes in the process. The line in the story reads 'all the rest of Tom's clothes came off on the way down'. The publisher wanted to change the line to 'nearly all', but Potter refused. Not wanting to alienate one of their best-selling authors, the publisher relented (Linder 1987: 187).

One author who openly violated many of the taboos associated with children's literature was Mark Twain. In both *The Adventures of Tom Sawyer* and *The Adventures of Huckleberry Finn*, Twain portrayed adults in a negative light and allowed his boy heroes to misbehave with impunity. Since these books were brought out by a subscription publisher rather than a standard publishing house, no one tried to censor these books before they were published. Soon after their publication, however, they became quite controversial. Many librarians refused to purchase Twain's books, and others removed them after reading them (Jordan 1948: 34–35). The librarians at the public library in Concord, Massachusetts, for example, decided to take *The Adventures of Huckleberry Finn* out of circulation, a move that received praise from the editor of the *Springfield Republican*. In an editorial reprinted in the *New York Times*, the editor noted:

> The Concord public library committee deserve well of the public by their action in banishing Mark Twain's new book, *Huckleberry Finn*, on the ground that it is trashy and vicious. It is time that this influential pseudonym should cease to carry into homes and libraries unworthy productions ... The trouble with Mr Clemens is that he has no reliable sense of propriety ... [*The Adventures of Tom Sawyer* and *The Adventures of Huckleberry Finn*'s] moral level is low, and their perusal cannot be anything less than harmful.
>
> West 1988a: 22

Twain's books sparked a great deal of controversy, but they were not the most frequently censored children's books published during the nineteenth or early twentieth centuries. That distinction belonged to a series of inexpensive publications that children generally purchased on their own. Known in Britain as 'penny dreadfuls' and in America as 'dime novels', these forms of popular culture emerged in the 1860s and remained on the scene until shortly after the turn of the century. The controversy surrounding them reflected the fact that they were written by people who cared more about meeting the demands of children than winning the approval of parents. Their authors tended to write about subjects that children found interesting even if the result was the breaking of certain taboos, for example, frequently portraying scenes of crime and violence and often depicting adults in a negative light. Because these forms of popular culture violated so many taboos, they often came under attack by self-appointed censors.

The attempts to suppress penny dreadfuls in Britain were tied to a fear that these publications might lead working-class youth to engage in anti-social behaviour. For the conservative critics who opposed the passage of Foster's Education Act of 1870 on the grounds that mass literacy could lead to social upheaval, the growing popularity of penny dreadfuls among working-class boys seemed to be an ominous development. These critics believed that the boys who read about crimes would be inspired to commit the same sorts of crimes in real life. Edward Salmon, one of the most virulent of these critics, went so far as to claim that the reading of penny dreadfuls could lead to madness. In an article published in the *Fortnightly Review*, Salmon wrote, 'Some time ago, a youth was so maddened by reading one of the tales provided for his entertainment that he shot dead his father and brother' (Salmon 1886: 255–256).

The opponents of penny dreadfuls often called for governmental suppression of them, and the police responded to this pressure on several occasions. In 1871 they forced the Newsagents' Publishing Office, one of the most prominent publishers of penny dreadfuls, to close its offices, albeit temporarily. A few years later, the police raided about a dozen news stands and seized the copies of the *Wild Boys of London*. In both of these cases, the police justified their actions by arguing that the publishers and retailers of penny dreadfuls could be prosecuted under Lord Campbell's Obscene Publications Act of 1857. This argument, however, did not hold up in court. Frustrated by their inability to eradicate the booklets, some critics launched a campaign in 1879 to enact legislation that would lead to the banning of them, but this effort never progressed much beyond the planning stages (Dunae 1979: 145). The controversy surrounding penny dreadfuls gradually subsided during the 1880s.

At the same time that the British were coming to accept penny dreadfuls, some Americans were sounding alarms about dime novels. The leader of the movement to suppress them was Anthony Comstock, the founder of the New York Society for the Suppression of Vice. Like his British counterparts, Comstock argued that this type of sensationalistic children's literature could cause children to become criminals. Comstock, however, added a religious element to his argument. In his book *Traps for the Young* (1883), he maintained that dime novels were traps that the agents of Satan created in order to corrupt children.

Comstock urged his supporters to work for the passage of laws that would prohibit or restrict their publication and distribution. Such legislation was enacted in several states, including California, Connecticut, Maine, New Hampshire, South Carolina, Tennessee, and Washington (Pivar 1973: 184). Although Comstock felt that passing such laws was the most desirable way to eliminate dime novels, he argued for the implementation of other methods of combating this 'evil' as well. He instructed parents to confiscate and burn all such books that their children brought home. He also suggested that parents apply economic pressure against businesses that sold them. 'The remedy lies in your hands,' he told his readers, 'by not patronising any person who offers these death-traps for sale ... Let your newsdealer feel that, just in proportion as he prunes his stock of that which is vicious, your interest in his welfare increases and your patronage becomes more constant' (Comstock 1883: 42).

During the first decades of the twentieth century, penny dreadfuls and dime novels gradually evolved into what became known as series books. Although series books cost more than their predecessors, they were still within the financial reach of many youngsters, and they were frequently sold directly to children. Most of the series books published in Great Britain were militaristic adventure stories in which young heroes battle the enemies of the British Empire. These books generated little controversy, but the same could not be said of their American counterparts.

Edward Stratemeyer, the leading author of series books in the United States, created numerous series, including the Rover Boys, the Bobbsey Twins, the Hardy Boys, and Nancy Drew. For the most part, Stratemeyer's books took the form of mystery stories in which youngsters solve crimes. His books were popular with children, but some adults found them objectionable and tried to discourage young people from reading them.

Librarians played a prominent role in the campaign against series books. During the early decades of the twentieth century, the *Library Journal*, the *Wilson Bulletin*, and other periodicals intended for librarians frequently published articles attacking them. The librarians who wrote these articles argued that they should be banned from public libraries because they gave children 'a false ideal of life'. These librarians especially disliked the unrealistically drawn child heroes, protesting time and again that series books' heroes were too adult-like. According to these librarians, reading about such characters aroused feelings of discontent in children, causing them to behave disrespectfully toward adults. Mary E. S. Root, a leading figure among American librarians, brought the movement to eliminate series books from public libraries to a head in 1929. She compiled a list of over sixty that she argued should 'not be circulated by standardised libraries' which appeared in the January 1929 issue of the *Wilson Bulletin*, and it sparked a lively debate in the pages of the the the *Bulletin* about whether or not librarians should attempt to censor children's reading materials (West 1988a: 27–30).

This controversy subsided in the 1930s, and there was not another major campaign to censor children's reading materials until the late 1940s when comic books came under fire. Fredrick Wertham, a New York psychiatrist, emerged as the central figure in the movement to restrict children's access to them. Wertham especially disliked horror and crime comic books, but he also disapproved of superhero comic books, such as Superman, Batman and Wonder Woman. Like the critics of penny dreadfuls and dime novels, Wertham argued that reading about violence and crime could lead children to engage in violent or antisocial behaviour. He also claimed that comic books were responsible for turning otherwise normal children into sadists and homosexuals. He first made these charges in an article published in the *Saturday Review of Literature* in 1948 and elaborated on them in his book, *Seduction of the Innocent* (1954).

Wertham called for the passage of state laws prohibiting the sale of crime comic books to children. In response to Wertham's campaign, several New York state legislators introduced a bill that would have made it a 'misdemeanour to publish or sell comic books dealing with crime, bloodshed or lust that might incite minors to violence or immorality'. In March 1952, this bill was approved by both the New York State Assembly and Senate, but the following month the governor vetoed it on the grounds that its wording was so vague that it bordered on being unconstitutional.

Although the publishers of comic books felt relieved that the New York bill did not become law, they realised that Wertham and his supporters might well succeed the next time such a bill was proposed. Hoping to defuse the campaign, the publishers of comic books adopted a programme of self-regulation. In September 1954, the Comics Magazine Association of America, an organisation representing nearly all of the major publishers of comic books, announced plans to adhere to a code of ethics, which was adopted the following month. This code prohibited the glorification of criminals and the depiction of all scenes of horror. A former judge was hired to enforce the code, and all comic books that met with his approval bore a seal which read 'Approved by the Comics Code Authority'. This system of self-censorship succeeded in dampening much of the controversy. (West 1988a: 43–53).

However, it had reverberations in Britain as well. In the years immediately following the Second World War, American comic books were often imported; many British adults disapproved of these publications, but they especially detested American horror comic books. Marcus Morris, a Lancashire vicar, spoke for many when he called these comic books 'deplorable, nastily over-violent and obscene'. In 1955, as a result of the campaign against horror comics, the importation of such comic books became illegal under the Children and Young Persons (Harmful Publications) Act (Carpenter 1983: 93).

The movement to censor comic books coincided with a period in American history often known as the McCarthy era. During this period, conservative activists called for the censorship of many forms of American culture, including movies, television programmes, and novels for adults. Works of children's literature, however, seldom attracted much attention from these would-be censors. The major way in which McCarthyism affected young people's reading experiences was through a campaign to ban certain adult novels from being taught in public high schools, which succeeded in excluding numerous works. Favourite targets of these censors included political novels that criticised America's government or economic system and books that contained profanity, such as J. D. Salinger's *The Catcher in the Rye* (Nelson and Roberts 1963: 182–183). These censors tended to ignore children's literature mainly because most children's books written in both America and Britain during this era were non-controversial and unquestionably supportive of the status quo.

During the 1960s and 1970s, American children's literature began to change. The tradition of self-censorship that had been honoured by most children's authors for decades gradually began to break down. As Americans became more accepting of sexuality and less confident in the infallibility of authority figures, a number of of authors and editors questioned the legitimacy of the taboos that had encumbered children's literature for so long. This development resulted in the emergence of a new breed of children's books. The works of Judy Blume, Norma Klein and Maurice Sendak dealt with the issue of sexuality, while other authors, such as Louise Fitzhugh, Paul Zindel, and Robert Cormier, depicted adult characters unflatteringly. At the same time, S. E. Hinton, Alice Childress, Isabelle Holland and several others wrote about controversial social issues, such as gang violence, drug abuse and homosexuality. A similar development occurred in British children's literature, but not until the 1980s. Scholars and critics began referring to many of these books as the 'new realism' in children's literature.

While several of these books raised eyebrows when they first appeared, few were actually censored during the first half of the 1970s. This situation started to change as the Moral Majority and other conservative religious and political groups gained power and influence. As the leaders of these organisations urged their followers to speak out against sex education, the teaching of evolution, and 'sinful' children's books, the new realism in children's literature came under serious attack. This trend accelerated dramatically in the early 1980s and has continued unabated into the 1990s. For the most part, however, the conservative backlash against works of new realism has been an American phenomenon.

One of the most frequently censored is Judy Blume. The censors have focused their attacks on five of her books: *Are You There God? It's Me, Margaret*; *Then Again, Maybe I Won't*; *Deenie*; *Blubber*; and *Forever*. During the first half of the 1980s, over sixty attempts to ban these works were reported to the *Newsletter on Intellectual Freedom*, and it is estimated that many more attempts went unreported. With the exception of *Blubber*, the censorship of Blume's books is the result of their sexual content. The censors dislike *Are You There God? It's Me, Margaret* because it discusses menstruation and breast development. *Then Again, Maybe I Won't* and *Deenie* are attacked for mentioning wet dreams and masturbation, and *Forever* gets into trouble because it deals with sexual intercourse and describes the use of birth-control devices.

Norma Klein, another children's author whose works are frequently targeted by censors, also comes under fire for including sexually related material in her books. Klein's first children's book, *Mom, the Wolf Man, and Me*, is sometimes censored because it contains an unmarried mother who remains sexually active. A number of Klein's other books are targeted for similar reasons. Critics attack *It's Not What You Expect* for including a character who has an abortion, *Naomi in the Middle* for explaining how conception occurs, and *It's Okay If You Don't Love Me* for portraying a teenage girl who initiates a sexual relationship.

Equally, Maurice Sendak's *In the Night Kitchen* is often censored because it contains pictures of a nude boy. *My Darling, My Hamburger* and *The Pigman*, both by Paul Zindel, are sometimes attacked by people who dislike Zindel's disparaging comments about parents and teachers. Robert Cormier's *The Chocolate War* and *I Am the Cheese* come under pressure from those who feel that they undermine parental, institutional, and governmental authority. Alice Childress's *A Hero Ain't Nothin' but a Sandwich*, is disapproved of for its discussion of drug abuse or its use of street language. These titles are only a few of the dozens of children's books that conservatives have tried to ban from libraries (West 1992: 53–54).

In addition to censoring individual children's books, many conservatives have also targeted textbooks some of which have no direct connections to children's literature. Science books, for example, have often been challenged if they contain extensive information about evolution. In some cases, however, the textbooks used in reading classes have also been subjected to censorship pressures, and these books frequently include short stories written for children as well as excerpts from children's books.

Initially, the campaign to censor reading textbooks was led by a Texas couple named Mel and Norma Gabler. In the 1960s, the Gablers began examining many of the most commonly used reading textbooks in an effort to ferret out material that they found objectionable. The Gablers felt that reading textbooks should reinforce the beliefs of conservative Christians. If the books that they examined contained stories or passages that failed their test, they would contact the books' publishers and demand that the 'objectionable' material be removed. If the publishers refused, the Gablers would urge their supporters on various school boards not to purchase the books (Noble 1990: 180–182).

The Gablers were soon joined by a host of other religious conservatives. Foremost among them were Revd Tim and Beverly LaHaye from San Diego, California. Tim LaHaye sharply criticised textbooks in *The Battle for the Public Schools*, one of a series of conservative manifestos he wrote in the early 1980s. While her husband was writing these tracts, Beverly LaHaye founded a conservative women's group known as Concerned Women for America (CWA). In 1983, CWA became a participant in a highly publicised court case that dealt with a dispute over the use of Holt, Rinehart and Winston's series of reading textbooks in Church Hill, Tennessee. While several other court cases involving conflicts over textbooks occurred during the 1980s, this case had the most direct impact on children's literature.

The Tennessee case began when Vicki Frost, a conservative fundamentalist and mother of four children who attended the Church Hill schools, complained about the opening story in *Riders on the Earth*, the reader used in her daughter's sixth-grade class. The story deals with telepathy, and Frost felt that this subject contradicted her religious beliefs. After filing her initial complaint, she went on to read the rest of the stories in the reader, and she found that she had religious objections to almost all of them. Many of the stories mention myths or non-Western religions, and she felt that these stories taught 'false religion'. Other stories include references to magic, and Frost saw this as being anti-biblical. Still others portray girls in non-passive roles, and this, according to Frost, violates the roles that God set forth for the sexes.

She decided to take her daughter out of class every time the book was used, but the school principal felt that such actions would be disruptive. Frost went ahead anyway, and she was eventually arrested for trespassing on school property. After Frost's arrest, several people in the community came to her support, one of whom contacted CWA. The leadership of CWA agreed to provide Frost with free legal assistance.

Michael Farris, the lawyer that CWA sent to Tennessee, hoped to turn this conflict into a test case and have it heard in federal court. Farris thought that the best way to accomplish this goal was to argue that the case involved constitutional issues. He decided to base his argument on the free exercise clause of the First Amendment, which guarantees the right to exercise one's religion without governmental interference. As Farris saw it, requiring students to read stories that offended their parents' religious beliefs could be interpreted as a violation of their and their parents' right to exercise their religion. He knew that if the court agreed to hear his argument, it would be a landmark case.

After many delays and complications, the case finally came to trial in 1986. The judge found in favour of Frost and her supporters. The school system, he wrote, 'burdened the plaintiffs' right to free exercise of religion' by requiring 'the plaintiffs' students to read from the Holt series'. The school board, however, appealed, and in August 1987 the United States Court of Appeals for the Sixth District overruled the original decision. As the chief judge for this court explained in his opinion, 'The requirement that public school students study a basal reader series chosen by school authorities does not create an unconstitutional burden under the Free Exercise Clause when the students are not required to affirm or deny a belief' (West 1988a: 85–96).

Even though Frost and the CWA did not ultimately win their case, the publicity and controversy surrounding the lawsuit succeeded in intimidating the publishers of the Holt series. Shortly after the case ended, Holt, Rinehart and Winston edited its reading series in an effort to make it more attractive to fundamentalists. In explaining this move, one of the publisher's representatives stated, 'When you're publishing a book, if there's something that is controversial, it's better to take it out.' Since the late 1980s, many other textbook publishers have joined Holt, Rinehart and Winston in this type of quiet censorship (Delfattore 1992: 120).

At the same time that conservatives attempted to censor the children's books and textbooks that they found offensive, some members of the political left also participated in efforts to censor certain works of children's literature. The leftists who sought to censor children's books generally had ties to the civil rights movement or the feminist movement. These people often argued that children's books with racist or sexist content should not be made available to children. The Council on Interracial Books for Children, for example, denounced numerous classic children's books for presenting Africans or African-Americans in a negative light. As a result of this campaign, many libraries stopped circulating such books as Helen Bannerman's *Little Black Sambo*, P. L. Travers's *Mary Poppins*, and Hugh Lofting's *The Story of Dr Dolittle* (MacLeod 1983: 35).

Another way in which leftists attempted to rid children's literature of racist or sexist content was by rewriting the passages that they found offensive. John Wallace, an African-American educator, engaged in this type of censorship when he removed the word 'nigger' from Mark Twain's *Adventures of Huckleberry Finn* and published his revised version under the title *The Adventures of Huckleberry Finn Adapted*. Similarly, Doug Larche rewrote many traditional nursery rhymes in an effort to make them less violent and sexist. In his book, entitled *Nursery Rhymes: The Equal Rhymes Amendment*, Humpty Dumpty is put back together by a coalition of horses, women and men, and Little Miss Muffet puts the spider in the garden to catch insects (Rollin 1992: 138).

The liberals and radicals in America were not alone: similar restrictions were attempted in Britain (Barry 1992: 234–238). A number of British feminists, for example, launched a campaign to ban Roald Dahl's *The Witches* from school libraries because Dahl's female witches are portrayed so negatively. During a discussion of this case, Dahl made an insightful observation about the censorship of children's literature:

> It seems to me that in England more censorship pressures are coming from the left than the right. We have a number of cities that are run by left-wing groups, and these people often try to take certain books out of the schools. Of course, right-wing people have been equally intolerant. It's usually the extremes on either side that want to ban books.
>
> West 1988b: 73

Dahl's observation that censors tend to be extremists applies to America as well as Britain. Throughout the history of children's literature, the people who have tried to censor children's books, for all their ideological differences, share a rather romantic view about the power of books. They believe, or at least profess to believe, that books are such a major influence in the formation of children's values and attitudes that adults need to monitor nearly every word that children read. Because the proponents of censorship invest books with so much power, they reject as too dangerous the idea that children should be exposed to a wide variety of books and be trusted to make their own selections. The people who seek to censor children's books may be practising intolerance, but in their own eyes, they are protecting innocent children and working for the benefit of society.

## References

Barry, P. (1992) 'Censorship and children's literature: some post-war trends', in Hyland, P. and Sammells, N. (eds) *Writing and Censorship in Britain*, London: Routledge.

Carpenter, K. (1983) *Penny Dreadfuls and Comics*, London: Victoria and Albert Museum.

Comstock, A. (1883) *Traps for the Young*, New York: Funk and Wagnalls.

DelFattore, J. (1992) *What Johnny Shouldn't Read: Textbook Censorship in America*, New Haven, CT: Yale University Press.

Dunae, P. (1979) 'Penny dreadfuls: late nineteenth-century boys' literature and crime', *Victorian Studies* 22, 2: 133–150.

Jordan, A. (1948) *From Rollo to Tom Sawyer and Other Papers*, Boston: Horn Book.

Linder, L. (1987) *A History of the Writings of Beatrix Potter*, London: Frederick Warne.

MacLeod, A. (1983) 'Censorship and children's literature', *Library Quarterly* 53, 1: 26–38.

Nelson, J. and Roberts, G. (1963) *The Censors and the Schools*, Boston: Little.

Noble, W. (1990) *Bookbanning in America*, Middlebury, VT: Eriksson.

Pivar, D. (1973) *Purity Crusade: Sexual Morality and Social Control, 1868–1900*, Westport, CT: Greenwood Press.

Rollin, L. (1992) *Cradle and All: A Cultural and Psychoanalytic Study of Nursery Rhymes*, Jackson, MS: University Press of Mississippi.

Rousseau, J. (1762/1974) *Emile*, London: J. M. Dent.

Salmon, E. (1886) 'What boys read', *Fortnightly Review* 45, 1: 255–256.

Smedman, S. (1990) 'Like me, like me not: *Gulliver's Travels* as children's literature', in Smith, F. (ed.) *The Genres of Gulliver's Travels*, Newark, DE: University of Delaware Press.

West, M. (1988a) *Children, Culture, and Controversy*, Hamden, CT: Archon Books.

—— (1988b) *Trust Your Children: Voices Against Censorship in Children's Literature*, New York: Neal-Schuman.

—— (1992) 'Teaching banned children's books', in Sadler, G. (ed.) *Teaching Children's Literature: Issues, Pedagogy, Resources*, New York: Modern Language Association.

## Further Reading

Baker, M. (1992) *A Haunt of Fears: The Strange History of the British Horror Comics Campaign*, Jackson, MS: University Press of Mississippi.

Burress, L. (1989) *Battle of the Books: Literary Censorship in the Public Schools*, Metuchen, NJ: Scarecrow Press.

Davis, J. (ed.) (1979) *Dealing with Censorship*, Urbana, IL: National Council of Teachers of English.

Hentoff, N. (1982) *The Day They Came to Arrest the Book*, New York: Delacorte.

Jenkinson, E. (1979) *Censors in the Classroom: The Mind Benders*, Carbondale, IL: Southern Illinois University Press.

Miles, B. (1980) *Maudie and Me and the Dirty Book*, New York: Knopf.

Tucker, N. (ed.) (1976) *Suitable for Children: Controversies in Children's Literature*, Berkeley, CA: University of California Press.

# 43

# Prizes and Prizewinners

## *Keith Barker*

Why award prizes? What importance is attached to them by writers, publishers, those selecting books and, probably most importantly, children themselves? What part of our personality desires perfection, discarding along the way the seemingly worthless? And in these days of sponsorship, what do organisations which help to fund the administration of an award and the glittering prizes themselves seek to gain from their involvement?

The awarding of prizes encapsulates many of the dilemmas of any adult-driven enterprise which is intended to benefit young people and helps to focus discussion on how far those who select reading material for children have to take into account the needs and desires of young people while also satisfying the adult's innate desire to improve children's tastes. Walter de la Mare's often quoted dictum that only the best is good enough for children would appear to be particularly applicable, despite the fact that this is now seen as something of an elitist viewpoint. But who should decide what is the best and what indeed that definition of best should be? Enid Blyton and Roald Dahl have almost certainly been the best children's writers to capture the child reader's attention and hold it; but would they be considered therefore in de la Mare's 'best' theory? The debate around children's reading habits has often circled around these very dilemmas and any discussion of the awarding of prizes needs to take these factors into account.

But what of the prizes themselves? The two oldest awards in the English speaking world bear striking similarities. The oldest, the John Newbery Medal, named after the publisher of *A Little Pretty Pocket Book*, which some see as the first work published specifically for children, was first mooted at the 1921 conference of the American Library Association. The publisher Frederick Melcher was highly impressed by the response to a talk he gave to a group of children's librarians:

> As I looked down from the platform at the three or four hundred people, I thought of the power they could have in encouraging the joy of reading among children. I could see that I was sure of having the librarians' cooperation in Children's Book Week, but I wanted to go further and secure their interest in the whole process of creating books for children, producing them, and bringing them to the children.

> Smith 1957: 36

This helped him very quickly (in fact, during the conference) to formulate the idea of presenting an annual prize for a children's book. It is interesting that he chose children's librarians as trustees of such an award at a time when their number was only slowly increasing. He did, however, have definite reasons for selecting such a group: 'their work had equal concerns with all age levels. They brought together every kind of reader on equal footing, whereas parents and teachers were bound to their specified age groups.' (36) After discussion, he made a spontaneous proposal to the gathering about the prize and was greeted with such a rush of enthusiasm that delegates there and then wished to make a presentation to Hugh Lofting's *The Story of Doctor Dolittle*. In the event, the award was first made the following year to one of the few non-fiction titles to win, Henrik Van Loon's *The Story of Mankind*.

Melcher did have definite reasons for introducing the Newbery Medal: as Smith (1957: 37) has said 'he thought children's librarians should find ways to encourage the creation of more that was worthwhile, by writers of outstanding ability'. A similar feeling lay behind the foundation of Britain's oldest children's book award, the Carnegie Medal. The first editorial of *Library Association Record*, the British Library Association's trade journal, in 1937, in announcing the medal, mentioned that one of its purposes was to encourage the improvement of standards, while W. C. Berwick Sayers, one of the architects of the award, defined the following criteria. An award-winner would be

> a book for a child somewhere between the ages of nine and twelve, but need not be absolutely within these age limits. Its appeal was to be universal, and therefore it was to be a book which appealed to both sexes equally, so far as any book could. It is possible that the greatest books for children do possess this equal appeal. In literary form it should be in the best English; its story should follow the line of the possible, if not the probable; its characters should be alive, its situations credible, and its tone in keeping with the generally accepted standards of good behaviour and right thinking.
>
> Sayers 1937: 218

Again, librarians were the main force behind this award, at a time when children's librarians were very rare and librarians themselves were not perceived as a group likely to be at the forefront of literary innovation.

It should not be assumed, however, that because the Newbery and Carnegie medals were low-key affairs, particularly in comparison with their modern, media-attracting counterparts, that they were left to pass unnoticed. From the beginning, their administrative decisions were questioned and the books chosen for honour were the source of much discussion. It should always be remembered that in its second year of existence, the year that *The Hobbit* was published, the Carnegie Medal went to Eve Garnett's *The Family from One End Street*. What indeed is more important: honouring innovative material, which at the time Garnett's book was, or trying to find a book which may (or more likely, may not) become a modern classic, as Tolkien's has?

The next awards both organisations established have been far less controversial. Both were for illustrated material and both were named after famous Victorian artists. The American Library Association's Randolph Caldecott Medal was first awarded in 1938 and the British Library Association's Kate Greenaway Medal followed in 1955. It is interesting that illustration should often be considered as of secondary importance to imaginative writing, as if it required less intellectual acumen. This is often how such awards are perceived today, even with the establishment of awards like the Emil Award (from 1982, administered by the British Book Trust) and the Mother Goose Award (from 1972, administered by Books for Children), designed specifically to honour illustrations. One problem is that many members of a selection panel feel at a loss at assessing illustration, particularly as it is such a personal reaction to the style of its creator.

But is this not the same with fiction? However much one tries to make book-selection objective, it is still very much personal reaction which is the major factor in deciding to recommend a title. Librarians are as guilty of this as any other group, although they do try to temper it with an overview of the requirements of their customers. But they can often be appalled by these very requirements. It should be remembered that one of the contributory factors in the setting up of both the Newbery and Carnegie Medals which were each established at a time when many children's books, both physically and in content, promised considerably more than they delivered, was dismay at the lack of quality children's publishing.

However, one controversy which has raged throughout the history of both awards is that the books selected by the adult members of the awards panels are not enjoyed by children:

> what has become quite obvious is that the chosen book need appeal only to more intelligent children and adults. The consideration that it might encourage or discourage young readers of average intelligence is, of course, not one of the criteria of choice, alas.
>
> Murison 1973: 144

This thinking is one of the reasons why in recent years there has been a great increase in the type of award known as 'children's choice'. Here the majority of the decisions are taken by child readers, although in many cases under adult supervision. There are a significant number of these awards in the USA, many of which appear to have been won mainly by Judy Blume whose name has not figured prominently in awards chosen by adults. She has been the recipient of the Texas Children's Choice Award every year since 1978 while three of her books have won the North Dakota Children's Choice Award. However, this prize has also been given to *Return of The Jedi: The Storybook* and the book of the film *ET.* It is also interesting to note that Judy Blume's most popular (and most controversial) book, *Forever*, has never won a children's choice award.

The most well-established such award in Britain is the Children's Book Award, administered by the Federation of Children's Book Groups, an organisation intended mainly for parents. Pat Thomson, one of the originators of the award, has discussed the differences between expected and actual attitudes of the child selectors:

> When it comes to the actual winners, however, it is surprising how unified the results can be and we adults have learnt to respect the children's judgement. They can be very strict. A book which is 'yeah, great, smashing' for a good read does not necessarily make it to the short list. The children demand a bit more from the actual winner. As one child said 'a really good book stays in your mind'.
>
> Thomson 1985: 24

Indeed, the winners of this award and similar British 'children's choice' awards are not that different from those of the established awards. The *Guardian* Award was established in 1966 as a direct reaction to the traditional winners of the Carnegie Medal. John Rowe Townsend, then the newspaper's literary editor, has said:

> We had a feeling that an award which was made and administered by a particular body of people might tend to go to the same kind of book. In the three years before we decided to start our award, the Carnegie, as it happened, had been awarded to three successive sound, elegantly written, beautifully produced, Oxford novels, and we wondered, perhaps, if a different perspective might conceivably produce a different kind of winner.
>
> Townsend 1978: 14

Just over ten years later, however, he was admitting: 'there has been rather more overlap between the Guardian and the Carnegie than I expected. Our winners and runners-up have frequently been winners or runners-up for the Carnegie as well' (14).

Similarly, The Other Award was established for non-biased books of literary merit in 1975, a year in which, as Rosemary Stones, the award's originator, observed, 'Mollie Hunter, a fine children's writer, was awarded the Carnegie Medal for a book that was nowhere near her best; nor was it the best piece of writing published for children that year' (Stones 1978: 182). That award was set up for a precise purpose, as indeed is the clumsily named A Book Can Develop Empathy Award (formerly the Kind Writers Make Kind Readers Award) designed to promote empathy for animals. The Other Award was established to honour writing which was intended to counteract the 'isms' in children's books (which were a topic of great debate in the 1970s and 1980s) and to highlight those books which attempt to portray positive images of minorities. It selected a list of four or five titles, none promoted above the others, honoured writers like Farrukh Dhondy and Bernard Ashley, announced its decisions in an intelligent manner (unlike the bland praise at so many awards ceremonies) and was then terminated in 1988 'not because all the "other" battles have been won but because it's time to think of new and imaginative ways of winning them' (Stones 1988: 22).

Other awards that try to highlight excellence in what is often a didactic type of literature include the Children's Peace Literature Award which is sponsored by the Psychologists for the prevention of war, a specialist group of the Australian Psychological Society. America also has several such awards, probably the most famous of which is the Coretta Scott King Award inaugurated in 1969. One English commentator has praised the presentation of this award:

> You do not have to be at this occasion long to sense that there is more at issue here than the celebration of good books. Librarians, who began and maintain it, writers, artists, publishers and sponsors are connected, in the act of making and celebrating this award, to a rich and complex strand of American life. For 'people of colour' the pain and the pride of their history, of their struggle for human and civil rights, is an ever-present and unfinished story.
>
> Triggs 1989: 16

Although English-speaking countries have a significant share in children's book prizes, particularly the USA and Australia, other countries also have a large number, most particularly India, Poland and France. There are also some international awards, the most famous of which is the Hans Christian Andersen Award, first awarded in 1956 by the International Board on Books for Young People (IBBY). Patricia Crampton, one of the British judges for a number of years, has spoken of the problems such an award causes, both practical and theoretical:

> One of the biggest problems in serving on the international jury is Getting the Books. We receive an average of 10 books by each nominee and there are usually about 32 nominations – 320 books. The jury meets in April, so we hope to start receiving the books in the previous September – little enough time one would think. Inevitably the ideal is not achieved. 1978 provides a classic illustration. The Russian juror did not receive the works of Alan Garner and Charles Keeping, all despatched in good time, until long after the meeting had taken place. The work of the internationally popular Janusz Stanny reached scarcely any jurors and was reluctantly dropped from the list. The Spanish nominees decided on air freight as their method of despatch; jurors found themselves with invitations from Customs to come and pay for the release of the books at the airport. When claimed, the books turned out to be only those of the author nominee, the illustrator's never arrived anywhere.
>
> Crampton 1984: 16

As for the criteria for the selection of an international award by a jury of ten who are unlikely to be proficient in all languages represented, Crampton feels:

> What is 'fair'? Should we stick to excellence as the first criteria? (I think that in fairness, ultimately, to all children we should.) Or should we to some extent at least cause the award to move around as a sort of congratulation for progress or to show our sympathy for effort (not the same thing!). Should we broaden the scope of the awards?
>
> Crampton 1984: 16

However, one American judge has praised the award for raising the profile of books which under normal circumstances would not be published in countries other than their origin:

> We have much to gain by reading and sharing the works of international authors and illustrators. Let's begin by learning who other cultures regard as their great writers, and then approaching them with the respect they deserve. The experience may be eye-opening.
>
> Garrett 1993: 314

So much for the prizes themselves, but what about the winning books and their authors and illustrators? It has to be said first of all that most are pleased to have been recognised by an award in the insecure world of creative writing (the reactions of the unsuccessful candidates are not usually reported, however). Whether a book's winning an award has a great effect on sales, however, is sometimes disputed, although it varies from country to country. Liz Attenborough, publishing director of Puffin, says

> The Japanese for example are wild about awards. When one of our books gets an award we get letters from publishers all over the world about foreign editions. And when *Sunshine* [by Jan Ormerod] won the Mother Goose Award the Australian publisher ordered an instant reprint of 5,000. That would never happen here.
>
> Bradman 1983: 4

The Newbery Medal has a far greater effect on the purchasing policy of American librarians than the Carnegie Medal does on their British counterparts. In the year immediately following its being awarded the Newbery Medal, a winning book is expected to sell 50,000 copies, with honour books selling between 10,000 and 20,000 copies. The apparent lack of sales in Britain is probably due to insufficient interest in award winning books on the part of British librarians, or more generously, to the fact that they have already purchased them: do British librarians set trends rather than follow them? The sales figures quoted for the Newbery Medal should also be seen in context, as one award-winning American publisher sees them:

> To look at the impact of the Newbery and Caldecott awards on the total hard cover trade children's book industry, we had to consult the invaluable tables and charts available in *Publisher's Weekly*. According to the February 19, 1979, issue ... the average price of a children's book in 1978 was $6.59. And for the same year, estimated publishing industry reports for hard cover children's book sales in the United States ... are $134,600,000. Using $7.95 as the average price of a winning or honour book published in 1978, that means that approximately $795,000 was spent on the winners and $349,000 on the four honour books, for a total of $1,444,800 – and that's less than 1 per cent of the total children's book sales last year?
>
> Kayden and Glazer 1979: 42

Penelope Lively has this to say about the effects of children's book awards on sales:

> Trying to determine the effect of literary prizes on book sales is a baffling exercise. Two of my children's books have won awards: *The Ghost of Thomas Kempe* won the Carnegie Medal for 1973, *A Stitch in Time* the Whitbread prize for 1976. *Thomas Kempe* has done well ever since, *Stitch in Time* has not distinguished itself particularly. But they are very different kinds of book, and I can't help feeling *Thomas Kempe* might have been more popular anyway, without the initial impetus of an award, though there's no doubt at all the Carnegie ... does a great deal to help a book on its way. *Thomas Kempe* was doing quite well even before the announcement of the award – 4,500 hardback in the first year – but this continued with another 5,500 in the next, followed by a startling (to me at least) 63,000 paperback in 1976 ...
>
> Lively 1979: 70–71

As Liz Attenborough has said in another context: 'If an award goes to a bad book it won't help it sell, and it won't help it last' (Bradman and Triggs 1983: 4).

One of the main dangers to prize-winning authors is if they try to reproduce that winning formula. Robert Westall has described how his writing was affected when he won an award for his first published work:

> And then *Machine Gunners* won the Carnegie, and it felt like the whole world was watching; for a month I couldn't write at all. The burden of all their expectations was totally flattening. My target figure had grown from one to thousands; how could I please them all. To my shame, I tried. Crawlingly and contemptibly, though unconsciously, I tried. The amount of swearing in my books dropped; the intellectual content, the scholarship and research grew. I began writing books for the children of publishers, librarians and the literary gent of *The Times* ... Now that I am at least conscious of what I was doing, I look around and see so many 'good' children's books written for the same bloody audience. Books that gain splendid reviews, win prizes, make reputations and are unreadable by the majority of children.
>
> Westall 1979: 37–38

Westall's final point is a criticism levelled frequently at the winners of children's book awards; particularly the more established ones. The early years of the Newbery Medal saw the selection committee asking itself such questions:

> The responsibility for the Medal was never held lightly. Were the award books too literary? too old in appeal? Were some indeed read more by the high-school ages? Were they running too much to the girls' side? Where were the strong red blooded books for boys?
>
> Smith 1957: 60–61

The Carnegie Medal was frequently criticised for similar reasons. One librarian called the winners 'the great unread', and critics have cited particular winners:

> *The God Beneath the Sea*, the Carnegie medal winner, is an outstanding book; but it is not for children. This award reflects the attitude of too many children's librarians who are so concerned with the elevation of literary taste that they are blind to effective methods of raising it.
>
> Murison 1971: 162

> Not one child enjoyed *City of Gold*, and in fact we received criticism about the way the stories were re-told in the book ... Surely one of the most important characteristics of a book put forward as a contender for the Carnegie award is that it should be stimulating and enjoyable for children to read?
>
> Bonfield and Hopkins 1981: 441

> [On *City of Gold*] As regards the awards in general, why does the committee so often choose something that no 'ordinary' child will read? Every year there are books really offering something new and fertile which give children opportunities for growing; every year they are passed by.
>
> Taylor 1981: 540

But who or what is this 'ordinary' child so often mentioned by critics of prizewinners? This would appear to be one of the most fundamental issues in selecting quality material for young people by adults, whether as award-winning books or for their normal reading matter? As John Rowe Townsend notes: 'It has been pointed out time and time again that children's books are written by adults, published by adults, reviewed by adults, and, in the main, bought by adults. The whole process is carried out at one, two, three, or more removes from the ultimate consumer' (Townsend 1980: 194). So should adults dictate their own preferences and prejudices to children? Or should they try to encourage young people to stretch their imaginations and vocabulary further than they would normally wish to do?

The ramifications of this argument have seen dramatic changes since the establishment of the Newbery and Carnegie medals. At that time the wildly held view encapsulated Walter de la Mare's 'only the best is good enough for children' view as well as C. S. Lewis's dictum that a good children's book is one that is worth reading by an adult as much as by a child. In the 1990s children have changed as much as their literature. Their attention span is said to be much shorter (due, it is argued, to new technologies and the influence of television which imposes much quicker response rates on their participants than reading traditionally does). There is a much stronger emphasis on egalitarianism and anything which rises above the norm is often regarded as tainted in some way. So is the 'only the best' viewpoint still valid?

Of course other prizewinners are criticised for the ideology of their books. A famous essay by Jason Epstein tackles a Newbery Medal winner, Elizabeth George Speare's *The Bronze Bow*, which seems to preach the virtues of conformity:

> It is thickly pious and its factitious historical setting is presented in language so drab and abstract and even, occasionally, illiterate, that it is impossible to adjust one's ear to it ('Prodded on by weary drivers, the camels swayed slowly'. 'The morsels of food had not begun to whet his hunger'.) But the trouble is less with the book's prose or even with its fake historical and religious paraphernalia than with the smugness of its doctrine.
>
> Epstein 1980: 80

A similar situation arose over K. M. Peyton's *Flambards* quartet. This was the winner of the *Guardian* award and one of the books, *The Edge of the Cloud*, was a Carnegie Medal winner (both in 1969). One critic, Dominic Hibberd, objected to the awarding of prizes to these books:

> It is my contention that the *Flambards* trilogy, though a lively and enjoyable story, is, if judged like any other group of novels, very definitely not of the first rank; and I shall suggest that, even if there are special standards to be invoked, the Carnegie judges do not seem to have used them in this case.
>
> Hibberd 1972: 5

Hibberd criticises the characterisation of the books' heroine, Christina, and the male characters, the avoidance of mediation about social issues raised by the plot and the author's style:

If you're a critic of the Carnegie kind you don't notice the bad style here. You don't wonder how pain can be shot through with stabs and seamed with chasms, how stabs can flick and shoot (or is it shot silk that we are supposed to think of), or how the whole weird concoction can be said to dog somebody. No, you seize upon those dear old chestnuts 'frustration and loneliness' and praise the author for 'raising issues'. Mrs Peyton's insight into Christina's relationship with Will 'raises issues of fundamental significance to adolescent self-awareness', according to the chairman of the Carnegie Medal committee. This dusty mouthful of cliches is supposed to be a compliment; but any book can raise an issue and far too many do.

Hibberd 1972: 6

He accuses Colin Ray, chairman of the selection committee, of 'using standards which in kind are the same as adult ones, but which in degree are lower and less demanding. If they were as high and as demanding he could not, for example, have praised Mrs Peyton's skill in characterisation or her evocation of atmosphere with such marked enthusiasm' (15). Colin Ray counters this:

What the committee seeks, in my experience, is a book, not necessarily breaking entirely new ground, but of the highest quality in its genre. And in considering quality, literary quality is only one aspect: its potential impact on the young reader, its ideas, its chances of being read, its individual aspects which make it stand out from the rest, are relevant.

Ray 1972: 6

To the critic, to whom 'literary quality' is the overriding aspect of giving awards to children's books, this is an unacceptable attitude and can explain why so many award winning books have not received the approbation of the purists. Lance Salway has observed that

worthy historical novels like Mollie Hunter's *The Stronghold* and amiable fantasies like Penelope Lively's *The Ghost of Thomas Kempe* hardly reflect the present state of children's literature? Barbara Willard's Mantlemass books – surely the finest historical novels for the young in recent years – did not even feature on the Honours list for the Carnegie Medal. Such outstanding and challenging novels as Jane Gardam's *The Summer after the Funeral* and William Mayne's *The Jersey Shore* have been ignored too.

Salway 1976: 888

However, is the rearranging of award winning books just an interesting party game? After all, the books Salway cites as unjustly neglected have hardly become timeless classics. Perhaps John Rowe Townsend is right when he says that

No sensible commentator would expect to find a list that fitted his own prescription exactly; everyone would agree that, with benefit of hindsight, it would be pleasant (though clearly impracticable) to reshape the list, remove the weaker titles, and bring in books that now seem to have been mistakenly passed over. No two people would agree on what should be discarded or introduced.

Townsend 1975: 152

So what is the value of awards to the children's book world? They often create controversy, they are a catalyst for discussion of what children read or what they should be reading. But if the awards were all to be dissolved, would children really suffer inordinately? As I have stated elsewhere in the context of just one award:

> it seems to me to be dangerous to attach too much importance to the presenting of any prize. The administering body of any award, from the Nobel Prize to a local flower show, is treading a dangerous path, for it is saying that one article is superior to another when one may be intrinsically different with a subtly unusual set of qualities. To dispense judgement from on high and class one better than another smacks of the ridiculous. Where children's book awards are vital is in bringing children and books together as often as possible: the goal for which we should all be working. If a child's life has been in some way altered by that child reading *Tom's Midnight Garden*, or even an 'unpopular' book like *The God Beneath the Sea*, then the ... years of the Carnegie Medal, with all its tribulations, turmoils and arguments, will definitely have been worthwhile.
>
> Barker 1986: 43

# References

Barker, K. (1986) *In the Realms of Gold: The Story of the Carnegie Medal*, London: MacRae.

Bonfield, G. and Hopkins, J. (1981) 'Carnegie criteria', *Library Association Record* 83, 9: 441.

Bradman, T. and Triggs, P. (1983) 'The awards business', *Books for Keeps* 20: 4–5.

Crampton, P. (1984) 'The Hans Christian Andersen Award', *Books for Keeps* 25: 16.

Epstein, J. (1980) 'Good bunnies always obey': books for American children, in Egoff, S., Stubbs, G. T. and Ashley, L. F. (eds) *Only Connect*, 2nd edn, Toronto: Oxford University Press.

Garrett, J. (1993) 'Far-away wisdom: three nominees for the 1992 Andersen Prize', *The Reading Teacher* 46, 4: 310–314.

Hibberd, D. (1972) 'The *Flambards* Trilogy: objections to a winner', *Children's Literature in Education* 8: 5–15.

Kayden, M. and Glazer, S. M. (1979) 'For whom the call tolls: the Newbery-Caldecott Awards from the publishers' viewpoint', *Top of the News* 36, 1: 35–42.

Lively, P. (1979) 'Winning reflections', *Author* 90, 2: 70–71.

Murison, W. J. (1971) 'Carnegie Medal', *Library Association Record* 73, 8: 162.

—— (1973) 'Carnegie Medal', *Library Association Record* 75, 7: 144.

Ray, C. (1972) '*The Edge of the Cloud*: a reply to Dominic Hibberd', *Children's Literature in Education* 9: 5–6.

Salway, L. (1976) 'Kids' Oscars', *Times Literary Supplement* 16 July: 888.

Sayers, W. C. B. (1937) 'The Library Association Carnegie Medal and Mr Arthur Ransome', *Library Association Record* 39, 5: 218–219.

Smith, I. (1957) *A History of the Newbery and Caldecott Medals*, New York: Viking.

Stones, R. (1978) 'The Other Award', in Library Association, *Study School and National Conference Proceedings*, London: The Library Association.

—— (1988) '13 other years: the Other Award 1975–1987', *Books for Keeps*, 53: 22.

Taylor, J. (1981) 'Extraordinary', *Library Association Record*, 81, 11: 540.

Thomson, P. (1985) 'The Children's Book Award', *Books for Your Children* 20, 2: 24.

Townsend, J. R. (1975) 'A decade of Newbery books in perspective' in Kingman, L. (ed.) *Newbery and Caldecott Medal Books 1966–1975*, Boston: The Horn Book.

—— (1978) 'Ten years of the *Guardian* Award' in *Federation of Children's Book Groups Year Book*, Birmingham: Federation of Children's Book Groups.

—— (1980) 'Standards of criticism for children's literature' in Chambers, N. (ed.) *The Signal Approach to Children's Books*, Harmondsworth: Kestrel.

Triggs, P. (1989) 'Book awards – American style', *Books for Keeps* 54: 16.

Westall, R. (1979) 'How real do you want your realism?', *Signal* 28: 34–46.

## Further Reading

Campbell, A. K. D. (1990) *Outstanding Children's Books*, Swansea: Librarians of Institutes and Schools of Education.

Jones, D. B. (ed.) (1988) *Children's Literature Awards and Winners*, Detroit: Neal-Schuman.

Manning, R. (1969) 'Whatever happened to Onion John?', *Times Literary Supplement* 4 December: 1383–1384.

Moransee, J. R. (1983) *Children's Prize Books*, Munich: Saur.

Morpurgo, M. (1992) 'When the best is not good enough', *Times Educational Supplement* 27 November: 10.

Powling, C. (1993) 'Contemplating Carnegie', *Books for Keeps* 82: 3.

# 44

# Translation

## *Ronald Jobe*

What would our lives and those of our children be like without translations of great pieces of literature such as the Bible, the Greek, Norse and Asian myths and legends – the *Iliad* and *Odyssey*, the fables of *Aesop*, and *The Ramayana*? Children continue to enjoy such classics as the *Arabian Nights* from the Arabic (1712), *The Swiss Family Robinson* from the German (1814), the Grimm's *Household Stories* from the German (1823), Andersen's *Fairy Tales* from the Danish (1846), *Heidi* from the German (1884) and *Pinocchio* from the Italian (1891). Thus, translations form a major part of our Western literary heritage.

Literature in translation enriches our lives by providing sensitive glimpses into the lives and actions of young people located in other parts of the world. Translated books become windows, allowing readers to gain insights into the reality of their own lives through the actions of characters like themselves. They frame experiences in other cultures vastly different from their own. Children's lives would be considerably less rich if they could not rejoice in the antics of Pippi Longstocking, see the splendour of the Alps through Heidi's eyes, experience the itchy noise of Pinocchio, or laugh at the blunderings of Robber Hotzenplotz, and the foibles of Mrs Pepperpot.

The tradition of translating literature for young people is a long-standing one in Europe. Surrounded by many languages, Europeans accept translations as a daily part of life. European publishers use translations to complement their own lists: between 30 and 70 per cent of the children's books published in Europe are translated, and it is considered important to have books from many countries available for children to read.

The same welcoming tradition of translations has not been evident in English-speaking countries. A few committed editors and publishers, such as Klaus Flugge of Andersen Press, Dorothy Briley of Clarion Books, and Margaret McElderry of McElderry Books, have tried to increase the numbers of translated titles but the overriding view in publishing seems to be that because the national output includes every genre and is of high standard, only English language books are necessary.

## The Translation Process

The translation of a work of literature from one language into another is a most challenging and demanding undertaking. Although not recognised with either the same status or financial remuneration as scientific or technical translators, literary translators face a far more complicated process, especially in translating for young people. They require a knowledge of linguistics; an appreciation of literature for children; a writer's instincts; and an awareness of the interests of English-speaking children.

One of the reasons why publishers are reluctant to include books in translation on their lists is the complex nature of the translation process and the difficulty of finding highly qualified people to translate the literature successfully. Unless the editor reads the original language, the translator's judgement proves to be vital, and the editor is dependent upon it for the success of the publication.

Translators are faced with the dilemma; do they produce a literal, word for word rendering of the story or do they flow with the spirit of the story. There are dangers inherent in both positions, for a lack of vitality and readability may result from being too literal, and an adapted version may easily be far removed from the author's original intent. These adaptations become particularly bothersome when they are oversimplified for younger children. In the purest form, then, translating literature for children presents a complex challenge wherein the translator tries to retain the original sense and meaning of the story in another language.

What is the process of translating? How is one work of art transformed into another? Several translators have distinctive views on their role as the process applies to themselves. American writer and translator of many Greek novels for young people, for example, Edward Fenton:

> The first and foremost aspect of translation is, of course, that of meaning. The translator must know both languages well enough to know what is meant in the original language and then to dredge from the depths of his experience and judgement in the second language the most effective, most suitable, and most evocative equivalent word or phrases. In addition to this, translation is not merely a matter of shifting linguistic gears. It is also a shift from one culture to another, from one way of thought into another, from one way of life into another. What may be strange and exotic must be made to seem, if not familiar, at least rational and acceptable.
>
> Fenton 1977: 639

One of the most internationally recognised translators is Patricia Crampton of Britain. She translates from six languages and views the process not as a cultural mirror but as an active performance.

> You read a score and you do your very best to perform it in such a way that the audience understands what the composer meant.
>
> [The process has to be] ... totally faithful to what your author intended. Almost inevitably you will be dealing with an author who writes well. But writing well involves different rhythms. And certainly if we just take Swedish, German, and English, you have got three tremendously different rhythms. You have somehow got to be true to the artist in the author, his own creativity. While you hope to appeal to the English reader in the same way he appealed to the Swedish reader. Otherwise, that is a different kind of

unfaithfulness. You are betraying the author if you make him less appealing
to another readership.

Jobe 1988: 413

Paule Daveluy, a Canadian translator who is recognised and respected for her
quality French translations of English-Canadian children's books comments:

> I become automatically, the author. Translators have different techniques.
> Mine is simple: I translate mot-a-mot on a stenographer's pad – anywhere:
> in the car, under the dryer, on plane trips – then type the result and, last but
> not least, write back the text in neat clean French as if it were my own
> manuscript. And I enjoy every phase of the process. I discovered that I really
> liked 'playing with words', translating, correcting, revising. I have to love the
> book I translate to make a success of the work involved.

Personal communication, 6 January 1981

Like Daveluy, noted translator Maria Poluskin observes:

> My own view is that, first of all, a translator must be a reader – a
> sympathetic, analytic reader – and secondly, that she be a writer herself. I am
> beginning to suspect that my old image of a translator as a person bent over a
> huge array of dictionaries and obscure volumes on syntactical usage is not
> really what translation is all about. For me, translation is more like creative
> art than a science. I immerse myself in another writer's art, probing and
> analysing every nuance; and, then, I set about trying to re-react that work in
> what amounts to a different medium ... Once I was past my initial interest
> and excitement, the process of translation was one of intense anxiety and
> disorientation. For long periods of time, I felt like a person suffering from
> aphasia in two languages at once. But, a commitment had been made; there
> were promises to keep; and sometimes only the prospect of having to face my
> editor kept me going.

Another British translator, Anthea Bell, perceives herself as a chameleon or an
actor on paper.

> 'One is interpreting as an actor does, actually trying to be a clear piece of
> glass, so as not to let yourself show through, only to clarify a passage'. In her
> translations Anthea always aims to produce 'what the author might have
> written had he been writing in English in the first place'. She has usually
> read the book during the screening process ... [yet] once selected, she then
> rereads it to re-establish the sense of unity of the work. Anthea works chapter
> by chapter, but in a long work she may pause to review beginning parts of the
> text for consistency. She may have to change the name(s) of something in an
> earlier section based on what came later. She works straight from the
> computer keyboard onto the screen and does the revisions on the screen.
> The word processor is of crucial assistance in this process, as it allows her to
> print passages however many times are necessary for further revision.

> Anthea Bell finds that, initially, translating a work is a slow process
> because she has to set the style, try to put herself into the skin of the author,

and try not to let her natural writing style show through. When translating she often feels that she gets to know an author and their writing better than they do themselves. 'When I am translating, I go over something so many times that I have actually picked up a name which got changed in the course of a story, something the editor should have picked up.'

Jobe 1990: 433–434

Illustrations in a picture book provide an additional challenge to the translator. Noted Finnish translator, Riita Oittinen, observes that 'when the translator sees the original text with certain illustrations, the pictures influence solutions. This affects not only the choice of words, but also the style of writing throughout the book' (1991: 15).

The process of translation is as unique as the style of the individual translator. However, all translators would agree that they work from Bell's basic premise: 'what would the author have said if he or she had been writing English in the first place?'

## The History of Translation

Translations into English for children was sparse up to the nineteenth century: John Comenius' *Orbis Pictus or The World Illustrated* was translated in 1658; Charles Perrault's fairy tales, *Stories or Tales of Times Past, with Morals,* in 1697; *The Arabian Nights* in 1706; and Perrault's *Tales of Mother Goose* in 1729. During this time only tales found in chapbooks, primers, good godly books, didactic novels, and adventure books were considered appropriate and published.

A significant turning point in children's literature came about with the arrival of the Grimm's *Popular Stories* from German (1823). Together with Andersen's fairy tales (in various translations) from Danish (1846) they established a greater awareness of the importance of translations in children's literature. Notable translations that followed were of Heinrich Hoffmann's *Struwwelpeter* from German (1848), by Jules Verne's *Twenty Thousand Leagues Under the Sea* (1870) and *Around the World in Eighty Days* from French (1872), Johanna Spyri's *Heidi* from German (1894), and C. Collodi's (Carlo Lorenzini) *The Adventures of Pinocchio* from Italian (1891).

The new century started with several titles which still form part of any set of classics today. These include: Selma Lagerlohff's *The Wonderful Adventures of Nils* from Swedish (1907), Felix Salten's *Bambi* from German (1929), Erich Kastner's *Emile and the Detectives* from German (1930), and Jean de Brunhoff's *The Story of Babar* from French (1935).

The years following the Second World War marked a period of intense upheaval, international frustration, inward-focused reconstruction policies, and a general lack of literary communication. The raising of the Berlin wall as a symbol of the Iron Curtain halted the sharing of information about life in many Eastern European countries as well as consideration of their viewpoints regarding the struggles during the war years. The continuing effects of the war brought a need for titles that related to the concerns of the people. Undoubtedly the English translation of Anne Frank's *The Diary of A Young Girl* in 1953 gave an unparalleled opportunity for children and adults to gain an insight into survival; Anne's buoyant outlook provides an inspiration to many on the meaning of life itself. The fact that war affects everyone was shown through a German family's experiences in Margot Benary-Isbert's *The Ark* (German, 1953).

The ability to laugh at oneself and one's institutions is as important for children as for adults, and perhaps the best example is Astrid Lindgren's *Pippi Longstocking* (1950) and its sequels, and Edith Unnerstad's *Little O* (Swedish, 1957).

Through the 1960s and into the 1980s, a more stable atmosphere encouraged publishers to expand their horizons, resulting in a 'golden age' of translation. The vast majority of books translated into English during this period originated from Western European countries (White 1991), and included the emergence of writing about the war. Without question Anne Holm's *I am David* (Danish, 1965, translated by L. W. Kingsland) and Hans Peter Richter's *Freidrich* (German, 1970) are outstanding, the first a journey across wartime Europe, the other the account of two German boys, one of Jewish descent.

Richter has written two other outstanding accounts of life during the Third Reich: two friends, Heinz and Gunter witness the changing ethos in *I Was There* (1972) and a 17-year-old officer survives three disillusioning years in the army in a hauntingly realistic account, *Time of the Young Soldiers* (1976). The war is also reflected in Jap ter Haar's account of the siege of Leningrad in *Boris* (Dutch, 1970), of partisans in Yevgeny Ryss's *Search Behind the Lines* (Russian, 1974), and escape with a baby through enemy lines in Vasil Bykov's *Pack of Wolves* (Russian, 1981), a glimpse of war's impact on friendships in Evert Hartman's *War Without Friends* (Dutch, 1982) and Else Pelgrom's *The Winter When Time Was Frozen* (Dutch, 1980), life in the Polish Ghetto in Joseph Ziemian's *The Cigarette Sellers of Three Crosses Square* (Polish, 1975), and an overwhelming account of young boys in Athens during the Nazi occupation in Alki Zei's *Petros' War* (Greek, 1972). A novel which deals with war in Israel is Uiel Ofek's *Smoke Over Golan* (Hebrew, 1979), while the post-war scene there is dramatically portrayed in Uri Orlev's *The Island on Bird Street* (Hebrew, 1983), as a young boy hides out in a damaged building waiting for his father to return.

Two picture books, designed for older readers, have helped to show the impact of war on people. These are accounts of the bombing of Hiroshima in Toshi Maruki's *Hiroshima No Pika* (Japanese, 1882) and the changing war scene in a southern German town in Christope Gallanz and Roberto Innocenti's *Rose Blanche* (Italian, 1985).

During this period, many writers were beginning to address the social problems of the times. Although considered rather tame in comparison to their British and American counterparts, they did address such issues as: hiding a mentally challenged brother so he would not be placed in a home, as in Friis-Bastad's *Don't Take Teddy* (Norwegian, 1967); the growing pains of a girl (*Mia*, Swedish, 1974) and a boy (*A Room of his Own*, Swedish, 1973) by Gunnel Beckman; a mentally handicapped youngster in Bo Carpelan's *Dolphins in the City* (Swedish, 1976); a night time baby-sitter for a mother who is a nurse, in Maria Gripe's *The Night Daddy* (Swedish, 1971); an ageing grandparent in Peter Härtling's *Oma* (German, 1977) and Elfie Donnelly's *So Long, Grandpa* (German, 1981); and a changing family structure in Kerstin Thorvall's *And Leffe Was Instead of a Dad* (Swedish,

1974), Christine Nöstlinger's *Marrying Off Mother* (German, 1983), and Boris Zhitkov's *How I Hunted the Little Fellows* (Russian, 1979).

The appeal of history, fantasy and adventure was also shown in translations at this time. Young readers are shown insights into the fear of a Siberian tribe 4,000 years ago in changing their ways in A. Linevski's *An Old Tale Carved Out of Stone* (Russian, 1973), the excavation of ancient Mesopotamia in Hans Baumann's *In the Land of Ur* (German, 1969), the days of medieval Sweden in Marie Gripe's *The Glassblower's Children* (Swedish, 1973), the arrival of young women to marry the fur traders in New France (Quebec) in Suzanne Martel's *The King's Daughter* (French, 1980), the existence of a modern medieval-ages environment in Harry Kullman's *The Battle Horse* (Swedish, 1981), the immigration to the United States in Willi Fahrmann's *The Long Journey of Lukas B.* (German, 1985), and the fascist take-over of Greece in 1936 in Alki Zei's *Sound of Dragon's Feet* (Greek, 1979).

Characteristic adventure stories are Siny Rose van Iterson's two novels set in Colombia, *Pulga* (Dutch, 1971) and *The Curse of Laguna Grande* (Dutch, 1973), as well as Cecil Bödker's *The Leopard* (Danish, 1975), and Wolfgang Korner's *The Green Frontier* (German, 1977). Equally important was the fantasy *Finn Family Moomintroll* (Swedish, 1965) and its sequels; and others such as Hanelore Valencak's *When Half-Gods Go* (German, 1976) about the possibility of the statue of a Greek god coming to life, or Otfried Preussler's *The Satanic Mill* (German, 1973), in whose evil atmosphere trapped apprentices turn into ravens.

This period also reflects the introduction of powerful characters and relationships. The friendship of a Swedish boy with a tramp is the subject of Astrid Lindgren's *Rasmus and the Vagabond* (Swedish, 1960) and an old lady and a young girl become friends in Elfie Donnelly's *Offbeat Friends* (German, 1982). Humorous characters include the bungling thief in Otfried Preussler's *The Robber Hotzenplotz* (German, 1964), the child who is always late in Anatolii Aleksin's *A Late-born Child* (Russian, 1971) and the mail-ordered perfectly mannered boy in Christine Nostlinger's *Konrad* (German, 1977).

This golden era saw the rise of professionally translated picture books as an art form. These were represented by the books of renowned artists, such as Susi Bohdal's *Selina: The Mouse and the Giant Cat* (German, 1982), Max Bolliger's *The Giants' Feast* (German, 1975), Hans Baumann's *The Hare's Race* (German, 1976), Achim Broger's *Outrageous Kasimir* (German, 1976), Bodil Hagbrink's *Children of Lapland* (Swedish, 1978), Ruth Hurliman's *The Cat and Mouse Who Shared A House* (German, 1974), and Jürg Steiner's *Rabbit Island* (German, 1978).

Things changed in the mid-1980s; while in Europe, the exchange of titles in translation continued, in English-speaking countries the exchange was almost entirely with other English-speaking countries. The tight economic situation, past experiences of translations not selling, isolationist tendencies dominant in Britain and the strong sales between the USA and Britain combined to keep the number of translations being published low. This situation remains despite a more open attitude towards internationalism in the USA.

Although fewer titles have been translated, there have been several areas of development. There has been a dramatic increase in the number of information books being translated, especially ones with a natural history focus. These include such titles as: Christina Bjork's *Linnea in Monet's Garden* (Swedish, 1987) and *Linnea's Almanac* (Swedish, 1989); Wolfgang Epple's *Barn Owls* (German, 1992); Heiderose and Andreas Fischer-Nagel's *Birth of Hamsters* (German, 1985), *Life of the Ladybug* (German, 1986), and *The Housefly* (German, 1990); Elig Hansen's *Guinea Pig* (German, 1992); Hans-Heinrich Isenbart's *Birth of a Foal* (German, 1986); and Rosabianca Skira-Venturi's *A Weekend with Leonardo da Vinci* (French, 1993).

A sign of this period is that fiction titles did not sell well, even in English. Despite this a few novels are being translated, such as Tamar Bergman's *Along the Tracks* (Hebrew, 1991), showing the desperation of a young boy as he searches for his family in the Soviet Union; the changing friendships of a Dutch Jewish girl are described in Ida Vos's *Hide and Seek* (Dutch, 1991); the care of a crippled war veteran for a young refugee boy in Peter Hartling's *Crutches*; the upheavals of a young Romanian girl being evacuated to Palestine in Uri Orlev's *Lydia, Queen of Palestine* (Hebrew, 1993); a nuclear attack in Gudrun Pausewang's *The Last Children of Schevenborn* (German, 1988); and life in South Africa in Maretha Maartens' *Paper Bird* (Afrikaan, 1991).

Picture books in translation provide new insights. Some of these are Annemie Margriet Heymans' *The Princess in the Kitchen Garden* (Dutch, 1993); two Japanese views in Takaaki Nomura's *Grandpa's Town* (Japanese, 1991), and Harutaka Nakawatari's *The Sea and I* (Japanese, 1992); Max Velthuijs' *Frog in Love* (Dutch, 1989), and Monica Zak's *Save My Rain Forest* (Spanish, 1992).

A gradual trend, one which follows the interests of English-speaking publishers is the increase in interest in poetry. Until the 1990s it was limited, with *Cricket* magazine being one of the few strong supporters. Recently, Michio Mado's book, *The Animals: Selected Poems* (Japanese, 1992), translated by the Empress Michiko, has caused much interest.

The history of books translated into English although never having a major impact in the publishing trade, nevertheless continues to produce a steady stream of titles; quality translations are available if we look for them. Maureen White in her study of more than 58,000 entries in *Children's Books in Print 1989–1990* found that there were 572 translated children's books in print yet of these she counted only 131 to be successful (that is, they had been in print for more than four years or had had a positive review), while 25 of these were classics and 42 were folklore.

## Issues in Translating for Children

There is a prevailing attitude among amateur enthusiasts and commodity-driven publishers that anyone who speaks and reads another language can effectively translate children's books from that language into English. This is a myth. For example, picture books, although short by novel standards, require an especially accomplished translator to glean the essence of the writer's and illustrator's intent. Words are at a premium and each must be precise to convey the nuances of story and meaning. An example is the work of the German illustrator Helme Heine. His earlier works, recognised for exciting illustrations were widely criticised for the flatness of their English text. Initially an editor just 'cleaned up' raw translations provided by the German publisher, but later titles were done with a professional translator to much greater acclaim.

A major problem in terms of quality is that relatively few children's books receive critical attention, and even fewer translations. Perhaps as a result, fundamental questions – for example, does a particular translation do credit to the author writing in another language? – largely remain unanswered.

Costs are also important. Translations are expensive; while the cost of scientific translation is seldom questioned, a lack of perceived need and the size of the market for translations of children's literature warns publishers that they may not get a sufficient return on their money. Some countries, such as Germany, Sweden, and The Netherlands have agencies which will assist British publishers with translation costs. However, in recent years the administrative paperwork for the application process has become so extensive and complicated that it actually acts as a deterrent to increasing future translations because the cost remains so prohibitive.

The dominant belief amongst publishers is that translations do not sell – which may be a self-fulfilling prophecy. Why do translations not sell? What marketing strategies have been undertaken to assure that they will? Generally, English-speaking publishers do not expend much promotional effort on translations; awards for translations are either not publicised very extensively or, as in the case of the American Library Association's Batchelder Award for the best translation published in the USA, they are given to a publishing company rather than to the individual responsible. (This award is not even given with the prestigious Newbery or Caldecott Awards – but the morning after!) Only on rare occasions when a television series is based on a work in translation, such as the *Moomintroll* books is there an extensive promotion.

One side-effect of the dramatic increase in co-production of picture books from other countries is the fear that writers and illustrators will lower their cultural standards and create works for children so general in nature that they require little if any editorial change from one culture edition to another. With writers, this can result in the omission of specific place references, ordinary character names, careful use of ordinary objects, and limited specifics to cultural customs. Similarly, there is a concern that artists will produce works so bland that they not offend any reader – unfortunately neither will they be enriching or stimulating.

There are two major influences on the translation of children's books: book fairs, and the concept of co-production of books. The major purpose of a book fair is to provide an opportunity for publishers to buy and sell the rights to books. The largest book fair in the world is the Frankfurt Buchmesse, held each autumn, although there children's books are only one small aspect, and thus the impact is relatively minor. For children's books, the most important book fair is held in the Italian city of Bologna each spring. Exclusively for children's books, the Bologna Book Fair, Fiera del Libro per Ragazzi, attracts approximately 1,200 publishers from around the world. It is the showcase of new books as well as hosting one of the leading competitions for illustrators, and the selling process involves a tight schedule. Because of the limited time factor many galleys of fiction titles and folded-and-gathered editions of new picture book titles, accompanied by a rough translation of the text, are frequently sent in advance to facilitate the decision-making process.

The most successful titles to be sold for co-productions are picture books. The art sells the book! Without question, editors can make decisions quicker based on a sense of the art, the reputation of the artist, and the immediate emotional appeal; they do not worry about the quality of the translated text. A rough version will give the general idea and can be cleaned up later. Fiction requires that a reader be hired to read the book in the original language and write a report attesting to its potential success in the market; for this reason, the sale of fiction titles is significantly lower.

A special aspect of the Bologna Book Fair is that it is attended by many professionals in the field; editors, literary agents, professors, and critics. These individuals often take back reports to publishing houses of those books they see that offer potential to be translated and published. It also has one of the three major juried awards for illustrations in the world, the other two being the International Board on Books for the Young's (IBBY) Hans Christian Andersen Award and the Bratislava International Biennial of Illustration's (BIB) Gold Apple. The Bologna Illustrators of Children's Books (Illustratori di Eibri per Ragazzi) collection is shown at a special exhibition but also in a yearly catalogue. At the same time, the winners of several graphic and illustration prizes given by the fair are exhibited. These displays are important in the translation process as they are viewed by publishers and editors looking for new talent. Very often co-productions are developed on the basis of an editor viewing an illustration in this exhibition.

The single most significant development in the international children's publishing industry has been the dramatic increase in the co-production of books. European publishers have a long tradition of co-productions because this allows them to print picture books of high quality: the size of the print run is directly related to the per unit cost of the book; but it is only in the last fifteen years that English-speaking countries have implemented co-productions more extensively. With the current printing technology, it is now possible to do large run, five-colour separations, with only a pause to change the black-and-white film for language texts. Thus, one of the costs of translation is considerably reduced.

There is often the feeling that translators are the unsung heroes of the international children's literature scene. Rarely do they receive the credit and recognition that is due them, although there are several awards. The Translators' Association in London administers four major awards: The Schlegel-Tieck Prize given annually for the best translation of a twentieth-century German literary work published by a British publisher; the John Florio Prize for a work from Italian; the Scott Moncrieff Prize for a work from French; and the Bernard Shaw Prize for a work from Portuguese. Other prizes include the PEN translation prize (USA), the Swedish Academy Prize for translation, and the Canada Council translations prize. Rarely do children's works receive serious attention or are their translators recognised.

The only major award given to an individual for the translation of a children's book is the Astrid Lindgren Translation Prize. This award is sponsored by the International Federation of Translators and is given every three or four years for either a single translation of outstanding quality or for a translator's body of work. The winners have included Ake Holmber (Sweden) (1981), Patricia Crampton (Britain) (1984), Liselotte Remane (German Democratic Republic) (1987), Anthea Bell (Britain) and Lyudmila Braude (USSR) (1990).

IBBY recognises translators as part of its IBBY Honour Books; each of its over sixty national sections can nominate an individual whose translation of a children's book is regarded as outstanding, for the IBBY Honour List Certificate. In 1994 translators from Argentina, Austria, Belgium, Brazil, Bulgaria, Colombia, Czech Republic, Denmark, Estonia, France, Germany, Greece, Indonesia, Iran, Israel, Italy, Japan, Mexico, Norway, Portugal, Russia, Slovak Republic, Slovenia, South Africa, Spain, Sweden, Switzerland, United States and Venezuela were honoured. Each translator received a certificate at IBBY's World Congress in Berlin. A special catalogue of the IBBY Honour Books is produced, and distributed worldwide.

The importance of translations for young people is increasingly being given consideration, but within the field itself there are many issues which must be addressed by writers, translators, publishers, educators and librarians. A professional translator must be valued and considered worth the additional costs in order to achieve a quality translation, marketing strategies must be improved, diversity should be more widely supported, and translators need to be more widely recognised for their contribution.

## Conclusion

The political changes of the 1990s created not only uncertainty in the world among adults, but a sense of uneasiness in young people. It is difficult to comprehend and understand the strong sense of cultural nationalism which exists at the same time when market economies are insisting on larger and larger political units. How do young people learn to experience what it is like to live in other cultural areas of the world? How will children learn what it is like to live in a global community? Never has there been a time when children need to be able to read books from other areas of the world. Michael Kerrigan, a columnist for the *Times Higher Educational Supplement*, reported that while 67,704 titles were published in Britain in 1991, shockingly, only 1,689 or 2.4 per cent were translations! This suggested to him that in Britain, 'we remain, it seems, a nation of cultural Eurosceptics with little interest in looking outward for our reading matter' (Kerrigan 1993: 15). Even though the situation in other English-speaking countries is not quite as dramatically isolationist, the fact is that there are too few translations being published. Ideally, children need to read the best literature other countries have to offer. Unless we meet this challenge by respecting and providing the best in translation they will be cheated out of a part of their global heritage. All of us who labour on the promotion of quality children's literature must stand up and support the increased availability of expert translations.

## References

Bell, A. (1980) 'Ten years of parcels', *Signal* 11, 31: 20–28.
Fenton, E. (1977) 'Blind idiot: the problems of translation, Part II', *The Horn Book Magazine* 53, 6: 633–641.
Jobe, R. (1988) 'Profile: Patricia Crampton', *Language Arts* 65, 4: 410–414.
—— (1990) 'Profile: Anthea Bell', *Language Arts* 67, 4: 432–438.

Kerrigan, M. (1993) 'Words lost in a new landscape: why are so few translations of foreign books popular in English?', *Times Higher Educational Supplement* 1065: 15.

Oittinen, R. (1991). 'On the situation of translation for the child: the dialogue between text and illustration', *USBBY Newsletter* 16, 1: 13–18.

Polushkin, M. (1974) 'A few words on translation', *The Horn Book* 50, 4: 256–259.

## Further Reading

Carus, M. (1980). 'Translation and internationalism in children's literature', *Children's Literature in Education* 11, 4: 171–179.

Corsaro, J. (1994) 'Through others' eyes: contemporary translated books', *Book Links* 3, 3: 39–42.

Hood, R. and Jobe, R. (1987) 'Moral decision making in children's translated European war novels', *International Review of Children's Literature and Librarianship* 2, 2: 95–110.

Jobe, R. (1983) 'Reflections of reality: literature in translation for young people', *English Journal* 27, 1: 22–26.

Lynch-Brown, C. (1991) 'Translated children's books: voyaging to other countries', *The Reading Teacher* 44, 7: 487–492.

McElderry, M. K. (1973) 'The hazards of translation', *The Horn Book* 49, 6: 565–569.

Nist, J. (1988). 'Cultural bonds and serious themes in US translated children's books: a study of the first twenty years 1968–1987 of the Mildred L. Batchelder Award', *Bookbird* 17, 4: 5–8.

Oittinen, R. (1993) *I Am Me – I Am Other: On the Dialogics of Translating for Children* [Acta Universitatis Tamperensis ser A vol 386], Tampere: University of Tampere.

Rudnik, M. (1981) 'The winter when time was frozen and the art of translating', *Top of The News* 38, 1: 91–95.

White, M. (1992) 'Children's books from other languages: a study of successful translations', *Journal of Youth Services in Libraries* 5, 3: 261–275.

# 45

# Radio, Television, Film, Audio and Video

## *Michael Rosen*

Children's reading is now integrated into a multimedia world. That is to say, systems of communication other than books have a great bearing on what, how and why children read. Looked at in terms of flow, various routes to the child with a book in its hand can be discerned. Book (for example, a children's classic like *The Secret Garden* (1911)) → film script → film (1949, 1993) → child in the cinema → child with the book and/or adaptation; script → television series (for example, Bernard Ashley's *Running Scared* (1986)) → watched by child → Ashley simultaneously writes a book (1986) → child with the book; book (for example, Rosemary Sutcliff's *The Eagle of the Ninth* (1954)) → radio adaptation (1955) → child as listener → child with book ... and so on. To take a classic example, Collodi's *Pinocchio* (1883) was adapted by Disney (1940) and made into the cartoon film that millions of people go to see, some of whom read the various Disney Corporation's book versions or some other edition of Collodi. The reading of *Pinocchio* by any one child is thus embedded in other processes, for example film scripting, the Disney publicity machine, social film going, video hire, family and peer-group discussion of 'what's on', family and peer-group discussion of the film, comparisons made by critics, teachers, family and friends between the book and the film and so on. So when a child approaches a librarian and asks for dinosaur books/love stories/horror books and so on it will be in part because that area of interest has made itself felt on the child through the multimedia world. The simple opposition of one electronic form and children's literature will not bear close examination.

It can also be argued that this integration of books within other media has now come to affect all children's reading, no matter whether a specific book has or has not been adapted and presented in another media. Traces of this can be found in the visual, linguistic and stylistic aspects of children's literature. In several of her picture books, Fiona French uses a cinematic intertextuality, in particular her *Snow White in New York* (1986) that evokes 1930s musicals. Jon Scieszka takes the traditional tale of the Three Little Pigs, re-writes it from the point of view of the wolf, investing him with the voice of gangster movies and television series (*The True Story of the 3 Little Pigs! by A. Wolf* (1989)). Robert Cormier, with such books as *The Chocolate War* (1974), and *After the First Death* (1979) uses a cinematic style of writing in short scenes with little digression. The Australian children's writer Morris Gleitzman has said (in interview on BBC Radio's *Treasure Islands* (1993)) that he follows the scriptwriter's rule: always begin a scene as late as you possibly can; meaning that if one can avoid scene setting, plot recapitulation, narrative commentary, then avoid it! This approach can be found both in his work and in other writers. Perhaps the writer whose textual approach is most affected by television and film is again an Australian, Paul Jennings, who with a series of books (for example, *Unreal! Eight Surprising Stories* (1985), *Unbelievable! More Surprising Stories* (1987)) has perfected a snappy style that seems to owe a lot to the swift cross-cutting of visual images in television and film, and as a consequence, has become something of a cult figure among young teenagers.

The problems of the relation of reading to other media has a history virtually as long as there have been films to see, radio programmes to listen to and television to watch – and, as it happens, children have been included in each of these media almost right from their respective beginnings. In America, L. Frank Baum was making silent films of his book *The Wonderful Wizard of Oz* (1900) in the early 1900s. In Britain, radio programmes aimed at children were broadcast virtually from the inception of public broadcasting (from 1922 until 1964 and fitfully since). On television, in both America and Britain, children's programmes appeared at the start of full nationwide service. In fact, it was a Mickey Mouse cartoon that was stopped in midstream when the British television service closed down for the war in September 1939 – and the same cartoon re-opened the service in June 1946 (Home 1993: 17).

Anxiety on the part of people keen to support reading has been expressed for many years. In *The World Radio and Television Annual. Jubilee Issue* (1946), there is an article called 'Children and Radio' by Ruth Adam. She situates herself in what was already a long history of anxiety: 'Magistrates used to grieve constantly over the influence of films. I've heard teachers blame the inaccuracy and lazy thinking of an entire school on the cinema habit' (79). Then, in what is a defence of radio – a medium that 'is accessible from before the time the household is stirring until bedtime' (79) – Adam concedes that 'the radio habit makes for careless listening. In homes where the radio is a continual background noise, children cultivate protective deafness' (80). But she goes on to point out how radio widens horizons and 'lifts lessons like Literature, History and Geography onto a plane which most of us – if we were fortunate – may have experienced just once in our school career' (80). She finishes by putting in a plea for learning how to listen and hoping that children will not do their homework with the radio on.

Here, in incipient form, are many of the battles that have been fought throughout most of the twentieth century around issues of children's literature and the other media. There is now a whole canon of anti-television-for-children critiques (see Goldsen 1977; Postman 1983; Winn 1985) from either left- or right-wing perspectives, the origins of which have been traced back to Plato who proposed to ban the dramatic poets from his ideal Republic, for fear that their stories about the immoral antics of the gods would influence impressionable young minds (Buckingham 1993: 7). Radio has now become the good fairy in the debate and is praised for its appeal to the imagination, unlike the visual media which, it is often claimed 'leave nothing to the imagination', prevent children from thinking, turn them into passive couch potatoes, render them subject to consumerism, turn them into atomised, separate non-collective, non-communitarian individuals.

Clearly, it is hard to disentangle a series of quite different concerns here: moral, aesthetic, educational, cognitive, developmental, political, among others, in which the totality of reading is counterpoised to the totality of (usually) television but also 'video nasties' and rock music. Children are often seen as fairly helpless and passive receivers in the midst of the cacophony unless they have been weaned off it by sensible parents and teachers and re-directed towards the healthy pursuit of reading. In Britain in 1993, the Secretary of State for Education and Prince Charles made appeals to parents and teachers to get children to turn off television sets.

Specialist children's radio, television and film programmes are caught up in this crossfire and so, like Ruth Adam above, practitioners and even critics frequently put themselves in an awkward position. It is as if they are saying, yes, too much radio/television/film is a bad thing but we produce quality programmes and if we didn't children would only be watching rubbish. Leaving aside the aesthetic and value judgements made, this neatly sidesteps the role children's productions play in helping to produce the viewers, film-goers and listeners of those other apparently awful programmes either now or in the future. That is to say, listening to the radio and watching visual productions are as much learnt activities as reading.

Because we say that learning to read takes place within an obviously pedagogical context, the process is measured, assessed and seen as 'work' both by teachers and children. On the other hand, listening and viewing are not taught to very young children. Children are simply and usually exposed to many hours of transmission. By the time they are articulating their wishes and desires, we hear from most of them that they know and understand large amounts of what they receive. It seems at first glance that in fact there was nothing to learn; watching television or listening to the radio is 'natural', and – more significantly – this is because these media are apparently 'real'.

On closer examination, none of this is the case. Taking the visual media first, the processes of cutting from one person or from one scene to another; the moving of cameras within one shot (panning, crabbing, tilting, zooming); the use of framing (close-ups, mid-shots, wide-shots) all have to be learnt to be understood. Consider the simplest: Jane is talking to Jill. A film-maker does not have to show Jane and Jill in the same frame talking. We will understand that they are talking to each other if in shot one Jane stands on the right side of a frame and looks left (with Jill not present in the frame) followed by shot two of Jill standing on the left side of a frame and looking right (with Jane not present in the frame). In actual fact it is not necessary for the two characters to have met for us to believe that a 'conversation' is taking place. Notice here that the camera does not even imitate the action of the human eye, panning from one person to the other. The film (that is, the editor) cuts from one person to the other from two stretches of film or video intermixed. Yet, when this happens we are quite happy to call this 'real' or 'naturalistic' (especially if various, but arbitrary, elements, are adopted like contemporary clothes or non-standard dialects). But it is also clear that for children to make sense of these and hundreds of other visual conventions, they have to learn them in order to buy the idea, as here, that two people are 'really' talking to each other.

But of course, if all that children were doing when learning to read was learning letters, and all that children were doing when they were learning visual media was learning how shots work, we would be describing fairly impoverished processes. Every watching act involves many learnings and many incorporations of the already learnt. Consider a popular children's series set around two main characters – *The Lone Ranger*. If the Lone Ranger or his assistant do not appear in the first minute or so, we are not usually perturbed, nor do we think that the wrong film has been tagged on to the titles. For a variety of reasons we recognise that we are being given material that our heroes will have to deal with. These reasons will be in part to do with our familiarity with the locale, language, pace of cutting, camera angles and music that we associate with this series but also because, in general terms, we have learnt the conventions of the 'tease' at the front of such a programme.

The argument here then is that watching and viewing are not lazy, unimaginative acts but ones that involve learning and cognition analogous to reading. Merely because when Alice appears in a film she moves and talks across a screen (1933, 1951, 1972), does not mean that when we read *Alice's Adventures in Wonderland* (1865) (where she does not move) that the brain is working less hard. What is actually taking place is that other forms of interpretation are taking place.

Radio is much reduced in significance but recorded sound for children is, of course, now available in cassette tapes and compact discs. Without labouring the point, once again we are presented with a whole series of conventions, some of which are nearer to literature. The phrase 'Once upon a time' coming at the beginning of a piece, whether read on the page or said in any number of voices near or far from a microphone or with any number of sound effects in the background or foreground is likely to be understood by someone listening as the introduction to something we call a fairy tale. On the other hand, these tones of voice, acoustic settings, sound effects and musical interventions have all been put there on the understanding that listeners will make knowing interpretations: this is a scary story, this is a sad story. However, simply because these forms cannot be dismissed as inherently and inevitably inferior to reading, it will not be claimed here that all films, tapes, videos, and television programmes are of equal value – though the claim is sometimes made for reading ('So long as they're reading something – I'm happy.')

Historically, children's films have always offered a diet that mixed versions of the classics with new specially scripted material. A film of *Alice in Wonderland* was made in 1903, while in the 1890s the French film-maker Georges Melies was making fantasies about such things as the man in the moon (though not made only and expressly for children). On the other hand, when cartoon films were first made for children, new characters were invented, notably Felix the Cat (1921), but then in 1923 Walt Disney also turned to *Alice* with his *Alice's Wonderland*. It combined live human figures with drawing. The new invention of Mickey Mouse (drawn animation) first appeared in 1928. What has become known as the Disney classic cartoon – full-length, musical cartoon adaptations of traditional or classic literary material – began with *Snow White and the Seven Dwarfs* in 1937. But the Disney Corporation has also been responsible for many live-action films, also offering a mix of adaptations of classics, such as *Treasure Island* (1950) and new, specially written material, notably *Davy Crockett, King of the Wild Frontier* (1956). This drew on a hotch-potch made up of a version of an autobiography, old dime novels and legends about an American hunter, Colonel David Crockett (1786–1836). *Old Yeller* (1957), also specially written, was set on a Texan farm in 1869; a young boy adopts a stray yellow dog but is then exposed to trials of loyalty and maturity.

A film, popularly regarded as the classic children's film of all time, *The Wizard of Oz* (1939) shows that in reality such films are received by families – the 'family film'. Then, in ways quite distinct from the reception of children's literature, the film is viewed, reviewed, extracted by adults in subsequent generations with or without their children. Stylistically, *The Wizard of Oz* reveals what for many years in America was thought to be an essential ingredient of a full-length feature film for children – music and song. In fact, one film – a cartoon film – *The Jungle Book* (1967) rests almost entirely on animation shaped and cut to fit some witty song writing, rather than following much that Rudyard Kipling had to say in *The Jungle Book* (1894) and *The Second Jungle Book* (1895). It shows quite clearly, that audiences initiated in a given children's book, cannot expect what are called 'faithful' reproductions in the cinema.

*Mary Poppins* (1964) and *Chitty-Chitty-Bang-Bang* (1967) (the latter taken from *Chitty-Chitty-Bang-Bang: The Magical Car* (1964) by Ian Fleming) were two films that continued the tradition of what is in effect the Hollywood musical comedy form. P. L. Travers's books about Mary Poppins started to come out in 1934, with quirky illustrations by Mary Shepard. Though they were fairly well-known up until the 1950s, the Disney film made the character and a version of the stories popular with millions of people. Such films are then integrated into the television and video systems and are watched by millions more. In this way, the Mary Poppins concept is diversified into many different conditions of reception: child and the book at home, child and the book at school, child with or without adults in the cinema, child at home with a video and so on. In this way, children have come to take hold of Mary Poppins, possess the character in a variety of ways, by far the most popular being to sing and re-sing the songs that Julie Andrews sings in the film.

Incidentally, this process is then incorporated into a version of the star structure, whereby children who like Julie Andrews can (and do) follow her to other films – like *The Sound of Music* (1965) – even if they are not expressly made for children. Christmas viewing in Britain usually finds a place for one or more of these films where they are seen and re-seen by several generations of people.

A question arises here about risk. The film industry as a whole frequently makes challenging, awkward and dangerous films for adult audiences. Can the film industry do the same with films that they put out as children's entertainment? If not, why not? In Britain, the Children's Film Foundation put out many films through the late 1940s and 1950s that were shown in cinemas on Saturday mornings and even now occasionally turn up on satellite television stations. These were generally low-budget knock-about comedies, thrillers or both. Occasionally they graduated to the role of being B-movies (support acts) to comedy films such as those acted in by the English actor Norman Wisdom. With the blockbuster children's films such as *Mary Poppins*, which has a mildly subversive tone to it concerning behaviour and greed, the children's film becomes a kind of sanitised zone, where the film industry puts on its decent-family-values face. Meanwhile for the rest of the year it can show its normal round of adultery, murder and horror.

With television and video, children see most of these films too. So what has grown up, at least since the 1970s, is a strange schizophrenic viewing structure. Film makers, publicity managers and critics create something everyone calls a children's film like *ET The Extra-Terrestrial* (1982), but which cannot really be defined as such on the basis of audience alone, for just as many children will see *The Terminator* (1984) or *Ghostbusters* (1984) which are classified by the film boards as adult, and needing parental supervision, respectively. Television and video sales and rentals defy age rank and age genre. It is almost as if the genre 'children's film' can be defined as a film by virtue of certain elements (for example, nakedness, sawn-off limbs) *not* being present. The structuring of one of the television audiences as 'family' may have something to do with all this: it being an area that satisfies criteria laid down by the agendas of religious organisations, right-wing political parties and various so-called 'moral' ginger groups. All this has a great bearing on what kind of risks children's films can take.

Two film adaptations of Roald Dahl books, *Danny* (1988) (from *Danny, The Champion of the World* (1975) and *The Witches* (1990) (from the book of the same name, 1983) highlight this issue. In *Danny, The Champion of the World*, Danny narrates a series of clashes with authority that he and his father go through. The boy narrator makes clear that this is in order to show the importance of his relationship with his father. The film uses the objective camera mode, the boy is not particularly favoured by the camera, and there is no sound-over narration from him. In other words, the film shifts the focus of the book away from the child. The book might be considered dangerous because it supports a child's eye view of subversive behaviour, the boy expresses solidarity with his father's defiance of authority – and acts upon it. The film shows the father as performing the same subversive acts but we do not see it from the child's point of view or with his commentary. Quite subtly, the danger of children identifying quite so whole-heartedly with adult illegality has been lessened and the anti-authoritarianism is made just more acceptable. Is there a problem that children in children's films cannot be seen to be as much in charge or as much in control as Roald Dahl presented them? With *The Witches* the film-makers changed the ending. In the book, the boy hero remains transformed as a mouse, in the film he is restored to human form.

In both cases, Dahl, as writer, chose the least conventional (more subversive?) approach. With Danny he allows the child to celebrate the anti-authoritarian episodes, and in *The Witches* Dahl upsets a golden rule of children's fiction – restoration after conflict or transformation. The film-makers could not live with it. Perhaps these two examples show that though there is no scope at all for claiming the superiority of *all* reading over *all* films, there are grounds for saying, that the commercial film industry, constructed as it is, is not yet able to be as unconventional as the children's publishing industry.

Television for children in America and Britain began with cartoons and puppets, the latter being a curious choice given that puppetry was not at that time a deeply embedded form in British popular culture. Perhaps it was derived in part out of the pseudo-puppetry of many children's book illustrations of the previous thirty years, as with Mabel Lucy Attwell or the illustrations for Enid Blyton's 'Noddy' books (beginning 1949); and also in part out of the highly popular children's radio series 'Toytown' (1929–1964). Puppetry and cartooning have proved to be great survivors in children's television. Cartooning, a highly labour-intensive process, is sustained by multinational deals which help determine the films' aesthetic to be either American or 'mid-Atlantic' or non-local. In recent years the Japanese have very successfully entered the market with a series of warrior fantasies derived in part from the ancient Greeks (there has been a modernised sequel to *The Odyssey*) and ideas derived from Japanese horror films. In fact there is an international marketplace for cartoons where television companies bid for silent versions of cartoons which are then dubbed for sound in their respective countries. This explains the strange crocodile-jaw motions of most of the characters' mouths which bear very little relation to the phonetics of the words that the characters speak. The plot-lines of most cartoon films follow a very traditional pattern: quest and/or test. Heroes go out on quests where they are tested by baddies, dangers and evil forces. Cartoon comedy, especially non-Disney from the 1940s or 1950s sustains a greater variety of ideas, tricks, ruses and disasters. Various modes of behaviour, other forms of entertainment, figures of authority – and, it should be said, ethnic minorities especially native Americans – are held up to ridicule (see especially *Popeye* (first shown 1933) and *Bugs Bunny* (first shown 1938).

Puppetry saw a huge renaissance from 1969 onwards at the hands of Jim Henson who was responsible for two major changes. The humble glove puppet, which had become rather characterless and restricted to mere bobbing up and down became, with some ingenious engineering, startling contemporary characters with features capable of expressing a much wider range of emotion; he also introduced animatronics, the electronically operated puppet, shown to great effect with talking mice in *The Witches* – the adaptation of Roald Dahl's novel mentioned above.

Children's television in Britain operates under its own budgets separate from 'Light Entertainment' departments and offers a variety of material all with its equivalents in (and frequently derived from) children's literature. The output includes drawn cartoons, stop-frame animation, puppets, specially commissioned drama series, adaptations of classic children's novels, quizzes, information and news programmes, magazine programmes, and large amorphous mixed pro-grammes, usually screened on Saturday mornings mixing elements of all these, along with performances by live bands. Much of this matches the adult output, so it is interesting to see what adult programmes are not matched: live sport and live comedy being the most obvious. In the USA children's television is largely a choice between drawn cartoons and *Sesame Street* (first broadcast 1969) a show founded on the premise of compensatory learning and behaviouristic teaching methods – for example, if you could make the alphabet seem as groovy as an advertisement or a piece of rock music, and as relevant to audiences regarded as 'disadvantaged' (for example, African-Americans and Hispanics), then a 'good thing' was being done. In actual fact, the programme's main contribution has probably been through its inventive puppetry (thanks originally to Jim Henson), great wit, top-flight showbiz performers, and an array of presenters who defy Western stereotypic conventions of race, appearance and age for children's television.

The BBC's adaptations of classic children's books (Burnett's *The Secret Garden*

(1952), Bawden's *Carrie's War* (1974), Masefield's *The Box of Delights* (1984) and many other productions) were for many years part of a particular BBC aesthetic, dominated by a theatrical use of cameras and framing. That is to say, the camera rarely moved, and if it did, it was slowly and on tracks – that is smoothly and unobtrusively); people tended to deliver their lines from within carefully composed frames, while sets, locations and costumes played as important roles as the characters. The direction allowed the viewer plenty of time to take in these physical aspects; the busy, rushing camera of *cinema verité* was thought inappropriate for such material. However, recently the television adaptation (1993) of Mary Norton's *The Borrowers* has used all the tricks of colour inlay to reduce and increase the size of characters, objects and landscape and the camera has followed the action in a much more active, less reverential way.

The history of children's programming on the radio is more fitful. In America it was often seen as part of populist, family listening with a strong use of American folksong, with performers such as Burl Ives. In Britain, *Children's Hour* was placed on the Home Service network, and was dominated by speakers, ideas and tones of the middle and upper classes. It was as if the nation's children could only be entrusted to such people – popular entertainers (frequently working-class in origin) were not thought to be suitable. That said, the programmes offered up a variety of classic serials, newly written dramas, information programmes, quizzes, and paternalistic chats. *Children's Hour* was taken off the air in 1964, unable to compete with television, it was claimed.

The dramatisation of children's books continues apace, however, with educational output of radio and television, occasional slots in the mainstream programming, and now, more importantly in cassette tape form. Sometimes in part-work form, bought each week from supermarkets or local newspaper stores, sometimes packaged in with the books themselves, sometimes free-standing, and sold by virtue of the fame of the name (*Peter Pan*, Enid Blyton), children's tapes are now very widely available. The companies making the tapes do not have the resources to produce full-scale dramatisations so what is usually on offer is a reading performed by someone with a range of voices with a variety of electronic music and noises accompanying. It is an interesting case of the technology (the portable cassette player) reviving what many had thought was a near extinct artistic form. It will have been seen that it is not easy to pluck what we call children's literature out of what is transmitted as children's television and radio, or distributed as film or sold as videos and tapes. In spite of all that is written about television and film being *visual* media, it is always worth bearing in mind that most of what we see and hear on television and films has started as words on a page; children's programmes are, much more often than is acknowledged, derived from the totality of children's literature. Equally, with the use of song, poetry, puppets, story-telling, story-reading and short dramatisations, there is often a two-way feeding of literature into television and television into books. In Britain the figure of John Cunliffe has proved to be one of the most successful with the invention of such characters and series as *Postman Pat* (1981 onwards) supported by merchandise such as hardback, paperback and mini-books, puppets, games, clothes, mobiles, friezes, stamps, posters, annuals, model vans, soft toys, pencils, rubbers, pens, key-rings, notebooks, notepaper and so on.

It is of course impossible to predict the future relationships between these media and the printed page. It is possible to see a future for the CD-ROM that integrates the printed word, still visual images, moving images and sound and which can be accessed in new sequences (but at present, not in unlimited ways). There does not appear to be any reason why either the children's literature of the past or the future should not be adapted and shaped within this format. Will children in a few year's time be walking about with small portable CD-ROM players, reading, viewing and listening to a musical, choose-your-own-adventure version of *Peter Pan*? Will it be possible for them to integrate themselves with the use of micro-cameras and sound-equipment into such adventures – *Peter Pan Meets Me*? Whatever happens, children's literature will flow into the new technologies just as it has always done, partly because children are seeing, feeling, responding human beings with desires for representations of their own lives, imaginations and emotions; but also because the makers of the new technologies will be especially anxious that young audiences are initiated into lifetime buying patterns.

## References

Adam, R. (1946) 'Children and radio' in Pedrick, G. (ed.) *The World Radio and Television Annual. Jubilee Issue*, London: Sampson Low.

Buckingham, D. (1993) *Children Talking Television: the Making of Television Literacy.* London: Falmer Press.

Goldsen, R. K. (1977) *The Show and Tell Machine*, New York: Dial.

Home, A. (1993) *Into the Box of Delights: A History of Children's Television*, London: BBC Books.

Postman, N. (1983) *The Disappearance of Childhood*, London: W. H. Allen.

Winn, M. (1985) *The Plug-In Drug*, rev. edn, Harmondsworth: Penguin.

## Further Reading

Eyles, A. (1985) *The World of Oz: An Historical Expedition Over the Rainbow*, Harmondsworth and New York: Viking.

Finch, C. (1975) *The Art of Walt Disney: From Mickey Mouse to the Magic Kingdoms*, Burbank, CA: Harry N. Abrams.

# 46

# Story-telling

## *Mary Medlicott*

Story-telling is often regarded as the 'Ur' form, the base of all the arts. It combines the art of the tale, regarded in the Irish proverb as 'worth more than all the wealth of the world', with the fundamental human propensity for seeing life in the form of stories. As Isaac Bashevis Singer put it, 'Today, we live, but by tomorrow today will be a story. The whole world, all human life, is one long story' (Singer 1976: 5).

For children as for adults, the oral tradition was originally the basis of all knowledge, and the way in which this material was communicated was also significant; it involved direct contact with whoever was the story-teller, sometimes as part of special celebrations, often in the course of ordinary life.

The oral tradition consists of three main sorts of material. First are the inherited stories which include myths, legends, folk-tales and fairy tales and all the proverbs, riddles and songs which traditionally accompany them. Second are life stories, accounts of personal, family and tribal events. These are the building blocks of history and the cement of social living. Third is the new material story-tellers create, sometimes weaving it so seamlessly into the old that its newness can scarcely be recognised except as creating the topicality and freshness which help tradition to survive. As well as providing entertainment, these materials carry enormous educational potential. In *The Ordinary and the Fabulous*, an influential book on using traditional literature with children, Elizabeth Cook argues that: 'a grown-up understanding of life is incomplete without an understanding of myths, legends and fairy tales' (Cook 1969: vii).

### Co-existing Traditions

In the past, key places such as castle, church, square, kitchen and bedroom provided the focus for different story-telling traditions, the nature of each determined by the type of venue, the kind and size of audience and the expectations surrounding the story-teller.

In courtly traditions, story-tellers entertained the chief or king, his entourage and guests. Normally highly trained, they undertook a long apprenticeship. In medieval Wales, such a story-teller was known by the name *cyfarwydd*, the one who knows the way. In contemporary West African countries such as The Gambia, comparable traditions are still upheld by the *griot* trained from childhood in the ancient stories, the music to which they are sung, and the history and genealogy of whoever is the *griot*'s patron.

Story-telling also played an important part in esoteric and religious traditions, the simplicity, wisdom and depth of stories providing a form of teaching as important for the adult on the peaks of spiritual search as for the child on the foothills of knowledge. Buddha, Mohammed, Christ and other great religious teachers spoke in the form of stories. Preachers of all kinds have maintained their example. In the West, Sunday school is one of the few venues where the telling of stories survived even in the period of its general decline. In some religious traditions, such as Sufism, the pithy wit of the teaching stories has attracted non-believers; in others, as with Hasidic Jews, stories are specifically not to be shared with outsiders.

Celebration and accord are the keynotes of community story-telling. In Ireland, the ceilidh is the time for music, dancing and stories. For the Xhosa in South Africa, *intsomi* is the term for the well-loved tales told on such occasions. In West Africa, dilemma tales are a speciality, a way of communally sorting out complex issues of psychology, ethics and imagination. Wherever the venue – Indian verandah, Maori *marae* or Scottish traveller's tent – stories have traditionally been central in marking the community's seasonal life.

Although children were typically present until they went to sleep, community story-telling occasions were rarely specifically for them. They had other times, especially bedtime, with grandmothers playing a vital role in many different cultures. However, domestic story-telling encompasses more than children. The Egyptian writer, Huda Shaarawi, describes the flower-water seller's visits to the women's household as especially enjoyed: the flower-water seller was a story-teller (46). In other cultures, spinning and dress making were aspects of women's lives closely linked with story-telling. The figure of Mother Goose, now best-known in connection with children's rhymes, probably derived from the elderly women who ruled the kitchens of the European past and told the servant-girls stories.

## The Variety of Story

Magic is a universal ingredient of different oral traditions, a central representation of the transformative power which stories and story-telling possess. However, different traditions also reflect the distinctive ways of life of the peoples who created them. Special characters and types of story emerge, often much loved by children. The Arabic world of the Middle East has Nasruddin Hodja, the wise man often regarded as a fool by others. Ghana has Ananse, half-man, half-spider, whose stories travelled with slavery to the Caribbean. America has Brer Rabbit. England has Jack. Russia has Baba Yaga, the witch both loved and feared. Almost everywhere, animals are important: taking on different aspects of human personality, they are also reminders of the mythical time, where stories often begin, when humans could talk to animals and animals could talk to each other.

Such bodies of story could scarcely have emerged without long passage of time and anonymity. Anonymity is particularly important. From Homer onwards, oral stories coming into written literature acquired tellers who became closely associated with them. Hans Christian Andersen, well-known in his own circle as a brilliant story-teller, especially with children, drew deeply on Scandinavian oral traditions in producing his own stories. Yet they are generally not easy to tell. Nor would it be easy to contemplate telling the Lake Wobegon stories of the contemporary American story-teller, Garrison Keillor, unless you were the man himself. Some stories become integral with particular people. However, the stories of genuine oral tradition are characteristically the property of no one.

Anonymity differentiates the oral from the literary tradition and raises the many problems which it has faced since the development of printing. Writing stories down tends to harness them to the phrasings and viewpoint of the particular writer. The great European folk-tale collectors such as Perrault in France, the Grimm brothers in Germany, Afanasiev in Russia, Asbjørnsen and Moe in Norway, performed the great service to humanity of recording many stories which might otherwise have disappeared. (Loss is still acute today as parts of the world experience the change away from the traditional that happened earlier in Europe.) At the same time, the publishing of folk-tales inevitably changed some of the central facts of the oral tradition. When a story is written down, it no longer needs to be remembered. Furthermore, what works in speech does not always work on the page.

## The Decline of Oral Tradition

Literacy and mass publishing were major reasons behind the worldwide decline of the oral tradition. As collectors, such as Pitré in nineteenth-century Sicily, noticed, many of the best story-tellers with the biggest repertoires were themselves illiterate. The advance of literacy undermined the traditional tellers, taking away from the respect they were accorded. The coming of television quickened the process. A story is told of a story-teller in a pub in Ireland, in the middle of telling a tale when the television was switched on. He stopped in the middle of what he was saying and never told again.

Changes in social structures furthered the processes of decline. As people moved into cities, they left behind the natural venues for story-telling. As family units became smaller they often no longer included grandmothers and other mainstays of domestic tradition. The writing down of folk stories and myths, which was eventually to bear fruit in the current renewal of story-telling, also had the great disadvantage that it led to a misunderstanding of the stories themselves. When a story is written down, not only the choice of words but also the choice of audience assumes a fixed and long-term importance. Many collectors, such as Perrault with Cinderella, not only adopted an over-literary style but decided that folk-tales and fairy tales were meant for children. Some stories became typecast whereas, told and re-told orally, they are free to alter to take account of different audiences, atmospheres and changing times.

## The Renewal of Story-telling

The contemporary revival of story-telling can be traced to a number of developments, including the rise of psychoanalysis and the new understanding of symbol and myth brought about by Jung and other writers such as Joseph Campbell and Bruno Bettelheim. After a revulsion against myths and fairy tales on the part of many parents and teachers on the grounds that they are too violent, the new understanding of their psychological value is currently helping to change attitudes about their suitability.

Another factor behind the revival is the great increase in mobility in the twentieth century with the consequent interspersing of peoples across the world and the new valuation of ethnicity and culture. In Britain, during the 1970s and early 1980s, for example, new cultural needs were felt – for instance for children to learn why the celebration of Diwali is an important part of Indian life. This created a demand for story-tellers from different cultures to tell the religious stories and folk-tales of their peoples. Over a similar period, a developing awareness of ecology was combining with new regard for the knowledge of primitive peoples to create an increased interest in traditional ways of life and the wisdom enshrined in the world's oral traditions. The growth in the children's book market, too, began making widely available, often in colourful picture-book format, traditional stories which had previously languished in obscure collections. Gail E. Haley's version of an Ananse tale, *A Story, A Story*, and Joanna Troughton's version of the Aboriginal story of Tiddalik are examples of what has become an important genre.

In Britain, revival was apparent in such developments as the forming of Common Lore, a multicultural troupe of story-tellers and musicians, the foundation of the now-defunct College of Story-tellers and the organisation of major Story-telling Festivals for adults, the first taking place in Battersea in 1985. Story-telling gained ground in schools, libraries and adult story-telling clubs, reminiscence work was done with elderly people and story-telling therapy with disabled and ill people. In education, the National Oracy Project was influential, with numerous projects and publications drawing attention to the importance of story, the abundance of techniques for working with it and the value of encouraging children to see themselves as tellers.

A new breed of professional story-teller has emerged. The renewal also gained immensely from bringing fresh opportunities to traditional tellers like Duncan Williamson, a Scottish traveller who claims to know more than 2,000 stories, some of which have been transcribed in *Fireside Tales* and other collections. In Scotland and Ireland, a new connection was made with oral traditions which were still surviving. In America, ethnically a fertile ground, the same process had begun rather earlier. There, the formation of NAPPS (The National Association for the Preservation and Perpetuation of Story-telling) gave focus to a renewal evidenced in regular story-telling programmes in libraries and museums, numerous festivals and conferences, college courses, and a flourishing market of books and cassettes related to story-telling. Canada too has made a distinguished contribution.

The revival was not a sudden one. In Britain, the poet John Masefield, had had a passionate interest although he failed to get a planned Guild of Story-tellers off the ground. The librarian, Eileen Colwell, was a pioneer, instituting regular story-telling sessions as a feature of England's first children's libraries in the 1920s. In *A Story-teller's Choice* and other books, she created useful collections of good stories for telling with notes about how to tell them. In the USA, Marie Shedlock, author of *The Art of the Story-teller*, and Ruth Sawyer, author of *The Way of the Story-teller* were both influential, drawing particular attention to the value of story-telling with children.

Similar revivals are now gaining momentum in countries across the world. In

Australia, the stories of the Dream-time are assuming new importance as part of the Aboriginal fight for political and cultural rights. Similar things are happening with American Indian story-telling. In France, through the work of Abbi Patrix and others, considerable experiment is taking place in story-telling as a performance art. In England, the formation of a Society for Story-telling gives the opportunity to establish strong international links as well as bringing greater public attention to the value and possibilities of the art.

## The Art of Story-telling

Story-telling is a live, expressive form in which story-tellers have a number of instruments: voice, facial expression, body movement, eye contact and, where these are used, musical instruments and props. Setting, too, is important and, as in the theatre, arrangement of the venue can also be part of the art.

Voice is the major instrument. Use of it varies enormously between tellers and cultures. Sometimes the emphasis is on an evenly paced narrative style, sometimes more on dialogue and mimicry, for example of animal sounds and birdsong. Some tellers use the actor's ability to put on different voices; others rely on change of tone and pitch rather more than accent. Ability to draw on dialects is almost always admired. As well as pace, rhythm and dynamics of speech, the story-teller draws on the value of silence. Pausing is essential to give the audience time to move through the mental images summoned by the tale. The length and weight of a pause is as vital as in music.

Use of facial expression and body movement also varies greatly. Some tellers enact; others recount. Much also depends on venue. In the glow of a fireside telling, voice assumes unique importance; large gestures will seem out of place. In other settings, hand gestures, for example, may play as expressive a part as in the associated art of shadow-play.

With children, eye contact is the aspect which most strongly differentiates story-telling from story-reading. It gives a host of advantages ranging from the freedom to observe which children are restless to being better able to establish rapport and communicate emotions. Some story-tellers use cloths or interesting objects to focus interest or enhance the story. Sound-making instruments may also be used either for effects within a story or to punctuate the telling. Where props are used, it is vital to consider the size and arrangement of the audience. Whether people will be able to see is greatly affected by whether the teller sits, stands or moves about. With children, it is important not to adopt a position which might feel intimidating. For seated tellers, a low seat is often ideal and, considering the arm movements that may be used, a stool is often preferable to an armchair.

## Preparing to Tell

Preparation involves attending to the story as well as the circumstances in which it may be told, the nature of the event and the kind of audience. Getting to know the story is the greatest challenge and is easiest when the story has been heard and not read. Being able to remember a story that has been heard probably means that the previous story-teller has told it in a memorable way, the words, sounds and meaning already shaped and patterned for telling. With a story found in a book, the work of bringing it to life has to be done from scratch. In either case, preparation involves considering how to make the story your own.

Imagination is crucial and strongly linked with memory. Remembering a story requires making a relationship with it and visualisation, essentially the act of making pictures in the mind, is an important technique. (Significantly, story-tellers have often been blind). The mental pictures, on which the story-teller subsequently draws during the telling, may be formed from all kinds of information, visual, aural, olfactory and textural. They may also be fed by research.

Another primary technique involves getting to know the story's underlying shape and structure, a task which is also helpful in identifying different types of stories and their inter-relationships. In America, Margaret Read Macdonald has published a source-book for story-tellers giving motif indexes and guides to tracing variants.

Words are also important. In traditional story-telling, freshness and beauty are important requirements but so is the reassurance of phrasings which sound well-settled, honed by time and repeated use. According to Alan Garner, the writer and collector of folk-tales, 'folktale is no dull matter that anyone may touch, but more a collection of patterns to be translated with the skill, bias and authority of the craftsman, who, in serving his craft, allows that craft to serve the people' (Garner 1980: 10).

The word stock of oral tradition consists of a wealth of phrases, refrains, formulaic runs, dialect words and proverbs and riddles. Alliteration is a frequent feature: 'There wasn't a stone but was for his stumbling, not a branch but beat his face, not a bramble but tore his skin'. Metaphor, too, is common. A person may disappear 'into the night of the wood' or run 'as swift as the thoughts of a woman caught between two lovers'. Also available are patterned beginnings and endings. 'Crick!' says the West Indian story-teller. 'Crack!' the audience replies. 'There was, there was not ...' may be a starter in Ireland. Other starters summon another kind of time: 'When birds made nests in old men's beards ...'

Endings soften the return to reality: 'They lived happily, so may we. Put on the kettle, we'll have a cup of tea.' One common Armenian ending reminds the audience of the nature of the oral tradition: 'three apples fell from heaven: one for the story, one for those who listened and one for those who first told this story long, long ago.'

Particularly important with children are refrains and chants encouraging participation. 'Run, run, as fast as you can. You can't catch me, I'm the gingerbread man': chanted or sung, such choral forms are also a peg for memory. Where they have not been handed on, it is worth making new ones. Where research can dig them out, it is good to bring them back into currency, adapted or in their original form.

Bringing stories to life in these ways is something which children can enjoy just as much as adults.

# References

Colwell, E. (1963) *Story-telling*, London: Bodley Head.

Cook, E. (1969) *The Ordinary and the Fabulous*, Cambridge: Cambridge University Press.
Garner, A. (1980) *The Lad of the Gad*, London: Collins.
Macdonald, M. R. (1982) *The Story-teller's Sourcebook*, Detroit: Neal-Schuman/Gale Research.
Sawyer, R. (1942/1962) *The Way of the Story-teller*, New York: Viking Press/London: Bodley Head.
Shaarawi, H. (1986) *Harem Years*, London: Virago.
Shedlock, M. L. (1915/1951) *The Art of the Story-teller*, New York: Dover.
Singer, I. B. (1976) *Naftali the Story-teller and his Horse, Sus*, New York: Farrar, Straus and Giroux.
Troughton, J. (1992) *What Made Tiddalik Laugh*, London: Penguin.
Williamson, D. (1983) *Fireside Tales*, Edinburgh: Canongate.

## Further Reading

Colwell, E. (1980) *Story-telling*, South Woodchester: Thimble Press in association with Westminster College, Oxford.
Macdonald, M. R. (1993) *The Story-teller's Start-Up Book*, Little Rock, AR: August House.
Mellon, N. (1992) *Story-telling and the Art of Imagination*, Rockport, MA: Element.

# 47

# Libraries and Research Collections

## Karen Nelson Hoyle

### Introduction

Books written especially for children have comprised an increasingly large and important segment of the book publishing industry ever since the mid-1940s. During these years of rapid growth in the field private collectors discovered children's literature as a promising speciality for their efforts. At the same time student researchers, other scholars, and individual writers and illustrators began to find studies of original materials for the creation of books for children rewarding topics for serious investigation.

Fortunately at this same time the growth of children's librarianship and the teaching of children's literature throughout colleges and universities led to the establishment of special collections of materials for research in this field and the development of numerous private collections with the same goal. The result is that today there are many collections, both public and private, where such scholars may find a wealth of valuable material for their investigations.

One large problem, however, remains before these resources can come close to fulfilling their maximum potential. That is the lack of a comprehensive and up-to-date source of information about where the early works and corrected manuscripts and sketches for book illustrations for any specific author or illustrator may be located (useful volumes are cited at the end of this article).

Scholarship is on the rise. Research methods vary, so a number of researchers are dependent on books, while others require access to related materials such as manuscripts, studies for book illustration, or correspondence. While some collections may duplicate others to a large extent, there are a few collections which focus mainly on very specific contents found nowhere else. Several libraries compared their holdings to Jacob N. Blanck's *Peter Parley to Penrod: A Bibliographical Description of the Best-loved American Juvenile Books* (1938) published in the USA from 1827 to 1926.

Libraries and research collections specialising in the field of children's literature for more than a century include the Free Library of Philadelphia and New York Public Library. Abraham S. Wolf Rosenbach's *Early American Children's Books, 1682–1847* (1928) proved to be a well-respected publication. The dramatic increase in number is a largely post-1945 phenomenon in the USA. Several – including the International Youth Library in Munich, Germany, the Kerlan in Minneapolis, Minnesota and the Osborne in Toronto, Canada – began in 1949.

These three represent categories of international, academic, and focused special collections respectively.

Characteristics of special collections are that they are kept apart physically from the general collection, usually are non-circulating, and more often than not depend financially on private donors. Some are open to the general public, while others, such as the Pierpont Morgan, limit use to qualified scholars who are given special permission.

Collectors often become donors to special collections. For example, d'Alte Welch collected Americana privately and soon amassed 2,800 volumes including two-thirds of the books printed in America before 1821; after his death these became part of the American Antiquarian Society in Worcester, Massachusetts.

Elisabeth Ball divided her collection among the Pierpont Morgan Library, the Lilly Library at Indiana University, and the Free Library of Philadelphia. The last of these received 150 hornbooks.

Special collections may be international or national, historical or contemporary, general or specific, and be in academic, public or private institutions.

## International

Today at least two well-known collections attempt to span the international output of children's books; most countries have national libraries which actually are often internationally comprehensive, while others deal with a more narrow national scope. Outside the city of Munich is the International Youth Library. It has moved from close proximation to the University of Munich to a castle in the town of Passing, easily accessible by electric train from downtown Munich. This collection of half a million volumes has books from around the world. Established in 1949, it attracts scholars, editors, writers, translators, and illustrators and offers three-month stipends on a competitive basis. A staff of language experts both catalogue the books and assist the visitors.

The Osaka (Japan) Children's Book Institute opened in 1984, with a similar intention to be international in scope. Its building was converted to its current library use after the Expo '70 and has a stunning setting next to an artificial lake. While the first floor is a working children's library and has an auditorium for such activities as Boy Scout assemblies, the upper floor is devoted to the children's literature research centre. Professor Shin Torigoe's historic collection of nineteenth- and twentieth-century Japanese books and periodicals provides the keystone to the collection. Among holdings are books from the Meiji and Taisho Periods. A staff of Japanese bibliographers specialising in languages collects and catalogues books in languages such as English, Finnish and German.

## National

The British Library exhibits its children's books on occasion. This prestigious national library owns the Caxton *Aesop's Fables*, the manuscript for Lewis Carroll's *Alice's Adventures Underground* (1865) and the first edition of *Little Goody Two-Shoes* (1765).

The Library of Congress, in Washington, DC serves as the national library for the USA. Not until the enactment of the Copyright Law of 1870 was it ensured that the national library would receive each year a copy of every book printed in the country. Efforts were begun in the 1920s to identify and separate out some children's books. In 1963, a Children's Book Section in the General Reference and Bibliography Division of the Reference Department was organised. It was re-named the Children's Literature Center. It houses the largest collection of non-English language children's books in the USA.

Meanwhile, the Rare Book Collection of the Library of Congress attracted subject collections, too. The Jean Hersholt Collection of Hans Christian Andersen has original manuscripts and correspondence. Not surprisingly, the Danish Royal Library also collects H. C. Andersen editions in all languages. Staff members there have compiled bibliographies of his books published in each of numerous foreign languages. For example, in the English language alone it lists more than a thousand editions.

Most countries today have library special collections devoted to children's books. In Wales, the Welsh National Centre for Children's Literature is located in Aberystwyth.

Each Scandinavian country has a book centre. These include the Swedish Children's Book Institute in Stockholm, the Finnish Institute for Children's Literature in Tampere, the Norwegian Institute for Children's Literature in Oslo, and the Danish Pedagogical Library in Copenhagen. Early in its development the founding director of the Swedish Institute made a list of all Swedish children's books published and then began to acquire them. Now the Institute is the place for the Swedish copyright copy of each new children's title to come directly from the publisher. Every doctoral dissertation on children's literature in the country is co-published by a commercial firm and the Institute. It collects Swedish language books published in other countries as well as Swedish books translated into other languages. The Institute has been a leader in international cooperation on issues such as cataloguing and subject headings for children's literature and its book collection is on the university library's on-line computerised catalogue system. It is also notable for its reference works and scholarly periodicals. Among the specialities in the Swedish Institute for Children's Books is a collection by Astrid Lindgren, best known for her *Pippi Longstocking* books; she was the second recipient of the Hans Christian Andersen Award, given to her in 1958 by the International Board on Books for Young People (IBBY).

The comparable Finnish Institute holds a remarkable collection of work by the internationally famous Tove Jansson, author of *Moomintroll* books.

Dromkeen, 'a home for Australian Children's Literature', is located in Riddells Creek, Victoria. Collected there are first editions of early Australian children's literature, such as Ida Rentoul Outhwaite's *Fairyland* (1926) and manuscripts by contemporary Ivan Southall and Patricia Wrightson who received the Hans Christian Andersen Award for the body of her work in 1986.

## Historical

Founded by Isaiah Thomas in 1812, the American Antiquarian Society's collecting scope emphasises books published in America up to 1820. It now has more than

3,000 primers, catechism and school books printed in America from 1700 to that date. It also has files of several children's periodicals published early in the nineteenth century, such as *Juvenile Magazine* (1802–1806).

In Salem, Massachusetts, the Peabody and Essex Museum (formerly the Essex Institute) owns over 5,000 children's titles, excluding textbooks, from the eighteenth century to 1875. Its periodical holdings include *The Nursery* (1867–1880).

The Osborne Collection in Canada, collected by Edgar Osborne in England, became a part of the Toronto Public Library. The donor was promised a catalogue, the first volume of which *The Osborne Collection of Early Children's Books 1566–1910: A Catalogue*, was published in 1958. A Japanese publisher recently printed facsimiles of a selection of early English books using originals from this collection. Selected early books from the Osborne have been exhibited in Tokyo on several occasions.

The Bethnal Green Museum of Childhood in London, England now owns the 75,000 volume Renier Collection of early English children's books reflecting Britain's political and social history of the period from 1780 to 1840. In Oxford is the Bodleian Library, with a recent acquisition of the Opie Collection of Folklore and Nursery Rhymes. An international fund-raising effort helped bring the collection to the Bodleian; staff and volunteers have now organised it. These libraries have excellent representation of Randolph Caldecott, Walter Crane and Kate Greenaway illustrated books, engraved and printed by Edmund Evans.

The Book Trust (formerly the National Book League) in Wandsworth near London holds several collections; some 280 original drawings by Beatrix Potter are in its Linder Collection.

## Contemporary

The Mary L. Schofield Collection of Children's Literature, at Stanford University in Palo Alto, California, totals more than 10,000 volumes. Along with the historic Thomas Day's *The History of Sanford and Merton* (1786–1789), it holds a complete Tasha Tudor Collection.

At Wheaton College in Illinois is the Wade Collection. Begun in 1965, it holds works, papers, and related materials of C. S Lewis, J. R. R. Tolkien, and nineteenth-century writer George MacDonald. Even the wardrobe from Lewis's home, an inspiration for his book *The Lion, the Witch and the Wardrobe* (1950), is among the artefacts in the Wade Collection.

Ezra Jack Keats's books, manuscripts and illustrations including *The Snowy Day* (1952) are in the extensive de Grummond Collection at the University of Southern Mississippi.

The University of Minnesota's Kerlan Collection houses manuscripts by Carol Ryrie Brink, Marguerite Henry, Newbery Award recipients Katherine Paterson (for *Jacob Have I Loved* (1980) and *Bridge to Terabithia* (1977)) and Lois Lowry (for *Number the Stars* (1989) and *The Giver*, (1993)) and several hundred other authors. In addition, there are thousands of illustrations by Wanda Gág, Marie Hall Ets, Caldecott Award recipient Barbara Cooney, and hundreds of other artists.

The Walter de la Mare Collection at Temple University in Philadelphia has more than 500 volumes and 1,000 letters.

## General versus Specific

Some children's collections are within huge umbrella organisations, such as those in the research library at the University of California Los Angeles (UCLA), while others are focused. The UCLA collection has more than 200 books published by John Newbery or his successors, and a large number of nineteenth-century children's books.

The Clement Moore Collection at the State University of New York at Albany has 200 volumes of twentieth-century English-language editions of the poem, 'A visit From St Nicholas'.

The May Massee Collection at Emporia State University in Kansas holds all the books she edited for both Doubleday, Page and Company from 1922 to 1932 and for Viking Press for the next three decades. By the end of her career, she had been involved with the publishing of nine books which received the Newbery Award and another four Caldecott Medalist titles. In her first year as an editor she published Charles B. Falls's *ABC Book* (1923). Later she published her own translation of Erich Kästner's *Emil and the Detectives* (1929). In addition to books in the collection, there are manuscripts, illustrations and correspondence accompanying a number of them.

Baylor University in Waco, Texas has the original manuscript with illustrations by William McCready for 'The Pied Piper of Hamelin' by Robert Browning, and 150 different editions of the poem. An exhibition of its Pied Piper materials was held in 1969, and an accompanying catalogue was produced.

## Genre and Format

The John M. Shaw Collection of Poetry at Florida State University in Tallahassee holds more than 25,000 volumes. A keyword index provides access to the 200,000 poems.

The Parker Collection of Early Children's Books in Birmingham (England) holds 105 games from the seventeenth century on, in addition to more than 10,000 books.

Small and Alternative Press books covering the years since 1970 are collected by the Co-operative Children's Book Center (CCBC) at the University of Wisconsin in Madison; by 1994 it contained over 1,600 books from American and Canadian publishers. Harry B. Hudson gave his boys' series books and dime novels to the University of South Florida. Girls' series books are a speciality of the Hess Collection at the University of Minnesota.

While the Library of Congress holds the largest number of foreign children's books in the USA, in more than sixty languages, many other research libraries also have rich collections. For example, Butler Library at Columbia University has non-English books published as early as the seventeenth century. The University of New Mexico, Arizona State University and El Paso Public Library in Texas have strong Spanish and bilingual English–Spanish book collections.

Publishing companies, too, place their business papers at educational institutions. For example, Indiana University at Bloomington has the papers of the Bobbs-Merrill Company covering the years 1885 to 1957, while the University of California at Berkeley holds the Parnassus Press records. The publishing house of Farrar, Straus and Giroux gave its editorial papers from 1946 to 1980 to the New York Public Library, with plans to donate more as they acquire archival status; among them is correspondence from Isaac Bashevis Singer, the Nobel Prize winner who wrote stories and re-wrote folk-tales for children.

At the de Grummond Collection in Mississippi there are more than 250 magazine titles, including one published in 1788.

George Hess of Saint Paul willed some 60,000 dime novels, story papers and children's series books to the the University of Minnesota. Likewise, author Albert Johannsen after collecting 8,000 dime novels for his book *The House of Beadle and Adams and Its Dime and Nickel Novels: The Story of a Vanished Literature* (1950, 1962) donated his collection to Northern Illinois University in deKalb. In more specialist vein, Indiana University holds a complete run of the *Amazing Spider Man* (1963–1972) comic book.

## Geographic Area

The Northeastern Collection at the University of Connecticut Library in Storrs collects materials by and about area authors and illustrators. Well-represented are Natalie Babbitt (including her *Tuck Everlasting* (1975)) manuscripts, Ruth Krauss and husband Crockett Johnson, and James Marshall. Avi also donated his collection of 1,600 historical children's books. The Voorhees Rutgers University Art Museum in New Brunswick, New Jersey holds the art of several artists in the state, including Roger Duvoisin.

An increasingly common practice today is the designation of some institution in each state to collect first or early editions of the children's books by the state's authors and those with a setting in the state. The Iowa Collection in the Public Library of Des Moines in Iowa is one such example. Another is the Phoenix Public Library, which collects work by Arizona authors. One treasure is the manuscript dummy for Marguerite Henry's *Brighty of the Grand Canyon* (1953), her book about a burro.

## Academic/Universities and Colleges

The Lilly rare-book library at the University of Indiana in Bloomington holds a considerable number of first editions. In the Lilly and many other libraries are the publications of the leading American publisher of toybooks in the nineteenth century, McLoughlin Brothers. Among its unique holdings is *The Brownies' Book*, a 'monthly magazine for the children of the sun', a magazine for African-American children edited in 1920–1921 by W. E. B. Du Bois.

The Mugar Memorial Library, one of the Boston University Libraries in Massachusetts, holds manuscripts by such notables as the science fiction novelist Isaac Asimov and the boys' sports writer John R. Tunis. In addition, it has manuscripts of several authors and poets of African-American heritage, such as Rosa Guy, and Eloise Greenfield.

The Ruth Baldwin Collection at the University of Florida in Gainesville was inaugurated in 1982, 40,000 of its 70,000 volumes were published before 1900.

## Public Libraries and Private Institutions

The strengths in the collection of the Philadelphia Free Public Library, Pennsylvania, include early imprints of the American Sunday School Union and tract society, for the city was a publishing centre for this type of material. Lloyd Alexander donated his manuscripts, including the Prydian cycle, while Evaline Michelow Ness donated her art for the Caldecott winning *Sam Bangs and Moonshine* (1966). Other area donors to this collection include Katherine Milhous, who described the Pennsylvania Dutch ethnic group.

A number of private special collections have highlighted their children's literature book holdings during the last two decades. Some of them are at work on special projects to identify and catalogue these materials to make them more accessible to researchers.

The Pierpont Morgan Library in New York City stages magnificent exhibits for the public. In 1988 after the extended original showing at the Tate Gallery in London, an outstanding Beatrix Potter: Artist and Storyteller exhibition moved to the Pierpont Morgan. The beautifully printed catalogue is a treasure in itself. In 1993 the Morgan exhibited its Antoine de Saint-Exupéry holdings for his *The Little Prince* (1943); the illustrations, on onion-skin type paper, correspondence and photographs enhanced the exhibit. Harcourt Brace published a facsimile edition from this exhibit for the fiftieth anniversary of the book's original publication.

At the Henry E. Huntington Library, located in San Marino, California it is possible to obtain facsimiles of its rare holdings. Among them are *Cinderella*, *Old Mother Hubbard and Her Dog* and a reprint of Lafcadio Hearn's *The Boy Who Drew Cats* published in Tokyo in 1898.

The Rosenbach Museum and Library in Philadelphia, Pennsylvania, has long been known for its holdings of early children's books. It published one of the first catalogues of historic collections of children's books, and today it is known for its almost exhaustive holdings of Maurice Sendak, including his Caldecott Award winning *Where the Wild Things Are* (1963).

Homes and Museums for children's literature figures abound in America. One can visit the Joel Chandler Harris home in Atlanta, Georgia, and the house in which Wanda Gág grew up in New Ulm, Minnesota. In Hannibal, Missouri is Mark Twain's Home and Museum, while in Hartford, Connecticut is the home he built in the last part of the nineteenth century. The Laura Ingalls Wilder/ Rose Wilder Lane Museum is located in Mansfield, Missouri. The year 1994 was the 100th anniversary of Wilder's arrival in Missouri, her home state for sixty-two years. The first in her series of pioneer books, *Little House in the Big Woods* (1932) was set near Menomonie, Wisconsin, where another homestead site is preserved.

## Research in Special Collections

Recent research has made much use of the special collections in the USA. In some cases, major collections may satisfy individual research topics – Ezra Jack Keats or Kate Greenaway at the de Grummond Collection, for example – while recent volumes in the Twayne Authors series were researched by Gary D. Schmidt (May Massee Collection for his *Robert McCloskey* (1990)), George Shannon (Kerlan Collection for *Arnold Lobel* (1989)) and Deidre Johnson (Hess Collection for *Edward Stratemeyer and the Stratemeyer Syndicate* (1993)).

Occasionally a researcher must travel to several collections for one assignment. For *American Picture Books: From Noah's Ark to the Beast Within* (1976), Barbara Bader used more than ten special children's collections.

Some author collections are widely scattered – for example, Laura Ingalls Wilder original materials. The handwritten manuscript for *Little House on the Prairie* (1935) is at the Pomona Public Library in California, manuscripts for *The Long Winter* (1940) and *These Happy Golden Years* (1943) are at the Detroit Public Library in Michigan; and the early correspondence between Laura and Almanzo Wilder published in 1974 by Harper as *West From Home: Letters of Laura Ingalls Wilder to Almanzo Wilder, San Francisco, 1915* is in the Herbert Hoover Presidential Library in West Branch, Iowa. The Carol Ryrie Brink manuscripts for *Caddie Woodlawn* (1935) are at the Kerlan Collection in Minnesota, while the illustrations for the first edition by Kate Seredy are at the University of Oregon.

## Organisations, Publications

Articles deriving from work in the special collections can be found in the major journals. The American Library Association (ALA) and its Association for Library Service to Children (ALSC) and Young Adult Library Services Association (YALSA) jointly provide the *Journal of Youth Services in Libraries*, which has occasional articles related to special children's literature collections. Specialist publications include the de Grummond's *Juvenile Miscellany*.

The two most up-to-date reference works for the USA are *Children's Authors and Illustrators: A Guide to Manuscript Collections in the United States Research Libraries* (1980) compiled by James H. Fraser, and the 1982 edition of *Special Collections in Children's Literature*. In the latter's Collections by Subject section, for example, a researcher finds that Maurice Sendak's inscribed books and original art work are held by Indiana University in Bloomington, University of Minnesota, and the Rosenbach Museum and Library. The Directory of Collections section is organised geographically by the name of the state. For example, under the heading 'Pennsylvania', eleven different collections are listed. An address telephone number, and list of holdings follows each entry. For the Rosenbach Museum and Library, three individual holdings are named – Lewis Carroll, Maurice Sendak and John Tenniel. Two appendices provide additional information. The Reference to Collections section lists publications including descriptive catalogues, guides, brochures, newsletters, and journal articles. The second appendix is entitled, 'Authors and illustrators in major collections not listed in body of work'. For example, Newbery Award winner for *Island of the Blue Dolphins* (1960), author Scott O'Dell's name does not appear in the Collections by Subject section. His name is listed under both the University of Oregon Library and the Free Library of Philadelphia.

Lance Salway's *Special Collections of Children's Literature* (1972) and Tessa

Chester's *Sources of Information about Children's Books* (1989) provide lists of collections in Britain.

## References

Blanck, J. N. (1938) *Peter Parley to Penrod: A Bibliographical Description of the Best-loved American Juvenile Books*, New York: R. R. Bowker.

Chester, T. R. (ed.) (1989) *Sources of Information About Children's Books*, South Woodchester: Thimble Press.

Fraser, J. H. (comp.) (1980) *Children's Authors and Illustrators: A Guide to Manuscript Collections in the United States Research Libraries* (Phaedrus Bibliographic Series, 1), New York: K. G. Saur.

Johannsen, A. (1950) *The House of Beadle and Adams and Its Dime and Nickel Novels: The Story of a Vanished Literature*, 2 vols and supplement, Norman: University of Oklahoma Press.

Johnson, D. (1993) *Edward Stratemeyer and the Stratemeyer Syndicate*, New York: Twayne.

Rosenbach, A. S. W. (1928) *Early American Children's Books, 1682–1847*, Portland, ME: Southworth Press.

St John, J. (ed.) (1958) *The Osborne Collection of Early Children's Books 1566–1910: A Catalogue*, Vol. 1, Toronto: Toronto Public Library.

Salway, L. (1972) *Special Collections of Children's Literature*, Birmingham: Library Association Youth Libraries Group.

Schmidt, G. D. (1990) *Robert McCloskey*, New York: Twayne.

Shannon, G. (1989) *Arnold Lobel*, Boston: Twayne.

## Further Reading

Jones, D. B. (ed.) (1995) *Special Collections in Children's Literature, an International Directory*, Chicago: American Library Association.

Williams, M. I. (ed.) (1985) *A Directory of Rare Books and Special Collections in the United Kingdom and the Republic of Ireland*, London: Library Association.

# 48

# What the Authors Tell Us

## *Peter Hunt*

'A lot of discussion about children's literature', the author Nina Bawden observed, 'suffers from pompous inflation' (Bawden 1987: 68), but on the whole children's authors display a down-to-earth concern with the complex situation in which they find themselves. They are commonly reluctant to theorise: Lucy Boston expressed the extreme view: 'I'm against all theoreticians. No original writing could result from a theory, could it?' (Wintle and Fisher 1974: 284). Joan Aiken is a little more tolerant:

> I suppose one ought to have theories about writing for children, but with me the theories seem to come second to the writing. However ... what I believe is that children's books should never minimise the fact that life is tough; virtue ought to triumph in the end, because even the best-regulated children's lives are so insecure that they need reassurance, but there's no point in pretending that wickedness and hardship don't exist. And one should never, never write down to a hypothetical children's level or reduce one's vocabulary ... But I'm sure, really, that the main thing is just to shove all theories aside and enjoy the writing; that's the only way to produce good work.
>
> Townsend 1971: 25

None the less, children's authors have continually to confront questions of quite who their audiences are and how they can entertain and influence them; they have to make decisions in terms of language and content, and this in the context of pressure from publishers, parents, the educational establishment and would-be censors. This chapter brings together comments from over fifty authors, throwing light on many such issues.

It is common, for example, to find that people have a low opinion of the children's authorship as a profession – as K. M. Peyton said, 'My mother asks me, "When are you going to write a proper book?" ' ('On not writing a proper book' in Blishen 1975: 123). Ivan Southall has questioned the suggestion that writing for children is a 'lesser' activity:

> The viewpoint mystifies me – that works for children must necessarily be minor works by minor writers, that deliberately they are generated and projected at reduced voltage, that they evade truth, that they avert passion and sensuality and the subtleties of life and are unworthy of the attention of

the serious artist or craftsman ... Adult scaling-down of the intensity of the child state is a crashing injustice, an outrageous distortion of what childhood is about.

'Sources and responses' in Haviland 1980: 85

They might, of course, be consoled by C. S. Lewis's robust defence in 'On three ways of writing for children':

Critics who treat *adult* as a term of approval, instead of merely a descriptive term, cannot be adult themselves. To be concerned about being grown up, to admire the grown up because it is grown up, to blush at the suspicion of being childish; these are the marks of childhood and adolescence ... The modern view seems to me to involve a false conception of growth ... surely arrested development consists not in refusing to lose old things but in failing to add new things?

Lewis 1966: 25

A preliminary question is, who do children's authors write for? A specific child or an abstract child or a specific age-group – or for themselves? One school of thought can be traced at least to Robert Louis Stevenson. In writing about *Treasure Island* to W. E. Henley, he said: 'It's awful fun, boys' stories. You just indulge the pleasure of your heart, that's all; no trouble, no strain' (Colvin 1911: 49). Arthur Ransome famously quoted these lines, in a letter to H. J. B. Woodfield, editor of *The Junior Bookshelf* in 1937:

That, it seems to me, is the secret. You just indulge the pleasure of your heart. You write not *for* children but for yourself, and if, by good fortune, children enjoy what you enjoy, why then you are a writer of children's books ... No special credit to you, but simply thumping good luck. Every writer wants to have readers, and than children there are no better readers in the world.

Crouch and Ellis 1977: 6

Ransome then went on to a much-imitated dictum:

I do not know how to write books for children and have the gravest doubts as to whether anybody should try to do any such thing. To write *for* children seems to me to be a sure way of writing what is called a 'juvenile', a horrid, artificial thing, a patronising thing, a thing that betrays in every line that author and intended victims are millions of miles apart, and that the author is enjoying not the stuff of his book but a looking-glass picture of himself or herself 'being so good with children' ...

Crouch and Ellis 1977: 6

This view can be refined, as by Lucy Boston: 'If you write for the child that was, in your own mind there's no division between that child and yourself now, so that it should be valid for both' (Wintle and Fisher 1974: 283). Equally, writers feel that when they are absorbed in the act of writing, audience ceases to be a problem; Susan Cooper's first book was started as a competition entry, but rapidly became something else:

Now I was no longer writing for a deadline or for money; I was writing for me, or perhaps for the child I once was and in part still am. I dismissed all thought of the . . . prize and I sat there with my back against the sofa and my head in a private world.

Cooper 1990: 20

There are dissenting voices, however. Betsy Byars:

Now I know that there's a theory today that we must never write for children and, after all, we're all just big kids, but I don't believe that. It's partly because I refuse to think of myself as a large wrinkled child, but also because, through my children, I have come to see that childhood is a special time, that children are special, that they do not think like adults or talk like adults. And even though we adults sometimes feel that we are exactly the same as when we were ten, I think that's because we can no longer conceive of what ten was really like, and because what we have lost, we have lost so gradually that we no longer miss it.

Byars 1982: 6

Meindert DeJong develops this:

You may try to go back [to childhood] by way of memory, but that memory is an adult memory, an adult conception of childhood for adults – and not for children . . . When you write for children from adult memory, you satisfy only the other adults who have also forgotten their inner childhood, and have substituted for it an adult conception of what the child needs and wants in books.

Townsend 1971: 75

Certainly there seems to be common agreement that writing with a particular aim or an age group in mind is a route to disaster. Sheena Porter observed that 'it is definitely wrong to write any book with the conscious aim of making it suitable for a particular type of child. The good book must make itself' (Crouch and Ellis 1977: 132). Rumer Godden concurs:

I think children's books should be either information, straight, or else they should be for entertainment. I think you find this worst of all in pony books – they teach a child how to look after a pony through a story. And I always think that's pretty horrid . . . As soon as anyone tries to write a novel with a target, he's bound to fail . . .

Wintle and Fisher 1974: 293

Similarly, John Rowe Townsend:

I think insofar as one has any of the instincts of the artist . . . or craftsman . . . one must write first for oneself with the aim of making something. I think that the book comes first and the audience comes afterwards . . . You are both a craftsman and communicator, and you must carry out each function with proper respect for the other. But as soon as you start thinking in terms of *catering* – a word I particularly detest – for a special readership, then I think you are heading for disaster.

Wintle and Fisher 1974: 239–240

Therefore, although there is a very distinctive market, authors are generally cautious about writing directly 'for' it. Ivan Southall, in a striking diatribe, castigated bad writers who 'do not judge themselves by the best; they shut their souls to that; they read the worst and say "I can do better than that" (Haviland 1980: 87). He distinguishes between the 'honest' second-rate and the 'blatantly commercial second-rate'. 'We are giving them what they want is the alleged doctrine of these people. I believe they do not want it for a moment and would never miss it if it were not there' (90). C. S. Lewis was equally scathing about 'manufacturing' a book: if your story sprang from telling a story to an individual child,

> There is no question of 'children' conceived as a strange species whose habits you have 'made up' like an anthropologist or a commercial traveller. Nor, I suspect, would it be possible, thus face to face, to regale the child with things calculated to please it but regarded by yourself with indifference or contempt.

Lewis 1966: 23

And he goes on to observe that the only way that he can write stories 'consists in writing a children's story because a children's story is the best art-form for something you have to say' (23).

Thus you must write *for* children, not covertly for two different audiences. As Roald Dahl observed: 'What narks me tremendously is people who pretend they're writing for young children and they're really writing to get laughs from adults. There are too many of those about. I refuse to believe that Carroll wrote *Alice* for that little girl. It's much too complex for that' (Wintle and Fisher 1974: 110).

He is not alone. The artist John Burningham said: 'I think there's a horrendous movement of people who think there's a formula: "let's draw everybody in party hats", but really they're appealing to adults while the children are actually bored' (Heaton 1988: 2).

Of course, not everyone agrees. W. E. Johns, who wrote over a hundred books about his flying hero, Biggles, was clear about his aims:

> I give boys what they want, not what their elders and betters think they ought to read. I teach at the same time, under a camouflage. Juveniles are keen to learn, but the educational aspect must not be too obvious or they become suspicious of its intention.

Trease 1964: 80

All writers for children must, naturally, find themselves in a position of teaching, and our perception of what constitutes authorial intention changes. For example, William Makepeace Thackeray wrote in 1846 in *Fraser's Magazine*,

> One cannot help looking with secret envy on the children of the present day, for whose use and entertainment a thousand ingenious and beautiful things are provided which were quite unknown some few scores of years since, when the present writer and reader were very possibly in the nursery state. Abominable attempts were made in those days to make useful books for

children, and cram science down their throats as calomel used to be administered under the pretence of a spoonful of current jelly.

'On some illustrated books for children', Salway 1976: 286–287

If the majority of writers do not see their role as specific to a child or to education or manipulation, why do they write for children? Some, like Alan Garner, follow Ransome: 'Simply, children make the best audience. Connect with a child and you really connect. Adolescence is the same only more so' (quoted in Philip 1981: 154). Other writers take an even more noble position: Paula Fox ('Some thoughts on imagination in children's literature'):

When you read to a child, when you put a book in a child's hands, you are bringing that child news of the infinitely varied nature of life. You are an awakener.

Hearne and Kaye 1981: 24

Some, like Paul Zindel and Ralph Steadman have a high sense of mission: Zindel:

You realise the enormity of the responsibility that you've brought children into the world, and if you don't like life and what you've given them is something you don't like, then it's a terrible thing. So I think there is a big responsibility that you pass on to the children a sense of faith, that life is good, that it's an adventure and that it's something to be chosen over oblivion.

Clark 1989: 15

Steadman:

Each child has a unique view of our world. Our world, that is, for now.

In the meantime, we have a duty, a clear duty to help sustain the openness of a child's pure vision and its wholesome acceptance of what it sees and feels in the world around it and within its own private world ...

In a child we're presented with the raw material, the clean slate, the possessor of potent senses, the ready absorber of the slightest whim. We must realise that every confrontation, every spark of human intention and every touch is registered by this miracle, and the life force within it will use whatever it can grasp to further the motives of a tender captive mind.

The best of children's books are secret doors [which you can only enter if you believe what is on the other side] ... They are readily available with a child to help you and yet inaccessible if you spurn the child's natural delight in the possibility of everything impossible.

Steadman 1990: 25

Others have a more specific intention, notably Roald Dahl, here quoted from two interviews with Mark West:

The person who is what I call a fit reader has a terrific advantage over people who are not readers. Life becomes richer if you have the whole world of books around you, and I'll go to practically any length to bring this world to children.

West 1988: 74

When I'm writing for adults, I'm just trying to entertain them. But a good children's book does more than entertain. It teaches children the use of words, the joy of playing with language. Above all it teaches children not to be frightened of books ... If they are going to amount to anything in life, they need to be able to handle books. If my books can help children become readers, then I feel I have accomplished something important.

West 1990: 65–66

Consequently, it is a task to be taken seriously, especially in the light of Joan Aiken's dictum that 'A children's book should be written ... remembering how few books children have time to read in the course of a childhood and that the impact of each one is probably equivalent to a dozen, or twenty, encountered at a later age' ('Between family and fantasy' in Haviland 1980: 63.)

As to the more profound motivations, Gillian Rubenstein has a theory 'that most people who end up writing for children [had] some kind of trauma which makes them feel that age emotionally for the rest of their lives because that's where they experienced their strongest emotions' (Nieuwenhuizen 1991: 232). Equally, there is a certain scepticism about anyone who claims an easy relationship with childhood, as expressed by E. L. Konigsberg: 'It seems to me that people who profess to love *children* really love *childhood* and, what's more ... they really love only one childhood – their own – and only one aspect of it, called *innocence*.' ('Ruthie Britten and because I can' in Hearne and Kaye 1981: 68). Lloyd Alexander also comments on this:

With all the best intentions in the world many adults have a very peculiar view of childhood. It's strange, because we were all children at some point, though we've forgotten that. We sentimentalise childhood. We look upon it very often as a happy golden age. There are a great many writers for children, and splendid writers for children, who are perhaps more interested in recapturing their own childhood; whereas I am trying to come to terms with my adulthood ... I speak to the child as a growing person.

Wintle and Fisher, 212, 213

The next question that authors confront is: what changes do you make for a child audience? A large majority of authors do not feel inclined to make changes, even under pressure from publishers. To journey-person writers, some of these stances may seem idealistic or privileged. Richard Adams:

From de la Mare I derived early the idea that one must at all costs tell the truth to children, not so much about mere physical pain and fear, but about the really unanswerable things – what Thomas Hardy called 'the essential grimness of the human situation'.

Adams 1974: 92

David Martin:

People in the children's book world ask ... 'Is it suitable?' 'Is it the right age level?' 'Is it about a contemporary problem?' These are important questions, but *not* of primary importance. The primary question should be '*Is this a good book?*', or '*Is this a good writer, writing a good book?*'

Nieuwenhuizen 1991: 173

Yet you can be optimistic, as is John Rowe Townsend:

> I don't think one ought to worry too much about corrupting children, so long as one's books are honest. It has always seemed to me (and this may sound unduly inspirational) that what is honestly intended, and done as truthfully as the author is able to do it, cannot intrinsically be regarded as harmful. On the whole I am inclined to think that children will pass unharmed over what they do not understand. The objection to the heavy sex novel is not that it is going to corrupt them, but that it is going to bore them stiff – by elaborating on experiences that are beyond meaning for them.

Wintle and Fisher 1977: 245

But reality does bite. C. S. Lewis made what he saw as limitations into advantages:

> Writing 'juveniles' certainly modified my habits of composition. Thus it (a) imposed a strict limit on vocabulary (b) excluded erotic love (c) cut down reflective and analytical passages (d) led me to produce chapters of nearly equal length, for convenience in reading aloud. All these restrictions did me great good – like writing in strict metre.

Meek *et al.* 1977: 158

Out in a less cloistered atmosphere, Jean Ure, an accomplished and committed writer of teenage novels, gives the example of using 'four-letter-words' in her book *One Green Leaf*, and its fate in the USA:

> I finally made a stand ... I gave the good and defensible reasons, heard no more, and thought with smug satisfaction that here was *one* author who couldn't be bullied into submission.

> Poor innocent fool! On receiving my advance copies from the States, what did I find? In the face of my bold authorial intransigence, the whole speech had been wiped out entirely.

> I could, of course, have got back to the publishers and made tremendous waves ... but equally of course I didn't. I bowed in the end to the inevitable economic pressures.

Ure 1989: 19

This whole question of what adults allow writers to give children opens up many curious questions about adults' approach to childhood. As Penelope Lively points out, childhood itself is a gross oversimplification:

> One of the oddest things we do to children is to confront them with someone else who is also eight, or ten, or seven, and insist that they be friends ... What concerns me is the misconception that people are fossilised at any particular point in a lifetime. We are none of us 'the young' or 'the middle-aged' or 'the old'. We are all of these things. To allow children to think

otherwise is to encourage a disability – a disability both of awareness and communication.

'Children and memory' in Heins 1977: 229–230

Consequently, it is a mistake ever to underestimate the child reader: Ann Fine:

I don't underestimate children, especially those who read a lot. They will have come across many ideas through books and through talking with intelligent people. They are more sophisticated and advanced in their thinking even though they may not be able to articulate these ideas. Just because they can't reproduce ideas at an adult level is no reason to think they can't take them on board.

Bierman 1991: 16

Shirley Hughes, in a Woodfield Lecture in 1983, 'Word and image' linked this idea to the role of the illustrator:

With a child audience you can never *assume* any level of literacy. But it is a great mistake to think that an unlettered audience is necessarily an unperceptive one, or that their visual reactions are crude or undeveloped. I suspect that children are at their most perceptive in this way before they start to read, and that after they have acquired this thrilling and prestigious skill their visual awareness tends to drop a little ... Our job as illustrators probably starts from that wonderful moment when a baby gets hold of a book and suddenly realises that the image on one page *connects* with the one overleaf. ... What we are after is to build on this excitement ...

Fearne 1985: 74

For all this faith in the reader, questions like – should books be frightening? – constantly arise. Catherine Storr, in an article, 'Things that go bump in the night' in the *Sunday Times Magazine* (March 1971), wrote:

I believe that children should be allowed to feel fear ... Walter de la Mare ... believed that children were impoverished if they were protected from everything that might frighten them ... Once one has answered this basic question ... the second problem arises of how it is to be presented. This is really a technical problem which has to be faced by every writer for children ...

Meek *et al.* 1977: 123

What is *fear*, in this context? Jan Mark:

It is debatable whether or not fear of the unknown is greater than fear of the known, but in childhood so much is unknown that a child, in order to make sense of fear, must isolate and identify it; only the known can be dealt with.

Mark 1986: 9

Or, as Lloyd Alexander put it, 'Children ... have the same emotions ... They may be not as complex ... but as primary colours, fear is fear, happiness is happiness, and love is the same sense for a child as it is for any other' (Wintle and Fisher 1974: 212). His answer is that 'the child ... can experience and come to terms with unsettling emotions within the safety of a work of art' (Alexander 1982: 67). In some senses, as Bernard Ashley notes, the problem has to be resolved through technique:

> We will want to share things with older children, argue a case, show what evil is before it's conquered by good ... Walter de la Mare ... said that a child who has not experienced fear will never be a poet. It isn't what we include, I suggest, it's how we include it.
>
> Ashley 1986: 27–28

Much of this argument becomes bound up with our concepts of 'rubbish'. Mollie Hunter is characteristic of those who take their position of responsibility seriously:

> There is a need for heroes in children's literature ... There is no particular harm in children's reading rubbish as long as they also have plenty of good stuff available for comparison. But it has to be recognised that the [Superman-type] presentation of the concept of hero could also be pernicious rubbish in that its equation of might with right elevates the use of force to a prime ethos.
>
> Hunter 1983: 146

But perhaps the most important and suggestive comment was Peter Dickinson's, in his 'A defence of rubbish'. His sixth defence of children's 'unrespectable' reading-matter was:

> it may not be rubbish after all. The adult eye is not necessarily a perfect instrument for discerning certain sorts of values. Elements – and this particularly applies to science fiction – may be so obviously rubbishy that one is tempted to dismiss the whole product as rubbish. But among those elements there may be something new and strange to which one is not accustomed, and which one may not be able to assimilate oneself, as an adult, because of the sheer awfulness of the rest of the stuff; but the innocence – I suppose there is no other word – of the child's eye can take or leave in a way that I feel an adult cannot, and can acquire valuable stimuli from things which appear otherwise overgrown with a mass of weeds and nonsense.
>
> Dickinson 1970/1976: 76

After all, this is the same argument as that used by Lewis Carroll, who wrote of *The Hunting of the Snark*: 'As to the meaning of the *Snark* I'm very much afraid I didn't mean anything but nonsense! Still, you know, words mean more than we mean to express when we use them: so a whole book ought to mean a great deal more than the writer meant' (Carroll 1973: 22).

What, then, should be changed? Of form and content, the simplification of language might seem to be the less problematic, but here again, authors express great faith in their audience, and a reluctance to bow to simplistic arguments. Eleanor Cameron takes a firm view of this: 'A writer ... should feel himself [*sic*] no more under the necessity to restrict the complexity of his plotting because of differences in child understanding ... than he feels the necessity of restricting his vocabulary' (Cameron 1969: 87), and E. B. White, himself an expert on style, links this with 'writing down':

Anyone who writes down to children is simply wasting his time ... Some writers deliberately avoid using words they think the child doesn't know. This emasculates the prose, and, I suspect, bores the reader. Children are game for anything. They love words that give them a hard time, provided they are in a context that absorbs their attention.

Haviland 1974: 87

That context is a matter of craft and skill, as Jill Paton Walsh points out:

The children's book presents a technically more difficult, technically more interesting problem – that of making a fully serious adult statement, as a good novel of any kind does, and making it utterly simple and transparent ... The need for comprehensibility imposes an emotional obliqueness, an indirection of approach, which like elision and partial statement in poetry is often a source of aesthetic power.

'The rainbow surface,' in Meek *et al.* 1977: 192–193.

Consequently, we may assume that many writers will continue to tackle such problems; as Chris Powling, author, and editor of the British children's book magazine, *Books for Keeps* put it: 'We could be in for some real advances in children's writing. The most significant writing for children always takes risks!' (Mills 1992: 17).

Can such risks be taken with 'content items', where censorious adults are inclined to intervene? The historical novelist Ronald Welch, once a teacher: 'I know from my own experience that children detest people who talk or write down to them; they are eager to accept the challenge of a more adult approach' (Crouch and Ellis 1977: 77). And yet the position of the adult can be untenable, simply because of being an adult: Eleanor Cameron:

I think it is this sense of restriction – of not feeling perfectly free to express all he knows to be true of teenage sexual feelings and the teenagers' deepest attitudes toward them – that so often pulls the quality of a writer's work for this age down to the level of the bland and superficial.

'McLuhan youth and literature', in Heins 1977: 113

The main problem has generally been with 'realism' – usually equated with the less pleasant or socially acceptable aspects of realism. The movement towards political correctness has made matters more complex than they were in the days of H. Rider Haggard:

Personally, I hate war, and all killing ... but while the battle-clouds bank up I do not think that any can be harmed by reading of heroic deeds or of frays in which brave men lose their lives.

What I deem undesirable are the tales of lust, crime, and moral perversion with which the bookstalls are strewn by the dozen.

Rider Haggard 1926: 105

At the end of the century, it could be argued that the reverse pertains. Certainly the concept of truth-telling has shifted. One of the leaders of what might be called the 'ultra-realists' is Robert Cormier:

I don't think a happy ending should be one of the requirements of a children's book. Kids want their books to reflect reality. They know that the bully doesn't always get his comeuppance in the end.

West 1988: 30

I think there's a lot going on in today's world that we have a false view of. Television in particular is lying to us ... We know life isn't always fair and happy. There are enough books with happy endings. I think there's room for the realistic novel about things that really go on in the world. I try to write a warning about what's waiting out there.

Elkin *et al.* 1989: 13

This is not a new idea. The artist Edward Ardizzone:

I think we are possibly inclined, in a child's reading, to shelter him too much from the harder facts of life. Sorrow, failure, poverty, and possibly even death, if handled poetically, can surely all be introduced without hurt ... If no hint of the hard world comes into these books, I'm not sure that we are playing fair.

'Creation of a picture book', in Egoff 1980: 293

Realism, in short, presents writers with a difficult problem. Here is Ursula Le Guin, one of the major fantasy and science fiction writers of the twentieth century (101–113):

I agree that children need to be – and usually want very much to be – taught right from wrong. But I believe that realistic fiction for children is one of the very hardest media in which to do it ... You get 'problem books'. The problem of drugs, of divorce, of race prejudice ... and so on – as if evil were a problem, something that can be solved, that has an answer, like a problem in fifth grade arithmetic. If you want the answer, you just look at the back of the book.

*That* is escapism, that posing evil as a 'problem' ...

But what, then, is the naturalistic writer for children to do? Can he present the child with evil as an *insoluble* problem ... To give the child a picture of ... gas chambers ... or famines or the cruelties of a psychotic patient, and say, 'Well, baby, this is how it is, what are you going to make of it' – that is surely unethical. If you suggest that there is a 'solution' to these monstrous facts, you are lying to the child. If you insist that there isn't, you are overwhelming him with a load he's not strong enough yet to carry ...

'The child and the shadow', in Haviland 1980: 112–113

Not only that, but 'realism' as a genre has become a site for fashionable angst. John Rowe Townsend noted in 'An elusive border':

I remember thinking how refreshing it would be to read a book about young people who enjoyed life, did well at school, had happy relations with their parents, and neither became nor made anybody pregnant. But fictionally, I suppose, that would be a dull life.

Heins 1977: 49

It would also be tactically difficult. Gillian Rubenstein:

> It's partly a children's book convention that you write from the kids' point of view, so you cannot be entirely fair to the parents as well. If you are going to write about children of twelve and thirteen who have totally understanding and marvellous parents, there'll be nothing to write about.
>
> Nieuwenhuizen 1991: 243

But parents, and other adults, are very sensitive, and this brings us to that constant problem of children's literature, censorship. A rationalist approach has been voiced by Joan Aiken in 'Between family and fantasy': 'Exercising any degree of control over the kind of books written for or read by children is a highly doubtful policy ... What terrifies one child may seem merely comic to another, or may be completely ignored; one can't legislate for fear' (Haviland 1980: 63). This is all very well in theory, but writers who push at the edges of acceptability are confronted with practical censorship. Judy Blume:

> Adults have always been suspicious of books that kids like. It seems as if some adults choose to forget what mattered to them when they were children ... Many adults do not trust children.
>
> West 1988: 11

> I think that a lot of adults in our society are uncomfortable with their own sexuality, and therefore their children's sexuality is a threat to them ...
>
> Wintle and Fisher: 315

> The most frightening thing about censors is their complete sense of self-righteousness.
>
> West 1988: 36

One answer, adopted by the political novelist James Watson, is confrontation:

> I'm particularly interested in noting where an accusation of bias is used – it says as much about the accuser as the person accused ... the very perception of impartiality is so soaked in ideological notions that there is no way to be impartial. So why pretend to be? If I'm accused of bias in my books – tough! I *am* biased – biased for certain value systems.
>
> Nettell 1989: 17

While realism attracts much general attention, it is fantasy, where children's literature has made such a major contribution, that much authorial theoretical attention has been focused. Susan Cooper:

> In 'realistic' fiction, the escape and the encouragement come from a sense of parallel: from finding a true and recognisable portrait of real life. In these pages we encounter familiar problems, but they're *someone else's problems* ... Fantasy goes one stage beyond realism; requiring complete intellectual surrender, it asks more of the reader, and at its best may offer more. Perhaps

this is why it is also less popular, at any rate among adults, who set such store by their ability to think.

'Escaping into ourselves', in Hearne and Kaye 1981: 14, 15

Jill Paton Walsh concurs:

If a book has a dragon in it, then maybe one dismisses it as rubbish ... There are no dragons in the world, but there are ferocious, greedy and destructive keepers of goldhoards. And there is greed in one's own soul. A work of fantasy compels a reader into a metaphorical state of mind. A work of realism, on the other hand, permits very literal-minded readings, even downright stupid ones ... Even worse, it is possible to read a realistic book as though it were not fiction at all ...

'The art of realism', in Hearne and Kaye 1981: 38

As Le Guin asked in the title of a famous paper, 'Why are Americans afraid of dragons?' (Le Guin 1992: 34–40). But the common-sense of Terry Pratchett might be allowed to have the last word here.

So let's not get frightened when children read fantasy. It is the compost for a healthy mind. It stimulates the inquisitive nodes. It may not appear as 'relevant' as books set firmly in the child's environment, or whatever hell the writer believes to be the child's environment, but there is some evidence that a rich internal fantasy life is as good and necessary for a child as healthy soil is for a plant, for much the same reasons ... Like the fairy tales that were its forebears, fantasy need no excuses.

Pratchett 1993: 5

Writers have other matters to contemplate, from Paul Jennings's view that 'Some academics and judges on panels consider that a book has more substance if it is difficult to read' (Nieuwenhuizen 1991: 131) to Nadia Wheatley's dismissal of the classification of books as for adults or for children: 'wouldn't it be better to stop fussing about definitions of genre, and simply put a copy of each into two sections of the library?' (Nieuwenhuizen 1991: 299]

On the whole, they are optimistic about childhood, as is Mary Norton:

Children nowadays are encouraged to invent, but still in ways devised by adults. 'Clear-up-that-mess' has destroyed many a secret world. As the Borrowers' house was destroyed by Mrs Driver. This particular incident, oddly enough, worries grown-ups far more than it does children. Children are used to repeated small destructions – in the name of punctuality or tidiness – and have learned to accept them. If raw materials are there to hand, they simply build again.

Crouch and Ellis 1977: 69

or, like Aidan Chambers, optimistic about the role that adults can take. Having cited Kafka's view that 'a book must be the axe which smashes the frozen seas' he goes on:

the hands that best wield those axes will belong to sympathetic and knowledgeable adults who wield for themselves, with enormous pleasure and skill, axes of their own size and weight.

Chambers 1985: 33

Children's authors have also written a great deal about the act of writing, a topic which seems to be of perennial interest to those who attend conferences. Interesting as those accounts can be, they are rarely generally applicable, and the ultimate anti-account, by William Mayne – might serve for all:

After the idea was there I wrote the book, a statement that, though short, is completely adequate. There is nothing particularly interesting about writing a book. In fact, it is rather a bore for everyone, and generally spoils the idea that was there in the first place.

Crouch and Ellis 1977: 95

Indeed, Mayne may be allowed the last word, standing, as he does, for the child before the adult, and, one suspects, the writer before the critic:

Adults can read my books if they like, it doesn't matter. I'm not interested in what they think.

Nettell 1990: 15

## References

Adams, R. (1974) 'Some ingredients of *Watership Down*', *Children's Book Review* 4, 3: 92–95.

Alexander, L. (1982) 'Sex, violence, passion, misery and other literary pleasures', *The Advocate* 1, 2: 65–70.

Ashley, B. (1986) 'TV reality – the dangers and the opportunities', *International Review of Children's Literature and Librarianship* 1, 2: 27–32.

Bawden, N. (1987), 'Through the dark wood', in Harrison, B. and Maguire, G. (eds) *Innocence and Experience: Essays and Conversations on Children's Literature* 68–75, New York: Lothrop, Lee and Shepard.

Bierman, V. (1991) 'Authorgraph No. 69: Anne Fine', *Books for Keeps* 69: 16–17.

Blishen, E. (1975) *The Thorny Paradise: Writers on Writing for Children*, Harmondsworth: Kestrel (Penguin).

Byars, B. (1982) 'Writing for children', *Signal* 37: 3–10.

Cameron, E. (1969) *The Green and Burning Tree*, Boston: Atlantic, Little, Brown.

Carroll, L. (1973) *The Hunting of the Snark*, Gardner, M. (ed.), Harmondsworth: Penguin.

Chambers, A. (1985) *Booktalk. Occasional Writing on Literature and Children*, London: Bodley Head.

Clark, M. 'Authorgraph No. 54: Paul Zindel', *Books for Keeps* 54: 14–15.

Colvin, S. (ed.) (1911) *Letters of Robert Louis Stevenson*, Vol. 1, London: Methuen.

Cooper, S. (1990) 'How I began', *The New Welsh Review* 2, 4: 19–21.

Crouch, M. and Ellis, A. (1977) *Chosen for Children*, 3rd edn, London: The Library Association.

Dickinson, P. (1970/1976) 'A defence of rubbish', in Fox, G. *et al.* (eds), *Writers, Critics and Children*, New York: Agathon/London: Heinemann Educational.

Egoff, S., Stubbs, G. T. and Ashley, L. F. (eds) (1980) *Only Connect: Readings on Children's Literature*, 2nd edn, Toronto: Oxford University Press.

Elkin, J. *et al.* (1989) 'Cormier talking', *Books for Keeps* 54: 12–13.

Fearne, M. (1985) *'Only the Best is Good Enough'. The Woodfield Lectures on Children's Literature, 1978–1985*, London: Rossendale.

Haviland, V. (ed.) (1974) *Children's Literature: Views and Reviews*, London: Bodley Head.

—— (ed.) (1980) *The Openhearted Audience: Ten Authors Talk About Writing for Children*, Washington DC: Library of Congress.

Hearne, B. and Kaye, M. (1981) *Celebrating Children's Books*, New York: Lothrop, Lee and Shepard.

Heaton, C. (1988) 'On the child's side', *British Book News Children's Books* June: 2–5.

Heins, P. (ed). (1977) *Crosscurrents of Criticism. Horn Book Essays 1968-1977*, Boston: Horn Book.

Hunter, M. (1983) 'A need for heroes', *The Horn Book Magazine* 59, 2: 146–154.

Le Guin, U. (1992) *The Language of the Night, Essays on Fantasy and Science Fiction*, rev. edn, New York: HarperCollins.

Lewis, C. S. (1966) *Of Other Worlds*, London: Geoffrey Bles.

Mark, J. (1986) 'Children writing', *Bookquest* 9, 2: 4–11.

Meek, M., Warlow, A. and Barton, G. (eds) (1977) *The Cool Web: The Pattern of Children's Reading*, London: Bodley Head.

Mills, C. (1992) 'Authorgraph No. 75: Chris Powling', *Books for Keeps* 75: 16–17.

Nettell, S. (1989) 'Authorgraph No. 58: James Watson', *Books for Keeps* 58: 17.

—— (1990) 'Authorgraph No. 63: William Mayne', *Books for Keeps* 63: 14–15.

Nieuwenhuizen, A. (1991) *No Kidding. Top Writers for Young People Talk About Their Work*, Chippendale, NSW: Sun (Pan Macmillan).

Philip, N. (1981) *A Fine Anger: A Critical Introduction to the Work of Alan Garner*, London: Collins.

Pratchett, T. (1995) 'Let there be dragons', *Books for Keeps* 83: 6–7.

Rider Haggard, H. (1926) *The Days of My Life*, Vol. 1, London: Longman.

Salway, L. (ed.) (1976) *A Peculiar Gift: Nineteenth Century Writings on Books for Children*, Harmondsworth: Kestrel (Penguin).

Steadman, R. (1990) 'What is a child? . . . and what is a children's book?', *Books for Keeps* 62: 25.

Townsend, J. R. (1971) *A Sense of Story. Essays on Contemporary Writers for Children*, Harmondsworth: Longman Young Books (Penguin).

Trease, G. (1964), *Tales Out of School*, rev. edn, London: Heinemann.

Ure, J. (1989) 'Who censors?', *Books for Keeps* 58: 19.

West, M. I. (1988) *Trust Your Children*, New York: Neal-Schuman.

—— (1990) 'Interview with Roald Dahl', *Children's Literature in Education* 21: 61–66.

Wintle, J. and Fisher, E. (1974) *The Pied Pipers: Interviews with the Influential Creators of Children's Literature*, London: Paddington Press.

## Further Reading

Chevalier, T. (ed.) (1989) *Twentieth-Century Children's Writers*, 3rd edn. Chicago and London: St James Press.

Commire, A. (ed.) (1971– ) *Something About the Author: Facts and Pictures About Authors and Illustrators of Books for Young Children*, Vol. 1, Detroit, MI: Gale Research.

de Montreville, D. and Crawford, E. D. (eds) (1978) *Fourth Book of Junior Authors and Illustrators*, New York: H. W. Wilson.

—— and Hill, D. (eds) (1972) *Third Book of Junior Authors and Illustrators*, New York: H. W. Wilson.

Fuller, M. (1969) *More Junior Authors*, New York: H. W. Wilson.

Hildick, W. (1970) *Children and Fiction*, London: Evans Brothers.

Hopkins, L. B. (1974) *More Books by More People: Interviews with Sixty-Five Authors of Books for Children*, Englewood Cliffs, NJ: Scholastic.

Kingman, L. (ed.) (1965) *Newbery and Caldecott Medal Books 1956–65*, Boston: Horn Book.
—— (ed.) (1975) *Newbery and Caldecott Medal Books 1966–75*, Boston: Horn Book.
Kunitz, S. J. and Haycraft, H. (eds) (1951) *The Junior Book of Authors*, New York: H. W. Wilson.

# Part IV

## Applications of Children's Literature

# 49

# Reading and Literacy

## Geoffrey Williams

### Introduction

Over the past decade or so children's literature has assumed a new status in the teaching of reading in the first years of school. Previously, though enthusiastic teachers read to children during story time, actual instruction in reading 'skill' was largely carried out through specially written materials, in the form of reading schemes and comprehension exercises. The result was that for very many children Janet and John, Dick and Jane were more familiar figures of fiction than Rosie, Alfie or Tom Long. There have, of course, always been teachers who understood that the texts through which children learned to read were important for the kinds of readers they became, but these exceptions were the more remarkable because the dominant practices were so strong.

Some features of recent changes in literacy pedagogy which give children's literature a new status in reading pedagogy are explored in this chapter. There are two aspects of particular interest: appreciation of the significance of the semiotic patterning of literary texts; and explorations of effects of ways of talking about literary texts. Certain ways of talking about narrative in some families have profoundly influenced the teaching of reading, but these pedagogic strategies rest on specific images of relations between home and school reading practices, which it is therefore important to examine closely. In particular, the metaphor of an essential partnership between home and school literacy practices will be under focus. The chapter also considers different forms of classroom work which develop through the metaphors of personal response to, and collaborative exploration of, literary text, and concludes with an image of a class of 11-year-old children using metasemiotic tools, in this case linguistic tools, to talk about a book they enjoyed greatly. For reasons of space the discussion is restricted to the early periods of children's literacy development in primary school, a selection which is perhaps justified by the fact that far greater critical attention is usually given to adolescents' reading.

### Texts in Reading Development

When children learn to read, they do so by reading *something*, texts, in fact. Despite this truism the effects of texts have been very little studied in reading pedagogy. A typical formulation is that 'Children learn to read', and it is the agent 'children' and the process 'read' which have attracted most attention from analysts. Even when children have been studied, it has typically not been children in some actual context of lived experience but individual, displaced acts of perception and cognition which experimenters have probed. Margaret Meek comments, on the basis of a lifetime's interest in children's literature and reading development,

> In all of the books I have read about reading and teaching reading there is scarcely a mention about what is to be read. Books are, as the saying goes, taken as read in the discussions about reading teaching. The reading experts, for all their understanding about 'the reading process', treat all text as the neutral substance on which the process works, as if the reader did the same thing with a poem, a timetable, a warning notice.
>
> Meek 1988: 5

Only in the last decade has a different formulation, 'Texts construct children's reading', entered discussions about how children learn to read, although understanding of the agency of texts in the making of readers has now become an important aspect of the children's literature field. Scholars such as Meek and Nodelman (1988) cross the established boundaries of academic disciplines to develop their accounts of the subtlety and significances of literary texts written for children, often surprising readers by how transdisciplinary the reach of such work is, and needs must be. Such studies draw on research in semiotics, socio-cultural theories of children's mental development, histories of literacy and, increasingly, anthropological and sociological studies of cultural differences in narrative practices.

Meek writes in particular of the 'untaught lessons' in reading, those which readers experience only through deep involvement in what they read and through sharing readings with others (1988: 7). These accounts of untaught reading lessons rest on the textuality of the literature children read, and they therefore require careful investigation of how meanings are built up by the patterning of visual and linguistic elements of individual texts. It is worth taking a few moments with the detail so that the specific resources for these signifying practices are made visible.

Since *Where the Wild Things Are* (Sendak 1970) counts as an example of a text which many children become deeply involved with, it is a useful 'test case' for the argument. Some economy can be achieved by asking a specific question about children's reading of narrative: how does a child reader learn about the development of plot from the semiotic patterning of this text? This is surely one crucial aspect of being able to read like a 'model reader', in Eco's (1994) sense.

Perhaps the most obvious source of understanding of plot relations is the excitement of the depicted events, from which comes the necessity to turn the page. But that is not all there is to say about the resource of the text for this learning. How is the sense of event and, perhaps more importantly, the significance of event, given by the patterning of the resources of language and image?

Consider those images in which Max looks directly at the viewer/reader, in contrast with those in which his gaze is directed 'within' the represented world. There are three such images. The first occurs just after the bedroom begins to become a forest, and just before Max begins to take advantage of it. He looks directly at the viewer, with a smile which seems to invite complicity. As readers we appear to be instructed that something slightly different is about to happen as we turn the page. Perhaps it will seem akin to one of those moments when somebody makes momentary eye contact, in a classroom or at a party, from which it is evident that more will follow. That is to say, at this point the text 'asks' us to begin to adopt a slightly different relationship with Max through the form of the image.

How does the image 'ask' something new of the reader? In a recent analysis of the semiotic resources of visual images, Kress and van Leeuwen (1990) describe direct gaze from the depicted figure to the viewer as the means through which demands, in comparison with offers, are made. Following their lead we might say that prior to this point the text has offered information, but in this image it makes a first demand on a reader to adopt a particular orientation of expectation to the sequent events. We might predict that what follows will therefore have some particular significance for the narrative development, as indeed it does as Max begins to act in the transformed world of his room.

The next moment of 'demand' comes soon after. It is the image in which Max sets out in his private boat to begin his voyage to the Wild Things. Max's gaze here is very clear, very direct – in some contrast with the furtiveness of the earlier image. The combination of the gaze, the disposition of the arms, the smile and the frontal angle of Max's body all seem to suggest a request which is something like 'come and play this game with me'.

There is one last image in which a demand is made. The wild rumpus has begun at Max's command and, of course, the following three images assume the full volume of the page. In the first of these Max dances in parallel with the wild things, but below them; in the second, he swings in the tops of the trees, equal with them; and in the third, he is on top of them, riding triumphantly, mace in hand. It is in the second that the new demand is made, just prior to his ascendancy to a position of total domination.

Direct gaze from the depicted character to the reader is, of course, just one of the many meaning resources which contribute to a sense of the plot. Going back through the images we can see many other ways in which subtle variation cues readers to adopt a variable role relationship with Max, or with the other participants. Consider just one further example of the significance of variation, the vertical angle at which the characters are depicted. As viewers we are positioned at eye level in the first image, at a slightly higher angle in the second, and at a much higher angle again through the images of Max in his bedroom, but then the angle drops back to eye level as he sails off through night and day, and then to a much lower angle as he encounters the first Wild Thing (cf. Nodelman 1988: 183).

Again, what is the significance of this variation? In Western European visual semiotic resources, angle of view is the primary means through which a relation of power between viewer and represented image is construed. (Consider, for example, the variable construal of a politician's power through press photographs shot at various vertical angles.) In this text the images instruct us to adopt variable power relations with Max as part of the plot development – first, we are more or less his equal; then, in his moment of abandonment we become 'superior' in power – or, perhaps more accurately, Max is relatively diminished in power; and then, as the plot develops, our power diminishes relative to the participants in the ensuing monstrous clash.

The significance of variation in the patterning of meanings might equally be pursued with regard to language. For example, we might ask how, linguistically, readers *initially* are given a sense that this night – the night of Max's transgression, journey and restoration – is a night with singular qualities.

Grammatically, the text has an unusual beginning which 'foregrounds' the particularity of the night. This comes about because of the choice the author has made for the initial element of the first clause of the text. Halliday (1994) describes how English gives readers a choice as to which constituent is placed in first position in a clause. As a consequence there is a meaning significance attaching to the initial element, which gives information about the textual organisation of the message by indicating the speaker/writer's 'point of departure'. Speakers may begin a clause with the grammatical Subject, as the writer of the publisher's introduction did in the Puffin edition:

*Max's wonderful adventure* began the night he put on his wolf suit.

Alternatively, a speaker might begin with an atypical choice or marked choice as Sendak did when he brought to the foreground not Max, nor his adventure, but instead

*The night Max wore his wolf suit and made mischief of one kind and another* his mother called him 'WILD THING!'

Notice, too, that grammatically a good deal of information about the particular night is built up immediately around the noun 'night' itself. Technically this is achieved through embedded clauses in the noun group, which are constituted by all the words in italics after 'night'. The physical distribution of the language on the page also supports this marking of the moment in time since the noun group is extended over the first two pages. Grammar and orthography together draw attention to the particularity of the moment.

To return, then, from the detail of the particular text to the general argument. The point to which Meek and others draw attention is this: many literary texts written for children enable readers to take up ways of meaning relevant to literary readings of text through the patterning of semiotic resources in both language and visual image. On this account children do not become 'literary' readers by first developing a bank of skills in 'decoding' and 'comprehension', and then apply these skills to literary (and other) texts. They learn how to act as literary readers partly because the resources of the texts they care about make it possible for them to act as literary readers.

The sense of 'act' is important. It draws attention to the fact that literacy is constructed in action, in and through the reading of texts and through engaging in the forms of interpretation which these texts make possible. The selection of verb here in fact owes much to Vygotsky's insight into the resources which mediate meaning in interaction and over time become part of a child's ways of meaning (Vygotsky 1986).

Literary texts are thus a necessary requirement for the development of literary readers. They are not, though, a sufficient condition. In Meek's formulation there are two conditions, the second being the necessity of 'sharing our readings with others'. The benefits of sharing readings have been so widely discussed in the children's literature field they may appear to require no further analysis, but this is not so.

Since for children the two main sites for this sharing are families and schools, relations between ways of sharing readings in these sites are crucial for development. Since sharing is always by definition with socially situated others, whose locations in socio-cultural practices vary, there is an important potential for different forms of interpretive practice to develop in and around literary text. Therefore, how readings are shared in classrooms, and how these classroom ways of saying relate to ways of meaning that children have developed in their families, have a deep significance for literacy pedagogy and are the focus of the next section. In the following discussion I will initially consider changes to early school literacy pedagogy which are based on observations of family reading practices, then raise some questions about the effects of the notion of a close partnership between home and school in literacy education.

## Story Reading and Early Literacy Pedagogy

From case studies of precocious readers (for example, Clark 1976; Durkin 1966), and correlational studies of early development of schooled literacy (for example Wells *et al.* 1981; Wells 1985; 1987), there have been consistent findings of strong associations between joint book reading in families and early success in school literacy. The findings have been widely used in Australia, Britain, Canada, New Zealand and the USA to fashion literacy education in the early years of schooling. In Australia, joint book reading has become one of the orthodoxies of the 'whole language' approach.

In classroom joint book reading, teachers have been encouraged to simulate family interaction by reading 'big book' versions of children's literature with whole classes of young learners (Holdaway 1979). Interaction during school joint book reading usually takes the form of an initial reading of a text and discussion of story features based on children's individual responses to it, then further readings in which children progressively take more responsibility for reading the written language aloud.

However, the foregrounding of continuity in reading practices between home and school, tending to universalise the practice of joint book reading in the home, comes at a high price for some young learners. In contrast with the universalising tendency of much of the pedagogical literature, a significant body of evidence points to the relativity of literacy practices in different social locations, including ways in which caregivers read to their children and hence the orientations which children develop to different 'ways with words' (Heath 1983). Since only some of these practices are selected into school discourse, even those children who are read to extensively at home may experience significant discontinuity between home and school literacy practices.

In fact, even in the early correlational studies of early reading achievement, important differences in family story-reading practices were evident. This was so in Wells's Bristol study (1985, 1987), and in a range of small-scale studies, for example Tizard and Hughes (1984) and Teale (1986). Researchers such as Wells have been clear that certain characteristics of linguistic interaction during the reading of text are related to school literacy development. He comments:

> it is not the reading of stories on its own that leads children towards the reflective, disembedded thinking that is so necessary for success in school, but the total interaction in which the story is embedded. At first they need a competent adult to mediate, as reader and writer, between themselves and the text; but even when they can perform the decoding and encoding for themselves, they continue to need help in interpreting the stories they hear and read and in shaping those that they create for themselves. The manner in which the adult – first parent and later teacher – fulfils this latter role is almost as important as the story itself.
>
> Wells 1985: 253

Despite the strength of these assertions, repeated frequently in both research reports and pedagogic handbooks, only rarely has linguistic interaction during joint book reading been a topic of intensive analysis. Among such detailed studies, Heath's ethnographic comparison of literacy events in three communities in the south-east of the USA is the most widely known. With respect to joint book reading specifically, Heath found crucial variation in interaction between caregivers and children in the white fundamentalist Christian community of 'Roadville' and the 'maintown' middle-class social location of 'Gateway'. (The practice was found to be virtually non-existent in the third community, 'Trackton'.) The Gateway variant was the only one which approximated school practices. Heath argues that the variants signify different historico-cultural literacy traditions in these communities.

Additional to Heath's study of 'inter-cultural' variation, intra-cultural variation by social class locations was considered by Williams (1995). Many hours of interaction between mothers and 4-year-old children, and between teachers and kindergarten classes in the first two months of schooling, were audiorecorded. Semantic features of each clause of this interaction were analysed to describe typical semantic patterning during talk about books. Findings from the study confirm the sensitivity of literacy practices to social location and, additionally, indicate that it is aspects of the practices of only one social class group which are projected into school pedagogy.

The sensitivity of joint book reading practices to social location represents a radical challenge to the image of naturalness in interaction around children's literature which strongly typifies teaching handbooks. In these environments children become, in Bernstein's phrase, the 'imaginary subjects' of instruction (Bernstein 1990) and the account of the complexity of what they have to learn for success in school literacy is significantly reduced.

One of the most important current challenges for early literacy educators is to find ways of talking about books which can be made genuinely inclusive of children, or at least genuinely clear to them. Another is to avoid impressions that literacy differences are simply educational differences in another guise, and therefore successfully 'treated' by parent education strategies. Both challenges will have to be addressed through greater knowledge about both the subtlety and effects of meaning variations in relation to different socio-cultural locations.

## Talking About Literary Texts and their Meanings in Classrooms

The metaphor of *personal response* to story currently dominates thought about the function of children's literature in education. Under this metaphor children are involved in a wide range of activities which amount either to forms of retelling the constructs of the text, for example by mapping the plot, or by recreating elements of a scene (draw a picture of Terabithia), or to acting imaginatively within the constructs of the text (write to Gilly Hopkins to encourage her in her new life with her grandmother). What is specifically encouraged is an individual response which effectively takes the fictive world as given.

At its best this work can be interesting for children, particularly by creating opportunities to explore the internal coherence of a fictive world. But, in so far as these approaches to 'using' children's literature dominate classroom work, they actually create significant problems for many children. ('Using' literature is by far the most common verb representing these processes in literacy pedagogy.) Activities of the imagination are refracted through the metaphor of personal response as though they were universal features of childhood rather than specific forms of interpretive activity which are learned through specific social practices. Consequently, because textual meaning and modes of interpretation are taken as given under this metaphor, the longer-term significances of classroom work based on it remain opaque for many learners. They may appear to participate willingly, and certainly to enjoy themselves, but their understandings of *why* they are engaging in such work are likely to be another matter.

A rather different approach is taken by teachers who include explorations of the nature of literary text itself in classroom work, even with emergent readers. In this approach teachers position children as apprentice collaborators in the investigation of meanings and how they are made, rather than as reactors to given meanings. Such teachers find in the textual play of books like Browne's *Bear Hunt* and *Piggybook*, Burningham's *Granpa* and Scieszka's and Smith's *The Stinky Cheese Man and other Fairly Stupid Tales* resources which enable them to encourage children to investigate literary meaning-making as textual practice.

Experienced readers sometimes fear that such explorations of how meanings are made will destroy embryonic reading pleasure through disturbing the 'magic of narrative', no doubt with memories of their own experiences of interminable and arbitrary classroom readings of texts still vivid. However, children do appear to be able to learn to read variably. Much in the way that Barthes describes in his introductory discussions in *S/Z* (1974) children can learn to read, on the one hand, as though for the moment a character were a real psychological entity and there were such places as midnight gardens and, on the other hand, as though there was nothing but the patterning of language which was the source of their pleasure. It is the integration of these two forms of pleasure which makes pedagogies which include investigation of how meanings are made so distinct: different ways of reading, each with its own satisfactions. What is importantly changed is the level of abstraction at which children learn to think about the nature of literature, and language.

In such approaches the search is always for the patterning of meaning, and never for the isolated textual instance of a felicitously used adjective or some other 'good word'. It is, after all, the patterning of relations which gives a literary text the kind of distinctive significance which Culler (1977) accords it. Although classroom readings begin by taking the figures of a text as given, it is usually not very long before children can be helped to notice features such as intertextual play and the repetitions and parallel structures of wordings which are the very basis of how literary texts mean.

One interesting example of such work is given by Aidan Chambers (Chambers 1985, 1993). Chambers's provocative question, first raised in *Booktalk* (1985) was this: are children critics, where the work of critics is understood in the terms Auden proposed in *The Dyer's Hand and Other Essays* (1948)? His evidence suggests that they may be. Chambers and his teacher collaborators describe children's participation in three types of 'sharing': sharing enthusiasms, sharing puzzles and sharing connections. The third is subtitled 'discovering patterns', and includes a framework of discussion through which sharing of ideas might take place, including the highly significant question 'Were there any patterns – any connections – that you noticed?' As with any proposal for a general framework, there is a danger that such a methodology might come to restrict what might be talked about with a particular text. Chambers himself warns repeatedly against this (for example, 1993: 87). But it is a danger which is a problem for any specific pedagogical proposal, and therefore not a criticism of the approach itself. Pedagogical proposals which avoid the specific transmit their own invitations to rigidity.

In investigating the patterning of text it eventually becomes necessary to say something about what it is that is patterned. This requirement leads directly to a need for metasemiotic tools: a language to talk about language, or about other meaning systems. Here we come full circle to the beginnings of this discussion, to ask a question which it has only been possible to raise within reading pedagogy during the last few years. The question is this: as people with an interest in various facets of children's literature learn more about the nature of textuality by using a range of metasemiotic tools (Doonan 1993), is it possible that children might also learn to participate in such explorations through accessible metasemiotic tools?

To exemplify, and in a sense to offer a test case, I will describe a specific, exploratory instance of work of this kind as the final movement of this chapter. The work was with a class of 11-year-olds and forms part of a research project concerned with children's development of knowledge about language being conducted at the University of Sydney. The teacher, Ruth French, is part of the small research group. The general purpose of this work is to explore children's understandings of the significance of variation in language. So far as literary text is concerned, the children were encouraged to investigate effects of variation in the patterning of certain kinds of meaning within a specific text. It is important, though, in order to place the literary work in the more general context to begin by describing aspects of the work on language variation.

The children knew well, from sharing between various members of the class, that languages themselves vary. The majority had a language other than English as their mother tongue, including Tamil, Mandarin, German and Italian, and their knowledge was an important resource for the rest of the class. For example, Giridhar taught the class something of the Tamil alphabet, Cathy showed them how difficult it is to write Mandarin, Eric talked about differences between his (Austrian) German and the German spoken in Germany itself. Since all of the children were learning to speak Italian they could make their own comparisons with English. They also knew that English varies in different contexts of use, and that this variation comes about partly because of the role language plays in making meaning.

The specific metasemiotic tools they were learning to use derived from a functional grammar of English (Halliday 1994), which describes English from the perspective of language as a resource for meaning rather than as a set of prescribed grammatical rules. Observations about grammatical patterning, and the significance of variation in patterning, were a prominent aspect of this work. The children knew, for example, that typically texts which give people instructions about how to do something are linguistically organised in a way different from texts which argue for a particular point of view: they are different genres, in Bakhtin's (1986) sense. Their knowledge of semiotic design generally, and linguistic variation more specifically, were then important bases for further insight into how literary texts mean.

A literary text which particularly attracted the children's attention was Anthony Browne's *Piggybook*. They laughed loudly as Ruth read it to them, exclaiming as they noticed the transformation of the setting through the occurrence of the pigs in wallpaper, light switches and lampshades. Their conversations about the book extended over several lessons. They began with the details of the represented figures, but soon extended their discussion to notice the patterning of colours, especially the colour selections and relative saturation. They also began to make some tentative observations about the different perspectives from which the images were drawn.

Their enthusiasm was so great that Ruth extended their observations to features of the language. They focused initially on Mr Piggott and the two sons, noticing that these figures *do* a lot of physical action, but their actions do not extend to anything else. So they learned some new descriptive terms of a functional grammar to further their observations. They learned, for example, that in a clause such as 'he went off to his very important job' Mr Piggott is the grammatical actor in the process 'went'. In contrast, in a clause such as 'Mrs Piggott washed all the breakfast things', Mrs Piggott is the grammatical actor and the process 'washed' extends to the goal 'all the breakfast things'. They found many similar examples in the first movements of the text and discovered that the males were never involved in physical processes which extended to anything else. In contrast, Mrs Piggott was almost always involved in physical processes which had some aspect of housework as goal, not only washing the dishes but also making the beds, vacuuming the carpets and so on. They played extensively with this new idea, discovering that a character can be made to seem very different by the types of physical process in which they are made to participate and the goals to which the processes extend. 'Janet made a new dress', or 'Janet made a mess' or 'Janet built a tree house'. All of this, they knew from their play, was a matter of a writer's choice, however unconsciously, in effecting specific meanings.

Finally, they went back to *Piggybook* to look at the last movement. They had, of course, already realised that the family relations were different by this time. That had been clear from their understanding of the sense of the characters and plot on the first reading. Their teacher's further question suggested that a different type of understanding might be possible. She asked: how does variation in the language itself make the family relations different now from the beginning of this book? After much further discussion and practical mapping of grammatical differences this is what the children themselves recorded about their discovery.

## What we learnt about the grammatical patterns in *Piggybook*

### *Beginning*

All the goals Mrs Piggott did were to do with housework.

Only Mrs Piggott had goals. This shows she is the only one doing something *to* something else.

Mr Piggott and the boys only did things for themselves; they did not do work in the home. This is shown by the fact that they didn't have any goals. They were the only characters that talked. They told Mrs Piggott to hurry up.

### *Resolution*

At the end, everyone did an action to something – to benefit the whole family, not just themselves. Everyone had goals at the end.

Now the goals for Mrs Piggott included more than housework.

She mended the car.

Just one moment in one class with one text and one particular teacher. But perhaps there is a suggestion here that children might be able to participate, with enthusiasm, in the search for linguistic patterning and its significances.

Margaret Meek observes that 'Children read stories they like over and over again; that's when they pay attention to the words – after they've discovered what happens' (1988: 36). What we have yet to find more about is the means through which children can be assisted to attend to 'words'. Heath's work, and that of others who have followed her lead, suggests there is nothing natural about these processes. Indeed Vygotsky's meticulous analysis of the ontogenesis of voluntary attention shows just how deeply social these apparently natural processes of attention are (Vygotsky 1981). It seems that offering children some access to semiotic tools which enable them to describe visual and verbal patterning in literary text may have some potential to develop a different reading pedagogy, remaking it to include the possibility of children delighting intelligently and critically in the nature of a text's composition without excluding their enjoyment of the constructed story.

# References

Auden, W. H. (1948) *The Dyer's Hand and Other Essays*, London: Faber.

Bakhtin, M. (1986) *Speech Genres and Other Late Essays*, trans. C. Emerson and M. Holquist, Austin: University of Texas Press.

Barthes, R. (1974) *S/Z*, trans. R. Miller, New York: Hill and Wang.

Bernstein, B. (1990) *Class, Codes and Control*, Vol. 4, London: Routledge and Kegan Paul.

Browne, A. (1986) *Piggybook*, London: MacRae.

Chambers, A. (1985) *Booktalk: Occasional Writing on Literature and Children*, London: Bodley Head.

—— (1993) *Tell Me: Children, Reading and Talk*, South Woodchester: Thimble Press.

Clark, M. M. (1976) *Young Fluent Readers: What Can They Teach Us?*, London: Heinemann Educational.

Culler, J. (1977) *Structuralist Poetics: Structuralism, Linguistics and the Study of Literature*, London: Routledge and Kegan Paul.

Doonan, J. (1993) *Looking at Pictures in Picture Books*, South Woodchester: Thimble Press.

Durkin, D. (1966) *Children who Read Early: Two Longitudinal Studies*, New York: Teachers College Press.

Eco, U. (1994) *Six Walks in the Fictional Woods*, Cambridge, MA: Harvard University Press.

Halliday, M. A. K. (1994) *An Introduction to Functional Grammar*, 2nd edn, London: Edward Arnold.

Heath, S. B. (1983) *Ways with Words: Language, Life and Work in Communities and Classrooms*, Cambridge: Cambridge University Press.

Holdaway, D. (1979) *The Foundations of Literacy*, Sydney: Ashton Scholastic.

Kress G. and van Leeuwen, T. (1990) *Reading Images*, Victoria: Deakin University Press.

Meek, M. (1988) *How Texts Teach What Readers Learn*, South Woodchester: Thimble Press.

Nodelman, P. (1988) *Words About Pictures: The Narrative Art of Children's Picture Books*, Athens, GA: University of Georgia Press.

Sendak, M. (1970) *Where the Wild Things Are*, Harmondsworth: Penguin.

Teale, W. H. (1986) 'Home background and young children's literacy development', in Teale, W. H. and Sulzby, E. (eds) *Emergent Literacy: Writing and Reading*, Norwood, NJ: Ablex.

Tizard, B. and Hughes, M. (1984) *Young Children Learning: Talking and Thinking at Home and at School*, London: Fontana.

Vygotsky, L. S. (1981) 'The genesis of higher mental functions', in Wertsch, J. V. (ed.) *The Concept of Activity in Soviet Psychology*, New York: M. E. Sharpe.

—— (1986) *Thought and Language*, ed. and trans. A. Kozulin, Cambridge, MA: MIT Press.

Wells, C. G. (1985) 'Pre-school literacy-related activities and success in school', in Olson, D. R. Torrance, N., and Hidyard, A. (eds) *Literacy, Language and Learning: The Nature and Consequences of Reading and Writing*, Cambridge: Cambridge University Press.

—— (1987) *The Meaning Makers: Children Learning Language and Using Language to Learn*, London: Hodder and Stoughton.

——, Bridges, A., French, P., MacLure, M., Sinha, C., Walkerdine, V. and Woll, B. (1981) *Learning Through Interaction: The Study of Language Development*, Cambridge: Cambridge University Press.

Williams, G. (1995) *Joint Book Reading and Literacy Pedagogy: A Socio-Semantic Examination*, Ph.D. dissertation, School of English and Linguistics, Sydney: Macquarie University.

# 50

# Teenagers Reading: Developmental Stages of Reading Literature

## *Jack Thomson*

Why did I succeed at High School English? I could play the game. My inability to experience any pleasure in literature was offset by articulating the pleasures of the teacher or the critics. The game skill was to paraphrase their gems of wisdom so that they sounded freshly discovered.

A tertiary student training to become an English teacher

In a research investigation of the stages of teenagers' reading development and the strategies they use to construct meaning from literary text, in secondary schools in a rural town in eastern Australia, I found that all the students who couldn't read and all of those who could but chose not to, had a common history in infants' and primary school (Thomson 1987). They had all used phonics-based readers and had experienced teaching methods that emphasised reading skills in isolation from meaningful contexts and interest in story. In circumstances like these many children never discover that 'reading is worth the trouble it takes to learn' as Margaret Meek puts it (Meek 1983: 224). Literary competence is not acquired from reading phonics-based readers that break the reading process down into subsets of technical skills which are seen as more important than meaning, but from reading real stories.

## The Research Project: Understanding Teenagers' Reading

The starting points for the research that led to the construction of a developmental model of teenagers' processes of reading literature were four assumptions about reading habits and the teaching of literature derived from observation and personal experience as a reader and teacher:

1 Reading literature is not important in the lives of most people. Few read much either at school or when they have left, and of those who do see reading as an important activity only a minority read what school syllabuses have tried to make them value as good literature. Mills and Boon and Virginia Andrews out-sell Joseph Conrad and T. S. Eliot despite the fact that the former pair don't get the large captive readership that being prescribed on school and university reading lists ensures.

2 Under the influence of New Critical literary theory we have emphasised aesthetics rather than enjoyment in our teaching of literature.

3   We haven't matched readers and books very well. We haven't started where our students are and progressed from there. We haven't started where the students are, I believe, for two reasons. The public examination has been the major influence on our teaching, rather than the needs of students. We expect them to arrive without having travelled, so many students move from Blyton *et al.* in upper primary to Shakespeare *et al.* in upper secondary without passing through Nadia Wheatley, Rosemary Sutcliff, Alan Garner, Betsy Byars, Robert Cormier, Aidan Chambers, Jan Mark, Peter Dickinson and so on, on the way. Second, we haven't started where our students are because we don't know where our students are. Are there developmental stages? Can they be identified? What do readers at each of these stages do when they read? Can we help them to progress from one stage to the next, increasing their enjoyment rather than destroying it in our attempts?

4   Instead of teaching students how to read better and with more enjoyment we have concentrated on explaining in detail how a few expert readers called 'critics', have read specific texts. We haven't passed on what Jonathan Culler calls 'literary competence' (Culler 1975), and we haven't done so because we haven't identified the reading activities or strategies that constitute such competence.

The aims of the research were, therefore, to see if clear staging points could be identified in students' literary development (towards greater control over texts), and to identify the strategies used at each stage.

## Value to Teachers

A developmental model that enables teachers to work out fairly easily each student's level of reading should be very useful in indicating what it is that each student already does competently. At present, teachers are more aware of what young readers don't understand rather than what they do understand. Students are far more likely to progress in situations in which teachers build on the constructive strategies they do possess – and which they are shown they possess – rather than in 'remedial' situations which emphasise their inadequacies and draw their attention to them. In the Bathurst workshops many reluctant readers found how easy it was to enjoy reading and to learn new reading strategies when they started to believe in their own abilities and to concentrate on meaning and their own interests in a story rather than on what they had come to see as teacherly concerns.

## A Developmental Model

In the developmental model set out below (influenced by the work of D. W. Harding 1937/1972, 1962 and 1967), the kinds of satisfaction readers experience are ordered in successive stage of increasing complexity of reading. These satisfactions are also cumulative: a good reader who reads at the highest levels also experiences enjoyments at earlier levels. The pleasure that comes from reviewing a whole text as an author's construction does not supersede, but rather supplements, the pleasures of empathising and analogising, for example. Similarly, the strategies of reading which students use at each staging point or level of development are also progressive and cumulative. As a reader progresses from one level to the next s/he does not, snake-like, shed old strategies like a worn out skin, but develops those strategies for increasingly complex purpose, as well as adopting new strategies. For example, the reader's predictive and interpretative activity can range from merely anticipating what might happen next, to a continual questioning of the text at each reading moment, reinterpreting the significance of short- and long-term past events and modifying expectations of possible alternative short- and long-term outcomes. Similarly, the mental images readers form range from pictorial stereotypes to complex emotional associations; the literary and cultural repertoires readers draw on vary according to the range and complexity of their reading and cultural experiences; and the reader's active hermeneutic process of filling in textual gaps involves formulating connections (between events, characters and narrative points of view) of increasing subtlety and complexity.

## Reading Literature: a Developmental Model

| *Process stages: kinds of satisfaction* (requirements for satisfaction at all stages: enjoyment and elementary understanding) | | *Process strategies* |
|---|---|---|
| 1 | Unreflective interest in action | i | rudimentary mental images (stereotypes from film and television) |
| | | ii | predicting what might happen in the short term |
| 2 | Empathising with characters | iii | mental images of affect |
| | | iv | expectations about characters |
| 3 | Analogising: deriving insights from fiction for understanding oneself | v | drawing on the repertoire of personal and cultural experiences; making connections between characters and one's life |
| 4 | Reflecting on the significance of events (theme) and behaviour (distanced evaluation of the characters) | vi | generating expectations about alternative possible long-term outcomes |
| | | vii | filling in textual gaps |
| | | viii | formulating puzzles, enigmas, accepting larger textual hermeneutic challenges |
| 5 | Reviewing the whole work as a construct or fabrication | ix | drawing on literary and cultural repertoires |
| | | x | interrogating the text to match the world view offered by the text with one's own |
| | | xi | recognition of implied author[1] |
| 6 | Consciously considered relationship with the text, recognition of textual ideology, and understanding of self (identity theme) and of one's own reading processes | xii | recognition of implied reader in the text, and the relationship between implied author and implied reader[2] |
| | | xiii | reflexiveness, leading to understanding of textual ideology, personal identity and one's own reading processes |

1  The implied author is Wayne Booth's term for the 'real author's second self' (Booth 1961), the kind of person the text implies the author is, and possessing the kinds of values the text implies that author has. The implied author represents the ideal aspirations of the real author.

2   The implied reader (Iser 1978) is the kind of reader the real reader is invited by the implied author
    to become, at least temporarily, so as to participate in the production of the text's meaning.

As can be seen from the table, specific reading strategies were clearly
identifiable at each developmental level. Each kind of reading satisfaction or
source of interest was found to be associated with particular strategies used by all
students reading at that level.

### Level 1: unreflective interest in action

Students reading at this level enjoy books with cut-and-dried plots and
characters tailored to fit them. An interest in characters goes no further than
concern for the success or failure of the actions they are engaged in. Characters
are enjoyed as stereotypes, sympathised with if they are 'goodies' and not
sympathised with if they are 'baddies'. ('You take sides with the good guy and
hope he wins.')

Hermeneutic puzzles and subtleties of motivation perplex and bore such
readers rather than arouse their curiosities. Their attention is fragile and requires
the constant excitement of dramatic action for its maintenance. The characteristic
reading strategies of this level are forming simple mental images and anticipating
what might happen next in the short term. The mental images are mainly
visualisations of place and character, together with stereotypic feelings about the
characters and events, with both the pictorial and affective elements influenced
substantially by film and television. In generating expectations about what might
happen ahead in a text, action-level readers are actively interested in the outcomes
of events beyond the present moment but not in the long-term implications or
significances of them. That a character succeeds or fails is the object of concern,
not why s/he succeeds or fails, nor what view of the world his or her success or
failure might imply.

Because of their lack of experience and satisfaction in the reading of fiction,
students at this level have limited understanding of literary conventions. For
example, a 16-year-old girl shows how her restricted literary repertoire led to her
failure to understand Robert Cormier's novel, *The Chocolate War*:

> In *The Chocolate War* it was wrong that Jerry got bashed up. It should have
> ended in good feelings, not bad. Brother Leon and all the boys should visit
> Jerry in hospital and be sorry for all they've done, and look after him and
> forgive and forget so that life will be better after.

Her narrow literary repertoire caused her to read the novel according to her
internalised conventions of the 'forgive-and-forget-and-live-happily-ever-after'
novel. To her this was the *only* kind of novel.

Associated with the appeal to these students of fiction that formulates their
fantasies or portrays the world as they would like it to be, is their dismissive
evaluation of most of their school texts as boring. For example, here is what a 16-
year-old boy says about Alan Paton's *Cry the Beloved Country*:

> *Cry the Beloved Country* was boring compared with *Star Wars*. There were
> long sections of description of people and places when nothing was
> happening.

What boredom really means to these students is an inability or unwillingness to participate in the creation of textual meaning, a failure to comprehend texts by filling in their gaps. To me, comprehension really means that the text answers the questions readers ask in their heads as they read. For many of the readers at this level boredom arises because they don't ask appropriate questions or generate any expectations; or because they find the gaps between textual details and events so wide they don't know which questions to ask and are, therefore, confused; or because they don't realise that the questions they do ask are not intended to be immediately answerable, that the information required for formulating an answer is deliberately withheld for some time and disclosed only gradually. Here are two examples of this from 15 to 16-year-old students:

> If the starts don't have enough action I don't read them. It's boring when writers go into great details on one event. When there's a lot of stuff about a character's feelings and the way he sees things it's boring ... If it's got nothing to do with the proper story it bores me.

> In *The Bridge to Terabithia* there were lots of boring bits that dragged on and on, and had nothing to do with the story, only descriptions of the house and people and what they thought.

In other words, to these young readers characters' thoughts and feelings are seen to be irrelevant to the action of a novel.

### Level 2: empathising

Readers at this level see characters as real people rather than as fictional constructs. They are more deeply interested in characters and more sensitive to their feelings, and are thus beginning to consider their motivations. Consequently, their mental images encompass more complex feelings about characters, and their expectations include not only what happens in action but the implications of the action for characters involved. For example, here is a 14-year-old girl's comment on her favourite fictional character:

> In the *Nancy Drew* books I always feel very close to Nancy herself. In all the adventures and troubles she got into I felt I was there with her and feeling with her. When she was frightened I felt frightened for her.

### Level 3: analogising and searching for self-identity

At the level of analogising, readers' satisfactions include not only an interest in characters like themselves, but a consideration of the implications of characters' behaviour for their own lives, and so conscious connections are made between what happens in fiction and personal experience. For example, here a 13-year-old boy explains how he learned about himself through his feelings of empathy with a character, Prince Arren, in Ursula le Guin's *The Farthest Shore*:

> I felt closer to Arren than to Sparrowhawk because I felt I was like him. It made it easier to imagine what it would be like in his position. He's like me because he's a boy, and he's with a powerful wizard, which is sort of like

being with a teacher you like and trust. You're young and inexperienced like him, and you can learn about yourself from his mistakes just like you can learn from your own mistakes in life if there's a kind and experienced person to help you.

### Level 4: reflecting on the significance of events and behaviour

By the stage of reflection the process of decentring (from 'me' to 'outside me') is well under way, and the growing capacity for detachment leads to deeper understanding of other people, their motives and aspirations, and of the human condition. The strategies associated with evaluating characters and interpreting themes include reconciling increasingly complex textual viewpoints, filling in larger textual gaps, and entertaining a range of alternative possible long-term outcomes.

Readers at this level are able to make generalisations about the themes of fiction they have read and these generalisations show an awareness of the significance and implications of action and behaviour. Such readers see literature as making complex statements about the human condition, and they recognise that these statements can only be understood by considering literary works as wholes. This kind of understanding is exemplified on the following comments of students, the first a 15-year-old boy and the second a 16-year-old girl:

> To Kill a Mockingbird had a strong effect on me. It showed what the truth was at the time it was set. It shows the prejudice white people felt about black, and the way truth and justice are distorted where there is hatred between people. I relate to To Kill a Mockingbird and its truth about the treatment of black people in the southern states of America with the treatment of aborigines in Queensland and the Northern Territory which are our versions of the American deep south.

> The main character in The Collector (by John Fowles) is representative of a range of people in our society, people without much individuality or strength of character who are always wanting to be accepted and who treat other people as objects because of their own inadequacies.

### Level 5: reviewing the whole work as a construct or fabrication

At the fifth stage of seeing the whole work as a construct and matching one's world view with that presented by the text, readers not only recognise that the text offers an evaluation of behaviour but they go on to actively evaluate that textual evaluation of behaviour. Readers at this level are aware that the values underpinning a text can be accepted or rejected, as illustrated by this comment from a 14-year-old boy:

> The author shows his feelings about the world from his experience. The author's view dictates what happens. The important thing is not just what the characters do but what the author tries to show about people by what he has them do. You're thinking about what you read in the book. Your view might be the same as the author's, but it may be the opposite.

Here is an example of a 16-year-old girl resisting the cliched values of a genre of fiction she feels she has outgrown:

> The teenage romances I've read all end up the same way. The girl gets the boy or, from the boy's point of view, the boy gets the girl. If it begins with a girl saying to herself 'I've loved Joe for so long', you know she'll get him in the end, or someone better. If they were more true to life and had a more varied story line I'd like them better.

*Level 6: consciously considered relationship with the text, recognition of textual ideology, and understanding of self and of one's own reading processes*

At this stage readers are not only interested in analysing the text as a construct, but also in considering the ideological implications of its constructedness and in reflexively exploring their own identities and their own reading processes. This reflective and reflexive thinking about the way texts work as structures of cultural transmission, and about the way they work on texts to interpret them, confers considerable power on readers. They can direct and control their own thinking when they are conscious of it, and control over their own thinking and over the rhetoric of texts gives them more power to operate effectively in their society as makers of culture rather than as passive receivers of it.

Here is an example of a 14-year-old analysing and arguing against the textual ideology of C. S. Lewis's Narnia books. He shows that he sees the whole work as a construct, and there is an explicit recognition of the implied author and of the relationship between the implied author and the implied reader.

> C. S. Lewis's Narnia books are good for young readers because of the happy endings, but he leaves out rational analysis of the characters. Edmund does bad things in *The Lion, the Witch and the Wardrobe*, but he always makes up for them by rescuing people out of the clutches of evil and becomes completely good. Eustace in *The Voyage of the Dawn Treader* is *all* bad and then he becomes *all* good. It is not believable. He's too bad and then too good. C. S. Lewis is saying to you, 'This kid is bad but if he learns to be good, that is good in the way I think – through taking on Christian values – he will become all good and never do any more bad things'. C. S. Lewis is too obviously directing your sympathies about what you should admire.

## Teaching Reflexiveness

One of the most productive and unanticipated findings of the research interview/ workshops is that conscious understanding of one's own productive reading strategies – or reflexiveness – can be taught at each stage of reading development. In retrospect, it can be seen as a function of the one-to-one relationship between student and interviewer and of the form of the enquiry into reading processes. The purposes of the interview were made explicit to each student at the outset, and the activities organised to identify students' reading strategies promoted students' interest in, and awareness of, their own reading processes. The students saw themselves as co-researchers, and formulated many of the productive findings of the research for the researcher. At the end of the interview/workshop all the students expressed some satisfaction in their newly acquired knowledge of their own reading powers.

Most of the more passive and unreflective readers did learn the pleasures and productivity of generating expectations, and expressed both surprise and satisfaction that some of their earlier attitudes to both stories and their own competencies as readers might have to be modified. In response to two of the questions about their reading strategies ('What is going on in your head while you are listening?'; 'What do you think might happen in this story?') most of these students expressed surprise at the notion that they should be actively doing anything. They thought that text operated on readers rather than that readers had to operate on text; that the minds of good readers automatically processed print into understanding; and the fact that their minds didn't seem to do this too well indicated that they were bad readers because they were unintelligent. The act of asking students what questions they were asking of the text read aloud to them led them to ask productive questions, and the enabling security of the interview situation led them to think aloud while doing so.

For example, here is the response of a 14-year-old non-reader to the opening section of Betsy Byars's novel, *The Cartoonist*. In the passage, a comic strip being drawn by Alfie, the central character, is described as follows:

In the first square a man was scattering birdseed from a bag labelled 'Little Bird Seed'. In the next square little birds were gobbling up the seeds.

In the third square the man was scattering birdseed from a bag labelled 'Big Bird Seed'. In the next square big birds were gobbling up the seeds.

In the fifth square the man was scattering huge lumps from a bag labelled 'Giant Bird Seed'. In the last square a giant bird was gobbling up the little man.

Byars 1978/1981: 5–6

The listener's response to this was a surprised laugh and the following unprompted comment:

I expected the giant birds to eat up the giant food instead of the man, and I thought it would go on to have super-giant seeds for a super-bird to eat. But that's great. I really like that, the way you expect one thing and it gets turned round on you. It gives you a surprise and it's very funny. I really like jokes like that. Are there lots more like that in the book?

Later on, he speculated that as Alfie would rather draw cartoons in his room than watch television with his mother, he might be a boy who 'does things on his own and mightn't get on with other kids'. This student has taken the first step to become an active reader. As with all the other non-readers and reluctant readers his developing consciousness of his own reading strategies is turning him into a real reader.

What I think is most interesting about almost all of the unsuccessful readers in the research is that at the end of the interviews/workshops they said things like 'I didn't know so much happened in my mind when I read', and 'I've never been much good at reading, but I know some of the ways to make it more interesting now'. The importance of the supportive and secure interview/workshop situation is, I think, that in it the students became conscious of the constructive strategies that the questions led them to use. It was not that these students were intellectually incapable of reading with enjoyment and understanding but, rather, that they had previously not been placed in situations in which they could learn how to go about it successfully. They possessed the capacity for reading productively, but seem not to have experienced situations that called on them to use that capacity. In the interviews they also gained an inkling that their consciousness of their own productive reading strategies is a powerful educational tool.

All students have internalised some of the conventions of reading and, therefore, have a potential 'literary competence'; but what they possess they often don't use because they don't know they have it or how to use it. Knowing what you know and knowing how you came to know it is very powerful knowledge. People can control and direct their own thinking when they are reflexively conscious of the productive moves they make when engaged in it.

## Teaching Adolescents to Question the Text

Students can be taught to interrogate, argue with and fill in the gaps of literary texts if they understand the point and experience the rewards of doing so. The productive reading strategies can be taught when students are encouraged to formulate their own questions arising from their own puzzlement, rather than being directed to answers set by the teacher. When students are reading to answer other people's questions they inevitably see the text as an object and the reader's role as one of extracting meaning. They become passive ciphers rather than active and reflective meaning-makers. They also experience boredom. Furthermore, when answers to other people's questions are assessed as being right or wrong, the textual puzzles and problems become sources of anxiety rather than of pleasure, and reinforce students' feelings of their own inadequacy as readers. The construction of textual meaning requires the correlation of details to form patterns, the holding of unresolved questions in the head and the constant generation and modification of expectations – all tough, vigorous mental activities which are certainly not encouraged by the kinds of 'comprehension' exercises demanding instant and 'correct' answers. Speculating and hypothesising, so essential to the construction of meaning from literary text, as well as to the development of language and thinking, are stifled by methods which penalise 'error'. You don't make guesses when you are likely to be penalised for being wrong.

In order to become more active readers, students need help during the process of reading. It is possible to develop in students the habit of asking questions while they are reading, and to help them to realise that the answers they formulate at one reading moment are provisional and will almost certainly require subsequent modification. The Bathurst research shows that students can find it liberating to discover that in guessing ahead you are likely to be wrong, and if you are, the text is far more interesting than if you are right. Formulating and solving puzzles us a source of pleasure when the rewards are so great, so long as the penalties are not imposed for perfectly productive 'wrong' answers. These are the kinds of questions that students can learn to ask of texts and can find considerable enjoyment in so doing:

1   What is the significance of this particular detail, event, form of words?
2   How does it connect with other details, episodes?
3   What is this preparing us for? What kinds of things might happen?
4   How does this event affect my interpretation of what has gone before.
5   What am I learning about this character and his or her relationship with others? Why was the character included in the story at all?
6   Whose point of view is being presented here? Why is this author offering this character's view at this stage?
7   What is the implied author's view of this character, that particular behaviour, the human condition as a whole? How is the author making me feel about this character, that behaviour, the human condition? How is she or he doing this? Is my world view changing when I match it with that offered by the text?

## References

Booth, W. (1961) *The Rhetoric of Fiction*, Chicago: University of Chicago Press.

Byars, B. (1978/1981) *The Cartoonist*, Harmondsworth: Penguin.

Culler, J. (1975) *Structuralist Poetics*, London: Routledge and Kegan Paul.

Harding, D. W. (1937/1972) 'The role of the onlooker' (*Scrutiny* 6, 3), in Cashdan, A. (ed.) *Language in Education: A Source Book*, London: Routledge and Kegan Paul/Open University Press.

—— (1962) 'Psychological processes in the reading of fiction', *British Journal of Aesthetics* 2: 133–147.

—— (1967) 'Considered experience: the invitation of the novel', *English in Education* 2, 1: 7–15.

Iser, W. (1978) *The Act of Reading: A Theory of Aesthetic Response*, London: Routledge and Kegan Paul.

Meek, M. (1983) *Achieving Literacy: Longitudinal Studies of Adolescents Learning to Read*, London: Routledge and Kegan Paul.

Thomson, J. (1987) *Understanding Teenagers' Reading*, Sydney: Methuen; New York: Nichols; London: Croom Helm. (Republished 1992, Urbana, IL: National Council for the Teaching of English.)

## Further Reading

Corcoran, B. and Evans, E. (1987) *Readers, Texts, Teachers*, Upper Montclair, NJ: Boynton/Cook.

Corcoran, B., Hayhoe, M. and Pradl, G. M. (eds) (1994) *Knowledge in the Making. Challenging the Text in the Classroom*, Portsmouth, NH: Boynton/Cook, Heinemann.

Hayhoe, M. and Parker, S. (1990) *Reading and Response*, Milton Keynes: Open University Press.

McCormick, K., Waller, G. and Flower, L. (1987) *Reading Texts: Reading, Responding, Writing*, Lexington, MA: Heath.

Mellor, B., Patterson, A. and O'Neill, M. (1991) *Reading Fictions*, Scarborough, Western Australia: Chalkface Press.

Protherough, R. (1983) *Developing Response to Fiction*, Milton Keynes: Open University Press.

Reid, I. (1984) *The Making of Literature: Texts, Contexts and Classroom Practices*, Norwood, South Australia: Australian Association for the Teaching of English.

Thomson, J. (ed.) (1992) *Re-Constructing Literature Teaching*, Norwood, South Australia: Australian Association for the Teaching of English.

# 51

# Teaching Fiction and Poetry

## *Geoff Fox*

The history of teaching English literature in schools has been marked by a series of controversies. The most durable arguments have focused less on *how* literature should be taught and more upon *what* should be taught.

In the mid-nineteenth century in Britain, however, the question was *whether* English literature should be taught at all. The influential public schools preferred the literature of Greece and Rome to that of Britain. Matthew Arnold however, as one of Her Majesty's Inspectors of Schools (HMIs), pressed for the study of English literature in the curriculum. He argued that if schools were to be humanising influences, then great literature (especially poetry) offered a powerful means to that end. All children should be given access to the sustenance of the native culture; and, Arnold insisted in *Literature and Dogma* (1873), the poor required culture as much as the rich.

The argument over the use of Classical or English texts had not been resolved when the Newbolt Report on *The Teaching of English in England* was published in 1921. The committee's fourteen members included several eminent literary figures, among them Sir Arthur Quiller-Couch, George Sampson, Caroline Spurgeon and John Dover Wilson, HMI. Sir Henry Newbolt, the committee's chairman, is best remembered for 'Drake's Drum', and 'Vitai Lampada' (There's a breathless hush in the close tonight . . . '). Perhaps Newbolt himself was the author of this section of his report:

> If we explore the course of English literature, if we consider from what sources its stream has sprung, by what a current it has come down to us, we shall see that it has other advantages not to be found elsewhere. There are mingled in it, as only in the greatest of rivers there could be mingled, the fertilising influences flowing down from many countries and from many ages of history. Yet all these have been subdued to form a stream native to our own soil. The flood of diverse human experience which it brings down to our own life and time is in no sense or degree foreign to us, but has become the national experience of men of our own race and culture.
>
> Newbolt 1921: 13

The sustained imagery may be too rich for contemporary taste, but the committee's thinking was driven by a passionate belief in the power of literature and an equally committed concern for children. Given a choice (which they increasingly feel they are not) most teachers at the close of the twentieth century might prefer Newbolt's ringing declaration of faith to the language and principles of recent reports on the teaching of English, whose writers have been severely constrained by their masters in government.

The committee saw literature as a means of unifying the country across class barriers – 'pride and joy in the national literature [should] serve as a bond' (Newbolt 1921: 21). Their recommendations concerning the selection of texts and teaching methods are eclectic:

> No fixed rule of treatment should be followed. Variety of treatment is an advantage and a stimulus, but serious study should be kept quite distinct from rapid reading, though the same book may well afford material for both. To harp on the same method lesson after lesson, to read in class minute fragments of a whole which the class may well be relied on to read for themselves without assistance and at their leisure, to work in successive terms at one and the same book – all these make staleness in class and teacher inevitable ... All good methods have this in common, that they aim at focussing attention on the living word of the author.
>
> Newbolt 1921: 112

The argument over Classical or English literature which had so troubled Arnold and Newbolt may now have been laid to rest, but other disagreements about texts have continued. This section does not allow a detailed rehearsal of those debates, but no discussion of current practice in the teaching of literature can be divorced from them. These disagreements are outlined below in a more polarised way than might be evident in schools day by day; although it is worth noting that the media, and those with political rather than educational priorities, have often presented the arguments in extreme terms, avoiding the complexities of how children actually read and learn.

There has been a continuing debate concerning the purposes of teaching literature in schools. Arnold's conviction about its humanising power is still shared by many literature teachers. In attempts to establish whether reading novels and poems *does* in some way make 'better' people, researchers have tried to determine what effect literature actually has upon behaviour. For example, one experiment in the USA probed the effects on adolescent readers of several books which reaffirmed the value of honesty; disconcertingly, groups exposed to these texts sometimes proved simply more adept at lying than parallel groups given a free choice of reading. George Steiner famously cast doubt on the power of literature 'to civilise our gentlemen' in pointing out that murderers of Jews in concentration camps are known to have been devotees of Goethe and Rilke when off duty (Steiner 1967: 55). The problem for researchers in this field is always that there are so many variables to take into account; readers can be offered texts which contain all kinds of 'humanising' elements – what they make of them is another matter.

The humanising teacher has often been at odds with colleagues who adopt a more utilitarian approach. Literature is sometimes employed as a means of teaching skills: passages are mined from novels for comprehension or dictation, or even to teach spelling and syntax. Teachers (particularly in primary schools) working on 'The Romans' might inject their children with a shot of Rosemary

Sutcliff; or a project on arachnids might include some snippets from E. B. White's *Charlotte's Web* (1952). Critics of this kind of work argue that to treat literature in this way is to run the risk of students perceiving books of fiction and poetry as little more than alternative textbooks.

The utilitarian approach is also evident in the separation of content and form, which devalues work with older students. They may find themselves in the hands of teachers who focus exclusively on content, seizing on novels as pretexts for the discussion of issues which might just as readily arise in humanities lessons. Characters in novels are sometimes discussed as if they were people with fully developed personalities and lives 'off the page'; equally, other students might be taught poetry with a concentration on form and technique which precludes discussion of the experiences of the students alongside those of the poet.

There are also divisions among teachers who might, ironically, all subscribe to Arnold's faith in literature's humanising powers. Perhaps the most enduring of these is the tension between those who see literature as a means of handing down a culture from generation to generation and those who believe that literature can foster the emotional and intellectual growth of the individual in a changing society. Those who favour the 'transmission of a cultural heritage' model often wish to promote a canon of texts or authors which all should share. The unsurprising difficulty with this notion is that no two readers can agree upon a canon. Those concerned with the individual reader's growth believe that teaching must start with the student's interests, whatever they may be; the task is then to draw them into reading which both expands and reflects their growing concerns.

The 'canon debate' resurfaces so frequently partly because it is often political rather than purely literary in its impulsion. Is literature to be taught because of its power to provoke, to disturb, to nurture individuals, with the possible consequence that they might become agents of change? Or should literature reinforce established authority – even to promote a view of a past which, though it may never have existed, is supportive of a regime in the present? Various groups have seen themselves as excluded by attempts to impose specific books or authors upon schools: women have noted how often reading lists are dominated by male writers; ethnic minorities (who may feel their very identities are under attack by the dominant culture) believe constant vigilance is needed to ensure their literature retains a place in classrooms.

In its most extreme forms, control by authority in the twentieth century may have been most evident in the burning of books in Nazi Germany or Bible Belt America. But authoritarian periods of government in Britain have usually been reflected by more muted forms of censorship. There have been parental objections to specific titles (even those as seemingly innocuous as Barry Hines's *Kes* (1968) or Raymond Briggs's *Father Christmas* (1973) with its hero's deeply satisfying visit to his outside lavatory); and, more recently, there has been the heavy-handed attempt of government to impose prescribed reading lists and the 1993 anthology of extracts for examination work including, notoriously, an extract from Johnson's *Rasselas* (1759) for the consideration of the nation's 13-year-olds.

## A Reading Community

The basis for successful teaching of literature is the same, whether the group is a primary-school class or an undergraduate seminar. The students need to become a community of readers, and the experienced teacher will probably plan to establish such a community in the early weeks of a class's life together.

The aim is to create a context in which stories, picture books, novels and poetry are regularly and unselfconsciously talked about, celebrated or criticised, both in and out of normal class time. Teachers have learned many strategies towards that end; although the one unalterable prerequisite is not a strategy at all, but the commitment of the teacher to literature. Enthusiasm for stories, novels and poems is not readily simulated, and in the best literature classrooms, many of the most effective moments of teaching take place in spontaneous conversations between teachers and individual children.

Resources, inevitably, are crucial. In 1931, The Board of Education's *Report on the Primary School* insisted that every class should have its own library, stocked with a variety of books ('mainly story books, but they should be widely chosen. Care should be taken not to press upon children books of a kind not likely to be attractive.') There were to be books for oral reading; individual, group and class study; and silent reading for enjoyment, along with a range of information books. Literature teachers in both primary and secondary schools would still argue that a class library is essential – or at least portable book boxes or mobile trolleys, and display stands. Especially in primary schools, teachers try to establish a comfortable, often half-enclosed, corner where children can retreat at odd moments in the day. This will also be the space where stories are told and read aloud. Beyond the classroom, in fortunate schools, there will be a well-stocked school library, where students are made welcome. It is now rare to find such libraries in Britain staffed by a teacher librarian.

The *Report*'s recognition of the importance of silent reading was far-sighted. Many schools at both primary and secondary levels try to maintain a daily (or at least a regular) period of silent reading. The practice is known by a variety of acronyms, from USSR (Uninterrupted, Sustained, Silent, Reading) to DEAR (Drop Everything And Read); the widespread experience is that the teacher must be seen to be a reader by the children during these sessions (rather than a marker, a compiler of assessment forms or a patrolling guard). Another support to individual reading can be the provision of tapes and headsets; professionally made tapes are available but, notably in the case of poems which have become popular in a particular class, tapes made by the teacher or a 'special guest reader' are often invaluable in creating a class's positive view of itself as a community of readers. In an overcrowded curriculum, a teacher's belief in silent reading time has to be strong if it is to be preserved.

Teachers also excite interest in books through ensuring that students frequently talk about their individual reading with them and with other students. Book recommendation sessions are conducted, sometimes as a class, sometimes in small groups; older readers may engage in more developed 'book exchanges', in which they talk about a book and give prepared readings of a couple of pages or a poem. Often, their comments are based on entries made in their 'reading journals', in which students record their questions and comments on books as they journey through them. Other students discuss common texts, from picture books to classics, in small groups with or without a teacher present, although sometimes the teacher will have left an agenda for the group to address.

Children's novelists, poets and picture book artists are invited into schools, and may engage in subsequent correspondence with their young readers. Book Weeks include speakers, story-tellers and writers along with events for parents, sometimes presented by the children themselves. Local bookshops, or the school's own bookshop, provide displays and a sales counter. Radio and TV programmes about books for children, which have improved markedly in recent years, are also used.

The enthusiastic teacher may also subscribe to reviewing journals, or attend local group meetings of like-minded teachers, to stay abreast of new titles and to share a pleasure in children's books. Cuts in funding and curriculum pressures have sometimes sapped the energy of teachers. Nevertheless, a resilience sustained by the books themselves and a concern to introduce them to students mean that much excellent work continues.

## Story-telling

For many children, their first encounter with literature in school may not in fact be through print or pictures, but through listening to stories. Advice on how to tell stories – including how to take a printed text and turn it into a told story – has been remarkably consistent throughout the century. Marie Shedlock's classic *The Art of Storytelling* (1915) is currently available in paperback and is used on story-telling courses in North America.

In recent times, there have been exciting developments in this field. The National Oracy Project argues (in *Common Bonds* (Howe and Johnson 1992)) that story-telling should be an important feature of classroom practice for students right through to school-leaving age. Professional story-tellers visit schools. There are training courses and weekend gatherings where teachers learn that there need be no mystique about becoming an effective classroom story-teller.

Telling has some qualities which set it apart from reading, though it is clearly facile to regard one activity as superior to the other. Oral story-tellers have a special immediacy available to them; they can 'play' their audiences, draw them into the tale through pace and inflection, the use of the eyes, the hands, the posture of the body. Adults as well as school students of all ages report a sense of community, of sharing gifts even, as they hear stories together over a period of time. Teachers find their story-telling becomes a particularly positive way of establishing bonds of trust and affection between themselves and their classes.

There is a parallel here with the way in which early peoples used stories to bind their communities together, to explain to themselves who they were, where they came from, their relationships with each other and with their environments; similarly, cultural minorities may preserve their identities through stories in the present day. Classes which become a community of listeners move, by a short stride, to a community which reads, writes and tells stories. One story leads to another – a story heard prompts a recalled anecdote from a listener; teachers such as Betty Rosen in Britain (1988) and Bob Barton in Canada (1986) have shown the value of working along a continuum in which listeners become tellers.

It is no surprise, given the value of stories to early communities, that traditional tales are especially well received in the classroom. (There is, in any case, little point in taking a carefully crafted written story and turning it into a spoken tale, losing much of its linguistic subtlety along the way.) Since a traditional tale has already been told by many voices, there is a fitness in a teacher taking that tale and making it her own to tell to her classroom community of listeners. A class working on the Greeks, for example, might hear the adventures of Odysseus or Herakles as a daily serial. Teachers concerned to introduce a multi-ethnic dimension might tell a series of Anansi adventures or Raven the Trickster tales from North America. Story-tellers soon find a distinctive personal style, a kind of signature which marks their stories and which listeners come to expect and relish.

## Picture Books

The potential value of picture books in the classroom remains far short of full realisation. The belief in the worth of picture books in upper primary and secondary schools is more honoured in theory than in practice, while teachers of younger children sometimes have such a commitment to 'enjoyment' that the idea of studying picture books is greeted with misplaced hostility.

Clearly, simply reading a picture book can be a delight in itself; but the form may also offer much to literature students in understanding how other literary forms work. Picture books have suffered from a lack of critical exposition, especially of the interrelationship of words and pictures; and from a failure of experts in pedagogy to suggest how they might best be explored. The work of critics such as Jane Doonan in Britain (1993) and Perry Nodelman in Canada (1988) has begun to provide a better sense of how picture books are made; as yet, we have not enough evidence of the mental activity of young readers as they read them, and what they take from them.

Writer-artists have to be conscious of how pictures and text work together, unless they are content merely to illustrate what is already evident in words (sometimes described as 'decorating' the text). Maurice Sendak is clear about the interplay of word and image when he writes:

> You ... must not ever be illustrating exactly what you've written. You must leave a space in the text so the picture can do the work. Then you must come back with the word, and now the word does its best and the picture beats time.

Sendak 1988: 185

He demonstrates that belief in books such as *Where the Wild Things Are* (1967) and *Outside Over There* (1981).

Certain books recur as exempla of this dynamic interplay between words and pictures, such as Anthony Browne's *Gorilla* (1983) or *Hansel and Gretel* (1981). It has to be admitted that, initially, children do not always share adult enthusiasm for such books where the reader is required to 'work' to fill the gaps between words and pictures. The answer is not to abandon Browne as too difficult, but to encourage readers to see and hear more of him, to accustom themselves to his idioms – much as teachers would expect to help older students to attune themselves to the ironic voice of Jane Austen. Once children taste the rewards of their 'work', they are eager for more.

Picture books which require a reader to work hard (or, better, to play hard, since it is a lively act of the imagination that is needed) offer much to almost all ages of school students. Picture books have been very helpfully used in the early weeks of literature courses for older students, since they raise certain issues about reading with particular clarity; the relationship between author and reader, how readers come to know what kind of a text they are handling, how readers need to move back and forth within a text, how endings are anticipated, for example.

Picture books can give younger readers insights into how narrative is structured. Teachers have given groups separate photocopies of each page of wordless picture books such as Raymond Briggs's *The Snowman* (1978) and asked them to sort them into a 'correct' sequence. Again, students can readily understand how irony works through certain picture books, since it is at the root of the satisfactions offered by some books where there is a seeming dissonance between pictures and words. In Pat Hutchins's classic *Rosie's Walk* (1968), the print constitutes a single 32-word sentence. The delight for readers is that they are 'in the know' as Rosie the Hen takes her circuitous farmyard stroll without noticing (or does she?) that a fox is in hot pursuit, thwarted from his supper only by a series of painful calamities. The sentence makes no mention of the fox, and the irony emerges as the reader puts words and pictures together.

Many picture books require a reading not unlike that of shorter, complex poems and an understanding of how they ask to be read may be a helpful step on the way towards reading poetry. The reader needs to move around within the text, checking picture against picture, connecting patterns of one element of the book with patterns elsewhere; much as the reader of a poem discovers how images or rhymes, for example, work together throughout a poem. The superb *The ox-cart man*, by Donald Hall and Barbara Cooney (1980), invites a reader to explore the pictures in following the rhythms of the year as they dictate the work and life of a nineteenth-century farm in rural New England. Bit by bit, we see the family grow and craft the goods they sell at Portsmouth Harbour market each year in order to sustain them through the next. Visual images work in ways similar to verbal images in that they are often multi-faceted and ambiguous of interpretation. Picture books present puzzles, and they refuse to be hurried over. They demand to be read more than once, just as many poems do, and as parents soon discover, young readers regularly insist that favourites are read many times. We still need to discover more precisely what is the function of rereading for these young children, and how their numerous return visits differ from each other.

A further value of picture books is simply that they promote searching discussion among pairs or groups, often between students of quite different abilities. Those who are 'visually literate' may not be the most fluent of readers or writers of words. Visual images prompt verbal interpretations, often provoking differences of opinion. The book is 'out there', a focus away from the students and argument is thus 'safer' or less confrontational; indeed, there is usually a sense of shared exploration, leading to the creation of a reading which the group agrees upon.

Older students have been invited to create their own picture books, usually with a readership of younger children in mind. This has been a widely successful activity since the 1960s and it usually begins with lengthy browsing among a pile of picture books for models and inspiration. These sessions are especially interesting for teachers in allowing insights into their students' early, and often formative, experiences as readers. Young adolescents recognise favourites from their childhood with glee, or meet classic picture books for the first time, often expressing surprise at the sophistication they find. Students who are familiar with a book insist on sharing it with others; while others become censorious about its suitability for younger children. This stage is usually followed by the creation of a draft version of students' own books, a visit to read them to a captive audience at a nearby primary school, and a return to their own classroom drawing boards for subsequent modification and completion.

Finding a vocabulary to describe picture books is a difficulty which still needs to be overcome to facilitate better teaching in this field. However, because critical work about picture books is still uncertain, the field has particular excitements for teachers who enjoy genuine exploration and discovery with their students. Many young readers carry fewer assumptions about books than adults and this can be illuminating. Six-year-old Michael, when asked by a student-teacher if he enjoyed sharing picture books with grown ups, confounded the received wisdom of the educational establishment about the value of young children reading with 'a trusted adult': 'Not really,' he said, 'they don't know how to read the pictures.'

## Teaching Fiction

Current teaching of fiction – and poetry – in schools has been much influenced by reader response or reception theory. This is not surprising, since teachers are interested in the education of readers and the effects of reading upon them, as well as the texts they introduce to them.

Opposition to work which values children's responses focuses on two areas. First, there has been criticism that teachers influenced by reception theory praise almost any response, no matter how naïve or distant it seems from the words on the page; students' personal responses have been dismissed as 'mere emoting'. Arguments over this issue were central in the evolution of the national curriculum in England and Wales in the early 1990s. The second group of opponents has been more concerned with older students, fearing that teaching stemming from reader response theory tends to concentrate on the individual reader, leaving aside consideration of the cultural context of the reader and the circumstances of the text's production. Elsewhere, especially in Australia, genre theorists have also exerted some influence upon the teaching of fiction, though their major interest has been in the area of information books.

In practice, teachers who are successful in developing a strong commitment to reading in their students tend to be eclectic rather than rigid in their theoretical thinking; they have a keen awareness of how texts shape readings *and* of how readers shape texts by their own reading styles.

Much teaching of novels, especially in the lower age ranges, concentrates on drawing young readers and listeners into stories with strong narrative lines. Few classroom experiences match the daily serial reading of a novel which the class awaits each day with hungry anticipation. In such a circumstance, it seems foolish to delay a group's pleasure by extensive work on what has been read so far. Usually, some brief talk to draw threads together and to whet appetites suffices; afterwards, some moments' discussion ensures understanding and throws interest forward to the next lesson's instalment.

As students grow older, however, they may be asked to study novels on their own, in pairs or groups, or as a class. Since reading tastes are idiosyncratic, it makes sense to allow space for those tastes to be exercised. Readers need to feel control over what they read and how they read. When this is *not* allowed – even at post-16 or undergraduate levels – the probability is that, the course once completed, students may scarcely open a book for themselves again. They do not become readers.

A well-tried structure to help students in their work is to plan in terms of 'before, during and after' the reading of a novel.

Some novels grab their readers' attention on the first page; others gain from some preparation *before* the book is started. Teachers might spend a lesson around a topic which will prove important in the early stages of a novel, without revealing that work on the novel is about to begin. Groups may speculate on what kind of a book is suggested by a cover or a title; or about what kind of a book might follow this particular opening sentence or paragraph, perhaps photocopied for work before the book is issued. Useful touchstones for this kind of work are that it should be suggested and shaped by the book itself, that it should be brief, and that it should draw readers in by thoroughly intriguing them.

Activities devised by teachers *during* the reading of a novel are important in keeping students engaged with the book along the way. There can be a need to refocus a class from time to time, to check that essential elements in the plot are clear, that relationships between characters are firmly established in readers' minds. Where characters are on journeys, as they often are in children's novels, student-made maps which can be added to day by day are usefully displayed on walls or included in individual folders. Occasionally, a tactic such as the teacher taking on a role as a character, available for questioning, is valuable in heightening anticipation about what might happen next and confirming what has gone before.

A wealth of approaches has been developed for work *after* completion of the first reading of a novel. There can be a temptation for the project-minded teacher to move swiftly away from the text to concerns raised incidentally in the novel. The test is to ask whether a proposed activity takes readers more closely into the book, requiring them to re-read sections, to look carefully at the language, the characters, the ideas which this book offers. Classroom displays where this principle has been applied are often characterised by wallcharts, maps, alternative designs for book covers, friezes, collages reflecting major themes or events in the book, and writing of all kinds from rapid notes to character studies, from reviews to letters to the author, sometimes with a reply. Groups might re-create aspects of the novel as radio plays, dramatised episodes or monologues. To work in this way is to understand the sources of readers' pleasure, and to design work which will enhance that pleasure through close reading.

## Teaching Poetry

The range of poetry accessible to younger children and to the whole ability range in secondary schools expanded considerably in the 1980s. Writers such as Michael Rosen, Gareth Owen, Roger McGough, Allan Ahlberg, Grace Nichols, John Agard and Shel Silverstein were widely read in schools. Often their themes are close to children's own daily lives at home or school. It was perhaps inevitable that in the enthusiasm for these newer voices there was some neglect of poets from earlier ages. The balance may have been restored, so that students now may enjoy an immense diversity of work, from poets such as Edward Lear and Lewis Carroll, to Walter de la Mare and Eleanor Farjeon, and to some of the most impressive writers of the present such as Ted Hughes and Charles Causley.

The newer, often comic voices were invaluable in giving an impetus to a revival in poetry teaching; and in disabusing students of the notion that poems are invariably sentimental in thought or remote in language. There has also been an increased awareness of how different kinds of poems ask to be read, from the narrative of a ballad to the compressed thought of a sonnet. Some poems require that readers walk about inside and around them, as it were, considering the words from different angles much as they might walk around a sculpture, seeing how the light falls. Other poems, where story predominates, invite a reading closer to prose fiction in its essentially linear movement. Most poems require readers to visit them again, sometimes at once, sometimes after an interval. Arising from such awarenesses, there has been an increasing belief that poems should be experienced before they are analysed. It is much less common now to encounter the kind of practice in which poems were read as if they were prose comprehension passages, a method which took classes through line by line, confronting a series of riddles which only the teacher knew how to solve 'correctly'.

Rather more frequently than with novels, teachers are concerned to prepare a class to meet poems, especially those where the density of thought or the multi-faceted nature of the images pose questions which a reader must address. Sometimes teachers ask students to sit quietly with eyes closed while, in a technique familiar in drama classes, they are 'talked into' the context of the poem so that they are ready for a first meeting. Whatever means is employed, it is important that the preparation is not so long or so involving in itself that the poem arrives as an afterthought rather than a climax.

Since poems must make an impact upon that first meeting – even if it is to demand a second, more reflective, reading – teachers are often concerned with how a first encounter should be arranged. It may be that the teacher reads the poem aloud; other means might be a well-prepared reading by several members of the class, a visiting reader, a taped version, or a silent reading where the physical shape of the poem on the page is crucial to its reception. The nature of a poem dictates how it is best introduced to the class or a group.

Once met, a wide range of means of deepening and enhancing a reader's response is available. It may be that, to help students feel the rhythms of a poem on their own pulses, groups will be asked to prepare readings of the poems themselves, using several voices and even sound effects. Primary and lower secondary teachers sometimes link mask work, movement and music to the presentation of poems, often culminating in carefully prepared 'poetry shows' for assemblies, parents, younger children, or outside audiences such as homes for the elderly. First encounters with other poems which demand reflection might be followed by individual jotting around the poem on the page noting patterns of words within the poem, similarities with personal experience, questions perhaps. This particularly useful approach precludes a dominant reading from another student or the teacher coming between the reader and the poem; each student has the basis for something to say. It also defers the expression of judgements upon a poem; 'I like it' or 'I hate it' are equally effective at closing down sustained reflection on poems, at best setting up defensive or hostile debate (often with the teacher cast as interrogator – '*Why* don't you like it, then?') rather than a circumstance where ideas can be played with and alternatives considered.

Various ways of re-exploring poems, once two or three readings are experienced, have been developed. Writing remains the most frequent means of response. Teachers use essays alongside more exploratory approaches; pastiche, for example, can take older students inside the techniques of a poet more revealingly than evaluative comment. Thoughts about poems might be translated into visual form – collages to represent the interplay of images, or an episodic series of illustrations to narrative poems. Usually students introduce such work to the rest of the class alongside a reading of the original poem as a way of organising their thinking about a poem so far; it is the quality of that thinking, not the quality of the art work, which needs to be emphasised.

The future of the teaching of children's literature in schools is uncertain. Teaching methods such as those outlined in this section acknowledging, as they do, the part a reader plays in the process of reading, might seem to offer the hope that students would leave school to become lifelong readers. Yet the future of the book itself as the means of bringing stories and poems to their audience may not be at all secure – and the implications of changes in the media have not yet been thought through by literature teachers who, hardly surprisingly, tend to cherish books as physical objects and to resent any suggestions of change in their field. Enthusiastic literature teachers have not, in the main, moved readily into media studies.

A more sinister threat has become evident, in different forms, to those teachers who would assert the old values of stories and poems and their essential function as bearers of knowledge of self and community. As long ago as 1970, Ted Hughes warned of the dangers of the reflective inner life becoming separated from, or suppressed by, the outer world of action. He spoke of his own *The Iron Man* as one myth which might help to arm children against such dangers. In recent years, the literature curriculum in schools has been invaded by governments driven by a utilitarianism which has seemed philistine in its intensity. This may have been most evident in Britain, but delegates to international conferences report similar pressures in their own contexts. The struggle against these forces has hardly begun.

## References

Barton, B. (1986) *Tell Me Another*, Markham: Pembroke.
Doonan, J. (1993) *Looking at Pictures in Picture Books*, South Woodchester: Thimble Press.

Howe, A. and Johnson, J. (1992) *Common Bonds: Storytelling in the Classroom*, London: Hodder and Stoughton.

Hughes, Ted (1968) *The Iron Man*, London: Faber.

Newbolt Report (1921) *The Teaching of English in England*, London: HMSO.

Nodelman, P. (1988) *Words About Pictures*, Athens, GA: University of Georgia Press.

Rosen, B. (1988) *And None Of It Was Nonsense*, London: Mary Glasgow.

Sendak, M. (1988) *Caldecott & Co.*, London: Reinhardt.

Shedlock, M. (1915) *The Art of Storytelling*, London: John Murray.

Steiner, G. (1967) *Language and Silence*, New York: Atheneum.

## Further Reading

Allen, D. (1980) *English Teaching since 1965: How Much Growth?* London: Heinemann Educational.

Benton, M. and Fox, G. (1985) *Teaching Literature 9–14*, Oxford: Oxford University Press.

Fenwick, G. (1990) *Teaching Children's Literature in the Primary School*, London: David Fulton.

Merrick, B. (1987) *Exploring Poetry 5–8*, Sheffield: NATE.

—— (1991) *Exploring Poetry 8–13*, Sheffield: NATE.

Shayer, D. (1972) *The Teaching of English in Schools, 1900–1970*, London: Routledge and Kegan Paul.

# 52

# Teaching Children's Literature in Higher Education

## *Tony Watkins*

Children's literature is taught at all levels of education, from kindergarten to doctoral level. However, this article is concerned solely with the teaching of children's literature at university undergraduate and graduate (or postgraduate) level.

At one time, children's literature would have been dismissed in university departments, particularly some English departments, as 'kiddie lit' and unworthy of academic study, research and teaching. However, with the radical changes in the nature of English studies during the 1970s and 1980s, including the increasing influence of literary theory, the situation has changed. For example, the growth of feminist literary theory and the realisation that many children's books are forms of women's writing, has contributed to the serious study of children's literature and makes it possible to explore more thoroughly the 'important role played by women in shaping the two major traditions of Anglo-American children's literature' (Knoepflmacher 1992: 4).

By the mid-1990s, a variety of courses in children's literature had developed in the USA, Britain, Canada, Australia and New Zealand, and the number of such courses continued to grow. Some of them were specifically literary in nature and taught children's literature as another form of literature, although with an awareness of the dual nature of the child/adult readership. Others were literary within the context of an education degree course, or part of multi-disciplinary courses on, say, the history and construction of 'childhood'.

Those involved with constructing and teaching courses on children's literature obviously face a number of problems. Above all, perhaps, which books to teach and, which critical and theoretical approaches to adopt in the teaching? Other literary critical issues which the teacher of children's literature must come to terms with include: issues related to particular genres or forms (for example, to realism, fantasy or folktales); the relationship between children's books and adult books written by the same author and, above all, the nature of children's literature itself and its relationship to childhood (see for example, Rose 1984; Hunt 1991; Myers 1992). The Modern Language Association of America's survey of courses in children's literature also includes problems such as 'the student's frequent sentimental distrust of taking any critical approach at all to the subject', ethnocentrism in children's literature; the question of censorship; and 'the child–adult response to classic children's books' (Sadler 1992: 145). The last involves getting students to recognise a potential conflict in the positions taken by adult readers of books written for children, especially with books which students may have read when they were children. In the adult response to such children's books, 'wishfulness and enchantment ... coexist with an acceptance of adult realities' (Knoepflmacher 1992: 1).

Defining the canon of children's literature is of great importance to those defining, validating and teaching the field because the concept of canonicity implies the kind of authority empowered to exclude as well as include certain works (Knoepflmacher 1992: 1). But in trying to establish the canon, it is important to recognise what one critic and teacher calls 'the historical and ideological (cultural, political, sexual, racial) relativity of the definition' of the concept (Stahl 1992: 13). Canons of literature, including children's literature, become centres of debate and ideological struggle. For example, cultural, ideological and historical considerations clearly enter into the constitution of the various national canons of children's literature such as the 'British canon' or the 'American canon', for such terms are 'a means by which a certain version of reality validates a given power arrangement' (Ronda 1992: 32).

Canons provide cultural frameworks for selecting and excluding works of children's literature and, as such, they are historically and socially constructed, and many 'speak for the values and interests of relatively well-to-do educated whites, males, Christians, northern Europeans' (Griffith and Frey 1992: 23). Again, the argument that 'classics' such as *The Wind in the Willows*, or *Peter Pan* 'revolve so imperiously around questions of male self-sufficiency', may help to account for their status, 'since the place and pressure of male domination is itself a canonical topic'. For such critics, reading the novels in this ideological way is not an argument for ceasing to teach them, but, rather, that teaching such works should become 'more responsive to the evolving life of our culture'. Such responsiveness, it is hoped, will lead teachers to 'teach the canon more critically and the noncanon more seriously' (Griffith and Frey 1992: 26, 28, 30).

As literary critical theory developed, so did the variety of critical approaches used in the teaching of children's literature in higher education. By the early 1990s, in English-speaking countries, many courses in children's literature included genre criticism; structural analysis; Jungian and other mythic and archetypal criticism; reader-response criticism; psychoanalytic, feminist and socio-historical criticism; narratology; and the semiotics and aesthetics of picture books. Some courses specialised in particular areas of children's literature: for example: romanticism, the nature of childhood and the relationship to gender; particular genres of story, for example, fairy tales; or particular forms of story, for example, fantasy. (For American examples of courses, see Sadler 1992; for British examples, see Watkins 1987 and the series of articles in the journal, *Signal*, 1984– ).

Children's literature as a subject for teaching in higher education in the USA developed considerably after 1969 when the first Modern Language Association seminar on children's literature was held. In 1979 children's literature was given a permanent place as an MLA group and in 1980, it became an MLA division. Twelve years later, it was argued that the subject was beginning to be accepted in most English departments as a valid part of the undergraduate curriculum, although, in fact, many departments did not accept a course in children's literature for credit towards the major in English.

The Children's Literature Association (many of whose members were professionals working in the field of children's literature) was founded in the USA in 1973 and twenty years later had over 1,200 members (Sadler 1992: 144). In 1992, an MLA survey claimed that courses in children's literature in higher education reflected the

> eclectic nature of the subject both for instruction and research. The range is very widespread in orientation and in methodology. One finds under-graduate introductory courses, studies of myth and folklore, and historical approaches to the classics, as well as genre courses on fantasy and fairy tales, the picture book, and related studies, such as the linking of children's literature to composition, Third World literature, and feminist criticism.
>
> Sadler 1992: 144

The wide range of courses is best illustrated by some examples. A course at the University of Massachusetts, Amherst, on 'Myth, folktale and children's literature' drew upon narrative, semiotic, and reader-response theories of literature combined with models drawn from cognitive psychology, cultural anthropology and folklore studies. Each of the twenty-eight sessions involved a lecture and discussion of four to six traditional tales or myths and seven or eight children's books related to the tales in theme, structure, or character (Moebius 1992). The course at the University of Pittsburgh, 'Children's literature: great books', one of the three core courses in an interdisciplinary children's literature programme involving the English department and the School of Library and Information Science, covered a range of books from myths and legends to picture books, fantasy, fiction and poetry. The Fantasy unit, for example, involved study of the *Alice* books, *The Wizard of Oz*, *The Wind in the Willows*, and *Charlotte's Web* (Meek 1992).

Some of the courses described were in the form of seminars and workshops, linking the study of children's literature to the practice of learning to write it. The Graduate Seminar in Children's Literature in the English Department, Iowa State University, for example, was a two-week seminar in which the mornings were devoted to the history of children's literature and the afternoons were devoted to writing an original piece of children's fiction (Mendelson 1992). The history strand ran from the work of John Newbery, Maria Edgeworth and Mrs Barbauld via nineteenth-century fairy tales, Lewis Carroll, Louisa May Alcott, Frances Hodgson Burnett, R. L. Stevenson, Rudyard Kipling, Beatrix Potter and Kenneth Grahame to E. B. White, C. S. Lewis and Maurice Sendak. The creative writing strand took students from the initial plan of the narrative, through characters, point of view, to sharing their manuscripts with other members of the class.

Graduate study programmes in children's literature (that is, those involving study and research at master's and doctoral level) expanded considerably in the USA from the mid-1980s to the early 1990s. (Such programmes are called 'postgraduate courses' in Britain.) The Children's Literature Association's *Directory of Graduate Studies in Children's Literature*, published in 1992, listed 200 graduate schools in the fields of Education, English and Library Science which offered courses in children's literature. They ranged from those who offered only one course to those, like Eastern Michigan University, which offered eight courses and Simmons College, Boston, Massachusetts, which offered nine courses for their MA in children's literature. The Eastern Michigan MA in English with concentration in children's literature consisted of courses such as major genres in children's literature, history of children's literature, comparative mythology, literature for adolescents, literature for early childhood and children's literature: criticism and response. The MA programme at Simmons College which ran over two semesters plus one summer was not a professional programme: it conferred 'an MA in children's literature comparable to an MA in English' (Bloom and Mercier 1992: 207). The first semester consisted of a cycle of history and criticism courses including criticism of children's literature, the picture book, and Victorian children's literature; the second semester included courses on fantasy and science fiction, and contemporary realistic fiction. Institutes and symposias were held in alternate summers.

Courses in children's literature in Britain developed from the beginning of the 1970s in institutions such as Colleges of Education, and a series of occasional articles which appeared in the British journal *Signal* during the 1980s and into the 1990s gave details of some of the work within initial and in-service teacher education. (For an overview of some of this work, see Watkins 1987). The picture that emerged was a contradictory one. On the one hand, universities and colleges had suffered severe restrictions on finance and resources over the previous years: faculty staff who left were not replaced, institutions were restricted to training teachers for work in *either* primary schools *or* secondary schools, but not for both, and so on. Within the field of children's literature, resource limitations meant that it was very difficult to continue to run some courses, and therefore contraction rather than expansion was more normal. But, paradoxically, activity was increasing.

There are two main ways of becoming a teacher in Britain: by taking either a four-year bachelor of education degree (B.Ed.), or a three-year degree in sciences, arts or humanities followed by a one-year postgraduate certificate in education (PGCE). In the B.Ed. programmes of those institutions enthusiastic about children's literature, faculty members ran courses for all undergraduates, whatever their specialist subject (see for example, Watson 1985; Fox 1985; Butts and Watkins 1985). Students specialising in English within the B.Ed. within such institutions had the chance to study even more children's literature: for example, at the University of Exeter, English students devoted a term in year two of their degree to a course which considered a range of topics from fairy tales and myths, to poetry, fantasy, series books, and realistic adolescent fiction. (Fox 1985: 114–115). At Bulmershe College, English specialists could take courses in children's literature for 5 to 8-year-olds, or for 7 to 11-year-olds, nineteenth-century children's literature, and a course called children and literature which discussed topics as various as the nature of story, children's television, poetry and folk-tales and myths (Butts and Watkins 1985: 178–180). In the 1990s, the main B.Ed. English course at Westminster College, Oxford, combined the study of children's literature with aspects of literary theory. For example, the first year covered such topics as 'picture books and their implied readers; codes; intertextuality; narrative modes; metafictive picture books; text and illustrations; reading children's novels as adults; the nature of the reader's response'. The second year covered topics such as 'ideology; literature in translation; ... introduction to history of children's books; classics; literary fairy tales', and so on (Sutcliffe 1995: 136). The emphasis in the course was on 'personal response while developing an appreciation of technical qualities and their effect on meaning' (Sutcliffe 1995: 137).

In the twelve-month PGCE courses, the problem was one of time, not lack of enthusiasm. At the University of Exeter, for example, postgraduate English specialists could only be introduced to children's literature through workshops on novels/short stories/poems in the classroom; at the University of Birmingham students read a core of books by modern authors such as Leon Garfield, Philippa Pearce, Rosemary Sutcliff, Alan Garner and Ursula Le Guin (Evans 1984: 105–106).

Outside teacher education at undergraduate level, there was, as we have seen, resistance (especially in University English Departments) to recognising children's literature as a valid area for study. However, the University of Wales Institute of Science and Technology (later to merge to become University of Wales, Cardiff) was the first in Britain to introduce (in the form of an option in the third year) a course on children's literature within a university BA degree in English. Critical concepts of narrative, genre, psychological and literary development provided an introduction to a historical survey of children's literature from the eighteenth century to the present, followed by special study of major nineteenth- and twentieth-century children's authors (Hunt 1990). As this university's courses have been modularised, this forty-four (teaching) hour course has been replaced by, initially, three fifteen-hour modules: an introduction to children's literature, the golden age of children's literature, and twentieth century children's literature. The University of York offered a term's course (ten weeks) on modern fiction for children to students taking a combined degree consisting of a main subject from the sciences, social sciences or humanities with education. The course introduced students to a wide range of modern fiction of a high literary standard for children, and, at the same time, discussed issues that arose from the study of such literature. Students specialising in English at York could write an independent essay on children's literature as a substitute for one of the nine examination papers making up the final degree (Bailey and Hollindale 1986). At Roehampton Institute, London, the modular BA degree offered three modules in children's literature: nineteenth-century children's literature considered a range of texts in their historical, social political, economic and philosophical contexts; twentieth-century developments in children's literature examined sub-genres such as animal stories and fantasy; and contemporary children's literature considered a range of narrative strategies used by contemporary writers.

The University of Reading offered an option course on twentieth-century children's literature within the English BA degree. The first part of the course examined pre-1950 texts by authors such as J. M. Barrie, Kenneth Grahame, E. Nesbit and J. R. R. Tolkien; the second part of the course ranged more widely in post-1950 children's literature: it included authors and author-illustrators, such as Anthony Browne, Margaret Mahy, Philippa Pearce, Ursula Le Guin, Alan Garner, Robert Cormier, John Burningham, Maurice Sendak, William Mayne and Gillian Cross. In Library Studies, the College of Librarianship Wales, Aberystwyth, ran a major children's literature course called literature and libraries for young people which could be taken in the undergraduate programme or on the postgraduate diploma course. A substantial part of the students' work concerned contemporary stories and novels, poetry and plays. (Lonsdale and Spink 1987: 203–204).

At the postgraduate and in-service level, the study of children's literature consolidated and strengthened its position in Britain during the 1980s and early 1990s. Again, most work was done within teacher education, but there were also major developments elsewhere. In the 1980s, Worcester College ran a diploma in professional studies in education focused on children's fiction – a two-year part-time course examining the importance of children's literature within the professional context of teaching (Croxson 1985). At the University of Birmingham, the developing M.Ed. provided opportunities to discuss genres of children's literature alongside general approaches to the theory and practice of teaching literature, with reader-response criticism as an important element. Wolfgang Iser's work was important, too, within a major unit of the University of Southampton's MA (Ed.) degree. There, the emphasis was on the role of literature (including children's literature) as the central imaginative discipline of English. The unit examined issues such as the nature of literary experience, criticism and ideology and elements of reader response, combined with an examination of children's growth through picture books, fairy tales, poetry and fiction. At the University of Bristol, one component of the M.Ed. degree related the close reading of novels written for children over the past century to three theoretical topics. The first, a theory of narrative, started from a theory of fiction making as the defining property of the imagination and moved on to reader-response and reception theory. The second, the social production of children's literature, analysed the composition and world views of authors, critics, editors, teachers and parents who make up the social formation that produces children's literature. The third, cultural history and cultural theory was an attempt to study the 'many ways in which men, women and children create their fictions in order to interpret experience' (Inglis quoted in Watkins 1987: 46).

The first MA in Britain devoted exclusively to the study of children's literature was started at Bulmershe College of Higher Education in 1984. The approach to children's literature was from a literary and cultural perspective. The first year of this part-time degree combined the study of twentieth-century children's literature (with the main emphasis on literature published since 1950) with a course on the theory of children's literature, drawing upon a variety of literary theories. In the second year, theoretical problems and issues which had been raised in the first year (for example, the nature of story, in particular its structural, cultural and developmental aspects; the nature of the reading process; issues around gender and ethnicity in children's literature), were refocused within four courses: 'Popular forms of children's fiction', which studied comics and television for children as well as popular fiction; 'The oral tradition and after', which covered folk- and fairy tales as well as oral verse and the work of modern poets for children who draw upon the oral tradition; 'A brief survey of children's literature from 1700 to 1850'; and a longer course entitled 'Genre and period 1850–1914', which examined children's literature in relation to literary and historical developments during this period (Watkins 1987). After institutional merger, the MA degree was offered in a new form at the University of Reading and the degree could be taken either full-time or part-time. There were six taught modules; three core modules: nineteenth-century children's literature; twentieth-century children's literature; and the theory of children's literature; and three additional modules drawn from the following list: eighteenth-century children's literature, Commonwealth children's literature; popular forms of children's fiction; myth and folk-tale in children's literature; North American children's literature; and children's radio, film and television.

Three other MAs in children's literature were started in Britain in the 1990s. The University of Warwick's MA offered nine modules including, text and readers, twentieth-century literature for children, reading images, the rise of literature for children, and versions of fictions. It raised questions about historical and contemporary concepts of childhood and child readers and considered 'the narrative and semiotic contents of texts which include pictures, televisual, filmic and written materials'. The MA in children's literature at Roehampton Institute was designed to promote critical debate and enquiry in the field of children's literature. The subject was studied 'both as a literary genre and in terms of its social, cultural and historical constructions'. It consisted of eight taught modules: critical theory; adaptation and performance; book illustration; experimental narration; subcultures and subversion; literature past and present; and literature in the curriculum. An MA similar in construction to that at Reading began at Trinity College, Carmarthen, in 1995.

In Australia, Canada and New Zealand, courses in children's literature at undergraduate and postgraduate level also developed during the 1980s and 1990s.

In Australia, programmes developed at several universities in New South Wales. For example, in the Faculty of Education of the University of Sydney, the aim was 'to establish enthusiasm for children's literature and an understanding of what enjoyed texts can do for literacy development', through introducing students to contemporary titles such Anthony Browne's *Hansel and Gretel* (Williams 1988: 134). Later in the degree, students intensified their study through a 'theory of children's literature in education [which] requires a theory of language, especially a theory of language which produces insight into relationships between texts and their contexts of production and reception' (Williams 1988: 136). The university also offered a Master's degree in language in education which included some children's literature. Macquarie University offered a graduate diploma and Master's degree in children's literature with the following units: sources of children's literature (which examined the relationship of children's literature to 'pre-texts found in mythology, legend and romance, folk and fairy story and fable'); language and verbal arts; development of children's literature; narrative: theory and method; Australian children's literature; and the picture book. Courses in both education and English have flourished at several other universities and colleges in the state, such as the University of Wollongong.

In Victoria, Deakin University, Geelong, pioneered the distance teaching and learning of children's literature through course units and radio broadcasts, to students living at considerable distance from the university. In South Australia, programmes developed at several universities, including Flinders University, which taught the subject at honours level. In the mid-1990s, the University of

South Australia launched a major in children's literature within the BA degree. A number of units were offered including: Australian children's literature, adolescent literature, literature and the media, picture books, fantasy, realism, history of children's literature, and children's literature and popular culture.

In New Zealand, where interest in children's literature generally flourished, the Auckland College of Education had developed courses in children's literature during the 1970s and in 1990, the first graduate course to be offered within an English department in New Zealand was started at the University of Waikato in Hamilton (Cochrane 1991).

In Canada, at the University of New Brunswick, for example, several courses on children's literature were offered in the Faculty of Education: children's literature (a general course), the literature of early childhood, the junior novel, young adult literature, children's literature in the classroom and a graduate course called children's literature and literary theory (Paul 1989: 43). Graduate courses in Children's Literature at Master's and Doctoral level, also developed in, for example, the English departments of the University of Alberta, the University of Calgary, the University of Western Ontario and the University of Guelph; and the School of Library, Archival and Information Studies of the University of British Columbia (Children's Literature Association 1992: 39–41).

Children's literature courses at universities around the world – although their status is still very frequently questioned – attract very large classes, and seem set to expand. As their scholarly backing becomes more extensive, and as the divisions between traditional subjects break down, so the essentially interdisciplinary nature of the subject and its appeal to many groups of people should ensure its continued growth.

# References

Bailey, J. and Hollindale, P. (1986) 'Children's books in teacher education at York University', *Signal* 51: 156–171.

Bloom, S. and Mercier, C. M. (1992) 'Center for the Study of Children's Literature, Simmons College', in Sadler, G. E. (ed.) *Teaching Children's Literature: Issues, Pedagogy, Resources*, New York: Modern Language Association of America.

Butts, D. and Watkins, T. (1985) 'Children's books in teacher education at Bulmershe College of Higher Education', *Signal* 48: 176–181.

Children's Literature Association (1992) *Directory of Graduate Studies in Children's Literature*, Battle Creek, MI: Childrens Literature Association.

Cochrane, K. (1991) 'Children's literature in New Zealand: new initiatives in higher education', *Signal* 64: 25–32.

Croxson, M. (1985) 'Children's books in teacher education at Worcester College of Higher Education', *Signal* 45: 173–179.

Evans, E. (1984) 'Children's books in teacher education: the University of Birmingham', *Signal*, 44: 103–111.

Fox, G. (1985) 'Children's books in teacher education at the University of Exeter', *Signal* 47: 112–119.

Griffith, J. and Frey, C. (1992) 'On teaching the canon of children's literature', in Sadler, G. E. (ed.) *Teaching Children's Literature: Issues, Pedagogy, Resources*, New York: Modern Language Association of America.

Hunt, P. (1990) 'Examining Children's Literature: Children's Books at the University of Wales College of Cardiff', *Signal* 62: 147–158.

—— (1991) *Criticism, Theory and Children's Literature*, Oxford: Blackwell.

Knoepflmacher, U. C. (1992) Introduction to Sadler, G. E. (ed.) *Teaching Children's Literature: Issues, Pedagogy, Resources*, New York: Modern Language Association of America.

Lonsdale, R. and Spink, J. (1987) 'Children's books in the education of librarians at the College of Librarianship Wales, Aberystwyth', *Signal* 54: 203–209.

Meek, M. E. (1992) 'Children's literature: great books', in Sadler, G. E. (ed.) *Teaching Children's Literature: Issues, Pedagogy, Resources*, New York: Modern Language Association of America.

Mendelson, M. (1992) 'Graduate seminar in children's literature', in Sadler, G. E. (ed.) *Teaching Children's Literature: Issues, Pedagogy, Resources*, New York: Modern Language Association of America.

Moebius, W. (1992) 'Myth, folktale and children's literature', in Sadler, G. E. (ed.) *Teaching Children's Literature: Issues, Pedagogy, Resources*, New York: Modern Language Association of America.

Myers, M. (1992) 'Little girls lost: rewriting romantic childhood, righting gender and genre', in Sadler, G. E. (ed.) *Teaching Children's Literature: Issues, Pedagogy, Resources*, New York: Modern Language Association of America.

Paul, L. (1989) 'Teaching children's literature in Canada', *Signal* 58: 39–50.

Ronda, B. A. (1992) 'An American canon of children's literature', in Sadler, G. E. (ed.) *Teaching Children's Literature: Issues, Pedagogy, Resources*, New York: Modern Language Association of America.

Rose, J. (1984) *The Case of Peter Pan: Or, the Impossibility of Children's Fiction*, London: Macmillan.

Sadler, G. E. (ed.) (1992) *Teaching Children's Literature: Issues, Pedagogy, Resources*, New York: Modern Language Association of America.

Stahl, J. D. (1992) 'Canon formation: a historical and psychological perspective', in Sadler, G. E. (ed.) *Teaching Children's Literature: Issues, Pedagogy, Resources*, New York: Modern Language Association of America.

Sutcliffe, M. (1995) 'Children's books in teacher education at Westminster College, Oxford', *Signal* 77: 134–150.

Watkins, T. (1987) 'Mapping the magnetic field', *Children's Literature Association Quarterly* 12, 1: 44–46.

Watson, V. (1985) 'Children's books in teacher education at the University of Cambridge', *Signal* 46: 27–33.

Williams, G. (1988) 'Children's books in teacher education at the University of Sydney', *Signal* 56: 133–141.

# 53

# Librarianship

## *Ray Lonsdale with Sheila Ray*

Although children's literature is now regarded as a subject of cross-disciplinary interest, the first group of professionals to take a systematic and knowledgeable interest in what children read consisted of librarians.

Although isolated examples of school libraries date back to the seventh century, and of libraries serving the general public to the early nineteenth century, libraries for children were a comparatively late development. Their appearance in English-speaking countries and elsewhere was motivated by improvements in educational provision, with the resultant increase in literacy, and to some extent governed by book publication for children. After the establishment of the American Library Association (ALA) in 1876, and the Library Association (LA) in Britain in 1877, progress was sure but very slow, with the Americans always at least a decade ahead.

In 1877, Minerva L. Saunders, Librarian at Pawtucket, Rhode Island, set aside a corner of her library for children, provided special chairs, and began lending them books. In 1882, Caroline M. Hewins, Librarian of Hartford Public Library in Connecticut, presented a report on library work with children to the American Library Association. It became increasingly difficult to exclude children from public libraries and in 1894, a *Report on Reading for the Young*, presented at the ALA Conference at Lake Placid, seems to have been a landmark in the development of library work with children, arousing 'the librarians present to a clear conviction of the desirability of abolishing age limitations in the public library, and of providing special rooms for children with special attendants designed to serve children' (Meigs 1969: 386).

In 1906, Anne Carroll Moore, who had been in charge of the children's room in the Pratt Institute Library since 1896, was invited to organise the children's department of the New York Public library, and she soon became the leading player in the development of children's librarianship. She had already, in 1898, pressed the need for specialised professional education for librarians working with children, and had launched a series of classes at the Pratt Institute. Similar classes at the Carnegie Library in Pittsburg led to the establishment, in 1901, of the Training School for Children's Librarians, which placed its graduates throughout the country. The Section for Children's Librarians of the American Library Association (now the Association for Library Services to Children), formed in 1900, held its first conference in the following year, with Anne Carroll Moore in the chair. Moore also became a leading critic of children's literature, contributing regular articles to *The Bookman* and demonstrating that criticism can distinguish 'between the merely average and the genuinely great; that it can discover books of quality and can define the quality; that it can stimulate creative writing and creative illustration' (Meigs 1969: 389).

Cooperation between librarians and the American Booksellers Association, whose secretary was Frederic G. Melcher, resulted in a national Children's Book Week in 1919. Booksellers, publishers and public and school librarians were all involved, and Children's Book Week became an annual event, its influence gradually increasing, with the Children's Book Council (originally organised for the purpose) taking over responsibility for publicity and publications.

Soon after the first Children's Book Week, the family of Frederic G. Melcher endowed the John Newbery Award for the 'most distinguished contribution to children's literature' published during the preceding year, to encourage original and creative work in the field of children's books and to emphasise that children's literature deserved recognition. Administration of the award was placed in the hands of the Section for Children's Librarians of the ALA and the first award made in 1922. The Randolph Caldecott Award for the most distinguished picture book for children followed in 1938.

In 1924, the first issue of the first magazine to specialise in the reviewing of children's books, *The Horn Book Magazine*, edited by Bertha Mahony and Elinor Whitney of the Bookshop for Boys and Girls in Boston, was launched, and was used primarily by librarians, many of whom became reviewers.

In the 1920s, after the publication of *Certain Standards*, schools in the USA increasingly employed librarians who were qualified in librarianship as well as having teaching qualifications; this helped to create an additional market for books for children and young people.

By the 1930s, children's librarianship in the USA had set the pattern for developments worldwide. As will be seen, British libraries followed the American pattern closely, and British influence subsequently shaped developments in the countries of the British Empire. Canada, Australia and New Zealand, however, were also directly influenced by America, and Lillian H. Smith of Toronto, Canada, and Dorothy Neal White of Dunedin, New Zealand, were among the notable early pioneers of children's librarianship, both emphasising the importance of quality in children's reading. Lillian H. Smith had trained at the Carnegie Library in Pittsburgh and under Anne Carroll Moore at the New York Public library, before being invited in 1912 to return to Canada to organise a boys' and girls' division at the Toronto Public Library; she thus became the first trained children's librarian in the British Empire. During the 1950s a number of young British librarians held one-year internships at Boys' and Girls' House in Toronto.

The American influence reached further: in the 1930s, some Scandinavian librarians trained at Pittsburgh, showing particular interest on their return in establishing imaginative areas for story-telling within the children's library. These ranged from an old-fashioned chimney-piece and fireplace to a whole room entered through bookshelves which swung back when the child knocked three times, as at Malmö, in Sweden. These developments were in turn influential, the earliest example in Britain being the story-hour room at Luton Public Library in England, opened in the late 1950s.

In France, the development of public libraries (as known in the English-speaking world) was comparatively late, but in 1924, an American committee established a children's library in Paris, L'heure Joyeuse; this was run by three librarians who developed it on the American model, attaching great importance to book selection and the introduction of extension activities (Ray 1983: 44). Later, other children's libraries were established along the same lines, including, in 1965, La Joie par les Livres in the Paris suburb of Clamart; this became a focal point for the belated development of children's libraries throughout France.

After the Second World War, the establishment of a specialist section for children's librarians within the International Federation of Library Associations enabled librarians working with children in countries around the world to meet together to discuss matters of common concern.

## The Special Contribution of Children's Librarians to Children's Literature

During the first half of the twentieth century, librarians were the pre-eminent professional experts on children's literature, having both a good knowledge of the books, and skills to promote them to children, both within and outside libraries. This expertise was acknowledged by publishers and booksellers, and later came to be valued by parents and teachers, as groups and courses were set up to improve awareness of children's reading materials.

The high standard of work by early librarians such as Anne Carroll Moore ensured a substantial market for quality children's books, which were bought in large quantities, the bigger public library systems usually providing at least one copy of approved titles to each branch library, and supported high-quality backlists. It is significant, in Britain for example, that the 'second golden age' of children's literature in the late 1960s coincided with a rapid expansion in both school and public libraries, while the decline in hardback publishing for young adults coincided with the decline in public library spending in the late 1980s.

Librarians, from Caroline M. Hewins, 'compiler of one of the first authoritative booklists for children, *Books for Boys and Girls*' (Meigs 1969: 385) onwards have been enthusiastic producers of recommended books, locally and nationally, and have written significant books about children's literature, such as Dorothy Neal White's *About Books for Children* (1946), Lillian H. Smith's *The Unreluctant Years* (1953), Marcus Crouch's *Treasure Seekers and Borrowers* (1962) and Mary Thwaite's *From Primer to Pleasure in Reading*.

Courses in children's librarianship, which included the study of children's literature, were established in the USA early in the twentieth century; in Britain, the Library Association offered a qualification in children's librarianship which required extensive knowledge of children's books, for some years before including children's literature as an optional paper in the Fellowship Examinations in the 1950s. When a two-year full-time course leasing to the Registration examination of the Library Association was established in 1964, the syllabus included optional papers in both children's literature and librarianship; these proved to be very popular and during the 1960s and early 1970s hundreds of librarians graduated from these courses with a good working knowledge of children's literature. Such courses preceded by some years courses on children's literature for trainee teachers or in literature degree courses.

Because of their economic power (in the 1960s and 1970s it was said that about 90 per cent of children's books published in hardback were bought for libraries), children's librarians have influenced publishing; for example the publication of young adult or teenage books and books for the very young was stimulated by and evolved from librarians' concerns. Similarly, non-racist, non-sexist, multi-cultural, dual-language books, books for the mentally or physically disabled, as well as books of high interest for readers with low reading skills have all been suggested and encouraged by librarians. As project work became more common in schools, so they pressed for simple information books.

As the *Unesco Public Library Manifesto of 1973* stated:

> It is in early life that a taste for books and the habit of using libraries and their resources are most easily acquired. The public library has therefore a particular duty to provide opportunity for the informal and individual choice of books and other material by children. Special collections and if possible separate areas should be provided for them. The children's library can then become a lively stimulating place, in which activities of various kinds will be a source of cultural inspiration.
>
> Quoted in Ray 1979: 7

Children's librarians have also had a profound influence on children's literature which has only declined with a general rise in interest in the subject, and its acceptability as an academic study.

The following detailed account of the development and present state of library services to children and young people in Britain may be paralleled in many countries, the current situation being dependent on educational, economic, political, and social circumstances.


## Public Library Services to Young People in Britain

### *The early years*

Prior to the first Public Libraries Act of 1850, library provision for children in the United Kingdom was sparse, facilitated by a small number of day schools, Sunday schools and collections in the Mechanics Institutes. It was with the passing of the Public Libraries Acts of 1850 and 1855 that the public library service to children was created, the earliest known provision being a reading department for boys in Manchester Public Library in 1862. The Elementary Education Act, 1870, provided an important stimulus and, during the remaining years of the nineteenth century, children's collections were established in other provincial towns. By 1898, however 'only 108 out of more than 300 libraries in England and Wales had made provision for young people' (Ellis 1971: 14).

Developments were due not to any national plan, but to the dedication and enthusiasm of individual librarians. Among early pioneers were John Ballinger

(Cardiff), J. Potter Briscoe (Nottingham), L. Stanley Jast (Manchester) and W. C. Berwick Sayers (Croydon). In Scotland, Ernest A. Savage of Edinburgh took a particular interest in provision for children and included chapters on children's literature in *A Librarian Looks at Readers* (1947). Several of these librarians were aware of the impressive developments on the other side of the Atlantic and tried to emulate their American counterparts.

Provision took a variety of forms. Perhaps the most outstanding was the Library for Boys and Girls in Nottingham, which was regarded as a pioneer in respect of its accommodation, its balanced collection of contemporary children's fiction, furnishings and general ethos (Kelly 1977: 79). Although there were rare examples of imaginative and progressive provision of this kind, many collections contained inappropriate stock and were on 'closed access' whereby each book had to be asked for unseen. It was not uncommon for children under the age of 12 to be denied access, and in a few instances segregation of the sexes was practised.

One of the primary problems was a limitation on the amount of money which local authorities could spend on libraries and books. This was used by many authorities as an excuse for not providing a library service. Another factor responsible for the slow and restricted evolution of children's libraries was the fact that county councils, which controlled large rural areas of Britain, were not empowered to provide a public library service. The Public Libraries Act of 1919 helped to overcome both these problems but did not immediately lead to significant developments in library provision for children.

In the 1920s and 1930s, however, more public libraries recognised the need to reflect the increasing output of children's publishing in their stock, and the new county libraries brought provision to small communities. Libraries began to shake off the constraints of former years, introducing open access, extending the eligibility of membership to younger children, looking outward to providing services to children in hospitals and youth clubs. In 1926 the Library Association became involved in publishing lists of books recommended for young people when it was asked to prepare lists for the guidance of club leaders engaged in spending Carnegie United Kingdom Trust grants made to boys' and girls' clubs. The Library Association lists of 'core' books for children's collections continued to appear until the early 1960s – at which point the large number of books in print made the production of the lists impracticable.

Some libraries provided 'extension activities'. Lantern slide shows had become transformed into film shows, and story hours, reading circles, quizzes, talks by authors and other activities were slowly becoming popular. Such activities were given an unprecedented boost and a national focus with the establishment in 1925 of the National Book Council (later the National Book League and now the Book Trust), which inaugurated a national Boys' and Girls' Book Week during the 1930s. This brought together children's librarians, parents and teachers for a range of activities and later spawned similar events at a local level throughout the country.

The 1930s saw major developments in the infrastructure of children's librarianship. In 1937, H. J. B. Woodfield, formerly one of the first county librarians, who worked for the library supply firm of Combridge in Birmingham, and who later set up his own firm of library suppliers, Woodfield and Stanley, established *The Junior Bookshelf*, modelled on *The Horn Book Magazine*, as the first British specialist reviewing journal for children's books. In the same year, the Library Association established the Carnegie Medal to be awarded annually to an outstanding children's book: the first award was made to Arthur Ransome, for *Pigeon Post*.

Teaching in both primary and secondary schools was still very formal and comparatively little attention was paid to the quality of children's recreational reading. However, in 1936 both the School Library Association and the School Libraries Section of the Library Association were established (they merged as an independent organisation in 1947), and, although the early issues of their journals seem to indicate that they were biased towards the academic school and that the main aim should be to get young people reading adult classics at the first opportunity, they gradually took on the reviewing of a wider range of books for the young. In 1937 an Association of Children's Librarians was formed; this was subsumed into the Library Association in 1947 as the Youth Libraries Section (now the Youth Libraries Group).

During the period immediately after 1945, the critical importance of appointing staff who had a specific remit for working with children was at last acknowledged by many library authorities. Many of these individuals were imaginative and innovative and characterised by their strong conviction, and dedication to the needs of the young. The overwhelming majority were women, a fact that characterised children's librarianship for half a century and which some believed to be detrimental to the development of the specialism.

Eileen Colwell, who, very unusually for the period, had trained full-time for a Diploma in Librarianship at University College, London, in the 1920s, was appointed to organise a library service for children in Hendon, a north London suburb. In 1928, Hendon organised the first Children's Book Week, and Colwell went on to be a major figure in many areas of children's librarianship and story-telling.

In 1942, the McColvin Report *The Public Library System* was a 'watershed in public library thinking' which drew the nation's attention to the importance of children's libraries, recognised the deficiencies of collections, and underlined the need for children's librarians to hold appropriate qualifications and possess the appropriate personal qualities (Whiteman 1986: 42–43). The 1944 Education Act led to a marked improvement in education and stimulated library services for children generally.

Publishing for children, both fiction and non-fiction flourished, but the children's library movement grew slowly. A survey undertaken by the Library Association in the late 1950s reflected a depressing level of service with few designated posts for children's librarians.

## Developments After 1964

The passing of a new Public Libraries Act in 1964 and the re-organisation of local government over the next decade consolidated the status of public libraries generally and paved the way for an unprecedented expansion of children's libraries. The 1964 Public Library and Museums Act obliged local authorities to encourage young people to make use of the public library, but while the provision of a public library service by local authorities was enabled by the 1964 Act, the nature and extent of that service was not prescribed. An authority is only required to provide a 'comprehensive and efficient' service, and the place of services for children and young people within the core of public library services has never been defined. This anomaly has led to contentious debate in recent years.

Although no new legislation is anticipated, three publications have recently appeared which are likely to affect significantly the future shape of British library services to young people. In 1991 influential guidelines for children's librarians were published by The Library Association (Library Association 1991). These constitute the only national guidance on the provision of services to children and young people, setting out service philosophy and offering pragmatic advice to librarians. They have proved to be an invaluable document, and since their publication a number of authorities have formally adopted them as the basis of their library policy.

In 1995, the Department of National Heritage (the governmental body responsible for public libraries) published its findings of a study of public libraries in England and Wales, the first major examination since the seminal McColvin Report of 1942 (Aslib 1995). While the report, The *Public Library Review*, focuses largely upon adult services, it reiterates in the strongest terms that services to the young should be 'at the head of a list of prime purposes at the core of public library provision'. Such a statement is a welcome confirmation of the importance of children's services. The *Public Library Review*'s discussion of children's services is cursory but any disappointment must be tempered by the knowledge that another, perhaps more important, study into public library and school library services to young people was being undertaken at the same time.

*Investing in Children: The Future of Library Services for Children and Young People* (Department of National Heritage 1995), the report of the Library and Information Science Council (LISC) Working Party on Library Services for Children and Young People, is a most comprehensive and impressive document touching on all aspects of provision. It is this document, with its highly significant recommendations, which is likely to strengthen the place of children's library services in the next millennium and determine their nature. The report recognises that until legislation is strengthened to ensure that children's libraries are a *core* public library service, provision will remain piecemeal, with some examples of excellent practice, but also some dire ones.

## The structure of public library services

Within Britain, Scotland and Northern Ireland each have their own administrative structure. Traditionally there has been a close rapport between the public library service and education in the five Education and Library Boards of Northern Ireland and in the regions of Scotland. In England and Wales there are three administrative structures: the metropolitan authorities composed of large urban conurbations, the county authorities which are predominantly rural but which may embrace some large towns, and the library authorities of London.

Library authorities differ in the way they structure and deliver services to the young – indeed, there are one or two authorities which still do not recognise the importance of separate specialist provision. The most common structure is characterised by a central department staffed by specially trained and qualified children's librarians who are responsible for services to the young throughout the authority. A variation of this is evident in many areas where there is a designated senior post overseeing children's services but where their delivery rests with community, team or area librarians responsible for both adult and children's services within the regions. Usually the staff will not have specialist training in children's work. There are some authorities in which no central specialist control or support is available, and the development of services locally depends upon the expertise, interest and enthusiasm of individuals.

During the last decade, the wide variety of provision which exists among authorities has been influenced by significant political events. The 1980s and 1990s have been marked by swingeing cuts in the public sector, and very few authorities have escaped the resultant effects. There have been library closures, reductions in opening hours, staffing cuts, slashed bookfunds and little refurbishment of the older library buildings. Market forces, one of the hallmarks of Conservative philosophy, have pervaded children's libraries, with the spectre of charges being imposed for certain facilities – something quite alien to the ethos of the free public library movement. The growth of citizen's charters as part of a move towards greater accountability and user entitlement in public life, has prompted public libraries to establish customer charters and service specifications, some specifically for young people. These documents set out the nature of service entitlement indicating the importance of library services.

### The value and importance of children's libraries

Viewed historically, there has been a shift in the philosophy underpinning the British children's library service. While acknowledging the traditional and fundamental right of young people to have access to a service (as enshrined in the United Nations Convention on the Rights of the Child, 1990), contemporary children's librarianship perceives children as an 'investment' and 'at the *heart* of the core services':

> The role of the public library in meeting the needs of children and young people is of paramount importance in the future economic and cultural health of this country ... [C]ontinuation of its service to them ... is a critical factor in the future development of the public library service as a whole.
>
> Department of National Heritage 1995: 64

Traditionally, the library has been perceived as a major contributor to the development of literacy, and this remains a primary aim of the service. Through its collections, and ultimately through reading, the public library supports children's leisure needs and contributes to their intellectual, emotional, social, educational and language development. In this way the library can create the habitual *adult* reader and user, instilling a positive view of reading and libraries throughout adulthood. The emergence of the new technologies has extended the concept of literacy to embrace, for example, computer, visual and aural literacies, and children's libraries are beginning to acknowledge and respond to this challenge.

Public libraries also seek to create at an early age an understanding of the power and importance of information in society, and to help equip the child with the skills necessary to locate and handle that information.

Today, the public library fulfils complementary social and cultural functions through its programmes of activities, promoting social interaction among young people, between children and other groups in the community, while fostering an awareness of the culture of others. These aims and values are reflected in the nature of the collections and services offered by authorities, each authority having its own interpretations.

### Library collections and users

With over 7,000 new children's books published each year in Britain, and several thousand new audiovisual, computer and multi-media titles, selection is a critical and exacting responsibility at the heart of the librarian's work. Most children's libraries have created policies designed to reflect the needs of the users within their local community and to support the development of a dynamic and pertinent collection. Nationally there are several acknowledged deficiencies – reference collections, non-book materials, comics and magazines – but in general terms, British libraries attempt to offer objective and balanced representations of the best of British publishing with collections tailored to support the variant needs of their users.

There are approximately ten million children aged under 16-years-old currently living in Britain, and the public library service believes that irrespective of background, culture, ethnic or social group children should have right of access. Central to this philosophy is the belief that libraries have a responsibility to serve the whole child population and not just current users who account for little more than about 30 per cent of the child population. While recognising that children's libraries have a remit to serve all children, certain groups receive particular attention.

Historically, the most neglected group has been pre-school children, the under-5s. There was an unprecedented growth in services to this sector throughout the 1970s prompted by a marked improvement in the publishing of picture books and easy readers, both fiction and non-fiction. The Plowden Report on primary education (Department of Education and Science 1967), a growing awareness of the contribution of books to the social and emotional development of the younger child (Butler 1980), and the rise of movements such as the Pre-school Playgroup Association (now Pre-school Learning Alliance), dedicated to non-statutory provision for pre-school children and the training of their carers, were other major contributory factors. Children's libraries responded by developing their collections and introducing specialist accommodation and furnishings for this age group. Some authorities appointed specialist librarians who were trained to work with pre-school children and their carers. The provision of nursery education is very much to the fore in current political and educational debate, and although public service cuts have led to an erosion of some specialist posts, collections continue to develop, reflecting the myriad of pre-school publications, from bath books to CD-ROM technology. Among a number of recent initiatives is a major long-term project, Bookstart. This was launched in 1992 by Birmingham children's libraries and the Children's Book Foundation, and is designed to promote the sharing of books with babies of new parents and to monitor the impact on the development of literacy among pre-school children (Coleman 1994).

Many libraries have recognised the importance of housing collections of material on parenting, child development, reading and associated subjects in children's libraries to support the information needs of carers. Some even hold small collections of popular adult fiction to accommodate parents' leisure reading.

During the 1970s, the public library service began to respond to the needs of the many multicultural groups which comprise British society. Again, this was prompted by a corresponding increase in the availability of children's books in languages other than English, and dual-language material, and children's library collections began to reflect the rich diversity of publications. While these collections support the needs of multi-ethnic communities, they also create an awareness of multi-culturalism among children in general. Specialist posts have also been established in some of the library authorities serving large multi-ethnic populations. These librarians possess the requisite language competencies to select material and promote services usually in close collaboration with local community leaders.

Until the 1970s children with special needs were also neglected by many librarians. The Chronically Sick and Disabled Persons Act of 1970 required public libraries to provide services for individuals with special needs. Later, the development of 'mainstreaming' (the integration of children with certain physical, mental or behavioural disabilities in state schools), gave impetus to a wider publishing base of material for and about children with special needs. Children's libraries sought to respond, by providing easier physical access, and relevant materials. Their efforts were stimulated by the sterling work and publications of Margaret Marshall (Marshall 1991), the establishment of the National Library for the Handicapped Child (Spiers 1994), and the Toy Library Association which, since 1972, has promoted the development of toy libraries for families of children with special needs throughout the country (Head and Phillipa 1987). Alongside these developments has been a growing recognition of the value of bibliotherapy for young children and the role which children's librarians can play in the process (Matthews and Lonsdale 1992). Since the nineteenth century children's libraries have acknowledged the importance of supporting young people in hospital, and yet today this remains the Cinderella of the service – neglected by many public libraries and dependent largely upon the contribution of individuals within the health service (Matthews and Lonsdale 1991). The problems of dyslexic children are at last beginning to be addressed by the profession.

Throughout the history of British children's librarianship, one group of user has commanded particular attention: teenagers or young adults. The concepts of childhood and adolescence are not new and pervade the history of childhood and libraries. Debate about the need for specially tailored services was common from the 1920s onwards, and there were isolated examples of separate provision. Post-war concern about adolescence and youth culture, the growth of a market economy centred on the teenager, and the emergence of a discernible young adult literature during the 1960s and 1970s served to revitalise the debate surrounding the nature of provision in libraries. Today, however, provision remains uncoordinated, and authorities reflect different ideologies, with collections, separate sections and examples of separate libraries dedicated to young adults. The Xchange in Bradford and the Johnstone Information and Leisure Library in Renfrew, Scotland, are services which exemplify some of the most progressive thinking with accommodation, furnishing, collections, services, activities and staffing tailored to contemporary youth culture.

During the past two decades there has been particular concern for the information needs of teenagers. Dublin libraries in the Republic of Eire were among the first in Europe to establish a specialist information service in conjunction with other information providers in the fields of education, health, social services, employment and housing. This venture became an inspiration for many librarians in the United Kingdom. Recently, an exciting partnership has been created between the National Youth Agency, which has developed 'information shops' for teenagers in various premises throughout the country, and the children's libraries in an attempt to foster the development of information provision (Read 1992 and 1994). However, the issue of teenage provision, and its planning and monitoring, remains live and contentious.

In keeping with national concern for the socially disadvantaged, many children's libraries have been targeting their services accordingly in both urban and rural areas. Itinerant populations such as travellers and gypsies constitute other potential users who have been neglected until recent years. Given that British libraries reach less than half of the child population, there is disquiet that a significant proportion of non-users are from these sectors. There is a belief among some authors and librarians that service development alone is insufficient to attract these young people. What is required they argue, is a more fundamental change to the professional ethos, and especially to our library collections. Robert Leeson, among others, maintains that children's libraries still tend to reflect a privileged, middle-class literature which does not reflect the tastes and interests of many children (Leeson 1986). This sentiment is refuted by others who maintain that collections do offer a broad array of writing for children, including popular titles and series as well as media inspired literature and non-book material.

A popular misconception which has now been dispelled is that the clientele of children's libraries is confined to the young: parents, carers, teachers, educational and local civic officials, and members of the book trade are now among the range of groups targeted and served by children's librarians.

### Library activities

To facilitate the educational, recreational, social and cultural needs of a large and diverse child population, children's libraries, as well as lending materials engage in a broad spectrum of activities which has widened considerably over the past twenty years with each library authority setting its own programme based on a specific philosophy (Ray 1979; Eyre 1994). The promotion of activities is viewed as an integral part of service delivery and most libraries offer a programme which responds to events in the local, regional or national calendar, such as religious festivals, National Book Week, school and national holidays.

Current national concern about falling levels of literacy among the young has led to many libraries prioritising their support for the development of reading, and appreciation of children's literature. Reading clubs, reading games and trails, talks and readings from authors and illustrators, story-telling (now being offered to young adults), and family reading programmes are the staple fare.

Supporting the formal educational needs of the child remains a contentious issue and one which has been brought into sharper focus with the cuts in educational provision. There are increasing demands from schools for the public library to offer curriculum related material and information skills programmes designed to develop the child's ability to identify, locate and exploit relevant information. Such services may be provided but deep concern has been expressed about the ability of the public library to sustain these demands without introducing charges.

To help satisfy their social and cultural aspirations, children's librarians invite a diverse range of individuals and groups into the library to work with children – local personalities, the emergency services, theatre and music groups, local radio companies who broadcast with the help of children, children's zoos are just a few examples. Some libraries have established in-residence schemes whereby craftsmen and women, artists, actors, musicians, writers may be appointed to run workshops throughout the authority for the young.

Another manifestation of the library's social and cultural remit is taking services beyond the confines of the library's walls and into the community. This was manifest even during the early years of the children's library movement in embryonic services to schools, children's homes and youth clubs. Since then, the concept of 'outreach' has extended to embrace the whole spectrum of society. Activities and collections of materials are taken into shopping centres, cinema complexes, health clinics, factories, playgrounds, swimming pools and a variety of other locations. One authority even has its own canal boat for story-telling, and the British railway system has been used for activities as part of a national book festival. During the 1980s, urban aid funding was used by a number of library authorities to establish book buses which became the primary medium for their outreach activities. The buses were specially decorated and equipped to appeal to the young, and their vibrant image succeeded in attracting many new patrons.

Many libraries offer programmes of activities which serve no other purpose than to entertain, to fulfil the recreational and leisure interests of the young. The range is huge – puppet shows, fancy dress parties, entertainers of all kinds, Teddy Bears' picnics for the very young and video, computer and music clubs for the older child. In some authorities, recreational activities are not viewed as part of the 'core' service, and it is thought that children should pay to participate.

The financial constraints imposed on many authorities in recent years has led to a re-awakening of the arguments which were put forward in the 1930s, suggesting that libraries should prioritise their activities and focus on what many still view as the primary aim, supporting the development of reading.

Whatever the mode of promotion, children's libraries have developed a valuable rapport with many other library and non-library organisations to undertake these activities. In this way crucial links are made with like-minded bodies, resources are maximised and the expertise of other specialist groups can be used. National organisations such as The Library Association (Library Power promotion scheme for children), the Young Book Trust (National Children's Book Week), The Federation of Children's Book Groups (National Story-telling Week), together with regional and local organisations interact to support the work of individual authorities. The mass media, too, are used widely to promote their services, particularly local radio and the local press.

Central to the success of many library activities has been the use of sponsorship and grants from commercial and charitable bodies and from the regional Arts Councils which operate in Britain. Although initially a contentious issue for many librarians, the financial cuts in public service have made sponsorship a matter of expediency.

### Information technology

Writing in 1984, the Canadian academic Adele Fasick drew attention to the need for children's librarians to respond to the age of new technologies (Fasick 1984). Collections, she argued, should contain the media-inspired literature such as film and television tie-ins, choose-your-own story books, novelisations and multi-media packages. These are now commonplace in the majority of collections. However, it is with respect to the availability of audiovisual, computer and multi-media software that British children's libraries are deficient in contrast with their counterparts in North America (Bergiarusso 1990). A major study undertaken in the early 1990s revealed a worrying picture (Lonsdale and Wheatley 1990, 1991). The provision of even established audiovisual formats such as videos and audiocassettes is piecemeal, with nearly a third of children's library authorities making no provision at all. However, the availability of computer materials is significantly worse, with fewer than one third of authorities offering largely outmoded hardware and software (Lonsdale and Wheatley 1992). Services are correspondingly sparse, and tensions were detected about whether the public library should provide computer material, despite an unprecedented growth in the publishing of software for young people and the availability of hardware in the home (Clyde 1993). While there is a general recognition of the need to develop skills to exploit the new technologies, there is little evidence that libraries are supporting this through their promotional and information skills programmes. The appearance of new interactive CD-ROM multi-media and the development of Internet during the past five years has largely gone unheeded in children's libraries (although not in school libraries), and unlike the United States and many other countries, there is a danger that the current revolution in information technology could pass British children's libraries by.

### Staffing of children's libraries

Since the 1880s the importance of having a specially qualified and trained staff for library work with children has been recognised, but only within the past thirty years has there been a significant demand for staff with specialist training and expertise, and it was not until the late 1970s that minimum levels for professional and non-professional staff were recognised. Today, the need for specialists who possess expertise and knowledge beyond library skills *per se* and children's literature, has been re-affirmed. To meet the challenges of collection and service development in the twenty-first century, the children's librarian should ideally possess a knowledge of child development, educational trends, a familiarity with contemporary child culture, promotional and teaching skills, and personal qualities including empathy with children and confidence in relating with and to them.

It is ironic that at the moment when there is a national consensus about the importance of specialist training, specialist posts are in decline. Some senior librarians with a remit for children's work have had to accept responsibility for a wider range of services and to develop a broader range of skills. This has usually been to the detriment of the young people's service.

The other potential threat has been the decline of specialist courses in children's literature and librarianship in university departments of library and information studies in Britain (Elkin 1992). The halcyon years of the 1970s and mid-1980s have gone, and there are now few specialist modules on offer in those departments. There is little prospect that this situation is going to alter in the near future and it is likely that individual public libraries will have to provide good quality in-service training for their staff in a time of marked economic constraint.

Children's librarians do, however, have the support of a professional body, the Youth Libraries Group of the Library Association. From its inception in the 1940s it has grown into an influential body supporting training programmes, professional publications, and publicity material. At a national level it liaises with professional and non-professional organisations concerned with children, and is a mouthpiece for children's librarians; it administers the Carnegie and Greenaway Medals. At a local level, its regional committees do much to enhance the rapport amongst staff within the local authorities.

### Library accommodation

A wide variety of approaches are evident with respect to the design and planning of children's libraries (Dewe 1995). The most common form is the separate children's room which offers the advantage of creating a suitable space and ambience with which the child can identify, and which allow the sort of noise levels associated with the young and their activities. During the 1970s, open plan libraries became fashionable, offering easy access between the young people's and the adults' sections, and often permitting an intermediate area for the teenage collection. Problems of noise do exist, although some libraries use screens to partition off the children's area during the more riotous events.

Dual purpose or dual use libraries as they are variously called are another manifestation, with the public library sited usually in a secondary school. The idea of drawing communities together in this way gained popularity in Europe and North America during the 1960s and 1970s but later waned as a result of conflicting ideologies, and few dual use libraries have been established in recent years. Separate mobile libraries for children are quite common in some

Scandinavian countries and across the Atlantic but in Britain they normally comprise holiday mobiles or book buses which are used for special events.

Purpose built activity areas are found in the larger libraries, comprising story-telling wells and arenas, rostra for staging plays, and facilities for parents with babies and young children. The advent of information technology is occasioning some fundamental re-designing to accommodate workstations, although there is little evidence of the SciFi hypermedia centres now found in some South-east Asian children's libraries, such as in Malaysia.

Whatever the form of provision, it is important to create the right atmosphere. To achieve this and to cater for the varied physical requirements of a diverse range of children, specially designed, highly colourful and imaginative shelving and furnishings are provided. It is not uncommon to see display equipment in the shape of space ships, trains, castles and other exotic forms, akin to those found in children's bookshops. During the 1990s there has been a decline in new library building projects but a continued appreciation of the importance of sound design, of attractive and functional accommodation and furnishing.

### Library services to children in education

The history of British public library services to young people is inextricably linked with library provision to children in schools. These may take two forms, school libraries and a centralised school library support service.

Throughout their long history, school libraries have been shaped and influenced by many official educational and library reports, the work of two professional bodies, the School Library Association and the Schools Library Group of the Library Association, and to a lesser extent by legislation (Ray 1982; Office of Libraries and Arts 1984; Kinnell 1995). Unlike Northern Ireland and Scotland, there has never been a statutory obligation for schools in England and Wales to establish a library or to appoint a qualified librarian. The absence of legislation and of official standards for funding and resourcing has resulted in considerable variation of provision amongst the English and Welsh authorities. This diversity has been exacerbated by the widely differing perceptions held by headteachers about the importance of the library and the priority given to its funding.

Although a growth in the appointment of qualified librarians is discernible, many secondary school libraries are staffed by teacher-librarians or teachers who hold no formal qualifications in librarianship. Qualified librarians are rarely found in primary schools. Funding of the library is determined by the headteacher usually in collaboration with the governors of the school. While bodies such as the Library Association have published guidelines for school libraries, the standards of provision to pupils and teachers remain diverse.

Since the 1970s changes in the curriculum, combined with new teaching and learning theories, and the emergence of information technology have led to the development of a new concept – the learning resource centre, which has been established in many secondary schools. The library is no longer seen simply as a repository of materials but as a medium for learning – at the heart of the education process. Although viewed with suspicion by some, one outcome of this concept is a new partnership between librarians and teachers in selecting, creating and exploiting learning and teaching resources, and designing and delivering information skills training for children. Another significant development has been the response of the school library to national information technology initiatives, with school libraries establishing computer facilities, integrated learning systems, networking systems and most recently, provision for interactive multi-media.

In both primary and secondary education there is a deep interest in the role of libraries to support reading and the newer literacies, and a growing recognition that library collections and services are fundamental to the educational process. In general, stocks reflect the formal educational demands of the National Curriculum, but many libraries also support the leisure reading of children with a complementary array of contemporary children's fiction and non-fiction. In many schools there are small scale programmes of promotional activities similar to those in public libraries. There is genuine concern that the absence of official standards of provision, exacerbated by national financial cutbacks in education and ideological divisions, pose a serious threat to those endeavours.

### School library services

The origins of school library services lie in the early public library movement when schools were permitted to borrow material from public libraries. Historically, after the Public Libraries Act of 1919, the English and Welsh county authorities were the first to develop this central support service to primary and secondary schools. For many primary schools this constituted a vital complementary source of books, and for some, the only source. School library services were later established in the London boroughs, and following local government re-organisation in the early 1970s many of the new metropolitan library authorities introduced such services. Traditionally, they were operated by the library department of the local authority as an agent of the education department, with costs normally being met from the education budget. As with school libraries, there is no statutory obligation in England and Wales to offer a central support service. In Northern Ireland, however, where the five education and library boards are responsible for both education and library services, the school library service is a statutory function. In Scotland too, the school library services are for the most part provided as a statutory function of the regional education service.

At their zenith in the 1970s and early 1980s, schools library services provided crucial support with an array of services including the loan of materials to supplement school library collections, collections designed to support project work, centralised purchasing and processing services which enabled teachers and teacher-librarians to select material using their own library budget, to aid selection and promotion, exhibitions, information skills programmes for pupils and teachers and an advisory service for school librarians and teachers.

School library services in England and Wales have been subject to fundamental changes in recent years resulting from the passing of the 1988 Education Reform Act and the introduction of Local Management of Schools. Funding is now devolved to schools giving headteachers the choice of buying back centralised services or spending the money unilaterally. Consequently many school library services have been forced to cut or reorganise their services to make themselves financially viable. In a growing number of authorities, alternative structures have been introduced, such as management of the schools library service by the local education authority, or the creation of an independent business unit. In a few authorities insufficient schools chose to 'buy back' into the central schools library service which became economically unviable, and subsequently closed.

The future for school library services remains uncertain, but what cannot be denied is that they have played a critical role in supporting the formal and non-formal education needs of many children. The contraction of these services together with the constraints witnessed within school libraries has led to new and ever increasing pressures on the public library.

### *Towards the twenty-first century*

What of the future? Public expenditure cuts, the threat of charges for children, the ideological concerns surrounding market forces and sponsorship, rationalisation and reductions in staffing and the precarious future of specialists are issues which led to a lack of confidence during the 1980s and will continue to impact on the development of services in the foreseeable future. Writing in the mid-1980s, one eminent children's librarian, Jennifer Shepherd, wrote:

> What of the future? If there is light on the horizon it is this, that children's work is at last growing up. There is an awareness of the need for aims and objectives to clarify what ought to be done and why; policies and programmes to identify how and when; monitoring and evaluation to look at results; accountability to ensure achievement in line with objectives and a *fair* distribution of total resources.
>
> Shepherd 1986: 30

A decade on, there is much to be positive about. Many libraries have established charter service policies, and performance indicators and sophisticated management techniques are being put in place; collections reflect the rich output of children's book publishing; the proactive marketing of collections, services and of children's libraries in general are bearing fruit. National aims and objectives and a clear philosophy are now manifest in the guise of the Library Association guidelines and recent reports. With their publication, new debate has been awakened which, given continued perseverance and dedication of children's librarians, could lead to a restored confidence and an optimistic future.

## References

Aslib (1995) *Review of the Public Library Service in England and Wales for the Department of National Heritage: Final Report*, London: ASLIB.

Bergiarusso, M. (1990) 'Public library services for children in the United States', *International Review of Children's Literature and Librarianship* 5, 3: 198–218.

Butler, D. (1980) *Babies Need Books*, London: Bodley Head.

Clyde, L. A. (1993) 'Computer based resources for young people: an overview', *International Review of Children's Literature and Librarianship* 8, 1: 1–21.

Coleman, P. (1994) 'Libraries and literacy: how public libraries should respond', in Barker, K. and Lonsdale, R. (eds), *Skills for Life: The Meaning and Value of Literacy*, pp 75–88, London: Taylor Graham.

Colwell, E. H. (1947) 'Twenty eventful years in children's books', *Papers and Summaries of Discussions at The Brighton Conference of the Library Association*, 55–59.

Department of Education and Science (1967) *Children and their Primary Schools*, 2 Vols, London: HMSO.

Department of National Heritage (1995) *Investing in Children: The Future of Library and Information Services for Children and Young People: Library and Information Services Council (England). Working Party on Library Services for Children and Young People*, London: HMSO.

Dewe, M. (1995) *Planning and Designing Libraries for Children and Young People*, London: Library Association Publishing.

Elkin, J. (1992) 'The education and training of children's librarians', *International Review of Children's Literature and Librarianship* 7, 3: 151–154.

Ellis, A. (1971) *Library Services for Young People in England and Wales 1830–1970*, Oxford: Pergamon Press.

Eyre, G. (1994) *Making Quality Happen: A Practical Guide to Promoting Your Library*, London: Youth Libraries Group.

Fasick, A. M. (1984) 'Moving into the future without losing the past: children's services in the information age', *Top of the News* 40, 4: 405–413.

Head, J. and Phillipa, B. (1987) *Toy Libraries in the Community*, London: Eltan.

Kelly, T. (1977) *A History of Public Libraries in Great Britain*, London: The Library Association.

Kinnell, M. (1995) 'Policy for secondary school library provision in England and Wales: an historical perspective' *Journal of Librarianship and Information Science* 27, 1: 17–26

Leeson, R. (1986) *Reading and Righting*, London: Collins.

Library Association (1991) *Children and Young People: Library Association guidelines for public library services*, London: Library Association Publishing.

Lonsdale, R. and Wheatley, A. (1990) 'The provision of audiovisual and computer services to young people by British public libraries: nature, range and availability of materials', *International Review of Children's Literature and Librarianship* 5, 3: 159–179.

—— (1991) 'The provision of audiovisual and computer services to young people by British public libraries: collection management and promotion of services', *International Review of Children's Literature and Librarianship* 6, 1: 31–55.

—— (1992) 'The provision of computer materials and services to young people by British public libraries', *Journal of Librarianship and Information Science* 24, 2: 25–37.

McColvin, L. R. (1942) *The Public Library System of Great Britain: A Report on its Present Condition with Proposals for Post-War Reorganisation*, London: The Library Association.

Marshall, M. (1991) *Managing Library Provision for Handicapped Children*, London: Mansell.

Matthews, D. A. and Lonsdale R. (1991) 'Children in hospital: I. Survey of library and book provision', *Health Libraries Review* 8, 4: 210–219.

—— (1992) 'Children in hospital: II. Reading therapy and children in hospital', *Health Libraries Review* 9, 1: 14–26.

Meigs, C. (ed.) (1969) *A Critical History of Children's Literature*, rev. edn, Toronto: Macmillan.

Office of Arts and Libraries (1984) *School Libraries the Foundations of the Curriculum*, London: HMSO.

Ray, C. (ed.) (1983) *Library Service to Children: An International Survey*, new edn, London: K. G. Saur.

Ray, S. G. (1979) *Children's Librarianship*, London: Clive Bingley.

—— (1982) *Library Service to Schools*, London: Library Association.

Read, L. (1992) 'Shopping for information: a National Youth Agency initiative', *Youth Library Review* 13: 8–12.

—— (1994) 'The use of the youth information shops', *Youth Library Review* 18: 14–21.

Shepherd, J. (1986) 'A crisis of confidence: the future of children's work', *International Review of Children's Literature and Librarianship*, 1, 1: 22–32.

Spiers, D. (1994) 'Literacy, education and the needs of the disabled child', in Barker, K. and Lonsdale, R. (eds) *Skills for Life: The Meaning and Value of Literacy*, London: Taylor Graham.

Whiteman, P. (1986) *Public Libraries since 1945: The Impact of the McColvin Report*, London: Clive Bingley.

## Further Reading

Fasick, A. M., Johnston, M. and Osler, R. (1990) *Lands of Pleasure: Essays on Lillian H. Smith and the Development of Children's Libraries*, Metuchen, NJ: Scarecrow Press.

Herring, J. (1988) *School Librarianship*, 2nd edn, London: Clive Bingley.

Kinnell, M. (1994) 'Far horizons: international perspectives on libraries and reading for teenagers', *International Review of Children's Literature and Librarianship* 9, 2: 73–87.

Lowrie, J. E. and Nagakura, M. (1991) *School libraries: international developments*, 2nd edn, Metuchen, NJ: Scarecrow Press.

Shepherd, J. (1992) 'Children's, young people's and school library services' in Bromley, D. W. and Allott, A. M. (eds) *British Library and Information Work 1986–90. Vol. 1: General Libraries and the Profession*, London: Library Association Publishing.

# 54

# Bibliotherapy and Psychology

## *Hugh Crago*

*Bibliotherapy* is one of an enormous range of methods for helping human beings in distress. The word itself suggests a specific therapeutic modality (as in 'art therapy' 'occupational therapy' or 'dance therapy' – all of which were developed specifically to meet the needs of patients perceived to be wholly or partly beyond the reach of mainstream psychotherapeutic methods). In fact, bibliotherapy has not remotely established its claim to such status, and may never do so, but it still has a direct, though peripheral, relationship to the whole field of *psychotherapy*.

However, because the printed text (*biblio-*) is the medium through which the helping/healing is considered to occur (whereas, the concept should really cover non-printed 'texts' such as oral story-telling and the viewing of visual narratives like films and picture books), bibliotherapy must also be considered in relation to the study of literature as received by its audience, a field now categorised as reception theory (Tabbert 1979) and reader response. With these bibliotherapy once again enjoys a presently tenuous but potentially significant connection.

Indeed, we may as well say clearly at the outset that both the theory and the practice of bibliotherapy have suffered from a failure fully to explore (or even in many cases to recognise) these connections. Few advocates of bibliotherapy have had much knowledge of reader-response theory – much of which postdates the pioneering work in bibliotherapy. Even fewer have had much personal acquaintance with the wider fields of psychology and psychotherapy. For their part, most psychologists have simply avoided dealing with a subject as complex and difficult to quantify as the potential effects of narrative on human lives. Much of what purports to be received wisdom on the subject of bibliotherapy is thus of dubious value, and perhaps it is not surprising that bibliotherapy has not been taken seriously by many people.

In so far as bibliotherapy has been seen as particularly relevant to children and adolescents, its proponents have been influenced by misleading assumptions about the nature of childhood, in particular, the Rousseau-derived belief that children are especially susceptible to suggestion through print in comparison with adults, and ignorance of the real similarities and differences between child readers and adult readers (outlined briefly in Crago 1979) In fact, as we shall see, there is little difference between children and adults at the level of reading where lasting 'influence' is most likely to occur.

## What Psychotherapy Is

Psychotherapy comprises a body of knowledge about what goes wrong with human beings, along with a set of practices designed to improve happiness and competence in the face of life's inevitable stresses. Lay people commonly assume that such work is the province of psychologists, but the academic discipline of psychology has no compelling claim on the practice of psychotherapy, and many 'scientific' psychologists eschew psychotherapy except in extremely restricted forms. Psychiatry, because of its association with mental illness, is the other profession most often associated with psychotherapy, but once again, psychiatrists need not necessarily practice it.

Psychotherapy, which Freud called 'the talking cure', is best understood as something which may be practised by nurses, social workers, family therapists, doctors, marriage counsellors and occupational therapists, as well as by psychiatrists and psychologists. In non-Western cultures, shamans and other traditional healers operate out of a totally different conceptual framework from that employed by European psychotherapists, but at a fundamental level satisfy the same needs in their troubled clientele – needs for reassurance, meaning and healing confrontation. This makes it clear that there is no universally 'true' system of psychotherapeutic theory, and that no single professional guild in our own, or any other, culture, 'owns' psychotherapeutic practice.

## The Co-Evolution of Story and Consciousness

In pre-literate cultures, narrative has always functioned in multiple ways, preserving accumulated knowledge, articulating meaning, offering cathartic release and pleasure, and promoting 'healing' in the broad sense of reassurance as to each listener's place in the scheme of things. A single myth or ceremony may embody all of these functions simultaneously. We can reasonably assume that the prehistoric antecedents of our own culture were similar. The earliest written versions of oral narratives that we possess appear to have operated in much the same way as prime time television does today: offering their audiences culturally central messages that confirmed listeners in their existing understandings of what was right and wrong, acceptable and unacceptable, heroic and ignoble.

In the European Middle Ages, where story-telling occurred – whether in church, or around the hearth at night – it would probably have been experienced in the same shared way, and with the same multiple dimensions, as myth and bardic epic. One reason why it has been possible for scholars in our own century to 'discover' the therapeutic potential of traditional folk tales (for example, Bettelheim 1976) is precisely because it has always been there. Those tales formed part of a collective, oral culture which spoke to a collective psyche, not a collection of individual psyches, and which inevitably embodied messages of broad relevance to the community in general.

The coming of print to Western Europe, followed a few centuries later by the spread of mass literacy, formed part of a process of gradual individualisation of consciousness. Jaynes (1976) and Wilber (1986) have independently constructed speculative overviews of the evolution of consciousness which differ in details, but agree on a shift from a collective consciousness in which individuals were embedded in a 'group mind' (brilliantly simulated in William Golding's *The Inheritors* (1955)) to the form of consciousness we know today, where people experience themselves as 'separate', and in which the 'private space inside the head' is experienced as under the control of the individual, and inaccessible to other individuals except under certain conditions. John Fowles's extraordinary novel *A Maggot* (1985) presents one of the best descriptions of this shift from pre-modern to modern consciousness.

There are some grounds for believing that the concept of 'private thoughts' was actually assisted by the development of diary-writing among the Protestant middle class in the seventeenth century (Stone 1976). Private writing enhanced the individual's awareness of his or her own uniqueness, just as the private documentation of the development of one's own children, which seems to have commenced during the nineteenth century (Steedman 1982), enhanced parental consciousness of those children's individuality. Simultaneously, an increasing life span, and a better standard of living (including the possibility of a 'room of one's own') for a larger proportion of the population in the centuries following the industrial revolution supported the movement to value the lives of individual human beings other than the famous and powerful.

The Romantic movement, coinciding as it did with the first phase of industrialisation, was a powerful cultural stimulus to the emergence of the individual sensibility, setting the tone for almost two centuries in which the individual mind, personality and emotions would become the central subject for poets, novelists, dramatists and (ultimately) film makers. As human beings increasingly experienced themselves as separate and even isolated ('I am a rock, I am an island', sang Paul Simon in the 1960s, explicitly contradicting Donne's seventeenth-century 'No Manne is an Islande'), it became doubly important for literature to offer validation for that individuality, by opening windows into the private worlds of other individuals, and by increasingly portraying a whole range of highly specialised subjects, which would of necessity appeal only to particular audiences who could identify with them. 'Bardic' literature had by contrast offered only matter that appealed to the common denominator, and had spoken only to the values which all its listeners possessed in common. Thus highly individualised fictions support and extend the development of highly individualised consciousness.

The emergence of individual psychotherapy as practised by Freud, and as elaborated vastly throughout this century, can also be seen as part of the development of an individualised consciousness, setting up a relationship similar to that of the confessional, but extending its scope to deal with the entire realm of emotional, existential and behavioural distress, now conceived in more secular than spiritual terms. Psychotherapy at its inception and still predominantly today deals explicitly with the inner world of the individual. It is commonly assumed that a highly individualised relationship must be established between client and therapist in order for any intervention strategy to work. The client or patient must first feel understood, valued and empowered before he or she is likely to accept challenge to existing habits of thought and feeling.

The encounter between a modern reader and a printed text is similar in many ways to the therapeutic encounter we have just examined. What happens between reader and printed text is a mystery – unless the reader chooses to tell us about it, and even then, there will be much that has occurred in the reading process that will have been below the level of consciousness. Once again, it is a question of a very 'private' transaction, in which an exquisite degree of 'matching' is required between the external agent (book) and the individual if any self-insight or change on the reader's part is to be elicited. The whole notion of bibliotherapy rests on the possibility of such matching.

The growing popularity of psychotherapy has in turn influenced narrative, which has become increasingly confessional (dealing explicitly with aspects of inner life hitherto considered entirely private), and increasingly concerned with abnormal mental and emotional states. This has been true equally in adult and in young people's fiction, where 'problem novels' for adolescents have been a burgeoning area in publishing over the past twenty years. The existence of such novels, dealing with highly individualised problems (such as anorexia nervosa, see Pantanizopoulos 1989), appears to be the most recent fictional manifestation of the individualisation of consciousness.

## Bibliotherapy: a Twentieth-century Notion

In its broadest historical context, the concept of 'bibliotherapy' forms part of the ancient *dulcis et utile* debate, in which some scholars advocated a role for literature as 'useful' or 'instructive' in some moral sense, while others maintained that stories and books existed primarily or even purely to give pleasure. Since Greek and Roman times, one side or the other has prevailed for periods of a century or more, but the weight of evidence has always suggested that people continued to listen and read regardless of what the 'experts' thought. Within the field of children's literature, the debate has focused in particular on the ambiguous category of fairy tales, originally oral narratives which, having been appropriated by 'child culture' from the nineteenth century, have been at varying times attacked as dangerous, defended as 'pure escapism', and re-conceptualised as 'morally instructive' or psychologically growthful.

In fact, there are few examples of successful and popular literature which do not offer both delight and 'instruction' in some form or other. The debate seems rather to reflect a continuing moral uneasiness, in which the intensity with which humans have always immersed themselves in 'story' has prompted us to seek justification for an involvement so seemingly unrelated to the hard business of daily life.

Simsova (1968), Hatt (1976) and Nell (1988) all draw attention to the extraordinary work of Nicholas Rubakin in the USSR in the 1920s, work which anticipates by nearly half a century the claim of reader-response theory that readers experience texts in their own images (Holland 1975). Rubakin also argued for something akin to Piagetian 'schemas' as facilitating comprehension, and recognised the possibility of 'scientifically' matching types of readers with types of books (the typology of reader personalities being broadly based on Jung's system). Such an enterprise of social engineering was likely enough to appeal to a revolutionary government, but Rubakin's ideas were never fully operationalised even in the USSR, and in the West (like his fellow Russians Vladimir Propp and

Kornei Chukovsky) Rubakin achieved no recognition until many years after the first appearance of his work.

Rubakin's pioneering efforts were not strictly directed towards 'therapy'. The idea of bibliotherapy as such seems to have originated in Germany and the USA in the early years of the century, but in Britain the term 'reading therapy' has been preferred until relatively recently. Jean M. Clarke (in Clarke and Postle 1988) summarises the development of this practice in Britain from the initial stage in which the provision of libraries for patients in mental hospitals was vaguely seen as 'a good thing' and reading as vaguely 'curative' without any apparent grasp of the dynamics involved (or the manifest potential difficulties). Much later in the century, librarians working in hospitals were joined by a handful of social workers who had independently concluded that reading might be a source of insight and cure.

In the idealistic and therapeutically oriented culture of the USA, the idea of bibliotherapy has enjoyed a somewhat wider constituency (Pardeck 1984). Fader and McNeil's *Hooked On Books* (1969) directed attention to a single client group (alienated and anti-print teenagers) and their enthusiastic anecdotal evidence of triumphant success in transforming teenagers into bookaholics inspired a generation of teachers. The idea that reading was in itself a 'wonder drug' with the power to 'transform lives' was not new, but it led to a number of attempts to use books to alleviate individual and social ills; thus Manning and Casbergue (1988) outline 'Bibliotherapy for children in step families'. In Pittsburg, Elizabeth Segal and Joan Friedberg set up a modestly-conceived but eventually nationally influential programme to bring quality picture books into the homes of the city's poor, in order to encourage early literacy and to promote cultural enrichment (Segal 1989). More strictly 'therapeutic' was Butler's work in New Zealand. *Cushla and Her Books* (Butler 1979) argues that picture books were instrumental in the rehabilitation of a multiple handicapped child.

The basic idea of bibliotherapy, as established by (predominantly) librarians runs approximately as follows. A child or adult has a problem. A skilled librarian, teacher or (Clarke would prefer) 'reading therapist', suggests a story which in some way bears on that problem. If the intervention is successful, the reader recognises that the book has something personally significant to say to him/her, perhaps becomes conscious of the dimensions of his/her own problem, and sometimes perceives potential solutions to it. The reader then returns the book to the professional, perhaps wishing to discuss it (and through it, his or her own problems), perhaps asking for more books 'like that one', which the professional then sensitively provides on the basis of feedback as to the reader's reception of the first.

The practical obstacles to the widespread employment of such a process, as opposed to the broader applications of 'reading as enrichment' mentioned above, are considerable. With the possible exception of staff in small private mental institutions or private boarding schools, few librarians are likely ever to know their constituents well enough, or have time enough, to play such a role, which requires both intimate knowledge of the individual and wide knowledge of literature. Moreover, bibliotherapy is open to ethical objections if it is foisted upon mental patients or older children without their having requested it, and (more pragmatically) will in such cases almost certainly be resisted openly or covertly. Worse still, existing bibliotherapeutic theory seems inadequately informed as to how narratives actually interact with human lives.

## How Stories Affect Individuals

Pre-literate children in our own and other cultures spontaneously compose songs, chants, monologues and other forms of 'phatic' expression, often to the accompaniment of motor play, and apparently in rough imitation of adult talk, song and story. Children who grow up with television emulate its manner and matter in their compositions (Sutton-Smith *et al.* 1981); those brought up on oral stories are influenced by that mode, and print-soaked children imitate the mode of print (Crago and Crago 1983). There are, however, distinctive structural principles in children's compositions which mark them off from adult models, and which suggest some innate paradigm that modifies direct imitation.

Later in life, such spontaneous story-making 'goes underground', taking the form of the 'inner newsreel' discussed by Becker (1972) and Klinger (1971). Adults do not normally chant aloud as they make beds, tee off on the golf course or type at their computer station, but their minds do run an endless stream of loosely arranged images, thoughts and inner dialogues – a waking version of dreaming.

All of this evidence suggests that story-telling, or at least, arranging the raw material of experience into some sort of pattern, is a process almost as fundamental to human life as breathing. In these ur-narratives, we are both 'creators' and 'audiences', both 'participants' and 'spectators': the roles are not substantially distinguished.

'Absorbed' or 'ludic reading', as investigated by Victor Nell (1988) is virtually a trance state, where readers willingly become oblivious to the world around them. Normal consciousness is put on hold and the print seems to guide the 'inner newsreel's' production of highly personalised images. Thus the reader 'merges' with the characters and events of the work. Nell, one of the few mainstream psychologists to offer anything useful on the affective dimension of reading, points out that it is useless to distinguish fiction from non-fiction or popular fiction from 'good literature' where ludic reading is in question. However, it is unlikely that ludic reading would normally occur unless in response to narrative material. It is as if there is something intrinsically consciousness-altering about the narrative form itself. Ludic readers are skilled in seeking out texts which will offer them the experience they desire, and can often successfully select on the basis of only small samples of writing (a process akin to that by which we 'instinctively' assess strangers after a few minutes' acquaintance).

If deep absorption in narrative has nothing to do with literary quality, then adult ludic readers are probably functionally identical with child readers/listeners, for whom aesthetic sophistication has little to do with enjoyment. Schlager (1977) found that children's preferences among award-winning children's books had more to do with 'matching' between the themes of the books and the developmentally appropriate themes of middle childhood than with literary sophistication or level of textual difficulty.

Together, these findings suggest that the optimal conditions for 'bibliotherapy' would be when a reader (child or adult) already capable of ludic reading (many readers do not read in this deeply absorbed manner) encounters a text (fiction or non-fiction, pot-boiler or classic) which matches his or her personal criteria for 'a good read', and where the themes are in some way appropriate to his or her developmental stage and inner world.

But whereas the bibliotherapists have proposed a fairly crude model in which the reading therapist seeks for a literal correspondence between the content of the text and the reader's own 'problem' or life situation, it is far more likely that the 'merging' of reader and text will occur when the correspondence is partly or wholly metaphorical rather than literal.

Human addiction to 'story' is an aspect of our symbol-making nature: our very language is strongly metaphorical and our dreaming almost always uses the language of symbol and analogy. When we read a story that is obviously very similar in its characters and events to our own life experience, we may read it with enjoyment and appreciation, consciously appreciating the parallels; but if our life experience is painful, then we may reject such a story altogether.

Thus when offered a short text (Wild's *Beast* (1993)) featuring a protagonist with obsessive-compulsive symptoms, three early adolescent boys with similar symptoms read only a few pages, or failed to read the novel at all, although their reading skills were more than adequate for the task, because, as they said, the protagonists were too much like themselves. Daniels (1992), on the other hand, describes an orphaned Vietnamese adolescent living in Britain who was deeply affected by a novel about a porpoise who becomes separated from its mother and is cruelly treated by its human captors.

The emergence of ur-narrative so early in human life strongly suggests that story is indeed a 'natural' mode of self-expression and self-healing. But for a print text to 'plug into' the inner newsreel and temporarily replace it as an ongoing source of images, feelings and self-talk, exquisitely fine unconscious matching must occur, so that the reader 'recognises' something of high personal significance, while simultaneously failing to pin down its precise meaning. I maintain (Crago 1993) that such matching is akin to 'falling in love'. In both cases, an instinctive, largely unconscious recognition of similarity occurs, while consciously, the individuals concerned are aware only of a powerful emotional 'pull' and a sense of 'rightness' or 'fitness' in being with the other person (or text). Texts that are self-selected on such a basis are likely to be read and re-read with total absorption.

In this 'systemic' model of reader–text interaction, readers 'influence' books, rather than the other way around (Holland 1975) But when preferred texts are read again and again, or are brooded over in memory, they become, in turn, potent shaping influences over the reader's future self concept and life path. Key texts then become 'potentiating devices', eliciting from individuals the full development of what is already latent within them, but which might never flower otherwise. Needless to say, such potentiation can occur both for good and for ill. *Der Ring des Niebelungen* and *Also Sprache Zarathustra* may have 'potentiated' Hitler's grandiose and paranoid fantasies; Wagner and Nietzsche are not therefore responsible for the Holocaust or the Second World War.

Here the theory of literary response begins to converge with recent developments within the field of psychotherapy where, quite independently of the bibliotherapy movement, the 1980s brought a new consciousness of the power of 'therapeutic story-telling' as an intervention device. Probably originating in Jay Haley's (1973) lively account of the therapeutic 'wizardry' of Milton Erickson, the concept of therapeutic story-telling has been picked up and popularised. Cameron-Bandler (1978), Gordon (1978), and Mills and Crowley (1986) all emphasise the power of metaphor to 'slip past' the defences of the conscious mind.

Such practitioners have little acquaintance with literary history – otherwise they would surely have recognised that their 'therapeutic metaphor' amounts to little more than a re-tooling of the time-honoured genres of allegory and fable. However, what is new is their highly individualised focus. Stories, they maintain, must be constructed specifically to suit the emotional dynamics of individuals. Also worth noting is their insistence that 'the unconscious does not recognise negatives' ('whatever you do, please don't smoke' becomes 'smoke!'); thus stories attempting to be 'curative' through the language of symbol and metaphor must be positive in intent and in the specific propositions they employ.

Not to be confused with 'therapeutic metaphor' is the development of so-called 'narrative therapy' (Epston and White 1989). A variant of strategic psychotherapy, but employing Foucauldian notions about power, language and meaning, 'narrative therapy' invites clients to become aware of how they have been participants in the construction of a 'dominant story' of their own life (for example, 'my life is a total failure') and instead to consider alternative ways in which they might have constructed their stories. This encourages the noticing and valuing of instances when the person subverted or resisted the 'dominant story' – and the construction (for example) of an alternative self-narrative of success and heroic resistance.

## Whither Bibliotherapy?

The sobering truth about bibliotherapy is that such a form of healing is more likely to occur through the reader's own unconscious selection of texts that will 'speak' to her or him than through the planned recommendations of a professional mediator. This is not to say that bibliotherapy in its existing form cannot offer modest contributions. First, the reading of narratives that literally or symbolically parallel one's own condition can provide a language in which a child or adult may begin to talk about what has previously been inchoate. Thus the intense interest shown by many adolescent girls in accounts of anorexia, drug addiction and sexual abuse even when they themselves do not have such problems, suggests that these stories provide a way of articulating their own sense of alienation, aggression or low self esteem.

Second, the reading of books can provide the comfort of knowing that one is not alone, and thus function as a 'safer', more private version of a psychotherapy or self-help group. Third, reading can provide vicarious insight into one's problems, and even a measure of integration of previously disowned feelings. In the sense that it is entirely private, reading is thus far safer than seeking an interview with a therapist or counsellor; but on the other hand, it is far easier to put a book down than to walk out of a therapist's office at the mention of an uncomfortable truth. Fourth, reading can, at a metaphorical level, and sometimes even at a literal one, provide suggestions, akin to hypnotic suggestions, for ways of resolving the reader's problems – suggestions which may bypass conscious resistance on the sufferer's part.

On the other hand, reading by itself, like any other form of 'therapeutic' activity, from painting to gardening or sport, is not likely to embody the element of caring confrontation that seems fundamental to much successful psychotherapy. If the theory of emotional 'matching' is correct, then readers will nearly always reject a text that contains too painful a self-confrontation; and they will be drawn again and again to those narratives which will encourage them to construct their lives much as before, albeit, perhaps, in a more vivid, enriched way.

This leaves a heavy onus on the bibliotherapist to provide what the text itself cannot, and while a sensitive librarian may do as well as a professional therapist with a relatively 'easy' client, it is likely that clients (child or adult) with more deeply-rooted dysfunctions will prove far beyond even a well trained teacher or librarian's ability to help.

If bibliotherapy is to fulfil its promise, its practitioners must learn to diagnose their clients' patterns of preferred reading through careful observation and questioning over time. Personally significant texts, which are read again and again, are the most efficient indicators of those patterns. The professional could then recommend further texts which embody the same patterns, or seek to engage the client in discussion of one of his or her existing 'special books'. If bibliotherapy is understood as a way of affirming and extending an individual personality rather than as a way of 'curing' or 'changing' a person, then its chances of being useful will be far greater. In her Earthsea quartet, Ursula le Guin's Mages can call up a magical wind to fill their sails if required; but they cannot magically compel an existing wind to blow in the opposite direction.

## References

Becker, E. (1972) *The Birth and Death of Meaning*, 2nd edn, Harmondsworth: Penguin.

Bettelheim, B. (1976) *The Uses of Enchantment: The Meaning and Importance of Fairy Tales*, New York: Knopf.

Butler, D. (1979) *Cushla and Her Books*, London: Hodder and Stoughton.

Cameron-Bandler, L. (1978) *They Lived Happily Ever After: A Book About Achieving Happy Endings in Coupling*, Cupertino, CA: Meta Publications.

Clarke, J. and Postle, E. (eds) (1988) *Reading Therapy*, London: Clive Bingley.

Crago, H. (1979) 'Cultural categories and the criticism of children's literature', *Signal* 30: 140–150.

—— (1993) 'Why readers read what writers write', *Children's Literature in Education* 24, 4: 277–290

Crago, M. and Crago, H. (1983) *Prelude to Literacy: A Preschool Child's Encounter with Picture and Story*, Carbondale, IL: Southern Illinois University Press.

Daniels, J. (1992): 'Stories we tell ourselves: stories we tell others', in Styles, M., Bearne, E. and Watson, V. (eds) *Exploring Children's Literature*, London: Cassell.

Epston, D. and White, M. (1989) *Literate Means to Therapeutic Ends*, Adelaide: Dulwich Centre Publications.

Fader, D. and McNeil, E. (1969) *Hooked on Books*, London: Pergamon.

Gordon, T. (1978) *Therapeutic Metaphors: Helping Others Through the Looking Glass*, Cupertino, CA: Meta Publications.

Haley, J. (1973) *Uncommon Therapy: The Psychiatric Techniques of Milton H. Erickson, MD*, New York: Norton.

Hatt, F. (1976) *The Reading Process: A Framework for Analysis and Description*, London: Bingley.

Holland, N. (1975) *Five Readers Reading*, New Haven: Yale University Press.

Jaynes, J. (1976) *The Origin of Consciousness in the Breakdown of the Bicameral Mind*, Boston: Houghton Mifflin.

Klinger, E. (1971) *The Structure and Function of Fantasy*, New York: Wiley-Interscience.

Manning, D. and Casbergue, R. (1988) 'Bibliotherapy for children in stepfamilies', *Clearing House* 62, 3: 124–127.

Mills, J. and Crowley, R. in collaboration with Ryan, M. (1986) *Therapeutic Metaphors for Children and the Child Within*, New York: Brunner-Mazel.

Nell, V. (1988) *Lost in a Book: The Psychology of Reading for Pleasure*, New Haven: Yale University Press.

Pantanizopoulos, J. (1989) 'I'll be happy when I'm thin enough': the treatment of anorexia nervosa in adolescent fiction', *ALAN* 17, 1: 9–10.

Pardeck, J. and Pardeck, J. (1984) *Young People With Problems: A Guide to Bibliotherapy*, New York: Greenwood Press.

Segel, E. (1989) 'Collaborations: putting children's literature to work for children at risk', in Gannon, S., Thompson, S. and Thompson, R. (eds), *When Rivers Meet: Selected Papers from the 1989 International Conference of the Children's Literature Association*, West Lafayette, IN: Children's Literature Association.

Schlager, N. (1977) 'Predicting children's choices in literature: a developmental approach', *Children's Literature in Education* 9, 3: 136–142.

Simsova, S. (ed.) (1968) *Nicholas Rubakin and Bibliopsychology*, Hamden, CT: Archon/ London: Bingley.

Steedman, C. (1982) *The Tidy House: Little Girls Writing*, London, Virago.

Stone, L. (1977) *The Family, Sex and Marriage in England, 1500–1800*, London: Weidenfeld and Nicholson.

Sutton-Smith, B. *et al.* (1981) *The Folkstories of Children*, Philadelphia: University of Pennsylvania Press.

Tabbert, R. 'The impact of children's books: cases and concepts', *Children's Literature in Education* 10, 2: 92–102.

Wilber, K. (1986) *Up From Eden: A Transpersonal View of Human Evolution*, Boston: Shambhala.

## Further Reading

Appleyard, J. (1990) *Becoming a Reader: The Experience of Fiction from Childhood to Adulthood*, Cambridge: Cambridge University Press.

Crago, H. (1985) 'The place of story in affective development: implications for educators and clinicians', in Curry, N. (ed.) *The Feeling Child*, New York: Haworth.

Holland, N. (1975) *Five Readers Reading*. New Haven: Yale University Press.

Lesnik-Oberstein, K. (1994), *Children's Literature: Criticism and the Fictional Child*, Oxford: Oxford University Press.

# 55

# Publishing for Special Needs

## Beverley Mathias

There has long been an awareness of the need for specialised reading materials for children who have difficulty in learning to read and then maintaining a reasonable reading ability. Some attempts, successful and unsuccessful, have been made to produce series and individual titles which would appeal to these children: one of the difficulties has always been their wide-ranging ages, abilities and interests.

What was not addressed until recently was the fact that for some children print is not the means by which they will be able to enjoy reading, and for others, reading is complicated by some intellectual, sensory or physical problem. Some children find it extremely difficult or even impossible to use print at all, and therefore no matter how many series are made available, some of these children will never aspire to be 'readers' in the commonly accepted sense.

When the National Library for the Handicapped Child (NLHC) was established in Britain in 1985, one of the problems addressed was the lack of understanding of the reading needs of the child who has special needs in other areas. It is in the areas of reading for children with hearing and visual loss, emotionally and behaviourally disturbed children, children with intellectual handicaps, children with physical difficulties, and children who simply fail to learn to read that the major advances have been made since then.

To understand these needs it is important to first understand some of the difficulties which the child must overcome. All parents and educationalists know that children find it easier to learn to read when offered material which is interesting, stimulating and arouses enough curiosity in the child for that child to *want* to read (Bennett 1991). In addition, children will have difficulty learning to read unless they have enough internalised language to have an understanding of the meaning and use of communication and language. Similarly, to read a child must be able to communicate with reasonable fluency with those around her and understand the language in which she is being taught. It is accepted that children learn language by watching and listening then imitating sound, and by learning that communicating can result in an approving response. However, this is not so with all children. Approximately 37 per cent of infant and junior school aged children will at some time have a reading or language difficulty serious enough to need supporting help. These children include those who have a learning problem related to reading, a sight or hearing difficulty, or who use a language other than speech for communicating. They may not be print users and will therefore need some other form of access to the printed word. It is these areas of book use and publishing development that this article addresses.

## Dual Language Signed and Written Text

Until the early 1980s most deaf children were taught using the oral method, which meant signed language was not used in the classroom. As the majority of deaf children learn language through observation not hearing, this meant that for many, their language was severely underdeveloped even at the time they reached school-leaving age. Often they left school with only functional reading and writing skills. A major change in thinking and philosophy in the mid-1980s resulted in the introduction of 'total communication' – the use of spoken and signed language, lip reading, writing, body movement, gesture – in combinations suited to the child and the moment. With the introduction of signed language (the fourth largest indigenous language group in the UK), these children were given a means of communicating on a level with their peers. It meant that language could develop through sign as naturally as speech. Despite some comments to the contrary, the use of signed language did not inhibit the development of speech, in fact in some cases, speech was enhanced. In Australia a language programme based on picture books has been developed expressly for deaf children (NSW 1990).

As a result of the introduction of 'total communication' many of these children were beginning to communicate fluently at around the same time as hearing children, and a need developed for the provision of materials which showed signed language in printed form. To this end, the National Deaf Children's Society, the Royal National Institute for the Deaf, the NLHC and one or two publishers began looking at the problem. The result was a series of five alphabet books by Beverley Mathias and Ruth Thomson in 'Sign supported English', such as *A to Z Food* (1988), each based on a particular area of understanding, and three picture books about two well-known children's book characters, Eric Hill's Spot and John Cunliffe's Postman Pat. Since then there have been other successful publications which incorporate signed language. This opened up signed language to hearing children, to the parents of deaf children and to the deaf children themselves, who for the first time, saw their preferred means of communication written in a book. Publishing in such a specialised area is a commercial risk, and deaf children in Britain are not as fortunate as their counterparts in the USA. Through the publishing company of Gallaudet University, Washington DC, which teaches through the medium of signed language, American children have an ever increasing range of picture books available in dual signed and written English. This level of publishing for deaf children is not available in Britain. Other countries have also experimented with dual signed and written texts, but in small quantities and low numbers of individual titles – examples are the work of Lothian Publishing, Port Melbourne, Australia; and Aschehough in Oslo. As the reading fluency of children using signed language has increased, so has their ability to read print, so that today the dual-language books are used not only by deaf children learning to read, but also by mainstream schools for support during the teaching of the communication units within the British National Curriculum. An ever-increasing number of deaf children are now reading print at or around the same level as hearing children of the same chronological and educational levels.

## Braille and ClearVision Books for Children

Children with visual impairment have always been provided with some materials, particularly if they are braille users, but have suffered from the theory that if they are blind, the school will provide. Children using braille first learnt the alphabet, then the various contractions, usually mastering level one before being introduced to independent reading of braille in story form. Schools provided some fiction in braille, but it was often books for older children and very rarely books which would interest and enthuse a newly independent reader aged between 7 and 10. The Royal National Institute for the Blind tried to maintain a reasonable service, but brailling is time-consuming and until recently, not automated to a great degree.

In order to try and increase the fluency of readers, and to lower the age at which blind children became independent readers, some schools, together with the Royal National Institute for the Blind, introduced a process which placed braille on the same page as print in trade produced books. To begin with a self-adhesive strip was brailled then stripped into existing trade publications. While this was helpful to the child who could already read braille, and it allowed sharing between blind and sighted readers, it did not overcome the difficulties of the child learning to read through the medium of braille. At Linden Lodge School in London a further development took place which has changed the way in which blind children learn to read. Following on from developments in Australia, Canada and America, staff at Linden Lodge began to experiment with brailling sheets of clear plastic which could be inserted into trade books. In other countries this method was already in use, but the braille was placed on special paper, not plastic – a method which made the book bulky, broke up a double page spread and made reading tedious and frustrating. By using clear plastic, the page was not disfigured in any way and both sighted and blind readers could share the same book. This project became 'ClearVision' which now supplies brailled picture books and non-fiction to a growing number of schools, libraries and individuals. By giving blind children access to trade picture books through ClearVision braille, they now learn to read using the same books as sighted children. This has increased the demand for more books for younger fluent braille readers and in turn created a subscription market for the brailling of early independent reading titles. In addition the development of microelectronic reading aids such as the Kurzweil Reading Machine has opened up a new world of literature to blind children.

## Large Print for Children

Until the mid-1980s there was virtually no large print available for children with visual difficulties. If they had sufficient sight to learn to read print, by the time they were reading with some degree of fluency, the children found that the books they wanted to read were printed in too small or dense typefaces and narrow margins. This was because publishers in their wisdom reduced the size of type in fiction for fluent readers in the mistaken belief than once a child can read, the size of print becomes immaterial. One exception to this has been the London publisher Cape, who have published many of Roald Dahl's titles in a large clear type face, with plenty of vertical and horizontal spacing therefore making the books much easier to read.

With the decision of two companies, Chivers and Isis, to introduce new series of children's books in large print, suddenly the range of reading available mushroomed. The peak came late in the 1980s during Children's Book Week, when *The Bookseller* listings for that week showed that the number of new titles published for children in large print, was greater than the number of new titles published for children in 'normal' print. Unfortunately this bonanza for children has been halved as Isis, having published themselves, and brought in from American a great number of outstanding children's titles, was forced by economics to retire from the field. This marvellous increase in the quality and quantity of large print for children from just two companies also had an effect on the stocks of public and school libraries. The use of these books is not limited to children with visual difficulties. The books are attractive, include illustrations where appropriate and are the same titles as 'everyone else' is reading. Libraries discovered that by interfiling large print into their fiction collections it was selected by a wider range of children, some of whom had not previously had the patience or the skills needed to cope smaller print sizes.

## Picture Books

The area of reading need which has traditionally caused the most concern is that of post-primary aged children who have failed to become fluent readers. Although one or two companies are producing specially designed and written series which are geared towards assisting these children to recover and increase their reading ability, the material varies greatly in format and content, and does not always appeal to the very children who need it. In 1981 with the publication of Elaine Moss's *Picture Books for Young People 9–13* came the realisation that this development in publishing offered an opportunity for older children to learn to read using books which were of interest to them, stimulating, approachable and within their language ability. These books offer a text which is comparatively easy to manage because of the format, and also help the older learner to develop good visual discrimination and scanning skills. It is important that these children should have the opportunity to read books which are thought-provoking. Humour in its various forms is also a valuable asset to these older children, particularly anarchic humour and black comedy. Public and school libraries are now beginning to see the very real difference between the two forms of picture story presentation and are shelving them according to interest level rather than format.

A further development which has considerably assisted children with reading difficulties has been the introduction into Britain of large-format picture books. These vary in size, but most are approximately 30 × 20 inches and are soft bound. They have been in use in Australia and New Zealand for some years, in Canada and the USA for a shorter period. Many trade titles are now available in this format, making reading easier for children with visual difficulties, children who have poor fine motor skills, and enabling signed story-telling with visual backup. An

increasing number are trade picture books which are photographically enlarged
and reset with large type face and these allow children who have visual difficulties
to read the same book as their peer group without the need for mechanical or
microelectronic assistance.

## Tactile Books

Probably the best known format is the pop-up or movable book, of which a vast
number have been published. Attempts have been made by some publishers to add
a third dimension to the printed page by giving a tactile surface to illustrations, not
always successfully. A partially tactile illustration can be more misleading than no
tactile surface at all. One of the more successful and also most expensive was Eric
Carle's *The Very Busy Spider* (1985) which has a tactile web. Cloth books have a
long history, but until recently these tended to be for babies, and were sometimes
not particularly well presented. The quality has been improved by the introduction
of stitched-in sheets of foam to bulk out the book and slightly stiffen the pages, and
other titles include pockets containing removable dolls. Bath books are another
innovation: made of plastic and usually highly coloured, they have the advantage of
being waterproof and washable. A newer addition which incorporates the
ubiquitous micro chip has been books with sounds. These range from books of
children's songs together with a keyboard, through those which operate on
opening and play a tune, to a more sophisticated development which allows the
child to interact with the story by pressing the appropriate illustration to produce
noise as a part of the story itself. On the whole, the noises produced are realistic
and can help a child who needs assistance with sound discrimination. Children
with poor fine motor control, severely handicapped children and those for whom a
multi-tactile approach is important, have found all of these forms of printed book
invaluable.

## Images of Children

It is difficult to pinpoint any dramatic change in the way children with difficulties
have been shown as book characters. Non-fiction, in particular series which look at
children with specific physical or sensory problems, is often the beginning of
change. While in fiction, the positive images of minority ethnic and cultural
groups of children and the mix of children within school classes also has
increasingly been realistically shown, the inclusion of children with visible
difficulties must be done with understanding and knowledge of the reality of
school life. American writers and publishers (for example, Albert Whitman) have
led the way: Marc Brown's Arthur series, beginning with *Arthur's Nose* in 1976 –
has always included children who have special needs; among them have been a
child in a wheelchair, a child wearing hearing aids, children wearing glasses;
Lorraine Henriod's *Grandma's Wheelchair* (1982) presents a child's view of a loved
grandparent who is still a companion and friend despite the wheelchair. When
Wendy Lohse's *Something Else* (1990) was first published there was a certain
amount of unease, as the main character is a child born without legs. The image
she presents is of a determined child who wants to attend school and make her own

way despite the typically short-sighted comments of some of her school mates. Books illustrated by Caroline Birch have presented Afro-Caribbean children with two wonderful role models: *Amazing Grace* by Mary Hoffman (1991) and *Hue Boy* by Rita Phillips Mitchell (1992). Among other areas which are now being more satisfactorily covered in children's fiction are the difficulties of teaching children about street safety and stranger danger, understanding intellectual handicap, children with learning difficulties, physical disability, loss of sight or hearing, death, AIDS, differences in home and family life, terminal and life threatening illness. My collection of specially commissioned short stories *The Spell Singer and other Stories* (1991) presents positive images of a wide range of children for whom learning and even living is a daily battle.

## Non-Print Books

Reading with eyes, ears, hands and fingers is a concept which is comparatively new to parents and some teachers. For some years provision has been made for blind people to listen to taped books, but this often required the use of special equipment which was not portable. Therefore listening to, or reading a book was limited to a specific geographic space, which meant that, unlike the printed word, the sound book was not fully portable. The developments in small personal tape and disc players, and the market demands for books on sound tape, has now reached most corners of the world and for a child who is blind this is one of the few ways of enjoying the printed word. Sound is also a more accessible form of reading for children with severe print reading difficulties and for those who cannot physically handle a printed book. The companies producing large print now offer boxed sound editions of a number of titles either as an alternative, or as an adjunct to large print editions.

As videotape recorders have proliferated in home and school life, another form of 'reading' has become accessible to children who cannot manage print and also to those who find reading print a long and laborious task. In addition, many commercial videos now carry a small symbol which indicates that they have been subtitled by the National Captioning Institute, and with the use of a decoder, deaf children can watch or read a book on film. The development of computer disk interactive (CDI) and CD-ROM is still in its infancy, but there is potential for the presentation of literature in a way which will assist children with reading difficulties: some books are available in print, braille, signed language, audio tape and video tape.

The NLHC, which is located in Britain, provides a resource centre and information service to anyone with a problem relating to children who have difficulty with reading.

While all of these developments are exciting they are also frustrating. Each new area opens up more need, every child helped leads to another who needs assistance. There is unfortunately a long lead time between the development of a new initiative and the take up by schools, libraries and the general public. That lead time can be the breaking point between the commercial release of some worthwhile and needed materials and the burial of the same idea. In the late 1980s some experimentation was done by the Royal College of Art on the use of holograms in the presentation of signed language in the hope that it would be commercially viable. Unfortunately the cost of research and the needs of the market did not coincide and although a good idea, it was not developed for commercial publishing. The production of braille in commercially viable quantities within standard trade editions of picture books is a technical problem which so far has not been solved. Using signed language in printed books is viable in the USA, but in Britain the demand is not yet great enough for companies to be interested in pursuing the market.

The need is still there, and will remain until all children leaving school are reading to their full potential, regardless of the medium used. Probably the most important developments over the past decade have been the recognition of the need for good quality reading for children with special needs regardless of their ability, the timely reminder that there is a book for every child at every stage of reading development, and the realisation that print is not the only way of presenting literature to children.

Note: At the time of writing, the NLHC was about to undergo a name change to REACH: National Resource Centre for Children with Reading Difficulties, but no date had been set for the change.

## References

Bennett, J. (1991) *Learning to Read with Picture Books*, South Woodchester: Thimble Press.
Moss, E. (1981) *Picture Books for Young People 9–13*, South Woodchester: Thimble Press.
NSW Department of School Education (1990) *Hands Up for A Story! A Literature Program for Young Hearing Impaired Children*, Sydney: State of New South Wales.

## Further Reading

Butler, D. (1979) *Cushla and her Books*, London: Penguin.
Chambers, A. (1991) *The Reading Environment*, South Woodchester: Thimble Press.
Mathias, B. and Spiers, D. (1982) *A Handbook on Death and Bereavement: Helping Children to Understand*, Wokingham: National Library for the Handicapped Child.
—— (1993) *'My Tummy has a Headache': Helping Children Understand Illness*, Wokingham: National Library for the Handicapped Child.
Waterland, L. (1988) *Read With Me: An Apprenticeship Approach to Reading*, South Woodchester: Thimble Press.

## Useful Addresses

ClearVision, Linden Lodge School, Princes Way, Wandsworth, London SW18.
National Captioning Institute, Thurston House, 80 Lincoln Road, Peterborough PE1 2SN.

# Part V

The World of Children's
Literature

# The World of Children's Literature: An Introduction

## *Sheila Ray*

In the world of children's books, there are certain factors which are common to all literatures. The need for stories is universal, and there can be few children, even in the most deprived circumstances, who do not have the opportunity from a very early age, to listen to people telling them stories. In some countries and in many ethnic groups, the custom of oral story-telling continues into adulthood and, even in the most developed countries, as late as the nineteenth and early twentieth centuries it was possible for many people to learn all they needed to know by listening to others.

Worldwide, at the end of the twentieth century, there is a belief that literacy is essential. Even in those societies where information technology is advanced, good reading skills are essential to exploit it, and it is generally thought that the best way to acquire fluency is through reading practice; children's books are thus a practical necessity.

The development of children's literature everywhere has followed a similar pattern, although in individual countries the stages in this development have come at different times in the last five hundred years. In the early stages of a printed literature, there are few or no books published specifically for children. There are perhaps a few books intended for broadly educational purposes, such as the courtesy or behaviour books printed in the fifteenth or sixteenth centuries in European countries, or the twentieth-century textbooks published to support the formal school curriculum in developing countries. In this situation children, as they learn to read, also take over adult books which appeal to them, a process helped by the fact that the early printed literature in any society is likely to draw on traditional stories which contain elements which appeal to every age group. Religion is also an important factor in the development of printed literature and many of the earliest books intended specifically for children are simplified versions of religious books or publications designed to support religious and moral instruction. As European influences spread to other parts of the world many of the books taken there by missionaries and teachers were of a religious nature.

Poetry and verse, ballads and nursery rhymes or their equivalent, also manifest themselves at an early stage in the development of a printed literature for children, but gradually stories written specially for children begin to appear. As the number of titles being published increases, demands for books to meet a variety of interests and special needs emerge. One of the problems which face developing countries in the twentieth century is that they are expected to go through all the stages in a relatively short space of time – thirty or forty years at most – whereas European countries have taken five hundred years over the same process. At the same time, modern technology has provided different ways of meeting the universal need for story. Should these societies, which have little tradition of a written literature, move straight to the use of audio and video tapes to record stories told since the beginning of time and to create new ones?

The development of children's literature is linked to social, educational and, above all, economic factors. Around the world, conditions in which children's books flourish or otherwise range widely. In some western countries children's book production is so high in terms of the number of titles published each year that it suffers from success; books are taken for granted, and concerns about quality and standards are expressed by a relatively small group of teachers, librarians, parents and critics, often dissipating their efforts through a large number of different organisations. At the other end of the scale there are poor countries ravaged by war and famine where strivings for a printed children's literature must seem to be very low on the national agenda. In between there are countries where there is official involvement, where there are one or two supportive central organisations and where there is a steady rise both in the number of children's books published annually and in their quality.

Every country has its own collection of traditional stories. Myths developed as a way of explaining natural phenomena such as the creation of the earth, the changing seasons, day and night, and floods and drought. Hero legends grew up around charismatic characters, who frequently acquired supernatural powers as time passed. Fables were a way of fleshing out useful advice and everyday truths. Folk- and fairy tales provided psychological satisfaction through their simplified system of reward and punishment, or as a way of working out relationships and fears in safety. These traditional tales reflect such basic truths that the same stories crop up all over the world, the details adapted to local circumstances. Such stories transplant easily and at the end of the twentieth century, many children are acquainted with the traditional stories of countries and ethnic groups other than their own. The popularity of this kind of story led, as children's literature developed in the nineteenth century, to the writing of modern fantasy stories.

Traditional stories, although they began as, and in many places still are, entertainment for the whole community, have in recent times come to be regarded as being something for children alone. In countries where literacy is at an early stage of development or where other imaginative literature may be suspect (as has been the case in totalitarian countries), traditional tales in printed form are an easy way of providing already familiar and uncontroversial stories for reading.

Although most European countries can claim one or two isolated examples of books published specifically for children in the sixteenth century, children's literature began to flourish generally in the nineteenth century at a time when population was growing rapidly, when educational opportunities were increasing and when technological developments made both paper and the printing process available at a reasonable price. This was also the period when land elsewhere, including many of today's less developed and poorer countries, was being settled and exploited by European nations and into which European teachers and missionaries were importing books from their country of origin. The results of these influences can still be seen at the end of the twentieth century.

During the five hundred years that have passed since the invention of printing by movable type in fifteenth-century Germany, children's literature has developed in much the same way and at much the same speed in most European countries. The influence of individuals, developments due to social and economic factors, and technological progress have all been shared experiences. Most countries can claim examples of books for children from a period soon after the invention of printing, the widespread use of traditional tales for books intended to entertain, the advent of literary magazines as a cheap and effective way of getting reading material into the hands of as many children as possible, the existence of a creative and imaginative literature by the mid to late nineteenth century and a flowering in the years after the Second World War. Thus the influence of Locke and Rousseau, and later the ideas of the Romantics fed through to children's books in many European countries; during the nineteenth century there was a general move throughout Europe towards universal education, and the size of the middle class increased; both helped to create a reading public with a viable market for children's books; while towards the end of the century, technical advances made the production of full-colour picture books possible, at an economic price.

Until the end of the nineteenth century, Europeans were divided almost as much by class as by nationality. Despite constant wars and the resulting changes in national boundaries, royalty, the aristocracy and the growing middle classes moved around comparatively easily, familiar with the major languages and receptive to new ideas. In this environment, children's books were translated and transferred from country to country with amazing ease.

The recognised father of the children's picture book is John Amos Comenius, born in Bohemia, now part of the Czech Republic. His book, *Orbis Sensualium Pictus*, published in Nuremburg in 1658, with a Latin and High German text, was rapidly taken up by other countries. It reached England only a year after its first publication, the High German text translated into English. The French fairy tales written down by Charles Perrault and published in Paris in 1697 were soon translated and published in most other European countries: in England, they appeared in 1729. The German folk-tales collected by the Brothers Grimm and published in German in 1812–1814 were translated into English and published as *German Popular Stories* in 1823. Meanwhile, literary works such as *Robinson Crusoe* and *Gulliver's Travels* swept across Europe in translations from the English. The close links of many European countries with the United States meant that American influences fed back from there. For example, Harriet Beecher Stowe's *Uncle Tom's Cabin* (1852) and Louisa M. Alcott's *Little Women* (1868) were quickly imported into many European countries.

In the twentieth century, children's literature in Europe has been more seriously affected by politics and by war. The First World War probably affected it little, but the period of dictatorships in Germany, Italy, Spain and Portugal certainly had a significant influence on the content of the children's books in those countries, as did the 1917 Revolution in the USSR. The Second World War had repercussions at the time on the production of children's books because of paper shortages, the absence on war service of publishing personnel, and the bombing of publishing houses and warehouses. It served as a watershed in children's literature; many children's books which had been steadily reprinting for years finally disappeared at this time.

Later, the war influenced the content of children's books, particularly from the 1960s onwards when writers who had themselves been children during the war began to produce stories based on their own childhood experiences. Authors wrote from different viewpoints; some had been refugees, some had been evacuated to safe areas, some had lived under occupation and some had experienced at close quarters the treatment of the Jewish population. Anne Frank's *Diary*, published in The Netherlands in 1947, with its account of day-to-day life hiding from the Nazis during the occupation, has captured the imagination of young people worldwide.

From 1945 until the late 1980s, the countries of Eastern Europe shared similar views about children's books, which were particularly subject to political pressure. However, nations which have re-emerged in the last ten years such as Bosnia, Croatia, the Ukraine and Latvia can trace an independent children's literature; the Czechs and Slovaks had always maintained their own literature and so the break up of Czechoslovakia into its two constituent parts after the 'velvet' revolution of 1989 made little difference.

A few European nations share the same language. In Great Britain and Ireland the common language is English; writers have moved easily between Ireland, England, Scotland and Wales, having their books published in London or in Glasgow or Edinburgh, whatever their roots. C. S. Lewis whose Chronicles of Narnia seem to be archetypal English fantasy was born in Northern Ireland; J. M. Barrie, whose Peter Pan seems another very English fantasy figure, was very much a Scot. Similarly, Germany, Austria and much of Switzerland share a common language and books and authors move freely from one to another.

In many European countries minority languages were actively suppressed until comparatively recently but, partly because of the existence of traditional stories, have been kept alive and are now being encouraged and supported. Trans-border alliances are being forged, for example among the Celtic languages and the Nordic languages. In 1982 the European Bureau for Lesser Used Languages, financed by the European Commission, was set up, with an office in Dublin, Eire, a Children's Publishing Secretariat, currently in Brittany, and an information centre in Brussels. This seeks to conserve and promote the lesser-used indigenous languages of the European Union, such as Welsh, Gaelic, Breton, Basque, Ladin, Occitan, Sorbian, Frisian and Cornish. The spread of democracy in the last quarter of the twentieth century has helped: for example, Catalan was recognised as an official language after Spain became a democracy in 1978 and with the founding of the Catalan Biblioteca de Catalunya in Barcelona in 1987, came the Catalan Institute of Children's Literature.

The market for children's books in some of the lesser-used languages is very limited and precludes the printing of any title in large quantities, and hence at low prices. In 1968 an easy reader, *Gaelg trooid Jallooghyn* by Brian Macstoyll, showing a brother and sister engaged in a variety of activities, was published in Manx and the famous fictional dog, Spot, the creation of Eric Hill, has made his contribution by appearing in a Cornish language version. Children's books in Manx and Cornish are rare but those in Welsh, Gaelic and Catalan have gone from strength to strength.

European children share a common literary heritage – the Moomintrolls (Finland), Heidi (Switzerland), Struwwelpeter (Germany), Babar (France), Pippi Longstocking (Sweden) and Alice (England) are all characters known to many children in different countries. From Hans Christian Andersen onwards, there are authors who are universally recognised and loved. Indeed, children's literature has always had an international dimension: certain themes and plots enjoy international popularity. The earliest datable Cinderella story appears in a book written in China in the ninth century; the 'desert island' motif, famously used by Daniel Defoe in *Robinson Crusoe* (1719), was quickly embraced by children, and Defoe's book spawned so many imitations that 'Robinsonade' became a recognised term in European literature: in the twentieth century there have been countless variants for children from Scott O'Dell's. *Island of the Blue Dolphins* (USA, 1960), to Ivan Southall's *To the Wild Sky* (Australia, 1967) and Monique Peyrouton de Ladebat's survival novel *The Village that Slept* (France, 1963).

Children in the English-speaking world also share a common literary heritage. The USA and English-speaking Canada, Australia and New Zealand all exchange books happily with each other and with Britain, and have done so since each began to produce their own children's books. The work of Louisa M. Alcott, L. M. Montgomery, Ivan Southall and Margaret Mahy may all be as familiar to British children as that of Lewis Carroll and Robert Louis Stevenson. Since the 1960s West Indian writers such as John Asgard and James Berry have become part of the British children's literature scene. In India, English-speaking Africa and elsewhere, English is a common language in which it is often more economic to publish than in the wide range of local, indigenous languages. In the period between 1950 and the late 1980s both the USSR and China recognised the international standing of English in the world of children's books and produced quantities of English language books which were exported and sold cheaply. In India, for example, in the early 1980s, English language picture books originating in Russia were more readily accessible in many places than the excellent books published by the Children's Book Trust in Delhi, because the cost of production was subsidised.

While countries with small local production may turn to translation, in the USA and Britain there are so many books available that there is little incentive for publishers to pay for translations. Although in the 1960s a number of British publishers made a point of publishing translations of prize-winning books from other European countries, relatively few were widely bought even by libraries, in the belief that children are easily deterred by foreign names, footnotes and explanations. Nevertheless many children's books, as we have seen, have appeal which crosses national boundaries; it is sad, therefore, that the number of translated titles may fall as authors are able to meet the needs of their own countries. Even worse is the feeling in some quarters that in the 1990s children everywhere read far less imaginative literature than they once did.

Spain and Portugal have influenced those countries settled by their adventurers in previous centuries, and export children's books to Central and South America. A strong Portuguese influence can also be seen in Angola. Similarly, children's books produced in France enrich the range available in French-speaking Canada and Africa.

Many of the countries along the north coast of Africa are, as far as children's literature is concerned, linked to the Arab world. Elsewhere in Africa, countries share the common problems of post-colonialism – continuing links with European countries, poverty, low literacy levels, conflict between cultural groups and problems of production and distribution which make it difficult to produce good quality children's books suited to local needs. While English, French or Portuguese may be the language of business, hundreds of local languages and dialects at once preserve the oral tradition and exacerbate the difficulties of producing printed text. The English-speaking colonies were generally left with a basic network of public libraries, much of which has been maintained. Before independence, major British publishers were involved in producing educational texts for local needs, and in Nigeria and Ghana, for example, texts by local writers were being produced as early as the 1920s (Segun 1992: 26–27). Equally, some benefits came in the 1960s from the interest of British publishers in producing stories which reflected life in the newly independent African nations, partly to meet the needs of immigrants into Britain.

There were different attitudes in French-speaking Africa: there was not the same network of public libraries, and there seems to have been much less effort to provide books relevant to African children. A Peace Corps volunteer working in Senegal in the 1970s commented on the lack of motivation amongst Senegalese children when faced with French texts about rosy-cheeked, blond French children (Melching 1981: 7).

Of the Portuguese-speaking countries, Angola, which became independent in 1975, seems to be the most advanced in terms of children's literature. A National Institute for Books and records was set up in 1977 and after 1980 attention began to focus on children's books. The need to encourage the local languages is recognised, and workshops have been organised to encourage Angolan writers to write for children. As early as 1980, a book in Portuguese, *As Aventuras de Ngunga* (1980) by Pepetela – a story about a young Angolan orphan boy, who goes to live in a guerrilla camp and becomes involved in the fight against Portuguese colonialism – was imported from Brazil. *Sagrada Esperanca* [Sacred Hope], a book of poetry by Agostinho Neto, is known to every Angolan child.

In Africa, as elsewhere, magazines for children have played a part in providing attractive reading material at a reasonable price. In the 1970s, the Centre d'Etude des Civilisations in Senegal launched a magazine, *Demb ak Tey* [Yesterday and Today] to promote the traditions of black Africa and to provide poems and stories related to the lives and interests of African children for as wide a public as possible. *Rainbow* was started in Kenya in 1976 with similar aims – to publish non-imperialistic English language reading material for children; locally produced material has gradually replaced imported writing. *Ngouvou* [Hippopotamus], founded in 1988, is both educational and entertaining – but the only such magazine published in the Congo.

Great encouragement has been given to African publishers by the Noma Award, founded in 1979 by the late Shoichi Noma of Kodansha Limited, a Japanese publishing firm. Despite many problems, an indigenous African children's literature is developing slowly but surely.

Children's picture books are particularly subject to economic pressures. The costs of originating full-colour illustrations are high and need to be spread over as many copies as possible. Even those countries with high book sales find it advantageous to produce co-editions, where publishers in a number of countries agree to publish a book simultaneously. The addition of the text in the appropriate language constitutes a very small part of the total production costs. The USA, Britain, Germany, Japan and the Scandinavian countries are predominant in this market but the practice of co-editions is appropriate everywhere and can be particularly beneficial for countries which share the same social and cultural patterns. One such scheme operates in Southeast Asia under the auspices of the Asian Cultural Centre for UNESCO (ACCU).

Perhaps the ultimate in international children's literature production is represented by *All in a Day* (1986), devised by Mitsumasa Anno, the Japanese author-illustrator. Published in International Peace Year, the book shows how, although we live on the same planet (and share the same sun and moon), climate, customs and language differ from one country to another. With eight double-page spreads, each of which takes the reader through a complete day in the life of a different child and its family, the book is about the concept of time. Anno himself illustrated an imaginary uninhabited island in the South Pacific, situated on the International Date Line. Prize-winning illustrators, Raymond Briggs (Britain), Leo and Diana Dillon (East Africa), Akiko Hayashi (Japan), Ron Brooks (Australia), Gian Calvi (Brazil), Eric Carle (USA) , Zhu Chenglian (China) and Nikolai Popov (USSR) all contributed to this book. The complexities of producing an international children's book, however, mean that such a publication is likely to be rare (Hickman 1987: 5–6). Co-production may also lead to a dilution of both text and illustrations to meet the needs of an international market. For example, Pat Hutchins's *The Wind Blew* (1974) shows a national flag that appears to be a cross between the British Union flag and the American Stars and Stripes, and an important building which is a combination of Buckingham Palace and the White House.

The other kind of children's book in which coloured illustrations are essential is the non-fiction or information book. Until comparatively recently such books have been significantly outnumbered by fiction but lavishly illustrated non-fiction is a recent specialisation in international publishing, although the subject must, of course, be of equal interest and relevance to all the participating countries. This form of publishing is known as 'packaging'. A packager buys in the services of illustrators and writers and is responsible for producing a master copy which is then sold to publishers in as many countries as possible. The illustrations are identical in all editions, and as in the case of picture story books the text may be translated or adapted as appropriate. Such economies in production can only be achieved in those books which contain a significant number of full-colour illustrations.

Even in comparatively rich countries, there are problems in providing children's books in minority languages. In developing countries there may be a conflict between the language of general use and the indigenous community languages or mother tongues. It is generally recognised that children acquire literacy skills most readily if they first become fluent readers in the language spoken in the home. How can this be achieved? A handful of books is not the answer; all children need to be able to choose from a wide range of titles, and children's books must compete on a level playing-field. Poorly produced books on shoddy paper, with little or no colour, unsophisticated illustrations and turgid, if well-meaning, texts are unlikely to be favoured in preference to glossily produced, well-illustrated and well-written books. Text in the appropriate language does not compensate for an unattractive appearance: Children are not motivated to support worthiness. It is only in the last twenty years or so that Welsh-language children's books have been able to compete fairly, in terms of both quantity and quality, with English-language books. How much more difficult is the problem for countries in the less developed parts of the world.

Belief in the value of, and need for, children's books has led to the setting up of children's book publishing programmes in the most remote and undeveloped parts of the world. These include workshops for potential authors and illustrators, subsidies for publishers and support for distribution methods which get books to children. This happens even in countries where the casual observer might suppose that there are more important basic needs such as food, water, health and peace to be met first.

Because of the book activities of various international organisations, certain trends in children's books are to be found worldwide. From the 1960s onwards, there has been general concern about racism, sexism and even ageism in children's books. There has been a wish to cater for children with special needs, whether these are due to outstanding gifts, learning difficulties or physical handicap. Ideas have been shared about provision for children of ethnic minorities or whose first language is a minority language in the country where the child lives. There has been international interest in the production of dual-language picture books, where the text appears in the main language of the country alongside a minority language. In Australia, for example, there was pressure from librarians and teachers in the late 1970s and early 1980s for books to meet the needs of young 'new' Australians. However, books produced specifically to meet special needs must be well supported by parents, teachers and librarians if their publication is to be commercially viable.

Many of these ideas have been promoted through the conferences and publications of the International Board on Books for Young People (IBBY), particularly through its quarterly journal, *Bookbird*. The publications and activities of the International Youth Library in Munich (such as its regularly issued booklist, The White Ravens), whose foundation by Jella Lepman predated her establishment of IBBY, are also invaluable in identifying international trends.

To support the production and reading of children's books there must be good systems of distribution. Few children, whatever their social and economic circumstances, have access to a well-stocked bookshop or can afford to buy all the books they want; good libraries and programmes to get books into children's hands are essential. For this reason, the publications of organisations such as the International Federation of Library Associations (IFLA) and the International Association of School Librarianship (IASL) also throw interesting light on children's literature and its availability and standing in individual countries.

The USA and Canada led the way in developing the infrastructure essential to both the successful promotion and sale of the books, and the scholarly study of them. By the 1920s, children's librarians, led by Anne Carroll More in New York, and Lillian H. Smith in Toronto, had begun to exercise strong leadership, sending out a positive message about the need for high standards. They saw the role of public libraries as essential, and when the family of Frederick G. Melcher endowed the Newbery Medal (the first prize for children's books anywhere in the world) in 1922, it was administered by the Association of Library Services to Children within the American Library Association. (A companion prize, the Caldecott Medal, the first award for distinguished work in picture-books, was established in 1938.) Other notable contributions of North America in this field have been the first specialist reviewing periodical for children's books – *The Horn Book Magazine* established by Bertha M. Miller and Elinor W. Field in 1924, the Children's Book Section of the Library of Congress, with Virginia Haviland, a former children's librarian at its head, and the Osborne Collection, presented by a British librarian, Edgar Osborne, to Toronto in 1949.

The complexity of the development of children's literature, which is traced in the following chapters, can be demonstrated by a case study, which illustrates the importance of cultural and political influences.

Cyprus provides a convenient bridge between Europe and the Middle East. Geographically close to Turkey, its children's literature has strong connections with Greece, and most of the available information comes from the southern, Greek part of the island which, in 1984, hosted the nineteenth IBBY Congress.

A literature for children first appeared in Cyprus at the beginning of the twentieth century when newspapers, magazines and books were produced for use in schools. A few books for children's leisure reading appeared before the Second World War, such as *Our Son* by Tefkros Anthias in the late 1930s, but a literature really began to develop a few years before independence in 1960. In 1959 the Elementary School Teachers' Union began to publish a literary magazine, *Pediki Chara* [Children's Joy]. The establishment in 1974 of a Cyprus National Section of IBBY was an important landmark.

As Cyprus has a relatively small population, it cannot support a significant publishing programme and children's books have always been imported from Greece. Reading surveys show that *Aesop's Fables*, *The Iliad* and *The Odyssey* feature in children's reading but so do the fairy tales of *Snow White* and *Little Red Riding Hood* as well as classics from Western Europe and the USA. Most of the stories for children published in Cyprus itself were, until the mid-1970s, fairy tales.

Cyprus was divided in 1974 after President Makarios was overthrown and troops from Turkey invaded the island, and this coincided with the introduction of a realistic note into the literature for children. *The Wasp Nest and Other Stories* (1976) by Spyros Epaminondas is a humorous story in which the children learn through adventures and mishaps, but many books reflect the country's recent and turbulent history. *Joys and Sorrows* (1977) by Philisa Hadjihanna is about the difficulties of a displaced family who are forced to take shelter in a tent and then a refugee camp; each member of the family recalls the good old days when Greeks and Turks lived happily side by side.

In the 1980s this trend continued. Cypriot writers for children, while pleading for peace and international understanding, also recorded the conflicts of the past.

For example, in *Mikroi Ston Agona* [Too Young to Fight] (1986), the story is set in the period before independence. In *O Theodores* [Theodore] (1989) Renos Prenzas tells a story about young boys protesting against the British occupation by throwing stones at the soldiers, but when the British finally leave the island, Theodore does not know whether to be glad or sorry; *Letters to My Lonely Brother* (1987), by Maria Abraamides deals with the events of the Turkish invasion and the subsequent war. Alongside these realistic stories, however, there are folk-tales and fairy stories, stories about animals and entertaining stories of everyday life. Maria Luka's *Istories tes Mikres Philios* [Stories of Little Philio] (1989) consists of Philio's accounts of her daily life, told with great humour, while Amarante Adler-Seta's *Ta Paramythia tes Sophias* [Sophie's Tales] (1989) is a collection of folk-tales based on recent oral tradition, which have been assiduously recorded by the author.

The pioneering New Zealand Librarian, Dorothy Neal White pointed out in her *About Books for Children* (1946) that 'Children read comparatively few books ... If one estimates one book a fortnight from seven to fourteen years (and actually this [is] a generous figure) the number read during that period is 416. These four hundred books often influence a child far more powerfully than parents realise' (11). Even if this seems a generous estimate in the days of television and computer games, the influence of those texts seems undeniable: when it is multiplied across the world, as the essays which follow demonstrate, showing as many common features as differences, some sense of the global importance of children's literature may be gained.

## References

Hickman, D. (1987) 'Anno's *All in a Day*: an international picture book', *Bookbird* 25, 3: 5–6.

Melching, M. (1981) 'Working with children and books in Senegal', *Bookbird* 2: 7–11.

Segun, M. D. (1992) 'Children's literature in Africa: problems and prospects', in Ikonne, C. *et al.*, (eds), *Children and Literature in Africa*, Ibadan: Heinemann Educational.

White, D. N. (1946) *About Books for Children*, London: Oxford University Press.

## Further Reading

Pellowski, A. (1968) *The World of Children's Literature*, New York: R. R. Bowker.

Pick, M. (1992) 'Co-editions of children's books: international but not (yet) global', *Logos* 3/4: 186–191.

St John, J. (1958) *The Osborne Collection of Early Children's Books, 1566–1910*, Toronto: Toronto Public Library.

# 57

# Culture and Developing Countries

## *Anne Pellowski*

Culture has many definitions, but here the term will be defined as the means people use to structure and express their experience conceptually so that belief, knowledge, or information can be transmitted from one generation to the next. One of the chief means is day to day behaviour, but this essay will concentrate on hand-made or machine-produced objects (or a combination of the two), all of which have a three-dimensional physical reality, with a 'double' or 'spirit world' or 'psychic' reality often implied within the same object. It will also consider at some length such means as oral story-telling or information sharing, often accompanied by body movements, music, or creation of pictures that are immediately erased or dissolved. These ephemeral means often have their own kind of permanence, depending on such factors as the number of times they occur and the way in which the next generation is trained to recreate them.

Developing countries are usually defined in economic terms such as per capita income or gross national product. Here they are defined as those countries in the process of using more and more machine-based methods of structuring and expressing culture, instead of, or together with, those methods that involve hand-made objects and direct interpersonal contact. This definition does not imply that technological media such as printing, film, video and radio are *per se* superior to oral and/or visual story-telling and information sharing. Indeed, there are some cultures that insist on the superiority of the oral, even though they have print available to them. What is implied is the movement toward the 'new' that seems to pull many cultures. And the definition also implies that each of these media is different, as are the cultural effects of ideas and information expressed by means of each of them.

Virtually all peoples have transmitted part of their culture to the children in their groups by means of language play, story and what can be called enhanced information. Language play here includes those forms such as nonsense rhymes or tongue twisters that occur in most languages, and that appear to have little meaning or purpose other than playfulness. It has been shown that infant babbling is a prerequisite for language development. The playful speech that follows, usually after the age of two, may well be another necessary step toward full language competence, but probably it is expressed also simply because it is fun.

Story is defined here as an account of a connected series of events, not necessarily in a linear order. Story includes tales, myths, legends, parables, sacred explanations, drama, biography, autobiography, and even much of what is often called non-fiction in English. The lifecycle (story) of a plant or animal, for example, can be as dramatic as that of a human person. Story can be sung, chanted in poetic form, spoken prose, or a combination of any of those.

Enhanced information is information conveyed by means of short bursts of symbolic, poetic, or special language, such as that found in proverbs, sayings, riddles, and the like. Language play, story and enhanced information form the basis of much of the world's children's literature.

To cite some specific examples from the country of Nigeria, the myth of 'Why the sky is far away' as written down in *My Father's Daughter* (Segun 1965) is a belief story within the story of the author's childhood. The styles in which both of these stories are presented, as well as their contents and contexts, tell us something of the culture out of which that book comes, and most particularly, how the culture is changing because it is in the process of developing, as defined above. An example of enhanced information from Nigeria would be this riddle: 'I pass the living, they are silent; I pass the dead, they speak to me.' The answer: leaves. This conveys information about the physical properties of leaves in a symbolic way. The fact that this information is encoded in a riddle and the contexts in which such a riddle would be used by adults with children tell us something about the culture of the people using the riddle.

Much of playful language, story and enhanced information was and still is expressed in oral formats in direct exchanges among two or more persons. In some cultures these oral expressions were/are accompanied by body movements, by playing of musical instruments, by drawing or sketching or moulding of images, by manipulation of objects. In some cultures there was less oral expression, and more body movement (dance or mime or acting out), or more pictorial expression.

Some of these cultures transformed their pictorial images or objects into recording systems. Relatively quickly, a few cultures developed long-lasting formats (clay tablets, smooth stones, papyrus scrolls, palm leaf pages, cloths strips, wood boards, leather strings, parchment sheets, paper) on which they could record many things. For even fewer of these cultures, record-keeping soon developed into fully-fledged writing systems that could record all types of human speech, including oral performance speech. Gradually, specialists in these cultures moved from composing and performing orally to a process in which they composed, wrote down, corrected, re-composed, re-wrote, re-corrected and hence we arrive at literature and children's literature.

In the twentieth century came the modern media of radio, television, film and video. Some cultures began to use all these means, as each developed, to add to the oral and printed versions of story and enhanced information they gave to their children.

Other cultures continued to exist and regenerate themselves chiefly through oral and mimetic means, either by choice or because of economic forces that pushed for development in other technological areas. These cultures sometimes used the same types of stories and enhanced information as the cultures in which writing systems and the modern media flourished, but the form and content were different. Each presentation was unique. This meant that those responsible for passing down culture had to develop extensive memory. In some places, memory aids such as vines or strings, beads, notched sticks or coded boards were devised to help retain a greater amount of story and/or information. Most of these memory aids are not considered writing systems, but they are certainly parallel recording systems, and it is now becoming clear that such memory aids were used in many cultures. But it was chiefly such language devices as rhythmic speech, formulaic expressions, repetition, alliteration, onomatopoeia and the like that were used to keep orature alive in memory.

There is much disagreement among scholars as to what differences have evolved in cultures that have used writing to keep factual information, story and enhanced information available to them, and those cultures that have relied chiefly on the limits of human memory, assisted sometimes by physical objects as aids. This brief essay can review only a few theories.

In his book *Visible Speech*, John de Francis postulates that there is an essential oneness in all attempts at human writing systems, applicable even to some of the mnemonic devices. Writing begins, he believes, as an extension of the 'picturing' humans do in the mind when they think or speak. But he insists that all true writing systems have a phonetic component, because that is the way to represent the sounds of human speech. Even Chinese, which so many believe to be chiefly 'ideographic', he convincingly shows to be highly phonetic.

Walter J. Ong (1982) finds that there are vast differences in the expressions of cultures that rely on orality and those that rely on literacy. The term 'oral literature' in his view is preposterous – a contradiction in terms. Because he believes the human voice is the most effective way for one person to reveal interior thoughts and feelings to another, he finds orality in many cultures more important and influential than literacy. Many other scholars agree with this view and believe that oral performances result in what should be called 'orature' and not 'literature', even when the texts of such performances are written down in some way. The term 'orature for children' will be used here to designate story and enhanced information passed on to children by persons who may be aware of writing and/or print, but do not use them in any significant way.

Very few societies today remain totally untouched by the printed word. A common misconception about society in developing countries is that the majority of their peoples have not had a history of significant literacy and literature. But as Jack Goody (1968) and others have pointed out, literacy has had an impact on many of these peoples for decades, and even, in some cases, centuries. Many of them have had texts from their orature written down for a long time, and many also have a written, composed literature, or translations of texts from other literatures of the world.

Translations often are not adequate for the task of conveying full cultural significance, particularly not in children's books, where the text is often very simple and concise. For example, Melching has pointed out that in Senegal, children had access to many books of French origin, in which polite phrases such as 'Please' and 'Thank you' were given great importance, as they often are in Western cultures. But they are:

> of no particular significance in Wolof. They certainly are not indications of whether or not a child is considered polite. However, there are words and expressions in Wolof that children must learn to apply ... in order to

become respected members of the community. These words and expressions are found in the traditional oral stories, proverbs, and anecdotes that have been transmitted orally.

Melching 1979: 109–111

It is possible to trace much of what is oral in texts that have come down through the centuries, as well as recently recorded texts. Milman Parry (Parry 1971) developed a method for identifying texts (such as *The Iliad* and *The Odyssey*) that were recordings of oral performance. His work has been expanded by subsequent scholars, and most 'epics' have now been scanned and studied using the method he suggested. Okpewho (1979), for example, finds that African oral epics use musical rhythm and formulaic language in much the same way Homer did.

Eric A. Havelock (1986) synthesised a theory that has gradually gained strength in many academic circles: that the effects of writing systems were so profound, that they created different brain (thinking) patterns. In Havelock's view, cultures using the Greek alphabet as the basis of writing had the simplest system to learn and manipulate; it could record human speech and thought in such a way that even little children could learn to decode the messages. The human brain did not have to use most of its space for memory, but was free to think of other things. This resulted, he contended, in a complete change in the mode of thinking among humans using such writing systems, the so-called 'logical' or 'categorical' mode of thinking. Havelock himself did not claim superiority for this mode of thinking over any other mode, but a number of other scholars and writers have used his theories to do so.

McLuhan (1964) put forth the theory that it was not the process of merely writing down things, or composing in a written form, that changed human ways of thinking; rather, it was the technology of printing that brought about a visually based way of thinking. And, in the present age, he believed that similar drastic changes were occurring with the spread of modern media such as radio, television, film and video, because orality had returned in these media, often simultaneously with visuality of a direct type only partially mediated by print.

The effect of narrative picturing on the permanence of cultures has not been studied much, apart from the early forms of picturing that led to alphabets or other language symbols. This is especially true for ephemeral forms such as Napaskiak story-knifing or Australian Aborigine story drawing in the sand. More permanent forms such as the tessellated cloth scrolls of India or Chinese picture scrolls have probably had an enormous impact, historically, on literature and orature for children in Asia, but they have hardly been mentioned in that light. Victor Mair's review (1988) of some of these widespread forms of picture story-telling or 'recitation' is one of the few studies that even mentions their impact on children. One has only to note the special forms of Indian film-making, and the widespread popularity of viewing films in that country, to realise that the cultures of India represent very special cases of visual response to story. However, there is only limited published research on the Indian child's response to all this visuality.

The study of the present-day child's response to printed picture books, with or without text, is just getting under way in developing countries. Segall *et al.* (1966)

and Kennedy (1974) reviewed and summarised early research on the human response to pictures, and part of that research included the child's response. Later studies tended to include more children as subjects and most often came to the conclusion that these children see or 'read' pictures in very different ways (Fuglesang 1982; Bellman and Bennetta 1977; Fussel and Haaland 1976; Forge 1970). Forge, for example, points out that for some groups in New Guinea, there is no word for colour, only a word for 'paint' because of the ritual significance of painting. And only white, black, red and yellow are used in these paintings (on the body, on buildings, artefacts, and so on). Therefore, when a child paints a picture and indiscriminately mixes blue and black in the same area, it does not necessarily mean that the child does not 'see' the difference between blue and black; it is more likely that the difference has no real meaning.

But only in rare cases did the above mentioned researchers use a series of sequential or 'story-telling' pictures, or even entire picture books, to test the children's responses. That type of picture 'reading' has yet to be studied cross-culturally.

Do all the theories mentioned above hold up when examined in the light of children's literature and orature in developing countries? Is there even a surviving orature in most of these cultures? Do they distinguish separate types of orature for children, or is all orature for general audiences of all ages? Is there a special language used with and/or by children? Does one find, in the literature and orature for children commonly found in developing countries today, a mixture of the oral and the visual? Does the physical entity that 'holds' children's literature today (book, magazine, film, cloth sheet or scroll) look different in developing countries than it does in countries with advanced printing and reproducing technologies? If there are differences, is it because of cultural forces or economic forces? What constraints on children's literature occur in cultures where the language exists in written form but in several different orthographies? What happens in those cultures where written language is very far removed from the spoken language of ordinary people?

These questions can be taken up in only the sketchiest fashion, because there have been so few studies of comparative children's literature, and even fewer of orature for children, that include examples from many cultures. For example, the extensive work of Iona and Peter Opie in collecting the playful language of English-speaking children encompasses much orature for children, and their notes often compare or contrast items from a few European cultures. But English is now the first language for children in many cultures, and the orature of British children (particularly the nursery rhymes and cumulative tales) was written down and transformed into fixed literary forms that were often exported in book form to other countries. Few scholars have taken the research of the Opies one step further, comparing and contrasting how the British children's orature they recorded has ended up in the children's literature of other cultures. And no one has yet taken this body of work and, using the theories of Parry and his followers, attempted to identify what parts of it can be classified as pure orature and what parts were kept alive mostly through print.

Orature does seem to be surviving in most cultures of the developing world, but it is more and more a recorded orature, except for cultural groups who are still very isolated from urban areas. And even such groups are coming increasingly under the scrutiny of folklorists, ethnologists, anthropologists, botanists and others.

A number of African cultures (among them the Ewe and the Mbiti) can identify specific orature that is aimed at children, as do some of the Native American cultures (Pellowski 1990: 67–68). Based on personal observation, one can say that orature performed by children (and passed on chiefly from child to child without adult intervention) is probably even more specific to them, but there are so few persons who have collected orature from children in developing countries that this must remain for now a highly speculative conclusion. The Kenyan writer Ngugi wa Thiong'o (1986), recalling his own Kikuyu upbringing, has noted that his appreciation of language was reinforced by word games, an approach so similar to the English-language orature recorded by the Opies that one is tempted to equate them without a closer comparative look (or hearing).

A change in the adult's tone of voice when talking to children has been noted in many cultures. But there are some cultures, notably the Thai, that use not only a special voice but also special linguistic expressions and devices when performing orature for children (Thai IBBY 1991). Such devices give a signal to the child listener that can be likened to the children's room in a public library, where children are shown by a specific sign and physical location that this is 'their' literature.

It has been noted by a number of scholars that orature often survives longer among the children than it does among the adults in a culture. Also, it is accepted as a truism that the children's literature of today, in all cultures, has more elements surviving from orature than does the general, adult literature in those same societies. However, children's literature has not been examined for traces of orality in the same way that adult literature has been scrutinised. It will first be necessary to cite many more specific examples before one can unequivocally accept the truism.

A very clear-cut example of orature pervading a modern piece of literature for children can be found in the works of D. O. Fagunwa of Nigeria. Fagunwa's works were written in Yoruba, and the largest number of persons who could read them was to be found among school children. The adventures of his protagonists were of the type that appeals strongly to children. Whether he intended them as children's literature or not, his novels became part of Nigerian children's literature, much as *Robinson Crusoe* and *Gulliver's Travels* were usurped by English-reading children.

The best-known of Fagunwa's works, *Ogboju Ode Ninu Igbo Irunmale*, first published in 1938, has been translated by Wole Soyinka as *Forest of a Thousand Daemons*. On the very first page, the reader is given a direct instruction to treat the book as though the author were a drummer performing the story and they, the listeners, were dancing out the appropriate responses. In other words, they must act as though they were at a traditional story-telling session. He exhorts his readers (listeners) not to dance like a mosquito but 'with joy and laughter' and he further requests two things:

> Firstly, whenever a character in my story speaks in his own person, you must put yourselves in his place and speak as if you are that very man. And when the other replies, you must relate the story to yourselves as if you, sitting

down, had been addressed and now respond to the first speaker. In addition
... you will yourselves extract various wisdoms from the story as you follow
its progress.

Fagunwa 1982: 1

Fagunwa senses that his printed words cannot possibly convey the give and take
of a Yoruba story-telling session, with its music, audience response (even takeover
of the narrator's role at times) and onomatopoeic, proverb-packed speech. His
novels are episodic rather than linear. As Soyinka, his translator, points out 'he is
both the enthusiastic raconteur and the pious moralist, and the battle of the
inventive imagination with the morally guided is a constant process in much of his
work' (Fagunwa 1982: 2).

*Pilgrim's Progress* by John Bunyan was translated into many African and Asian
languages in the late nineteenth century or the early twentieth. Some critics feel
that it was the ready availability of such works that influenced the first writers in
many of those languages, including Fagunwa. They see in the pious moralising a
direct attempt on the part of those early writers to combine what they knew of
printed literature with what they knew and felt of their orature. Other critics
believe that this same seriousness of purpose can be found in the proverbs and
aphorisms of orature and that it was quite natural to weave this into written genres.
However, most studies of the novels of Fagunwa (and those of his contemporaries
and followers) do find in that writing a unique combination of orature and
literature.

Another Nigerian writer, Chinua Achebe, has written some books specifically
for children as well as a number of novels for adults. Achebe, too, takes very
seriously this commonly accepted requisite for stories aimed at children in his
culture: they must pass on wisdom, be educative, in some way. He has specifically
stated that he does not wish to be excused from this task: 'Perhaps what I write is
applied art as distinct from pure. But who cares? Art is important, but so is
education of the kind I have in mind' (Achebe 1975: 72).

Apart from a few skilled writers (of the Fagunwa and Achebe calibre), this
preoccupation with message overwhelms much of the writing for children in
developing countries. It is parallel to the didacticism in European children's
literature of the nineteenth century. It often prevents writers from allowing the
exuberance and spontaneity of orature to be carried over into the texts they create
for children. And those who publish and promote reading for children in
developing countries often show a subtle bias against oral cultures, even while
professing to be interested in creating literature for them. A recent manual from
Bolivia states: 'We use the term "bridge-book" to define a new type of reading
material, destined for newly literate populations, whose cultural roots reveal
themselves to be very different from those of more advanced populations'
(*Promocion de la Lectura* 1985: 95).

An illustrated children's book represents quite well the linear, 'rational' aspects
of many Western cultures, and even some of the Asian ones with fairly long
traditions of writing. Whether the lines move from left to right, right to left, or up
and down, they are essentially all paced in the same way, with words or characters
separated from each other in easily recognised repeating patterns. The story

contained within the book generally also is very linear, moving from one action or event to the next, most often with cause expressed or implied before effect.

But many cultures have stories (and other cultural artefacts) that are expressed chiefly in circular or spiral terms. There might be a 'beginning' but there is no real 'middle' or 'end'. Cumulative stories in some cultures do not have a climactic event that then triggers actions moving the story to a final conclusion, as in the English 'The old woman and her pig'. Instead there is a continuing series of events that can go on *ad infinitum*; they can begin or end at almost any point.

Or there is far more ambiguity in the ending, as in the dilemma stories common among the Nkundo and other African cultures. Such stories are not really comparable to the 'choose your own adventure' type of book published in North America and Europe which are linear in pattern regardless of the 'path' one has selected. Such a physical format would not suit the 'circular' stories of some cultures. A format that might fit them better is that of the 'turnaround' books, in which the child reads the words (and sometimes pictures) while holding the book in one direction and then turns the book over and reads a different set of words (and often the same pictures, but seen from a different perspective). No publisher in a developing country seems to have attempted such a format for some of the circular stories common to their language.

Iran is one place in which the physical design of children's books was very definitely shaped by strong local cultural forces. Because Islamic culture precludes the use of pictures for certain types of literature, children's books in which that kind of literature is published had to be designed using only script and space. Even with these limitations, the Institute for Intellectual Development of Children succeeded in publishing a number of books attractive to children despite their lack of pictures (Pellowski 1980).

On the whole, the physical shape, the illustrations, the size and quality of type, the overall design of published children's literature in developing countries has not yet shown much experimentation in matching local cultural expression with print. Nor, with only a few exceptions, have there appeared numerous forms of popular print literature (such as broadsheets, chapbooks, penny theatres) of the type that were common in Europe in the centuries after the invention of printing by movable type. Some of the inexpensive pamphlet-format versions of illustrated folk-tales in developing countries (for example, those produced in Onitsha, Nigeria) come close to chapbooks, but most of them lack the vividness, the raffishness, the local colour needed to make them truly popular. This may well be due to the cost of paper; it became relatively cheap in Europe where it could be produced out of local wood pulp, but it is relatively expensive in many developing countries, where it usually must be imported. The same is true of printing inks.

Even in societies influenced by strong colonial cultures, it was usually the didactic that won out over the popular. As Maggi points out for Venezuela,

> it is not likely that there existed among us a popular literature written for children ... but it is possible for us to imagine that children read with pleasure, and at times in secret, the broadsheets, wall posters, and handbills [from Spain] of a humorous character that circulated in some of our cities during the nineteenth century and also that they began to be attracted by the

pictures and characters and typographic ostentations of our first almanacs and weeklies. In any case, supposing there had existed a printed literature for children of a popular nature, it was not preserved; the only books that have been saved are those containing educational or didactic reading.

Maggi 1992: 11

Maggi is specifically writing about printed literature and therefore makes no reference to the orature of the indigenous populations nor to that of the groups descended from European and African peoples who settled in Venezuela. Some current Venezuelan publishers, notably Ediciones Ekare, are attempting to produce children's books that not only go beyond the didactic but also reflect, in the stories and illustrations, the numerous peoples and cultures that make up the current population of that country. But although these books use portions of recorded texts from orature and design motifs from the hand-made artefacts of some of the indigenous peoples, the books have to be regarded as mere translations of the central meaning those texts and motifs have in the lives of their original creators and users. As David Guss has pointed out, to really 'tell' and understand *Watunna*, the oral creation epic of the Yekuana and other indigenous peoples of the Orinoco region, one must learn to weave baskets and decorate one's body, to construct one's house and one's garden, all the time re-living the creation cycle. One must learn 'to weave the word', symbolically and actually (Guss 1989).

Two concrete examples of an attempt to experiment with new formats are the picture books printed on large cloth rectangles, known as *kanga* in East Africa and *pagne* in Mali and other West African countries. Traditionally, these cloths have been put to use as clothing, baby carriers, head coverings, blankets, and for many other purposes. In East Africa, they were (and still are) usually printed with colourful designs and intriguing Swahili sayings. The Children's Literature Association of Kenya and the Operation Lecture Publique of Mali have each experimented with versions that could be called 'picture books for children' that can be worn, hung up on a wall, spread on the ground and displayed in other ingenious ways so that children can read them. Only experience and time will tell whether rural persons, with little exposure to printed pictures, will find such a format more approachable and easier to read than a picture book printed on paper.

Another unusual example of picture book publishing adapted to a local cultural situation are the picture books produced by Somboon Singkamanen of Thailand for distribution at Buddhist ceremonies honouring a recently deceased family member. In the past, *ted nitarn* (sermon stories) were read or told at such gatherings. Ever since the availability of widespread printing, it has been common for a few of these *ted nitarn* to be printed up and distributed to those attending. Most often they were in inexpensive, unattractive formats. Since many of these sermons contain stories from the *Jatakas* that are appealing to children, Singkamanen had the idea (first begun at the ceremony honouring her deceased mother) of making up an attractive children's picture book version of one of these stories. All who gathered to honour her mother were given a copy, and encouraged to take it home and read it to children, or give it to children to read. This very culturally appropriate method of promoting children's reading in Thailand is only one of many advocated by Singkamanen.

Based on experiments he has carried out to determine how orally centred persons tend to read pictures, Fuglesang contends that the illustrator of children's books for such cultures must be more aware of the difference between a memory-picture and a two-dimensional picture printed on paper. For the person living in a mostly oral culture, he says,

> A lorry has a clear, concrete visual gestalt characterised by the high valence of the four wheels. For a person who experiences his inner picture with concrete qualities, it is logical and meaningful to make all four wheels visible. There is no clear distinction between the real and the apparent, between the memory-picture and the here-and-now visual expression.
>
> Fuglesang 1982: 199–200

There is no question that the illustration and design of children's books in developing countries present challenges, but an even greater one is the language used in children's literature. There are still quite a number of cultures in which the everyday speech of people, even fairly educated persons, is very different from the generally accepted written forms of the language. Most notable in this category is Arabic, spoken by nearly 200 million people. Kaye and Zoubir find that

> Classical Arabic, in its written form, is of an almost hallucinatory imprecision. Hence its difference from many other classical languages, and hence also the fact that, unlike other written languages of power, it has not altered the basically oral quality of cultures where it has a privileged place. It needs to be read aloud but all such readings can only ever be variations on the many-layered textual possibilities. In addition, Arabic calligraphy is quite unlike the rectangular uniformities of print. It is, therefore, aurally and visually variable.
>
> Kaye and Zoubir 1990: 21

Many writers for children are well aware of the fact that their young readers understand only a small percentage of texts written in classical Arabic, yet they hesitate to write in colloquial style. Their hesitations come partly from fear of being accused of downgrading the importance of classical Arabic, of denigrating the language of the Koran, of helping to cause the disappearance of the great classical Arabic traditions. But lack of model children's books, written in good but colloquial Arabic, is also a factor.

Many children learn by rote the verses of the Koran in classical Arabic, even though in their homes they speak an Arabic dialect or another language altogether. This linking of language with sacred texts sometimes creates what Jack Goody (1968) calls 'religious literacy'. In his view, in societies where children first become literate in this manner, general reading of secular literature is often restricted or discouraged. Such children have very different expectations of books and other printed matter.

Another factor that has created difficulties for many writers is orthography. So many of the world's languages were written down in orthographies that were only partially successful. Ngugi wa Thiong'o has made a conscious decision to write only in Gikuyu, his mother tongue. He believes that writers should compose in their home languages rather than in one inherited from colonial times. But when he began writing in Gikuyo, he encountered a problem. 'The distinction between the short and the long vowel is very important in Gikuyu prose and poetry. But the prevailing orthography often left the reader to guess whether to prolong or shorten the vowel sound' (Ngugi 1986: 11).

Recently, the Peruvian section of the International Board on Books for Young People (IBBY) decided to publish a series of of bilingual picture books. When it came to producing a picture book in Spanish and Quechua, it was found that no single rendering could, in all likelihood, be read or understood by all Quechua-speaking children. The orthography, the vocabulary, and the mode of expression are so different for the different branches of Quechua speakers in Peru, that the picture book was printed in four different versions.

Many of these languages have speakers numbering in hundreds of thousands rather than millions; nevertheless, each group has its own culture and its own distinct orature. These minority groups are often ignored in the professional writing about children's orature and literature. By using such sources as the IBBY publications, *Bookbird* and *Children's Literature Abstracts*, and past issues of *Phaedrus*, one can locate general reviews about children's literature in quite a number of developing countries, but these are invariably limited to majority languages. Also, the descriptions also tend to be modelled on European or North American views of children's literature. Orature for and by children in the developing countries is scarcely mentioned. Until there is more research and discussion about the specific ways in which local or national cultures of the developing countries find expression in the children's literature and orature of the past and present, it will remain difficult to compare and contrast children's literature and orature in a truly international and multi-cultural manner.

# References

Achebe, C. (1975) *Morning Yet On Creation Day*, London: Heinemann.

Akivaga, S. A. and Gachukiah, E. (1974) *The Teaching of African Literature in Schools*, Nairobi: Kenya Literature Bureau.

Bellman, B. L. and Bennetta, J.-R. (1977) *A Paradigm for Looking: Cross-Cultural Research with Visual Media*, Norwood, NJ: Ablex.

de Francis, J. (1989) *Visible Speech: The Diverse Oneness of Writing Systems*, Honolulu: University of Hawaii Press.

Fagunwa, D. O. (1982) *Forest of a Thousand Demons*, trans. from the Yoruba by W. Soyinka, New York: Random House.

Forge, A. (1970) Learning to see in New Guinea', in Mayer, P. (ed.) *Socialization, the Approach from Social Anthropology*, London: Tavistock Publications.

Fuglesang, A. (1982) *About Understanding: Ideas and Observations on Cross-Cultural Communication*, Uppsala: Dag Hammarskjold Foundation.

Fussel, D. and Haaland, L. (1976) *Communicating with Pictures in Nepal*, Kathmandu: UNICEF.

Goody, J. (1968) *Literacy in Traditional Societies*, Cambridge: Cambridge University Press.

Guss, D. M. (1989) *To Weave and Sing: Art, Symbol, and Narrative in the South American Rain Forest*, Berkeley: University of California Press.

Havelock, E. A. (1986) *The Muse Learns to Write*, New Haven: Yale University Press.

International Board on Books for Young People (1985) *Proceedings, 19th Congress, 9–14 October 1984: Children's Book Production and Distribution in Developing Countries*, Nicosia: Cyprus Association on Books for Young People.

International Federation of Library Associations, Children's Libraries Section and Round Table of Children's Literature Documentation Centers (1973– ) *Children's Literature Abstracts* (place of publication varies).

Kaye, J. and Zoubir, A. (1990) *The Ambiguous Compromise: Language, Literature and National Identity in Algeria and Morocco*, London: Routledge.

Kennedy, J. M. (1974) *Psychology of Picture Perception*, New York: Jossey-Bass.

McLuhan, M. (1964), *Understanding Media, the Extensions of Man*, New York: McGraw-Hill.

Maggi, M. E. (1992) 'Estudio preliminar: En los inicios de la literatura infantil venezolana', in reprint of 1865 edition of *Amenodoro Urdaneta, El Libro de la Infancia*, Caracas: Biblioteca Nacional and Fundacion Latino: 11–42.

Mair, V. (1988) *Painting and Performance: Chinese Picture Recitation and its Indian Genesis*, Honolulu: University of Hawaii Press.

Melching, M. (1979) 'Meeting children on their own terms', *Wilson Library Bulletin* 54, 2: 109–111.

Ngugi wa Thiong'o (1986) *Decolonising the Mind: The Politics of Language in African Literature*, Nairobi: Heinemann/London: James Curry.

Okpewho, I. (1979) *The Epic in Africa: Towards a Poetics of Oral Performance*. New York: Columbia University Press.

Ong, W. J. (1982) *Orality and Literacy: The Technologizing of the Word*, New York: Methuen.

Opie, I. and Opie, P. (1959) *The Lore and Language of School Children*, London: Oxford University Press.

—— (1962) *The Oxford Dictionary of Nursery Rhymes*, London: Oxford University Press.

Parry, A. (ed.) (1971) *The Making of Heroic Verse: The Collected Papers of Milman Parry*, London: Oxford University Press.

Pellowski, A. (1980) *Made to Measure: Children's Books in Developing Countries*, Paris: UNESCO.

—— (1990) *The World of Storytelling*, rev. edn, New York: H. W. Wilson.

*Phaedrus* (1973–1988) 'International reports', in Vols 1–13, 1988, Madison, NJ: Fairleigh Dickinson University.

*Promocion de la Lectura, una Experiencia en Bolivia* (1985) Geneva: Fundaciones Simon I. Patino and Pro Bolivia.

Segall, M. H., Campbell, D. T. and Herskovits, M. J. (1966) *The Influence of Culture on Visual Perception*, New York: Bobbs Merrill.

Segun, M. (1985) *My Father's Daughter*, Lagos: African Universities Press.

Thai IBBY (1991) *The Story: A Report on the Sub-Regional Seminar on Reading Animation, Bangkok, August 12–17*, Bangkok: Thai IBBY.

## Further Reading

Abd al-Tawab, Y. (1987) *Wa-adab al-tifl al-Arabi: Maa qaimah bibliyujrafiyah li-intajihi al-fikri*, Cairo: al-Hayah al-Misriyah al-Ammah lil-Kitab.

Abidi, Syed Ameer Haider (1987) 'Creation, publication and distribution of reading materials in Africa', *Proceedings of the Third International Jerusalem Symposium on Encouraging Reading*, Thirteenth Jerusalem International Book Fair: 58–78.

Bravo-Villasante, C. (1966) *Historia y antologia de la literatura infantil iberoamericana*, 2 vols, Madrid: Doncel.

Bynum, D. E. (1978) *The Daemon in the Wood: A Study of Oral Narrative Patterns*, Cambridge, MA: Harvard University Press.

Ikonne, C., Oko, E. and Onwudinjo, P. (eds) (1992) *Children and Literature in Africa*, Ibadan: Heinemann Educational Books.

Delgado Santos, F. (1989) 'Ecuador: obras, cambios, esperanzas',, *Casa de las Americas* 30: 175–181.

Devasare, Hari Krishna (1969) *Hindi balasahitya: eka adhyayana*, Delhi: Atmarama.

Egypt IBBY Section (1992) *Integrated Care Society International Symposium on Reading for All: Proceedings, Future Look*, Cairo: General Egyptian Book Organization Press.

Fayose, P. O. (1991) 'Children's literature and research in Africa: problems and prospects', in International Youth Library (ed.) *Children's Literature Research, International Resources and Exchange, First International Conference, 5-7 April 1988*, Munich: K. G. Saur.

Gerard, A. S. (1981) *African Language Literatures: An Introduction to the Literary History of Sub-Saharan Africa*, Washington: Three Continents Press.

Holmes, A. C. (1966) *A Study of Understanding of Visual Symbols in Kenya*, London: OVAC.

Jafa, M. (1991) 'Children's literature and research in India, Bangladesh, Sri Lanka and Nepal', in International Youth Library (ed.) *Children's Literature Research, International Resources and Exchange, First International Conference, 5-7 April 1988*, Munich: K. G. Saur.

Netzorg, M. J. (1985) *Backward, Turn Backward*, Manila: National Book Store.

Patte, G. and Hannesdottir, S. (1984) *Library Work for Children and Young Adults in the Developing Countries*, Munich: K. G. Saur.

Pena Munoz, M. (1982) *Historia de la Literatura Infantil Chilena*, Santiago: Editorial Andres Bello.

Scott, D. H. (1980) *Chinese Popular Literature and the Child*, Chicago: American Library Association.

Thai IBBY (1989) *Report of the Third Reading Animation Workshop, 23-25 June, Surat Thani*, Bangkok: Thai IBBY, Children's Reading Development Association and UNESCO Regional Office for Book Development.

Wahdan, Nadra Abd el-Halim (1972) *Literatura infantil en Egipto*, Madrid: Instituto Hispano-Arabe de Cultura.

# 58

# British Children's Literature:
# A Historical Overview

## *John Rowe Townsend*

The modern history of children's books in Britain is commonly regarded as beginning in the 1740s, when John Newbery opened a shop in London and began to publish and sell books for 'little masters and misses'. The first serious historian of the subject, Harvey Darton, wrote in *Children's Books in England* of 'Newbery the Conqueror', and (with tongue firmly in cheek) described the year 1744, in which Newbery published his first title, *A Little Pretty Pocket-Book*, as 'a date comparable to the 1066 of the older histories'.

Darton admitted that the assigning of a specific date to a development that took place over a number of years was merely a convenience, and that Newbery was not alone in the field; but there is no doubt that the mid-eighteenth century was the time at which children's books as a serious branch of the book trade got under way. Stable political conditions, the spread of literacy, the rise of the respectable middle class and the growing domesticity of its life, were combining with a new view of childhood to make the production of books for children an economic and psychological possibility.

However, if one accepts the age of Newbery as, conventionally, the beginning of children's-book history, one must acknowledge and briefly glance at a sizeable prehistory. This may be said to have two branches, which were, broadly, story material handed down over the centuries but not meant specially for children, and material that was meant specially for children but was not story. The former branch is the larger. It includes legend and romance (tales of King Arthur, Robin Hood, Guy of Warwick, Bevis of Hampton, the Seven Champions of Christendom and many others), fable (Aesop, Reynard the Fox) and folk-tale: a great mass of stuff, of varied nature and quality. Much of it was put into print by the early printers of the late fifteenth and the sixteenth centuries; much was passed on by word of mouth, circulating in the population at large.

The audience for story was seen as universal. Sir Philip Sidney wrote in his *Defence of Poesie* (posthumously published in 1595) of the poet as story-teller: 'With a tale forsooth he cometh unto you, with a tale which holdeth children from play and old men from the chimney-corner.' A tale was for young and old alike. But with the advance of the Renaissance, educated people were already turning to the classics, and the old tales were increasingly looked down on by the literate. They were also condemned on moral grounds, especially by the sixteenth- and seventeenth-century Puritans. In his *Book of Nurture* (1554), Hugh Rhodes alleged that 'feigned fables, vain fantasies and wanton stories and songs of love' brought much mischief to youth – a complaint which in one form or another has been echoed at many times and in many places.

The other branch of children's-literature prehistory is instructional: school books, courtesy books (which told children how to behave in a seemly manner) and didactic and religious books which aimed to instil virtue and devotion. The notorious 'godly books' of seventeenth-century Puritans ranged from the relatively mild such as James Janeway's *A Token for Children* (1671), telling of the 'holy and exemplary lives and joyful deaths of several young children', to grim and lurid threats of hellfire for the impious.

## A Clean Slate

The writers who, with the best of intentions, warned their readers that they were 'not too little to go to hell' believed that children were steeped in original sin. But around the start of the eighteenth century a new view was becoming widely held. It was associated with the Enlightenment and especially, in England, with the philosopher John Locke. This saw the child as being born in a state of innocence, and the young mind as a *tabula rasa* – a clean slate, waiting to be written on.

Locke perceived the possibility of combining pleasure with instruction. In his *Thoughts Concerning Education* (1693) he suggested that children could be 'cozened into a knowledge of their letters' and could 'play themselves into what others are whipped for'. A child who had learned to read could be given 'some easy, pleasant book' which would reward his pains in reading yet not 'fill his head with perfectly useless trumpery, or lay the principles of vice and folly'. Locke's prescription, in his own view, ruled out the old tales and romances, and he could find nothing to recommend, outside the Scriptures, but *Aesop* and *Reynard the Fox*.

This was an invitation to producers of books to fill a gap. Newbery – a great admirer of Locke – was not the first or the only one to respond, but he was the most successful and the most important. His many titles brought together the pleasurable and the instructive, frequently between the same covers. The two aims – to teach and to please – have remained twined together ever since, and publishers today tend to bring out both recreational and instructional books. A clear distinction is drawn between them on the publishers' lists; but the urge to instruct the young is deeply built into human nature, and at all times there have been supposedly recreational books which have had, consciously or unconsciously, a didactic element. This remains true today.

The present essay will concern itself with books that have been specially written and published for children and are designed, at least in part, to give them pleasure: essentially fiction, poetry and picture books. It will not examine schoolbooks or information books. Also outside the scope of this study is the continuation of the old unregenerate line of popular fiction which can be traced, in a rough and ready way, through the chapbooks that used to be hawked from door to door by pedlars, the penny dreadfuls and Victorian horror sheets and the modern comic.

## Landmarks of Fiction

During or just after John Locke's lifetime, three major works of fiction were published, none of which was written specially for children but all of which were adopted, or adapted, as children's books. They were John Bunyan's *Pilgrim's Progress* (1678), Daniel Defoe's *Robinson Crusoe* (1719) and Jonathan Swift's *Gulliver's Travels* (1726). All three incorporate archetypal story themes which have been in constant use ever since: the perilous journey in the first, the desert island in the second, the miniaturised or magnified world and imaginary society in the third. These three belong to the general history of English literature rather than that of children's books, but they have always been present as features of the landscape and have inspired many works that were undoubtedly meant for children.

The titles published by Newbery and his contemporaries were not of comparable significance. The best known Newbery title was the anonymous *Goody Two-Shoes* (1765), often attributed on doubtful evidence to Oliver Goldsmith. It is the story of a poor orphan who manages to learn her letters, become a teacher, make a good marriage and grow rich. It was reprinted well into the nineteenth century, and pantomimes bearing its title are still performed, though they have little or no resemblance to the original. Newbery's books are notable mainly for a relaxed and cheerful good-humour; he described himself to his readers as 'your old friend in St Paul's Churchyard' and liked his (occasionally corny) little joke. But Newbery and his contemporaries were no more tolerant of the old folk-tales than had been the previous century. 'People stuff children's heads with stories of ghosts, fairies, witches and such nonsense when they are young, and so they continue fools all their days', wrote the author of *Goody Two-Shoes*.

Newbery's successors and their competitors were less relaxed than Newbery himself. Didactic influences of different kinds remained powerful. The educational philosophy of Locke was followed by that of Jean-Jacques Rousseau, who preached that civilisation had overlaid natural virtue with idleness, inequality and indulgence. His British followers seized on the concepts of simplicity and usefulness, notably in the children's stories of Maria Edgeworth and in *Sandford and Merton* (1783–1789) by the eccentric Thomas Day. This inserts a number of stories intended to 'express judicious views of nature and reason' into the framework of the friendship of spoiled, rich Tommy Merton and honest farmer's son Harry Sandford, and of their education under the wise, Rousseauite eye of their tutor, Mr Barlow. The emphasis is on the goodness of the natural and rational, as opposed to the corrupting influence of idle wealth.

Among other moralising writers around the close of the eighteenth century were Mrs Sarah Trimmer, in whose *History of the Robins* (1785) 'the sentiments and affections of a good father and mother are supposed to be possessed by a nest of redbreasts', and Hannah More, who launched in the 1790s the Cheap Repository Tracts, intended to help the poor to be virtuous and know their place. Hellfire still smouldered: the last of the major preachers in children's fiction was Mrs Mary Martha Sherwood, in whose *Fairchild Family* (1818) Henry, Lucy and Emily undergo some gruelling experiences for the good of their souls. (Significantly, this book was toned down in later editions.)

## Verse with a Purpose

The beginnings of verse for children parallel the beginnings of story. There was verse that children heard and knew, though it was not specially meant for them: ballad, popular song, nursery rhyme. (Many nursery rhymes are not as old as is supposed, but Iona and Peter Opie estimated in the foreword to their *Oxford Dictionary of Nursery Rhymes* that approximately half of them date from before 1700; some are much older.) There was also verse used as an aid to memory, or to sweeten the instructional pill; the old courtesy books were often rhymed. Some austere Puritans deigned to write in verse, among them John Bunyan, though his *Book for Boys and Girls* (1686), later reissued as *Divine Emblems*, was hardly designed to delight the youthful heart. It offered, for instance, the following thoughts 'upon Death':

> Death's a cold Comforter to Girls and Boys
> Who wedded are unto their Childish Toys:
> More grim he looks upon our Lustful Youth
> Who, against Knowledge, slight God's saving Truth . . .

Isaac Watts, in his *Divine Songs* (1715) was no less concerned than Bunyan with religious instruction, and Hell was still a serious threat; but Watts's tone was the gentler one of the new century, and his verses were easy to remember; many indeed, such as 'Hush, my dear, lie still and slumber' and 'How doth the little busy bee' are still familiar today. Moral tales in verse, in which good children were rewarded and bad ones punished, sometimes with untimely death, continued to be produced through the eighteenth century and on into the nineteenth. More amiably, Newbery gave new currency to old rhymes in *Mother Goose's Melody* (1765). But the great name in eighteenth-century poetry for children was that of William Blake. The *Songs of Innocence* (1789) clearly stated their intended audience – And I wrote my happy songs/Every child may joy to hear – though they subsequently reversed the usual process by which adult books come to be adopted by children, and, in company with the *Songs of Experience* (1794), were recognised by adults as classic poetry for the world at large.

## Adornment with Cuts

The history of illustration goes back further than that of printing. Early printers could not match the pictorial glory of medieval manuscript – nor, for that matter, can modern ones – but from the days of Caxton onward printed books have been illustrated. The early medium was woodcut, which continued to be largely employed until the late nineteenth century and is still quite often used, though nowadays not printed directly from the wood block.

In their early days, children's books as defined here were commonly 'adorn'd with cuts'. To modern eyes those cuts are extremely crude, but clearly their customers loved them: Leigh Hunt, lamenting in 1848 the 'little penny books, radiant with gold and rich with bad pictures' of his childhood, confessed that 'we preferred the uncouth coats, the staring blotted eyes and round pieces of rope for hats, of our very badly drawn contemporaries to all the proprieties of modern embellishment'. Many significant eighteenth-century artists, including Thomas Bewick and William Blake himself, illustrated children's books, and this tradition continued in the nineteenth century with William Mulready, George Cruikshank, Richard Doyle, John Tenniel and many others.

## Fairy Tale, Fantasy and Adventure

In the early nineteenth century, the output of books for children continued to grow, but emphasis was still largely on the didactic and instructional. Fiction stood at a discount to fact and was represented largely by a flow of wishy-washy moral stories which presumably children found acceptable in the absence of anything more stimulating. Catherine Sinclair, in a preface to *Holiday House* (1839), complained that 'imagination is now carefully discouraged, and books written for young persons are generally a mere dry record of facts, unenlivened by any appeal to the heart, or any excitement to the fancy'. She wished to write about 'that species of noisy, frolicsome, mischievous children' which was (she alleged) 'now almost extinct'; and *Holiday House*, though now forgotten, is in fact a refreshing contrast to its more leaden contemporaries.

The most interesting development of the early nineteenth century was the gradual rehabilitation of the folk-tales. They had been under a series of clouds: regarded by the Tudor and Stuart literati as peasant absurdities, by the Puritans as dangerous and immoral nonsense, and by the eighteenth century as contrary to reason. But they were still at large in the population. Their emergence into respectable print is probably associated with the rise of Romanticism, the greater esteem for imagination that had followed the Age of Reason, and the replacement to some extent of classical influences by Nordic ones. In the early years of the century, Benjamin Tabart, owner of a children's bookshop, produced several collections of 'popular fairy tales'; and from this time onward the old tales gradually gained acceptance, the greatest stimulus coming from translation of the Grimm brothers' *German Popular Stories* in 1823–1826.

By the mid-nineteenth century, imagination was in favour among the more forward-looking writers. John Ruskin put his stamp of approval on fairy tales by publishing his well-known and popular *King of the Golden River* in 1851. Conditions were now favourable to the production of children's books. The population was growing rapidly, literacy was increasing, publishing was becoming a profession. A great deal of the material published remained didactic: the work of third- and fourth-rate writers turning out what the market demanded. The Victorian ideal of childhood, in brief, was that children should be good and do as they were told. Piety, often to an unrealistic degree, was approved of; the activity of tract societies and the growing trade in Sunday School 'rewards' resulted in a torrent of 'goody-goody' books. To look at the Victorian children's books still familiar today is in one way misleading but in another way illuminating: the survivors are far from representative of the entire output and come almost invariably from the minority that ignored, bent or broke the rules.

In the 1860s – a key decade – two major fantasies appeared: Charles Kingsley's powerful and urgent, but muddled, *The Water Babies* (1863), and the book which many would call the greatest English children's book of all: Lewis Carroll's *Alice's*

*Adventures in Wonderland* (1865), to be followed in 1871 by *Through the Looking-Glass*. The *Alice* books, though not always successful with children themselves, have endless fascination for commentators and have been analysed from a variety of standpoints. Arguably however, the most imaginative of mid-Victorian fantasy writers was George Macdonald, author of *At the Back of the North Wind* (1871) and *The Princess and the Goblin* (1872).

But fantasy was not the only or the numerically dominant genre of that era. The adventure story, from its base in adult fiction with *Robinson Crusoe* and the novels of Walter Scott, Fenimore Cooper and others, crossed over to children's literature with the children's books of Captain Marryat in the 1840s. There followed the long runs of 'boys' stories' by R. M. Ballantyne, W. H. G. Kingston, G. A. Henty and others, offering as role models for those growing out of childhood the upright, clean-living, Empire-building young men who were seen as Britain's, and therefore the world's, best. This line of development led eventually to Robert Louis Stevenson, who acknowledged in his prefatory verses to *Treasure Island* (1882) the influence of 'Kingston, and Ballantyne the brave' – while, paradoxically, writing a book whose power derives in part from its lordly disregard of conventional ethics.

For girls a different kind of book was thought appropriate: the domestic dramas of such writers as Charlotte M. Yonge, Mrs Molesworth, Mrs Ewing and others, now forgotten by all except a few enthusiasts. Frances Hodgson Burnett has sometimes been bracketed with this group of writers, but should properly be placed above them. Her reputation has suffered from the notoriety of *Little Lord Fauntleroy* (1885), whose eponymous hero has been much maligned: he is actually a friendly, unaffected small boy who would surely have detested the 'Fauntleroy suit' in which the artist dressed him. Mrs Burnett's *A Little Princess* (1905) and *The Secret Garden* (1910) are still living books.

It was acknowledged even by Victorians that girls disliked 'goody-goody' books, preferring their brothers' adventure stories. This preference may be assumed to have extended to school stories, which were almost invariably set in boarding schools, to which only boys went. School was in fact a promising setting: an enclosed world within which the boy was a fully participating citizen. The school story sprang to prominence with Thomas Hughes's *Tom Brown's Schooldays* (1857) and F. W. Farrar's *Eric, or Little by Little* (1858), a passionately moral tear-jerker which now seems preposterous but went through some thirty editions by the end of the century. The classic school stories were written by Talbot Baines Reed in the 1880s and 1890s, but their values were fatally undermined by Kipling's *Stalky and Co* (1899) which portrayed – though not quite at full length – the unregenerate young male animal.

Kipling's contribution to children's literature was rich and various: it included the much-loved *Jungle Books* (1894–1895), more fantasy than animal story, but in fact defying classification; the sounding and memorable *Just-So Stories* (1902), which could be described as beast fables for the very young, and *Puck of Pook's Hill* (1906), a time fantasy celebrating the land and people of England. Edith Nesbit also resists pigeon-holing; her best-known books are three family stories about the Bastable children, beginning with *The Story of the Treasure-Seekers* in 1899, and three that are about a family of children but also introduce magical creatures: the furry, bad-tempered Psammead in *Five Children and It* (1902) and *The Story of the*

*Amulet* (1906), and the Phoenix which hatches in the fire in *The Phoenix and the Carpet* (1904). The characters in Kenneth Grahame's many-layered classic *The Wind in the Willows* (1908) are people, although lightly disguised as animals. For children, the adventures of the incorrigible Mr Toad have ensured continuing popularity; adults surely are seduced in part by an air of poetic nostalgia. The play of *Peter Pan* (1904), by J. M. Barrie, has been a lasting success on the stage, but in book form it has a whiff of coyness and condescension and an after-taste of saccharine.

## Poems and Pictures

Nineteenth-century verse for children begins with the innocuous but long-remembered verses of Ann and Jane Taylor, authors respectively of 'My Mother' and 'Twinkle, Twinkle, Little Star' among much else, and the pleasantly non-didactic 'The Butterfly's Ball', by William Roscoe (1807), which owed much to illustrations by William Mulready. Robert Browning's *Pied Piper of Hamelin* has survived through the years since its first publication in 1842. Lewis Carroll's best-known verses are in the *Alice* books; Edward Lear's are in *Nonsense Songs* (1870) and *Laughable Lyrics* (1877), and the best of them are at the same time comedy and strange, sad poetry. Christina Rossetti published *Goblin Market*, an original fairy story in verse, in 1862, and *Sing-Song*, a collection of short poems for young children, in 1872, and in 1885 came Robert Louis Stevenson's still-popular *Child's Garden of Verses*.

In graphic art, the great Victorian innovation was the 'quality' picture book in colour: not an illustrated text but a work in which the pictures were of the essence and usually the dominant feature. Edmund Evans was a printer and engraver who brought colour printing to a fine art, developed the picture book concept, and found the artists to put it into effect. The leading names were those of Walter Crane, brilliant as a pictorial designer and decorator, Randolph Caldecott, notable for a strong and wiry line and gift for showing action, and Kate Greenaway, whose pretty, prettily-dressed children created a new dream of childish innocence. A few years later, Beatrix Potter produced a score of small masterpieces, portraying and telling the tales of Peter Rabbit, Tom Kitten, Jemima Puddle-Duck and other very human animals.

## Between Two Wars

The fifty or sixty years leading up to the outbreak of the First World War have been called the golden age of children's literature. In comparison with their richness, the two decades between the end of that war and the beginning of the Second World War seem impoverished. Children's books had little status, and writing them professionally was not an attractive pursuit for anyone who sought to be a serious writer. The perception in the USA that children's literature was a part of the national culture, and the corresponding development of library work with children and use of recreational books in schools, was slow to spread to Britain. It was beginning to do so by the mid-1930s; the Carnegie Medal for an outstanding children's book was instituted in 1937, fifteen years after its American equivalent and inspiration, the Newbery. But routine publishing for children ran to cheap 'rewards', bumper books, series books, annuals and endless production lines of the tired old school and adventure stories. Financially, the great successes were those writers whose books came in series about the same protagonists, were easy and readable and made no demands on their readers.

The highlights of the 1920s and 1930s resulted from inspirations that struck individual authors: most of them people who had not particularly meant to write for children. Most successful of all were the *Winnie-the-Pooh* stories of A. A. Milne, which not only established a still thriving literary industry but added to the small stock of books that can be quoted or alluded to in the confidence that every literate adult will be familiar with them. In this respect the Pooh books are probably second only to *Alice*.

Other memorable books of the two decades did not set clear trends. Hugh Lofting's Dr Dolittle series, beginning in 1922 and originally inspired by the sufferings of horses in the First World War, was a popular continuance of the age-old tradition of the humanised-animal story, neatly reshaped around the benign, innocent figure of the Doctor himself. John Masefield brewed two rich mixtures of magic and adventure in *The Midnight Folk* (1927) and *The Box of Delights* (1935); P. L. Travers introduced the magic nursemaid Mary Poppins – already a figure from a bygone age – in 1934; Arthur Ransome let some fresh open air into children's books with *Swallows and Amazons* (1930), first of a series that continued to appear until 1947 and is still in print and widely read in the 1990s. The most influential book of the 1930s – though this could not have been predicted at the time – was J. R. R. Tolkien's *The Hobbit* (1937). In conjunction with *The Lord of the Rings*, published after the Second World War on an adult list, this gave rise to a fashion for books about wizards, dragons and other creatures of lore and legend, set in lands far away in space and time, which has persisted and even strengthened over many years.

Walter de la Mare was the outstanding poet writing for children in the first half of the twentieth century; he was also a fine writer of often-haunting, often-poetic short stories. He was at the height of his powers in the inter-war period, though his *Collected Rhymes and Verses* were not published until 1944 and his *Collected Stories for Children* until 1947. Edward Ardizzone, with his gentle, traditional and instantly recognisable style, was perhaps the most distinguished English artist and picture book creator to work in the children's field in the first three-quarters of the twentieth century. *Little Tim and the Brave Sea-Captain*, the first of his picture-story books about the young seafarer Tim, appeared in 1936, and the Tim series continued after 1945.

## A New Age

The stresses of war and post-war shortages restricted publishing during the Second War, as they had done in the First, and the decade of recovery was the 1950s. In that decade the standard of children's books coming from main-line publishers improved greatly. The reasons were partly institutional. School and library work with children, benefiting from American example, were expanding, and those in charge of it demanded work of literary merit. Publishers were appointing specialist children's editors, some of whom were exceptional individuals. 'Quality' paperbacks for children were establishing themselves under the leadership of Puffin Books, a Penguin imprint. In the new and more encouraging atmosphere a new generation of writers came to the fore.

At the same time – and intensifying in the decades that followed – there was a move to widen the readership of children's books. Traditionally children's fiction had been produced by middle-class writers for middle-class children and was largely about middle-class children. Many intermediaries, especially teachers, felt that this prevented the books from appealing to 'ordinary' children. There was some division between the 'book people' who drew attention to the excellent books available and the 'child people' who pointed to the large numbers of children who did not willingly read them. In succeeding years, because divisions in society have lessened or at any rate been played down, and because both writers and their fictional characters and settings have been drawn from a broader stratum, the class divide in the books themselves has become less visible. But in spite of all efforts the aim of extending the readership base has not been achieved as fully as might be hoped. Book buying and reading remain largely characteristic of middle-class homes.

Oddly, perhaps, it was several years before the war itself as a subject of fiction for children and young people gave rise to books of much interest. Ian Serraillier's *The Silver Sword* (1956), about the trek of three children across war-torn Europe in search of their parents, was probably the first. Later came Jill Paton Walsh's *The Dolphin Crossing* (1967) and *Fireweed* (1969), Nina Bawden's *Carrie's War* (1973), Robert Westall's *The Machine-Gunners* (1975) and *Blitzcat* (1989), and Michelle Magorian's immensely popular *Goodnight, Mister Tom* (1981).

In general, the adventure story has had a hard time in the post-war years, perhaps because of its vulnerability to competition from television. In former times, books were a way to travel in the imagination, to see different places, meet different people; now television puts distant lands and peoples vividly before our eyes. Similarly, the essence of adventure is physical action, which films and TV can show with maximum immediacy. Books still have their advantages, even when dealing with action: they can more effectively than TV tell how it felt and what people thought about it, help the reader to become involved rather than merely watch from outside, and raise moral, social and philosophical issues. Writers who have explored these possibilities while at the same time keeping their readers turning the page include Peter Dickinson, an author with an energetic and speculative mind, in *The Blue Hawk* (1976), *Eva* (1988) and other titles, and Gillian Cross, with *Born of the Sun* (1983), *On the Edge* (1984) and *Wolf* (1990).

The historical novel achieved great prestige and prominence in the early post-war years. The dominant figure in this field was Rosemary Sutcliff, whose novel of Roman Britain *The Eagle of the Ninth* (1954) was the first to appear in a sequence of books which remained the core of her work and whose theme was the making of Britain. There were many other writers of sound, traditional historical fiction. The Sutcliff protagonist was nearly always male and of what would now be called 'officer class'; but there was a new tendency, initiated by Geoffrey Trease before the Second World War and continued after it, to see events from a point further down the social scale and to consider their impact on the common people. There was also fiction set in a past created by the writer rather than reported upon: notably the highly personal eighteenth century in which Leon Garfield set his larger-than-life novels. And there was unhistory, as in the James III books of Joan Aiken, set in a Britain ruled over by that previously unknown monarch, with the Hanoverians plotting to bring Bonnie Prince Georgie to the throne. 'Straight' historical or period novels have to some extent lost ground in recent years; there is a self-fulfilling belief at large that 'children don't like history, so we won't give it to them'. But there are counter-instances: Jill Paton Walsh's *A Parcel of Patterns* (1983) and *Grace* (1992) and Geraldine McCaughrean's *A Little Lower than the Angels* (1987) among them.

Fantasy, long a speciality of British writing for children, has held its place through the post-war years. Traditional themes have continued to give good service: miniaturisation, for instance, in Mary Norton's *The Borrowers* (1952) and its successors, about the small people who live in odd corners of old houses and survive by 'borrowing' from the human occupants, and Pauline Clarke's *The Twelve and the Genii* (1962) which brings to life the toy soldiers of the young Brontës. At the other end of the scale of size were the imagined secondary worlds, greatly stimulated by Tolkien. The Narnia books of Tolkien's friend C. S. Lewis began in fact to appear before *The Lord of the Rings*, with *The Lion, the Witch and the Wardrobe* in 1950; but Lewis was conversant with Tolkien's work in progress and learned in some of the same fields. He was also learned in medieval allegory, and the Narnia books are Christian allegory.

A form of fantasy of special interest, developed mainly in Britain since 1945, is what might be called minimal or marginal fantasy, in which the fantasy element is so elusive that one wonders whether anything supernatural has 'really' happened. In L. M. Boston's *The Children of Green Knowe* (1954) and *The Chimneys of Green Knowe* (1958), a present-day small boy hears the voices of, and seems to meet, children who have lived in the same house in the past: but do these encounters actually occur or are they imagined? We do not know, and perhaps it doesn't matter. In *Tom's Midnight Garden* (1958), by Philippa Pearce, Tom plays at night, in a garden that no longer exists, with a little girl who turns out to be the old lady now living on the top floor of the house in which he is staying. We learn that she has been dreaming him into her past life: does this mean that he has been dreaming it too? A similar question arises in Penelope Lively's *A Stitch in Time* (1976). In *Stig of the Dump* (1963), by Clive King, does the cave-boy Stig 'really' exist, or is he imagined by a lonely child? There is nothing to prevent the reader from accepting either alternative, or both. The rumoured Beast in Janni Howker's *The Nature of the Beast* (1985) has a symbolic existence but probably not a real one. In Alan Garner's *The Owl Service* (1967), where the power of ancient myth breaks dangerously through to the present in a Welsh valley, the possibility that nothing abnormal actually happens can barely be entertained, and in any case it is the old myth that powers the book; but there is an eerie sense that the fabric separating our world from some other is thin and flimsy, and could tear. This is also a feature of Garner's *Red Shift* (1973).

Contemporary realism in the 'let's-face-it' sense has been much less dominant in Britain than in the USA, and tends to self-destruct or at best decline to the status of a period piece when it ceases to be contemporary. Realistic fiction in the more general and catch-all definition of fiction set in the present or recent past and not making use of the exotic or the supernatural has been written with distinction by authors as various as Nina Bawden, Jane Gardam and Jan Mark; Farrukh Dhondy and James Berry have been among the (too few) writers whose work for the children's list has been a reminder that modern British society is multi-racial and multi-cultural.

Most of the post-war titles mentioned above are likely to appeal mainly to 11-year-olds and upwards, with perhaps some bright 10-year-olds. As award committees discover year after year, it is hard to find outstanding literary distinction in books for younger readers of, say, 7 to 9. Young children's lack of experience and, possibly, their limited reading ability restricts what can be done in writing for them, and many authors find it difficult. But they are not a less valuable audience. Most of the writers mentioned above have written for them, and often very well, although the titles are not the authors' best-known books. The age-group is one to which humanised-animal stories often appeal, ranging from Michael Bond's *A Bear Called Paddington* (1958) and its successors to the farmyard dramas of Dick King-Smith in *The Sheep-Pig* (1983) and other titles. And then there are the Roald Dahl books, immensely popular but disliked by many commentators for an underlying unpleasantness and appeal to the less likable of childish characteristics.

Last to be mentioned here of contemporary prose writers for children is William Mayne, perhaps the most distinguished of them all: bewilderingly prolific and protean. He has written, it seems, in every genre and for every age group, and a small selection from his more than one hundred titles must be arbitrary and subjective: a possible sampler would be *A Swarm in May* (1955), *No More School* (1965), *The Jersey Shore* (1973) and *Drift* (1985).

## From Garden to Street

Most books of poetry for children published since 1945 have been anthologies, selected with children in mind but drawn from the body of poetry at large. Some poets however have written specially for children. In 1950 and 1952 James Reeves published *The Wandering Moon* and *The Blackbird in the Lilac*, containing some of the best children's verse of the post-war period. Ted Hughes wrote the comic *Meet My Folks!* in 1961, and in more serious vein *Season Songs* in 1976 and the mysterious and haunting moon poems which were brought together in *Moon-Whales* (1988). Charles Causley, a poet with a vigorous narrative gift, did much for children over the years, both as writer and anthologist; his collection of short poems with Cornish settings, *Figgie Hobbin* (1970), showed him continually at his best. In the 1970s and 1980s came a wave of 'urchin verse', representing a childhood of the street rather than the garden and inspired particularly by Michael Rosen's *Mind Your Own Business* (1974).

For many years the picture book as a distinctive contemporary art form developed more strongly in the USA than in Britain; but in 1962 Brian Wildsmith, essentially a painter, opened many eyes with his rich and glowing *ABC*. Later in the same decade came the early books of Charles Keeping, an uncompromising artist with a strong and increasingly sombre line, thought by some to be too stark for young children, but clearly a powerful talent. Several artists – John Burningham and Raymond Briggs notable among them – created picture books that looked like, and perhaps were, comedy, but beneath whose surfaces there were serious concerns. Shirley Hughes drew solid, flesh-and-blood children, and understood what adventures can be contained in a small child's ordinary day; Quentin Blake used a light sketchy style to create visual fantasy; Janet and Allan Ahlberg appealed to the very smallest with *Each Peach Pear Plum* (1978), *Peepo!* (1981) and *Bye Bye Baby* (1989) and were among many picture book creators to exploit the physical properties of the book in gaining their effects. Paper engineering, well known to the Victorians, though not under that name, became part of the vocabulary of the trade.

Many good artists were active in the field besides those mentioned, and at the start of the 1990s the picture book seemed to be in a reasonably healthy state. Children's fiction was less so; it had for some years been having a hard time in Britain, as schools and libraries had less money in real terms to spend on recreational reading, while the price of books rose remorselessly and was driven higher in a vicious spiral by the shortening of print runs. The chill economic wind seemed to cause, or at any rate to be accompanied by, a fall in the numbers of good new writers. The wealth of talent that had emerged in the third quarter of the century was not matched in the years that followed. It remained to be seen whether this trend was cyclical and would be reversed with better times or whether it was the new reality. Books were being hit by television, videotape, computer games and various social and educational developments; and multimedia was advancing over the horizon. But there were favourable signs: among them the growth of a serious interest in children's literature in colleges and elsewhere, and the arrival in parenthood of a generation young enough to have grown up on good books itself. It was still possible to look hopefully to the future.

## References

Darton, F. J. H. (1932/1982) *Children's Books in England: Five Centuries of Social Life*, 3rd edn, rev. Brian Alderson, Cambridge: Cambridge University Press.

Opie, I and Opie, P. (1955) *The Oxford Nursery Rhyme Book*, Oxford: Oxford University Press.

# 59

# Scotland

## *Stuart Hannabuss*

Scotland has a distinctive place in the history and development of British children's literature. Peter Pan (J. M. Barrie) and Henry Baskerville (Arthur Conan Doyle), Mr Toad (Kenneth Grahame) and Kevin and Sadie (Joan Lingard) were all created by Scottish writers. Writing and publishing for children in Scotland has been active for several hundred years, arising in the beginning out of a unique tradition with three languages (Scots, Gaelic and English) and two cultures (Highland and Lowland). Writing for children both merges with and diverges from writing for adults, and before the thirteenth century flows from a rich oral tradition of sung ballads and chivalric romance. Best known are the 'border ballads' which Sir Walter Scott, among others, brought together in the nineteenth century. Joseph Jacobs's collections of Celtic fairy tales (1892 and 1894) are still favourites with children.

Many ballads and folk-tales, on subjects like Robin Hood and King Arthur, appeared in chapbooks between the sixteenth and the eighteenth centuries. Many were for readers of all ages, although some publisher/booksellers specialised in cheap entertaining works for children. Among them were James Lumsden (1750–1830) of Glasgow (the Newbery or Harris of Scotland), whose nursery tales and stories were popular, some making known the work of writers like Berquin and Thomas Day. The fairy and folktale tradition emerges through George MacDonald and, today, in writers like Winifred Finlay and Iris MacFarlane, as well as in compilations by Norah and William Montgomerie. A characteristic of Scottish children's literature is the closeness of its writers to oral story-telling and the story-tellers' relationship with their audience.

Education has been another distinctive strand in Scottish writing for children. Some 'books of nurture' (early works on how young people should behave) found their way to Scotland or were translated there (for example, Sir Gilbert Hay's *Buke of the Governance of Princes* in the fifteenth century). Grammars, like Lily and Murray, remained in print and in use in schools up to the eighteenth century, and as the educational market grew such works became a major source of revenue and copyright contention among publishers. Many works were distributed from London into Scotland by way of Edinburgh. Thomas Ruddiman (1674–1757) produced a famous grammar in 1714 and also introduced the ideas of John Locke to Scotland. Later traditions of educational publishing for children and young people developed with firms like Nelson and Blackie in the nineteenth century, particularly after the Education Acts of the 1870s.

Many early chapbooks were 'small godly books' and found their way into children's hands. There were simplified versions of Bunyan's *The Pilgrim's Progress*, for example, those published by James Orr of Glasgow in 1800 and by Blackie in 1820. Two of Isaac Watts's works had been translated into Gaelic by 1795, and his *Divine Songs* had gone through numerous editions. Thomas Nelson started in Edinburgh by publishing religious works, including children's hymnals, and went on to publish evangelical writers like Kingston, Ballantyne, and 'A.L.O.E.' (Charlotte Maria Tucker). He also published many religious magazines for family and children's reading, like *The Children's Paper* (1855–1925). Throughout the nineteenth century, too, the SPCK through its Scottish branch promoted Christian knowledge in Sunday schools; other bodies like the Glasgow Religious Tract Society were also active. Many local publishers like John Ritchie, motivated by the urge to combat the immoral effects of reading fiction, produced evangelical books and periodicals for children, such as *The Young Watchman*.

The nineteenth century saw major children's writers like George MacDonald (1824–1905) emerge. His powerful religious and allegorical works for adults (for example, *Lilith*, 1895) and for children (for example, *At the Back of the North Wind*, 1871) reveal both the Celtic and religious traditions of Scottish writing, as well as German Romanticism. Tales like 'Sir Gibbie' (1879) also show realistic Scottish settings. His influence on the fantasy of C. S. Lewis, who edited an anthology of his work in 1946, is well known. Another writer drawn to the fantasy tradition was Andrew Lang (1844–1912), whose 'colour' fairy books (from *The Blue Fairy Book*, 1889, to *The Lilac Fairy Book*, 1910) and stories such as 'Prince Prigio' (1889) are still of interest to both children and scholars.

Inspired by Sir Walter Scott's (1771–1832) stirring historical tales like *Rob Roy* (1818) and *Guy Mannering* (1815), with their feel for the romance and character of Scotland, later Scottish writers returned to historical themes. Robert Louis Stevenson (1850–1894) set *Kidnapped* (1886), and the more mature *The Master of Ballantrae* (1888) against the 1745 Jacobite Rebellion. Naomi Mitchison (b.1897) draws on history and classical mythology in many of her children's books.

A second major development through the nineteenth century leads off from Tobias Smollett's picaresque nautical tales, such as *Roderick Random* (1748) and the work of Captain Marryat. This can be seen most obviously in the extensive work of R. M. Ballantyne (1825–1894), whose *The Coral Island* (1858) was one of seven titles he published with Nelson before moving to James Nisbet, in R. L. Stevenson's *Treasure Island* (as a book 1883), and in the output of Gordon Stables (1849–1910). Writers for adults, John Buchan and Arthur Conan Doyle have both offered much for young readers in the adventure genre. Kailyard writer Samuel Rutherford Crockett (1859–1914) moved into this area with *The Raiders* (1893), in the style of Stevenson.

There has been a sentimental streak to the Scottish characterisation of children and childhood, perhaps best known in J. M. Barrie's Peter Pan. Barrie's view of childhood and the psychological dimensions of this in his life are explored by a number of his biographers. The distinct theme of 'childhood' trots alongside mainstream reading for children, in works like J. J. Bell's *Wee Macgreegor* (1902) with its humorous and sentimental sketches of a boy in a working-class Glasgow family, in novels about childhood by writers such as J. F. Hendry and Robin

Jenkins, and in autobiographies of Scottish authors such as Compton Mackenzie, Naomi Mitchison and Neil Gunn. Gunn's evocation of boyhood in *Morning Tide* (1931) and *Highland River* (1937) is memorable, as is the 'Reachfar' world of Jane Duncan (1910–1976) which, though adult, led to some interesting children's books. One of the themes of Lewis Grassic Gibbon's Scots Quair trilogy (especially *Sunset Song*, 1932) is the sexual growth from girlhood to maturity of the heroine, Chris Guthrie, portrayed with Hardyesque intensity.

Scottish children's literature in the twentieth century has a number of distinctive features and personalities. Joan Lingard's Maggie series (1974–1977) moves between Glasgow and Edinburgh and the Highlands. *The Clearance* shows powerful relationships and the effect of history; *The Resettling* the world of the Glasgow tenement, *The Pilgrimage* is about teenage choices in the Highlands, and *The Reunion* follows Maggie as she moves to womanhood. Her Kevin and Sadie quintet (from *The Twelfth Day of July* (1970) to *Hostages to Fortune* (1976)) about Northern Ireland and love in the midst of religious division, is deservedly famous, not least for school curricula.

Mollie Hunter is another internationally known writer, especially for her semi-autobiographical *A Sound of Chariots* (1975) and well-researched historical fiction. Others include the Edinburgh writer Iona McGregor, picture book story-teller Mairi Hedderwick, illustrator of joke-books Scoular Anderson, Aileen Paterson for her Maisie series (published by Musselburgh publisher The Amaising Publishing House Limited), adventure writer Allan Campbell McLean, and Lavinia Derwent (for Tammy Troot). There is also the fertile tradition of comics from D. *c.* Thomson of Dundee, for example, *The Beano* and *The Dandy.*

Kathleen Fidler (1899–1980) has a special place, not only for impressive stories like *The Boy with the Bronze Axe* (1968) but also for the award named after her for a first novel for children between 8 and 12. Blackie Books, co-founder of the award, publish the winning entry, and Book Trust Scotland administers the award. A second important initiative has been the Canongate/BBC Radio Scotland 'Quest for a Kelpie' prize, christened from the first winning entry by Frances Mary Hendry. Canongate of Edinburgh publish a series called 'Kelpies' which includes original works and reprints for children of works by writers like Eric Linklater, Lavinia Derwent, Kathleen Fidler, and Mollie Hunter. There are also many works from other sources with Scottish settings.

Scotland is a rich culture drawing on several linguistic traditions, and one of these is Gaelic. Early literature draws on the oral and ballad tradition, while later works like those of Bunyan and Watts appeared in Gaelic (the Church and bodies like the Scottish SPCK have been major disseminators). More dominant were grammars and primers and religious works. Today, 90 per cent of the sale of children's books in Gaelic occurs in the Western Isles and the Highlands of Scotland. A major influence on Gaelic speakers has been the integration of Gaelic into the school curriculum for its literature and as a teaching medium. Gaelic publishing has had a renaissance with the work of An Comunn Gaidhealach (The Highland Association, 1891– ) and the Gaelic Books Council (1968– ) at the University of Glasgow, which advises on the spending of Scottish Arts Council funding to support Gaelic publishing. The largest Gaelic publisher today is Gairm Publications (1958– ), whose backlist includes children's books like Iain Mac a'Ghobhainn's version of Little Red Riding Hood. A short-lived Gaelic comic, *Sradag*, was published in Glasgow in the early 1960s. The Stornoway publisher Acair (Gaelic for 'anchor') started in 1977 and publishes mainly for the Western Isles school market. Some works are translations from other publishers. There is an active Gaelic children's books culture with writer story-tellers like Anne Lorne Gillies, Mairead Hulse and Fionnlagh Macleoid. A few, like Lisa Storey, are publishers in their own right: Storey's Inverness-based Leabhraichean Beaga, publishes Gaelic primary school works, some illustrated by Mairi Hedderwick. There is also an active tradition, both oral and printed, among Gaelic-speaking emigrant communities in countries like Canada.

Scottish writers have made a distinctive mark on the world of children's literature and publishing out of all proportion to their numbers. Writing in many forms, they show the capacity of the Scots to think in English but to feel in Scots, and this binds them successfully to the story-telling tradition.

## Further Reading

Lindsay, M. (1992) *A History of Scottish Literature*, rev. edn, London: Hale.

# 60

# Wales

## *Menna Lloyd Williams*

It is believed that the first Welsh language book for children was *Anrheg i Blant* (1816), a translation of James Janeway's *A Token for Children*. In the nineteenth century there were very few books for children in Wales apart from religious tracts, pamphlets and catechisms designed to save children's souls. Between 1823 and 1891, many religious magazines appeared, for example *Yr Addysgydd* (1823), *Yr Oenig* (1857–1959), *Trysorfa y Plant* (1862–1965), and *Y Winllan* (1848–1965).

At the end of the century, Owen Morgan Edwards, a history don and fellow of Lincoln College, Oxford, and afterwards His Majesty's Inspector of Schools had a new vision of what children's literature should be. He believed that the children of Wales should be familiar with the historical and literary heritage of their country and their mother tongue. In 1892 he published *Cymru'r Plant*, a monthly magazine for children. His aim was to educate children through the magazine by discussing subjects such as nature, science, history, geography, music and literature. From then the motive behind publishing books for children changed from the religious to the educational and many classroom 'readers' and 'learners' were published.

During the 1920s and 1930s some authors began to write adventure and history stories for children. In 1925, *Llyfr y Bobl Bach* was published, the first bumper book for children. Another milestone in the field was the publication in 1931 of *Llyfr Mawr y Plant*, a sumptuous and colourful publication. One of the main characters in this book was Wil Cwac Cwac, who is still popular with children today.

In the early 1940s, Welsh-medium primary schools were established, followed by Welsh-medium secondary schools. This development created a new demand for Welsh-language books for children and the response to this demand can be seen in the pattern of publishing for children over the last forty years. The late 1950s and 1960s saw the setting-up of the Welsh Joint Education Committee and the Welsh Books Council, two institutions which support children's books.

Publishing in a minority language results in relatively small print runs, thus the granting of subsidies becomes a major factor. Until about 1978, the Welsh Joint Education Committee was the only institution to operate a children's book publishing programme on the basis of guaranteed sales to local education authorities. Over the years this scheme has ensured the publication of many original Welsh fiction and non-fiction, and translations of numerous colourful picture books. A further source of grant aid was the Arts Council, whose Literature Committee established a Children's Book Panel in 1976. Through this panel, ambitious projects such as *Y Mabinogion, Culhwch ac Olwen, Lleuad yn Olau, Llyfr Hwiangerddi y Dref Wen* have been published. In 1979, the Welsh arts Council established, with the College of Librarianship, Wales, the Welsh National Centre for Children's Literature, which amalgamated with the Welsh Books Council in 1990.

The year 1978 proved to be a landmark in the history of publishing for children when the Council for the Welsh Language published a report, *Publishing in the Welsh Language*. In 1979, as a result of this report, direct government grant aid was made available for children's publishing for the first time, and the Welsh Books Council was asked to administrate this new grant and to have the authority to commission books for recreational reading. This led to studying the provision for children and arranging to fill the gaps. As well as administrating grants to Welsh publishers, the Welsh Books Council's Commissions Panel meet twice a year to discuss possibilities and to suggest a specific programme. The first book to emerge was an original, full-colour ABC book, *Llyfr ABC* (1981); since then, we have seen many picture books for children such as *Congrinero* (1983), *Ben y Garddwr* (1988) and *Drama'r Nadolig* (1989). This panel is alert to the gaps in the market, and for example commissioned 'Cyfres Corryn' (1983–1992), a series of novels for children aged 7–10 years; over forty titles have appeared in this series. As one gap is filled another always becomes evident, and in 1991 a series of lively novels for the 9–12 age group, 'Cyfres Cled', was launched to bridge the gap between the readers of 'Cyfres Corryn' and young adult novels. 'Llyfrau Lloerig' is another example, a series of books for the 6 to 9-year-olds. In recent years, the Welsh Books Council have worked closely together in order to finance ambitious projects such as *Gwyddoniadur Mawr y Plant* (1991), a translation of *Macmillan's Children's Encyclopedia*; 'Llyfrau Llygad-dyst' (1993– ), translations of some of Dorling Kindersley's 'Eye Witness Guides'; and D. Geraint Lewis's *Geiriadur Gomer i'r Ifanc* (1994) an illustrated dictionary with over 22,000 Welsh definitions. In 1995 the Curriculum and Assessment Authority for Wales (ACAC) began commissioning projects to produce educational material both bilingual and in Welsh, by tendering for subvention costs. In 1983, Clwb Sbondonics, the Book Council's Welsh-language book club for 6 to 11-year-old children was launched, and books are commissioned to meet the needs of the club.

In 1976 the Tir na n-Og Awards (named after the land of eternal youth in Irish mythology) were established. Their main purpose is to raise the standard of children's and young people's books and to encourage the buying and reading of good books. Prizes are awarded annually to acknowledge the work of authors and illustrators in three categories: Welsh fiction – original Welsh-language novels, stories and picture books; Welsh non-fiction – every other Welsh-language books published, with the exception of translations; and the English section – the best English-language book with an authentic Welsh background. Both fiction and non-fiction originated in English are eligible, but translations from Welsh or any other language are not. The prize for each category (currently £1,000) is sponsored by the Welsh Arts Council, the Welsh Library Association and the Welsh Books Council. Some major Welsh authors who have won the Tir na n-Og Welsh prize include T. Llew Jones, Emily Huws, J. Selwyn Lloyd, Mair Wynn Hughes, Gweneth Lilly, Angharad Tomos and the late Gwenno Hywyn and Irma Chilton.

In 1985, the Mary Vaughan Jones award was established and is available for presentation every three years to a person who has made an outstanding contribution to children's literature in the Welsh language over a considerable period of time. Mary Vaughan Jones (1918–1983) was one of the main benefactors of children's literature in Wales for over thirty years. She wrote nearly forty books for children, one of the most popular is *Sali Mali* (1969). She was also a translator, her best work perhaps being the Welsh version of Tamasin Cole's *Fourteen Rats and a Rat Catcher* and Pat Hutchins's *Rosie's Walk*. The award is a silver trophy depicting scenes from Vaughan Jones's books.

Children's books are reviewed in various periodicals. *Llais Llyfrau/Books in Wales*, a quarterly magazine published by the Welsh Books Council has a Children's Books section where Welsh-language books and English books about Wales are reviewed regularly.

Another important category of children's literature in Wales are English books with a Welsh background. Among the winners of the English Tir na n-Og prize are *The Grey King* and *Silver on the Tree*, by Susan Cooper; *The Blindfold Track*, *Region of the Summer Stars* and *Who Stole a Bloater?* by Frances Thomas; *The Prize* by Irma Chilton; *The Snow Spider* by Jenny Nimmo, *Steel Town Cats* by Celia Lucas; *Bluestones* by Mary John; *Time Circles* by Bette Meyrick; *Denny and the Magic Pool*, by Pamela Purnell, and *The Candle Man* by Catherine Fisher.

In 1992, Pont Books, an imprint of Gomer Press, was established with the aim of offering young readers a range of literature – novels, stories and poetry written in English but set in Wales, and/or concerned with Welshness. Over thirty titles have been published.

In March 1995, the Welsh Books Council, with the support of the ACAC published a Catalogue of Welsh Books and Educational Resources for Children. Over 3,000 items are listed, which reflects the revolution that has taken place in Welsh-language publishing for children in recent years.

# 61

# Ireland

## *Valerie Coghlan*

Ireland has a long tradition of literary creativity, but this has focused mainly on adult literature, and until very recently Irish children and adolescents looked mainly to Britain and the USA as their source of reading material, particularly in relation to contemporary matters.

Reasons for this may be speculated upon. Perhaps it was due to political and religious unrest in Ireland which did not encourage the flow of writing for children which took place elsewhere in the late nineteenth century and early twentieth century. Indeed, much of the best adult Irish literature rebels against and frequently rejects the constraints of the society in which many authors grew to maturity, and until very recently this questioning spirit would not have been acceptable in contemporary Irish children's books.

To a large extent, what was read by Irish children in the eighteenth and nineteenth centuries and earlier, paralleled the literary diet available to children in England. While not specifically written for children, *Gulliver's Travels* (1726) by Jonathan Swift was widely read by them and may claim to be the first children's novel by an Irish writer. Later in the eighteenth century, Maria Edgeworth's was an influential voice in the tradition of Mrs Barbauld, with publications including *The Parent's Assistant* (1796) and *Early Lessons* (1801).

During this period the chapbook trade flourished. John Newbery's publications were widely available and a number of his children's books were edited or revised by Oliver Goldsmith. The founders of the Kildare Place Society, a philanthropic organisation dedicated to the education of the poor, recognising a need for reading material for the children whom it sought to educate, began to publish books specifically for the young, and were probably the first Irish publishers to do so. Their first publication was *The History of Joseph* in 1817 and between 1817 and 1827 their Literary Assistant, the Reverend Charles Bardin, wrote a number of books about travel and natural history that were original or loosely adapted from existing works.

For many centuries, the fertile ground of myth and folk-tales was a vital element in fostering the imaginative development of Irish children. Mostly these stories were passed on by *seanchaithe* or story-tellers until the latter part of the nineteenth century, when a renewed interest in Celtic folklore encouraged retellings by, among others, W. B. Yeats (*Irish Fairy Tales* (1892)) and Ella Young (*Celtic Wonder Tales* (1910)). More recent collections include *Irish Sagas and Folk Tales* (1954) by Eileen O'Faolain, who also wrote several novels for children, Liam MacUistin's *The Táin*

(1989), Michael Scott's *Irish Hero Tales* (1989) and Carolyn Swift's *Irish Myths and Tales for Young People* (1990). Scott has also written several fantasy novels which reflect his interest in Irish mythology.

Folk-tales also provided inspiration for the blind Donegal author, Frances Browne whose *Granny's Wonderful Chair* appeared in 1857, for Padraic Colum with *The King of Ireland's Son* (1916) and for several collections by Sinead de Valera. Fantasy worlds also inspired Oscar Wilde to write *The Happy Prince and Other Tales* (1888).

In a different vein, two prolific writers of the later nineteenth century whose novels were widely read outside Ireland, were Thomas Mayne Reid, the author of rollicking adventure stories, and L. T. Meade, writer of school stories for girls.

Patricia Lynch wrote over fifty books, many of them, such as *The Turf-Cutter's Donkey* (1934), set in a rural Ireland which at times becomes a land of magic. Rural life was a popular background for writers in the mid-twentieth century, such as Maura Laverty with *The Cottage in the Bog* (1945), and the western landscape is evoked by Walter Macken in *The Island of the Great Yellow Ox* (1966) and *The Flight of the Doves* (1967). Her native west of Ireland is used by Eilis Dillon as the background for many of her novels, such as *The Lost Island* (1952) and *The Coriander* (1963), and more recently, *The Island of Ghosts* which won the 1990 Bisto Book of the Year Award. However, in *The Children of Bach* (1993) she has written with considerable sensitivity about children faced with personal and political conflict in central Europe. Janet McNeill who was born in Dublin, has also produced a considerable number of titles, among them those featuring her eponymous hero, Specs McCann.

Belfast-born C. S. Lewis set his children's novels in the fantasy Land of Narnia, but Ulster itself is the setting for most of the historical novels of Meta Mayne Reid. Irish history is also the focus for most of the novels of Michael Mullen, although it may be argued that his best works are the magical *Magus the Lollipop Man* (1981) and *The Caravan* (1990) which has a contemporary background of social and economic deprivation. In 1991 Marita Conlon-McKenna won the International Reading Association Award for *Under the Hawthorn Tree* (1990), which describes some of the misery of the nineteenth-century potato famine. A detailed historical background characterises the historical novels of Morgan Llywelyn and a strong sense of the past is also evoked in John Quinn's *The Gold Cross of Kiladoo* (1992), but he displays a more sensitive interpretation of events gone by in *The Summer of Lily and Esme* (winner of the 1991 Bisto Book of the Year Award).

Martin Waddell is the author of over ninety books, ranging from picture books for the very young to works for older readers, which he writes under the name of Catherine Sefton. In a number of these, such as *Starry Night* (1986), his characters resolve tensions in their own lives against the background of conflict in Northern Ireland. The northern troubles are also the background for Belfast born Joan Lingard's Kevin and Sadie novels, but while it is also set in Ulster, this conflict is just hinted at in Sam McBratney's *Put a Saddle on a Pig* (1992), in which he moves from books like the Jimmy Zest series for younger readers, to writing for a teenage audience.

The central characters in the Giltspur trilogy by Cormac MacRaois move between the present and pre-historical times as good and evil battle for supremacy in the County Wicklow landscape. Moral battles with an environmental theme are the focus for Tom McCaughren's Fox series, the first of which, *Run With the Wind* (1983), won a Bisto Book of the Decade Award. McCaughren is also the author of a number of adventure stories as are Tony Hickey and Margrit Cruickshank, also author of *Circling the Triangle* (1991), a novel of teenage unrest and rebellion.

Poetry, picture books and non-fiction have all suffered the constraints of the small local market. Both the poetry and novels of Donegal poet Matthew Sweeney have been published in Britain, as has the outstanding work of artist P. J. Lynch who has illustrated the works of Oscar Wilde and W. B. Yeats among others.

Sculptor Rosamond Praeger created several picture books, including *Billy's Garden Plot* (1918) and the posthumously published *The Young Stamp Collectors* (1965). *The Sleeping Giant* (1991) was written and illustrated by Marie-Louise Fitzpatrick, whose Irish language picture book, *An Chanáil* (1988), won a Reading Association of Ireland Award and a Bisto Book of the Decade Award. This was published by the state-funded publishing house, An Gúm, which was founded in 1945 as a means of promoting the Irish language. An Gúm has published a number of picture books and other books for children, some of these translations or co-editions of titles originally published abroad, as well as original work.

Overall, the development of Irish language writing for children has paralleled that of English. The work of authors such as Padraig Pearse in the early part of this century and other more recent writers reflected a very traditional way of life, and it was not until the 1980s with the advent of publishers such as Cló Iar-Chonnachta that Irish language writing for young people has begun to adopt a more contemporary note.

The 1980s was the decade which saw a major upsurge in both writing and publishing for children, and also a growing appreciation of the importance of children's literature. In 1981 the Fourteenth Loughborough International Conference on Children's Literature took place in Dublin. The Children's Press publishing house was founded in 1980, and other publishers, notably O'Brien, Poolbeg and Wolfhound, began to pay serious attention to the juvenile market, supported on occasion by funding from the Arts Council of Ireland. Since then other publishers too have turned their attention in this direction. Production standards have improved considerably and increasingly books published in Ireland are marketed abroad.

The publishing of information books still lags behind fiction, both in terms of output and of quality. Exceptions to this include *Exploring the Book of Kells* (1988) and other titles by George Otto Simms, and some recent publications by An Gúm. Some Irish publishers have also begun to produce co-publications of non-fiction titles from abroad for the Irish market.

Ireland has provided a setting for writers from abroad too, such as Peter Carter's *Under Goliath* (1977), David Rees's *The Green Bough of Liberty* (1979) and Elizabeth Lutzeier's *The Coldest Winter* (1991), who have all captured the spirit of the country in their work.

Organisations active in promoting children's literature include the Youth Libraries Group of the Library Association of Ireland, The Reading Association of Ireland which offers a biennial award for outstanding books of Irish interest for children, the Children's Literature Association of Ireland (CLAI) and the Irish

Children's Book Trust. CLAI was founded in 1987 and through its Annual Conferences and seminars and twice-yearly publication, *Children's Books in Ireland*, provides a lively and pertinent commentary on the state of children's literature in Ireland and elsewhere. The Irish Children's Book Trust, established in 1989, published the *Irish Guide to Children's Books 1980–1990* (1990). The Trust is involved with both the selection of the Bisto Books of the Decade and the annual Bisto Book Awards for books by Irish authors or illustrators or which have been published in Ireland, and in creating the Irish Children's Book Room in the Dublin Writers' Museum. In 1991 the last two of these organisations combined to hold the first of a series of annual summer schools on children's literature. CLAI and the YLG also combine to compile a list of recommended reading for young people. This is published annually by the Booksellers Association during Children's Book Fortnight, a nationwide event which promotes reading by children and young people, mainly through events in libraries, bookshops and schools.

Traditionally, the school curriculum in both Irish and English did not encourage a wide range of reading by pupils, and school libraries are very considerably underresourced. This, however, is changing due to the advent of new curricula and a growing appreciation of the value of encouraging children to enjoy books, and allied to other developments discussed above, indicates an exciting future for the development of children's literature in Ireland.

## Further Reading

*Children's Books in Ireland* (1989– ) Ongoing.
Reece, L. and Rosenstock, G. (comp.) (1990) *Irish Guide to Children's Books. The Decade 1980–1990*, Dublin: Irish Children's Book Foundation.

# 62

# The Nordic Countries

## Boel Westin

Children's literature in the Nordic countries is comparatively well thought of. There are special Institutes for children's books in Finland, Norway and Sweden. Criticism and research are growing and several dissertations have been published since the 1970s, mainly in Sweden. Since 1983 there has been a special Chair of Children's Literature at the University of Stockholm. Children's reading has been stimulated in various ways through collaboration between schools and the public libraries. As a cultural export children's literature has been quite successful and many Nordic children's authors are internationally well-known. Among those who have been awarded the prestigious H. C. Andersen Medal are Astrid Lindgren and Maria Gripe (Sweden), Tove Jansson (Finland), Cecil Bødker, Ib Spang Olsen and Svend Otto S (Denmark) and Tormod Haugen (Norway).

The history of Nordic children's literature displays some obvious similarities between the countries; there are differences, partly due to various political conditions. In Finland and Norway children's books have played a part in the struggle for a national identity. Finland was an integral part of Sweden for 600 years (until 1809), then a duchy within the Russian Empire, and gained its independence in 1917. Since its children's literature had for a long time been written in Swedish, the production of a Finnish children's literature became of vital importance. Norway achieved independence from Denmark in 1814 but then became part of a union with Sweden until 1905. The struggle for a national identity as well as a native literary language is clearly reflected in children's books. They have became a vital feature of the nation's cultural life.

The first books for children in the Nordic countries were published in the sixteenth century and into the early nineteenth century there was a strong reliance on imported books (and pictures), mostly translations and adaptations of religious texts, courtesy books and fables, generally from Germany and France. In Iceland, where children's literature is a late phenomenon, generally dating from after the Second World War, the first children's book appeared in 1780.

The national awakening during the romantic period in the nineteenth and early twentieth centuries paved the way for national children's literatures; collections of folk-tales, rhymes and songs were published in the mid-nineteenth century, and the first picture books appeared around the 1880s. The century ended in a wave of fairy tales, often issued in annuals, short story collections and magazines. Elementary school reforms, the improved printing techniques, new ideas about child-rearing and society's growing interest in children's social upbringing prepared the ground for an expanding literary market. Children's literature began to respond to the needs of children rather than adults.

During the twentieth century, realism has been dominant, although the most original and well-known authors are to be found at the interface between fantasy and realism. The tradition of fairy tales has also been strong, prompted by authors like H. c. Andersen in Denmark, Zachris Topelius in Finland and Astrid Lindgren in Sweden. In the period between the wars the output relied heavily on traditional girls' and boys' stories. Modern child psychology and literary modernism of the 1930s and 1940s encouraged experiments and artistic innovations in children's books; the most obvious examples are found in Denmark and Sweden. Later mutual trends are the problem-oriented novel for young adults in the 1970s, succeeded by the renaissance of fantasy and fairy tales in the 1980s. The most interesting developments in recent years have been made in the field of the picture book. One could even say that the basic idea of compartmentalising children's literature according to different ages is being called into question. Nordic picture books in the 1980 and 1990s are often visually advanced and poetically narrated, based on a close interaction between text and picture, and on the whole, they seem to reject the traditional conception of a specific readership.

## Denmark

The first children's book in Danish was *Bøorne Spiegel* [The Child's Mirror] by Niels Bredal (1568), an adaptation of Erasmus's courtesy book *De Civilitate Morum Puerilium*. The romanticist Adam Oehlenschläger introduced the Grimms' tales in 1816. A first collection of Danish folk-tales appeared in 1823, but the major edition of Danish folk-tales, rhymes and songs was initiated by the folklorist Svend Grundtvig in the mid-nineteenth century. A children's collection of fables was made by H. V. Kaalund, *Fabler for Børn* (1845). Original picture books appeared quite early. Of fundamental importance are Johan and Pietro Krohn's *Peters jul* [Peter's Christmas], a verse tale with black and white pictures (1866) and *Hvorledes Dagen Gaaer for Lille Lise* (1863) by Lorenz Frølich, a delightful depiction of the everyday life of a little girl. As Frølich lived in France the book first appeared in French, *La Journée de Mlle Lili* (1862).

In 1835 Hans Christian Andersen (1805–1875) published his first fairy tales, *Eventyr fortalte for Børn* [Fairy Tales told for Children]. Up until 1874 he produced more than 150 tales and stories. Selections appeared in English in 1846. Andersen later dropped 'told for children' from the title, thus indicating an audience of all ages. These ambivalent tales were originally based on folk motifs, but Andersen soon created a fairy tale canon of his own. The usual order of events in the traditional folk-tale is reversed – objects of everyday life are humanised. Andersen's stylistic synthesis of oral and written language also formed a new narrative discourse. Among the most popular of his tales throughout the world are 'The tinder box', 'The princess and the pea', 'The little mermaid', 'The swineherd', 'The ugly duckling', 'The little match girl', and 'The snow queen'. Apparently Andersen was well aware of his future world fame; he once wrote to a friend that the fairy tales would make him immortal. His impact on children's literature in the Nordic countries has been exceptional.

In order to introduce low-price quality literature for children, 'Børnenes Bogsamling', a publisher's series (of classics, fairy tales and so on), was founded in 1896 (Sweden followed the example a few years later). A number of children's periodicals, magazines and annuals also emerged.

Teachers have played an important role in Danish children's literature during the twentieth century, both as critics and authors; indeed, the relationship between children's books and the school system is a characteristic feature of Danish children's literature. Children's novels between 1900 and 1945 contain three myths, all connected to the attitudes and aims of the school: the myth of the good man, the myth of the family without inner problems and the myth about the fair and righteous society (Winge 1976). Books were written in a traditional and often didactic mode, aimed either for girls or boys. Among the popular writers were Bertha Holst (girls' stories) and Walter Christmas (boys' stories). Karin Michaëlis (1872–1950), considered as the most innovative writer, created a girl's *Bildungsroman* with her widely translated Bibi series, beginning with *Bibi: A Little Danish Girl\**, in 1927. (An asterisk indicates that the book has been published in English.)

In the field of picture books a naïvistic and child-oriented pictorial style developed in the 1930–1940s, influenced by Russian poster design and its use of bright colours and clear line-drawing technique. The issue at stake was the little child's needs and inner yearnings. Among the most famous books are *Palle alene i Verden* [Palle Alone in the World] by Arne Ungermann (pictures) and Jens Sigsgaard (text) in 1942 and Egon Mathiesen's *Mis med de blå Øjne* [The Cat with the Blue Eyes] (1949). Mathiesen (1907–1976) published a number of picture books with the deliberate aim of creating a rhythmic interaction of text, pictures and colours. Two highly influential names in the picture book genre are Ib Spang Olsen (b.1921), with his experimental forms, one artistic highlight is *Det lille lokomotiv* [The Little Train\*] (1954) and Svend Otto S. (b.1916), a popular illustrator of fairy tales, who also has published a string of picture books of his own. Both have been active into the 1990s and their work has influenced the richness and variation of pictorial style in modern Danish picture books. Erik Hjorth Nielsen (b.1937) works in the naturalistic tradition, Jan Mogensen (b.1945) has reinterpreted the tales of H. C. Andersen; others have revitalised the naïvistic concept of the 1930s. Notable in the new generation of illustrators are Dorte Karrebæk (b.1946) and Lilian Brøgger (b.1950), both showing an obvious interest in developing the picture as a narrative medium.

Society was consciously involved in children's reading in the late 1960s. The close relationship between children's literature and the school and library systems has resulted in the publication of a lot of easy-to-read books and depictions of children's everyday life in contemporary society. Thøger Birkeland (b.1922) is one of the most prominent contemporary realists, several of his books being accounts of daily family life. The year 1967 proved a milestone, both in terms of motif and literary expression. Preben Ramløv (1919–1988) examined slavery in the West Indies in the nineteenth century by means of magic realism in the novel *Massa Peter*. Cecil Bødker (b.1927), one of Denmark's internationally best known modern children's authors, published her first book in the historical series about the boy Silas: her protagonist is both good and bad, which was something new. The very same year Ole Lund Kierkegaard (1940–1979), writer of popular humorous stories in a somewhat hyperbolic style, also made his debut.

Problem-oriented realism and social criticism dominated books for young adults in the 1970s, while a shift towards a more fantastic and historical perspective came in the 1980s. Among the foremost in the historical genre is Gerd Rindel (b.1941), notably with her chronicle of the life of a Jewish family around the year 1900. The Second World War has been a recurrent theme in historical novels. One notable depiction of the struggle of the resistance during the German occupation is *Lulu* (1988), written by a 15-year-old girl, Cæcilie Lassen.

Modern Danish books for young adults are to some extent more outspoken than in the other Nordic countries. Earlier taboos (sexuality, criminality, violence) are deliberately broken and traditional moral values are questioned. The most controversial writer is Bernt Haller (b.1946), author of both adventure stories and novels of social criticism. His first book *Katamaranen* (1976), focusing the relationship between two boys, aroused the ire of both critics and librarians (it was banned from the libraries) with its comparatively unmitigated violence and sexuality. Criticism of modern civilisation and society has become intense in recent years, and in the 1980s and 1990s several terrifying visions of the future have appeared. However, probably the most remarkable novel of the 1980s is *Shamran* (1985) by Bjarne Reuter (b.1950). Written in a mythological mode, this novel displays a boy's mortal struggle in a battle between good and evil in a world filled with oppression. Reuter has written a number of books both for children and young adults in different genres. In the context of modern Danish children's literature he is one of the most widely read authors.

## Finland

A primer written in Finnish, *ABC-kiria*, was published in 1543, but up until the mid-nineteeth century only a 100 or so books for children (in Finnish and Swedish) appeared. Of fundamental importance to the vivid fairy tale tradition in Finnish children's literature is *Suomen kansan Satuja ja Tarinoita* [The Folk and Fairy Tales of the Finnish People] (1852–1866), a collection of Finnish folk-tales and stories by the folklorist Eero Salmelainen. The national epic *Kalevala* (1835), by Elias Lönnroth, later appeared in an abridged version for children. The emerging interest in creating a truly national culture for Finnish children was revealed in two picture books, *Kuvia Suomen lasten elämästä* [The Finnish Picture Book] in 1882 and *Suomalainen kuvakirja lapsille ja nuorisolle* [The Finnish Picture Book for Children] in 1894.

Through the work of the Finno-Swedish author Zachris Topelius (1818–1898) children's literature became established as an independent genre with artistic quality. First influenced by H. C. Andersen, Topelius soon developed a child-oriented style of writing of his own, and his first collection of stories was published in 1847. Topelius aimed directly at children and displayed a strong feeling for the Finnish nature. His numerous fairy tales, poems and plays are collected in *Läsning för barn* [Reading for Children] (8 vols, 1865–1896). He also wrote historical novels. Topelius has been translated into some twenty languages and for decades he remained the number one Finnish children's writer.

The work of Anni Swan (1875–1958), the first classic children's writer in Finnish, is closely linked to the world of fairy tales (6 vols, 1901–1923). The narrative is lyrical, often symbolic, but places the child at the centre. Her many books for young adults feature both boys and girls. *Pikkupappilassa* [In the Small Vicarage] (1922) and *Ulla ja Mark* [Ulla and Mark] (1924) are two highlights. Notable works of their day were the fantastic and burlesque stories about 'the Kiljunen family' (1914–1925) written by Jalmari Finne (1874–1938). After independence in 1917, the production of children's books in Finnish increased, although it mainly consisted of traditional boy's and girl's stories.

Among the more innovative Finno-Swedish authors during the first half of the century was Nanny Hammarström (1870–1953) who published several animal stories; internationally known is *Två myrors äventyr* [The Adventures of the Two Ants] (1906). Of interest in the 1920s and 1930s are the nonsense stories by Lisa Cawén-Heikkinen and the lyrical fairy tales by Viola Renvall, both probably influenced by Finno-Swedish literary modernism. A popular and lyrical fairy story in Finnish was *Pessi ja Illusia* [The Earth and the Wings] (1944), by Yrjö Kokko.

The foremost name in Finnish children's literature is however Tove Jansson (b.1914), one of the great modern Swedish-language authors. The nine Moomin books (1945–1970) with their closely observed psychology, wisdom and humour have been translated into more than thirty languages. They all play on a basic theme of order and chaos. The first books are marked by the apocalyptic mood of the post-war era although in the end life emerges triumphant. The lightest in spirit is *Trollkarlens hatt* [Finn Family Moomintroll*] (1948); the later *Trollvinter* [Moominland Midwinter*] (1957) is darker and deals with questions of identity. The dreamlike finale of the profoundly original Moomin world is *Sent i november* [Moominvalley in November*] (1970). Since then Jansson has written mainly for adults. Her work for children is based on a close interaction of text and illustration. Most visually elegant of her picture books is *Hur gick det sen?* [The Book about Moomin, Mymble and Little My*] (1952). The world-famous Moomin comics, based on the books, began in the early 1950s.

Fantasy and fairy tale have by tradition had a great impact on Finnish children's literature, and this phenomenon did not change after the war – rather the contrary. Aila Nissinen (1916–1973) and Marjatta Kurenniemi (b.1918) are two representatives of the 1950s. Writers have contributed in different ways to the innovations of these two genres but the foremost names are Irmelin Sandman Lilius (b.1936), a Finno-Swedish author, and Kaarina Helakisa (b.1946). In Tulavall, the literary universe of Sandman Lilius, reality interacts with supernatural forces: it may be described as an amalgamation of fairy tale, myth and fantasy. A central work is the trilogy about the mythical queen Mrs Sola (1967–1971), including *Gullkrona gränd* [Gold Crown Lane*], *Gripanderska gården* [The Gold-Maker's House*] and *Gångande grå* [Horses of the Night*]. A deliberate female perspective is revealed in the writings of Kaarina Helakisa, as in the adapted folk-tale *Olena ja Vassuska* [Olena and Vassuska] (1979). Her fantastic stories often include surrealistic elements. Since the 1970s Leena Krohn (b.1947) has been a popular writer of literary fairy tales, while fantasy and humour are the tools of Hannu Mäkelä (b.1943).

Realistic books, however, did not become important until the 1960s. Among the notable Finno-Swedish authors for smaller children are Bo Carpelan (b.1926) and Marita Lindquist (b.1918), both depicting children's experiences of everyday life. Books for young adults, focusing on social and psychological problems, have been written in Finnish: for example, the drug problem was discussed in *Tabut* [The Pills] (1970) by Margareta Keskistalo (b.1921). A typical protagonist is the male anti-hero, as in the novel *Sigmund Freudin kaamea flunssa* [The Fatal Cold of Freud] (1972) by Uolevi Nojonen (b.1939).

In the field of picture books, there was a revival in the 1980s: the number of books published was many times that of the previous decade. Clear colours, and a sometimes ascetic but highly visual aesthetic unite many of the new illustrators: Kaarina Kaila, Hannu Taina and Kristina Luohi are known abroad, Luohi with her portrayal of daily life in the *Aino* books. The modern picture books must be considered as the most interesting feature in the 1980s and 1990s.

## Iceland

Few books were published in Iceland until the twentieth century. The first children's title was Vigfus Jonsson's poems for children (1780). Influenced by H. C. Andersen, the poet Jonas Hallgrimsson published children's stories in the first half of the nineteenth century. In the early twentieth century Sigurbjörn Sveinsson (1858–1950) with his childhood memories, *Bernskan* (1907–1908) introduced a highly influential genre in Icelandic children's literature. Memories by Jon Sveinsson (1857–1944), one of the few writers of children's books known abroad, followed a few years later. His books were originally published in German, the first as *Nonni: Erlebnisse eines jungen isländers* (1913). Children's books mainly consisted of short stories, memories and fairy tales. The first author to publish a children's novel was Gunnar M. Magnuss (1898–?) in the 1930s. The foremost name in modern Icelandic children's literature is Gudrun Helgadottir (b.193?), author of popular books for smaller children. Notable is her picture book story about the love story of a female giant, *Astarsaga ur fjöllunum* [The Tale of Flumbra] (1981), with pictures by Brian Pilkington.

## Norway

Willum Stephanson's *Lommebog for Børn* (1798) was an early attempt to create a non-didactic book for children, but an independent children's literature did not develop until the middle of the nineteenth century. Of literary interest is the children's tale *Lille Alvilde* (1829) by the romanticist Maurits Hansen. The epoch's foremost author, Henrik Wergeland (1808–1845), interpreted European children's literature for Norwegian children. In 1840 he launched his classical collection of verses, *Vinterblommor i Barnekammaret* [Winter Flowers in the Nursery]. Folk-tales were collected by Jørgen Moe and P. Chr. Asbjørnsen in the 1840s. Of importance is also Moe's *I Brønden og i Kjærnet* [In the Well and in the Pond] (1850), regarded as an artistic precursor to the realistic tradition of the twentieth century. It is characteristic that the greatest authors of the epoch wrote for children as well as for adults. In Norway writing for children is generally said to be the literary equivalent of 'crop-rotation' (Vold 1989).

Children's literature in Norway is also connected with the maintenance of a national identity. The first picture book, *Norsk Billedbog for Børn* [Norwegian Picture Book for Children] (1888) deliberately emphasised nationalism. Wergeland was one of the text contributors, the pictures were by the later well-known illustrator Eivind Nielsen.

The period from the 1890s until the First World War, is usually referred to as the Golden Age in Norwegian children's literature. Folk-tales and fairy stories were illustrated and published for children by famous artists like Erik Werenskiøld and Theodor Kittelsen. The new authors, often writing in a realistic mode, focused on the condition of children in the family and society, and depicted the peasants, fishermen and shepherds of the Norwegian countryside. A couple of books by Hans Aanrud were translated to German, but the most well-known author of the period is Dikken Zwilgmeyer (1853–1913), one of the many practitioners of the Norwegian literary 'crop-rotation'. As a founder of the Norwegian girl's story she is a classic. The twelve books about the active and independent girl Inger-Johanne, starting in 1890 with *Vi Børn* [What Happened to Inger-Johanne*], launched a new kind of female protagonist.

The inter-war years were long regarded as a period of stagnation, but new research will probably re-assess this rather gloomy view. Serials aimed for either boys or girls flourished. A couple of picture books of political interest were published during the years of German occupation. Using the children's book as a camouflage (the Nazi regime had enforced censorship) the main purpose was the hidden message of resistance. Well-known is *Snorre Sel* (1941) by Fridtjof Sælen, a fable about a little seal and a grampus.

A renewal of children's literature came in the early 1950s, when three highly innovative authors became prominent. They all gained a unique popularity due to their appearance in the radio. Anne-Cath. Vestly (b.1920), author of more than forty books, began with realistic stories about children in urban surroundings; one classic is *Ole Aleksander Filibom-bom-bom* (1953). She later moved towards contemporary realism in discussing family and sex-role problems, mostly ending in positive solutions. The many-sided authorship of Thorbjørn Egner (1912–1990) consists of songs, plays, tales, prose and short stories. With his imaginative and deliberately fictional universes he broke with the powerful realistic tradition. Classics in this category are the animal society depicted in *Klatremus og de andre dyrerne i Hakkebakkeskogen* (1953) and the dynamic society of robbers and common people in *Folk og Røvere i Kardemomme by* [The Singing Town*] (1955). Egner has appeared in around twenty languages and is one of the most translated Norwegian authors for children. Alf Prøysen (1914–1970), whose writing consists of both songs and stories, worked with fantastic elements, often derived from the folk-tales. The stories are mainly set in the countryside, as in his well-known stories about Mrs Pepperpot, the woman who shrinks without warning. The first book *Kjerringa som ble så lita som ei teskje* came out in 1957. A visual and musical direction in children's poetry was introduced by an established poet for adults, Inger Hagerup (1906–1985) in the early 1950s.

The realistic tradition was continued well into the 1970s, but the several new writers are characterised by their desire to explore the narrative possibilities of children's literature. Significantly, most of them also write for adults. Tor-Åge

Bringsvaerd (b.1939) is the foremost exponent of a new fantastic literature, combining the fantastic elements with social concerns. Rune Belsvik (b.1956) has examined the inner lives of teenagers in books for young adults. The historical novel was revitalised by Torill Hauger (b.1943): the Viking Age is one of her specialities. Most prominent in children's poetry is Einar Økland (b.1940), who has experimented with free verse. Picture books, an expanding field in the 1980s, have equally developed a poetical kind of narrative. Books by Fam Ekman (b.1946) and Wenche Øyen (b.1946) have won international recognition.

Children's literature in the 1980s has been described as an area where authors can find linguistic and generic challenges. Significantly, one of the most prominent names in modern children's literature has rejected the tradition of 'crop-rotation'. Tormod Haugen (b.1945), author of books both in the realistic and the fantastic mode, has declared that he deliberately writes for young readers. Among the highlights are the novels *Dagen som försvann* [The Lost Day*] (1983) and *Vinterstedet* [The Winter Residence*] (1984). Haugen's blend of different genres and his deliberate experiments with various narrative techniques has made him a children's postmodernist. His sensitive exploration of childhood, *Skriket fra jungelen* [The Cry from the Jungle*] (1989), was awarded the H. C. Andersen medal in 1990.

## Sweden

The history of Swedish children's books began with an adaptation of a German homily on maidenhood for young women, *En sköön och härligh jungfrw speghel* [A Pretty and Splendid Maiden's Mirror] (1591). A children's magazine appeared as early as 1766. The teachers of the future Gustavus III wrote fables, and Carl Gustaf Tessin's witty collections of letters (1751), dedicated to the crown-prince, became important for a literature of Swedish origin. An English version, *Letters from an Old Man to a Young Prince*, was published in 1756. During the Romantic period German cultural life became highly influential. Collections of folk-tales and songs were made in the 1830s and 1840s. The first classic is *Lille Viggs äfventyr på julafton* [The Adventures of Little Vigg on Christmas Eve*] (1871) by Viktor Rydberg (1828–1895), an ambiguous dream narrative about a boy's moral growth. The picture book began to develop in the 1880s, partly as a reaction against the import of mass-produced illustrations. The aim was to depict children in settings that were recognisably Swedish, and the texts were borrowed from Swedish folklore. Female artists like Jenny Nyström (1854–1946), with *Barnkammarens bok* [The Nursery Book] (1882) and *Svenska barnboken* [The Swedish Children's Book] (1886) led the way, but with the debut of Elsa Beskow (1874–1953) in 1897 a new picture book era began. Beskow wrote thirty books over fifty-five years, which are still in print. Her texts and pictures reveal a strong affection for children and family, but adult authority is seldom questioned. The forest became an important setting, as in *Puttes äfventyr i blåbärsskogen* [Peter in Blueberry Land*] (1901) and *Tomtebobarnen* [The Little Elves of Elf Nook*] (1910). The plots may well be fantastic, but the depictions of nature are always botanically accurate. The five books about Aunt Green, Aunt Brown and Aunt Lavender (1918–1947) present a collective of females and broadens the conventional family perspective. One classic is also *Kattresan* [The Cat Journey] (1909) by Ivar Arosenius.

In 1900, when Ellen Key issued her internationally influential appeal *Barnets Århundrade* [The Century of the Child*] the modern child-oriented era began. Teachers launched various projects to promote reading: a publishers' series of quality literature (*Barnbiblioteket Saga*), annuals, magazines, collections of fairy tales, rhymes and short stories. The illustrations, by Swedish artists like John Bauer, became important. Furthermore, the epoch's foremost authors were engaged in writing for children. The world famous tale *Nils Holgerssons underbara resa genom Sverige* [The Wonderful Adventures of Nils*] (1906–1907) by Selma Lagerlöf (1858–1940) was part of a reader project for the elementary schools, initiated by the teachers. The first naturalistic children's novel, *Barnen ifrå Frostmofjället* [Children of the Moor*] (1907) by Laura Fitinghoff (1808–1908), also belongs to this first golden era of children's literature.

The period between the wars has been regarded as a time of retrospection, but new research is about to change that picture. Some of the girls' stories reveal a surprisingly radical and feminist view in describing girls' development, maturity and plans for the future. Among the interesting authors are Jeanna Oterdahl and Ester Blenda Nordström.

Modern child psychology and literary modernism had great impact on the new authors that emerged after the Second World War. The 1940s witnessed a pluralism in both motifs and genres. Earlier idyllic realism gave way to a more credible approach to reality, but mention of the war (Sweden was neutral) is conspicuously lacking. The old didactic concept of children's literature was challenged, and, in fact deconstructed. Astrid Lindgren's (b.1907) literary breakthrough came in 1945, with the first book about the strong and independent girl Pippi Longstocking. Lindgren's diverse and extensive output is based on well-known genres, but the familiar genre-patterns are twisted and changed into new contexts. Existential problems are tackled through myth and fairy tale in *Mio, my Mio* (1954), while the adventure story forms an allegory over life and death in *Bröderna Lejonhjärta* [The Brothers Lionheart*] (1973). Her novel, *Ronja rövardotter* [Ronia, the Robber's Daughter*] (1981), an allegory of love and family dynamics, expresses a powerful plea for life against violence. Lindgren's impact on Swedish children's literature, both as an author and a publishing editor, is exceptional. She is the most widely read Swedish author of our time, and her books have been translated into more than sixty languages.

The modification of earlier forms also marks the poetry of Lennart Hellsing (b.1919), whose extensive output of poems, lyrics, verses and short tales began in the mid-1940s and continues in the 1990s. The texts oscillate between nonsense, modernistic experiments and concentrated poetic imagery. One experimental book is *Summa summarum* (1950), a multi-media art project bringing together text and picture, music and movement.

A shift towards social and contemporary realism marks the output of the 1960s and 1970s. Inger (b.1930) and Lasse Sandberg (b.1924) have produced a number of picture books, focusing on the small child's view of reality. Gunilla Wolde (b.1939) addressed the not yet talking children with several brief and simply-drawn picture books such as *Thomas Goes Out* (1969). New family situations are reflected in

Gunilla Bergström's (b.1942) series of picture books about Alfie Atkins and his single father (from 1972).

Books for young adults focused on social and political (often global) injustices, family problems, death, sex roles and sexuality. Gunnel Beckman's (b.1910) *Tillträde till festen* [Admission to the Feast*] (1969) combines typical motifs. She also examined from the viewpoint of young women hitherto forbidden subjects such as fear of pregnancy, and abortion. Maria Gripe (b.1923) writes on contemporary realism as well as fantasy-oriented novels for young adults, often centring on problems of identity. One major work is the sequence of four novels set around the time of the First World War, beginning with *Skuggan över stenbänken* [The Shadow over the Stone Bench*] (1982). The work of Barbro Lindgren (b.1937) ranges over nonsense stories, poetry and information books.

The greatest changes during the 1980s occurred in the field of the picture book. Its increasing share of the children's literary market is due to several factors: growth of interest in the picture as a narrative medium, a new awareness of the interaction between the text and the illustrations, and a new generation of artists who have been influenced by such media as films and comics. Eva Eriksson (b.1949) has developed an expressive style, inspired by the artistic language of cartoons, Anna Höglund (b.1958) has worked within a symbolic mould and Anna-Clara Tidholm (b.1946) has developed a poetically evocative imagery. A noted debut was made by Pija Lindenbaum (b.1955) with her provocative and humorous tale *Else-Marie och småpapporna* [Else-Marie and the Seven Fathers*] (1990). Notable is also *Linnea in Monet's Garden* (1985), an art book for children, by Christina Björk and Lena Anderson.

In the 1980s children's prose has shown a clear retrospective tendency, manifested in historical novels and depictions of childhood. A book in this retrospective vein is *Janne, min vän* [Johnny, my Friend*] (1985) by Peter Pohl (b.1940). This book about adult society's exploitation of children was the outstanding novel of the decade, innovative both in its disregard of traditional narrative techniques and in its lack of a happy ending. Mats Wahl (b.1945) is one exponent of the new historical novel with its camouflaged discussion of ethical values and ideologies. His contemporary novels equally question traditional moral values, as in *Vinterviken* (1993). Ulf Stark (b.1944) and Viveca Sundvall (b.1944) represent different aspects of the new comic approach in the prose of the 1980s and 1990s, and the last decades have generally been characterised by the search for new forms of literary expression.

# References

Vold, K. B. (1989) 'Contemporary Norwegian writing for children', *News from the Top of the World. Norwegian Literature Today* 2.

Winge, M. (1976) *Dansk børnelitteratur 1900–1945*, Copenhagen: Gyldendal [English summary: Danish Children's Literature 1900–1945].

# Further Reading

## Denmark

*Roots in Denmark: Danish Children's Literature Today* (1992) Copenhagen: Danish Literature Centre.

Sønsthage K. and Eilstrup, L. (ed.) (1992) *Dansk Børnelitteratur Historie* [History of Danish Children's Literature], Copenhagen: Høst and Søn.

## Finland

Lehtonen, M. and Rajalin, M. (eds) (1987) *Barnboken i Finland förr och nu*, Stockholm: Rabén and Sjögren [English summary: Children's Books in Finland].

Westin, B. (1988) *Familjen i dalen. Tove Janssons muminvärld*, Stockholm: Bonniers [English summary: The Family in the Valley. The Moomin World of Tove Jansson].

## Iceland

Adalsteinsdottir, S. (1981) *Islendskar barnabækur 1780–1979*, Reykjavik: Mal og Menning.

## Norway

Breen, E. (1988) *Slik skrev de. Verdi og virkelighet i barnebøker, 1968–1983*, Oslo: Aschehoug.

Hagemann, S. (1964–1970) *Barnelitteratur i Norge*, Oslo: Aschehoug: I. –1850, II. 1850–1914, III. 1914–1970 [English summary: Children's Literature in Norway].

## Sweden

Edström, V. (1992) *Astrid Lindgren – vildtoring och lägereld*, Stockholm: Rabén and Sjögren [English summary: Astrid Lindgren – Campfire Rebel].

Klingberg, G. (1964) *Svensk barn- och ungdomslitteratur 1591–1839. En pedagogisk och bibliografisk översikt*, Stockholm: Natur och Kultur [English summary: Swedish Literature for Children and Adolescents 1591–1839].

von Zweigbergk, E. (1965) *Barnboken i Sverige 1750–1950*, Stockholm: Bonniers [English summary: Children's Books in Sweden 1750–1950].

Westin, B. (1991) *Children's Literature in Sweden*, Stockholm: The Swedish Institute.

# 63

# The Netherlands

## Anne de Vries

### The Origin of a Separate Children's Literature

Until recently it was commonly thought that a separate children's literature in The Netherlands emerged at the end of the eighteenth century, when Hieronymus van Alphen published his famous poetry for children (1778). This view was slightly adjusted by the appearance of *De hele Bibelebontse berg* [The Whole Meeny-Miny Mountain] (Heimeriks and van Toorn 1989) – 'The History of Children's Books in The Netherlands and Flanders from the Middle Ages until now'. However, the authors do not name any children's books from the Middle Ages; and from the sixteenth and seventeenth centuries they mention mainly didactic literature: schoolbooks, catechisms, and so on. There are only a few exceptions, such as the collection *Kinderliedekens* [Songs for Children] (1630).

At the end of the eighteenth century one can see a distinct watershed. There was an explosive increase in the number of books for children, with fiction becoming dominant. In other words, children's literature as we know it came into being, and that is exactly how it was perceived at the time. In 1779, the author Elisabeth Wolff, famous for her epistolary novels for adults, wrote in an essay on education: 'In one respect, our era can be distinguished very well from all previous times. This is the era, in which one writes for children.'

But one thing became very clear thanks to *De hele Bibelebontse berg*: a separate children's literature did not come into being suddenly at the end of the eighteenth century: it was the result of a process which took more than two hundred years, and which was connected to the discovery of childhood as a separate stage of life (Ariès 1960).

### Eighteenth and Nineteenth Centuries: From Morality to Entertainment

This process was accelerated during the Enlightenment. The doctrine of empiricism, implying that man was moulded completely by experience and that virtue was the natural result of knowledge, stimulated great interest in education. This led to the creation of a separate children's literature: children's books were considered as an outstanding way of expanding knowledge: learning through playing. Hardly any attention was paid to the needs of children; although the authors applied themselves to using simple language and a childlike presentation, everything was concentrated on the moral content, the 'lesson'.

Hieronymus van Alphen's *Kleine gedigten voor kinderen* (3 volumes, 1778–1782; English translation: *Poetry For Children*, 1856) fits this description completely. Apart from a few poems about God's love and the love of father and mother, he put model children on the stage. In poem after poem, virtues are shown to the reader: gratitude, modesty, honesty, patience, obedience, inquisitiveness, diligence.

The reviews were unanimously laudatory: the poems were praised for the profitable lessons they contained, articulated in a language that children could understand. The collection appeared to fulfill exactly the needs of the cultivated public, as was proven by seven printings of the first volume in 1778. But that was not all: the poems were written with a rare literary talent, because of which they survived until the beginning of the twentieth century, and acquired a place in the literary history of The Netherlands, as very few children's books did.

This success stimulated other authors to make an effort as well. Within one year there was such a large supply of children's books that they were considered a separate literary category; besides poetry, other genres appeared. But for a very long time Van Alphen remained the example for authors and the standard for critics. For more than half a century, he overshadowed his followers: they could imitate his moral lessons, but not his talent.

As far as we know, the needs of children were not taken into account before 1830, for a thorough inventory of nineteenth-century children's books has not been made yet: to a large extent, our knowledge of this period consists of stereotypes. Although this period did not produce real classics, as it did in England and Germany, a serious investigation might unearth some attractive, childlike books, which were forgotten because they did not fulfil the pedagogical demands of their time.

After 1850 several new genres emerged. School-teachers, like P. J. Andriessen and P. Louwerse, covered almost the complete history of The Netherlands in numerous children's novels. And around 1880 the girl's novel (in imitation of Louisa May Alcott's books) and the boy's novel came into vogue.

## 1900–1945: The Republic of Childhood

At the turn of the century children's literature began to bloom, partly because of the increasing interest in children. By that time it was generally accepted that children's books should first of all offer diversion. Moral considerations were still applied, but the emphatic moral had been replaced by self-censorship by the authors. The nursery no longer had an outlook on the adults' world: children lived in their own *jeugdland*.

Even in historical surveys authors often react against this 'segregation', but it can also be interpreted in a positive way. Child labour had been abolished, compulsory education had just been adopted. In this 'century of the child' children were to enjoy their childhood years in peace. In children's literature this notion was reflected by a growing attention to the emotions of children, their play and their leisure. And although the image of childhood was sometimes too happy for today's taste, the increasing interest in children also became apparent from the fact that accredited artists were recruited to illustrate children's books. The happy world of children can still be seen on the pictures of Rie Cramer and Henriëtte Willebeek Lemair (who also illustrated a number of English children's books).

In children's poetry of that period one finds the influence of nursery rhymes, and themes such as dolls' tea-parties, the arrival of a baby brother or sister, and small children's worries. In prose 'domestic realism' came into vogue, in which the world was reduced to the children's immediate surroundings (mainly countryside – the big city was not considered a suitable setting in which to enjoy your childhood years). This genre produced one of the first classics: *Afke's tiental* (1903) [Afke's Ten (1936)] by Nienke van Hichtum: a story about a working-class family with ten children, kept together by a loving, self-effacing mother.

Another classic was published a decade earlier: C. Joh. Kieviet's *Uit het leven van Dik Trom* [From the Life of Dik Trom] (1891) is the portrait of a 'real Dutch boy', who plays all possible pranks, but has a heart of gold. Initially, it was praised as a revitalising and refreshing boy's novel, but when its success resulted in innumerable imitations and the 'rascal's story' grew into an extensive genre, more and more objections were made: boyish pranks were assumed to set bad examples; some people predicted that the genre would create a lawless generation.

## 1945–1960: The Revolt against Isolation

After the Second World War one may observe an increasing interest in children's books. At that time, there was great concern about an alleged cultural and social 'decay' among children and young people; and good children's books were considered as a means to stop this process. This was why money was provided for the creation of the Bureau Boek en Jeugd (Book and Youth Bureau) in 1952 to give information about children's books. At the opening of the first Children's Book Week, in 1955, the first Children's Book of the Year award was presented (since 1971 this award has been continued as the *Gouden en Zilveren Griffel* (Gold Pencil and Silver Pencil) (literally, Slate Pencil)).

The tone of children's literature itself gradually changed, especially in the work of the generation that made its debut after the war. The most striking example is Annie M. G. Schmidt (1911–1995), who is generally recognised as the most versatile and most talented children's book author in The Netherlands. Her influence has been great and the writers of the 1970s and 1980s are particularly indebted to her.

From the very beginning, her children's books showed a happily anarchistic world, which was completely new in Dutch children's literature. She showed not even a vestige of moralism, and there was often a rebellion against decorum. She began with poetry (from 1947 in the newspaper *Het Parool*, and from 1950 in books). The form of her poems has much in common with nursery rhymes: for instance, many repetitions, alliteration and a great richness of sound. In content there are analogies as well, especially in the many nonsense poems with mysterious formulae and illogical associations. We meet eccentric characters, such as the mayor who paints ducks on the walls of the town hall, but overcomes this habit in the end: 'now he paints tigers on the walls'. There are also subdued poems, about major events in a child's life ('The loose tooth') or a lullaby for a little porcupine. An anthology from her poetry, *Pink Lemonade*, was published in English in the USA in 1981.

She also wrote stories for young children, which two generations of Dutch children have now grown up with: *Jip en Janneke* (8 vols, 1953–1960) [Mick and Mandy, 3 vols, 1961; *Bob and Jilly,* 3 vols, 1976–1980]. But the highlights of her work are fantasy stories: *Minoes* (1970) [Minnie, 1992], *Pluk van de Petteflet* [Pluk and his Breakdown Lorry] (1971) and *Otje* (1980). These novels have a realistic, modern setting, but the world is 'enchanted' and includes with fairy tale elements, for example talking animals, who assist the protagonists in their fight against injustice. The structure shows the author's mastery; although the story appears to be told in a casual way, all threads come together in the end and every detail has a meaning.

In realistic stories for older children the main development was that the world grew larger, in more than one sense: more and more stories were set in other countries, often far away; while the border between the world of children and the world of adults was disappearing as well. Two authors stood out in this genre: An Rutgers van der Loeff-Basenau (1910–1990) and Miep Diekmann (b.1925).

The work of Rutgers van der Loeff contained educational elements within traditional literary forms, for instance in *De kinderkaravaan* (1949) [Children on the Oregon Trail, 1961] and *Lawines razen* (1954) [Avalanche, 1958].

Diekmann broke new ground in many other respects: she paid more attention to the psychology of her characters, explored new literary forms, and pushed back thematic frontiers. Many of her novels are situated at Curaçao (Netherlands Antilles), where she spent her childhood years. In *De boten van Brakkeput* (1956) [The Haunted Island, 1959] we first meet a recurrent theme: a protagonist who has to fight his environment, alone. This theme emerges even more strongly in *Marijn bij de Lorredraaiers* (1965) [Slave Doctor, 1974]: the story of a 16-year-old white boy in the seventeenth century, who gradually realises the injustice of slavery. Another remarkable book is *De dagen van Olim* [Long, Long Ago] (1971), which is autobiographical and builds a bridge towards adults' literature, in both form and theme. Diekmann also wrote lively poetry for young children – genuinely modern nursery rhymes (*Wiele wiele stap* [Wheely Wheely Step], 1977).

## The 1960s: Further Growth and Consolidation

There were no really new developments in the 1960s, but an important moment for the acknowledgement of children's literature was the establishment of a triennial National Award for Children's Literature (since 1988, the Theo Thijssen Award). This was awarded to Annie M. G. Schmidt (1965), An Rutgers van der Loeff (1967) and Miep Diekmann (1970), the three leading authors of the decade.

The most important new author of this period was Paul Biegel (b.1925). Since 1962, he has written a large oeuvre, mainly consisting of fantasy stories. One can distinguish three types, progressing – according to the age of the intended reader – from amusing stories for younger children to more complex novels. There are adventure stories abounding in action (such as *De kleine kapitein* (1971) [The Little Captain, 1971]; fairy tales about kings, robbers, dwarfs and magicians (for example, *De Rode Prinses* [The Red Princess, 1987]; and symbolic novels with philosophical or moral themes (for example, *De tuinen van Dorr* (1969) [The Gardens of Dorr, 1975]). However, simple or complex, his work is always entertaining, not least because of a large dose of humour.

Tonke Dragt (b.1930) also creates a new detailed fantasy world with every new book, which she always illustrates herself. Her oeuvre shows a development from exciting adventures in a historical setting to stories with a more philosophical character. Her magnum opus is *Zeeën van tijd* [Oceans of Time] (vol. 1, 1992), a fascinating story of voyages in space and time to a 'mirror world', in which one can discover elements from the theory of relativity, science fiction, fairy tales and other literary sources.

Max Velthuijs (1923), who started as an illustrator in 1962, has become one of the most outstanding Dutch picture book artists. In his recent work – books for young children, consisting of exquisite paintings with very few words – he manages to incorporate the great themes of the world literature in a subtle, poetic way (*Kikker is verliefd* (1989) [Frog in Love, 1989]; *Kikker en het vogeltje* (1991) [Frog and the Birdsong, 1991]).

## The 1970s: The Great Revolution?

In the 1970s, there was an explosive increase of interest in children's literature. Between 1970 and 1980 more books and brochures on this subject were published than in the preceding century, largely because of the heated discussion about children's books and the rapid social changes which were taking place. Pressure groups demanded books in which the traditional divisions of the roles of men and women were broken down, in which sex was no longer taboo and discrimination was combated by a positive attitude towards other races and other cultures. Their wishes were met by a flow of books emphasising all kinds of social themes. Most of these have been forgotten. At the same time, however, a few authors did emerge who often incorporated the same themes in their work, but coloured them with a personal view and paid much more attention to literary quality.

One of these was the poet Willem Wilmink (b.1936), who wrote many songs for children's television programmes. In his opinion, an important function of children's literature is that it should comfort children, and therefore, the emotions and fears of children are among the main themes in his work. Like no other writer, he manages to immerse himself in the psyche of a child who is a slow learner or a bed-wetter. The comfort often arises from a comical and topical twist (suggesting, for example, that Johan Cruyff and other famous football players also used to wet their beds when they were small). Apart from that, one finds subdued and idyllic songs, although Wilmink does not avoid difficult subjects like sex or discrimination.

Guus Kuijer (b. 1942) became famous first of all as the author of five lively books about *Madelief* [Daisy]. The first volume, *Met de poppen gooien* (1975) [Daisy's New Head, 1980] was recognised immediately as a very special children's book. It fitted into the tradition of stories about the everyday experiences of children, but the tone was surprisingly new. In the short, sketchy stories, emotions emerged which had not been presented in children's books before. Kuijer did not try to portray children as sweet and endearing, and the adult characters are not always protective and sensible, but sometimes troublesome or unreasonable. In other words, he drew an image of children and adults which had only previously been found in adults' literature; in children's books, and especially in books for young children, conflicts had been more concealed.

Wim Hofman (b.1941) began with an absurdist fairy tale, and has alternated between light-hearted fantasy and realism. *De Stoorworm* [The Disturbing Worm] (1980), in which a friendly monster accidentally causes a flood, appears to be pure fantasy. However, it was inspired by memories of the flood of 1953, a theme returning in *Het Vlot* (1988) [The Raft, 1994], in which Hofman described his childhood years in Flushing (Zeeland), after the Second World War. So, the border between fantasy and reality may not be as strict as it appeared to be: both belong to the same world, shaped by Hofman in a lively language and 'primitive', child-like pictures, showing the influence of the painters from the Cobra group.

The popular genre of children's books dealing with the German occupation of The Netherlands during the Second World War, was renewed by the appearance of books based upon autobiographical facts, written by authors who were children at that time. An example is a book by Els Pelgrom (b.1934): *De kinderen van het Achtste Woud* (1977) [The Winter when Time was Frozen, 1980), describing the experiences of an 11-year-old girl during her evacuation in the last year of the occupation. It has an almost idyllic character: the child from the city experiences her stay at a farm as a long holiday. However, the war is always present in the background, and sometimes it comes grimly close.

Pelgrom also attracted much attention with *Kleine Sofie en Lange Wapper* (1984) [Little Sophie and Lanky Flop, 1987), which relates the dreams of a little girl, who is terminally ill. In those dreams, symbolising her situation in reality, she performs a play in a cardboard toy theatre, together with her dolls, about 'What life has to offer'. This book, greatly appreciated by the critics, is considered one of the highlights of Dutch children's literature in the 1980s.

## After 1980: The Literary Emancipation of Children's Literature

Looking back, we can say that the pressure groups of the 1970s did not have a lasting influence; the emphasis on social themes has disappeared, and in the 1980s critics began to pay more attention to literary aspects of the books.

One of the most remarkable young authors is Joke van Leeuwen (b.1952): a very individual and playful talent. She illustrates her books herself, with smooth transitions from words to pictures, using letters in all kinds of handwriting or even in code, rebuses and other mysterious elements, which challenge the reader in an attractive way. Her books are full of surprises: every word may have an association which leads to a story within the story. These features symbolise what seems to be the central theme of her work: a child being baffled in a world which has become self-evident for adults. High points in her work have been *Deesje* [Daisy] (1985) and *Het verhaal van Bobbel die in een bakfiets woonde en rijk wilde worden* (1987) [The Story of Bobble who Wanted to be Rich, 1990].

Toon Tellegen (b.1941) has published five collections of surprising, short stories about animals. In the wood he has created, only one specimen is found of every species; they have hardly any personal features and are all the same height, and they ignore their normal behaviour. And so it can happen that the sperm whale dances with the seagull, the elephant disappears behind the clouds, and the hippopotamus retires from the wood to live in the air, where the other animals bring him a pond for his birthday. The most remarkable titles are *Toen niemand iets te doen had* [When Nobody had Anything to Do] (1987) and *Langzaam, zo snel als zij konden* [Slowly, as Fast as They Could] (1989).

Imme Dros (1936) works in very heterogeneous genres, which makes it difficult to briefly classify her work. She published her first children's book in 1971, but gained her greatest recognition in recent years. The book taking a central place in her work is *Annetje Lie in het holst van de nacht* (1987) [Annelie in the Depths of the Night, 1991]. Rather like Els Pelgrom's *Kleine Sofie en Lange Wapper*, it relates the dreams of a little girl, symbolising her situation in reality. Annelie's father leaves her with her grandmother without any explanation. Her confusion, later increased by a feverish illness, reveals itself in frightening dreams about mysterious, threatening characters from her grandmother's stories and songs. The story is written in evocative language, full of the whimsical, associative jumps of thought which are characteristic of dreams. Because of these qualities the book is very complicated, unless one reads it like poetry, without trying to comprehend it from beginning to end. In her subsequent works Imme Dros shows the same mastery in simpler stories, in which the emotions are expressed more directly.

Dutch children's literature has achieved a very high level, as the many translations and foreign awards show. Because of the increase of artistic freedom and the emphasis on literary aspects, children's books have become more interesting for adults as well, but as the borderline between children's and adults' books fades the question has to be asked – are there any borders at all?

# References

Ariès, P. (1960) *L'enfant et la vie familiale sous l'Ancien Régime*, Paris: Editions du Seuil.
Heimeriks, N. and van Toorn, W. (eds) (1989) *De hele Bibelebontse berg. De geschiedenis van het kinderboek in Nederland en Vlaanderen van de middeleeuwen tot heden*, Amsterdam: Em. Querido.

# Further Reading

Bekkering, H. (1993) De emancipatie van kinder- en jeugdliteratuur, in Schenkeveld-van der Dussen, M. A. (ed.), *Nederlandse literatuur; een geschiedenis*, Groningen: Martinus Nijhoff.
Boonstra, B. (1993) 'Er was eens een waseens; de jeugdliteratuur', in Matsier, N. *et al.* (eds) *Het literair klimaat 1986–1992*, Amsterdam: De Bezige Bij.
de Vries, A. (1989) *Wat heten goede kinderboeken? Opvattingen over kinderliteratuur in Nederland sinds 1880*, Amsterdam: Querido.
Holtrop, A. (1986) 'Eenvoudig is niet hetzelfde als simpel; over kinderliteratuur', in van Deel, T., Matsier, N. and Offermans, C. (eds) *Het literair klimaat 1970–1985*, Amsterdam: De Bezige Bij.
*Lexicon van de jeugdliteratuur* (1982– ) Alphen aan den Rijn: Samsom/Groningen: Wolters-Noordhoff.
Linders, J. (1990) *An Rutgers van der Loeff. Een biografie*, Baarn: De Prom.
Salverda, M. (ed.) (1991) *Altijd acht gebleven. Over de kinderliteratuur van Annie M. G. Schmidt*, Amsterdam: Em. Querido.

# 64

# France

## *Jean Perrot*

### From Stereotypes to Real-Life Publishing

The spread of French children's literature to English-speaking countries may seem surprising. The shelves of bookshops in Britain or in the USA carry only a few translations portraying Jean de Brunhoff's little elephant King Babar or Saint Exupèry's *The Little Prince* (published in New York in 1943, before being published in Paris in 1945). And yet, stories from the *Histoires ou Contes du Temps Passé*, published in 1697 by Charles Perrault are in print in innumerable adaptations, and some have been transformed into Walt Disney's galaxy myths: Cinderella and Sleeping Beauty are the best known; others are part of British pantomime tradition, such as Puss in Boots – while others such as Riquet with the Tuft or Hop o' my Thumb are less well-known. These stories are set in the *ancien régime*, but refer to bourgeoisie's ideal of social advancement as it climbed to power. Has this ideal become an integral part of the initiation rites of children throughout the world, and become no longer specifically French?

It should also be noted that the first time Perrault's complete collection was introduced in England it was used as an introduction to the language: the publication in French in 1884 of *Contes de fées*, with notes and complete vocabulary by G. F. Fasnacht, in Macmillan's Illustrated Primary Series of French Readings actually preceded the famous edition by Andrew Lang, *Perrault's Popular Tales* (1888). One may wonder why this literary reception was so slow: was this due to resistance from the national folklore or insularity? However, the works of the Comtesse de Ségur and Jules Verne in the nineteenth century were translated more quickly: *Les Anglais au Pôle Nord* published in French in 1864 was published by Routledge and Sons in 1874 in London and New York, perhaps because this was the epoch of industry, of exploration of the world by a science at full stretch, and also of the beginnings of mass culture. But similarly, in another register, the works of Madame de Genlis in the eighteenth century were published almost simultaneously in both French and English: a volume such as *Théâtre á l'usage des jeunes personnes* (1781) appeared in London in the same year under the title *Theatre of Education* and *Adèle et Théodore ou Lettres sur l'education* (1782) appeared a year later under the title *Adelaide and Theodore, or Letters on Education*, reflecting the common concerns of educationalists. Has there been a change, and have our two cultures now moved further apart? What characterises children's publishing in France at this time of a uniform worldwide culture imposed in a positive fashion by the 1989 Declaration of Children's Rights and, more dubiously, by contemporary co-publications and co-productions?

This article cannot, therefore, ignore publishing conditions; it must be remembered that the number of titles published in France in the children's sector has increased steadily to reach 4,850 in 1988; in the same year, 31,000 titles were published in the general sector, compared to 55,000 in Great Britain, 24,200 in Italy, and 38,000 in Spain (Bouvaist 1990: 71). Half of the new titles in the children's sector consist of translations or adaptations mainly from English-speaking countries: for example, in 1988, Bouvaist identified 355 titles in this category compared to fifty-five from German and thirteen from Italian or Japanese (30). Is this a sign of cultural domination or of openness? Will French creativity be marginalised by its publishing system, which is too rigidly bound to literature and school? Will television and the new computerised media result in a world crisis of book reading, which will be overtaken by films and video cassettes? These questions are intended to justify my approach to this presentation of our literary archipelago: I shall concentrate on contemporary work after considering the classics.

## Training the Mind, Education in Language: Story-Telling to Children

I shall briefly discuss the centuries prior to the reign of Louis XIV, during which children's literature developed simultaneously with growing awareness of childhood (Ariès 1960). Before this, children's culture was identified with an oral culture and religious instruction: saws, stories and tales belonged to this tradition, whereas almanacs, holy pictures, tales of chivalry, *The Roman de Renart*, the Chronicles of Gargantua and the Lives of the Saints made up the main aspects of the culture of the chapbooks, which were read aloud in families and which complemented the practice of rhetoric, Latin texts and Aesop's fables in the schools.

In fact, children's literature in France was born (noting the prelude of the La Fontaine *Fables* written for the Dauphin in 1668) with the publication of *Histoires ou Contes du temps passé* by Charles Perrault in 1697, when a centralised state, unifying linguistic practices had come into being. On the one hand, Perrault's work was close to and almost an extension of popular literature and as such was exposed to the sarcastic criticism of literary circles. In *Le Dictionnaire de l'Académie Française* of 1694, prefaced by Charles Perrault himself, fairy tales are described as 'ridiculous fables, such as those which old people tell to amuse children'.

This marginalisation of the fairy tale, banished to old age and childhood, was part of an approach which was adopted by educators for centuries. From 1696, the second version of the treatise *Instructions for the Education of a Daughter* by Fénelon left no doubt about the definition of the tale as a horizon of expectation for young readers and a model for writing for authors. The prelate, tutor to the Duke of Burgundy, wrote:

> Children passionately love ridiculous tales; we can see them every day transported with joy or weeping tears at the tale of the adventures recounted

to them; do not fail to exploit this tendency; when you see that they are ready
to listen to you, tell them a short and pretty tale.

Author's translation, Fénelon 1983: 114

Here we note a historic codification of the properties specifically attributed to
tales for children: what is involved is indeed telling 'tales' to children for
educative and moral purposes, but also to move a public consisting also of adult
educators. This strategy was adopted by the Counter-Reformation and was
apparent in the religious works of Jean-Baptiste de la Salle, who spoke to the
mind through the emotions, and was related to baroque aesthetics, which were
still triumphant in contemporary operas and court entertainments. Thus, the
fairy from Cinderella has been transposed to the childhood imagination from the
enchantments of Circe, the sorceress. The 'fairies' of Charles Perrault indicate
extravagance, irregularity (baroco in Portuguese means an irregular pearl) which
is that of the marvellous in the order of classical Reason (Perrot 1991: 26). All the
major writers of the period pay homage to this aesthetic. We should refer first to
*The Adventures of Telemachus, the Son of Ulysses* of 1699 by Fénelon (1651–1715),
which was to be published in hundreds of editions in many languages during the
following century: this didactic novel was animated by the 'machines' of baroque
opera such as those, for example, in Lully's *Atys* (1676) and shows Venus on her
chariot ascending to the heavens. Baroque stage productions also figure in *La
Tour ténébreuse et les jours lumineux* (1701) by Marie-Jeanne Lhéritier de
Villandon (1664–1734), Charles Perrault's niece, who was famous for her *Les
Enchantements de l'Eloquence*, published in her *Oeuvres Meslées* in 1696. We should
also mention the publication in 1698 of several collections: *Contes nouveaux ou les
Fées à la mode* by Marie-Catherine Le Jumel, baroness of Aulnoy (1650–1705),
the best known stories of which are 'The bluebird', 'The white cat' and 'The
yellow dwarf'; *Contes de fées* by Henriette-Julie de Castelnau-Murat (1670–1716);
and *Les fées, contes des contes* by Charlotte-Rose de la Force (1654–1754),
reflecting the literary jousting and the fashion which predominated in the Salons
of the time. This fashion was led towards exoticism by Antoine Galland's
translation of *A Thousand and One Nights* between 1704 and 1717, and the finest
flowers of the eighteenth century were *Mille et un quarts d'heure contes tartares*
(1723), by Thomas-Simon Gueulette (1683–1766) and those tales published by
Madame Leprince de Beaumont in *Magasin des enfants* and particularly in *Beauty
and the Beast* (1757). The fame of the best stories was ensured during the
eighteenth century by their inclusion in *Cabinet des fées* which gradually grew to
forty-one volumes by 1783 and their systematic use by educators: notably by
Arnaud Berquin (1747–1791), who also published plays in one of the first
magazines for children, a much admired work, *L'Ami des enfants* (1782–1785).
This appeared in England as *The Children's Friend* from 1783. A collection of
tales translated from *L'Ami des enfants* was published by E. Newberry in 1787:
*The Looking Glass for the Mind or Intellectual Mirror, being an elegant collection of
the most delightful little Stories and interesting Tales* (Escarpit 1983: 37). In *L'Ami
de l'adolescence* (1784–1785), Berquin used the theatre as Jean Racine had done in
*Esther* (1689) and *Athalie* (1691), plays written for the girls of Saint Cyr, the
school set up by Madame de Maintenon, in the same way as the Jesuits and Mme

de Genlis had resorted to theatricals in their educational programmes. The linguistic drilling of children was under way.

## The Perspective of a Message Situated between Text and Image

Beyond this convergence between fashion and pedagogy, the power of images was highlighted, with the same aim of attracting, by the philosopher John Locke in his *Some Thoughts Concerning Education*, translated into French in 1695 by Pierre Coste under the title of *Education des Enfants*. This power of images, which is crucial in holding children's attention, was to be taken into account in the revolutionary system of Jean-Jacques Rousseau, which is based on a realistic observation of play and the behaviour of real children: it governs the education of Julie's children in *Eloisa* (1761), and doubtless the reader will remember the intimate scene in which Julie is shown with her children looking at a collection of pictures, the elder explaining the engravings to his younger brother (Rousseau 1761/1964: 581). This is a symbolic attitude on which the educator in *Emile, ou, de l'Education* (translated into English by M. Nugent as *Emilius, or an Essay on Education* (1763)), too busy fighting against the damage of the feverish reading of his childhood, was to maintain a prudent silence, restricting his pupil to the reading of *Robinson Crusoe*. (Of course, many editions of that novel were at the time decorated with splendid plates and thus glorified the pleasures of the imagination as much as the joys of concrete good behaviour.) In Rousseau's outlook on the world, pictures are the ideal channel which allow the child to pass from the world of 'nature' to that of 'culture'.

A picture is what appeared in the 'window' of the painter Alberti in the Renaissance or which burst out fantastically in the 'lens' of Nathanël in Hoffmann's *Sandman*, published at the time the kaleidoscope was invented (1816): it is the unexpectedness of the body which disturbs the vision by the 'alarming strangeness' identified by the Freud in this story (Milner 1982: 123). It forms the basis of a more ambiguous narrative than the discourse which it underlies or unravels. Significantly, its eruption into the culture of children corresponds to the developments of modern optics at the time when Comenius was publishing his *Orbis Sensualium Pictus* (1658), which combined text and illustration, and the scene from *Eloisa* which we referred to above followed close behind the improvements made to the telescope by John Dollond in 1757. It is true that Venus, ascending back to Olympus at the beginning of Book Eight of Fénelon's *The Adventures of Telemachus* already shared a view of our world which can be explained only by the overturn of the baroque vision through the use of astronomical lenses developed by Galileo as early as 1609. As a result,

> The most innumerable peoples and most powerful armies are only like ants quarrelling with each other over a blade of grass on this bit of mud. The immortals laugh about the most serious affairs which agitate weak mortals and which appear to them to be as children's games.
>
> Author's translation, Fénelon 1983: 114

Through the implicit handling of the astronomical lens, we are present at a subversion of the adult vision which is treated as a child's game. We know that the applications of optics devised to entertain adults – 'the shadow theatres', entertainments invented in 1772 by Dominique Seraphic at Versailles – were later to be included in books. Similarly, the drawings of Rodolph Töpffer (1799–1846), a great admirer of Rousseau, were introduced into France in 1860, the year in which Heinrich Hoffmann's *Struwwelpeter* was translated and one year before the famous illustration of Perrault's *Contes* by Gustave Doré. These contributions widened the scope of fantasy, freeing the expression of desire and referring back to the process described by Philippe Ariès in which cultural objects of adults are handed over to children after they have outlived their usefulness for adults. The same discrepancy can be seen following the introduction of the trends in illustration and painting in children's culture: it was only in 1969 that François Ruy-Vidal and Harlin Quist dared to take up a surrealist aesthetic to illustrate Eugène Ionesco's *Contes*. Today, the art of photography, the first photograph having been taken by Niepce in 1822, and the art of the cinema, are just beginning to influence books for children (*Vent Latéral* by Pef illustrated by Frédéric Clement, 1988 shows the influence of Wim Wenders to whom it is dedicated) at the same time as laser discs and other computerised gadgets from the MacLuhan firmament.

## Revolution and Romanticism: Literature and Academic Laws

The 1789 Revolution fostered a new way of looking at children through its concern to bring into being a new citizen: *Emile* includes a study of the *Social Contract*. However, after the Revolution, on the one hand we see the development of a cult of heroic childhood, a symbol of the regeneration of the social body, and the juridical liberation of children (who were now subject to a less draconian mortality than during the *ancien régime*) while on the other hand, factory work became widespread. In this context, the republican school was involved in developing reading and civic awareness: the revolutionary 'catechisms', the alphabetical primers, together with books of civilities, collections of tales and moral stories were all intended to construct the New Man. This was reflected in an article published in the *Journal de Paris*, on the sixteenth *vendémiaire*, year IV, which advised that children should be given *L'Ami des Enfants*, together with 'small works', such as *Lolotte et Fanfan*, published in 1793 by Ducray-Duminil (1761–1819) and specifies that a single method is involved, that is good and holy morality put into practice, incorporated in the stories which 'appeal to children' (Manson 86–87). The moralists of the Republic therefore transferred the narrative techniques of the educationalists of the *ancien régime* to the modern context.

However, the beginning of romanticism, seen in *Das Knaben Wunderhorn* (1806–1808) by Achim von Arnim and Clemens von Brentano, by the works of Canon Schmid, by the publication of Grimms' fairy tales in Germany, and those of Fenimore Cooper, J. D. R. Wyss, and later of Andersen and Dickens, was marked in France by a return to stories rooted in popular culture. This corresponded to the rise of nationalist feelings in European countries, and was illustrated by stories such as Charles Nodier's *La fée aux miettes* in 1831, the year following the appearance of *Notre-Dame de Paris* by Victor Hugo. (Hugo's *Les Misérables* was begun in 1845, but was published only in 1862, heralding Gavroche). Romanticism also faced the turbulence of adolescence in *The Three Musketeers* (1844) and the other works of Alexandre Dumas. In addition, the turbulence of childhood itself was taken into account in the cult of its eccentricities in *Les aventures de Jean-Paul Choppart* (1934) by René-Louis Desnoyers (1802–1868), a version of which had appeared in *Le Journal des enfants* in 1832 (Caradec 1977: 119). This magazine, like *Le Journal des Jeunes Personnes*, edited by Julie Gouraud, corresponded to a desire to develop reading formulated in the Guizot law of 1833 on primary education.

Following the 1860 amnesty, the same ideas led Pierre-Jules Hetzel (who had set up the *Nouveau Magasin des Enfants* in 1843, and who was also a politician exiled by Napoleon III after the 1851 *coup d'Etat*), launched *Le Magasin d'Education et de Récréation* in 1864. This periodical set out to further the aims of science, and Jean Macé, who founded the Ligue de l'Enseignement, was responsible for the educative section. It was here that Jules Verne (1828–1905) published most of his writings and here too that *The Little Weakling* (1868) and *Letters from My Mill* (1869) by Alphonse Daudet, *L'art d'être grand-père* by Victor Hugo, Hetzel's adaptations (published under the pseudonym of P. J. Stahl) of Louisa May Alcott's *Little Women* and Marco Woyzog's *Maroussia*, and other stories appeared. The project of exploring the realities of contemporary France proposed to Hector Malot in 1869 led to nothing in the short term, but *Sans Famille* [Nobody's Boy] by this author was published in 1878, and Bruno's *Le Tour de France de deux enfants* in 1886. This female educationalist, author of *Cours de Morale et d'Instruction Civique* and other works, incarnates the republican spirit which was expressed in the Jules Ferry laws on the obligatory and secular nature of the French school. *Le Tour de France de deux enfants*, which was to appear in 300 editions within thirty years, drew the lessons of patriotism following the French defeat after the 1870 war against the Germans and was intended to stimulate national sentiments (as did Selma Lagerlöf's account of Nils Olgersson's wonderful travels through Sweden, published in 1907).

A sign of the educational project of Hetzel was Verne's ambition to write 'the science novel', to make use of the changes in the contemporary world and to invent the fiction of the future. The writer used new hypotheses: navigation of submarines in *Twenty Thousand Leagues under the Sea* (1870), propeller propulsion in *The Clippers of the Clouds* (1886), astronautics in *From the Earth to the Moon* (1865), and so on. However, his fictional writings appeal initially because they are in advance of their time and allow the reader to experience the adventures of modern discoveries in 'extraordinary voyages': *Five Weeks in a Balloon* published in 1862, was the first of a series of initiation and training stories in which information and entertainment are evenly balanced. In over forty novels, the whole social and political history of a period is considered with its international conflicts (*Floating Island*, 1896) and its utopias (*L'éternel Adam*, 1910).

The work of Sophie, Countess de Ségur (1799–1874), daughter of the governor Rostopchin who faced Napoléon at Moscow, had as much success amongst girls as Verne did among boys. It shows the other side of the ideology of the period: in the conflict which opposed secular morality epitomised in the republican school and religious morality. Her novels, written like lives of the saints, were inspired by the conservative militantism which led the author to publish *Livre de messe des petits enfants* (1857) and *A Life of Christ for Children as told by a Grand-Mother* (1859).

*Les petites filles modèles* (1857) may seem to be highly moralistic, since the aim was to produce docile children and ideal Catholics. This would be to fail to take into account the imagination of a novelist, who portrays her own childhood and who appeals through her descriptions of 'transgressions and pranks' rather than of well-behaved children, as shown by the heroine of *Les Malheures de Sophie* (1864) (which was translated into English as *The Misfortunes of Sophie* by Edgar Skinner as late as 1936). English readers responded to a spirit of adventure in the adaptations of *François le Bossu* (1863) [*The Little Hunchback* (1884)] and of the *Mémoires d'un âne* (1860) [*The Ups and Downs of a Donkey's Life* (1891)]. However, the most celebrated propagator of the ideas of Rousseau in the nineteenth century was George Sand in *Contes d'une Grand-Mère* first published in the *Revue des Deux Mondes* in the 1870s and then in a single volume in 1879 which achieved worldwide celebrity.

## The Two Images of France

The twentieth century is marked by the changes which have followed the world wars. The first change occurred in the 1930s. Culture was rooted in rural France, which responded to the Rabelaisian spirit of *La guerre des boutons* (1912) by Louis Pergaud (1882-1919), to *Le Grand Meaulnes* [The Wanderer] (1913) by Alain-Fournier (1886-1914) and to the satirical vision of farm animals in *Gédéon* (1923) by Benjamin Rabier (1864–1939). In the 1930s, this world was expanded by the use François Faucher (1898–1967) (who set up L'Atelier du Père Castor in 1931) made of the theories of 'New Education' inspired by Frantisek Bakulé, Havranek, Claparède, Piaget, and of Russian art in the Rozhankovsky collections (Parmegiani, 1989: 262). Similarly, Paul Hazard's reading of international children's literature in *Les Livres, les Enfants et les Hommes* (1932) opened new vistas. Lewis Carroll's *Alice* thus inspired *Fattypuffs et Thinifers* by André Maurois and Jean Bruller (1930), whereas Jean de Brunhoff's *Histoire de Babar* (1931) revealed a mythical Africa, as did Blaise Cendrars's *Petits contes nègres pour les enfants des Blancs* (1928).

. However, rural France was still haunting the Catholic periodical *La Semaine de Suzette* (1905–1960), which was famous for the adventures of Bécassine, a caricature Breton female character invented in 1905 by Caumery and drawn by Pinchon as a cartoon strip. It also made a return in the equally famous cartoon strip drawn by René Goscinny and André Uderzo, *Asterix le Gaulois* (1961). This spirit was present in *L'Ile rose* (1930), *Les lunettes du lion* (1932), and *Bridinette* (1930), tales by Charles Vidrac, who wrote for the Primary School Teachers' Union; in the novel by Henri Bosco, *L'âne Culotte* (1937); in Marcel Aymè's *The Wonderful Farm* (1950); in Colette Vivier's *La maison des petits bonheurs* (1938) and in Robert Desnos's *Trente chantefables pour enfants sages* (1944); and after the war in *Le Pays où l'on n'arrive jamais* (1955) by André Dhotel and in *Le Château de ma mère* by Marcel Pagnol (1958), in which the authors sang the praises of their home regions of the Ardennes and Provence.

The years following the Second World War were characterised by the more socially militant attitude of Amitié publications, which published the novels of René Guillot, who in 1964 became the only French writer to be awarded the Andersen prize (*Au pays des bêtes sauvages*, 1948). Guillot knows how to develop fine plots and real suspense. He has been stimulated by African landscapes and people to some of his best writing, such as *Sama, Prince des éléphants* (1950); most of his books have been translated, and have won prizes abroad. One should also mention the collection Plein Vent, started in 1966 by André Massepain; and by the éditions de la Farandole and the considerable success of *Pif* magazine (published by Vaillant), which was also famous for its cartoon strips.

The growing influence of detective magazines should also be underlined. Paul Berna (b.1910), for instance, wrote his celebrated *Cheval sans tête* [A Hundred Million Francs] (1955), which won the Award of the Salon de l'Enfance for that year. The story was based on a real mystery, set in a working-class suburb, and used working-class language. *Millionaires en herbe* (1958) is among his best books, and Berna's style influenced René Guillot, Paul-Jaques Bonzon, and other writers.

## Humour and the Spirit of Childhood of the New Story-Tellers

However, the real change in children's literature was due to the power of images with the L'école des Loisirs publishing house in 1965, which was set up on the fringe of the academic world to develop the sense of aesthetics and creative fantasy (Perrot 1987: 182–183). The introduction of foreign artists such as Sendak, Lionni, Lobel and more recently Chris van Allsburg, was accompanied by the discovery of French artists such as Tomi Ungerer, in *Les trois brigands* (1968), *Le geant de Zéralda* (1971) and numerous illustrators inspired by the spirit of childhood such as Philippe Dumas in *Victor Hugo s'est égaré* (1986), Michel Gay (*Biboundé*, 1986), and Yvan Pommaux (*John Chatterton détective*, 1993). Gallimard developed the use of pictures with their collections of cartoon-strip documentaries, such as *Mes premières Découvertes* (1981) and *Les Yeux de la Découverte* (1992). The events of May 1968 also saw the development of a school of the absurd, of caustic humour and of anarchist claims with, among others, Ionesco's *Contes* (1969–1976), the fourth of which was illustrated by Nicole Claveloux. This artist, the most productive of her generation, proposed a modernist manifesto with her illustrations of the French translation of *Alice in Wonderland*, published as *Aventures d'Alice au pays des merveilles* by Grasset-Jeunesse in 1974. She has illustrated numerous books by Christian Bruel, of the *Sourire qui mord* (*Les dessous du sable*, 1986). She was involved in the editorial adventure of Harlin Quist from 1967 to 1977 in France, illustrating John Galwaithe's *Dracula Spectacular* in 1975, and in the Editions des Femmes with her illustration of *Brise et Rose* (1977), an adaptation of a feminist tale by George Sand, whose heiress she can be considered. The aesthetic current is well represented by the Ipomée books by Nicole Maymat (*Maco des grands bois*, illustrated by Claire Forgeot, 1986), with picture books by Frédéric Clément, at the Ecole des Loisirs (*Le luthier de Venise*, text by Claude Clément, 1986) and with the work of Georges Lemoine, published by Gallimard (*Comment Wang Fu fut sauvé* by Marguerite Yourcenar, 1979), or by Le Centurion (*Leila*, by Sue Alexander, 1983).

The three great illustrator-authors of the last decade are, however, Jean Claverie, Pef and Claude Lapointe. The first is distinguished by the subtlety of his vision in *Riquet with the Tuft* (Albin Michel, 1989), by the diabolic turbulence of his creations (*Little Lou, La batterie de Théophile*, Gallimard, 1990), and by excellent pop-up books such as *Peekaboo* (Matthew Price, 1985). The second is a humorist who is more tender than Roald Dahl, but equally talented: we should mention his *La belle lisse poire du prince de Motordu* (1980), *Noël, Père et Fils* (1985) (Perrot, 1991: 221–241). The third made his name through his illustrations of works by Gripari and in his *Le Petit Poucet* published by Grasset-Jeunesse in 1974.

In the field of the novel, the reputation of *Vendredi ou la vie sauvage* by Michel Tournier has extended far beyond the frontiers of the country, and the stories of J. M. G. Le Clézio (*Peuple du ciel*, illustrated by G. Lemoine, Gallimard, 1991), of Claude Roy, who is a distinguished poet (*Enfantasques*, Gallimard, 1974) and story-teller (*C'est le bouquet*, 1964) and Daniel Pennac (*Kamo*, Gallimard, 1991) are in the first rank. Novels less closely linked to education, including those of Susie Morgenstern (*L'amerloque*, L'Ecole des Loisirs, 1992), of Marie-Aude Murail (*Nos amours ne vont pas si mal*, L'Ecole des Loisirs, 1992), of Nadine Garrel (*Le pays du grand condor*, *Les Princes de l'exil*, Gallimard, 1986), and of Jean Alessandrini (*Le labyrinthe des cauchemars*, Rageot, 1991), have a regular readership. However, it is difficult here to distinguish between works which children themselves demand, with no pressure from adult critics, and to pick out the future classics: the history of contemporary French children's literature remains to be written.

## References

Ariès, P. (1960) *L'Enfant et la Vie familiale sous l'Ancien Régime*, Paris: Plon.

Bouvaist, J. M. (1990) *Les enjeux de l'édition-jeunesse à la veille de 1992*, Montreuil: Salon du Livre de jeunesse.

Caradec, F. (1977) *Histoire de la Littérature enfantine en France*, Paris: Albin Michel.

Escarpit, D. (1983) *Arnaud Berquin (1747–1791)*, Pessac: Nous Voulons Lire.

Fénelon (1983) *Oeuvres 1*, Paris: Bibliothèque de la Pléiade, Gallimard, NRF.

Manson, M. (1989) *Les livres pour l'enfance et la jeunesse sous la Révolution*, Paris: INRP.

Milner, M. (1982) *La fantasmagorie*, Paris: PUF, Ecritures.

Parmegiani, C. A. (1989) *Les Petits Français illustrés*, Paris: Edition du Cercle de la Librairie.

Perrot, J. (1987) *Du jeu, des enfants et des livres*, Paris: Edition du Cercle de la Librairie.

—— (1991) *Art baroque, art d'enfance*, Nancy: Presses Universitaires.

Rousseau, J.-J. (1761/1964) *La Nouvelle Héloïse* in *Ouvres Complètes*, 2, Paris: Gallimard.

## Further Reading

Diament, N. (1993) *Dictionnaire des écrivains français pour la jeunesse (1914–1991)*, Paris: L'Ecole du Loisirs.

Fourment, A. (1987) *Histoire de la Presse des jeunes et des journaux d'Enfants (1708–1968)*, Paris: Edition de l'Ecole.

Hazard, P. (1932) *Les Livres, les enfants et les hommes*, Paris: Flammarion.

Jan, I. (1969/1972) *On Children's Literature*, (ed.) Storr, C., London: Allen Lane.

Soriano, M. (1968) *Les contes de Perrault, culture savante et tradition populaire*, Paris: Gallimard.

—— (1976) *Guide de littérature de jeunesse*, Paris: Flammarion.

# 65

# Spain

## Carmen García Surrallés and Antonio Moreno Verdulla with Marisol Dorao

Until the end of the nineteenth century there was no literature, properly speaking, for children in Spain, but only books with the sole purpose of moralising and instructing children and young people. Two exceptions are Padre Coloma and Fernán Caballero. After this long pre-history the first attempts to introduce European tales into Spain were made. Andersen was translated for the first time by Julius Nombela in 1871–1872; José S. Viedma translated the Grimm tales in 1879, while the tales by Perrault had been known since the previous century, due to the influence that France had on Spanish literature.

In 1876 the publishing house Calleja was founded, lasting until the end of the civil war (1936–1939). This publishing house contributed greatly to the diffusion of the stories by Perrault, Schmid, Andersen, Nesbit, as well as *The Arabian Nights*, and traditional Spanish tales and others by unknown authors, and the classic adventure books (Defoe, Swift). A similar task was carried out by the publishing house Sopena.

Around this time, magazines for adults, such as *Estampa* and *Blanco y Negro* started to have pages devoted to children's stories, with illustrations by the famous Salvador Bartolozzi. *Blanco y Negro* published *Gente Menuda*, a supplement for children which later became an independent magazine.

Narratives based on reality, with children as protagonists, and no didactic intentions, started to appear in the 1920s. The atmosphere in which these children live is mostly upper-middle-class, such as in the case of *Celia*, a series created by Elena Fortún and which was in some ways imitated after the war by Borita Casas with *Antoñita la fantástica*, and by Emilia Cotarelo with *Mari-Pepa*.

After the civil war, the government of the dictatorship gave an impulse to children's books, and the recommended themes were mainly heroic and fantastic (but with a moral), and they drew their inspiration from both Spanish folk literature and classical literature. The work of the publishing house Araluce, which presented well adapted and illustrated 'masterpieces within the reach of children' is worthy of note.

During the 1950s, new names appeared, such as José María Sánchez Silva, Monserrat Del Amo, and Joaquín Aguirre Bellver.

More realistic and problematic social themes appeared in the 1960s, such as life in the slums and the problems of immigrants. It is important to mention here Ángela Ionescu, and, from adult literature, Carmen Kurtz and Ana María Matute.

In the 1960s too, there was a magazine for girls, *Bazar*, which had a very important role. The main collaborators were Monserrat Del Amo, Ángela Ionescu, Consuelo Armijo and Gloria Fuertes.

Before 1962 it was forbidden to publish anything in any of the other languages spoken in Spain, such as Catalan, Galician and Basque but after that date there was a flourishing of literature in these languages, particularly in Catalan.

During the 1970s a great change can be detected in children's literature as a result of political changes. On the one hand, numerous translations allowed the Spanish to become acquainted with new European trends; on the other, there was an increasing number of original books in Galician, Basque, and, mainly, Catalan. Many of the Catalonian authors, such as Josep Vallverdú, Mercé Company and Joan Manuel Gisbert also wrote in Spanish, or were translated.

In the last twenty years, the themes in children's literature in Spain have dealt not only with of rural life seen from a nostalgic point of view versus life in the city, but also with new themes, mainly related to ecology, and to the countryside, and even some themes never before mentioned in books for children, such as racism and xenophobia, divorce, poverty, mental illness, and so on. Many of these themes, which may in fact be assimilated with difficulty by children, had to be treated with humour, in order to make them more accessible. But humour itself also took on new forms, with eschatological references which had not been allowed before, and with the demystification of witches and dragons, as well as the creation of new characters of fantasy. The influence of Rodari, Tolkien and Ende can be felt here. In this way a new style appeared, called 'fantastic realism' and seen in works by J. M. Gisbert, Mercé Canela and Pilar Mateos.

With reference to theatre, at the beginning of the century some well-known modernists, and authors of the Generation of 98, started to write for children. Here we must mention Ramón del Valle Inclán, who in *Farsa infantil de la cabeza del dragón* [The Children's Farce of the Dragon's Head] presented the first ideas of what would later be known as 'esperpento' and also Jacinto Benavente, who, with his touches of irony and social satire (and showing himself as dogmatic as in his works for adults), wrote *El nietecito* [The Grandchild] and *El príncipe que todo lo aprendió en los libros* [The Prince who Learnt Everything from Books]. The brothers Serafín and Joaquín Álvarez Quintero, used music in *La muela del rey Farfán* [King Farfan's Tooth], written with the sole intention of amusing children.

Later, during the Republic (1931–1936), the Government gave Alejandro Casona the task of undertaking a mission for children similar to that which García Lorca undertook with his travelling theatre 'La barraca'. In the 1960s, during the dictatorship, the government subsidised theatrical companies. We may mention Lauro Olmo, Alfonso Sastre and Carlos Muñiz, who both in their children's plays and in their adult works dealt mainly with social themes.

Nowadays authors, more closely connected to the world of children, tend to make children fully participate in the plays they write.

In poetry, before the civil war there were collections of folklore for children, fables, and anthologies of classical writers, but there was no proper children's poetry until sometime after the war. Exceptions are the poems of Alejandro Casona, Josefina Bolinaga and Carmen Conde. It took some time after the war to realise that this genre could also be enjoyed by children, and various authors such as Celia Viñas, Pura Vázquez and Gloria Fuertes started to write poetry for children. Nevertheless, even now there are not many books of poetry published for children. There are some folkloric collections of songs and games edited by the Teacher's Training College in Madrid, Arturo Medina (1915–1995) and the eminent researcher Carmen Bravo-Villasante (1922–1994).

## Children's Authors Before the Civil War

Salvador Bartolozzi (1882–1840) was the author and illustrator of the famous series *Pinocho y Chapete* and *Pipo y Pipa*. In the first, the protagonists act as hero and faithful servant in the style of Don Quixote and Sancho Panza.

Elena Fortún (1886–1952) was the celebrated author of the series of books about Celia: *Celia lo que dice, Celia novelista*, and others. She also published several plays for children to act: *Moñitos, La bruja Piñonate*, and so on, collected in *Teatro para niños*.

Antoniorrobles's (1897–1983) publications began with *Ocho cuentos de niñas y muñecas* [Eight Stories of Girls and Dolls], and received the National Award for his book *Hermanos monigotes* [Brother Puppet] in 1932. He discovered that modern characters can be full of fantasy and of humour, and is considered to be the creator of contemporary children's literature. His book *La bruja Doña Paz* [Mrs Peace, the Witch] was awarded the prize of the Anglo-American Committee of the United Nations.

Alejandro Casona (1903–1965) was a teacher and famous playwright for adults; his plays combine fantasy and reality, as in *El lindo Don Gato*, [Beautiful Mr Cat] and *A Belén, pastores!* [To Bethlehem, Shepherds!]. With *La flauta del sapo* [The Toad's Flute] with its light and easy style, he gave new life to poetry for children.

These last three authors went to exile for political reasons and continued writing after the civil war.

## From the End of the Civil War (1939) to the Present

In 1952 José María Sánchez Silva (b.1911) published the book which would make him famous: *Marcelino, pan y vino* [Marcelino, Bread and Wine] which has been reprinted and translated many times, eventually being made into a film. In 1968 he was awarded the Andersen Prize for his complete works.

Carmen Kurtz (1911) also wrote for adults. In 1962 she published *óscar cosmonauta* which was a runner-up for Andersen Prize, and which started the series of óscar novels: *óscar espeleólogo, óscar espía atómico* and others. She has also received the CCEI (Comisión Católica Española de la Infancia) on four occasions: three times for books in the óscar series, and once (1981) for *Veva*, the story of a little girl who discovers her inner self. She has also received the Lazarillo Prize for *Color de fuego* [Colour of Fire], which is the story of a boy who is 'tamed' by a horse.

Gloria Fuertes (b.1918). After her success as a poet for adults, she has been fully accepted by the youngest children. Her distinctive style reflects children's speech in a very colourful way. She has given her name to a Prize for poetry written by children. Among her works we can mention: *Don Pato y Don Pito*, poems for children, *La princesita que quería ser pobre* [The Little Princess who Wanted to be

Poor], a play, *El hada acaramelada, cuentos en verso* [The Caramel Fairy, Tales in Verse], *Las tres reinas magas, cuento teatro* [The Three Wise Women, a theatre story].

Ana María Matute (b.1925) started to write for children about 1956, after publishing *El país de la pizarra* [The Country of the Blackboard]. Other short stories are 'El saltamontes verde' ['The Green Grasshopper'] and 'El aprendiz' ['The Apprentice']. She has also written several novels including *Paulina, Sólo un pie descalzo* [Just a Bare Foot], and *El polizón del 'Ulises'* [The Stowaway of the 'Ulises'] which won the Lazarillo Prize. She has always been strongly attracted to the world of children, and very often presents children as narrators.

A playwright, Lauro Olmo (1925–1994), has had great success in collaboration with his wife, Pilar Enciso, with *La maquinita que no quería pitar* [The Little Engine which Wouldn't Whistle], *Asamblea general* [General Meeting], and *El raterillo* [The Little Pickpocket], for different ages. With the last he won the Prize of the Círculo de la Crítica del Uruguay.

Monserrat Del Amo (b.1927) has received many prizes for her works: the Lazarillo Prize for *Rastro de Dios* [Traces of God], the CCEI for *Chitina y su gato* [Chitina and her Cat], and the National Prize for Children's Literature for *El nudo* [The Knot]. Her style is attractive and appropriate both for small children and for adolescents. Following the trend of collective protagonists in the adventure novel, she created the series *Los Blok* [The Bloks], about a family, and *Zuecos y naranjas* [Wooden Shoes and Oranges] about emigration. As a playwright, in 1970 she was presented with the AETIJ (Spanish Association of Theatre for Children and Youngsters) Award, for her play *Fiesta*.

Jaime Ferrán (b.1928) received the Lazarillo Prize for *Ángel en Colombia*, which is the second book of his Angel series. His contribution to poetry comprises *La playa larga* [The Long Beach] and *Cuaderno de música* [The Music Notebook] among others. His poetry is directed towards children of over 12 years of age, with the intention of introducing them to adult poetry.

Ángela Ionescu (b.1937) discovered her literary vocation when telling tales to her children. Her most important work, translated to many languages, is *De un país lejano* [From a Distant Country], which has received the Doncel and Lazarillo Prizes, and has appeared in the List of Honour of IBBY. Other works are: *El país de las cosas perdidas* [The Country of the Lost Things], *Donde duerme el agua* [Where Water Sleeps], and *La misma piedra* [The Same Stone].

Concha López Narváez (b.1939) was awarded the Lazarillo Prize for *El amigo oculto y los espíritus de la tarde* [The Hidden Friend and the Evening Spirits], the CCEI for *La colina de Edeta* [The Hill of Edeta] and *Memorias de una gallina* [The Story of a Hen]. Her name was on the IBBY List for *La tierra del sol y la luna* [The Land of the Sun and the Moon], a historical novel. Her books range from short tales for the youngest, to adventure or historical novels for older children.

Fernando Alonso (b.1941). His book *El hombrecillo vestido de gris y otros cuentos* [The Little Man in Grey and other Stories] gained him the Lazarillo Prize, and his name has been on the Honour Lists of the Andersen Prize and IBBY. He has also written *Feral y las cigüeñas* [Feral and the Storks], *El hombrecillo de papel* [The Little Paper Man] and other books. One of his characteristics is a curious sense of humour which may seem bitter to grown-ups.

Fernando Almena (b.1943). His works are full of ironic humour, which adults may consider criticism: *Pocachicha*, *Un solo de clarinete* and *Tartesos*, a historical novel. As a playwright he was awarded a Prize in 1990 for his play *El cisne* [The Swan].

João Manuel Gisbert (b.1949) received the CCEI Prize for his first book, *Escenarios fantásticos*, [Fantastic Scenery], and the Lazarillo with *El misterio de la isla de Tökland* [The Mystery of Tökland Island]. His works transport us to mysterious, far away worlds, and to the world of dreams.

Many other authors deserve also to be mentioned: in poetry, Marina Romero, Concha Lagos; in narrative prose: Juan Antonio de Laiglesia, Carlos Murciano, Juan Farias, Pilar Molina, Juan Muñoz, Marta Osorio, Pilar Mateos, José Antonio del Cañizo, Consuelo Armijo, Carmen Vázquez-Vigo and José González Torices. The last three have also worked in drama, together with Juan Cervera, Luis Matilla and Ángeles Gasset.

## Further Reading

Bravo-Villasante, C. (1962) *Historia de la literatura infantil española*, Madrid: Doncel.
Cervera, J. (1981) *Historia crítica del teatro infantil español*, Madrid: Editora Nacional.

# 66

# Portugal

## *Natércia Rocha*

In Portugal, as in other countries, the first books for children had their roots in the oral tradition. It is only later that English and French stories were translated. Books specifically aimed at young readers first appeared during the second half of the nineteenth century, and their authors all pursued the same ideal: always to teach something. In the last 150 years one can distinguish three main periods in this world of children's books: the early period, from the eighteenth century to the late 1920s; the period of the dictatorship, from 1928 to 1974, and from then on, when democracy made it possible for writers to work on topics previously considered as unacceptable.

During the first period, poetry and traditional stories dominated, with translations in a distant second place. In the second period, the dictatorship made itself felt by imposing political values and propaganda on the books; short stories on colonial situations were quite frequent, although they took only the colonialist point of view. The third period can be seen as allowing new trends to develop, inviting writers to approach real-life situations such as divorce, war, extreme poverty, death and delinquency; in novels, psychological problems, adventure, mystery and history play a larger role now: in poetry, well-known authors attract children by writing specially for them.

From the first period, some names and titles are not completely forgotten although they can be considered somewhat dated. Famous writers who wrote for children only occasionally left books that are still read. The best example is *O romance da raposa* [The Fox's Story] (1924), by Aquilino Ribeiro, one of the best Portuguese writers. *Bonecos falantes* [Talking Toys] (1925), by Carlos Selvagem, was a great favourite at the time. Some other books were very popular when they first appeared, such as *O mundo dos meus bonitos* [The World of My Toys] (1920), by Augusto de Santa Rita, *O tesouro poético da Infância* [Treasures of Children's Poetry] (1883) by Antero do Quental, a great poet; and also the poems by João de Deus included in *Versos para as crianças e para o povo* [Poems for the Children and the People] (1883). From Jaime Cortesao there is a very interesting book about the Azores, *O romance das ilhas encantadas* [The Story of the Enchanted Islands] (1926); Carlos Amaro wrote a single book, a lovely long poem, *S João subiu ao trono* [St John Sat on the Throne] (1927). For children, Afonso Lopes Vieira wrote a charming book of verses under the title *Os animais nossos amigos* [Our Friends, the Animals] (1911). From the long bibliography of Emilia de Sousa Costa, *Aventuras da Carochinha Japonesa* [Adventures of the

Little Japanese Beetle] (1928) can be selected as one of the most engaging stories.

However, the most interesting writer among these is Ana de Castro Osório who wrote and translated more than thirty books, directed a series of books for the very young, worked for the Just Born Press for children and fought for quality and beauty in books for this new public of young readers. Henrique Marques Junior, besides being a writer, was the first researcher on literature for children, publishing *Algumas achegas para uma Bibliografia Infantil* [Some Notes for a Bibliography] (1928), a very valuable and unique work on the subject. Many famous painters used to illustrate books for children; one can find the signatures of Benjamin Rabier, Eduardo Malta. Milly Possoz, Francisco Valença, Roque Gameiro, Alfredo Moraes, Guida Ottolini, Raquel Roque Gameiro, Carlos Carneiro and others.

During the second period the number of titles published goes up, but the topics are greatly limited by a strong and always present dictatorial power. Poetry gives us some great names whose books have been reprinted several times since then. Matilde Rosa Araújo wrote *O livro da Tila* [Tila's Book] (1957), her first poems for children, which are still in print. Other notable books included Sidónio Muralha's *Bichos, bichinhos e bicharocos* [Pets, Small Pets, Little Pets] (1949) and Maria Alberta Menéres's *Figuras figuronas* [Geometric Figures] (1969). Books on historical events, and biographies made Adolfo Simões Muller well known among children; he wrote more than thirty books including novels, poems and plays. Sophia de Mello Breyner Andresen published her first two novels, *A fada Oriana* [Fairy Oriana] (1958) and *A menina do mar* [The Little Girl from the Sea] (1959), which remain favourites with young readers. Ricardo Alberty is a great writer of short stories of which the best known are 'A galinha verde' [The Green Hen] (1957) and 'Os quatro corações do coração' [The Four Hearts of the Heart] (1968). Aquilino Ribeiro wrote two new books: *Arca de Noé, terceira classe* [Noah's Ark, Third Class] (1936) and *O livro da Marianinha* [Little Mariana's Book] (1967). Two novels set in Africa are *Kurika* and *Impala* (1946) by Henrique Galvão. Matilde Roda Araújo was the author of one of the most cherished books of this period, *O palhaço verde* [The Green Clown] (1962). Two books have remained in great demand: one written by a poet, Papiniano Carlos: *A menina gotinha de água* [Little Miss Waterdrop] (1965); the other is *Constantino, guardador de vacas e de sonhos* [Constantino, Guardian of Cows and Dreams] (1962) by Alves Redol. This was also the golden period for the press; magazines for children, such as *O senhor Doutor, O Papagaio, O Mosquito* and *O Cavaleiro Andante* were very popular and helped many authors to fame.

Since the end of the dictatorship in 1974, literature for children has bloomed, both in the quality of text and of illustration. Some authors from the previous period now explore humour, nonsense and social conflicts more openly. The best known are Matilde Rosa Araújo, Luisa Ducla Soares, António Torrado, Maria Alberta Menéres, Mário Castrim, Luisa Dacosta and Ilse Losa, all of them with long lists of short stories, novels and plays to their names. The following titles must be mentioned: *As Fadas* [The Fairies] (1994) by Matilde Rosa Araújo; *A vassoura mágica* [The Magic Broom] (1986) by Luisa Ducla Soares; a series of traditional stories retold by António Torrado as *Histórias tradicionais portuguesas contadas de novo* [Retold Portuguese Traditional Stories] (from 1992); *Uma palmada na testa* [Slapping the Forehead] (1993) by Maria Alberta Menéres; *A caminho de Fátima* [On the Road to Fátima] (1992) by Mário Castrim and *A menina coração de pássaro* [The Little Girl with a Bird's Heart] (1978) and *O quadro roubado* [The Stolen Picture] (1977), one of the most reprinted books by Ilse Losa.

Agustina Bessa-Luis, another great name in Portuguese literature, has occasionally written for children and one of her first books for them was *Contos Amarantinos* [Stories from Amarante] (1990). Alice Vieira, previously a journalist, is nowadays one of the most read authors by young people; her first book was published in 1979; *Rosa, minha irmã Rosa* [Rose, my Sister Rose], dealing with the interests of urban teenagers, has been translated into several languages.

Other books which should be mentioned are *O soldadinho e a pomba* [The Little Soldier and the Pigeon] (1981), dealing with military discipline, by Leonel Neves, *O virus diabólico* [The Diabolic Virus] (1991), centred on computers, by Carlos Correia and *Um segredo ... dois segredos* [One secret ... Two secrets] (1993), the amusing story of a family sharing their secrets, by Natércia Rocha. A biography of Olympic Champion Carlos Lopes is the last book Carlos Pinhão wrote for children.

The younger generation is represented by José Jorge Letria who has been publishing poetry and short stories such as *Teia de um segredo* [The Web of a Secret] (1993), by Catarina Fonseca, still in her early twenties, whose first book *A herança* [The Heritage] (1990) a quiet amusing story won her a prize from the Association of Writers. António Mota also won a prize with a moving story about rural life, *Pedro Alecrim* (1988). Alvaro Magalhões who has shown a remarkable sense of humour published a curious collection of very short stories named *Histórias pequenas de bichos pequenos* [Little Stories of Little Pets] (1985). *Gosto de ti. R.* [I Love You. R.] (1992) is a novel about love by Graça Gonçalves. A historical novel *O filho do trovão* [The Son of Thunder] (1991) is one of the most arresting stories told by Alexandre Honrado. Sérgio Godinho, best known as singer and composer, published *O pequeno livro dos medos* [The Little Book of Fears] (1991) as his second work for children. A writer with a fast growing list is Violeta Crespo de Figeiredo who recently published a book of poetry for very small children, *Fala bicho* [Talking Beast] (1991).

Several anthologies of poems have appeared, the most recent being *Verso aqui ... Verso acolá* [A Verse Here ... A Verse There] (1990) compiled by Natércia Rocha including poems that were not written especially for children; another has been compiled by Sophia de Mello Breyner Andresen, *Primeiro livro de poesia* [First Book of Poetry] (1991). Famous poets have written for children as Eugénio de Andrade did in his book *Uma nuvem e outras* [A Cloud and Others] (1989).

Adventure and mystery also have an important place, often being published in series, such as *Uma aventura* [One Adventure] (started in 1982) by Ana Maria Magalhães and Isabel Alçada, *1001 Detectives* (started in 1987) by Carlos Correia, Maria Alberta Menéres and Natércia Rocha and another series named *Club das Chaves* [Keys Club] by Maria Teresa Maia Gonzalez and Maria do Rosário Pedreira.

The importance of illustration has been recognised and editors are paying more attention to its quality. Several illustrators are outstanding: Manuela Bacelar, João

Machado, Maria Keil, António Modesto, Carlos Barradas, Romeu Costa, Cristina Malaquias, Soares Rocha and Vasco Colombo.

There are very few 'home-grown' Portuguese comics because of the success of well-established foreign material. Magazines about music which are very much in demand by young adults have replaced the magazines for young children, who are thus being pushed to accept teenagers' tastes much sooner than before. Because of grammatical and lexical differences, Portuguese authors are scarcely known in Brazil; both Portuguese and Brazilian writers are now publishing local versions with the necessary alterations.

## Further Reading

Gomes, J. A. (1994) *A Poesia na Literatura para a Infância*, Oporto: Asa.

Pires, M. L. B. (1990) *História da Literatura Infantil em Portugal*, Lisbon: Vega.

Rocha, N. (1981) *Bibliografia Geral da Literatura Portuguesa para Crianças*, Lisbon: Editorial Communicão.

—— (1984/1992) *Breve história da literatura para crianças em Portugal*, 2nd edn, Lisbon: Ministério da Educão.

# 67

# Germany

## 1 German Children's Literature from the Eighteenth to the Twentieth Century

### *Hans-Heino Ewers*

In Germany, as in England and France, children's literature in the modern sense begins only in the eighteenth century. A separate market for literature aimed at children and young people arose, and was carefully watched by the educational and, to some extent, by the literary community. From the mid-century on, the liberal educational ideas of John Locke were influential. They led to greater adaptation of the material to the child's grasp, but development of the intellect and mediation of knowledge were still expected to begin at an early age. Into the 1770s children's literature was dominated by compendia and encyclopaedic works, packed with facts and omitting no area of knowledge; there was no feel for child-friendly contents. Most of the corpus consisted of textbooks for private tuition, spiced with fables and moral exemplary tales. Many such works were translations from the French; the most outstanding German work is Johann Peter Miller's (1725–1789) *Historischmoralische Schilderungen zur Bildung eines edlen Herzens in der Jugend* [Improving Tales to Edify a Noble Heart in Youth, 5 vols, 1753–1764].

France was the great model for German literature, and children's literature was no exception. As well as encyclopedias, the weeklies and magazines were translated (thus Marie Leprince de Beaumont's *Magasin des enfants* (1756, German 1758) including the fairy story 'La belle et la bête'). Not until 1772 did the first independent German children's magazine appear, the *Leipziger Wochenblatt für Kinder* [Leipzig Children's Weekly] (1772–1773) of Johann Christoph Adelung (1732–1806). A little later Lessing's friend Christian Felix Weiße (1726–1804), a renowned comedy-writer of his time, published the *Kinderfreund. Ein Wochenblatt* [Children's Friend, a Weekly] (1775–1782), which was continued as *Briefwechsel der Familie des Kinderfreundes* [Correspondence of the Children's Friend's Family] (1784–1792) in the style of the English moral weeklies. This is one of the high points of eighteenth-century German children's literature, famous not least for the many dramas for children it incorporates. C. F. Weiße was also responsible for the first poetry anthology in German for children, *Lieder für Kinder* [Songs for Children] (1766).

The effect of Rousseau's philosophy of childhood was especially great in Germany; in educational theory it led to a new movement, Philanthropism, whose exponents set out to reform not only education but also children's literature. Their first spokesman, Johann Bernhard Basedow (1724–1790), still used the old form of the encyclopedia: *Elementarbuch für die Jugend* [Young People's Elementary Book] (3 vols, 1770), extended under the title *Elementarwerk* [Elementary Work] (4 vols, 1774). But its layout is adapted to the child's need for stimuli: it is accompanied by a magnificent collection of copper etchings after drawings by the celebrated Daniel Chodowiecki (1726–1801). Another climax of children's illustration two decades later was the first volume of the *Bilderbuch für Kinder* [Picture Book for Children] (1790–1830, 12 vols in all) by the Weimar publisher Friedrich Justin Bertuch (1747–1822).

The younger philanthropic authors undertook a more thorough reform of children's literature: notably Joachim Heinrich Campe (1746–1818), the most outstanding and most modern German children's writer of the late eighteenth century. This reform is based on Rousseau's view that childhood represents a qualitatively self-contained mode of human being. To cram children full of knowledge that will only be of use to them later as adults can result merely in empty verbal learning. Children's literature must divest itself of its mass of erudition and restrict itself to what is of immediate importance for the child. Why give the child a teaching that concerns only adults? asks Campe in 1779; he demands that children's literature take its cue not only – as was already the case – from the intellectual understanding potential of the child, but also from its moral needs. Here the mainsprings of the philanthropic reform of children's literature are clear: restriction to the child's concerns and concentration on the child's environment. A new paradigm was born: that of children's literature as being strictly literature suited to children. His *Robinson Crusoe* adaptation of 1779–1780, inspired by the relevant passages of Rousseau's *Emile* and entitled *Robinson der Jüngere* [Robinson Junior], puts the reform programme into practice with thoroughness and verve; it was one of the most successful German children's books, translated into numerous languages and reprinted into the twentieth century (122nd legitimate printing 1923). Goethe remarks of Campe, 'He did incredible service to children; he is their delight and, so to speak, their gospel' (to Eckermann, 29 March, 1830).

A further reforming idea traceable to Rousseau's *Emile* is the conviction that childhood can only be understood on its own terms. The adult is stripped of all authority *vis-à-vis* the child: child's world must be respected in its autonomy. Literature deriving from this concept would not just deal with children's concerns, but would also put itself in the child's shoes and adopt the child's perspective. Such anti-authoritarian children's literature would present children's experiences independently of, and uninfluenced by, adults' values; it would aim to express children's feelings and perceptions with as little distortion as possible. This is a view of children's literature which at first glance seems to belong to the late twentieth century; but the demand for an anti-authoritarian children's literature, one starting from the child, has been voiced since the beginnings of reformed children's literature in the early modern social era.

Repeated attempts at reform, always with the same basic tenor, were needed, it is true, before this reforming impulse could gain broad-based acceptance – something not thinkable before the mid-twentieth century. Yet the late eighteenth century already provides the first anti-authoritarian children's book in German: Christian Adolf Overbeck's (1755–1821) collection of poems *Frizchens Lieder* [Freddie's Songs] (1781), where a child as lyrical subject is allowed to express itself extraordinarily freely for the time. In the preface the author announces with visible pride, 'Here, if I have done my job well, it really is a child speaking. Overbeck's volume, however, remained alone. The philanthropists' reform does attach children's literature to the child's world; but it conceives of this world less as a free space, rather as a sanctuary, a didactic province where educationalists have a definite place – and the final authority. The frame of Campe's *Robinson Junior* with the father as narrator and authority figure combined, or the frame of the *Moralisches Elementarbuch* [Moral Primer] (1782–1783) of the second great philanthropic children's writer, Christian Gotthilf Salzmann (1744–1811), are examples of such sanctuaries.

With the philanthropic reform, German children's literature freed itself from dependence on the great French and English models (the latter generally known via French intermediaries). Indeed, it can be argued that from this time, the history of European children's literature was largely written in Germany. German ideas radiated to France and England, and to Scandinavia and eastern Europe. Even Jewish children's literature is indebted to the German Enlightenment. German children's literature retained this primacy for the next historical age: that of the Romantic reform of children's literature, which also started in Germany. Prepared by the young Herder, its programmatic principles were first put forward in stray utterances, particularly by Ludwig Tieck and Friedrich von Hardenberg (Novalis) – a form which effectively prevented contemporaries from noticing them. Then in the first two decades of the nineteenth century the great works appeared: the supplement of children's songs to the third volume of Achim von Arnim and Clemens Brentano's *Des Knaben Wunderhorn* [The Boy's Magic Horn] (1808), Brentano's *Italienische Märchen* [Italian Fairy Tales] (*c.*1805–1811), and in the second decade the fairy tales for children by Tieck, Contessa, Fouqué and E. T. A. Hoffmann, and finally the *Kinder- und Hausmärchen* [Fairy Tales for Children and Home] of the brothers Grimm (1812–1815). What a mass of immortal works – appearing in a time of war and confusion, when literary production was not the least of the things which almost entirely ceased!

The romantics too started by recognising the self-sufficiency of childhood; they too demanded strictly child-orientated children's literature, but they had a quite different concept of both these criteria. What modern societies have produced and separated out and designated as the space of childhood is actually, said the Romantics, the remains of a past state of the world, just as children themselves are nothing but humans who are close to their divine origin. To adopt the child's standpoint meant, for the Romantic, to transport oneself back into the past, which the child by its nature embodies; in respect of children's literature it meant to have recourse to the kinds of creative art which originated in that past. Romanticism declared traditional national folklore, particularly the popular children's rhyme and the fairy tale, to be the true reading matter for children. The brothers Grimm put this into practice by insisting that the poetry handed down should reach its child recipients as far as possible in an unaltered form – that only rhymes and tales, legends and humoresques of proven antiquity should be placed before them. All additions from a more recent age were regarded as impurities.

The Romantic creative writers, on the other hand, believed that each age, however far it may be from the beginnings, commanded a sufficient poetic gift to renew the traditional genres creatively. The late-Romantic fairy tale was from the outset a genre that mixed the old and the modern. It deals with a distant world of miracles, a child-like and poetic existence; but it deals with the present too. This latter is done in Brentano's *Italian Fairy-Tales*, an adaptation of a number of tales by Basile for German children, particularly in the narrative mode; though perception of the pervasive irony here is perhaps possible only for the adult reader. In Tieck's children's fairy tale *Die Elfen* [The Elves] (1812) the modern world is made explicit on the level of the action – though only in allegorical form. In the popular fairy tale, our world and the wondrous world co-exist unproblematically. Tieck sees them as being in an antagonistic relationship, which he endows with a new function: it is the metaphoric representation of the antagonistic contrast in modern life between the child's sense of the numinous and the rationality of the adult. Together with E. T. A. Hoffmann's elf-story *Das Ffremde Kind* [The Little Stranger] (1817), Tieck's tale inaugurates modern fairy tale literature for children. These writings, copious in the nineteenth and even stronger in the twentieth century, generally express the abyss between poetic child mentality and prosaic reality in a symbolic or allegorical manner.

In E. T. A. Hoffmann's tale *Nußknacker und Mäusekönig* [The Nutcracker and the King of the Mice] (1816), realistically shown modern actuality replaces the conventional ordinary world of the traditional fairy story, and a psychologically realistic child figure takes the place of the child-like fairy tale hero. The child's continuing belief in the wondrous remains unsatisfied until the potential experience of a second, an other world, is turned into reality. In a temporary stay in such an other world, or in the temporary presence of a figure from the other world in our world, all the limitations that the child's imagination (in particular the sense of the wondrous) suffers in modern actuality are removed. E. T. A. Hoffmann makes the child an inhabitant of two worlds; and thus he enables the young reader to sharpen his sense of reality without having to suppress his pleasure in the improbable and the fantastic which co-exists with his sense of reality. With his children's story *Nußknacker und Mäusekönig*, Hoffmann founded the genre of the fantastic children's story, a genre which was to become the central component of children's literature in the late nineteenth and the first half of the twentieth century.

In German children's literature from 1770, the year of *Basedow's Elementarwerk*, to 1819, the date of the second, much altered edition of the *Kinder- und Hausmärchen*, the basic patterns of modern, child-orientated children's literature, which remained dominant into the late 1960s, are found already developed and to some extent exemplified in classic works. But an oddity of the development of German children's literature in the nineteenth and early twentieth centuries is that the heritage both of the philanthropic and of the Romantic reforms was to a considerable degree squandered.

With the regrowth of literary production from the end of the 1820s, children's literature in Germany largely ceased to be a vehicle of programmatic intentions and reforming ideas; it became increasingly a pure business matter and thus had to adapt to the traditionalistic, in some cases decidedly anti-modern, ideas of the buyers. Children's poetry almost succeeds in being an exception to this rule. The rhymes, songs and poems for children by Friedrich Rückert (1788–1866), Wilhelm Hey (1789–1854), Hoffmann von Fallersleben (1798–1874), Robert Reinick (1805–1852) and Friedrich Güll (1812–1879) show a blossoming of the Romantic spirit in children's poetry between the 1830s and 1850s. In fairy tales, on the other hand, a sense of reality which is inhibited in its dealings with the numinous becomes predominant. Yet there are still examples of lasting children's stories: first and foremost the fairy tale yearbooks of Wilhelm Hauff (1826–1828), then the tales of Eduard Mörike (*Das Stuttgarter Hutzelmännchen* [The Wrinkled Manikin of Stuttgart] (1853)), Gottfried Keller (*Spiegel, das Kätzchen* [Kitten Mirror] (1856)), Theodor Storm (*Der kleine Häwelmann* [Little Häwelmann] (1849); *Die Regentrude* [Wet Weather Trude] (1864)), and Victor Blüthgen (*Hesperiden* [Hesperides] (1878)). There is no continuation in German children's writing of the nineteenth and early twentieth century of the extremely modern narrative pattern used by E. T. A. Hoffmann in *Nußknacker und Mäusekönig*, and no major German contribution to children's literature of the fantastic. Here of course other nations filled the gap. The decisive mediating role fell here to the Dane Hans Christian Andersen, who learnt from the Grimms as well as from Tieck and E. T. A. Hoffmann. The heritage of German Romanticism in the field of children's literature reached Europe and the world only indirectly, in the form of Andersen's tales. This inheritance then bore fruit in English children's literature with Kingsley, Carroll and George MacDonald.

The following of the brothers Grimm was much greater in Germany. The number of collections of popular fairy tales and legends for children published during the nineteenth century is immense; let us mention only the highly successful compilations by Ludwig Bechstein (1801–1860), *Deutsches Märchenbuch* [German Fairy Tale Book] (1845) and *Deutsches Sagenbuch* [German Legend Book] (1859). In Germany, since the Grimms, this editing of traditional lore went hand in hand with uncompromising enmity toward the writing of up-to-date children's books. The attitude was that the present lacked any capacity to produce a really child-like poetry, so that only traditional folklore could be considered suitable reading for children. Modern children's literature was to the Grimms and their followers a contradiction in terms; anything that declared itself as such must be mercilessly opposed. In the history of German children's literature not the modern, but the highly anti-modern side of the Romantic movement sets the tone; this has had lasting consequences. From this point, the educated elite refused to engage critically and productively with newly written children's literature, which thus, deprived of any official esteem or critical challenge, degenerated more than ever into a purely commercial enterprise – sinking to the level of the trivial or colportage. Virtually none of the innumerable moral or historical tales and travel and adventure stories for children from German pens, with a few exceptions such as Theodor Storm's *Pole Poppenspäler* [Paul the Puppeteer] (1874), have survived. That the Biedermeier (from the 1840s to the 1860s), despite this, is thought of as a golden age of children's literature is essentially due to brilliant illustrators: Ludwig

Richter (1803–1884), Franz Pocci (1807–1876), Theodor Hosemann (1807–1875), Otto Speckter (1807–1871) and many others. Not by chance are the German children's classics of the nineteenth century picture books: Heinrich Hoffmann's *Struwwelpeter* [Shock-Headed Peter] (1845), C. Reinhardt's *Sprechende Tiere* [Talking Animals] (1854) and Wilhelm Busch's *Max und Moritz* [Max and Moritz] (1865).

It is not surprising that mass entertainment literature for children, whether sensational and adventure-based or sentimental and kitschy – the work of such authors as Gustav Nieritz (1795–1879), Franz Hoffmann (1814–1882), Sophie Wörishofer (1838–1890) and Karl May (1842–1912) – succumbed, towards the end of the century, to the fascination of nationalism, chauvinism, colonialism and militarism. Here we see children's literature as a major medium of ideological mobilisation. But at the same time fresh literary and educational demands were brought to bear on children's literature. Richard (1863–1920) and Paula Dehmel (1862–1918) with their collection *Fitzebutze* (1900, illustrated by Ernst Kreidolf) renewed German children's poetry. Here we find a child's impulsive, uncensored lyrical self-expression. In Paula Dehmel's *Singinens Geschichten* [Singine's Stories] (1903, book publication 1921) modern first-person narration by a child appears: the child is made the centre of perception and value-judgement, and no adult interference occurs. The Dehmels' works bring back consistently anti-authoritarian children's literature. Around the turn of the century the children's verses of Christian Morgenstern (1871–1914), only collected and published posthumously (*Klein Irmchen* [Little Irma] (1921), were written; his nonsense poems (*Galgenlieder* [Gallows Songs] (1905)), however, do not come under consideration as children's literature until the 1960s. In fairy tale, Otto Julius Bierbaum's (1865–1920) free adaptation of Pinocchio, *Zäpfel Kerns Abenteuer* [Adventures of Zäpfel Kern] (1905) and Gerdt von Bassewitz's (1878–1923) *Peterchens Mondfahrt* [Peterkin's Trip to the Moon] (1911–1915) stand out. The turn of the century is also noted for a new growth of the picture book, under heavy English influence (Caldecott, Greenaway, Crane). As well as Ernst Kreidolf (1863–1956) artists like Carl Hofer (1878–1955), Karl F. E. von Freyhold (1879–1944) or the Austrians Heinrich Lefler (1863–1919) and Joseph Urban (1872–1933) should be mentioned.

While Social-Democratic children's literature starts with fairy tales (Lorenz Berg: *König Mammon und die Freiheit* [King Mammon and Freedom] (1878)), teachers committed to reforming movements in education wrote sketches and stories of the city, aimed at children beginning school. These on the one hand hold firmly to the child's experiential perspective and thus to the principle of starting from the child, but on the other hand go beyond the child's world and focus attention on the city, the industrial world of work and the social problems of industrial society. This trend, partly naturalistic and partly impressionistically tinged, started with Ilse Frappan's (1852–1908) *Hamburger Bilder für Kinder* [Hamburg Pictures for Children] (1899), Fritz Gansberg's (1871–1950) *Streifzüge durch die Welt der Großstadtkinder* [Exploring the World of the City Children (1904) and Heinrich Scharrelmann's (1871–1940) *Ein kleiner Junge* [A Little Boy] (1908), and culminates in Carl Dantz's (1884–1967) penetrating portrait of the circumstances of a working-class boy, *Peter Stoll* (1925). Parallel with this arose the tradition of city novels for children, generally with a plot consisting of a detective or crime novel; this includes Wolf Durian's (1892–1969) *Kai aus der Kiste* [Kai from the Crate] (1927), Erich Kästner's (1899–1974) *Emil und die Detektive* [Emil and the Detectives] (1928) and *Pünktchen und Anton* [Dot and Anton] (1931), and Wilhelm Matthießen's (1891–1965) *Das rote U* [The Red U] (1932). Proletarian children's literature had a voice here too with Alex Wedding's (1905–1966) *Ede und Unku* (1931), which, however, also clings to fairy tale conventions. Hermynia Zur Mühlen (1883–1951) wrote *Proletarische Märchen* [Proletarian Fairy Tales] (from 1921), Lisa Tetzner *Hans Urian* (1929). Karl Aloys Schenzinger (1886–1962) produced a National Socialist city novel for children, *Der Hitlerjunge Quex* [Quex, the Hitler Youth] (1932). After the National Socialists took power socially critical children's literature was forced into exile; from this phase of production Lisa Tetzner's children's Odyssey *Die Kinder aus Nummer 67* [The Children from Number 67] (9 vols, 1933–1949) and Kurt Held's (1897–1959) *Die rote Zora und ihre Bande* [Red Zora and her Gang] (1941) stand out.

The post-war situation in West Germany and Austria is characterised by a paradox. On the one hand a withdrawal into the private and unpolitical domain occurred, explicable as a reaction to the way children's literature was forced into propaganda service in the Third Reich; thus socio-critical traditions failed to re-establish themselves and critical treatment of recent German history was prevented. On the other hand there was unprecedented openness to the children's literature of other nations, particularly the Anglo-American area and Scandinavia. The English and American classics of fantasy literature were read; Scandinavian authors, especially Astrid Lindgren and Hans Peterson, became influential. Thus German children's literature was confronted with its own traditions as mediated by England and Scandinavia. This could not have occurred had not Germans reversed that negative attitude of principle – characteristic of a large section of the German educated elite since the nineteenth century – toward all writing specifically for children. This anti-modernism in the field of children's literature reached its climax in the *völkisch* and National Socialist camps' propagation of true Germanic folk poetry as the sole legitimate reading matter for children. One may see in this one of the most serious hindrances to the development of German children's literature. For the first theoretical attempt to put specific children's literature on a footing of legitimacy since the Philanthropists and the Romantics, we have to wait for the 1950s and the work of the literary scholar Anna Krüger (1904–1991), whose approach has been followed by most contemporary theorists. She opened up the whole field; the fifteen years from 1955 or so were one of the most productive eras of German children's writing ever. Here Germany caught up with all the elements of modern children's literature, both in the philanthropic or reforming educational trend and in the romantic tendency, that it had so far missed or been prevented from exploring. A literature that set out from the experiential perspective and the viewpoint of the child, that allows infant wishes to have their way, and that largely refrains from didacticism and over-protectiveness, flourished: a literature of sanctuaries for children situated outside society.

First we may mention an apogee of modern German children's verse. Joining the traditions of Biedermeier and turn-of-the-century verse, this poetry is naïve and expressive in style; it is nature-lyric too in the sense that only nature is capable of reflecting the childlike spirit. On one hand the new verse is very close to popular traditional rhymes (Friedrich Hoffmann: *Ole Bole Bullerjahn* (1857)), on the other hand it picks up elements of the modern adult (nature) lyric (Josef Guggenmos: *Lustige Verse für kleine Leute* [Happy Verses for Little People] (1956), *Was denkt die Maus am Donnerstag* [What does the Mouse Think on Thursday] (1967); Christine Busta: *Die Sternenmühle* [The Starmill] (1959); Elisabeth Borchers: *Und oben schwimmt die Sonne davon* [And the Sun floats away on Top] (1965)). Another thread, traceable back to Erich Kästner (*Das verhexte Telefon* [The Bewitched Telephone] (1932)), consists of comic, sometimes gruesomely grotesque poems, primarily those of James Krüss (*Spatzenlügen* [Sparrows' Lies] (1957) and *Der wohltemperierte Leierkasten* [The Well-Tempered Hurdy-Gurdy] (1961)). Krüss also encourages nonsense poetry and lyrical plays on words, but these only really became popular in the mid- to late 1960s (Hans A. Halbey: *Pampelmusensalat* [Grapefruit Salad] (1965); Jürgen Spohn: Der Spielbaum [The Play Tree] (1966); Michael Ende: *Das Schnurpsenbuch* [The Schnurps Book] (1969); Josef Guggenmos: *Gorilla, ärgere dich nicht* [Sorry, Gorilla] (1971)).

On the narrative front, James Krüss stands out. His Heligoland cycles (*Der Leuchtturm auf den Hummerklippen* [The Lighthouse on the Lobster Cliffs] (1956) and *Mein Urgroßvater und ich* [My Great-Grandfather and Me] (1959)) bring old-fashioned story-telling back into children's writing. Alongside him is Otfried Preußler, whose literary children's fairy stories and 'kasper' (Punch and Judy) stories (*Der kleine Wassermann* [The Little Water Man] (1956), *Die kleine Hexe* [The Little Witch] (1957), *Der Räuber Hotzenplotz* [Robber Hotzenplotz] (1962), *Das kleine Gespenst* [The Little Ghost] (1966) have become internationally successful classics, as have the Jim Knopf books (1960–1962) of Michael Ende. The realistic children's narratives of the period (Heinrich M. Denneborg: *Jan und das Wildpferd* [Jan and the Wild Horse] (1957); Ursula Wölfel: *Der rote Rächer* [The Red Avenger] (1959), *Feuerschuh und Windsandale* [Fireshoe and Windsandal] (1961)), the adventure literature (Kurt Lütgen: *Kein Winter für Wölfe* [Not a Winter for Wolves] (1951)), and the children's historical novel (Hans Baumann: *Der Sohn des Kolumbus* [Son of Columbus] (1951)) have all dated by comparison. In the 1960s first attempts at critical treatment of German history, particularly that of the Third Reich, appeared (Hans Peter Richter: *Damals war es Friedrich* [Then it was Friedrich] (1961); Hans Georg Noack: *Stern über der Mauer* [Star over the Wall] (1962)).

A new era began at the end of the 1960s for the west German language area (including Switzerland and Austria); one might speak of its entry into a second modern period. The modern children's literature of the preceding epoch aimed to autonomise childhood as an other, an alternative world. In the free spaces or play spaces of the child the (market) laws of the modern world were suspended. The children's literature reform of 1970 on the other hand transferred modern basic principles, in this case basic rights, to children too: they are not to possess other rights, but the same rights as adults. The new trend from 1970 is a literature of equal rights for children, claiming general human rights for them. The concept of childhood on which it is based emphasises the similarities of children and adults. Children are removed from their sanctuaries, their worlds of play and adventure and exoticism, and set down in real life, where they are expected to stand up for their human rights. They are taken seriously, they are left scope for making decisions, their decisions are respected, they are granted the right to speak in discussions and to vote, and they are seen not as recipients of instructions but as negotiating partners. In the so-called anti-authoritarian children's literature (*c.*1968–1972), the children themselves struggle for all this against the resistance – sometimes embittered, sometimes ineffectual – of the adults, especially fathers (Christine Nöstlinger: *Wir pfeifen auf den Gurkenkönig* [We Don't Give a Toss for the Cucumber King] (1972)). The children become inhabitants of a real world undivided between children and adults, a reality with no idyllic features left. 'We don't have our children just being happy on sunny playgrounds and in airy classrooms', said Ursula Wölfel in 1972. 'They live with adults in a world full of conflicts and dissonances.' This author's pioneering collection of short stories, *Die grauen und die grünen Felder* [The Grey Fields and the Green Fields] (1970), confronts the young reader with this world's multiplicity of social and political problems – even at the risk of having a depressing effect.

Adults too, and their existential problems, can now become a subject for children's literature, opening up a series of new themes: problems in the parents' relationship, divorce, the mother's striving for emancipation and career, the father's unemployment, aggressiveness, alcoholism and other forms of dependence, finally disability, sickness and death, to name just a few of the new topics (Peter Härtling: *Das war Hirbel* [That was Hirbel] (1973), *Oma* [Grandma] (1975), *Fränze* [Francie] (1989); Ursula Fuchs: *Wiebke und Paul* [Wiebke and Paul] (1982). Then again the child's subjectivity – its inner life, mood-swings, feelings, dreams and fears – is now taken seriously. Being declared responsible for themselves is a considerable psychological challenge and stress for the children, so it is unsurprising that their interior life is unbalanced, tense and dissociated. The place of the unworried, extrovert, generally cheerful and balanced childish spirit in the previous literary era is now taken by the introverted child, experiencing its own interior life and its rifts with some self-awareness, able even to describe its inner life in a rudimentary way with the aid of psychological terms it has picked up (Peter Härtling: *Ben liebt Anna* [Ben loves Anna] (1979); Gudrun Mebs: *Das Sonntagskind* [Sunday's Child] (1983); Christine Nöstlinger: *Olfi Obermeier und der Oedipus* [Olfi Obermeier and Oedipus] (1984)).

A final element of equality is the right of children to a literature that is no different in principle from that of adults. Since the 1970s authors have essayed a style very similar to that of adult writing. The familiar demand that children be treated as human beings is joined by the new one that one should write for them, basically, just as one would for adults. The new narrative children's literature of the 1970s views itself as cognate in form and style with the modern novel. It takes over the complex techniques developed by the latter in the nineteenth century. The psychological novel, with its predominance of interior events and its themes of ego-stabilisation and self-finding, has become the preferred form for new children's narrative.

Thus the children's literature of the western German-speaking countries has, since the 1950s, increasingly joined the trends of north-west European and North American children's literature, in a way returning to its own beginnings in the early nineteenth century.

## 2 The German Democratic Republic

*Bernd Dolle-Weinkauff*

After 1945 children's and youth literature in the area of the Soviet Zone of Occupation – from 1949 the German Democratic Republic (GDR) – went its own way. In the 1940s and 1950s a system of literary production and distribution characteristically distinct from that of the other German-speaking countries soon developed, following the Soviet cultural-political model. In this system, state support and direction of the literary industry played a vital role – as seen not least in the dominant position of two publishing houses: Neues Leben (New Life) founded in 1946 under the name Verlag der Jungen Generation (New Generation Publishers), and Der Kinderbuchverlag (Children's Book Publishers), established in 1949 as the publishing arm of the Junge Pioniere [Young Pioneers] youth organisation.

At all points – in the printing and distribution process, the system of awards, the organs of criticism, and involvement in education through schools and other institutions – society had a pervasive, visible and effective influence on the children's writer. The history of East German children's and youth literature is largely a story of adaptation to and interaction with official cultural-political criteria and desirable role models. This interaction can be discerned even in changes of literary-theoretical viewpoints and of style, in authors' modes of writing and rhetorical strategies, and in the choice of particular genres and subjects.

It is, however, not right to regard GDR children's and youth literature as a more or less successful imitation of that of the Soviet Union. Admittedly the Soviet military administration went to great pains immediately after the war to secure publication of translations. Up to 1949 alone about eighty titles appeared, including major works of the Soviet youth literature canon such as Nicolai Ostrovsky's *How the Steel was Hardened* (German 1947) and Arkady Gaidar's *Timur and his Band* (German 1947). Such works as Nicolai Nossov's school stories (*I was a Bad Pupil*, German 1955) or the fantasies of Alexander Volkov (*The Magician of the Emerald City*, German 1963) inspired by L. Frank Baum also gained considerable popularity in ensuing years. Trends of Soviet literary and cultural politics also influenced the East German publishing scene – particularly its organisational structure – considerably at all periods. However, the constant official demand to follow the model of the Soviet Union in all ways, and in particular to imitate its children's writing, was never whole-heartedly espoused; at any rate, no great wish to imitate Russian texts is discernible in the relevant East German writings themselves.

GDR children's literature attempted to produce an independent tradition by carrying on from the proletarian children's literature of the Weimar Republic and the work of the emigrants driven from Germany after 1933, not a few of whom returned to East Germany; to some extent it also looked to representatives of the 'inner emigration'. Thus it was not chance, but a statement of policy, that one of the earliest significant publications was Hans Fallada's (pseud. of Rudolf Ditzen, 1893–1947) *Geschichten aus der Murkelei* [Stories from Murkelei] (1947) and Bertolt Brecht's (1898–1956) *Der verwundete Sokrates* [Wounded Socrates] (1949).

Among the most important texts published or republished by the mid-1950s which entered the GDR canon were Alex Wedding's (pseud. of Grete Weiskopf, 1905–1966) story of class struggle in the city, *Ede und Unku* [Ede and Unku] (1954, first published 1931), and Auguste Lazar's (1887–1970) *Sally Bleistift in Amerika* [Sally Pencil in America] (1948, first published 1935), about the solidarity of a group of children asserting themselves in a racist environment.

For the rest, the GDR did share with West Germany the heritage of a kind of children's literature that supplied comfort by fleeing from reality or by excluding problematic aspects of real life, whether that meant the inimical conditions of the National Socialist regime or the privations of the post-war period. Over against this, officially propagated writing defining itself as contemporary and socialist could provide only an affirmative concept of literature, in which traditionally conceived stereotyped figures were linked with baldly stated convictions about the correct behaviour in developing socialist society. The early works of successful East German children's writers, such as Ilse Korn (1907–1975) with *Mit Bärbel fing es an* [It started with Bärbel] (1952), Horst Beseler (b.1925) with *Die Moorbande* [The Swamp Gang] (1952), or Benno Pludra (b.1925) with *Ein Mädchen, fünf Jungen und sechs Traktoren* [One Girl, Five Boys and Six Tractors] (1951), exemplify this.

But experiments in, and discussions about, children's writing were not confined to topical political themes. Debates went on about classical types of received bourgeois literature for their young and their potential adoption. Then from the 1960s attempts were made to make available the tradition of national and world literature, beginning with Franz Fühmann's (1922–1984) adaptations of Greek and medieval epics (*Das hölzerne Pferd* [The Wooden Horse] (1968); *Das Nibelungenlied* [The Lay of the Nibelungs] (1971)) and of Shakespeare's plays *Shakespeare-Märchen* [Shakespeare Fantasies] (1968). But at first, fairy tales, girls' literature and adventure stories were the especial objects of a critical discussion on the national heritage. The adventure story – historical or contemporary – was then to become one of the strengths of GDR children's literature, since this genre lent itself to the current concept of literary realism and at the same time allowed particular reader expectations to be fulfilled. Great names in this context are Ludwig Renn (pseudonym of Arnold Friedrich Vieth von Golßenau, 1889–1979), who in *Trini* (1954) dealt with an episode of the Mexican revolution of 1910–1920, and Liselotte Welskopf-Henrich (1901–1979) with her series of novels *Die Söhne der großen Bärin* [The Sons of the Great She-Bear], begun in 1951, a history of the North American Indians and their struggles up to the present.

Children's fantasy literature on the other hand remained a genre of marginal interest, meaning mainly long stories by the dramatist Peter Hacks (b.1928) [for example, *Das Windloch* [The Wind Hole] (1956); *Das Turmverlies* [The Dungeon] (1962), inspired by the West German James Krüss. But the 1970s brought a more intensive preoccupation with fantasy, both in theoretical considerations and in actual texts. A new acceptance of the play character of children's literature is represented for instance in Franz Fühmann's language-play book *Die dampfenden Hälse der Pferde im Turm von Babel* [The Steaming Necks of the Horses in the Tower of Babel] (1978) and Christoph Hein's (b.1944) *Das Wildpferd unterm Kachelofen* [The Wild Horse under the Stove] (1986). Fairy tale fantasy also sometimes rose to critical and satirical mirroring of social circumstances in the last years of the GDR, as in Reinhard Griebner's story of silly townspeople *Das blaue Wunder Irgendwo* [The Big Surprise Somewhere] (1980), or Christa Kozik's (b.1941) plea for reform, scantily disguised in the story *Kicki und der König* [Kicki and the King] (1990), which was only published after the political situation altered.

GDR narrative literature for children was characterised throughout by its aim of integrating the recipient into the socialist order. Protagonists, not only in contemporary and topical books, are therefore as a rule individuals who are looking for something, often insecure personalities whose relationship with the collective has to be clarified. Through identification the reader is to be enabled to recognize the 'correct' solution or behaviour and to incorporate this knowledge in his mentality. The dilemma arising from this is reflected in literary and educational discussions as early as the 1950s. On the one hand direct moralising and cliché-ridden treatment of conflicts are criticised, a greater degree of literary sophistication demanded. On the other hand narratives with literary ambitions, such as Erwin Strittmatter's (1912–1994) village novel *Tinko* [Tinko] (1954), were criticised because – as the influential Alex Wedding claimed – they lacked educative exemplary quality. Thus writers often found it more important to demonstrate socially relevant decision-situations than to portray contradictory characters with complex perceptions and reactions.

Gradually, differentiations of this scheme – and eventually the development of narrative models opposed to it – appeared, as sensibility toward the changing nature of children's and youth literature grew, and as new montage-type multi-perspective modes of narration took their place alongside conventional modes. Admittedly no decisive watershed like that of the other German-speaking countries around 1968 can be discerned; but between the mid-1960s and mid-1970s there was a widespread movement towards new forms and subjects. These developments are to be seen particularly in the works of Uwe Kant (b.1936), Joachim Nowotny (b.1933), Gerhard Holtz-Baumert (b.1927), Alfred Wellm (b.1927) and Wolf Spillner (b.1936).

For a while, the limits of the 'break out from the world of habit' noted by GDR literary scholars in this phase were set by Ulrich Plenzdorf's (b.1934) *Die neuen Leiden des jungen W* [The New Sorrows of Young W.] (1972). Then in the final phase of the GDR a previously unheard-of social-analytic sharpness was reached in Jurij Koch's (b.1936) *Augenoperation* [Eye Operation] (1988). Children's authors joined in the general process of exploring afresh the conflicts inherent in the social milieu, trying in particular to define more specifically the experience-spaces of their young protagonists. The previously unquestioned security of the child in the socialist society was replaced by awareness of discords, even injuries. A good example is the works of Benno Pludra, from *Lütt Matten und die Weiße Muschel* [Little Matten and the White Seashell] (1963) through to *Insel der Schwäne* [Island of Swans] (1980) and *Das Herz des Piraten* [The Pirate's Heart] (1985).

## Further Reading

*Almanach zur Kinder- und Jugendliteratur der DDR* (1989) Hamburg: Katholische Akademie.

Brüggemann, T. and Brunken, O. (eds) (1987) *Handbuch zur Kinder- und Jugendliteratur. Von Beginn des Buchdrucks bis 1570*, Stuttgart: Metzler.

—— (1991) *Handbuch zur Kinder- und Jugendliteratur. Von 1750–1800*, Stuttgart: Metzler.

Brüggemann, T. and Ewers, H.-H. (1982) *Handbuch zur Kinder- und Jugendliteratur von 1750–1800*, Stuttgart: Metzler.

Dahrendorf, M. (1980) *Kinder- und Jugendliteratur im bürgerlichen Zeitalter*, Königstein: Scriptor.

Dolle-Weinkauff, B. and Peltsch, S. (1990) 'Kinder- und Jugendliteratur der DDR', in Wild, R. (ed.) *Geschichte der deutschen Kinder- und Jugendliteratur*, Stuttgart: Metzler.

Ebert, G. (1975) *Ansichten zur Entwicklung der epischen Kinder- und Jugendliteratur der DDR von 1945 bis 1970*, Berlin: Kinderbuchverlag.

Emmrich, C. (ed.) (1982) *Literatur für Kinder und Jugendliche in der DDR*, Berlin: Kinderbuchverlag.

Ewers, H.-H. (ed.) (1980) *Kinder- und Jugendliteratur der Aufklärung. Eine Textsammlung*, Stuttgart: Reclam.

—— (1984) *Kinder- und Jugendliteratur der Romantik. Eine Textsammlung*, Stuttgart: Reclam.

—— (1995) *Kinder- und Jugendliteratur. Von der Gründerzeit bis zum Ersten Weltkrieg. Eine Textsammlung*, Stuttgart: Reclam.

Haas, G. (1984) 'Kinder- und Jugendliteratur in der DDR', in Haas, G. (ed.) *Kinder- und Jugendliteratur. Ein Handbuch*, Stuttgart: Reclam.

Mattenklott, G. (1989) *Zauberkreide. Kinderliteratur seit 1945*, Stuttgart: Metzler.

Wallesch, F. (ed.) (1977) *Sozialistische Kinder- und Jugendliteratur der DDR*, Berlin: Volk und Wissen.

# 68

# Switzerland

## *Verena Rutschmann*

Switzerland is a country with four national languages: German (spoken by 63.6 per cent of the population), French (19.2 per cent), Italian (7.6 per cent) and Rhaeto-Romanic (0.6 per cent). The three larger linguistic areas look culturally to the neighbouring countries with the same language, so that the main reading matter of children and young people in Switzerland consists of what is available in these countries: Germany and Austria, France, and Italy. Native Swiss writing of children's books is found only in Francophone and German-speaking Switzerland, and most particularly when foreign texts do not meet the expectations of the Swiss public or cover subjects in demand.

The Italian-speaking population was so small as not to develop a children's literature of its own. The same is true of the Rhaeto-Romanic area, except that here no recourse to foreign works was possible, and religious books and school textbooks were occasionally produced. In French-speaking Switzerland, on the other hand, there has been since the nineteenth century a children's literature of strongly protestant tone, not only for religious education but also for leisure reading. And in German-speaking areas the appearance of a true national children's literature, proud to diverge (politically or linguistically) from German writings, underlined Switzerland's separateness.

Swiss children's literature developed in line with trends across Europe. Here as elsewhere, the second half of the eighteenth century saw a children's and youth literature which, in the spirit of late enlightenment educational theories, set out to mediate bourgeois virtue and useful facts of the era of industrialisation to the young in an entertaining and concrete manner. But unlike the children's writers of the neighbouring countries, Swiss authors also stressed the development of attitudes of responsible citizenship and republicanism among their readership. Prominent men in public life addressed themselves to young people, for instance Isaak Iselin (1728–1782), Joseph Anton Felix Balthasar (1737–1810), Johann Caspar Lavater (1741–1801), and later Frédéric César de Laharpe (1754–1838) in Lausanne. Swiss history was one of their favourite subjects. The forces working for a renewal of the old confederation at the end of the eighteenth century – the ambitious bourgeoisie, politicians, writers – not only created schools and educational associations, but also formulated their ideas of popular improvement in educational writings for the young. In *Lienhard und Gertrud* [Lienhard and Gertrud] (1781) Heinrich Pestalozzi had presented a model of economic and social improvements to the people at large.

The Bernese pastor Johann David Wyss (1743–1818) presumably also saw himself as primarily an educator rather than an author, when with his four sons he wrote his tale in the manner of *Robinson Crusoe*, *Der Schweizerische Robinson oder der schiffbrüchige Schweizer Prediger und seine Familie* [The Swiss Robinson or the Shipwrecked Swiss Pastor and his Family] (translated as The Swiss Family Robinson). The plot offered the pastor unlimited opportunity to provide his children with scientific and technical knowledge and at the same time to show them 'how reason and unremitting toil conquer all'. His son Johann Rudolf Wyss published the story, the first two volumes appearing in 1812 and 1813. As early as 1814, before publication of the third (1826) and fourth (1827) volumes, the Vaud writer Isabelle de Montolieu (1751–1832) published a French translation of the first two volumes together with a continuation by herself. She made Wyss's didactic tale into an adventure story, which proved a great success. Her version, not that of J. R. Wyss, is the basis of most English translations and adaptations of the book.

For a long time no other Swiss story approached the popularity of *The Swiss Family Robinson*. The attempt of Jeremias Gotthelf, a great educator of the common people, to create a 'Swiss republican' story for German-speaking Swiss youth in *Der Knabe des Tell* [Tell's Boy] (1845) failed because of its epic length and copious philosophical digressions. The outstanding work of the painter-author August Corrodi (1826–1885) failed to exude the desired seriousness and didactic purpose: Corrodi's fantasies with their leaning to absurd humour were apparently alien to the Swiss public. But with Johanna Spyri's *Heidi's Lehr- und Wanderjahre* [Heidi's Apprenticeship and Journeyings] (1880) and *Heidi kann brauchen, was es gelernt hat* [Heidi Uses What She has Learnt] (1881) we find a work that entered the canon of world children's literature. The image of the alpine pasture as a 'pedagogic island', where the little girl Heidi is given a simple upbringing in harmony with nature, was certainly influenced by the renewed interest in Rousseau in the late nineteenth century. But Johanna Spyri (1827–1901), as a middle-class woman hedged about by conventions, also expressed in this story her personal nostalgia for the lost freedom of childhood. This celebration of simplicity and harmony with nature, with its evocative scenery, matched so completely the image of Switzerland dear both to the Swiss themselves and to foreigners that *Heidi* became the 'Swiss' book par excellence. Spyri wrote sixteen books for 'children and also for those who like children'; only *Heidi* achieved world fame and continuing success.

*Heidi* is the beginning of a whole series of realistic portrayals of childhood which are still read by German-speaking Swiss children but have never really travelled. Among them are for example *Die Turnachkinder im Sommer* [The Turnach Children in Summer] (1906) and *Die Turnachkinder im Winter* [The Turnach Children in Winter] (1909) by Ida Bindschedler, Elisabeth Müller's *Vreneli* [Little Verena] (1916) or *Theresli* [Little Theresa], (1918), and Olga Meyer's *Anneli* [Annie] (1918).

These stories also mark the onset of a consciously 'Swiss' children's literature as counterweight to the increasing nationalism of German writings. The authors, including Fritz Brunner and Josef Reinhart as well as Elisabeth Müller and Olga Meyer, were almost all teachers, which may explain the didactic nature of German-language Swiss children's literature well into the twentieth century. Education for citizenship remains an important theme of this literature, as exemplified by *Der Schmied von Göschenen* [The Smith of Göschenen] (1920) by the pastor Robert Schedler (1866–1930), a tale about the improvement of the Gotthard pass and the first liberation movements of the pioneer cantons of Switzerland in the twelfth century.

The provinciality of Swiss children's literature is cut across by the work of the two emigrants Lisa Tetzner (1894–1963) and Kurt Held (1897–1959). Emigrating from Germany to Switzerland in 1933, they lived in Ticino canton, collaborating closely on young people's books that were quickly to become classics: *Die Kinder aus Nummer 67* [The Children from Number 67] (9 vols, 1933–1949), *Die schwarzen Brüder* [The Dark Brothers] (2 vols, 1940–1942), *Die rote Zora und ihre Bande* [Red Zora and her Gang] (1941), the four-volume cycle *Giuseppe and Maria* (1955–1956) and others. These stories express the hope that young people will succeed in building a better world, with fairer social circumstances and no wars. Their mixture of adventure, social commitment and lifelike description of milieu is close to the German tradition of the 1920s.

The writers who worked to develop a native Swiss literature for the young continued to determine its character into the 1960s. In the 1970s a generation of authors arose who published their books in West Germany again. German-Swiss children's literature was reintegrated into German-language children's literature with the works of Eveline Hasler, Franz Hohler, Hanna Johansen, Hans Manz, Regine Schindler and others. At the same time a trend towards play and imagination can be discerned, writing for children had broken out of the schoolroom and opened new fields for itself. By word-play or unaccustomed uses of language the new texts sharpened perception of reality. Fantasy was the new form for critical discussion of social reality, most particularly the destruction of the environment.

With few exceptions narrative literature for children circulates only within Switzerland, indeed only within its own language area. In contrast, the making of picture books has found international recognition. Ernst Kreidolf (1863–1956) as an exponent of *Jugendstil* is the first major name here. His picture books, almost exclusively filled with personified plants and animals, show great technical skill and precise botanical and zoological knowledge. The imaginative mixing of man, plant and animal corresponded both to the mood of the time with its longing for communion with nature, and to the idea that children enjoy particular closeness to all creatures.

The Second World War and the following years are the classical age of the Swiss picture book. Alois Carigiet (1902–1987), Hans Fischer (1909–1958) and Felix Hoffmann (1911–1975) produced books of world rank. Carigiet's landscapes with their impressive bold perspective, Fischer's playfully sketched animal fables, and Hoffmann's individualistic combination of fairy tale fantasy and everyday reality, all share – despite their differences – outstanding mastery of technique and deep insight into the workings of a child's mind.

Alongside painting as 'fine art', poster art had a great share in picture book art. As well as Carigiet and Fischer, other illustrators had made their name with posters: Herbert Leupin (b.1916), Celestino Piatti (b.1922), later Etienne Delessert (b.1941). Fischer had at an early date incorporated cartoon film techniques in his presentation of sequences of movement. In the 1980s techniques of film and comic strip appeared in picture books, for instance by Jörg Müller (b.1942) and Etienne Delessert. Both these illustrators, under changed circumstances, repeat the quest for nearness to nature which was a vital aspect of Ernst Kreidolf's work almost a century before. French-speaking and German-speaking Switzerland share equally in the general internationalisation of picture book making.

## Further Reading

Gros, C. (1989) 'Heidi de Dörfli ou la Suissesse missionnaire de la pureté alpestre', in Crettaz, B. (ed.) *Terres de femmes*, Genève: Musée d'ethnographie.

Hurrelmann, B. (1993) 'Heidi: Mignons erlöste Schwester', *Neue Sammlung* 33, Heft 3: 347–363.

Keckeis, P. (1993) 'Zur Entstehungsgeschichte des Schweizerischen Robinsons', in Diederichs, R. *et al.* (eds) *Bern und sein Beitrag zum Buch- und Bibliothekswesen*, Bern: Haupt.

Mooser, A. (1992) ' "Heidi" de Johanna Spyri et son adaptation française, ou L'aliénation d'une liberté', in Institut suisse de littérature pour la jeunesse (ed.) *Modernité et Nostalgie: La nature utopique dans la littérature enfantine suisse*, Zurich/Lutry: Institut suisse de littérature pour la jeunesse.

Müller, H. (1989) 'Pädagogik in Johanna Spyris Heidi-Büchern: Literaturgeschichtliche Koordinaten eines Bildungsromans', *Schweizer Monatshefte* 69, Heft 11: 922–932.

Ribaupierre, C. (1992) 'Pour que naisse le roman. L'affirmation du désir chez Madame de Montolieu', in Institut suisse de littérature pour la jeunesse (ed.) *Modernité et Nostalgie. La nature utopique dans la littérature enfantine suisse*, Zurich/Lutry: Institut suisse de littérature pour la jeunesse.

Ris, R. (1994) 'Vom "Verbrüderungs" au-des-Konzept Johanna Spyris zur "Geistigen Landesverteidigung". Schweizerisch-deutsche Kulturbeziehungen im Spiegel der Sprache schweizerischer Jugendbuchautorinnen', in Schweizerisches Jugendbuch-Institut (ed.) *Horizonte und Grenzen*, Zurich: Schweizerisches Jugendbuch-Institut: 33–74.

Weilenmann, C. (1993) *Annotierte Bibliographie der Schweizer Kinder- und Jugendliteratur von 1750 bis 1900 – Bibliographie annotée de livres suisses pour l'enfance et la jeunesse de 1750 a 1900*, Stuttgart: Metzler.

# 69

# Austria

## *Lucia Binder*

Although German-speaking countries have in the past had, and still have, much in common in their literatures, and mutual influences can be clearly discerned, Austria has a distinct literature for children and young people.

The beginnings of an Austrian literature specially written for children can be traced to the time of the empress *Maria Theresia* and her son *Josef II*, when great educational reforms took place. Two authors dominated the children's book market and were widely read – the catholic teacher *Leopold Chimani* (1774–1844) and the Protestant *Jakob Glatz* (1776–1831). Their writings reveal the influence of the Enlightenment besides a religious touch.

During the Romantic period, the first collections of fairy tales were published. Swashbuckling and wild west adventure stories began to appear towards the middle of the nineteenth century, and of course some children's books that glorified the Habsburg dynasty and national ideals could also be found.

The most important influence on the development of literature came from the German children's book movement advocated by Heinrich Wolgast, who wished to give the young readers the best quality literature. For Austria this meant that texts by well-known authors for adults like Peter Rosegger, Marie von Ebner-Eschenbach or Franz Karl Ginzkey were adapted and published for young readers.

Also characteristic in the development of Austrian children's literature were the series of inexpensive, but well-illustrated books published by Jugend und Volk publishing house. The best known of these series, which also in some ways represented a breakthrough in artistic illustration was *Gerlachs Jugendbücherei* (1901). It contained sagas, poems, legends and was designed in Art Nouveau style. (Today collectors pay high prices for these books.) Another series, Science for Children (from 1937) contained true-to-life stories and science fiction.

In the first third of the twentieth century, many well known illustrators worked with children's books, for instance Oskar Laske, whose late-impressionistic, imaginative illustrations were quite famous. One of the best examples are the famous colour-lithographs to the Leporello *Noah's Ark* (1925).

During the Second World War, most children's books in Austria derived from Germany, but there were also some easy-to-read books by the Austrian teacher Annelies Umlauf-Lamatsch, illustrated by Ernst Kutzer, which were widely read by elementary schoolchildren. The stories by Umlauf-Lamatsch were simple and mostly located in imaginative worlds such as a cat's town or among dwarfs in a wood. They were far away from the political life in the period and are still reprinted.

After the war, in 1949, the Austrian Children's Book Club was founded, offering authors and publishers a wide readership and encouraging the development of a distinctively Austrian children's literature.

Characteristic authors in the 1950s and 1960s were Mira Lobe, Vera Ferra-Mikura and Karl Bruckner; all three were concerned with social problems, war and peace and problems of living together. Mira Lobe (1913–1995) is considered to be one of the leaders of children's literature in Austria: she wrote highly imaginative books (*Die Omama im Apfelbaum* [The Granny in the Apple Tree]), texts for picture books (*Das kleine Ich bin ich* [The Little Me is Me]) and also turned to such controversial themes as violence against children (*Die Sache mit dem Heinrich* [The Thing that Happened to Heinrich] (1989)).

Vera Ferra-Mikura (b.1923) is an important figure in the development of children's poetry (*Lustig singt die Regentonne* [The Water-Butt Sings Merrily]). Her series of picture books about *Die drei Stanisläuse* has been widely read by many generations of Austrian children.

Karl Bruckner became world-famous with *Sadako will leben* [The Day of the Bomb] (1961) which was one of the very first books dealing with the Second World War. It describes the sad story of the Japanese girl Sadako, who dies about ten years after the first atomic bomb fell on Hiroshima. This book has been translated into twenty-seven languages.

The problems of the war have also been dealt with in later books. In 1963 Winfried Bruckner published *Die Toten Engel* [The Dead Angels], which tells the story of a group of children in the Warsaw ghetto. *Das Schattennetz* [The Net of Shadows] (1965) by Käthe Recheis is set in Austria and deals with the break-up of a concentration camp and the destinies of the people involved. The book is based on the author's own experience – she had helped her doctor father care for the people released from a camp; it was criticised for its sharp focus on one particular viewpoint, and today is reprinted under the title *Geh' heim und vergiß alles* [Go Home and Forget Everything] and recognized as one of the most interesting contributions of children's literature about World War II. In a later book, also partly autobiographical, *Lena: Mein Dorf und der Krieg* [Lena: Our Village and War] (1987), Recheis describes how a young girl and her village in Upper Austria experience hardship during the war, but also shows the fascination that Hitler's regime had for young people. Renate Welsh's *In die Waagschale geworfen* [Thrown into the Scales] (1988) consists of stories about the resistance movement and recreates the atmosphere of fear and uncertainty and the suffering experienced during the war by both adults and children. These stories are often criticised for providing too little information about events and for not being sufficiently objective. They are, however, literary works and are not intended to be textbooks stuffed with facts; it is the emotional impact which is important.

In the 1970s and 1980s there is hardly any topic which has not found its way into Austrian children's books. Authors write about social conditions, war and peace, and the problems of everyday life.

Two collections of short stories, *Mädchen düren pfeifen – Buben dürfen weinen* [Girls may Whistle, Boys may Cry] (1981), and *Omageschichten* [Grandma Stories] (1988), were published as the result of a competition sponsored by the Austrian Office for Women's Affairs and the Jugend und Volk publishing house. This was held at a time when gender roles were being questioned in Austria as in other countries. The stories explore male and female stereotypes and look at still-prevalent prejudices, but also try to paint an authentic and vivid picture of the social background, and do not aim to be didactic.

Foremost among the writers of this period is Christine Nöstlinger, whose new and unconventional style, based on the picturesque Viennese dialect, swept away a number of traditional taboos. She has achieved great success with her many realistic stories set against a carefully described background. She drew on her own experiences for *Maikäfer Flieg* [Fly Away Home] (1973), a story of the last weeks of the Second World War from the viewpoint of an 8-year-old girl living in Vienna. In *Rosa Riedl Schutzgespenst* [Guardian Ghost] (1979), a timid girl is befriended by Rosa, an anti-authoritarian ghost who figures in a number of situations in which the authority figure is either ridiculed or overruled; past and present are brought together by the fact that Rosa was run over by a tram when she went to help a Jewish shopkeeper during the war. One of Nöstlinger's greatest successes was *Wir pfeifen auf den Gurkenkönig* [We Don't give a Toss for the Cucumber King] (1972) which tells about a fantastic creature full of arrogance and claims to power, who succeeds in deceiving a whole family and gaining authoritarian control over it, with the exception of the child and the grandfather. Christine Nöstlinger's books have been translated into many languages. In 1984, she was the winner of the International Hans Christian Andersen award.

Another author who has broken quite a lot of taboos in children's literature is Renate Welsh, who has been writing for children since 1970. Her books are characterised by contemporary social themes and an ability to sympathise with young people's problems and their surroundings. She does careful research and one of her best-known books is *Johanna* (1979), a story about a servant girl, set in the 1920s. She also writes about the disabled, drug problems, and the problems of young delinquents, subjects which were avoided in children's books until comparatively recently. For *Johanna* she was awarded the German Children's Literature Award. Other topics she deals with are problems of handicapped children, the difficulties of children of migrant workers, and gender roles.

Austrian children's literature, however, is not only concerned with problems, but also offers excitement and entertainment. Humour and playing with language is characteristic, and one of the most outstanding examples is *Das Sprachbastelbuch* [The Language Craft Book] (1975), a collaboration by nearly all the well-known children's books authors in Austria; it was edited by Hans Domenego (Helmut Leiter) who himself has written several ironical and satirical children's books. The *Sprachbastelbuch*, which encouraged the enjoyable acquisition of experience through having fun with the language, represented a trend in Austrian children's literature. Ernst A. Ekker is another author who works with children, playing with words and making nonsense rhymes with them.

Children's poetry developed and showed elements of humour and play and elements of traditional Austrian poetry. The most important authoress of children's poems is Friedl Hofbauer, who created rhymes for very small children, and poetry with a lot of atmosphere for older ones. *Der Brummkreisel* [The Humming Top] is one of her best-known works.

Lene Mayer-Skumanz has brought fresh interest and new ideas to stories with a religious background. Her books are full of imagination, warmth, humour and understanding of how children experience life. Some of her stories are open-ended, inviting readers to find their own solutions, guided by principles of Christian thinking. *Hanniel kommt in die Stadt* [Hanniel is Coming to Town] (1989) is typical of her work, the tale of a guardian angel who appears in human form and helps a child to solve her problems.

Wolf Harranth has a special place in Austrian children's literature, as writer and translator and he is very important for his work in training and encouraging young authors by means of writing workshops. He himself writes mostly fantasies with a social edge, but also realistic narratives with excellent dialogue and a comic touch. One of his best-known books *Mein Opa ist alt und ich hab ihn sehr lieb* [My Grandpa is Old and I Like him a Lot] (1981) tells of the relationship between child and grandfather when the grandfather comes from the country to the town for a visit and is not comfortable there. The little boy understands the old man, who secretly tends the roses in the park and would rather tell stories than watch television.

Engendering understanding across generation barriers, as practised by Wolf Harranth, is a particular concern of Austrian authors.

Martin Auer, who writes mainly poetry and short stories for children, and Edith Schreiber-Wicke, popular with her fantastic stories, must also be mentioned.

After a period of artistic picture books in the first third of the twentieth century, illustration began to flourish again about twenty years after the Second World War. Since 1960, there have been three main types of illustration in children's books: one is influenced by commercial considerations, the second reflects a very personal and committed style of interpretation and drawing, and the third is the kind of picture one draws for one's own children. Helga Aichinger, in books such as *Ein Körnchen fur den Pfau* [A Kernel for the Peacock] (1970), which was awarded the 1971 BIB Medal in Bratislava, creates a world of highly differentiated colours, using a crayon technique with which she manages to produce incredible nuances of colour. Angelika Kaufmann is one of Austria's most important picture book artists, combining drawing and painting: she has colourful surfaces, with brush and ink drawings to show contours and details, and she also uses collage techniques in some of her books. She has illustrated many prize-winning books by Mira Lobe, as did Winfried Opgenoorth.

Erwin Moser has a special place in illustration. He writes his own stories, and his works are full of fantasy and humour; he draws in both black and white and colour and many of his characters have become very popular also outside of Austria. His Philipp Schnauze [Philip Bigmouth] (1982) for instance, a witty little mouse, is highly appreciated by German children.

Another famous Austrian mouse is Hanne Turk's Max, whose wordless adventures in a series of small books (describing the adventures of little Max going to take a holiday or trying to bake biscuits for Christmas and so on) have appeared in English too.

One artist, whose black and white drawings and etching technique is much appreciated by art critics is Susi Bohdal, who also publishes many of her books in Germany; she has won many Austrian awards, and was twice specially distinguished at BIB.

One of the most distinguished younger illustrators is Lisbeth Zwerger, awarded the International Hans Christian Andersen Award for illustration in 1990. Her ink and watercolour illustrations are unmistakable in their style and expressiveness. Her characters are shown in dance-like movements, suggestive of pantomime, a style particularly suitable for the many fairy tales she has illustrated. Beginning in 1977 with *Das fremde Kind* [The Strange Child], a fairy tale by E. T. A. Hoffmann, she has been inspired by the works of the Grimm Brothers, Hans Christian Andersen and Oscar Wilde to produce her characteristic illustrations, which are familiar in many countries.

In Austria, a flourishing children's literature is supported by a comprehensive network of institutions. The Children's Book Award of the city of Vienna, (1954– ) and the Austrian National Children's and Juvenile Book Award (1955– ) were both established to encourage high standards in publishing for children, and have been given for both fiction and non fiction to books written for various age groups. The International Institute for Children's Literature and Reading Research was established in 1965. It actively promotes children's books through special events, provides guidance in book selection for teachers and librarians and organises exhibitions.

The Austrian Children's Book Club was founded in 1949 to fill an urgent educational need; its main object is to stimulate interest in reading amongst young people. It operates throughout the Austrian school system and also covers pre-school groups, publishes magazines and annuals about books, recommends specific titles, issues literary anthologies and cooperates with publishers and booksellers to make recommended books available at discounted prices.

## Further Reading

Barker, K. (1992) 'Standing your own company: the novels of Christine Nöstlinger', *The School Librarian* 40, 1: 6–7.

Binder, L. (1979) 'World War II in books read by Austrian children: from propaganda to experience', *Bookbird* 3: 8–13.

—— (nd) *Österreichische Kinder- und Jugendliteratur*, Vienna: International Institute for Children's Literature and Reading Research, with assistance from the Austrian Ministry for Education and Arts.

*Bücher haben ihren Preis. 30 Jahre Hösterreichischer Kinder- und Jugendbuchpreis* (1985), Vienna: Austrian Ministry for Education, Art and Sports.

*Freiheit ist besser als Speck. Text für Mira Lobe, zusammengestellt zu ihrem 80. Geburtstag* (1993), Vienna: Jugend und Volk; Mödling: St Gabriel.

International Institute for Children's Literature and Reading Research (ed.) (1994) *Lexikon der österreichischen Kinder- und Jugendliteratur. Vol 1: Autoren und Übersetzer. Vol 2: Illustratoren*, Vienna: Buchkultur-Verlagsgesellschaft (including short summaries in English).

# 70

# Italy

## Laura Kreyder

The stories children have read for centuries, such as Phaedrus's fables, Ovid's myths and Aeneas's adventures, come from Italy. Later there were medieval Christian legends, collected by Jacopo da Varagine, and chivalrous romances. Then, from the sixteenth century onwards, story writers like Straparola with *Le piacevoli notti* [Pleasant Nights] or Giulio Cesare Croce with *Le sottilissime astuzie di Bertoldo* [The Very Subtle Tricks of Bertoldo] took inspiration from popular oral sources, some of them probably meant for children. The sub-title of *Lo cunto de li cunti, ovvero lo Trattenimiento de li peccerille* [The Tale of the Tales, or How to Entertain Little Girls] (1634–1636), a collection of tales edited in Neapolitan dialect by Giambattista Basile stands out as the first work in which little girls play an important role. But, like Perrault's *Fairy Tales*, it was intended for adult readers.

Other critics (Fanciulli and Monaci 1935) have seen in Domenico Soresi's *Novelle piacevoli e istruttive* [Instructive and Pleasant Tales] (1768) the first text written specifically for children. The date is meaningful (a few years after *Emile*) since it is without doubt thanks to the spread of liberating ideas that books intended expressly for children came into being in Italy. They are collections of passages: the childhoods of famous persons, heroic deeds taken from history, and tales (like those of the Venetians Gasparo and Carlo Gozzi, modelled on the Grimm brothers).

In the first half of the nineteenth century, partly out of hatred for the Austrians and Bourbons, and partly out of admiration for Napoleon, a patriotic line was added, carried along by the rising wave of Romanticism. It was obvious to campaigners in the battle against illiteracy (which at that time involved three quarters of the population) that there was a need for literature for schools, and so prize-winning competitions were set up for the creation of children's books. In 1837 Luigi Alessandro Parravicini (1799–1880) wrote *Giannetto*, a compendium of knowledge and fiction for children, 'a universal primer' (Faeti 1977: 62). Pietro Thouar (1809–1861), after a restless childhood in Florence, undertook to write many *Racconti pei giovanetti* [Short Stories for Young People] and *Letture di famiglia* [Family Readings] and created the *Giornale per i fanciulli* [Children's Journal] which was banned on account of the patriotic stand taken by a writer for whom 'politics was not a profession but a creed' (Montazio 1862: 24). However, Catholic educators also played their part, for example, Giulio Tarra (1832–1889), a priest and head of the Deaf and Dumb Institute in Milan, who translated and reworked many stories in his moralising prose.

The golden age of children's literature in Italy, as throughout Europe, came with the latter half of the nineteenth century. As a phenomenon it was accentuated by the achievement of national unity in 1860 and the setting up of a state independent of the Church in which the institutions, and schools in particular (education became obligatory with the Casati law of 1859) were called upon to promote the use of a national language and creation of a sense civil responsibility and conscience. It was no coincidence that the two masterpieces of Italian children's literature, Collodi's *Pinocchio* (1883) and De Amicis's *Cuore* [Heart] (1886) should have come out almost simultaneously, in Florence and Turin respectively, the first capitals of united Italy.

Fervently republican and anticlerical, Carlo Lorenzini (alias Collodi, 1826–1890) was a journalist and pamphleteer, with a great talent for brief character sketches and comedies of manners. He also translated Perrault's tales and, in 1876, published *Giannettino*, a reworking of Parravicini's classic. He gave the first episode of *La storia di un burattino* [A Puppet's Story] to Ferdinando Martini, who issued a new children's paper (*Il Giornale per i bambini*). He broke off Pinocchio's adventures, having him hanged (the detail is important since it excluded any moralising intent), but the success of his creation obliged him to bring the puppet back to life and a happy end. The tale was published by Felice Paggi in 1883, with illustrations first by Enrico Mazzanti, then by Carlo Chiostri. Pinocchio, a typical variation of the trickster, a rebel against the established order, speaks the Tuscan tongue that was to become standard Italian, without eclipsing the many dialects which remained mother tongue to countless schoolchildren all over Italy. Ancient themes recurrent throughout literature – stories of the whale and the prodigal son, talking animals and the human turned into an ass, the land of Cockaigne and other wanderings – are all taken up and worked into the context of a little Italy consisting of village and artisan life. Besides, all over the peninsular masks and puppet shows were popular entertainment even amongst the cultured elite, having been kept alive through the centuries (as witnessed by the continual exporting of the repertoire and the widespread popularity in Europe of the various Punches and Harlequins, all the way back to the seventeenth century).

More obviously inspired by an ideology, *Cuore* is the diary of a boy who enters secondary school and discovers the great differences that exist between people as individuals and between social conditions – great gaps that can be bridged through human solidarity and a sense of belonging to a country and a culture, all brought about thanks to the school. Edmondo De Amicis (1846–1908), a militant socialist, holds up a mirror to the institution that above all others had the task of encouraging the spread of reading. Between its publication and the outbreak of the first World War nearly a million copies of his novel were sold, a feat that was only made possible by the strengthening of publishing houses nationwide, such as Paravia in Turin, Treves, Hoepli and Vallardi in Milan, Salani in Florence and Sandron in Palermo. Children's magazines also started to proliferate. In 1881, the first girls' paper, *Cordelia*, came into existence. The *Corriere dei piccoli* [Children's Post] was launched in 1908 and published the first comic strips, in an original format, that is pictures without balloons but with the text underneath in octosyllabic verse (which could easily be learnt by heart owing to its distinctive rhythm). Sergio Tofano, called Sto, the most inventive illustrator of the period, imagined the adventures of *Il signor Bonaventura*, who ends up as a millionaire.

By the turn of the century the industry was crying out for writers to fill column after column of special features. Influenced by Jules Verne, Emilio Salgari (1861–1911) invented exotic plots and in particular the Black Jungle cycle with a Malay hero, *Sandokan*, which enjoyed a huge success in spite of which its author, hounded by debts and predatory publishers, committed suicide. By now every kind of genre had made its appearance, from sentimental humility (*Il racconto del piccolo vetraio* [The Story of a Little Glassmaker] by Olimpia De Gasperi), to folklore, rediscovered now that tales from the oral and dialect tradition were being collected and transcribed (Costantino Nigra for Piedmont, Giuseppe Pitré for Sicily).

Professional writers found it easier, however, to invent new characters, closer to the child's world. Vamba (Luigi Bertelli, 1860–1920) published the diary of an enfant terrible, *Il giornalino di Gian Burrasca* [Gian Burrasca's Diary] (1912), which he illustrated himself. Unlike *Cuore*, Gian Burrasca's tricks make fun of provincial manners and deflate the sentimental image of the good child.

Fascism was keen to build up its widespread support (Cannistraro 1975) and actively promoted children's literature with that aim in view. As a result *Il giornale del balilla* (the Young Fascist's paper) came into being, as did stories about young people seen in scenes of communal and paramilitary life and ritual. The country's literary avant garde expressed their approval (Marinetti 1939).

The post-war generation promoted children's literature as the Risorgimento and Fascism had done. In wondering what kind of books its children should read, it found itself divided into two camps (as happened within Einaudi, the major publisher of general literature). On one side were the realists, who set up models to follow such as working-class hero's sons, and on the other those more sensitive to the popular and cultural heritage, who favoured fantasy, dream and narrative. Italo Calvino, in particular, promoted the publication of collections of tales, and even wrote some himself, such as *Marcovaldo* or the *Cosmicomiche* [Cosmicomics] which have become children's classics. Gianni Rodari, clearly Communist in ideology, tried to reconcile the two opposing positions, writing a *Grammatica della fantasia* [A Grammar of Imagination] (1973) on one side, and nursery rhymes, stories and poems containing such theories as the superiority of manual work, class solidarity and the search for freedom on the other. Besides, in the 1960s, even Catholics decided to review their attitude to education, as can be seen in Don Milani's *Lettera ad una professoressa* [Letter to a Teacher] (1967), which attacks the injustices and authoritarianism of middle-class teaching methods. All these themes, taken up and expanded in 1968, brought about great changes in children's literature in the following decades. Feminism, with the work of Elena Gianini Belotti, *Dalla parte delle bambine* (which was to give its name to a publishing house), produced texts that tried to alter gender stereotypes (Belotti 1976).

At the present time, less than 50 per cent of book production is of native extraction (Li.B.eR 1993). What with the gap between North and South, between a rich literary tradition and a crisis offset by an unexportable language, between a *laissez-faire* attitude in the field of communication and an ideological and moralising discourse in the field of criticism, Italy still to a large extent imports children's literature and culture. It is by no means coincidental that it is in new media like the cinema (from the children of neo-realism to Luigi Comencini's entire output) and comic strips (from Jacovitti and Altan, with *Pimpa*, to Bonelli's productions) that the most original ideas for and about children are being expressed. Other encouraging signs are the important annual Children's Book Fair that takes place in Bologna, the inclusion of the teaching of children's literature in the universities, and the emergence of young writers like the wistful Roberto Piumini (*Lo stralisco*) or the witty Bianca Pitzorno (with her funny, fighting heroines as in *L'incredibile storia di Lavinia* [The Incredible Story of Lavinia].

## References

Belotti, E. G. (1976) *What are Little Girls Made Of? The Roots of Feminine Stereotypes*, New York: Schocken.

Cannistraro, P. V. (1975) *La fabbrica del consenso*, Bari: Laterza.

Faeti, A. (1977) *Letteratura per l'infanzia*, Florence: La nuova Italia.

Fanciulli, G. and Monaci, E. (1935) *La letteratura per l'infanzia*, Turin: SEI.

Li.B.eR, Quaderni di (1993) *Libri per ragazzi, selezione 1992*, supplemento 3, gennaio–marzo.

Marinetti, F. T. (1939) 'Prefazione-Manifesto della letteratura giovanile', *Convegno nazionale per la letteratura infantile e giovanile*, 7–10, Rome.

Montazio, E. (1862) *Pietro Thouar*, Turin: Unione Tipografica editrice.

## Further Reading

Bertacchini, R. (1993) *Il padre di Pinocchio*, Milan: Camunia.

Beseghi, E. (ed.) (1990) *La valle della luna. Avventura, esotismo, orientalismo nell'opera di Emilio Salgari*, Florence: La nuova Italia.

Faeti, A. (1983) *La 'camera' dei bambini*, Bari: Dedalo.

——— (1985) *La bicicletta di Dracula*, Florence: La nuova Italia.

——— (1986) *I tesori e le isole*, Florence: La nuova Italia.

——— (1990) *Le notti di Restif*, Florence: La nuova Italia.

Marcheschi, D. (1990) *Collodi ritrovato*, Pisa: ETS.

Pallottino, P. (1988) *Storia dell'illustrazione italiana*, Bologna: Zanichelli.

Tibaldi Chiesa, M. (1945) *Letteratura infantile*, Milan: Garzanti.

Visentini, O. (1936) *Libri e ragazzi*, Milan: A. Mondadori.

# 71

# Greece

## *Vassilis D. Anagnostopoulos*

### The Beginnings

The quest of the first roots of the Greek children's literature leads us to the depths of antiquity, to the Homeric era and the classical times (fourth and fifth centuries BC). During the ancient Greek, Roman and Byzantine eras, and during the Turkish domination of Greece (1453–1821) 'children's literature' comes under the heading of oral and written tradition.

To the oral tradition belong the popular myths, tales, and children's songs, such as 'the swallow's song', a song for the coming of spring, variants of which are preserved today. It appears that children also liked, besides Aesop's myths, excerpts from Homeric epics and other popular stories. The oral tradition was enriched, especially during the Byzantine epoch, by heroic narratives about the Akrites (the guardians of the eastern borders), prayers, and (mainly) by folk songs. During the period of the Turkish occupation, the enslaved Greeks preserved their ethnic consciousness and the mother tongue through lullabies, lyric verses, popular songs, tongue-twisters, and so on. These constitute the first beginnings of children's poetry. The oral children's literature continued unimpaired until recently, when it seems to have gone into decline.

During antiquity the best-loved reading-matter for children consisted of texts such as the Homeric epics, Aesop's myths and the comic poem *The Battle of Frogs and Mice*. During Byzantine times the main reading was the Bible, hymns, and legends. Metrical 'novels' which had as heroes animals or plants, such as *Poulologos* [Bird watcher], were popular although they were not intended for children.

During the period of Turkish and Viennese occupation, ignorance and poverty prevailed, and children's reading-texts were scarce. School texts such as Catechism, the Psalter, and Primers, as well as texts not intended for schools, such as the Lives of Saints, or the story of the Macedonian Alexander (first published in 1529) the *Characters* of Theophrastos, and Homer's *Iliad* and *Odyssey* were circulating.

During the second half of the eighteenth century the Greeks elsewhere in Europe (Vienna, Trieste, London, Budapest, Venice and so on) published children's books which were sent to schools in Turkish-occupied Greece. These books were largely translations of such writers as Fenélon, Kampe and De Beaumont; in this way Greek children's literature was touched by the European Enlightenment.

## The Nineteenth Century

After the liberation of Greece, the rebuilding of the educational, political and economic structures of the free Greek state began. Pioneers in the provision of educational texts for children (written in purest Greek) included Alexandros Rizos Rangavis (1809–1892), Elias Tantalidis (1818–1876) and Alexandros Katakouzinos (1824–1892). The first magazine for children *Children's Storeroom* was founded by D. Pantazis in 1836. With translations of such books as Stowe's *Uncle Tom's Cabin* complementing the native product, the foundations of Greek children's literature were laid.

The work which marks the true starting point of children's books in Greece is *Old Stathis or The Memories of my Childhood* (1858) by Leon Melas (1812–1879). *Old Stathis* together with Rangavis's *Greek Virtuous Learning* also defined the educational and aesthetic framework within which children's books developed through the nineteenth century. Ethical, religious, and national instruction was the basis of children's literature well into the twentieth century.

As interest grew in educational matters, children's literature benefited. Among children's magazines, such as *Children's Journal* and *Children's Paper of Markouizos*, there was one which can be regarded as a turning point, *The Fashioning of Children* [Diaplasis ton Pedon] (1879) founded by N. Papadopoulos with Gregorios Xenopoulos (1868–1952) as chief editor. This is one of the pillars of Greek children's literature; it had great influence over the next seventy years, and rallied around itself prestigious authors who have supported with promoted children's work.

Among the first poets for children were Georgios Vizyinos (1848–1896) (*Children's Songs* (1877-1884)), Demetrios Kambouroglou (*Myths and Dialogues for the Use of Youth*, 1881) and Alexandros Pallis (1851–1935), with his collection *Ditties for Children* (1889). Equally, many accomplished poets published poems for children in the magazines of the period, and anthologies of children's poems, mainly for school use, began to circulate around this time. In prose, there were many original short stories such as *Tromaras* by Vizyinos, and *Fire-Raiser* by Kourtidis; Kourtidis also wrote books such as *Children's Dialogues, Children's Short Stories*. Xenopoulos's first children's novel, *My Little Sister*, was published in *The Fashioning of Children*, in 1891. Meanwhile, works taken from international children's literature were being translated and adapted, notably Verne, Dickens, and Twain. In general terms, around the end of the nineteenth century Greek children's literature began to be conscious of its beneficial role and a literary tradition was created.

## The Twentieth Century

In the first twenty years of the twentieth century, national and international events (the First World War, the Balkan Wars, the discord, the Asia Minor catastrophe and others) as well as the struggles for the language deeply influenced Greek education. At that time Penelope Delta (1874–1941) through her works *For the Motherland* (1909), *A Tale Without a Name* (1910) and *At the Time of Bulgaroktonos* (1911) showed that children's literature could be a distinctive genre, and pioneered the historical novel. She was followed by Julia Dragoumis (1885–1937) (*Tales of a Greek, Under the Skies, Three Children*) and Arsinoe Papadopoulou (1853–1943), creating a tradition in the field of children's books of women authors. The production of poems and plays was limited. Nevertheless, some collections and anthologies of poetry were produced, such as those by I. Kambouroglou, Arist. Kourtidis, Polyx. Melandinou, Leon. Maroulis, Ioannis Laios, and I. Polemis and of others. Children's song anthologies were also being published, such as those of Kleovoulos Artemidis and A. G. Argyropoulos. The production of children's books was reinforced by the initiative of the Educational Group (1910) to publish a series of 'Books for Young Greeks Written in their own Language'.

A landmark is *The High Mountains* (1918), a literary reading book for primary school children in their third year, largely written by Zaharias Papandoniou. It expressed the new linguistic, aesthetic and educational concept of the Education Reform of 1917. Children's poetry was given new life by Papandoniou's collection of poems, *The Swallows* (1920). Both the Society for the Spreading of Greek Letters and the Society for Spreading of Useful Books helped to consolidate the position of children's books.

In the period between the wars (1920–1940) special attention was given to the 'object lesson narratives', related to nature, the motherland, books of knowledge, covering the cognitive needs of children. Many works of this genre are to be found in the Children's Library of Dimitrakos, the Green Books series, and in individual works by M. Papamavrou, Steph. Granitsa, Athens Vlachou and others. Also a considerable number of authors produced short stories, mainly with historical, social and ethnographic content. Children's theatre became established, with books of plays for children by authors such as Arist. Kourtidis, Greg. Xenopoulos and Dem. Kambouroglou. Two significant events promoted children's theatre: the foundation of the Theatrical Organisation of Children's Theatre in 1931, by Efrossini Londou-Dimitrakopoulou, and the foundation of the Children's Theatre School, in 1932, by Antigoni Metaxa. The performances of both companies lasted until 1941.

Traditional tales, and original stories in similar form were adapted or written by writers such as Evdokia Athanasoula, Alexandra Delta, A. Melachrinos, K. Varnalis, Marianthi Kambouroglou, Takis Kondos, G. Megas and G. Perialitis. Poetry was less important, although there were anthologies by P. Kalogerikou, and others, and a few novels appeared (I. Boukouvala, Stratis Myrivilis, P. Pikros).

During the period of the Occupation (1941–1944) the circulation of children's books was minimal and only after 1945, within the climate of national reconstruction was there a move towards providing children's reading.

Immediately after the war, two conflicting currents may be observed: the comics, illustrated classics, popular editions and 'marginal' literature, and the Hellenocentric movement, an effort for the offer to Greek children of Greek books alongside the translations of foreign works. Thematically, this literature used both the traditional themes, such as family, school, motherland, religion and nature and new themes such as the Albanian War, the Occupation, the Cypriot Struggle, the idea of cooperation. In the 1950s over 300 books of tales – containing 6,000 items were produced; there was a considerable number of books of short and simple stories, and over 300 books of drama, written by over 140 writers. Poetry and the novel declined, and translations outnumbered Greek novels by five to one. On the other hand, religious books became prominent, and if children's theatre mainly covered school needs, there were some impressive theatrical productions.

In 1958 the Women's Literary Company was founded, representing the start of a new epoch for children's books. Since then, the Company gives annual Panhellenic awards for children's books 'within the context of Greek reality'. Other factors which affected the evolution of children's literature have been political and social events such the rise of the Centre Union Party, the educational reform of 1964, the migrations to Western Europe, the dictatorship of 1967 and others. The most important genres have been books with historical, social, religious and naturalistic content, and stories and biographies of prominent men of history and of science. There was also a revival in the novel.

Children's books have continued to blossom since then. The Circle of the Greek Children's Book was founded in 1969, as part of IBBY (International Board on Books for Young People) and contributes to the promotion of children's books (announces awards, establishes libraries, inaugurates seminars for children's literature and so on). Contemporary children's literature is free from instruction, is more realistic, and deals with social and political events of recent history and contemporary universal problems, such as technology, space, natural environment, drugs, divorce and so on. Short stories tend to outsell novels. In poetry, there are traditionalists, expressionists and modernists, and numerous poetic children's song, stories anthologies circulate. The theatre now offers entertainment to children, rather than satisfying educational needs. In Athens alone there are over seventy children's stages in operation and the authors are numerous.

In general, the appearance of books has improved, and a considerable number of artists are occupied with illustration, with impressive results. Criticism of children's books first appeared in the 1970s, and since 1980 systematic studies have been made. The journal *Diadromes [Routes] to Literature for Children and Young Adults* has, since 1986, offered quarterly updates to parents, educationists and students and traces the circulation of children's books in Greece and abroad. Annual guides such as *Review of Children's Literature* (from 1987) are also being published. Children's literature is also being taught in universities as an autonomous academic subject.

Broadly speaking, children's literature in Greece today has matured and does not address only Greek children but all the children of the world.

## Further Reading

Anagnostopoulos, V. D. (1991) *Greek Children's Literature during the Postwar Period (1945– 1985)*, Athens: Kastaniotis.

Giakos, D. (1990) *History of Greek Children's Literature from XIX Century until Today*, Athens: Kastaniotis.

Petrovitch-Androutsopoulou, L. (1990) *Children's Literature in Our Times*, Athens: Kastaniotis.

Stavropulos, A. (ed.) (1991) *Wegweiser dürch die Internationale, Kinder und Jugendliteratur 2: Griechenland und Zypern*, Munich: International Youth Library.

# 72

# Russia

## Ben Hellman

The first Russian books explicitly addressed to children were primers, with Ivan Fyodorov's *ABC-Book* (1571) as the earliest sample. The birth of the picture book was *The Illustrated Primer* (1694), in which Karion Istomin with the help of poems and pictures gave young people maxims and scattered facts about the surrounding world. Peter the Great favoured books on courtesy, like *A True Mirror for Youth* (1717), which served the Europeanising process of Russia. Correspondingly foreign literature dominated children's reading all through the eighteenth century.

The Enlightenment and the pedagogy of Rousseau introduced new ideals into children's literature during the reign of Catherine II. The Empress's own didactic allegories constituted the first attempts to write fiction for children in Russia. The ideals of the period found expression in the first children's magazine, *Detskoe chtenie dlya serdtsa i razuma* [Children's Reading for the Heart and the Mind, 1785–1789]. The editor Nikolai Novikov offered 6 to 12-year-old children a wide range of informative material in an engaging form while publishing fiction only sparingly.

The figures for children's books published in the eighteenth century vary, according to the principle of definition, from fifty to four hundred. The number steadily grew in the nineteenth century, when the importance of periodicals (which could most easily reach the scattered readership) increased. The first illustrated magazine appeared in St Petersburg in 1813–1814.

The main epic genre of Romanticism was the fairy tale. Anonymous folk-tales and songs had always occupied a prominent place in oral children's culture, but it was only in the nineteenth century that they were systematically collected. The children's magazines introduced folk-tales on a broader scale in the middle of the century, and Aleksandr Afanasyev's classical collection *Russian Folk Tales* (1855–1864) also dates from this period. Afanasyev compiled a special edition for children in 1871.

Much earlier – in the 1830s – fairy tales in verse had been composed by Russian Romantics. Originally written for adults, they gradually also gained a place in children's literature. Aleksandr Pushkin, Vasily Zhukovsky and Pyotr Ershov took subjects, motifs and literary devices mainly from Russian folklore, but as Zhukovsky's *The Sleeping Tsarevna* (1831) and *Puss in Boots* (1845) and Pushkin's *The Tale About the Fisherman and the Fish* (1835) show, west European fairy tales were also known in Russia. Ershov's *The Little Hump-Backed Horse* (1834) was a folk-tale pastiche, in which a peasant boy rises to riches and power with the help of a magic horse.

In prose, Vladimir Dahl produced revisions of folk-tales, while Antony Pogorelsky wrote an original fantasy story, *The Black Hen, or The Subterranean Inhabitants* (1829), in which a Petersburg schoolboy gets to know the secret world of some Lilliputians and thereby learns fidelity and diligence. Vladimir Odoevsky also combined a realistic and a fantasy layer, when he acquainted the children with the mechanics of a music box (*The Little City in a Snuffbox*, 1834). His Moroz Ivanovich from *Uncle Irinei's Fairy Tales and Stories for Children* (1838) was a variation of Cinderella, while the prototype for Sergei Aksakov's *The Scarlet Little Flowers* (1858) was the French fairy tale *Beauty and the Beast*.

Romanticism also brought with it growing interest in the national past. Pyotr Furman's biographical tales about the great men of Russia were popular reading up to the early twentieth century. Aleksandra Ishimova, the first prominent woman writer in Russian children's literature, popularised Russian history (1837–1840) and biblical tales (1841) with due concern for the readers' fondness for dramatic events. Ishimova was also influential as the editor of two girls' magazines. The extensive literary output of Boris Fyodorov is full of praise of Christian virtues, as his favourite subheading, 'Moral examples', reveals. Viktor Buryanov specialized on geography, taking the children on 'walks' in a popular trilogy (1836–1838).

Poetry was widely included in children's magazines, but only by the mid-nineteenth century was a significant artistic level reached. Vasily Zhukovsky wrote small, charming poems with bird- and animal-motifs, but more to the liking of children were the Russian imitations of Heinrich Hoffmann's *Struwwelpeter*. The first translation had been published in 1849, only four years after the original.

The realistic novel brought fame to Russian literature in the nineteenth century. The development of children's literature was not as remarkable, even if leading critics early attached importance to this field of literature and worked for the birth of a realistic school. With his numerous reviews, Vissarion Belinsky laid a basis for a theory of children's literature. Writers had to give a truthful picture of the society and awake a civic spirit, without forgetting, however, the readers' literary taste. Belinsky's endeavours were continued in the 1850s and 1860s by Nikolai Chernyshevsky and Nikolai Dobrolyubov. Out of the existing Russian children's literature, only magazines like *Novaya biblioteka dlya vospitaniya* [The New Library for Education] (1847–1849) and *Podsnezhnik* [Snowdrop] (1852–1862) were approved by these utilitarian critics.

Realism became dominant in children's literature in the 1860s. Many prominent writers of adult literature made sporadic attempts to write for youth. Another factor of importance was the broadening and democratisation of the readership through a network of schools. For the elementary schools the prominent pedagogue Konstantin Ushinsky edited two influential readers, *Children's World* (1861) and *The Native Word* (1864), and he preferred to use fictional narratives in information texts. A central place was given to poetry, folk tales, riddles and proverbs.

Lev Tolstoi founded a school for peasant children in 1859, and compiled *The New Primer* (1875) and *A Russian Reader* (1875–1885) for the use of the pupils. Recommended by the Ministry of Education, these books were widely used in

Russia until the October revolution. Apart from non-fiction material on natural science and history, *A Russian Reader* included stories, fairy tales and fables. Features in common were a short form, a stylised content and an objective style. Tolstoi did not include much original material, but he revised all the texts to suit his ideals. For young people he wrote a tale of adventure, *A Captive in the Caucasus* (1872) which he saw as exemplary in its form.

In a semi-fictional novel, *The Childhood of Bagrov-Grandson* (1858), Sergei Aksakov depicted the life of a child of the gentry in the 1790s. The narrator is only 10-years-old, as he looks back at his early years. Nikolai Garin-Mikhailovsky traced in a trilogy, starting with *Tyoma's Childhood* (1892), the spiritual development of a boy from an officer's family. The strict upbringing generates attempts at revolt.

The 1870s and 1880s saw the rapid development of the Russian girl's story. Evgeniya Tur pictured a carefree childhood in the families of rich landowners, while Aleksandra Annenskaya was the first to write about middle-class girls who are forced to earn their living and thus have a social role outside the family. Others, like Elizaveta Kondrashova, Nadezhda Lukhmanova and Vera Zhelikhovskaya, wrote about their own childhood and youth at home or in boarding schools.

Populism with its emphasis on social justice and moral duty strongly influenced children's literature. The writers chose as heroes children who live in poverty and hunger, and the hard life of the common people was depicted with compassion. By comparing the everyday life of rich and poor children, the lack of equality was made visible, as in Dmitry Grigorovich's *The Gutta-Percha Boy* (1883) and Vladimir Korolenko's *The Cave Children* (1886). Pavel Zasodimsky's *Heartfelt Stories* (1883–1884) were based on the author's solid knowledge of rural life. Zasodimsky also developed the genre of sentimental Christmas tales. In the 1880s and 1890s Dmitry Mamin-Sibiryak wrote stories about children, who are deprived their childhood through heavy work. A field of his own – stories of naval life – was found by Konstantin Stanyukovich. One of the first to write nature tales for children was Dmitry Mamin-Sibiryak. In *Emelya, the Hunter* (1884) he combined a love of the Siberian nature with a humanitarian view of man.

All the fairy tale writers of the period acknowledged their debt to Hans Christian Andersen. The most original was Nikolai Wagner, a professor of zoology, who under the pseudonym Kot-Murlyka published a collection of philosophical fairy tales in 1872. 'Eternal questions' were treated in a pessimistic mood which many critics found more suitable for an adult audience. More traditional were the allegorical fairy tales of Vsevolod Garshin. The realist Mamin-Sibiryak surprised with the excellect collection *Alyonushka's Fairy-Tales* (1894–1896). Animals are personified in the tradition of the folk tale, but simultaneously Mamin-Sibiryak also gave true facts about their life.

Much importance was attached to non-fiction; for example, Russian children first learned about Puskhin and Gogol from novelised biographies by Vasily Avenarius. Leading scientists popularised their fields of knowledge in books or special magazines, like *Vokrug mira* [Around the World] (1891–1916). A major endeavour was the publication of a children's encyclopedia in ten parts in 1913–1914.

Statistics show the continuing growth of children's literature before the October revolution. During the first half of the nineteenth century, twenty-two magazines were published, in the second sixty-one, whereas in 1909 Russian children could chose between nineteen titles. Among the most popular were *Semeinye vechera* [Family Evenings] (1864–1890) and *Zadushevnoe slovo* [The Heartfelt Word] (1877–1918). The ideals of the realistic school were upheld by *Detskoe chtenie* [Children's Readings] (1869–1905) and *Yunaya Rossiya* [Young Russia] (1906–1918). Small children also had their own magazines.

At the beginning of the twentieth century, around 500 children's books appeared per year; at the threshold of the First World War, the number had been doubled. Unprecedentedly popular was Lidiya Charskaya, the prolific writer of melodramatic stories for girls about life in boarding schools, and adventures in the Caucasus or in historical times. In the shadow of Charskaya, Klavdiya Lukashevich wrote sentimental works for a wide range of readers.

While women writers did not fear romance and adventures, a gloomy naturalism and an insufficient adaptation to children's tastes were characteristic of many men. The new generation of realists loved to depict maltreated children from the lower strata of society – or maltreated animals. For Nikolai Teleshov it was important to show that his homeless heroes nevertheless encounter much kindness. Using his own experiences, Aleksei Svirsky portrayed in *Ginger* (1901–1902) an orphan, who roams around Russia until he finds his place in the community of workers. In Ivan Shmelyov's stories, children and adults with different social backgrounds are brought together, while Aleksandr Kuprin praised the friendship between children and animals in moving tales like 'The white poodle' (1904) and 'The elephant' (1907). The favourite reading of the Russian boys were, however, weekly detective magazines with Sherlock Holmes, Nick Carter and Nat Pinkerton as the heroes.

The modernists also took an interest in children's literature. Leading artists attributed to the development of the picture book. The magazine *Tropinka* [The Path] (1906–1912) was close to the symbolists. With a linguistic and rhythmic brilliance they brought nature to life in their children's poems and cultivated mystical themes. In two small books of children's verse, Aleksandr Blok revealed an interest in folk poetry. Love of childhood and children's imaginations characterised the poetry of Mariya Moravskaya and Sasha Chorny. Even as an émigré, Chorny continued to write cheerful children's verse.

The interest that Russian pedagogues took in children's literature at the beginning of the twentieth century indicates a growing prestige. The first substantial book on the history and theory of Russian children's literature appeared in 1907. Special journals offered recommendations for children's reading. The critic Kornei Chukovsky tried to awake an awareness of the 'dangers' of mass produced children's literature. Ten years later he was himself to set up a new standard for children's literature under completely different circumstances.

Only a few months after the October revolution, the first demands were made that children's literature should be put in the service of communist ideology. The state was to take responsiblity for children's reading and replace private publishing houses and 'bourgeois' magazines with revolutionary institutions. The Bolsheviks received valuable support from Maksim Gorky, editor of the first Soviet children's magazine, *Severnoe siyanie* [Northern Lights] (1919–1920).

The New Economic Politics gave writers a breathing space. For a few years it was possible to pursue an independent literary policy. When *Raduga* [The Rainbow] published a verse tale by Kornei Chukovsky in 1923, this marked the beginning of a decade which can be called the Golden Age of Russian children's literature. A group of talented Leningrad writers and artists gathered around *Raduga*, the Studio for Children's Literature and the magazine *Novyi Robinzon* [The New Robinson] (1923–1925). The central name was Samuil Marshak, who for children's literature recruited not only acclaimed poets like Osip Mandelshtam and Boris Pasternak but also the Oberiuts, a group of absurdists, who had been banished from adult literature.

The Oberiuts found refuge in the Marshak-led section for children's literature of the state publishing house *Gosizdat* and in the artistically outstanding children's magazines *Yozh* [Hedgehog] (1928–1935) and *Chizh* [Siskin] (1930–1941). Simultaneously the Communist Party strengthened its hold on the growing generation through the foundation of political children's organisations. A prominent goal of magazines like *Murzilka* and *Pioner* (1924– ) was to mould the readers into communists.

The greatest name in Russian children's verse is Kornei Chukovsky. His output was not large, but his popularity and influence have been immense. A recurrent theme in his fairy tales in verse, like *The Crocodile* (1917), *The Great Cockroach* (1923) and *The Fly's Wedding* (1924), is the revolt against usurpers of power. Evil shrinks as it meets resistance. The same theme was used in a didactic fairy tale like *Wash 'Em Clean* (1923). Characteristic of Chukovsky's verses is a lingustic and rhythmic virtuosity and a whimsical humour and fantasy, features which most clearly stand out in the nonsense-poem *The Telephone* (1926). A source of inspiration for Chukovsky was the English nursery rhyme.

Samuil Marshak was a leading name both as a writer and as an organizer in Soviet Russian children's literature for over forty years. In the 1920s he was part of the avant-garde, publishing in cooperation with Vladimir Lebedev excellent picture books (*Circus*, 1925) and anecdotal, funny poems (Oh what an absent-minded man, 1928). In his didactic poems, Marshak taught respect for work.

Chukovsky and Marshak influenced the Oberiuts, above all Daniil Kharms. Typical of Kharms's poems and short prose texts (*Firstly and Secondly*, 1928) was a childlike humour, play on words and the use of unexpected points of view. Another approach represented ideologically committed poets, like Vladimir Mayakovsky, who wanted to prepare children for the political struggle.

Prose works were written about children in the civil war and their involvement in the building of socialism. A social problem that was reflected strongly was the situation of the homeless waifs and the attempts to integrate them into the society. In the autobiographical *The Shkid Republic* (1927), L. Panteleev and Grigory Belykh depicted life in a Soviet juvenile reformatory. A satirical picture of the pre-revolutionary school was offered by Lev Kassil in *The Grade Book* (1929) and *The Land of Shvambraniya* (1931).

A talented author of books on popular science was the engineer M. Ilyin, while the description of nature found its master in Vitaly Bianki. His experimental *A Forest Newspaper* (1928) consisted of 'news-items' about events in nature. Of Bianki's many successors, Evgeny Charushin, Mikhail Prishvin and Ivan Sokolov-Mikitov deserve mention. Boris Zhitkov's principal genre was short, dramatic adventure stories with the sea or exotic countries as the setting. Quick reactions and courage are demanded of his heroes. The posthumously published *What I Saw* (1939) is a novel encyclopedia for preschoolers, in which Soviet reality is presented from the viewpoint of an inquisitive little boy.

Fairy tales were written by Aleksandr Grin (*Scarlet Sails*, (1923)) and Yury Olesha. The latter's *Three Fat Men* (1928) illustrated the class struggle and revolution using fairy tale figures. The first professional Russian writer of science fiction was Aleksandr Belyaev, who revealed an extraordinary ability to combine exciting plots, scientific knowledge and political orthodoxy.

In the 1930s the struggle to create a Soviet children's literature was brought to fruition. It was preceded by a violent debate about fairy tales. Many influential critics advocated strict realism, based upon a materialistic world view and almost all leading children's writers became the target of attacks, when even antropomorphism was perceived as a suspect device.

In 1932 the Union of Soviet Writers was formed with a special section for children's literature. In the same year a critical monthly, *Detskaya literatura* [Children's Literature] was set up, followed a year later by a publishing house with the same name. At the first congress of Soviet writers in 1934, socialist realism was made the obligatory method for all creative work. A major problem, often to be discussed but never to be solved, was how to unite ideological demands with an acceptable literary standard. Books were again published at around 1,000 titles a year, but the number of copies had risen decisively. On the other hand, children's literature had now also become the concern of the security police, and many a writer's career was cut short in the purges.

Industrialisation and the collectivisation of farming, solidarity with the international communist movement, and military readiness were popular themes in the children's literature of the 1930s. Biographical literature about Russian revolutionaries, especially Lenin, was encouraged, and Pavel Morozov, a country boy who denounced his own father for resistance against Soviet power, was made into a hero.

Marshak and some of the Oberiuts adjusted their poetry to the demands of the time. Marshak's famous *Mister Twister* (1933) was directed against American racism. A new name was Agniya Barto, an ideologically committed poet who also wrote satirical portraits of children and scenes from the nursery. Sergei Mikhalkov's hyperbolically depicted, always helpful adult hero *Uncle Styopa* (1936) became a favourite among small children, and during his long career, Mikhalkov added several sequels.

Classic realistic works of prose were written by Valentin Kataev (*A Lone Sail Gleams White*, 1936) and Venyamin Kaverin (*Two Captains*, 1938–1944). Ruvim Fraerman's girl's story *Wild Dog Dingo; or, A Story about First Love* (1939) initially met with criticism, as young love was not considered a suitable subject for Soviet youth. More typical of the period were the books by Arkady Gaidar, a veteran from the civil war: *Military Secret* (1935), *The Fate of a Drummer* (1939) and *Timur and his Team* (1940) have the qualities of adventure stories, but the ideological aspects always remain dominant. The bonds between the world of the children and the norms of Soviet society are perpetually stressed.

As the official attitude to fairy tales grew more liberal, there appeared in the 1930s three books which have remained favourite reading ever since: Aleksei Tolstoi's *The Little Golden Key, or the Adventures of Buratino* (1935–1936), Lazar Lagin's *The Old Man Khottabych* (1938) and Aleksandr Volkov's *The Wizard from the Emerald Town* (1939). All were adaptions of foreign literature, a fact which reflects both the increasing isolation of Soviet children's literature and the claims that the literature of the capitalist countries as such had become incomprehensible for the Soviet child.

The whole of the Soviet society was affected by the Second World War. The main task of literature was to strengthen will to victory. Writers depicted children participating in the fighting (Kataev's *The Son of the Regiment*, 1945; Aleksandr Fadeev's *The Young Guard*, 1945) or in work at home (Lev Kassil's *My Dear Urchins*, 1944). The hero of Lyubov Voronkova's *The City Girl* (1943) has lost her parents in the war but finds a new home in the countryside. After the war, many semi-documentary works were written about young martyrs of the war (Kassil's *The Street of the Youngest Son*, 1949). During the whole Soviet period, the theme of war was to occupy a prominent place in juvenile reading, partly compensating for the lack of adventure stories.

The return to peace was darkened by an ideological tightening up with, among others, Chukovsky being used as a warning example. The decade after the war meant an unprecedented state of humiliation for literature. Ideal heroes and trifling conflicts dominated children's literature. Most writers also contributed to the apotheosis of Stalin.

In 'kolkhoz' novels for young adults (Aleksei Musatov's *Stozhary Village*, 1948), the educative function of physical labour was stressed. A popular genre was the school story, in which an individualistically minded pupil gets corrected by the class collective (Mariya Prilezhaeva's *The Comrades Are With You*, 1949; Nikolai Nosov's *Vitya Maleev in School and at Home*, 1951). Also the Cold War left its mark on children's literature. N. Kalma pictured racism in American schools and the joyless life of children under capitalism. Poetry was in the service of topical needs, as the political verses of Sergei Mikhalkov show.

Against this gloomy background two humorists stood out clearly. Nikolai Nosov's and Yury Sotnik's curious and lively schoolboys perpetually end up in difficult situations. Nosov added to the humour by letting the children themselves narrate their small adventures in an innocent tone.

The criticism of Stalinism at the party congress in 1956 signified a turning point in Soviet history. The cultural 'thaw' brought with it some new children's magazines, like *Vesyolye kartiny* [Funny Pictures, 1956– ] and many important translations. New writers appeared, enriching children's literature both thematically and stylistically. Young, innovative poets like Boris Zakhoder, Emma Moshkovskaya, Irina Tokmakova and Genrikh Sapgir cultivated play on words, the use of the child persona and humorous verse.

A movement towards greater realism occurred within prose. Writers like Nikolai Dubov, Grigory Medynsky and Anatoly Kuznetsov treated ethical conflicts in families, at school, or at work. Also subjects like orphanhood, divorce and juvenile crime were touched upon. The heroes stand on the threshold of adult life, searching for lasting values. Less exterior drama, but a deeper psychological analysis were characteristic of Anatoly Aleksin, Yury Yakovlev, Rady Pogodin and Vadim Zheleznikov.

The most popular writer of adventure novels was Anatoly Rybakov. In *The Dirk* (1948) and *The Bronze Bird* (1956) pioneers expose the plans of Soviet enemies. The young heroes are on the side of the revolution, but more important was Rybakov's excellent handling of the standard devices of the genre. Also science fiction was revived through the novels of Arkady and Boris Strugatsky. Viktor Dragunsky composed amusing stories about the imaginative boy Deniska, while Nosov taught diligence and honesty in a popular fairy tale trilogy about the Lilliputian Neznaika [Dunno] (1954–1965). Vladimir Suteev's fairy tales with the author's own illustrations represent the Russian story book at its best.

The Brezhnev years were a period of stagnation in children's literature. While poetry declined, prose for young people, however, saw some new names, like Albert Likhanov, Vladimir Amlinsky and Vladislav Krapivin. Yury Korinets won international fame with the novels *Far Away, Beyond the River* (1967) and *In the White Night By the Bonfire* (1968). Readers were attracted by the friendship across the generation gap and the lyrical description of nature, but Korinets's principal concern was to celebrate the spirit of the October Revolution. In his main work, *The Wisest Horse* (1976), he poignantly portrayed an orphan and his horse. Vladimir Zheleznikov's school story *Scarecrow* (1981) with its analysis of the cruelty of the collective, received much attention.

Yury Koval's ambiguous *Yearling Fox* (1974), in which an arctic fox heads for freedom with the help of children, was translated into many languages. Soviet favourites were Kir Bulychov's humorous science fiction tales about little Alisa in the world of tomorrow and the series of fairy tale books with which Aleksandr Volkov followed up of his pirate version of *The Wizard of Oz*. The most famous Russian fairy tale figure is Cheburashka from Eduard Uspensky's *Gena the Crocodile and His Friends* (1966). Here and in *Uncle Fyodor, the Dog, and the Cat* (1974) Uspensky praised the spirit of solidarity. The weak and small but good-hearted defeat the narrow-minded bureaucrats. Uspensky's humour ranges from the absurd to linguistic puns and situation comedy.

The end of the Soviet era and the abandonment of the socialist ideals put children's literature in a radically new situation. A big part of the literary legacy was rejected, while undeservedly forgotten names were brought to life. A more liberal attitude towards religion emerged with reprints of pre-revolutionary books with biblical tales for children. Simultaneously a flood of western light reading and comics challenged the traditional stress on serious literature. The birth of a new Russian children's literature has only just begun.

## Further Reading

Akimova, A. and V. (1989) *Semidesyatye, vosmidesyatye ... Problemy i iskaniya sovremennoi detskoi prozy*, Moscow: Detskaya literatura.

Babushkina, A. P. (1948) *Istoriya russkoi detskoi literatury*, Moscow: Uchebno-pedago-gicheskoe izdatelstvo.

Chekhov, N. (1909) *Detskaya literatura*, Moscow: Polza.

Hellman, B. (1991) *Barn- och ungdomsboken i Sovjet-Ryssland. Från oktoberrevolutionen 1917 till perestrojkan 1986*, Stockholm: Rabén and Sjögren.

Lifschutz-Loseff, L. (1981) 'Children's literature, Russian', in *The Modern Encyclopedia of Russian and Soviet Literature*, Vol. 4, Gulf Breeze: Academic International Press.

Lupanova, I. P. (1974) *Sovetskaya detskaya literatura 1917–1967. Ocherki.* Moscow: Detskaya literatura.

Setin, F. I. (1990) *Istoriya russkoi detskoi literatury*, Moscow: Prosveshchenie.

Sokol, E. (1994) *Russian Poetry for Children.* Knoxville: University of Tennessee Press.

# 73

# Eastern Europe

## *Sheila Ray*

From 1945 until the end of the 1980s, most publishing for children in the countries within the Russian sphere of influence in Eastern Europe followed a common pattern. Publishing houses were state owned, first editions of new books were very large, sold well and went out of print very quickly. There was a sameness of appearance and writing style. Most countries established centres for children's books where publishers, authors, illustrators and editors could meet with librarians, teachers and children, and books were produced to meet perceived needs and requirements. Children's library services were generally well developed and generously staffed so that there was a clearly defined market for books. Publishers made good use of traditional material and editions with new and attractive illustrations were frequently published. Paperback books and magazines and comics were widely available through schools and youth organisations and in shops and markets. It is interesting to note, however, that even before the break up of the Soviet Union and the former Yugoslavia, the constituent nations had their own traditions and pre-1940 literatures for children on which to draw, and this led to national differences even in the fifty years of communist domination.

With the arrival of the free market, however, came the problem of publishing books at a price which children and those who buy books for children can afford. In the days of state publishing, the production costs of many books were subsidised. Publishers in a monopoly situation could afford to publish good books; everything that was printed was readily bought.

There are now fears that in a free market, with commercial interests involved, more trivial literature will appear and flood the market. Comics of the kind previously only available in Western Europe are now produced in the East and, in addition, books have to compete with more attractive and entertaining television programmes. While production costs rise steadily, publishers who used to be subsidised by central government now have to compete on the open market.

## The Czech and Slovak Republics

Even before the establishment of two separate republics after 1989, there were separate children's literatures for the two parts of Czechoslovakia, each of which had its own state publishing house.

Created in 1920 in the wake of the First World War, Czechoslovakia inherited a tradition of picture books which had manifested itself in what is generally accepted as the first picture book for children, the *Orbis Sensualium Pictus* of Comenius, published in 1658. Jan Amos Komenský (Comenius) was born in Bohemia, now part of the Czech Republic. He believed in the importance of pictures in children's books and *Orbis Sensualium Pictus* was a small pictorial encyclopedia with each object pictured and described in words in both Latin and the vernacular. Mikoláš Aleš, working in the late nineteenth and early twentieth centuries, is regarded as the founder of modern Czech children's book illustration, while the work of Jivři Trnka in the twentieth century enjoys a well deserved international reputation. In 1992, Květa Pacovská won the Hans Christian Andersen Award for illustration, praised for the dynamic quality of her books and the fact that she turns her children's books into rare works of art.

In the mid-nineteenth century, Karol Jaromír Erben began to collect Czech traditional tales systematically, while Božena Němcová recorded these stories as he had heard them in childhood. In the late nineteenth century Alois Jirásek wrote stories and novels about legendary and historical figures, many of which became popular with young people. *Broučci* by Jan Karafiát, published in the early 1870s, became a classic. Two outstanding Czech writers for children emerged in the inter-war period, Josef Lada and Josef Čapek. Lada's first book, *Moje Abeceda* [My ABC] (1911), was followed by illustrated books of nursery rhymes and proverbs but in 1934 he published *O Mikešori* [Mikeš the Cat], in which he combined ancient fable with modern fairy tale and added a humorous dimension through his comic illustrations, which are deceptively simple in appearance. Lada does not simplify essentials, but strips his pictures of irrelevant detail. Josef Čapek showed his interest in children in his early art ventures but not until he was thirty did he write specially for children. In 1918 he contributed a story called 'My fat grandfather and the brigands' to a collection, *A Basketful of Fairy Tales*, edited by his brother, Karel. The tale moves at a brisk pace with a profusion of comic situations and songs to vary the prose. After 1923, when his daughter was born, children began to play a more important part in his work. His *Tales of the Dog and the Cat* (1929), which grew out of a series of animal cartoons published in a newspaper, soon became his most famous children's book.

During the Second World War, many beautiful editions of traditional tales were published: these were popular because they helped to preserve the national and ethnic elements of Czech culture. After 1949, when Albatros, the state publishing house, was established, modern fairy tales and traditional tales from other countries continued to appear in significant quantities. Although realistic stories were published, notably those of Marie Majerová, Jaroslav Foglar's *Výprava na Yucatan* [The Expedition to the Yucatan] (1990) was the kind of the book that could only be published after 1989. The author, through excerpts from the diary of a Boy Scout, gives a picture of young people and their experiences in Czechoslovakia from 1926 to 1973.

In nineteenth-century Slovakia, moral tales, fiction, poetry and fairy tales were all published for children in a country seeking for a national identity. After its inclusion in the new and independent Czechoslovakia in 1918, Slovakia developed a tradition of illustrated books. Slovak folk-tales were a source of inspiration for many artists such as Ludovít Fulla and Martin Benka and both of them continued to illustrate children's books after the Second World War.

The Czech and Slovak special interest in illustration is reflected in the establishment of the Biennale of Illustration Bratislava (BIB), an international competition for picture book artists.

## Poland

In the nineteenth century, the Polish language was banned in schools in most of the country but this only increased the wish of parents to teach their children about their cultural heritage. One book which was read by nearly every girl was a journal fashioned out of the life of the Countess Françoise Krasinska by Klementyna Tanska Hofmanowa, which provided a detailed picture of life during the eighteenth century and which was just the kind of literature which appealed to the nationalistic spirit of the oppressed Poles. In the late nineteenth century, Adolf Dygasiński wrote stories with animals as central characters and these were much enjoyed by children. Maria Konopnicka and Julian Tuwim, both lyricists of great imagination, were amongst the most successful poets for children. After Poland regained its independence in 1918, children's writers were in the forefront of educational and social reform, and included authors who continued in the pattern already set such as M. Dombrowska (1889–1964) and more radical writers such as Helen Bibinska (1887–1968). A major figure at this time was Janucz Korczak (1878–1942), an early children's rights activist who produced a classic children's novel, *Krol Macius Pierwzy* [King Matt the First] (1923).

Children's books continued to be published during the German occupation, some of those produced by the underground press calling for resistance. After the war many children's books used a wartime setting and this practice has continued. Krystyna Siesicka (1928– ), who edited *Filipinka*, a magazine for young girls, wrote novels dealing with the problems of young people. Although her popularity reached a peak in the late 1960s, her finest achievement is considered to be *Moja droga Aleksandro* [My Dear Alexandra] (1983). This depicts the lives of four generations of women and shows the importance of family traditions in Poland. Through letters supposed to be written in 1944 and the retrospective memories of the narrator, she depicts life during the Second World War and the German occupation.

Since 1989 publishing for children has boomed. Fairy tales, now in luxury editions, are still popular but Bible stories and other religious literature have reappeared. Marian Murawski's work as an illustrator is an indication of the quality of modern Polish picture books; in 1989 he won the BIB Grand Prix. As a child, he lived in eastern Poland where Polish traditions mixed with Byelorussian and Jewish legends. He has illustrated both Byelorussian tales, *Niewyczerpany dzban* [A Bottomless Jug] and *Ksiegabajek Polskich* [A Book of Polish Fairy Tales], enriching the traditional stories through the pictures based on his own memories and experiences.

## The Former Yugoslavia

The six republics or provinces which make up the former Yugoslavia each has its own literature; each has a long history of national heroes celebrated in folk-tale epics and ballads. Before the Second World War, there was a distinction between the poorer and the richer areas of the country, the poorer, southern republics having relatively fewer books.

Immediately prior to the break up of Yugoslavia, children's books were being published in Zagreb, Belgrade, Sarajevo and Ljubljana, and titles indicate that children there enjoyed the same kind of books as children anywhere – humour, fantasy, family stories, adventure and animal stories as well as a range of information books. In the 1992 edition of *The White Ravens*, the list of recommended books published by the International Youth Library in Munich, the former Yugoslavia was represented by entries from Croatia and Slovenia; in the same year *Bookbird* published an article about children's books in Croatia ('Mesić and Vlahović', 1992). This shows that although publishers of children's books face new problems, there is still a range of picture books, information books, teenage novels and magazines being produced. Mladost, a leading Zagreb publisher, publishes a wide selection of titles including *Price iz Davnine* [Stories of Yesterday] by Ivana Brlic-Mazuranic, who is described as the Croatian Hans Christian Andersen. Mladost has responded to the new situation in the former Yugoslavia by publishing *Ubili su mi Kucu* [They have Killed my House) by M. Kusec, in which children who have had to leave their homes because of the war 'cry for help'. *Moj tata spava s andelima* [My Father is Sleeping with the Angels] by S. Tomas is written in the form of the diary of a young girl, showing all the horrors of a war-torn city in a state of siege. Alongside books like these are translations of Enid Blyton's *Famous Five* stories, teenage romances and, of course, folk- and fairy tales long known and told in Croatia.

In the 1992 edition of *The White Ravens*, Slovenia is represented by a book of modern fairy tales, Niko Grafenauer's *Mahajana in druge pravljice o Majhnici* [Mahayana and other Fairy Tales about Piccolina] (1990). Grafenauer is a popular Slovene poet whose style and themes are reminiscent of a more romantic age. The Bosnian poet, Josip Osti, discussed the role of books in the lives of the children of Sarajevo in an interview published in 1994 (Kordigel 1994). Despite the war, publishing for children has continued. Osti emphasises the value of the 'national' literatures in this situation and the way in which the Serbs and Croats in Bosnia-Herzegovina turn to them more than before.

## Hungary

Despite years of occupation by foreign powers, Hungary, where the official and literary language was Latin until the nineteenth century, produced its first children's book in 1538 and was open to the developments seen elsewhere in Europe. There were translations of Campe's *Robinson* by 1787 and of Defoe's *Robinson Crusoe* by 1844. Folk-tales formed the basis of most of the vernacular children's literature. Elek Benedek (1859–1929) played a similar role to that of the Brothers Grimm in Germany and his collection of traditional tales is the basis for many of the numerous modern editions such as *Világszép Nádszál Kisasvzony* [The Most, Beautiful Miss Rushes] (1990). Hungarian children's books now considered as classics were written by Móra Ferenc, probably Hungary's first true children's author, and Zsigmond Moricz.

After the Second World War, a network of children's libraries and the reading camps, which were an essential part of public education, created an environment in which children's literature flourished. As elsewhere in eastern Europe, literary periodicals were a way of providing stories and poems for young people at a low cost. One of these, *Kincskereső* [Treasure Hunter] sponsored events at which children could meet authors. Some authors have achieved international success, notably Éva Janikovszky, whose delightful picture books have been translated into many languages. She has also written short stories and novels for older children and teenagers, such as *Az úgy volt* [It All Started When ... ] (1980) and *A Nagyzuhe* [When it Rained Cats and Dogs] (1976). Her picture books, which never lose sight of everyday life and the relationships between children and adults, owe much to their illustrator, László Réber. Two of her books, translated as *Happiness* and *Even Granny was Young Once*, were published in Britain in 1970. The latter, illustrated with a combination of child-like drawings and old family photographs, is a graphic explanation of family relationships.

István Csukás published popular stories for adolescents from the late 1960s onwards. Very prolific, he also produced picture books written in verse, and humorous tales for younger children. *Vakacio a Halott Utcaban* [Holiday in Death Street] (1976), an exciting detective story, and the more romantic *Hogyan Lettem Filszinesz* [How I Became A Movie Star] (1981) are adventure stories for older children. Csukás also created favourite cartoon characters in Süsü the Dragon and Pom Pom. Both Éva Janikovszky and István Csukás worked for many years for Mora Konyrkiado, the major children's publishing house in Budapest, which continues to dominate the scene after the political changes of 1989.

More recently, Pál Békés has attracted attention with his badger stories, *Borz a Samlin* [Badger on the Stool] (1986), and novels such as *A. Kétbalkezes Varázslo* [The Fumble-Fisted Wizard] (1983). His books are a combination of the modern and the fabulous while his messages are universal. The story about the fumble-fisted wizard, for example, demonstrates the need for people to find each other even within the labyrinths of dull, modern high-rise housing units.

## Romania

Many Eastern European countries seem to have had one individual committed to the cause of children's literature during the 1920s. In Romania this was Apostol Culea. The modern Romanian language dates to the nineteenth century: Ion Creanga and Mihail Sadoveanu wrote short stories which appealed to young people. Another influential figure in Romanian children's literature was Carmen Sylva, the literary pseudonym of Queen Elizabeth, wife of King Carol I. Her book, *Poveștile Peleșului* [The Tale of Pelesch Castle] was first published in Romanian in 1882. This is a collection of fairy tales woven around Pelesch Castle in the Carpathians and was very popular. During the communist period it was banned because of its royalist connections but its lasting role in Romanian children's literature is shown by the fact that a new edition was published in 1991, after the political changes of 1989.

# Bulgaria

Bulgaria was under Ottoman domination for five centuries and only emerged as a separate nation in 1878; this situation hampered both educational and cultural development. Nevertheless, Peter Beron's *Primer with a Fish*, the first Bulgarian book produced specifically for children, appeared in 1824. Poetry was also written for children in the nineteenth century, with a view to encouraging love of their country, and patriotism has continued to be an important theme in Bulgarian children's literature.

During the 1970s, there were many children's books set during the Second World War, about war orphans joining the army, particularly as musicians as in Petar Neznakomov's *Barabantchika na Polka* [Drummer of the Regiment] (1978), and boys fighting against fascism. Maria Grubeshlieva's *Gemia v. Moreto* [A Small Ship at Sea] (1972) tells of Petko, a boy who helps the crew of a Russian submarine to fight for freedom when they arrive in his small seaside town.

Among outstanding modern writers, the work of Assen Bossev and Valory Petrov should be mentioned. Assen Bossev was one of the generation of writers who shaped children's poetry in the 1960s and had far-reaching influence. He set and maintained high standards, addressed modern social issues and emphasised the theme of peace. Valery Petrov wrote stories, modern fairy tales, poetry and drama which have appealed to several generations of young people. *Thumbkin*, written soon after the establishment of the communist government, remained popular for forty years. Petrov moved easily between various literary forms. *Pet Prikazki* [Five Fairy Tales] (1986) consists of stories which were originally created as plays for children; in story form, prose and verse complement each other and the stories, with a strong nonsense element, have a cheerful air.

Short stories continue to be popular with Bulgarian children. *Čudnite Raboti* [Strange Jobs] (1990) by Vladimir Zelengorov is a collection of tales ranging from an adventure story set in Tibet to humorous tales about everyday life.

# Lithuania, Latvia and Estonia

Even before the political upheavals of 1989, some of the Republics within the USSR had their own clearly defined literatures. Children's literature in Lithuania began in 1547 when a catechism with a rhymed preface by Martynas Mazvydas encouraging children to read the book appeared. Through the following centuries primers and catechisms, rudimentary forms of writing for children, were published, but the 'golden age' of Lithuanian children's literature came at the turn of the nineteenth century. Later it came under the influence of Soviet authors such as Agnia Barto and Kornei Chukovsky. The influence of fairy tales continued to be important; the stories of Aldona Liobyte are full of irony, about queens and princesses whose lifestyles and behaviour conform to present day conventions. Modern fairy tales are used as an allegorical way of putting forward solutions to modern social problems. However, there are also realistic stories for teenagers by writers like Vytautas Bubnys whose *Baltas Vejas* [White Wind] (1974) is typical in the way it explores the maturing personality of the teenager and the process of self-discovery.

Latvia too has a long and rich tradition of book publishing, with traditional material predominant in children's books. The work of writers in pre-Soviet Latvia was re-introduced to young people in the 1960s through anthologies such as *Solar Years* (1965), which contained folk songs and poetry of the pre-Soviet and Soviet periods. *Stories of Sunny Years* (1966), which included folk-tales, performed the same service for prose. *Children's Folklore of Latvia*, compiled by V. Greble, was published in 1979.

An account of children's literature in Estonia shows how the now independent republic provided for children during the period of Soviet rule, and how quickly things began to change with the coming of perestroika. In 1990 ten children's books were published in Estonian, which included translations – one of these was *Winnetou*, an adventure story by the German Karl May. The magazine *Pioneer*, has begun to 'correct' the history of Estonia. The fairy tale was important in 'socially complicated' times, as it was possible to deal with taboo themes which could not have been tackled in any other way. Fairy tales were written in a multi-layered style and works of artistic value emerged. E. Raud's *Nakgitrallied* [Three Jolly Fellows] is a good example. Traditional Estonian tales, and stories about Estonia in the first half of the twentieth century also helped to correct the impressions created by the 'official' teaching of history.

The way in which children's literature has developed in Eastern Europe in the twentieth century shows how it can be exploited for what is seen as the national good, but it also clearly demonstrates just how resilient it is, an important instrument of freedom and democracy.

## References

Kordigel, M. (1994) 'Children's culture under siege: a conversation with the Bosnian poet Josip Osti', *Bookbird* 32, 1: 6–10.
Mesić, D. and Vlahović, V. (1992) 'Literature despite the war: children's books in Croatia', *Bookbird* 30, 4: 9–12.

## Further Reading

Auryla, V. (1986/87) 'Lithuanian children's literature: an historical sketch', *Phaedrus* 12: 28–30.
Bode, A. (1991) 'Children's book publishers in Eastern and Southeastern Europe and their prospects for the common market', *Bookbird* 29, 2: 12–15.
Krusten, R. (1991) 'The situation of children's literature in Estonia', *Bookbird* 29, 4: 14–15.

# 74

# Turkey

## *Sheila Ray*

Folk-tales and epics have been told in Turkey as long as they have been told elsewhere and the humorous tales about the Hodja, for example, are enjoyed by children worldwide. The history of Turkish children's literature goes back to the 'Tanzimat' (Reform) period between 1839 and 1876, when Turkish society was Europeanised. Authors typical of this early period are Çaylak Tevfik (1843–1892), Ahmet Mithat Efendi (1844–1912) and Şemsettin Sami (1850–1904).

At the beginning of the twentieth century, when books for children were required to support educational developments, the need for a Turkish written language based on the vernacular became increasingly urgent. The spread of children's books, particularly amongst the poorer classes, was hindered by the use of the Arabic alphabet which has few vowels and does not suit the Turkish language which has many. The modern Turkish Republic dates from 1923 when it came into being under the leadership of President Kemal Ataturk. A Turkish alphabet, based on the Roman one, was adopted in 1928 and this helped the fight against illiteracy although progress was slow and the problems have not yet been entirely overcome.

However, children's literature did begin to develop, albeit slowly, after 1928, with authors like Ahmet Rasim (1864–1932) and Ziya Gökalp (1876–1924). Ali Ulvi Elöue (1881–1975) produced some of the first Turkish poetry written especially for children; the main themes of his work are freedom, patriotism and the heroism of the Turkish people. Writers of stories, who later included Elfâtun Cem Güney and Peyani Safa, used folk-tales and legends but also wrote about everyday life. There was praise for the new republic but little criticism of conditions; literature mainly reflected life in the towns and cities and there were few stories about the harsher conditions in rural areas.

Turkey's European links have in one sense hindered rather than helped the development of children's literature – Turkey (and other Middle Eastern countries) have been flooded by poorly produced translations of European and American books, the settings and characters of which bear little relationship to the experiences of local children.

By 1950, when a multi-party political system was introduced in Turkey, there were signs of changes in the content of books for young people. Themes such as the fight for freedom, the problems of farmers and the differences between poor and rich began to appear. Poets like Nasim Hikmet (1902–1963) and the humorist Aziz Nesin (1915– ) were pioneers of this new kind of literature. Talip Apaydin (1926– ) and Fakir Baykurt (1929– ), who came from a rural background, were part of the Village Institute movement, whose aim was to provide education and training for the children of farmers.

After changes to the Turkish constitution in 1961, more writers from rural and working-class backgrounds appeared. Outstanding are Rifat Ilgaz (1911– ), whose humorous tale, *Hababam Sinifi*, was both dramatised and filmed with great success, and Gülten Dayioglu (1935– ) who in her later work abandoned her characteristically naïve outlook and began to write more realistically. In the 1970s she took up the theme of foreign workers from a female standpoint, and in the 1990s she is one of the most widely read children's writers in Turkey. In *Journey to the Other Side of the Ocean*, she writes in a lively and exciting way about her journey to South America. Another popular author is Can Göknil who produces picture story books about children's everyday life. *Fiti Fiti Tek Basina* [Fiti Fiti All Alone] (1991) about a small girl and her pets, and *Kardes Kardese* [Brother and Sister] (1991) about a little girl who suddenly discovers that her younger brother is now old enough to be a real playmate, are typical of her work.

The poet, Yalvaç Ural (1945– ) has won international recognition, having been awarded L'Ordre du Sourire, a Polish prize which had previously been given to Astrid Lindgren and Tove Jansson, in 1986. At the time of the award he also edited a monthly magazine for children, *Milliyet*, and much of his poetry was published in magazines before being published in collected editions. Of his collections, his own favourite is *Bir Gök Dolusu Güvercin* [A Sky Full of Pigeons], in which the poems are about children growing up in a small town and in which he tries to show the powers of children's imaginations when they play make-believe games. His poems are mostly based on true stories or are designed to make learning fun. *Tekir Noktalama Isaretlerini Öğnetiyor* [The Pussycat Teaches Punctuation] is designed to make the rules of punctuation comprehensible by making a game out of them. *Zipir Bilmeceler* [Crazy Puzzles] (1988) is a collection of entertaining pictures, each with a question which is then answered in a humorous way.

Traditional tales are published in new editions and Turkish children are also being introduced to the folk-tales of other countries. *Bengiboz ve Küçük Sehzade* [Bengiboz and the Young Prince] (1985) is a Turkish folk-tale retold and illustrated for young children by Cagla Erdoğan; a special feature of this is that all the illustrations are based on the traditional patterns of Turkish embroidery.

Turkish authors are being encouraged to write both poetry and prose for children, and the quality of picture books and of illustrations in books for older children has risen considerably with the work of such artists as Isa Çelik and Mehment Sönmez. The future for children's literature in Turkey looks hopeful.

## Further Reading

Alpay, M. (1980) 'A survey of Turkish children's and juvenile literature', *Bookbird* 4: 10–11.

# 75

# Hebrew and Israeli

## *Zohar Shavit*

The history of Hebrew children's literature, dating back to 1779, is the history of an ideological attempt to build a new literary system and to invent its consumers and producers simultaneously. It is a history characterised by strong ideological inclinations, and delayed developments and regressions, until Hebrew children's literature attained the conditions typical of the European children's systems which it sought to emulate. Its peculiar circumstances of development involved the special status of the Hebrew language as the language of high culture rather than the native language of its child readership, as well as the multi-territorial existence of Hebrew culture: a situation which ended only when the centre of Hebrew culture was transferred to Eretz-Israel in the mid-1920s.

The emergence and crystallisation of the concept of childhood was a precondition for the development of Hebrew children's literature, as was the case with other European children's literatures; but Hebrew children's literature also required a substantial modification of the basic views of Jewish society, especially those concerning children's education and Jewish attitudes towards the outside world, in order to enable the initial development of a system of children's books. Only when such a change occurred at the end of the eighteenth century within the framework of the Haskalah (Jewish Enlightenment) movement in Germany, was there culturally room for Jewish books for children.

The Haskalah movement firmly believed that shaping a new mode of Jewish life could be achieved through changes in educational orientation and curriculum, making them rational and secular. Such changes were implemented in the new school network, where the demand for new and different books was created. This demand meant that a system of books for children had to be established from the very beginning. The close relations between the Jewish Haskalah and the German Enlightenment movement, made German children's literature an ideal model for the newly established system to imitate. Hebrew children's literature endeavoured to follow German children's literature both in its stages of development, and in the structure of its repertoire. However, Hebrew children's literature could not adapt itself to the present stage of development of German children's literature, given the former's ideological underpinnings. Thus, unlike German children's literature, Hebrew children's literature was characterised by the rather monolithic nature of its texts. Even in its later stages of development, Jewish writers adhered to a limited number of textual models and seldom deviated from this fixed repertoire during the entire Haskalah period.

Since the Haskalah ideology provided legitimisation for Jewish children's literature in Hebrew, ideological constraints determined the nature and selection of some texts – whether original or translated – for inclusion in the system, as well as the exclusion of others.

This ideological hegemony resulted in the Hebrew children's literature system remaining incomplete for a considerable period, lacking some of the sub-systems existing in other European children's literatures at the time. The lack of popular texts was particularly noticeable: the existence of literature for pure amusement was unthinkable in terms of Jewish culture. In fact, Hebrew children's literature managed to liberate itself from the exclusive hegemony of ideology only much later in Eretz-Israel where Hebrew children's literature become a 'native literature'.

When the centre of Hebrew culture was transferred to Eastern Europe, Hebrew texts for Jewish children were still published in the German-speaking countries, but more significant developments occurred in Eastern Europe. Even there, Hebrew children's literature continued to be dependent on German children's literature for quite a long time, in contradistinction to the adult system, where the Russian system had begun to dominate. Only subsequently in Eretz-Israel was the German system gradually replaced by the Russian as a mediating system.

In Eastern Europe, writers for children continued to regard Hebrew children's literature as an educational tool and consequently wrote texts with a didactic bearing. At this stage in its development, Hebrew children's literature tolerated only one criterion for the rejection or acceptance of texts for children: the extent of their conformity to their didactic and/or ideological role. Since the educational programme endorsed strong contacts with the surrounding and neighbouring cultures, Hebrew children's literature tended to translate extensively from these languages as well as to use translated texts as a model for original Hebrew texts.

In Europe, Hebrew children's literature never managed to become 'native literature' as it was written for children whose mother tongue was not Hebrew. As a result Hebrew children's literature could not transform its rather superficial existence, and was unable to release itself from the various ideological frameworks in which it was generated. Furthermore, even later on, when its circumstances of existence indeed changed in Eretz-Israel, its traditional ideological inclination still remained very strong, and long years of cultural battles were required before Hebrew children's literature managed to liberate itself from the bonds of ideology.

In Eretz-Israel the urgent need to construct *all* components of the Hebrew culture led to the creation of an entire cultural conglomerate for children, including children's literature, whose products ranged from children's songs to fairy tales; from the ceremonies in schools and kindergartens to schoolbooks; from poems to stories, novels, non-fiction prose, and so on.

Hebrew literature in Eretz-Israel addressed children who spoke Hebrew, sometimes as their first and only language, and gradually came to address a readership which had all its schooling in Hebrew. The change of the nature of the readership into a real and authentic one resulted in a new course of development, which culminated in Hebrew children's literature gaining an 'independent' status. Nevertheless, the process involving the decline of the ideological domination of the system in favour of commercial and educational factors probably only came to an end in the late 1960s.

In Eretz-Israel Hebrew children's literature was no longer part of a cultural enclave, but belonged to a single sovereign culture. Yet its history and tradition could neither be ignored, nor easily utilised. Because of its drastically different circumstances of development, the European Hebrew children's literature tradition could be used only partially. Unlike the case of Hebrew literature for adults, where the transfer to Eretz-Israel implied at least some degree of continuity, Hebrew children's literature, facing excessive new needs, had to repeat initial processes of development based on new and different motivations and legitimisations.

The needs of the children's system in Eretz-Israel were the principal determinants of the nature of its repertoire. The needs and demands of the educational system enjoyed first priority. The use of Hebrew as the natural language of education created an urgent need for books suitable for the first generation of Hebrew speakers. The scarcity of school books overshadowed any other deficiencies of the children's system. Given the necessity, however, of creating a children's culture from scratch, school texts also included original poems and stories. These texts can be seen as the first original texts of Hebrew children's literature in Eretz-Israel. Many of them answered the need for a curriculum for everyday life, as well as for festive days. From Hanukkah poems, to Tu Bi-Shevat and Passover songs, the curriculum urgently required texts suitable for the celebration of these festivals.

Behind this undertaking were some of the most prestigious writers for adults, who readily accepted the task of providing texts. They regarded writing for children as a national task, an indispensable component of the creation of the new nation. Such writers even included the national poet Bialik. For the first time in the history of Hebrew children's literature, texts for children were written in great quantities by writers known primarily as writers for adults. Simultaneously, quite a few books were written by teachers and educators within an educational framework. Thus at its outset, Hebrew children's literature had few, if any, writers who could be viewed as professional writers for children.

The discrepancy between prestigious writers for adults who wrote for children, and non-professional writers who wrote in the framework of their educational pursuits, was typical of the irregular situation of Hebrew children's literature at this stage of its development (though not exclusive to Hebrew literature alone; a similar situation pertained in Italy). As Hebrew children's literature in Eretz-Israel evolved and prospered, this gap was gradually filled; one aspect of the 'normalisation' was the creation of a specific group of writers who wrote solely or mostly for children. This process of differentiation was only fully manifested in the 1950s.

Urgent cultural demands on the one hand, and the inability of original writers to respond to them fully on the other, virtually forced many publishing houses to produce translations in large numbers. The motivation behind translating so many books was rooted both in ideology and the inability of original Hebrew writers to supply as many texts as were required. By translating into Hebrew, the editors of various publishing houses wished to prove that all a child's educational and cultural needs could indeed be supplied in Hebrew. This motivation, as well as the desire to fill up the system as quickly as possible and thus to approximate the condition of European cultures, made the translation of the so-called children's 'classics' a priority mission. Thus in its early years, the Hebrew children's literature system in Eretz-Israel was filled by translations rather than original texts.

The process of liberating Hebrew children's literature from its formative stages and acquiring an 'independent' status was manifested primarily in the growth of a group of writers who wrote exclusively for children, as well as in the increase in the number of original texts written for children. Consequently the relations between, and the proportion of translated and original texts began to change: translations were still published in great quantities, but many original texts produced as literature *per se*, rather than on educational or didactic pretexts, were published.

Still the ideological grip on Hebrew children's literature in Eretz-Israel was very strong. In fact, during the 1940s and 1950s, the pre-State, or late Yishuv stage, children's literature was simply transformed to meet new ideological claims rooted in the ideology of the labour parties who subsidised almost all the big publishing houses. Publishing policy, determined by the labour parties, demanded that books comply with the ideological demands of the political parties, and this affected translated as well as original texts, especially in thematic and evaluative terms, but also in characterisation and illustration. Due to the strong link with the Soviet Union and Russian culture, most of the texts were translated from the Russian.

The entire attitude towards Hebrew children's literature was extremely earnest: it was children's books which were entrusted with the heavy burden of building new and healthier Hebrew children as opposed to the weak Jewish children of the *Gola* (Diaspora). The expectations of Hebrew children's literature were high, and so were the limitations imposed on it. As far as original books were concerned, it was almost taboo to write popular children's literature, such as detective stories.

Towards the end of the 1950s, for the first time in the history of Hebrew culture, Hebrew children's literature was no longer exclusively the result of the ideological yearnings of publishers and cultural agents. Not only did private publishing houses enter the field, but the publishing policy of the labour parties also gradually changed. Publishing policy was now put on a commercial foundation in its broadest sense. That is to say, books were chosen for publication either because they were believed to be valuable, or saleable, or both. Children's literature began to flourish, especially from the 1960s onward both in terms of the number of published books and the number of copies sold. It became central to the activity of the publishing houses; some original and translated books even became best-sellers in Israel. Most of the large publishing houses appointed editors specifically for children's literature, and children's libraries or book clubs were formed.

Since the 1960s, Hebrew children's literature has experienced a tremendous boom.

The system of children's literature managed to become a full system consisting both of popular and high literature. No fewer than 480 children's books were published in 1976, among them 194 new titles and 286 reprints. The number of books published more than doubled between 1965/6 and 1979/80, and almost tripled in the twenty years between 1965/6 and 1986.

Poetry for children was allotted enormous space. Prose writing developed as well. Gone was the almost exclusive focus on realistic fiction about the history and life of the people of Israel and the history of the Jewish people. The door was opened to themes which had previously been banned, such as first love, friendship, childhood, children's adventures, as well as the Holocaust, death in war, the death of family members, divorce, and family crisis. The range of topics covered by children's literature has expanded greatly both as a result of the 'normalisation' of the system and because of its relationship with European children's literatures, which underwent a similar process. For instance, Raya Harnik's, *Achi Achi* [Oh My Brother] (1993), Uri Orlev's *Chayat Hachosech* [The Beast of Darkness] (1967) and Yaacov Shavit's *Nimrod Kelev Zayid* [Nimrod Hunting Dog] (1987) deal with a child's response to the death of a father or brother. Other writers depict conflicts between the individual and society, notably Gila Almagor (*Etz Ha-Domim Tafus* [Our Tree on the Top of the Hill] (1992)), Ofra Gelbart-Avni (*Kirot Shelo Roim* [Invisible Walls] (1992)), Roni Givati (*Mishalot Choref* [Winter Wishes] (1993)), Nira Harel (*Kova Chadash* [A New Hat] (1995)), Israel Lerman (*Ha-Yeled MiGdat Hanachal* [The Child from the Other Bank of the River] (1992)), Yona Tepper (*David Chatzi Chatzi* [David Half-and-Half] (1990)) and Nurit Zarchi (*Yaldat Chutz* [Outsider] (1978) and *Wolfinea Momi Blum* (1988)).

Much of the prose writing is devoted to original realistic fiction about the history and life of the Yishuv in the pre-State period, and the history of the Jewish people. Among the prominent authors to publish such works are Ehud Ben-Ezer (*Geda, Sipuro Shel Avraham Shapira* [Geda, the story of Avraham Shapira] (1993)), Sami Michael (*Pachohim Ve-Chalomot* [Shacks and Dreams] (1979)), Dorit Orgad (*Ha-Chatufim Li-Tzva Ha-Tzar* [Kidnapped by the Czar's Army] (1986)), Devorah Omer (*Pitom Be-Emtza Ha-Chayim* [Suddenly in the Midst of Living] (1984)), Galila Ron-Feder (*Moshe Dayan: Hanaar Mi-Nahalal* [Moshe Dayan: The Boy From Nahalal (1984)), Yael Roseman (*Ha-Roman Sheli Im Ben-Gurion Ve-Im Penina* [My Affair with Ben-Gurion and with Penina] (1986)), Esther Streit-Wortzel (*Ha-Bricha* [The Escape] 1969)) and Binyamin Tene (*Hechazter Ha-Shlishit* [The Third Courtyard] (1982)).

The silence about the Holocaust, previously characteristic of Israeli books for children, has been broken. In this connection, it is worth mentioning that the sudden and intense production of Holocaust writing is typical not only of the generation of survivors, but of the second generation as well. Such writers include: Tamar Bergman (*Ha-Yeled Mi-Sham* [The Boy from 'Over There'] (1983)), Ruth Ilan-Porath (*Kurt Achi* [Kurt, My Brother] (1983)), Rivka Keren (*Kaitz Atzuv, Kaitz Meushar* [Bittersweet Summer] (1986)), Irena Liebman (*Sus Etz U-Shmo Zariz* [A Wooden Horse called Zariz] (1988)). These books either describe the Holocaust very directly, or indirectly describe its consequences, as for instance in Gabriel Zoran's *Morad Hazami* [Nightingale Lane] (1986), which describes the life of a Jewish-German family who immigrated to Eretz-Israel.

Extensive development in picture books and books for the very young took place. In the pre-State period, and even during the first decades of the State of Israel, picture books were poorly produced. From the 1960s onward great improvements took place in the design and graphics of books for children, especially books for the very young. Israeli children's literature has been able to attain the very highest international standards of production.

Efforts to encourage writing for children by raising the status of children's authors bore fruit. The change in the status of the children's writer manifested itself in the fact that by 1978 three authors had received the highly prestigious Israel Prize for their life's work in children's literature.

This change is also manifested by the fact that successful adult writers began writing for children as well. They include Ruth Almog (*Rakefey, Ahavati Ha-Rishona* [Rakefet, my First Love] (1992)), Yizhak Ben-Ner (*Beikvot Mavir Ha-Sadot* [On the Trail of the Field Firebug] (1980)), David Grossman (*Yesh Yeladim Zigzag* [The Zigzag Child] (1994)), Yoram Kaniuk (*Yiuv, Chaluk-Nachal Ve Ha-Pil* [Job, Pebble and the Elephant] (1993)), Shulamit Lapid (*Naarat Ha-Chalomot* [The Girl of Dreams] (1985)), Amos Oz (*Sumchi* (1977)), Meir Shalev (*Aba Ose Bushot* [Shame on You, Daddy] (1988)), Yaacov Shabtai (*Ha-Massa Ha-Mufla Shel Ha-Karpad* [The Wonderous Journey of the Toad] (1965)), and Dan Tsalka (*Mari Ben Amtel* (1992)).

Translations and re-translations of children's classics (most of them dating back to the end of the nineteenth and the beginning of the twentieth centuries) predominated. The most important of these appeared in the framework of the Kitri series, by the Keter publishing house, which published new translations of, among others, Spyri's *Heidi*, George Sand's *La Petite Fadette*, Stowe's *Uncle Tom's Cabin*, Edmondo de Amicis's *Cuore*, and Waldemar Bonsels's *Die Biene Maja und Ihre Abenteuer*.

Hebrew children's literature has undergone tremendous changes over the last two hundred years. Starting as a literature with no natural reading public, it acquired a large and stable reading public. Although it was believed to serve as a tool for other purposes, it managed to liberate itself from ideological and didactic constraints to become a full and 'normal' system, having a 'normal' reading public and functioning on the same basis as any other national literature in the Western world. In an extremely short period of time, Hebrew children's literature has attained the highest possible standards of Western children's literature.

## Further Reading

Ariès, P. (1962) *Centuries of Childhood*, London: Cape.

Elboim-Dror, R. (1986–1990) *Hebrew Education in Eretz Israel, Vol. 1: 1854–1914; Vol. 2: 1914–1920*, Jerusalem: Yad Yizhak Ben-Zvi [Hebrew].

Eliav, M. (1960) *Jewish Education in Germany in the Period of Enlightenment and Emancipation*, Jerusalem: Jewish Agency Publications, 1960.

Even-Zohar, I. (1990) *Polysystem Studies. Poetics Today*, Special Issue, 11. 1. Durham, NC: Duke University Press.

Moore, O. (1991) *The Ideology of the Jewish National Movement in Hebrew Children's Literature, 1899–1948*, unpublished doctoral dissertation, Cambridge: University of Cambridge.

Ofek, U. (1979) *Hebrew Children's Literature: The Beginning*, Tel Aviv: University Publishing Projects [Hebrew].

Rapel, D. (1986) 'Jewish education in Germany in the mirror of school books', *Sefer Aviad* Jerusalem: Mossad ha-Rav Kuk: 205–216 [Hebrew].

Shavit, Z. (1986) *Poetics of Children's Literature*, Athens, GA: University of Georgia Press.

—— (1988) 'From Friedländer's Lesebuch to the Jewish campe: the beginning of Hebrew children's literature in Germany', *Leo Baeck Year Book* 33, 385–415.

—— (1992) 'Literary interference between German and Jewish-Hebrew children's literature during the Enlightenment: the case of Campe', *Poetics Today* 23, 1: 41–61.

# 76

# The Arab World

## *Julinda Abu-Nasr*

The richness in the tales of the Arabian Nights, which included stories of Aladdin, Ali Baba and Sinbad, were brought back to Europe in the eighteenth century by travellers to the Middle East. These stories are as familiar to most European children as those about Cinderella and Hansel and Gretel, and yet there is almost no tradition of a special literature for children in the Arab World.

Positive initiatives to encourage native authors and illustrators to produce children's books, reflecting their own environment and interests, mostly date from the 1920s and so far few of the books published as a result of these efforts have reached other parts of the world. There are various reasons for this late start. First, there was an unwillingness to appreciate children's needs and interests. Although Arab countries are rich in folk-lore, with stories about characters such as El-Shater Hassan, buffoons like Goha and epics about heroes of the past such as Abu Zaid El-Hilali Antar and El-Khalifa, as well as the famous tales from the Arabian Nights, such tales were opposed by educators who believed they had no educational value. Second, writers chose not to use a simple Arabic language. Third, early providers of children's books relied too much on translations of European works, which tended to describe situations and settings alien to Arab children. (This inclination to translate irrelevant foreign works continues despite efforts to encourage native writers.)

Interest in children's literature in the Arab world started in Egypt in the late nineteenth century, and a little later in Lebanon. One of the first writers for children was Othman Jalal (1828–1898) who wrote fables in the manner of Aesop and La Fontaine. The poet Shawqi (1889–1932) published fables, songs and poems for children. The real revolution, however, came with the Egyptian Kamel Kilani (1897–1959), who was the first writer to specialize in producing children's literature in Arabic. Between 1930 and 1950, he was responsible for a long series of children's books which drew on Arabian folk-tales and fiction from Western countries, and were distributed throughout the Arab world. Although they were quite attractive in appearance, the contents had a certain uniformity. None the less he was well liked in his day; his books abound in description and are less popular today with a generation used to television and the comic strip. After his death, his publisher Dar al-Ma'aref branched out and began to publish picture books, original and translated fiction for children of different ages, historical and religious stories, biographies of famous Arabs and humorous tales.

Among writers who succeeded Kilani were Al-Ourian, Al Barkuki and

Al-Abrashi, all of whom contributed to the modernization of Arabic children's stories. Al-Tawab is recognized for his religious stories. Ahmed Naguib, who received the State Prize for Children's Literature, published several children's books, including *Tales of the Blue Bird*, *Adventures of Shater Hassan* and *Tales for the New Generation*. He is the most modern and popular of Egyptian story writers today.

Meanwhile, between 1940 and 1960, the Arabic language was evolving in Lebanon, developing a new, simpler style, which broke away from some of the complexities of traditional Arabic and introduced newly created vocabulary and words borrowed from the colloquial. These changes helped to pave the way for the creation of modern children's literature.

In the early part of the twentieth century, a few poets from Egypt, Lebanon and Iraq produced poems for children. With the availability of a simpler style of Arabic, Lebanese writers began to produce poems, stories and songs for the young. Folk-tales and folk-tunes, with their simplicity, local colour and imaginative elements, were a valuable basis for children's literature. The revival of colloquial poetry known as 'Zajal' encouraged writers to use colloquial expressions in these songs and stories for children.

In 1948 a collection of original songs, written and set to music by Rose Ghurayyib, was published in Lebanon. Some were written in colloquial Arabic, while others were classical. The colloquial songs proved to be the more successful and popular, and this encouraged the further use of colloquial Arabic in children's literature. Lebanon has continued to make an important contribution to the development of children's books in the Arab world because of its central position, openness to foreign cultures and the comparatively high rate of literacy. In the 1990s, it has a large number of well-equipped printers, and publishers capable of producing books of high quality.

Rose Ghurayyib was a very popular children's writer with over eighty books to her credit. Other pioneers of children's literature in Lebanon include Habbouha Haddad, who began to tell stories for children on the radio in the 1940s, Lauren Rihani, who retold folk-tales, and Rashad DarRouth, the author of *Bedtime Stories*, told first to his own children. Edvich Shyboub wrote a series of illustrated books for young children in the 1950s and then wrote realistic stories for young people.

Dramatic changes came in the 1960s. Foreign publishing houses became aware of the Arab market and a flood of poor translations which used a sophisticated classical Arabic far beyond the comprehension of most children, provoked a strong reaction. Research centres and Institutes for children's literature were set up in Egypt, Lebanon and Syria. The defeat of the Arab countries in the 1967 war also seems to have led to a recognition of the need for national literatures that will take positive action to improve the quality of children's books and a combination of events led to conferences and workshops designed to bring this about.

In 1981 the Institute for Women's Studies in the Arab World at Beirut University College in Lebanon, together with the Lebanese Section of IBBY, evaluated Arabic books for children available in Lebanon. This revealed a plethora of poor translations which had no bearing on the lives and culture of Arab children. Despite the earlier efforts, there was a scarcity of good books that addressed the needs of the young. In 1983, a programme of research and action was launched by the Institute which involved research into the vocabulary, language structures, style, and concepts familiar to children between the ages of 2 and 12 and also into their reading preferences, which proved similar to children universally.

Workshops were organized for writers and illustrators, and manuscripts suitable for publication were produced. In 1994 the Institute received the IBBY Asahi Award for its efforts in promoting reading among children in Lebanon.

In the 1980s developments also took place in Egypt and children's books benefited from the involvement of Mrs Suzanne Mubarak, wife of the Egyptian President, who became Chair of the Egyptian Section of IBBY when it was formed in 1987. She established the Suzanne Mubarak Awards for children's books to encourage a new generation of writers. Winners include Sameh Moussa El Shandouly, Farid Mohamed Awad for *The Sun Always Rises* and Taher Said Thabet for *The Princess and the Bride of the Nile*. These are all collections of short stories, published by the Egyptian National Book Organization, which has the facilities, financial resources and staff to print and distribute children's books. Awards have also been made to poets writing for children.

The same intellectual-political climate that prevailed in Lebanon in the 1960s was also to be found in Syria. Suleiman El Issa, writer of poems, plays and stories, wanted to arouse national consciousness among the young. Other Syrian writers such as Abdullah Abd, Adel Abu Shanab and Zacharia Tamer were more concerned about the messages they intended to convey as opposed to the language and style. Consequently their writings were difficult for children to read and understand. Iraq saw a boom in children's literature in the following decade when foreign experts were called in to advise local writers on how to produce good books for children. All this unfortunately came to a halt at the time of the Iran–Iraq war in 1980, followed by the Gulf war and the blockade imposed on Iraq.

Egypt and Lebanon, therefore, continue to make the major contribution to children's literature throughout the Arab world while Iraq, Jordan, Tunis, Algeria and Kuwait encourage their own local authors. The revenue from the oil industry has been used to finance publishing houses, some specifically devoted to publishing for young people. There is a general recognition of the need for information books written in a stimulating and creative way, although from 1987 onwards there have been more books about science and technology, encyclopedias of the arts, craft books and compilations of general knowledge, as well as books on religious themes.

The need to encourage more writers and illustrators to work in the field of children's books remains, and there is also a need for a good network of children's libraries if books are to reach all children. Meanwhile, there are many magazines which are a comparatively low-cost way of getting good quality material to as many children as possible. *Sandouk El Donia*, founded in Egypt in 1978, offers the Arab child a magazine promoting national ideals and providing general knowledge. *Majalati*, established in Iraq in 1969, is a general-interest magazine for 5 to 14-year-olds. The Syrian *Ousama* [Boys], also founded in 1969, contains both fiction and information. *Majed*, a weekly periodical published in Abu Dhabi in the United Arab Emirates for 6 to 16-year-olds since 1979, is available in most Arab countries and aims to raise a generation of mature readers who 'believe in God and a unified Arab world'.

The cooperative attitude which appears to prevail in Arab countries is a great advantage, opening up a viable market for the publication of children's literature. One can conclude that children's literature in the Arab world is attracting significant attention locally and internationally.

## Further Reading

Abdel Razzak, J. (1993) 'Children's literature in Syria', *Arab Childhood* 26: 22–30 [Arabic].

Abou Said, A. (1979) *Development of Writing for Children in the Arab World*, Beirut: Lebanese Writers Union [Arabic].

Abu Nasr, J. (1986) 'Results of the evaluation of 826 children's books', *Arab Childhood* 6: 9–11; 7: 9–11 [Arabic].

—— and Nassar, A. (1987) 'Children's literature project in the Arab World', *Bookbird* 25, 4: 8–9.

Carus, M. (1990) *Children's Magazines: An International Survey*, New York: Carus Publishing.

Ghurayyib, R. (1981) 'Children's literature in Lebanon and the Arab World', *Bookbird* 4: 17–19.

Kuwait Society for the Advancement of Arab Children (1988) 'Writers and illustrators of children's books in the Arab World', *Arab Childhood* 24: 26–9 [Arabic].

Ramadan, K. (1988) 'Children's books in Kuwait', *Bookbird* 26, 2: 8–9.

## A Note on Iran

As a more detailed example of the development of children's literature in the Arab states, we can consider Iran.

Iran had a head start over most of its neighbouring countries in the establishment of schools but progress was slow and there were comparatively few books written for children in Persian (Farsi). About fifty such books are recorded as having been published before 1950. There was a heavy reliance on translations from foreign languages, and Iranian children were introduced to Western heroes such as the Italian Pinocchio in this way. There was felt to be a need for books which reflected the lives and experiences of Iranian children, and in 1962 a Children's Book Council was established. The great leap forward, however, came with the foundation of the Institute for the Intellectual Development of the Children and Young People of Iran in 1965 under the direction and patronage of the Empress of Iran, Farah Pahlavi. One of its most important aims was to improve the quality of children's literature by giving encouragement and support to writers, illustrators and publishers. In 1966 a publishing section was set up and the first publication was *La Fille de la Mer*, written by the Empress herself. Despite the deposition of the Shah, and the Islamic Revolution of 1979 with its subsequent political changes, and then the long-running conflict with Iraq, the activities of both the Institute and the Book Council have continued.

A magazine for children, *Keyhan Bacheha* [Children's Keyhan] began publication in 1956. At first most of the stories were translated from foreign magazines and bore little relation to the needs of Iranian children but after the Islamic Revolution, it began to include stories by Iranian authors about life and problems in both urban and rural Iran. Articles and illustrations also reflected the hardships of the war years.

A series of magazines known as *Roshd* are produced for very specific age groups; the earliest of these date back to 1964 and were intended to encourage the reading habit among children in rural areas. The content is closely geared to the abilities and interests of the target age group, and includes stories, legends, poems and information. *Ayesh*, founded in 1984 and published by the Institute for Intellectual Development especially for young people who are interested in literature and art, includes outstanding contributions from its readers. It also introduces past and present Iranian literature. In the 1990s, magazines, published by both government institutions and private organisations, are still an important source of leisure reading for Iranian children.

One of the first Iranian writers or illustrators to win international recognition was Farshid Mesghali (1943– ), who was the winner of the Hans Christian Andersen Award for illustration in 1974. He began his association with the Institute for Intellectual Development in 1967, illustrating both fantasy stories and folk-tales, and making animated films. His illustrations for *The Little Black Fish* by Samad Behrangi (1968) won the Graphic Prize at the Bologna Children's Book Fair and an Honorary Diploma at the Biennale Illustratione Bratislava (BIB) in 1969. Another distinguished book illustrator is Noureddin Zarrinkelk (1937– ) who, after illustrating a number of books such as *Amir Hamzeh*, a folk-tale, and *The Crows*, for which he won a Golden Apple at BIB in 1971, began to write and illustrate his own texts, *The Story of Silkworm* and *When I was Little*.

Iranian writers encouraged by the Institute for the Intellectual Development were at first very much influenced by traditional stories. *Kaleteh-Non* by Gholamhosein Saedi (1973) is the story of how the hard life of a farmer teaches a rich and lazy girl that it is necessary to work and earn one's living.

After the Islamic Revolution, fiction began to deal with the revolution, the war, poverty and the struggle against oppression. Despite the war, which led to publishers experiencing problems with equipment and to paper shortages, 359 books were published for children in 1980–1981. A title typical of this period was *Ai, Ebrahim!* [Oh, Abraham!] by G. Emami (1981), the story of an old shoemaker who cannot go to war but does his bit by repairing soldiers' boots. His work emphasises his faith and his devotion to his country.

H. Moradi Kermani has emerged as one of Iran's most important children's writers; he received the Children's Book Council of Iran's Award in 1980. *Quesehaye Majid* [The Stories of Majid], published in five volumes between 1979 and 1987, consists of short stories about a boy who lives with his old and wise grandmother. The hardships they experience and their struggle to preserve some of the old social values are humorously described. *Bachehaye Qalibafkhaneh* [The Children of the Carpet Weaving Mill] (1980) was an IBBY Honour book in 1982, and Kermani was highly commended for his contribution to writing for children in the 1992 Hans Christan Andersen awards. His work for children, including short stories, describes the hardships of the poor and village and rural life in Iran. His style is dynamic and colourful. He reflects universal and permanent values, and he challenges his readers with his readable stories.

Poetry is also enjoyed by Iranian children. In 1988, to celebrate the six-hundredth anniversary of Hafiz, a great mystical poet, six of his most famous odes were printed in a fine edition, illustrated by Bahram Khaef, another artist who has received much encouragement from the Institute for Intellectual Development, who began to publish his work in 1987. In 1990 *Shesh Gazal az Hafiz* [Six Odes from Hafiz] was included in the IBBY Honour List for illustration.

# 77

# Africa

## English-Speaking Africa

### *Jay Heale*

In the broadest outline, the history of much of Africa could be said to fall into three phases: original identity; dominant colonisation; independence. The same broad framework can be seen in Africa's literature for children: an original oral tradition of story-telling; the arrival of literacy and literature from abroad; and the growth (or not) of a new indigenous youth literature.

The British desire for empire brought the English language to such west African countries as Nigeria and Ghana, to Kenya, Uganda and Tanzania in the east, and to Zambia, Zimbabwe, Botswana and South Africa in the south.

Education was the key to employment in the British Empire. So literacy (in English) meant social and economic advancement. Schools were British-run, books were printed in Britain, and the benevolent white man knew best. It is little wonder that in shaking off the colonial yoke, some African countries have even considered ejecting that imported idea the 'book' (and the library) to return to their long-established oral tradition. For any institution to play an important role in society it must be legitimate and relevant. According to Adolphe Amadi, the dominant ethos of African society is at variance with the aims of libraries (Amadi 1981: 68–69). There is opinion that most Africans do not wish to continue with reading once their formal education has been completed 'they derive more pleasure from the oral and performing arts – talking, singing, dancing, socialising – than from the rather private and individual reading of a book' (Chakava 1984: 348).

However, as the present universal emphasis is for literacy, it would seem that the young people of Africa (even if not their parents) will be steadily introduced to more books. Must literacy arrive before there is 'literature'? For in the same way that children's literature includes the ability to 'read' pictures, so the first recording of African literature came in graphic style. Cave painting, rock engraving, woodcarving, painted pottery, delicate beadwork – all form part of African tradition and culture. They all have stories to tell.

## Oral tradition

Story-telling itself began beside the fire. Though no one sat down to analyse them, these tales told aloud probably had three main intentions: to preserve local history, to emphasise correct behaviour, and to entertain. Here were the stories of Anansi the story-spinning spider, the half godlike Mantis of the Bushmen, the unhurried and wise Tortoise, imperious Lion, and mischievous Hare 'the patiently tolerated, fiercely hated, yet beloved vagabond of all the peoples of Africa' (Savory 1990: 14). Crossing the Atlantic with the slave trade and finding new life as Brer Rabbit (in the *Uncle Remus* stories), the trickster Hare was one of Africa's early literary exports.

The first indigenous publishing for children was ardently didactic. This gave rise to the bitter joke: 'When the missionaries came, we had the land and they had the Bible. They then taught us to close our eyes in prayer. When we finally opened our eyes, we found that they had the land and we had the Bible.' So early literature for African children was confined to moralistic primers with a few safe folk-tales with a strong (inserted) moral flavour. Christian missionaries to 'darkest Africa' were frequently appalled at the approval of deceit and the casual cruelty of the folklore they encountered. In making the first written versions of African stories, these pious authors frequently reshaped the story to provide more suitable morals. Yet the stories were thus preserved, and (though the original tales were not specifically for young listeners) African children's literature had been launched.

## An unknown world

The English-speaking colonisers brought with them, naturally, English education. 'Fiction was intended to aid Christianisation and the teaching of literacy' (Schmidt 1981: 23). Into the missionary school came the 'English reader' book preaching the benefits of European lifestyle and values. All were written and published overseas. The situation is little changed today. As recently as 1988, Gloria Dillsworth (1988: 19) could write of the book scene in Sierra Leone: 'A wide range of fiction can be found in the children's library and the most popular authors are Enid Blyton, Susan Coolidge, Louisa May Alcott, Richmal Crompton, Franklyn W. Dixon, Carolyn Keene, Capt. W. E. Johns'. Then she does mention two Sierra Leonean authors, Clifford Fyle and Thomas Decker, but adds 'There are only a few children's books written by Sierra Leoneans and those which are in print can be found in the children's library though not in adequate numbers.'

The great age of the English adventure book resulted in a fictionalised picture of Africa. Such titles as R. M. Ballantyne's *The Settler and the Savage* (1877) indicate clearly the British-based bias. A few authors wrote from a brief acquaintance of Africa – like Sir Henry Rider Haggard, whose *King Solomon's Mines* (1885) was partly inspired by his visit to the Sudwala caves in South Africa – but many created a stereotyped Africa in which the residents were 'sometimes described as hideously scarified, naked, superstitious, bloodthirsty, and un-changing in their ways, and are called vagabonds, rascals, pagans, cannibals, ignorant brutes and "niggers"' (Schmidt 1981b: 64). Better informed writers, perhaps after a tour of duty in Colonial Africa, created kinder images of the inhabitants either as noble savages or dutiful servants.

Meanwhile, the popularity of such heroic tales as Edgar Rice Burroughs's *Tarzan of the Apes* (1914) continued to portray Africa as a land of jungle, inhabited mostly by animals. The many stories of Rene Guillot (written in French in the 1950s and 1960s but widely available in English translations) are factually correct, since he lived in Africa for over twenty years, but still perpetuate the atmosphere of savage beasts, witch doctors and naked warriors.

Almost the only genuine indigenous African story-telling to reach European readers was in the field of animal legend. There still remains a world interest in quaint folk-tale. So the Ashanti tales from Ghana by Peggy Appiah (for example, *The Pineapple Child* (1969)), the Nigerian folk-tales retold by Chinua Achebe (for example, *How the Leopard got his Claws* (1972)), and the Swazi, Zulu and Xhosa tales collected in southern Africa by Phyllis Savory (for example, *The Best of African Folklore* (1988)) have retained their popularity – as well as capturing in print some products of the dying oral tradition.

### Africa of the Africans

Those working with African children today can be in little doubt of the need for relevant local material. If books reflect a world that is foreign to children, then the concept of reading (and enjoying) books must also be foreign. Sheer 'book love' is not the only target of African authors, however. The Kenyan author Asenath Odaga emphasises the point that 'In Kenya, one of the writer's tasks is to decolonise the thinking of his readers ... He tries to make them discover and recover their dignity and honour which they had lost during colonial suppression' (Odaga 1988: 32).

But hard economics are often against such noble intentions. If so few people buy books, there is no profit in either writing them or printing them. Only in countries whose education system guarantees sufficient sales does local publishing thrive. (Many of those education systems are heavily controlled by the state, with a resulting pressure on authors to toe the official line.) This results in the oft-repeated cliché that in Africa books = school. At the IBBY Congress of 1984, devoted to children's book production and distribution in developing countries, a whole day was devoted to Africa. Francis Nyarko from Ghana emphasised: 'Most children in Africa see and handle books for the first time only in the classroom ... In most African countries the only books young people have access to are textbooks' (Nyarko 1985: 53).

The production of imaginative indigenous fiction, divorced from the textbook or school reader field, has emerged in appreciable quantity only in Nigeria, Ghana, Kenya, Zimbabwe, South Africa and (very recently) Namibia. Efforts there have begun to be supplemented by international publishers who produce an 'African' series of stories featuring black boys and girls in genuine localised adventures. Such series as the Heinemann Junior African Writers Series (JAWS) or the Macmillan English Language Teaching Services (MELTS) offer the advantage of an Africa-wide readership to indigenous authors. In this way, a young reader in (say) Kenya can meet stories about children in west or southern Africa. The difficulty in marketing books with a small print-run to a huge continent has been solved to a certain degree by a sponsored, non-profit organisation African Books Collective (in Oxford, England) which warehouses and publicises books from Africa. Among the children's section of their Catalogue No. 4, 1992, are five publishers from Nigeria, and one each from Kenya, Ghana and South Africa.

It is cheaper and therefore easier to produce books for older children, where black ink on fairly white paper (with perhaps a colour cover) is sufficient. Young children, who so *need* to be attracted to books, seldom find more than an extra single colour to enliven their picture books, and often the standard of illustration is not high. It is impossible in Africa to earn a living by writing for children, so the published authors are either writers for adults taking time off to write a junior story, or part-time (often mostly amateur) authors. In many countries, the infrastructure is missing. As Tötemeyer has noted: 'The considerable potential writing talent in Africa is being frustrated by a totally depressed publishing industry owing to a lack of foreign exchange to buy printing paper, machinery, film, chemicals, plates and spare parts. Financial institutions in most African countries do not as yet consider publishing a viable industry to lend money to' (10).

Add to this the lowest literacy rate of all the continents in the world. Then add to that the multiplicity of languages. In Nigeria alone there are 395 languages. Ghana has over forty and has attempted to produce books in eleven of these. Kenya has forty or more languages, with Swahili as the official luguage, though few Swahili books have been published. Zambia has seven official languages. South Africa now has eleven officially recognized languages; most children receive their first two years of schooling in their mother tongue. Who is to blame education authorities for using with relief the huge reservoir of children's literature available in English? Indeed, soon after independence, Namibia (which has the largest number of Afrikaans speakers of any country in Africa) opted for English as the official language for all education. Zambia too chose English as the language of instruction in education since it was seen as a neutral language which would give no undue advantage to any one ethnic group. However, it has now been found that English has created 'a dichotomy between those who can, by virtue of their education participate, and those who cannot, for lack of it' (Siachitema 1992: 19). The prominence given to English has made the local languages valueless in terms of career advancement. In the face of such linguistic problems and present economic recession, one can only praise the creators of the books which *have* been published.

## West Africa

Among the titles which have attracted international acclaim from West Africa are *The Brassman's Secret* by Meshack Asare, *How the Leopard Got His Claws* by Chinua Achebe, while the IBBY Honour List for 1992 includes author Abenaa Korama for *The Cats and the Mice* and illustrator Therson Boadu for *Island of No Return* (both from Ghana).

Nigerian society is harshly polarised (as in so many African countries) into the literate minority and the illiterate majority. So it is not surprising to find the young heroes and heroines portrayed as ambitious, eager children 'whose main ambition is to go to school' (Lawal 1989: 11). The pioneer series in Nigerian children's literature is the African Reader's Library, where readers encounter such redeeming adventures as *Akpan and the Smugglers* by Rosemary Uwemedimo in which a boy struggling to restore his family's good name, receives a large reward for exposing a smuggling syndicate which saves his family from poverty *and* pays his own school fees.

One of the most prolific writers in Nigeria is Cyprian Ekwensi and his children's books have proved very popular. *The Drummer Boy* (1960) is about a blind boy in modern Nigeria, *Trouble in Form Six* and *Juju Rock* (1966) are set in high school, and the dramatic *Samankwe and the Highway Robbers* (1975) concerns the struggle to survive in the days after the Nigerian Civil War. A series of books about *Mr B* by Ken Saro-Wiwa (1987) reached wide popularity when they were used as the basis of a Nigerian television comedy series *Basi and Company.*

It is interesting to note that though many books of folk-tales have been published – including *The Drum and the Flute* by Chinua Achebe, *Stories My Mother Told Me* by Remi Adedeji, and *The Hunter and the Hen* by Oladele Taiwo – according to local expert Mabel Segun, 'While folktales are recognised as vehicles for teaching traditional values, librarians have found that most children do not *read* folktales although they enjoy listening to them being told' (Segun 1989: 8).

The stories of Geraldine Kaye (for example, *Kwasi and the Parrot* (1961), and *Kofi and the Eagle* (1963)) stem from her years spent in Ghana. Popular books by Ghanaian authors include D. K. Kwarteng's *My Sword My Life* (1972), J. O. deGraft-Hanson's *The Little Sasabonsam* (1972) and the picture story book *Tawia Goes to Sea* by Meshack Asare (1970).

Both Ghana and Nigeria are member countries of the International Board on Books for Young People (IBBY).

## East Africa

The 'wild animal safari' has become the cliché of East African children's books. Usually published in England, such stories perpetuated Africa as a land full of animals. Willard Price continued the genre with *Safari Adventure* (1966) and *Lion Adventure* (1967).

More realistic indigenous writing has come from the Kenyan teacher, Asenath Odaga, with such stories as *The Angry Flames* (1968) and *The Villager's Son* (1971). *Mweru the Ostrich Girl* (1966) by Charity Waciuma is by an author whose books have a Kikuyu setting. In a lighter vein has been *The Hippo Who Couldn't Stop Crying* (1972) by Susie Muthoni. Kenya has been a member of IBBY since 1988. Such previous English-colonial countries as Uganda and Tanzania rely mostly on imported children's books.

## Southern Africa

Botswana had the great benefit of having author Naomi Mitchison resident there for many years, and her children's stories (for example, *The Family at Ditlabeng* (1970)) have been rightly popular there. Modern publishing in Botswana has not progressed much beyond locally printed staple-stitched paperbacks, but Mary Kibel has had several stories published in such series as Oxford's 'Leopard readers' (for example, *Folk Tales from Botswana*).

Such adventurous publishers as Baobab Press and Anvil Press are producing good books in Zimbabwe. *Stories from a Shona Childhood* by Charles Mungoshi (1989), *The Village Bridge* by Andre Proctor, and several picture books by Margaret Tredgold (for example, *The Hare in the Moon*) have proved popular. The internationally accepted 'Jafta' books by Hugh Lewin originated with the Zimbabwe Publishing House.

Publishing for children in Namibia is a fairly recent innovation, but the vigorous support of the Namibian Children's Book Forum has led to a growing number of indigenous picture books, easy readers and folk-tales. Notable among these have been *Leonard the Land-Rover* (1984) by Liz McClain and Ginny Brain, *Monyenyane* (1992), an African Cinderella story by Jennifer Davis, and the surge of inexpensive little books created by a workshop collective (using local writers and illustrators) called New Namibia Books.

The country which has been the most prolific publisher of books for children in the African continent is South Africa. For political (as well as economic) reasons, these have not become available in other African countries. Though for years South Africa might be thought to produce only white-written books for white children, this has not been totally true. The English-speaking white population has been among the most liberal thinking in that country, and many fine books with a genuine African setting have been published there. For example, the percentage of children's fiction with a black central character in recent years has been: 1990: 43 per cent, 1991: 49 per cent, 1992: 54 per cent, with a marked increase of black authors writing for children (Heale 1993: 12). In the latter field are such acknowledged names as Es'kia Mphahlele (for example, *Father Come Home* (1984)) and Njabulo Ndabele (for example, *Bonolo and the Peach Tree* (1992)). Many South African authors and illustrators have had children's books published internationally, including Niki Daly, Marguerite Poland, Paddy Bouma, Lesley Beake and Maretha Maartens.

South African children's publishing in English reached a peak with 134 titles published during 1987, and has been sliding back each year since (1990: 104; 1991: 82; 1992: 68). The major publishers are Tafelberg, Human and Rousseau, Daan Retief, Maskew Miller Longman and David Philip, and quite a few children's books are optimistically published privately each year. Jenny Seed has remained the most prolific writer, with many acclaimed historical novels (for example, *The Great Thirst* (1971) and *Place Among the Stones* (1987)). Other local favourites have included *The Mantis and the Moon* (1979), new folk-style animal tales by Marguerite Poland; *The Strollers* (1988), about the street children of Cape Town by Lesley Beake; *Not So Fast, Songololo* (1985), a picture book about a modern urban African boy by Niki Daly, and *Child in Darkness* (1985), a poignant subterranean fantasy by Robert Hill. Stories written by the accomplished story-teller Gcina Mhlophe (for example, *The Singing Dog*) have found wide readership. Coverage of Southern African children's literature is kept up to date by the magazine *Bookchat* which was founded in 1976 by Jay Heale. The acceptance (in 1992) of South Africa as a national section of IBBY – represented by the Southern African Children's Book Forum – has done much to boost local publishing pride.

South Africa is on the brink of a new constitution and a fresh educational dispensation. There is already a strong emphasis on literacy (for non-literate adults as well as underprivileged children) and local publishers are hoping that money will be found for improved library provision as well. The READ Organisation having already done admirable work in providing libraries in black schools, has now launched its own 'Little Library' kit (1993) with ten carefully workshopped, full colour picture books, and a programme of teacher training to support its use.

One hopes that a greater cultural interchange will grow between the English speaking (or using) countries of Africa. As Professor Eldred Jones, of the University of Sierra Leone, has so rightly stated 'In ideal circumstances, the majority of books used at all stages of education in Africa should be produced in Africa. They would then most fittingly reflect the environment of the readers and be most relevant to their needs' (Dillsworth 1988: 21).

## French-Speaking Africa

### *Marie Laurentin*

After their independence around the 1960s, twenty African countries kept – from their colonial past – French as their official language and as their language in education. Benin, Burkina Faso, Burundi, Cameroun, Central African Republic, Comoros, Congo, the Ivory Coast, Djibouti, Gabon, Guinea, Madagascar, Mali, Mauritania, Niger, Rwanda, Senegal, Chad, Togo and Zaïre therefore have a common ground from which a literature for youth is beginning to emerge, despite the diversity of their culture, of their history, of the people that are part of them and the multiplicity of their spoken tongues. It is singular that this literature is developing, with very few exceptions, in a language which is not normally used by the children.

A UNESCO conference in 1968 on the development of books in Africa marked the first specific attention given to African children in this field. Despite this move, these independent countries have seen the development of a literature for adults, while for children, only heavily Westernised books for learning to read have been available. Education is in fact the priority for most states; the only books for entertainment originate in Europe, have no links with the local environment or culture, and are found (and then rarely) in parish libraries or schools.

Since the last decades of the nineteenth century, religious materials were produced and distributed, often in great numbers, by the Christian missionaries. They have not been studied in detail, but the evidence suggests that they had a considerable impact on the young, and reinforced the 'sacred' character of the printed page. Traditional oral tales were also transcribed and distributed by the missionaries.

The mission school is therefore the best place to approach textbooks for children. Since the 1930s, some books attempted 'Africanisation' by including 'selected pieces' from the rich stock of tales. However, the expression of the imagination remained linked to the oral, while the written page was linked to education, and so written texts kept their didactic and moralising character. Even the books first written for use outside schools did not escape this influence.

African conceptions of the child's personality, psychology, family relationships and place in society differ profoundly from those of the Western world. Traditionally, children are taught by their mothers in their early years. In rural areas, they are expected to contribute to the family income and join in adult social life. In this context, in the rare cases where the book is present, it represents a form of individual and 'anonymous' communication which does not fit easily into a culture where the oral tradition is strong and there is a keen sense of collectivity. Its content can be frightening, and it can threaten to separate the reader from society. 'If the act of reading becomes a solitary act, and if those who practise it are treated as "whites" it is because it also symbolises a certain power, that which comes from appropriating the foreign culture' (Traoré 1987: 5). So the book may well be perceived as a means of social advancement and as a tool for learning rather than as a means of escape and enjoyment.

Youth literature began at the time of the greatest social change. With decolonisation came modernisation, a rural exodus and its corollary urbanisation, the disruption of traditional structures and values, and variable access to education. Children's books can only flourish in the right economic conditions; books which do not generate large profits are not a priority. Today, there are few places, such as libraries, where books can be read without charge (although these are increasing). But the most significant element remains the degree to which the child has access to the French language, which depends on the location, literacy, education, social situation and country. In the majority of cases, the first contact with French would be at the elementary school, at about 6 to 7-years-old. But despite this, when books were available, the thirst to read shown by the young was remarkable.

The first real writing for children, at the beginning of the 1970s, came largely from a handful of famous publishing houses: Nouvelles Editions Africaines of Senegal, the Ivory Coast and Togo, Les Editions Ceda of the Ivory Coast, St Paul in Zaïre, Clé in Cameroon, Présence Africaine in Paris and Senegal, the Ivory Coast, Cameroon, and Zaïre. They produced a small but significant number of publications, especially picture books and tales.

Today, the picture is much the same – a small number of countries produce the majority of titles. In 1994, a glance at the catalogues shows that the publishing leap between 1975 and 1985 has been followed by stagnation, caused by the fragility of the publishing houses, by the price of books being more than ever out of reach for families, by the unequal promotion of reading, by the lack of distribution structures and perhaps by a lack of will to write and illustrate for children. There are, however, some new trends. New publishers have emerged, with new publishing strategies – cooperatives, self-publishing, co-publishing ventures using public or private finance – often motivated to produce an affordable, truly local product.

The survey, *Livres Africains pour la Jeunesse* (1994) initiated by La Joie par les Livres, uses the following criteria: books must have been designed for children, but not be schoolbooks; they must either have been published by African countries or have an African author and/or illustrator, or derive from the traditional African oral heritage. The limited number of these works (about 300), together with the diverse origins of their authors, publishers, and where they were printed underlines the heterogeneous character of African literature for children. The survey lists forty-two picture books, nine comic books, twenty-three illustrated stories, seventy-two novels, fifteen books of poetry, forty-one illustrated tales, forty-two books of tales, and sixty works of non-fiction. To these must be added a very small number of works in national languages (for example in Senegal, Mali and Zaïre) which have very limited distribution, and those published by missionary organisations, whose numbers are not known precisely.

There has been a paradoxical disproportion between the number of books published for children and books published for adults. In 1982, according to Kotei, about 50 per cent of the population was under 15 years of age, but only 5 per cent of the publications were designed for them. Ninety per cent of African publishing was utilitarian non-fiction. These figures have not changed much since that date.

Recent, heterogeneous, and usually little-known, literature for children in francophone black Africa has been until recently the object of little research, but it is gradually gaining ground.

The first identifiably African books for the young are schoolbooks, but ones which broke with Western tradition; African writers were preferred, and the oral heritage was drawn on. Examples are *La belle histoire de Leuk-le-lièvre – cours élémentaire des écoles d'Afrique noire* [The Beautiful Story of Leuk the Hare – elementary course for the schools of black Africa] (1953) by L. S. Senghor and A. Sadji, or the reading book by A. Davesne and J. Gouin, *Contes de la brousse et de la forêt* [Tales of the Bush and the Forest] (1936) which remain reference points. These books, and others which were not for schools had a role in safeguarding oral literature. Animal fables have been illustrated in a variety of ways: the Senegalese illustrator G. Lorofi used a cartoon form for the adventures of the same Leuk, the clever hero of the West African tales, adapted from the work of Senghor and Sadji; T. T. Minan gathered the tales of Tôpé, the crafty spider (*Les aventures de Tôpé-l'araignée* (1985)); Amadou Hampâté Bâ gives us initiation tales in *Petit Bodiel* (1976). The tale, rightly or wrongly assimilated into children's literature, provides an inexhaustible source inspiration for anthologies, illustrated books, or original works such as *La chanson de la vie* [The Song of Life] (1990) of which V. Tadjo is both the author and the inspired illustrator. This leaves little room for illustrated stories depicting every-day life and reflecting the young child's familiar world, such as J. de Cavilly's *Papi* (1978), O. Akpaka and T. Midiohouan's *Connais-tu Riga?* [Do you know Riga?] (1990), and R. Fadiga and D. Marteaud's *La case* [The Hut] (1975). Customs, social life and beliefs find their expression more in the form of the novel: they form the framework (*Le mineur détourné* [The Miner Led Astray] (1988) by B. Sy, *Halimatou* (1987) by A. Kanta, and A. Banto Djerzon's *Ouly la petite danseuse* [Ouly the Little Dancer] (1980)), or become the subjects of contention (*Quatre semaines pour grandir* [Four Weeks to Grow Up] (1992) by M. S. Diakité), being close to what can be called 'educational' novels (*L'enfant noir* [The Black Child] (1994) by L. Camara; *L'aventure d'Albarka* [The Adventures of Albarka] (1981) by A. Clair and B. Hama). The social upheavals (*Pain sucré* [Sweet Bread] (1983) by M. L. Martin-Koné), the onset of modernity (*Le voyage d'Hamado* [Hamado's Journey] (1981) by B. M. Say), the urban universe as place of all dreams and all dangers (*Le réveillon de Boubacar* [Boubacar's Christmas Eve] (1981) by J. de Cavally), and the struggle to survive (*Les enfants de la cité* [The Children of the City] (1987) by S. Njami) are a source of constant inspiration, while the references to the past, such as the evocation of slavery or the colonial period, have a few echoes. There are some new subjects, which, although rarely approached, show new trends: delinquency (*La mauvaise passe* [The Bad Pass] (1990) by A. Diouri), political repression (*Un matin pour Loubène,* [A Morning for Loubène] (1991) by P. N. Nkashama), and the place of women (*L'oiseau en cage* [The Bird in the Cage] (1984) by D. Zanga-Tsogo). Non-fiction has been the poor relation: examples are the historical *La fin héroïque de Babemba, roi du Sikasso* [The Heroic End of Babemba, King of Sikasso] (1980) by C. O. Diong, or accounts of every day life (*Moussa et Amina au village* [Moussa and Amina in the Village] (1985) by J. H. Kihm. More scientific books are still very rare, but a new, simple and cheap encyclopedia, which covers scientific themes in a well-organised manner, has appeared: the *Encyclopedia Afrique Jeunes.* Some books are on the borderline, using traditional tales to convey, for example, a message about health.

Comics are read widely; African comics have asserted themselves and are very diverse – from the life story of a great person to police adventures (*L'ombre de Boy Melakh* [The Shadow of Boy Melakh] (1989) by S. Fall). In a style sometimes reminiscent of the West, but with an inspiration and a humour which is entirely African, writers such as B. Baruti in Zaïre, S. Fall or G. Lorofi in Senegal have been very successful.

Many writers, such as J. de Cavally, F. Ndiaye Sow, Th. Ndiaye, J. M. Adiaffi and T. Boni, come from the world of teaching: more knowledge about children's wants, needs, interests and difficulties has allowed entertaining books to be written. Recent books are more realistic and simpler, and make more use of dialogue. This new generation of writers is without doubt closer to the public (for example, V. Tadjo, S. Njami and N. Thiam); similarly, the illustrators have broken away from tradition, and have used more personal styles (M. Seka Seka, J. Daïkou). Many important writers for adults have written for this new public – L. S. Senghor, A. Hampâte Bâ, J. M. Adiaffi, W. Sassine, B. Dadié, G. Menga, P. Ngandu Nkashama, F. Bebey, although usually in a single piece of work.

Reading networks have evolved, the 'non-school' book has entered the school (sometimes thanks to national programmes); children's books are acquiring recognition and are written by 'real' writers for children. Professionalisation, courses in creative writing, international exchanges, book exhibitions, visits by writers to schools, the creation of bilingual works or books in national languages, competitions and literary prizes are all indicators of the vitality – against all odds – of this literature. New editions, often less 'luxurious' than before, but produced locally, open new perspectives. The two objectives – education and entertainment – although still linked, are becoming more distinct.

It is the cost and the poor distribution of the books both inside and outside their countries of origin which remain the main impediment to development.

# References

Amadi, A. (1981) 'The emergence of a library tradition in pre- and post-colonial Africa', in *International Library Review* 13: 68–69.

Chakava, H. (1984) 'Reading in Africa: some obstacles', in *IFLA Journal* 10, 4: 348–356.

Dillsworth, G. (1988) 'Children's and Youth Literature in Sierra Leone', in *African Youth Literature Today and Tomorrow*, Bonn: Deutsch UNESCO-Kommission.

Heale, J. (1993) *SACBIP 93: South African Children's Books in Print (Supplement)*, Grabouw: Bookchat.

Kotei, S. I. A. (1982) *Le livre aujourd'hui en Afrique* [African Books Today], Paris: Les Presses de l' Unesco.

Lawal, O. O. (1989) 'Children in fiction: the Nigerian perspective', in *Bookbird* 27, 2: 9–12.

*Livres africains pour la jeunesse* [African Books for the Young] (1994) Paris: Les amis de la Joie par les livres.

Nyarko, F. (1985) 'The production and distribution of children's literature in Africa: a diagnostic survey', in *Children's Book Production and Distribution in Developing Countries* (19th Congress of the International Board on Books for Young People), Nicosia: Cyprus Association on Books for Young People.

Odaga, A. B. (1988) 'The job of a writer and book production in Kenya', in *African Youth Literature Today and Tomorrow*, Bonn: Deutsch UNESCO-Kommission.

Savory, P. (1990) *The Little Wise One: African Tales of the Hare*, Cape Town: Tafelberg.

Schmidt, N. J. (1981) *Children's Fiction about Africa in English*, New York: Conch Magazine.

Segun, M. (1989) 'The image of old age in Nigerian children's literature', in *Bookbird* 27, 2: 5–8.

Siachitema, K. (1992) 'When nationism conflicts with nationalist goals', in *Democratically Speaking*, Salt River, South Africa: National Language Project.

*Takam tikou. Le bulletin de la Joie par les livres* [The Bulletin of the Joy of Books] (1989, 1992, 1993, 1995), 1, 2, 3, 4, 5 1995 Paris: Les amis de la Joie par les livres.

Tötemeyer, A.-J. (1992) 'Speaking from a book: the transfer of de-recorded information to the information starved', *Newsletter* 12, 9, Pretoria: South African Institute for Librarianship and Information Science.

Traoré, R. (1987) *La litterature d'enfance et de jeunesse en Afrique. L'exemple de la Côte d'Ivoire* [The Literature of Childhood and Youth in Africa. The example of the Côte d'Ivoire], Abidjan: Cerav.

## Further Reading

Brunot-Derioz, M. (1992) *Une littérature francophone d'Afrique noire pour la jeunesse?* [A Francophone Black African Literature for the Young?], Paris: Universite Paris XII.

Chevrier, J. (1986) *L'arbre à palabres. Essai sur les contes et récits traditionnels d'Afrique Noire* [The Tree of Palavers: An Essay on the Tales and Traditional Stories of Black Africa], Paris: Hatier.

—— (1992) *Ecrivains de langue française. Afrique noire, Maghreb, Caraïbes, Océan Indien* [Writers in the French Language. Black Africa, Maghreb, Caribbean, Indian Ocean], Paris: Club des lecteurs d'expression française.

Cilliers I. (ed.) (1988) *Towards Understanding*, Cape Town: Maskew Miller Longman.

Jenkins, E. (1993) *Children of the Sun: Selected Writers and Themes in South African Children's Literature*, Johannesburg: Ravan Press.

Konaté, S. (1993) *La littérature d'enfance et de jeunesse en Afrique noire francophone: Burkina Faso, Côte d'Ivoire et Sénégal. L'impérialisme culturel à travers la production et la distribution du livre pour enfants* [The Literature of Childhood and Youth in Francophone Black Africa: Burkina Faso, Côte d'Ivoire and Sénégal. Cultural Imperialism through the Production and Distribution of Children's Books], Ottawa: Bief.

Ormerod, B. and Volet, J. M. (1994) *Romancières africaines d'expression française* [African Women Writers in French], Paris: L'Harmattan.

Patte, G. and Hannesdottir, S. K. (eds) (1984) *Library Work for Children and Young Adults* in the Developing Countries/*Les enfants, les jeunes et les bibliothèques dans les pays en voie de développement*, Munich: K. G. Saur.

Pellowski, A. (1980) *Sur mesure. Les livres pour enfants dans les pays en développement* [Made to Measure. Books for Children in the Developing Countries], Paris: Unesco.

# 78

# The Indian Sub-Continent

## *Manorama Jafa*

The Indian sub-continent comprises five major countries: India, Bangladesh, Nepal, Pakistan and Sri Lanka; all except Nepal were part of the British Empire until the 1940s. Though politically independent today, these countries have over one sixth of the world's population and are related to each other geographically, historically and culturally. Apart from English, these countries share at least one major language with India.

The sub-continent is extraordinarily rich in tales and folklore and this vast reservoir of traditional literature has been an important source of stories for children. The oral tradition of children's literature goes back more than five thousand years, and the world's oldest collection of stories for children, India's *Panchatantra*, derives from this.

In these countries, the child has remained an integral part of the family, the nucleus of community life, and art and literature have developed for the enjoyment of the entire family. Only in recent times has the child gained a separate identity and this is reflected in modern literature for children. The concept of children's literature as a separate discipline has come from the West; contact with European countries, and particularly with England and the English language, has led to the growth of modern literature for children. The English language still enjoys a privileged status in these countries.

The development of children's literature in the sub-continent has passed through three distinct phases. Initially, the stories from the oral tradition, mythology, religion, folk-tales, legends and classics were adapted and rewritten. Then there were translations and adaptations of material already published in England and other European countries and also in different native languages. Original creative writing has appeared only in recent years.

With improving literacy levels and the setting up of new schools, demand for textbooks has increased over the years, and supplementary reading material has also developed alongside. The reasons for the slow growth of modern literature for children were the preoccupation of the publishers with the production of school textbooks and supplementary readers, the multiplicity of languages, lack of demand, poor purchasing power and high production costs. Moreover, these books continue to be treated, by and large, as an appendage to the textbook programme. Libraries for children are few, and institutional and individual purchases are small. Besides, the promotion of reading is not a very high priority for parents.

The books have to have low prices, and most of the books are therefore available in soft cover. There are also problems with the availability of appropriate skills in writing, and facilities for illustration, book design, printing and production. In spite of these limitations there is growing consciousness of the importance of children's books for reading pleasure.

The increased interest in the development of indigenous literature for children has led to the organisation of seminars, conferences and training programmes in the sub-continent. Institutions and organisations to promote literature for children have been established, and delegates from these countries have also participated in seminars, conferences and book fairs in other countries, availing themselves of opportunities for interaction. India and Sri Lanka are members of the International Board on Books for Young People (IBBY) and participate in the Bologna International Children's Book Fair.

The Asian Cultural Centre for UNESCO (ACCU) in Japan has made a valuable contribution to the growth of children's literature in these countries since 1983 by organising training programmes, recruiting experts from the developing countries themselves, who have a better understanding of local problems, and encouraging production of better books for children. The ACCU's Noma Concours for Picture Book Illustration, given to picture book illustrators from developing countries since 1978, has promoted children's book illustrations and picture books.

## India

India has a rich heritage of ancient oral tradition, of which the *Panchatantra* is part. These stories were compiled by Vishnu Sharma to teach *Niti*, which could be roughly translated as 'the wise conduct of life', to three sons of a king. In all, there are eighty-four stories and many more interpolated anecdotes – which was a typical Indian way of story-telling to keep the interest alive. Before the *Panchatantra* came to be written, the stories had already been disseminated from India with travellers to west Asia and also to European countries. Today, these tales have been translated and adapted in over two hundred languages around the world: 'The monkey and the crocodile', 'The blue jackal', and 'The flight of pigeons' are widely known.

India is a large country with an area of 3.28 million square kilometres, and 880 million people. The country is divided into twenty-five states, with seventeen main languages and 1,652 dialects. The literacy rate is 53 per cent. There is an abundance of tales, folklore, myths, legends and also tales connected with festivals, cities, rivers and mountains. India is the birthplace of four major religions – Hindu, Buddhist, Jain and Sikh – and home to many other religious groups: religiously orientated stories are therefore plentiful. Besides, *Kathasarit Sagar*, *Jatak*, *Puran*, epics of *Mahabharat* and *Ramayan* and other classics have also been a perennial source of stories.

Books for children, as a separate genre made a beginning after the establishment of the School Book Society by the Christian missionaries in Calcutta in 1817. Several well-known books published in English were translated into Indian languages and traditional Indian tales were rewritten and adapted for children.

Soon the writers in Indian languages began to publish stories for children and the publication of magazines in different Indian languages promoted new writing. Early in the twentieth century it was recognised that children needed special reading material. By 1930 illustrated story books for children started appearing in the Indian languages, and today, an increasing number of books are being published, although the publication of original and creative writing is still in a low key. A large number of books continue to draw upon traditional and already published material. Some good plays, nursery rhymes, biographies and information books are also being published.

### English

The quality of writing, illustration, book design and overall production in English-language books has reached an excellent level. Despite the support from central and state governments, the regional language publications have not been able to match the quality of books in English; even if the manuscripts are rich in content, the production quality is far from satisfactory. This is happening despite the fact that the sale of books in some Indian languages is higher than of books in English and the market is growing every year.

The present day book scene owes much to the setting up of the Children's Book Trust (CBT) in 1957. Founded by K. Shankar Pillai, a political cartoonist, CBT is an exclusive children's book publisher and has long been a trend setter. CBT brought out its first set of two illustrated books in 1961: *Kings Choice* (English) written by K. Shiv Kumar and illustrated by Reboti Bhushan, and *Varsha Ki Boond* (Hindi) by Kusmawati Deshpande and illustrated by K. K. Hebbar. India's first picture book *Home* (English) written by Kamla Nair and illustrated by K. S. Kulkarni was published by CBT in 1965. The same year CBT also published *Life with Grandfather* and *Sujata and the Wild Elephant*, both written and illustrated by Shankar. The first picture book for pre-school children *Three Fish* written by Dolat Doongaji and A. K. Lavangia, and illustrated by Pulak Biswas was published by CBT in 1966.

CBT set up its own printing facilities and also engaged artists on its staff. The quality of writing, art work, book design, printing and binding was better than books published by any other Indian publisher. Most of the titles published by CBT were in English and translations were brought out later in some major Indian languages, using the same illustrations and the same format. Almost all the picture books were of 18 cm × 24 cm size, a size chosen to avoid waste of paper. The books were in soft cover and were low-priced in order to reach a wider audience. This is an excellent example of publishing in a multi-lingual environment. CBT's publications took note of the requirements for different age groups of children and brought out books with suitable text, typography and illustrations.

CBT looked for new talent in writing and illustration, endeavoured to upgrade skills, and remained open to new ideas. To encourage new writing they organised an annual competition for writers in English (from 1978) and published selected manuscripts. The first adventure story in an Indian setting in English for teenagers was *Kaziranga Trail* by Arup Kumar Dutta, published by CBT in 1979. To develop skills in writing, CBT established a Workshop for writers and later published a book *Writing for Children* by Manorama Jafa. In 1979, they organised the First International Children's Book Fair in New Delhi, which provided a welcome exposure to children's books from different countries.

Among other publishers in the English language is the National Book Trust (NBT), a government-owned institution, publishing common reading material in Indian languages including English and Hindi since 1969 under the Nehru Bal Pustakalaya Scheme. The National Council of Educational Research and Training (NCERT), another government organisation, established in 1961, has also been bringing out supplementary reading material along with textbooks for schools.

The Year of the Child, 1979, saw a sudden spurt in children's publishing. India Book House and Thompson Press published excellent books in the early 1980s but have since ceased to publish children's books. The main publishers in English apart from the above are Anada, Delhi Press, Dreamland Publishers, Frank Brothers, Hemkunt, Penguin, Ratnabharati, Ratna Sagar, Rupa and Co. and Vikas. An interesting feature of English book publishing is that it is largely based in the capital city of Delhi.

There are several magazines for children in English and the prominent ones are *Children's World*, *Champak*, *Junior Quest*, *Tamasha*, *Tinkle* and *Target*. *Cub* is a well produced specialist magazine on wild life. *Science Reporter* is also a specialist magazine. Another milestone in the development of children's literature was the establishment of the Association of Writers and Illustrators for Children (AWIC) in 1981 in New Delhi. Founded by K. Shankar Pillai, AWIC has contributed immensely to the development of better books for children. It has provided a vibrant forum for debate and discussion. It organises workshops for writers, evaluates their work, provides guidance and also assists in the publication of their work. AWIC has published a quarterly journal *Writer and Illustrator* since 1981. They have also published a catalogue, *Indian Illustrators 1960–1992*. AWIC has organised a chain of children's libraries and was awarded the IBBY-Asahi Reading Promotion Award in 1991. It organised the first national exhibition of picture books in 1993 and will host the 26th Congress of the International Board on Books for Young People (IBBY) in 1998.

Among the well-known writers in English are Ruskin Bond, Mulk Raj Anand, Shankar, Manorama Jafa, Arup Kumar Dutta, Nilima Sinha, Kavery Bhatt, Pratibha Nath, Vernon Thomas, Dilip Salwi, Ira Saxena, Deepa Agarwal and Manoj Das. Some of the well-known illustrators of children's books are Reboti Bhushan, Jagdish Joshi, Mrinal Mitra, Mickey Patel, Pulak Biswas, Ramesh Bagchi, Niren Sengupta, Atanu Roy, Phalguni Das Gupta, Subir Roy and B. G. Verma.

### Hindi

Hindi is the national language of India and is spoken by about 45 per cent of its people. The history of children's literature in Hindi can be traced back to the riddles in verse written by Amir Khusro in the fourteenth century. In the nineteenth century, Raja Shivprasad wrote many books: the better-known ones are *Bachchon Ki Kahani* (1867) *Raja Bhoj Ka Sapna* (1876) and *Larkon Ki Kahani* (1876). The Hindi writers took full advantage of the source material like the *Panchatantra*, *Ramayan*, *Mahabharat* and the legends. Bharatendu Harishchandra wrote a humorous book *Andhernagari*. Besides, translations of *Robinson Crusoe* and many other English books for children were also published.

In the early twentieth century, a number of well-known writers began to write for children. Premchand wrote *Kutte Ki Kahanian* and *Jungle Ki Kahanian*, Sohan Lal Dwivedi's collection of poems, *Balbharti*, and *Bigul* and other patriotic poems earned instant popularity. During this period, several magazines also came out; the foremost of these were *Vidyarthi* (1914), *Shishu* (1915) and *Balsakha* (1917). The first full-length fiction for children was *Khar Khar Mahadev* by Narain Dixit, which was serialised in *Balsakha* in 1957.

At present, well known children's magazines are *Nandan, Champak, Balbharti, Balhans* and *Chakmak*. Two of the most popular magazines *Parag* and *Balmela*, after publishing for more than a decade stopped publication a few years ago. The Children's Book Trust started a competition for writers in Hindi in 1987 and also the Writers's Award. The winning manuscripts are published by CBT.

Some of the best known Hindi writers are Shyam Narayan Pande, Ram Naresh Tripathi, Subhadra Kumari Chauhan, Nirankar Dev Sewak, Vishnu Prabhakar, Vyathit Hridaya, Harikrishna Devsare, Swarna Sahodar, Manohar Verma, Sri Prasad, Shakuntala Sirothia, Jai Prakash Bharti, Nilima Sinha, Ira Saxena and Manorama Jafa. Many new young writers are also entering the field.

Today, the foremost publishers in Hindi are Arya Book Depot, Shakun Prakashan, Atmaram, Children's Book Trust, Delhi Press, Kitab Ghar, Parag Prakashan, Pitambar Publishing Company, Mishra Bandhu Karyalaya, Mishra Brothers, the National Book Trust, the National Council of Educational Research and Training, Sasta Sahitya Mandal, Umesh Prakashan and Vikas Publishing Company. Most of the Hindi book publishing is now centred in Delhi.

### Bengali

Bengali is spoken in the state of West Bengal and is a rich language in children's literature. The first magazine for children in India, *Digdarshan* was published in Bengali under the editorship of John Clerk Marshman, by Serampore Press in 1818. An important tradition in Bengali is that a large number of those writing for adults have also written for children, unlike writers in any other Indian language. Nineteenth-century children's literature was based largely on traditional and oral literature. In 1847, Ishwarchandra Vidyasagar, a teacher by profession, translated *Betal Pancabinsati* [Hindi: Betal Pachchisi]. He wrote several books for children. At this time translations of Hans Andersen's stories and Western masterpieces also appeared: 'The little mermaid' was translated by Madhusudan Mukhopadhyaya as *Matsaya Narir* (1857). In 1878, the magazine *Balak Bandhu* and in 1885, *Sakha* and *Balak* opened further avenues for both creative writers and illustrators. Rabindra Nath Tagore, a Nobel Prize-winner in literature wrote his famous poem for children *Bisti Pade Tapur Tupur, Nadey Eloban*, which was published in *Balak*. *Birpurus* an action-packed long poem by Rabindra Nath Tagore was published in a booklet form. It was colourfully illustrated by Nandlal Bose, a celebrated graphic painter. Tagore also wrote stories, poems and plays for children. In 1919, Abanindranath wrote *Barngtarbratn*, Sukumar Ray wrote and illustrated a collection of nonsense rhymes, *Abol Tabol*. His father had launched a children's magazine *Sandesh*, which was discontinued after Sukumar Ray's death. His son Satyajit Ray, the well-known film maker, restarted and edited *Sandesh*, and encouraged almost all the modern writers for children. It is one of the most reputed magazines in Bengali. He edited *Sandesh* together with Lila Majumdar and Nalini Das. Satyajit Ray wrote and illustrated a number of books and liked to illustrate his own stories. His notable books are *Gupi Gayen Bagha Bayen, Sonar Kalla* and *Prof Sanku*.

Bengal also produced many artists for children's books who have also illustrated books in other languages. During the last decade there has been a rapid growth of children's literature in Bengali. *Hasir Galpa*, written by Ashapurna Debi is very popular with children. In 1961, Shishu Sahitya Parishad was established, followed later by other organisations for the development of children's literature. Among well-known publishers in Bengali are Shishu Sahitya Samsad, Anand Publishers, Signet Press, M. C. Sarkar and Sons and Calcutta Publishers.

### Gujarati

Gujarati is spoken in the state of Gujarat and has an abundance of literature for children based on folklore. There are also plenty of translated books from other languages. In 1860, *Batris Putlini Virta* was written by Baji Bhai Amichand. During the third decade of the twentieth century, Giju Bhai Badheka started two periodicals, *Sikshan Patrika* and *Dakshinamurthi*. Through these periodicals Badheka promoted new authors. He himself published 150 books for children of which eighty books were published in the series *Bal Sahitya Mala*. Badheka's stories are very popular even today.

In Gujarati, writers have developed humorous characters. Gijubhai has written anecdotes of Advo. Hariprasad Vyas wrote *Bakore Patel* (1938). Jivram Joshi created humorous stories around new characters and published *Miyan Fuski* and *Chhako Ane Mako*. Among other well-known writers are Uma Shankar Joshi, Panna Lal Patel, Labhuben Mehta, Nagardas Patel, Mulshankar Bhatt and Hansaben Mehta. Many other writers also contributed to children's literature through children's magazines. Some of the important publishers are Ratnabharti, Anada Book Depot, S. S. V. Karyalaya, Lok Milap Trust, R. R. Seth and Company, Sanskruti Prakashan, Harihar and Sahitya Publishers.

### Marathi

Marathi is spoken in the state of Maharashtra. *Panchopakhyana*, a translation of *Panchatantra* was published in Marathi in 1825 by Mumbai Hind Shikshan Mandali. Later, a number of translations and adaptations of children's books from other languages and English were published. Children's literature in Marathi was influenced mainly by works in English; H. K. Damle translated several books from English. V. K. Oke wrote many original books – *Hindusthan, Katharaja* and *Mahamanimala*.

The American mission published a magazine, *Balabodhmewa*, in 1872, catering for Christian children, which contained mainly biblical stories. Several other magazines were also published in the late nineteenth century and early twentieth century. *Baljivan* was started by Ramanlal Shah in 1918 and later *Kishore* came out. These magazines promoted original and creative literature. N. D. Tamhankar's

*Gotya* (1940), a novelette, was published in the magazine *Khelgadi*. Tarabai Modak wrote original nursery rhymes and stories, Sane Guruji's *Shamachi Aai* is considered an outstanding book.

Since 1952, original writings have developed at a faster pace. There is the unique annual event, Pustak Yatra, when the writers of children's books in Maharashtra travel to different cities and towns and interact with children, and to publicise children's books.

B. R. Bhagwat's best-known titles are *Chandravara Swari*, and *Jaichinaval Kahani*, D. S. Desai wrote *Saha Sahase* and Jayant Narlikar wrote several books of science fiction. *Antaril Visphot* is Narlikar's most recent book. R. K. Atre wrote a play, *Guru Dakshina*. Ratnakar Matkari, Sai Paranjpe and Sudha Karmarkar have also written plays. Among popular writers are Sane Guruji, Tara Bai Modak, Jayant Narlikar, N. D. Tamhankar, V. G. Apte, B. R. Bhagwat and his wife Durga Bhagwat. The most well-known publishers in Marathi are Ghanshyam Prakashan, Adarsha Prakashan, Anada Book Depot, Rajhans, Sahitya Saurabh and Shree Harihar Pustkalaya.

### Kannada

Kannada is spoken in the state of Karnataka. In Kannada, children's literature began with the translation of *Panchatantra* stories from the Sanskrit by Durga Simha in AD 1035. Translations and adaptations from Sanskrit and European literature are an integral part of Kannada children's literature. About sixty years ago, an encyclopedia for children, *Balaprapanch* by S. Karanth was published.

From 1945 onwards, children's literature has taken great strides and creative literature has also developed. *Petemathenaji* by M. S. Puttana is a good example from this period. In 1940, *Makkala Pustaka*, a monthly illustrated magazine for children was brought out. *Bal Bharati*, another monthly magazine, publishes the work of new authors. An organisation called the Rashtrothana Parishat has a scheme for publishing biographies and other children's books.

### Malayalam

Malayalam is spoken in the southern state of Kerala where literacy has always been higher than in other states: the state has now achieved nearly total literacy. In 1876, a collection of Bible stories, *Balbodhini*, was published. Starting with re-told tales, translated and adapted books from traditional literature, children's books have been published in plenty. *Bilathivisesham* by K. P. Kesava Menon is one of the earliest travelogues in this century. Mathew M. Kuzhiveli has written about a hundred books for children, including translations, adaptations and abridgements from Indian and foreign languages. *Balan* (1948) a children's monthly, published works of new writers. Although there are good writers, such as V. Madhavan Nair and Sumang, many other writers prefer to translate and adapt children's books from other languages, and so the development of indigenous modern literature is still in a low key. Almost all picture books in Malayalam are translations from English. The State Institute of Children's Literature and D.C. Books have brought out original titles for teenagers in Malayalam. Some of the important publishers are D.C. Books, Kerala Sahitya Academy, Southern Languages Book Trust and the State Institute of Children's Literature.

### Oriya

Oriya is spoken in the state of Orissa. The first effort was made by Balkrishna Kar during the early 1930s when he prepared an encyclopedia for children, *Shishu Sarkhali*. Nandkishore Bal wrote Oriya lullaby songs *Nanabaya Gita* in two parts, in 1934. Children's literature in Oriya has largely developed in the last decade. The most well-known writers of children's books are Ramakrishna Nanda, Jagannath Mohanty, Balkrishna Kar and Manorama Mahapatra, and the main publisher is J. Mohapatra.

### Tamil

Tamil is spoken in the state of Tamil Nadu. In Tamil, *Avivekapurana Kurukathai* by Veeramamuniver is the earliest humorous story for children and was written in the eighteenth century. The development of children's literature was facilitated by the early arrival of printing presses. In 1940, the Christian Society of Nagercoil published a quarterly magazine for children, *Bala Deepihai*, to which Tamil writers from Sri Lanka and Malaysia also contributed. Later, many popular magazines for adults in Tamil included a separate section for children. The development of children's literature received great encouragement when an illustrated monthly magazine *Ambulimama* was started by A. V. Subba Rao at Madras in 1947. At present this magazine is published in eleven Indian languages simultaneously. This is an example of a successful magazine publishing in a multi-lingual society. Children's literature in Tamil is very rich in poetry and short stories based on traditional material. Novels, plays and biographies have also been written. In recent years two of the Tamil writers Al Valliappa and Kalvi Gopalakrishnan have made valuable contributions. Al Valliappa started the Association of Tamil Writers for children, which promotes children's literature and also awards prizes to Tamil writers.

### Urdu

In Urdu, Amir Khusro (1253–1325) wrote many riddles for children and his book *Pahelian* could be regarded as the first book for children in Urdu. *Rani Ketaki Ki Kahani* by Insha Alla Khan was published in 1893. Nazir Akbarabadi wrote a number of books for children on many subjects. Well-known writers of adult books contributed to children's literature in Urdu. *Abbukhan Ki Bakri* by Zakir Hussain has been translated in many Indian languages. Urdu has very rich humorous literature for children: *Chacha Chakkan*, stories by Syed Imtiaz Ali are delightful reading, and *Lambi Dahri* by G. P. Srivastava and Azim Beg Chugtai's story *Cricket Match* are classic examples. *Payam-E-Taleem*, a monthly magazine for children, started publishing in 1926. In the 1980s the Bachchon Ka Adbi Trust was set up which has published a number of picture books and enriched Urdu children's literature.

Among the most important writers in Urdu are Syed Imtiaz Ali, Qudsia Zaidi, H. G. Haider, Abdul Wahid Sindhi, M. S. Nayyar, Mushtaq Ahmed and Chugtai. Nurul Hasan Maktaba Jamia is one of the oldest publishers, and others include the Bureau for the Promotion of Urdu, the Urdu Academy and the Bachchon Ka Adbi Trust.

### Telegu

Telegu is spoken in the state of Andhra Pradesh. Christian missionaries published an illustrated book, *Pedda Balasiksha* in 1864, and since then, translations and adaptations from English and other Indian languages have been published. Kandukuri Veeresalingan translated and adapted Aesop's tales with illustrations, *Neeti Kadha Manjari* (1898) and also a volume of moral verses, *Neeti Deepika*. *Balageetavali* (1912) by V. P. Kavulu is the earliest collection of folk-songs for children. V. Venkatappaiah has collected 500 rhymes in *Pilla Patalu* (1982). Writing of novels for children started only after 1947 and among the popular ones are *Chandram* by Sabha, *Veedhi Gayakudu* by Narla Chiranjeevi and *Ratanala Loya* by R. Bharadwaja. The first magazine for children, *Bala Kesari* was started by a schoolteacher in 1941, and was followed by *Bala* in 1945, *Bala Mitra* in 1949, and later *Bala Chandrika*

In 1976, the Balala Academy was set up to promote children's literature and also to channel the creative energies of children. In 1979, the Academy produced a series of books including picture books.

### Punjabi

Children's literature in Punjabi has developed only since 1949 when Punjabi was accorded the status of an official language of the state of Punjab. Behari Lal Puri (1830–1885) was the earliest to write books for children. He wrote *Buddhi di Vadiayee*, *Vidya Da Ada*r and *Chup Rahne De Gun*. These books were, however, all didactic in nature.

Punjabi translations of Tarzan and Betal stories have been published and some rewritten tales are also available. Some of the better-known books are *Chirhi De Chonchle* by Dhanwant Singh, *Pappu Te Pari* by Rajendra Singh Atish, and *Tukk Khoh Laya Kanvan* by Gurdial Singh.

At present, the Punjab Text Book Board is the leading publisher of children's books. A cultural and literary society, Sarang, has created a separate wing for publishing children's books. Rama Rattan's Bal Preet Milnee (Kafla) is a unique organisation designed to introduce books to children by sending teams to different cities and towns every year.

*Pankhrian* is a well-produced children's magazine which promotes new writing in Punjabi; *Primary Sikhia* is another popular magazine for children.

## Bangladesh

Bangladesh became an independent country in 1971. Earlier, it was the part of British India's Bengal province and in 1947, it became the eastern wing of

Pakistan. Bangladesh has an area of 143,999 square kilometres and a population of 109.6 million. Bangla is the state language and is spoken by 95 per cent of the population; the literacy rate is 33 per cent.

Children's literature in Bangladesh has its roots in the oral literature of the sub-continent, and folk-tales and *Panchatantra* stories were an integral part of early childhood literature. Before the division of British India, children's literature in the Bangla language was shared with the Indian state of West Bengal. At the time of partition, many writers migrated from India, while several publishers shifted to India.

Betweeen 1955 and 1970, only a few books for children were published in Bangla language. These too were mostly based on the oral tradition. *Madhumati*, edited by Al Kamal Abdulla Chaba, an assorted collection of stories, poems and jokes for children was published in 1964. Several information books based on science were published between 1948 and 1968. *Bijananer Rajya* and *Abak Prithibi* by Abdullah Aalmuti are well known. In the past twenty years about 120 volumes of fairy tales have been published: *Sanjher Belar Rupkatha* by Ataur Rahman and *Bijan Baner Rajyakanya* by Habibur Rahman deserve special mention. *Bangla Shishu Sahitya Granthapanji* (1946–1971), a bibliography of children's books was compiled by Shamshul Huque and was published in 1974.

After the establishment of the Bangladesh Shishu Academy in 1976, the children's book scene has been changing. Supported by the Bangladesh government, the Academy has started publishing quality children's books, with low prices to keep them within the reach of children and they have been very popular throughout the country. *Golap Photo Khuker Hate* (1975) by Shamsur Rahman and illustrated by Rafikun Nabi, and *Khuki Kathberalee* (1977) are good examples of picture books published by the Academy. Since 1980, the National Book Centre and the Bangla Academy have also supported the development of children's literature.

Until recently, attention was paid only to publishing textbooks. Even the school libraries stocked either textbooks or books of religious and classical nature and biographies, written mostly in didactic form. Children's literature mainly developed in the form of supplementary readers. The available literature abounds in biographies, nursery rhymes, poetry, short stories and plays. The Central Public Library of Dhaka has a special collection of children's books, but library services are otherwise poor and individual buying is limited.

An interesting phenomenon on the Bangladesh book scene is that the total number of books published by the authors themselves outnumber those published by the publishing houses. The ratio of such books is 70:30 for fiction and 60:40 for other books. Among the writers of children's books are Shamsher Rahman, Kazi Abdul Quasem, Hossain Mir Musharraf, Mustassir Mamoon, Jobeda Khanam, Kazi Nazrul Islam, Abdul Hafiz, Tahera Huq and Abdul Al Muti. The best known illustrators of children's books are Hashem Khan, Rafikum Nabi, Kazi Abdul Quasem, Sitara Abraham, Qayyum Chowdhury, Asem Ansari and Abdul Bark Alvi. The active publishers are Bangladesh Shishu Academy, Muktadhara, Bohi Ghar and Adeylebros and Co.

UNICEF and the Asian Cultural Centre for UNESCO (ACCU), Tokyo have been assisting in training and other book-development programmes for children's books. These have helped immensely in the advancement of better literature for children.

## Nepal

Nepal is located on the southern slopes of the Himalayas and is the only country in the Indian sub-continent which has remained independent of foreign rule. Nepal has an area of 147,181 square kilometres of which 77 per cent consists of high mountains. The population of 18.8 million lives largely in the rural areas and the literacy is 29 per cent. Nepal was virtually closed to the outside world until 1951; however, the cultural links between Nepal and India have been close since ancient times. The bulk of the population is Hindu and the Hindu tradition and culture is shared with India. Nepali is the main language and is spoken by 58 per cent of the population. The Devanagri script of Nepali is also shared with India's national language Hindi. Besides Nepali, there are about fifty other languages and dialects spoken in Nepal.

Nepal has a rich tradition of oral literature in the form of tales, folk-tales, lullabies, tongue twisters and children's songs. Since literacy came late, most of the children's literature was confined to the oral tradition for a long time. The earliest children's literature is based on stories from *Panchatantra* and *Jatak* tales. The first books for children, in 1901, were in the form of alphabet books, and textbooks were brought out by Prithvi Bahadur Singh. During the 1920s poet laureate Lekhanath Paudyal wrote many poems for children.

In the 1950s, several publishers became interested in publishing reading material for children. Books of poems of this period are particularly notable, and the most well-known of these are *Putali* and *Sunko Biham* by Laxmi Prasad Devkota, *Gham pani* by Madhav Ghimire and *Ramaila Nani* by Krishna Prasad Parajuli. Some books of fables, folk-tales, biographies and information books were also published. Books of poems continue to have a prominent place: among other popular titles are *Tirmir Tara* by Sidhi Charan Shrestha (1988), and *Gaukhane Kavita* by D. R. Neupane.

In 1951, Sajha Prakashan, a cooperative publishing house, under the supervision of L. K. Devkota, started publishing children's books and encouraged new writers. The same year another publishing house Janak Shiksha Samagri Kendra also started publishing textbooks and supplementary reading material. In 1965, the first children's magazine, *Kopala*, came out; in the same year Nepal Bal Sangathan brought out some books and a magazine, *Balak*. Another organization, Bal Pustak, started publishing children's books in 1966. The movement for publishing children's books was further activated when the first seminar on children's books was organised in Kathmandu in 1966. Soon after, Ratna Pustak Bhandar brought out children's books under their scheme Bal Sahitya Prakashan.

The celebration of the International Book Year in 1972 included a seminar on Book Development and Reading Habits where the state of children's books was discussed. At the same time, a survey of reading habits of school children was conducted by the Sigma Mu society of Kathmandu. The survey results showed that one of the main causes of poor reading habits among students was the lack of suitable books.

Sajha Prakashan published several titles, including two volumes in 1977 under the co-publication programme of the Asian Cultural Centre for UNESCO (ACCU), Tokyo. In 1979, the Year of the Child, a few more publishers brought out new titles. *Ganesh Ko Laddu*, written by P. Sapkota and illustrated by R. Vajracharya was a popular picture book. A monthly magazine, *Bal Posh* was started and later, another bi-monthly *Bal Koshi* was launched in 1981. In 1982, *Kalilo*, a news magazine for children was also published. Today, the most popular children's magazine is *Balak*, which has been running for over twenty-five years. By 1983, the importance of illustrations in children's books was well recognised.

Exposure to quality books from other countries, participation in training programmes organized by the ACCU and interaction with writers, illustrators, editors and publishers from other countries influenced the further development of children's literature. Illustrators from Nepal regularly take part in the Noma Concours of Picture Book Illustrations of ACCU.

Books on science have also appeared in recent years; for eaxmple, *Pani Ka Thopa* by Kavita Ram introduces basic lessons in science and is one of the best known titles. The Royal Academy of Nepal gave encouragement to publishing better books for children. They have published *Balvigyan*, a book on science, by T. B. Shrestha and Bimal Man, and they have plans to publish information books for children.

The year 1987 could be regarded as a landmark in the development of children's literature in Nepal. The Royal Nepal Academy, with the support of UNESCO, organised a workshop for writers and illustrators of children's books. At this workshop, twenty dummies of picture books with texts were prepared and later on the Royal Academy undertook the responsibility of publishing these titles. On this occasion, two hundred children's books in Nepali were displayed. To keep the momentum alive, in 1987 Dr C. M. Bandhu and other interested persons formed Nepal Bal Sahitya Samaj (Nebasas) [Nepalese Society for Children's Literature (NESCHIL)], and they publish the NESCHIL newsletter on children's literature in both the Nepali and English languages. The most prominent writers of children's books are Ramesh Bikal, Churamani Bandhu, T. B. Shrestha, Dhruba Ghimire, M. L. Karmacharya, Dhruba Sapakota, Bhupa Hari Paudyal, Krishna Prasad Parajuli, Kalpana Bista and Parashu Pradhan. Some of the eminent illustrators are Tek Bir Mukhiya, Milan Shakya, Ratna D. Rajracharya, Mohan Khacka, Kul Man Singh Bhandari, Abha Mishra and Ram Kumar Pande.

## Pakistan

In 1947, when the British left India, Pakistan appeared as a new country on the world map, its two wings separated by more than one thousand miles of Indian territory. The western and eastern wings had little in common except the religion Islam, and in 1971, the eastern wing separated and became another independent country, Bangladesh. Pakistan has an area of 796,095 square kilometres and a population of 109.2 million. Urdu is the national language, although Sindhi and a few other languages and dialects are also spoken. The literacy rate is 26 per cent and is growing.

Pakistan has paid attention mainly to textbooks for schoolchildren and books for reading pleasure have not developed adequately. The slow development of children's literature in Pakistan is largely due to children's books being considered as an extension of textbooks. In 1964, the National Book Council of Pakistan published a bibliography of children's books and lists 1,288 titles; another bibliography published in 1973 lists 3,400 titles. The supplementary readers form the bulk under the category of children's literature. Most of the children's books comprise of biographies, stories from religious sources and some creative writing in Urdu.

The National Book Council of Pakistan, established in 1960, has promoted children's literature by organising workshops for writers and publishers. Recently some good titles have been published: *Batashay* (1979) by Abdul Ali Absar is a book of poems with colourful illustrations. *Beej Aur Boond* (1975) was published by the National Book Foundation and won the 1975 National Council Award for illustrations. *Hum Suraj Chand Sitare*, a collection of songs by Rais Farogh, and illustrated by S. Sajid Rizvi won the National Book Council Award for book production in 1978.

*Ek thi Jheel* (1973) by Meher Nigar Masroor, illustrated by Naheed Jafri, is profusely illustrated in colour and won the National Book Award and the 1973 UBL Literary Award for book production in 1972–1973. The National Book Foundation also published a humorous book for children, *Mulla Nasiruddin* (1975) by Mahmud Sham. The National Book Foundation in Pakistan has taken up the task of publishing low-cost illustrated children's books. They also get the books translated into regional and national languages and up to 1988 had produced 215 titles. In addition, another project was under way to bring out 90 titles in the next three years. Some leading private publishers like Ferozsons have undertaken publishing joint ventures with foreign collaboration.

The prominent writers in Pakistan are Meher Nigar Masroor, Ibne Insha, Muhammad Iqbal, Qamar Ali Abbas, Sharif Kamal Usmani, Mahmud Sham, Lakhat Saeed and Nazar Qayyum. The prominent illustrators for children are Naheed Jafri, A. Mansoor, Zaki Meer, Syed Sultan Akbar, B. A. Najmi, Samina Shahabuddin, Talat, Sajid Rizvi and Zahimeer. The prominent publishers of children's books are Ferozesons, Saeed Kitab, Tahir Sons and the government-supported National Book Council of Pakistan.

## Sri Lanka

Sri Lanka is an island country, separated from the Indian sub-continent by the narrow Palk Strait. With an area of 61,610 square kilometres and 16.9 million population, it is a mixed society of which 72 per cent of the population is Sinhala and 20 per cent Tamil, with other smaller communities making up the remaining 8 per cent. It is also a multi-religious society in which 67 per cent of the people are Buddhists, 17 per cent Hindus, 8 per cent Christians and 7 per cent Muslims.

Sri Lanka was part of the British Empire until it became an independent nation in 1948. The history and culture of Sri Lanka has close links with its neighbour, India. Sinhala and Tamil are the main languages and English is widely spoken. In addition, there are fifty other dialects. The most remarkable feature in Sri Lanka is its literacy rate of 87 per cent which is the highest in the Indian sub-continent. In spite of such a high literacy rate, Sri Lanka suffers from lack of indigenous children's literature.

The early literature for children comprised folk-tales, rhymes and songs in the form of oral literature. When the British ruled the island, the medium of instruction in the better schools was English; the textbooks and supplementary readers were imported from England and the books in Tamil were imported from India. The Sinhala-speaking children who comprised the bulk of schoolchildren were too poor to buy other books, with the result that for a long time no publisher came forward to publish books for children in Sinhala. The first books for children in Sinhala were written by Munidasa Kumartunga, Martin Wickramasinghe and G. B. Senanayake.

The government made education free for all from kindergarten to university in 1943 which led to a rapid increase in the number of school children. The adoption of Sinhala as the language of instruction in schools created the demand for books in that language and supplementary readers for use in school were developed.

Children's books of this period often contained questions and exercises for use in classrooms, although the quality of writing remained indifferent and unrelated to the interests of children or the requirement for different age groups.

Illustration, book design and book production also did not match the quality of imported books. Measures taken by the government to raise the level of literacy had an unintended adverse effect on the development of books. Thus, in 1956, schools were instructed not to ask children to buy more than one basic reader, and in 1963, the government decided to issue all textbooks free. These factors have depressed the demand for children's books. Besides, the high cost of production made children's books a luxury item.

Over the years, publishing techniques have improved immensely but good-quality literature is still a rarity. Most children's books draw on the oral tradition and are didactic. The number of books for reading pleasure have been increasing and about two hundred books in Sinhala and about fifty titles in English are now available. An example of the good-quality books now being produced is *Umbrella Thief*, written and illustrated by Sybil Wettasinghe, which was originally published in Sinhala in 1956. The English translation later won Japan's Maruzan Award in 1986. Sybil Wettasinghe has published several other books. She is also the secretary of the Sri Lankan Section of IBBY and an active member of the Children's Book Foundation. *Mihibata Surapura* (1974) written by K. Jayatilaka won the literary award as the best children's book of the year. *Labu Kiribath* (1975) written by K. G. Premaratna and illustrated by Sunil Jayaweera won the Academy of Letters award in Sri Lanka. *Deeptha Lama Maga* [Children's Bible in Sinhala] won an award for the illustrations in 1989. The Nirmana Institute, an organisation for the promotion of children's literature in Sri Lanka has taken up the publication of children's books to raise funds to assist writers.

Several children's magazines have been published: *Miniral* published by Lake House, *Wijaya* (1980) by Wijaya, *Suratmala* (1984) for pre-school children by Wijaya, *Bindu* (1986) for under twelves by Upali newspapers, and *Handamama* (1987) published by Little Rose are the prominent ones.

In 1983, ACCU supported a writers' workshop in Colombo. Later, the Nirmana Institute conducted two workshops on illustration for children's books, and the participants in these workshops joined together and formed the Colombo Book Association to promote children's books.

The best-known author-illustrators in Sinhala are Sybil Wettasinghe, Sunil Jayaweera and Mahagma Sekara. Some of the well known authors are K. Jayatilaka, H. D. Sugathapala and W. A. Abeysinghe. Among the publishers Gunasena, Hansa and Pradeepa publishers have made good contributions to children's books.

## Further Reading

### The Indian Sub-Continent

ACCU (1969–1993) *Asian Book Development Newsletter*, Tokyo: Asian Cultural Centre for UNESCO.
—— (1980) *Bibliography of Children's Books from Asia*, Tokyo: Asian Cultural Centre for UNESCO.
—— (1984) *Development of Writing for Children*, Tokyo: Asian Cultural Centre for UNESCO.
—— (1984) *Development of Educational Publishing for Children*, Tokyo: Asian Cultural Centre for UNESCO.
—— (1985) *Development of Illustrating for Children*, Tokyo: Asian Cultural Centre for UNESCO.
—— (1988) *Publishing in Asia/Pacific Today*, Tokyo: Asian Cultural Centre for UNESCO.
—— (1988) *Development of Children's Book Translation*,Tokyo: Asian Cultural Centre for UNESCO.
Carpenter, H. and Prichard, M. (1984) *The Oxford Companion to Children's Literature*, Oxford: Oxford University Press.
Jafa, M. (1982) *Writing for Children*, New Dehli: Children's Book Trust.
—— (ed.) (1981–1996) *Writer and Illustrator*, New Delhi [Quarterly Journal of the Association of Writers and Illustrators for Children (AWIC)].
—— (1991) 'Children's literature and research in India, Bangladesh, Sri Lanka and Nepal', in International Youth Library (ed.) *Children's Literature Research*, Munich: K. G. Saur.
Khorana, M. (1991) *The Indian Sub-Continent in Literature for Children and Young Adults*, New York: Greenwood Press.
Pellowski, A. (1980) *Made to Measure: Children's Books in Developing Countries*, Paris: UNESCO.

### India

Bharti, J. (ed.) (1985) *Who's Who: Children's Writers Editors, Illustrators*, New Delhi: Indian Council of Child Education.
CBT (1983) *Bibliography of Children's Books Published in India*, New Delhi: Children's Book Trust (CBT).
Devsare, H. K. (1980) *Who's Who of Indian Children's Writers*, New Delhi: Communication Publishers.
Hasan, A. (1977) *Promoting Books in South East Asia*, Madras: Sheshchalam and Co.
Jamuna, K. A. (ed.) (1982) *Children's Literature in Indian Languages*, New Delhi: Publications Division, Ministry of Information and Broadcasting, Government of India.
NBT (1992) *Select Children's Books 1989–1990*, New Delhi: National Book Trust (NBT).
Pattanayak, D. P. (1976) *Trends in Juvenile Literature in India*, Mysore: Central Institute of Indian Languages.

Tawney, C. H. (1927) *The Ocean of Story* [Translation from the Sanskrit of Somdev's *Katha Sarit Sagar*], Delhi: Motilal Banarsidas.

### Bangladesh

Huque, S. (1974) *Bangla Shishu Sahitya Granthapanji*, Dhaka: Jatha Grantha Kendra.
Ministry of Education (1983) *Education in Bangladesh*, Dhaka: Ministry of Education, Government of Bangladesh.
National Book Centre of Pakistan (1964) *Shishu Sahitya Granthapanji*, Dhaka: National Book Centre of Pakistan (NBCP).

### Nepal

Bandu, C. M. (1986) 'Children's literature in Nepali: creation and methods', Paper presented at the twentieth IBBY Congress, Tokyo, 1986.
Bandhu, C. M., Narhari, A. and Victor, P. (1985) *Survey of Nepali Children's Literature*, Kathmandu: Tribhuvan University (unpublished).
Karmacharya, M. L. (1985) *The Publishing World in Nepal*, Kathmandu: Laliguram Prakashan.
NESCHIL (1988, 1989) *Bal Sahitya, Journal of the Nepalese Society for Children's Literature*, Kathmandu: NESCHIL.
Royal Nepal Academy (1987) *Children's Books and Reading in Nepal*, Report on the proceedings of the Seminar on Children's Books and Reading in Nepal, Kathmandu, 19-22 August 1987, Kathmandu: Royal Nepal Academy.

### Pakistan

Hashmi, S. (1980) *Book Illustrations*, Karachi: National Book Foundation of Pakistan.

### Sri Lanka

IBBY (1990) *Sri Lanka Centre Newsletter*, Colombo: IBBY.
Jafa, M. (1984) 'Children's literature in Sri Lanka: the current scene', in *Writer and Illustrator*, New Delhi: AWIC: 3, 4: 14–18.
Sugathapala, H. D. (1978) 'Development of children and young people's literature in the Democratic Socialist Republic of Sri Lanka, in *Printed for Children*, Munich: K. G. Saur.

# 79

# The Far East

## Sheila Ray

In the diverse countries of the Far East, attitudes to the reading and publishing of children's books vary widely. Levels of literacy are generally related to the wealth of the country. Some countries have been swamped by British and American children's books, and have had to struggle against this flood of imports to produce indigenous children's literature. This is particularly true of Malaysia and Singapore where the influence of writers such as Enid Blyton is apparent. Political climates vary too. China, Mongolia and Vietnam, for example, have a very positive attitude towards children's books, and reading is seen as a popular activity. In the wealthiest countries, such as Japan and Singapore, life is earnest and children's books are assessed in terms of the contribution they make to the educational process. Japan has long imported and translated Western books, and now, in return, exports its own books to the West, where the work of Anno, the picture book author/illustrator, for example, is well known and admired. Singapore imports so many English and American children's books, with no need for translation, that local publishers see little point in trying to compete.

However, there are some notable examples of cross-border cooperation which try to overcome some of the problems involved in publishing books of high quality. The Asian Co-Publication Programme (ACP), which began its programme in 1973, is coordinated by the Asian Cultural Centre for UNESCO (ACCU) in Tokyo. The aim is to involve as many Asian countries as possible in producing low-priced picture books for areas that suffer from book shortages. Titles are planned by experts from twenty-three countries who pool their knowledge and suggest suitable topics and themes. Manuscripts with illustrations are submitted to ACCU in English and an English edition is prepared, which serves as a master. ACCU then produces duplicate sets of film which are distributed to the national agencies in the participating countries, who then organise the translation of the text into one or more of their indigenous languages, and publish and distribute the books in their own countries. By 1990, twenty-two titles had been published in twenty-six countries and thirty-eight languages. The topics chosen for the books include festivals, folk-tales and contemporary stories.

Thailand, the Philippines, Singapore, Malaysia, Indonesia and Brunei Darussalem also cooperate on a smaller scale within the Association of Southeast Asian Nations (ASEAN) through the Project on Children's Books and Source Materials, which is coordinated in Thailand by the Book Development Centre, part of the Ministry of Education in Bangkok. *Water, Water Everywhere* (1985) and

Doll's Party (1985) are good examples of ASEAN productions. Well produced, with information relevant to each of the six countries involved colourfully illustrated, they cover topics of interest to children. Through reading *Doll's Party*, children can learn about the different kinds of houses, foods and clothes to be found in each country, and learn the words of greeting used there. *Water, Water, Everywhere* describes how water is used in industry and in water sports, includes legends and descriptions of festivals connected with water, and tells the reader about the plant and animal-life.

In most countries of the Far East, despite the problems, there is a promising future for children's literature.

## Mongolia

In Mongolia there is a long tradition of oral story-telling and at an early age most children hear the popular tales of 'The White Mare of Tsut' or 'The White Little Orphan Camel', or the poem, 'The Young Hare', in which the hare describes his sufferings as he grows up with the threat of being hounded by dogs, shot by a hunter or snatched by a bird of prey.

*The Secret History of Mongolia*, containing the historical and literary oral tradition of the Mongols, which was first written down in the thirteenth century, includes a wide variety of stories about the origins of the Mongols, the life and deeds of Genghis Khan, fairy tales, and stories which contain gems of popular wisdom. One story which finds parallels elsewhere is the tale of Mother Alan Ghua who summons her five sons and demonstrates the idea that 'together we stand, divided we fall' by showing them that although each of them can break a single arrow, none of them can manage to break a whole bunch. Since it was translated from Old Mongolian into the modern Mongolian literary language in the middle of the twentieth century by Céndijn Damdinsürén, editions of *The Secret History* intended for children have appeared regularly. A new edition, illustrated in colour by S. Mižiddorž and with silhouettes by S. Torburam, was published in 1990. In the same year an illustrated edition of *Altan Tovč* [The Golden Summary] written in the seventeenth century and providing the same kind of stories as *The Secret History*, was also published for children.

The founder of modern Mongolian literature was Natsagdorge Dashdorge who wrote the *Pioneer's Hymn* for children in 1925. Since the 1950s writers who specialise in writing for children have emerged. For example, Ts. Damdinsürén whose titles include *Pioneer Camp* and *A Tale of Wishes*, and U. Basanjar, author of *The Golden Swallow*, are amongst the many authors whose books have found a ready response among readers.

Animals have always played a major role in Mongolian literature and sheep, dogs, horses, camels and cattle frequently feature in stories for children. Most children can recite the poem, 'My Tardy Lamb', which is said to appeal to all Mongolian children who are the descendants of cattle breeders. Although books by Hans Christian Andersen, Mark Twain, Astrid Lindgren and others are known in Mongolia, it is thought to be important to have books which contain images and characters familiar to Mongolian children. L. Tudeǔ, winner of a State prize for Literature, in *Vanity is Worthless* (1977) and *Discovering the World* (1987), uses autobiographical material to entertain children with stories about his boyhood, both at school and in the outdoor world amongst the Mongolian mountains. P. Horloo's *The Snap of the Whip* (1981) consists of three stories about the life of Mongolian nomads and their children. To encourage the creation of artistic works for children, a prize, The Golden Colt, is awarded every two years for outstanding work in writing, illustrating or making films for young people.

## Vietnam

In Vietnam children's literature has a clearly defined purpose; this is to prepare children for maturity by encouraging them to learn and work, and to love their country.

Books intended for pre-school and younger children make use of animal stories, folk-tales, legends and myths, to inspire a love of beauty, justice and honesty. *Chep Con Trong Ruong Lua* by Nguyen Quynh is a notable example.

The main characters in realistic fiction for older children are children who excel in their studies or who join their elders in fighting the enemy and helping to build their country, and adults who are good role models such as exemplary parents, excellent teachers or dedicated and loyal soldiers. In books intended to inspire patriotism a popular character is the brave and resourceful child who serves as runner for the army, but as well as emphasising the child's bravery authors are at pains to describe the beautiful countryside and its customs. Good examples of books set during the wars against the French and Americans are *Doi du Kich Thieu Nien Dinh Bang* [Little Guerrillas at Dinh Bang] by Kuan Sach, and Ho Phuong's *Khau Sung Nguoi Ong* [Grandfather's Gun].

There are also stories about school life such as *Mai Truong Than Yeu* [My Beloved School] by Le Khao Hoan, which describe children working hard and overcoming difficulties, emphasising the joy of making progress.

## Malaysia

Malaysia, like most countries, has a strong oral tradition. Story-tellers called *penglipurlana* used to travel from village to village telling stories. These might be animal tales about the witty mouse deer, Sang Kancil, humorous folk-tales about the dull-witted simpleton, Pak Pandir, or the luckless Mosque caretaker, Lebai Malang, or romantic folk-tales many of which take their plots from the Hindu epics, the Ramayana and the Mahabharata.

When the exploitation of natural resources began, the Chinese came to work in the mines and the Indians to work on the rubber plantations, and teachers came from China and India, bringing their own books with them.

After independence in 1957, Malaysia began to pursue an active policy to create a national language, culture, ideology and image. Traditional Malaysian folk-tales, including legends about the ancient Malay heroes such as Hang Tuah, Hang Jebat, Tun Perak and Panglima Away, were promoted. Bahasa Malaysia (Malay) became the official language although English, Chinese and Tamil are also still widely spoken.

The National Literacy Agency believed that an indigenous literature would help to create a national identity. Children's books were needed to promote patriotism, understanding amongst the various ethnic groups, social responsibility towards the less fortunate, and international goodwill. Children themselves needed stories which would help them to understand what was happening around them and to create a positive self-image.

Local publishers, however, needed a lot of encouragement to bring about this vision. There was a tendency to translate English children's books, with unsatisfactory results. For example Enid Blyton's books about the Famous Five were translated and Malaysianised to the extent of changing the names of the characters, but the cultural setting was untouched so that Mohammed, Ibrahim and Fatimah, apparently good Muslims, were described as eating bacon and eggs for breakfast!

However, there were some good examples of enterprise. For example, an attractive, full-colour picture book, *Burung Bermata Satu* [The Bird Hunter] (1972) an Indonesian folk-tale, was published in both English and Malay.

Despite a high literacy rate, Malaysia is not really a reading society, and it faces problems in that there is an overemphasis on textbook learning and a lack of book distribution networks in rural areas.

## Singapore

Singapore is an island republic with an ethnically diverse population made up of Chinese (76 per cent), Malays (15 per cent), Indians (7 per cent) and Eurasians and other minorities (2 per cent). Nearly a quarter of the population is under 15-years-old. There are relatively high levels of prosperity and literacy. English is the language of administration, but Chinese, Malay and Tamil are also recognised as official languages.

Locally produced children's books have a very low profile. Many books are imported; in Chinese from Taiwan, Hong Kong and China; in Tamil from South India; in Malay from Malaysia and in English from Britain and the USA, and these are easily available in bookshops and public libraries. While easy access to imported books does not help the situation, the lack of indigenous publishing is also due to the small, multilingual population and the fact that parents are mostly interested in buying books which have an obvious educational value. The standards of the children's books published in Singapore are generally low, both in the matter of content and in appearance.

The major exception to this observation is children's books in Chinese. Singapore participates in the Asian Co-Publication Programme and English texts have been translated into Chinese. The Moongate Collection, picture books in the Chinese language and based on folk-tales, was launched in 1972. Books in this series have attractive, high quality formats and lay-out, and make good use of colour. *The White Elephant*, an adaptation of a Burmese folk-tale, received honourable mention at the Biennale Illustratione Bratislava in 1973. In 1974, *Xie Gei Hai Zi Men De Shi* [Poems for Children] by Chew Kok Chan, a collection of poems in Chinese, mostly about the sights and sounds of Singapore, and illustrated in colour, won the National Book Development Council of Singapore's National Book Award for Children's Books in Chinese. *Tian Luo Zi* [The Fairy Snail] (1979) is one of a number of Asian folk-tales retold by Huang Yue Zhu (Olive Lee) in Chinese and subsequently translated into English and Malay.

Four generations of Singaporeans have enjoyed Enid Blyton's books and local writers have been inspired to produce similar stories just because they are so popular. *Pipi Kirinya Bercalar* [The Scar on the Left Cheek] (1974), written in Malay by Muhammed Ariff Ahmad, is about a gang of children who help the police to arrest a man who is responsible for a series of thefts in the district.

The Spider series, written by two of Singapore's most prominent children's writers, Jessie Wee and Bessie Chuah, is intended for 2 to 12-year-olds. It consists of books of short stories about the same gang of children, written in English to a formula with predictable plots. The gang is made up of one Malay, Ali, one Indian, Siva, and two Chinese children, Su Chong and Boon Liong; they have adventures in abandoned dwellings or on a Malay kampong, inhabiting an old-fashioned world which is quite foreign to the experience of modern children in Singapore, most of whom live in high-rise flats on housing estates.

Children's writers seem to be constrained by the requirements of the publishers who, in turn, are influenced by the expectations and demands of parents. Didactic elements are injected even into the most light-hearted fiction. However, there are examples of good quality children's books in English. Jessie Wee has also written some picture books for pre-school children. *A Home in the Sky* (1992) and *A Friend in Need* (1992), illustrated by Lee Kowling and sponsored by American Express International, are both stories set in high-rise flats. David Loy has written some very good fantasies. *Patrick and the Animal Bushes* (1981) is the story of the topiary works in Singapore Botanical Gardens coming alive and *The Last Troll in Singapore* (1983) is about a young boy helping his father in a bumboat business.

The National Book Development Council of Singapore recognises that children have special reading needs, but there seems to be little in the way of positive encouragement to authors, illustrators or publishers to motivate them to produce high quality children's books locally.

## Thailand

Although the country is rich in oral tradition, Thailand's first books for children appeared only in the early years of the twentieth century when the first schools were established and European printing techniques were introduced into the country. Real interest in children's literature, however, dates back only to 1972, designated International Book Year by UNESCO, and developments since then are largely due to a small group of people, one of the most prominent of whom is Somboon Singkamanon of Srinakharinwirot University in Bangkok, and the determination to make as much use as possible of outside agencies such as UNESCO, UNICEF and the International Federation of Library Associations (IFLA). By 1987, about 200 children's books were being published each year, including poetry, folk-tales, stories taken from Buddhist texts, simplified versions of the classical literature of Thailand made attractive through illustration, and some realistic stories.

In 1989 courses in children's literature were being offered at eight out of the ten universities and at twenty-one out of the thirty-six teacher training colleges. The Book Development Centre of the Ministry of Education is closely involved with the Asian Co-publication Programme (ACP), in which Thailand participates fully, and Thailand is at the centre of the ASEAN Project on Children's Books. CREDA (The Children's Reading Development Association) is very active and the Portable Library project, set up in 1989 to get books to schools in remote villages, received the IBBY Asahi Reading Promotion Award. This scheme has been so successful that it has been adopted by neighbouring Laos. Magazines such as *Children's Voice*, *Children's Garden*, *Kiewkoy* and *Chaiyapruk Cartoon* provide cheap and accessible reading material for many children.

The majority of the books published each year are for young children, and translations account for almost half the titles, but workshops and seminars are held to encourage local authors and illustrators. The didactic element is still strong in Thai children's literature. S. Rojanasaroj's poem, 'School for Crickets', for example, is about the advantages of listening to an adult who can teach children how to survive among possible dangers. *The Origin of Tiger's Stripes and Rabbit's Shortened Tail* by Thepsiri Suksopa (1984), a title which has overtones of a 'Just-So' story by Kipling, reflects the popularity of animal stories. Modern writers, however, have also realised the importance of including modern messages in their fiction. Charoen Malarochana, author of *Kheaw-Sua Fire* [The Fang of the Fire Tiger] (1988), is one of the most distinguished of these. In this 1990 IBBY Honour Book, he tells the story of Kaewhuan, who is very much braver than most girls, and Kamkong, her brother, who is shy and loves solitude; their parents are afraid that as they are so different from most children of their sex, they will encounter difficulties and problems as they grow up. Kaewhuan has got a fang of the Fire Tiger which people believe is a sacred talisman, and with it her uncle teaches her the magic which will calm her down and strengthen her brother, and so the two children learn to behave in the way society expects. Chotiwat Punnopatham's illustrations for *Tod Sorb Sa-Hai* [To Test the Friends] (1989) by Suwanna Kriengkraipetch, won the IBBY Honour book nomination for illustrator in the same year. This is the story of Tukammanik, whose millionaire father has taught him not to make friends with bad people; when his father dies, he decides to test this, finds that his father's advice was perhaps wise and all ends well.

The great enthusiasm for children's literature in Thailand is geared not only to encouraging the publication of good books, but also to ensuring that the results are distributed as widely as possible. Despite economic problems, it seems likely that children's literature will continue to develop at an impressive rate.

## Korea

Korea has a recorded history of 2,000 years but for much of this time it was part of the Chinese Empire. It was annexed by Japan in 1910, and Japanese literature has also been a strong influence. However, nationalism was kept alive during the long period of foreign occupation by the traditional folk literature. Pang Chong-hwan manipulated his Japanese education to meet Korean needs. He believed that Korean children should be educated in their own language and, realising that folk rhymes and songs were popular, he put Korean words to one of the most rhythmic

Japanese songs. Yun Sok-chung was influenced by this and his poems and rhymes constituted the first true Korean literature for children.

After 1945, when the country was divided, North Korea adopted the Russian pattern of education and book provision, while South Korea was influenced by the USA. In 1962 an important literary event in South Korea was the publication of *Hanguk Adong Munhak Tokpon* in ten volumes. This contains nursery rhymes, short stories, drama, poetry and even short novels and is attractively illustrated. A Korean Modern Children's Literature Institute was established in Seoul in 1978.

## Indonesia

Until independence in 1949, Indonesia was a Dutch colony, and Dutch and English were the main languages of instruction in the schools. The official language is now Bahasa Indonesia, a form of Malay.

The classical literature of Indonesia was influenced by Sanskrit, Arabic and Persian, and only recently have classical stories been written down in a form suitable for children. Apart from traditional rhymes and some songs, children's literature has been slow to develop. However, the country participated in the ASEAN cooperative publishing project and in 1987 Murti Bunanta suggested that strong action was needed to improve and promote children's books and a Society for the Advancement of Children's Literature was founded in the following year; this became a National Section of IBBY in 1971.

Hardiyono, who began to illustrate books for children in 1971, was the first winner of the Indonesian IBBY Competition for Illustrations in 1991. Toety Maklis is a pioneer in writing for small children and frequently uses environmental themes. Suyadi both writes and illustrates: *Gua Terlarang* [The Forbidden Cave] and *Made Dan Empat Teman* [Man and His Four Friends] are typical of his work. Salim M. felt the need to provide children's books with illustrations that are typically Indonesian. Dwianto Setyawan began by writing for adults but was motivated to write for children when he saw the flood of translated books coming on to the Indonesian market, particularly those by Enid Blyton. He subsequently wrote short stories, adventure serials and picture books, but catered mainly for 11 to 13-year-olds.

With these, and other promising writers and illustrators ready to produce books for children, the children's literature scene in Indonesia is set to develop rapidly.

## Further Reading

Dashdondog, J. (1991) 'When did children's literature appear in Mongolia?', *Bookbird* 29 3: 3–6.

Ho Leina (1993) 'Of morals, misguided writing and commercialism: the essence of children's literature in Singapore', *International Review of Children's Literature and Librarianship* 8, 3: 181–189.

Hoang Nguyen (1984) 'Literature for young people in Vietnam', *Bookbird* 1: 24–26.

Muniandy, T. (1982) 'The changing social context', in *Story in the Child's Changing World. The Papers and Proceedings of the 18th Congress of the International Board on Books for Young People, 1982*, Cambridge: IBBY.

# 80

# China

## Wong Yoon Wah and Laina Ho

China is the oldest continuous civilisation in the world and in its four thousand years of history Chinese literature flourished, rich and diverse in its themes, genres and collections. Yet it was only in the twentieth century that the special educational and recreational needs of children were recognised and provision made for them. Until then, children were able to enjoy a literature meant for adults. To understand why this was possible it is necessary to have an understanding of the social life of the Chinese from ancient times.

### Socio-Cultural Life of Children in Relation to Literature

From a very early age most Chinese children became familiar with a wide range of myths, legends, folk-tales, short stories with heavy moral values, as well as classic tales of romance, adventures, mysticism, supernatural, and even stories of crime and detective work, told to them by their elders, mostly to entertain but very often to explain the reasons behind every Chinese festival that was celebrated. The festivals which were, and still are, celebrated throughout the thirteen-month Chinese calendar have as their origins Chinese fables, folklores, historical figures and incidents which had an impact on the political scene in China. For instance, a festival such as the Dragon Boat race originated in the death of a famous court official and poet, Qu Yuan (340–278 BC) who drowned himself when he became disillusioned with the follies of his King. The making of rice dumplings to feed the soul of Qu Yuan, and the race of the dragon boats sent out to rescue him, have been carried on by the Chinese for centuries. Over the years the tragic story of Qu Yuan, with much elaboration, has been romanticised to appeal to children. On the other hand, a piece of romantic folklore, 'The cowherd and the weaving maid', became the reason why unmarried women and men celebrated the seventh day of the seventh month.

In Imperial China children's literary experiences were enriched by professional story-tellers who continued with their trade up to modern times. It was customary for children to accompany their elders to public places such as the market and the tea-houses where they were treated to soap-opera style stories told in many segments. This oral tradition became highly professional during the Song period (960–1279). This kind of story-telling could sustain the interest of children because it used a simple narrative style. The narration was rich in rhyme, and was often punctuated by bamboo clappers, drums, cymbals, and the use of two or three musical instruments so that it became half-narration, half-singing.

Chinese children also had the opportunity of watching open-air theatres during festivals and fairs. These plays or operas are characterised by visually stunning costumes and actors' make-up and impressive displays of acrobatics, and Chinese martial arts. This was one reason why classical works of literature could be appreciated by everyone, literate or non-literate, including children. When theatres or operas were not available, children often had the choice of watching puppet shows or shadow plays, which were frequently held during festival times.

In formal education children were taught the Confucian classics as these were the basic grounding to a civil service career. Children were taught these through rote-learning and memorising without understanding them. Until the early twentieth century, Chinese classical literature was the traditional material for primers in schools. Children who went to school could recite highly literary works such as poems, songs, historical chronicles, works of philosophy, moral sayings, and ceremonial and religious rituals, from the Confucian classics. The ease with which children could memorise and chant such serious literature was facilitated by the literary techniques of the classical works – the conciseness of the Chinese language in four-, five-, or seven-character-line couplets, and the rhythm and tonal quality. *The Analects*, is an example of a classical piece of literature considered very heavy reading material for adults, let alone children – yet children in ancient China had only these texts as literature.

However, many of the earliest versions of myths and legends were incorporated into these philosophical writings and historical chronicles. Fables, folklore, humorous anecdotes, including folk-songs, nursery rhymes, cumulative story rhymes and proverbs were culled from as far back as the Classical period, and taught to children in the oral tradition.

Although there are records of literature from the earliest times of Chinese civilisation (1765 BC) it can be said that literary works – the Classics – were written during the times of the sages. Confucius (551–479 BC) and his teachings of morals and familial values had a profound influence on the life of the Chinese. Confucianism moulded the Chinese character and pervaded every aspect of Chinese society, the family and the arts. In a broad sense, much of Chinese literature is Confucian literature. Influenced by Confucian ethics, the Chinese were especially strong in their sense of right and wrong, which naturally found expression in literature, both written and oral. To the majority of Chinese writers in post- and pre-modern China, literature has been a vehicle for the communication of the aim of Confucian doctrine: to teach and influence people to be good. Thus, there is always a moral lesson in a work of Chinese literature.

Despite the pervasiveness of didacticism, Chinese literature is enjoyed tremendously by children and adults alike. Its appeal lies in drawing accurate accounts of historical events and figures, mostly of the romantic, imaginative kind. For instance, the notorious Qin dynasty (221–207 BC) and its first emperor, Shihuangdi, famous for building the Great Wall of China, were the sources of many a romantic tales about heroism and honour. Similarly, the period of the warring factions (480–221 BC) became the source for the epic tale, *Romance of the Three Kingdoms*, with its countless tales of glowing military exploits, cunning strategies and magnificent bravery. *Men of the Marshes* or *The Water Margin*, written in the Song dynasty, was another great Chinese literary work based on the adventures of bandits, criminals and stories of knights-errant. The spread of Buddhism to China in the seventh century led to another grand epic tale about a Chinese monk travelling to India. *Journey to the West* used incidents from this famous journey, combining tales of fantasy, the supernatural, demons and monsters. At the other end of the scale, the classic work, *Dream of the Red Chamber* written in the Qing (Manchu) dynasty (1644–1908), a treatise on the social life of a wealthy Chinese family in the seventeenth century, could be enjoyed by children because of the tragic romance of the main protagonists.

It can be seen why epic tales like these had such enormous appeal to children, and why these works could be translated into theatrical art. Whether it was oral or written, Chinese literature was readily and abundantly available to children. Therefore, no conscious efforts were made to write a literature specially for children. In Chinese society children were often treated as adults, doing adult labour and shouldering adult responsibilities, and education for children from wealthier homes, was only a means to an end – to pass the Imperial civil service examination.

The term 'children's literature' came to the fore only at the beginning of the twentieth century when China was invaded by Western powers, and subjected to numerous humiliating demands from the West with the result that the educated Chinese populace clamoured for revolutionary reforms. Especially important among these was China's education system. The civil service examination was abolished, vernacular language teaching was implemented, and the school system was modelled on that of the USA.

## Post Imperial China and Children's Literature

The movement of Chinese literature in the past seventy years has often been called a 'renaissance'. It was a departure but not a complete break from tradition, and the force that gave impetus to the new literature had come from abroad. This movement was closely linked with the political developments in China with the fall of the Qing dynasty, the First World War and the Chinese Revolution.

The new social developments had the unexpected effect of arousing Chinese interest in and admiration for Western accomplishments in science and technology as well as literature. Never before in China's history were Chinese authors exposed so much to a culture alien to them. As translations of Western literary works became fashionable in China, the earliest works of children's literature at the turn of the twentieth century were mostly translated works from the West. Most popular among these translated works were *Aesop's Fables*, the fairy tales of the Grimms and Andersen, and *The Arabian Nights*. The term *Tong-hua* (children's tales) was coined for the first time.

The underlying reason why Western literature had so much appeal and popularity with the Chinese readership was that this was the first time that literature had been free from Confucian ideology and morals. It was also the first time that the Chinese readership had access to reading materials with a wide range of subjects, setting, themes, including animal characterisation and its very imaginative appeal. A unique feature of contemporary Chinese literature is therefore the all-pervasive influence of the West on forms and techniques, on spirit and ideology, even up to the present time.

The new awareness in a literature for children came about after the establishment of the Commercial Press in Shanghai in 1902, which promoted children's literature by launching a number of children's periodicals and magazines, such as *Shao Nian Za Ji* [Youth Magazine], *Er Tong Jiao Yu Hua* [Educational Pictures for Children] and *Tong Hua*.

The other factor that gave impetus to children's literature was the efforts of some educationists. Foremost among these were Lu Xun (1881–1936) and his brother Zhou Zouren who advocated translations of foreign children's literature. Lu Xun's role in Chinese children's literature was not his many translated works of Western classics into Chinese, but his stress on need for writing for children. He revolutionised children's literature and with it the whole approach to fiction and to stories for children. Lu Xun encouraged the revival of woodcut illustrations which later gave rise to picture books for children. His major contribution rests in his deep insight into the mind of the child and his passionate desire for a new and more equitable society. Lu Xun's brother continued to translate Western fiction and recommended the use of literature in primary schools.

Similarly, a children's editor in the Commercial Press, Sun Yuxiu (editorship 1909–1916), became the first writer of children's literature when he wrote 'The Kingdom Without a Cat'. This is the first children's tale written in the vernacular language, about a child labourer and his cat; the cat redeems a king's dignity, and the hero is rewarded with a successful scholarship. Sun Yuxiu encouraged another fellow writer by the name of Shen Dehong (1896–1981) to write for children. As a result, Shen, known by his pen-name, Mao Dun, wrote twenty-eight tales, many of which were stories re-written from the traditional Chinese short stories of the Tang, Song, Yuan and Ming dynasties. Prominent among these were tales of love, chivalry and the supernatural that characterised the Tang period (618–906); stories of murder and law suits, sword fights, the martial arts, and religious tales (mostly Buddhist), of the Song period; stories about love and intrigue, religious and supernatural, historical and pseudo-historical, domestic and social, of the Yuan (Mongol) period (1260–1368), and stories of Chinese ghosts, Taoist magic and wizardry from the Ming period (1368–1644).

As a result of the efforts of people like Shen Dehong, classical Chinese literature became even more accessible to children. On the other hand, modern Chinese poetry for children had little appeal for children because of the use of vernacular language and the free-verse style. This compares unfavourably with classical Chinese in poetry of the Tang and Song periods, for example, because the use of vernacular language and free verse is less rhythmic and more difficult to memorise.

As the publications of the Commercial Press continued to flourish and children's tales were becoming increasingly popular, more and more writers were encouraged to write for children's magazines. Two children's short stories were written by Ye Shengtao (1894–1988) called *The Scarecrow* (1923) and *The Statue of an Ancient Hero* (1931). The first story tells about a scarecrow who witnesses the social life of the Chinese people, but is helpless to prevent the tragic events unfolding before his eyes. The second story is allegorical, presenting a very moralistic view of the importance of the unimportant and insignificant compared to the pretentiousness and snobbery of the high and mighty.

The first full-length children's novel, *Big Lin and Little Lin* by Zhang Tianyi was published in 1932. This was a politically motivated novel for children, the story about two brothers, separated from each other when their village was destroyed and they were each sold into different families. Big Lin, the more fortunate boy was brought up by a wealthy family, and became corrupt, suppressing the suffering poor, but died later by drowning; little Lin became a train driver, led an uprising against his unsympathetic employer and even joined the Chinese Revolution. Zhang Tianyi himself was a leftist living in the times of the feudal warlords when the peasantry suffered under their corruption. However, Zhang was recognised as a successful children's writer.

## Children's Literature from 1949

The founding of the People's Republic of China in 1949 changed the course of Chinese children's literature. The central feature of the new literature was its accordance with a set of theoretical principles laid down by Mao Zedong and Marxist ideology. All literature and the arts were for the people and therefore had to reflect the lives of the workers, peasants and soldiers, as well as revolutionary struggles. These principles of literary creation undermined the works of children's writers. Children's literature, like all literary works for adults, had to depict reality and had to take as its goal the raising of the socialist consciousness of the people.

After 1949, many veteran writers of children's literature of the 1920s and 1930s were discredited and heavily criticised, and as a result, stopped writing. Zhang Tianyi and Ye Shengtao were among the few who continued to write. Zhang, in particular, wrote mostly tales, short stories and plays for juvenile readers as he was encouraged by the Communist leaders. His children's fiction was stereotyped and full of communist clichés, and he even revised and changed many of the endings in his children's stories in line with Mao's ideology, and in order to be accepted for publication by government-owned publishers.

Younger professional writers nurtured by the communist regime began to churn out children's stories in the 1950s and 1960s. Among them were Jin Jin, Qin Zhaoyang, He Yi, Bao Lei and Ge Cuilin. With their writing, Chinese children's literature became truly proletarian. With works of traditional and universal themes no longer available, those with highly propagandist themes and poor quality writing flooded the market. From the 1950s to the 1970s earlier children's literature was criticised because 'the sky is overcast with ancient people and animals, while the workers, peasants and soldiers are pitifully lonely (Hong Xuntao 1986: 306). As a result, works of both Chinese and foreign writers were banned, and creativity in Chinese writing in both adult and children's fiction was suppressed.

The death of Mao Zedong and the fall from grace of the Gang of Four in 1976 brought about great changes in politics and in children's literature. Many writers discredited during the Cultural Revolution were rehabilitated. Literary works, especially those of the 1920s and 1930s became readily available. The publication of the *General Anthology of Modern Children's Literature of China* (1990) shows that new variations in contents, techniques and themes are now allowed. This fifteen-volume anthology contains children's tales, short stories, essays, poetry, drama, novels and studies of children's literature since the 1920s. The concept of the superiority of politics over pure aesthetics as well as the necessity for 'correctness' in ideology continues to be taken into account, but the rigid application of these two criteria is now not so important.

According to the *Encyclopedia of Children's Literature of the World* (Jiang Feng 1992) many publishers, organisations and research institutes are actively supporting and promoting the development of Chinese children's literature. Prominent among these are the Chinese Writers' Association: Children's Literature Committee, and China's Children's Literature Research Association, both in Beijing. There are about a hundred existing periodicals devoted to children's literature and eight major awards for children's books. The recognition for children's literature in the People's Republic of China today is seen in the annual Children's Literary Works Award of China awarded by the National Committee of Children's Literary Works Assessment, comprising such government bodies as the Ministry of Education, Ministry of Culture and the National Publication Office.

Although children's literature in China is enjoying an immense popularity and gaining recognition as literary works, much of what is published these days are stories that imitate Western literature. Fantasy and animal characters are popular, whereas realistic fiction depicting the Chinese way of life, and the struggle against poverty and natural disasters for example, is too starkly realistic and depressing for children.

The Chinese attitude to children has changed in recent years, with the implementation of the one-child family policy, and the result is that children are now more pampered and treated as children, rather than as sources of family income. The education of children and their reading needs is now fully recognised. However, Chinese children's literature can still be considered as being in its infancy, although the next decade will surely see a new movement in its writing. An impetus to this may come from the demand for children's books from the Chinese readership in the predominantly Chinese-populated countries of Taiwan and South East Asia.

## References

Hawkes, D. (trans.) (1974) *The Story of the Stone [Dream of the Red Chamber]*, Harmondsworth: Penguin.

Hong Xuntao (1986) *Tong Hua Xue [A Study of Chinese Tales]*, He Fei: Anhui Children's Literature Publishing House.

Jackson, J. H. (trans.) (1976) *The Water Margin [Shui Hu Chuan]*, Shanghai: Commercial Press.

Roberts, M. (trans.) (1976) *Three Kingdoms: China's Epic Drama*, Pantheon: New York.

Waley, A. (1985) *Monkey [Journey to the West]*, London: Allen and Unwin.

# Further Reading

## In English

Hsia, C. T. (1962) *Modern Chinese fiction 1917–1957*, New Haven: Yale University Press.
Liu Wuchi (1966) *An Introduction to Chinese Literature*, Bloomington: Indiana University Press.
Lu Xun (1976) *A Brief History of Chinese Fiction*, trans. Yang Xian Yi and G. Yang, Westport, CT: Hyperion Press.
Scott, D. H. (1980) *Chinese Popular Literature and the Child*, Chicago: American Library Association.
Ye Shengtao (1978) *The Scarecrow: Stories for Children*, Beijing: Foreign Language Press.

## In Chinese

Jiang Feng (ed.) (1992) *Encyclopedia of Children's Literature of the World*, Tai Yuan: Xi Wang Publishing House.
Yee Zhishan (ed.) (1990) *General Anthology of Modern Children's Literature of China*, 15 vols, Tai Yuan: Xi Wang Publishing House.

## Chinese Literature and Children's Literature in Translation

Birch, C. (trans.) (1958) *Stories from a Ming Collection*, London: Bodley Head.
—— (ed.) (1961) *Chinese Myths and Fantasies*, New York: Walck.
—— (ed.) (1972) *Anthology of Chinese Literature from the 14th Century to the Present*, New York: Grove.
Chang, H. C. (1973) *Chinese Literature: Popular Fiction and Drama*, Edinburgh: Edinburgh University Press.
Lin Yutang (1959) *Famous Chinese Short Stories*, New York: John Day.
Yang Xian Yi and G. Yang (1957) *The Courtesan's Jewel Box: Chinese Stories of the 10th–17th Centuries*, Beijing: Foreign Language Press.

# 81

# Japan

## Teruo Jinguh

### Edo Era: 1603–1868

The establishment of the Tokugawa government in 1603 marked the beginning of 250 years of peace, the Edo Era. It was also the starting point for books for children.

In the middle of the seventeenth century, a few lesson books for children were published: the best of them was *Kin mo Zui* [The Illustrated Encyclopedia for Children] (1666) by Tekisai Nakamura (1629–1702). Basing his work on a Chinese book, Nakamura produced an illustrated book for his daughter, and its success stimulated the production of similar books. Another notable work of this period was *Wazoku Dôji Kun* [The Popular Book on the Upbringing of Children] (1710) by Ekiken Kaibara (1630–1714) a celebrated Confucian, naturalist, and educationalist, which was the first book of systematic thought on child care.

The appearance of these books suggests the existence of a fair number of literate children, and the adults' concern for children. The private elementary school, the *terakoya* (temple school), which had been started for the education of the children of the common people in the middle of the Muromachi Era (1336–1573), became popular in the middle of the Edo Era.

The literacy rate for children was, therefore, quite high even before the beginning of compulsory education in 1872, and many kinds of books such as *kana zôshi* (story books written in Japanese syllabary) and *otogi zôshi* (entertainment books) were published for the amusement and instruction of both adults and young people. These books generally had pictures of a higher standard than those in European books of the same period, a standard which may have derived from the famous *Chôjû Giga* (Picture Scrolls of Frolicking Animals) which were published anonymously at the end of the twelfth century and the beginning of the thirteenth.

Story books especially for children came into being as early as the 1670s; they were called *Akahon* (Red Books), as they were books of myth, legend, folk or fairy tales in red bindings.

### Meiji Era: 1868–1911

After the fall of the Tokugawa Dynasty in 1867, the new government began to promote Westernisation in every aspect of life. Compulsory elementary education meant more literate children, and more children's books. The first step, just as in the Edo Era, was to produce children's versions of traditional literature. The most successful writer was Sazanami Iwaya (1870–1932). His contribution to children's literature can be divided into three genres: children's versions of myths and tales, literary fairy tales, and realistic short stories. The most celebrated of them all was *Koganemaru* [Koganemaru, the Dog who Avenged his Parents] (1891), generally reputed to be the starting point for modern Japanese children's literature. Most of Sazanami's characters were active, cheerful and full of a strong sense of justice, and the story is simple, straightforward and full of action, with a very clear theme.

## Taishô Era: 1912–1926

The First World War brought remarkable changes even to a small island country in the Far East. Japan was reconstructed as a capitalist country, and became relatively prosperous. During this Indian summer, which might be compared with the Edwardian period in Britain, the urban educated classes became liberal and democratic in their views. Naturally, Sazanami's work, with its practical but rather old-fashioned morals based on a feudal way of thinking was severely criticised, and new writers began to look for different kinds of stories; they were influenced by literary fairy tales such as Andersen's *Eventyrs* and Wilhelm Hauf's *Kunstmärchen*.

In 1910, Mimei Ogawa (1882–1961) published *Akai Fune* [A Red Ship], including short stories of children's everyday life, an adventure story and literary fairy tales, in which he attempted to explore children's thoughts and actions. In all, he wrote around a thousand tales for children, the best of which were included in *Kin no Wa* [The Golden Hoop] (1919) and *Akai Rôsoku to Ningyo* [A Little Mermaid and Red Candles] (1921). His fairy stories are full of vivid and stimulating images which symbolise his themes, and he was very influential before 1945. Since then, however, his work has been severely criticised on social and political grounds.

Hirosuke Hamada (1893–1973) was well known for stories such as *Mukudori no Yume* [Dream of the Little Grey Starling] (1920) and *Taishô no Dôzô* [The Statue of a General] (1920). He was regarded as an innovator of literature for small children for whom most of his stories were written; his real achievement was to make stories with major themes accessible to a younger audience.

A poet and agricultural chemist, Kenji Miyazawa (1896–1933) wrote stories in the fairy tale mode partly to propagate the doctrine of the Lotus Sutra. One of his masterpieces, *Ginga Tetsudô no Yoro* [A Night Train in the Milky Way] (1924–c.1932), which tells of a boy's dream journey, has a large-scale setting reminiscent of Hans Andersen, and vivid, poetic and symbolic images reminiscent of George MacDonald. The simple and original characters and the clear imagery mark him as a gifted fantasy writer.

The market for boys' and girls' magazines expanded with economic growth. One of the most celebrated, *Akai Tori* [Red Bird] (1918–1936) was published by the novelist Miekichi Suzuki (1882–1936) with the cooperation of the poet Hakushuh Kitahara (1885–1942). This poet, holding the view that 'the child is father of the man', published many poems and verses for children, encouraged promising young poets, and was largely responsible for a golden age of poetry for children. Shôzô Chiba (1892–1975), editor of another magazine, *Dôwa*

(1920–1926) wrote nostalgic stories based on his own boyhood, and was skilled in depicting children's actions and feelings in everyday life. *Torachan no Nikki* [A Summer Diary of a Village Boy Tora] (1925) and *Tote Basha* [A Story of an Old-Fashioned Coach] (1929) were highly regarded as first steps towards realism.

## Shôwa Era, before the Second World War: 1925–1944

The worldwide panic of 1929, and the deepening shadow of war forced people to turn to practicalities, and although the movement towards proletarian literature for children was immediately suppressed, it strongly influenced many writers. The books of Kenjiro Tsukahara (1895–1965), Daiji Kawasaki (1902–1980), Taku Shimohata (1916–1944), Yoshio Okamoto (1919–1963), and Hideo Seki (1912– ) show children who come to understand the realities of life.

The most distinguished author of the period was Jôji Tsubota (1890–1982). As well as many novels for adults, he contributed to the growth of realistic novels for children with *Kaze no naka no Kodomo* [A Family Against the Wind] (1936) and *Kodomo no Shiki* [A Family's Four Seasons] (1937). The two novels tell the story of a small family business, involving the children. All the characters are lifelike, although the author idealised children, and the family's problems are solved through their innocence.

## Shôwa Era after the Second World War: 1945–

The defeat and occupation of Japan in 1945 brought revolutionary changes (although, looking back, some of these were actually superficial) and children's literature was no exception.

Released from wartime controls, there was a temporary boom in publishing books and magazines for children; many of these books lacked charm and only a few have survived. Momoko Ishii (1907– ), translator of A. A. Milne's *Pooh* books, wrote a family chronicle of pre-war Japan, which not only showed her sense of humour, but which is permeated with Western democratic spirit: *Nonchan Kumo ni Noru* [Nobuko and her Family] (1947). Another authoress, Sakae Tsuboi, told of children growing up before, during, and after the war in *Nijûshi no Hitomi* [The Story of Twelve Boys and Girls] (1954). It is a very good anti-war novel, as is *Biruma no Tategoto* [A Harp in Burma] (1949) by Michio Takeyama (1903–1984), then a professor of German literature.

The 1950s was really a preparatory decade. The Japanese economy was still weak, the market for children's books was small, and young writers were searching for an appropriate technique. The novel was thought to be the best way of writing about the situation of boys and girls in disordered post-war Japan, and writers looked to translations of British and American books for models.

### Realistic fiction

The first of the young writers to make an impression was Hisashi Yamakana (1931– ) with *Akagne no Pochi* [Katsuko and her Dog, Pochi] (1960). The heroine is the daughter of a part-time coal miner in the early 1950s. Through her growing awareness of social problems, the author succeeded in presenting not only an individual child, but a member of a rapidly changing society.

As society changed, so genuine historical novels began to appear. Sukeyuki Imanishi's *Higo no Ishiku* [A Stonemason of Higo] (1965), is a story of feudal Japan, in which the stonemason attempts to keep his bridge-building techniques secret so that they will be used for peaceful, rather than military purposes. *Uragami no Tabibitotachi* [Exiles of Uragami] (1969), is another fine example of this author's work, a fictional record of the sufferings of Christians in Nagasaki early in the Meiji Era. Yasuo Maekawa (1921– ) published a remarkable book, *Majin no Umi* [The Bewitched Sea] in 1968. It tells the story of the Ainu people who lived on a small island between Russia and Japan in the last decade of the eighteenth century, and their tragic struggle for independence. The author's intention was to discuss the meaning of nationality in a complicated world.

The turning point for realistic fiction was *Bokuchan no Senjô* [The Battlefield of a Naïve Boy] (1969) by Tsuguo Okuda (1934– ). The characters in this novel, which deals with the compulsory evacuation of elementary school children during the last stage of the Pacific war, differ from their counterparts in the novels of the 1950s and the first half of the 1960s. They are no longer model children; childhood was changing with the high growth rate of the economy.

### Young adult novels

The growth of the young adult novel was one of the characteristics of the 1970s. In his most famous work, *Bonbon* [A Boy From a Good Family] (1973), Yoshitomo Imae (1932–) wrote a successful modern *bildungsroman* around the protagonist's childhood during the Japanese–Chinese war. Kenjiro Haitani's *Usagi no Me* [Rabbit's Eye] (1974) showed the realities of children who were unsuccessful in the examination-centred education system, making clear the terrible lack of compassion in all levels of society. Other outstanding new writers of this period were Yumiko Izawa, Tatsuya Saragai and Keiko Takada.

A striking feature of realistic works in the 1980s was the fact that the borderline between works for adults and for children became less clear: many young writers wrote for readers in general, rather than especially for children. They tried to treat both adults and children as human beings. Fresh and noteworthy examples are *Mama no Kiiroi Kozô* [Mother's Little Yellow Elephant] (1986) by Akiko Sueyoshi, *Samâ Taimu* [Summer Time] (1990) by Takako Satô, *Watagashi* [Candyfloss] (1991) by Kaori Ekuni, and *800* [800 Metre Race] (1992) by Makoto Kawashima.

### Fantasy and imagination

Epoch-making imaginative works also appeared, under the influence of British and American fantasy, and humorous and nonsensical novels with individual characters were written. Typical is the story of an English dwarf family's life in Japan before, during, and after the war, Tomiko Inui's *Kokage no Ie no Kobitotachi* [Little Men in a House Under the Big Tree] (1959). But the really innovative work was *Daremo Shiranai Chiisana Kuni* [My Little People and Their Country] (1959) by Satoru Satô (1928– ). The exciting story of the hero's encounter with native little people, and the rediscovery of them after the war appealed to readers of all generations; it has grown to a five-volume series, and commands a wide audience even now.

Miyoko Matsutani's *Tatsunoko Taro* [Taro, Dragon's Son] (1960) was very significant in two ways. It was one of the first original stories based on folk and fairy tale materials, and one of the first long stories for younger children with a strong storyline, a simple plot and characters and an easily understandable theme. Toshiko Kanzawa's *Chibikko Kamu no Bôken* [The Adventure of Little Cam] (1961) was also a folk-tale-based adventure for younger children.

If the 1960s were the period of innovation, the next ten years were the period of expansion. The revival of epic fantasy in Britain and the USA may have encouraged such work in Japan, and there were two ambitious works in the genre in 1972 (which did not, however, rise above the level of the experimental). *Gin no honoo no Kuni* [The Story of the Country of Silver Flame] by Kanzawa tells of the rebirth of the great legendary reindeer Hayate and his struggle to recover his lost kingdom of silver flame from the barbarous blue wolves; *Hikariguruma yo Maware* [Spin Round, Oh Wheels of Light!] is the story of the quest for a symbol of life by boys and girls.

Eniji Shôno (1915–1993) was well-known as the author of *Hoshi no Makiba* [The Meadow of Stars] (1963), a novel about the dream world of Momiichi, who was wounded in the war and suffers from a memory defect. *Arufabetto Guntô* [The Alphabetical Archipelago] (1977) is a story of nonsensical voyages to twenty-six islands with their names in alphabetical order. His work is full of wit, humour and the joy of life, with sad undertones of his serious experiences in wartime.

Eiko Kadono (1935– ) began to write for children rather late, and her first successful nonsense story *Ôdorobô Bula Bula shi* [The Robber Bla-Bla] (1981) and her most popular work of fantasy *Majo no Takkyubin* [Young Witch Kiki's Express Delivery Service] (1985) are very near to the spirit of the 1960s in their wit and optimism.

The post-war generation was free of both pre-war didacticism and the rigid idealism of the 1950s, and they began to enlarge the possibilities of children's literature. *Poppen Sensei no Nichiôbi* [Dr Pitter-Patter's Strange Sunday] (1973) by Yoshihiko Funazaki (1945–) is a fantasy of an assistant professor's experiences in the world of a riddle picture book. Other promising examples of fantasy are *Nonbiri Kobuta to Sekaseka Usagi* [A Carefree Little Pig and a Restless Bunny] (1974) by Tadashi Ozawa (1937– ); *Kiri no Mukô no Fushigina Machi* [A Wonderful Small Town Beyond the Mist] (1975) by Sachiko Kashiwaba (1954), and *Inemuri Jiizelkâ* [A Sleepy Diesel Train] (1977) by Sumiko Horiuchi.

More mature original fantasies include Noriko Ogiwara's (1959– ) first book, *Sorairo Magatama* [Crescent Jade] (1989). Like most works of fantasy in the west, this is a story of the struggle between light and dark, but it is based on Japanese mythology. (It was published in the USA as *Dragon Sword and Wind Child* (1993)). Yôko Tomiyasu's *Kunugi bayashi no Zawazawaso* [The Rustling Apartment in the Oak Wood] (1991) and Katsuno Shigeta's *Furusato wa Natsu* [Father's Village in Summer] (1991) are pleasant attempts to create a native animistic world close to the hearts of Japanese readers.

But the richest harvest has been in the fairy tale, thought by some critics to be old-fashioned, and the foremost writers are Erika Tachihara (1937– ), Kimiko

Aman (1931– ) and Naoko Awa (1943–1993). Tachihara's main theme is love, and Aman's is kind-heartedness, and they both express strong anti-war feelings. Awa's most celebrated books for young people, *Shiroi Ômu no Mori* [The Forest of White Parrots] (1973) and *Gin no Kujaka* [Silver Peacock] (1975) demonstrate her penetration into human nature and are reminiscent of the work of E. T. A. Hoffmann.

## Further Reading

Kami, S. (ed.) (1992) *Fukusei Edo-ki Dowa Kenkyu Sosho* [Studies of Children's Literature in the Edo Period, 1603–1868], 4 vols in 6, Tokyo: Kyuansha.

Knuth, R. (1993) 'Japan and Malaysia: how two countries promote the reading habit', *International Review of Children's Literature and Librarianship* 8, 3: 108–180.

Reynolds, K. A. (1992) 'Children's books and motherhood in Japan', *Literature and Hawaii's Children*, Canham, S. (ed.) Honolulu: University of Hawaii.

Richard, O. and MacCann, D. (1990) 'The Japanese sensibility in picture books for children', *Wilson Library Bulletin* 65, 2: 23–27.

Shimi, T. (1987) *Japanese Children's Books at the Library of Congress: a Bibliography of Books from the Postwar Years, 1946–1985*, Washington: Library of Congress.

# 82

# Australia

## Rhonda M. Bunbury

### Aboriginal Narratives

Children's narratives in Australia might be said to have begun 40,000 years ago when oral telling of stories was an integral part of Aboriginal daily living. People who live tradition-oriented lives in Australia confirm that ancient stories are retold today with strict ownership customs ensuring their continuity and accuracy. Both adults and children were the intended audience for stories and for these public or 'outside versions of the stories, there is no distinction. Collections of traditional stories do exist in both contemporary and historically significant editions, and writers and collectors have made varying degrees of effort to reproduce accurate written translations of the oral stories. Notable examples are Mary Ann Fitzgerald's *King Bungarees Phyalla: Stories, Illustrative of Manners and Customs that Prevailed among Australian Aborigines* (1891), Langloh Parker's *Australian Legendary Tales: Folklore of the Noongahburrahs, as Told to the Piccaninnies* (1896, 1978), Daisy Bates's *Tales Told to Kabbarli* (collected in the 1930s and retold by Barbara Ker Wilson, 1972) and Catherine H. Berndt's *Land of the Rainbow Snake: Aboriginal Children's Stories and Songs from Western Arnhem Land* (1977). The 'inside stories, which are not intended for children, are not at issue here as they are secret and sacred. In the 'Western world of contemporary Australia, it is the advent of print which begins to enable non-Aboriginal cultures of Australia to focus on Aboriginal stories which can be said to be specifically for children.

Today, however, Kooris (Aboriginal in south-eastern Australia) object to the idea that publication of these 'outside traditional stories is relevant to their life in contemporary Australia. What can traditional stories say about the life of the young Koori footballer in the heart of Sydney? Stories written by Kooris about contemporary Koori life are needed, and it is here that the most striking gap in Australian publishing exists. One contemporary Koori story-teller, Maureen Watson, reminds her listeners that Captain Cook did not 'discover Australia and it is no accident that such stories which reflect Australia's origins still receive a mixed reception in a land which has just begun to acknowledge that the country was not *terra nullus* (empty land) when the Caucasian explorers arrived, which has only recently passed an Act of Parliament granting its Aboriginal citizens land rights (1994), and which debates whether or not its constitution ought to become republican, hence formally severing its remaining links to the monarchy and to

Britain. In a very real sense, the publication of children's literature in Australia is a reflection of the voices of power in the land.

Early works of children's fiction are noted for their poor treatment of Aborigines and Aboriginal themes, characters are stereotypical, non-Aboriginal viewpoints are dominant and the 'strange and 'exotic are emphasised. Mary and Elizabeth Durack's *Way of the Whirlwind* (1941) was an exception, although even this book was a fantasy, meant to entertain the children who lived on the Durack's remote cattle station.

There are books about Aboriginal lifestyles today and these are published by small community printeries in any one of the fifty known Aboriginal languages which survive (with more than one thousand speakers). Those which are published in English by the commercial publishers are usually written by non-Aboriginal writers; for example, Jeanie Adam's picture book *Pigs and Honey* (1989) reflects with warmth and understanding the family life of people living in Aurukun, a tradition-oriented community, and her books have been endorsed by the community. Similarly, Bill Scott, befriended by the Kabi tribesmen in southern Queensland has published his version of Murrie (Aboriginal in north-eastern Australia) stories in *Boori* (1978) and other titles. It is with the permission of the community that the stories have emerged in published form but still he is an interpreter of a culture not his own. Australian publishers of children's books need to find and foster writers and illustrators who are themselves Aboriginal and who do not need these interim interpreters. Successful examples for older readers are *Wild Cat Falling* (1965/1992) by Mudrooroo (Colin Johnson), *The First Born and Other Poems* (1970) by Jack Davis. A very positive development is the steady output by Magabala Books, which was established in north western Australia exclusively to publish works by Aboriginal people. From this source has emerged titles such as Narelle McRobbie's *Bip the Snapping Bungaroo* (1990) and Gracie Green, Joe Tramacchi and Lucille Gill's *Tjarany/Roughtail* (1992). Bold illustrations, original to Aboriginal people intensify meaning and design impact for readers, young and old. Local languages and information about today's customs and cultures add further insight.

## The Development of Colonial Publishing

The origins of published children's literature in Australia actually lie within the efforts of the monocultured, class-bound English who were conscious of the need to bring civilisation to children of a convict colony – a colony of 'mother England'. No evidence is to be found of stories written during the first half century of the colony's struggle for survival but in 1820 there were 6,688 children (23 per cent of the total population) who had been born in the colony (Bigge 1823: 80). Free settlers, along with those holding pardons, expirees and 'ticket of leavers' began to make their mark in the colony during the 1830s. Shipbuilding was established; there were the beginnings of the prosperous pastoral industry; the colony was almost self-sufficient in foodstuffs (in the short term) and the transportation of convicts to New South Wales had ceased by the time the first (known) children's book emerged from the colony: *A Mother's Offering to Her Children: By a Lady Long Resident in New South Wales* (1841). It was a book in question and answer format written by a governess, Charlotte Barton. The didactic intention was uppermost, as the young reader learned about the struggles within the colony along with natural science, geology, anthropology and morality, amidst occasional adventures and shipwrecks.

There followed many titles, particularly adventure stories set in the colonies amidst pioneering struggles, hazardous explorations, encounters with 'blacks', bushrangers and escaped convicts; although the distinction between adventures for adolescent boys and adults' adventure stories was not always clear. (Niall's focus on book characters, their values and adventures gives a good coverage of the period (1984)). Some of the publications of this time were essentially travel documents by people who visited the colonies for a brief period: one such book was William Howitt's *A Boy's Adventures in the Wilds of Australia: Or Herbert's Note Book* (1854) which contains descriptive details of the colonies, their flora and fauna, amid adventurous activities. The colonies were at least ten months' sailing time from Europe, but the cultural ties remained strong.

As the six colonies became more settled, democratically elected members entered parliament, and free immigration from Britain ended for all time the transportation of England's convicts; wealth from gold, the sale of wool and then wheat, strong trade union stands and the evolution of a Labour Party, over protectionism and free trade, together prompted the Federation of States. For fifty years this 'rising spirit' of democracy was given voice in various ways until the Commonwealth of Australia was proclaimed in 1901. The idealism of this period was strong and the nation's writers and educators were receptive to the influence of educational philosophers of Europe – Rousseau, Pestalozzi, and Dewey – who were responsible for the development of a child-centred approach to education. Indirectly, their impact was felt on the processes of cultural reproduction in the newly declared nation.

At this time, the literature for children which reflected the stable environment and which developed from strength to strength, was the family story. Its antecedents were clearly established in the USA and Britain, and Australian family stories emerged in response to these and the lively competition in publishing. Australia's best and most enduring example of the family story is Ethel Turner's *Seven Little Australians* (1894). Fun, affection, trouble, strife and authoritarian paternalism set the tone for books about family events in the city. Turner wrote over thirty novels for children and adolescents, and so earned a significant place in Australian literary history. Mary Grant Bruce and her fifteen Billabong novels (from *A Little Bush Maid* (1910) to *Billabong Riders* (1942)) are equally important in the world of Australian children's fiction, although she writes of 'mateship' and life on a well established pastoral property (Alexander 1979; Niall 1979). Reading with today's values, critics (and perhaps child readers) object to the chauvinism and racism which reflected the values of their day, but the books retain their popularity and have appeared in edited editions which omit the offending segments of text. Debate continues, questioning the appropriateness of such editions.

As in England, so too in Australia, school stories developed during this period, exploring the interpersonal friendships between young girls: Louise Mac's *Teens* (1897) and its sequels were set in Sydney. The nation's writers, compelled by the spirit of optimism in the new nation, were beginning to write for their own young readers – rather than all that was good and wholesome being seen as having to come from England.

Books which broke from the didactic tradition and which sought primarily to entertain emerge as distinctive contributions to Australian children's literature. An early example is *Cole's Funny Picture Book: The Funniest Picture Book in the World* (1876), a collection which includes the humorous the tragic and the guilty through many different genres: poems, stories, black and white engravings, puzzles, riddles, teasers and which has been a family favourite for many years. (Annotations of the many collections of Australian short stories and poems – both historical and contemporary – are to be found in the research catalogue *Through Australian Eyes* which accompanied the 1988 European exhibition of Australian children's literature, now housed in the International Youth Library in Munich, Germany (Bunbury *et al.* 1988).) Outstanding among more lengthy humorous tales, is a book known for its fun, its fighting, its endless supply of food, and its tricky central 'character' – *The Magic Pudding* written and illustrated by Norman Lindsay (1918) – an acclaimed artist of the time. Dorothy Wall's Australian animal characters and the koala *Blinky Bill* in particular, dominated in the publishing scene from 1933 to 1942 and her books are still read today.

## A Continent-Wide Market

The period between Federation and the great depression also saw the development of a 'continent-wide market' with a background of strong clashes between capital and labour, arbitration, an emerging middle class, child endowment, hopes for a new social regeneration devoid of class privilege, inequality and poverty. Pride in an egalitarian democratic society was firmly established – at least in the hearts of the people.

> There'll be higher education for the toilin', starvin', clown,
> And the rich an' educated shall be educated down'.
>
> Henry Lawson, *For'ard* (1893)

A broad cultural background has always been valued by teachers in Australia. When schooling by correspondence became possible across the vast expanses of the country (1916), and free secondary education became a reality along with technical education and kindergartens, the child and adolescent reading population grew. Literature generally reflected an egalitarian society and a positive commitment to social regeneration. The new nation was prosperous and – as it thought – far from the troubles of war.

Australia's first involvement in war (1914–1918) had re-affirmed yet simultaneously strained the links with Britain. Post war, there was a call to turn to sources of inspiration other than the 'bush' and the 'outback' – particularly as the majority of Australians had become city dwellers. Commercial broadcasting, the movies and the motor car were a regular part of suburban life. Mass-produced 'popular children's literature emerged – a sign that the publication of children's books had become a flourishing business.

Nevertheless, there emerged fine works in the fairy tradition, by the Rentoul sisters, Annie and Ida (the latter becoming Rentoul Outhwaite), May Gibbs and

Pixie O'Harris. They focused on fairy tales and animal fantasies: gumnut babies met and played with creatures of the bush. The stories made their impact largely because of inspiration from art nouveau and the quality of reproduction. Ida Rentoul Outhwaite's *Elves and Fairies* (1916) was notable because the reproduction of watercolour illustrations was so lavish and because the book was completely published in Australia. Most Australian children's books prior to this period had been published in Britain. (Muir and Holden (1985) explore the details of originals which are to be found in the Hardie Collection, Sydney NSW.) Bicentennial celebrations confirmed that May Gibbs's 'gumnut babies' from *Snugglepot and Cuddlepie* (1918) have become Australian icons – while the 'banksia men' remained in hidden adult fears remembered from childhood.

The Second World War was a strategic point of development for many facets of Australian life. People realised, probably for the first time, that the Commonwealth of nations could not meet Australia's needs, although Britain continued to be important for the purposes of industrialisation, markets for primary produce and as a source of culture. Australians realised they had to become more self-reliant, yet for the sake of security, military and strategic links were developed with the USA; links were also sought with emerging nations of Asia, Australia's northern neighbours; and the country began to play its own role in the international arena of the United Nations. These were difficult and contradictory political threads to weave. Similarly, the sense of national identity ebbed and flowed in the cross currents of a society experiencing rapid change.

Within the nation, at a level identifiably closer to the future of children's literature, there was a post-war 'baby boom'. Librarians became the self-appointed custodians of literature for children – many gave their time voluntarily to bring children and books closer together. They were responsible for the Children's Book Council of New South Wales which was established in 1945, and which in 1946 began the Children's Book Awards. From these modest beginnings the Australian Children's Book Council was formed in 1959. The awards (listed in Prentice and Bennet 1992) are highly valued by authors and publishers, and have done much to foster children's literature – though not without controversy.

The world of children's literature during the post-war period, into the 1950s and beyond, was clearly focused, with the emergence of a number of women writers who not only wrote stories of family life, but who combined this with a strong sense dawning self-awareness in childhood and adolescence and the beginnings of a questing after a sense of belonging in the land: Nan Chauncy, Mavis Thorpe Clark, Joan Phipson, Patricia Wrightson, Eleanor Spence and Hesba Brinsmead remain significant writers of the period. In writing about such works Maurice Saxby, an early influential critic of children's literature in Australia dismissed them as being 'as predictable as those of the adventure stories of a hundred years earlier' (Saxby 1969: 194). In retrospect, few would agree and such comments are now recognised as part of the cultural cringe of the times (where things Australian were less valued than those which came from overseas) as much as alignment against the value of subject matter (usually domestic, family or romance) said to be chosen by women writers.

Wrightson has subsequently become Australia's best known writer for children internationally, as was confirmed by the prestigious Hans Christian Andersen award in 1986. She has been publishing books for children for more than forty years and has courageously broken new ground with her trilogy, *The Song of Wirrun* (1993) – comprising *The Ice is Coming* (1977), *The Dark Bright Water* (1979) and *Behind the Wind* (1981). Drawing her inspiration from the 'folk-spirits of Aboriginal Dreamtime', she has created a contemporary fantasy where ancient folk-spirits (not of the secret-sacred variety) meet and work with a young fringe-dwelling Aborigine. She does not claim 'inside knowledge' of Aboriginal cultures but her work's poetic resonance appeals to her readers for its inclusion of folklore which originates from the Australian continent, rather than those far away lands of Europe. Such creative endeavours have prompted Driver (1993) to compile a register of Aboriginal folk-spirits for use by future readers and scholars. One section of the volume lists folk-spirits whose existence has been confirmed by Aboriginal people in touch with their 'country and customs of origin'; the appendix, almost as large, lists folk-spirits represented in the writings of Causcasian Australia which are yet to be confirmed – or denied – by specific tribal groups.

Ivan Southall and Colin Thiele (both translated into many languages) were also writing during this period. Southall's narratives grew from the post-war excitement of flight (and space flight) in his Simon Black books, to explorations of the hazards of children facing the natural disasters of the land. His exacting and introspective works such as *Josh* (1971) were yet to come. Thiele drew on a German background and his engaging humour provoked by incidents as innocent as a possum in the kitchen were embedded in a rich appreciation of language. The wonder of the intense interaction between a boy and a pelican are known internationally through the book and film, *Storm Boy* (1974).

By 1967, Australian children's literature was able to parody the nation's eulogising of its rogues and thieves – the Wild Colonial Boy and the bushrangers – in the work of Randolph Stow's *Midnite*. Ironic treatment of a national hero is surely a sign of a nation self-consciously reflecting on its history and its identity. This was in fact, happening in a political sense, when in 1966 Australia entered the Vietnam conflict. The students who were present at the mass demonstrations against Australia's involvement in Vietnam, and who joined the activities of Amnesty International, became the scholars of children's literature in the universities during the 1970s, humanitarian ideals being the thread as much as literary scholarship.

Educational authorities were obliged to respond to the post-war increase in the birth rate and the influx of immigrants: more schools were built, returned servicemen entered the teaching force, studentships became available thus increasing voluntary school retention rates (to year twelve) of secondary schooling. These young people became librarians and teachers who graduated from the rapidly expanding Teachers Colleges and Colleges of Advanced Education. Tertiary courses gradually added the study of children's literature as an integral part of their training programmes. The Library Association of Australia required the study of children's literature of all its graduates. Public libraries and school libraries gradually increased with the Commonwealth government subsidising secondary schools libraries (from 1968). This political endorsement effectively increased young people's access to books. The national research project, *Children's*

*Choice* (Bunbury 1995), which explored children's reading preferences, at school and at home, reported that the most important source of books for young people's reading was not those so lovingly presented as gifts at home, but the school library. In the 1990s, when Australia consciously strives to become 'a clever country', government sponsorship still seeks ways of increasing the youthful reading public; an example is to be found in the 'book gigs' at St Martin's Youth Theatre, organised by Agnes Nieuwenhuizen, where authors meet their readers after youthful actors have staged sequences from published literary works (see her related annotated lists of adolescent fiction (1992a, 1992b) and her interviews with writers for youth (1991)).

## Contemporary Developments

It was not until the 1970s, that universities took up the serious academic study of children's literature. Many undergraduate courses evolved to meet the needs of the growing numbers of teachers who were graduating. Masters degrees by course-work, both on campus and in distance mode, exist in several Australian universities and Masters by research and Doctorates occur spasmodically but in growing numbers. Research collections which feed academic endeavour are housed in the Bailleau Library (Morgan Collection) University of Melbourne, the State Libraries of Victoria, South Australia and Western Australia and The Lu Rees Archives at Canberra University.

Conferences in the field of children's literature, both national and international, are now a regular event with published proceedings providing an informed readership with critical insights into major preoccupations in the field (Trask 1972, 1973, 1975; Robinson 1977; Saxby 1978; Lees 1980; Murphy 1980; Noel 1981; Alderman and Harman, 1983; Stodart, 1985; Alderman and Reeder, 1987; Children's Book Council of Australia 1992, 1994; Stone 1991, 1993; Parsons and Goodwin 1994).

Basic bibliographic data have been compiled (Muir 1970, 1976) and historical surveys are in place (Saxby 1969, 1971, 1993; Niall 1984; Lees and MacIntyre 1993; Bayfield 1994) thus the groundwork has been laid for fuller critical consideration of Australian children's literature (for example, McVitty 1981; Thomson 1987; Stephens 1992). There is, however, a marked schism between those who consider children's books within the context of awards and library promotions, and those whose task it is to place children's literature within the context of general literary studies. Children's literature needs the energies from both sources.

Unless one writes for *Meanjin* and similar mainstream outlets for literature in Australia, publication outlets for scholarly articles in children's literature are largely confined to the journal *Papers: Explorations into Children's Literature*. Journals of professional interest to teachers, librarians and publishers are available in richer supply through: *Access* (formerly *Australian School Librarian*), *The Australian Author*, *Australian Book Review*, *Australian Journal of Reading*, *Curriculum Exchange*, *Editions*, *English in Australia*, *Idiom*, *Journal of the School Library Association of Queensland*, *Lines*, *The Literature Base*, *The Lu Rees Archives*, *Magpies*, *Orana* (formerly *Children's Libraries Newsletter*), *Reading Time* (formerly

*New Books for Boys and Girls*), *Review Point*, *Rippa Reading*, *Teacher and Librarian*, and *Viewpoint*. The wide range of journals is a reflection of the growing children's literature industry in Australia.

A boom in children's book publishing occurred again in the prosperous 1980s. Even during the international recession of the early 1990s, publishers of children's and adolescents' books were expanding – as though hope could only be sustained through youth. Yet it is through the literature for young people that many social problems were confronted so that the 'problem novel' has become a sustained genre in publishing: single parent families, divorce, drug addiction, teenage pregnancies, are typical themes. As in many nations of the world, post-holocaust fiction is a genre which has also emerged, Victor Kelleher's *Taronga* (1986) and Gillian Rubenstein's *Beyond the Labyrinth* (1989) are complex and compelling examples. Romance fiction sustains its popularity with its role in the lives of young women now being critically scrutinised (Gilbert 1991). Undoubtedly, however, the authors most sought after in the 1990s are those who write humorous fiction for children and adolescents, although writers such as Paul Jennings, Robin Klein and Margaret Clark receive little critical attention. Ironically, such writers are very serious about their humour, often seeing it as a vehicle for social comment. Klein's narratives sustain an ideology sympathetic to working class youth; Clark's indirectly address social issues such as bulimia and significant roles for young women; Jennings's are a pure indulgence of black humour – endorsed by youth, if not by custodians of youth.

Books which include illustrations have existed throughout Australia's publishing history and examples of these early works are now available on microfiche (*Pre-1890 Australian Children's Books* (1994) from the State Library of South Australia). Books which depend for their meaning on illustrations are a more recent development and have become a publishing phenomena, maturing in the 1970s. This was a time when the mineral boom brought a sense of hope and great prosperity to the country. As a nation Australia saw itself as a thriving independent nation – no longer subservient to or dependent on Britain. Along with the general feeling of independence, wealth and prosperity, came the development of lithographic techniques, the removal of import restrictions on books, 'off-shore printing, cooperation between publishing companies (both nationally and internationally), a diversifying of media and subject matter, a broadening of the audience for picture-books; and the influence of visual communication in television and film. High-quality books diverse in subject matter, design and medium intricately explored the subtle interaction between illustration, print and the reader. These trends have been intensified during the 1980s and 1990s as picture books have increasingly been identified as a source of aesthetic interest for child, adolescent and adult. It has, however, been a matter of contention that far too often the picture book section of the Children's Book Council of Australia Book of the Year Award has not been awarded. This has led to the Australian Book Publishers Association Book Design Awards Best – Designed Illustrated Children's Book (from 1969). There is also the Crichton Award (from 1988) for new illustrators in the field of picture books. Through the Macmillan Award (from 1990), one publisher even seeks out unpublished manuscripts for picture books. Titles which have captured the market both nationally and internationally are the alphabet puzzle book, *Animalia* by Graeme Base (1986), and the entertaining family story *Possum Magic* by Mem Fox and Julie Vivas (1983), with *Waltzing Matilda* by Desmond Digby (1970) proving to be a significant pictorial representation of the melody. More than half the books nominated for the book of the year award are now picture books with the styles and artistic techniques becoming increasingly sophisticated. Variation in artistic technique and impact is to be found in the detailed pen and ink work of Peter Pavey, the fine cross hatchings of Ron Brooks, the droll humorous characters of Pamela Allen and quick impressionistic line of Bob Graham; the witty, pointed characters of Terry Denton, the very funny line drawings of Craig Smith, the delicate pastel collage of Patricia Mullins, the robust painterly drawings of Donna Rawlins, the soft, realistic pastel detail of Jane Tanner and many more. Robert Ingpen's classical engraving style is probably the best known since he won the coveted Hans Christian Andersen award in 1986. Muir (1977) and Holden (1988) give details of the many illustrators active in Australia.

Collections of original illustrations for children's books have become the subject for curators, exhibitions and sales. A home for Australian children's books and original illustrations was established in 1973 by Joyce and Courtney Oldmeadow at Dromkeen, a rambling old house in rural Victoria, and is now visited by international visitors who seek exhibitions of historical and contemporary works. Books Illustrated, housed in Melbourne exhibits contemporary works and offers some for sale. Both places also organise workshops and meetings of authors and artists with visiting public and groups of schoolchildren.

Television came to Australia along with the Olympic Games in 1956, yet this medium did not undermine the extraordinary growth of children's literature. The 1960s saw both a qualitative and quantitative increase in the publication of Australian children's literature. Australian publishing houses opened; British publishing houses established Australian branches; printing in Hong Kong and Singapore reduced publication costs; publishers began appointing editors such as Joyce Saxby, Barbara Ker Wilson and Anne Bower Ingram whose task it was to specialise in children's literature; and the book trade began actively to seek translation for their holdings. Literary adaptations to film, television, video, hypertext and multimedia outlets continue to be significant features of the 1990s, with the potential demise of the book posing a substantial threat to many in conventional book publishing. Once again, children's literature, its writers, producers, readers and promoters see the need to come to grips with technological change.

Australia was once known critically as 'white Australia as the immigration schemes following the First World War and again following the Second, accepted immigrants only from Britain and continental Europe. The incentive was seen by politicians of the time as: 'We must populate this country or we will never be able to hold it (Greenwood 1955: 315). The core of government policy was a forced pace of development with the assistance of sponsored migration and land settlement, but at the grass roots level the workers and ordinary suburban people feared the influx of cheap labour at a time when unemployment levels were rising. This conflict endures, but strenuous efforts are being made to redefine and celebrate national identity through the recognition of difference. Around one hundred different languages, plus the Aboriginal languages are now spoken, apart from English; current ideology has moved away from assimilation and endeavours to recognise 'difference within the society and its cultures and to encourage all to sustain pride in their origins, while making their first commitment to Australia.

How the political and social can motivate the literary can be seen in the evolution of the Multicultural Children's Literature Award which is funded by the Office of Multicultural Affairs within the Department of the Prime Minister and Cabinet. In 1990 there were five titles eligible for the award and by 1993 this had grown to forty-nine titles. Understandings of the concept of multiculturalism differ but award-winners are those stories in which the different races and cultures merge as a natural course of events as in Libby Gleeson's *Big Dog* (1991) where a Vietnamese dragon (street festival costume style) helps two Australian children overcome their fear of a savage dog. However, most of the multicultural books for youth written in Australia are written by long-resident Anglo-Celtic Australian writers, whose acute observations of cultural morés articulate and try to soften or provide alternative resolutions to the conflicts they observe; and who believe in the capacities of literature to foster respect and knowledge about other cultures: Allan Baillie and Nadia Wheatley are such writers.

*The Bibliography of Australian Multicultural Writers* (Gunew *et al.* 1992) lists 900 writers but very few of them have published for a child audience. David Martin, born in Hungary, is one such writer whose literature for youth is listed alongside his adult publications. Published narratives, written for children by people from within the many different ethnic minority groups are still quite rare: *Looking for Alibrandi* (1992) by Melina Marchetta explores the subjectivity of a young Italian girl, her family and friends and lays open the conflicts between the generations of immigrant Australians. Current trends suggest that such books could be the new growth area for Australian Children's literature, particularly as the *Access to Excellence* Report calls for market research: 'with a view to develop new markets in the literary field within Australia (Papastergiadis *et al.* 1993: 49).

With at least thirty publishers and more than a thousand active writers and illustrators of children's books in a population of 17.8 million, the competition for the promoters', selectors' and readers', attention is considerable – particularly in a nation where sunshine and outdoor sports dominate the way of life.

# References

Alderman, B. and Harman, L. (eds) (1983) *The Imagineers: Writing and Illustrating Children's Books*, Canberra: Children's Book Council.

Alderman, B. and Reeder, S. O. (eds) (1987) *The Inside Story: Creating Children's Books*, Canberra: Children's Book Council.

Alexander, A. (1979) *Billabong's Author*, Sydney: Angus and Robertson.

Bayfield, J. (comp.) (1994) *Pre-1890 Australian Children's Books* (Microfiche), Adelaide: State Library of South Australia, Children's Literature Research Collection.

Bigge, J. T. (1823) 'Report of the Commissioner of Enquiry on the State of Agriculture and Trade in the Colony of New South Wales in Clark, C. M. H. (ed.) (1950) *Select Documents in Australian History 1788–1850*, Sydney: Angus and Robertson.

Bunbury, R. (ed.) (1995) *Children's Choice*, Geelong, Victoria: Deakin University Press.

—— et al. (1988) *Through Australian Eyes. Kinderbücher aus Australien*, Geelong, Victoria: Deakin University.

Children's Book Council of Australia (1992) *At Least They're Reading. Proceedings of the first National Conference of the Children's Book Council of Australia*, Sydney: D. W. Thorpe.

Children's Book Council of Australia (1994) *Ways of Seeing. Proceedings of the second National Conference of the Children's Book Council of Australia*, Melbourne: D. W. Thorpe.

Driver, B. R. L. (1993) *Aboriginal Folkspirits in Australian Children's Literature*, MA thesis, Adelaide: Flinders University.

Gilbert, P. (1991) *Girls, Popular Culture and Schooling*, Sydney: Allen and Unwin.

Greenwood, G. (1955) *Australia: A Social and Political History*, Sydney: Angus and Robertson.

Gunew, S., Houbien, L., Karakostas-Seda, A. and Mahyuddin, J. (eds) (1992) *A Bibliography of Australian Multicultural Writers*, Geelong, Victoria: Deakin University Centre for Studies in Literary Education.

Holden, R. (1988) *Koalas, Kangaroos and Kookaburras: 200 Australian Children's Books and Illustrations 1857–1988*, Granville, NSW: James Hardie.

Lees, S. (ed.) (1980) *A Track to Unknown Water: Proceedings of the second RIM Conference on Children's Literature*, Victoria: Melbourne State College Department of Librarianship.

Lees, S. and MacIntyre, P. (1993) *The Oxford Companion to Australian Children's Literature*, Melbourne: Oxford University Press.

McVitty, W. (1981) *Innocence and Experience: Essays on contemporary Australian children's writing*, Melbourne: Nelson.

Muir, M. (1970) *A Bibliography of Australian Children's Books*, Vol. 1., London: André Deutsch.

—— (1976) *A Bibliography of Australian Children's Books*, Vol. 2, London: André Deutsch.

—— (1977) *Australian Children's Book Illustrators*, South Melbourne, Victoria: Sun Books.

Muir, M. and Holden, R. (1985) *The Fairy World of Ida Rentoul Outhwaite*, Sydney: Craftsman House.

Murphy, B. (ed.) (1980) *Readings in Children's Literature: Proceedings of the second national seminar on Children's Literature*, Frankston, Victoria (Australia): Frankston State College.

Niall, B. (1979) *Seven Little Billabongs: The World of Ethel Turner and Mary Grant Bruce*, Melbourne: Melbourne University Press.

Niall, B. (assisted by O'Neil, F.) (1984) *Australia Through the Looking Glass 1830–1980*, Melbourne: Melbourne University Press.

Nieuwenhuizen, Agnes (1991) *No Kidding: Top Writers for Young People Talk about Their Work*, Chippendale, NSW: Pan Macmillan (Sun).

—— (1992a) *Good Books for Teenagers*, Port Melbourne, Victoria: Mandarin.

—— (1992b) *The Written Word: Youth and Literature*, Port Melbourne: D. W. Thorpe.

Noel, E. (ed.) (1981) *Able to Enjoy: Books and the Young Disabled. Papers Presented at the Australian National Section of the International Board on Books for Young People (IBBY)*, Sydney: IBBY Publications.

Papastergiadis, N., Gunew, S. and Blonski, A. (1993) *Access to Excellence – Review of Issues Affecting Artists and Arts from Non English Speaking Backgrounds: Writers*, Geelong, Victoria: Centre for Studies in Literary Education.

Parsons, W. and Goodwin, R. (eds) (1994) *Landscape and Identity: Perspectives from Australia. Conference Proceedings*, Blackwood, South Australia: University of South Australia Centre for Children's Literature.

Prentice, J. and Bennett, B. (1992) *A Guide to Australian Children's Literature*, Port Melbourne, Victoria: D. W. Thorpe.

Robinson, M. (ed.) (1977) *Readings in Children's Literature. Proceedings of the first National Seminar on Children's Literature*, Frankston: Frankston State College.

Saxby, H. M. (1969) *A History of Australian Children's Literature 1841–1941*, Sydney: Wentworth Books.

—— (1971) *A History of Australian Children's Literature 1941–1970*, Sydney: Wentworth Books.

—— (ed.) (1978) *Through Folklore to Literature. Papers presented at the Australian National Section of the International Board on Books for Young People (IBBY)*, Sydney: IBBY Publications.

—— (1993) *The Proof of the Puddin' 1970–1990*, Brisbane: Ashton Scholastic.

Stephens, J. (1992) *Language and Ideology in Children's Fiction*, London: Longman.

Stodart, E. (ed.) (1985) *Writing and Illustrating for Children, Australian Capital Territory (ACT) Seminars 1975–1980*, Canberra: Children's Book Council of Australia.

Stone, M. (ed.) (1991) *Children's Literature and Contemporary Literary Theory*, Wollongong, NSW: New Literatures Research Centre, University of Wollongong.

—— (ed.) (1993) *Australian Children's Literature: Finding a Voice*, Wollongong NSW: New Literatures Research Centre, University of Wollongong.

Thomson, J. (1987) *Understanding Teenagers Reading*, London: Croom Helm; Melbourne: Methuen.

Trask, M. (ed.) (1972) *Fantasy, Science Fiction, Science Materials*, Kensington, Sydney: University of New South Wales.

—— (ed.) (1973) *Picture Books*, Kensington, Sydney: University of New South Wales.

—— (ed.) (1975) *A Sense of History*, Kensington, Sydney: University of New South Wales.

# 83

# New Zealand

## *Betty Gilderdale*

The first book for children with a New Zealand setting was *Stories About Many Things: Founded on Facts* (1833), in which an anonymous author tells stories about New Zealand to an enquiring small boy. They feature descriptions of flora and fauna as well of the indigenous people – the Maori. The same ingredients were to appear in a number of early books especially those written about the North Island and largely giving a missionary perspective.

Early books from the South Island were dominated by the experiences of mainly middle-class women settlers and were compiled from diaries and letters sent "Home' to England. They graphically recorded how, deprived of the household help they were accustomed to in Britain, gently nurtured ladies had to learn how to bake their own bread, wash their own dishes, attend to poultry and the vegetable garden and bear their children miles away from medical expertise.

The most entertaining of the early writers was Lady Barker, whose accounts of a three-year sojourn on a sheep station in Canterbury, *Station Life in New Zealand* (1870), is a classic for adults, but her lively stories for children, *Stories About...* (1870), *A Christmas Cake in Four Quarters* (1871) and *Boys* (1874), also contain amusing domestic detail.

In the North Island, however, disputes between Maori and settlers eventually erupted into the Land Wars, and overseas writers such as Jules Verne, G. A. Henty and Reginald Horsley were quick to seize upon the opportunity for fast-paced adventure stories set in this strange volcanic country where hitherto unknown native peoples posed a threat to the new wave of European immigrants.

These novels were published in London or Paris by writers who were not directly involved in the conflict. European New Zealanders who subsequently drew upon the same material were at pains to emphasise the tragedy of what was virtually a civil war, where individual friendships between Maori and European sometimes triumphed over tribal and national affiliations. The best known of these novels is William Satchell's *The Greenstone Door* (1914), but the friendship between Maori and European in times of conflict was re-visited thirteen years later by Mona Tracy in *Rifle and Tomahawk* (1927), and more recently by Anne de Roo in *Jacky Nobody* (1983).

By the end of the century a new generation of children had been born in New Zealand and there was a sudden flurry of activity to provide stories for them with a local setting. Unfortunately, instead of honest non-fiction to tell children about the local flora and fauna, this information was clothed in "flower fairy' tales which were condescending and sentimental. One writer, however, emerged from the morass as an excellent and prolific story-teller. This was Edith Howes, a science teacher who was anxious that children should know more about the natural world. Her most famous book at the time was *The Cradle Ship* (1916), in which she was daring enough to explain "the facts of life' to children through showing them how first fish, then reptiles, birds and mammals give increasing protection to their young from conception to maturity, finally finishing with drawing parallels with human beings. The book was enormously successful, not only in New Zealand but in Britain and Australia and it was translated into French, Italian and Danish. Nevertheless it has not stood the test of time, and it is her adventure story *Silver Island* (1928), which is still enjoyable and which became the forerunner of numerous New Zealand "survival' stories.

Edith Howes worked in the South Island, and another Christchurch writer, journalist Esther Glen, was one of her contemporaries. Both authors profited from the favourable climate for children's literature which was developing at the time. A library conference in Dunedin in 1910 had advocated the establishment of juvenile libraries and reading rooms in all municipal libraries, and children's reading was greatly encouraged. Local authors were also finding a publisher in the Christchurch firm of Whitcombe and Tombs and were not always forced to send their manuscripts to London for publication. In the spirit of the times, Esther Glen established a children's supplement in the *Christchurch Sun* where she published the work of aspiring young writers. She was eager to encourage a body of work for New Zealand children and felt particularly challenged by Australian Ethel Turner's *Seven Little Australians* (1894) so in answer she wrote *Six Little New Zealanders* (1917).

The novel, with its sequel *Uncles Three at Kamahi* (1926), is reminiscent of Lady Barker's witty accounts of life on a New Zealand sheep station, as six city children from Auckland spend a summer with three bachelor uncles in Canterbury. The children are unused to the country and the uncles are unused to children so the resulting mixture of misunderstandings and mishaps makes for amusing reading.

The distinctive way of life on large sheep-stations was picked up again thirty years later in a number of novels written by Joyce West in the 1950s, beginning with *Drover's Road* (1953). Although she depicts a North Island farm, there is still much in common with earlier books which have a rural setting. Food is plentiful, events such as agricultural shows and point-to-points dominate the social calendar, and human relationships are predominantly cheerful and uncomplicated, the drama occurring in battles with nature – flash floods, drowning stock, bush fires or hurricanes.

Books set in the country are less dominated by the vagaries of human behaviour than those by the Auckland writer Isabel Maud Peacocke, who offers a more unhappy picture of urban life in the 1920s and 1930s. Her world is one of ex-servicemen returning from the First World War to a country where unemployment and poverty are commonplace and where children, often orphaned, are subject to custody disputes. It is a world where people die because they cannot afford medical treatment and where social snobbery is rife. Her adults are frequently irresponsible, but her children are always well-intentioned and are generally tolerant of aberrant adult behaviour. Her many novels are variable in style, at best incisive and satirical, at worst sentimental and banal, but her acute portrayal of life in Auckland at the time is unrivalled.

Unfortunately children's literature in a country with a population of only three million people is particularly vulnerable to economic fluctuations. The Great Depression of the 1930s, followed closely by six years of war severely affected the publication of books for children. Not only were few published locally or imported from overseas, but the body of literature which had gradually been accumulating was not kept in print and was consequently forgotten.

The result of more than a decade of neglect was a re-awakening in the 1950s to the fact that there were few local books for children and there was an immediate stampede to produce some. Oblivious of the Edith Howes stories of the 1920s, authors such as Avis Acres produced similar "flower fairy' picture books to tell children about local flora and fauna, and by the 1960s there was a rash of photographic books to tell New Zealand children about their country, with an abundance of titles such as *Kuma is a Maori Girl* (1961) by Pat Lawson, or *David, Boy of the High Country* (1964) by David Kohlap.

The desire to develop a strong New Zealand identity, separate from the British, also saw a return to the preoccupation with the land itself, a preoccupation which is never far below the surface of New Zealand literature. The early settlers had marvelled at the strangeness of the forested mountainous country where rivers flooded, volcanoes erupted and daily routines could be disrupted by earthquakes, but they met its challenges by cutting down trees and trying to tame unruly nature into something like the benign English landscape. The challenge of the land in the 1960s, however, was met in adventure stories whose protagonists were lost in the bush (forest), nearly drowned in floods or cut off in inaccessible mountains by massive land slips resulting from earthquakes. During their adventures they were likely to encounter smugglers who were attempting illegally to export either Maori artefacts or rare and endangered animal species. Both Phyl Wardell, in novels such as *Hazard Island* (1976), and Joan de Hamel in *X Marks the Spot* (1973), show a strong sense of conservation as their characters foil the theft of paua shell in the former and smugglers of the rare kakapo parrot in the latter.

The 1960s and 1970s also saw a return to the "early settler' theme, but now the emphasis was upon less wealthy immigrants to New Zealand who were having to make their way in a harsh and uncaring society. Elsie Locke in *The Runaway Settlers* (1965) and Ruth Dallas in *The Children in the Bush* (1969) both depict women left on their own to be the sole support of their families, while in *Green Gold* (1976) and its sequels, Eve Sutton described how young immigrant boys had to make their way alone in the tough conditions of early nineteenth century Auckland.

The 1960s and 1970s, with their emphasis on establishing a New Zealand identity, were not encouraging to writers of fantasy, who failed to conform to the prevailing contemporary ethos. So it was that when a young librarian, Margaret Mahy, submitted her stories of archetypal witches, wizards and dragons to local publishers they were rejected as being "too English'. Fortunately the *School Journal*, a publication funded by the Department of Education and distributed free of charge to all schools, did publish her stories, and when the *Journals* were exhibited in the USA they were noticed by an editor of the Franklin Watts publishing house. Joint publication with Dents of Britain was arranged and in 1969 five picture books appeared, illustrated by leading artists. They were an instant success and since then Margaret Mahy has received numerous local and international awards for picture books, collections of stories such as *The First Margaret Mahy Story Book* (1972) and novels for older children like *The Haunting* (1982), which won the British Carnegie Medal.

Although Mahy's books have international and timeless appeal there are, nevertheless, strong New Zealand components in her work. Her settings are recognisably New Zealand landscapes and seascapes, and the sea which surrounds the islands is featured in many stories including *The Man Whose Mother Was a Pirate* (1972), and *Sailor Jack and the Twenty Orphans* (1970). Earthquakes occur in a number of stories and volcanoes erupt in *Aliens in the Family* (1986).

One of the most noticeable components in New Zealand children's literature is the number of elderly, and often idiosyncratic, characters who appear in stories. One of the most celebrated was the old sailor Falter Tom in Maurice Duggan's *Falter Tom and the Water Boy* (1958), but Margaret Mahy continues the tradition with the poetic tale of old Phoebe in *The Wind Between the Stars* (1976), with Great Uncle Magnus Pringle in *Ultra Violet Catastrophe* (1975), who refuses to be cosseted like a pot plant, and, most recently in the remarkable portrait of Sophie, a sufferer from Alzheimer's disease in *Memory* (1987), who is treated with discerning sympathy and manages, in spite of a chaotic existence, to retain her dignity.

This respect and tolerance for the elderly may well stem from the Maori veneration of grandparents, and since the 1970s there has been a considerable revival in Maori culture. One of the first picture books to be published in full colour in New Zealand was Jill Bagnall's *Crayfishing with Grandmother* (1973), which was also the first picture book to feature both Maori and English texts. It was another grandmother in *The Boy and the Taniwha* (1966), who initiated her grandson into Maori legends and customs. The book was the first to be published by Auckland author R. L. Bacon, a teacher who felt that his pupils were lacking in knowledge of the Maori, and who also insisted that his well-told stories should be equally well illustrated by Maori artists. He later broke new ground with three books, *The House of the People* (1977), *The Fish of our Fathers* (1984) and *The Home of the Winds* (1986), which explain how the first Maori meeting house, war canoe and fortified *pa* were constructed, and which are outstandingly interpreted by R. H. Jahnke's rhythmical stylised pictures. Since then a number of Maori artists, including Robyn Kahukiwa and Gavin Bishop have both written and illustrated picture books which have added richness and variety to the canon of New Zealand illustration.

The 1970s saw a number of developments which were favourably to influence children's literature. In 1969 a Children's Literature Association had been formed in Auckland which drew together parents, teachers and librarians and which received much encouragement from Dorothy Butler, a specialist children's bookseller, and one of her staff, Ronda Armitage, later to become the author of *The Lighthouse Keeper's Lunch* (1977). The Association exerted pressure on newspapers and journals to review children's books – something never previously attempted – and in 1973 the *New Zealand Herald* became the first newspaper in the country to give reviewing space to children's literature.

The growing interest in the genre also led to critical examination and in 1980 J. B. Ringer's *Young Emigrants, New Zealand Juvenile Fiction 1833–1918* was published followed two years later by Betty Gilderdale's *A Sea Change, 145 Years of New Zealand Junior Fiction* (1982), a comprehensive survey of the subject from 1833–1978.

While literary critics were discussing the merits of local writers, Professor Marie Clay of Auckland University's Education department was discovering that children learn to read more quickly if they are given "real' books rather than graded readers. This method of teaching reading was so successful that educational publishers such as Ashton Scholastic, Shortland and Heinemann commissioned well-known writers to write short stories which were then attractively illustrated and offered to schools for the teaching of reading. At present not only New Zealand schools but English-speaking countries overseas, including the USA, import these stories and use the Clay method of teaching reading.

During the same period a number of international publishers had become established in Auckland, bringing with them greater expertise in colour reproduction. This factor, added to the use of picture books in the schools, led to an explosion in the production of local picture books. Two of the best known New Zealand writers of books for the young, however, are no longer domiciled in New Zealand. Pamela Allen lives in Australia and Ronda Armitage and her illustrator husband David live in England.

The most internationally successful author/illustrator who remains firmly in New Zealand is Lynley Dodd, whose cumulative rhyming texts relate the exploits of *Hairy Maclary from Donaldson's Dairy* (1983, and sequels), with his canine and feline friends. Text and lively pictures are totally complementary; Dodd never stoops to anthropomorphism and her animals are characters in their own right, with names that are as expressive as their actions; who can forget Schnitzel von Krumm the dachshund or Scarface Claw, the terrible tom cat?

Lynley Dodd's animals have international appeal and during the 1980s there appeared to be less of an obsession with portraying New Zealand in print. Those books which, in fact, convey a vivid picture of life in New Zealand do so unselfconsciously, for example, the novels of Aucklander Tessa Duder, which depict strong female characters sailing on the harbour, playing in an orchestra or, in her popular *Alex* (1987) series, becoming a swimming champion.

The New Zealand preoccupation with winning at sport is satirised in William Taylor's *The Worst Soccer Team Ever* (1987) and its sequels, and these amusing school stories explore a genre which has been generally neglected in New Zealand. In the late 1920s and 1930s Phillis Garrard had written *Hilda at School, a New Zealand Story* (1929) and its three sequels which featured a country day-school, while in the 1940s and 1950s Clare Mallory depicted an exclusive South Island girls' boarding school in *Merry Begins* (1947) and subsequent novels. In general, however, adventures in New Zealand seem to take place outside the classroom and even in the William Taylor novels much of the action is outside school hours.

Taylor has written a number of novels for older readers which offer a less happy picture than that of the ebullient pupils of Greenhill Intermediate School. In *Possum Perkins* (1987) he sensitively explores the subject of incest, and other novels have characters who tangle with the law, growing marijuana, stealing hub caps or even holding up a bank. They reflect a society which has growing social problems and an economic climate which does not favour the poor.

With the honourable exception of Margaret Mahy's work, fantasy has always been the weakest genre in New Zealand writing for children, but since the 1980s some of the most able authors have turned to science fiction. They include Barry Faville, Maurice Gee, Gaylene Gordon, Sheryll Jordan, Jack Lasenby and Caroline Macdonald.

Apart from Gaylene Gordon, who explores aspects of mind control, novels by the other writers are frequently set in the future, after some holocaust, but where New Zealand has escaped through its isolation from the rest of the world. The theme offers an appropriate opportunity to examine systems of government, the use and abuse of power and indirectly to caution young people to avoid the mistakes of their elders and prepare for a different world.

Because of the quality of their prose style and their skill as story-tellers, these writers have managed to avoid overt didacticism, but in lesser writers throughout the 160 years briefly discussed in this survey, didacticism and condescension have been the major faults, and the worst books in New Zealand literature are those which attempt to deliver information.

Joy Cowley, however, is one contemporary author whose stories for young children certainly contain messages but they are so charmingly recounted that the charge of didacticism could scarcely be levelled against them. Books such as *The Duck in the Gun* (1969) and *The Fierce Little Woman and the Wicked Pirate* (1984) deflect violence with humour as they point out the absurdities of armed conflict in the former and the underlying motives of aggressors in the latter.

Anthony Holcroft is another writer who uses timeless fairy tale and mythical themes, but places them within a deeply felt and acutely observed South Island landscape. His overall message in collections of short stories like *Tales of the Mist* (1987), is that greed and possessiveness not only destroy human relationships but even threaten the land itself, which becomes barren.

As we have seen, the land has always taken a central place on the stage of New Zealand literature and the challenges afforded by these mountainous islands, isolated in the Pacific and vulnerable to the vagaries of oceanic weather, have shaped the New Zealand character. Over the past century-and-a-half children's literature has reflected the development of the country from a colonial outpost to a multi-cultural nation in its own right. The best contemporary writers are no longer trying self-consciously to establish a national identity. They are dealing with universal subjects of interest and in consequence are increasingly recognised in international literary circles. Nevertheless, children's books are peculiarly vulnerable to economic variations, depending as they do upon government funding to schools and libraries. It would be ironic if, owing to the current economic climate, the renaissance of children's literature in the 1990s were to suffer the fate of writers in the 1920s and 1930s, whose books were lost after Depression and War. At present, however, New Zealand authors have achieved international success out of all proportion to the size of the population, a success which could never have been visualised when the first halting tales in *Stories About Many Things* were first penned.

## Further Reading

Gilderdale, B. (1982) *A Sea Change, 145 Years of New Zealand Junior Fiction*, Auckland: Longman Paul.
—— (1987) *Introducing Margaret Mahy*, Auckland: Viking Kestrel.
—— (1991) *Introducing Twenty-One New Zealand Children's Writers*, Auckland: Hodder and Stoughton.
Ringer, J. B. (1980) *Young Emigrants, New Zealand Juvenile Fiction 1833–1919*, Hamilton: Privately Published.
Sturm, T. (ed.) (1991) *The Oxford History of New Zealand Literature*, Auckland: Oxford University Press.

# 84

# Canada

## English-Speaking Canada

### Alexandra West

#### Background

Children's literature in English-speaking Canada parallels, though it does not always mirror, the cultural development of Canada from a colony to the post-confederation nation which celebrated its centennial year in 1967. Canada's early dependence on British and American culture, and the struggle to waken from a long post-colonial sleep and to achieve a composite national character reflecting the multi-ethnic nature of Canada's population, are well demonstrated in English-language Canadian children's literature.

The title of the first Canadian children's book, Catharine Parr Traill's settler survival tale, *The Canadian Crusoes: A Tale of the Rice Lake Plains* (1852) intertextually linked Canada with Robinson Crusoe's island domain and thus linguistically asserted its colonised status. Scotsman R. M. Ballantyne's *Snowflakes and Sunbeams; or, The Young Fur Traders* (1856) helped to invent Canada's north as an exotic literary landscape for generations of British schoolboy readers of adventure books, reflecting an Occidentalism no less problematic than the Orientalism common elsewhere. Certainly, from the 1850s, Canadian children's literature has made some advances in developing its national character. For instance, between the 1890s and the 1920s, Sir Charles G. D. Roberts, Ernest Thompson Seton and L. M. Montgomery produced, among their other work, three still-famous Canadian children's books: *Red Fox* (1905), *The Biography of a Grizzly* (1900) and *Anne of Green Gables* (1908). Nevertheless, though many Canadian books for children have been written, very few of those written before 1967 have survived as classics, though Farley Mowat's *Lost in the Barrens* (1956) and James Houston's *Tikta'liktak* (1965) rightly occupy places of honour with Canadian readers at least.

After 1967, however, Canadian children's literature in English has reflected the significant expansion of Canadian adult literature in English and has helped to educate readers into an awareness of Canada's complex cultural identity which is trying to honour equally its aboriginal peoples, its new immigrants and its European and Asian forebears. In the past twenty years, Canadian educators have tried to increase the numbers of home-grown school texts and to expand students' experience of Canadian literature in the classroom. In effecting this, federal money supporting Canada Council publishing grants and literary awards, and the establishment of small presses and publishing houses, have been crucial.

The symbiotic relationship between the cultural health of a previously-colonised country and the commercial means to disseminate its art has been confirmed in the recent success of small Canadian publishing houses and presses that specialise in children's books. Tundra Books, Orca Books, Kids Can Press, Annick Press, Groundwood Books and Harbour Publishing, to name only a few, are vital to this process. After many years in which Canada's cultural identity in print was tightly bound up with British publishing in a postcolonial relationship, to the detriment of a strong national children's literature, the growing presence of Canadian publishing houses since the 1970s has greatly encouraged and enhanced the production of high-quality children's books in Canada.

### Major Writers

In the usual definition of the word 'major', that is with respect not only to crafting and influence but also to an international reputation, Canada has only a few major children's writers. L. M. Montgomery, perhaps the most famous, has a place beside Alcott and Burnett because of *Anne of Green Gables*, if not for her other books in the Anne series, her *Emily of New Moon* trilogy and *Pat of Silver Bush*, all published between 1908 and 1935. Roberts, Thompson, Mowat, Houston, Dennis Lee, Robert Munsch and Monica Hughes are all known internationally, as are the illustrators Ted Harrison, Ann Blades, Michael Martchenko and William Kurelek. Though it is hard to predict the staying power of the newer novel writers, literary fame often being the result of odd quirks of reader loyalty, Brian Doyle, Jan Truss, Janet Lunn, Kevin Major, Joan Clark, Mary-Ellen Lang Collura, Maria Campbell and Beatrice Culleton have all produced at least one novel that may survive.

### Fiction

The novel for young adults is the most flourishing of forms, encompassing psychological realism, animal realism, adventure, mystery and detection, domestic realism, growth, fantasy, science fiction and history. Since the 1970s there has also been a great growth of illustrated texts for younger children. Crossovers among the categories are common, realism often being combined with fantasy and history, as for example in Janet Lunn's excellent *The Root Cellar* (1981).

Probably because Canada's small population has always had to live close to its vast and dangerous landscape, right from the beginnings of Canadian children's fiction one feature has threaded its way through all the categories: the presentation of various faces of the natural world. Whether Canadian writers are composing fictionalised animal biographies, such as Seton's *The Biography of a Grizzly* (1900), or Roberts's *Red Fox* (1905); adventure survival tales such as Roderick Haig-Brown's *Starbuck Valley Winter* (1943), Farley Mowat's *Lost in the Barrens*

(1956) or James Houston's *Frozen Fire* (1977); stories in which teenagers, troubled by domestic conflict, run to the wilds for comfort, as in Jan Truss's *Jasmin* (1982) or Kevin Major's *Hold Fast* (1978); or anthropomorphic animal adventures, as in Sheila Burnford's *The Incredible Journey* (1960); awe and admiration for the natural world (tinged with a healthy respect) and anthropomorphism, reflected often in the trope of prosopopeia, are characteristic notes. Solid biological, botanical and geographic knowledge is also a feature of such works, which frequently have environmental concerns as a hidden agenda. Of course, pathetic fallacy, a very common device in all children's literature, shows up in Canadian texts too. In *Anne of Green Gables* (1908), Anne Shirley's state of mind is reflected in the trees and flowers who are pictured as her supporters and friends who rejoice and thrive when she does, while in Barbara Smucker's *Underground to Canada* (1977) Jullily, even in the midst of her terrible despair as a slave, sees her future rescue in a gorgeous sunset. When the natural world is a dominant feature of a Canadian children's book, it is rarely pictured as mere background or setting but often has the force of a character interacting with humans.

Since the late 1970s, many novels have appeared in which teenagers struggle to come to terms with life crises, particularly familial in origin, and sometimes cultural too. Whether the book is set on the West Coast, as is Elizabeth Brochmann's *What's the Matter, Girl?* (1980), or Alberta, as are both Mary-Ellen Lang Collura's *Winners* (1984) and Marilyn Halvorson's *Cowboys Don't Cry* (1984), or Ontario, as are Janet Lunn's *The Root Cellar* and *Shadow in Hawthorn Bay* (1986), or Newfoundland, as are Kevin Major's *Hold Fast* (1978), *Far From Shore* (1980), *Thirty-six Exposures* (1984) and *Dear Bruce Springsteen* (1987), alienation, anger, struggle and winning through are depicted against backdrops of social or familial injustice and conflict. These books are well crafted and psychologically acute and are likely to last as excellent examples of their type.

Pure fantasy and science fiction are not common in Canadian children's literature, (though fantasy in particular tends to crop up across the categories) but existing texts are often very readable, and at least in the case of Monica Hughes's eight novels are among the more important futuristic children's fiction being written anywhere today. Hughes's *Beyond the Dark River* (1979), *The Tomorrow City* (1978), *Ring-Rise, Ring-Set* (1982), *Devil on My Back*, (1984) and *The Dream Catcher* (1986) and the trilogy, *The Keeper of the Isis Light* (1980), *The Guardian of Isis* (1981), and *The Isis Pedlar* (1982), are both entertaining and thought-provoking in their concern with moral choices and humane values.

In fantasy, Monica Hughes's *Sandwriter* (1985), Janet Lunn's *The Root Cellar* and *Shadow of Hawthorn Bay*, Mordecai Richler's *Jacob Two-Two Meets the Hooded Fang* (1987), Margaret Laurence's *The Olden Days Coat* (1979), and Joan Clark's *Wild Man of the Woods* (1985) and *The Moons of Madeleine* (1987), aimed at a variety of ages, are all enjoyable. Catherine Anthony Clark's six fantasies are of historical as well as literary interest, being the first identifiably Canadian fantasy for children. *The Golden Pine Cone* (1950), *The Sun Horse* (1951), *The One-Winged Dragon* (1955), *The Silver Man* (1958), *The Diamond Feather: or, The Door in the Mountain: A Magic Tale for Children* (1962) and *The Hunter and the Medicine Man* (1966) are quest tales in fantasised Canadian settings, as are Ruth Nichols' *A Walk Out of the World* (1969) and *The Marrow of the World* (1972) which are also much concerned with the inner symbolic life and inner knowledge of self. Fantastical elements appear as subordinate threads in novels that are otherwise psychologically realistic or historical, as, for instance, happens in Collura's *Winners* or Lunn's *The Root Cellar*.

Given Canada's history, one might have expected historical fiction to be a strong feature of the national children's literature, but the typical features of such fiction in which events are privileged over character in an attempt to achieve accuracy, and in which an instructive tone is adopted towards the reader, produce the same stilted and didactic work in Canadian literature as in other national literatures. Besides, the growing recognition that the term 'historical fiction' is a tautology, and that all history is no more than the fictions we tell ourselves about the past, has begun to blur the lines between so-called history and an imaginative rendering of the past. Of the more traditional kind of historical fiction, John Hayes' six books on events in Canada's past, such as *Treason at York* (1949) and *Rebels Ride at Night* (1953), present a standard approach to historical 'accuracy'. More interesting because they deal with a subject less than common in children's literature, labour troubles and union politics, Bill Freeman's *Shantymen of Cache Lake* (1975) and *Trouble at Lachine Mill* (1983) manage to be both informative and entertaining at the same time. Whether set in a recognisable previous time period, in the current era looking back, or in a constructed present, rendering the varieties of Canadian culture, the ethnic groups and their reaction to each other – and the contact between the native peoples and white Canadian culture – has been the kind of 'history' that interests Canadian writers of children's literature. James Houston and Farley Mowat are writers of this kind, as are Roderick Haig-Brown in *The Whale People* (1962), Edith Sharp in *Nkwala* (1958), and Barbara Smucker in *Underground to Canada*. Jan Hudson's *Sweetgrass* (1984), on a year in the life of a young Blackfoot woman in the nineteenth century, has become recognised as a novel of note. And Shizuye Takashima's illustrated *A Child in Prison Camp* (1971), though not strictly speaking historical fiction since it uses her own family's story, skilfully and plainly evokes a child's view of the Canadian government's internment of Japanese Canadians during the Second World War. Telling the history of Canada as story rather than as event will probably continue to be an important aspect of the mirroring and the making of national identity for Canadian children.

## Illustrated Texts

Since the 1970s there has been a proliferation of excellent illustrated texts for children under the age of 10, including single fairy tales and myths, alphabet books, poetry and stories. So numerous now are Canadian illustrated books for children that it is impossible to list more than a few. However, in their highly recommended critical guide to Canadian children's literature, *The New Republic of Childhood* (1990), Sheila Egoff and Judith Saltman include a fifty-one page chapter, 'Picturebooks and Picture-Storybooks' that provides a wealth of detail about categories, titles, authors and illustrators, many of whom have won awards for their work. Another source of help in sorting out this extremely rich field of work, up to 1988, lies in *Canadian Books for Children: A Guide to Authors &*

*Illustrators* (1988), by Jon C. Stott and Raymond E. Jones. Besides concise short articles on individual authors, Stott and Jones list award-winning books and authors, and the names of the prizes they have won, by year, as well as suggestions of books suitable for specific ages of children.

From among the many outstanding alphabet picturebooks for very young children one might name Elizabeth Cleaver's *ABC* (1984), Ted Harrison's *A Northern Alphabet* (1982), Ann Blades's *By the Sea: An Alphabet Book* (1985) and Allan Moak's *A Big City ABC* (1984). In the category of picture storybooks for school-age children Ann Blades's *Mary of Mile 18* (1971) and *A Boy of Taché* (1973) and William Kurelek's *A Prairie Boy's Winter* (1973), *A Prairie Boy's Summer* (1975), and *A Northern Nativity* (1976) stand out. Of many recent publications, *Mr Kneebone's New Digs* (1991), by Ian Wallace, presents readers with a challenging text about urban poverty. *Waiting for the Whales*, by Sheryl McFarlane and Ron Lightburn (1991), present very poignant text and pictures, and the myth-poem *Last Leaf First Snowflake to Fall* (1993), by Native artist Leo Yerxa, pictures intensely and lovingly a Canadian annual experience like no other, the first snowfall just after the autumn colours. Informed by the Egoff/Saltman and Stott/Jones guides, readers of the Canadian illustrated text have a feast waiting for them.

### Native myths, legends and stories

There is a growing awareness among English-speaking Canadians that in a multi-ethnic society, the cultures of all ethnic groups should be honoured. Thus a reluctance to be seen as appropriators of Native culture has diminished the amount of work on native subjects by non-Native writers that began to appear infrequently early this century and more frequently between 1955 and the mid-1980s. In 1955 Cyrus Macmillan's *Glooscap's Country*; in the 1960s Robert Ayre's *Sketco the Raven* (1961), Kay Hill's *Glooscap and His Magic* (1963), Dorothy Reid's *Tales of Nanabozho* (1963), Christie Harris's *Once Upon a Totem* (1963), and William Toye and Elizabeth Cleaver's *The Mountain Goats of Temlaham* (1969) and *How Summer Came to Canada* (1969); in the 1970s Harris's *Once More Upon a Totem* (1974) and her *Mouse Woman* series, and Toye and Cleaver's *The Loon's Necklace* (1977) and *The Fire Stealer* (1979); and in the 1980s Alden Knowlan's *Nine Micmac Legends* (1983), appeared as examples of successful literary retellings for children, by non-Natives, of Indian oral stories. Versions of Inuit material by non-Natives are much scarcer, the work of James Houston (who lived for a decade in the Arctic in the 1950s) being by far the most important: his *Tikta'liktak* (1965), *The White Archer* (1967), *Akavak* (1968), *Wolf Run* (1971), *Kiviok's Magic Journey* (1973), *Long Claws* (1981) and *The Falcon Bow* (1986) all reflect Houston's knowledge of and empathy for his material.

Although Native writers of adult text are growing in numbers, in children's literature this is happening more slowly, though there are some notable exceptions. Basil Johnston is an Ojibway, an ethnologist, some of whose work, though intended for adult Natives, is accessible to children, especially *How the Birds Got Their Colours* (1978) and *Tales the Elders Told: Ojibway Legends* (1981), both of which are illustrated by Native artists. George Clutesi's *Son of Raven, Son of Deer: Tales of the Tseshaht People* (1967) and *Potlach* (1969) were the work of a man dedicated to restoring to primary importance cultural values that had been almost swamped by white traditions. *Tales From the Longhouse* (1973), the work of Native children on Vancouver Island, and some picturebooks, such as Freda Ahenakew and George Littlechild's *How the Birch Tree Got Its Stripes* (1988), and *How the Mouse Got Brown Teeth* (1988), and Jacquelinne White's *Coyote Winter* (1991) are excellent Native literary retellings of myths.

In fiction, books by Natives are few, though the Inuit Markoosie's 1970 *Harpoon of the Hunter*, Maria Campbell's *People of the Buffalo* (1975), *Little Badger and the Fire Spirit* (1977) and *Riel's People* (1978), and Beatrice Culleton's *In Search of April Raintree* (1983) and *Spirit of the White Bison* (1986) are very strong examples of the type.

### Poetry

Although there is only a limited amount of poetry specially written for children in Canadian literature, what there is, often illustrated by noteworthy artists, is of some merit. Also, adult Canadian poetry suitable for children has been published in two children's anthologies, *The Wind has Wings* (1968) and *The New Wind Has Wings* (1984), edited by Mary Alice Downie and Barbara Robertson, and illustrated by Elizabeth Cleaver. Probably the best known books of Canadian children's poetry are by Dennis Lee, a winner of the Governor General's Award for Poetry. His nursery rhymes in *Wiggle to the Laundromat* (1970), and his witty, psychologically perceptive poems in *Alligator Pie* (1974), *Nicholas Knock and Other People* (1974) and *Garbage Delight* (1977), all illustrated by Frank Newfeld, *Jelly Belly* (1983), illustrated by Juan Wijngaard, and a single-poem book *Lizzy's Lion* (1984), illustrated by Marie-Louise Gay, have been important to the growth of reader interest in Canadian children's literature. Some children's poetry has been written by Canadian poets better known for their adult poetry. Among these works are Desmond Pacey's *The Cat, the Cow and the Kangaroo: The Collected Children's Verse of Desmond Pacey* (1968), Irving Layton's *A Spider Danced a Cosy Jig* (1984) and B. P. Nichol's *Moosequakes and Other Disasters* (1981), *Giants, Moosequakes and Other Disasters* (1985) and his three single-book poems for younger children: *Once: A Lullaby* (1983), *To the End of the Block* (1984) and *On the Merry-Go-Round*, published posthumously in 1991. Other illustrated books of poetry of some note include Phoebe Gilman's *Jillian Jiggs* (1985), Robert Heidbreder's *Don't Eat Spiders* (1985), and Sean O Huigan's *Scary Poems for Rotten Kids* (1982), *The Ghost Horse of the Mounties* (1983), *The Dinner Party* (1984) and *Atmosfear* (1985). Apart from O Huigan's free verse, most Canadian children's poetry to date is marked by strong rhythm and rhyme, and much of it is humorous or nonsense verse.

Those who spend their lives dealing with children's literature are aware that a nation's cultural and political past and the growth in its civilised values are often more acutely reflected in its children's literature than in its traditional history books. The way a culture treats its young is inevitably displayed in its children's books, and that treatment also demonstrates, usually unconsciously, what the general populace accepts as important in its national character. Contrary to the common perception that children's literature is 'just' for kids, those who work in the field know that it is a major conveyor of cultural and political ideologies. This is specially important in Canadian children's literature, given Canada's cultural and political history.

## French-Speaking Canada

### *Elvine Gignac-Pharand*

French Canadian children's literature is constantly developing, and scholarly research in this area is expanding. During the latter part of the nineteenth century, children in French-speaking Canada were exposed to an oral literature that had been handed down from generation to generation by story-tellers. Apart from a few translations and imports arriving from France, books written by authors Philippe Aubert de Gaspé, Patrice Lacombe, Joseph Marmette, Pierre-Georges Boucher de Boucherville and Laure Conan were given as school prizes. Children were subjected to what Louise Lemieux in *Plein feux sur la littérature de jeunesse au Canada français* (1972) describes as *une littérature spontanée* or *récupérée* as opposed to *intentionnelle* (32). According to her, such literature only appeared in the 1920s. In 1923, Claire Daveluy's book, *Les adventures de Perrine et de Charlot*, first serialised in *L'Oiseau bleu* was published. The principal characters of this pioneer story were orphan children who settle in New France. Other works followed such as *Le Petit Page de Frontenac* (1930) by Maxine, *Aux quatre coins des routes canadiennes* (1921) by Eugène Achard and *L'ABC du petit naturaliste canadien* (9 vols) by Harry Bernard.

In the twentieth century certain events influenced children's literature in French Canada. The Second World War brought with it a scarcity of children's books coming from Europe, and Canadian publishers tried to fill the gap with national publications. These consisted largely of fairy tales and legends, written by Achard, and Marius Barbeau whose *Les Contes du grand-père sept-heures* (1950–1953) filled 12 volumes. Félix Leclerc also produced his trilogy of fables and poems, *Adagio* (1943), *Allegro* (1944), and *Andante* (1944), while Guy Boulizon and Ambroise Lafortune wrote adventure stories about Boy Scouts. Public interest in children's books soon diminished, and changes were needed to reflect new societal attitudes. Thus was born *l'âge d'or* (1955–1964) of children's literature. Some of the writers who became well-known included Paule Daveluy (*L'Été enchanté*) (1958), Yves Thériault (*Alerte au camp 29*) (1959), Claudine Vallerand (*Chante et joue*) (1957), Monique Corriveau (*Le Secret de Vanille*) (1958), and Suzanne Martel (*Quatre Montréalais en l'an 3000*) (1971). Other popular children's books were Claude Aubry's *Le Loup de Noël* (1962), and Andrée Maillet's *Le Marquiset têtu et le mulot réprobateur* (1944).

Surprisingly, after this successful period there was a drastic decline. In fact, very few books were published from 1965 to 1970, and only seven were published in the latter year. Books were no longer given as school prizes. Teaching in Québec was secularised and the province's editors chose to concentrate on the production of textbooks. At the same time, the *Révolution tranquille* in that part of French Canada caused the reassessment of traditional values. The numbers of books published diminished, leaving the door wide open to French and Belgian imports which resurfaced in the children's book market.

This dramatic slump was followed in the 1970s and 1980s by an increase in production which has continued into the 1990s. Created in 1971, a corporation known as Communication-Jeunesse has remained a key element in the promotion and distribution of Canadian children's books written in Québec. It publishes a répertoire of people with an interest in children's literature, and biographies of the *créateurs et créatrices de livres québécois pour la jeunesse.* The list includes illustrators Hélène Desputeaux and Paul Roux, writers Michel Cailloux, Henriette Major, Raymond Plante, Michèle Marineau, Robert Soulières, Bernadette Renaud, Daniel Sernine, Francine Pelletier, Denis Côté, Cécile Gagnon, Mireille Levert, Christiane Duchesne and Gilles Tibo. The last four are also successful illustrators.

Québec still produces the vast majority of francophone books written for children. Well-established publishers are Fides (1937), Paulines (1947), Pierre Tisseyre (1947), Boréal (1963), Héritage (1968), Québec-Amérique (1974) and La Courte Échelle (1978). Some of the more recent publishers are Ovale (1987), Michel Quintin (1983), Raton Laveur (1984), Chouette (1987), Coïncidence Jeunesse (1989), and in 1994, Les 400 Coups. Efforts are also made in other parts of Canada where French-speaking communities exist. Among these are Ontario (Les Éditions Prise de Parole, Les Éditions du Vermillon), New Brunswick (Les Éditions d'Acadie) and Manitoba (Les Éditions des Plaines). In the field of publishing, there is at present a demand for well-translated books initially written in French or in English. These products are favourably received by both linguistic groups: Québec writers tend to prefer North American involvement as opposed to European, while Canadian English writers are happy to discover that their books are in demand everywhere in the country, including Québec.

Some of the main educational, social and political factors contributing to the success of today's children's book industry can be summed up as follows. New programmes being implemented in the education system call for a better usage of what have been described as *livres de loisir* or pleasure books in order to achieve a more holistic approach to children's learning of their mother tongue. There is now a greater variety of children's books located in the classroom (coin de lecture). School libraries have become resource centres and in French Ontario these centres are pivotal in providing young students with a friendly place to find a good variety of books intended for pleasure and learning. In Québec, teacher training programmes often include methodology on the proper understanding and use of children's literature.

Throughout French Canadian schools, children are now writing their own stories, and local writers give workshops in school settings. Such exchanges have demystified writing and it is hoped that this will produce a new generation of creators. University research has resulted in a greater awareness and a better acknowledgement of children's literature and the many forms it can take.

Socially and politically, French Canadian children's literature has slowly reflected a change in the traditional role of women and minorities in our society. Interestingly, in French Canada the feminist movement of the early 1970s did not have much impact on the books written for children until the 1980s. If in many of the earlier books the child was often portrayed as a model child, the more recent publications offer a more balanced picture of today's children.

Political correctness has also found its way in both the writing and the evaluating of children's literature. The criteria for judging the current literature while taking into account the intelligence and the creativity of young readers restrict moralising and any form of sexism, racism, or other unacceptable discriminating.

## Further Reading

Doolittle, J. and Barnieh, Z. (1979) *A Mirror of Our Dreams: Children and Theatre in Canada*, Vancouver: Talonbooks.

Egoff, S. and Saltman, J. (1990) *The New Republic of Childhood. A Critical Guide to Canadian Children's Literature in English*, Toronto: Oxford University Press.

Gignac-Pharand, E. (1986) 'L'évolution de la littérature de jeunesse au Canada français', *Cultures du Canada français* 3: 5–17.

Lemieux, L. (1972) *Pleins feux sur la littérature de jeunesse au Canada français*, Ottawa: Leméac.

Potvin, C. (1982) *Le Canada français et sa littérature de jeunesse*, Moncton: CRP.

Pouliot, S. (1991) 'La littérature d'enfance et de jeunesse québécoise (1970–1990)', *Nous voulons lire*, 90: 9–18.

Saltman, J. (1987) *Modern Canadian Children's Books*, Toronto: Oxford University Press.

Stott, J. C. and Jones, R. (1988) *Canadian Books for Children. A Guide to Authors & Illustrators*, Toronto: Harcourt Brace Jovanovich.

# 85

# Children's Literature in the USA: A Historical Overview

## *Jerry Griswold*

### Before 1800

It is only by contrivance that we can divide what is a seamless thread and declare some arbitrary episode the Alpha – the moment when children's literature began in the USA. Were the legends and oral stories of its aboriginal peoples (Indians or Native Americans) the first stories? If Ernesto Rodríguez – a Spanish soldier stationed in Santa Fe, New Mexico, in 1625 – told his daughter an anecdote from *Don Quixote*, would that be the first children's tale? Even if America's early history is reckoned by the fact that it was an English colony, and even if the search for an origin is limited to stories in print, it is difficult to discover a discrete beginning because, along with shiploads of furniture and material goods of all kinds, religious refugees and spiritual colonists brought with them or had imported texts of all kinds – English chapbooks, alphabet books, books of manners, Isaac Watts's poems, the fairy tales of Perrault, the fables of Aesop, stories of Cock Robin and Dick Whittington, etc.

Even so, among the earth-changing events that occurred in the first half of the seventeenth century – the announcement of Galileo's heliocentric conclusions in his *Dialogue* in 1632, the founding of Harvard University in 1636, and the publications of Descartes's summary cogitations in his *Discourses* in 1637 – among these events one is not likely to find the publication of John Cotton's *Spiritual Milk for Boston Babes* (1646). None the less, though it was printed in London, this slender volume was probably the first book especially prepared for North American youth. Part catechism and part schoolbook, Cotton's work was part of a genre that eventually reached its apogee in *The New England Primer*, America's most popular educational text, more than six million copies of which were printed between 1680 and 1830. This genre's yoking of church and school – that is, education as salvation and vice versa – is suggested in *The Primer*'s alphabet, which begins: In Adam's fall,/We sinned all.

Milton's Adam, however, fell in *Paradise Lost* in 1667. Ten years later, mapping a way to regain paradise, the ambulatory John Bunyan issued the first part of *Pilgrim's Progress*. Understanding these two books, one would understand the flavour of the first work actually printed in America for minors: Cotton Mather's wonderfully titled *A Token for the Children of New England; or some Examples of Children in whom the Fear of God was remarkably budding before they dyed; in several parts of New England* (1700). Mather's funereal work is an anthology of biographies of woebegone but pious ephebes, and each biography follows a predictable plot ending with the Protestant Pieta: a child contracts some terminal illness, readies himself or herself for the afterlife through secret prayer and fasting, then (from its deathbed) offers pithy counsel to the living about how they might also reform their lives, and then – depending upon the reader's taste – this juvenile exemplar either dies commendably or commendably dies.

Mather's work is an example of genre we might call 'juvenile martyrology'. The product of a religious refugee community, the Puritans, this book drew its inspiration from a long tradition of earlier adult works which featured the persecutions of righteous Protestants (for example, Foxe's *Book of Martyrs*). In the case of these books, however, colonial children were brought down by dreaded illnesses, not by dreaded Papists. Other religious refugee communities, however, were not ready to cede the moral high ground to the Puritans, who otherwise seemed to have a monopoly on youthful saints blessed in the tubercular virtues. Others, too, insisted that they, too, had their juvenile saints – their woebegone but prescient minors. In Philadelphia in 1717, for example, the Quakers published *A Legacy for Children: Last Words and Dyeing Expressions of Hannah Hill, aged 11 years and near three months.*

Hannah was a Good Girl and, for all that, a little boring. On the other hand, evil females (Eve's daughters) had already been featured in adult circles and were found to be more entertaining: in 1692, for example, colonists in Salem, Massachusetts, took to burning witches; and in 1722, Defoe introduced the world to the enterprising Moll Flanders. Interestingly enough, *The Prodigal Daughter* (Boston: *c.*1737) showed that children's stories needn't lag behind. While this short work contains the familiar scenario of deathbed pronunciamentos, *The Prodigal Daughter* differed – as its introductory summary makes clear – in its focus on a Bad Girl, its Faustian melodrama, and its Edgar-Allan-Poe-like special effects: 'showing, how a Gentleman of a Vast Estate ... had a proud and disobedient Daughter, who because her parents would not support her in all her extravagance, bargained with the Devil to poison them. How an Angel informed her parents of her design. How she lay in a trance four days; and when she was put in the grave, she came to life again, and related the wonderful things she saw in the other World.'

The era of *The Prodigal Daughter* marked a change, and the blame can be put on John Locke. In 1690, Locke published his *Essay on Human Understanding.* Confident at having tackled that subject, the bachelor philosopher turned three years later to the subject of child-raising and offered his experience and sage advice in *Thoughts Concerning Education.* Locke's views gained currency in succeeding years. He became, in fact, the 'Dr Spock' for the parents who raised the generation of American revolutionaries born in the 1730's: among them, John Adams, Paul Revere, Patrick Henry, John Hancock, Thomas Paine *et al.* – bad boys all, or prodigal sons, at least as far as Britain's paternal and civil authorities were concerned.

Among other things, Locke's ideas turned prior Protestant child-raising practices on their head: instead of original sin, Locke stressed the vision of the child as *tabula rasa*; instead of Cotton Mather's sickrooms, Locke championed the outdoors; instead of prayer and secret fasting, Locke advocated fresh air and exercise; and instead of exemplary biographies with tearful accounts of youthful martyrs, Locke endorsed a stiff upper-lip and Aesop's *Fables*. The result of this last endorsement was a shift from sanctimonious, deathbed reading to a new kind of vigorous, ethical, Aesopian literature.

This shift is evident in the anonymous *A New Gift for Children* (1750), perhaps America's first secular storybook, and its tales of children who are good and merit rewards, and tales of children who are otherwise and receive their comeuppances. In other words, while adult readers – busy with Candide and Werther and Tom Jones – were viewed as consumers to be diverted or titillated, their juvenile counterparts were regarded as empty-vessels-into-which-lessons-should-be-poured. This vision of the-child-as-learner is implicit in the didactic stories of *A New Gift*: when Miss Polly aids a stranger, for example, he later rescues her from a mad dog; when Master Billy parades about town to show off his fine clothes, robbers strip him and he comes home naked; and so forth.

One noticeable difference between these tales and their religious antecedents is the fact that justice does not wait for the afterlife but is immediate and Aesopian. When, for example, George snubs a poor boy in the morning in *The Grateful Return* (1796), he cannot share in the gift the boy brings that very afternoon. 'You should have recollected,' his priggish brother instructs him, 'the Fable you read this morning of the Mouse that released the Lion from the net.'

Well, the mouse roared in 1776 – the year Gibbon published *The Decline and Fall of the Roman Empire* – when Americans declared their independence from England. That and two other events can be said to mark the end of the eighteenth century, *vis-à-vis* children's literature. In 1798, in England, William Wordsworth published *Lyrical Ballads*, and children were romanticised and forever afterwards had to trail 'clouds of glory'. The following year Bronson Alcott was born; he would later father four little women, one of them Louisa who would write.

## A National and Secular Literature (1800–1865)

Parson Weems's famous biography *The Life of Washington the Great* (1806) is most remembered for its celebrated incident where, in a fit of patriotism, the young George chops down his father's favourite English cherry tree: 'I cannot tell a lie,' America's future leader says, when he confesses to the crime. Strangely, his father forgives him because of this candour; such honesty, it would seem, is a rare and exculpatory virtue in future American presidents.

In any event, Weems's book can serve as a touchstone and representative example of American children's books of the first half of the nineteenth century. We can begin by noting the honorific of its title. That's not surprising. Heroes were in the air. That same year Beethoven finished the 'Eroica'. It was, after all, the Napoleonic era.

Weems's hagiography, then, is not surprising. What is remarkable is his substitution of a civil saint into the role heretofore reserved for a pious Protestant ephebe. Even more remarkable was its implicit assertion: not even a generation after the founding of the USA, the country's history had already become the stuff of legends.

Consider the dilemma American writers faced in the early part of the nineteenth century: how could such a young country (no more than a generation old) present its own mythology or offer any sense of historicity? While the Romantic Movement was all the fashion in Europe, while the Grimm Brothers were huddled around peasant fires and ventilating ancient German myths and legends and tracing them back to some medieval *Volk*, while English poets swathed in velvet could wax melancholic in the ruins of abbeys and castles, while the French could vacillate between *nostalgie de' la boue* and nostalgia for the *ancien régime* – in the midst of all this, what history had these young United States to offer? This land of sun-baked prairies so unsuitable for Byronic brooding in black velvet clothing, this outback devoid of castles and cathedrals and colourful babushkas doing folkloric dances? What past did this young country have that could be painted on the canvas and then given an antique, golden patina? Well, if the answer could be given telegraphically, it would be this: in answer to Sir Walter Scott's Scottish kilts in *Ivanhoe* (1819), Fenimore Cooper offered Indian loincloths in *Last of the Mohicans* (1826). Of course, such syncretism takes explaining.

Of all American writers, Washington Irving was probably most aware of the dilemma his countrymen faced. As diplomat and bohemian, Irving had travelled widely on the European continent, amongst its capitols and castles. We might take as a symbol of this American hunger for culture and history the remarkable fact that Irving even took up residence for some time not just in Granada but in the Alhambra. Of course, in the late twentieth century it has become fashionable to eschew America's Eurocentrism; in the nineteenth century, however, anyone observing that the USA was Eurocentric would have been treated like the village idiot who offered as a significant discovery the observation that the sea tastes salty. It was obviously so. Say it again: in cultural matters, most residents of the USA slavishly aped European ways.

Understanding that, we should then see Irving's tales about early Dutch settlers in New York's Hudson Valley – memorable characters like Rip Van Winkle and Ichabod Crane – as attempts to make America's modest, rural history into something passably European, legendary and urbane. And these tales – in *A History of New York, by Dietrich Knickerbocker* (1809) and his *Sketch Book* (1819–1820) – would soon became schoolroom favourites. Though not intended exclusively for children, the young prized them; and these stories are, perhaps, the first great works in the conventional canon of American juvenile literature.

In the first half of the nineteenth century, the American schoolroom was, in fact, a forge for literary patriotism and the place where canons were made. Weems's *The Life of Washington the Great* provides an example, Irving's stories another. At the same time, Young America was learning its national history by memorising passages from poems by Henry Wadsworth Longfellow ('The Village Blacksmith', 'Evangeline', 'The Song of Hiawatha', 'The Courtship of Miles Standish', and 'Paul Revere's Ride') or by reading the quasi-historical prose of (to mention just a few examples) Fenimore Cooper's *The Last of the Mohicans* (1826), Samuel Griswold Goodrich's *The Tales of Peter Parley about America* (1827), *The Life of Davy Crockett* (1834), and Daniel Pierce Thompson's *The Green Mountain Boys* (1839).

When Rufus Wilmot Griswold – in his *Poets and Poetry of America* (1842) and *Prose Writers of America* (1847) – astonishingly asserted that there was something called 'American Literature', that seemed a specimen of audacity. Be that as it may, the actual enterprise of fashioning a national literature had started as much as a decade earlier in country schoolrooms, in inspired textbooks like McGuffey's *First Eclectic Reader* (1836 *et seq.*) which contained passages from what was slowly being recognised as this country's literature – among them: Whittier's 'Snow-bound', Poe's 'The Raven', and Bryant's 'Thanatopsis'.

To be honest, this young country had not quite generated enough literature to fill an anthology. This explains why American authors were also busy co-opting the work of others. In his *Wonder Book* (1852) and *Tanglewood Tales* (1853), Nathaniel Hawthorne made the Greek myths American by retelling them in a New England setting – keeping royalties otherwise due Ovid. In *The Night Before Christmas* (1823), Clement Moore appropriated Dutch customs (gift-giving, Santa, reindeer) and passed them off as American (later they would, in fact, become so). And in *Mother Goose's Melodies* (1833), publishers Munro and Francis pirated a British book of nursery rhymes and made it American by substituting the word 'Boston' for every appearance of the word 'London' – a bit of nationalistic revisionism which would result in a curious and entirely spurious claim made at mid-century that Mother Goose had actually been a dame living in seventeenth-century Boston; indeed, to this day, Boston tour guides – apparently unaware that 'Mother Goose' derives from a French expression for a type of tale (*Conte de la mère oye*) – point out Mother Goose's grave in a Boston churchyard.

Besides schoolrooms, churches were also busy centres in the children's literature business. In the first half of the nineteenth century, religious institutions created the genre known as the 'Sunday School book' – small tracts offered by the American Sunday School Union (1824–1860) and similar religious organisations. By means of them, countless young Americans learned to read and be good – two sometimes unrelated skills. Unabashedly didactic, Sunday School books were likewise formulaic: boys who fail to go to church on Sunday morning are invariably struck by lightning in the afternoon; those who climb trees to steal apples, inevitably fall and break their arms.

We might exaggerate and say that the demise of the Sunday School book can be associated with the birth in 1835 of Samuel Clemens, who would finally bury the genre in 1876 with his parody and celebration of the Bad Boy in *The Adventures of Tom Sawyer*. In truth, the demise of the Sunday School book was the result of a much slower process of secularisation. By the mid-1830s, lessons still remained at the centre of juvenile books but now they concerned history and geography not behaviour. Instead of ministers, America's authors for juveniles were now schoolteachers. Jacob Abbott provides an example. In his Rollo books (1835 *et seq.*), Abbott – after showing *Rollo Learning to Read* and *Rollo at School* – took his literary lad on journeys around the world in travelogues that were thinly disguised geography lessons.

The next step in the process of secularisation might be marked by the commercial success of William Taylor Adams' Oliver Optic series (1855 *et seq.*). Inexpensive printing techniques had given rise to 'pulp fiction', and publishers suddenly became more intent on increasing sales than in imparting lessons to the young. In 1860, Irwin Beadle and Co. became the first American publisher to offer mass-market fiction in the equivalent of today's comic books – in 'dime novels' that told of outlaws, pirates, and damsels; Deadwood Dick, Horatio Alger's newsboys, and Frank and Jesse James.

As we approach the middle of the century, we can also begin to glimpse the rise of vague gender distinctions in reading materials for the young. From the dime novels, would eventually come the 'boy's book' – adventure stories set in the Great Outdoors. The 'girl's book' drew its inspiration from elsewhere (from sentimental and domestic fiction) and offered emotional stories occurring in the Great Indoors.

For an example of the 'girl's book' we can turn to Susan Warner's *The Wide, Wide World* (1851) where Ellen Montgomery, a poor girl harmed by uncaring adults and an indifferent world, nearly drowns in a sea of tears but is buoyed up by her Christianity. Maria Susanna Cummins's *The Lamplighter* (1854) provides another example; this is a Dickensian tale of young Gerty adrift in the streets of Boston. These were works of a group of authors that scholars would later refer to as the 'lachrymose ladies' – an injudicious sobriquet. In truth, their work is akin to Harriet Beecher Stowe's *Uncle Tom's Cabin* (1852), a novel with which they shared best seller status and which also became a favourite among the young.

As for Mrs Stowe, it is said that at their first meeting President Abraham Lincoln greeted her with: 'So, this is the little lady who wrote the big book' – the implication being that Stowe's touching anti-slavery novel had kindled America's Civil War. That may be too grand a claim, but beginning in 1861 America's two great regions (the North and the South) were locked in bloody internecine warfare until a peace accord could be signed at Appomattox in 1865, the year Tolstoy's *War and Peace* was published. Elsewhere, that same year, juvenile literature was taking different turns: to the East (across the Atlantic) Lewis Carroll published *Alice in Wonderland*, and in the West (in California) an author by the name of Mark Twain wrote hilariously about Jumping Frog contests.

## The Golden Age (1865–1914)

The Golden Age of American Children's Books occurred between the conclusion of America's Civil War and the start of the First World War. It was a remarkable time that saw the publication of many of America's most famous children's novels: *Little Women*, *The Adventures of Tom Sawyer*, *The Wonderful Wizard of Oz*, *Tarzan of the Apes*, *The Secret Garden*, and others. Major authors (Mark Twain, Louisa May Alcott and others) wrote for minors. And, extraordinarily, children's books headed the best seller lists because adults, too, were eagerly turning to these stories.

The epoch was, as some historians have said, the Era of the Child. Some of this attention was fuelled by nostalgia; following the horrors of the Civil War, many authors were eager to recall the agrarian bliss of their pre-war childhoods and turned to the Child as a symbol of the Always Vernal Past. Other authors seized on the figure of the Child as a symbol of a Promising Future in a post-war America illuminated by the incandescent light bulb, taking wing with the flights of the Wright Brothers, hastening along on railroads and steamships, and engaged in angelic communications via transcontinental and oceanic telegraph cables.

Legions of reformers, however, were not interested in the Child as Symbol. Instead, they saw the Child as Class. These argued that children, *per se*, had their own unique needs. So, ministers, politicians, and reformers of all kinds ministered to these special needs by creating orphanages, kindergartens, playgrounds, child labour laws, and mandatory schooling. By way of example, we might note that Pediatrics became in the 1880s a recognised medical speciality and a field taught at Harvard.

All this social attention paid to the child may explain the great interest during the period (even among adults) in children's literature. Among the most flourishing periodicals of the time were magazines meant for the young: *The Youth's Companion* (1827–1929), *Our Young Folks* (1865–1873), *The Riverside Magazine for Young People* (1867–1870), and *Harper's Young People* (1879–1899). Foremost among these was *St Nicholas* (1873–1943), ably edited by Mary Mapes Dodge and whose contributors included virtually every literary notable of the time.

Besides her editorial skills, Dodge is best known for *Hans Brinker, or the Silver Skates* (1865), her story about a hardluck and impoverished but hardworking and loving Dutch family. Change the setting from The Netherlands to New England and this description might easily fit another classic domestic novel, the one Louisa May Alcott once thought of titling 'The Pathetic Family' – that is, *Little Women* (1868). Pathos was, in fact, all the rage whether one turned to Martha Finley's aggrieved *Elsie Dinsmore* (1867) or Horatio Alger's pitiable *Ragged Dick* (1867).

Some found this interest in pathos pathetic and, tired of the good boys of Sunday School books and the pitiable children of popular fiction, Thomas Bailey Aldrich published his own antidote: *The Story of a Bad Boy* (1870). Six years later Samuel Clemens would publish his own bad boy story, *The Adventures of Tom Sawyer*. But that same year (1876), Tom Sawyer's nemesis would be engendered with the birth of Vivian Burnett to author Frances Hodgson Burnett; Vivian would later become the model for the Exemplary Boy in *Little Lord Fauntleroy*.

In fact, just a few years later, Frances Hodgson Burnett would spend the summer at Nook Farm (a neighbourhood in Hartford, Connecticut) and her next-door neighbour was Clemens; Burnett was a guest of Harriet Beecher Stowe and stayed in a bungalow financed by the sales of *Uncle Tom's Cabin*. The following summer, Clemens published *The Prince and the Pauper* and sent Burnett a copy. Several years later, upon publication of *Little Lord Fauntleroy* (1885), Clemens would consider a lawsuit against Burnett, believing she had plagiarised from his novel to create her own.

But Clemens was too busy to begin legal proceedings. Following the success of James Otis Kaler's story about a runaway boy in *Toby Tyler* (1881), Mark Twain wrote about another conscience-stricken escapee in that milestone book of American literature the *Adventures of Huckleberry Finn*. At the end of that book, Huck advises that he's about to 'light out' to the wilderness but, in truth, the wilderness was fast disappearing; about the time the book was published (1884–1885), the last buffalo herd was slaughtered. Then, too, wilderness of another kind disappeared in 1899 when Freud's *The Interpretation of Dreams* was published.

In the very first year of the new century, Frank L. Baum published another milestone book: *The Wonderful Wizard of Oz* (in subsequent printings, 'wonderful' was dropped from the title). The success of Baum's book (cleverly illustrated by W. W. Denslow) as well as the success of its sequels suddenly made visible America's fledgling fantasy industry. Until the Oz books, authors of fantasy laboured in near obscurity since America's rough-and-ready taste seemed to require the gravitas of facticity. There were, however, exceptions – among them: Joel Chandler Harris's animal *fabliaux* in his Uncle Remus stories (1878 *et seq.*), Howard Pyle's illustrated 'fairy stories' (1886 *et seq.*), and Palmer Cox's Brownies (1887 *et seq.*).

Still, in the interval between *The Wizard of Oz* and the First World War, America seemed settled in a pastoral bliss. To be sure, plucky girls faced problems: Baum's Dorothy and (later) his Princess Ozma wrestled with aunt-like witches in a place far from Kansas, while heroines in Kate Douglas Wiggins's *Rebecca of Sunnybrook Farm* (1903) and Eleanor Porter's *Pollyanna* (1913) dealt with witch-like aunts in New England. Still, it was a Green and Pastoral World that was the setting for these books.

Another nature, however – one red of tooth and claw – could be glimpsed elsewhere: in boys' books published on the eve of war; in novels that eschewed the feminine and boasted of a gritty, dog-eat-dog, Darwinian-survival-of-the-fittest kind of realism; in Jack London's books, for example, *The Call of the Wild* (1903) and *White Fang* (1905). Atmospherically, then, the pre-war world of 1913 seemed poised somewhere between Igor Stravinsky's fey 'Rites of Spring' and D. H. Lawrence's feral *Sons and Lovers*; or, analogously, the world of American juvenile literature was atmospherically poised between Frances Hodgson Burnett's *The Secret Garden* (1911) and Edgar Rice Burroughs's *Tarzan of the Apes* (1914).

## The Modern Period (after 1914)

Across the Atlantic, in 1916, James Joyce published an account of a hyperesthetic Irish youth named Stephen Daedalus in *Portrait of the Artist as a Young Man*. The same year, on the western side of the Atlantic, Booth Tarkington published *Seventeen*, his story about an awkward Indiana adolescent named Sylvanus Baxter. The next year Dorothy Canfield Fisher published her novel about a neurotic Vermont child in *Understood Betsy*. Each of these books can serve as heralds of a particularly twentieth-century phenomenon in American children's literature – the 'YA' or young-adult novel that features adolescents suffering maturation or puberty. We might say, in fact, that these three begat: Holden Caulfield (in J. D. Salinger's 1951 *Catcher in the Rye*), M. C. Higgins (in Virginia Hamilton's 1974 *M. C. Higgins the Great*), Jody Baxter (in what may be the most remarkable Y.A. novel of the twentieth century, Marjorie Kinnan Rawlings's 1938 *The Yearling*), Harriet (in Louise Fitzhugh's 1964 *Harriet the Spy*), a dozen heroines in Judy Blume's books (1970 *et seq.*), and countless other pubescent solipsists.

Beyond the literature of brooding teens, regional and historical fiction also found its markets. A Will Rogers lookalike (Will James) published his paean to the American Cowboy in *Smoky, the Cowhorse* in 1926. In the midst of the Depression (1929–1939), Laura Ingalls Wilder offered her own histories of midWestern pioneer prowess in her successful Little House books (1932 *et seq.*). Akin to these is Lois Lenski's *Strawberry Girl* with its remarkable portrait of backwoods life in the Florida scrub country. Other examples of historical and regional fiction might be found Esther Forbes's story of colonial America in *Johnny Tremain* (1943) or, even later, in Scott O'Dell's account of Indian or Native American life off California's coast in *Island of the Blue Dolphins* (1960).

Other children's novels were an admixture of realism and fantasy. Many examples might be pointed to, but three volumes stand out above the rest. E. B. White's *Charlotte's Web* (1952), a story of a friendship between a pig and a writer, is a near-perfect children's book and written in a familiar tone of voice that is at once wise and witty and nostalgic. Randall Jarrell's *The Animal Family* (1965) is a haunting and trim and archetypal story, a Kiplingesque tale of humans and animals living in adopted families. Russell Hoban's *The Mouse and his Child* (1967) is a horse of a different colour: a fantasy that is also an existential fable for children and adults, a story of refugee animals whose no-exit lives are occasionally made efflorescent by unexpected epiphanies and episodes of hope.

But novels only compose one category. We can turn to another genre, the picture book, to witness an equally incredible efflorescence. Certainly one of America's most remarkable productions of this kind is Wanda Gag's *Millions of Cats* (1928), the work of an artist born of Eastern European immigrants and a story that tells of an elderly couple inundated with feline émigrés. What was striking about Gag's book was its advanced compositional techniques and its *moderne* style; here was the Museum of Modern Art between the covers of a children's book.

Another example of this modernity might be seen in the work of yet another (Austrian) immigrant to the USA, in Ludwig Bemelman's Picasso-like sketches for his *Madeline* books (1939 *et seq.*). Madeline, of course, is a resident of Paris and, for a time, it seemed the best of American picture books were imbued with a certain European flavour. To be sure, between the wars, Europe was all the rage in certain artistic circles; Ernest Hemingway was only the most conspicuous of Americans who saw themselves as writers-in-residence in (variously) Paris, London, Spain, Italy, Gstaad, and elsewhere. But unlike Hemingway's ambulance-chasing novels, the glories of war were not celebrated in children's books; in Robert Lawson's *The Story of Ferdinand*, published at the outset of the Spanish Civil War (1936), the hero is a Spanish bull who is a pacifist.

A picture book published the next year (1937) set a new course for the genre. Dr Seuss's *And to Think I Saw It on Mulberry Street* brought jangling verse and a new kind of incantatory musicality to this otherwise visual medium. Like this is another extraordinary and kinetic book: Margaret Wise Brown's playful *Goodnight Moon* (1947). Some years later – but still two years before Ginsberg's *Howl* and one year before Kerouac's *On the Road* and Ferlinghetti's *Coney Island of the Mind* – Dr Seuss published *The Cat in the Hat* (1957) and introduced one of America's hippest pranksters.

A third stage of development of the picture book occurred in 1963 when Maurice Sendak took forward this incantatory musicality and added a new psychological dimension – in his story of Max's struggles with parental demons in *Where the Wild Things Are*. This kind of psychological depth and insight would characterise Sendak's subsequent and brilliant work. It would also characterise the work of many other gifted artists – for example, William Steig, especially in his 1969 *Sylvester and the Magic Pebble*.

Of course, it is impossible to cast a net (however wide) around the whole twentieth century. Works and authors easily slip through; mention should be made, for example, of Madeline L'Engle's science-fiction series that began with *A Wrinkle in Time* (1962) and of the unrecognised genius behind D. Manus

Pinkwater's whimsical novels. Even so, time will point out (and later generations will lament) our short-sightedness in not recognising other contemporary authors whose genius will, subsequently, be so manifest. Then, too, despite the size of our nets, entire seas have gone unfished in this short essay; to mention just one: in 1937 Walt Disney released his best-known animated feature *Snow White*, and upon her frail and white shoulders was built a canon-making kingdom of children's cinema that still has not received the attention it deserves as a seminal force in story-telling that would also eventually beget, for example, George Lucas's *Star Wars* and Shelley Duvall's television tales.

But before exiting the late twentieth century, we should note (however briefly) a relatively recent phenomenon in the USA during the last two decades: the extensive adult interest in children's literature. While the number of children in the population has dropped precipitously (for example, total births in 1987 were only 58 per cent of what they were in 1958), children's books have been selling in extraordinary numbers (for example, sales quadrupled between 1982 and 1990) and marketing surveys indicate that as many as a third of all sales are made to childless customers in their 20s or 30s who don't mean to pass these purchases along to a minor. In a similar vein, courses in children's literature are now among the most popular electives at American universities and, since 1960, the number of universities offering courses in the field has mushroomed. Likewise, adults are now revisiting the fairy tales in theatricals like Stephen Sondheim's *Into the Woods* or in National Book Award winning books like Bruno Bettelheim's study of the fairy tales *The Uses of Enchantment*. Add to this another item of news: in the 1980s, picture books by Dr Seuss (*The Butter Battle Book* and *You Only Grow Old Once!*) had a long run on adult bestseller lists. We can see something when we note that Stephen Spielberg's recent film *Hook* is about adults restoring their youth by means of children's books, about reliving Barrie's *Peter Pan*.

It may be difficult to know just what, in the USA is fuelling this resurgence of interest in childhood, especially among adults. One explanation may be found, however, in a number of social critics who have noted (in the words of a title of a book by Neil Postman) 'the disappearance of childhood'. Noting how taboos are disappearing (how television programmes were routinely addressing subjects from hermaphroditism to spouse swapping once deemed too sensitive for tender years); noting how child actors were no longer waif-like Shirley Temples but (from Gary Coleman to Brooke Shields) transistorised adults; noting how the distinction between juvenile and adult court systems seems arbitrary (once the label 'gang member' is no longer applied to Al Capone-like adults but to metropolitan youths not yet old enough to vote) – noting all this and other evidence, social critics have sent up their wail and insisted that the concept of childhood (invented in the sixteenth century, according to historian Phillipe Ariès) is being dismantled before our eyes. These same critics (besides Postman, Marie Winn in *Children Without Childhood*, David Elkind in *The Hurried Child*) predict a return to an earlier time when 'children' were not separated from 'adults', when those cultural concepts and divisions did not even exist. They predict a return to conditions seen, for example, in the paintings of Breughel where young and old alike are carousing together, equally besotted and groping each other with abandon.

These pessimistic and conservative views may explain the late twentieth century's increasing fascination with 'childhood': if the cultural notion of childhood is disappearing into some Spenglerian void, then we have grown nostalgic in its twilight. American films of the 1980s and 1990s, however, suggest a more centrist explanation. With Spielberg's *Hook* (where a workaholic adult played by Robin Williams is redeemed when he is stripped of his cellular phone and every other vestige of maturity and made a kid again, a kid who even engages in a food fight), with Tom Hanks's reincarnation from adult into child in the movie *Big*, with George Burns in *Eighteen Again*, with Dudley Moore in *Like Father, Like Son*, with these (and a dozen other cultural or shared dreams seen on the Big Screen) we can detect the anxieties of the middle-aged and a wish for rejuvenation. Whatever the explanation then, whether the loss of childhood is seen as cultural or personal phenomenon, America's late twentieth century and acute interest in children's literature reminds us how much the subject is entwined with presentiments of mortality and sentiments of nostalgia.

## Further Reading

Attebery, B. (1980) *The Fantasy Tradition in American Literature: From Irving to Le Guin*, Bloomington, IN: Indiana University Press.

Blanck, J. (1956) *Peter Parley to Penrod: A Bibliographical Description of the Best-Loved American Juvenile Books*, Providence, NJ: Bowker.

Griswold, J. (1992) *Audacious Kids: Coming of Age in America's Classic Children's Books*, New York: Oxford University Press.

Jordan, A. M. (1949) *From Rollo to Tom Sawyer*, Boston: The Horn Book.

Kelly, R. G. (1974) *Mother Was a Lady: Self and Society in Selected American Children's Periodicals 1865–1890*, Westport, CT: Greenwood.

MacLeod, A. S. (1975) *A Moral Tale: Children's Fiction and American Culture 1820–1860*, Hamden, CT: Archon Books.

Meigs, C. (ed.) (1969) *A Critical History of Children's Literature*, New York: Macmillan.

Rosenbach A. S. W. (1933) *Early American Children's Books*, Portland, ME: Southworth Press; reprinted 1966, New York: Kraus.

Welch, d'A. (1972) *A Bibliography of American Children's Books Printed Prior to 1821*, Worcester, MD: American Antiquarian Society/Barre Publishers.

# 86

# Central and South America and the Caribbean

*Enrique Pérez Díaz*

The history of children's literature in Latin America could never be isolated from the five-century history of the continent, a New World, a meeting-place of two cultures. In 1492, when Christopher Columbus's three caravels sighted land, the area was populated by peoples having cultural and scientific wealth as rich as that possessed by any country of the Old World. Unfortunately, due to the economic requirements of the budding capitalist society, then just emerging from feudalism, America was viewed as a huge store of raw materials, riches that the European kingdoms wanted to finance their wars.

In the course of a few years splendid civilisations – the Mayas, the Aztecs, the Incas, to mention only the more advanced –were reduced to slavery; their palaces, religious centres and scientific institutions were sacked and destroyed, their cultures practically obliterated.

In the wake of conquest and colonisation another process, more rapid and more complex, was under way: that of transculturation, especially accentuated by millions of African slaves imported by the colonies to supplement the reluctant native labour force. South America soon became a mosaic of cultures, religions and races that created a culture that was heterogeneous, diverse, rich and ultimately unique. The European powers imposed their creeds using the whip and the sword, and their main purpose was indoctrination. But the mixture of races – Indian, African, Chinese and Spanish – produced a collective nationality, peoples whose history makes them kindred even if their languages may differ.

In the development of this new world its culture was dialectically enriched; the legends that settlers and missionaries brought from old Europe were added to those told by native priests and also to images evoked in their prayers and lamentations by the African slaves. Figures of Latin folklore appear in the American folklore; myths, cosmographia, the explanation of natural phenomena which always awed primitive peoples are blended in an amalgam that is reiterated all over the continent.

With the invention of printing, the Creoles – natives conscious of their origin who looked askance at their Old World ancestors – developed new oral and written forms, which although strongly traditional – an oral tradition of myths and legends – looked forward to literary forms.

Every critic, theorist, essayist and researcher interested in the subject agrees that literature specifically for children first appeared in the Latin American and Caribbean countries only between the middle of the nineteenth century and the beginning of the twentieth. Teachers, tutors and a few authors produced largely moralising and dogmatic books intended to create a model child in a perfect world, contrasting with the real world, and full of explicit and implicit schemes, dogmas and prohibitions.

In the twentieth century, countries such as Brazil, Argentina, Venezuela and Cuba have been outstanding in the development of literature for children; other countries have isolated major authors, while in the English- and French-speaking Caribbean, this literature is practically non-existent. Its basic sources are tradition, oral folklore, fairy tales, lullabies, and myth, and there is a nineteenth-century flavour to the writing.

In the more developed countries, authors are more receptive to the new trends, and they meet the requirements of children and youngsters conditioned by the cinema, television and computer games. South American literature remains insular and thematically undeveloped, but authors exist of undeniable quality. In Brazil, for example, Lygia Bojunga Nunes (winner of the Andersen Award 1982) is an outstanding representative of this new literature that espouses the cause of young people. Cuba and Argentina have been represented at important events such as the Bologna Children's Book Fair: Cuba by Dora Alonso, and Argentina by Elsa Isabel Bonnerman; both writers have been included in the honours list of the Hans Christian Andersen Award and the White Raven selection of the International Youth Library.

Children's literature in this continent has been afflicted by lack of support; with the exception of isolated attempts in some countries, or the support accorded to culture in Cuba (in spite of stringent economic conditions for many years). Education, literature and art have been deprived of resources. Writers can hardly develop if publishing houses are not willing to consider their works; or, if the few books produced with great personal effort do not find specialised outlets or must compete with comics and commercial literature; if libraries have no funds, and if illiteracy is endemic and just as real as poverty and lack of sanitation.

However, many voices strive to be heard, and more than a few spread the seeds of nonconformity. Such nonconformity inspired the life and work of Hans Christian Andersen, that in turn inspired José Martí to write his *La Edad de Oro* [The Golden Age] while being immersed in preparing a war of independence.

Brazil, Argentina, Venezuela and Cuba show a strong, consistent movement in the realm of literature for children, and a few individuals have continent-wide reputations, such as Chilean Marcela Paz (*Papelucho*), and the Costa Rican Joaquín Gutiérrez (*Cocorí*). But elsewhere, children's literature lacks official backing, and there are no specialist bookstores, publishers or sponsoring.

There are isolated examples of serious critics, such as the Uruguayan Sylvia Puentes de Oyenard, the Peruvian Jesús Cabel, and the Ecuadorian Francisco Delgado Santos. Similarly, occasional books may be found; for example, in Honduras there has been *El caracol de cristal* by Rubén Berrios; in Belize, *Shave my song* by Corinth I. Lewis; in Surinam, *Anasi* by R. Dobrú and *Zik en ik* by M. Th. Hijlaard, and *The Love Song of Boyse B. and Other Poems*, by Anson González; in Barbados, *Fen Lach En Een taa*, by Gerrit Barron; and in Guadeloupe, *Ti-Chika*, by Sylviane Tachild. Other West Indian authors are discussed in the final section.

Communication between countries in the continent is poor, even between countries having the same language and a common frontier. The Caribbean countries are strangers to each other due to their languages and societal differences. The Casa de las Américas (with its permanent seat in Cuba) has attempted to improve matters through its literary awards.

## Argentina

The earliest literature was folklore; each region evolved its particular tradition from myths, legends and other forms largely inherited from the indigenous races. One of the first texts of literature for children was by Eduardo García Mantilla, *Cuentos*, written about 1880. The pioneer of Argentinian children's literature is considered by critics to be Ada María Elflein, whose stories were published in dailies and magazines, especially *Leyendas Argentinas*, from 1906. She revived the epics and the legends and rewrote the myths. Similar books of that period were *Cuentos Patrióticos* and *Episodios Históricos* by Varela Oro.

Especially significant is the work of an Uruguayan author who wrote and published his entire production in Argentina: Horacio Quiroga. In his *Cuentos de la Selva* (1921), Quiroga turned out literature of continent-wide importance. In the early years of the century, Álvaro Yunque with *Barcos de Papel* (1925) and Benito Lynch with *El Potrillo Roano* (1924), are equally important.

The magazine *Billiken*, founded 17 November 1919 by Constancio C. Vigil, was for many decades a valuable vehicle for this literature.

Also significant is that many great authors of the end of the nineteenth century and the beginning of the twentieth century also wrote for children. One of them was Bartolomé Hidalgo, originator of gaucho literature; another, Esteban de Luca. Domingo de Azcuénaga was an outstanding writer of fables.

Between 1880 and 1920 – during the boom of modernism and realism – there were several publishing houses and many books dedicated to children. Besides Quiroga – a modernist influenced by naturalism – the writings for children by Alfonsina Storni, Alfredo Bufano, Juan Burghi and Arturo Marasso are worthy of note. Other authors around that period were Leopoldo Marechel (*El Niño y Dios*), Jorge Luis Borges with a few pieces adapted to children's tastes, Leónidas Barletta, Aristóbulo Echegaray and Gustavo Riccio (poetry), José Pedroni, Conrado Nalé Roxlo, the great poet José Sebastián Tallón (renowned for his work *Las Torres de Nüremberg*), Luis Franco, Roberto Ledesma, Luis Cané, Rafael Jiménez Sánchez, and others.

The years 1935 to 1963 are crucial to the production of Argentinian children's books, with the emergence of a woman who, from her earliest books was an absolute favourite among children. María Elena Walsh provided a fresh approach, unrestrained, untraditional, more playful and enriching. Her most famous books include *Tutú Marambá*, *El Reino del Revés*, *Cuentopos de Gulubú*, *Zoo Loco*, and *Dailan Kifki*.

Another outstanding writer of the period was the globetrotter Javier Villafañe, the author of important poetic and theatrical works which he promoted on his travels.

During that time the activities of critics and essayists were superbly represented by Fryda Schultz de Mantovani, who studied children's literature from many angles. Martha Salotti, founder of the Summa Institute and of the first department of children's literature in the country's universities, is another significant figure, as is Dora Pastoriza de Etchebarne, who succeeded Salotti as director of the Institute.

Argentina (together with Brazil and Venezuela) is the most important country for the production of children's literature, thanks to the tradition established by Jacobo Peuser and Guillermo Craft, who started the first specialised collections, and Atlántida, Sigmar, Kapelusz, Codex (the first national publishing house), Sudamericana, Difusión, Fausto, Orión, Plus Ultra, Guadalupe and others.

There was a time when Argentina benefited from the contribution of a number of important Spanish publishers who took refuge in this country during the Spanish civil war of 1936–1939. Aguilar, Espasa Calpe, Losada, Pedro García (Ateneo), and others moved their businesses to Buenos Aires and their know-how was an important addition to the trade.

Since the 1970s, other publishers have appeared in the form of cooperatives – not so powerful as the great houses but noteworthy for the aggressiveness of their projects. Colíhue and Libros del Quirquincho have published works by Laura Devetach, Gustavo Roldán, Ricardo Mariño, Ana María Ramb, Graciela Montes, Ema Wolf, Elsa Bonnerman, and others who were previously unable to publish for political or economic reasons. Great names of the past have also been revived, such as the remarkable narrator José Murillo, the singer of the hills of Jujuy.

This healthy situation is sustained by more than twenty specialist bookshops, and a number of libraries and reading rooms that facilitate the access by children to works written for them.

## Brazil

Folklore has been an excellent source of inspiration for writers, with roots in the Portuguese, African and indigenous traditions. Up to the second half of the nineteenth century the lore was transmitted within the family circle by the Portuguese granny figure. Celso de Magalhaes, José de Alençar, Pereira da Costa, and General Couto de Magalhaes were among the first writers who collected these tales, but the credit for putting them into the hands of children must go to Alexina de Magalhaes Pinto (1870–1921), professor and musician. She was an assiduous collaborator in the *Almanaque Brasileiro Garnier*; conducted research on children's games and toys, and published a list of recreational books, 'Esboço provisório de una biblioteca infantil', which was included in her book *Proverbios, máximas e observaçoes usuais*. She also published many writings based on her experiences, rejected spelling primers, and experimented with a process that was later called the global method of teaching letters.

At this early stage, important folklore figures included the one-legged Saci, who wears a red cap and has an ever-smoking pipe, immortalised in the book *O Saci* by Monteiro Lobato (1882–1948), an author who is considered a classic and an innovator in the art of writing for children.

The year 1822 was crucial for Brazilian culture. The Portuguese royal family left Lisbon for Rio de Janeiro, with its retinue of servants and noble followers, and this brought about the import of many previously banned books. Don Joao IV launched the National Library and the Royal Printing House and children were soon reading stories by the Grimms, Perrault, Andersen, Verne, Amicis, Salgari, the Countess of Ségur, and other classics. These, however, did not meet the demand. A few publishers issued collections and the first periodicals for children appeared, among others *O Dico-Tico*, founded in 1905 by the Minas journalist Luis Bartolomeu de Souza e Silva. For several decades this magazine was a source of fun and learning for generations of children.

In 1921, the publication of *A menina do narizinho arrebitado*, edited by Monteiro Lobato *et al.*, inaugurated a new phase of books for children, which critics consider more 'literary. Lobato created the figure of Donna Benta, a superlative narrator and a leading character in his celebrated book *La granja del pájaro amarillo* where half-real, half-fantastic characters enrapture children and make them think; for in his books Lobato includes historical events, makes literary intertextualities, and so on. His works were intended to enrich the language and the world view of Brazilian children. He also made use of folklore, approached in various ways by his different characters – some lower-class, such as Donna Benta, others highbrow, such as Aunt Anastasia and Uncle Bernabé. Lobato believed that children should be exposed to real facts; he believed in their intelligence and perceptive powers, hence the multitude of subjects in his books. His works are still alive, partly due to the fact that he was not oblivious of the problems of his time, fantasy notwithstanding.

After Lobato, realism was a major current, featuring formerly taboo subjects such as sex, death, war, homosexuality, family quarrels and social problems. Writers in this group include Wander Piroli, Henry Correia de Araujo, Luis Fernando Emediato, among others. There is also a sub-group of authors not entirely committed to realism, but who use it as a starting point; Carlos Marigny and Odette de Barros retake a line initiated by Viriato de Correa in 1920. But the most successful genre was magical realism where fantasy is used to illuminate or transform facts. The Italian Gianni Rodari (1920–1980) initiated the idea of modifying fairy tales: among other writers in the same genre are Fernanda Lopes de Almeida, Eliardo Franca, Ana María Machado, Ruth Rocha, and Bartolomeu da Queiroz.

Lygia Bojunga Nunes is a leading fantasist, perhaps the most widely known writer for children within Brazil and abroad since 1982 when IBBY awarded her the Andersen medal. She has written two kinds of books: animist works such as *Los compañeros, Angélica, El sofá estampado*, modern fables in which human-like animals use irony to denounce the evils of society; and works where magical realism goes hand in hand with the oneiric and the extra-sensory, exploring the psyche without disregarding social reality. Among these are *La casa de la madrina*, where a child undertakes a mystic journey to flee from poverty; *El bolso amarillo*, the story of a girl who keeps in her purse frustrations, longings, and disillusionments that keep her from dealing with real life; *La cuerda floja*, where a girl has to uncover her parents' story; *Juntos los tres*, where three human beings are confronted by an incredible and dreadful situation; and *Mi amigo el pintor*, in which a boy investigates the suicide of his friend, a painter.

Lygia Bojunga Nunes is typical of the way in which contemporary Latin-American authors are exploring more universal, yet untraditional, themes.

In Brazil, there is a strong group of author-illustrators, and around forty publishers, some producing up to fifty titles annually. Among the more outstanding are Melhoramentos and Atica (São Paulo), Miguilim (Belo Horizonte), and Salamandra (Rio de Janeiro).

## Cuba

The earliest Cuban children's literature was related to education and dates from the beginning of the nineteenth century; texts include catechisms, primers and other texts which contained poetry and stories. *Libro de lectura para niños* (1846), by Manuel Coatales, *El librito de los cuentos y las conversaciones* (1847) by Cirilo Villaverde, and other writings by Eusebio Guiteras, José María de la Torre and Juan Bautista Sagarra stand out, but their names are now largely forgotten.

As in other countries, Cuban children appropriated reading matter not originally written for them, such as Miguel Teurbe Tolón's *Leyendas cubanas* (1857), or the fables of Gabriel de la Concepción Valdés (1856) and Aurelia Castillo González (1879). Altruistic people sponsored publications such as *El álbum de los niños*, *El periquito*, *La infancia*, and *La niñez*, while Francisco Javier Balmaseda's *Fábulas morales* was reprinted more than fifteen times before the turn of the century.

The Cuban text par excellence, a benchmark which upset the prevailing ideas on language intended for children, was *La Edad de Oro*, by José Martí, published in instalments in a periodical in 1889.

Very few books for children were published in Cuba in the first half of the twentieth century. Works by the poets Mariano Brull and Emilio Ballagas, the *Romancero de la Maestrilla* by Renée Potts, *Niña y el viento de mañana* by Emma Pérez Téllez, *El caballito verde* by Anita Arroyo and Antonio Ortega, and *Los cuentos de Apolo* by Hilda Perera stand out. *Cuentos de todas las noches* (a collection of traditional stories made into fables) by Emilio Bacardí Moreau, was published in 1950, and in the 1950s a young journalist, Dora Alonso made her debut as a playwright.

The year 1959 was important not only for the social changes of the revolutionary period that followed, but also for the impulse given to education and culture. Ample resources were invested in children's books and in 1962, a Spanish teacher Herminio Almendros established the Editora Juvenil both to republish classics and stimulate local talent. Characteristic of this period were Dora Alonso's *Las aventuras de Guille* (translated into many languages), *Dos niños en la Cuba colonial*, with which Renée Mendez Capote initiated a type of book for children referring to national history with a fluent, entertaining style; and *Nuestro Martí*, by Herminio Almendros, a biography of Cuba's national hero. Other writers who joined this movement include Onelio Jorge Cardoso, a great story-teller, who has written some of his best stories for children: *Caballito Blanco*, *Negrita*, and others.

Following the campaign against illiteracy, numerous public and school libraries were established, and in the Juvenile Department of the National Library, the Department of Literature and Stories for Children was founded, under the guidance of the experienced librarian María Teresa Freyre de Andrade and poet Eliseo Diego. Here space was set apart for 'La hora de cuento' [Time for Stories] and many young authors showed their ability as raconteurs. Well-known figures in the promotion of children's literature have emerged from this seedbed, one being Alga Marina Elizagaray.

In 1967, Editora Juvenil closed, and since then practically all children's books have been published by its successor, Editorial Gente Nueva. Occasionally, other institutions organise literary contests which give awards for children's books, such as Casa de las Américas, Abril, Pueblo y Educación (school texts), Unión, Letras Cubanes, and the University of Havana.

The La Edad de Oro Award was established in the 1970s. Sponsored by the Ministry of Culture and the José Martí Pioneers Organisation (a children's institution), this award promoted the production of literature for children. Many writers have been honoured with this award, but only a comparatively few became fully fledged writers. An important Forum for Children's Literature was held under the guidance of writer Mirta Aguirre, during which policies were discussed and the foundations were laid for a movement that is today an important province of Cuban culture.

Three groups of writers can be distinguished since 1959. First, writers who had published books before then, and who have continued to do so: these include Onelio Jorge Cardoso; Eliseo Diego (adaptations of English classics and the book of poems *Soñar despierto*); Renée Méndez Capote with *Memorias de una cubanita que nació con el siglo* (a text for adults enjoyed by children); Félix Pita Rodríguez with *Niños de Viet Nam*; Mirta Aguirre with her paradigmatic *Juegos y otros poemas*; Nícolas Guillén with his book of poems *Por el mar de las Antillas anda un barco de papel*; and, of course, Dora Alonso, whose name was included in the Honours Roll of the Andersen Award for 1984. Alonso has published books of poems, novelettes, books of stories, memoirs and quite a number of plays.

There is a transitional group, of writers born before 1959 who gained recognition through periodicals and literary contests: Rafaela Chacón Nardi, Hilda de Oráa, Anisia Miranda, Lourdes Díaz Canto, Adolfo Martí Fuentes, Adolfo Menéndez Alberdi, Edwigis Barroso and others.

The third group of younger writers has a different approach to realism. Literary contests have been instrumental in what is published – only award-winners can be assured of publication. Memorable works and promising authors are: Julia Calzadilla (two Casa de las Américas awards for *Cantares de la América Latina y el Caribe* and *Los chichiricú del charco de la jícara*); Nersys Felipe (with the same awards for *Cuentos de Guane* and *Román Elé*); Enid Vian (same award for *Las historias de Juan Yendo*); Emilio de Armas (same award for *Junto al álamo de los sinsontes*); Aramís Quintero for his poetic collections *Días de aire*, *Maíz regado*, and *Arca*; Omar Felipe Mauri (13th March Award for *Un patio así*, *Amigos del patio*, and *Lunar*; and La Edad de Oro Award for *Alguien borra las estrellas*); Luis Cabrera Delgado (UNEAC and White Rose Awards for *Tía Julita*, *Mayito*, and other titles); Antonio Orlando Rodríguez (UNEAC, La Edad de Oro and White Rose Awards for *Abuelita Milagro*, *Pues señor este era un circo*, *Mi bicicleta era un hada y otros secretos por el estilo*); Froilán Escobar (*Ana y su estrella de olor*, *Secreto caracol*, *El monte en el sombrero*); Ivette Vian (*Mi amigo Muk Kun*, *La Marcolina*, *El telescopio de David Sietecuentinos*); Excilia Saldaña (*Kele Kele*, *La noche*); Alberto Yáñez (*Cuentan que Penélope*); and also David Chericián, Alberto Serret, Chely

Lima, Denia García Ronda, Mirta Yáñez, Waldo González López, Julio M. Llanes, Emilia Gallego, Omar González, José Antonio Gutiérrez, Olga Fernández, Rodolfo Pérez Valero and Daisy Valls.

There is also a new generation of authors, the publication of whose works has been limited due to the shortage of paper and other materials in the last few years. They win awards, and approach literature more critically and less conservatively. Poets, story-tellers and most novelists of the previous generation viewed the book for children as a plaything, and the act of writing as a form of beautiful speech. They neglected real life, and if their stories were splendid, imaginative, humorous and most articulate, they lacked conflict. Among these younger authors who also write for adults and explore difficult subjects are Luis Carlos Suárez (*Claro de Luna*), Eric González Conde and his saga of *La familia Tosco*, Ricardo Ortega, the unconventioneal poetess Emma Artiles, and my own short novels and stories of fairies and witches who break all the rules, such as *Inventarse un Amigo* [To Invent a Friend] (1993) and *Cuentos y mincuentos ae hadas* [Fairy Tales and Mini Tales] (1991).

Criticism and theoretical studies are inadequate, although Eliseo Diego's pupil, Alga Marina Elizagaray has both promoted Cuban books abroad, and more advanced foreign literature in Cuba. Her books include adaptations of folklore, surveys, essays (*En torno a la literatura infantil, El poder de la literatura para niños y jóvenes*) and other works. Another important critic of the same kind was Waldo González López, who wrote *Escribir para niños y jóvenes*. More recently, several young writers have contributed to criticism and research, either tracing origins or analysing present literature, among them, José Antonio Gutiérrez, Joel Franz, Sergio Andricaín, Antonio Orlando Rodríguez and myself.

## Venezuela

Although this country has a wealth of oral literature, a systematic compilation of its folklore was undertaken only when the Servicio de Investigaciones Folclóricas was started in 1947 (it was later renamed Instituto de Folclor). The Poet Rafael Olivares Figueroa gathered an important collection of popular rhymes for children, published in his *Antología infantil de la nueva poesía venezolana* (1942), and *Folclore Venezolano* (1948). The latter includes two chapters of interest for this discipline: children's folklore and mothers' folklore. Javier Villafañe, an Argentinian writer and puppeteer living in Venezuela, made the collections *Los cuentos de Oliva Torres* and *La gallina que se volvió serpiente y otros cuentos que me contaron*, among others. However, the first book specifically edited for children did not come from folklore, it was the didactic *Lecciones de buena crianza, moral y mundo o educación popular*, written by Feliciano Montenegro and printed in Caracas in 1841. Of the same kind, but perhaps more entertaining was *El libro de la infancia* (1865), published by Amenodoro Urdaneta.

The first periodicals appeared early in the twentieth century. *El Amigo de los Niños* was the more stable and regular, and was followed by *Onza, Tigre y León* (1938–1949) and *Tricolor*, founded at that time and still publishing. *El Cohete* (1979-1981) was a periodical that approached children from a fresh angle.

Among successful authors, one of the first was Rafael Rivero Oramas, who compiled and adapted popular stories that appeared on the radio and in periodicals. In 1965 he published an adventure novel for children, *La danta blanca*, and in 1973 *El mundo de Tío Conejo* one of the best collections ever made of this character's exploits. Eduado Egui included three stories of Tío Tigre and Tío Conejo in his *Cuentos para niños*, while Pilar Almoina de Cabrera also uses this character in *El camino de Tío Conejo*. Other authors known for their excellent stories, occasionally based on folklore or on traditional tales are, besides Pilar Almoina (*Este era una vez*), Lola da Angeli (*Los cuentos de Mamá Lola*), Ida Gramcko (*Juan sin Miedo*) Reyna Rivas (*El perico asado*), and Hernán Hedderich (*Trece cuentos para niños de ayer y de hoy* and *Cuentos de la negra Dominga*).

Writers for adults who have written for children include Luis Manuel Urbaneja (*Ovejón Pantaléon y el mulatero*), José Rafael Pocaaterra (*La I latina*, and *De cómo Panchito Mandefue cénó con el Niño Jesús*), Pedro Emilio Coll (*El castillo de Elsinor*), Julio Garmendía (*Manzanita*), Orlando Araujo (*Miguel Vicente, pate caliente* and *Los Viajes de Miguel Vicente, pata caliente*), and Oscar Guaramato (*La niña vegetal*).

New authors have appeared, among others Daniel Borbot, Hernán Hedderich Arismendi, Carlos Izquierdo, Kurusa and his celebrated story *La calle es libre*, Teresa de la Parra and her books *Memorias de mamá Blanca* and *Ifigenia*. Also outstanding are Marisa Vannini (*El oculto, La fogata*) and Francisco Massiani (*Piedra del mar*).

Rafael Olivares Figueroa and Efraín Subero are notable verse collectors (*Antología infantil para la nueva poesía venezolana* and *Poesía infantil venezolana*). There are many books of poems written by Fernando Paz Castillo, author of *La huerta de Doñana* (1920), regarded by critics as the first book of verses for children: other poets are Aquiles Nazoa, Manuel Felipe Rugeles, Ana Teresa Hernández, Beatriz Mendoza Sagarzazu, Velia Bosch, Marita Carrillo, and Jesús Rosas Marcano.

Literature for children has been published by Fundación Eugenio Mendoza (1952–1960), the Ministry of Education (Tricolor Collection, 1965–1971), and the Instituto Nacional de Cultura y Bellas Artes (INCIBA). The first specialist children's book publisher was Churum-Merú (1967–1968), and in 1977 the Banco del Libro founded Ekaré, its publishing house. Part of the Ministry of Education, the Centro de Capacitación Docente 'El Macaro', a training centre for teachers, has made several collections for children, among them *La voz del maíz*. Monte Avila Editores and María di Mase also cater for the little ones.

Since 1975 public library services have expanded: in 1983 there were 380. Institutions such as the Banco del Libro have spread their networks in the capital city and the provinces. Special libraries for children are short-lived, except those backed by the Banco del Libro. The Banco has also made an important contribution to the criticism and promotion of children's literature by publishing the theoretical journal *Parapara*.

## The West Indies

In the islands of the Caribbean, with the exception of Cuba, the development of indigenous children's literature has been slow, mainly because in most of them the colonial power exercised such a strong influence on the educational system and in the related area of children's books that, even thirty years after independence, the influence has been slow to disappear. Apart from the islands which were colonised by the British, there are islands where Dutch, French, and American influences are strong. Most children's books are imported from Britain, The Netherlands, France, and the USA; children in the British-colonised islands, for example, read books by Enid Blyton and W. E. Johns, apparently oblivious of the racist attitudes of these authors, or the unfamiliar landscapes and situations.

Since 1960, respect for indigenous literatures and languages has begun to make itself felt. A British West Indian children's literature has developed, but the books have been largely written by emigrants and published in Britain or the USA. Books published in Jamaica include Christine Craig's *Right On*, Carmen Manley's *The Land of Wood and Water*, and Dennis Ranston's *The Kite and Petchary*. *The Third Gift* by Jan Carew was published in mainland Guyana and *Step by Step* by Maria Gonzalez in Trinidad–Tobago.

Writers such as Philip Sherlock, C. Everard Palmer and Andrew Salkey were among the first authors to produce books which, although published in Britain, reflected the West Indian landscape and provided West Indian children with a positive self-image.

Philip Sherlock retold traditional West Indian folk-tales, first in *Anansi the Spider Man* (1956) which contained fifteen Anansi stories of the kind originally told in West Africa, and then in *West Indian Folk-Tales* (1966). Andrew Salkey, a Jamaican, was one of the first to set stories in the West Indies. Beginning with *Hurricane* (1964), his early books are all concerned with natural disasters. C. Everard Palmer, another Jamaican, in *The Cloud with the Silver Lining* (1967) uses the theme of children restoring the family fortunes: two young boys make enough money to buy a buggy for their crippled grandfather. In his *Big Doc Bitter Root* (1968) the story is told by a girl, Misty; she describes how a quack doctor comes to the village and deceives nearly everyone except her father.

In the 1970s, authors and illustrators who had either emigrated to Britain themselves, or were the children of emigrants began to emerge. Grace Hallworth, a librarian who became a professional story-teller, has published several traditional collections, such as *Listen to this Story* (1977). Errol Lloyd, a distinguished author-illustrator sets *Nini at Carnival* (1978) in London, but the pictures conjure up all the bustle, excitement, and colour of a Caribbean carnival. Jenny Stow used a vibrant Caribbean setting for *The House that Jack Built* (1992).

James Berry grew up in Jamaica and arrived in Britain in 1948. His *A Thief in the Village* (1987) is a collection of atmospheric and humorous short stories about children and young people in present-day Jamaica. His retelling of Anansi stories, some recalled from childhood, uses the traditional West Indian spelling of the name: *Anancy Spiderman: Twenty Caribbean Folk Stories* (1988). John Agard was an established poet in Guyana when he emigrated to Britain in 1977, publishing his first book for children, *Letters for Lettie* in 1979. He writes in both standard English and Creole. Another poet is Grace Nichols, from Guyana (*Come into my Tropical Garden* (1988)).

These writers and illustrators have won distinction in the world of children's books: Rita Phillips Mitchell's *Hue Boy* (illustrated by Caroline Binch) won the 0–5 category of the Smarties Prize in 1992.

Authors look at the West Indies from various angles. Anne Marie Linden's

*Emerald Blue* (1994) is based on her childhood memories of living in rural Barbados with a much-loved grandmother. Kate Elizabeth Ernest also draws on her own experience both of rural Jamaica and urban England in *Hope Leaves Jamaica* (1993). Caroline Binch's *Gregory Cool* (1994) reverses the situation. British-born Gregory visits his grandparents and cousin in Tobago – dislikes the food, and prefers to play with his pocket video game than feed goats or swim in the sea.

One of the most distinguished of West Indian writers is Rosa Guy, who left Trinidad for New York, and sets her fiction, such as *The Friends* (1974), and *Paris, Pee Wee and Big Dog* (1984) there.

This recent development in West Indian children's literature seems to be unparalleled elsewhere. Having moved to an environment sympathetic to books, and with mainstream publishers willing to consider their work, these writers have proved that they can hold their own in any company.

## Further Reading

Andricaín, S., Marín de Sásá, F. and Rodríguez, A. O. (1993) *Puertas a la lectura*, San José: Ministerio de Cultura, Juventud y Deportes de Costa Rica.

Asociación española de Amigos del Libro Infantl (eds) (1990) *Corrientes actuales de la narrativa infantil y juvenil española en lengua castellana*, Madrid: Asociación Española de Amigos del Libro Infantil y Juvenil.

Asociación Española de Amigos del Libro Infantl (eds) (1991) *El continente americano en los libros infantiles y juveniles*, Madrid: Asociación Española de Amigos del Libro Infantil y Juvenil.

Cabel, J. (1984) *Literatura infantil y juvenil en el Perú*, Lima: Centro de Investigación de la Literatura Infantil y Juvenil en el Perú.

Delgado Santos, F. (1984) *Ecuador y su literatura infantil*, Quito: Subsecretaría de Cultura del Ministerio de Educación.

Elizagaray, A. M. (1975) *En torno la literatura infantil*, Havana: Ediciones Unión.

—— (1979) *El poder de la literatura para niños y jóvenes*, Havana: Editorial Letras Cubana.

—— (1981) *Niños, autores y libros*, Havana: Editorial Gente Nueva.

Fundacíon Germán Sánchez Ruipérez (eds) (1992) *Catálogo de libros infantiles y juveniles iberoamericanos*, Salamanca: Junta de Castilla y León.

Gallelli, G. (1985) *Panorama de la literatura infantil-juvenil argentina*, Buenos Aires: Editorial Plus Ultra.

Galván, F. (1984) *La literatura infantil en México*, Mexico City: D. F.

González López, W. (1985) *Escribir para niños y jóvenes*, Havana: Editorial Gente Nueva.

International Youth Library (eds) (1991) *Children's Literature Research*, Munich: K. G. Saur.

Layolo, M. and Zilberean, R. (1984) *Literatura Infantil Brasileira. História. Histórias*, São Paulo: Atica.

Nikolajeva, M. (1988) *The Magic Code: The Use of Magical Patterns in Fantasy for Children*, Stockholm: Almqvist and Wiksell International.

Peña Muñoz, M. (1982) *Historia de la literatura infantil chilena*, Santiago de Chile: Editorial Andrés Bello.

Piñeiro de Rivera, F. and Freire de Matos, I. (1983) *Literatura infantil caribeña*, Dominican Republic: Boriken Libros.

Puentes de Oyenard, S. (1982) *Literatura infantil uruguaya*, Montevideo: Ediciones García.

Uribe, V. and Delón, M. (eds) (1984) *Panorama de la literatura infantil en América Latina*, Caracas: Banco del Libro.

# Index

Abanindrath 811
Abbott, Jacob 344
Abd, Abdullah 791
Abrams, M.H. 71–2
Al-Abrashi 790
Absar, Abdul Ali 819
Abu Dhabi 791
academics 9–12; and collections 546;
    feminism 108
Achebe, Chinua 669, 789, 799
Acres, Avid 857
*Action* (comic) 251–2
Adam, Jeanie 844
Adam, Ruth 531
Adams, Richard 560; *Watership Down* 292
Adams, William Taylor 478, 875
adolescents 387–96; assumptions about
    reading 584–5; developmental stages of
    reading 584–93, 585–90; empathy 588;
    engaging 7; family relationships 391–3;
    friendships 393–4; happiness-binding
    77; issues of development 64; perceived
    boredom 587–8; pregnancy 391; school
    stories 357–8; sexuality and love 388–91;
    six stages of response 77; social problems
    395–6; teaching to question text 592–3
adoption and adaption 422–31; adventure
    stories 423–4; common cultural pool
    424–5; criteria for differentiating 423;
    genre fiction 425–7; mediation and
    adaption 428–31
adults *see also* authors: as audience 17;
    colonisation of children 120; imbalanced
    power relationship 132
adventure stories: adopted by children
    423–4; folk elements 332; the genre
    330–4; historical 369; origins 326–30;
    ponies 360; Robinsonnades 326–7, 328;

science fiction 336; Scotland 689;
    twentieth century 334–7
*The Adventures of Tom Sawyer* (Twain)
    478–9, 877
*Aesop's Fables* 143, 162, 234, 282, 761; early
    translations 410; Richardson's
    translation 412
Afanasyev, Aleksandr 765
Africa: book design 670, 671; cultural
    differences 668–9, 802; English-speaking
    796–801; French-speaking 801–4;
    journals 495; languages 658; storytelling
    539–40
Agard, John 203, 891
age groups *see also* adolescents: birth to five
    378–9; criticism 384–5; five to seven
    379–81; seven to ten 381–4; 'suitability'
    arguments 377–8; younger readers
    377–85
Agee, H. 84
Aguirre, Mirta 888
Ahlberg, Allan 380, 381, 687; intertextuality
    5, 133; metafiction 399; picture books
    234; poetry 203
Ahlberg, Janet 378–9, 380, 687; book design
    466; intertextuality 133; picture books
    234
Ahmad, Muhammed Ariff 827
Aichinger, Helga 755
Aiken, Joan 20, 555, 560, 685
Aikin, Lucy 195
Ainsworth, W. Harrison 263–4
Akbarbadi, Nazir 814
Akpaka, O. 803
Akrill, Caroline 367
Aksakov, Sergei 767
Alcott, Louisa May 478; *Good Wives* 345;
    *Little Women* 103–4, 345, 655, 877

Alderson, Brian 115, 125
Aleman, Fernando 730
Ale, Mikolás 775
Alexander, Cecil Frances 193–4
Alexander, Lloyd 560, 562
Alger, Horatio 877
Ali, Syed Imtiaz 814
*Alice's Adventures in Wonderland* (Carroll)
    680–1; illustrations 226; influence 377;
    multimedia forms 533; publications
    473–4, 479
Allan, Mabel Esther 355, 357
Allen, Pamela 851, 859
Allingham, William 198
Allsobrook, Marian 5
*Ally Sloper* (Ross) 244
Almendros, Herminio 887
Almonia de Cabrera, Pilar 890
A.L.O.E. (Charlotte Maria Tucker) 284
Alonso, Dora 883, 887, 888
Alonso, Fernando 729
von Alphen, Hieronymous 710, 711
Aman, Kimiko 842
American Antiquarian Society 547, 548–9
American Libraries Association 488
Amichand, Baji Bhai 812
Andersen, Hans Christian 106, 522, 700;
    brilliant storyteller 540; *Eventyr* 127;
    fairy tales 159; Hersholt collection 548;
    illustrations by Robinson 228–9
Andersen (Hans Christian) Award 233, 512,
    527
Anderson, Lena 708
de Andrade, María Teresa Freyre 887
*Androcles and the Lion* 216
da Angeli, Lola 890
Angola 658
animals 282–93, 824; anthropomorphic 120,
    123, 289–90, 360; appeal to different ages
    427; pony books 292, 360–7; realistic,
    wild stories 288–9; roots in realism
    291–3; talking 284–8, 425; used
    symbolically 292–3
*Anne of Green Gables* (Montgomery) 862,
    863
Anno, Mitsumaso 234; *All in a Day* 659
Anstey, F. 299; *Vice Versa* 297–8
anthropology: new ethnography 36
Anyon, J.M. 54
apartheid 395
Apaydin, Talip 782

Appiah, Peggy 797
Appleton, Victor: *Tom Swift* 318
*Arabian Nights* 156
Arabic language 789–2; book design 672;
    folk-tales 789; magazines 453
Araújo, Matilde Rosa 732
Araujo, Orlando 890
archetypes 91–3, 169
Ardizzone, Edward 232, 565, 683
Argentina 884–5
Ariès, Philippe 18–19
Aristotle 46, 171
Armitage, Ronda 858, 859
Arnheim, Rudolph 121
von Arnim, Achim 737
Arnold, Edward 475
Arnold, Matthew 594, 595
art: defining children's literature 18; history
    of styles 122; transforming social order
    38; visual arts 80
Arthur, King 170–1, 305–6; retellings 174,
    308
Arundel, Honor 389
Asare, Meshack 789
Ashley, Bernard 563
Asia 823–9
Asimov, Isaac 320
Association of Booksellers for Children
    482–3
*At the Very Edge of the Forest* (Fox) 3
Atish, Rajendra Singh 815
Atkinson, J. 76
Attenborough, Liz 513, 514
Aubry, Claude 868
audience: authors aims 556–60; writing up
    or down to 20–1, 563–4
audio *see* multimedia
Auerbach, Nina: *Communities of Women* 104
d'Aulnoy, Mme Marie-Catherine 153–4,
    156; *Yellow Dwarf* 152, 153
Australia 843–52; collections 548; cultural
    response 82; higher education 612–13;
    journals 487, 494–5; magazines 457;
    myth and legend 167, 169; native culture
    666, 843–4, 848; storytelling 542, 543
Australian Children's Picture Book of the
    Year Award 233
Austria 444–5, 752–6
authors: aiming at the audience 556–8;
    anonymity and traditional verse 178–9;
    censorship 499; changing relationship

with implied reader 83–4; creation of child in book 11; creation of readers 71; effect of prizes 513–14; effect of war and politics 656; information books 436–7; intentions 48; intrusions into story 309; 401–2; magazines for young authors 444; major authors' work for children 410–20; market forces 9; not in dialogue with reader 89–90; prizes 512; reader response to 10–11; school visits 598; series 80; speak out on children's literature 555–68; symmetrical communication 20–1; and texts 131; therapeutic release 89, 90; translation 520–2; working with publishers 465; on writing 555–60; young 365–6

Avery, Gillian 21, 127, 371
Awa, Naoko 842
Awad, Farid Mohamed 791
Awdry, Rev. W.: *Thomas the Tank Engine* 6–7
Axton, Richard 212
Ayckbourn, Alan 217
de Azcuénaga, Domingo 884

Bâ, Amadou Hampâte 803
*Babar* series (de Brunhoff) 232, 290
Babbitt, Natalie 25–6, 301
Baby-Sitters Club 53
Bacardí Moreau, Emilio 887
Bach, Richard 423
Bacon, R.L. 858
Bagnall, Jill 858
Bagnold, Enid: *National Velvet* 363
Baker, Jannie 234
Baker, Julius Stafford 248
Bakhtin, Mikhael 131, 132
Baldwin (Ruth) Collection 551
Ballaga, Emilio 887
Ballantyne, R.M. 328, 329, 330–1, 422, 681, 689, 862
Balmaseda, Francisco Javier 887
Bangladesh 807–8, 815–17
Bankert, Birgit 22
Banks, Lynne Reid 389
Barbauld, Anna 148, 193
Al Barkuki 789–90
Barne, Kitty 365
Barnes, D. 76
Barrie, J.M. 682, 688, 689; *Peter Pan* 207, 208, 215–17
Barron, Gerrit 883

Barthes, Roland: circular memory of reading 135; lost codes 131–2, 133; polysemous texts 51
Bartolozzi, Salvador 726, 728
Barton, Charlotte 844–5
Basanjar, U. 824
Base, Graeme 293, 851
Batchelder Award 526
Baum, L. Frank 531; *The Master Key* 315–16; *Wizard of Oz* 479; *The Wizard of Oz* series 877
Bawden, Nina 46, 374, 555, 684
Baxendale, Leo 251
Baykurt, Fakir 782
Beach, R. 80, 82
Beadle, Erastus Flavel 259–60
Beake, Lesley 800
*The Beano* (comic) 249
*A Bear Called Paddington* (Bond) 296
Beardsley, M. 73
de Beaumont, Jeanne Marie Leprince 273
Bechstein, Ludwig 155, 739
Beckman, Gunnel 389, 708
Behrangi, Samad 793
Békés, Pál 778
Belgium 445
Belinsky, Vissarion 766
Bell, Anthea 521–2
Bell, George 473
Bell, R. 76
Belloc, Hilaire 199
*Bell's Life in London and Sporting Chronicle* 242–3
Belotti, Elena Gianini 759
Belsey, Catherine 47; characters as authors of actions 48; construction of the reader 50; on history 32–3; popular literature 52
Belykh, Grigory 769
Bemelman, Ludwig: *Madeline* series 879
Ben-Ezer, Ehud 787
Benavente, Jacinto 727
Benedek, Elek 777
Benjamin, Walter 46
Benton, Michael 10, 76, 77, 80, 83–4; ethnographic approach 81
*Beowulf* 174, 304
Berg, Leila 280
Berger, John 119
Bergman, Tamar 787
Berna, Paul 724
Beron, Peter 779

Berrios, Rubén 883
Berry, James 203, 891
Beskow, Elsa 706–7
Bessa-Luis, Agustina 733
Bethnal Green Museum of Childhood 549
Bettelheim, Bruno: *The Uses of Enchantment*
   91, 332, 541, 880
*Bevis: The Story of a Boy* (Jefferies) 333
Bewick, Thomas 223, 225
Bhadheka, Giju Bhai 812
Bhagwat, B.R. 813
Bhushan, Reboti 809
Bianki, Vitaly 769
Bibles: catechisms 271–2; children's
   versions 269–72; hieroglyphic 270–1;
   stories 268–9, 277–8
bibliotherapy 634–42; development 637–9;
   story and consciousness 635–7
Biegel, Paul 713
*Biggles* series (Johns) 334–5
*Billy Bunter* stories (Hamilton) 250, 353–4
Binch, Caroline 892
Bisenieks, Dainis 306
Björk, Christina 708
*Black Beauty* (Sewell) 284–5, 360
Blackwell, Basil 475
Blades, Ann 863, 866
Blake, Quentin 234–5
Blake, William 5, 151, 194, 679
Blanck, Jacob N. 546
Bleich, D. 73–4
blind children *see* special needs
Blish, James 320
Blok, Aleksandr 768
Blonsky, Marshall 116, 117
Bloom, Harold 98
Blos, Joan W. 368
Blount, Margaret 289
Blume, Judy 383, 566; censorship 503, 504;
   *Forever* 389–90; prizes 510
Blyton, Enid 43, 49, 277, 354–5; characters
   46; criticism 384; family stories 340;
   ideology and contradictory readings 52
Boadu, Therson 789
Bobbs-Merrill Company 550–1
Bødker, Cecil 701
Bodleian Library 549
Bohdal, Susi 755
Bojunga Nunes, Lygia 883, 885, 886
Bolivia 457

Bologna Children's Book Fair 233, 475, 483,
   526–7
Bologna Illustrators of Children's Books
   Award 527
Bond, Michael: *A Bear Called Paddington*
   296
Bond, Nancy 300
Bonnerman, Elsa Isabel 883
book design 461–70 *see also* illustration;
   blockbooks 461–2; books which do things
   467; comic strip format 468; cultural
   difference 660–72; designers not
   illustrators 463; history 473; information
   books 468–9; jackets and binding
   469–70; layout of pages 467–9; in
   practice 463; reading and typography
   464–7
book fairs 474–5, 483; translations 526;
   USA 479
bookselling 9, 127; book fairs *see* book fairs;
   book tokens 475; effect of awards 512–13;
   international promotion and sales 660–2;
   libraries 618; in USA 482–3, 880
*The Borrowers* (Norton) 381
Bossev, Assen 779
Boston, Lucy 556, 685
Botswana 453, 799
Bowers, Fredson 128
boys' stories 317–18; rascals 712
Bradbury, Ray 320
Brantlinger, P. 35
Bratislava Illustrators award 233, 527
Bratton, J.S. 47, 49, 275
Brazil 457, 885–7
Brazil, Angela 351
Breary, Nancy 355
'Brenda' (Mrs G. Castle Smith) 277
Brent-Dyer, Elinor M. 352, 353
Brentano, Clemens 737, 738
Brett, Edwin J. 264
Briggs, J. 127
Briggs, Raymond 235, 425, 687; *Father
   Christmas* 383; nursery rhymes 379;
   *Where the Wind Blows* 394
Britain: critical journals 485–6, 487, 492–3,
   493; cultural materialism 36; fairy tales
   155–60; family stories 338–42; higher
   education in children's literature 609–12;
   historical overview 676–687; imperialism
   and adventure stories 327–30, 332;
   library history 616, 618–20; library

services 620–31; magazines (English and Welsh) 447; New Historicism and cultural materialism 34; publishing 472–6, 656; retellings of myths and legends 173–4; storytelling revival 542, 543; twentieth century poetry 201–4
British Arts Council 208
British Library 547
Brlic-Mazuranic, Ivana 777
Brooke, Leslie 229, 473
Brooks, Ron 851
Brown, J. 76
Brown, Marcia 235–6
Brown, Margaret Wise 879; *Good Night Moon* 95–6, 481
Browne, Anthony 46, 235, 293; metafiction 400, 403; *Piggybook* 580–2
Browne, Tom 245–6
Browning, Elizabeth Barrett 198
Browning, Robert 198, 415, 682
Bruce, Dorita Fairlie 352, 356
Bruce, Mary Grant 845
Bruckner, Karl 753
Brull, Mariano 887
Bruna, Dick 378
Brunei Darussalem 823
de Brunhoff, Jean: *Babar* series 232, 290, 522, 723
Bubnys, Vytautas 779
Buckeridge, Anthony 354
Büdinger, Moses Mordecai 269
Bufano, Alfredo 884
Bulgaria 445, 779
Bunbury, R. 82
Buntline, Ned (Edward Judson) 260–1
Bunyan, John 141; *Pilgrim's Progress* 144, 272, 277, 678; verse 192, 679; works for children 411
Burghi, Juan 884
Burnett, Frances Hodgson 207, 208, 216, 681
Burnford, Sheila 289, 864
Burningham, John 236, 380, 558, 687; intertextuality 5; *Mr Gumpy's Outing* 113–23
Burns, Robert 180
Burns and Oates 279
Burroughs, Edgar Rice 317, 797
Burton, Hester 372, 374
Buryanov, Viktor 766
*Buster Brown* comic strip 254, 255

Butler, Dorothy 378
Butler Library 550
Butts, Dennis 128
Byars, Betsy 557, 591
Byelorussia 445

Caballer, Fernán 726
Cabel, Jesús 883
Cadogan, Mary 292
Caldecott, Randolph 226–7, 549, 682
Caldecott (Randolph) Medal 233, 480, 509, 513, 616
Calhoun, Frances Boyd 344
*Call of the Wild* (London) 288–9
Calvino, Italo 759
Camara, L. 803
Cameron, Eleanor 300, 563, 564
Campbell, John W. 319–20
Campbell, Joseph 541; *The Hero with a Thousand Faces* 171, 332
Campe, Joachim Heinrich 736
Canada: English-speaking 862–68; French-speaking 868–70; higher education in children's literature 613; journals 487, 494; libraries 616, 627; magazines 450–1; Native writing 866–7
Canada Council prize 527
Cannan, Joanna 360, 363–4
canon: debate about 596; and New Historicism 34; retellings 53; teaching in higher education 607; women in 108
Čapek, Josef 775
Cardell, William 343
Cardoso, Onelio Jorge 887, 888
Caribbean literature 882–4, 890–2; poetry 203; storytelling 540
Carigiet, Alois 750
Carle, Eric 236; *The Very Hungry Caterpillar* 466
Carlos, Papiniano 732
Carnegie (Andrew) Medal 440, 509; criticized 513–16; effect on sales 513; introduction 510, 682
Carpenter, Humphrey 286, 288, 428–9
Carrington, Noel 475
Carroll, Lewis 180, 680–1; animals 285; moves imaginative writing to foreground 377; parodies Watts 272; verses 682; wants low price 473–4; on writing 563
Carter, Angela: reclaimed fairy tales 106, 110

Carter, Nick 261–2
Casona, Alejandro 727, 728
de Castro Osório, Ana 732
Catalan language 656
*Catcher in the Rye* (Salinger) 64, 503
Causley, Charles 686
de Cavilly, J. 803
Caxton, William 143, 410, 472
Celtic lore 152, 167; fairy tales 159;
    Hallowe'en 182; influence on fantasy
    305; Ireland 695–6; retellings 174;
    Scotland 688; Tolkien 310; Wales 300–1
censorship 498–507, 596; authors on 560–1;
    dime novel guidelines 260; at editorial
    level 506; evolution versus creation
    504–6; legislation 501, 502;
    McCarthyism 503; penny dreadfuls 265;
    sexuality 503–4; Soviet Union 770, 771;
    various motives 498; violence and crime
    501–3; Wertham writes against comics
    258
Central America 882–4
Chaba, Al Kamal Abdulla 816
Chambers, Aidan 357, 567–8; characters 46;
    children's participation 580; implied
    readers 82, 83; intertextuality 5;
    metafiction 406; *The Present Takers* 384;
    stories about sexuality 390; textual
    devices 50
Chambers, E.K. 211–12, 213
Chambers, Nancy 108
chapbooks 677; adventure tales 326; folk-
    tales 162; illustrations 222; religion 274;
    religious writing 271; Scotland 688, 689;
    seventeenth century 410–11
*Charlotte's Web* (White) 97, 291, 299, 481,
    879
Charskaya, Lidiya 768
Châteillon, Sebastian 271
Chaucer, Geoffrey 410
Chear, Abraham 143
Cherland, Meredith Rogers 53
Chester, Tessa 126, 128
Chew Kok Chan 826
Chiba, Shôzô 838–9
childhood: attitudes in the USA 876–7,
    880–1; authors on childhood 561–2;
    blank or naïve 109; changing view of
    710–11, 718–19; defence and attack in
    traditional verse 183–4; defining the
    child 21–2, 24–6; focusing on life

experiences 378; historical revelation 26;
    Romantic ideal within nature 35; social
    relationships 381–2
*The Children of the New Forest* (Marryat)
    327, 331, 369
Children's Book History Society 127
Children's Book Trust 809
Children's Film Foundation 534
*Children's Hour* (radio) 537
children's literature *see also* drama; poetry:
    adopted by children 422–31; authors'
    viewpoints 555–68; bibliography and
    history 125–8; defining 17, 18–19, 23–7,
    423; defining the reader 19–22, 24–6;
    early texts 142; in higher education
    606–13; history 141–51; humanising
    power 595–6; international scene
    653–62; by major authors 410–20;
    suitability 560–1; symmetrical
    communication with author 20–1
Children's Peace Literature Award 511
*Children's Theatre* (Goldberg) 208–9
Childress, Alice: censorship 503, 504
Chimani, Leopold 752
China 455, 830–5
Chiranjeevi, Narla 815
Chodorow, Nancy 97
Chorny, Shasha 768
Chorpenning, Charlotte 216
Christian-Smith, Linda K. 49, 51, 52–3, 54
Christianity *see also* religion: Africa 796,
    800; catechisms 271; and Darwinism 315;
    evangelist literature 273–81; festivals and
    holidays 279–80; folk-tales 162; oral
    tradition and customs 182–3; Puritans
    155–6, 871–2; Quakers 872; roots of
    drama in Catholic Church 211–12, 213;
    saints in mythology 168
Christopher, John 322–1
Chuah, Bessie 827
Chugtai, Azim Beg 814
Chukovsky, Kornei 769
Cinderella stories 101, 157
Clapham, Henoch 269
Clark, Margaret 850
Clarke, Arthur C. 320
Clarke, Jeane M. 638
Clarke, Pauline 685
classics: defining 430; relation to the child
    26; 'tellings gaps' and 'implied readers'

83–4; translated works 519; translations 522–5

Claverie, Jean 724–5

Cleary, Beverly 382, 388

Clemens, Samuel *see* Twain, Mark

Clement Jr, William 242–3

Cleveland-Peck, Patricia 381

closure 80, 398

Co-operative Children's Book Centre 550

Cocking, Percy 246

Cody, William F. ('Buffalo Bill') 260–1

cognitive development 18

Cohen, Adir 27

Cole, Babette: *Mummy Laid an Egg* 5–6

Cole, Elisha 270–1

Cole, Henry 223–4

Coleridge, Samuel Taylor 194–5

Coleridge, Sara 197

Coll, Pedro Emilio 890

collections 126–7, 546–7; academic/ universities and colleges 550–1, 551–2; contemporary 549; general versus specific 550; genre and format 550–1; historical 548–9; locations 546–8, 551; organisations and publications 553–4; public libraries and private institutions 552; research 552–3

Collodi (Carlo Lorenzini) 522, 757

Coloma, Padre 726

colonialism 22; adventure stories 327–30; Australia 843–5; education 796; language 658, 672–3; new ethnography 36; redirecting 109

Colwell, Eileen 542

Comencini, Luigi 759

Comenius, Johann Amos: coincides with optics 720; *Orbis Sensualium Pictus* 220, 410, 434, 462, 522, 655; place in Czech literature 775

comics: American 252–8; Britain 242–52; censorship 502–3; and science fiction 319

commodification 6–7

computers *see* information technology

Comstock, Anthony 501

Confucius 831

Connolly, Joseph 128

Cook, Elizabeth 539

*The Cool Web* (Meek) 79

Coolidge, Susan 351; *What Katy Did* 345

Cooney, Barbara: *The Ox-Cart Man* (with Hall) 600

Cooper, C.R. 77–8

Cooper, James Fenimore 326, 874

Cooper, Mary 145–6

Cooper, Susan 373, 556–7; *The Dark is Rising* 134–5; on realism 566–7; use of *The Mabinogion* 300–1

Cormier, Robert 356, 530; censorship 503, 504; *The Chocolate War* 393; *We All Fall Down* 393–4; on writing 564–5

Cotton, John 871

Coughlin, Ellen K. 101

Cowley, Joy 859

Cox, C.B. 77–8, 80

Crago, Hugh 101–2

Craig, Patricia 292

Crampton, Patricia 512, 520–1

Crane, Walter 226, 227, 549

Creanga, Ion 778

Cresswell, Helen 342

Crichton, James 249

crime and detective fiction 261–2, 263

criticism: applying adult criticism 47; concept of ideology 37–8; defining the literature 22–3; feminist 101–10; implied reader 83–5; information books 440; journals 485–7, 491–3; 'milk bottle versus Grimm' controversy 480–1; New Criticism 44–5, 48, 73, 584; psychoanalytical 89–98; reader response 71–4, 79; reading and writing 'rubbish' 563; teaching adolescents to question 592–3; teaching children's literature in higher education 606–13; younger readers' literature 384–5

Croatia 656

Crompton, Richmal: *Just William* series 127, 345

Cross, Gillian 684

Crossley-Holland, Kevin 383, 429

Crouch, Marcus 361, 366, 423

Crouch, Nathaniel 270, 272

Cruikshank, George 158–9, 223, 224, 276

Crumb, Robert 252

Csukás, István 778

Cuba 883, 887–9

Culea, Apostol 778

Culler, Jonathan 131, 132

cultural materialism 34, 47–9

cultural poetics 34

*Cultural Studies* (Inglis) 38

culture: American isolationism 482, 524;
  assumptions 117; child within the book
  25; China 830–2; cross-cultural
  influences 82–3; defining audience 21–2;
  developing countries 663–73; difference
  which affects reading 802; families and
  learning reading 577–8; and history 33;
  and ideology 121; individual identity 54;
  justice 80–1; libraries and
  multiculturalism 624; popular 37; reader
  response studies 81–3; shifts 19; values
  within tradition 24; Williams defines
  35–6
Cumming, Primrose 360, 364–5
Cutt, M. Nancy 128
Cyprus 661–2
Czech and Slovak Republics 774–6 see also
  Comenius; magazines 445–6

Dahl, Roald 686; characters 46; film
  adapatations 535; implied author and
  reader 83; The Witches 506; on writing
  558, 559–60
Dahl, Vladimir 766
Dallas, Ruth 857
Dalta, Penelope 762–3
Daly, Niki 800
Damdinsürén, Ts. 824
Damle, H.K. 812
Dan Dare 250–1
The Dandy (comic) 249
Dankert, Birgit 24
Danny, the Champion of the World (Dahl)
  535
Danto, Arthur 115
Danziger, Paula 64–5, 392
Darch, Winifred 352–3
The Dark is Rising (Cooper) 134–5
Darton, F.J. Harvey 23, 42, 104, 126, 472
Darton, William 145, 221, 222
Dashdorge, Natsagdorge 824
Daveluy, Paule 521, 868
Davesne, A. 803
David, Linda 127
Day, Thomas 149
Day Lewis, Cecil 418–19
Dayioglu, Gülten 782
D.C. Thomson: comics 257, 258; penny
  dreadfuls 265; science fiction 317
De Amicis, Edmondo 757
de Hamel, Joan 857

de la Mare, Walter 200, 277, 683
de la Mare (Walter) Collection 549
de Roo, Anne 855
deaf children see special needs
Debi, Ashapurna 812
Defoe, Daniel 872; Robinson Crusoe 326,
  655, 678
Dégh, L. 305
Dehmel, Richard and Paula 740
DeJong, Meindert 557
Del Amo, Monserrat 726, 727, 729
Delgado Santos, Francisco 883
Dell Publications 256
Demers, Patricia 297
Denmark 699; collections 548; magazines
  446; overview of literature 700–2;
  translated works 523, 524
Dennison, Dorothy 278
Denton, Terry 851
Desai, D.S. 813
Deshpande, Chris 281
Deshpande, Kusmawati 809
determinism and agency 54
developing countries 663–73, 669
Dey, Frederick Marmaduke Van
  Rennsselaer 261–2
Dhanwant Singh 815
Diakité, M.S. 803
dialogue: style 67–9
Diary of a Young Girl (Frank) 522–3, 656
Dias, P. 76, 80, 82
Dickens, Charles 276, 414–15
Dickinson, Peter 323, 402, 563, 684
dictionaries 434
didacticism 678 see also information books;
  catechistical and Biblical writing 267–72;
  defining children's literature 23; drama
  218; early publishing 478; ideology 49,
  53; poetry 191; pony stories 361, 362;
  purpose of literature 41–2; religion
  338–9; splits critics 26–7
Diego, Eliseo 887, 888
Diekmann, Miep 713
Digby, Desmond 851
dime novels 262–3; censorship 500–1;
  science fiction 317
Diong, C.O. 804
Diouri, A. 804
Dirks, Rudolph 253, 254, 255
discourse 58; defining 59

Disney productions 880; adaptations 533–4; for all ages 427; comics 249; intertextuality 133–4

Dixit, Narain 811

Dixon, Bob: representation and bias 43, 44

Dixon, J. 76

Dixon, Paul 22

Dobrú, R. 883

*Doctor Dolittle* series (Lofting) 291, 506, 509

Dodd, Lynley 859

Dodge, Mary Mapes: *Hans Brinker, or the Silver Skates* 478, 877

Doherty, Berlie 391

Dollimore, J. 34, 38

Domenego, Hans 754

Donenfield, Harry 256, 257

Doongaji, Dolat 809

Dorset, Catherine Ann 195

Doubleday Publishing 480, 550

Doyle, Arthur Conan 317, 688

Dragt, Tonke 714

drama 206–19; devotional 273; education 208–10, 214; Elizabethan 212; history up to *Peter Pan* 210–15; mystery plays 212; pantomimes 210, 214–15; *Peter Pan* and after 215–19; theatre 208–10

Dromkeen collection 548

Dros, Imme 176

drug abuse 503, 504

Duder, Tessa 859

Duggan, Maurice 858

Dulac, Edmund 227, 228

Dumas, Alexandre 426, 722

Dupasquier, Philipe 236

Durak, Mary and Elizabeth 844

Dutta, Arup Kumar 809

Dwivedi, Sohan Lal 811

Dygasiski, Adolf 776

Eagleton, Terry 47, 51–2

*Earthsea Revisioned* (Le Guin) 104–5

*Earthsea* series (Le Guin) 168

Eco, Umberto 51, 116

Edgeworth, Maria 35, 104, 149, 413–14, 678; plays 214, 273

education 28 *see also* information books; academic research 546; bibliography 126; book budgets 439–40; changing attitudes towards younger readers 377–8; classroom practices 75, 601–2, 603–4; cognitive issue 18; colonialism 796;

debate over Leavisite paradigm 45–6; defining children's literature 18; Denmark 701; developmental model for adolescent readers 585–90; drama 208–10, 214; early texts 142; expanding literacy 329; family role 577–8; feminism 108; Germany 735, 736, 740; graduate studies 608–9, 611–12; ideology 54; journals and reviews 489–91; learning skills books 438; librarians 617–18; libraries 629–30; literacy 226, 573–82; literature in higher education 606–13; National Curriculum 73; National Defense Education Act 481–2; personal response to texts 579–82; publishing 475; religious 267–72; response criticism 73; school libraries 597, 630–1; school stories 348–58; Scotland 688; special needs readers 644–50; storytelling 598–9; teacher education 609–10; teaching fiction and poetry 594–604; teaching reflexiveness 590–2; theorists and early texts 147–9; typefaces and letter recognition 465–6; women distancing selves from romance 412–13

Education Acts 226, 228, 329, 348; increases market 349; stimulates publishing 472

Egan, M. 91

Egner, Thorbjørn 705

Egoff, Sheila 26–7, 324, 865

Egypt 453, 540, 789, 791

Ekker, Ernst A. 754

Ekwensi, Cyprian 790

Elflein, Ada María 884

Eliot, T.S. 201; *Old Possum's Book of Practical Cats* 417

Elizagaray, Alga Marina 888, 889

Elöue, Ali Ulvi 781

Emami, G. 793

Emerson, Hunt 252

Enciso, Pilar 729

encyclopedias 434–5

Ende, Michael 742

English language: cross-cultural influences 82–3; international publishing 657; isolationist 528; metasemiotic tools 580–2; patterns of meaning 576; publishing economics 474

enjoyment 18

environment: information books 435–6

*The Epic of Gilgamesh* 171

epics 169–72; influence on fantasy 305–6
Epstein, Jacob 515
Erikson, Erik 64
Ernest, Kate Elizabeth 892
Ershov, Pyotor 765–6
escapism: from bourgeois capitalism 48; versus didacticism 23; early fun texts 149–51
Escarpit, Robert 464
Estonia 446, 780
*ET The Extra-Terrestrial* 535
ethnography 36
Evans, Clifford: *Where the Rainbow Ends* (with Ramsey) 216
Evans, Edmund 81, 549
Ewing, Juliana Horatia 339–40

fables 161, 163; animals 282–4; Swift and Gay 413; universality 654
Fadiga, R. 803
Fagunwa, D.O. 668–9
Fairfax-Lucy, Brian 342
fairy tales 6, 152–63, 428, 654; audience 160–1; Cinderella and feminism 101; Disney adaptations 134; eighteenth century publishing 146; feminism 106; folk- tales 161–3; gender 161; Ireland 695–6; monsters and menace 95; moral stories to frighten children 152; retellings 241; Scotland 688, 689; storytelling 539; used by major authors 414–15, 418
Falkner, J. Meade 333
Fallada, Hans (Rudolf Ditzen) 744–5
families 18–19, 338–47; black families 347; divorce 347; domesticity 342–3; novel breaks free of 44–5; orphans and problem parents 338, 339, 342–4, 413; reading at home and literacy 577–9; social realism for adolescents 391–3
*Famous Five* series (Blyton): ideology and contradictory readings 52
fantasy 59, 685; animal characters 285; authors on 566–8; crosses age groups 424; defined 303–4; domestic 295–302; Finland 703; high 303–12; historical settings 300; language 60; limits of high fantasy 312; magic discovered by or hidden from parents 296; the *Märchen* 305, 310; metafiction 402–3; pulp magazines 262–3; read by all age groups 309; versus realism 79; science 322;

secondary worlds 303–4; social relationships 382
Farjeon, Eleanor 201, 277
Farmer, Penelope 356
Farogh, Rais 819
Farquharson, Martha (Martha Finley) 343–4
Farris, Micheal 505
*Father Christmas* (Briggs) 383
Fawcett Publications 258
Felix, Monique 236–7
Felperin, H. 33, 34
feminism 101–10, 759; fairy tales 106; new ethnography 36; psychoanalytic criticism 97–8; reclaiming 105–8; redirection 108–10; redressing the balance 7–8; rereading 103–5; second wave 102, 105, 108; theory 101–2
Fénlon, François de Salignac 718–19, 720
Fenn, Eleanor 148, 157
Fenton, Edward 520
Ferenc, Móra 777
Ferguson, Ruby 365
Ferra-Mikura, Vera 753
Ferrán, Jaime 729
fiction and non-fiction division 4
Fidler, Kathleen 690
Field, Eugene 198
Fielding, Sarah 42, 148, 348; fairy tales 153, 156
Fienberg, Anna: *Ariel, Zed and the Secret of Life* 63–4
films *see* multimedia
Fine, Anne 357, 392, 562
Finland 174, 446, 548, 699, 702–4
Firth, Barbara 237
Fischer, Hans 750–1
Fish, Stanley 72, 73–4
Fisher, Bud 256
Fisher, Dorothy Canfield 343, 878
Fisher, Margery 2, 23, 45, 438, 440
Fisk, Nicholas 323
Fisk, Pauline: *Midnight Blue* 278
Fitinghoff, Laura 707
Fitzhugh, Louise 382; *Harriet the Spy* 210
*Five Children and It* (Nesbit) 299
Florida State University 127
Florio (John) Prize 527
flying stories 334–5
focalisation 66–7, 69
Foglar, Jaroslav 775

folk-tales 161–3, 428, 654 *see also* under
individual countries; adventure stories
332; American slaves 287; and
consciousness 635–6; Nordic countries
699–700, 703; retellings 241; Scotland
688; storytelling 541, 544
Fontaine, Nicolas 268
Forbes, Esther 878
Ford, H.J. 229
Foreman, Michael 237
Forest, Antonia 280, 355–6, 374
Fortescue, Sir John 289
Fortún, Elena 726, 728
Foucault, Michel 33
Fox, Carol: *At the Very Edge of the Forest* 3
Fox, Geoff 51, 77, 441
Fox, Paula 405; *How Many Miles to
Babylon?* 66; *The Slave Dancer* 22, 374
Foxe, John 272
Foxwell, Herbert S. 248
France: awards 512; comics 253; drama 214;
effect of Revolution 721; fairy tales 152,
161; international publishing 657;
magazines 446–7; oral tradition 541;
overview of literature 717–25; public
libraries 617; storytelling 542; translated
works 524, 525
de Francis, John 664–5
Frank, Anne: *Diary of a Young Girl* 522–3,
656
*Frankenstein* (Shelley) 314
Frankfurt Book Fair 475, 526
Franklin Watts Publishers 481
von Franz, Marie Louise 93
Fraser, Gordon 246
Fraser, James 126
*Freaky Friday* (Rodgers) 297–8
Freedman, K.: cultural response 82
Freeman, Bill 865
Fremont, Jessie Benton 260
French, Fiona 237
French language: in Africa 658; magazines
453
Freud, Sigmund 94
Freudian criticism 90–1
Freund, E. 73
Fritz, Jean 371–2
Frost, Arthur Burdett 253
Frost, Vicki 505
Fry, D. 80; cultural response 82
Frye, Northrop 45, 46, 93

Fuertes, Gloria 727, 728–9
Fuglesang, A. 672
Funazaki, Yoshihiko 841
Furman, Pyotr 766
Fyodorov, Boris 766
Fyodorov, Ivan 765

Gabler, Mel and Norma 504–5
Gaelic language 690–1
Gág, Wanda 552, 879
Gaidar, Arkady 744, 770
Gaines, Max 256
Galda, L. 75
games: gender 186–7; rhymes of oral
tradition 186–8
Gardam, Jane 110
Garfield, Leon 269, 401, 402, 685
Garin-Mikhailovsky, Nikolai 767
Garmendía, Julio 890
Garner, Alan 279–80, 390, 559, 685; on folk-
tales 544; *The Owl Service* 134–5; *Red
Shift* 407; use of Welsh mythology 301
Garrard, Phillis 859
gay and lesbian relationships 103, 390
Gedike, L.F. 474–5
Geertz, Clifford 38
gender: adventure stories 331–2; boys' and
girls' stories 349–50, 681; and culture 35;
games 186–7; ideology 54–5; ideology
and contradictory readings 52; interest in
information books 438; maternality of
fairy tales 158; origins of ideological
construction 107; politics in *Earthsea*
104–5; pony stories 360–1, 367;
representation and bias 43–4; roles 52–3;
sex roles 102; sexism 102; tomboys 52;
visual codes 118; women distance selves
from romance 413; women's and
children's literature 25
Genette, Gérard: transtexuality 132
de Genlis, Madame 214, 717–18
genres: adoption by different age groups
425–7; collections 126
Geras, Adèle 280
German language: international publishing
656
Germany 475, 735–46; cultural response 82;
eastern literature 744–6; effect of
National Socialism 741; fairy tales 154–5;
journals 495; magazines 447; oral

tradition 541; Romanticism 154, 737–9; translated works 523–5
Gernsback, Hugo 263, 314
Ghana 453, 540
ghost stories 181–2
Ghurayyib, Rose 790
Gibbs, May 846–7
Gilbert, Pam 54–5
Gilbert, S. 98
Giovanni, Nikki 204
Gisbert, João Manuel 727, 730
Glatz, Jakob 752
Glazer, Joan 23–4
Gleeson, Libby 406
Gleitzman, Morris 530–1
Glen, Esther 856
Godden, Rumer 557
Godwin, William 214, 413
Göknil, Can 782
Goldberg, Moses: *Children's Theatre* 208–9
Golden Books 481
*Goldengrove* (Paton Walsh) 135
Golding, William: *Lord of the Flies* 387
Goldsmith, Evelyn 121
Goldsmith, Oliver 412
González, Anson 883
*Good Night Moon* (Brown) 95–6
Goodrich, Samuel G. 434, 478, 874
*Goody Two-Shoes* (anonymous) 678
Goodyer, George 242
Gopalakrishnan, Kalvi 814
Gottlieb, Gerald 127
Gouin, J. 803
Grafenauer, Niko 777
Graham, Eleanor 475
Grahame, Kenneth 682, 688; *The Wind in the Willows* 46–7, 216, 287–8
Gramcko, Ida 890
*Grange Hill* (television) 357
Grant, C.J. 243
Gray, Nicholas Stuart 217
Greece 447–8, 523, 524, 761–4; literature 594–5
Greek myths 167, 169–70, 172–3, 305, 761
Green, Evelyn Everett 422
Green, Phyllis 383
Greenaway, Kate 197, 226, 227, 473, 549, 552, 682
Greenaway (Kate) Medal 233, 440, 509
Greene, Graham 418
Grice, Frederick 372

Griebner, Reinhard 746
Grimm, Albert Ludwig 155
Grimm Brothers (Wilhelm and Jacob) 106, 153, 154–5, 522, 655; folk-tales 163; readership 161; Romanticism 737–8, 739
Grin, Aleksandr 770
Gripe, Maria 708
Griset, Ernest 225
Grubeshilieva, Maria 779
de Grummond Collection 127, 552
Guaramato, Oscar 890
*Guardian* Award 511
Guatemala 457
Gubar, S. 98
Guillot, René 723–4
*Gulf* (Westall) 136
*Gulliver's Travels* (Swift) 326, 422, 499, 695
Güney, Elfâtun Cem 781
Gutiérrez, Joaquín 883
Guy, Rosa 892

Hacks, Peter 745
Haddad, Habbouha 790
Hade, D.D. 78
Hafiz 793–4
Haig-Brown, Roderick 863, 865
Haitani, Kenjiro 840
Hale, Kathleen: *Orlando the Marmalade Cat* 232, 290, 466
Hale, Lucretia 344
Hale, Sarah Josephus 179, 198
Hall, Donald: *The Ox-Cart Man* (with Cooney) 600
Hall, Major Sam 261
Hall, Stuart 36
Hallack, Cecily 279
Haller, Bernt 702
Halliday, M.A.K. 576
Hallworth, Grace 891
Halsey, Harlan P. 261
Hamada, Hirosuke 838
Hamilton, Charles 353–4
Hampson, Frank 250–1
Harcourt Brace Publishers 480, 481, 483
Harding, D.W. 28, 51, 72, 585–90
Hardiyono 829
Hardy, Thomas 416
Harishchandra, Bharatendu 810
Harmsworth, Alfred 245, 246–7, 251, 264–5, 329–30
Harnett, Cynthia 370

Harnik, Raya 787
Harper Brothers 480, 481
Harranth, Wolf 755
*Harriet the Spy* (Fitzhugh) 210
Harris, Aurand 216, 218
Harris, Benjamin 270
Harris, Joel Chandler: *Uncle Remus* stories
    163, 287, 478, 552, 878
Harris, John 221, 222
Harris, Mary K. 355
Harrison, Harry 321, 426
Harrison, Ted 863, 866
Harvey, F.J. 1
Harwood, John 125–6
Hauff, Wilhelm 155
Haugen, Tormod 706
Hautiz, Deborah 390
Havelock, Eric A. 666
Hawthorne, Nathaniel 875
Haydon, A.L. 353
Hayes, John 865
Hayhoe, M. 76, 80, 82
Hazard, Paul 170
Hearst, William Randolph 254, 255
Heath, William 243
Hebbar, K.K. 809
Hedderich, Hernán 890
*Heidi* (Spyri) 749
Heine, Helme 525–6
Heinlein, Robert A. 320, 426
Helgadottir, Gudrun 704
Hemans, Felicia 196–7
Henderson, James 243–4, 245, 247
Henson, Jim 536
Hentoff, Nat 43
Henty, G.A. 329, 330, 331–2, 422, 681
Hergé: *Tintin* series 232
Herm, Gerhard 310
Herriman, George 253
Hersholt (Jean) Collection 548
Hess Collection 550, 553
Hibberd, Dominic 515–16
Hickman, J. 79
Hidalgo, Barolomé 884
*Higglety Pigglety Pop!* (Sendak) 62–3
Hijlaard, M.T. 883
Hikmet, Nasim 781–2
St Hildegard of Bingen 168
Hill, Douglas 323–4, 336
Hill, Robert 800
Hissey, Jane 237

historical fiction 368–75; adventure stories
    335–6; characters and events in
    traditional verse 179–80; real or
    imaginary characters 268; sense of place
    268–9; use of language 368
historicism *see* New Historicism
history: of children's literature 127; colonial
    heritage 22; culture 33; defining
    children's literature 18; in domestic
    fantasy 300; formerly seen outside
    literature 32; libraries and collections
    548–9; metafiction 407; new
    ethnography 36; reconceptualisation
    32–3; as storytelling 33
Ho Phuong 825
Hoban, Russell 381, 405; age group 423;
    animals 293; *The Mouse and His Child* 97,
    879; picture books 235
*The Hobbit* (Tolkien) 61, 169, 422
Hofbauer, Freidl 754
Hoffman, E.T.A. 155, 737, 738, 739
Hoffman, Felix 750
Hoffman, Heinrich 522, 720, 721, 740
Hoffman, Mary 383
Hofman, Wim 715
Hofmanowa, Klementyna Tanska 776
Holcroft, Anthony 859
Holland, N.N. 73–4, 80
Hollindale, Peter 11, 49, 53, 81
Holt, Rinehart and Winston 505–6
Holtz-Baumert, Gerhard 746
Holub, R.C. 72–3
Homer 304; *The Iliad* 172; influence on
    fantasy 306; *The Odyssey* 172; oral
    performance 666
Horloo, P. 825
Horney, Karen 93–4
Horowitz, Carolyn 370
horror 52, 425; registers 63–4
Houston, James 862, 864, 865
*How Many Miles to Babylon?* (Fox) 66
Howes, Edith 856
Howitt, Mary 196
Howitt, William 845
Howker, Janni 685
Huang Yue Zhue 827
Hübner, Johann 268
Huck, Charlotte 23
*Huckleberry Finn* (Twain) 210, 423, 877;
    appeal to all ages 430; censorship 500,
    506

Hughes, Felicity 44, 46
Hughes, Monica 323, 863, 864
Hughes, Shirley 237, 380, 384, 562, 687
Hughes, Ted 419; inner life 604; *The Iron Man* 8; plays 218
Hughes, Thomas: *Tom Brown's Schooldays* 349, 681
Hugo, Victor 721, 722
humanism: historical ideals 24; ideological approach to criticism 47–9; liberal consensus 45
Hume, Kathryn: *Fantasy and Mimesis* 303
humour: poetry 191, 202–4; seven to ten years 382
*The Hundred and One Dalmatians* (Smith) 291
Hungary 777–8
Hunt, Irene 371
Hunt, Peter 10, 45, 63, 404, 407
Hunter, Mollie 60–1, 372–3, 563, 690
Hunter, Norman 319
Huntington (Henry E.) Library 552
Hurst, K. 76
Huse, Nancy 108
Hutchins, Pat 237–8, 380; *Rosie's Walk* 293, 600, 659
hymns 193–4

Iceland 448, 704
identity 27–8; adolescents 588–9; and culture 54; ironic 82; real verus implied readers 51; transforming social order 38
ideology: China 832–3; circumstances of production 49–50; the common sense 42–3; contradictory readings 51; and criticism 37–8; and culture 121; feminism 103–5, 109–10; gender 54–5; ground of value 47–9; higher education teaching 607; historical contexts 35; Hollindales's three levels 49; not necessarily undesirable 116; polysemous texts 51; purpose of literature 41–2; reader identification 51; reader response 81; Romantic 35; structuralism on character and action 46–7; subjective position 119; uncontrollable factor 11
Ilan-Porath, Ruth 787
Ilgaz, Rifat 782
*The Iliad* (Homer) 172
illustration: American publishing 480; Britain 679–80, 682; collections 549;
colour printing 246; cultural differences 667; engraving and woodcuts 220–3; etching 224; history 461–3; lithography 223, 233, 243; magazines 443–4; prizes 509–10; wordless books 468
Imae, Yoshitomo 840
Imanishi, Sukeyuki 840
Immel, Andrea 127
imperialism 661–2
*In the Night Kitchen* (Sendak) 383
India 807–15; awards 512; Bengali publishers 811–12; Diwali storytelling 542; Hindi publishers 810–11; Kannada publishing 813; magazines 455; Malayalam publishing 813–14; Marathi publishing 812–13; myth and legend 167, 168; Oriya publishing 814; Punjabi publishing 815; Tamil publishing 814; Telegu publishing 815; Urdu publishing 814–15; visual response to story 666
Indonesia 21–2, 457, 823, 829
information books 433–41; criteria 436–7; criticism 440; defining 433; design 468–9; as the fact bank 434–5; narrative style 481, 482; practical guides 436; publishing 439–40; purposes 434–7; readership 437–9; trends 441
information technology 627; abstracts and indexes 496; non- print books for special needs 649–50
Ingelow, Jean 428
Inglis, Fred 20, 38, 45
Ingpen, Robert 238, 851
Ingraham, Prentiss 261
Inokum, Yoko 27
International Board on Books for the Young (IBBY) 527, 528, 660
International Youth Library 495, 546–7, 547
interpretation: Fish on 72
intertextuality 131–7 *see also* metafiction; Anthony Browne 235; game even for the young 11–12; metafictive 4–5; multimedia 530–1; narrative techniques 401; overreferential 136; picture books 231; reader response 83; three main categories 132–3
Inui, Tomiko 840
Ionescu, Ángela 726, 727, 729
Iran 454, 670, 792–4
Iraq 454

Ireland 394–5, 695–8 *see also* Celtic mythology; Irish language 697; libraries 625; storytelling 540
*The Iron Man* (Hughes) 8
irony 68
Irving, Washington 874
Iser, Wolfgang 50, 73–4, 74, 83–5, 440
Ishii, Momoko 839
Ishimova, Alksandra 766
Israel 454, 783–8 *see also* Jewish and Hebrew literature; translated works 523, 525
Italy 757–60 *see also* Latin literature; fairy tales 159, 160; magazines 448; translated works 523
Iwaya, Sazanami 838

Jackson, D. 77, 79
Jackson, Mary V. 126
Jadedeji, Remi 799
Jafri, Naheed 819
Jahnke, R.H. 858
Jalal, Othman 789
James, Henry 44, 46, 71, 430
James, Will 360
Jan, Isabelle 427
Janeway, James 143, 272, 677
Janikovszky, Éva 778
Jansson, Tove 548, 703
Japan 823, 837–42; magazines 455–6; translated works 523, 525
Jarrell, Randall 879
Jayatilaka, K. 820
Jefferies, Richard: *Bevis: The Story of a Boy* 333
Jenkinson, A.J. 438
Jennings, Paul 531, 567, 850
Jewish and Hebrew literature 418, 783–8; Bible stories 269; catechistical writing 268; contemporary fiction 280; effect of war and politics 656; influence of Germany 737, 784; religious storytelling 540; translated works 523, 525
Jirásek, Alois 775
Johns, W.E. 321–2; *Biggles* series 334–5; on writing 558
Johnson, Jane 127
Johnston, D.C. 252
Johnston, Ethel: *Tatterhood and Other Tales* 106
*Jolly Postman* (Ahlberg) 133

Jones, Diane Wynne 403, 404; *The Ogre Downstairs* 297–8
Jones, Mary Vaughan 693
Jones, Terry 401
Jones, Toekey 395
Jonson, Ben 213
Joshi, Jivram 812
journals: abstracts and indexes 496; critical 491–3; education 489–91; history of reviewing 485–7; international 495–6; libraries 485, 488–9; recent 493–4
Jungian criticism 91–3, 541
*The Jungle Book* (Kipling) 285; film adaptation 534
justice 80

Kadono, Eiko 841
*Kalevala* 174, 702
Kambouroglou, Emetrios 762
Kant, Uwe 746
Kanzawa, Toshiko 841
Karafiát, Jan 775
Kästner, Erich 522, 741
Katakouzinos, Alexandros 762
Kaufmann, Angelika 755
Kaye, Geraldine 799
Keach, Benjamin 143
Keary, Annie 339
Keats, Ezra Jack 238, 549, 552
Keeping, Charles 238, 686
Kelleher, Victor 850
Kemp, Gene 357, 382, 383, 401–2
Kenya 453, 799
Keppler, Joseph 253
Kere, Rivka 787
Kerlan Collection 546–7, 549, 553
Kermani, H. Moradi 793
Kermode, Frank 74
Kerrigan, Michael 528
Key, Ellen 707
Khan, Insha alla 814
Kharms, Daniil 769
Khusro, Amir 814
*Kidnapped* (Stevenson) 332–3
Kihm, J.H. 804
Kilani, Kamel 789
Kilner, Dorothy 149, 194, 284
Kilner, Mary Ann 149
King, Clive 685
King (Coretta Scott) Award 511
King-Smith, Dick 291–2

*King Solomon's Mines* (Haggard) 330
Kingsley, Charles 276, 680; *Water Babies*
    160, 314–15; *Westward Ho!* 329
Kingston, W.H.G. 681
Kintgen, E.R. 78
Kipling, Rudyard 200, 328, 416–17, 681;
    animal fables 285; appeal to all ages 427;
    *The Jungle Book* 285, 534; *Puck of Pook's
    Hill* 300, 369; science fiction 316; *Stalky
    and Co.* 350–1
Kirkpatrick, Robert 128
Kitahara, Hakushuh 838
Kitamura, Satoshi 238
Klein, Melanie 93, 94–5
Klein, Norma 503, 504
Klein, Robert 850
Knight, Eric: *Lassie-Come-Home* 423
Kohlap, David 857
Kolodny, A. 81
Komensky, Jan Amos *see* Comenius, Johann
    Amos
Konigsberg, E.L. 560
Konopnicka, Maria 776
Korama, Abenaa 789
Korea 456, 475, 828–9
Korinets, Yury 772
Kot-Murlyka (Nikolai Wagner) 767
Kourtidis, Arist. 762
Koval, Yury 772
Kowling, Lee 827
Krauss, Ruth 481
Kreidolf, Ernst 750, 751
Kriengkraipetch, Suwanna 828
Kristeva, Julia 131
Krüss, James 742
Kuan Sach 825
Kuijer, Guus 714
Kulkarni, K.S. 809
Kumar, K. Shiv 809
Kumartunga, M. 820
Kurelek, William 863, 866
Kurtz, Carmen 726, 728
Kusec, M. 777
Kushkin, Karla 204
Kuzhiveli, Mathew M. 813
Kuznets, Lois 108, 309

Lacan, Jacques 96–7
Lada, Josef 775
Ladybird Publishing 134
Lagerlöf, Selma 522, 707

Lagin, Lazar 771
LaHaye, Tim and Beverly 505
Lamb, Charles and Mary 348, 413
Lancelyn Green, Roger 215, 216, 299
Landsberg, Michele 17
Lane, Allen 472
Lang, Andrew 159, 689
language: colonialism 672–3; creating
    historical atmosphere 368; figurative
    66–7; ideology of 43; play 90, 663–4;
    representation of experiences 59–60;
    represented conversation 67–9; social
    semiotic 60, 62; speech communities 58,
    59; storytelling 544; unconscious aspects
    96–7
languages: minority 656, 672–3, 688, 697,
    727; Switerland's many 748
Lapointe, Claude 724–5
Laske, Oskar 752
Latin literature 213, 271, 594–5, 757
Latvia 656, 780
Lavangia, A.K. 809
Lavender, Ralph 439
Lawrence, Don 250
Lawrence, Louise 323, 336, 394
Lawson, Pat 857
Lawson, Robert: *The Story of Ferdinand*
    232, 879
Le Guin, Ursula: *Earthsea Revisioned*
    104–5; *Earthsea* series 168; on high
    fantasy 304; on narrative 3; on problems
    and escapism 565; on style 306; *A Very
    Long Way from Anywhere Else* 390–1, 430
Le Khao Hoan 825
Leaf, Munro: *The Story of Ferdinand* (with
    Lawson) 232
Lear, Edward 198–9, 682
Leavis, F.R. 36; characters and action 46–7;
    judging literary merit 53; Leavisite
    paradigm 44–6; Marxist critics 47
Lebanon 790–1
Lee, Dennis 863, 867
Leeson, Robert 28, 43, 47, 48, 49
Leitch, Patricia 360, 366–7
L'Engle, Madeline 879
Lenski, Lois 878
Lerner, Laurence 72
Lessing, G.E. 122
L'Estrange, Roger 282
Letria, José Jorge 733
Lévi-Strauss, Claude 47

Levy, Jonathan 214
Lewis, Corinth I. 883
Lewis, C.S. 382, 549, 556, 590, 685; Narnia Chronicles 278, 311–12; on writing 558, 561
lexical set 58, 61, 69
libraries and librarians 126–7, 615–31; accommodation 628–9; activities 625–7; bibliography 126; bibliotherapy 638; in Britain 488–9; censorship 502; censorship or restricting access 498; collections 547–53, 552; criticism and reviews 616; Elementary and Secondary Education Act 482; force behind prizes 509; future prospects 631; history 615–17; importance and value of children's libraries 622–3; information books 433, 437, 439; information technology 627; international promotion and sales 660; journals 485, 488–9; multi-culturalism 624; National Defense Education Act 481–2; prizes 513; Public Libraries Act (1964) 620–1; publishing economics 475; rise of 228; school 597; schools 630–1; special contribution to literature 617–18; staffing 627–8; storytelling 542, 626; structure of services 621–2; in USA 488; users and public collections 623–5; working with schools 629–30
libraries and libraries: organisations and publications 553–4
Library of Congress 548, 550
Liebman, Irena 787
Lilly Rare Book Library 127, 551
Linden, Anne Marie 891–2
Lindenbaum, Pija 708
Lindgard, Joan 394, 688, 690
Lindgren, Astrid: collection 548; Pippi Longstocking 523, 707, 741
Lindgren (Astrid) Prize 527
Lindsay, Norman 846
Lingard, Joan 696
literacy 4, 78, 79; creates market for publishers 349; expanding 329; falling rate 626; family reading and social location 577–9; international view 654; and oral tradition 664–8; and reading development 573–82; religious worries about vulgar chapbooks 274; undermines oral tradition 541; and vulgarisation 46; writing systems of different cultures 664
Lithuania 448, 779
A Little Princess (Burnett) 207, 208
Little Women (Alcott) 103–4, 345, 655, 877
Lively, Penelope 342, 561–2, 685; on awards 513; The Ghost of Thomas Kempe 300; historical fiction 374
Lloyd, Edward 263
Lloyd, Errol 891
Lobato, Monteiro 885, 886
Lobe, Mira 753
Lobel, Arnold 380
Locke, Elsie 857
Locke, John 26, 143, 677, 720; against fairy tales 152; international influence 735, 872–3; Some Thoughts Concerning Education 147–8, 149
Lofting, Hugh 318–19, 683; Doctor Dolittle series 291, 506, 509
London, Jack 317, 427, 878; animal stories 288–9
Longfellow, Henry Wadsworth 198, 874
Lönnroth, Elias 702
López Narváez, Concha 729
The Lord of the Rings (Tolkien) 309–12
Lorofi, G. 803
Low, A.M. 319
Low Tide (Mayne) 61–2, 67
Lowry, Lois 405
Loy, David 827
Lu Xun 833
de Luca, Esteban 884
Luks, George 254
Lumsden, James 688
Lunn, Janet 864, 865
Lurie, Alison 286
Lutterworth Press 278
Lydgate, John 410
Lynch, Benito 884
Lynch, Patricia 696
Lynn, Ruth Nadelman 311
Lyppy, Maria 20–1

The Mabinogion 174, 300–1
Mac, Louise 845
Macaulay, David 404
McCann, Jerome J. 2
McCarthyism 503
McCaughrean, Geraldine 685
McCready, William 550

McCullers, Carson: *The Member of the Wedding* 430
MacDonald, George 127, 160, 276, 680–1, 688, 689
Macdonald, Margaret Read 544
McDowell, Myles: child in the book 25
McGough, Roger 202, 203, 384
Macherey, P. 50, 51
McKee, David 238–9
Mackey, Margaret 6–7
MacLean, Alistair 426
McLean, Ruari 462
McLuhan, Marshall 666
Macmillan Publishers 473–4, 480
McNeill, Janet 280
*Madeline* series (Bemelman) 879
Maekawa, Yasuo 840
Maeterlinck, Maurice 216
de Magalhaes Pinto, Alexina 885
magazine: European 444–50
magazines 262–3, 473; adventure stories 329–30; Africa 453–4; appeal, aims and achievements 443–4; Asia 455–7; Australasia 457; Central and South America 457; effect of Education Act 349; *Horn Book* 490–1, 492; Middle East 454; North America 450–2, 478; reviewing and scholarly journals 485–96; Russia 452–3; science fiction 317–18
Maggi, M.E. 670–1
magic: storytelling 540
Magorian, Michelle 342, 684
Mahy, Margaret 382, 391, 857–8
Maillet, Andrée 868
Majerová, Marie 775
Maklis, Toety 829
Malarochana, Charoen 828
Malaysia 823, 825–6
Mallory, Clare 859
Malta 448
Mamin-Sibirayk, Dmitry 767
Mantilla, Eduardo García 884
Many, J. 77–8, 80
Mao Dun (Shen Dehong) 833
Marasso, Arturo 884
Marchenko, Michael 863
Marchetta, Melina 851
Mark, Jan 393, 402, 562
marketing 472
Marryat, Captain Frederick 331, 681; *The Children of the New Forest* 327, 331, 369

Marshak, Samuil 769, 770
Marshall, James Vance: *Walkabout* 430
Marteaud, D. 803
Martel, Suzanne 868
Martin, David 560–1
Martin-Koné, M.L. 803
Martineau, Harriet 348–9
Marxism 47, 49–50
*Mary Poppins* (Travers) 296–7, 506, 534
Maschler (Emil/Kurt) Award 463
Masee (May) Collection 550
Masefield, John 417–18, 683
Maslow, Abraham 93, 94
Masroor, Meher Nigar 819
Massee (May) Collection 553
Mather, Cotton 268, 271–2, 871–2
Mathis, Sharon Bell 22
Matsui, Tadashi 22, 24
Matsutani, Miyoko 841
Matute, Ana María 726, 729
May, Karl 334
May, Sophie (Rebecca Clarke) 344
Mayer-Skumanz, Lene 754–5
Mayne, William 279–80, 342, 354, 686; characters 46; *Earthfasts* 300; *Low Tide* 61–2, 67; metafiction 402, 405; on writing 568
Meade, L.T. 350
meaning 72
Meek, Margaret 84; on appreciation of reading 384–5; *The Cool Web* 79; cultural response 82; on repeated reading 582; on teaching reading 574; on Willard 372; on *The Wind in the Willows* 288; women in the canon 108
Melas, Leon 762
Melbourne, Sydney 25
Melcher, Frederick G. 479, 480, 508–9, 616, 661
Melwood, Mary 218
Méndez Capote, Renée 887, 888
Menon, K.P. Keseva 813
Mesghali, Farshid 793
metafiction 136–7, 397–408 *see* intertextuality; authorial intrusions 401–2; defining 300–400; historiographic 407; linguistic construction of texts 405–6; multistranded and polyphonic 406–7; narrative techniques 400–5; readers 398–9; strategies 397–8
metonymy 65, 135

Metz, Christian 119
Michael, Sami 787
Michaèlis, Karin 701
Middle East 540, 657
Midohouan, T. 803
Mikhailov, Sergei 770
Miller, Johann Peter 735
Miller, Olive 108
Miller, William 179
Milne, A.A. 201, 683; animals 285; humour
    382–3; plays 217
Minan, T.T. 803
*The Mirror and the Lamp* (Abrams) 71–2
Mitchell, Adrian 202, 203; plays 217
Mitchell, Elyne 360
Mitchell, Rita Philips 891
Mitchell, W.J.T. 115, 122
Mitchison, Naomi 689, 799
Miyazawa, Kenji 838
Modak, Tarabai 813
Moebius, William 45
Molesworth, Mary Louisa 340
Moncrieff (Scott) Prize 527
Mongolia 456, 824–5
Montgomery, L.M. 862, 863
de Monval, Maurice Boutet 229
Moore, Clement 875
Moore, Patrick 322
Moore (Clement) Collection 550
*Moorland Mousie* (Wace) 362–3
moral tales 157, 158–9; fairy tales 152,
    153–4; genre fiction 425–7; illustrated
    books 222; Maria Edgeworth 413–14;
    parodies 428–9; poetry 191, 194; villain
    as hero 263
morality 24; ideology 53; and narrative 3
Moravskaya, Mariya 768
More, Hannah 274
Morgan, Helen 380
Morgan (Pierpont) Library 546–7, 552
Moricz, Zsigmond 777
Morris, Marcus 250, 503
Morris, William 306–7
Morrow (William) Publishers 483
Moser, Erwin 755
Moss, Anita 102, 401
Moss, Elaine 361
Moss, Gemma 52
*Mother Goose* 179–80; Newbery's 150
*The Mouse and His Child* (Hoban) 97
Mowat, Farley 862, 863–4, 865

Mozley, Harriet 339
Mphahlele, Es'kia 800
*Mr Gumpy's Outing* (Burningham) 113–23
Mudrooroo (Colin Johnson) 844
Mugar Memorial Library 551
Muir, M. 126
Mukerji, Dhan Ghopal 289
Mullins, Patricia 851
multimedia 209, 530–8; adaptions of books
    430–1; codes and reality in visual media
    532–3; competition with theatre 218–19;
    distribution 537; early days of puppets
    and cartoons 535–6; *Grange Hill* 357;
    integration of books and anxiety 530–2;
    merchandise 537–8; protective deafness
    and careless listening 531; science fiction
    427; Spielberg 215; technology 537–8
*Mummy Laid an Egg* (Cole) 5–6
Munghoshi, Charles 800
Munro, George P. 260
Munsch, Robert 863; *The Paper Bag
    Princess* 106
Munsey, Frank A. 262
Murawski, Marian 776
museums *see* collections
Muthoni, Susie 799
*Mutt and Jeff* comic strip 255
Myers, Mitzi 34–5, 104
myth and legend 6, 166–75; Britain 676;
    catharsis 170; definition and function
    166–7; historical figures 169; influence
    on high fantasy 305–6; intertextuality
    134–5; Jungian archetypes 91–3; modern
    Denmark 701; monsters and menace 95;
    relation to nature 167; storytelling 539;
    universality 654

Nabi, Rafkun 816
Naidoo, Beverly 81
Nair, Kamla 809
Nair, V. Madhavan 813
Nakamura, Tekisai 837
Namibia 800
Narnia Chronicles (Lewis) 278, 311–12
narrative: changing identities 38; disruption
    and discontinuity 403–4; familiarity in
    adventure stories 332; focalisation 66–7;
    historical 33; linguistic level 59;
    matching individual consciousnesses
    635–7; metafiction 300, 397–8, 400–5;
    *mise en abyme* and self-reflective devices

404–5; multistranded and polyphonic
406–7; mystery, fantasy, games and
readers 402–3; narrator's presence in
story 115–16; represented conversation
67–9; and storytelling 2–4; subjective
position 118–19; ur-narrative 639–40;
use of present tense 65; voice 66–7;
working out problems 94
National Book Trust 809
National Library for the Handicapped
Child 644
*National Velvet* (Bagnold) 363
National Youth Theatre 210, 218
nature 154, 167
Ndabele, Njabulo 800
Needle, Jan 336, 395; *Wild Wood* 48, 288,
401
Neilson, Kay 227, 228
Nell, Victor 639
Nelson, Claudia 107
Nelson (Thomas) Publisher 689
Nepal 807–8, 817–18
Nesbit, E. 382, 681–2; family stories 340;
*Five Children and It* 299; parodies
moralising 428–9; *The Railway Children*
279, 340; science fiction 316; *The Story of
the Amulet* 315; *The Story of the Treasure
Seekers* 401
Nesin, Aziz 781–2
the Netherlands 449, 656; overview of
literature 710–16; translation 523, 524,
525
Neupane, D.R. 817
New Historicism 32–5; British and
American schools 34; five-point
definition 34
New Zealand 855–61; higher education in
children's literature 613; magazines 457;
Maori culture 858
Newbery, Elizabeth 145
Newbery, John 141, 143, 146–7, 149–50;
animal stories 282; collection at UCLA
550; illustrations 221; information books
434; published in USA 478; publishing
472–3, 676, 677; religious writing 268,
272; reviews 485
Newbery (John) Medal 440, 480;
administered by librarians 661; effect on
sales 513; historical fiction 370, 371;
introduction 508–9, 510, 616
Newbolt, Sir Henry 594–5

Neznakomov, Petar 779
Nguyen Quynh 825
Nicholls, Christine 101–2
Nicholls, Helen 381
Nicholls, Peter 324
Nicholson, William 232
Nigeria 453, 664, 789–90
Njami, S. 803
Nkashama, P.N. 804
Nodelman, Perry 97
non-fiction books *see* information books
Nordic countries 475, 699–708
Nordinoff, Nicolas 239
Norse myth: Tolkien 310
Norse myths 159; influence on fantasy 305;
landscape 167; retellings 173
Northeastern Collection 551
Norton, André (Alice) 321
Norton, Donna 27
Norton, Mary 567, 685; *The Borrowers* 381,
537
Norway 449, 699, 704–6; collections 548;
oral tradition 541; translated works 523
Nossov, Nicolai 744
Nöstlinger, Christine 754
Nourse, Alan 321
Nowotny, Joachim 746
nursery rhymes 177–80, 379; censorship
506; early English 679; fitting history to
179–80

Odaga, Asenath 799
O'Dell, Scott 878
Odoevsky, Vladimir 766
*The Odyssey* (Homer) 172
Oedipus complex 91
Ogawa, Mimei 838
Ogiwara, Noriko 841
*The Ogre Downstairs* (Jones) 297–8
O'Hara, Mary: *My Friend Flicka* 289, 423
O'Harris, Pixie 847
Oittinen, Riita 522
Oke, V.K. 812
O'Keefe, Adelaide 195
Okuda, Tsuguo 840
Olesha, Yury 770
Olivares Figueroa, Rafael 889, 890
Olmo, Lauro 727, 729
Omer, Devorah 787
*The Once and Future King* (White) 308
*Once Upon a Time* (Prater) 133

Oneal, Zibby 405
Opie, Iona 2, 191, 667
Opie, Peter 126–7, 667
Opie Collection 126, 549
Opper, Frederick Burr 253, 255
oral tradition 21–2, 177–89; Africa 796, 800;
    appealing to common consciousness 636;
    Asia 830; authority of rhyme and
    assonance 184; cultural values 24; decline
    541; developing countries 664–8; fairy
    tales 153; Far East 824; Greece 761;
    Indian subcontinent 816, 817–18; versus
    literary storytelling 540–1; lullabies 177;
    nursery rhymes 177–80; playground
    rhymes 180–6; skipping rhymes and
    games 186–8; storytelling 539–44; young
    readers and stories 379
Orbis Sensualium Pictus (Comenius) 220,
    410, 434, 462, 522, 655
Orgad, Dorit 787
Orlando the Marmalade Cat (Hale) 232, 290,
    466
Orlev, Uri 787
Ormerod, Jan 380, 513
Oro, Varela 884
Orwell, George 218, 348
Osaka Children's Book Institute 547
Osborne Collection 127, 546–7, 549
Osti, Josip 777
Ostrovsky, Nicolai 744
The Other Award 511
O'Toole, John 206, 207
Al-Ourian 789–90
Outcault, Richard F. 253, 254, 255
Outhwaite, Ida Rentoul 548, 846–7
Overbeck, Christian Adolf 737
Owen, Gareth 203
The Owl Service (Garner) 134–5
Oxenbury, Helen 239
Oxenham, Elsie Jeanette 351–2, 356
The Oxford Companion to Children's
    Literature 2
Oxford University Press Juvenile Library
    126

Paconska, Kveta 239
Pagit, Eusebius 271
Pakistan 807–8, 818–19
Pakovská, Kvta 775
Pallis, Alexandros 762
Palmer, C. Everard 891

Pantelev, L. 769
pantomime: and Peter Pan 216
Papandoniou, Zaharias 763
The Paper Bag Princess (Munsch) 106
A Parcel of Patterns (Paton Walsh) 135–6
Paris, Bernard 94
Parishad, Shishu Sahitya 812
Parker Collection of Early Children's Books
    550
Parnassus Press 551
Parravicini, Luigi Alessandro 757
Patmore, Coventry 190
Paton Walsh, Jill 373, 567, 684, 685;
    Goldengrove 135; A Parcel of Patterns
    135–6, 373; on writing 564
Patten, Brian 202, 203
Paul, Lissa 8, 25
Pavey, Peter 851
Paz, Marcela 883
Paz Castillo, Fernando 890
Peabody and Essex Museum 549
Peacocke, Isabel Maud 856–7
Pearce, Philippa 46, 341–2, 382, 685
Pelgom, Els 715
Pellerin, Jean-Claude 319
PEN Translation Prize 527
Penguin Books 472; USA 483
Pennac, Daniel 725
penny dreadfuls 500–1
Pérez Téllez, Emma 887
Perkins, David 32, 33
Perrault, Charles 153–4, 655, 717, 718;
    gender dynamics 106; translations 146,
    156, 522
Perrott, Reg 248, 249
Persian language see Iran
Peru 673
Pestalozzi, Henrich 748
Peter Pan (Barrie) 207, 208, 215–17
Peterson, Hans 741
Petrov, Valory 779
Peyton, K.M. 280, 515–16, 555; historical
    sea stories 373; pony books 360, 366;
    romantic realism 388–9
Phaedrus (journal) 126
Philadelphia Free Public Library 552
Philip, Neil 128, 190
the Philippines 823
picture books 113–23; alphabet and
    counting books 378; board books 379;
    contemporary authors and illustrators

233–41; early engravings and woodcuts 220–5; effect of rising literacy 226; gap between illustration and text 599–600; historical development 220–9; iconic representation 114, 116; implied readers 118; information books 441; intertextuality 231–2; metafiction 400; modern development 231–3; psychoanalytical criticism 121–2; psychology of perception 121; right to gaze 119; semiotics 123; signed language and written 645–6; teaching 599–601; 'toy' books 224–5; translations 525–6, 527; visual arts 80; visual codes 117–18, 119, 121, 122–3; for visually impaired 647–8

Pienkowski, Jan 239, 381, 467
*Piggybook* (Browne) 580–2
*The Pilgrim's Progress* (Bunyan) 144, 272, 277, 429, 678
Pilkington, Mary 148
Pillar, A.M. 80
Pinkwater, Daniel Manus 879–80
*Pinocchio* 757
*Pippi Longstocking* (Lindgren) 523, 707, 741
Pita Rodríguez, Félix 888
Pitzorno, Bianca 759
Piumini, Roberto 759
Plath, Sylvia 419
Plato 171, 531
playground rhymes 180–6
Pocaaterra, José Rafael 890
poetry 190–204, 653; authority of rhyme and assonance 184; Britain 679, 682, 686; Canada 867–8; defining that for children 190–2; Eliot 417; international 204; nonsense 198–9; nursery rhymes 177–80; pre-twentieth century 192–200; reader response studies 76; Romantic movement 195; Russia 766, 768, 769; teaching 603–4; twentieth century 191–2, 200–4
Pohl, Peter 708
Poland 776; awards 512; magazines 449; translated works 523
Poland, Marguerite 800
*Political Shakespeare* (Dollimore and Sinfield) 34
politics and war 759, 764; effect on children's books 661–2; effect on

publishing 655–6; Vietnamese war 848; violence 394–5
*Pollyanna* (Porter) 344
Poluskin, Maria 521
pony books 360–7; appeal to all ages 427; formula 361; four categories 360; plot formula 292; social class 361–2; young authors 365–6
popular fiction: Robinsonnades 862
popular literature *see also* comics: censorship 500–1; conflict within the middle class 49; dime novels, pulps and penny dreadfuls 259–65; gulf between school and leisure 430; ideology and contradictory readings 51–2; pony books 360–7; reactionary values 52
Porter, Eleanor Hodgson: *Pollyanna* 344
Porter, Sheena 557
Portugal 731–4; fairy tales 160; international publishing 657; language in Angola 658
Postman, Neil 431
postmodernism 400, 407
poststructuralism 101
Potter, Beatrix 127, 284, 285–7, 473, 682; allays childhood fears 380–1; censorship 499–500; illustrations 228; versions 134
Potts, Renée 887
Powling, Chris 382
Pownall, David 217
*Practical Criticism* (Richards) 72
Prasad, Krishna 817
Prasad, Laxmi 817
Pratchett, Terry 403, 405–6, 422, 567
Prater, John 133
Premaratna, K.G. 820
Prest, Thomas Peckett 263
Preussler, Otfried 742
Price, Willard 799
Prince, Alison 288
printers 462 *see also* typography
prizes and prizewinners 508–17; children's choice 510–11, 514–15; criteria 509, 514–17; problems and fairness 512; purpose and introduction 508–9; translations 526, 527
Proctor, Andre 800
production: literature as a product 49–50; processes 58
*The Promise of Happiness* (Inglis) 45
Propp, Vladimir 46, 47, 332

Protherough, Robert 51, 77, 79
Prøysen, Alf 705
psychoanalytic criticism 89–98;
    displacements, substitutions and gaps 89,
    90–1; ego psychology and object relation
    theories 93–6; feminist critique 97–8;
    implied author 89; Jungian 91–3;
    Oedipus complex 91; storytelling 541–2;
    unconscious content 89, 90; visual
    images 121–2
psychology 28; affective aspects of literary
    experience 72; bibliotherapy 634–42;
    defining children's literature 18;
    development of consciousness 635–7;
    developmental 90; faith in books to cure
    problems 380–1; historical revelation of
    childhood 26; identification 27–8;
    picture perception 121
psychotherapy: defined 635
Public Libraries Act 488
publishers: chapbooks 150; labelling
    adolescent fiction 387–8
publishing see also comics: Africa 797–8;
    book design 461–70; Britain 472–6;
    censorship at editorial level 498, 506;
    changing attitudes 9–10; chapbooks 145;
    collections 550–1; developing countries
    669–73; early texts 141–51, 220–5,
    654–5; economics 473–5, 513, 526;
    editors 463, 465, 476, 479–81;
    educational 688; France 718; India 809;
    information books 439–40; international
    655–60; market for lighter reading
    145–6; market forces 8–9, 49; modern
    picture books 232–3; Net Book
    Agreement 475; packagers 659; religion
    271–2, 278–9; restructuring for juvenile
    market 479; small presses and niche titles
    484, 550; territorial rights 474;
    translation 519–22, 525–6; in USA
    478–84
Puck of Pook's Hill (Kipling) 369
Puentes de Oyenard, Sylvia 883
Puffin Books 232, 475–6, 684
Pullein-Thompson sisters 360, 364
pulp magazine 262–3
Punnopatham, Chotiwat 828
Puri, Behari Lal 815
Puritans 280
Purves, D.C. 76
Pushkin, Aleksandr 765

Puttana, M.S. 813
Pyle, Howard 307–8, 334

Quakers 280
Quayle, E. 126
Quiroga, Horacio 884

race and ethnicity 19; identification 27–8;
    King (Coretta Scott) Award 511; need for
    storytelling 542; new ethnography 36;
    poetry 203, 204; reader response studies
    81–2; redressing the balance 8;
    representation and bias 43–4
racism: adventure stories 336; censorship
    506; school stories 357; varying
    judgements of books 22
Rackham, Arthur 227–8, 229
radio see multimedia
Rahman, Shamsur 816
The Railway Children (Nesbit) 279, 340
The Rainbow (comic) 247–8
Ramsey, John: Where the Rainbow Ends
    (with Evans) 216
Random House Publishers 481, 483
Rands, William Brighty 199
Rangavis, Alexandros Rizos 762
Ransome, Arthur 127, 335, 417–18, 556,
    683
Raud, E. 780
Rawlings, Majorie Kinnan 289
Rawlins, Donna 851
Ray, Colin 516
Ray, Satyajit 811–12
Ray, Sukumar 811
Raymond, Harold 475
reader response 71; academic research 10;
    active judgements 69; affective fallacy 73;
    bibliotherapy 634; creation rather than
    discovery 73–4; criticism 71–4; culturally
    oriented studies 81–3; development in
    reading 78–9; experience 72; interaction
    with author 20–1; intersubjectivity 95–6;
    likes and dislikes don't determine quality
    24; process of responding 75–8;
    responding-aloud protocols 80; text-
    oriented studies 83–5; texts 74–5; types
    of behaviour 80–1
readers: comparison of experiences 59–60;
    construction of 50–3; implied 50–3, 71,
    83–5, 118; metafiction 398–9; not in
    dialogue with authors 89–90

reading: absorbed or ludic 639–40; books as
  potentiating devices 640; a community of
  readers 597–8; cultural acceptability 802;
  development of response 78–9; early
  appreciation 384–5; influence of libraries
  620; letter recognition 465; process of 37,
  71; repetition 582; silent reading 597; as
  therapy 637–9; typography and design
  464–7
realism 59; adolescent romances 388–91;
  authors on 564–6; and censorship 503–4;
  family relationships for adolescents
  391–3; versus fantasy 79; Germany
  742–3; harsh aspects 25; identification
  27; illustration 114; metonymic mode
  65–6; post-war Italy 759
Rebecca of Sunnybrook Farm (Wiggins) 344,
  878
Réber, László 778
reception theory 72–3
Recheis, Käthe 753
Redmond, Phil 357
Redol, Alves 732
Reed, Talbot Baines 349
Reed, W. Maxwell 481
Rees, David 373
Reeves, James 201, 686
register 63–5
Reid, Captain Mayne 328
religion 24 see also Christianity; Jewish and
  Hebrew literature; adaptation and
  mediation of adult books 428; adventure
  stories 329, 331–2; catechistical and
  Biblical writing 267–72; censorship 498;
  devotional literature 272–3; didacticism
  338–9; diversity in literature 280–1;
  drama 273; early American literature
  871–2; early publishing 478; evangelism
  428; evangelism in 18th and 19th century
  273–7; evolution versus creation
  controversy 504–6; Greek literature 761;
  historical fiction 371; illustrated books
  222; India 808; international importance
  653; Lewis 685; poetry 192–3; Puritans
  429, 676–7, 679; saints and martyrs 272;
  Scotland 689; seventeenth century
  chapbooks 411; storytelling 539; Sunday
  school prize books 277, 278, 377, 875;
  20th century 277–81; themes in adult
  and children's books 424; using Arabic
  language 672

Religious Tract Society 274, 278, 329, 429,
  689
Renier Collection of Historical and
  Contemporary Children's Books 126,
  549
Renn, Ludwig 745
Rentoul, Annie 846–7
responding-aloud protocols (RAPs) 76, 80
Reuter, Bjarne 702
Reynolds, George William MacArthur 264
Reynolds, Kimberley 107
Ribeiro, Aquilinio 731, 732
Rice, Alice Hegan 345
Richards, I.A. 72
Richardson, Samuel 411–12; domesticity
  413
Richmond, Legh 275
Richter, Hans Peter 373–4, 523, 742
Rider Haggard, H. 331, 564, 796; King
  Solomon's Mines 330
Rigby, Elizabeth 42, 485
Rihani, Lauren 790
Rippere, V. 76
rite of passage 424
Rivas, Reyna 890
Rivero Oramas, Rafael 889–90
Rizvi, S. Sajid 819
Roberts, Sir Charles G.D. 862, 863
Robinson, Barbara 279
Robinson, William Heath 228–9
Robinson Crusoe (Defoe) 326, 655, 678;
  adapted for children 428; adopted by
  children 422
Rodari, Gianni 759
Rodgers, Mary: Freaky Friday 297–8
Rogers, Bruce 462
Rojanasaroj, S. 828
Roman Catholics 271, 279, 280
romances 417, 676; realistic 388–91
Romania 778
Romanticism: fantasy 306; German
  influence 737–9; poetry 195; Russia
  765–6
Ron-Feder, Galila 787
Root, Mary E.S. 502
Roscoe, William 195
Rose, Jacqueline 11, 19, 50, 120
Roseman, Yael 787
Rosen, Michael 202, 203, 239, 381, 686
Rosenbach, Abraham S. Wolf 429, 546
Rosenbach Museum and Library 552

Rosenblatt, Louise: *Literature as Exploration* 72; transactional theory 74, 76

Rosenthal, L. 299

*Rosie's Walk* (Hutchins) 293, 600, 659

Ross, Charles Henry: *Ally Sloper* 244

Ross, Tony 239

Rossetti, Christina 197, 428, 682

Rousseau, Jean-Jacques 26, 149, 498–9, 678, 720; *Emil* 736; international influence 735, 765

Routledge, George 473

Roy, Claude 725

Rubakin, Nicholas 637–8

Rubenstein, Gillian 560, 566, 850

Rupert the Bear 232

Rushdie, Salman 419–20

Ruskin, John 115, 159–60, 415, 486, 680

Russia 765–72; magazines 452–3; oral tradition 540, 541; translated works 523, 524

Rybakov, Anatoly 772

Rydberg, Viktor 706

Saalburg, Charles 254

Sabha 815

Sadji, A. 803

Sadler, Allen 357

Sadoveanu, Mihail 778

Safa, Peyani 781

Said Thabet, Taher 791

de Saint-Exupéry, Antoine 322

St John, Patricia 278

Salgari, Emilio 759

Salinger, J.D.: *Catcher in the Rye* 64, 387–8, 503

Salkey, Andrew 891

Salmon, Edward 103–4, 501

Salten, Felix 289, 522

Saltman, Judith 865

Salway, Lance 516

Salzmann, Christain Gotthilf 737

Sanchez Silva, José María 726, 728

Sapkota, P. 817

Sarland, C. 52, 82

Saro-Wiwa, Ken 790

Satchell, William 855

Satô, Satoru 840–1

Sawyer, Ruth 542

Say, B.M. 803

Sayers, W.C. 509

Scandanavia *see* Nordic countries or individual countries

Schaefer, Jack: *Shane* 427

Schlegel-Tieck Prize 527

Schmidt, Annie M.G. 712–13

Schofield (Mary L.) Collection of Children's Literature 549

school stories 348–58, 681; Girl Guides 353; teenaged characters 387; transition to day schools 354

schools: information books 438

science fiction 314–24; adventure stories 336; appeal to all ages 426; comics 251, 319; magazines 317–18; pulp magazines 262–3; Russian 772

Scotland 688–91; Gaelic language 690–1; historical fiction 372–3

Scott, Sir Walter 326, 414, 426, 681, 688, 689

Scudder, Horace E. 344, 486

Seaby, Allen W. 362

Sedgwick, Catharine Maria 342–3

Sedley, Sir Charles 179

Seed, Jenny 800

de Ségur, (Sophie) Countess 722–3

semiotics 117, 123; learning to read 574–6; and Leavisite paradigm 46; picture books 116

Senanayake, G.B. 820

Senarens, Louis 317

Sendak, Maurice 239–40, 481, 552; censorship 503, 504; characters 46; *Higglety Pigglety Pop!* 62–3; *In the Night Kitchen* 383; semiotics 574–6; on space between illustration and text 599; *Where the Wild Things Are* 5, 879

Senegal 803; French language 658

Senghor, L.S. 803

series books: censorship 501–2

Serraillier, Ian 336, 371, 684

*Sesame Street* (television) 536

Seton, Ernest Thompson 289, 862, 863

Setyawan, Dwianto 829

Seuss, Dr (Theodore Geisel) 480, 879

Sewell, Anna: *Black Beauty* 284–5, 360

Sewell, Elizabeth 339

sexism: censorship 506; fairy tales 158

sexuality: adolescent romances 388–91; adult and children's literature 430; AIDS and changing attitudes 391; censorship

503–4; pregnancy 391; psychoanalytical criticism 91; school stories 357–8

Shaarawi, Huda 540

Shakespeare, William 212

Sham, Mahmud 819

Shanab, Adel Abu 791

El Shandouly, Sameh Moussa 791

*Shane* (Schaefer) 427

Sharp, Evelyn 350

Shavi, Yaacov 787

Shavit, Z. 84

Shaw, George Bernard: *Androcles and the Lion* 216

Shaw (Bernard) Prize 527

*Shaw Childhood in Poetry Collection* (FSU) 127

Shaw (John M.) Collection of Poetry 550

Shedlock, Marie 542

Shelley, Mary: *Frankenstein* 314

Shepard, Ernest 226

Sherlock, Philip 891

Sherwood, Mary Martha 275–6; *The History of the Fairchild Family* 338–9

Shivprasad, Raja 810

Shmelyov, Ivan 768

Shôno, Eniji 841

Shrestha, Sidhi Charan 817

Shukovsky, Vasily 765

Shultze, Carl ('Bunny') 254–5

Shuster, Joe 257

Shyboub, Edvich 790

Sidney, Margaret 345; *The Five Little Peppers* series 478

Sidney, Sir Philip 676

Siegel, Jerry 257

Siesicka, Krystyna 776

signed language: and picture books 645–6

signs and referents 61–3, 97

Silver, Norman 395

Silverberg, Robert 426–7

Silverstein, Shel 203–4

Simha, Durga 813

Simon & Schuster Publishers 483

Sinclair, Catherine 339, 680

Sinfield, A. 34, 38

Singapore 456, 823, 826–7

Singer, Isaac Bashevis 418, 539, 551

skipping rhymes and games 186–8

*The Slave Dancer* (Fox) 22

Slemon, Stephen 109

Slovak language 450

Slovenia 450

Smart, Christopher 193

Smith, Charlotte 196

Smith, Dodie: *The One Hundred and One Dalmatians* 291

Smith, Lane 240

Smollett, Tobias 689

Snorri Sturluson 310

social class 19, 28, 35; middle-class bias 341, 345–6, 684; Orwell on schools 348; pony stories 361–2

social issues: information books 435–6

Society for Promoting Christian Knowledge 278–9, 429, 689

sociolinguistic codes 60–2

sociology 18, 28

Soresi, Domenico 757

South Africa 453–4, 800–1; translated works 525

South America 882–7, 889–90

Southall, Ivan 548, 555–6, 558, 848

Spain 449, 525, 657, 726–30; fairy tales 160; myth and legend 175

Speare, Elizabeth George 280, 371, 515

special needs 644–50, 660; characters in books 648–9; dual signed and printed books 645–6; non-print books 649–50; tactile books 647–8; use of libraries 624; for visually impaired 646–8

Spielberg, Steven 422, 880, 881

Spillner, Wolf 746

Spyri, Johanna 522; *Heidi* 749

Squire, J.R. 75, 76–7

Sri Lanka 807–8, 819–21

Srivastava, G.P. 814

Stables, Dr Gordon 318

*Stalky and Co.* (Kipling) 350–1

Standing Conference of Young People's Theatre 209

Steadman, Ralph 559

Steig, William 292–3

Steiner, George 595

Stephens, John 10, 44, 51, 84; constructing the reader 50; ideologies 53, 116; reader only within text 84; subjective position in text's ideology 119

Stevenson, Robert Louis 199–200, 332–3, 387, 681, 689; verses 682; on writing 556

Storni, Alfonisa 884

Storr, Catherine 562

storytelling 2–3, 539–44; art of 543; audio
cassette technology 537; Australia 843–4;
bibliotherapy 641; cultural continuation
542; fairy tales 160–1; history 33;
libraries 626; Nigeria 668–9; oral
tradition 540–1; picture books 231;
preparation 543–4; renewal of
storytelling 541–3; in schools 598–9;
storytellers 539–40, 542
Stow, Jenni 891
Stowe, Harriet Beecher: *Uncle Tom's Cabin*
655, 876
Strachan, Ian 395
Strang, Herbert (G.H. Ely and J.
L'Estrange) 333, 334
Stratemeyer, Edward 218, 501
Streatfeild, Noel 280, 340–1
Streit-Wortzel, Esther 787
Stretton, Hesba (Sara Smith) 276
Strittmatter, Erwin 746
structuralism 46–7
Strugatsky, Arkady and Boris 772
style 58, 69; discourse 59; methodologies 60;
sentence structure 67; speech
communities 59
Styles, Morag 107
Subero, Efraín 890
Suddaby, Donald 322
Sufism 540
Suksopa, Thepsiri 828
Sullivan, C.W. 301
Sun Yuxiu 833
Sunindyo 21–2
*Superman* (comic) 257–8
Sutcliff, Rosemary 20, 335–6, 368, 370–1,
429, 684
Sutton, Eve 857
Suyadi 829
Suzuki, Miekichi 838
Svirsky, Alekei 768
Swan, Ani 703
Swan, Gerald G. 250
Sweden 449–50, 706–8; collections 548;
history 26, 699; religion and morality 24;
translated works 523, 524, 525
Swedish Academy Prize 527
Swift, Jonathan 695; censored 499;
*Gulliver's Travels* 326
Swindells, Robert 394, 395–6
Swinnerton, James 255

*Swiss Family Robinson* (Wyss) 326–7, 428,
749
Switzerland 450, 748–51
Sylva, Carmen (Elizabeth of Romania) 778
symbols 94
syntax 58, 69
Syria 454, 791

Tabart, Benjamin 680
Tabbert, R. 82, 83
Tachihara, Erika 842
Tachild, Sylviane 883
Tadjo, V. 803
Tagore, Rabindra Nath 811
Taiwan 457, 475
Taiwo, Oladele 799
Takashima, Shizuye 865
Takeyama, Michio 839
Tamer, Zacharia 791
Tamhankar, N.D. 812–13
Tanner, Jane 851
Tanzania 453
*Tarka the Otter* (Williamson) 289
Tarkington, Booth 345, 878
Tate, Binnie 22
Taylor, Ann 195, 682
Taylor, Jane 179, 195, 199, 682
Taylor, John 270, 272
Taylor, Sandra 54–5
Taylor, Susan 53
Taylor, William 859–60
Teasy, J. 76
teenagers *see* adolescents
Teleshov, Nikolai 768
television *see* multimedia
Tellegen, Toon 715–16
Tene, Binyamin 787
Tenniel, Sir John 226
Tetzner, Lisa 750
textuality: children's participation 580–2;
constructing the reader 50; early 141–51,
180; and history 33; image of
unconscious structured like language
96–7; lessons in reading 574; multiple
versions 6–7; new representational forms
4; polysemous 51; power of images
720–1; production 58; reader response
74–5, 83–5; restrictive 69; telling gaps
83–4, 84, 136; true history 128
Thackeray, William Makepeace 414, 558–9
Thailand 457, 671, 823, 827–8

theatre 208–10, 216–17 *see also* drama;
Greece 763, 764
*Theatre in Education* (O'Toole) 206, 207
themes: adult and children's books in
common 424; comparing adult and
children's books 430; picture books 232
*Theory of Literature* (Warren and Wellek) 73
Thériault, Yves 868
Thiel, Colin 848
Thijseen (Theo) Award 713
Thiong'o, Ngugi wa 668, 672–3
Thomas, Isaiah 271
*Thomas the Tank Engine* series (Awdry) 6–7
Thompson, Denys 36
Thompson, Judith 27–8
Thomson, D.C. 249
Thomson, J. 77, 79
Thwaite, M.F. 126
Tieck, Johann Ludwig 737, 738
*Tintin* series (Hergé) 232
Tir na n-Og Award 693
Todd, F. 76
Todorov, Tzvetan 46
Tofano, Sergio (Sto) 759
Tolkien, J.R.R. 549, 683; on *Beowulf* 304;
*The Hobbit* 61, 169, 308–12; *The Lord of
the Rings* 309–12; on secondary world
304; *The Simarillion* 309
Tolstoi, Aleksei 771
Tolstoi, Lev 766–7
*Tom Brown's Schooldays* (Hughes) 349
*Tom Swift* (Appleton) 318
Tomas, S. 777
Topelius, Zachris 702
Torigoe, Professor Shin 547
Tournier, Michel 725
Townsend, John Rowe 17, 515; on awards
511; criteria for judgement 45; disputes
among critics 28; on Georgian lady
novelists 104; *Gumble's Yard* 341; on
prizes 516; on realism 565; on writing
557–8, 561; *Written for Children* 1–2, 32
toys 296
Tracy, Mona 855
tragedy and catharsis 170
translation 519–28; costs 526; the Far East
823–4; history of 522–5; issues and
developments 525–8; number of titles
falling 657; picture books 525, 527;
process of 519–22

translations: isolationism of English-
language countries 528
transtextuality: Anthony Browne 235
Travers, P.L. 20, 683; *Mary Poppins* 296–7,
506
Treadgold, Mary 365
Trease, Geoffrey 9, 43, 280, 684–5;
adventure stories 335; historical fiction
369
*Treasure Island* (Stevenson) 332–3
Treece, Henry 371
Trevor, Meriol 280
Trimmer, Sarah 148, 157–8, 270, 428, 678;
*Fabulous Histories* 283–4; reviews 486
Tring, A. Stephen 354
Trnka, Jivi 775
Tsuboi, Sakae 839
Tsubota, Jôji 839
Tucker, Charlotte Maria 276, 689
Tucker, Nicholas 20, 21, 79, 286
Tudev, L. 824–5
Tur, Evgeniya 767
Turk, Hanne 755
Turkey 454, 781–2
Turner, Elizabeth 195–6
Turner, Ethel 845
Tuwim, Julian 776
Twain, Mark 415–16, 552, 875; *The
Adventures of Tom Sawyer* 334, 478–9,
877; censorship 500, 506; *Huckleberry
Finn* 210, 423, 430, 877
typography: book design 464–7; book
jackets and binding 469; metafiction 397,
406

Udall, Nicholas 213
Ukraine 450, 656
Umlauf-Lamatsch, Ammelies 752
*Uncle Remus* stories (Harris) 287, 478, 878
*Uncle Tom's Cabin* (Stowe) 876
Ungerer, Tomi 724
United Arab Emirates 454, 791
United States 871–81; before 1865 871–6;
Civil War to present 876–81; critical
journals 491–2; cultural isolation 482,
524; cultural poetics 36; education
journals 489–91; Elementary and
Secondary Education Act 482; fairy tales
160; faith in books to cure problems
380–1; family stories 342–7; folk-tales
163; higher education in children's

literature 606–9; historical fiction 369–70, 371, 374; journals 486–7, 493–4; library history 615–17; magazines 451–2, 478; 'milk bottle versus Grimm' critical controversy 480–1; National Defense Education Act 481–2; New Historicism and cultural poetics 34; twentieth century poetry 201–2

University of California at LA 127; Newbery collection 550

Ural, Yalvaç 782

Urbaneja, Luis Manuel 890

Ure, Jean 357, 390; on writing 561

Uruguay 457

*The Uses of Enchantment* (Bettelheim) 91, 332, 880

Uspensky, Eduard 772

Ussaie, Zakir 814

utopia and dystopia 425

Uttley, Alison 289–90

Uwemedimo, Rosemary 790

Vajracharya, R. 818

del Valle Inclán, Ramón 727

Vallerand, Claudine 868

Valliappa, Al 814

values 117

Vamba (Luigi Bertelli) 759

Van Allsburg, Chris 240

van Leeuwen, Joke 715

van der Leoff, Rutgers 713

Van Loon, Henrik 480, 509

Veeser, H. Aram 34

Velthuijs, Max 714

Venezuela 457, 670–1, 889–90

Verne, Jules 316, 317, 522, 717, 722

*The Very Hungry Caterpillar* (Carle) 466

*Vice Versa* (Anstey) 297–8

Victor, Orville J. 259

Vietnam 825

Viking Press 550

Villafañe, Javier 884, 889

violence and crime 52, 393–4; censorship 500–3; political troubles 394–5

Vipont, Elfrida 280, 355

*The Virginian* (Wister) 427

visual codes 600–1

visual presentation: picture books 5–6; and textuality 4

Vives, Juan Luis 24

*Viz* (comic) 252

Vizyinos, Georgios 762

vocabulary 26

Voight, Cynthia 392–3

Volkov, Aleksandr 744, 771

Volosinov, V.N. 43

Voorhees Rutgers University 551

Vyas, Hariprasad 812

Vygotsky, L.S. 576, 582

Wace, Muriel: *Moorland Mousie* 362–3

Waciuma, Charity 799

Waddell, Martin 237, 395, 696

Wade, B. 76

Wade Collection 549

Wales: collection 548; fantasy literature 300–1; magazines 447; overview of literature 692–4; storytelling 539; Welsh language 656, 660

Walker, Sebastian 473

Walkerdine, Valerie 106

Wall, Barbara 21, 26

Wall, Dorothy 846

Wallace, Jo-Ann 109

Walsh, María Elena 884

Walters, Hugh 322

Walton, Mrs O.F. 276–7

war 395, 684; historical fiction 370–5; nuclear 394

Wardell, Phyl 857

Warne, Frederick 473

Warner, Gertrude Chandler 346

Warner, Marina 109

Warren, W.P.: *Theory of Literature* (with Wellek) 73

*Water Babies* (Kingsley) 160, 314–15, 680

*Watership Down* (Adams) 292

Watkins, Dudley D. 249–50

Watson, James 395, 566

Watson, John 243

Watts, Isaac 144–5, 193, 268, 269, 272, 411, 679, 689

Webster, Jean 344

Wedding, Alex (Grete Weiskopf) 745

Wee, Jessi 827

Weems, Parson 873

Weisner, David 240

Welch, Ronald 371

Wellek, René 73

Wellm, Alfred 746

Wells, C.G. 577–8

Wells, H.G. 316–17

Wells, Rosemary 293, 356
Welsh, Renate 753
Welsh National Centre of Children's
    Literature 548
Wertham, Frederick 258, 502
Wesley, Charles 193
West, Joyce 856
Westall, Robert 336, 395, 684; on awards
    514; *Gulf* 136; historical fiction 373; *The
    Scarecrow* 392
Westerman, Percy F.C. 334
westerns 259–61; appeal to all ages 427
Westin, Boel 26
*Westward Ho!* (Kingsley) 329
Wetherell, Elizabeth (Susan Warner) 343
Wettasinghe, Sybil 820
Whalley, J.I. 128
*What Katy Did* (Coolidge) 345
Wheatley, Nadia 567
Wheeler, Edward L. 261
Wheeler-Nicholson, Major Malcolm 256–7
*Where the Wild Things Are* (Sendak) 5,
    574–6, 879
White, Dorothy Neal 379
White, E.B.: animal stories 291; *Charlotte's
    Web* 97, 291, 299, 481, 879; on writing
    563–4; on writing up to children 20
White, T.H. 322; *The Once and Future King*
    308
*White Fang* (London) 288–9
Whitehead, F. 79
Wickramasinghe, Martin 820
Wiesner, David 400
Wiggins, Kate Douglas: *Rebecca of
    Sunnybrook Farm* 344, 878
*Wild Wood* (Needle) 48, 288
Wilde, Oscar 416
Wilder, Laura Ingalls 346, 369, 480, 552,
    553, 878
Wildsmith, Brian 233, 240, 468, 686
Willard, Barbara 280, 372
Williams, Gurney 23–4
Williams, Raymond 35–6, 36
Williamson, Henry: *Tarka the Otter* 289,
    423
Wilmink, Willem 714
Wilson, Roy 248, 250
Wilson, William Carus 274
Wimsatt, W.K. 73
*The Wind Blew* (Hutchins) 659

*The Wind in the Willows* (Grahame) 216,
    287–8; characters 46–7; liberal humanist
    criticism 47–8
Winner, Septimus 179
Winnicott, Donald W. 93, 95–6
Winterbottom, Mrs Ann Sophia 259
Wiseman, D. 78
Wister, Owen: *The Virginian* 427
*The Witches* (Dahl) 506; film adaptation 535,
    536
*Wizard of Oz* (Baum) 479
*The Wizard of Oz* (Baum): film adapatation
    534
*The Wizard of Oz* series (Baum) 531, 877
Wodehouse, P.G. 417
Wolde, Gunilla 707
Wolfe, Gary K. 303–4
Wölfel, Ursula 743
Wollstonecraft, Mary 104, 148–9, 412–13
*The Wood Beyond the World* (Morris)
    306–7
Woodard, Gloria 27–8
Wordsworth, Dorothy 196
Wordsworth, William 194–5
Wright, Elizabeth 95, 96
Wright, Kit 203
Wrightson, Patricia 548, 847–8
The Writers and Readers Publishing
    Cooperative 43–4
*Written for Children* (Townsend) 1–2
Wyndham, John 322
Wyss, Johann: *Swiss Family Robinson* 326–7,
    428, 749

Xenopoulos, Gregorios 762

Yale University 126
Yamakan, Hisashi 839–40
Ye Shengtao 833–4
Yeats, W.B. 695
Yonge, Charlotte M. 276, 422, 681; family
    stories 339; school stories 349–50
Yugoslavia (former) 450, 776–7
Yun Sok-chung 829
Yunque, Álvaro 884

Zambia 789
Zancella, D. 78
Zanga-Tsogo, D. 804
Zarrillo, J. 78
Zarrinkelk, Noureddin 793

Zhang Tianyi 834
Zhitkov, Boris 770
Zhou Zouren 833
Zhukovsky, Vasily 766
Ziefert, Harriet 381
Zimbabwe 453, 800

Zimet, S.G. 43
Zindel, Paul 391, 503, 504, 559
Zipes, Jack 51–2
Zoran, Gabriel 787
Zwerger, Lisbeth 241, 755–6
Zwilgmeyer, Dikken 705